New Perspectives on

CREATING WEB PAGES WITH HTML AND DYNAMIC HTML

Comprehensive

PATRICK CAREY
Carey Associates, Inc.

Contributor:
SHIRLEY E. KAISER, M.A.
SKDesigns

COURSE TECHNOLOGY
THOMSON LEARNING

Australia • Canada • Mexico • Singapore • Spain • United Kingdom • United States

New Perspectives on Creating Web Pages with HTML and Dynamic HTML—Comprehensive Edition is published by Course Technology.

Managing Editor	Greg Donald
Senior Editor	Donna Gridley
Series Technical Editor	Rachel Crapser
Associate Product Manager	Melissa Dezotell
Editorial Assistant	Rosa Maria Rogers
Developmental Editor	Mary Kemper
Production Editor	Daphne Barbas
Text Designer	Meral Dabcovich
Cover Art Designer	Douglas Goodman

ISBN 0-619-01969-7
Printed in the United States of America

4 5 6 7 8 9 10 BM 04 03 02

PREFACE

The New Perspectives Series

About New Perspectives

Course Technology's **New Perspectives Series** is an integrated system of instruction that combines text and technology products to teach computer concepts, the Internet, and microcomputer applications. Users consistently praise this series for innovative pedagogy, use of interactive technology, creativity, accuracy, and supportive and engaging style.

How is the New Perspectives Series different from other series?

The **New Perspectives Series** distinguishes itself by **innovative technology**, from the renowned Course Labs to the state-of-the-art multimedia that is integrated with our Concepts texts. Other distinguishing features include **sound instructional design**, **proven pedagogy**, and **consistent quality**. In each tutorial, students learn features in the context of solving a realistic case problem rather than simply learning a laundry list of features. With the **New Perspectives Series**, instructors report that students have a complete, integrative learning experience that stays with them. They credit this high retention and competency to the fact that this series incorporates critical thinking and problem solving with computer skills mastery. In addition, we work hard to ensure accuracy by using a multi-step quality assurance process during all stages of development. Instructors focus on teaching and students spend more time learning.

Choose the coverage that's right for you

New Perspectives applications books are available in the following categories:

Brief — 2-4 tutorials

Brief: approximately 150 pages long, two to four "Level I" tutorials, teaches basic application skills.

Introductory — 6 or 7 tutorials, or Brief + 2 or 3 more tutorials

Introductory: approximately 300 pages long, four to seven tutorials, goes beyond the basic skills. These books often build out of the Brief book, adding two or three additional "Level II" tutorials.

Comprehensive — Introductory + 4 or 5 more tutorials. Includes Brief Windows tutorials and Additional Cases

Comprehensive: approximately 600 pages long, eight to twelve tutorials, all tutorials included in the Introductory text plus higher-level "Level III" topics. Also includes three or four fully developed Additional Cases. The book you are holding is a Comprehensive book.

Advanced — Quick Review of basics + in-depth, high-level coverage

Advanced: approximately 600 pages long, covers topics similar to those in the Comprehensive books, but offers the highest-level coverage in the series. Advanced books assume students already know the basics, and therefore go into more depth at a more accelerated rate than the Comprehensive titles. Advanced books are ideal for a second, more technical course.

Office — Office suite components + integration + Internet

Office: approximately 800 pages long, covers all components of the Office suite as well as integrating the individual software packages with one another and the Internet.

Custom Editions

Choose from any of the previous options to build your own Custom Editions or CourseKits

Custom Books: The New Perspectives Series offers you two ways to customize a New Perspectives text to fit your course exactly: *CourseKits*™—two or more texts shrink wrapped together. We offer significant price discounts on *CourseKits*™. *Custom Editions*® offer you flexibility in designing your concepts, Internet, and applications courses. You can build your own book by ordering a combination of topics bound together to cover only the subjects you want. There is no minimum order, and books are spiral bound. Contact your Course Technology sales representative for more information.

What course is this book appropriate for?

New Perspectives on Creating Web Pages with HTML and Dynamic HTML—Comprehensive can be used in any course in which you want students to learn all the most important topics of HTML and DHTML, from creating multimedia Web pages with hypertext links, tables, frames, and forms, to using cascading style sheets, programming with JavaScript, working with dynamic content and layout, controlling mouse and keyboard events, and creating new frames and windows. It is particularly recommended for a full-semester course on creating Web pages using HTML and DHTML. This book assumes that students have learned basic operating system and browser skills.

Proven Pedagogy

CASE

Tutorial Case Each tutorial begins with a problem presented in a case that is meaningful to students. The case turns the task of learning how to use an application into a problem-solving process.

45-minute Sessions Each tutorial is divided into sessions that can be completed in about 45 minutes to an hour. Sessions allow instructors to more accurately allocate time in their syllabus, and students to better manage their own study time.

1.

2.

3.

Step-by-Step Methodology We make sure students can differentiate between what they are to *do* and what they are to *read*. Through numbered steps—clearly identified by a gray shaded background—students are constantly guided in solving the case problem. In addition, the numerous screen shots with callouts direct students' attention to what they should look at on the screen.

TROUBLE?

TROUBLE? Paragraphs These paragraphs anticipate the mistakes or problems that students may have and help them continue with the tutorial.

Read

"Read This Before You Begin" Page Located opposite the first tutorial's opening page for each level of the text, the Read This Before You Begin Page helps introduce technology into the classroom. Technical considerations and assumptions about software are listed to save time and eliminate unnecessary aggravation. Notes about the Data Disks help instructors and students get the right files in the right places, so students get started on the right foot.

Quick Check Questions Each session concludes with meaningful, conceptual Quick Check questions that test students' understanding of what they learned in the session. Answers to the Quick Check questions are provided at the end of each tutorial.

RW

Reference and Design Windows Reference Windows and Design Windows are succinct summaries of the most important tasks and design concepts covered in a tutorial.

TAG REFERENCE

Tag Reference A table at the end of the book, the Tag Reference contains a summary of how to perform common tasks using the most efficient method.

End-of-Chapter Review Assignments, Case Problems, Internet Assignments, and Lab Assignments
Review Assignments provide students with additional hands-on practice of the skills they learned in the tutorial using the same case presented in the tutorial. These Assignments are followed by three to four Case Problems that have approximately the same scope as the tutorial case but use a different scenario. In addition, some of the Review Assignments or Case Problems may include Exploration Exercises that challenge students and encourage them to explore the capabilities of the program they are using, and/or further extend their knowledge. Each tutorial also includes instructions on getting to the text's Student Online Companion page, which contains the Internet Assignments and other related links for the text. Internet Assignments are additional exercises that integrate the skills the students learned in the tutorial with the World Wide Web. Finally, if a Course Lab accompanies a tutorial, Lab Assignments are included after the Case Problems.

New Perspectives on Creating Web Pages with HTML and Dynamic HTML— Comprehensive Instructor's Resource Kit (IRK) contains:

- Sample Syllabus
- Data Files
- Solution Files
- Course Labs
- Course Test Manager Testbank
- Course Test Manager Engine
- Figure Files
- HTML files for the Faculty Online Companion (includes Lecture Notes)
- WebCT Content

These supplements come on CD-ROM. If you don't have access to a CD-ROM drive, contact your Course Technology customer service representative for more information.

The New Perspectives Supplements Package

Electronic Instructor's Manual Our Instructor's Manuals include tutorial overviews and outlines, technical notes, lecture notes, solutions, and Extra Case Problems. Many instructors use the Extra Case Problems for performance-based exams or extra credit projects. The Instructor's Manual is available as an electronic file, which you can get from the Instructor Resource Kit (IRK) CD or download it from **www.course.com**.

Data Files Data files contain all of the data that students will use to complete the tutorials, Review Assignments, Case Problems, and Additional Cases. A Readme file includes instructions for using the files. See the "Read This Before You Begin" page at the beginning of each level for more information on how students should set up their Data Disks.

Solution Files Solution Files contain every completed file students are asked to create or modify in the tutorials, Review Assignments, Case Problems, Extra Case Problems (which can be found in the Instructor's Manual) and Additional Cases. A Help file on the Instructor's Resource Kit includes information for using the Solution files.

Course Labs: Concepts Come to Life These highly interactive computer-based learning activities bring concepts to life with illustrations, animations, digital images, and simulations. The Labs guide students step-by-step, present them with Quick Check questions, let them explore on their own, test their comprehension, and provide printed feedback. Lab icons at the beginning of the tutorial and in the tutorial margins indicate when a topic has a corresponding Lab. Lab Assignments are included at the end of each relevant tutorial. The Labs available with this book and the tutorials in which they appear are:

TUTORIAL 1   TUTORIAL 10   ADDITIONAL CASES

Figure Files Many figures in the text are provided on the IRK CD to help illustrate key topics or concepts. Create traditional overhead transparencies by printing the figure files. Or, create electronic slide shows by using the figures in a presentation program such as PowerPoint.

Course Test Manager: Testing and Practice at the Computer or on Paper Course Test Manager is cutting-edge, Windows-based testing software that helps instructors design and administer practice tests and actual examinations. Course Test Manager can automatically grade the tests students take at the computer and can generate statistical information on individual as well as group performance.

Online Companions: Dedicated to Keeping You and Your Students Up-To-Date Visit our faculty sites and student sites on the World Wide Web by browsing www.course.com. Instructor's can browse this text's password-protected site to obtain an online Instructor's Manual, Solution Files, Data Files, and more. Students can also access this text's Student Online Companion, which contains Data files, assignments and other useful links.

Student Resource CD in the back of this book A special feature of this book! The CD contains Java applets, HTML Tag Reference, additional coverage, and other multimedia elements, such as shareware.

MyCourse MyCourse.com is a quick and easy way to put your course online. MyCourse.com is an easily customizable online syllabus and course enhancement tool. This tool adds value to your class by offering brand new content designed to reinforce what you are already teaching. MyCourse.com even allows you to add your own content, hyperlinks, and assignments. For more information, visit our Web site at: http://www.course.com/at/distancelearning/#mycourse

WebCT WebCT is a tool used to create a distance-learning course. The site is hosted on your school campus, allowing complete control over the course materials. WebCT has its own internal communication system, offers internal e-mail, a Bulletin Board, and a Chat room. Course Technology offers content for this book to help you create your WebCT class, such as a suggested Syllabus, Topic Reviews and Lecture Notes, Practice Test questions, and more. For more information, visit our Web site at: http://www.course.com/at/distancelearning/#webct

Blackboard Like WebCT, Blackboard is a management tool to help you plan, create, and administer your distance-learning class, without knowing HTML. Classes are hosted on Blackboard's or your school's servers. Course Technology offers content for this book to help you create your Blackboard class, such as Topic Reviews and Lecture Notes, Practice Test questions, a sample syllabus, and more.

Acknowledgments

This book would not have been started without the support and enthusiasm of Mac Mendelsohn and Christine Guivernau, who initially proposed the project. Special thanks to Mary Kemper, who improved the book with her editorial skill and valuable ideas, and to Donna Gridley, Senior Editor, who kept the project on track and on time and provided useful input. Other people at Course Technology who deserve credit are Daphne Barbas, Production Editor; Foxxe Editorial, copyeditors; and John Bosco and his team of QA testers. Feedback is an important part of writing any book, and thanks go to the following reviewers for their ideas and comments: John Chenoweth, East Tennessee State University; Romona Coveny, Patrick Henry Community College; Joseph Farrelly, Palomer College; Ralph Hooper, University of Alabama; Stuart Varden, Pace University; and Dr. Ahmed Zaki, College of William and Mary. I would also like to thank Shirley Kaiser for her assistance and artist's eye in creating the case for DHTML Tutorial 5. Finally, I want to thank my wife Joan for her encouragement, suggestions, and photographs (which I liberally used in creating my sample Web pages!) and my five sons: John Paul, Thomas, Peter, Michael, and Stephen, to whom this book is dedicated.

Patrick Carey

TABLE OF CONTENTS

Tutorial 2   **DHTML 2.01**

Working with Dynamic Content and Styles

Creating a Product Information Web Site

Tutorial 3 — DHTML 3.01

Working with Special Effects

Creating Rollovers, Menus, Filters, and Transitions

Tutorial 4 — DHTML 4.01

Working with the Event Model

Creating a Drag-and-Drop Shopping Cart for Games Etc.

Reference Window List

Reference Window List

Design Window List

Tutorial Tips

These tutorials will help you learn about creating Web pages using HTML The tutorials are designed to be worked through at a computer. Each tutorial is divided into sessions. Watch for the session headings, such as Session 1.1 and Session 1.2. Each session is designed to be completed in about 45 minutes, but take as much time as you need. It's also a good idea to take a break between sessions.

Before you begin, read the following questions and answers. They will help you use the tutorials.

Where do I start?

Each tutorial begins with a case, which sets the scene for the tutorial and gives you background information to help you understand what you will be doing. Read the case before you go to the lab. In the lab, begin with the first session of a tutorial.

How do I know what to do on the computer?

Each session contains steps that you will perform on the computer to learn how to use HTML. Read the text that introduces each series of steps. The steps you need to do at a computer are numbered and are set against a shaded background. Read each step carefully and completely before you try it.

How do I know if I did the step correctly?

As you work, compare your computer screen with the corresponding figure in the tutorial. Don't worry if your screen display is somewhat different from the figure. The important parts of the screen display are labeled in each figure. Check to make sure these parts are on your screen.

What if I make a mistake?

Don't worry about making mistakes—they are part of the learning process. Paragraphs labeled "TROUBLE?" identify common problems and explain how to get back on track. Follow the steps in a TROUBLE? paragraph only if you are having the problem described. If you run into other problems:

- Carefully consider the current state of your system, the position of the pointer, and any messages on the screen.

- Complete the sentence, "Now I want to…" Be specific, because identifying your goal will help you rethink the steps you need to take to reach that goal.

- If you are working on a particular piece of software, consult the Help system.

- If the suggestions above don't solve your problem, consult your technical support person for assistance.

How do I use the Reference Windows?

Reference Windows summarize the procedures you will learn in the tutorial steps. Do not complete the actions in the Reference Windows when you are working through the tutorial. Instead, refer to the Reference Windows while you are working on the assignments at the end of the tutorial.

How can I test my understanding of the material I learned in the tutorial?

At the end of each session, you can answer the Quick Check questions. The answers for the Quick Checks are at the end of that tutorial.

After you have completed the entire tutorial, you should complete the Review Assignments and Case Problems. They are carefully structured so that you will review what you have learned and then apply your knowledge to new situations.

Before you begin the tutorials, you should know the basics about your computer's operating system. You should also know how to use the menus, dialog boxes, Help system, and My Computer.

Now that you've read Tutorial Tips, you are ready to begin.

New Perspectives on

CREATING WEB PAGES WITH HTML,

2ⁿᵈ Edition

Read This Before You Begin

To the Student

Data Disks

To complete the Level I tutorials, Review Assignments, and Case Problems in this book, you need two Data Disks. Your instructor will either provide you with Data Disks or ask you to make your own.

If you are making your own Data Disks, you will need two blank, formatted high-density disks. You will need to copy a set of folders from a file server or standalone computer or the Web onto your disks. Your instructor will tell you which computer, drive letter, and folders contain the files you need. You could also download the files by going to http://www.course.com, clicking Data Disk Files, and following the instructions on the screen.

The following table shows you which folders go on your disks, so that you will have enough disk space to complete all the tutorials, Review Assignments, and Case Problems:

Data Disk 1

Write this on the disk label:
Data Disk 1: Level 1 Tutorial 1

Put these folders on the disk:
Tutorial.01

Data Disk 2

Write this on the disk label:
Data Disk 2: Level 1 Tutorial 2

Put these folders on the disk:
Tutorial.02

When you begin each tutorial, be sure you are using the correct Data Disk. See the inside front or inside back cover of this book for more information on Data Disk Files, or ask your instructor or technical support person for assistance.

Course Lab

Tutorial 1 features an interactive Course Lab to help you understand Web page concepts. There are Lab Assignments at the end of the tutorial that relate to this Lab. To start the Lab, Click the Start button on the Windows taskbar, point to Programs, point to Course Labs, point to New Perspectives Applications, and click creating Web Pages: HTML.

Using Your Own Computer

If you are going to work through this book using your own computer, you need:

- **Computer System** A text editor and a Web browser (preferably Netscape Navigator or Internet Explorer, versions 3.0 or higher) must be installed on your computer. If you are using a non-standard browser, it must support frames and HTML 3.2 or higher. Most of the tutorials can be completed with just a text editor and a Web browser. However, to complete the last sections of Tutorial 2, you will need an Internet connection and software that connects you to the Internet.

- **Data Disks** Ask your instructor or lab manager for details on how to get the Data Disk. You will not be able to complete the tutorials or exercises in this book using your own computer until you have Data Disks. The Data Disk Files may be obtained electronically over the Internet. See the inside back cover of this book for more details.

Visit Our World Wide Web Site

Additional materials designed especially for you are available on the World Wide Web. Go to http://www.course.com. For example, see our Student Online Companion that contains additional coverage of selected topics in the text. These topics are indicated in the text by an online companion icon located in the left margin.

To the Instructor

The Data Disk Files are available on the Instructor's Resource Kit for this title. Follow the instructions in the Help file on the CD-ROM to install the programs to your network or standalone computer. For information on creating Data Disks, see the "To the Student" section above.

You are granted a license to copy the Data Disk Files to any computer or computer network used by students who have purchased this book.

LAB

Web Pages & HTML

CREATING A WEB PAGE

Web Fundamentals and HTML

CASE

Creating an Online Resume

Mary Taylor just graduated from Colorado State University with a master's degree in telecommunications. Mary wants to explore as many employment avenues as possible, so she decides to post a copy of her resume on the World Wide Web. Creating an online resume offers Mary several advantages. The Web's skyrocketing popularity gives Mary the potential of reaching a large and varied audience. She can continually update an online resume, offering details on her latest projects and jobs. An online resume also gives a prospective employer the opportunity to look at her work history in more detail than is normal with a paper resume, because Mary can include links to other relevant documents. Mary asks you to help her create an online resume. You're happy to do so because it's something you wanted to learn anyway. After all, you'll be creating your own resume soon enough.

SESSION 1.1

In this session you will learn the basics of how the World Wide Web operates. Then you will begin to explore the code used to create Web documents.

Introducing the World Wide Web

The **Internet** is a structure made up of millions of interconnected computers whose users can communicate with each other and share information. The physical structure of the Internet uses fiber-optic cables, satellites, phone lines, and other telecommunications media that send data back and forth, as Figure 1-1 shows. Computers that are linked together form a **network**. Any user whose computer can be linked to a network that has Internet access can join the worldwide Internet community.

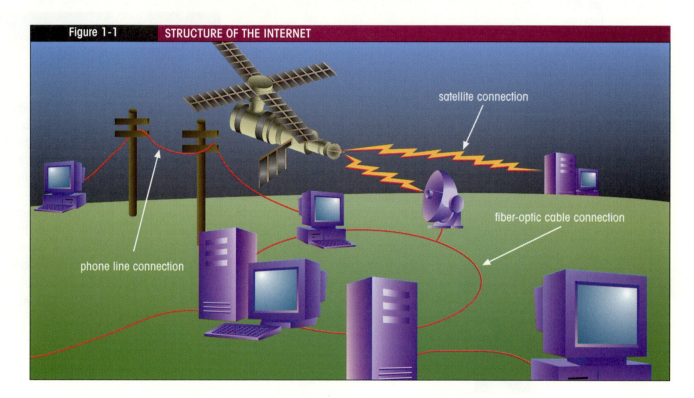

Figure 1-1   STRUCTURE OF THE INTERNET

satellite connection

fiber-optic cable connection

phone line connection

Before 1989, anyone with Internet access could take advantage of the opportunities the Internet offered, but not without some problems. New users often found their introduction to the Internet an unpleasant one. Many Internet tools required you to master a bewildering array of terms, acronyms, and commands before you could begin navigating the Internet. Navigation itself was a hit-and-miss proposition. A computer in Bethesda might have information on breast cancer, but if you didn't know that computer existed and how to reach it, the Internet offered few tools to help you get there. What Internet users needed was a tool that would be easy to use and would allow quick access to any computer on the Internet, regardless of its location. This tool would prove to be the World Wide Web.

The Development of the World Wide Web

The **World Wide Web** organizes the Internet's vast resources to give you easy access to information. In 1989, Timothy Berners-Lee and other researchers at the CERN nuclear research facility near Geneva, Switzerland, laid the foundation of the World Wide Web, or the Web. They wanted to create an information system that made it easy for researchers to locate and share data and that required minimal training and support. They developed a system of hypertext documents that made it very easy to move from one source of information to another. A **hypertext document** is an electronic file that contains elements that you can select, usually by clicking a mouse, to open another document.

Hypertext offers a new way of progressing through a series of documents. When you read a book, you follow a linear progression, reading one page after another. With hypertext, you progress through pages in whatever way is best suited to your goals. Hypertext lets you skip from one topic to another, following a path of information that interests you. Figure 1-2 shows how topics could be related in a hypertext fashion, as opposed to a linear fashion.

| Figure 1-2 | LINEAR VS. HYPERTEXT DOCUMENTS |

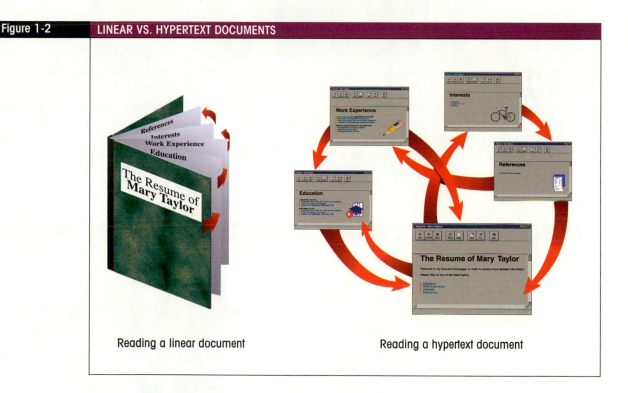

Reading a linear document   Reading a hypertext document

You might already be familiar with two common sources of hypertext: Windows Help files and Macintosh HyperCard stacks. In these programs, you move from one topic to another by clicking or highlighting a phrase or keyword known as a **link**. Clicking a link takes you to another section of the document, or it might take you to another document entirely. Figure 1-3 shows how you might navigate a link in a Help file.

Figure 1-3 **CLICKING A LINK IN A HELP FILE**

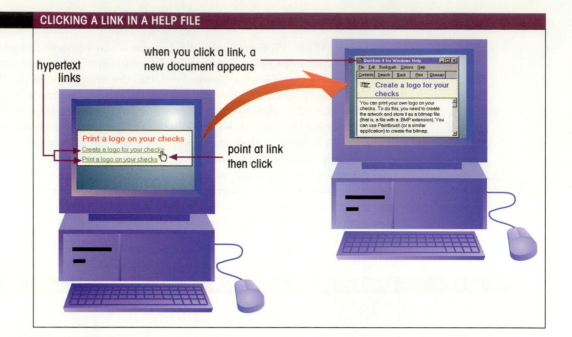

Hypertext as implemented by the CERN group involves jumping from one document to another on computers scattered all over the world. In Figure 1-4, you are working at a computer in Canada that shows a hypertext document on traveling in the United States. This document contains a link to another document located on a computer in Washington, D.C., about the National Park Service. That document in turn contains a link to a document located in California on Yosemite National Park.

Figure 1-4 **NAVIGATING HYPERTEXT DOCUMENTS ON THE WEB**

You move from document to document (and computer to computer) by simply clicking links. This approach makes navigating the Internet easy. It frees you from having to know anything about the document's location. The link could open a document on your computer or a document on a computer in South Africa. You might never notice the difference.

Your experience with the Web is not limited to reading text. Web documents, also known as **pages**, can contain graphics, video clips, sound clips, and, more recently, programs that you can run directly from the page. Moreover, as Figure 1-5 shows, Web pages can display text in a wide variety of fonts and formats. A Web page is not only a source of information, it can also be a work of art.

| Figure 1-5 | WEB PAGE FEATURING INTERESTING FONTS, GRAPHICS, AND LAYOUT |

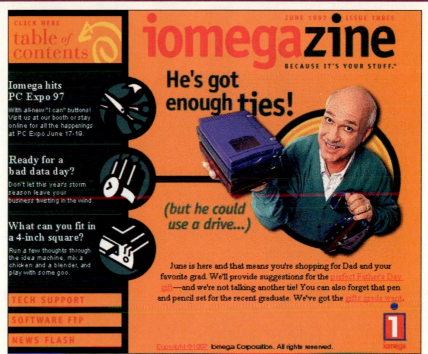

A final feature that contributes to the Web's popularity is that it gives users the ability to easily create their own Web pages. This is in marked contrast to other Internet tools, which often require the expertise of a computer systems manager. Figure 1-6 illustrates the growth of the world online population. In a space of six years, the online population is projected to more than triple in size. Is there any doubt why Mary sees the Web as a worthwhile place to post a resume?

Figure 1-6 GROWTH OF THE WORLD ONLINE POPULATION

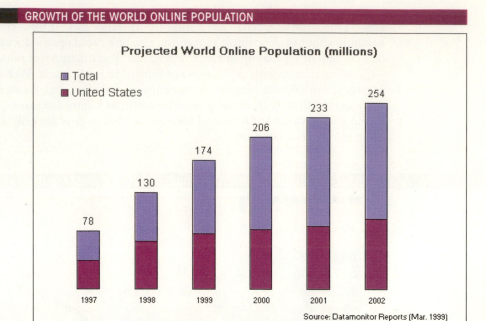

Projected World Online Population (millions)

■ Total
■ United States

Source: Datamonitor Reports (Mar. 1999)

Web Servers and Web Browsers

The World Wide Web has the two components, shown in Figure 1-7. The **Web server** is the computer that stores the Web page that users access. The **Web browser** is the software program that accesses the Web document and displays its contents on the user's computer. The browser can locate a page on a server anywhere in the world and display it for you to see.

Figure 1-7 USING A BROWSER TO VIEW A WEB DOCUMENT ON A SERVER

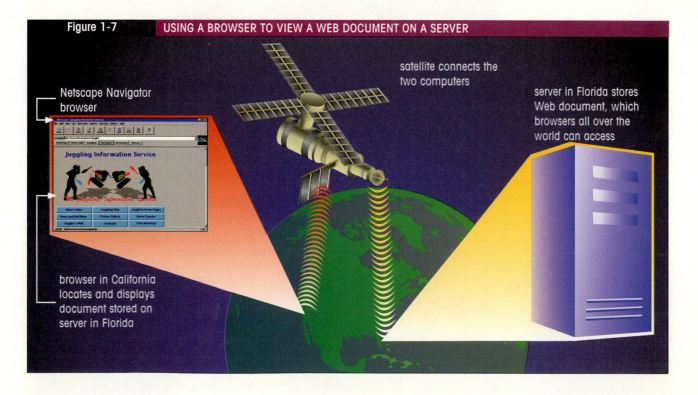

Netscape Navigator browser

satellite connects the two computers

server in Florida stores Web document, which browsers all over the world can access

browser in California locates and displays document stored on server in Florida

Browsers can either be text-based, like the Lynx browser found on UNIX machines, or graphical, like the popular Internet Explorer and Netscape browsers. With a **text-based browser**, you navigate the Web by typing commands; with a **graphical browser** you can use the mouse to move from page to page. Browsers are available for virtually every computer platform. No matter what kind of computer you have, you can probably use it to navigate the Web.

HTML: The Language of the Web

Web pages are written in a language called the **Hypertext Markup Language** or **HTML**. A **markup language** is a language used to describe the content and format of documents. HTML is only one example of a markup language. HTML has its roots in the **Standard Generalized Markup Language (SGML)**, a language used for large-scale documents. SGML though proved to be too cumbersome and difficult for use on the Internet, and thus HTML was created based on the principles of SGML.

The success of the World Wide Web is due in no small part to HTML. HTML allows Web authors to create documents that can be displayed across different operating systems and the HTML code is straight-forward enough that even non-programmers can learn to use it. Millions of Web sites are based on HTML, and there is every indication that HTML will continue to be the dominant language of the Web for a long time to come.

HTML formats a document in very general way. If you've used a word processor, you know that you control the appearance of text by the font you choose (such as Arial or Times Roman), or by an attribute (such as bold, or italic). Basic HTML doesn't describe how text looks. Instead it uses a **tag** describing the purpose that the text has in the document. Text appearing in the document's heading is marked with a heading tag. Text appearing in a bulleted list is marked with a list tag. A Web browser interprets these tags to determine how it will render the text. One browser might apply a Times Roman font to the text in the document's heading, while another browser might apply an Arial Font. Figure 1-8 shows how the same HTML file might appear on two different browsers.

| Figure 1-8 | TWO DIFFERENT BROWSERS DISPLAYING THE SAME HTML FILE |

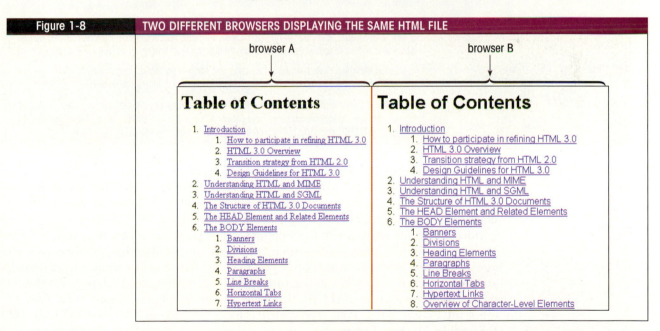

There are a couple of reasons to put the formatting choices in the control of the browser. Web pages must be **portable**, so that they can work well with all kinds of operating systems and applications. Because different operating systems and applications differ in how they code and render information, it would be a daunting task to create a page for all users. Portability frees Web page authors from this concern. HTML can also work with a wide range of devices, from clunky teletypes to high-end workstations. It also works with non-visual medium such as speech software. Web pages can even be rendered in Braille.

Of course portability does limit one's ability to exactly define the Web page's appearance. For this reason, HTML has allowed the use of **style sheets**, in which the Web page author can define the fonts and formats the Web browser should apply to the document's text. Style sheets are a topic that should be mastered only after one has become familiar with basic HTML.

A second reason to put the formatting choices in the browser's control is speed. Specifying the page's exact appearance could dramatically increase both the size of the document file and the time required to retrieve it. It is much quicker to render the document on the user's own computer. The downside of this approach is that you cannot be sure exactly how each browser and browser version will render your document. For this reason, it is important that you test your document code on several different browsers, and if possible, several different operating systems.

Versions of HTML

HTML has a set of rules, called **syntax**, that control how document code is to be written. There must be a consensus among the creators of Web browsers on these rules, or else there would be no guarantee that documents would be rendered correctly. It wouldn't do Mary much good to create a stunning online resume, unreadable by potential employers. This consensus appears as a set of **standards** or **specifications** developed by a consortium of Web developers called the **World Wide Web Consortium**, or more commonly known as the **W3C**. Figure 1-9 describes a history of the various versions of HTML that have been released by the W3C. For more information on the W3C, see their home page at http://www.w3c.org.

Figure 1-9		VERSIONS OF HTML
VERSION	**DATE**	**DESCRIPTION**
HTML 1.00	1989–1994	The first public version of HTML, which included browser support for inline images and text controls
HTML 2.00	1995	The version supported by all graphical browsers, including Netscape Communicator, Internet Explorer, and Mosaic. It supported interactive form elements such as option buttons and text boxes. A document written to follow 2.0 specifications would be readable by most browsers on the Internet.
HTML 3.20	1997	This version included more support for creating and formatting tables, and expanded the options for interactive form elements. It also allows for the creation of complex mathematical equations.
HTML 4.01	1999	This version adds support for style sheets, to give Web authors greater control over page layout. It adds new features to tables and forms and provides support for international features. This version also expands HTML's scripting ability and support for multimedia elements.

The world of Web browsers is a competitive one however, and over the years each browser has added **extensions** to HTML, supporting new features and tags. Netscape and Internet Explorer have added the most extensions to HTML, and often these extensions have been adopted in the next set of HTML specifications released by the W3C. These extensions have provided Web page authors with more options, but at the expense of fragmenting Web page development. Before using an extension, the Web page author has to determine which browser and browser versions support it, and then the author has to create a workaround for browsers that do not support the extension. All of this complicates Web page development, and betrays the properties of HTML that made it so integral to the success of the Web.

For this reason, future Web development is focusing more on XML and XHTML. **XML (Extensible Markup Language)** is used for developing customized document structures. With XML, Web authors can create their own tags and attributes for their documents. XML combined with style sheets, can provide the same functionality as HTML, with greater flexibility. **XHTML (Extensible HyperText Markup Language)**, is a stricter and cleaner version of HTML, designed to overcome some of the problems of competing HTML standards introduced by the various browsers. Any Web page written in XHTML will be automatically compatible with HTML 4.01.

Tools for Creating HTML Documents

HTML documents are simple text files. The only software package you need to create them is a basic text editor such as the Windows Notepad program. If you want a software package to do some of the work of creating an HTML document, you can use an HTML converter or an HTML editor.

An **HTML converter** takes text in one format and converts it to HTML code. For example, you can create the source document with a word processor such as Microsoft Word, and then have the converter save the document as an HTML file. Converters have several advantages. They free you from the occasionally laborious task of typing HTML code, and, because the conversion is automated, you do not have to worry about typographical errors ruining your code. Finally, you can create the source document using a software package that you might be more familiar with. Be aware that a converter has some limitations. As HTML specifications are updated and new extensions created, you will have to wait for the next version of the converter, to take advantage of these features. Moreover, no converter can support all HTML features, so for anything but the simplest Web page, you still have to work with HTML.

An **HTML editor** helps you create an HTML file by inserting HTML codes for you as you work. HTML editors can save you a lot of work. They have many of the same advantages and limitations as converters. They do let you set up your Web page quickly, but to create the finished document, you often still have to work directly with the HTML code.

Session 1.1 QUICK CHECK

1. What is hypertext?

2. What is a Web server? A Web browser? Describe how they work together.

3. What is HTML?

4. How do HTML documents differ from documents created with a word processor such as Word or WordPerfect?

5. What are the advantages of letting Web browsers determine the appearance of Web pages?

6. What are HTML extensions? What are some advantages and disadvantages of using extensions?

7. What software program do you need to create an HTML document?

SESSION 1.2

In this session you begin entering the text that will form the basis of your Web page. You will insert the appropriate HTML codes, creating a simple Web page that outlines Mary's work experience and qualifications.

Creating an HTML Document

It's always a good idea to plan the appearance of your Web page before you start writing code. In her final semester, Mary developed a paper resume that she distributed at campus job fairs. Half her work is already done, because she can use the paper resume as her model. Figure 1-10 shows Mary's hardcopy resume.

Figure 1-10 MARY'S PAPER RESUME

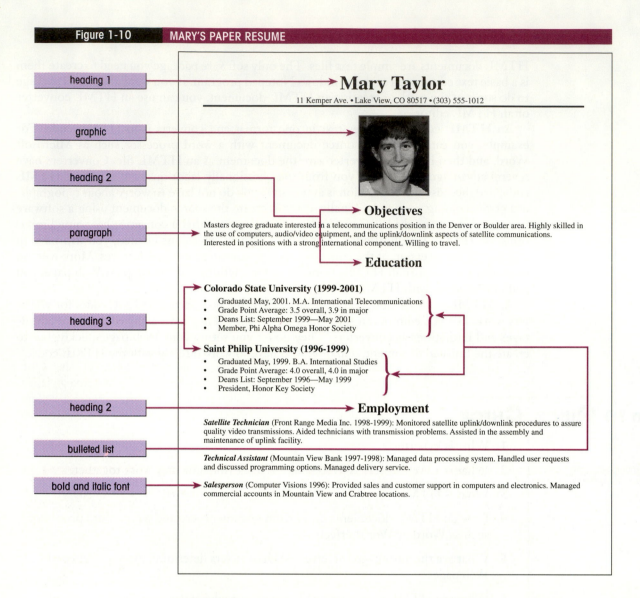

Mary's paper resume includes several features that she would like you to implement in the online version. A heading at the top prominently displays her name in a large font. Beneath the heading is her photo. Mary's resume is divided into three sections: Objectives, Education, and Employment. Within the Objectives section, a paragraph describes Mary's interests and future goals. Within the Education section, two smaller headings name the two universities she attended. Under each of these headings, a bulleted list details her accomplishments. The Employment section describes each position she's held, with the official title in boldface and italics. Mary's paper resume has three heading levels, bulleted lists, formatted characters, and graphics. When she creates her online resume with HTML, she wants to include these features. As you help Mary create this document for the World Wide Web, you will probably want to refer to Figure 1-10 periodically as the page develops.

HTML Syntax

An HTML document has two elements: document content and tags. **Document content** are those parts of the document that you want the user to see, such as text and graphics.

The HTML syntax for creating the kinds of features that Mary wants in her page follows a very basic structure. You apply a tag to document content using the syntax:

```
<Tag Name Properties> Document Content </Tag Name>
```

You can always identify a tag by the brackets (< >) that enclose the tag name. Some tags can include **properties**, or additional information placed within the brackets that controls how the tag is used. Tags usually come in pairs: the **opening tag** is the first tag, which tells the browser to turn on the feature and apply it to the document content that follows. The browser applies the feature until it encounters the **closing tag**, which turns off the feature. Note that closing tags are identified by the slash (/) that precedes the tag name. Not every type of tag has an opening and closing tag. Some tags are known as **one-sided tags** because they require only the opening tag. **Two-sided tags** require both opening and closing tags.

For example, look at the first line of Mary's resume, the name Mary Taylor, in Figure 1-10. You could format this line with the two-sided HTML tag as follows:

```
<H1 ALIGN=CENTER>Mary Taylor</H1>
```

Here the <H1 ALIGN=CENTER > opening tag tells the browser that the text that follows, Mary Taylor, should be formatted with the H1 style (H1 stands for Heading 1; you'll learn what this means later). This tag also includes a property, the **alignment property** (ALIGN), which tells the browser how to align the text: in this case, centered. After the opening tag comes the content, Mary Taylor. The </H1> tag signals the browser to turn off the H1 style. Remember that each browser determines the exact effect of the H1 tag. One browser might apply a 14-point Times Roman bold font to Mary's text, whereas another browser might use 18-point italic Arial—but in each case, the font would be appropriately larger than the normal font of the document. Figure 1-11 shows how three different browsers might interpret this line of HTML code.

| **Figure 1-11** | **EXAMPLES OF HOW DIFFERENT BROWSERS MIGHT INTERPRET THE HTML <H1> TAG** |

BROWSER INTERPRETING THE H1 TAG	**APPEARANCE OF THE DOCUMENT CONTENT**
Browser A	Mary Taylor
Browser B	**Mary Taylor**
Browser C	*Mary Taylor*

Tags are not case sensitive. That means that typing "<H1>" has the same effect as typing "<h1>". Many Web authors like to use only uppercase for tags, to distinguish tags from document content. We'll follow that convention throughout this book.

Creating Basic Tags

When you create your Web page, you first enter tags that indicate the markup language used in the document, identify the document's key sections, and assign the page a title.

In the steps that follow, type the text exactly as you see it. The text after the steps explains each line. To start entering code, you need a basic text editor such as Notepad or WordPad.

To start creating an HTML file:

1. Place your Data Disk in drive A.

   TROUBLE? If you don't have a Data Disk, you need to get one. Your instructor will either give you one or ask you to make your own. See the Read This Before You Begin page at the beginning of the tutorials for instructions.

   TROUBLE? If your Data Disk won't fit in drive A, try drive B. If it fits in drive B, substitute drive B for drive A in every tutorial.

2. Open a text editor on your computer, and then open a new document.

   TROUBLE? If you don't know how to locate, start, or use the text editor on your system, ask your instructor or technical support person for help.

3. Type the following lines of code into your document. Press the **Enter** key after each line (twice for a blank line).

```
<HTML>
<HEAD>
<TITLE>The Resume of Mary Taylor</TITLE>
</HEAD>

<BODY>
</BODY>

</HTML>
```

4. Save the file as **Resume.htm** in the Tutorial.01 folder on your Data Disk, but do not close your text editor. The text you typed should look something like Figure 1-12.

Figure 1-12	INITIAL HTML TAGS

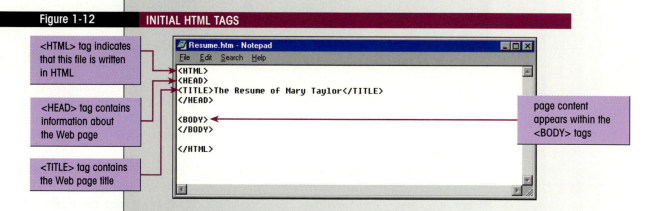

<HTML> tag indicates that this file is written in HTML

<HEAD> tag contains information about the Web page

<TITLE> tag contains the Web page title

page content appears within the <BODY> tags

TROUBLE? If you don't know how to save a file on your Data Disk, ask your instructor or technical support person for assistance.

TROUBLE? Don't worry if your screen doesn't look exactly like Figure 1-12. The text editor shown in the figures is the Windows Notepad editor. Your text editor might look very different. Just make sure you entered the text correctly.

TROUBLE? If you are using the Windows Notepad text editor to create your HTML file, make sure you don't save the file using the text document type (.txt), which Notepad automatically adds to the filename. This renders the file unreadable to the Netscape Navigator browser, which requires an .htm or .html file extension. So make sure you save the file using the All Files (*.*) type, and then add the .htm or .html extension to the filename yourself.

The opening and closing HTML tags bracket all the remaining code you'll enter in the document. This indicates to a browser that the page is written in HTML. While you don't have to include this tag, it is necessary if the file is to be read by another SGML application. Moreover, it is considered good style to include it.

The <HEAD> tag is used where you enter information about the Web page itself. One such piece of information is the title of the page, which appears in the title bar of the Web browser. This information is entered using the <TITLE> tag. The title in this example is "The Resume of Mary Taylor".

Finally, the portion of the document that Web users will see is contained between the <BODY> tags. At this point, the page is blank, with no text or graphics. You'll add those later. The <HEAD> and <BODY> tags are not strictly required, but you should include them to better organize your document and make its code more readable to others. The extra space before and after the BODY tags is also not required, but it will make your code easier to view as you add more features to it.

Displaying Your HTML Files

As you continue adding to Mary's HTML file, you should occasionally display the formatted page with your Web browser to verify that there are no syntax errors or other problems. You might even want to view the results on several browsers to check for differences between one browser and another. In the steps and figures that follow, the Internet Explorer browser is used to display Mary's resume page as it gradually unfolds. If you are using a different browser, ask your instructor how to view local files (those located on your own computer rather than on the Web).

To view the beginning of Mary's resume page:

1. Start your browser. You do not need to be connected to the Internet to view a file loaded on your computer.

    TROUBLE? If you try to start your browser and are not connected to the Internet, you might get a warning message. Netscape Navigator, for example, gives a warning message telling you that it was unable to create a network socket connection. Click OK to ignore the message and continue.

2. After your browser loads its home page, click **File** on the menu bar and then click **Open**.

    TROUBLE? If you're using Netscape Navigator, you will have to use a different command to open the file from your Data Disk. Talk to your instructor or technical support person to find out how to open the file.

3. Locate the **Resume.htm** file that you saved in the Tutorial.01 folder on your Data Disk, and then click Open. Your browser displays Mary's file, as shown in Figure 1-13. Note that the page title, which you typed earlier between the <TITLE> tags, appears in the browser's title bar.

| Figure 1-13 | THE INITIAL HTML FILE IN INTERNET EXPLORER |

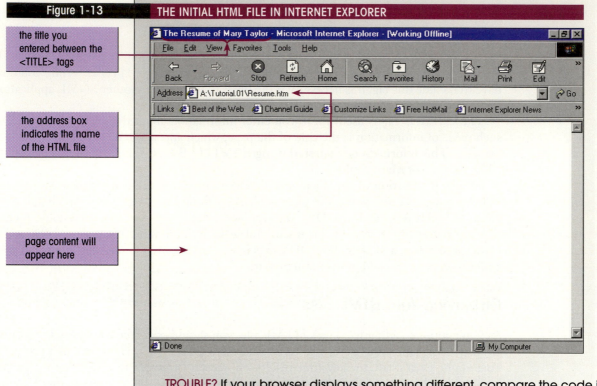

the title you entered between the <TITLE> tags

the address box indicates the name of the HTML file

page content will appear here

TROUBLE? If your browser displays something different, compare the code in your file to the code shown in Figure 1-12, and correct any errors.

4. Return to your text editor. You can leave your browser open.

Creating Headers, Paragraphs, and Lists

Now that the basic structure of Mary's page is set, you can start filling in the page content. One place to start is the headers for the various sections of her document. Her document needs a header for the entire page and headers for each of three sections: Objectives, Education, and Employment. The Education section has two additional headers that provide information about the two universities she attended. You can create all these headers using HTML heading tags.

Creating Header Tags

HTML supports six levels of headers, numbered <H1> through <H6>, with <H1> being the largest and most prominent, and <H6> being the smallest. Headers (even the smallest) appear in a larger font than normal text, and some headers are boldface. The general syntax for a header tag is:

```
<Hy>Heading Text</Hy>
```

where y is a header numbered 1 through 6.

Figure 1-14 illustrates the general appearance of the six header styles. Your browser might use slightly different fonts and sizes.

Figure 1-14	SIX HEADER LEVELS

This is an H1 Header

This is an H2 Header

This is an H3 Header

This is an H4 Header

This is an H5 Header

This is an H6 Header

REFERENCE WINDOW   **RW**

Creating a Header Tag
- Open the HTML file with your text editor.
- Type <H*y*> where *y* is the header number you want to use.
- If you want to use a special alignment, specify the alignment property setting after *y* and before the closing symbol, >.
- Type the text that you want to appear in the header.
- Type </H*y*> to turn off the header tag.

Starting with HTML 3.2, the header tag can contain additional properties, one of which is the alignment property. Mary wants some headers centered on the page, so you'll take advantage of this property. Although Mary's address is not really header text, you decide to format it with an <H5> tag, because you want it to stand out a little from normal paragraphed text.

To add headings to the resume file:

1. Return to your text editor, and then open the **Resume.htm** file, if it is not already open.

2. Type the following text between the <BODY> and </BODY> tags (type the address and phone number all on one line, as shown in Figure 1-15):

   <H1 ALIGN=CENTER>Mary Taylor</H1>

   <H5 ALIGN=CENTER>11 Kemper Ave. Lake View, CO 80517 (303) 555-1012</H5>

<H2 ALIGN=CENTER>Objectives</H2>

<H2 ALIGN=CENTER>Education</H2>

<H3>Colorado State University (1999-2001)</H3>

<H3>Saint Philip University (1996-1999)</H3>

<H2 ALIGN=CENTER>Employment</H2>

The revised code is shown in figure 1-15. To make it easier to follow the changes to the HTML file, new and altered text is highlighted in red. This will not be the case in your own text files.

Figure 1-15 ENTERING HEADER TAGS

```
<BODY>
<H1 ALIGN=CENTER>Mary Taylor</H1>
<H5 ALIGN=CENTER>11 Kemper Ave. Lake View, CO 80517 (303) 555-1012</H5>
<H2 ALIGN=CENTER>Objectives</H2>
<H2 ALIGN=CENTER>Education</H2>
<H3>Colorado State University (1999-2001)</H3>
<H3>Saint Philip University (1996-1999)</H3>
<H2 ALIGN=CENTER>Employment</H2>
</BODY>
```

3. Save the revised Resume.htm file in the Tutorial.01 folder on your Data Disk. You can leave your text editor open.

The section headers all use the ALIGN=CENTER property to center the text on the page. The <H3> tags used for the two university headers, however, do not include that property and will be left-justified because that is the default alignment setting. If a browser that displays Mary's page does not support HTML 3.2 (or above) or does not support the alignment property through an extension, the headers will appear, but all of them will be left-justified.

To display the revised Resume.htm file:

1. Return to your Web browser.

2. If the previous version of the file still appears in the browser window, click **View** on the menu bar, and then click **Refresh**. If you are using Netscape, you will need to click **View** and then click **Reload**.

The updated Resume.htm file looks like Figure 1-16.

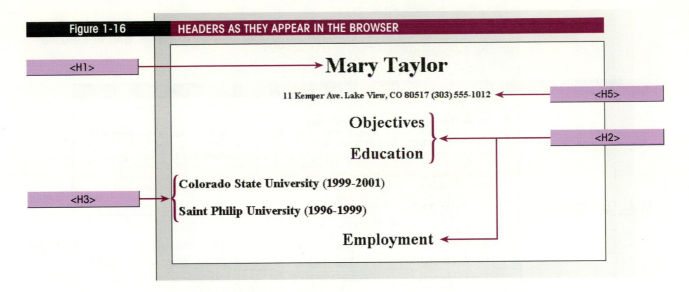

Figure 1-16 | **HEADERS AS THEY APPEAR IN THE BROWSER**

Entering Paragraph Text

The next thing that you have to do is enter information for each section. If your paragraph does not require any formatting, you can enter the text without tags.

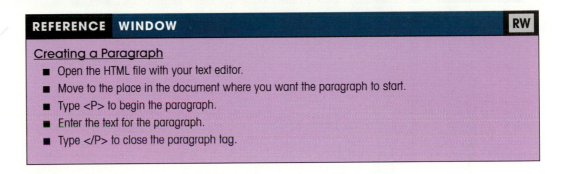

REFERENCE WINDOW | **RW**

<u>Creating a Paragraph</u>
- Open the HTML file with your text editor.
- Move to the place in the document where you want the paragraph to start.
- Type <P> to begin the paragraph.
- Enter the text for the paragraph.
- Type </P> to close the paragraph tag.

Mary's career objective, which appears just below the Objectives heading, does not require formatting, so you can enter that as paragraph text.

To enter paragraph text:

1. Return to your text editor, and then reopen the **Resume.htm** file, if it is not already open.

2. Type the following text directly after the line of code that specifies the Objectives heading:

   Masters degree graduate interested in a telecommunications position in the Denver or Boulder area. Highly skilled in the use of computers, audio/video equipment, and the uplink/downlink aspects of satellite communications. Interested in positions with a strong international component. Willing to travel.

Your text should be placed between the Objectives head and the Education head, as shown in Figure 1-17. Check your work for mistakes, and edit the file as necessary.

Figure 1-17 **ENTERING PARAGRAPH TEXT**

```
<BODY>
<H1 ALIGN=CENTER>Mary Taylor</H1>
<H5 ALIGN=CENTER>11 Kemper Ave. Lake View, CO 80517 (303) 555-1012</H5>
<H2 ALIGN=CENTER>Objectives</H2>
Masters degree graduate interested in a telecommunications position in
the Denver or Boulder area. Highly skilled in the use of computers,
audio/video equipment and the uplink/downlink aspects of satellite
communications. Interested in positions with a strong international
component. Willing to travel.
<H2 ALIGN=CENTER>Education</H2>
```

TROUBLE? If you are using a text editor like Notepad, the text might not wrap to the next line automatically. You might need to select the Word Wrap command on the Edit menu, or a similar command, so you can see all the text on your screen.

3. Save the changes you made to the Resume.htm file.

4. Return to your Web browser, and then reopen the **Resume.htm** file to view the text you've added. See Figure 1-18.

Figure 1-18 **PARAGRAPH TEXT IN THE BROWSER**

Mary Taylor

11 Kemper Ave. Lake View, CO 80517 (303) 555-1012

Objectives

Masters degree graduate interested in a telecommunications position in the Denver or Boulder area. Highly skilled in the use of computers, audio/video equipment, and the uplink/downlink aspects of satellite communications. Interested in positions with a strong international component. Willing to travel.

Education

5. Now enter the Employment paragraph text by returning to your text editor and reopening the **Resume.htm file**, if needed.

6. Go to the end of the file, and, in the line before the final </BODY> tag, type the following text:

Satellite Technician (Front Range Media Inc. 1998-1999): Monitored satellite uplink/downlink procedures to assure quality video transmissions. Aided technicians with transmission problems. Assisted in the assembly and maintenance of uplink facility.

Technical Assistant (Mountain View Bank 1997-1998): Managed data processing system. Handled user requests and discussed programming options. Managed delivery service.

Salesperson (Computer Visions 1996): Sales and customer support in computers and electronics. Managed commercial accounts in Mountain View and Crabtree locations.

Figure 1-19 shows the new code in Mary's resume file.

Figure 1-19 | **ENTERING EMPLOYMENT TEXT**

```
<H2 ALIGN=CENTER>Education</H2>
<H3>Colorado State University (1999-2001)</H3>
<H3>Saint Philip University (1996-1999)</H3>
<H2 ALIGN=CENTER>Employment</H2>
Satellite Technician (Front Range Media Inc. 1998-1999): Monitored
satellite uplink/downlink procedures to assure quality transmissions.
Aided technicians with transmission problems. Assisted in the assembly
and maintenance of uplink facility.

Technical Assistant (Mountain View Bank 1997-1998): Managed data
processing system. Handled user requests and discussed programming
options. Managed delivery service.

Salesperson (Computer Visions 1996): Sales and customer support in
computers and electronics. Managed commercial accounts in Mountain View
and Crabtree locations.
</BODY>
```

employment history →

7. Save the changes you've made to the file.

8. Return to your Web browser, and then reopen the **Resume.htm** file.

9. Scroll down to see how the new text looks (see Figure 1-20).

Figure 1-20 | **THE EMPLOYMENT HISTORY DISPLAYED BY THE BROWSER**

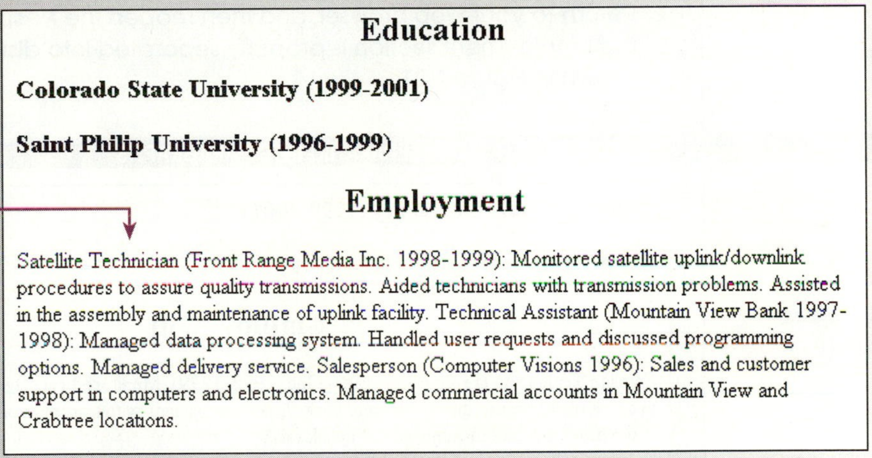

Education

Colorado State University (1999-2001)

Saint Philip University (1996-1999)

Employment

employment history is
not separated into
paragraphs →

Satellite Technician (Front Range Media Inc. 1998-1999): Monitored satellite uplink/downlink procedures to assure quality transmissions. Aided technicians with transmission problems. Assisted in the assembly and maintenance of uplink facility. Technical Assistant (Mountain View Bank 1997-1998): Managed data processing system. Handled user requests and discussed programming options. Managed delivery service. Salesperson (Computer Visions 1996): Sales and customer support in computers and electronics. Managed commercial accounts in Mountain View and Crabtree locations.

To your surprise, the text you typed into the HTML file looks nothing like what appeared on the browser, as you can see from Figure 1-20. Instead of being separated by blank lines, the three paragraphs are running together. What went wrong?

The problem here is that HTML formats text only through the use of tags. HTML ignores such things as extra blank spaces, blank lines, or tabs. As far as HTML is concerned, the following three lines of code are identical, so a browser interprets and displays each line just like the others, ignoring the extra spaces and lines:

```
<H1>To be or not to be. That is the question.</H1>
<H1>To be or not to be.   That is the question.</H1>
<H1>To be or not to be.
            That is the question.</H1>
```

At first glance, the Employment section seemed not to need any formatting; however, each paragraph needs to be separated by a blank line. To add this space between paragraphs, you need to use the **paragraph tag, <P>**, which adds a blank paragraph (the extra line you need) before text to separate it from any text that precedes it.

To add paragraph tags for blank lines:

1. Return to your text editor and the Resume.htm file.

2. Modify the Employment text, bracketing each paragraph between a **<P>** and **</P>** tag, so that the lines now read:

<P>Satellite Technician (Front Range Media Inc. 1998-1999): Monitored satellite uplink/downlink procedures to assure quality video transmissions. Aided technicians with transmission problems. Assisted in the assembly and maintenance of uplink facility.</P>

<P>Technical Assistant (Mountain View Bank 1997-1998): Managed data processing system. Handled user requests and discussed programming options. Managed delivery service. </P>

<P>Salesperson (Computer Visions 1996): Sales and customer support in computers and electronics. Managed commercial accounts in Mountain View and Crabtree locations.</P>

3. Save the revised text file.

4. Return to your Web browser, and then reopen the **Resume.htm** file. The text in the Employment section is properly separated into distinct paragraphs, as shown in Figure 1-21.

Figure 1-21   EMPLOYMENT HISTORY SEPARATED INTO PARAGRAPHS

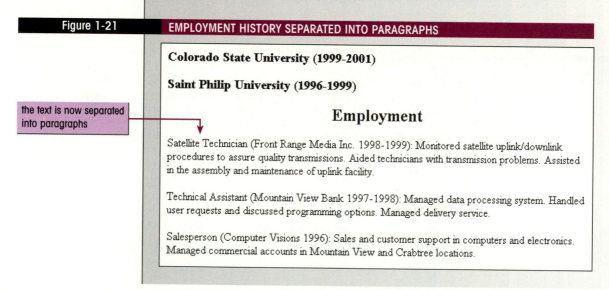

the text is now separated into paragraphs

Colorado State University (1999-2001)

Saint Philip University (1996-1999)

Employment

Satellite Technician (Front Range Media Inc. 1998-1999): Monitored satellite uplink/downlink procedures to assure quality transmissions. Aided technicians with transmission problems. Assisted in the assembly and maintenance of uplink facility.

Technical Assistant (Mountain View Bank 1997-1998): Managed data processing system. Handled user requests and discussed programming options. Managed delivery service.

Salesperson (Computer Visions 1996): Sales and customer support in computers and electronics. Managed commercial accounts in Mountain View and Crabtree locations.

If you start examining the HTML code for pages that you encounter on the Web, you might notice that the <P> tag is used in different ways on other pages. In the original version of HTML, the <P> tag inserted a blank line into the page. In HTML 1.0, <P> was placed at the end of each paragraph; no </P> tag was required. In versions 2.0 and 3.2, the paragraph tag is two-sided: both the <P> and </P> tags are used. Moreover, the <P> tag is placed at the beginning of the paragraph, not the end. Starting with HTML 3.2, you can specify the alignment property in a paragraph tag, but in HTML 1.0 and 2.0 you cannot; paragraphs are always assumed to be left justified. For the Web documents that you are creating in this book, you should use the style convention shown in the above example.

Creating Lists

You still need to enter the lists describing Mary's achievements at Colorado State University and Saint Philip University. HTML provides tags for such lists. HTML supports three kinds of lists: ordered, unordered, and definition.

An **ordered list** is a list in numeric order. HTML automatically adds the numbers once you display your Web page in a browser. If you remove an item from the list, HTML automatically updates the numbers to reflect the new order. For example, Mary might want to list her scholastic awards in order from the most important to the least important. To do so, you could enter the following code into her HTML document:

```
<H3>Scholastic Awards</H3>
<OL>
<LI>Enos Mills Scholarship
<LI>Physics Expo blue ribbon winner
<LI> Honor Key Award semifinalist
</OL>
```

This example shows the basic structure of an HTML list. The list text is bracketed between the <OL> and </OL> tags, where OL stands for ordered list. This tells the browser to present the text between the tags as an ordered list. Each list item is identified by a single <LI> tag, where LI stands for list item. There is no closing tag for list items.

A Web browser might display this code as:

Scholastic Awards

1. Enos Mills Scholarship

2. Physics Expo blue ribbon winner

3. Honor Key Award semifinalist

You can also specify the symbol used for the ordered list, using the **TYPE** property. The default, as you've seen, is a number. By setting the TYPE property to "a", you can use letters instead of numbers. For example, the code:

```
<OL TYPE=a>
<LI>Enos Mills Scholarship
<LI>Physics Expo blue ribbon winner
<LI> Honor Key Award semifinalist
</OL>
```

yields the following list:

a. Enos Mills Scholarship

b. Physics Expo blue ribbon winner

c. Honor Key Award semifinalist

Other values of the TYPE property are "A" for uppercase letters, "i" for lowercase Roman numerals, and "I" for uppercase Roman numerals. Be aware that the TYPE property is not supported by all browsers. It was not part of the HTML standards prior to HTML 3.0.

You can also create an **unordered list**, in which list items have no particular order. Browsers usually format unordered lists by inserting a bullet symbol before each list item. The entire list is bracketed between the <UL> and </UL> tags, where UL stands for unordered list. If Mary wants to display her awards without regard to their importance, you could enter the following code:

```
<H3>Scholastic Awards</H3>
<UL>
<LI>Enos Mills Scholarship
<LI>Physics Expo blue ribbon winner
<LI>Honor Key Award semifinalist
</UL>
```

A Web browser might display this code as:

Scholastic Awards

- Enos Mills Scholarship
- Physics Expo blue ribbon winner
- Honor Key Award semifinalist

As with the ordered list, you can use the TYPE property to specify the type of symbol used in the list. The default symbol is a bullet or "disc." Other values for the TYPE property are SQUARE for square bullets and CIRCLE for circles. This property was introduced with HTML 3.0, although Netscape has supported it since version 1.0. Internet Explorer does not support this property, although this may change with new versions. If symbol type is an important part of your document, you will probably want to test this feature on several different browsers.

A third type of list that HTML can display is a definition list. A **definition list** is a list of terms, each followed by a definition line, usually indented slightly to the right. The <LI> tag used in ordered and unordered lists for individual items is replaced by two tags: the <DT> tag used for each term in the list and the <DD> tag used for each term's definition. As with the <LI> tag, both of these tags are one-sided. The entire list is bracketed by the <DL> and </DL> tags, indicating to the browser that the list is a definition list. If Mary wants to create a list of her scholastic awards and briefly describe each, she can use a definition list, even though the items are not actually terms and definitions. To create a definition list for her awards, you could enter this code into her HTML file:

```
<H3>Scholastic Awards</H3>
<DL>
<DT>Enos Mills Scholarship<DD>Awarded to the outstanding
student in the senior class
<DT>Physics Expo blue ribbon winner<DD>Awarded for a research
 project on fiber optics
<DT>Honor Key Award semifinalist<DD>Awarded for an essay on
the information age
</DL>
```

A Web browser might display this code as:

Scholastic Awards

Enos Mills Scholarship

     Awarded to the outstanding student in the senior class

Physics Expo blue ribbon winner

     Awarded for a research project on fiber optics

Honor Key Award semifinalist

     Awarded for an essay on the information age

REFERENCE WINDOW .RW

Creating Lists
- Open the HTML file with your text editor.
- Move to the place in the document where you want the list to appear.
- Type <OL> to start an ordered list, <UL> to start an unordered list, and <DL> to start a definition list.
- For each item in an ordered or unordered list, type <LI> followed by the text for the list item. For each item in a definition list, type <DT> before the term and <DD> before the definition.
- To turn off the list, type </OL> for an ordered list, </UL> for an unordered list, and </DL> for a definition list.

On her paper resume (Figure 1-10), Mary's educational accomplishments are in a bulleted list. You can include this feature in Mary's online resume by using the <OL> and <LI> tags.

To add an unordered list to the resume file:

1. Return to your text editor and reopen the **Resume.htm file**, if it is not still open.

2. Type the following code and text between the headers "Colorado State University" and "Saint Philip University":

   <UL>

   <LI>Graduated May, 2001. M.A. International Telecommunications

   <LI>Grade Point Average: 3.5 overall, 3.9 in major

   <LI>Dean's List: September 1999-May 2001

   <LI>Member, Phi Alpha Omega Honor Society

   </UL>

3. Type these lines of code after the heading "Saint Philip University":

   <UL>

   <LI>Graduated May, 1999. B.A. International Studies

   <LI>Grade Point Average: 4.0 overall, 4.0 in major

   <LI>Dean's List: September 1996-May 1999

   <LI>President, Honor Key Society

   </UL>

   The new lines in the resume file should look like Figure 1-22.

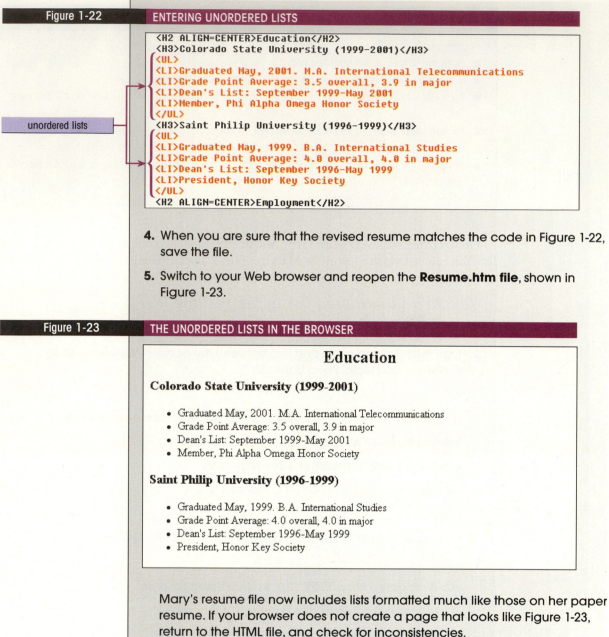

Figure 1-22   **ENTERING UNORDERED LISTS**

```
<H2 ALIGN=CENTER>Education</H2>
<H3>Colorado State University (1999-2001)</H3>
<UL>
<LI>Graduated May, 2001. M.A. International Telecommunications
<LI>Grade Point Average: 3.5 overall, 3.9 in major
<LI>Dean's List: September 1999-May 2001
<LI>Member, Phi Alpha Omega Honor Society
</UL>
<H3>Saint Philip University (1996-1999)</H3>
<UL>
<LI>Graduated May, 1999. B.A. International Studies
<LI>Grade Point Average: 4.0 overall, 4.0 in major
<LI>Dean's List: September 1996-May 1999
<LI>President, Honor Key Society
</UL>
<H2 ALIGN=CENTER>Employment</H2>
```

unordered lists

4. When you are sure that the revised resume matches the code in Figure 1-22, save the file.

5. Switch to your Web browser and reopen the **Resume.htm file**, shown in Figure 1-23.

Figure 1-23   **THE UNORDERED LISTS IN THE BROWSER**

Education

Colorado State University (1999-2001)

- Graduated May, 2001. M.A. International Telecommunications
- Grade Point Average: 3.5 overall, 3.9 in major
- Dean's List: September 1999-May 2001
- Member, Phi Alpha Omega Honor Society

Saint Philip University (1996-1999)

- Graduated May, 1999. B.A. International Studies
- Grade Point Average: 4.0 overall, 4.0 in major
- Dean's List: September 1996-May 1999
- President, Honor Key Society

Mary's resume file now includes lists formatted much like those on her paper resume. If your browser does not create a page that looks like Figure 1-23, return to the HTML file, and check for inconsistencies.

Creating Character Tags

Until now you've worked with tags that affect either the entire document or individual lines. HTML also lets you modify the characteristics of individual characters. A tag that you apply to an individual character is called a **character tag**. You can use two kinds of character tags: logical and physical. **Logical character tags** indicate how you want to use text, not necessarily how you want it displayed. Figure 1-24 lists some common logical character tags.

Figure 1-24	COMMON LOGICAL CHARACTER TAGS
TAG	**DESCRIPTION**
<EM>	Indicates that characters should be emphasized in some way. Usually displayed with italics.
<STRONG>	Emphasizes characters more strongly than <EM>. Usually displayed in a bold font.
<CODE>	Indicates a sample of code. Usually displayed in a Courier font or a similar font that allots the same width to each character.
<KBD>	Used to offset text that the user should enter. Often displayed in a Courier font or a similar font that allots the same width to each character.
<VAR>	Indicates a variable. Often displayed in italics or underlined.
<CITE>	Indicates short quotes or citations. Often italicized by browsers.

Figure 1-25 shows examples of how these tags might appear in a browser. Note that you can combine tags, allowing you to create boldface and italics text by using both the <EM> and the <STRONG> tags.

Figure 1-25	LOGICAL CHARACTER TAGS AS THEY APPEAR IN THE BROWSER

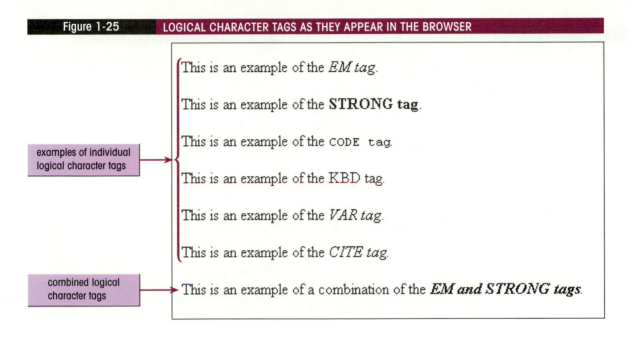

examples of individual logical character tags

This is an example of the *EM tag*.

This is an example of the **STRONG tag**.

This is an example of the `CODE tag`.

This is an example of the KBD tag.

This is an example of the *VAR tag*.

This is an example of the *CITE tag*.

combined logical character tags

This is an example of a combination of the ***EM and STRONG tags***.

HTML authors can also use **physical character tags** to indicate exactly how characters are to be formatted. Figure 1-26 shows common examples of physical character tags.

Figure 1-26	COMMON PHYSICAL CHARACTER TAGS
TAG	**DESCRIPTION**
<B>	Indicates that the text should be bold.
<I>	Indicates that the text should be italic.
<TT>	Indicates that the text should be used with a font such as Courier that allots the same width to each character.
<BIG>	Indicates that the text should be displayed in a big font. Available only in HTML 3.0.
<SMALL>	Indicates that the text should be displayed in a small font. Available only in HTML 3.0.
<SUB>	The text should be displayed as a subscript, in a smaller font if possible. Available only in HTML 3.0.
<SUP>	The text should be displayed as a superscript, in a smaller font if possible. Available only in HTML 3.0.

Figure 1-27 shows examples of how these tags might appear in a browser. Some browsers also support the <U> tag for underlining text, but other browsers might not show underlining, so use it cautiously.

Figure 1-27	PHYSICAL CHARACTER TAGS AS THEY APPEAR IN THE BROWSER

This is an example of the **B tag**.

This is an example of the *I tag*.

This is an example of the `TT tag`.

This is an example of the **BIG tag**.

This is an example of the SMALL tag.

This is an example of the $_{SUB\ tag}$

This is an example of the $^{SUP\ tag}$

Given the presence of both logical and physical character tags, which should you use to display some text in an italicized font: <EM> or <I>? Some older versions of browsers are text-based and cannot display italics. These older browsers ignore the <I> tag, so the emphasis you want to place on a certain piece of text is lost. If this a concern, you should use a logical tag. On the other hand, the physical character tags are more commonly used today and are easier to interpret. Some Web page authors believe that the use of logical character tags such as <EM> and <STRONG> is archaic and confusing.

Only one part of Mary's resume requires character tags: the Employment section, where Mary wants to emphasize the title of each job she has held. She decides to use a combination of the <B> and <I> tags to display the titles in boldface and italics.

To add character tags to the resume file:

1. Return to your text editor, and reopen the **Resume.htm** file if necessary.

2. Type the **<I>** and **<B>** tags around the job titles in the Employment section of the resume (just after the <P> tags), so that they read:

<I><B>Satellite Technician</B></I>

<I><B>Technical Assistant</B></I>

<I><B>Salesperson</B></I>

See Figure 1-28.

Figure 1-28	APPLYING CHARACTER TAGS

use the <B> and <I> tags to display this text in boldface and italics

```
<H2 ALIGN=CENTER>Employment</H2>
<P><I><B>Satellite Technician</B></I> (Front Range Media Inc. 1998–
1999): Monitored satellite uplink/downlink procedures to assure quality
transmissions. Aided technicians with transmission problems. Assisted
in the assembly and maintenance of uplink facility.</P>

<P><I><B>Technical Assistant</B></I> (Mountain View Bank 1997–1998):
Managed data processing system. Handled user requests and discussed
programming options. Managed delivery service.</P>

<P><I><B>Salesperson</B></I> (Computer Visions 1996): Sales and
customer support in computers and electronics. Managed commercial
accounts in Mountain View and Crabtree locations.</P>
</BODY>
```

3. Save the changes to your Resume file.

4. Return to your Web browser, and reopen the Resume file. The updated Employment section of Mary's page should look like Figure 1-29.

Figure 1-29	THE EFFECT OF THE CHARACTER TAGS IN THE BROWSER

boldface and italics

Employment

Satellite Technician (Front Range Media Inc. 1998-1999): Monitored satellite uplink/downlink procedures to assure quality transmissions. Aided technicians with transmission problems. Assisted in the assembly and maintenance of uplink facility.

Technical Assistant (Mountain View Bank 1997-1998): Managed data processing system. Handled user requests and discussed programming options. Managed delivery service.

Salesperson (Computer Visions 1996): Sales and customer support in computers and electronics. Managed commercial accounts in Mountain View and Crabtree locations.

5. If you are continuing to Session 1.3, you can leave your text editor and browser open. Otherwise, close your browser and text editor.

When you apply two character tags to the same text, you should place one set of tags completely within the other. For example, you would combine the <I> and <B> tags like this:

`<I><B>Satellite Technician</B></I>`

and not like this:

`<I><B>Satellite Technician</I></B>`

Although many browsers interpret both sets of code the same way, nesting tags within each other rather than overlapping them makes your code easier to read and interpret.

You have finished adding text to Mary's online resume. In Session 1.3, you will add special formatting elements such as lines and graphics.

Session 1.2 QUICK CHECK

1. Why should you include the <HTML> tag in your Web document?

2. Describe the syntax for creating a centered heading 1.

3. Describe the syntax for creating a paragraph.

4. If you want to display several paragraphs, why can't you simply type an extra blank line in the HTML file?

5. Describe the syntax for creating an ordered list, an unordered list, and a definition list.

6. Give two ways of italicizing text in your Web document. What are the advantages and disadvantages of each method?

SESSION 1.3

In this session you will insert three special elements into Mary's online resume: a special character, a line separating Mary's name and address from the rest of her resume, and a photograph of Mary.

Adding Special Characters

Occasionally you will want to include special characters in your Web page that do not appear on your keyboard. For example, a math page might require mathematical symbols such as β or μ. As Mary views her resume file, she notices a place where she could use a special symbol. In the address information under her name, she finds that the street address, city, and phone numbers all flow together. She decides to look into special characters that could separate the information.

HTML supports several character symbols that you can insert into your page. Each character symbol is identified by a code number or name. To create a special character, type an ampersand (&) followed either by the code name or the code number, and then a semicolon. Code numbers must be preceded by a pound symbol (#). Figure 1-30 shows some HTML symbols and the corresponding code numbers or names. A fuller list of special characters is included in Appendix B.

| Figure 1-30 | SPECIAL CHARACTERS AND CODES | | | |

SYMBOL	CODE	CODE NAME	DESCRIPTION
©	&#169;	&copy;	Copyright symbol
®	&#174;	&reg;	Registered trademark
•	&#183;	&middot;	Middle dot
º	&#186;	&ordm;	Masculine ordinal
TM	&#153;	&trade;	Trademark symbol
			Nonbreaking space, useful when you want to insert several blank spaces, one after another
<	&#60;	&lt;	Less than symbol
>	&#62;	&gt;	Greater than symbol
&	&#39;	&amp;	Ampersand

One solution for Mary's resume is to insert several **nonbreaking spaces** using the   character code. However, Mary decides it would look better to insert a bullet (•) between the street address and the city, and another bullet between the zip code and the phone number.

To add a character code to the resume file:

1. Make sure the **Resume.htm** file is open in your text editor.

2. Revise the address line at the beginning of the file, inserting the code for a middle dot, **·**, between the street address and the city, and between the zip code and the phone number, so that the line reads:

   <H5 ALIGN=CENTER>11 Kemper Ave. · Lake View, CO 80517 · (303) 555-1012</H5>

   TROUBLE? In your text editor this line probably appears as a single line.

3. Save the changes to your Resume file.

4. Return to your Web browser and reopen the Resume file. Figure 1-31 shows Mary's resume with the bullets separating the address elements.

| Figure 1-31 | SPECIAL CHARACTERS IN THE BROWSER | |

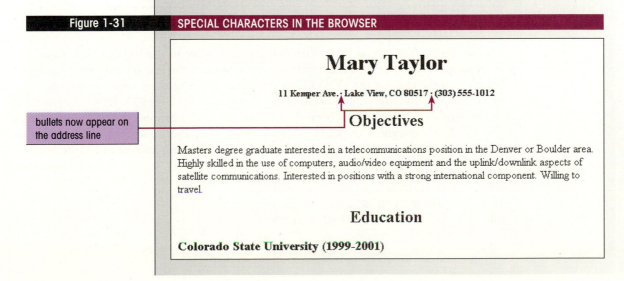

bullets now appear on the address line

Mary Taylor

11 Kemper Ave. • Lake View, CO 80517 • (303) 555-1012

Objectives

Masters degree graduate interested in a telecommunications position in the Denver or Boulder area. Highly skilled in the use of computers, audio/video equipment and the uplink/downlink aspects of satellite communications. Interested in positions with a strong international component. Willing to travel.

Education

Colorado State University (1999-2001)

The next thing Mary wants in her resume is a horizontal line separating the name and address information from the rest of her resume.

Inserting Horizontal Lines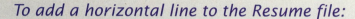

The horizontal line after Mary's name and address in Figure 1-10 lends shape to the appearance of her paper resume. She'd like you to duplicate that in the online version. You use the **<HR>** tag to create a horizontal line, where HR stands for horizontal rule. The <HR> tag is one-sided. When a text-based browser encounters the <HR> tag, it inserts a line by repeating an underline symbol across the width of the page. A graphical browser inserts a graphical line.

To add a horizontal line to the Resume file:

1. Return to your text editor and reopen the **Resume.htm** file if necessary.

2. At the end of Mary's address line, press the **Enter** key to insert a new blank line.

3. In the new line, type **<HR>**.

4. Save the changes to your Resume file.

5. Return to your Web browser and reopen the Resume file. The Resume file with the new horizontal line appears in Figure 1-32.

Figure 1-32   HORIZONTAL LINE AS IT APPEARS IN THE BROWSER

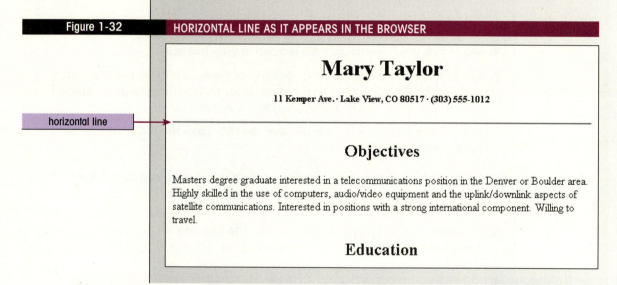

The <HR> tag has several properties that you may want to use in your Web page. The ALIGN property can be set to left, right, or center to place the line on the page (the default is center). You can also use the WIDTH property to tell the browser what percentage of the width of the page the line should occupy. For example, WIDTH=50% tells the browser to place the line so that its length covers half of the page. You can use the SIZE property to specify the line's thickness in pixels. A pixel, short for picture element, is ½-inch wide. Figure 1-33 shows how a browser would interpret the following lines of HTML code:

```
<HR ALIGN=CENTER SIZE=12 WIDTH=100%>
<HR ALIGN=CENTER SIZE=6 WIDTH=50%>
<HR ALIGN=CENTER SIZE=3 WIDTH=25%>
<HR ALIGN=CENTER SIZE=1 WIDTH=10%>
```

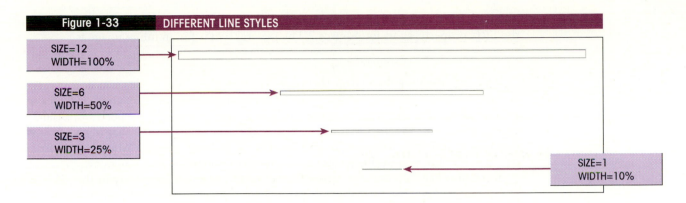

Figure 1-33   DIFFERENT LINE STYLES

Netscape Navigator and Internet Explorer also support properties specific to those browsers. As always, you should remember that using browser-specific extensions might produce wildly different results on browsers that do not support the extensions.

Inserting a Graphic

One feature of Web pages that has made the World Wide Web so popular is the ease of displaying a graphic image. The Web supports two methods for displaying a graphic: as an inline image and as an external image.

An **inline image** appears directly on the Web page and is loaded when the page is loaded. Two of the more commonly supported image types are GIF (Graphics Interchange Format) and JPEG (Joint Photographic Experts Group). Before you display a graphic image, you should convert it to one of these two types.

An **external image** is not displayed with the Web page. Instead, the browser must have a **file viewer**, a program that the browser loads automatically, whenever it encounters the image file, and uses to display the image. You can find file viewers at several Internet Web sites. Most browsers make it easy to set up viewers for use with the Web. External images have one disadvantage: you can't actually display them on the Web page. Instead they are represented by an icon that a user clicks to view the image. However, external images are not limited to the GIF or JPEG formats. You can set up virtually any image format as an external image on a Web page, including video clips and sound files.

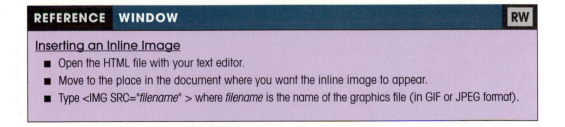

REFERENCE   WINDOW   RW

Inserting an Inline Image
- Open the HTML file with your text editor.
- Move to the place in the document where you want the inline image to appear.
- Type <IMG SRC="*filename*" > where *filename* is the name of the graphics file (in GIF or JPEG format).

Mary is more interested in using an inline image than an external image. **<IMG>** is the tag used for displaying an inline image. You can place inline images on a separate line in your document, or you can place the image within a line of text (hence the term "inline").

To access the image file, you need to include the filename within the tag. You do this using the SRC property, short for "source." The general syntax for an inline image is:

```
<IMG SRC="filename">
```

If the image file is located in the same folder as the HTML file, you do not need to include any folder information. However, if the image file is located in another folder or on another computer, you need to include the full path with the SRC property. Tutorial 2 discusses directory paths and filenames in more detail. For now, assume that Mary's image file is placed in the same folder as the HTML file. The image file that Mary has created is a photograph of herself in JPEG format. The name of the file is Taylor.jpg.

You'd also like to center the image on the page. There is no property in the <IMG> tag that would allow you to center it on a page, but you can nest the <IMG> tag within a paragraph tag, <P>, and then center the paragraph on the page using the ALIGN=CENTER property for the <P> tag. This has the effect of centering all of the text in the paragraph, including any inline images. Note that the ALIGN property was introduced in HTML 3.2; in browsers that do not support this convention, Mary's image may be left-justified.

To add Mary's photo to the online resume:

1. Look in the Tutorial.01 folder on your Data Disk and verify that both the Resume.htm file and Taylor.jpg file are there.

2. Return to your text editor with the Resume.htm file open.

3. At the end of the line with the <HR> tag that you just typed, press the **Enter** key to create a new line.

4. Type **<P ALIGN=CENTER><IMG SRC="Taylor.jpg"></P>** and then save the changes to the Resume file.

5. Print a copy of your completed Resume.htm file, and then close your text editor, unless you are continuing to the Review Assignments.

6. Return to your Web browser, and reopen the Resume file. Mary's online resume now includes an inline image. See Figure 1-34 for a view of the entire page.

Figure 1-34 | MARY'S COMPLETED RESUME PAGE

Mary Taylor

11 Kemper Ave. · Lake View, CO 80517 · (303) 555-1012

Objectives

Masters degree graduate interested in a telecommunications position in the Denver or Boulder area. Highly skilled in the use of computers audio/video equipment, and the uplink/downlink aspects of satellite communications. Interested in positions with a strong international component. Willing to travel.

Education

Colorado State University (1999-2001)

- Graduated May, 2001. M.A. International Telecommunications
- Grade Point Average: 3.5 overall, 3.9 in major
- Dean's List: September 1999-May 2001
- Member, Phi Alpha Omega Honor Society

Saint Philip University (1996-1999)

- Graduated May, 1999. B.A. International Studies
- Grade Point Average: 4.0 overall, 4.0 in major
- Dean's List: September 1996-May 1999
- President, Honor Key Society

Employment

Satellite Technician (Front Range Media Inc. 1998-1999): Monitored satellite uplink/downlink procedures to assure quality transmissions. Aided technicians with transmission problems. Assisted in the assembly and maintenance of uplink facility.

Technical Assistant (Mountain View Bank 1997-1998): Managed data processing system. Handled user requests and discussed programming options. Managed delivery service.

Salesperson (Computer Visions 1996): Sales and customer support in computers and electronics. Managed commercial accounts in Mountain View and Crabtree locations.

7. Use your browser to print a copy of Mary's online resume.

Compare the printout of the code, shown below, to the online resume on your browser. When you finish, you can exit your browser unless you're continuing to the Review Assignments.

```
<HTML>
<HEAD>
<TITLE>The Resume of Mary Taylor</TITLE>
</HEAD>
<BODY>
<H1 ALIGN=CENTER>Mary Taylor</H1>
<H5 ALIGN=CENTER>11 Kemper Ave. &#183; Lake View, CO 80517
&#183; (303) 555-1012</H5>
<HR>
<P ALIGN=CENTER><IMG SRC="Taylor.jpg"></P>
<H2 ALIGN=CENTER>Objectives</H2>
Masters degree graduate interested in a telecommunications
position in the Denver or Boulder area. Highly skilled in
the use of computers, audio/video equipment, and the uplink/
downlink aspects of satellite communications. Interested in
positions with a strong international component. Willing to
travel.
<H2 ALIGN=CENTER>Education</H2>
<H3>Colorado State University (1999-2001)</H3>
<UL>
<LI>Graduated May, 2001. M.A. International Telecommunications
<LI>Grade Point Average: 3.5 overall, 3.9 in major
<LI>Dean's List: September 1999-May 2001
<LI>Member, Phi Alpha Omega Honor Society
</UL>
<H3>Saint Philip University (1996-1999)</H3>
<UL>
<LI>Graduated May, 1999. B.A. International Studies
<LI>Grade Point Average: 4.0 overall, 4.0 in major
<LI>Dean's List: September 1996-May 1999
<LI>President, Honor Key Society
</UL>
<H2 ALIGN=CENTER>Employment</H2>
<P><I><B>Satellite Technician</B></I> (Front Range Media Inc.
1998-1999): Monitored satellite uplink/downlink procedures
to assure quality video transmissions. Aided technicians
with transmission problems. Assisted in the assembly and
maintenance of uplink facility.</P>
<P><I><B>Technical Assistant</B></I> (Mountain View Bank 1997
-1998): Managed data processing system. Handled user requests
and discussed programming options. Managed delivery
service. </P>
<P><I><B>Salesperson</B></I> (Computer Visions 1996): Sales
and customer support in computers and electronics. Managed
commercial accounts in Mountain View and Crabtree
locations.</P>
</BODY>
</HTML>
```

You show the completed online resume file to Mary; she thinks it looks great. You tell her that the next step is adding hypertext links to other material about herself for interested employers. You take a break while she heads to her desk to start thinking about what material she'd like to add. You'll learn about hypertext links in Tutorial 2.

Session 1.3 QUICK CHECK

1. How would you insert a copyright symbol, ©, into your Web page?

2. What is the syntax for inserting a horizontal line into a page?

3. What is the syntax for creating a horizontal line that is 70% of the display width of the screen and 4 pixels high?

4. What is an inline image?

5. What is an external image?

6. What is the syntax for inserting a graphic named Mouse.jpg into a Web document as an inline image?

7. What are two graphic file formats you can use for inline images?

REVIEW ASSIGNMENTS

After thinking some more about her online resume, Mary Taylor decides that she wants you to add a few more items. In the Education section, she wants you to add that she won the Enos Mills Scholarship contest as a senior at St. Philip University. She also wants to add that she worked as a climbing guide for The Colorado Experience touring company from 1994 to 1995. She would like to add her e-mail address, mtaylor@tt.gr.csu.edu, in italics at the bottom of the page. You tell her that adding a horizontal line to separate it from the rest of the resume might look nice. She agrees, so you get to work.

1. Open the **Resume.htm** file located in the Tutorial.01 folder on your Data Disk. This is the file you created over the course of this tutorial.

2. Save the file on your Data Disk in the Tutorial.01/Review folder with a new name: Resume2.htm, so that you will leave your work from the tutorial intact.

3. After the HTML line reading "President, Honor Key Society," enter a new line, "Winner of the Enos Mills Scholarship."
   Use the <LI> tag to format this line as an addition to the existing list.

4. Move to the Employment section of the Resume2.htm file.

5. After the paragraph describing Mary's experience as a salesperson, insert a new paragraph, "Guide (The Colorado Experience 1994-1996): Climbing guide for private groups and schools." Make sure you mark the text with the correct code for a two-sided paragraph tag.

6. Using the <I> and <B> tags, bracket the word "Guide" in the line you just entered to make it both bold and italic.

7. After the paragraph on Mary's climbing guide experience, insert a horizontal line using the <HR> tag. Set the thickness of the line to 6 pixels.

8. After the horizontal line, insert a new line with Mary's e-mail address.

Explore 9. Use the <CITE> tag to format her e-mail address as a citation:
   <CITE>mtaylor@tt.gr.csu.edu</CITE>

10. Save the changes to your Resume2.htm file and print it.

11. View the file with your Web browser.

12. Print a copy of the page as viewed by your browser.

PROJECTS

1. Creating a Web Page at the University Music Department   You are an assistant
to a professor in the Music Department who is trying to create Web pages for topics in classical music. He wants to create a page showing the different sections of the fourth movement of Beethoven's Ninth symphony. The page should appear as shown in Figure 1-35.

Figure 1-35

Beethoven's Ninth Symphony

The Fourth Movement

Sonata-Concerto Form

1. Open Ritornello
2. Exposition
    1. Horror/Recitative
    2. Joy Theme
    3. Turkish Music
3. Development
4. Recapitulation
    1. Joy Theme
    2. Awe Theme
5. Coda Nos. 1 2 3

The page needs an inline image, three headings, and a list of the fourth movement's different sections. Several of the sections also have sublists. For example, the Recapitulation section contains both the Joy and Awe themes. You can create lists of this type with HTML
by inserting one list tag within another. The HTML code for this is:

```
<OL>
<LI>Recapitulation
          <OL>
          <LI>Joy Theme
          <LI>Awe Theme
          </OL>
</OL>
```

1. Open a text editor program.

2. Type the <HTML>, <HEAD>, and <BODY> tags to identify different sections of the page.

3. Within the HEAD section, insert a <TITLE> tag with the text: "Beethoven's Ninth
   Symphony, 4th Movement".

4. Within the BODY section, create an <H1> header with the text "Beethoven's Ninth Symphony" and center the heading on the page with the ALIGN property.

5. Below the <H1> header, create an <H2> header with the text "The Fourth Movement" and then center the header on the page.

6. Below the <H2> header, create an <H3> header with the text "Sonata-Concerto Form", but this time do not center the header.

7. Create an ordered list using the <OL> tag, with the list items "Open Ritornello", "Exposition", "Development", "Recapitulation", and "Codas Nos. 1 2 3".

Explore ▶ 8. Within the Exposition list, create an ordered list with the items "Horror/Recitative", "Joy Theme", and "Turkish Music".

Explore ▶ 9. Within the Recapitulation list, create an ordered list with the items "Joy Theme" and "Awe Theme".

10. Before the <H1> header, insert the inline image LVB.jpg (located in the Projects folder of the Tutorial.01 folder on your Data Disk) centered on the page.

11. After the <H2> header, insert a horizontal line that extends the width of the page and is 1 pixel in height.

12. Save the file as Ludwig.htm in the Cases folder of the Tutorial.01 folder on your Data Disk, print it, and then close your text editor.

13. View the file with your Web browser, print it, and then close your browser.

2. Creating a Web Page for the Mathematics Department   Professor Laureen Coe of the Mathematics Department is preparing material for her course on the history of mathematics. As part of the course, she has written short profiles of famous mathematicians. Using content she's already written, Laureen would like you to create several Web pages to be placed on the university's Web server. You'll create the first one in this exercise. A preview of one of the pages about the mathematician Leonhard Euler is shown in Figure 1-36.

Figure 1-36

Euler, Leonhard

(1707-1783)

The greatest mathematician of the eighteenth century, **Leonhard Euler** was born in Basel, Switzerland. There, he studied under another giant of mathematics, **Jean Bernoulli**. In 1731 Euler became a professor of physics and mathematics at St. Petersburg Academy of Sciences. Euler was the most prolific mathematician of all time, publishing over *800 different books and papers*. His influence was felt in physics and astronomy as well. Euler's work on mathematical analysis, <u>Introductio in analysin infinitorum</u> (1748) remained a standard textbook for well over a century. For the princess of Anhalt-Dessau he wrote *Lettres à une princesse d'Allemagne* (1768-1772), giving a clear non-technical outline of the main physical theories of the time.

One can hardly write mathematical equations without copying Euler. Notations still in use today, such as e and π, were developed by Euler. He is perhaps best known for his research into mathematical analysis. Euler's formula:

$$\cos(x) + i\sin(x) = e^{(ix)}$$

demonstrates the relationship between analysis, trignometry and imaginary numbers, in one beautiful and elegant equation.

Leonhard Euler died in 1783, leaving behind a legacy perhaps unmatched, and certainly unsurpassed, in the annals of mathematics.

Math 895: The History of Mathematics

1. Start your text editor and then open the file **Eulertxt.htm**, located in the Cases folder of the Tutorial.01 folder on your Data Disk, and save it as Euler.htm.

2. Add the opening and closing <HTML>, <HEAD>, and <BODY> tags to the file in the appropriate locations.

3. Insert "Leonhard Euler" as a page title in the Head section of the document.

4. Insert the inline image **Euler.jpg** (located in the Tutorial 1 Projects folder on your Data Disk) at the top of the body of the document.

5. Format the first line of the page's body, "Euler, Leonhard", with the <H1> tag, and format the second line of the page's body, "(1707-1783)", with the <H3> tag.

6. Add the appropriate paragraph tags, <P>, to the document to separate the paragraphs.

7. Within the first paragraph, display the names, "Leonhard Euler" and "Jean Bernoulli" in boldface. Italicize the phrase "800 different books and papers", and underline the publication "Introductio in analysin infinitorum".

8. Replace the one-letter word "a" in "Lettres a une princesse d'Allemagne" with an *à*, using the character code &agrave, and then italicize the entire name of the publication.

9. In the second paragraph, italicize the notation "e" and replace the word "pi" with the inline image "**pi.jpg**" located in the Cases folder on your Data Disk.

Explore ▷ 10. Center the equation and italicize the letters "x", "i", and "e" in the equation. Display the term "(*ix*)" as a superscript, using the <SUP> tag.

Explore ▷ 11. Format the name of the course at the bottom of the page using the <CITE> tag.

12. Add horizontal lines before and after the biographical information.

13. Save the Euler.htm file, and then print it from your text editor.

14. View the file in your Web browser, and then print a copy of the page as displayed by the browser.

3. Chester the Jester   A friend of yours who performs as a clown named "Chester the Jester" wants to advertise his services on the World Wide Web. He wants his Web page to be bright and colorful. One way of doing this is to create a colorful background for the page. You create a background using a graphic image. Such backgrounds are called tile-image backgrounds because the graphic image is repeated over and over again, like tiles, until it covers the entire page. To create a tile-image background, you must have a graphic image in either GIF or JPEG file format. You insert the file in the background by adding the BACKGROUND property to the <BODY> tag with the syntax:

```
<BODY BACKGROUND= "filename">
```

Your friend gives you a JPEG file named Diamonds.jpg, which contains the pattern he uses in his clown costume. He also has a JPEG file named Chester.jpg, which shows him in his clown outfit. A preview of the page you'll create is shown in Figure 1-37.

Figure 1-37

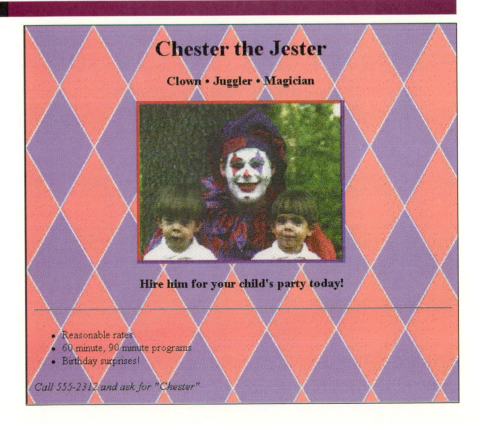

1. Start your text editor, open the file **Chestertxt.htm** from the Cases folder of the Tutorial.01 folder on your Data Disk, and save it as Chester.htm.

2. Insert the <HTML>, <HEAD>, and <BODY> tags in the appropriate locations.

3. Insert a <TITLE> tag in the Head section, giving the Web page the title "Chester the Jester".

Explore   4. Modify the <BODY> tag to read:

```
<BODY BACKGROUND="Diamonds.jpg">
```

5. Format the text "Chester the Jester" with the <H1> tag and center it on the Web page.

6. Format the text "Clown Juggler Magician" with the <H3> tag and center it on the page. Insert a middle dot, character symbol •, between each word.

7. Insert the inline image **"Chester.jpg"** (located in the Projects folder of the Tutorial.01 folder on your Data Disk) after the <H3> header. Center it on the page.

8. Format the text "Hire him for your child's party today!" with the <H3> tag, centered on the page.

9. Insert a horizontal line after the <H3> header.

10. Format the next three lines as an unordered list.

11. Format the text in the last line of document text, using the <I> tag.

12. Save the Chester.htm file and then print it from your text editor.

13. View the file in your Web browser and then print it in your browser.

4. Create Your Own Resume   After completing Mary Taylor's resume, you are eager to make your own. Using the techniques from this tutorial, design and create a resume for yourself. Make sure to include these features: section headers, bulleted or numbered lists, bold and/or italic fonts, paragraphs, special characters, inline graphic images, and horizontal lines.

1. Start your text editor, and then create a file called MyResume.htm in the Cases folder of the Tutorial.01 folder on your Data Disk. Type the appropriate HTML code and content.

2. Add any other tags you think will improve your document's appearance.

3. You could take a picture of yourself to your lab or a local office services business and scan it. If you do, save it as a GIF or JPEG file. Then place the graphic file in the Projects folder of the Tutorial.01 folder on your Data Disk. Add the appropriate code in your MyResume.htm file. If you don't have your own graphic file, use the file **Kirk.jpg** located in the Projects folder of the Tutorial.01 folder on your Data Disk.

4. You could use a graphics package that can store images in GIF or JPEG format to create a background image that you could insert as you did in Case Problem 3. If you do, use light colors so the text you place on top is readable. Add the appropriate code to your MyResume.htm file, using the steps in Case Problem 3.

5. Test your code as you develop your resume, by viewing MyResume.htm in your browser.

6. When you finish entering the code, save and print the MyResume.htm file from your text editor.

7. View the final version in your browser, print the Web page, and then close your browser and text editor.

Web Pages & HTML

LAB ASSIGNMENTS

This Lab Assignment is designed to accompany the interactive Course Lab called The Internet World Wide Web. To start the Internet World Wide Web Course Lab, click the Start button on the Windows taskbar, point to Programs, point to Course Labs, point to New Perspectives Applications, and click The Internet World Wide Web. If you do not see Course Labs on your Programs menu, see your instructor or technical support person.

The Internet World Wide Web Lab Assignment One of the most popular services on the Internet is the World Wide Web. This Lab is a Web simulator that teaches you how to use Web browser software to find information. You can use this Lab whether or not your school provides you with Internet access.

1. Click the Steps button to learn how to use Web browser software. As you proceed through the Steps, answer all of the Quick Check questions that appear. After you complete the Steps, you will see a Quick Check Summary Report. Follow the instructions on the screen to print this report.

2. Click the Explore button on the Welcome screen. Use the Web browser to locate a weather map of the Caribbean Virgin Islands. What is its URL?

3. A scuba diver named Wadson Lachouffe has been searching for the fabled treasure of Greybeard the pirate. A link from the Adventure Travel Web site leads to Wadson's Web page, called "Hidden Treasure". In Explore, locate the Hidden Treasure page and answer the following questions:
   a. What was the name of Greybeard's ship?
   b. What was Greybeard's favorite food?
   c. What does Wadson think happened to Greybeard's ship?

4. In the Steps, you found a graphic of Jupiter from the photo archives of the Jet Propulsion Laboratory. In the Explore section of the Lab, you can also find a graphic of Saturn. Suppose one of your friends wanted a picture of Saturn for an astronomy report. Make a list of the blue, underlined links your friend must click to find the Saturn graphic. Assume that your friend will begin at the Web Trainer home page.

5. Enter the URL *http://www.atour.com* to jump to the Adventure Travel Web site. Write a one-page description of this site. In your paper include a description of the information at the site, the number of pages the site contains, and a diagram of the links it contains.

6. Chris Thomson is a student at UVI and has his own Web pages. In Explore, look at the information Chris has included on his pages. Suppose you could create your own Web page. What would you include? Use word-processing software to design your own Web pages. Make sure you indicate the graphics and links you would use.

Quick | Check Answers

Session 1.1

1. Hypertext refers to text that contains points called links that allow the user to move to other places within the document, or to open other documents, by activating the link.
2. A Web server stores the files used in creating World Wide Web documents. The Web browser retrieves the files from the Web server and displays them. The files stored on the Web server are described in a very general way; it is the Web browser that determines how the files will eventually appear to the user.
3. HTML, which stands for Hypertext Markup Language, is used to create Web documents.

4. HTML documents do not exactly specify the appearance of a document; rather they describe the purpose of different elements in the document and leave it to the Web browser to determine the final appearance. A word processor like Word exactly specifies the appearance of each document element.

5. Documents are transferred more quickly over the Internet and are available to a wider range of machines.

6. Extensions are special formats supported by a particular browser, but not generally accepted by all browsers. The advantage is that people who use that browser have a wider range of document elements to work with. The disadvantage is that the document will not work for users who do not have that particular browser.

7. All you need is a simple text editor.

Session 1.2

1. The <HTML> tag identifies the language of the file as HTML to packages that support more than one kind of generalized markup language.

2. <H1 ALIGN=CENTER> *Header text* </H1>

3. <P> *Paragraph text* </P>

4. HTML does not recognize the blank lines as a format element. A Web browser will ignore blank lines and run the paragraphs together on the page.

5. Unordered list:
```
<UL>
    <LI> List item
    <LI> List item
</UL>
```
Ordered list:
```
<OL>
    <LI> List item
    <LI> List item
</OL>
```
Definition list:
```
<DL>
    <DT> List term <DD> Term definition
    <DT> List term <DD> Term definition
</DL>
```

6. <EM> *Italicized text* </EM>
   and
   ```
   <I> Italicized text </I>
   ```
   The advantage of using the <EM> tag is that it will be recognized even by older browsers that do not support italics (such as a terminal connected to a UNIX machine), and those browsers will still emphasize the text in some way. The <I> tag, on the other hand, will be ignored by those machines. Using the <I> tag has the advantage of explicitly describing how you want the text to appear.

Session 1.3

1. ©

2. <HR>

3. <HR WIDTH=70% SIZE=4>

4. An inline image is a GIF or JPEG that appears on a Web document. A browser can display it without a file viewer.

5. An external image is a graphic that requires the use of a software program, called a viewer, to be displayed.

6. <IMG ALIGN=LEFT SRC="Mouse.jpg">

7. GIFs and JPEGs

OBJECTIVES

In this tutorial you will:

- Create hypertext links between elements within a document

- Create hypertext links between one document and another

- Review some basic Web page structures

- Create hypertext links to pages on the Internet

- Understand the difference between and use absolute and relative pathnames

- Learn to create hypertext links to various Internet resources, including FTP servers and newsgroups

ADDING

HYPERTEXT LINKS TO A WEB PAGE

Developing an Online Resume with Hypertext Links

CASE

Creating an Online Resume, continued

In Tutorial 1 you created the basic structure and content of an online resume for Mary Taylor. Since then Mary has made a few changes to the resume, and she has ideas for more content. The two of you sit down and discuss her plans. Mary notes that although the page contents reflect the paper resume, the online resume has one disadvantage: prospective employers must scroll around the document window to view pertinent facts about Mary. Mary wants to make it as easy to jump from topic to topic in her online resume as it is to scan through topics on a one-page paper resume.

Mary also has a few references and notes of recommendation on file that she wants to make available to interested employers. She didn't include all this information on her paper resume because she wanted to limit that resume to a single page. With an online resume, Mary can still be brief, but at the same time she can make additional material readily available.

SESSION 2.1

In this session you will create anchors on a Web page that let you jump to specific points in the document. After creating those anchors, you will create and then test your first hypertext link to another document.

Creating a Hypertext Document

In Tutorial 1 you learned that a hypertext document contains **hypertext links**, items that you can select, usually by clicking a mouse, to instantly view another topic or document, often called the **destination** of the link. These links can point to another section in the same document, to an entirely different document, to a different Web page, and to a variety of other Web objects, which you'll learn about later in this tutorial.

In addition to making access to other documents easy, hypertext links provide some important organizational benefits. They indicate what points or concepts you think merit special attention or further reading. You can take advantage of these features by adding hypertext links to Mary's online resume.

At the end of Tutorial 1, the resume had three main sections: Objectives, Education, and Employment. You and Mary have made some additions and changes since then, including adding a fourth section, Other Information, which provides additional information about Mary that employers might find helpful in their job searches. However, because of the document window's limited size, the opening screen does not show any of the main sections of Mary's resume. The browser in Figure 2-1 shows Mary's name, address, and photograph, but nothing about her education or employment history. Employers have to scroll through the document to find this information.

Figure 2-1	OPENING SCREEN OF MARY'S ONLINE RESUME

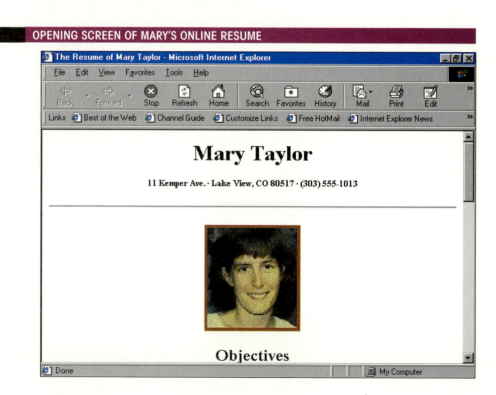

Without using hypertext links, you can do little to show more of Mary's resume in the browser except remove the image file or move it to the end of the resume, which Mary doesn't want you to do. However, you could place text for the four headings (Objectives,

Education, Employment, and Other Information) at the top of the document and then turn these headings into hypertext links. When readers open Mary's resume, they'll see not only her name, address, and photo, but also links to the main parts of her resume. They can then click any of the headings, and they will immediately see that section of the document. The hypertext links that you create here point to sections within the same document. You'll create such hypertext links in Mary's resume using three steps:

1. Type the headings into the HTML file.

2. Mark each section in the HTML file using an anchor. (You'll learn what this is shortly.)

3. Link the text you added in Step 1 to the anchors you added in Step 2.

You can accomplish the first step using techniques you learned in Tutorial 1. You need to open the Resume.htm text file in your text editor and then enter the text. You want the text to appear on the same line as Mary's photo in the browser, as in Figure 2-2.

| Figure 2-2 | ADDING TEXT FOR LINKS TO LATER SECTIONS IN THE RESUME |

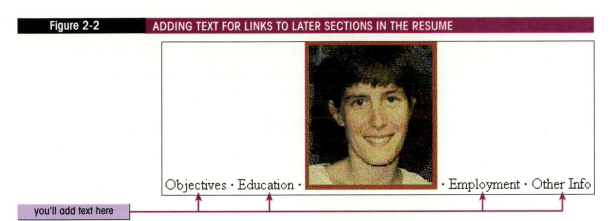

To achieve this, you place the text within the paragraph tags that already encompass the Taylor.jpg graphics file. You could type all the text into the HTML file on the same line, but to keep the HTML file as legible as possible, add the text in two lines instead. This way, when you add more tags to the text later, it will still be easy to read. Remember that because you format with markup tags in HTML, putting the text on different lines does not affect its appearance in the browser.

To add text to the document, indicating the different sections of the resume:

1. Open your text editor.

2. Open the file **Resumetxt.htm** from the Tutorial.02 folder on your Data Disk, and then save it as **Resume.htm** in the Tutorial.02 folder so you still have a copy of the original.

   TROUBLE? If you can't locate the Resumetxt.htm file in the Tutorial.02 folder in your text editor's Open dialog box, you might need to set the file type to All Files.

3. Before "<IMG SRC="Taylor.jpg">", type **Objectives · Education ·** (be sure to type the semicolons), and then press the **Enter** key so this new entry is on its own line.

4. Create a new line directly after "<IMG SRC="Taylor.jpg">" and then type **· Employment · Other Info** so this new entry is on its own line. See Figure 2-3. The new lines include the special character code · which inserts a bullet into the text to separate section headings.

Figure 2-3   INSERTING NEW TEXT IN THE RESUME PAGE

```
<BODY>
<H1 ALIGN=CENTER>Mary Taylor</H1>
<H5 ALIGN=CENTER>11 Kemper Ave. &#183 Lake View, CO 80517 &#183 (303) 555-
1013</H5>
<HR>

<P ALIGN=CENTER>
Objectives &#183; Education &#183;
<IMG SRC="Taylor.jpg">
&#183; Employment &#183; Other Info
</P>

<H2 ALIGN=CENTER>Objectives</H2>
```

5. Save the changes to the Resume.htm file, but leave the text editor open. You will revise this document throughout this tutorial.

6. Start your Web browser (you do not have to connect to the Internet), and open **Resume.htm** to verify the change. See Figure 2-4.

Figure 2-4   NEW RESUME PAGE TEXT

Mary Taylor

11 Kemper Ave. · Lake View, CO 80517 · (303) 555-1013

Objectives · Education ·   · Employment · Other Info

Creating Anchors

Now that you've created the text describing the resume's different sections, you need to locate each header and mark it in the document, using the <A> tag. The **<A> tag** creates an **anchor**, text that is specially marked so that you can link *to* it from other points in the document. Text that is anchored will become the *destination* of a link; it is *not* the text you click. You assign each anchor its own anchor name, using the NAME property. For example, if you want the text "Employment" to be an anchor, you could assign it the anchor name "EMP":

```
<A NAME="EMP">Employment</A>
```

Later, when you create a link to this anchor from the headings you just inserted at the beginning of Mary's resume, the link will point to this particular place in the document, using the anchor name, EMP. Figure 2-5 illustrates how the anchor you create will work as a reference point to a link.

Figure 2-5	ANCHORING TEXT

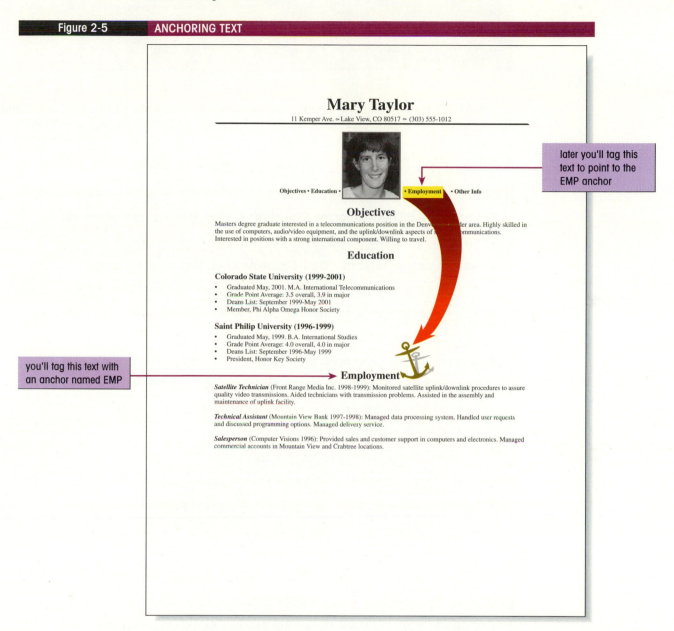

An anchor doesn't have to be just text. You can also mark an inline image using the same syntax:

```
<A NAME="PHOTO"><IMG SRC="Taylor.jpg"></A>
```

In this example, you anchor a photo. You can create a link to this photo from other points in the document by using the anchor name PHOTO. As you'll see, adding an anchor does not change your document's appearance in any way.

REFERENCE   WINDOW   RW

Creating Anchors
- Locate the text or graphic you want to anchor.
- Before the text or graphic, place the tag
  <A Name="*anchor_name*"> where *anchor_name* is the name you choose for your anchor.
- After the text or graphic, place a closing </A> tag to turn off the anchor.

For Mary's resume file, you decide to create four anchors named OBJ, ED, EMP, and OTHER for the Objectives, Education, Employment, and Other Information sections.

To add anchors to the resume's section headings:

1. Return to your text editor and open the **Resume.htm** file, if it is not already open.

2. Locate the H2 header for the Objectives section. This line currently reads:

   ```
   <H2 ALIGN=CENTER>Objectives</H2>
   ```

3. Add an anchor tag around the Objectives heading so that it reads:

   ```
   <H2 ALIGN=CENTER><A NAME="OBJ">Objectives</A></H2>
   ```

4. Locate the H2 header for the Education section. This line currently reads:

   ```
   <H2 ALIGN=CENTER>Education</H2>
   ```

5. Add an anchor tag around the Education heading so that it reads:

   ```
   <H2 ALIGN=CENTER><A NAME="ED">Education</A></H2>
   ```

6. Locate the H2 header for the Employment section, which reads:

   ```
   <H2 ALIGN=CENTER>Employment</H2>
   ```

   and add an anchor tag so that it reads:

   ```
   <H2 ALIGN=CENTER><A NAME="EMP">Employment</A></H2>
   ```

7. Locate the H2 header for the Other Information section, which reads:

   ```
   <H2>Other Information</H2>
   ```

   and add an anchor tag so that it reads:

   ```
   <H2><A NAME="OTHER"> Other Information</A></H2>
   ```

8. Save the changes you made to the Resume file.

9. Open your Web browser, reload the **Resume.htm** file, then scroll through Resume.htm to confirm that the Resume file appears unchanged. Remember that the marks you placed in the document are reference points and should not change the appearance of the resume in your browser.

   TROUBLE? If you see a change in the document, check to make sure that you used the NAME property of the <A> tag.

You created four anchors in the Web page. The next step is to create links to those anchors from the text you added around Mary's picture.

Creating **Links**

After you anchor the text that will be the destination for your links, you create the links themselves. For Mary's resume, you want to link the text you entered around her photograph to the four sections in her document. Figure 2-6 shows the four links you want to create.

Figure 2-6 | **LINKS YOU NEED TO CREATE**

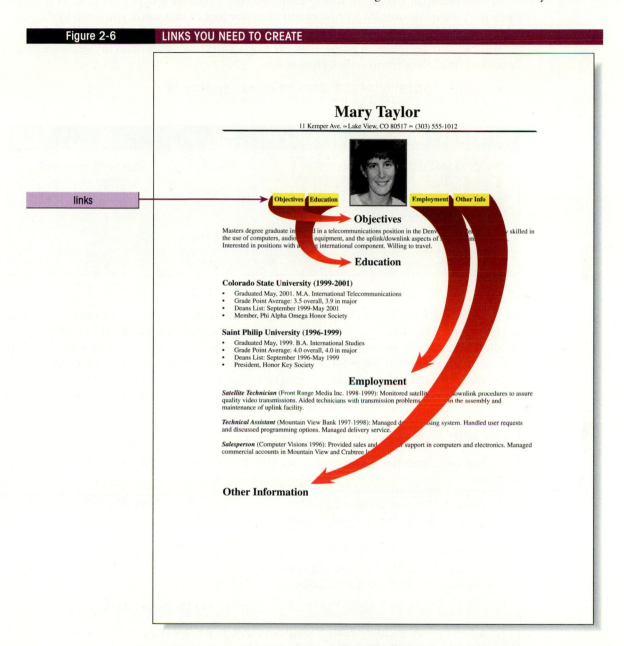

To create a link to an anchor, you use the same [A] tag you used to create the anchor. The difference is that instead of using the NAME property to define the anchor, you use the **HREF** property, short for Hypertext Reference, to indicate the location to jump to. HREF can refer to an anchor that you place in the document, or, as you'll see later, to a different Web page or a resource on the Internet. <A> tags that create links are called **link tags**.

You link to an anchor using the anchor name preceded by a pound (#) symbol. For example, to create a link to the Employment heading in Mary's resume, you use the anchor name EMP and this HTML tag:

```
<A HREF="#EMP">Employment</A>
```

In this example, the entire word "Employment" becomes a hypertext link. When you open the resume in your Web browser and click any part of that word, you jump to the location of the EMP anchor.

You can also designate an inline image as a hypertext link. To turn an inline image into a hypertext link, place it within link tags, as in:

```
<A HREF="#OTHER"><IMG SRC="Taylor.jpg"></A>
```

REFERENCE WINDOW   **RW**

Linking to Text Within a Document
- Mark the destination text with an anchor.
- Locate the text or graphic you want to designate as the link.
- Before the text or graphic, place the tag
  <A HREF="#anchor_name"> where anchor_name is the name of the anchor.
- Close the link tag with the </A> closing tag after the text or graphic you designated as the link.

Sometimes a link does not work as you expect. One common source of trouble is the case of the anchor. The HREF property is case sensitive. The anchor name "EMP" is not the same as "emp". You should also remember to make each anchor name unique within a document. If you use the same anchor name for different text, your links won't go where you expect.

In the current HTML document, you've created four anchors to which you can link. You're ready to place the link tags around the appropriate text in the HTML file.

To add link tags to the Resume.htm file:

1. Return to your text editor and make sure the Resume.htm file is open.

2. Locate the paragraph containing the four section headings and Mary's photograph at the top of the page. Within that paragraph you need to bracket each section heading with a link tag and the HREF property.

3. Change the line reading "Objectives · Education ·" to

   ```
   <A HREF="#OBJ">Objectives</A> &#183;
   <A HREF="#ED">Education</A> &#183;
   ```

4. Change the line reading "· Employment · Other Info" to

   ```
   &#183; <A HREF="#EMP">Employment</A> &#183;
   <A HREF="#OTHER">Other Info</A>
   ```

5. Compare your HTML file to Figure 2-7.

Figure 2-7	ADDING LINK TAGS

```
<BODY>
<H1 ALIGN=CENTER>Mary Taylor</H1>
<H5 ALIGN=CENTER>11 Kemper Ave. &#183 Lake View, CO 80517 &#183 (303) 555-
1013</H5>
<HR>

<P ALIGN=CENTER>
<A HREF="#OBJ">Objectives</A> &#183; <A HREF="#ED">Education</A> &#183;
<IMG SRC="Taylor.jpg">
&#183; <A HREF="#EMP">Employment</A> &#183; <A HREF="#OTHER">Other Info</A>
</P>

<H2 ALIGN=CENTER><A NAME="OBJ">Objectives</A></H2>
```

6. Save the changes you made to Resume.htm.

7. Open your Web browser and reload the **Resume.htm** file. The headings should now be a different color and be underlined—the standard formatting for links in most browsers. See Figure 2-8.

Figure 2-8	TEXT LINKS AS THEY APPEAR IN THE BROWSER

text links

Mary Taylor

11 Kemper Ave. · Lake View, CO 80517 · (303) 555-1013

Objectives · Education ·   · Employment · Other Info

TROUBLE? If the headings do not appear as text links, check your code and make sure that you are using the <A> tag around the text and the HREF property within the tag.

Before continuing, you should verify that the links work properly. To test a link, you click it.

To test your links:

1. Click one of the links. You should jump to the section of the document indicated by the link. If not, check your code for errors by comparing it to Figure 2-7.

2. Click each of the other links, scrolling back to the top of the page each time.

3. If you are continuing to Session 2.2, you can leave your browser and text editor open. Otherwise, close them.

If you still have problems, make sure you used the correct case and that you coded the anchor and link tags correctly. When you add an anchor to a large section of text, such as a section heading, make sure to place the anchor within the header tags. For example, you should write your tag as:

```
<H2><A NAME="EMP">Employment</A></H2>
```

not as:

```
<A NAME="EMP"><H2>Employment</H2></A>
```

The latter could confuse some browsers. The general rule is to always place anchors within other tag elements. Do not insert any tag elements within an anchor, except for tags that create document objects such as inline graphics.

You show the new links to Mary. She is excited to see how they work. She thinks they will quickly inform interested employers about her resume's contents and help them quickly find the information they want. In the next session, you'll create links that jump to other HTML documents.

Session 2.1 Quick Check

1. What is the HTML code for marking the text "Colorado State University" with the anchor name CSU?

2. What is the HTML code for linking the text "Universities" to an anchor that is named CSU?

3. What is wrong with the following statement?

   ```
   <A NAME="INFO"><H3>For more information</H3></A>
   ```

4. What is the HTML code for marking an inline image, Photo.jpg, with the anchor name PHOTO?

5. What is the HTML code for linking the inline image Button.jpg to an anchor with the name LINKS?

6. True or False: Anchor names are case insensitive.

SESSION 2.2

In Session 2.1 you created hypertext links to other points within the same document. In this session you will create links to other HTML documents.

Mary wants to add two more pages to her online resume: a page of references and a page of comments about her work from former employers and teachers. She then wants to add links on her resume that point to both these pages. Figure 2-9 shows what she has in mind.

Figure 2-9	MARY'S THREE WEB DOCUMENTS

Mary wants you to create links from her resume to her Comments page and her References page

References

View My Resume • Comments

Comments about my work

View My Resume • References

Mary Taylor

11 Kemper Ave. ∞ Lake View, CO 80517 ∞ (303) 555-1012

Objectives

Masters degree graduate interested in a telecommunications position in the Denver or Boulder area. Highly skilled in the use of computers, audio/video equipment, and the uplink/downlink aspects of satellite communications. Interested in positions with a strong international component. Willing to travel.

Education

Colorado State University (1999-2001)
- Graduated May, 2001. M.A. International Telecommunications
- Grade Point Average: 3.5 overall, 3.9 in major
- Deans List: September 1999-May 2001
- Member, Phi Alpha Omega Honor Society

Saint Philip University (1996-1999)
- Graduated May, 1999. B.A. International Studies
- Grade Point Average: 4.0 overall, 4.0 in major
- Deans List: September 1996-May 1999
- President, Honor Key Society

Employment

Satellite Technician (Front Range Media Inc. 1998-1999): Monitored satellite uplink/downlink procedures to assure quality video transmissions. Aided technicians with transmission problems. Assisted in the assembly and maintenance of uplink facility.

Technical Assistant (Mountain View Bank 1997-1998): Managed data processing system. Handled user requests and discussed programming options. Managed delivery service.

Salesperson (Computer Visions 1996): Provided sales and customer support in computers and electronics. Managed commercial accounts in Mountain View and Crabtree locations.

References page

Comments page

Resume page

You tell Mary that her ideas are good, but that before she starts thinking about how the documents will link to each other, she should understand the basics of Web page structures.

Web Page Structures

The three pages that will make up Mary's online resume—Resume, Comments, and References—are part of a system of Web pages. Before you set up links for navigating a group of Web pages, it's worthwhile to map out exactly how you want the pages to relate, using a technique known as storyboarding. **Storyboarding** your Web pages before you create links helps you determine which structure works best for the type of information you're presenting. You want to make sure readers can navigate easily from page to page without getting lost.

Linear Structures

You'll encounter several Web structures as you navigate the Web. Examining these structures can help you decide how to design your own system of Web pages. Figure 2-10 shows one common structure, the **linear structure**, in which each page is linked to the next and to previous pages, in an ordered chain of pages.

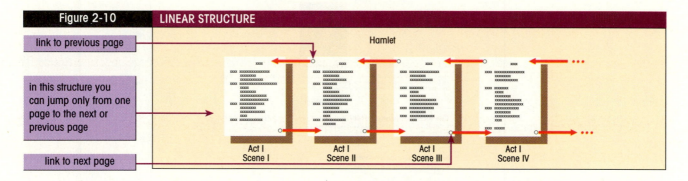

Figure 2-10   LINEAR STRUCTURE

link to previous page

in this structure you can jump only from one page to the next or previous page

link to next page

You could use this type of structure in Web pages that have a defined order. Suppose that a Web site of Shakespeare's *Hamlet* has a single page for each scene. If you use a linear structure for these pages, you assume that users want to progress through the scenes in order.

You might, however, want to make it easier for users to return immediately to the opening scene, rather than backtrack through several scenes. Figure 2-11 shows an **augmented linear structure**, in which you include a link in each page that jumps directly back to the first page, while keeping the links that allow you to move to the next and previous pages. This kind of storyboarding can reveal approaches to organizing the Web site that otherwise might not be noticed.

Figure 2-11 **AUGMENTED LINEAR STRUCTURE**

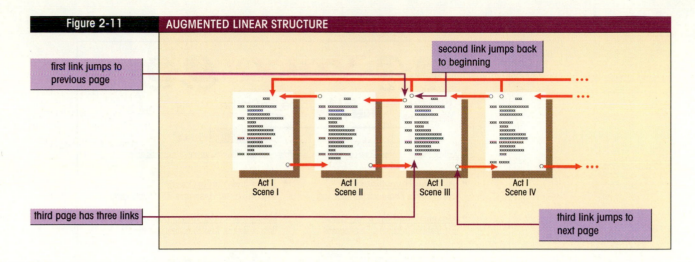

first link jumps to previous page

second link jumps back to beginning

third page has three links

third link jumps to next page

Act I Scene I   Act I Scene II   Act I Scene III   Act I Scene IV

Hierarchical Structures

Another popular structure is the hierarchical structure of Web pages shown in Figure 2-12. A **hierarchical structure** starts with a general topic that includes links to more specific topics. Each specific topic includes links to yet more specialized topics, and so on. In a hierarchical structure, users can move easily from general to specific and back, but not from specific to specific.

Figure 2-12 **HIERARCHICAL STRUCTURE**

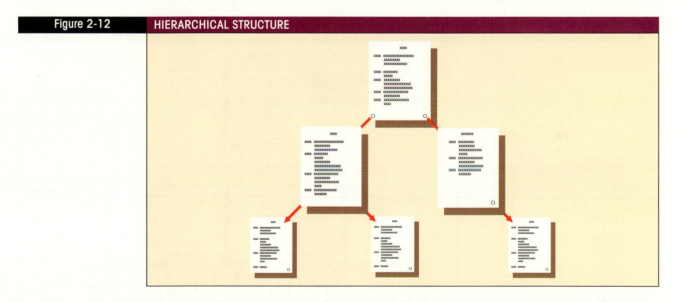

As with the linear structure, including a link to the top of the structure on each page gives users an easy path back to the beginning. Subject catalogs such as the Yahoo! directory of Web pages often use this structure. Figure 2-13 shows this site, located at *http://www.yahoo.com*.

Figure 2-13   HIERARCHICAL STRUCTURE ON YAHOO! WEB PAGE

Mixed Structures

You can also combine structures. Figure 2-14 shows a hierarchical structure in which each level of pages is related in a linear structure. You might use this system for the *Hamlet* Web site to let the user move from scene to scene linearly, or from a specific scene to the general act to the overall play.

Figure 2-14   COMBINATION OF LINEAR AND HIERARCHICAL STRUCTURES

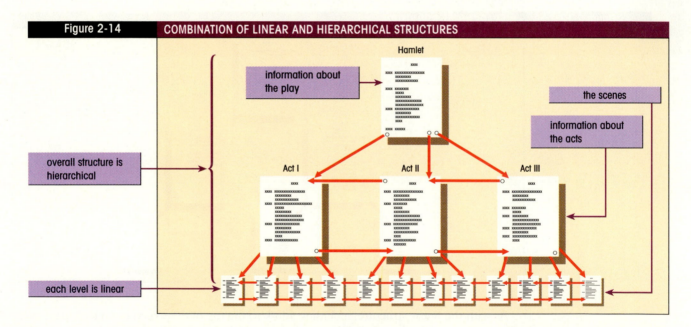

As these examples show, a little foresight can go a long way toward making your Web pages easier to use. The best time to organize a structure is when you first start creating multiple pages and those pages are small and easy to manage. If you're not careful, your structure might look like Figure 2-15.

Figure 2-15   MULTIPAGE DOCUMENT WITH NO COHERENT STRUCTURE

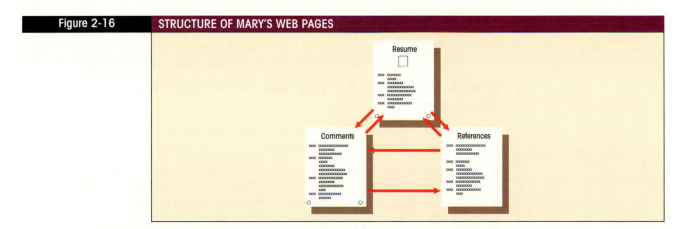

This structure is confusing, and it makes it difficult for readers to grasp the contents of the entire Web site. Moreover, a user who enters this structure at a certain page might not even be aware of the presence of other pages at the far end of the chain.

Creating **Links Between Documents**

Mary and you discuss the type of structure that will work best for her online resume. She wants employers to move effortlessly among the three documents. Because there are only three pages, all focused on the same topic, you decide to include links within each document to the other two. If Mary later adds other pages to her resume, she will need to create a more formal structure involving some principles discussed in the previous sections.

For her simple three-page site, the structure shown in Figure 2-16 works just fine.

Figure 2-16   STRUCTURE OF MARY'S WEB PAGES

Resume

Comments   References

Mary has given you the information to create two additional HTML files: Refertxt.htm, a page with the names and addresses of previous employers and professors; and Comtxt.htm, a page with comments from previous employers and teachers. You suggest that Mary include a graphic—a check mark–on the Comments page. You have just the file for her, Check.jpg. These three files are in the Tutorial.02 folder on your Data Disk. You should save these files with new names: Refer.htm and Comments.htm, to keep the originals intact.

To rename the Refertxt.htm and Comtxt.htm files:

1. Using your text editor, open **Refertxt.htm** from the Tutorial.02 folder on your Data Disk, and save it as **Refer.htm**.

2. With your text editor, open the file **Comtxt.htm** in the Tutorial.02 folder, and save it as **Comments.htm**.

Linking to a Document

You begin by linking Mary's Resume page to the References and Comments pages. You use the same <A> tag that you used earlier. For example, let's say you wanted a user to be able to click the phrase "Comments on my work" to jump to the Comments.htm file. You could enter this HTML command in your current document:

```
<A HREF="Comments.htm">Comments on my work</A>
```

In this example, the entire text "Comments on my work" is linked to the HTML file, Comments.htm. In order for the browser to be able to locate and open the Comments.htm file, it must be in the same folder as the Resume.htm file, the document containing the links.

REFERENCE WINDOW   **RW**

Linking to a Document on Your Computer
- Locate the link text or graphic (that is, the text or image you want to click to jump to the destination of the link).
- Before the text or graphic, place the tag
  <A HREF="*filename*">
  where filename is the name of the destination document.
- After the link text or graphic, place the tag </A>.

Unlike creating hypertext links between elements on the same page, this process does not require you to set an anchor in a file to link to it—the filename serves as the anchor.

To add links in the Resume page to the References and Comments pages:

1. If you closed your text editor, reopen it and open the **Resume.htm** file that you worked on in Session 2.1 of this tutorial.

2. Scroll down to the Other Information section near the bottom of the page. Three items are listed; you want the first, References, to link to the References page, and the second, Comments on my work, to link to the Comments page. (You'll link the third to a Web site in the next session.)

3. Change the line reading "<LI>References" to:

   ```
   <LI><A HREF="Refer.htm">References</A>
   ```

4. Change the line reading "<LI> Comments on my work" to read:

   ```
   <LI><A HREF="Comments.htm">Comments on my work</A>
   ```

See Figure 2-17.

| Figure 2-17 | TEXT LINKED TO OTHER FILES |

<A> tag creating a link to another file

```
<H2><A NAME="OTHER">Other Information</A></H2>
<UL>
<LI><A HREF="Refer.htm">References</A>
<LI><A HREF="Comments.htm">Comments on my work</A>
<LI>Go to Colorado State
</UL>

<H3> Interested? </H3>
Contact Mary Taylor at mtaylor@tt.gr.csu.edu

</BODY>
```

5. Save the changes to the Resume file.

6. Open your Web browser, if it is not open already, and view Resume.htm. The items in the Other Information section now appear as the text links shown in Figure 2-18.

| Figure 2-18 | NEW LINKS |

links in Mary's resume to other files

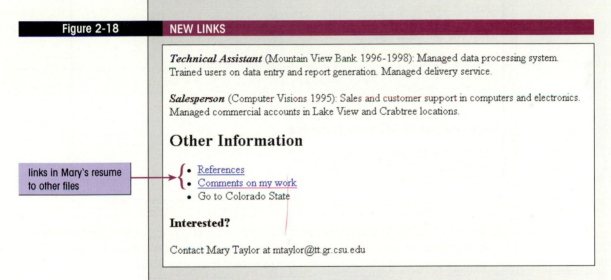

Technical Assistant (Mountain View Bank 1996-1998): Managed data processing system. Trained users on data entry and report generation. Managed delivery service.

Salesperson (Computer Visions 1995): Sales and customer support in computers and electronics. Managed commercial accounts in Lake View and Crabtree locations.

Other Information

- References
- Comments on my work
- Go to Colorado State

Interested?

Contact Mary Taylor at mtaylor@tt.gr.csu.edu

7. Click the **References** link to verify that you jump to the References page shown in Figure 2-19.

TROUBLE? If the link doesn't work, check to see that Resume.htm and Refer.htm are in the same folder on your Data Disk.

Figure 2-19   **REFERENCES PAGE**

References

View My Resume · Comments

Lawrence Gale, Telecommunications Manager

Front Range Media Inc.
1000 Black Canyon Drive
Fort Tompkins, CO 80517
(303) 555-0103

Karen Carlson, Manager

Mountain View Bank
2 North Maple St.
Lake View, CO 80517
(303) 555-8792

Trent Wu, Sales Manager

Computer Visions
24 Mall Road
Lake View, CO 80517
(303) 555-1313

Robert Ramirez, Prof. Electrical Engineering

Colorado State University
Kleindist Hall
Fort Collins, CO 80517

8. Go back to the Resume page (usually by clicking a Back button on the tool-bar of your browser), and then click the **Comments on my work** link to verify that you jump to the Comments page shown in Figure 2-20.

Figure 2-20   COMMENTS PAGE

Comments about my work

View My Resume · References

 Lawrence Gale, Telecommunications Manager, *Front Range Media Inc.*

"Mary is a highly professional technician who takes much pride in her work. She impressed me with her ability to learn the details of our sophisticated and complex hardware and software, especially given her lack of telecommunications experience when she first started with us. Mary works well in a team but also has the ability to take my suggestions and finish a project in a highly competent manner without further direction. As she closes out her work here, I find her to be an excellent and essential component in our operations. I have complete confidence that you will be very pleased with Mary's work and recommend her very highly."

 Karen Carlson, Manager, *Mountain View Bank*

"Mary assisted in the operations and development of a new database program we were setting up. I found Mary to be an enthusiastic and hard-working addition to our team. Mary is one of those people who gets things done and done right. She will excel in whatever she does. I think any company that hires her will be very happy that they did."

Next you want to add similar links in the Refer.htm and Comments.htm files that point to the other two pages. Specifically, in Refer.htm, you need to add one link to Resume.htm and another to Comments.htm; in Comments.htm you need one link to Resume.htm and another to Refer.htm. This way, each page will have two links on it that point to the other two pages.

To add links in the References page to the Resume and Comments pages:

1. Return to your text editor and then open the file **Refer.htm** from the Tutorial.02 folder on your Data Disk.

2. Locate the H4 header at the top of the page.

3. Change the text "View My Resume" to:

   ```
   <A HREF="Resume.htm">View My Resume</A>
   ```

4. Locate the text "Comments" on the same line. Change "Comments" to:

   ```
   <A HREF="Comments.htm">Comments</A>
   ```

5. Compare your code to Figure 2-21.

Figure 2-21

ADDING LINKS TO THE REFERENCES PAGE

new links

```
<BODY>
<H2 ALIGN=CENTER> References</H2>

<H4 ALIGN=CENTER> <A HREF="Resume.htm">View My Resume</A> &#183;
<A HREF="Comments.htm">Comments</A> </H4>
<HR>

<H4>Lawrence Gale, Telecommunications Manager</H4>
Front Range Media Inc.<BR>
1000 Black Canyon Drive<BR>
Fort Tompkins, CO 80517<BR>
(303) 555-0103
```

6. Save the changes to Refer.htm.

7. Open your Web browser, if it is not open already, and view Refer.htm. Your links should now look like Figure 2-22.

Figure 2-22

LINKS ON THE REFERENCES PAGE

new links

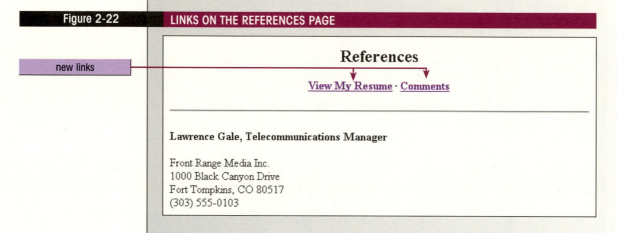

References

View My Resume · Comments

Lawrence Gale, Telecommunications Manager

Front Range Media Inc.
1000 Black Canyon Drive
Fort Tompkins, CO 80517
(303) 555-0103

8. Test the two links to verify that you jump to the Resume and Comments pages.

   TROUBLE? If the links do not work, check the spelling of the filenames in the HREF property of the <A> tag. For some Web servers, the case (upper or lower) is also important, so you should make sure that the case matches as well.

Now you need to follow similar steps so that the Comments page links to the two other pages.

To add links in the Comments page to the Resume and References pages:

1. Return to your text editor, and then open the file **Comments.htm** from the Tutorial.02 folder on your Data Disk (you can close Refer.htm).

2. Locate the H4 heading at the top of the page.

3. Change the text "View My resume" to:

   ```
   <A HREF="Resume.htm">View My Resume</A>
   ```

4. Change "References" on the same line to:

```
<A HREF="Refer.htm">References</A>
```

5. Save the changes to Comments.htm.

6. Open your Web browser, if it is not open already, and view Comments.htm. You should see the links shown in Figure 2-23.

| Figure 2-23 | LINKS ON THE COMMENTS PAGE |

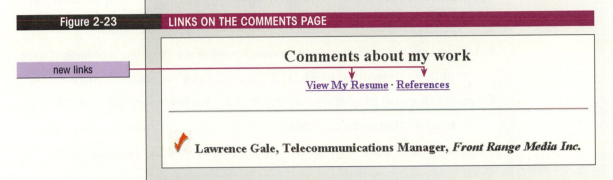

new links

7. Click the two links to verify that you jump to the Resume and References pages.

Now that all the links among the three pages are set up, you can easily move among the three documents.

Linking to a Section of a Document

You might have noticed in testing your links that you always jump to the top of the destination page. What if you'd like to jump to a specific location elsewhere in a document, rather than the beginning? To do this, you can set anchors as you did in Session 2.1 and link to an anchor you create within the document. For example, to create a link to a section in the file Home.htm marked with an anchor name of "Interests," you would create an anchor in the Home.htm file at the section on Interest, and then you would enter this HTML code in your current document:

```
<A HREF="Home.htm#Interests">View my interests</A>
```

In this example, the entire text, "View my interests," is linked to the Interests section in the Home.htm file. Note that the pound (#)symbol in this tag distinguishes the filename from the anchor name (that is why you included the # symbol earlier when linking to anchors within the same document).

Mary wants to link the positions listed in the Employment section of her resume to specific comments from employers on the Comments page. The Comments.htm file already has these anchors in place:

- **GALE**, for comments made by Lawrence Gale, Mary's telecommunications manager
- **CARLSON**, for comments made by Karen Carlson, manager of Mountain View Bank
- **WU**, for comments made by Trent Wu of Computer Visions

Now you need to link the names listed in the Resume file to these three anchors in the Comments page.

To add links to the Resume page that jump to anchors on the Comments page:

1. With your text editor, reopen the **Resume.htm** file (you can close the Comments file).

2. Locate the Employment section in the middle of the Resume file. You need to bracket each job title with link tags that point to the appropriate comment in the Comments page. Leave in place any tags that format the text, such as the <P>, <I>, and <B> tags.

3. Move to the first job description and replace the title "Satellite Technician" with:

   ```
   <A HREF="Comments.htm#GALE">Satellite Technician</A>
   ```

4. Move to the next job description and replace the title "Technical Assistant" with:

   ```
   <A HREF="Comments.htm#CARLSON">Technical Assistant </A>
   ```

5. Move to the final job description, and replace the title "Salesperson" with:

   ```
   <A HREF="Comments.htm#WU">Salesperson</A>
   ```

6. Save the changes to the Resume file.

7. Open your Web browser and open **Resume.htm**. The job titles in the Employment section should appear as text links, as shown in Figure 2-24.

Figure 2-24 **LINKS TO SPECIFIC LOCATIONS WITHIN THE COMMENTS PAGE**

Employment

Satellite Technician (Front Range Media Inc. 1998-1999): Monitored satellite uplink/downlink procedures to assure quality video transmissions. Aided technicians in the diagnoses and repair of transmission errors. Assisted in the assembly and maintenance of uplink facility.

Technical Assistant (Mountain View Bank 1996-1998): Managed data processing system. Trained users on data entry and report generation. Managed delivery service.

Salesperson (Computer Visions 1995): Sales and customer support in computers and electronics. Managed commercial accounts in Lake View and Crabtree locations.

Other Information

- References
- Comments on my work
- Go to Colorado State

links in the resume that point to specific locations within the Comments page

8. Click the three links to verify that you jump to the appropriate places in the Comments page.

   TROUBLE? If you have a problem with your links, remember that anchors are case sensitive. Make sure you typed GALE, CARLSON, and WU in all uppercase letters.

9. If you are continuing to Session 2.3, you can leave your browser and text editor open. Otherwise, close them.

With these last hypertext links in place, you have given readers of Mary's online resume access to additional information. In the next session, you will learn how to point your hypertext links to documents and resources on the Internet.

Session 2.2 QUICK CHECK

1. What is storyboarding? Why is it important in creating a Web page system?

2. What is a linear structure?

3. What is a hierarchical structure?

4. You are trying to create a system of Web pages for the play *Hamlet* in which each scene has a Web page. On each page you want to include links to the previous and next scenes of the play, as well as to the first scene of the play and the first scene of the current act. Draw a diagram of this multipage document. (Just draw enough acts and scenes to make the structure clear.)

5. What code would you enter to link the text "Sports info" to the HTML file Sports.htm?

6. What code would you enter to link the text "Basketball news" to the HTML file Sports.htm at a place in the file with the anchor name BBALL?

SESSION 2.3

In Session 2.2 you created links to other documents within the same folder as the Resume.htm file. In this session you will learn to create hypertext links to documents located in other folders and in other computers on the Internet.

Mary wants to add a link to her Resume page that points to the Colorado State University home page. The link gives potential employers an opportunity to learn more about the school she attended and the courses it offers. Before creating this link for Mary, you need to review the way HTML references files in different folders and computers.

Linking to Documents in Other Folders

Until now you've worked with documents that were all in the same folder. When you created links to other files in that folder, you specified the filename in the link tag, but not its location. Browsers assume that if no folder information is given, the file is in the same folder as the current document. In some situations you might want to place different files in different folders, particularly when working with large multidocument systems that span several topics, each topic with its own folder.

When referencing files in different folders in the link tag, you must include each file's location, called its **path**. HTML supports two kinds of paths: absolute paths and relative paths.

Absolute Pathnames

The **absolute path** shows exactly where the file is on the computer. In HTML you start every absolute pathname with a slash (/). Then you type the folder names on the computer, starting with the topmost folder in the folder hierarchy and progressing through the different levels of subfolders. You separate each folder name from the next with a slash. The pathname, from left to right, leads down through the folder hierarchy to the folder that contains the file. After you type the name of the folder that contains the file, you type a final slash and then the filename.

For example, consider the folder structure shown in Figure 2-25.

Figure 2-25	FOLDER TREE

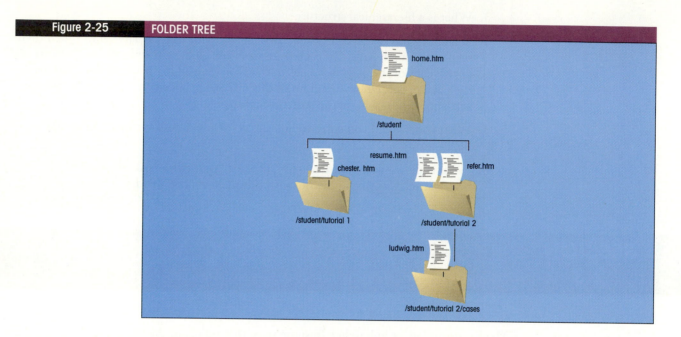

Figure 2-25 shows five HTML files contained in four different folders. The topmost folder is the student folder. Within the student folder are the tutorial1 and tutorial2 folders, and within the tutorial2 folder is the cases folder. Figure 2-26 shows absolute pathnames for the five files.

Figure 2-26	ABSOLUTE PATHNAMES

ABSOLUTE PATHNAME	INTERPRETATION
/student/home.htm	The home .htm file in the student folder
/student/tutorial1/chester.htm	The chester.htm file in the tutorial1 folder, a subfolder of the student folder
/student/tutorial2/resume.htm	The resume.htm file in the tutorial2 folder, another subfolder of the student folder
/student/tutorial2/refer.htm	The refer.htm file in the same folder as the resume.htm folder
/student/tutorial2/cases/ludwig.htm	The ludwig.htm file in the cases folder, a subfolder of the /student/tutorial2 folder

Even the absolute pathnames of files located on different hard disks begin with a slash. To differentiate these files, HTML requires you to include the drive letter followed by a vertical bar (|). For example, a file named "resume.htm" in the student folder on drive A of your computer has the absolute pathname "/A|/student/resume.htm".

Relative Pathnames

If a computer has many folders and subfolders, absolute pathnames can be long, cumbersome, and confusing. For that reason, most Web authors use relative pathnames in their hypertext links. A **relative path** gives a file's location in relation to the current Web document. As with absolute pathnames, folder names are separated by slashes. Unlike absolute pathnames, a relative pathname does not begin with a slash. To reference a file in a folder above the current folder in the folder hierarchy, relative pathnames use two periods (..).

For example, if the current file is resume.htm, located in the /student/tutorial2 folder shown in Figure 2-25, the relative pathnames and their interpretations for the other four files in the folder tree appear as in Figure 2-27.

Figure 2-27	RELATIVE PATHNAMES

RELATIVE PATHNAME	INTERPRETATION
../home.htm	The home.htm file in the folder one level up in the folder tree from the current file
../tutorial1/chester.htm	The chester.htm file in the tutorial1 subfolder of the folder one level up from the current file
refer.htm	The refer.htm file in the same folder as the current file
cases/ludwig.htm	The ludwig.htm file in the cases subfolder, one level down from the current folder

A second reason to use relative pathnames is that they make your hypertext links portable. If you have to move your files to a different computer or server, you can move the entire folder structure and still use the relative pathnames in the hypertext links. If you use absolute pathnames, you need to painstakingly revise each and every link.

Linking to Documents on the Internet

Now you can turn your attention to creating a link on Mary's resume to Colorado State University. To create a hypertext link to a document on the Internet, you need to know its URL. A **URL**, or **Uniform Resource Locator**, gives a file's location on the Web. The URL for Colorado State University, for example, is *http://www.colostate.edu/*. You can find the URL of a Web page in the Location or Address box of your browser's document window.

After you know a document's URL, you are ready to add the code that creates the link—again, the <A> code with the HREF property that creates links to documents on your computer. For example, to create a link to a document on the Internet with the URL *http://www.mwu.edu/course/info.html*, you use this HTML code:

```
<A HREF="http://www.mwu.edu/course/info.html"> Course
Information</A>
```

This example links the text "Course Information" to the Internet document located at *http://www.mwu.edu/course/info.html*. As long as your computer is connected to the Internet, clicking the text within the tag should make your browser jump to that document.

REFERENCE WINDOW RW

Linking to a Document on the Internet

- Locate the text or graphic you want to designate as the link.
- Before the text or graphic, place the tag <A HREF=*"URL"*> where ***URL*** is the URL of the Web page you want to link to.
- After the text or graphic, insert the </A> closing tag.

In the Other Information section of Mary's resume, she wants to link the text "Go to Colorado State" to the CSU home page. You're ready to add that link.

To add a link to the Colorado State University page from Mary's Resume page:

1. If necessary, open your text editor, and then open the **Resume.htm** file that you worked on in Session 2.2 of this tutorial.
2. Locate the Other Information section near the bottom of the page.
3. Change the line "<LI>Go to Colorado State" to:

```
<LI><A HREF="http://www.colostate.edu/"> Go to Colorado
State</A>
```

4. Save the changes to the Resume file.
5. If necessary, open your Web browser and connect to the Internet.
6. Open the file **Resume.htm**. The Go to Colorado State entry should look like the text link shown in Figure 2-28.

Figure 2-28 LINK TO ANOTHER PAGE ON THE WEB

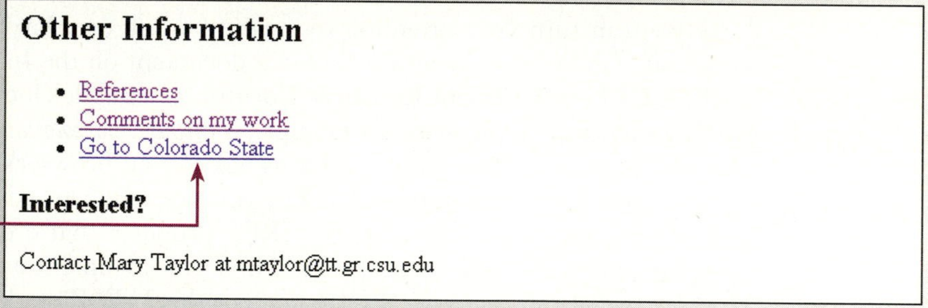

Other Information
References
Comments on my work
Go to Colorado State
Interested?
Contact Mary Taylor at mtaylor@tt.gr.csu.edu

link to Colorado State home page

7. Click the **Go to Colorado State** link. The Colorado State University home page shown in Figure 2-29 appears.

   TROUBLE? If the CSU home page doesn't appear right away, it might just be loading slowly on your system because it contains a large graphic. If the CSU home page still doesn't appear, verify that your computer is connected to the Internet.

Figure 2-29	COLORADO STATE UNIVERSITY HOME PAGE

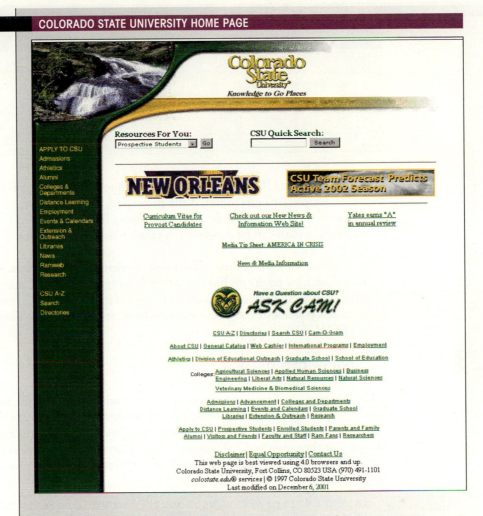

8. Click the **Back** button in your browser to return to Mary's resume.

Linking to Other Internet Objects

Occasionally you see a URL for an Internet object other than a Web page. Recall that one reason for the World Wide Web's success is that it lets users access several types of Internet resources using the same program. The method you used to create a link to the Colorado State University home page is the same method you use to set up links to other Internet resources, such as FTP servers to Usenet newsgroups (you'll learn what these are below). Only the proper URL for each object is required.

Each URL follows the same basic format. The first part identifies the **communication protocol**, the set of rules governing how information is exchanged. Web pages use the communication protocol **HTTP**, short for **Hypertext Transfer Protocol**. All Web page URLs begin with the letters "http". Other Internet resources use different communication protocols. After the communication protocol there is usually a separator, like a colon followed by a slash or two (://). The exact separator depends on the Internet resource. The rest of the URL identifies the location of the document or resource on the Internet. Figure 2-30 interprets a Web page with the URL:

```
http://www.mwu.edu/course/info.html#majors
```

Figure 2-30	INTERPRETING PARTS OF A URL

PART OF URL	INTERPRETATION
http://	The communication protocol
www.mwu.edu	The Internet host name for the computer storing the document
/course/info.html	The pathname and filename of the document on the computer
#majors	An anchor in the document

Notice that the URL for the Colorado State home page doesn't seem to have any path or file information. By convention, if the path and filename are left off the URL, the browser searches for a file named "index.html" or "index.htm" in the root folder of the Web server. Note that the path can be expressed in relative or absolute terms. This is the file displayed in Figure 2-29.

Before you walk Mary through the task of creating her final link, you take a quick detour to show her how to create links to other Internet resources, if needed. You might not be familiar with all the Internet resources discussed in these next sections. This tutorial doesn't try to teach you about these resources in detail; it just shows you how to reference them in your HTML files.

Linking to FTP Servers

FTP servers store files that Internet users can download, or transfer, to their computers. **FTP**, short for **File Transfer Protocol**, is the communications protocol these file servers use to transfer information. URLs for FTP servers follow the same format as those for Web pages, except that they use the FTP protocol rather than the HTTP protocol: ftp://*FTP_Hostname*. For example, to create a link to the FTP server located at ftp.microsoft.com, you could use this HTML code:

```
<A HREF="ftp://ftp.microsoft.com">Microsoft FTP server</A>
```

In this example, clicking the text "Microsoft FTP server" jumps the user to the Microsoft FTP server page shown in Figure 2-31. Note that different browsers will show the contents of the FTP site in different ways. Figure 2-31 shows what it might look like with Internet Explorer.

Figure 2-31	**FTP SERVER AT FTP.MICROSOFT.COM**

ftp.microsoft.com

Server: ftp.microsoft.com
User Name: Anonymous

This is FTP.MICROSOFT.COM. Please see the dirmap.txt file for more information.

Click here to learn about browsing FTP sites.

bussys deskapps developr kbhelp misc peropsys products

reskit services softlib dirmap.htm

Linking to Usenet News

Usenet is a collection of discussion forums, called **newsgroups**, that lets users send and retrieve messages on a wide variety of topics. The URL for a newsgroup is news:*newsgroup*. To access the surfing newsgroup, alt.surfing, you place this line in your HTML file:

```
<A HREF="news:alt.surfing">Go to the surfing newsgroup</A>
```

When you click a link to a newsgroup, your computer starts your newsgroup software and accesses the newsgroup. For example, if you have the Outlook Newsreader program installed, clicking the above link will open the window shown in Figure 2-32.

Figure 2-32	**ACCESSING THE ALT.SURFING NEWSGROUP**

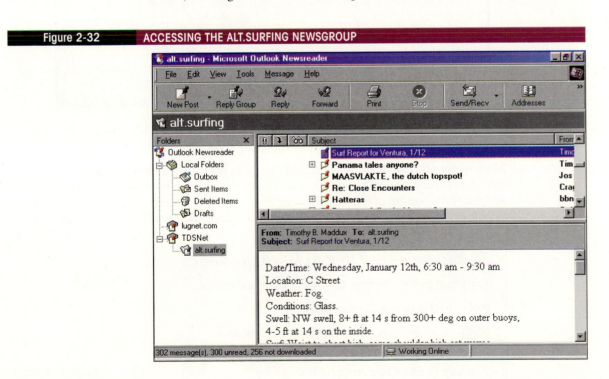

Linking to E-mail

Many Web authors include their e-mail addresses on their Web pages so that users who access these pages can easily send feedback. You can set up these e-mail addresses to act as hypertext links. When a user clicks the e-mail address, the browser starts a mail program and automatically inserts the author's e-mail address into the outgoing message. The user then types the body of the message and mails it. The URL for an e-mail address is mailto:*e-mail_address*. To create a link to the e-mail address davis@mwu.edu, for example, you enter the following into your Web document:

```
<A HREF="mailto:davis@mwu.edu">davis@mwu.edu</A>
```

If you click the text davis@mwu.edu and you have Microsoft Outlook installed as your default e-mail program, the window shown in Figure 2-33 appears.

Figure 2-33   **SENDING MAIL TO DAVIS@MWU.EDU**

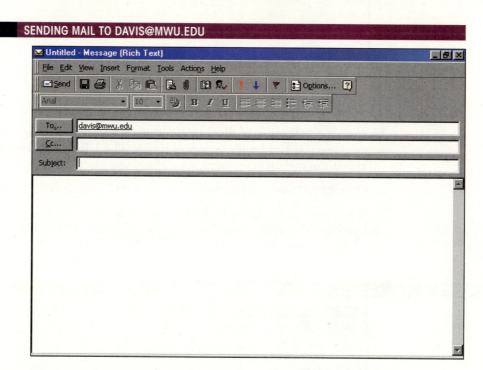

Adding an E-mail Link to Mary's Resume

Mary wants a final addition to her resume: a link to her e-mail address. With this link, an interested employer can quickly send Mary a message through the Internet. Mary placed her e-mail address at the bottom of the Resume page. Now you need to designate that text as a link so that when an employer clicks it, a window similar to the one shown in Figure 2-33 will open.

To add an e-mail link to Mary's resume:

1. Return to the Resume.htm file in your text editor.

2. Go to the bottom of the page.

3. Change the text "mtaylor@tt.gr.csu.edu" to

```
<A HREF="mailto:mtaylor@tt.gr.csu.edu">
mtaylor@tt.gr.csu.edu</A>
```

4. Save the changes to the Resume file.

5. Return to your Web browser and reload Resume.htm.

6. Move to the bottom of the page. Mary's e-mail address should look like the hypertext link shown in Figure 2-34.

   TROUBLE? Some browsers do not support the mailto URL. If you use a browser other than Netscape Navigator or Internet Explorer, check to see if it supports this feature.

Figure 2-34	MARY TAYLOR'S E-MAIL ADDRESS AS A HYPERLINK

Interested?

Contact Mary Taylor at <u>mtaylor@tt.gr.csu.edu</u>

Mary's e-mail address

7. Click the hypertext link to Mary's e-mail address. See Figure 2-35.

Figure 2-35	MAIL MESSAGE WITH MARY TAYLOR'S E-MAIL ADDRESS AUTOMATICALLY INSERTED

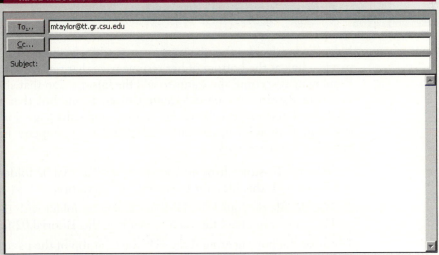

To...	mtaylor@tt.gr.csu.edu
Cc...	
Subject:	

   TROUBLE? Your e-mail window might look different, depending on the mail program installed on your computer.

8. Cancel the mail message by clicking the Close button in the upper-right corner of the window. Mary's e-mail address is fictional, so you can't send her mail anyway.

9. Close your Web browser and text editor.

You show Mary the final form of her online resume. She's really thrilled with the result. You tell her the next thing she needs to do is contact an Internet service provider and transfer the files to an account on their machine. When that's done, Mary's resume becomes available online to countless employers across the Internet.

Session 2.3 QUICK CHECK

1. What's the difference between an absolute path and a relative path?

2. Refer to the diagram in Figure 2-25: If the current file is ludwig.htm in the /student/tutorial2/cases folder, what are the relative pathnames for the four other files?

3. What tag would you enter to link the text "Washington" to the FTP server at *ftp.uwash.edu*?

4. What tag would you enter to link the text "Boxing" to the newsgroup *rec.sports.boxing.pro*?

5. What tag would you enter to link the text "President" to the e-mail address *president@whitehouse.gov*?

REVIEW ASSIGNMENTS

Mary Taylor decides that she wants you to add a few more items to her resume. She wants to add a link at the bottom of her resume page that returns readers to the top. Also, in the Employment section, she wants to add the information that she worked as a tutor for Professor Ramirez at Colorado State University and link that job title to comments Professor Ramirez made about her in the Comments page. Finally, she wants to add a link to Colorado State's Department of Electrical and Computer Engineering, where she did a lot of her graduate work.

1. Open the **Resume.htm** file located in the Tutorial.02 folder on your Data Disk. You worked with this file over the course of this tutorial.

2. Save the file on your Data Disk in the Review folder with the same name, Resume.htm. This will leave intact the version that is in the Tutorial.02 folder.

3. Add an anchor tag around the H1 header at top of the page (Mary's name). Give the anchor the name TOP.

4. After the HTML line at the bottom of the page containing Mary's e-mail address, and before the </BODY> tag, enter a new paragraph with the line "Go to the top of the page." Change this text to a hyperlink, pointing to the TOP anchor you created in Step 3.

5. Move to the Employment section. After the paragraph describing Mary's experience as a salesperson, insert this paragraph: "Tutor (Colorado State): Tutored students in electrical engineering and mathematics." Format this paragraph using the same <P>, <B>, and <I> tags you used for the other job descriptions in the resume.

6. Change the text "Tutor" to a hyperlink pointing to the RAMIREZ anchor in the Comments page (this anchor already exists).

7. Move to the Other Information section, and add a new list item to the unsorted list: "Go to Colorado State Department of Electrical and Computer Engineering."

8. Change the new list item to a hyperlink pointing to the URL: *http://www.lance.colostate.edu/depts/ee/*.

9. Save the Resume.htm file and print it.

10. View the Resume.htm file with your Web browser. Make sure you open Resume.htm in the Review folder of the Tutorial.02 folder. Verify that all of the new links work correctly.

11. Print a copy of the Resume page as displayed by the browser.

CASE PROBLEMS

Case 1. Creating Links to Federal Departments   As a librarian at the city library, you are creating a Web page to help people access the home pages for several federal government departments. Figure 2-36 lists each department's URL.

Figure 2-36

DEPARTMENT	URL
Department of Agriculture	http://www.usda.gov/
Department of Commerce	http://www.doc.gov/
Department of Defense	http://www.defenselink.mil/
Department of Education	http://www.ed.gov/
Department of Energy	http://www.doe.gov/
Department of Health and Human Services	http://www.dhhs.gov/
Department of Housing and Urban Development	http://www.hud.gov/
Department of Interior	http://www.doi.gov/
Department of Justice	http://www.usdoj.gov/
Department of Labor	http://www.dol.gov/
Department of State	http://www.state.gov/
Department of Transportation	http://www.dot.gov/
Department of Treasury	http://www.ustreas.gov/
Department of Veteran Affairs	http://www.va.gov/

You'll create an unsorted list containing department names, and then make each name a text link to the department's home page.

1. Start the text editor on your computer and open a new document.

2. Enter the <HTML>, <HEAD>, and <BODY> tags to identify different sections of the page.

3. Within the HEAD section, insert a <TITLE> tag with the text "Federal Government Departments".

4. Within the BODY section, create a centered H1 header with the text "A list of federal departments".

5. Create an unordered list of the department names shown in the first column of Figure 2-36. You can save yourself a lot of typing by using the Copy and Paste commands in your text editor (so that you don't have to type "Department of " each time).

6. Link each department name with its URL (shown in the second column of Figure 2-36).

7. Save the file as Depart.htm in the Cases subfolder of the Tutorial.02 folder on your Data Disk, print the file, and then close your text editor.

8. View the file with your Web browser, create a printout, and then close your browser.

Case 2. *Using Graphics as Hypertext Links* You are an assistant to a professor in the Music Department who is trying to create Web pages for topics in classical music. Previously you created a Web page for her that showed the different sections of the fourth movement of Beethoven's Ninth symphony. Now that you've learned to link multiple HTML files together, you have created pages for all four movements.

Explore

The four pages are in the Cases folder of the Tutorial.02 folder on your Data Disk. Their names are: Move1A.htm, Move2A.htm, Move3A.htm, and Move4A.htm. You'll rename them Move1.htm, Move2.htm, Move3.htm, and Move4.htm so that you'll have the originals if you want to work on them later. Figure 2-37 shows the page for the third movement.

Figure 2-37

Beethoven's Ninth Symphony

☜ The Third Movement ☞

Sectional Form

1. A-Section
2. B-Section
3. A-Section varied
4. B-Section
5. Interlude
6. A-Section varied
7. Coda

View the Classical Net Home page.

You now need to link the pages. You've already placed graphic elements—the hands pointing to the previous or next movement of the symphony—in each file. You decide to mark each graphic image as a hypertext link that jumps the user to the previous or next movement.

1. Start your text editor and then open the **Move1A.htm — Move4A.htm** files in the Tutorial.02/Cases folder on your Data Disk, and save them as Move1.htm — Move4.htm in the Cases folder.

2. Within each of the HTML files you created in Step 1, edit the inline images, Right.jpg and Left.jpg, so that the Right.jpg inline image is a hyperlink pointing to the next movement in the symphony, and Left.jpg points to the previous movement in the symphony.

3. Within each of the four HTML files, change the text "View the Classical Net Home page." to a hyperlink pointing to the URL *http://www.classical.net/*. Save and print all four HTML files and then close your text editor.

4. Open the pages in your Web browser and verify that all of the links work correctly.

5. Print each page in the Web browser, and then close your browser.

Case 3. Creating a Product Report Web Site   You work for Jackson Electronics, an electronics firm in Seattle, Washington. You've been asked to create a Web site describing the company's premier flatbed scanner, the ScanMaster. There are three Web pages in the site: a product report, a fact sheet, and a sheet of frequently asked questions (FAQs). Your job is to add the links connecting the pages.

1. Start your text editor and then open the files **SMtxt.htm**, **Factstxt.htm**, and **FAQtxt.htm** in the Tutorial.02/Cases folder of your Data Disk and save the files as: Scanner.htm, Facts.htm and FAQ.htm, in the Cases folder.

2. Open the **Scanner.htm** file in your text editor, and add anchor names to the five H1 headers after the table of contents. Use the following anchor names: PR, SALES, STANDARD, PLAN, and LINKS.

3. Link the entries in the table of contents to the anchors that you created in Step 2.

4. Change the text "e-mail" in the second paragraph of the "Products Report Go Online" section to a hyperlink pointing to the e-mail address "jbrooks@Jckson_Electronics.com".

5. Go to the Links section of the document, and link the text "View the ScanMaster fact sheet" to the Facts.htm file. Link the text "View the Product Summary" to an anchor named SUMMARY in the Facts.htm file. Link "View the Features List" to the FEATURES anchor in Facts.htm. Link "View Ordering Information" to the INFO anchor in Facts.htm. Finally, link the text "View the FAQ sheet" to the FAQ.htm file. Save your changes to Scanner.htm file. Print the Scanner.htm file from your text editor.

6. Open the Facts.htm file in your text editor. Create anchors for each of the H2 headers with the names SUMMARY, FEATURES, and INFO.

7. Change the text "Return to the product report." at the bottom of the page to a hyperlink pointing to the Scanner.htm file. Save your changes. Print the Facts.htm file from your text editor.

8. Open the FAQ.htm file in your text editor. Change the last line to a hyperlink pointing to the Scanner.htm file. Print the FAQ.htm file from your text editor.

9. Open the Scanner.htm file in your Web browser and verify that all of your links work correctly.

10. Print each of the three resulting Web pages from your browser.

Case 4. Create Your Own Home Page   Now that you've completed this tutorial, you are ready to create your own home page. The page should include information about you and your interests. If you like, you can create a separate page devoted entirely to one of your favorite hobbies. Include the following elements:

- section headers
- bold and/or italic fonts
- paragraphs
- an ordered, unordered, or definition list

Explore

- an inline graphic image that is either a link or the destination of a link
- links to some of your favorite Internet pages
- a hypertext link that moves the user from one section of your page to another

1. Create a file called Myhome.htm in the Cases folder of the Tutorial.02 folder on your Data Disk, and enter the appropriate HTML code.

2. Add any other tags you think will improve your document's appearance.

3. Insert any graphic elements you think will enhance your document.

Explore

4. Use at least one graphic element as either a link or the destination of a link.

5. Use your Web browser to explore other Web pages. Record the URLs of pages that you like, and list them in your document. Then create links to those URLs.

6. Test your code as you develop your home page by viewing Myhome.htm in your browser.

7. When you finish entering your code, save and print the Myhome.htm file, and then close your text editor.

9. View the final version in your browser, print the Web page, and then close your browser.

QUICK CHECK ANSWERS

Session 2.1

1. <A NAME="CSU">Colorado State University</A>

2. <A HREF="#CSU">Universities</A>

3. Anchor tags should be placed within style tags such as the <H3> header tag.

4. <A NAME="PHOTO"> <IMG SRC="Photo.jpg"> </A>

5. <A HREF="#LINKS"> <IMG SRC="Button.jpg"> </A>

6. False. Anchor names are case-sensitive.

Session 2.2

1. Storyboarding is diagramming a series of related Web pages, taking care to identify all hypertext links between the various pages. Storyboarding is an important tool in creating Web sites that are easy to navigate and understand.

2. A linear structure is one in which Web pages are linked from one to another in a direct chain. Users can go to the previous page or next page in the chain, but not to a page in a different section of the chain.

3. A hierarchical structure is one in which Web pages are linked from general to specific topics. Users can move up and down the hierarchy tree.

4. A company might use such a structure to describe the management organization.

5. <A HREF="Sports.htm">Sports info</A>

6. <A HREF="Sports.htm#BBALL">Basketball news</A>

Session 2.3

1. An absolute path gives the location of a file on the computer's hard disk. A relative path gives the location of a file relative to the active Web page.

2. ../../home.htm

   ../../tutorial1/chester.htm

   ../resume.htm

   ../refer.htm

3. <A HREF="ftp://ftp.uwash.edu">Washington</A>

4. <A HREF=news:rec.sports.boxing.pro>Boxing</A>

5. <A HREF=mailto:president@whitehouse.gov>President</A>

New Perspectives on

CREATING WEB PAGES WITH HTML,

2nd Edition

Read This Before You Begin

To the Student

Data Disks

To complete the Level II tutorials, Review Assignments, and Case Problems in this book, you need two Data Disks. Your instructor will either provide you with Data Disks or ask you to make your own.

If you are making your own Data Disks, you will need two blank, formatted, high-density disks. You will need to copy onto your disks a set of folders from a file server, or stand-alone computer, or the Web. Your instructor will tell you which computer, drive letter, and folders contain the files you need. You could also download the files by going to www.course.com, locating this book, clicking Data Disk Files, and following the instructions on the screen.

The following table shows you which folders go on your disks, so that you will have enough disk space to complete all the tutorials, Review Assignments, and Case Problems:

Data Disk 1

Write this on the disk label:

Data Disk 1: Level II Tutorials 3 and 4

Put these folders on the disk:

Tutorial.03 and Tutorial.04

Data Disk 2

Write this on the disk label:

Data Disk 2: Level II Tutorial 5

Put this folder on the disk:

Tutorial.05

When you begin each tutorial, be sure you are using the correct Data Disk. See the inside back cover of this book for more information on Data Disk files, or ask your instructor or technical support person for assistance.

Using Your Own Computer

If you are going to work through this book using your own computer, you need:

- **Computer System** A text editor (such as Notepad or Word) and a Web browser (preferably Netscape Navigator 4.7 or Internet Explorer 5.0) must be installed on your computer. If you are using a non-standard browser, it must support frames and HTML 3.2 or above.

- **Data Disks** You will not be able to complete the tutorials or exercises in this book using your own computer until you have Data Disks. The data files may be downloaded from the Internet. See the inside back cover for more details.

Visit Our World Wide Web Site

Additional materials designed especially for you are available on the World Wide Web. Go to http://www.course.com. For example, see our Student Online Companion, which contains additional coverage of selected topics in the text. These topics are indicated in the text by an Online Companion icon located in the left margin.

To the Instructor

The Data Disk Files are available on the Instructor's Resource Kit for this title. Follow the instructions in the Help file on the CD-ROM to install the programs to your network or standalone computer. For information on creating Data Disks, see the "To the Student" section above. You are granted a license to copy the Data Disk Files to any computer or computer network used by students who have purchased this book.

DESIGNING A WEB PAGE

Working with Color and Graphics

Announcing the Space Expo

MidWest University has one of the top departments in the country for the study of astronomy and astrophysics. The university is also home to the Center for Space Science and Engineering, which works with the government and with industry to create products to be used on the Space Shuttle, space probes, and communications and weather satellites. Tom Calloway is the director of public relations for the center.

One of the major events of the year is the Space Expo, held in late April, at which professors and graduate students showcase their research. The purpose of the Expo is to allow representatives from industry, academia, and the government to meet and discuss new ideas and emerging trends. In recent years, the Expo has caught the imagination of the general public, and Tom has made a major effort to schedule events for schools and families to attend. The Expo has become not only an important public relations event, but also an important fund-raiser for the department and the center.

It is early March, less than two months before the Expo, and Tom would like you to create a page advertising the Space Expo on the World Wide Web. The page should provide all the necessary information about Expo events, and it should also catch the eye of the reader through the use of interesting graphics and color.

SESSION 3.1

In this session you will explore how HTML handles and defines color. You'll learn how to add color to a Web page's background and text. You'll also see how to liven up your page with a background image.

Working with Color in HTML

The time of the Space Expo is drawing near, and Tom has called you to discuss the appearance of the Web page advertising the event. Tom has already written the text of the page, as shown in Figure 3-1.

Figure 3-1   **THE SPACE EXPO WEB PAGE**

The Space Expo

More than 60 exhibits and events await visitors at the Space Expo,
Looking Towards the Future
Friday-Sunday, April 24-26

The Space Expo is an annual, student-run event that showcases recent developments in astronomy and space sciences and demonstrates how these developments can be applied to everyday life. The event includes student, government and industrial exhibits, and features presentations from NASA, Ball Aerospace, Rockwell, and IBM.

The Space Expo will feature activities for the kids, including *Creating a Comet, Building a Model Rocket,* and *The Inter-Galactic Scavenger Hunt.* Friday is Students' Day, with school children in grades K-8 displaying astronomy and space science projects and competing for individual and school achievement awards.

Professor Greg Stewart's famous astronomy show is also coming to the Space Expo. Professor Stewart will show the wonders of the night sky and discuss the nature of quasars, exploding stars, and black holes. Presentations will be at the Brinkman Planetarium at 1 p.m. and 3 p.m., Friday through Sunday.

Please check out these other events:

- **Bryd Hall**   Rockwell representatives and graduate students will display some of the latest advances in robotics for use in the Space Shuttle missions.
- **Mitchell Theatre**   Famous astronomer and popular science writer, Kathy White, will present a talk, "Forward to Mars and Beyond," on Saturday at 7 p.m. Tickets for this very special event are $12. Seating is limited.
- **Astronomy Classrooms**   Graduate students and professors display the results of their research in atmospherics, satellite technology, climatology, and space engineering.

The Space Expo is located on the engineering and physics campus, north of Granger Stadium, and is open to the public on April 24 (Students' Day) from 10 a.m.-5 p.m., April 25 from 9 a.m.-7 p.m. and April 26 from 11 a.m.-5 p.m. Admission is $4.00 for the general public and $3.00 for senior citizens and students. Children four and under will be admitted free.

Sponsored by the Department of Astronomy and the Center for Space Science and Engineering.

Tom is satisfied with the page's content, but he wants you to work on the design of the page. He'd like you to add a colorful background or background image to the page for visual interest; modify the appearance of some of the text; and add some graphics to the document, including the official logo of this year's Expo and photographs of the Space Center. He wants the Web page to be as visually appealing as possible so that it catches the viewer's eye.

Tom leaves you with a list of files, images, and photos to work with. You decide to start by working on a color scheme for the page. First you should learn how to work with color in HTML.

If you've worked with color in a graphics or desktop publishing program, you've probably selected and identified your color choices without much difficulty, because those packages usually have graphical interfaces. When working with color in HTML files, however, you have to create color schemes using text-based HTML tags. Trying to describe a color in textual terms can be a challenge.

HTML identifies a color in one of two ways: either by the color's name or by color values. Both methods have their advantages and disadvantages. You'll first learn about color names.

Using Color Names

There are 16 **color names** that are recognized by all versions of HTML. These color names are shown in Figure 3-2.

Figure 3-2	THE 16 BASIC COLOR NAMES		
Aqua	Gray	Navy	Silver
Black	Green	Olive	Teal
Blue	Lime	Purple	White
Fuchsia	Maroon	Red	Yellow

As you can see, the list of color names is fairly basic. As long as you keep to these simple colors, you can rely solely upon these color names to set up color schemes for your Web pages, and those color schemes will be understood by all graphical browsers. The great advantage here is that you can be sure the colors you specify will be the colors viewers see on their computers.

However, a list of 16 color names is limiting, so some browsers (Netscape Navigator and Internet Explorer) support an extension to this list of color names. Figure 3-3 shows a partial list of these additional color names. The extended color name list allows you to create color schemes with greater color variation. A fuller list is provided in Appendix A, "Extended Color Names."

Figure 3-3	PARTIAL LIST OF EXTENDED COLOR NAMES		
Blueviolet	Gold	Orange	Seagreen
Chocolate	Hotpink	Paleturquoise	Sienna
Darkgoldenrod	Indigo	Peachpuff	Snow
Firebrick	Mintcream	Salmon	Tan

One problem with using a color name list is that, while it's easy to specify a blue background, "blue" might not be specific enough for your purposes. How do you specify a "light blue background with a touch of green"? To do so, you would have to look through a long list of color names before finding that Paleturquoise is close to the color you want. Even so, some users might try to access your page with older browsers that do not support the long list of color names. In that situation you would lose control over your page's appearance, and it might end up being unreadable on those browsers.

In cases where you want to have more control and more choices over the colors in your Web page, you must use a color value.

Using Color Values

A **color value** is a numerical expression that exactly describes a color's appearance. To understand how HTML uses numbers to represent colors, you have to examine some of the basic principles of color theory.

In classical color theory, any color can be thought of as a combination of three primary colors: red, green, and blue. You are probably familiar with the color diagram shown in Figure 3-4, in which the colors yellow, magenta, cyan, and white are produced by combining the three primary colors. By varying the intensity of each primary color, you can create any color and any shade of color that you want. This principle allows your computer monitor to combine pixels of red, green, and blue light to create the array of colors you see on your screen.

Figure 3-4	COMBINING THE THREE PRIMARY COLORS

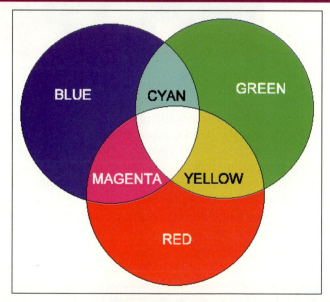

Software programs, such as your Web browser, use a mathematical approach to define color. The intensity of each of the three primary colors is assigned a number from 0 (absence of color) to 255 (highest intensity). In this way, 255^3, or more than 16.7 million, distinct colors can be defined—more combinations than the human eye can distinguish.

Each color is represented by a triplet of numbers, called an **RGB triplet**, based on its **R**ed, **G**reen, and **B**lue components. For example, white has a triplet of (255,255,255), indicating that red, green, and blue are equally mixed at the highest intensity. Gray is defined with the triplet (192,192,192), indicating an equal mixture of the primary colors with less intensity than white. Yellow has the triplet (255,255,0) because it is an equal mixture of red and green with no presence of blue. In most programs, you make your color choices with visual clues, usually without being aware of the underlying RGB triplet. Figure 3-5 shows a typical Colors dialog box in which you would make color selections based on the appearance of the color, rather than on the RGB values.

Figure 3-5	A TYPICAL COLORS DIALOG BOX

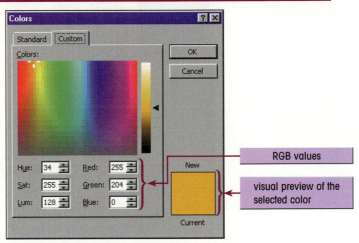

It is these RGB triplets that you have to enter into your HTML code if you want to express the exact appearance of a color. HTML requires that such color values be entered as hexadecimals. A **hexadecimal** is a number that is represented using 16 as a base rather than 10. In base 10 counting, you use combinations of 10 characters (0 through 9) to represent all of the integers, whereas hexadecimals include 6 extra characters: A (for 10), B (for 11), C (for 12), D (for 13), E (for 14), and F (for 15). For values above 15, you use a combination of the 16 characters; 16 is expressed as "10", 17 is expressed as "11", and so forth. To represent a number in hexadecimal, you convert the value to multiples of 16 plus a remainder. For example, 21 is equal to $(16 \times 1) + 5$, so its hexadecimal representation is 15. The number 255 is equal to $(16 \times 15) + 15$, or FF in hexadecimal format (remember that F = 15 in hexadecimal). In the case of the number 255, the first F represents the number of times 16 goes into 255 (which is 15), and the second F represents the remainder of 15.

Once you know the RGB triplet of a color you want to use in your Web page, you need to convert that triplet to hexadecimal format and express it in a single string of six characters. For example, the color yellow has the RGB triplet (255,255,0) and is represented by the hexadecimal string FFFF00. Figure 3-6 shows the RGB triplets and hexadecimal equivalents for the 16 basic color names presented earlier.

Figure 3-6   **COLOR NAMES, RGB TRIPLETS, AND HEXADECIMAL VALUES**

Color Name	RGB Triplet	Hexadecimal	Color Name	RGB Triplet	Hexadecimal
Aqua	(0,255,255)	00FFFF	Navy	(0,0,128)	000080
Black	(0,0,0)	000000	Olive	(128,128,0)	808000
Blue	(0,0,255)	0000FF	Purple	(128,0,128)	800080
Fuchsia	(255,0,255)	FF00FF	Red	(255,0,0)	FF0000
Gray	(128,128,128)	808080	Silver	(192,192,192)	C0C0C0
Green	(0,128,0)	008000	Teal	(0,128,128)	008080
Lime	(0,255,0)	00FF00	White	(255,255,255)	FFFFFF
Maroon	(128,0,0)	800000	Yellow	(255,255,0)	FFFF00

At this point you might be wondering if you have to become a math major before you can even start adding color to your Web pages. In practice, Web authors rely on several tools, such as the ones shown in Figure 3-7, to generate the hexadecimals HTML requires for specific colors. You might also choose to create your initial color scheme with a Colors dialog box similar to the one shown earlier in an HTML editor (a program that you can use to create Web pages without needing to know HTML code). Once you've chosen your colors, you can take the code that is generated and use your text editor to add the text and formatting you want.

Figure 3-7   **COLOR SELECTION RESOURCES AVAILABLE ON THE WORLD WIDE WEB**

TITLE	URL	DESCRIPTION
The Color Center	http://www.hidaho.com/colorcenter/	A Web page that allows you to interactively select page colors and textures and the corresponding fragments of HTML code
Color Browser	http://www.maximized.com/shareware/colorbrowser	A Windows program you can use to view and select colors and copy the corresponding HTML code
Two4U's Color page	http://www.two4u.com/color	Contains color databases and a color-composing program you can use to generate HTML code for colors you choose
Background Color Selector	http://www.imagitek.com/bcs.html	A Web page you can use to experiment with a wide variety of text and background color schemes

However you decide to work with color in your Web pages, it's important to understand how HTML handles color, if for no other reason than to be able to interpret the HTML code of the pages you'll find on the Web.

Specifying a Color Scheme for Your Page

After reviewing the issues surrounding color and HTML, you are ready to add color to the Web page that Tom has given you. Web browsers have a default color scheme that they apply to the background and text of the pages they retrieve. In most cases this scheme will involve black text on a white or gray background, with hypertext highlighted in purple and blue. When you want more or different colors than these, you need to modify the properties of the page, using the <BODY> tag.

REFERENCE   WINDOW   **RW**

Defining a Color Scheme
- Locate the <BODY> tag in your HTML file.
- Edit the <BODY> tag to read:

  `<BODY BGCOLOR=color TEXT=color LINK=color VLINK=color>`

  where BGCOLOR is the background color property, TEXT is the text color property, LINK is the color of hypertext links, and VLINK is the color of hypertext links that have been previously visited.
- For *color,* enter either the color name or the hexadecimal value formatted as "#hexadecimal_number."

In your work with HTML, you've used the <BODY> tag to identify the section of the HTML file containing the content that users would see in their browsers. At that point, the <BODY> tag had no purpose other than to separate the content of the Web page from other items such as the page's title and file heading. But the <BODY> tag can also be used to indicate the colors on your page. The syntax for controlling a page's color scheme through the <BODY> tag is:

`<BODY BGCOLOR=color TEXT=color LINK=color VLINK=color>`

Here, the BGCOLOR property sets the background color, the TEXT property controls text color, the LINK property defines the color of hypertext links, and the VLINK property defines the color of links that have been previously visited by the user. The value of *color* will be either one of the accepted color names or the color's hexadecimal value. If you use the hexadecimal value, you must preface the hexadecimal string with the pound symbol (#) and enclose the string in double quotation marks. For example, the HTML tag to create a background color with the hexadecimal value FFCO88 is:

`<BODY BGCOLOR="#FFCO88">`

After viewing various color combinations, Tom has decided that he'd like you to use a color scheme of white text on a dark green background. He also wants the hypertext links to appear in red, with previously visited links appearing in turquoise. Using color values he retrieved from a graphics program, Tom has learned that the RGB triplet for the dark green background is (0,102,0), which has a hexadecimal value of "#006600" in the <BODY> tag. He can use color names for the other items, since they are on the list of basic colors that all browsers use.

To change the color scheme of the Expo Web page:

1. Start your text editor, open the file **Expotext.htm** from the Tutorial.03 folder on your Data Disk, and then save the file in the same folder, as **Expo.htm**.

2. Within the <BODY> tag at the top of the file, type **BGCOLOR="#006600" TEXT=WHITE LINK=RED VLINK=TURQUOISE**.

   Your file should appear as displayed in Figure 3-8.

Figure 3-8   MODIFIED <BODY> TAG

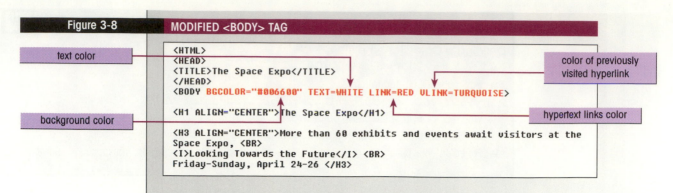

text color

color of previously
visited hyperlink

```
<HTML>
<HEAD>
<TITLE>The Space Expo</TITLE>
</HEAD>
<BODY BGCOLOR="#006600" TEXT=WHITE LINK=RED VLINK=TURQUOISE>

<H1 ALIGN="CENTER">The Space Expo</H1>

<H3 ALIGN="CENTER">More than 60 exhibits and events await visitors at the
Space Expo, <BR>
<I>Looking Towards the Future</I> <BR>
Friday-Sunday, April 24-26 </H3>
```

background color

hypertext links color

3. Save the changes to the Expo.htm file, but leave the text editor open. You'll be revising this file throughout this session.

4. Open your Web browser (you don't need to connect to the Internet) and view the Expo.htm file. See Figure 3-9.

Figure 3-9   THE SPACE EXPO PAGE WITH THE NEW COLOR SCHEME

The Space Expo

More than 60 exhibits and events await visitors at the Space Expo,
Looking Towards the Future
Friday-Sunday, April 24-26

white text throughout

dark green background

The Space Expo is an annual, student-run event that showcases recent developments in astronomy and space sciences and demonstrates how these developments can be applied to everyday life. The event includes student, government and industrial exhibits, and features presentations from NASA, Ball Aerospace, Rockwell, and IBM.

The Space Expo will feature activities for the kids, including *Creating a Comet*, *Building a Model Rocket*, and *The Inter-Galactic Scavenger Hunt*. Friday is Students' Day, with school children in grades K-8 displaying astronomy and space science projects and competing for individual and school achievement awards.

Professor Greg Stewart's famous astronomy show is also coming to the Space Expo. Professor Stewart will show the wonders of the night sky and discuss the nature of quasars, exploding stars, and black holes. Presentations will be at the Brinkman Planetarium at 1 p.m. and 3 p.m., Friday through Sunday.

Please check out these other events:

hypertext links
appear in red

- **Bryd Hall**   Rockwell representatives and graduate students will display some of the latest advances in robotics for use in the Space Shuttle missions.
- **Mitchell Theatre**   Famous astronomer and popular science writer, Kathy White, will present a talk, "Forward to Mars and Beyond," on Saturday at 7 p.m. Tickets for this very special event are $12. Seating is limited.
- **Astronomy Classrooms**   Graduate students and professors display the results of their research in atmospherics, satellite technology, climatology, and space engineering.

The Space Expo is located on the engineering and physics campus, north of Granger Stadium, and is open to the public on April 24 (Students' Day) from 10 a.m.-5 p.m., April 25 from 9 a.m.-7 p.m. and April 26 from 11 a.m.-5 p.m. Admission is $4.00 for the general public and $3.00 for senior citizens and students. Children four and under will be admitted free.

Sponsored by the Department of Astronomy and the Center for Space Science and Engineering.

The Expo page now appears with white text on a dark green background. Hypertext links will show up in red and turquoise (you'll need to scroll the window to see the hypertext links). By adding the color scheme to the <BODY> tag of the HTML file, you've superceded the browser's default color scheme with one of your own.

Modifying Text with the <FONT> Tag

Specifying the text color in the <BODY> tag of your Web page changed the color of all the text on the page. Occasionally you will want to change the color of individual words or characters within the page. Color that affects only a few sections of a page is called **spot color**. HTML allows you to create incidences of spot color using the <FONT> tag, which you attach to specific text.

REFERENCE WINDOW   **RW**

Modifying Text Appearance with the <FONT> TAG
- In your text editor, locate the text whose appearance you want to modify.
- Place the text within the <FONT> tag as follows:

      `<FONT SIZE=sizevalue COLOR=color FACE=fontname> Revised Text`
      `</FONT>`

   where SIZE is the actual size of the text or the amount by which you want to increase or decrease the size of the text; COLOR is the color name or color value you want to apply to the text; and FACE is the name of the font you want to use for the text.

You've already worked with some character tags that allow you to bold format or italicize individual characters. The <FONT> tag gives you even more control by allowing you to specify the color, the size, and even the font to be used for the text on your page. The syntax for the <FONT> tag is:

   `<FONT SIZE=size COLOR=color FACE=fontname> Revised Text </FONT>`

The <FONT> tag has three properties: size, color, and face. Your only concern right now is to use the <FONT> tag to change text color, but it's worthwhile exploring the other properties of the tag at this time.

Changing the Font Size

The SIZE property of the <FONT> tag allows you to specify the font size of the revised text. The SIZE value can be expressed in either absolute or relative terms. For example, if you want your text to have a size of 2, you enter SIZE=2 in the <FONT> tag. On the other hand, if you want to increase the font size by 2 relative to the surrounding text, you enter SIZE=+2 in the tag. What is the value "size" in absolute terms? Remember that in HTML we define things such as font size in a fairly general way and allow the browser to render the page. This means that text formatted with size 7 font in one browser might be slightly different in size than the same text in another browser. Figure 3-10 gives a representation of the various font sizes for a typical browser.

Figure 3-10   **EXAMPLES OF DIFFERENT FONT SIZES**

This is size 1 text
This is size 2 text
This is size 3 text
This is size 4 text
This is size 5 text
This is size 6 text
This is size 7 text

For comparison, text formatted with the <H1> tag corresponds by default to bold, size 6 text; the <H2> tag is equivalent to bold, size 5 text, and so forth. Figure 3-11 presents a complete comparison of header tags and font sizes.

Figure 3-11   **HEADER TAGS AND FONT SIZES**

TAG	FORMAT
<H1>	Size 6, Bold
<H2>	Size 5, Bold
<H3>	Size 4, Bold
<H4>	Size 3, Bold
<H5>	Size 2, Bold
<H6>	Size 1, Bold
Normal text (no <H*> tag)	Size 3, Not Bold

So, if you use the property SIZE=+1 to increase the size of text enclosed within an <H3> tag, the net effect will be to produce text that is size 5, and bold. Note that the largest font size supported by browsers is size 7.

Changing the Font Color

The COLOR property of the <FONT> tag allows you to change the color of individual characters or words. As when creating a color scheme, you specify the color by using either an accepted color name or the color value. For example, to change the color of the word "Expo" to the hexadecimal color value 8000C0, you would enter the following HTML tag:

```
<FONT COLOR="#8000C0"> Expo </FONT>
```

The text surrounding the word "Expo" would still be formatted in the color scheme specified in the <BODY> tag, or in the default scheme used by the Web browser.

Changing the Font Face

The final property of the <FONT> tag is the FACE property. You use the FACE property to indicate the font the text should be displayed in. The introduction of this property in HTML 4.0 (although it was supported by Internet Explorer 1.0 and Netscape 3.0) was a bit of a departure from earlier versions of HTML, in which the browser alone determined the font used in the Web page. With the FACE property you can override the browser's choice. For this to work, you must specify a font that is installed on the user's computer. But, because you have no way of knowing which fonts have been installed, the FACE property allows you to specify a list of potential font names. The browser will attempt to use the first font in the list; if that fails, it will try the second font, and so on to the end of the list. If none of the fonts listed matches a font installed on the user's computer, the browser will ignore this property and use the default font. For example, to display the word "Expo" in a font without serifs, you could enter the following HTML tag:

```
<FONT FACE="ARIAL, HELVETICA, SANS SERIF">Expo</FONT>
```

In this example, each of the three specified fonts is a nonserif font. The browser will first attempt to display the word "Expo" in the Arial font. If a user's computer doesn't have that font installed, the browser will try the Helvetica font, and after that it will try the Sans Serif font. If none of these fonts is installed on the user's computer, the browser will use its own default font.

DESIGN	WINDOW	

Formatting Text in a Web Page
- Do not overwhelm your page with different font sizes, colors, and font faces. Using a minimal number of font styles gives your page a uniform appearance that is easy to read.
- Avoid using the same color for normal text as you do for hypertext links, so that you do not confuse the reader.
- If you use a particular font face for your text, specify a list of alternate font names to accommodate different operating systems.

Using the <FONT> Tag for Spot Color

As you can see, the <FONT> tag gives you a lot of control over the appearance of individual blocks of text. At this point, though, you are only interested in using the <FONT> tag for spot color. Tom wants the name of this year's event, "Looking Towards the Future," to stand out on the page. To accomplish this, you'll format the line of text so that it appears in yellow.

To change the appearance of the Expo title:

1. Return to your text editor and the **Expo.htm** file, if necessary.
2. Enclose the title within the <FONT> tag as follows:

   <FONT COLOR=YELLOW> Looking Towards the Future </FONT>

   The Expo.htm file should now appear as shown in Figure 3-12.

Figure 3-12

USING THE <FONT> TAG TO CREATE SPOT COLOR

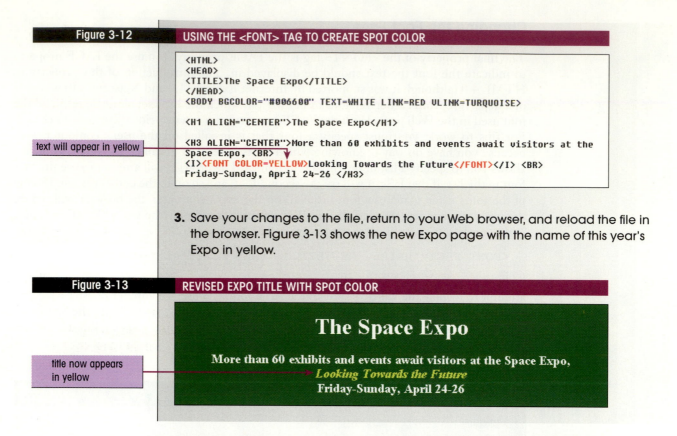

```
<HTML>
<HEAD>
<TITLE>The Space Expo</TITLE>
</HEAD>
<BODY BGCOLOR="#006600" TEXT=WHITE LINK=RED VLINK=TURQUOISE>

<H1 ALIGN="CENTER">The Space Expo</H1>

<H3 ALIGN="CENTER">More than 60 exhibits and events await visitors at the
Space Expo, <BR>
<I><FONT COLOR=YELLOW>Looking Towards the Future</FONT></I> <BR>
Friday-Sunday, April 24-26 </H3>
```

text will appear in yellow

3. Save your changes to the file, return to your Web browser, and reload the file in the browser. Figure 3-13 shows the new Expo page with the name of this year's Expo in yellow.

Figure 3-13

REVISED EXPO TITLE WITH SPOT COLOR

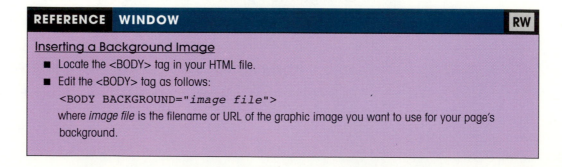

title now appears in yellow

You show the revised page to Tom. He likes the use of color in the page and the spot color, but feels that the background needs work. He's seen Web pages that have graphic images used for backgrounds, and he'd like you to try something similar.

Inserting a Background Image

Another property of the <BODY> tag is the BACKGROUND property. With this property you can use a graphic file as a background image for your page. The syntax for inserting a background image is:

```
<BODY BACKGROUND="image file">
```

Here, *image file* is the filename or URL of the graphic file you want to use. For example, to use a graphic file named "Bricks.gif" as your background image, you would use the tag:

```
<BODY BACKGROUND="Bricks.gif">
```

REFERENCE WINDOW   RW

Inserting a Background Image
■ Locate the <BODY> tag in your HTML file.
■ Edit the <BODY> tag as follows:
   ```
   <BODY BACKGROUND="image file">
   ```
   where *image file* is the filename or URL of the graphic image you want to use for your page's background.

When the browser retrieves your graphic file, it repeatedly inserts the image into the page's background, in a process called **tiling**, until the entire display window is filled up, as shown in Figure 3-14.

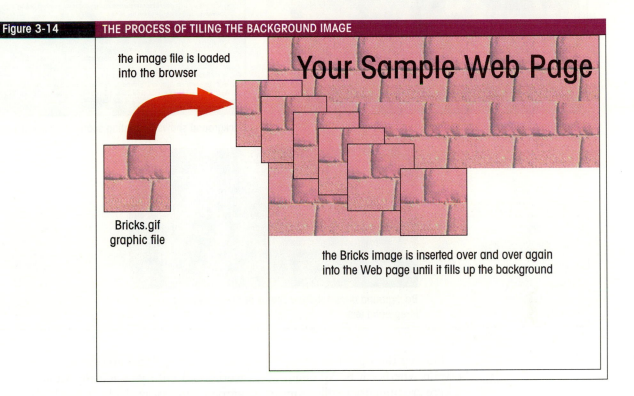

Figure 3-14   THE PROCESS OF TILING THE BACKGROUND IMAGE

the image file is loaded into the browser

Your Sample Web Page

Bricks.gif graphic file

the Bricks image is inserted over and over again into the Web page until it fills up the background

In choosing a background image, you should remember the following:

- Use an image that will not detract from your page's text, making it hard to read.
- Do not use a large image file (more than 20 kilobytes). Large and compli-cated backgrounds will cause your page to take a long time to load, and no matter how attractive the page's background is, it won't impress people who won't wait around to see it.
- The background should appear seamless to the user. Use images that will not show boundaries and grids when tiled.

Figure 3-15 shows examples of well-designed and poorly designed Web page backgrounds.

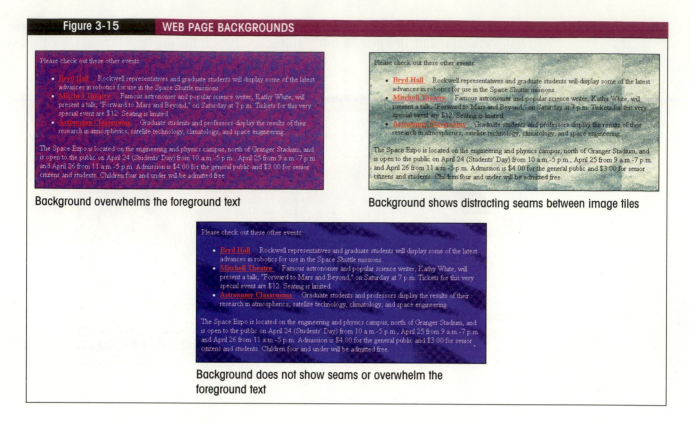

Figure 3-15 WEB PAGE BACKGROUNDS

Background overwhelms the foreground text

Background shows distracting seams between image tiles

Background does not show seams or overwhelm the foreground text

Finding the right background image is a process of trial and error. You won't know for certain whether a background image works well until you actually view it in a browser. There are numerous collections of background images available on the Web. You can copy many of these and use them on your own pages for free. The only restriction is that you cannot sell or distribute the images in a commercial product. Figure 3-16 provides a short list of these collections.

Figure 3-16 SOURCES OF BACKGROUND IMAGES

TITLE	URL	DESCRIPTION
3D Netscape Backgrounds	http://www.sonic.net/~lberlin/new/3dnscape.html	A collection of heavily textured and colored backgrounds
Founder's Background Samplers	http://www.mei-web.de/backgrounds/back_main.shtml	A collection of background images from around the world
Netscape's Background sampler	http://www.netscape.com/assist/net_sites/bg/backgrounds.html	A collection of backgrounds from Netscape
SBN Image Gallery	http://msdn.microsoft.com/downloads/images/default.asp	A collection of images and backgrounds from the Microsoft Site Builder Network
Cool Archive	http://www.coolarchive.com/	An archive of images, backgrounds, buttons, and icons
Imagine	http://imagine.metanet.com/	Background archive and search engine

After searching, Tom has found a graphic he thinks will work well for the Expo. The image, named Space.jpg, is shown in Figure 3-17.

Figure 3-17	SPACE.JPG BACKGROUND IMAGE

Next, you'll replace the dark green background of the Space Expo Web page with the Space graphic.

To add the Space.jpg graphic file to the background:

1. Return to your text editor and the **Expo.htm** file.

2. Modify the <BODY> tag, replacing the BGCOLOR property with:
   BACKGROUND="Space.jpg"

   The revised <BODY> tag should now appear as shown in Figure 3-18.

Figure 3-18	ENTERING SPACE.JPG AS THE BACKGROUND IMAGE

the <BACKGROUND> property of the <BODY> tag

```
<HTML>
<HEAD>
<TITLE>The Space Expo</TITLE>
</HEAD>
<BODY BACKGROUND="Space.jpg" TEXT=WHITE LINK=RED VLINK=TURQUOISE>

<H1 ALIGN="CENTER">The Space Expo</H1>

<H3 ALIGN="CENTER">More than 60 exhibits and events await visitors at the
Space Expo, <BR>
<I><FONT COLOR=YELLOW>Looking Towards the Future</FONT></I> <BR>
Friday-Sunday, April 24-26 </H3>
```

3. Save your changes to Expo.htm and then view the page in your Web browser. Figure 3-19 shows the new background for the Expo page.

Figure 3-19   THE EXPO PAGE WITH THE SPACE.JPG BACKGROUND

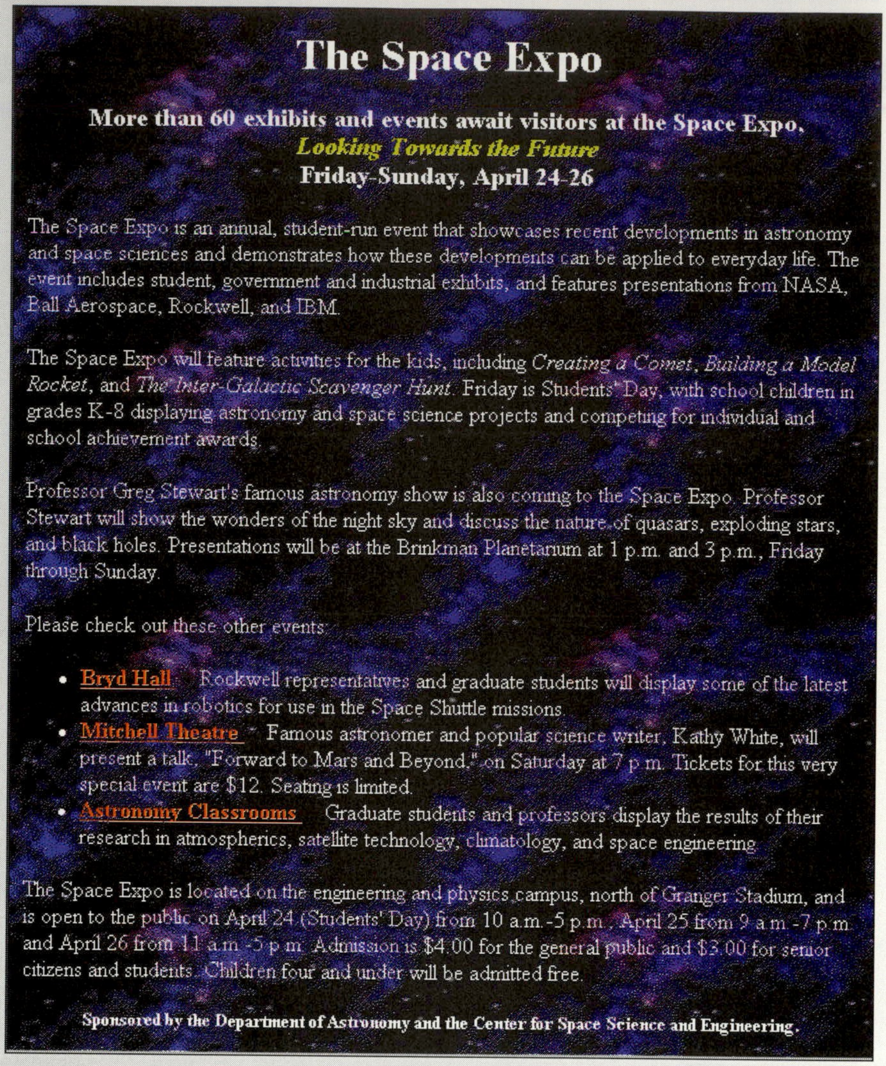

Tom is pleased with the impact of the new page background. He notes that the size of the image file is not too large (only 6 kilobytes) and that it does not show any obvious seams between the image tiles. Also, the background does not overwhelm the content of the Web page, and it fits in well with the theme of the Space Expo.

In the next session, you'll learn more about handling graphics with HTML as you add inline images to the Expo.htm file.

Session 3.1 QUICK CHECK

1. What are the two ways of specifying a color in an HTML file? What are the advantages and disadvantages of each?

2. What tag would you enter in your HTML file to use a color scheme of red text on a gray background, with hypertext links displayed in blue, and previously visited hypertext links displayed in yellow?

3. What is spot color?

4. What tag would you enter to format the words "Major Sale" in red, with a font of size 5 larger than the surrounding text?

5. What tag would you enter to display the text "Major Sale" in the Times New Roman font and, if that font is not available, in the MS Serif font?

6. What tag would you enter to use the graphic file "Stars.gif" as the background image for a Web page?

7. Name three things you should avoid when choosing a background image for your Web page.

SESSION 3.2

In this session you will learn about different graphic file formats and how you can use them to add special effects to your Web page. You'll explore the advantages and disadvantages of each format. You'll also learn how to control the size, placement, and appearance of your page's inline images.

Having finished adding color to the Expo Web page, you now turn to the task of adding graphics. The two image file formats supported by most Web browsers are GIF and JPEG. Choosing the appropriate image format for your graphics is an important part of Web page design. You have to balance the goal of creating an interesting and attractive page against the need to keep the size of your page small and easy to retrieve. Each graphic format has its advantages and disadvantages, and you will probably use a combination of both formats in your Web page designs. First you'll look at the advantages and disadvantages of GIF image files.

Working with GIF Files

GIF (Graphics Interchange Format) is the most commonly used image format on the Web. Web pages with GIF image files should be compatible with any graphical browser users have. GIF files are limited to displaying 256 colors, so they are more often used for graphics requiring fewer colors, such as clip art images, line art, logos, and icons. Images that require more color depth, such as photographs, often appear grainy when saved as GIFs. There are actually two GIF file formats: GIF87 and GIF89a. The GIF89a format, the newer standard, includes enhancements such as interlacing, transparent colors, and animation. You'll explore these enhancements now, and learn how to use them in your Web page design. First you'll look at interlacing.

Interlaced and Noninterlaced GIFs

Interlacing refers to the way the GIF file is saved by the graphics software. Normally, with a **noninterlaced GIF** the image is saved one line at a time, starting from the top of the graphic and moving downward. The graphic image is retrieved as it was saved: starting from the top of the image and moving down. Figure 3-20 shows how a noninterlaced GIF appears as it is slowly retrieved by the Web browser. If the graphic is large, it might take several minutes for the entire image to appear. People who access your page might find this annoying if the part of the image that interests them is located at the bottom.

Figure 3-20   NONINTERLACED GRAPHIC

top appears first

image appears one
line at a time

entire image is retrieved

With **interlaced GIFs**, the image is saved and retrieved "stepwise." For example, every fifth line of the image might appear first, followed by every sixth line, and so forth through the remaining rows. As shown in Figure 3-21, the effect of interlacing is that the graphic starts out as a blurry representation of the final image, then gradually comes into focus—unlike the noninterlaced graphic, which is always a sharp image as it's being retrieved, although an incomplete one.

Figure 3-21   INTERLACED GRAPHIC

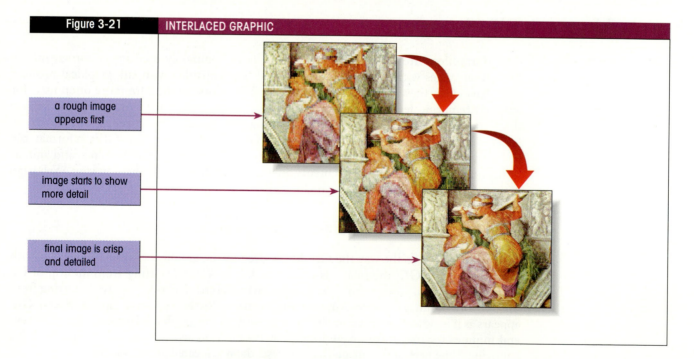

a rough image
appears first

image starts to show
more detail

final image is crisp
and detailed

Interlacing is an effective format if you have a large graphic and want to give users a preview of the final image. They get an idea of what the image looks like and can decide whether to wait for it to come into focus. The downside of interlacing is that it increases the size of the GIF file by anywhere from 3 to 20 kilobytes, depending on the image.

Transparent GIFs

Another enhancement of the GIF89a format is the ability to create transparent colors. A **transparent color** is a color from the image that is not displayed when the image appears in the browser. In place of that color, the browser will display whatever is on the page background, whether that is white, a background color, or a background image. This effect integrates inline images with the page background.

The process by which you create a transparent color depends on your graphics software. Many packages include extra options you can select when saving images in GIF89a format. One of these is to designate a particular color from the image as transparent. Other packages include a transparent color tool, which you use to click the color from the image that you want saved as transparent.

Tom has a graphic created in the GIF89a format that displays the official logo for the Space Expo. He wants you to replace the text heading from the Expo.htm file with the graphic image. The logo is shown in Figure 3-22.

Figure 3-22	THE SPACE EXPO LOGO

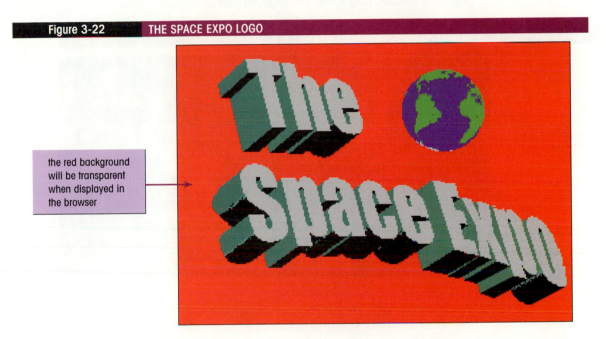

the red background will be transparent when displayed in the browser

When the graphic was created, the red background color was designated as transparent. This means that when you insert the graphic into your Web page, the background image you inserted in the previous session will show through in places where red now appears. To see how this works, you'll replace the text heading with the logo.

To insert the logo in your HTML file:

1. If you took a break after the previous session, start your text editor and reopen the **Expo.htm** file from the Tutorial.03 folder of your Data Disk.

2. Go to the top of the page and replace the text within the <H1> tag with the following <IMG> tag:

```
<IMG SRC="Logo.gif">
```

Figure 3-23 shows the modified section of the Expo.htm file.

Figure 3-23   REPLACING THE HEADER TEXT WITH THE LOGO FILE

tag for the logo image file

```
<HTML>
<HEAD>
<TITLE>The Space Expo</TITLE>
</HEAD>
<BODY BACKGROUND="Space.jpg" TEXT=WHITE LINK=RED VLINK=TURQUOISE>

<H1 ALIGN="CENTER"><IMG SRC="Logo.gif"></H1>

<H3 ALIGN="CENTER">More than 60 exhibits and events await visitors at the
Space Expo, <BR>
<I><FONT COLOR=YELLOW>Looking Towards the Future</FONT></I> <BR>
Friday-Sunday, April 24-26 </H3>
```

3. Save your changes and then load the file in your Web browser. The browser displays the revised page with the logo, as shown in Figure 3-24.

Figure 3-24   SPACE EXPO LOGO IN THE WEB PAGE

logo background is transparent

Note that the background image is visible beneath the graphic in those locations where red background appeared in the original image.

Animated GIFs

One of the most popular uses of GIFs in recent years has been to create animated images. Compared to video clips, animated GIFs are easier to create and smaller in size. An **animated GIF** is composed of several graphic images, each one slightly different. When the GIF image is displayed in the Web browser, the images are displayed one after another in rapid succession, creating the animated effect. To create animated GIFs, you need special software. Figure 3-25 provides a list of such programs available on the Web.

Figure 3-25	PROGRAMS YOU CAN USE TO CREATE ANIMATED GIFS		
TITLE	**URL**		**DESCRIPTION**
GifBuilder	http://download.cnet.com		Windows, Macintosh
Gif.glf.giF	http://www.peda.com		Windows, Macintosh
Gif Construction Set	http://www.mindworkshop.com		Windows
AniMagic	http://www.rtlsoft.com		Windows

Animated GIF software allows you to control the rate at which the animation plays (in number of frames per second) and to determine the number of times the animation will be repeated before halting. You can also set the animation to loop continually. Most of these packages will import and combine individual GIF files, but some also provide tools to create special transitions between one GIF image and another. For example, you could use the software to gradually fade from one image into another, using a process called **morphing**.

If you don't want to take the time to create your own animated GIFs, many animated GIF collections are available on the Web. Figure 3-26 lists a few of them.

Figure 3-26	ANIMATED GIF COLLECTIONS	
TITLE	**URL**	
Yahoo! List of Animated GIF Collections	http://dir.yahoo.com/Arts/Visual_Arts/Animation/Computer_Animation/Animated_GIFs/	
Gallery of GIF Animation	http://members.aol.com/royalef1/galframe.htm	
GIF World	http://www.gifworld.com/	
Animation Factory	http://www.eclipsed.com/	

Because an animated GIF is larger than the corresponding static GIF image, overusing animated GIFs can greatly increase the size of your page. You should also be careful not to overwhelm the user with animated images. Animated GIFs can quickly become a source of irritation to the user once the novelty has worn off, especially because there is no way for the user to turn them off! As with other GIF files, animated GIFs are limited to 256 colors, which makes them ideal for small icons and logos, but not for larger images.

To see whether an animated GIF will enhance the appearance of your Web page, you'll replace the existing Space Expo logo with an animated version of the logo.

To insert the animated logo in your HTML file:

1. Return to your text editor and the **Expo.htm** file.

2. Replace "Logo.gif" in the <IMG> tag at the top of the document with the file-name **"LogoAnim.gif"**.

3. Save your changes and then reload the file in your Web browser.

As shown in Figure 3-27, the revised logo now shows a spinning Earth superimposed on the Space Expo title. Note as well that animated GIFs, like static GIFs, can use transparent colors.

Figure 3-27   ANIMATED GIF LOGO

transparent background

a spinning globe is added to the logo

Not all Web browsers support animated GIFs. If a user tries to access your page with an older browser, only a static image of the first frame of the animation will be displayed.

The GIF Controversy

The future of GIFs as a preferred file format on the World Wide Web is in doubt. The problem is that GIFs employ an image compression method known as **Lempel-Ziv-Welch**, or **LZW**. When the GIF format became hugely popular, CompuServe released the format as a free and open file specification, meaning that people could create and distribute GIFs without purchasing the rights from CompuServe. Between 1987 and 1994, GIF became the most popular image format on the Internet, and later, on the World Wide Web. However, the LZW compression method at the heart of the GIF format is patented by the Unisys Corporation. At the end of 1994, Unisys and CompuServe announced that software developers would have to pay a license fee to continue to use LZW compression. This included software developers of GIFs.

Because the Web relies so heavily on free and open standards, the possibility that GIFs would be licensed caused an uproar. Unisys is not asking for any licenses for GIFs themselves, but only for software that incorporates the LZW algorithm. Most commercial programs that create GIF files already have a GIF/LZW license from Unisys, so users and Web authors creating GIF files with these programs do not need to worry about getting a separate license.

Still, uncertainty about the patent issue and how Unisys might try to enforce its patent in the future has caused many in the Web community to move away from GIFs as a preferred file format. In its place, a new file format called **PNG (Portable Network Graphics)** has been offered. PNG files use a free and open file format and can display more colors than GIFs. However, PNGs cannot be used for animated graphics. PNGs do allow transparent colors, but not all browsers support this feature. PNGs may eventually replace GIFs as the primary file format of the World Wide Web, but for the moment, to ensure compatibility across the widest range of browsers, GIFs are still the preferred standard. A detailed summary of this issue and its history can be found in the article "The GIF Controversy: A Software Developer's Perspective" at *http://cloanto.com/users/mcb/19950127giflzw.html*.

Working with JPEG Files

Another important image format supported by most Web browsers is the JPEG format. **JPEG** stands for **Joint Photographic Experts Group**. The JPEG format differs from the GIF format in several ways. With JPEG files you can create graphics that use the full 16.7 million colors available in the color palette. Because of this, JPEG files are most often used for photographs and images that cover a wide spectrum of color.

Another feature of JPEG files is that their image compression algorithm yields image files that are usually (though not always) smaller than their GIF counterparts. For example, in the previous session you used the JPEG file Space.jpg as your background image. The file is only 6 KB; however, if that image is converted to a GIF file, the size increases to 23 KB. There are also situations in which the GIF format creates a smaller and better-looking image—such as when the image has large sections covered with a single color—but as a general rule, JPEGs are smaller files.

Unlike GIFs, JPEG files allow you to control the amount of compression used. Increasing the compression reduces the file size, but it might do so at the expense of image quality. Figure 3-28 shows the effect of compression on a JPEG file. As you can see, the increased compression cuts the file size to one-sixth of the original, but leaves much of the image blurry.

Figure 3-28	THE EFFECTS OF COMPRESSION ON JPEG FILE SIZE AND IMAGE QUALITY

Minimal compression
File size = 23 KB

Moderate compression
File size = 11 KB

Medium compression
File size = 7 KB

Heavy compression
File size = 4 KB

By testing different compression levels with your graphics software, you can reduce the size of your JPEG files while maintaining an attractive image. Note that a smaller file size does not always mean that your page will load faster. The browser has to decompress the JPEG image when it retrieves it, and for a heavily compressed image this can take more time than retrieving and displaying a less compressed file.

There are some other differences between JPEGs and GIFs. You cannot use transparent colors or animation with JPEG files, and standard JPEG files are not interlaced, which means that they do not "fade in" gradually as do interlaced GIFs. In recent years a new format called **Progressive JPEG** has been introduced, which allows for interlacing without increasing the size of the graphic file. Not all graphics programs and Web browsers support progressive JPEGs, however.

Tom wants you to add a photograph of the Center for Space Science and Engineering to the Expo Web page. The photo has been saved as a JPEG file named Center.jpg on your Data Disk. You will insert the image below the title and date.

To insert the Center photograph into your Web page:

1. Return to your text editor and the **Expo.htm** file.

2. Locate the paragraph that begins "The Space Expo is an annual, student-run event" and then insert the following <IMG> tag after the paragraph's <P> tag:

   `<IMG SRC="Center.jpg">`

   Figure 3-29 shows the revised HTML code.

Figure 3-29

ADDING THE CENTER JPEG IMAGE TO THE EXPO WEB PAGE

image tag for the Center JPEG file

```
<H1 ALIGN="CENTER"><IMG SRC="LogoAnim.gif"></H1>

<H3 ALIGN="CENTER">More than 60 exhibits and events await visitors at the
Space Expo, <BR>
<I><FONT COLOR=YELLOW>Looking Towards the Future</FONT></I> <BR>
Friday-Sunday, April 24-26 </H3>

<P><IMG SRC="Center.jpg">The Space Expo is an annual, student-run event
that showcases recent developments in astronomy and space sciences and
demonstrates how these developments can be applied to everyday life. The
event includes student, government and industrial exhibits, and features
presentations from NASA, Ball Aerospace, Rockwell, and IBM.</P>
```

3. Save your changes and then reload the Expo.htm file in your Web browser. Figure 3-30 shows the revised page with the newly inserted JPEG graphic.

Figure 3-30   SPACE CENTER INLINE IMAGE

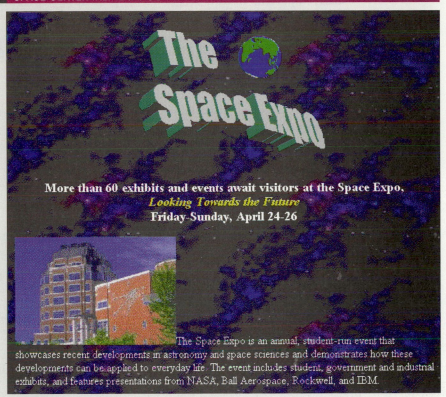

TROUBLE? If the graphic appears blurry or grainy, it could be because your monitor is capable of displaying only 256 colors, and not the full palette of 16.7 million colors.

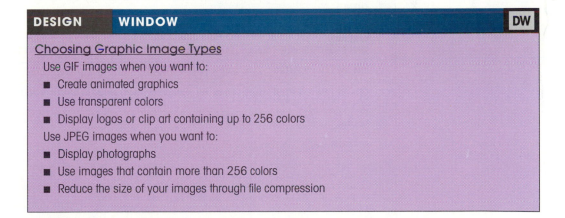

DESIGN   WINDOW   DW

Choosing Graphic Image Types

Use GIF images when you want to:
- Create animated graphics
- Use transparent colors
- Display logos or clip art containing up to 256 colors

Use JPEG images when you want to:
- Display photographs
- Use images that contain more than 256 colors
- Reduce the size of your images through file compression

Using the ALT Property

One of the properties available with the <IMG> tag is the ALT property. The ALT property allows you to specify text that will appear in place of your inline images, either temporarily or for the entire time a viewer has your page loaded. Alternate image text is important because it allows users who have nongraphical browsers to learn the content of your graphics. Alternate image text also appears as a placeholder for the graphic while the page is loading. This is particularly important for users accessing your page through a slow dial-up connection.

REFERENCE WINDOW   **RW**

<u>Specifying Alternate Text for an Inline Image</u>
- Locate the <IMG> tag for the inline image.
- Edit the <IMG> tag as follows:

  `<IMG SRC="`*image file*`" ALT="`*alternate text*`">`

  where *image file* is the filename or URL of the graphic image, and *alternate text* is the text you want to have displayed in place of the image.

The syntax for specifying alternate text is:

`<IMG SRC="`*image file*`" ALT="`*alternate text*`">`

You'll add the ALT property to the two <IMG> tags in your Expo Web page now.

To insert alternate image text into your Web page:

1. Return to the **Expo.htm** file in your text editor.

2. Within the <IMG> tag for the Expo logo (Logoanim.gif), insert the text: **ALT="The Space Expo"**.

3. After the <IMG> tag for the Center photograph, insert the text: **ALT="The MWU Center for Space Science and Engineering"**.

   Figure 3-31 shows the revised <IMG> tags for the Expo.htm file.

Figure 3-31   **SPECIFYING ALTERNATE TEXT FOR THE INLINE IMAGES**

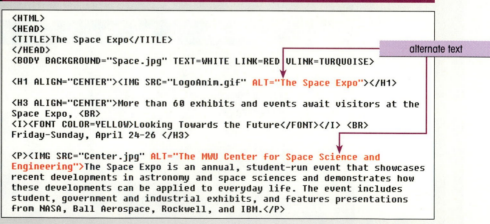

```
<HTML>
<HEAD>
<TITLE>The Space Expo</TITLE>
</HEAD>
<BODY BACKGROUND="Space.jpg" TEXT=WHITE LINK=RED VLINK=TURQUOISE>

<H1 ALIGN="CENTER"><IMG SRC="LogoAnim.gif" ALT="The Space Expo"></H1>

<H3 ALIGN="CENTER">More than 60 exhibits and events await visitors at the
Space Expo, <BR>
<I><FONT COLOR=YELLOW>Looking Towards the Future</FONT></I> <BR>
Friday-Sunday, April 24-26 </H3>

<P><IMG SRC="Center.jpg" ALT="The MWU Center for Space Science and
Engineering">The Space Expo is an annual, student-run event that showcases
recent developments in astronomy and space sciences and demonstrates how
these developments can be applied to everyday life. The event includes
student, government and industrial exhibits, and features presentations
from NASA, Ball Aerospace, Rockwell, and IBM.</P>
```

alternate text

4. Save your changes to the file. Figure 3-32 shows the appearance of your Web page with the alternate text replacing the image. (You can create this effect by turning off the display of inline images within your browser, or by interrupting the retrieval of the Expo page before the two images are rendered.)

Figure 3-32   **ALTERNATE TEXT IN THE WEB PAGE**

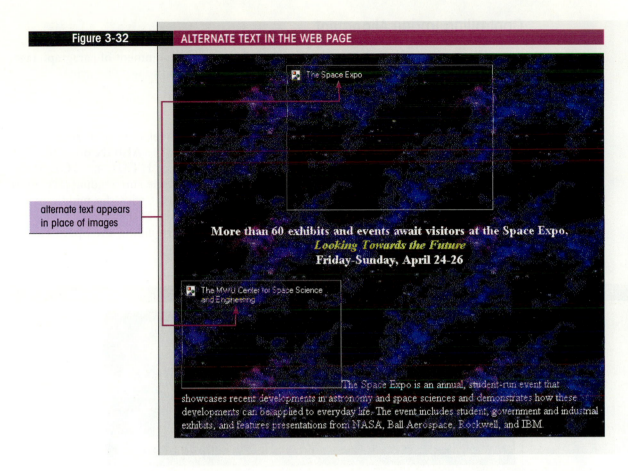

alternate text appears in place of images

Now that you've entered the images on the page, your next task is to control their placement and appearance.

Controlling Image Placement and Size

You show Tom the progress you've made on the Web page. Although he's pleased with the graphic image of the Center, he wants you to modify the placement of the image on the page. With the image's current placement, the page has a large blank space to the upper right of the image. Tom wonders if you could control the way text flows around the image so that there is less blank space. You can, using the ALIGN property of the <IMG> tag.

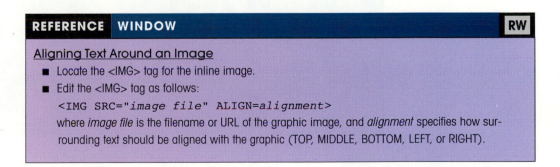

REFERENCE WINDOW   **RW**

Aligning Text Around an Image
- Locate the <IMG> tag for the inline image.
- Edit the <IMG> tag as follows:

  `<IMG SRC="image file" ALIGN=alignment>`

  where *image file* is the filename or URL of the graphic image, and *alignment* specifies how surrounding text should be aligned with the graphic (TOP, MIDDLE, BOTTOM, LEFT, or RIGHT).

Controlling Image Alignment

As you know, the ALIGN property can be used to control the alignment of paragraph tags. The ALIGN property fulfills a similar function in the <IMG> tag. The syntax for the ALIGN property is:

```
<IMG SRC="image file" ALIGN=alignment>
```

Here, *alignment* indicates how you want the image aligned in relation to the surrounding text. Different versions of HTML support different values for the ALIGN property. The three values for the ALIGN property accepted in all versions of HTML are TOP, MIDDLE, and BOTTOM. With the ALIGN property set to TOP, the surrounding text aligns with the top of the image; the MIDDLE setting aligns the text with the middle of the image; and the BOTTOM setting aligns the text with the bottom of the image.

Figure 3-33 shows the effect of each of these on text surrounding the Space Center image.

Figure 3-33   EFFECTS OF THE ALIGN PROPERTY

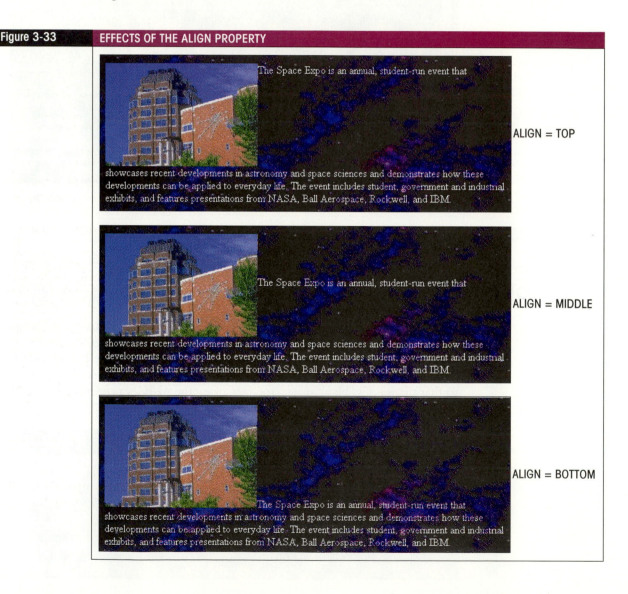

Inserting an image works fine if you have only one line of text, or if the image itself is very small. However, if you are trying to integrate a large image with several lines, you will invariably create a lot of blank space, as illustrated in Figure 3-33.

Versions of HTML 3.0 and above, as well as the Netscape Navigator and Internet Explorer browsers, support an extension to the <IMG> tag that aligns the image with either the left or right margin of the page and wraps text on the opposite side of the image. By using the values LEFT and RIGHT for the ALIGN property, you can remove the blank space problem that Tom was concerned about.

Next, you'll align the Center image with the left side of the page, wrapping the surrounding text around the image.

To align the Center photograph on the left side of the page:

1. In the <IMG> tag for the Center photograph, insert the following text after the ALT property: **ALIGN=LEFT**.

Your revised <IMG> tag should appear as shown in Figure 3-34.

Figure 3-34	USING THE ALIGN PROPERTY

align the image with the left page margin

```
<P><IMG SRC="Center.jpg" ALT="The MWU Center for Space Science and
Engineering" ALIGN=LEFT>The Space Expo is an annual, student-run event that
showcases recent developments in astronomy and space sciences and
demonstrates how these developments can be applied to everyday life. The
event includes student, government and industrial exhibits, and features
presentations from NASA, Ball Aerospace, Rockwell, and IBM.</P>
```

2. Save your changes and then reload the Expo page in your browser. Figure 3-35 shows the new page with the text wrapped around the Center photograph.

Figure 3-35	SPACE CENTER IMAGE ALIGNED WITH THE LEFT PAGE MARGIN

text wraps around the right edge of the image

Because the LEFT and RIGHT alignment values are not supported by all browsers, some older browsers might not display your page correctly. However, almost all of the newer browsers should be able to render the page properly.

Controlling Vertical and Horizontal Space

Wrapping the text around the image has solved one problem: the large blank space has been removed. A second problem now exists, however—there's not enough space separating the image and the surrounding text, which makes the page appear crowded. You can increase the horizontal and vertical space around the image with the HSPACE and VSPACE properties, as follows:

```
<IMG SRC="image file" VSPACE=value HSPACE=value>
```

The HSPACE ("horizontal space") property increases the space to the left and right of the image, and the VSPACE ("vertical space") property increases the space above and below the image. The value of the VSPACE and HSPACE properties is measured in pixels. As with the ALIGN property, the HSPACE and VSPACE properties might not be supported by older browsers, but all new browsers should support them.

REFERENCE   WINDOW   **RW**

Increasing the Space Around an Image
- Locate the <IMG> tag for the inline image.
- Edit the <IMG> tag as follows:

  ```
  <IMG SRC="image file" HSPACE=value VSPACE=value>
  ```
  where *image file* is the filename or URL of the graphic image, HSPACE is the space to the left and right of the image (in pixels), and VSPACE is the space above and below the image (in pixels).

You need to use the VSPACE and HSPACE properties to increase the space between the Center image and the surrounding text.

To increase the space around the Center image:

1. Return to the **Expo.htm** file in your text editor.

2. Within the <IMG> tag for the Center image, add the following properties and values: **VSPACE=5 HSPACE=15**.

   Your revised <IMG> tag should appear as shown in Figure 3-36.

Figure 3-36	USING THE HSPACE AND VSPACE PROPERTIES

set the vertical space around the image to 5 pixels and the horizontal space to 15 pixels

```
<P><IMG SRC="Center.jpg" ALT="The MWU Center for Space Science and
Engineering" ALIGN=LEFT VSPACE=5 HSPACE=15>The Space Expo is an annual,
student-run event that showcases recent developments in astronomy and space
sciences and demonstrates how these developments can be applied to everyday
life. The event includes student, government and industrial exhibits, and
features presentations from NASA, Ball Aerospace, Rockwell, and IBM.</P>
```

These property values will increase the gap to the left and right of the image to 10 pixels, and the gap above and below to 5 pixels.

3. Save your changes and then reload the Expo page in your browser. The revised page shows an increased gap between the image and the surrounding text. See Figure 3-37. The page does not seem so crowded now.

| Figure 3-37 | INCREASED SPACE AROUND THE CENTER IMAGE |

increased space around image

The Space Expo is an annual, student-run event that showcases recent developments in astronomy and space sciences and demonstrates how these developments can be applied to everyday life. The event includes student, government and industrial exhibits, and features presentations from NASA, Ball Aerospace, Rockwell, and IBM.

The Space Expo will feature activities for the kids, including *Creating a Comet*, *Building a Model Rocket*, and *The Inter-Galactic Scavenger Hunt*. Friday is Students' Day, with school children in grades K-8 displaying astronomy and space science projects and competing for individual and school achievement awards.

Controlling Image Size

The final properties you'll be setting for the image are the HEIGHT and WIDTH properties, which tell the browser how large to make the image. You can use these properties to increase or decrease the size of the image on your page. The syntax for setting the HEIGHT and WIDTH properties is:

```
<IMG SRC="image file" HEIGHT=value WIDTH=value>
```

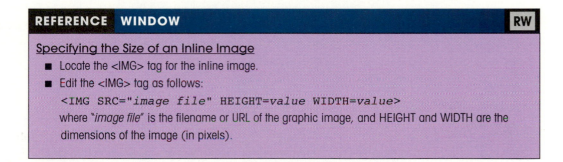

REFERENCE WINDOW   **RW**

Specifying the Size of an Inline Image
- Locate the <IMG> tag for the inline image.
- Edit the <IMG> tag as follows:
  ```
  <IMG SRC="image file" HEIGHT=value WIDTH=value>
  ```
  where "*image file*" is the filename or URL of the graphic image, and HEIGHT and WIDTH are the dimensions of the image (in pixels).

Generally, if you want to decrease the size of an image, you should do so in a graphics package, because then you will also be reducing the size of the graphics file. Changing the size of the image within the <IMG> tag does not affect the file size. Specifying the height and width of an image is a good idea, however, even if you're not trying to change the image's dimensions. Why? Because of the way browsers work with inline images. When a browser encounters an inline image, it has to calculate the image size and then use this information to format the page. If you include the dimensions of the image, the browser does not have to perform that calculation, and the page will be displayed that much faster. To determine the size of an image, use your graphics software and record the dimension of each graphic on your page in pixels.

The LogoAnim image is 296 pixels wide by 209 pixels high, and the Space Center image is 280 pixels wide by 186 pixels high. You'll enter this information into the <IMG> tags for each image.

To specify the width and height of the two images:

1. Return to your text editor.

2. Within the <IMG> tag for the LogoAnim image, add the following properties and values: **WIDTH=296 HEIGHT=209**.

3. Within the <IMG> tag for the Space Center image, add the following properties and values: **WIDTH=280 HEIGHT=186**.

   The revised Expo.htm file should appear as shown in Figure 3-38.

Figure 3-38   SPECIFYING THE WIDTH AND HEIGHT OF THE INLINE IMAGES

image WIDTH and HEIGHT properties

```
<H1 ALIGN="CENTER"><IMG SRC="LogoAnim.gif" ALT="The Space Expo"
   WIDTH=296 HEIGHT=209></H1>

<H3 ALIGN="CENTER">More than 60 exhibits and events await visitors at the
Space Expo, <BR>
<I><FONT COLOR=YELLOW>Looking Towards the Future</FONT></I> <BR>
Friday-Sunday, April 24-26 </H3>

<P><IMG SRC="Center.jpg" ALT="The MWU Center for Space Science and
Engineering" ALIGN=LEFT VSPACE=5 HSPACE=15 WIDTH=280 HEIGHT=186>
The Space Expo is an annual, student-run event that showcases recent
developments in astronomy and space sciences and demonstrates how these
developments can be applied to everyday life. The event includes student,
government and industrial exhibits, and features presentations from NASA,
Ball Aerospace, Rockwell, and IBM.</P>
```

4. Save your changes and then reload the Expo page in your browser. Confirm that the layout is the same as the last time you viewed the page, because you have not changed the dimensions of the inline images; you've simply included their dimensions in the HTML file.

General Tips for Working with Color and Images

You've completed much of the layout of the Space Expo page. When working with color and images in your Web page, keep in mind that the primary purpose of the page is to convey information. "A picture is worth a thousand words," and if an image can convey an idea quickly, by all means use it. If an image adds visual interest to your page and makes the user interested in what you have to say, include it. However, always be aware that overusing graphics can make your page difficult to read and cumbersome to display. With that in mind, this section provides some tips to remember as you work with color and images in your Web pages.

Reduce the Size of Your Pages

You should strive to make your page quick and easy to retrieve. If users will be accessing your page over a dial-up connection, the amount of material they can retrieve in a given time will be limited. For example, a user with a 56.8 Kbps modem can retrieve information at a rate of about 7 kilobytes per second. If you have about 100K of graphics and other information on your page, that user will wait, on average, 15 to 20 seconds to see the page. To get a feeling how long that can be, sit quietly and patiently count to 20. When users are used to quick responses from their computers, 20 seconds can seem like a long time. That's a problem when a user is a potential customer whose business you don't want to lose. A general rule of thumb is that the total amount of graphics on your Web page should be no more than 40 to 50 kilobytes. There are several ways to achieve this:

- Reduce the size of the images, using your graphics software (not by simply changing the WIDTH and HEIGHT properties in the <IMG> tag).
- Reduce the number of colors used. Instead of saving an image in a 16.7 million color format, reduce it to 256 colors.
- Experiment with different graphic format types. Is the file size smaller with the JPEG format or the GIF? Can you compress the JPEG graphic without losing image quality?
- Use **thumbnails**—pictures that are reduced versions of your graphic images. Place the thumbnail image within a hypertext link to the larger, more detailed image, so that clicking the reduced image loads the better image. This gives users who really want to view the more well-defined image the option to do so. Note that the thumbnail has to be a different, smaller file than the original graphic. If you simply use the HEIGHT and WIDTH properties to reduce the original graphic file, you won't be saving your browser any time in rendering the page.
- Reuse your images. If you are creating a Web presentation containing several pages, consider using the same background image for each page. Once a browser has retrieved the image file, it will store the image locally on the user's computer and will be able to retrieve it quickly to display it again, if necessary. Using the same images also gives your multipage Web site a consistent look and feel.

Finally, you should provide an alternate, text-only version of your Web page for those users who are either using a text-based browser or want to quickly load the information stored on your page without viewing inline images.

Manage Your Colors

Color can add a lot to your page, but it can also detract from it. Make sure that you have enough contrast between the text and the background. In other words, don't put dark text on a dark background or light text on a light background. Avoid clashing colors. A green text on a red background is not only difficult to read, it's an eyesore. Color is handled differently on different browsers, so you should try to view your page in most of the popular browsers. Certainly you should check to see how Netscape Navigator and Internet Explorer render your page.

You should also check to see how your page appears under different color depths. Your monitor might be capable of displaying 16.7 million colors, but users viewing your page might not be so lucky. View your page with your display set to 256 colors to see how it is rendered. When a 16.7 million color image is displayed at 256 colors, the browser must go through a process called **dithering**, in which the appearance of increased color depth is approximated. As shown in Figure 3-39, dithered images can sometimes appear grainy. Even if your computer is capable of displaying full-color images, you might want to consider creating all your images in 256 colors to control the effect of dithering.

Figure 3-39 | **IMAGE DITHERING**

original image dithered image

To completely eliminate dithering, some Web authors recommend that you use the Safety Palette. The **Safety Palette** is a palette of 211 colors that are guaranteed to be displayed accurately on all browsers without dithering.

By limiting your color selections to the colors of the Safety Palette, you can be assured that your images will appear the same in the users' Web browsers as they do in your graphics software. You can learn more about the Safety Palette at *http://msdn.microsoft.com/workshop/design/default.asp*.

You're finished working with the inline images on your Web page. You've learned about the different image formats supported by most browsers and their advantages and disadvantages. You've also seen how to control the appearance and placement of images on your Web page. In the next session you'll learn how to create an image that links to other Web pages.

Session 3.2 QUICK CHECK

1. List three reasons for using the GIF image format instead of the JPEG format.

2. List three reasons for using the JPEG image format instead of the GIF format.

3. What HTML tag would you enter to display the alternate text "MidWest University" in place of the graphic image mwu.jpg?

4. What tag would you enter to align the mwu.jpg image with the top of the surrounding text?

5. What tag would you enter to place the surrounding text on the left side of the mwu.jpg image? For which browsers might this tag not work?

6. What tag would you enter to increase the horizontal and vertical space around the mwu.jpg image to 10 pixels?

7. The mwu.jpg image is 120 pixels wide by 85 pixels high. Using this information, what would you enter into your HTML file to increase the speed at which the page is rendered by the browser?

8. What is dithering? What is the Safety Palette?

SESSION 3.3

In this session you will learn about different types of image maps, and you'll create an image map and test it for the Space Expo Web page.

Understanding **Image Maps**

Tom has reviewed your Space Expo Web page and is pleased with the progress you're making. He's decided that the page should also include a map of the center's floor plan (shown in Figure 3-40) so that visitors will know where to go for different exhibits.

Figure 3-40   MAP OF THE CENTER FOR SPACE SCIENCE AND ENGINEERING

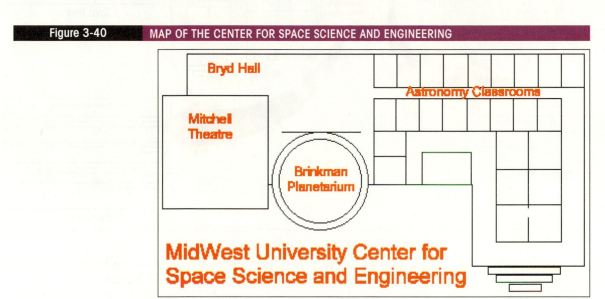

Tom wants the graphic of the map to be interactive, so that, for example, when a user clicks the text "Mitchell Theatre" on the floor plan, a page displaying events at the theatre will appear. If a user clicks the Brinkman Planetarium, a page about the planetarium will be displayed, and so forth. Figure 3-41 shows how these links will work on the map.

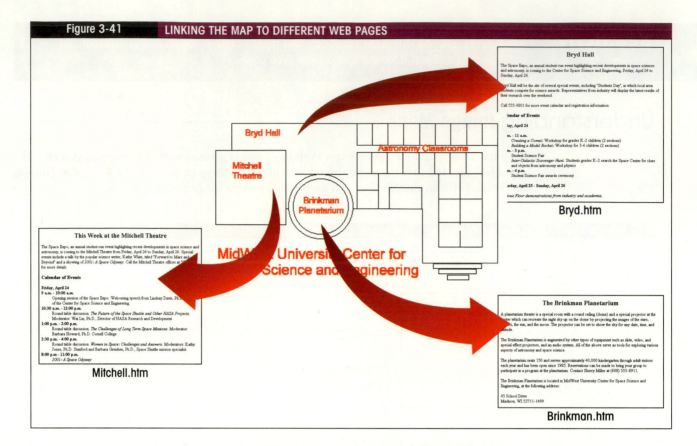

Figure 3-41   LINKING THE MAP TO DIFFERENT WEB PAGES

To use a single graphic to access multiple targets, you must set up hotspots within the image. A **hotspot** is a defined area of the image that acts as a hypertext link. One such hotspot for the floor plan of the Space Center would be the circular area that defines the location of the Brinkman Planetarium.

You define hotspots through the use of image maps. **Image maps** list the coordinates that define the boundaries of the hotspots on the image. Any time a user clicks inside those boundaries, the hyperlink is activated. As a Web author, you can use two types of image maps: server-side image maps and client-side image maps. Each has advantages and disadvantages.

Server-Side Image Maps

In a **server-side image map**, the server, which is the computer that stores the Web page, controls the image map. As shown in Figure 3-42, the Web author includes the coordinates of the hotspots within the Web page; whenever a user clicks the inline image, the appropriate coordinates are sent to a program running on the server, and the program uses them to activate the appropriate hyperlink.

Figure 3-42   SERVER-SIDE IMAGE MAP

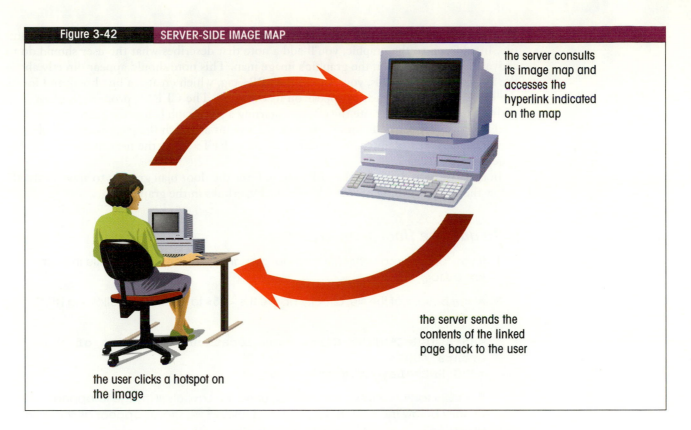

the server consults
its image map and
accesses the
hyperlink indicated
on the map

the server sends the
contents of the linked
page back to the user

the user clicks a hotspot on
the image

Server-side image maps are supported by most, if not all, graphical browsers, but there are limitations to server-side image maps. Because a program on the server must process the image map, you cannot test your HTML code using local files. Also, server-side image maps can be slow to operate, because every time a user clicks the inline image, the request has to be processed by the Web server. On most Web browsers the target of a hyperlink is indicated in the browser's status bar, giving valuable feedback to the user—but this is not done with the hotspots of a server-side image map. Because it is the server and not the Web browser that handles the hotspots, no feedback is given to the user regarding the location of the hotspots and their targets. These limitations can be overcome through the use of client-side image maps.

Client-Side Image Maps

In a **client-side image map**, you insert the image map into the HTML file, and the user's Web browser processes the image map locally. Because all of the processing is done locally, and not on the Web server, you can easily test your Web pages using the HTML files stored on your computer. Another advantage of client-side image maps is that they tend to be more responsive than server-side maps, because the information does not have to be sent over the network or dial-up connection. Finally, when a user moves the pointer over the inline image, the browser's status bar will display the target of each hotspot. The downside of client-side image maps is that older browsers do not support them. This is much less of a problem than it once was, so you can now use client-side image maps with confidence.

As you become more experienced with HTML, you may want to support both server-side and client-side image maps in your Web pages. For now, however, you will concentrate solely on working with client-side image maps.

The first step in creating the image map is to add the floor plan graphic to the Expo.htm file. In addition to the graphic, you'll add a note that describes what the user should do to activate hyperlinks within the graphic's image map. This note should appear directly above the image. To achieve this, you can use the <BR> tag, which creates a line break and forces the following image or text to appear on its own line. The CLEAR property is often used within the <BR> tag to create the effect of starting a paragraph below the inline image. The CLEAR property starts the next line at the first point at which the page margin is clear of text or images. For example, using <BR CLEAR=LEFT> starts the next line when the left page margin is clear.

In this case, you'll use just the <BR> tag to force the floor plan graphic to appear directly below the text describing how to activate the hyperlinks in the graphic.

To add the floor plan graphic:

1. If you took a break after the previous session, open the **Expo.htm** file in your text editor.

2. At the bottom of the file, directly above the <H5> tag, enter the following HTML code:

   ```
   <H5 ALIGN=CENTER> Click each location for a list of
   events <BR>
   <IMG SRC="Layout.gif"> </H5>
   ```

   The <BR> tag creates a line break, causing the Layout.gif image to appear directly below the explanatory text. Your revised file should appear as shown in Figure 3-43.

Figure 3-43   INSERTING THE LAYOUT IMAGE

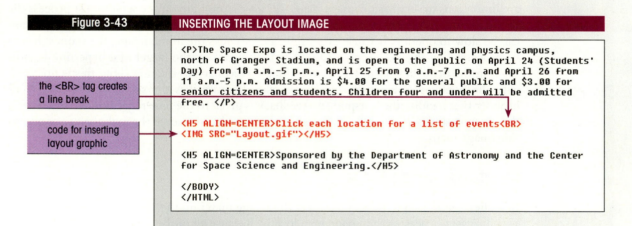

the <BR> tag creates a line break

code for inserting layout graphic

```
<P>The Space Expo is located on the engineering and physics campus,
north of Granger Stadium, and is open to the public on April 24 (Students'
Day) from 10 a.m.-5 p.m., April 25 from 9 a.m.-7 p.m. and April 26 from
11 a.m.-5 p.m. Admission is $4.00 for the general public and $3.00 for
senior citizens and students. Children four and under will be admitted
free. </P>

<H5 ALIGN=CENTER>Click each location for a list of events<BR>
<IMG SRC="Layout.gif"></H5>

<H5 ALIGN=CENTER>Sponsored by the Department of Astronomy and the Center
for Space Science and Engineering.</H5>

</BODY>
</HTML>
```

3. Save your changes to the Expo.htm file and then open the file in your Web browser. Figure 3-44 shows the Layout image as it appears in the Web page.

Figure 3-44	CENTER FLOOR PLAN AS IT APPEARS IN THE WEB PAGE

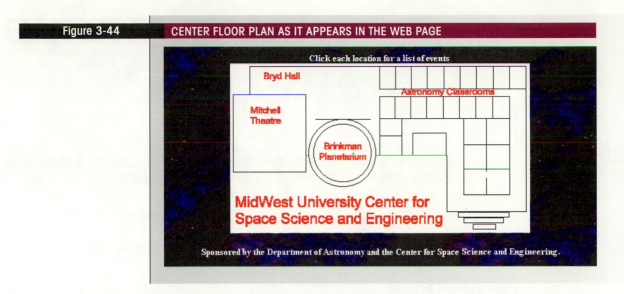

Your next task is to turn this image of the floor plan into an image map.

Defining Image Map Hotspots

To create the image map, you could open the image in a graphics program and record the coordinates of the points corresponding to the hotspot boundaries. In practice, this is difficult and time-consuming, so you'll typically use a special program to create image map coordinates for you. There are several different programs available for this purpose, some of which are listed in Figure 3-45.

Figure 3-45	PROGRAMS FOR CREATING IMAGE MAPS	
TITLE	**URL**	**PLATFORM**
Web Hotspots 3.0 S Edition	http://www.concentric.net/~automata/hotspots.shtml	Windows
LiveImage	http://www.mediatec.com/	Windows
Mac-ImageMap	http://weyl.zib-berlin.de/imagemap/Mac-ImageMap.html	Macintosh
Mapedit	http://www.boutell.com/mapedit/	Windows, UNIX
MapServe	http://www.spub.ksu.edu/other/machttp_tools/mapserve/mapserve.html	Macintosh

Most image map programs generate the coordinates for hotspots as well as the necessary HTML tags. To help you understand the syntax of image maps better, you'll be given the coordinates and then use that information to create your own HTML code.

Defining a Client-Side Image Map
- Create the <MAP> tag that defines the different hotspots on the image as follows:

  ```
  <MAP NAME="mapname">
  <AREA SHAPE="shape" COORDS=coordinates HREF=URL>
  ...
  </MAP>
  ```

  where *mapname* is the name you give the image map, *shape* is the type of hotspot (rectangle, circle, or polygon), *coordinates* are the locations of points that define the shape, and *URL* is the target of the hypertext link (the page that will open when a user clicks that part of your image map). You can have multiple <AREA> tags within each <MAP> tag, enabling you to have several hotspots for each image map.
- Once the image map is created, add the USEMAP property to the <IMG> tag for the inline image, as follows:

  ```
  <IMG SRC="image" USEMAP="#mapname">
  ```

  where *image* is the filename of the graphic, and *mapname* is the name you gave the image map defined in the <MAP> tag.

The general syntax for an image map tag is:

```
<MAP NAME="mapname">
<AREA SHAPE=shape COORDS="coordinates" HREF="URL">
</MAP>
```

The <MAP> tag gives the name of the image map. Within the <MAP> tag, you use the <AREA> tag to specify the areas of the image that will act as hotspots. You can include as many <AREA> tags within the <MAP> tags as you need for the image map.

The <AREA> tag has three properties: SHAPE, COORDS, and HREF. The SHAPE property refers to the shape of the hotspot: RECT for a rectangular hotspot, CIRCLE for a circular hotspot, and POLY for hotspots shaped like irregular polygons.

In the COORDS property, you enter coordinates to specify the hotspot's location. The values you enter depend on the shape of the hotspot. As you'll see, you need to enter different coordinates for a rectangular hotspot than you would for a circular one. Coordinates are expressed as a point's distance in pixels from the left and the top edges of the image. For example, the coordinates (123,45) refer to a point 123 pixels from the left edge and 45 pixels down from the top. If the coordinates of your <AREA> tags overlap, the browser uses the first tag in the list.

In the HREF parameter, you enter the URL for the hypertext link that the hotspot points to. You can use the value "NOHREF" in place of a URL if you do not want the hotspot to activate a hypertext link. This is a useful technique when you are first developing your image map, without all the hypertext links in place. The <AREA> tag then acts as a placeholder until the time when you have the hypertext links ready for use.

REFERENCE WINDOW **RW**

<u>Defining Image Map Hotspots</u>
- Locate the <MAP> tag that defines the image map.
- Within the <MAP> tag, enter the code for the type of hotspot(s) and the coordinates.
  The syntax for a rectangular hotspot is:
  ```
  <AREA SHAPE=RECT COORDS="x_left, y_upper, x_right, y_lower"
  HREF="URL">
  ```
  where *x_left, y_upper* are the coordinates of the upper-left corner of the rectangle, and *x_right, y_lower* are the coordinates of the lower-right corner.
  The syntax for a circular hotspot is:
  ```
  <AREA SHAPE=CIRCLE COORDS="x_center, y_center, radius" HREF="URL">
  ```
  where *x_center, y_center* is the center of the circle, and *radius* is the circle's radius.
  The syntax for a polygonal hotspot is:
  ```
  <AREA SHAPE=POLY COORDS="x1, y1, x2, y2, x3, y3, … " HREF="URL" >
  ```
  where *x1, y1, x2, y2, x3, y3,* … are the coordinates of the vertices of the polygon.

Before creating your <AREA> tags, you'll add the <MAP> tag to the Expo.htm file and assign the name "FloorPlan" to the image map.

To insert the <MAP> tag:

1. Return to the **Expo.htm** file in your text editor.

2. Go to the bottom of the file and enter the following directly above the </BODY> tag:

   ```
   <MAP NAME="FloorPlan">
   </MAP>
   ```

With the <MAP> tag in place, you must next determine what kinds of areas the image map will require. Tom wants the image to include hotspots for the Mitchell Theatre, the Brinkman Planetarium, and Bryd Hall. The locations of these three hotspots are shown in Figure 3-46.

Figure 3-46   HOTSPOTS FOR THE FLOOR PLAN IMAGE

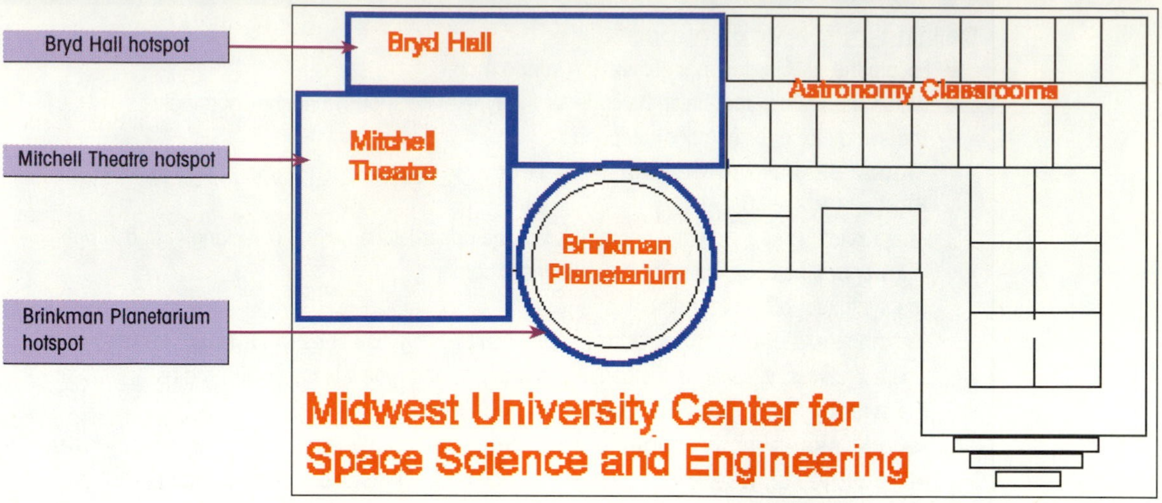

You'll define the hotspot for the Mitchell Theatre first. The hotspot for the Mitchell Theatre will be a rectangle.

Creating a Rectangular Hotspot

Two points define a rectangular hotspot: the upper-left corner and the lower-right corner. These points for the Mitchell Theatre hotspot are located at (5,45) and (108,157). In other words, the upper-left corner is 5 pixels to the left and 45 pixels down from the left and top edges of the image, respectively, and the lower-right corner is 108 pixels to the left and 157 pixels down. The hotspot will link to the file Mitchell.htm, a page with information on events at the Mitchell Theatre.

To insert the Mitchell Theatre <AREA> tag:

1. Insert a new blank line between the opening and closing <MAP> tags you just entered. The blank line is necessary only to make your code more readable.

2. Type the following in the new blank line:

```
<AREA SHAPE=RECT COORDS="5,45,108,157" HREF="Mitchell.htm">
```

Note that the coordinates are entered as a series of four numbers separated by commas. Because this is a rectangular hotspot, HTML expects that the first two numbers represent the coordinates for the upper-left corner of the rectangle, and the second two numbers indicate the location of the lower-right corner.

Next you'll enter the <AREA> tag for the Brinkman Planetarium, a circular hotspot.

Creating a Circular Hotspot

The coordinates required for a circular hotspot differ from those of a rectangular hotspot. A circular hotspot is defined by the locations of its center and its radius. The circle representing the Brinkman Planetarium is centered at the coordinates (161,130), and it has a radius of 49 pixels. The hotspot will link to the file Brinkman.htm. You need to enter this <AREA> tag into the Expo.htm file.

To insert the Brinkman Planetarium <AREA> tag:

1. Insert a new blank line directly below the Mitchell Theatre <AREA> tag.

2. Type the following in the new blank line:

```
<AREA SHAPE=CIRCLE COORDS="161,130,49" HREF="Brinkman.htm">
```

The final hotspot you have to define is for Bryd Hall. Because of its irregular shape, you have to create a polygonal hotspot.

Creating a Polygonal Hotspot

When you want to specify an irregular shape for a hotspot, you must use the POLY value for the SHAPE property. To create a polygonal hotspot, you enter the coordinates for each vertex in the shape.

The coordinates for the vertices of the Bryd Hall hotspot are (29,4), (29,41), (111,41), (111,78), (213,78), and (213,4). See Figure 3-47. The HREF for this hotspot is the file Bryd.htm.

Figure 3-47   COORDINATES FOR THE BRYD HALL HOTSPOT

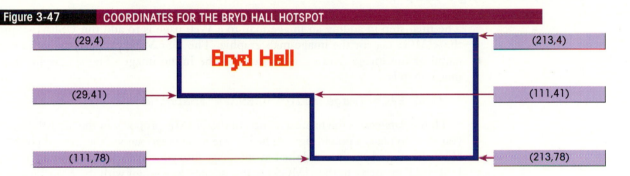

With the coordinate information in hand, you can create the final <AREA> tag for your image map.

To insert the Bryd Hall <AREA> tag:

1. Insert a new blank line directly below the Brinkman Planetarium <AREA> tag.

2. Type the following in the new blank line:

```
<AREA SHAPE=POLY COORDS="29,4,29,41,111,41,111,78,213,78,
213,4" HREF="Bryd.htm">
```

Figure 3-48 shows the completed list of <AREA> tags for the Layout image map. Compare these values with the ones you've entered to confirm that you entered them correctly.

Figure 3-48   LAYOUT IMAGE MAP AND HOTSPOTS

image map name

rectangular hotspot

circular hotspot

polygonal hotspot

```
<H5 ALIGN=CENTER>Click each location for a list of events<BR>
<IMG SRC="Layout.gif"></H5>

<H5 ALIGN=CENTER>Sponsored by the Department of Astronomy and the Center
for Space Science and Engineering.</H5>

<MAP NAME="FloorPlan">
<AREA SHAPE=RECT COORDS="5,45,108,157" HREF="Mitchell.htm">
<AREA SHAPE=CIRCLE COORDS="161,130,49" HREF="Brinkman.htm">
<AREA SHAPE=POLY COORDS="29,4,29,41,111,41,111,78,213,78,213,4"
 HREF="Bryd.htm">
</MAP>

</BODY>
</HTML>
```

With all of the <AREA> tags in place, you're finished defining the image map. Your next task is to instruct the browser to use the FloorPlan image map with the Layout inline image. Then you'll test the image to confirm that it works properly.

Using an Image Map

The final step in adding an image map to a Web page is to add the USEMAP property to the <IMG> tag for the image map graphic. The USEMAP property tells the browser the name of the image map to associate with the inline image. The syntax for accessing an image map is:

```
<IMG SRC="image file" USEMAP="#mapname">
```

Here, *mapname* is the name assigned to the NAME property in the <MAP> tag. Note that you have to place a pound sign (#) before the image map name. You named your image map "FloorPlan" and you inserted the Layout image into your Web page. Now you have to add the USEMAP property to the <IMG> tag to associate Layout.gif with the FloorPlan image map.

To assign the FloorPlan image map to the Layout graphic and test the image map:

1. Locate the Layout.gif <IMG> tag in the Expo.htm file.

2. Add the following property to the tag: **USEMAP="#FloorPlan"**.

   The completed <IMG> tag should appear as shown in Figure 3-49.

Figure 3-49   SPECIFYING THE IMAGE MAP TO USE

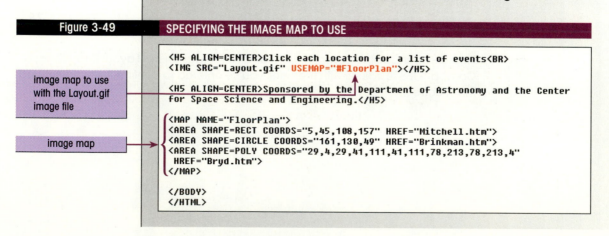

image map to use with the Layout.gif image file

image map

```
<H5 ALIGN=CENTER>Click each location for a list of events<BR>
<IMG SRC="Layout.gif" USEMAP="#FloorPlan"></H5>

<H5 ALIGN=CENTER>Sponsored by the Department of Astronomy and the Center
for Space Science and Engineering.</H5>

<MAP NAME="FloorPlan">
<AREA SHAPE=RECT COORDS="5,45,108,157" HREF="Mitchell.htm">
<AREA SHAPE=CIRCLE COORDS="161,130,49" HREF="Brinkman.htm">
<AREA SHAPE=POLY COORDS="29,4,29,41,111,41,111,78,213,78,213,4"
 HREF="Bryd.htm">
</MAP>

</BODY>
</HTML>
```

3. Save the changes to the Expo.htm file.

Now that you've created the image map, you're ready to test it in your Web browser.

4. Reload the Space Expo Web page in your Web browser.

5. Scroll down to the Layout graphic and place the pointer over the graphic. Note that the pointer changes to a hand when it is positioned over a hotspot. Note as well that the status bar displays the URL for that particular hotspot. See Figure 3-50.

| Figure 3-50 | PLACING THE POINTER OVER THE MITCHELL THEATRE HOTSPOT |

pointer changes to a hand as it passes over a hotspot

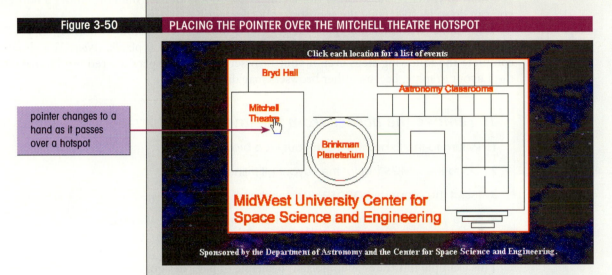

TROUBLE? If your image does not have a red border around it, don't worry. The border is created by some browsers and will be discussed in the section that follows.

6. Click within the Mitchell Theatre hotspot in the floor plan graphic. Your Web browser displays the page listing the events at the Mitchell Theatre over the Expo weekend.

7. Click the **Back** button in your Web browser to return to the Space Expo page.

8. Test the other hotspots in the graphic and confirm that they jump to the appropriate page of events. When you're finished working with those pages, return to the Expo page.

On some browsers you will notice that the floor plan image is surrounded by a red border that is not displayed when you view the image in a graphics program. Where did this border come from? The border is placed around the image by some browsers to identify the image as a hyperlink. If you are using Internet Explorer prior to version 5.0, you will not see this border. The border color is red because that is the color you specified earlier for hyperlinks. You can remove the border with the BORDER property.

Using the BORDER Property

The BORDER property allows you to create a border to surround your inline images. The syntax for changing the border width is:

```
<IMG SRC="image file" BORDER=value>
```

where *value* is the width of the border in pixels. An inline image that does not contain hyperlinks to other documents will, by default, not contain a border. However, if the image does contain hyperlinks to other documents, some browsers will create a border 2 pixels wide. If you want to either create a border (for an image that does not have one) or remove a border, you can do so by specifying the appropriate border width.

Tom thinks that the floor plan image would look better without a border, so you'll remove it from the floor plan by specifying a border width of 0 pixels. (*Note:* You should complete the following steps even if your browser does not display the red border around the Layout graphic, because other browsers may display it.)

To remove the border from the layout graphic:

1. Return to the **Expo.htm** file in your Web browser.

2. Go to the <IMG> tag for the Layout.gif inline image.

3. Insert the property **BORDER=0** within the <IMG> tag.

4. Save your changes to the file and then reload it in your Web browser.

This example illustrates an important principle of page design: you should examine your page in different browsers. If were using version 4.0 of Internet Explorer to view your page, you would not have learned of the border issue for the Layout graphic.

Note that the BORDER property works for both Internet Explorer and Netscape Navigator, although it is used differently with Internet Explorer. In the case of Internet Explorer, applying the BORDER property to an image without hyperlinks will create an invisible border around the image, whereas for images that contain hyperlinks, the border color will be the same as the link color.

Tom reviews the completed Space Expo page. He's pleased with the work you've done and will get back to you with any changes he wants you to make. For now you can close your browser and text editor.

To close your work:

1. Close your Web browser.

2. Return to your text editor, and then close the Expo.htm file.

Figure 3-51 shows the finished Web page of the Space Expo. Figure 3-52 shows the complete HTML code for this page.

Figure 3-51   COMPLETED SPACE EXPO WEB PAGE

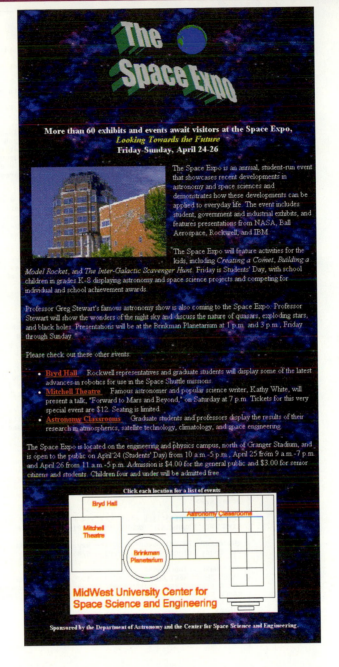

Figure 3-52   COMPLETED EXPO.HTM FILE

```
<HTML>
<HEAD>
<TITLE>The Space Expo</TITLE>
</HEAD>
<BODY BACKGROUND="Space.jpg" TEXT=WHITE LINK=RED VLINK=TURQUOISE>

<H1 ALIGN="CENTER"><IMG SRC="LogoAnim.gif" ALT="The Space Expo"
 WIDTH=296 HEIGHT=209></H1>

<H3 ALIGN="CENTER">More than 60 exhibits and events await visitors at the
Space Expo, <BR>
<I><FONT COLOR=YELLOW>Looking Towards the Future</FONT></I> <BR>
Friday-Sunday, April 24-26 </H3>

<P><IMG SRC="Center.jpg" ALT="The MWU Center for Space Science and
Engineering" ALIGN=LEFT VSPACE=5 HSPACE=15 WIDTH=280 HEIGHT=186>
The Space Expo is an annual, student-run event that showcases recent
developments in astronomy and space sciences and demonstrates how these
developments can be applied to everyday life. The event includes student,
government and industrial exhibits, and features presentations from NASA,
Ball Aerospace, Rockwell, and IBM.</P>

<P>The Space Expo will feature activities for the kids, including
<I>Creating a Comet</I>, <I>Building a Model Rocket</I>, and <I>The
Inter-Galactic Scavenger Hunt</I>. Friday is Students' Day, with school
children in grades K-8 displaying astronomy and space science projects and
competing for individual and school achievement awards.</P>

<P>Professor Greg Stewart's famous astronomy show is also coming to the
Space Expo. Professor Stewart will show the wonders of the night sky and
discuss the nature of quasars, exploding stars, and black holes.
Presentations will be at the Brinkman Planetarium at 1 p.m. and 3 p.m.,
Friday through Sunday. </P>

<P>Please check out these other events:</P>

<UL>
<B><LI> <A HREF="Bryd.htm"> Bryd Hall </A> </B>     Rockwell
representatives and graduate students will display some of the latest
advances in robotics for use in the Space Shuttle
missions.</LI>

<B><LI> <A HREF="Mitchell.htm"> Mitchell Theatre </A> </B>    
Famous astronomer and popular science writer, Kathy White, will present a
talk, "Forward to Mars and Beyond," on Saturday at 7 p.m. Tickets for this
very special event are $12. Seating is limited.</LI>

<B><LI> <A HREF="Class.htm"> Astronomy Classrooms </A> </B>    
Graduate students and professors display the results of their research in
atmospherics, satellite technology, climatology, and space engineering.
</LI>
</UL>

<P>The Space Expo is located on the engineering and physics campus,
north of Granger Stadium, and is open to the public on April 24 (Students'
Day) from 10 a.m.-5 p.m., April 25 from 9 a.m.-7 p.m. and April 26 from
11 a.m.-5 p.m. Admission is $4.00 for the general public and $3.00 for
senior citizens and students. Children four and under will be admitted
free. </P>

<H5 ALIGN=CENTER>Click each location for a list of events<BR>
<IMG SRC="Layout.gif" USEMAP="#FloorPlan" BORDER=0></H5>

<H5 ALIGN=CENTER>Sponsored by the Department of Astronomy and the Center
for Space Science and Engineering.</H5>

<MAP NAME="FloorPlan">
<AREA SHAPE=RECT COORDS="5,45,108,157" HREF="Mitchell.htm">
<AREA SHAPE=CIRCLE COORDS="161,130,49" HREF="Brinkman.htm">
<AREA SHAPE=POLY COORDS="29,4,29,41,111,41,111,78,213,78,213,4"
 HREF="Bryd.htm">
</MAP>

</BODY>
</HTML>
```

You've finished enhancing the Space Expo page with graphics. You've seen how to create an image map so that a single graphic can link to several different Web pages. You've also learned about some of the design issues involved in adding graphics to a Web page, and how to choose the correct graphic type for a particular image. Using the knowledge you've gained, you're ready to work on new design challenges that Tom has for you.

Session 3.3 QUICK CHECK

1. What is a hotspot? What is an image map?

2. What are the two types of image maps? List the advantages and disadvantages of each.

3. What HTML tag would you enter to define a rectangular hotspot with the upper-left edge of the rectangle at the point (5,20) and the lower-right edge located at (85,100)? If the user clicks the hotspot, the file Oregon.htm should be displayed.

4. What tag would you enter for a circular hotspot centered at (44,81), with a radius of 23pixels, that you want linked to the LA.htm file?

5. What tag would you enter for a hotspot that connects the points (5,10), (5,35), (25,35), (30,20), and (15,10) and that you want linked to the Hawaii.htm file?

6. What HTML tag would you enter to assign an image map named States to the graphics file WestCoast.gif?

7. What HTML tag would you enter to increase the border around the WestCoast graphic to 5 pixels?

REVIEW ASSIGNMENTS

After reviewing the finished Space Expo Web page, Tom made a few changes to its contents. He also has a few additional suggestions for you to implement. He would like you to add a hotspot to the Layout image that points to a page listing the talks given in various classrooms. He also would like you to work with the other Web pages to improve their appearance.

To implement Tom's suggestions:

1. In your text editor, open the **Mitchtxt.htm** file in the Review folder of the Tutorial.03 folder on your Data Disk, and then save the file as Mitchell.htm in the same folder.

2. Use the **Stars.jpg** file as your background image for this page. Change the color of the text on the page to white.

3. Change the font color of the heading "This Week at the Mitchell Theatre" to use the hexadecimal color value 00CC00. Use the Arial font for the same heading. If a user's computer does not have the Arial font, specify that the Helvetica font should be used instead, and then, finally, that the Sans Serif font should be used.

4. Change the color of "Calendar of Events" to the hexadecimal color value 00CC00.

Explore 5. Change the color of the day and date lines (for example Friday, April 24) to the RGB triplet (255,0,0).

6. Save your changes to the Mitchell.htm file.

7. Repeat Steps 2 through 5 for the **Brydtxt.htm** file in the Review folder, editing the "Bryd Hall" heading with the same color and font you applied to the Mitchell Theodore page. Save the file as Bryd.htm in the same folder.

8. Open the **Brinktxt.htm** file in the Review folder of the Tutorial.03 folder on your Data Disk, and then save the file as Brinkman.htm in the same folder.

Explore 9. Change the background color value of the Brinkman page to (0,153,204). (*Hint:* You will have to convert this RGB triplet to hexadecimal, using one of the resources mentioned in Figure 3-7.) Change the text color value to white.

Explore 10. Change the color of the heading "The Brinkman Planetarium" to (255,255,204).

11. Insert the inline image **Equip.jpg** file at the beginning of the first paragraph. Align the image with the right edge of the page so that the text wraps on the left side of the image. Increase the horizontal and vertical space around the image to 5 pixels. Enter "The Planetarium Projector" as alternate text for the image.

12. The inline image is 326 pixels wide by 201 pixels high. With this information, how could you increase the speed at which your Web browser loads this page? Implement your response to increase the speed.

13. Save your changes to the Brinkman.htm file.

14. Use your text editor to open the **Expotxt.htm** file in the Review folder of the Tutorial.03 folder on your Data Disk, and then save the file as Expo.htm in the same folder.

15. Add a polygonal hotspot to the Floorplan image map and connect the hotspot to the **Class.htm** file. The coordinates of the hotspot are (215,4), (215,132), (311,132), (311,213), (424,213), and (424,4).

16. Load the Expo.htm file into your Web browser and confirm that the hotspot to the Class.htm file works correctly. Use the links in the page to examine the appearances of the other Web pages for any errors.

17. When you are satisfied with the Web pages, save your work, print each page (Mitchell.htm, Bryd.htm, Brinkman.htm, and Expo.htm) from your text editor, and then close your Web browser and text editor.

CASE PROBLEMS

Case 1. Creating a New Products Page for Jackson Electronics   Paul Reichtman is a sales manager at Jackson Electronics in Seattle, Washington. He wants you to create a Web presentation that advertises three new products released in the last month: the ScanMaster scanner, the LaserPrint 5000 printer, and the Print/Scan 150 combination printer-scanner-copier.

The press releases for the three products and the general announcement have already been put into HTML files for you. The general announcement is shown in Figure 3-53.

Figure 3-53

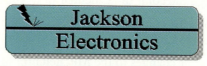

**Jackson Electronics Introduces
a New Line of Products**

Jackson Electronics announced this month a new line of small business printers, copiers and scanners. Designed to meet the growing need for economical scanning and printing solutions, the new products do not sacrifice quality or dependability.

The ScanMaster continues Jackson Electronics' leadership in the field of flatbed scanners. With the patented "Single-Pass" technology, the ScanMaster is fast, with image quality better than multiple-pass scanners.

Building on its popular line of laser printers, Jackson Electronics introduces the LaserPrint 5000. The LaserPrint 5000 prints b&w text at 12 ppm. and its memory expands up to 24 megabytes for graphic-intensive print jobs.

The new Print/Scan 150 combines the benefits of a printer, copier and scanner - all in one! And all without sacrificing quality. Save money (and space) with this three-in-one product.

Interested? Click one of the product names to the left for more information.

Paul would like you to enhance the appearance of this page and the other pages with special color and graphics. The pages should also be linked through an image map. A preview of the page you'll create is shown in Figure 3-54.

Figure 3-54

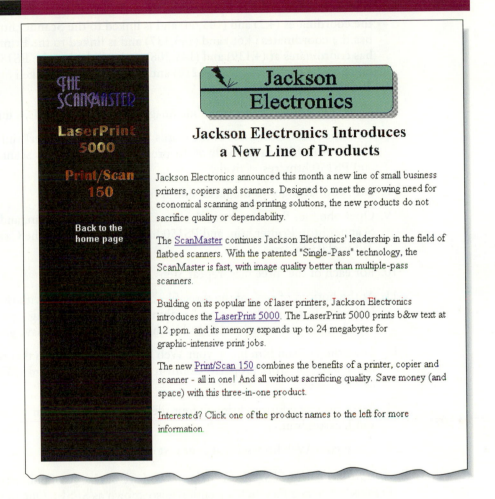

You'll create the left bar effect shown in the figure by using a background image consisting of a single line that is 1 pixel high and 1600 pixels wide. The first 180 pixels of the line are black, and the remainder of the line is white. The browser repeatedly inserts this image into the page background, but because the image is so wide, the bar is not repeated across the width of the page, only down the length of it. An inline image with a black background is placed on the left edge of the page to complete the effect. You'll use this background and image combination for all four of the documents that Paul gives you.

To create Paul's Web presentation:

1. In your text editor, open the **Newtext.htm** file in the Cases folder of the Tutorial.03 folder on your Data Disk, and then save the file as Jackson.htm in the same folder.

2. Change the background image to the **Bars.jpg** file.

3. Insert the file **Product.jpg** as an inline image at the top of the page. Align the image with the left edge of the page. Increase the space around the image to 5 pixels in all directions. Set the border width of the inline image to 0 pixels.

4. Create an image map named "Product_List."

5. Add four rectangular hotspots to the Product_List image map. The first rectangle has the coordinates (4,2) and (143,66) and is linked to the Scanner.htm file. The second has the coordinates (4,68) and (143,137) and is linked to the Printer.htm file. The third has coordinates at (4,139) and (143,208) and is linked to the PS150.htm file. The final hotspot has the coordinates (4,210) and (143,278) and is linked to the Jackson.htm file. You'll create these files in Step 9.

6. Specify that the Product.jpg inline image uses the Product_List image map.

7. Link the first occurrences of the words "ScanMaster," "LaserPrint 5000," and "Print/Scan 150" in the body of the press release to the files Scanner.htm, Printer.htm, and PS150.htm, respectively.

8. Save your changes to the Jackson.htm file.

9. Open the files **Scantext.htm**, **Printext.htm**, and **PStext.htm**, and then save them as Scanner.htm, Printer.htm, and PS150.htm, respectively, in the Cases folder of the Tutorial.03 folder.

10. For each of the three files, repeat Steps 2 through 6.

11. At the bottom of each of the three files, insert a single line with the text "Return to the Jackson Electronics home page." within an <H5> heading tag. Specify that the line of text should be centered and linked to the Jackson.htm file. Save your changes to the file.

12. Load the Jackson.htm file in your Web browser and confirm that the hypertext links in the image map work properly. Confirm that the hypertext links in the main text also work correctly.

13. Use your text editor to print all four files: Scanner.htm, Printer.htm, and PS150.htm, and Jackson.htm.

14. Close your Web browser and your text editor.

Case 2. Announcing the SFSF Convention.   You are in charge of publicity for the San Francisco Science Fiction Convention (also known as SFSF). One of your jobs is to create a Web presentation announcing the three guests of honor for the convention. You've decided to create a home page with three thumbnail photos of the guests combined into a single image map, which will then be linked to separate biography pages for each person. The biography pages will also contain the photos, but in a larger and more detailed format. A preview of the home page is shown in Figure 3-55, and a preview of one of the biography pages is shown in Figure 3-56.

Figure 3-55

the
San Francisco
Science Fiction
Convention

Welcome to the San Francisco Science Fiction Convention

The SFSF committee welcomes you to the annual San Francisco Science Fiction convention. The convention starts Thursday, August 19th at 8 p.m. with the Get-Together party in Derleith Hall. The fun doesn't stop until Sunday morning on August 22nd. Be sure to attend Friday's costume party and the *"You Don't Know Jack* trivia contest.

The guests of honor at this year's convention are: Philip Forrest, famous fan and fiction follower; Karen Charnas, author of the award-winning novel *The Unicorn Express*, and Jeffrey Unwin, critic and editor of *The Magazine of Speculative Fiction*.

Click the images above for guest biographies

Registration is $35 at the door, $30 in advance. It's worth it!

For more information and a calendar of events, contact:

SF SF
301 Howlitze Lane
San Francisco, CA 94201
(311)555-2989

Figure 3-56

Biography

Name: Philip Forrest
Age: 68
Occupation: Professional fan and editor of *Horizons*
Favorite Fish: Huh? What? Fried, I guess.
Comments: I'm thrilled to be selected fan guest of honor. I look forward to seeing everyone at SFSF.

Phil has been a fan favorite for forty years. His knowledge of science fiction is legendary, and anyone who has seen his immense magazine collection knows where that knowledge came from! As editor of *Horizons*, Phil has won two Tucker awards for the best fanzine of the year.

To create the SFSF Convention Web site:

1. In your text editor, open the **Forsttxt.htm** file in the Cases folder of the Tutorial.03 folder on your Data Disk, and then save the file as Forrest.htm in the same folder.

Explore ▶ 2. Change the background color to the RGB triplet (255, 255, 204).

3. At the top of the page, before the <H2> Biography heading, insert the **Forrest.jpg** inline image aligned with the left margin. Specify 10 pixels of horizontal space and 5 pixels of vertical space.

Explore ▶ 4. After the Comments line, use the CLEAR property of the <BR> tag so that it starts the next line below the inline image you inserted in Step 3. What would happen if you left the <BR> tag in its original position? Write your answer on the printout you create in Step 15.

5. Save your changes.

6. Open the file **Charntxt.htm** in the Cases folder of the Tutorial.03 folder and repeat Steps 2 through 5 using the graphic file **Charnas.jpg**. Save the file as Charnas.htm in the same folder. Then open the file **Unwintxt.htm** in the Cases folder and repeat Steps 2 through 5 using the graphic file **Unwin.jpg**. Save the file as **Unwin.htm**.

7. Open the **SFSFtxt.htm** file in the Cases folder of the Tutorial.03 folder on your Data Disk, and then save the file as SFSF.htm in the same folder.

Explore ▶ 8. Change the background color value to (255, 255, 204).

9. Within the <H2> heading at the top of the page, insert the inline image **SFSF.gif**. Place a <BR> tag after the image so that it resides on its own line. Color the heading text blue.

10. After the description of the guests of honor, insert a centered <H4> tag with the inline image **Guests.jpg** on one line, followed by a <BR> tag and then the text "Click the images above for guest biographies" on the second line. Color the text blue.

11. Create an image map named "Guests" with three rectangular hotspots. The first hotspot has the coordinates (0,0) and (70,70) and points to the Forrest.htm file; the second has coordinates at (71,0) and (140,70) and points to the Charnas.htm file; and the third has coordinates at (141,0) and (210,70) and points to the Unwin.htm file. Apply this image map to the Guests.jpg inline image.

12. For the first occurrences of the names of the guests of honor, create hypertext links that point to their biography pages.

13. Save your changes.

14. Open the SFSF.htm file in your Web browser and check all hypertext links to verify that they work properly.

15. Use your text editor to print the files Forrest.htm, SFSF.htm, Unwin.htm, and Charnas.htm.

16. Close your Web browser and your text editor.

Case 3. Creating an Online Menu for Kelsey's Diner   You've been asked to create an online menu for Kelsey's Diner, a well-established restaurant in Worcester, Massachusetts, so that patrons can order carryout dishes from the Web. The manager, Cindy Towser, shows you a text file with the current carryout breakfast menu, displayed in Figure 3-57. She wants you to spice it up with colors and graphics. She also wants you to create hyperlinks to the lunch and dinner carryout menus. A preview of the page that you'll create is shown in Figure 3-58.

Figure 3-57

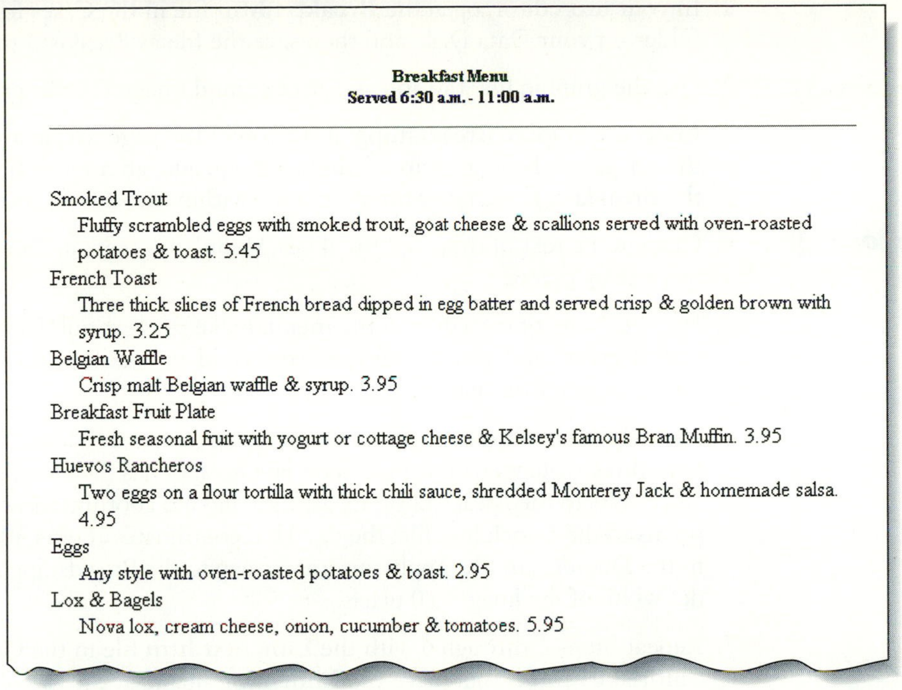

Breakfast Menu
Served 6:30 a.m. - 11:00 a.m.

Smoked Trout
Fluffy scrambled eggs with smoked trout, goat cheese & scallions served with oven-roasted potatoes & toast. 5.45

French Toast
Three thick slices of French bread dipped in egg batter and served crisp & golden brown with syrup. 3.25

Belgian Waffle
Crisp malt Belgian waffle & syrup. 3.95

Breakfast Fruit Plate
Fresh seasonal fruit with yogurt or cottage cheese & Kelsey's famous Bran Muffin. 3.95

Huevos Rancheros
Two eggs on a flour tortilla with thick chili sauce, shredded Monterey Jack & homemade salsa. 4.95

Eggs
Any style with oven-roasted potatoes & toast. 2.95

Lox & Bagels
Nova lox, cream cheese, onion, cucumber & tomatoes. 5.95

Figure 3-58

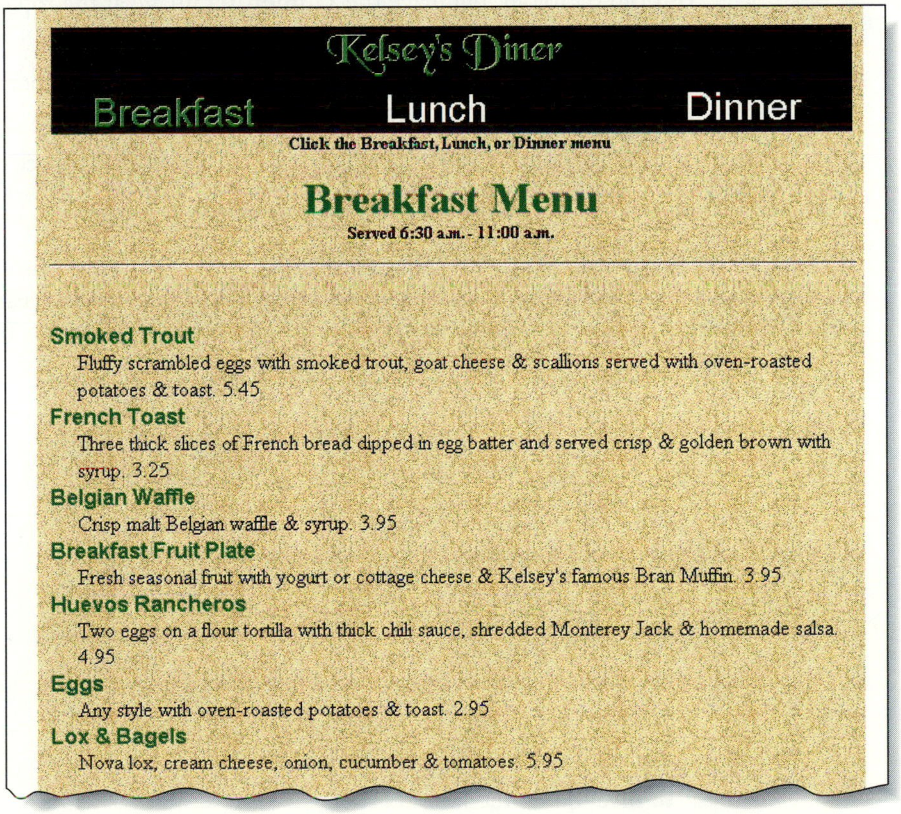

Kelsey's Diner

Breakfast   Lunch   Dinner
Click the Breakfast, Lunch, or Dinner menu

Breakfast Menu
Served 6:30 a.m. - 11:00 a.m.

Smoked Trout
Fluffy scrambled eggs with smoked trout, goat cheese & scallions served with oven-roasted potatoes & toast. 5.45

French Toast
Three thick slices of French bread dipped in egg batter and served crisp & golden brown with syrup. 3.25

Belgian Waffle
Crisp malt Belgian waffle & syrup. 3.95

Breakfast Fruit Plate
Fresh seasonal fruit with yogurt or cottage cheese & Kelsey's famous Bran Muffin. 3.95

Huevos Rancheros
Two eggs on a flour tortilla with thick chili sauce, shredded Monterey Jack & homemade salsa. 4.95

Eggs
Any style with oven-roasted potatoes & toast. 2.95

Lox & Bagels
Nova lox, cream cheese, onion, cucumber & tomatoes. 5.95

To create the Web menu for Kelsey's Diner:

1. In your text editor, open the **Breaktxt.htm** file in the Cases folder of the Tutorial.03 folder on your Data Disk, and then save the file as Breakfst.htm in the same folder.

2. Use the graphic file **Tan.jpg** as a background image for this page.

3. Insert the graphic **Breakfst.jpg** at the top of the page within a set of <H5> tags. Center the image on the page. Directly below the image, after a line break, insert the text "Click the Breakfast, Lunch, or Dinner menu" (within the <H5> tags used for the inline image).

Explore ▶

4. Change the text of the title "Breakfast Menu" to green, and increase the point size of the text by three.

5. For the name of each dish in the menu, make the text boldface, change the color of the text to green, and specify that the text should appear in either the Arial, Helvetica, or Sans Serif font (in that order).

6. At the bottom of the page, insert an image map named "Menu." The image map should have three rectangular hotspots. The first hotspot has the coordinates (20,40) and (156,77) and points to the Breakfst.htm file; the second has coordinates at (241,40) and (336,77) and points to the Lunch.htm file; the third has coordinates at (464,40) and (568,77) and points to the Dinner.htm file. Apply this image map to the Breakfst.jpg inline image. Set the border width of the image to 0 pixels.

7. Repeat Steps 2 through 6 with the **Lunchtxt.htm** file in the Cases folder of the Tutorial.03 folder, but place the **Lunch.jpg** image at the top of the page, and save the file as "Lunch.htm."

8. Repeat Steps 2 through 6 with the **Dinnrtxt.htm** file in the Cases folder of the Tutorial.03 folder, but place the **Dinner.jpg** image at the top of the page, and save the file as "Dinner.htm."

9. Open the Breakfst.htm file in your browser and test the hyperlinks. Verify that the pages look correct and that the inline image changes to reflect the change in the menu.

10. Print a copy of the Breakfast menu, and then print the source code for all three files.

11. Close your Web browser and your text editor.

Case 4. Creating a Listing for Tri-State Realty

Tri-State Realty is in the process of putting their listings on the World Wide Web. You've been asked to create some pages for their Web site. You've been given the following information for your first page, a listing describing property located at 22 Northshore Drive:

"This is a must see. Large waterfront home overlooking Mills Lake. It comes complete with three bedrooms, a huge master bedroom, hot tub, family room, large office or den, and three-car garage. Wood boat ramp. Great condition!"

In addition, the owners of the property have included the following main points that they want to be emphasized in the Web page:

- 2900 sq. feet
- 15 years old
- updated electrical, plumbing, and heating systems
- central air conditioning
- near school, park, and shopping center
- nice, quiet neighborhood
- asking price: $280,000

Finally, you've been given the following files (in the Cases folder of the Tutorial.03 folder on your Data Disk):

- **House.jpg**, which contains a photo of the property; size is 243×163
- **Tristate.gif**, the company logo; size is 225×100
- **Listings.gif**, a graphic image showing the various listing categories; size is 600×100
- **TSBack.gif**, the background texture used on all Tri-State Web pages

Using this information, you'll create a Web page for the property at 22 Northshore Drive. The design of the page is up to you, but it should include the following:

- an appropriately titled heading
- a paragraph describing the house
- a list of the main points of interest
- the photo of the house, the company logo, and the graphic of the different listing categories (use the company background file as your page's background)
- at least one example of spot color
- at least one example of a font displaying a different face and size from the surrounding text
- alternate text for the logo and house photo images
- height and width information for all inline images
- the listings graphic converted to an image map, with the following hotspots (target files are not included, so you should create blank HTML files that display the filename and nothing else):
  - rectangular hotspot at (5,3) (182,44) that points to the Newhome.htm file
  - rectangular hotspot at (12,62) (303,95) that points to the Mansions.htm file
  - rectangular hotspot at (210,19) (374,60) that points to the Business.htm file
  - rectangular hotspot at (375,1) (598,44) that points to the Family.htm file
  - rectangular hotspot at (378,61) (549,96) that points to the Apartmnt.htm file
- appropriately labeled hypertext links that point to the same files as indicated in the image map
- your name, as Web page author, in italics

Save the page as Tristate.htm in the Cases folder of the Tutorial.03 folder on your Data Disk, and then print a copy of your page and the HTML code. Close your Web browser and your text editor when you're finished.

QUICK CHECK ANSWERS

Session 3.1

1. Color names and color values. Color names are easier to work with but the color name may not exist for exactly the color you want to use. Also your color name may not be supported by all browsers. Color values allow you to exactly describe a color, but they can be difficult to work with.
2. <BODY BGCOLOR=GRAY TEXT=RED LINK=BLUE VLINK=YELLOW>
3. Spot color is color that affects only a few sections of a page such as a single character, word or phrase.

4. <FONT COLOR=RED SIZE=+5>Major Sale</FONT>

5. <FONT FACE="Times New Roman, MS Serif">Major Sale</FONT>

6. <BODY BACKGROUND="Stars.gif">

7. Overwhelming the page's text, using a large image file that will make the page take longer to load, and using an image that displays visible seams.

Session 3.2

1. When you want to use transparent colors, when you want to use an animated image, and when your image has only 256 colors or less.

2. For photographic images, for images that contain more than 256 colors, to reduce file size through compression, and to avoid the problem of the legal issues of using GIFs.

3. <IMG SRC="mwu.jpg" ALT="MidWest University">

4. <IMG SRC="mwu.jpg" ALIGN=TOP>

5. <IMG SRC="mwu.jpg" ALIGN=RIGHT>

   This tag will not work with browsers that don't support the RIGHT align property, such as versions of Netscape and Internet Explorer prior to 3.0.

6. <IMG SRC="mwu.jpg" HSPACE=10 VSPACE=10>

7. <IMG SRC="mwu.jpg" HEIGHT=85 WIDTH=120>

8. When an image with many colors is displayed on a monitor that does not support all those colors, the monitor will attempt to approximate the appearance of those colors. The Safety Palette is a palette of 211 colors that is guaranteed to be displayed on all browsers without resorting to dithering.

Session 3.3

1. A hotspot is a defined area of the image that acts as a hypertext link. An image map lists the coordinates on the image that define the boundaries of the hotspots.

2. Server-side and client-side. The server-side is the older, more accepted method of creating image maps and relies on the Web server to interpret the image map and create the hypertext jump. The client-side image map is newer and is not supported by older browser. Because the user's machine interprets the image map, the image map is interpreted more quickly, it can be tested on the local machine, and information about various hotspots appears in the status bar of the Web browser.

3. <AREA SHAPE=RECT COORDS="5,20,85,100" HREF="Oregon.htm">

4. <AREA SHAPE=CIRCLE COORDS="44,81,23" HREF="LA.htm">

5. <AREA SHAPE=POLY COORDS="5,10,5,35,25,35,30,20,15,10" HREF="Hawaii.htm">

6. <IMG SRC="WestCoast.gif" USEMAP="#States">

7. <IMG SRC="WestCoast.gif" BORDER=5>

OBJECTIVES

In this tutorial you will:

- Create a text table

- Create a graphical table using the <TABLE>, <TR>, and <TD> tags

- Create table headers and captions

- Control the appearance of a table and table text

- Create table cells that span several rows or columns

- Use nested tables to enhance page design

- Learn about Internet Explorer extensions for use with tables

DESIGNING A WEB PAGE WITH TABLES

Creating a Products Page

CASE

Middle Age Arts

Middle Age Arts is a company that creates and sells replicas of historic European works of art for home and garden use. The company specializes in sculpture, tapestries, prints, friezes, and busts that evoke the artistic styles of the Middle Ages and the Renaissance.

Nicole Swanson, an advertising executive at Middle Age Arts, is directing the effort to create Web pages for the company. She hopes that a Web page can improve the company's visibility, as well as make it easier for customers to place orders. The type of information she wants to provide on the Web includes a description of the company, contact information for individuals who want to place an order over the phone, a list of stores that distribute Middle Age Arts products, and a display of the company's merchandise.

Nicole has asked you to work on creating Web pages for the Gargoyle Collection, a new line of Middle Age Arts products featuring gargoyles recreated from the walls and towers of Gothic buildings and churches. The page should display the product name, item number, description, and price. Information of this type is best displayed in a table, so to create the page, you'll have to learn how to work with tables in HTML.

SESSION
4.1

In this session you will learn how to add tables to a Web page, starting with simple text tables and then moving to graphical tables, and you'll learn the advantages of each approach. You'll also learn how to define table rows, cells, and headings with HTML tags. Finally, you'll add a caption to your table and learn how to control the caption's placement on the page.

Tables on the World Wide Web

Nicole has been considering the prototype page she wants you to create for the Gargoyle Collection. She wants you to start out small. The page will eventually have to display more than 50 separate items, but for now she is only interested in a small sample of that number. With that in mind, Nicole has selected three products, shown in a table format in Figure 4-1, that she wants you to place on the Web page.

Figure 4-1   NICOLE'S PRODUCTS TABLE

Name	Item #	Type	Finish	Price
Bacchus	48059	Wall Mount	Interior Plaster	$95
Praying Gargoyle	48159	Garden Figure	Gothic Stone	$125
Gargoyle Judge	48222	Bust	Interior Plaster	$140

There are two ways to insert a table of information on a Web page: you can create either a text table or a graphical table. A **text table**, like the one shown in Figure 4-2, contains only text, evenly spaced out on the page in rows and columns. Text tables use only standard type-writer characters, so that even a line in a text table is created by repeating a typographical character, such as a hyphen, underline, or equals sign.

Figure 4-2   A TEXT TABLE

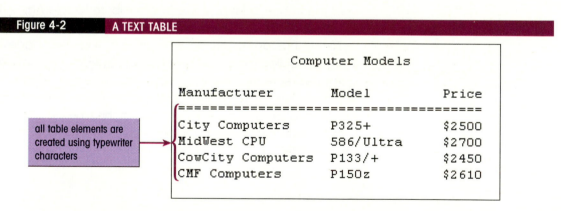

```
                    Computer Models


Manufacturer            Model           Price
========================================
City Computers          P325+           $2500
MidWest CPU             586/Ultra       $2700
CowCity Computers       P133/+          $2450
CMF Computers           P150z           $2610
```

all table elements are created using typewriter characters

A **graphical table**, as shown in Figure 4-3, appears as a graphical element on the Web page. A graphical table allows you to include design elements such as color, shading, and borders. Because of this, you have greater control over the table's appearance. You can control the size of individual table cells and text alignment. You can even create cells that span several rows or columns.

Figure 4-3 A GRAPHICAL TABLE

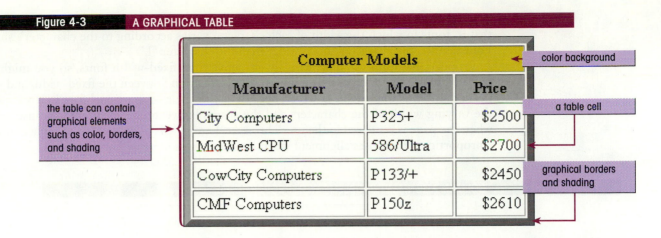

Graphical tables are more flexible and attractive than text tables. However, there are some situations in which you will want to use a text table. Some browsers, such as the text-based Lynx browser used on many UNIX systems, can display only text characters. Also, working with the tags for graphical tables can be complicated and time-consuming. For these reasons, you might want to create two versions of your Web page: one that uses only text elements and text tables, and another that takes advantage of graphical elements. This is the approach Nicole suggests that you take. First you'll create a text table of the products in the Gargoyle Collection, and then you'll start to work on the graphical version of the table.

Creating a Text Table

The beginning of the file you'll use for the text table version of the products page has already been created for you and is stored on your Data Disk as MAA.htm. To begin, you'll open this file and save it with a new name.

To open the MAA.htm file and then save it with a new name:

1. Start your text editor.

2. Open the file **MAA.htm** from the **Tutorial.04** folder on your Data Disk, and then save the file in the same folder as **MAAtext.htm**.

The page consists of two headings formatted with the <H1> and <H3> tags, followed by a paragraph of text that describes the Gargoyle Collection. You'll add the text table below the paragraph.

Using Fixed-Width Fonts

To create a text table, you have to control the type of font that is used. A text table relies on spaces and the characters that fill those spaces to create its column boundaries. You have to use a font that allots the same amount of space to each character and to the empty spaces between characters. This type of font is called a **fixed-width font**, or a **typewriter font**.

Most typeset documents (such as the one you're reading now) use **proportional fonts**—that is, fonts in which the width of each character varies according to the character's shape. For example, the character "m" is wider than the character "l."

Proportional fonts are more visually attractive than fixed-width fonts, so you might be tempted to use them for your text tables. The distinction between the fixed-width and proportional font is important, however, because if you use a proportional font in a text table, the varying width of the characters and the spaces between characters might cause errors when the page is rendered in the user's browser. Figure 4-4 shows how a text table that uses a proportional font loses alignment when the font size is increased or decreased.

Figure 4-4   **COLUMN ALIGNMENT PROBLEMS WITH PROPORTIONAL FONTS**

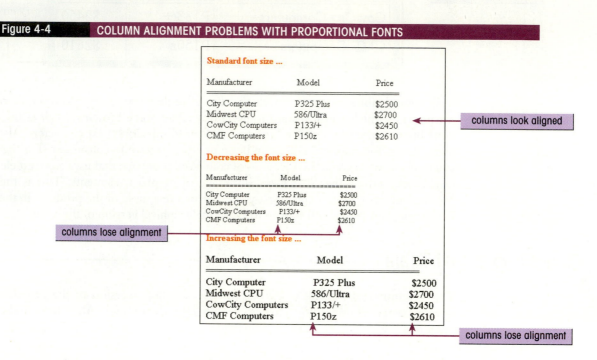

By contrast, the table shown in Figure 4-5 uses fixed-width fonts. Note that the columns remain aligned regardless of font size.

Figure 4-5   **COLUMN ALIGNMENT WITH FIXED-WIDTH FONTS**

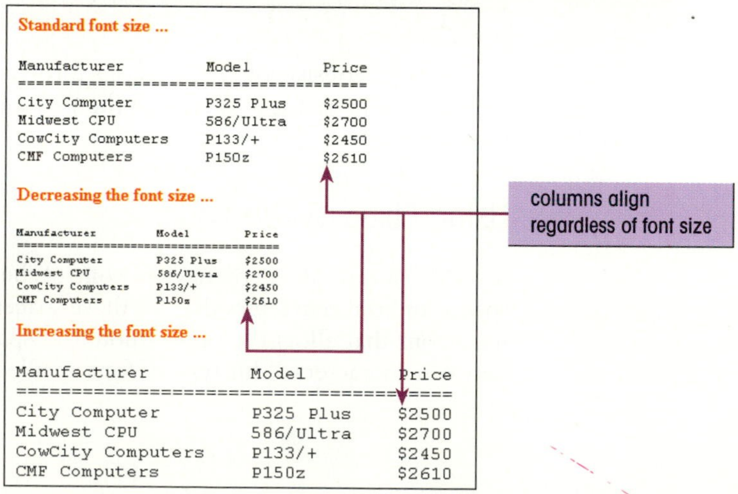

Different browsers and operating systems may use different font sizes to display text, so you should always use a fixed-width font to ensure that the columns in your text tables remain in alignment.

Using the <PRE> Tag

Recall that HTML ignores extra blank spaces, blank lines, or tabs; however, to control the appearance of a table, you need to use spaces and other characters. You can insert the <PRE> tag to display preformatted text, text formatted in ways that you want retained in your Web page. Any text formatted with the <PRE> tag retains those extra blank spaces and blank lines. The <PRE> tag also displays text using a fixed-width font, which is what you want for your text table.

REFERENCE WINDOW   **RW**

Creating a Text Table Using the <PRE> Tag
- Before the table, type the tag <PRE>.
- Enter the table text, aligning the columns of the table by inserting blank spaces as appropriate.
- Type </PRE> to turn off the preformatted text tag.

You'll use the <PRE> tag to enter the table data from Figure 4-1 into the MAAtext.htm file. When you use this tag, you insert blank spaces by pressing the spacebar to align the columns of text in the table.

To create the text table with the <PRE> tag:

1. Place the insertion point in the blank line directly above the </BODY> tag.

2. Type **<PRE>** and then press the **Enter** key to create a new blank line.

3. Type **Name** and then press the **spacebar** 15 times.

4. Type **Item #** and then press the **spacebar** 5 times.

5. Type **Type** and then press the **spacebar** 15 times.

6. Type **Finish** and then press the **spacebar** 15 times.

7. Type **Price** and then press the **Enter** key.

   Next you'll enter a series of equals signs to create a double underline that will separate the column headings you just typed from the text of the table.

8. Type a line of = signs to underline the column headings you just entered. End the line below the "e" in "Price," and then press the **Enter** key.

9. Complete the table by entering the following text, aligned with the left edge of the column headings (press the **Enter** key after each line):

```
Bacchus       48059    Wall Mount      Interior Plaster   $95
Praying       48159    Garden Figure   Gothic Stone       $125
Gargoyle
Gargoyle      48222    Bust            Interior Plaster   $140
Judge
```

10. Type **</PRE>** to turn off the preformatted text tag. Figure 4-6 shows the complete preformatted text as it appears in the file.

Figure 4-6 | **TEXT TABLE CREATED WITH THE <PRE> TAG**

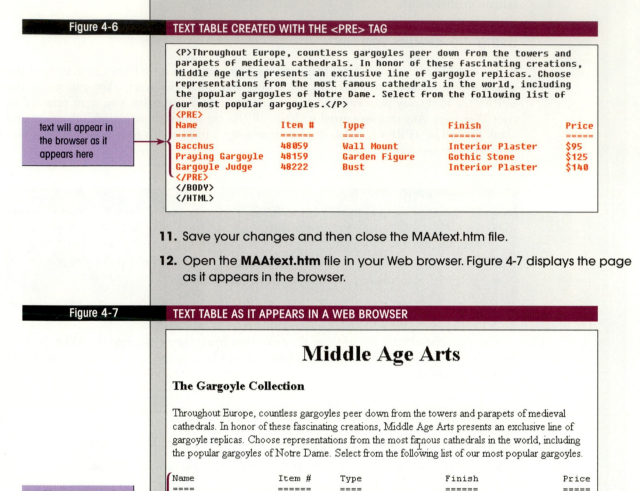

text will appear in the browser as it appears here

```
<P>Throughout Europe, countless gargoyles peer down from the towers and
parapets of medieval cathedrals. In honor of these fascinating creations,
Middle Age Arts presents an exclusive line of gargoyle replicas. Choose
representations from the most famous cathedrals in the world, including
the popular gargoyles of Notre Dame. Select from the following list of
our most popular gargoyles.</P>
<PRE>
Name                Item #      Type            Finish              Price
====                ======      ====            ======              =====
Bacchus             48059       Wall Mount      Interior Plaster    $95
Praying Gargoyle    48159       Garden Figure   Gothic Stone        $125
Gargoyle Judge      48222       Bust            Interior Plaster    $140
</PRE>
</BODY>
</HTML>
```

11. Save your changes and then close the MAAtext.htm file.

12. Open the **MAAtext.htm** file in your Web browser. Figure 4-7 displays the page as it appears in the browser.

Figure 4-7 | **TEXT TABLE AS IT APPEARS IN A WEB BROWSER**

table text appears in a fixed-width font

Middle Age Arts

The Gargoyle Collection

Throughout Europe, countless gargoyles peer down from the towers and parapets of medieval cathedrals. In honor of these fascinating creations, Middle Age Arts presents an exclusive line of gargoyle replicas. Choose representations from the most famous cathedrals in the world, including the popular gargoyles of Notre Dame. Select from the following list of our most popular gargoyles.

```
Name                Item #      Type            Finish              Price
====                ======      ====            ======              =====
Bacchus             48059       Wall Mount      Interior Plaster    $95
Praying Gargoyle    48159       Garden Figure   Gothic Stone        $125
Gargoyle Judge      48222       Bust            Interior Plaster    $140
```

By using the <PRE> tag, you've created a text table that can be displayed by all browsers, and you've ensured that the columns will retain their alignment no matter what font the browser is using.

You show the completed table to Nicole. She's pleased with your work and would like you to create a similar page using a graphical table. To create that table, you'll start by learning how HTML defines table structures.

Defining a Table Structure

Creating graphical tables with HTML can be a complicated process because you have to enter a lot of information to define the layout and appearance of your table. The first step is to specify the table structure: the number of rows and columns, the location of column headings, and the placement of a table caption. Once you have the table structure in place, you can start entering text and data into the cells of the table.

As with the text table page, the beginning of the page for the graphical table has already been created and stored on your Data Disk, as MAA2.htm. You need to open that file in your text editor and save it with a new name.

To open the MAA2.htm file and then save it with a new name:

1. Return to your text editor.

2. Open the file **MAA2.htm** from the Tutorial.04 folder on your Data Disk and then save the file, in the same folder as **MAAtable.htm**.

Using the <TABLE>, <TR>, and <TD> Tags

To create a graphical table with HTML, you start with the <TABLE> tag. The <TABLE> tag identifies where the table structure begins, and the </TABLE> tag indicates where the table ends. After you've identified the location of the table, you identify the number of rows in the table by inserting a <TR> (for table row) tag at the beginning of each table row, starting with the top row of the table and moving down. The end of each table row is indicated by a </TR> tag. Finally, within the <TR> tags you must indicate the location of each table cell with <TD> (for table data) tags.

HTML does not provide a means of specifying the number and placement of table columns. Columns are determined by how many cells are inserted within each row. For example, if you have four <TD> tags in each table row, that table has four columns. So if you want to make sure that the columns in your table line up correctly, you must be careful about the placement and number of <TD> tags within each row. The general syntax of a graphical table is:

```
<TABLE>
    <TR>
            <TD> First Cell </TD>
            <TD> Second Cell </TD>
    </TR>
    <TR>
            <TD> Third Cell </TD>
            <TD> Fourth Cell </TD>
    </TR>
</TABLE>
```

This example creates a table with two rows and two columns, displaying a total of four cells. Figure 4-8 shows the layout of a table with this HTML code.

| Figure 4-8 | A SIMPLE TABLE |

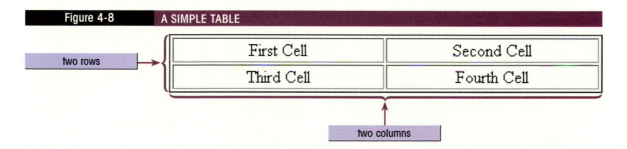

This example creates a table with two rows and two columns, displaying a total of four cells.

two rows

| First Cell | Second Cell |
| Third Cell | Fourth Cell |

two columns

Strictly speaking, the </TR> tag is not necessary at the end of rows that have rows below them, because the presence of the next <TR> tag will signal the browser to go to the next table row. It is still good practice to use the </TR> tag, at least until you become comfortable with the way HTML creates tables.

REFERENCE   WINDOW

Defining Table Structure with HTML
- Enter the <TABLE> and </TABLE> tags to identify the beginning and end of the table.
- Enter <TR> and </TR> tags to identify the beginning and end of each table row.
- Enter <TD> and </TD> tags to identify the beginning and end of each table cell.
- Enter <TH> and </TH> tags to identify text that will act as table headers.

Look at the table that Nicole outlined in Figure 4-1. Notice that the table requires four rows and five columns. However, one of the rows consists of column titles, leaving three rows and five columns for the body of the table. HTML provides a special tag for the column titles, called **table headers**, which you'll learn about shortly. You'll create the basic table structure first and then enter the table text.

To create the structure for the products table:

1. Place the insertion point in the blank line directly above the </BODY> tag.

2. Press the **Enter** key, type **<TABLE>** to identify the beginning of the table structure, and then press the **Enter** key again.

3. Type the entries for the first row of the table as follows:

```
<TR>
    <TD></TD>
    <TD></TD>
    <TD></TD>
    <TD></TD>
    <TD></TD>
</TR>
```

   Note that you do not need to indent the <TD> tags or place them on separate lines, but you might find it easier to interpret your code if you do so.

4. Press the **Enter** key and then repeat Step 3 twice to create the final two rows of the table. You might want to use the copy and paste functions of your text editor to save time.

5. Press the **Enter** key and then type **</TABLE>** to complete the code for the table structure. See Figure 4-9.

Figure 4-9 STRUCTURE OF THE PRODUCTS TABLE

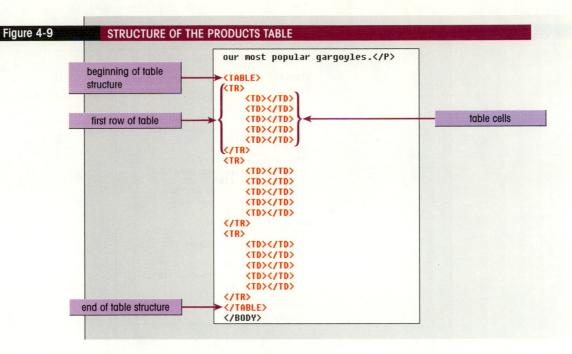

With the table structure in place, you're ready to add the text for each cell, inserted within the <TD> tags in each table row.

To insert the table text:

1. Go to the first <TD> tag in the table structure.

2. Within the first set of <TD> tags, type **Bacchus**.

3. Within the next four <TD> tags, type the remaining entries for the first row of the table as follows:

```
<TD>48059</TD>
<TD>WallMount</TD>
<TD>Interior Plaster</TD>
<TD>$95</TD>
```

4. Continue entering the text for the cells in the remaining two rows of the table. Figure 4-10 shows the completed text for the body of the table.

Figure 4-10   COMPLETED TABLE TEXT

```
our most popular gargoyles.</P>

<TABLE>
<TR>
    <TD>Bacchus</TD>
    <TD>48059</TD>
    <TD>Wall Mount</TD>
    <TD>Interior Plaster</TD>
    <TD>$95</TD>
</TR>
<TR>
    <TD>Praying Gargoyle</TD>
    <TD>48159</TD>
    <TD>Garden Figure</TD>
    <TD>Gothic Stone</TD>
    <TD>$125</TD>
</TR>
<TR>
    <TD>Gargoyle Judge</TD>
    <TD>48222</TD>
    <TD>Bust</TD>
    <TD>Interior Plaster</TD>
    <TD>$140</TD>
</TR>
</TABLE>
</BODY>
```

With the text for the body of the table entered, you'll next add the table headers.

Creating Headers with the <TH> Tag

HTML provides a special tag for cells that will act as table headers (or column headings): the <TH> tag. Like the <TD> tag used for table data, the <TH> tag is used for cells within the table. The difference between the <TH> and <TD> tags is that text formatted with the <TH> tag is centered within the cell and displayed in a boldface font. A table can have several rows of table headers. In fact, because the <TH> tag is a replacement for the <TD> tag, you can use the <TH> tag for any cell containing text that you want to be displayed in centered boldfaced type.

In the gargoyle products table, Nicole has specified a single row of table headers. You'll enter them using the <TH> tag.

To insert the table headers:

1. Go to the <TABLE> tag line and press the **Enter** key to create a new blank line below it.

2. Type the following:

```
<TR>
<TH>Name</TH>
<TH>Item#</TH>
<TH>Type</TH>
<TH>Finish</TH>
<TH>Price</TH>
</TR>
```

Figure 4-11 shows the <TH> tags as they appear in your file.

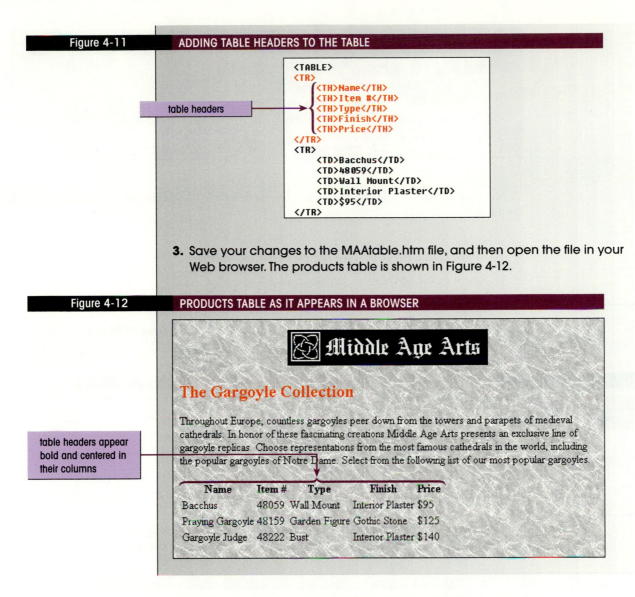

Figure 4-11 | ADDING TABLE HEADERS TO THE TABLE

```
<TABLE>
<TR>
    <TH>Name</TH>
    <TH>Item #</TH>
    <TH>Type</TH>
    <TH>Finish</TH>
    <TH>Price</TH>
</TR>
<TR>
    <TD>Bacchus</TD>
    <TD>48059</TD>
    <TD>Wall Mount</TD>
    <TD>Interior Plaster</TD>
    <TD>$95</TD>
</TR>
```

table headers

3. Save your changes to the MAAtable.htm file, and then open the file in your Web browser. The products table is shown in Figure 4-12.

Figure 4-12 | PRODUCTS TABLE AS IT APPEARS IN A BROWSER

table headers appear bold and centered in their columns

Note that the cells formatted with the <TH> tag appear in boldface and centered above each table column. Your next task is to add a table caption.

Creating a Table Caption

You create a table caption using the <CAPTION> tag. The syntax for the <CAPTION> tag is:

```
<CAPTION ALIGN=value>caption text</caption>
```

where *value* indicates the caption placement—either TOP (above the table) or BOTTOM (below the table). In either case, the caption will be centered in relation to the table. Because the <CAPTION> tag works only with tables, the tag must be placed within the <TABLE> tags.

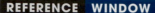

REFERENCE WINDOW   **RW**

<u>Creating a Table Caption</u>
- Within the <TABLE> tags enter the following tag:

  `<CAPTION ALIGN=value>caption text</CAPTION>`

  where *value* can be either TOP (to place the caption directly above the table) or BOTTOM (to place the caption directly below the table).

Nicole asks you to add the caption "Here is a sample of our products" centered above the table.

To add the caption to the products table:

1. Return to the MAAtable.htm file in your text editor.

2. Insert a blank line below the <TABLE> tag.

3. In the new line, type **<CAPTION ALIGN=TOP>Here is a sample of our products</CAPTION>**. See Figure 4-13.

Figure 4-13	INSERTING A TABLE CAPTION

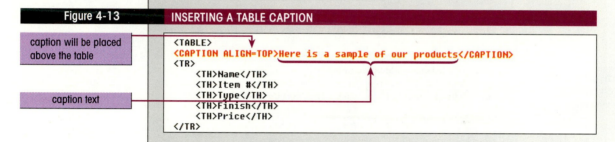

caption will be placed above the table

caption text

```
<TABLE>
<CAPTION ALIGN=TOP>Here is a sample of our products</CAPTION>
<TR>
     <TH>Name</TH>
     <TH>Item #</TH>
     <TH>Type</TH>
     <TH>Finish</TH>
     <TH>Price</TH>
</TR>
```

4. Save your changes to the MAAtable.htm file, and then reload the file in your Web browser. Figure 4-14 shows the table with the newly added caption.

Figure 4-14	PRODUCTS TABLE WITH THE TABLE CAPTION

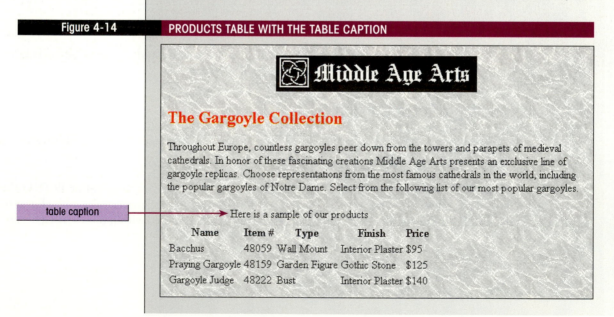

table caption

Middle Age Arts

The Gargoyle Collection

Throughout Europe, countless gargoyles peer down from the towers and parapets of medieval cathedrals. In honor of these fascinating creations Middle Age Arts presents an exclusive line of gargoyle replicas. Choose representations from the most famous cathedrals in the world, including the popular gargoyles of Notre Dame. Select from the following list of our most popular gargoyles.

Here is a sample of our products

Name	Item #	Type	Finish	Price
Bacchus	48059	Wall Mount	Interior Plaster	$95
Praying Gargoyle	48159	Garden Figure	Gothic Stone	$125
Gargoyle Judge	48222	Bust	Interior Plaster	$140

Captions are shown as normal text without special formatting. As with other tags in your HTML file, you can format table text by embedding the text within the appropriate tags. For example, placing the caption text within a pair of <B> and <I> tags will cause the caption to appear in a bold italicized font.

You've completed your work with the initial structure of the products table. Nicole is pleased with your progress, but she would like you to make some improvements in the table's appearance. In the next session, you'll learn how to control the appearance and placement of your table and the text in it.

Session 4.1 QUICK CHECK

1. What are the two kinds of tables you can place in a Web page? What are the advantages and disadvantages of each?

2. What is the difference between a proportional font and a fixed-width font? Which should you use in a text table, and why?

3. What tag can you use to create a text table?

4. Name the purpose of the following tags in defining the structure of a table:

   ```
   <TR>
   <TD>
   <TH>
   ```

5. How do you specify the number of rows in a graphical table? How do you specify the number of columns?

6. How does the <TH> tag differ from the <TD> tag?

7. What code would you enter to place the caption "Product Catalog" below a table? Where must this code be placed in relation to the <TABLE> and </TABLE> tags?

SESSION 4.2

In this session you will learn how to create table and cell borders and how to control the width of each. You'll learn how to specify the space between table text and the surrounding borders. You'll also work with the placement and size of the table on your Web page. Finally, you'll learn how to specify a table background color.

Modifying the Appearance of a Table

After viewing the products table in the browser, Nicole notes that the text is displayed with properly aligned columns, but that the format of the table could be improved. Nicole asks you to enhance the table's appearance with borders and color. She also wants you to control the placement of the table on the page as well as the table size. HTML provides tags and properties to do all of these things.

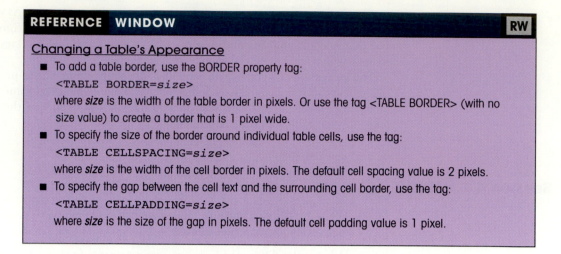

You'll begin enhancing the products table by adding a table border.

Adding a Table Border

By default, browsers display tables without table borders. You can create a table border by adding the BORDER property to the TABLE tag. The syntax for creating a table border is:

    <TABLE BORDER=size>

where *size* is the width of the border in pixels. The size value is optional; if you don't specify a size, but simply enter BORDER, the browser creates a border 1 pixel wide around the table. Figure 4-15 shows the effect on a table's border of varying the border size. Note that only the outside border is affected by increasing the size of the BORDER property; the internal borders between cells are not affected. You'll see how to change the size of these internal borders later on.

| Figure 4-15 | TABLES WITH DIFFERENT VALUES FOR THE BORDER PROPERTY |

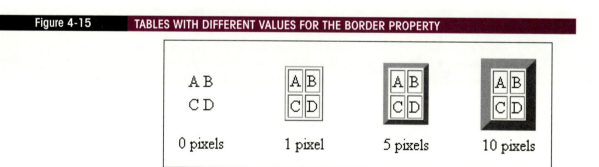

Nicole wants a good-sized border around the products table, so you'll format the table with a 10-pixel-wide border.

To insert a table border:

1. If you took a break after the previous session, start your text editor and open the **MAAtable.htm** file.

2. Go to the <TABLE> tag, and within the tag, type **BORDER=10**. See Figure 4-16.

Figure 4-16	ADDING A 10-PIXEL BORDER TO THE PRODUCTS TABLE

```
the popular gargoyles of Notre Dame. Select from the following list of
our most popular gargoyles.</P>

<TABLE BORDER=10>
<CAPTION ALIGN=TOP>Here is a sample of our products</CAPTION>
<TR>
    <TH>Name</TH>
    <TH>Item #</TH>
    <TH>Type</TH>
    <TH>Finish</TH>
    <TH>Price</TH>
</TR>
```

3. Save your changes and then open the **MAAtable.htm** file in your Web browser. Figure 4-17 shows the new border.

Figure 4-17	PRODUCTS TABLE WITH THE NEW BORDER

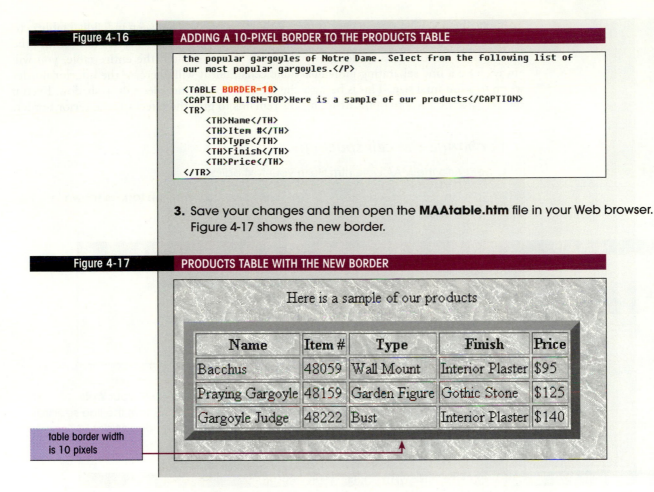

table border width is 10 pixels

You've modified the outside border of the table, but Nicole would also like you to change the width of the inside borders, between individual table cells. She feels that the table would look better if the interior borders were less prominent. This is done by adding the CELLSPACING property to the TABLE tag.

Controlling Cell Spacing

The CELLSPACING property controls the amount of space inserted between table cells. The syntax for specifying the cell spacing is:

```
<TABLE CELLSPACING=size>
```

where *size* is the width of the interior borders in pixels. The default cell spacing is 2 pixels. Figure 4-18 shows how different cell spacing values affect a table's appearance.

Figure 4-18	TABLES WITH DIFFERENT CELL SPACING VALUES

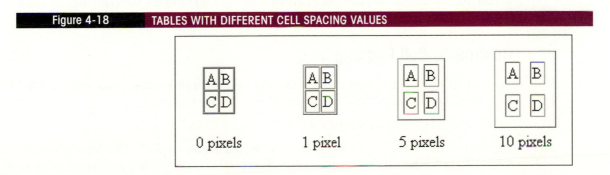

Nicole has decided that she wants the width of the borders between individual table cells to be as small as possible, so you'll decrease the width to 0 pixels. This will not remove the border between the cells (as long as you have a border around the entire table, you will always have a line separating individual table cells), but it will decrease the interior border width to a minimal size. This is because the interior border includes a drop shadow. Even if the cell spacing is set to 0, the drop shadow remains to give the effect of an interior border.

To change the cell spacing:

1. Return to the MAAtable.htm file in your text editor.

2. Go to the <TABLE> tag and type **CELLSPACING=0** within the tag, as shown in Figure 4-19.

Figure 4-19	SETTING THE CELLSPACING PROPERTY

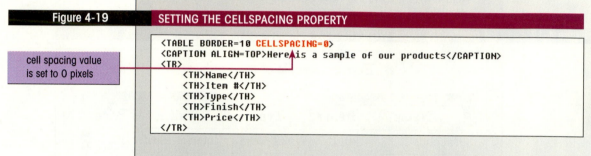

cell spacing value is set to 0 pixels

```
<TABLE BORDER=10 CELLSPACING=0>
<CAPTION ALIGN=TOP>Here is a sample of our products</CAPTION>
<TR>
    <TH>Name</TH>
    <TH>Item #</TH>
    <TH>Type</TH>
    <TH>Finish</TH>
    <TH>Price</TH>
</TR>
```

3. Save your changes and then reload the MAAtable.htm file in your Web browser. The new cell spacing is shown in Figure 4-20. Note that the line separating the cells has been slightly reduced, but has not totally disappeared (compare Figure 4-17 with Figure 4-20).

Figure 4-20	PRODUCTS TABLE WITH DECREASED CELL SPACING

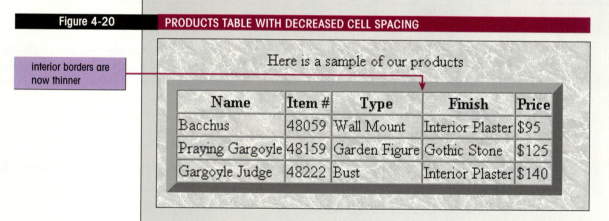

interior borders are now thinner

After viewing the modified table, Nicole points out that it now appears crowded. She would like you to increase the space between the table text and the surrounding cell borders. You can do this by increasing the amount of cell padding in the table.

Controlling Cell Padding

To control the space between the table text and the cell borders, you add the CELL-PADDING property to the TABLE tag. The syntax for this property is:

```
<TABLE CELLPADDING=size>
```

where *size* is the distance from the table text to the cell border, in pixels. The default cell padding value is 1 pixel. Figure 4-21 shows the effect of changing the cell padding value on a sample table.

Figure 4-21

Figure 4-21   TABLES WITH DIFFERENT CELLPADDING VALUES

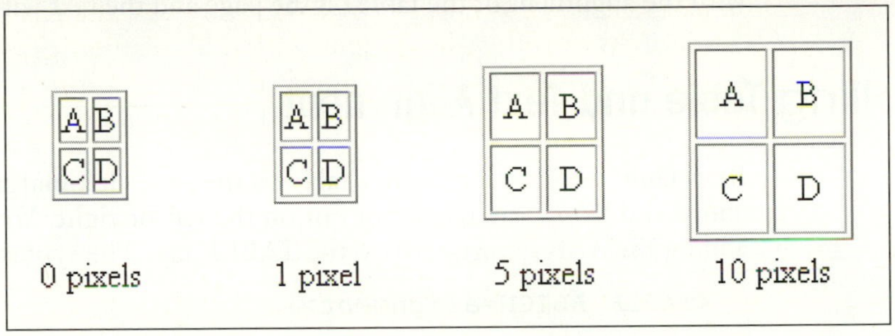

You might confuse the terms cell spacing and cell padding. Just remember that cell spacing refers to the space between the cells, and cell padding refers to the space within the table cells. You need to increase the amount of space within your table cells because the default 1-pixel gap is too small and causes the cell borders to crowd the cell text. You'll increase the cell padding to 4 pixels.

To increase the amount of cell padding:

1. Return to the MAAtable.htm file in your text editor.

2. Go to the <TABLE> tag and type **CELLPADDING=4** within the tag, as shown in Figure 4-22.

Figure 4-22   SETTING THE CELLPADDING PROPERTY

the value of the
CELLPADDING property
is set to 4 pixels

```
<TABLE BORDER=10 CELLSPACING=0 CELLPADDING=4>
<CAPTION ALIGN=TOP>Here is a sample of our products</CAPTION>
<TR>
        <TH>Name</TH>
        <TH>Item #</TH>
        <TH>Type</TH>
        <TH>Finish</TH>
        <TH>Price</TH>
</TR>
```

3. Save your changes and then reload the MAAtable.htm file in your Web browser. Figure 4-23 shows the table with the increased amount of cell padding.

Figure 4-23   PRODUCTS TABLE WITH INCREASED CELL PADDING

the space between the
cell text and the cell
borders has been
increased

Here is a sample of our products

Name	Item #	Type	Finish	Price
Bacchus	48059	Wall Mount	Interior Plaster	$95
Praying Gargoyle	48159	Garden Figure	Gothic Stone	$125
Gargoyle Judge	48222	Bust	Interior Plaster	$140

By increasing the cell padding, you added needed space to the table. Next you'll work with the alignment of the table on the page and the text within the table.

Controlling Table and Text Alignment

By default, the browser places a table on the page's left margin, with surrounding text placed above and below the table, but not on the left or right. You can change this placement by adding the ALIGN property to the TABLE tag. The syntax for this property is:

```
<TABLE ALIGN=alignment>
```

where *alignment* equals LEFT, RIGHT, or CENTER. The ALIGN property is similar to the ALIGN property used with the <IMG> tag, except that images have more alignment options. As with inline images, using left or right alignment places the table on the page's margin and wraps surrounding text to the side, as illustrated in Figure 4-24.

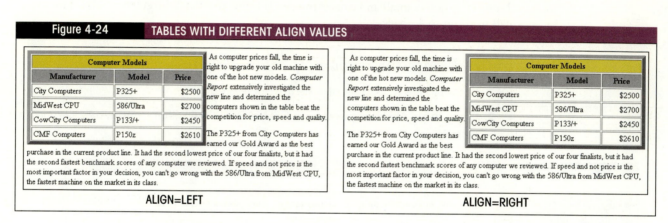

Figure 4-24   TABLES WITH DIFFERENT ALIGN VALUES

The ALIGN property is available only with browsers that support HTML 3.2 or later. Earlier browsers will ignore the ALIGN property and leave the table on the left margin without wrapping text around it.

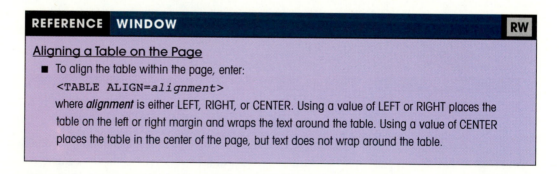

REFERENCE WINDOW   RW

Aligning a Table on the Page

■ To align the table within the page, enter:

```
<TABLE ALIGN=alignment>
```

where **alignment** is either LEFT, RIGHT, or CENTER. Using a value of LEFT or RIGHT places the table on the left or right margin and wraps the text around the table. Using a value of CENTER places the table in the center of the page, but text does not wrap around the table.

Nicole wants the products table to be centered, to balance the layout of the page.

To center the products table:

1. Return to the MAAtable.htm file in your text editor.

2. Within the <TABLE> tag (after "CELLPADDING=4") type **ALIGN=CENTER**.

3. Save your changes and then reload the file in your Web browser. The products table should now be centered on the page.

You can also add the ALIGN property to the <TD> tag to align text within table cells. By default, text is aligned with the left edge of the table cell, but you can use the ALIGN property to center the text within the cell or to align it with the cell's right edge. Another property, VALIGN, allows you to control the vertical placement of text within the table cell. By default, text is placed at the top of the cell, but with the VALIGN property you can align text with the top, middle, or bottom of the cell. Figure 4-25 shows how the combination of the ALIGN and VALIGN properties affects the placement of text within a table cell.

Figure 4-25   **VALUES OF THE ALIGN AND VALIGN PROPERTIES**

ALIGN=LEFT VALIGN=TOP	ALIGN=LEFT VALIGN=MIDDLE	ALIGN=LEFT VALIGN=BOTTOM
ALIGN=CENTER VALIGN=TOP	ALIGN=CENTER VALIGN=MIDDLE	ALIGN=CENTER VALIGN=BOTTOM
ALIGN=RIGHT VALIGN=TOP	ALIGN=RIGHT VALIGN=MIDDLE	ALIGN=RIGHT VALIGN=BOTTOM

Looking over the table, Nicole decides that the values in the Price column should be right-aligned so that the numbers align properly. Because of the way HTML works with table columns, if you want to align the text for a single column, you must apply the ALIGN property to every cell within that column.

To right-align the Price column values:

1. Return to the MAAtable.htm file in your text editor.

2. For each <TD> tag in the Price column, insert the text **ALIGN=RIGHT**. Figure 4-26 shows the revised HTML code in your file.

Figure 4-26   RIGHT-ALIGNING THE VALUES IN THE PRICE COLUMN

```
<TR>
    <TD>Bacchus</TD>
    <TD>48059</TD>
    <TD>Wall Mount</TD>
    <TD>Interior Plaster</TD>
    <TD ALIGN=RIGHT>$95</TD>
</TR>
<TR>
    <TD>Praying Gargoyle</TD>
    <TD>48159</TD>
    <TD>Garden Figure</TD>
    <TD>Gothic Stone</TD>
    <TD ALIGN=RIGHT>$125</TD>
</TR>
<TR>
    <TD>Gargoyle Judge</TD>
    <TD>48222</TD>
    <TD>Bust</TD>
    <TD>Interior Plaster</TD>
    <TD ALIGN=RIGHT>$140</TD>
</TR>
</TABLE>
```

3. Save your changes and then reload the page in your Web browser. The prices are now right-aligned. See Figure 4-27.

Figure 4-27   RIGHT-ALIGNED PRICES IN THE PRODUCTS TABLE

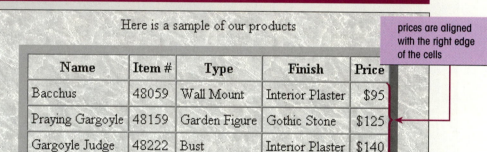

Here is a sample of our products

Name	Item #	Type	Finish	Price
Bacchus	48059	Wall Mount	Interior Plaster	$95
Praying Gargoyle	48159	Garden Figure	Gothic Stone	$125
Gargoyle Judge	48222	Bust	Interior Plaster	$140

prices are aligned with the right edge of the cells

You can also use the ALIGN and VALIGN properties with the <TR> tag if you want to align all the text within a single row in the same way. Your next task will be to work with the size of your table and table cells.

Working with Table and Cell Size

The size of a table is determined by the text it contains. By default, HTML places text on a single line. If you insert additional text in a cell, the width of the column and the table will increase up to the page edge, still keeping the text confined to a single line (unless you've inserted a break, paragraph, or header tag within the cell). Once the page edge is reached, the browser will reduce the size of the remaining columns to keep the text to a single line. The browser will wrap the text to a second line within the cell only when it can no longer increase the size of the column and table or decrease the size of the remaining columns. As more text is added, the height of the table automatically expands to accommodate the additional text.

If you want to have greater control over the size of the table and table cells, you can explicitly define the width and height of these elements.

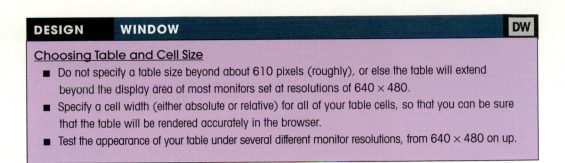

Defining the Table Size

The syntax for specifying the table size is:

```
<TABLE WIDTH=size HEIGHT=size>
```

Here *size* is the width and height of the table, either in pixels or as a percentage of the display area. If you want your table to fill the entire width of the display area, regardless of the resolution of the user's monitor, set the WIDTH property to 100%. Note that the percent value should be placed within double quotation marks (use WIDTH="100%" not WIDTH=100%). Similarly, to create a table whose height is equal to the height of the display area, enter the property HEIGHT="100%".

On the other hand, if you specify the size of a table exactly, its absolute size remains constant, regardless of the browser used. If you use this approach, remember that some monitors will display your page at a resolution of 640 by 480 pixels. If it's important that the table not exceed the browser's display area, you should specify a table width of less than 610 pixels (roughly) to allow space for other window elements such as scroll bars.

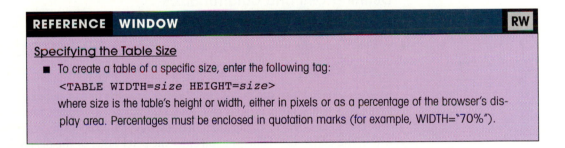

You'll set the width of the products table to 550 pixels. This will ensure that the table will not extend beyond the display area, but will also provide more room in the table cells if you want to insert additional text. You don't need to specify the height of the table, because the table's height will expand as additional products are added.

To increase the width of the products table:

1. Return to the MAAtable.htm file in your text editor and move to the <TABLE> tag.

2. Within the <TABLE> tag, type **WIDTH=550**, as shown in Figure 4-28.

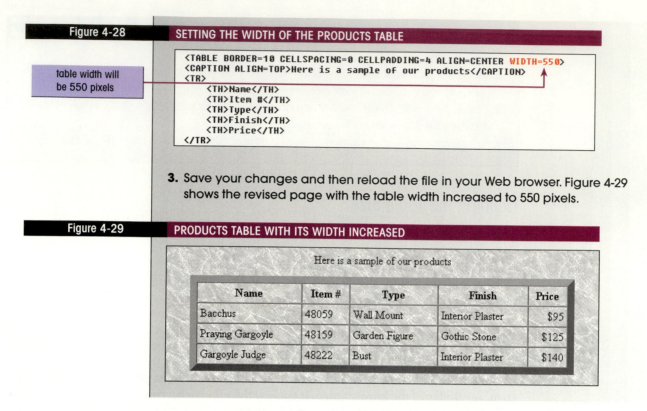

Figure 4-28   **SETTING THE WIDTH OF THE PRODUCTS TABLE**

table width will
be 550 pixels

```
<TABLE BORDER=10 CELLSPACING=0 CELLPADDING=4 ALIGN=CENTER WIDTH=550>
<CAPTION ALIGN=TOP>Here is a sample of our products</CAPTION>
<TR>
    <TH>Name</TH>
    <TH>Item #</TH>
    <TH>Type</TH>
    <TH>Finish</TH>
    <TH>Price</TH>
</TR>
```

3. Save your changes and then reload the file in your Web browser. Figure 4-29 shows the revised page with the table width increased to 550 pixels.

Figure 4-29   **PRODUCTS TABLE WITH ITS WIDTH INCREASED**

Here is a sample of our products

Name	Item #	Type	Finish	Price
Bacchus	48059	Wall Mount	Interior Plaster	$95
Praying Gargoyle	48159	Garden Figure	Gothic Stone	$125
Gargoyle Judge	48222	Bust	Interior Plaster	$140

Now that you've set the width of the table, you need to set the width of individual cells.

Defining Cell and Column Sizes

You can use the WIDTH property with the <TD> (table data) and <TH> (table headers) tags as well. To set the width of an individual cell, you add the WIDTH property to the TD tag:

    <TD WIDTH=*size*>

where *size* once again can be expressed either in pixels or as a percentage of the table width. For example, a width value of 30% displays a cell that is 30% of the total width of the table (whatever that might be). To create a cell that is always 35 pixels wide, you would enter WIDTH=35 within the <TD> tag. Whether you enter the pixel value or the percentage depends on whether you're trying to create a table that will fill a specific space or a relative space.

Specifying a width for an individual cell does not guarantee that the cell will be that width when displayed in the browser. The problem is that the cell is part of a column containing other cells. If one of those other cells is set to a different width or expands because of the text entered into it, the widths of all cells in the column change accordingly. Setting a width for one cell guarantees only that the cell width will not be less than that value. If you want to ensure that the cells do not change in size, neither increasing nor decreasing from the value you set, you must set the WIDTH property of all the cells in the column to the same value.

You can use the HEIGHT property in the TD (or TH) tags to set the height of individual cells. Like the WIDTH property, the HEIGHT property can be expressed either in pixels or as a percentage of the height of the table. If you include more text than can be displayed within that height value, the cell will expand to display the additional text.

Nicole decides that the widths of both the Item # and Price columns can be set to a specific size. Setting a width for these columns will make more space available for the remaining three columns. A width of 60 pixels for the Item # column and 50 pixels for the Price column should work well for the products table.

To set the column widths for the Item # and Price columns:

1. Return to the MAAtable.htm file in your text editor.

2. For the <TH> and <TD> tags in the Item # column, enter the property **WIDTH=60**.

3. For the <TH> and <TD> tags in the Price column, enter the property **WIDTH=50**.

   Figure 4-30 shows the revised HTML code in your file. Check your code carefully because it's easy to place the properties in the wrong columns or outside the tag brackets.

Figure 4-30   SETTING THE WIDTH OF THE ITEM # AND PRICE COLUMNS

```
<TR>
        <TH>Name</TH>
        <TH WIDTH=60>Item #</TH>
        <TH>Type</TH>
        <TH>Finish</TH>
        <TH WIDTH=50>Price</TH>
</TR>
<TR>
        <TD>Bacchus</TD>
        <TD WIDTH=60>48059</TD>
        <TD>Wall Mount</TD>
        <TD>Interior Plaster</TD>
        <TD ALIGN=RIGHT WIDTH=50>$95</TD>
</TR>
<TR>
        <TD>Praying Gargoyle</TD>
        <TD WIDTH=60>48159</TD>
        <TD>Garden Figure</TD>
        <TD>Gothic Stone</TD>
        <TD ALIGN=RIGHT WIDTH=50>$125</TD>
</TR>
<TR>
        <TD>Gargoyle Judge</TD>
        <TD WIDTH=60>48222</TD>
        <TD>Bust</TD>
        <TD>Interior Plaster</TD>
        <TD ALIGN=RIGHT WIDTH=50>$140</TD>
</TR>
```

4. Save your changes and then reload the page in your Web browser to verify that the column widths for the Item # and Price columns have been decreased.

You've completed your work with the layout, and now Nicole would like you to turn your attention to the table color. By default, the table background color is the same as the page background color, but some browsers allow you to change that.

Modifying the Table Background

One of the extensions supported by both Internet Explorer and Netscape Navigator is the ability to define the background color or image for a table. To change the background color of the entire table, insert the BGCOLOR property in the <TABLE> tag; to change the background color of individual cells, insert the same property into the <TR> (table row), <TH> (table header), and/or <TD> (table data) tags. You can use either the color name or the RGB color value. Your color choices might not show up on other browsers, so you should make sure that any design decisions you make work with the background color either on or off.

The process of setting color for the table follows a hierarchy. Using the BGCOLOR property for the <TABLE> tag sets the background color for all cells in the table. You can override this color choice for a single row by using the BGCOLOR property in the <TR> tag. You can also override the table or row color choices for a single cell by inserting the BGCOLOR property in a <TD> or <TH> tag. To set the background color for a column, you must define the background color for each cell in that column.

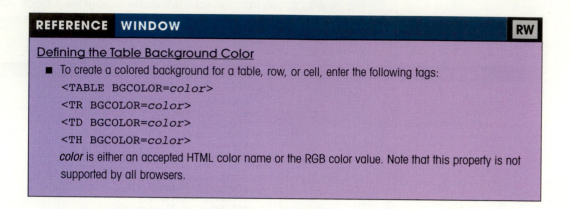

REFERENCE WINDOW   **RW**

Defining the Table Background Color

■ To create a colored background for a table, row, or cell, enter the following tags:

    <TABLE BGCOLOR=*color*>

    <TR BGCOLOR=*color*>

    <TD BGCOLOR=*color*>

    <TH BGCOLOR=*color*>

color is either an accepted HTML color name or the RGB color value. Note that this property is not supported by all browsers.

After considering many different colors, Nicole decides that she would like to have the background color of the header row set to green, the rows of the table set to white, and the background of the names of the products set to yellow. She asks you to make these changes now. You'll start by setting the table background color.

To define the table background color:

1. Return to the MAAtable.htm file in your text editor and go to the <TABLE> tag.

2. Type **BGCOLOR=WHITE** within the <TABLE> tag.

Now that you've set the background color of each cell to white, you'll override this option for the header row, setting the background for cells in that row to a shade of green. The RGB color value is (51,204,102), which translates to 33CC66.

To define the background color for the header row:

1. Go to the first <TR> tag in the products table (the row containing the <TH> tags).

2. Type **BGCOLOR="#33CC66"** within the <TR> tag.

Finally you'll change the background color of the three product names to yellow.

To define the background color for the cells in the first column:

1. Go to the <TD> tag for the Bacchus cell.

2. Type **BGCOLOR=YELLOW** within the <TD> tag.

3. Type the **BGCOLOR=YELLOW** property within the remaining two cells for the first column (the Praying Gargoyle cell and the Gargoyle Judge cell). Figure 4-31 shows the revised HTML code for your page.

Figure 4-31   **SETTING THE BACKGROUND COLOR FOR THE TABLE**

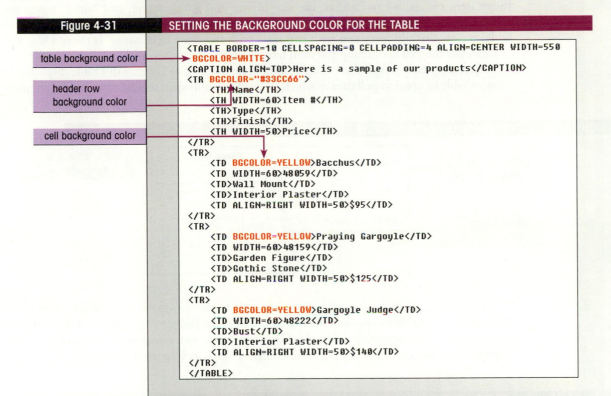

table background color

header row background color

cell background color

```
<TABLE BORDER=10 CELLSPACING=0 CELLPADDING=4 ALIGN=CENTER WIDTH=550
BGCOLOR=WHITE>
<CAPTION ALIGN=TOP>Here is a sample of our products</CAPTION>
<TR BGCOLOR="#33CC66">
      <TH>Name</TH>
      <TH WIDTH=60>Item #</TH>
      <TH>Type</TH>
      <TH>Finish</TH>
      <TH WIDTH=50>Price</TH>
</TR>
<TR>
      <TD BGCOLOR=YELLOW>Bacchus</TD>
      <TD WIDTH=60>48059</TD>
      <TD>Wall Mount</TD>
      <TD>Interior Plaster</TD>
      <TD ALIGN=RIGHT WIDTH=50>$95</TD>
</TR>
<TR>
      <TD BGCOLOR=YELLOW>Praying Gargoyle</TD>
      <TD WIDTH=60>48159</TD>
      <TD>Garden Figure</TD>
      <TD>Gothic Stone</TD>
      <TD ALIGN=RIGHT WIDTH=50>$125</TD>
</TR>
<TR>
      <TD BGCOLOR=YELLOW>Gargoyle Judge</TD>
      <TD WIDTH=60>48222</TD>
      <TD>Bust</TD>
      <TD>Interior Plaster</TD>
      <TD ALIGN=RIGHT WIDTH=50>$140</TD>
</TR>
</TABLE>
```

4. Save your changes and then reload the file in your Web browser. Figure 4-32 shows the revised table with the new color scheme.

Figure 4-32   **PRODUCTS TABLE WITH THE NEW BACKGROUND COLORS**

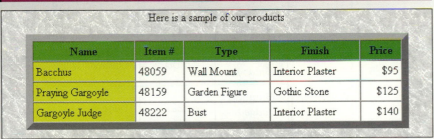

Here is a sample of our products

Name	Item #	Type	Finish	Price
Bacchus	48059	Wall Mount	Interior Plaster	$95
Praying Gargoyle	48159	Garden Figure	Gothic Stone	$125
Gargoyle Judge	48222	Bust	Interior Plaster	$140

TROUBLE? If your page looks different from the one shown in Figure 4-32, it could be because of your browser. Early versions of the Internet Explorer browser apply the table background color to the caption. Also, the Netscape Navigator browser might align the table text differently.

Spanning Rows and Columns

Nicole has reviewed your table and would like to make a few more changes. The Gargoyle Judge item comes in two finishes, interior plaster and gothic stone, and Nicole wants this information added to the table. You can add the information by inserting a new row in the table, but that would leave you with two rows with the same item name. Is there a way that you can use the cell containing the item name in both rows? Yes, with a spanning cell.

A **spanning cell** is a cell that occupies more than one row or column in a table. Figure 4-33 shows a table of opinion poll data in which some of the cells span several rows and/or columns.

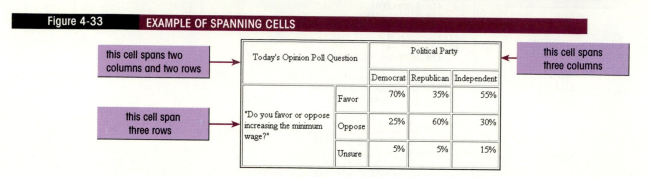

Figure 4-33   **EXAMPLE OF SPANNING CELLS**

Nicole wants to include similar spanning cells in the products table. She sketches how she expects the table to appear with the new Gargoyle Judge entry (Figure 4-34). She has indicated two new spanning cells: the Gargoyle Judge entry will span two rows, and the Type and Finish columns will be combined into a single cell spanning two columns.

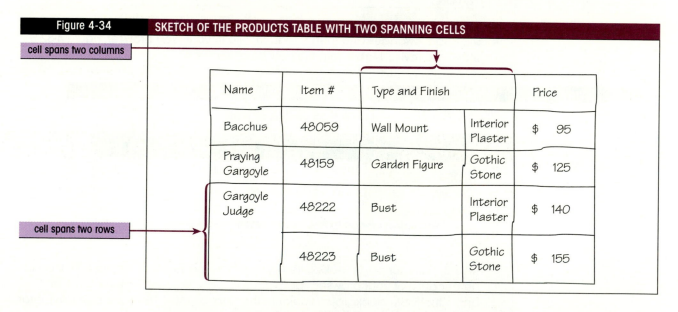

Figure 4-34   **SKETCH OF THE PRODUCTS TABLE WITH TWO SPANNING CELLS**

You can create spanning cells by inserting the ROWSPAN and COLSPAN properties in a <TD> or <TH> tag. The syntax for the <TD> tag is:

```
<TD ROWSPAN=value COLSPAN=value> Cell Text </TD>
```

where *value* is the number of rows or columns that the cell will span within the table. Spanning is always downward and to the right of the cell containing the ROWSPAN and COLSPAN properties. For example, to create a cell that spans two columns in the table, you would enter a <TD COLSPAN=2> tag. For a cell that spans two rows, the tag is <TD ROWSPAN=2>, and to span two rows and two columns, the tag is <TD ROWSPAN=2 COLSPAN=2>.

The important thing to remember when you have a cell that spans several rows or columns is that you must adjust the number of cell tags used in the table row. If a row has five columns, but one of the cells in the row spans three columns, you would only need to have three <TD> tags: two <TD> tags for the cells that occupy a single column, and the third for the cell spanning three rows.

When a cell spans several rows, the rows below the spanning cell must also be adjusted. Consider a table, shown in Figure 4-35, with three rows and four columns. The first cell in the first row is a spanning cell that spans three rows. You would need four <TD> tags for the first row, but only three <TD> tags for rows two and three. This is because the spanning cell from row one occupies the cells that would normally appear in rows two and three.

Figure 4-35	TABLE STRUCTURE WITH A ROW-SPANNING CELL

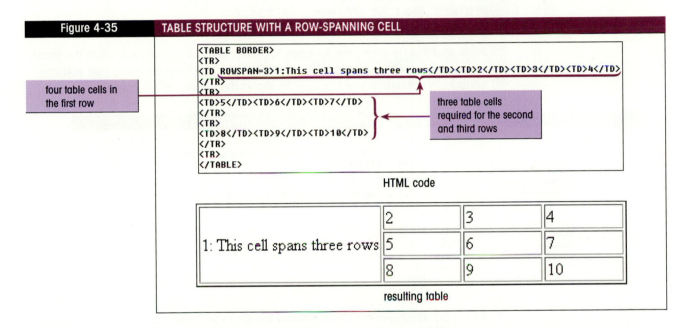

```
<TABLE BORDER>
<TR>
<TD ROWSPAN=3>1:This cell spans three rows</TD><TD>2</TD><TD>3</TD><TD>4</TD>
</TR>
<TR>
<TD>5</TD><TD>6</TD><TD>7</TD>
</TR>
<TR>
<TD>8</TD><TD>9</TD><TD>10</TD>
</TR>
<TR>
</TABLE>
```

four table cells in the first row

three table cells required for the second and third rows

HTML code

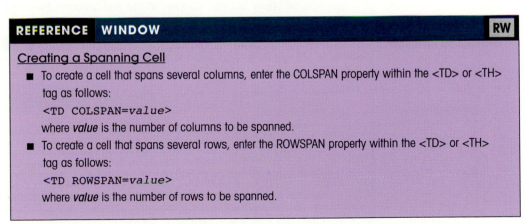

1: This cell spans three rows	2	3	4
	5	6	7
	8	9	10

resulting table

REFERENCE WINDOW	RW

Creating a Spanning Cell
- To create a cell that spans several columns, enter the COLSPAN property within the <TD> or <TH> tag as follows:

  <TD COLSPAN=*value*>

  where *value* is the number of columns to be spanned.
- To create a cell that spans several rows, enter the ROWSPAN property within the <TD> or <TH> tag as follows:

  <TD ROWSPAN=*value*>

  where *value* is the number of rows to be spanned.

To make the changes Nicole requested, you must first change the cell containing the text "Gargoyle Judge" to a spanning cell covering two rows, and then you need to add a new row to the bottom of the table.

To create a cell that spans two rows:

1. Return to the MAAtable.htm file in your text editor and locate the <TD> tag for the Gargoyle Judge cell in the last row of the table.

2. Type **ROWSPAN=2** within the <TD> tag.

3. Go to the </TR> tag at the end of the row, and then press the **Enter** key to create a new blank line below it.

4. Enter the following text, starting at the new line you just inserted:

```
<TR>
<TD WIDTH=60>48223</TD>
<TD>Bust</TD>
<TD>Gothic Stone</TD>
<TD ALIGN=RIGHT WIDTH=50>$155</TD>
</TR>
```

Note that this new row has four cell tags, not five like the other rows in the table, because one of the cell tags is being replaced by the spanning cell you created in the previous row. Figure 4-36 shows the revised HTML code.

Figure 4-36   CREATING A ROW-SPANNING CELL IN THE PRODUCTS TABLE

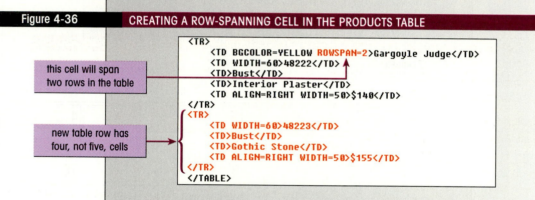

this cell will span two rows in the table

new table row has four, not five, cells

5. Save your changes and then reload the file in your Web browser. The Gargoyle Judge cell now spans two rows in the first column. See Figure 4-37.

Figure 4-37   ROW-SPANNING CELL IN THE PRODUCTS TABLE

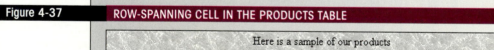

The text in the spanning cell is centered vertically, but it would look better if it were placed at the top of the cell. You can do this using the VALIGN property mentioned earlier.

To align the text with the top of the spanning cell:

1. Return to the MAAtable.htm file in your text editor.

2. Within the <TD> tag for the spanning cell you just created, type **VALIGN=TOP**.

Your next task is to merge the Type and Finish header cells into one cell. To do this, you can create a spanning cell to span across the Type and Finish columns.

To span a cell across the two columns:

1. Go to the <TH> tag in the first row of the table for the word "Type."

2. Within the <TH> tag, type **COLSPAN=2**.

3. Change the table header "Type" to **Type and Finish**.

Because this cell now spans two columns, you have to remove the Finish cell from the header row.

4. Delete the <TH> tags and enclosed text for the Finish table header. Figure 4-38 shows the revised HTML code.

Figure 4-38	CREATING A COLUMN-SPANNING CELL

this header cell will span two columns

the old Finish table header has been removed

```
<TABLE BORDER=10 CELLSPACING=0 CELLPADDING=4 ALIGN=CENTER WIDTH=550
  BGCOLOR=WHITE>
<CAPTION ALIGN=TOP>Here is a sample of our products</CAPTION>
<TR BGCOLOR="#33CC66">
     <TH>Name</TH>
     <TH WIDTH=60>Item #</TH>
     <TH COLSPAN=2>Type and Finish</TH>
     <TH WIDTH=50>Price</TH>
</TR>
```

5. Save your changes and then reload the file in your browser. Figure 4-39 shows the final layout of the gargoyle products table.

Figure 4-39   FINAL VERSION OF THE GARGOYLE PRODUCTS WEB PAGE

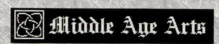

Middle Age Arts

The Gargoyle Collection

Throughout Europe, countless gargoyles peer down from the towers and parapets of medieval cathedrals. In honor of these fascinating creations Middle Age Arts presents an exclusive line of gargoyle replicas. Choose representations from the most famous cathedrals in the world, including the popular gargoyles of Notre Dame. Select from the following list of our most popular gargoyles.

Here is a sample of our products

Name	Item #	Type and Finish		Price
Bacchus	48059	Wall Mount	Interior Plaster	$95
Praying Gargoyle	48159	Garden Figure	Gothic Stone	$125
Gargoyle Judge	48222	Bust	Interior Plaster	$140
	48223	Bust	Gothic Stone	$155

You've completed your work on the appearance of the products table. You've learned how to control table size, alignment, border style, and color. You've also seen how to create cells that span several rows or columns in your table. In the next session you'll learn how to use tables to enhance the layout of an entire Web page.

Session 4.2 QUICK CHECK

1. What HTML code would you enter to create a table that has a 5-pixel-wide outside border with a 3-pixel border between table cells, and 4 pixels between the cell text and the surrounding cell border?

2. What code would you enter to align text with the top of a table header cell?

3. What code would you enter to center all of the text within a given row?

4. What are the two ways of expressing table width? What are the advantages and disadvantages of each?

5. What code would you enter to create a table that fills up half the width of the browser's display area, regardless of the resolution of the user's monitor?

6. What code would you enter to set the width of a cell to 60 pixels? Will this keep the cell from exceeding 60 pixels in width? Will this keep the cell from being less than 60 pixels wide? How would you guarantee that the cell width will be exactly 60 pixels?

7. What code would you enter to set the background color of your table to yellow? What are the limitations of this code?

8. What code would you enter to create a cell that spans three rows and two columns?

In this session you will work with tables to create a newspaper-style layout for a Web page. You'll create nested tables to enhance the page's design. Finally, you'll learn about some extensions supported by Internet Explorer that you can use on your tables.

Controlling Page Layout with Tables

In the first two sessions you used the <TABLE> tag to create a table of products that was part of a larger Web page. In practice, however, the table features of HTML are most often used to control the layout of an entire Web page. If you want to design a page that displays text in newspaper-style columns, or separates the page into different topical areas, you'll find tables an essential tool. One of the most useful features of tables is that within each table cell you can use any of the HTML layout tags you've learned so far. For example, you can insert an <H1> header within a cell, or you can insert an ordered list of items. You can even nest one table inside another.

Nicole is satisfied with your prototype page of Middle Age Arts products. She now wants you to create a home page for the Gargoyle Collection product line. The page will contain a list of links to other Middle Age Arts pages, a message from the company president, a few notes about the uses of gargoyles, and a profile of one of Middle Age Arts' artists. Nicole sketches a layout for the home page (Figure 4-40).

Figure 4-40	NICOLE'S SKETCH OF THE GARGOYLE COLLECTION HOME PAGE

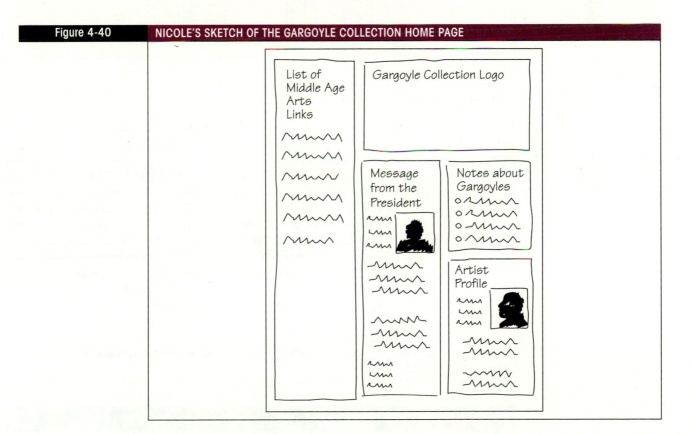

One way to create the layout specified in Nicole's sketch is to create two tables, one nested inside the other. The first table, shown in Figure 4-41, consists of one row with two columns. The first column will contain the list of hypertext links. The second column will contain the nested table along with the rest of the page material. You'll create the outer table first.

Figure 4-41   OUTER TABLE OF THE GARGOYLE COLLECTION HOME PAGE

1 row x 2 columns

hypertext links	the rest of the page

Creating the Outer Table

When designing a page that contains tables and other elements within tables, it's best to begin with the outer table and work inward. In the case of the Gargoyle Collection home page, you'll start by creating the outer table, which has one row and two columns. Because you want to control the layout exactly, you'll specify an overall width of 610 pixels for the table. This will preserve the layout of the various page elements and allow users with monitor resolutions of 640×480 to view the page correctly. You'll set the width of the first column to 165 pixels and the width of the second column to 445 pixels. As you design Web pages, you'll decide on column widths like these through trial and error, and whatever looks best.

The HTML code for pages like the one you're about to create can be long and complicated. One aid for you and for others who will be viewing the source code of your page is to include comments that describe the different sections of the page. The text entered into comments will not appear on the Web page. The format for a comment tag uses an exclamation point:

```
<! comment text>
```

Any text appearing within the tag after the exclamation point is ignored by the browser but can still be read in a text editor.

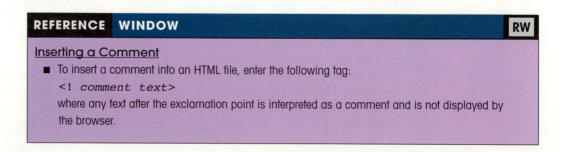

REFERENCE WINDOW   **RW**

Inserting a Comment
- To insert a comment into an HTML file, enter the following tag:

  ```
  <! comment text>
  ```
  where any text after the exclamation point is interpreted as a comment and is not displayed by the browser.

The initial file that you'll use for the Gargoyle Collection home page has been created for you. The file, named GHome.htm, contains no text but does have a page title and a background image consisting of a single maroon stripe. Now you need to open the file and create the outer table structure. You'll include comments along with the <TABLE> tags to help you document the different elements of the page layout. You'll add dashes to the comments to help the comment tags stand out a bit more.

To create the outer table and comments:

1. If you took a break after the previous session, start your text editor.

2. Open the file **GHome.htm** in the **Tutorial.04** folder of your Data Disk.

3. Save the file as **Gargoyle.htm**.

4. Between the <BODY> tags, enter the following:

```
<TABLE WIDTH=610 CELLPADDING=0 CELLSPACING=0>
<TR>
<!--List of Hypertext Links-->
<TD WIDTH=165 VALIGN=TOP>
</TD>
<!--Articles about the Gargoyle Collection-->
<TD WIDTH=445 VALIGN=TOP>
</TD>
</TR>
</TABLE>
```

The Gargoyle.htm file should look like Figure 4-42.

Figure 4-42   **TAGS FOR THE OUTER TABLE AND COMMENTS**

comment tag →

```
<HTML>
<HEAD>
<TITLE>The Gargoyle Collection Home Page</TITLE>
</HEAD>
<BODY BACKGROUND="RedBar.jpg" LINK=WHITE VLINK=WHITE ALINK=WHITE>
<TABLE WIDTH=610 CELLPADDING=0 CELLSPACING=0>
<TR>
   <!--List of Hypertext Links-->
   <TD WIDTH=165 VALIGN=TOP>
   </TD>
   <!--Articles about the Gargoyle Collection-->
   <TD WIDTH=445 VALIGN=TOP>
   </TD>
</TR>
</TABLE>
</BODY>
</HTML>
```

Note that in both cells of this outer table, you've set the vertical alignment to top, rather than using the default value of middle. This is because the cells in this table will act as newspaper columns, with text flowing from the cell top down. You'll follow this practice with other table cells on the page. You've also set the cell padding and cell spacing values to 0. This allows any text entered into those cells to use the full cell width. You won't be displaying any table borders in this layout.

Now you can enter data in the first cell, which will contain the list of Middle Age Arts hypertext links. A page with the filename Links.htm has already been created with this information, shown in Figure 4-43.

Figure 4-43	THE LINKS.HTM PAGE

links to other pages

To create the contents for the table's first column, you'll copy the information contained in the document shown in Figure 4-43 and paste it between the table cell tags. (If you don't know how to copy and paste with your text editor, ask your instructor or technical support person for assistance.)

To insert the first column's contents:

1. Insert a blank line between the first set of <TD> and </TD> tags in the Gargoyle.htm file.

2. Open the file **Links.htm** from the **Tutorial.04** folder of your Data Disk.

   TROUBLE? You might have to close your text editor if your operating system does not permit you to have multiple copies of the editor running at the same time. If so, save the changes to the Gargoyle.htm file before opening Links.htm.

3. Copy the HTML code within the <BODY> tags of the Links.htm file, but do *not* include the <BODY> tags themselves. Note that all the code you need to copy is indented in the file.

4. Return to the Gargoyle.htm file in your text editor.

5. Paste the HTML code you copied from Links.htm in the blank space you created between the first set of <TD> and </TD> tags. See Figure 4-44.

Figure 4-44	CODE FOR THE LIST OF HYPERTEXT LINKS

```
<TR>
    <!--List of Hypertext Links-->
    <TD WIDTH=165 VALIGN=TOP>
        <IMG SRC="MAA2.jpg" WIDTH=144 HEIGHT=25 ALT="Middle Age Arts">
        <H4><FONT COLOR=YELLOW>Middle Age Arts</FONT></H4>
        <FONT COLOR=WHITE>
        <A HREF="Index.htm">Home Page</A><BR>
        <A HREF="Catalog.htm">View the catalog</A><BR>
        <A HREF="Orders.htm">Place an order</A><BR>
        </FONT>
        <H4><FONT COLOR=YELLOW>About Gargoyles</FONT></H4>
        <FONT COLOR=WHITE>
        <A HREF="MAAtable.htm">Gargoyle Products</A><BR>
        <A HREF="MAAtext.htm">Gargoyle Products<BR>(text version)</A><BR>
        </FONT>
        <H4><FONT COLOR=YELLOW>Other Collections</FONT></H4>
        <FONT COLOR=WHITE>
        <A HREF="Vatican.htm">The Vatican Collection</A><BR>
        <A HREF="Rodin.htm">The Rodin Collection</A><BR>
        <A HREF="Masters.htm">Renaissance Masters</A><BR>
        </FONT>
    </TD>
</TR>
```

this new text should be pasted within the first <TD> tags

6. Save your changes and then open the **Gargoyle.htm** file in your Web browser. Figure 4-45 shows the current state of the Gargoyle Collection home page.

Figure 4-45	INITIAL GARGOYLE COLLECTION WEB PAGE

TROUBLE? Note that not all of the links on this page point to existing files. They are provided to create a complete picture of the Web page's appearance.

Notice that the contents of the original Links.htm file are contained within the boundaries of the first column of the outer table. You've completed the first half of the page. Now you'll turn your attention to the second half.

Creating the Nested Table

The material in the second column will be organized inside a second table. This inner, or nested, table has three rows and three columns, as shown in Figure 4-46. The first row contains a single cell with the Gargoyle Collection logo spanning the three columns. The first cell in the second row contains the president's message, spanning the second and third rows of the table. The second cell in that row will act as a gutter, which is a blank space separating the material between columns (in this case, between the first and third columns). The gutter will also span the second and third rows. Finally, the third cell in the second row contains the notes about gargoyles, and the third cell in the last row contains the artist's profile.

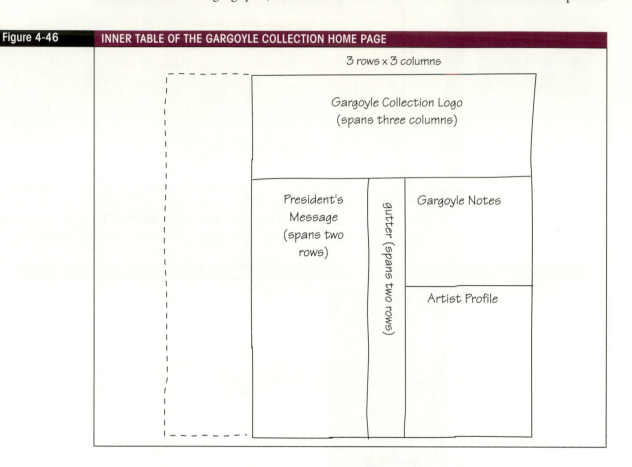

Figure 4-46   INNER TABLE OF THE GARGOYLE COLLECTION HOME PAGE

3 rows x 3 columns

Gargoyle Collection Logo
(spans three columns)

President's Message (spans two rows)

gutter (spans two rows)

Gargoyle Notes

Artist Profile

As with previous tables, you'll first enter the table structure and then enter the table text. Nested tables work in the same way as regular tables, except that they are inserted within the <TD> tags of a different table.

To create the nested table:

1. Return to the Gargoyle.htm file in your text editor.

2. Insert a blank line between the second set of <TD> and </TD> tags.

3. Enter the following text, indented three spaces in from the <TD> tag (to make the code easier to read):

```
<TABLE WIDTH=445 CELLSPACING=0 CELLPADDING=0>
<TR>
<!--The Gargoyle Collection Logo-->
<TD COLSPAN=3 VALIGN=TOP ALIGN=CENTER>
</TD>
</TR>
<TR>
<!--Message from the company president-->
<TD ROWSPAN=2 WIDTH=220 VALIGN=TOP>
</TD>
<!--The table gutter-->
<TD ROWSPAN=2 WIDTH=5></TD>
<!--Notes about gargoyles-->
<TD WIDTH=220 VALIGN=TOP>
</TD>
</TR>
<TR>
<!--Profile of an artist-->
<TD WIDTH=220 VALIGN=TOP>
</TD>
</TR>
</TABLE>
```

Your file should appear as shown in Figure 4-47. Note that by indenting the text for the nested table three spaces, you have improved the readability of the HTML code without affecting the code itself.

Figure 4-47   CODE FOR THE INNER TABLE

```
<!--Articles about the Gargoyle Collection-->
<TD WIDTH=445 VALIGN=TOP>
   <TABLE WIDTH=445 CELLSPACING=0 CELLPADDING=0>
   <TR>
      <!--The Gargoyle Collection Logo-->
      <TD COLSPAN=3 VALIGN=TOP ALIGN=CENTER>
      </TD>
   </TR>
   <TR>
      <!--Message from the company president-->
      <TD ROWSPAN=2 WIDTH=220 VALIGN=TOP>
      </TD>
      <!--The table gutter-->
      <TD ROWSPAN=2 WIDTH=5></TD>
      <!--Notes about gargoyles-->
      <TD WIDTH=220 VALIGN=TOP>
      </TD>
   </TR>
   <TR>
      <!--Profile of an artist-->
      <TD WIDTH=220 VALIGN=TOP>
      </TD>
   </TR>
   </TABLE>
</TD>
```

Before proceeding, you should study the HTML code you just entered and compare it to Figure 4-46. Make sure that you understand the purpose of each tag in the nested table.

The first item you'll enter in the nested table is an inline image, GLogo.jpg, which you'll place within the single cell that spans the three columns of the inner table's first row.

To insert the Gargoyle Collection logo:

1. Insert a blank line below the first <TD> tag in the nested table.

2. Type the following in the blank line, indented three spaces in from the <TD> tag, to make the code more readable:

```
<IMG SRC="GLogo.jpg" WIDTH=440 HEIGHT=220>
```

Figure 4-48 shows the revised HTML code.

Figure 4-48   **INSERTING THE GARGOYLE COLLECTION LOGO**

```
<!--Articles about the Gargoyle Collection-->
<TD WIDTH=445 VALIGN=TOP>
   <TABLE WIDTH=445 CELLSPACING=0 CELLPADDING=0>
   <TR>
      <!--The Gargoyle Collection Logo-->
      <TD COLSPAN=3 VALIGN=TOP ALIGN=CENTER>
         <IMG SRC="GLogo.jpg" WIDTH=440 HEIGHT=220>
      </TD>
   </TR>
```

With the logo in place, you'll insert the message from the company president next. The message has already been created for you in the file Oneil.htm. This page is shown in Figure 4-49.

Figure 4-49   **THE ONEIL.HTM PAGE**

From the President

This month Middle Age Arts introduces the Gargoyle Collection. I'm really excited about this new set of classical figures.

The collection contains faithful reproductions of gargoyles from some of the famous cathedrals of Europe, including Notre Dame, Rheims, and Warwick Castle. All reproductions are done with exacting and loving detail.

The collection also contains original works by noted artists such as Susan Bedford and Antonio Salvari. Our expert artisans have produced some wonderful and whimsical works, perfectly suited for home or garden use.

Don't delay, order your gargoyle today.

Irene O'Neil
President,
Middle Age Arts

As you did with the list of hypertext links, you'll copy and paste the contents of the page body into a table cell. The pasted text needs to be placed in the first column of the second row of the nested table.

To insert the message from the company president:

1. Insert a blank line below the first <TD> tag in the second row of the nested table.

2. Open the file **Oneil.htm** from the **Tutorial.04** folder of your Data Disk, saving and closing the Gargoyle.htm file if necessary.

3. Copy the HTML code between, but not including, the <BODY> tags in the Oneil.htm file. All of the code you need to copy is indented.

4. Return to the Gargoyle.htm file in your text editor.

5. Paste the HTML code you copied from Oneil.htm in the blank line you created in Step 1. See Figure 4-50.

Figure 4-50	INSERTING THE PRESIDENT'S MESSAGE

code for the cell in the second row, first column of the nested table

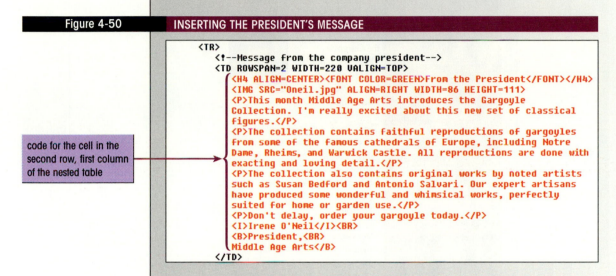

```
<TR>
    <!--Message from the company president-->
    <TD ROWSPAN=2 WIDTH=220 VALIGN=TOP>
        <H4 ALIGN=CENTER><FONT COLOR=GREEN>From the President</FONT></H4>
        <IMG SRC="Oneil.jpg" ALIGN=RIGHT WIDTH=86 HEIGHT=111>
        <P>This month Middle Age Arts introduces the Gargoyle
        Collection. I'm really excited about this new set of classical
        figures.</P>
        <P>The collection contains faithful reproductions of gargoyles
        from some of the famous cathedrals of Europe, including Notre
        Dame, Rheims, and Warwick Castle. All reproductions are done with
        exacting and loving detail.</P>
        <P>The collection also contains original works by noted artists
        such as Susan Bedford and Antonio Salvari. Our expert artisans
        have produced some wonderful and whimsical works, perfectly
        suited for home or garden use.</P>
        <P>Don't delay, order your gargoyle today.</P>
        <I>Irene O'Neil</I><BR>
        <B>President,<BR>
        Middle Age Arts</B>
    </TD>
```

6. Save your changes and then reload the file in your browser. The page now displays the column from the company president, as well as the Gargoyle Collection logo. See Figure 4-51.

Figure 4-51   LOGO AND PRESIDENT'S MESSAGE ON THE GARGOYLE COLLECTION PAGE

Before proceeding, read the code you copied from the Oneil.htm file; you should recognize and understand it.

The next cell in the nested table creates a space (gutter) between the first and third columns. You do not have to enter any text into this cell, but you should create a blank space between the <TD> and </TD> tags. The blank space ensures that the cell occupies the 5-pixel width set aside for it. Without anything in the table cell, some browsers will not display the cell, even if you have specified a width for it.

To insert a blank space into the gutter:

1. Return to the Gargoyle.htm file in your text editor.

2. Go to the <TD> tag after the table gutter comment tag.

3. Type the nonbreaking space symbol, ** **, between the <TD> and </TD> tags.

The blank space you inserted will help ensure that the column retains its 5-pixel width. The next cell in the table will include a whimsical list describing the "uses" of gargoyle products. The list has been saved in the GNotes.htm file, shown in Figure 4-52.

Figure 4-52	THE GNOTES.HTM PAGE

What do I do with a gargoyle?

Don't think you need a gargoyle? Think again. Gargoyles are useful as:

- Bird baths
- Wind chimes
- Pen holders
- Paperweights
- Bookends

Note that the background of this page is yellow. You want this color in the table cell as well, but you can't copy the code for it from the GNotes.htm file because in that file the color is a background for the entire Web page and is found in the <BODY> tag. You'll apply yellow to the cell by adding the BGCOLOR property to the cell tag. First you can copy the code for the uses of gargoyles.

To insert the gargoyle notes and apply yellow to the cell:

1. Make sure the Gargoyle.htm file is displayed in your text editor.

2. Insert a blank line between the <TD> and </TD> tags located directly below the "Notes about gargoyles" comment tag.

3. Open the file **GNotes.htm** from the **Tutorial.04** folder of your Data Disk.

4. Copy the HTML code between the <BODY> tags in the GNotes.htm file. Once again, do not include the <BODY> tags themselves.

5. Return to the Gargoyle.htm file.

6. Paste the HTML code in the blank line you created in Step 1.

   Next you'll change the color of the cell background to yellow.

7. Type **BGCOLOR=YELLOW** within the <TD> tag for the cell. The revised code is shown in Figure 4-53.

Figure 4-53 INSERTING NOTES ABOUT GARGOYLES

cell background color
is changed to yellow

```
<!--The table gutter-->
<TD ROWSPAN=2 WIDTH=5> </TD>
<!--Notes about gargoyles-->
<TD WIDTH=220 VALIGN=TOP BGCOLOR=YELLOW>
    <FONT COLOR="#800000">
    <H4 ALIGN=CENTER>What do I do with a gargoyle?</H4>
    Don't think you need a gargoyle? Think again. Gargoyles are
    useful as:
    <UL>
```

8. Save your changes and then reload the file in your browser. The revised
   Gargoyle Collection page is shown in Figure 4-54.

Figure 4-54 GARGOYLE NOTES ADDED TO THE WEB PAGE

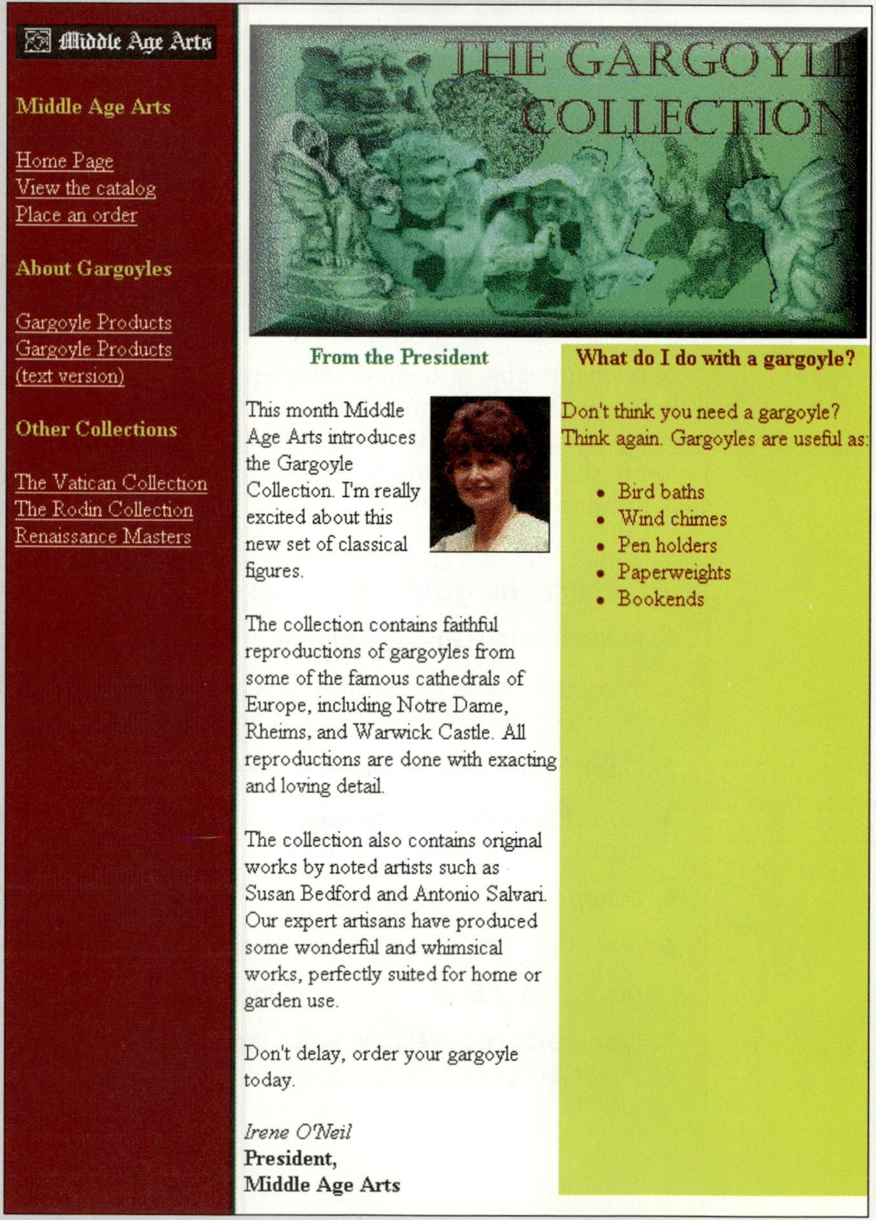

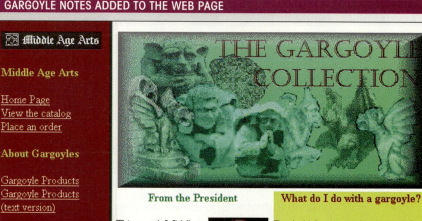

TROUBLE? The space between the columns might look different in your browser from what is shown in Figure 4-54. Different browsers handle column spaces and gutters in slightly different ways.

The last component of the page is the profile of the artist, Michael Cassini. The contents of this profile can be found in the Cassini.htm file, shown in Figure 4-55.

Figure 4-55	THE CASSINI.HTM PAGE

Profile of the Artist

This month's artist is Michael Cassini. Michael has been a professional sculptor for ten years. He has won numerous awards, including the prestigious *Reichsman Cup* and an Award of Merit at the 1997 Tuscany Arts Competition.

Michael specializes in recreations of gargoyles from European cathedrals. You'll usually find Michael staring intently at the church walls in northern France. His work is represented by the *Turin Gargoyle*, a great entry to our Gargoyle Collection.

You need to place the text for the profile in the last cell in the third row. Remember that the first two cells of the third row have been already filled in, being merely extensions of the spanning cells created in the table's second row.

To insert the profile of Michael Cassini:

1. Return to the Gargoyle.htm file in your text editor.

2. Insert a blank line below the final <TD> tag, located in the third row of the nested table.

3. Open the file **Cassini.htm** from the **Tutorial.04** folder of your Data Disk. Again, the HTML code is already indented.

4. Copy the HTML code between the <BODY> tags in the Cassini.htm file.

5. Return to the Gargoyle.htm file.

6. Paste the HTML code in the blank line you created earlier. See Figure 4-56.

Figure 4-56	INSERTING THE ARTIST PROFILE

```
<TR>
   <!--Profile of an artist-->
   <TD WIDTH=220 VALIGN=TOP>
      <H4 ALIGN=CENTER><FONT COLOR=GREEN>Profile of the Artist</FONT></H4>
      <IMG SRC="Cassini.jpg" ALIGN=RIGHT WIDTH=64 HEIGHT=74>
      <P>This month's artist is Michael Cassini. Michael has been a
      professional sculptor for ten years. He has won numerous awards,
      including the prestigious <I>Reichsman Cup</I> and an Award of
      Merit at the 1997 Tuscany Arts Competition.</P>
      <P>Michael specializes in recreations of gargoyles from European
      cathedrals. You'll usually find Michael staring intently at the
      church walls in northern France. His work is represented by the
      <I>Turin Gargoyle</I>, a great entry to our Gargoyle
      Collection.</P>
   </TD>
</TR>
</TABLE>
```

7. Save your changes and then reload the file in your browser. Figure 4-57 shows the final version of the page.

Figure 4-57   FINAL VERSION OF THE GARGOYLE COLLECTION WEB PAGE

Middle Age Arts

Home Page
View the catalog
Place an order

About Gargoyles

Gargoyle Products
Gargoyle Products
(text version)

Other Collections

The Vatican Collection
The Rodin Collection
Renaissance Masters

From the President

This month Middle Age Arts introduces the Gargoyle Collection. I'm really excited about this new set of classical figures.

The collection contains faithful reproductions of gargoyles from some of the famous cathedrals of Europe, including Notre Dame, Rheims, and Warwick Castle. All reproductions are done with exacting and loving detail.

The collection also contains original works by noted artists such as Susan Bedford and Antonio Salvari. Our expert artisans have produced some wonderful and whimsical works, perfectly suited for home or garden use.

Don't delay, order your gargoyle today.

Irene O'Neil
**President,
Middle Age Arts**

What do I do with a gargoyle?

Don't think you need a gargoyle? Think again. Gargoyles are useful as:

- Bird baths
- Wind chimes
- Pen holders
- Paperweights
- Bookends

Profile of the Artist

This month's artist is Michael Cassini. Michael has been a professional sculptor for ten years. He has won numerous awards, including the prestigious *Reichsman Cup* and an Award of Merit at the 1997 Tuscany Arts Competition.

Michael specializes in recreations of gargoyles from European cathedrals. You'll usually find Michael staring intently at the church walls in northern France. His work is represented by the *Turin Gargoyle*, a great entry to our Gargoyle Collection.

You've completed the design of the Gargoyle Collection home page. By using tables, you managed to create an interesting and attractive layout. This process illustrated several principles that you should keep in mind when creating such layouts in the future:

1. Diagram the layout before you start writing the HTML code.

2. Create the text for various columns and cells in separate files, which you'll insert later.

3. Create the table structure for the outer table first, and then gradually work inward.

4. Insert comment tags to identify the different sections of the page.

5. Indent the code for the various levels of nested tables, to make your code easier to follow.

6. Test and review your code as you proceed, in order to catch errors early.

DESIGN   WINDOW   DW

Using Tables to Control Page Layout
- Create gutters and use cell padding to keep your columns from crowding each other.
- Add background colors to columns to provide visual interest and variety.
- Use the VALIGN=TOP property in cells containing articles, to ensure that the text flows from the top down.
- Use row spanning to vary the size and starting point of articles within your columns. Having all articles start and end within the same row creates a static layout that is difficult to read.
- Avoid having more than three columns of text, if possible. Inserting additional columns could make the column widths too narrow and make the text hard to read.

You show the final version of the page to Nicole. She's pleased that you were able to create a page to match her sketch. She'll look over the page you created and get back to you with any additional changes. As you wait for her feedback, you can learn a little more about tables and HTML tags.

Extensions to Tables

Both Netscape and Internet Explorer support several additional tags you can use to enhance the appearance of your tables. These additional tags, or **extensions**, allow you to specify table border colors and control the appearance of cell boundaries. Although you won't apply them to any of the tables you've created so far, you might want to use them in tables you create in the future.

Specifying the Table Border Color

By default, a table's borders are displayed in two shades of gray, creating a three-dimensional effect. Both Internet Explorer and Netscape Navigator support an extension that allows you to choose the border color. The syntax of this extension is:

```
<TABLE BORDERCOLOR=color>
```

where *color* is either the color name or color value. Figure 4-58 shows examples of tables using the BORDERCOLOR property. Note that the two browsers display the table differently. Once again, this shows the importance of testing your code on different browsers and different browser versions.

Figure 4-58

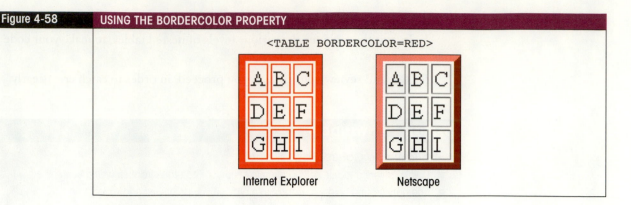

Figure 4-58   USING THE BORDERCOLOR PROPERTY

In Internet Explorer this tag applies the color to the entire border, which eliminates the three-dimensional effect of the default color scheme provided by Netscape. What if you want to keep the 3-D effect for Internet Explorer users? Internet Explorer provides two additional properties, BORDERCOLORLIGHT and BORDERCOLORDARK, which allow you to specify light and dark colors of the 3-D border. Note that Netscape does not support these properties. The syntax for specifying the light and dark border colors is:

```
<TABLE BORDERCOLORDARK=color BORDERCOLORLIGHT=color>
```

Figure 4-59 shows an example of the use of the BORDERCOLORDARK and BORDERCOLORLIGHT properties to create a 3-D border effect with shades of blue for Internet Explorer. The Netscape browser ignores these properties.

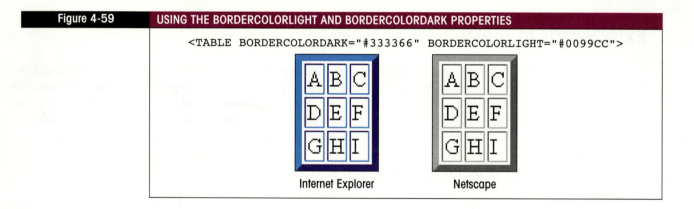

Figure 4-59   USING THE BORDERCOLORLIGHT AND BORDERCOLORDARK PROPERTIES

When using these extensions, be sure to view your page in browsers other than Internet Explorer, to verify that the table still looks good even when the color extensions are not supported.

Creating Frames and Rules

Two additional properties introduced in HTML 4.0 (and above) and supported by Internet Explorer, but not supported by Netscape, are the FRAME and RULE properties. As you've seen, when borders are displayed, they surround the entire table on all four sides. The FRAME property allows you to control which sides of the table will have borders. The syntax for the FRAME property is:

```
<TABLE FRAME=value>
```

where *value* is either BOX (the default), ABOVE, BELOW, HSIDES, VSIDES, LHS, RHS, or VOID. Figure 4-60 describes each of these values.

Figure 4-60   VALUES OF THE FRAME PROPERTY

FRAME VALUE	DESCRIPTION
BOX	Draws borders around all four sides
ABOVE	Draws only the top border
BELOW	Draws only the bottom border
HSIDES	Draws both the top and bottom borders (the horizontal sides)
LHS	Draws only the left-hand side
RHS	Draws only the right-hand side
VSIDES	Draws both the left and right borders (the vertical sides)
VOID	Does not draw borders on any of the four sides

Figure 4-61 shows the effect of each of these values on the table grid.

Figure 4-61   EFFECT OF DIFFERENT FRAME VALUES

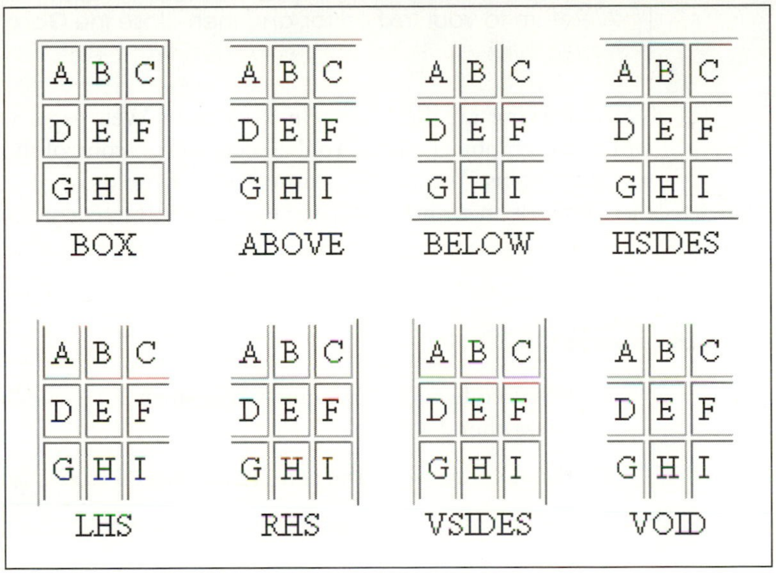

By default, borders are drawn around each cell in the table. The RULES property lets you control this by specifying how you want the table grid to be drawn. The syntax of the RULES property is:

```
<TABLE RULES=value>
```

where *value* is either ALL, ROWS, COLS, or NONE. The ALL value causes all cell borders to be drawn. The ROWS and COLS values cause borders to be drawn around only the table rows and columns, respectively. NONE suppresses the display of any cell borders. Figure 4-62 shows the effect of different RULES property values on a table's appearance.

Figure 4-62   EFFECT OF DIFFERENT RULES VALUES

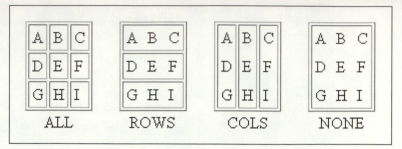

Once again, remember that when you use these Internet Explorer extensions, the effects you see will not be duplicated in other Web browsers, which will display tables with the usual grid layout. Therefore, you should always test under different Web browsers.

You've finished your work on the Web page and can now close your browser and text editor.

To close your work:

1. Close your Web browser.

2. Return to your text editor, and then close the **Gargoyle.htm** file.

By working on the Gargoyle Collection Web page, you've learned how to create text tables and graphical tables. You've seen how to control the appearance of your table and the text it contains. You've also learned one of the most powerful uses for tables—controlling the layout of an entire Web page to create attractive page designs.

Session 4.3 QUICK CHECK

1. What code would you enter to create a 2 × 2 table nested inside the upper-left cell of another 2 × 2 table?

2. What code inserts the comment "Nested table starts here"?

3. What code would you enter to change the border color of your table to yellow?

4. What code would you enter to use red for the light border color and blue for the dark border color?

5. What code would you enter to display only the top border of your table?

6. What code would you enter to create dividing lines around your table columns only?

7. What is the limitation of the code you created for Quick Checks 3 through 6?

REVIEW ASSIGNMENTS

Nicole has finished reviewing the pages you created for her. She has made a few changes and has a few additional suggestions that she wants you to implement. These involve updating the text table you created to reflect the changes made to the graphical table, altering the appearance of the graphical products table, and making some changes to the Gargoyle Collection home page.

To implement Nicole's suggestions:

1. In your text editor, open the **MAA4.htm** file in the Review subfolder of the Tutorial.04 folder on your Data Disk, and then save the file as GTable.htm in the same folder.

2. Align the Name header with the left edge of its cell.

3. Increase the size of the table border to 10 pixels. Increase the size of the cell spacing to 3 pixels.

4. Change the Bust cell in the third row of the table body to a spanning cell that spans two rows.

5. Align the text "Bust" in the spanning cell with the cell's top edge.

6. Add the following new item in a new row to the bottom of the products table: Item Name—Spitting Gargoyle, Item #—49010, Type—Garden Figure, Finish—Gothic Stone, Price—$110.

7. Change the color of the header row to a greenish-blue. The color value (in hexadecimal) is 33FFFF. Save the changes to the GTable.htm file.

8. Open the **MAA3.htm** file in the Review subfolder of the Tutorial.04 folder on your Data Disk, and then save the file as GText.htm in the same folder.

9. Add a fourth and fifth row to the text table body to match the items listed in the graphical table. Save your changes.

10. Open the **GHome2.htm** file in the Review subfolder of the Tutorial.04 folder on your Data Disk, and then save the file as GCollect.htm in the same folder.

11. Add a fourth row at the bottom of the nested table. The row should have one cell that spans three columns.

12. Within the cell, insert the text "View a table of gargoyle products". Format the text as a hypertext link to the Gtable.htm file.

13. Align the text in the cell with the top and center of the cell.

14. Change the background color of the table cell to the hexadecimal value #800000. Save your changes.

15. Print both the page and the HTML code for the Gtext.htm, Gtable.htm, and GCollect.htm files.

16. Close your Web browser and your text editor.

CASE PROBLEMS

Case 1. Creating a Calendar of Activities at Avalon Books You've been asked to create a Web page that displays a calendar of activities at the Avalon Books bookstore for the month of May. Updating the calendar is a monthly activity, so a page has already been created containing a graphical table of the days of the month. Your job will be to update this table with the May activities. You will also add a caption and title to the table and format it. The calendar should include the following activities:

- Every Monday: Noon story time with Susan Sheridan
- Every Friday: Noon story time with Doug Evans
- May 1st: Young authors' workshop from 1 to 4 p.m.
- May 5th: Ecology workshop with Nancy Fries from 9 to 11 a.m.
- May 15th: Ms. Frizzle teaches about science from 2 to 3 p.m.
- May 19th: Origami with Rita Davis from 2 to 3 p.m.
- May 22nd: Making a model of the solar system from 2 to 3 p.m.
- May 29th: Spenser Brown's Clown Show from 1 to 2 p.m.

To create the Avalon Books calendar:

1. In your text editor, open the **Avalon.htm** file in the Cases subfolder of the Tutorial.04 folder on your Data Disk, and then save the file as May_List.htm in the same folder.

Explore 2. Set the table width to use 100% of the display area.

Explore 3. Modify each cell in the table, changing the cell for Sundays to 16% of the table width, and changing the width of each of the remaining days to 14% of the table width. Align the text in each cell with the top of the cell border.

4. At the beginning of the table, insert a new row with a single spanning cell that spans the seven table columns. Set the width of this cell to 100% of the width of the table.

5. Within the spanning cell, insert the text "Children's Events in May". Center this text within the spanning cell and format it as an H3 header.

6. Insert the days of the week in the cells of the table header row, starting with Sunday.

7. Enter the activities listed earlier. Note that some of the activities are repeated throughout the month.

8. Insert the table caption "For more information call Debbie at 555-4892" aligned with the bottom of the table.

9. Increase the width of the table border to 5 pixels.

Explore 10. Save your changes and then view the page in your Web browser. If your monitor allows it, view the table at different screen resolutions (you might need to ask your instructor how to modify your monitor's resolution). How does the appearance of the table change under different resolutions?

11. Print the HTML code for the calendar page. Print the page itself; if you can change your monitor resolution, print the page at the 640×480 and 800×600 screen resolutions.

12. Close your Web browser and your text editor.

Case 2. Creating a Television Schedule at WMTZ   You're in charge of creating Web pages for WMTZ, a television station in Atlanta. One of these pages contains the weekly prime-time television schedule from 7:00 p.m. to 10 p.m. You'll create this schedule with a table broken down in half-hour installments. Because some programs in the schedule last longer than 30 minutes, you will have to include spanning cells to cover those time periods. Figure 4-63 shows the completed table.

Figure 4-63

Day	7:00	7:30	8:00	8:30	9:00	9:30
Mon.	The Nanny	Fred's Place	Old Friends	Cybill	Emergency Center	
Tue.	Babylon 5		Tonite!	911 Stories	Mission Impossible	
Wed.	Special: The Budget Crisis		Perfume		48 Hours	
Thu.	Mel's Diner	Alien World	Movie: Wayne's World III			
Fri.	Movie Special: Schindler's List					
Sat.	Dr. Quinn		Murder for Hire		New York Streets	
Sun.	Hey Dogs!	Wild Life	Movie: The Lost World			

To create the television schedule table:

1. In your text editor, open the **WMTZ.htm** file in the Cases subfolder of the Tutorial.04 folder on your Data Disk, and then save the file as TVList.htm in the same folder.

2. Create a table that has seven columns and eight rows, with one of the rows consisting of table headers.

3. Set the table border width to 5 pixels, the cell spacing to 3 pixels, and the cell padding to 5 pixels.

Explore ▶ 4. Using the Internet Explorer extensions, change the color of the dark part of the table border to the color value 0000FF and the color of the light part of the table border to CCCCFF.

5. Set the width of each cell in the first column to 50 pixels.

6. Set the width of the table header cells (aside from the first column) to 90 pixels.

7. Enter the table text. Create spanning cells as indicated in Figure 4-63.

8. For each half-hour program, set the cell width to 90 pixels; set the cell width of one hour programs to 180 pixels, of two-hour programs to 360 pixels, and of three-hour programs to 540 pixels.

9. Set the background color of the first row and first column of the table to yellow.

10. Center the table on the page.

11. Save your changes to the file.

Explore ▶ 12. View the page, if possible, in both Netscape and Internet Explorer. What are the differences between the way the page appears in the two browsers?

13. Print a copy of your HTML code and the finished Web page.

14. Close your Web browser and your text editor.

Case 3. Creating the Dunston Retreat Center Home Page The Dunston Retreat Center, located in Northern Wisconsin, offers weekends of quiet and solitude for all who visit. The center, started by a group of Trappist monks, has grown in popularity over the last few years, as more people have become aware of its services. The director of the center, Benjamin Adams, wants to advertise the center on the Internet and has asked you to create a home page. The page will include a welcoming message from Benjamin Adams, a list of upcoming events, a letter from one of the center's guests, and a description of the current week's events. The home page you'll create is shown in Figure 4-64.

Figure 4-64

Welcome

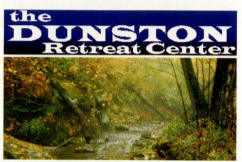

Welcome to the Dunston Retreat Center. Whether you are planning to attend one of our many conferences or embarking on a private retreat, we're sure that you will enjoy your stay.

Located in the northern woods of Wisconsin, the Dunston Retreat Center provides comfortable and attractive accommodations while you enjoy the rustic setting available just outside your door. The Retreat Center has 32 beds, large meeting rooms, a chapel, and kitchen facilities. If you want to get out, there are ample opportunities for hiking, canoeing and horseback riding in the surrounding area.

Throughout the year the center staff conducts retreats to accommodate the needs of various groups. We offer retreats for men, for women, and for couples. Please call about special needs retreats.

If you prefer, an individually directed retreat is possible. The retreat includes a time of daily sharing and guidance by a retreat director to supplement your private time of solitude and meditation.

At the Dunston Retreat Center we make everything as easy as possible, providing meals, towels, bedding - everything you need. Just bring yourself.

Benjamin Adams
Director,
Dunston Retreat Center

Next week at the Dunston Retreat Center

The annual meeting of the Midwest Marriage Encounter occurs at the Dunston Retreat Center, June 11-13. Registration is $50 and includes room and board. A boating trip on Lake Superior is planned for Saturday night ($10 fee).

Contact Maury Taylor at 555-2381 for reservation information.

Upcoming Events

June 11-13 Marriage Encounter

June 18-20 Recovering Alcoholics

June 25-27 Spirituality Workshop

July 2-4 Lutheran Brotherhood

July 9-11 Recovering Alcoholics

July 16-18 Duluth Fellowship

July 23-25 Special Needs Children

August 6-8 St. James Men's Group

August 13-15 St. James Women's Group

August 20-22 Recovering Alcoholics

August 27-29 Knights of Columbus

A letter from one of our guests

I'm writing to tell you how much I enjoyed my retreat at Dunston. I came to your center haggard and worn out from a long illness and job difficulties. I left totally refreshed. I especially want to thank Father Thomas Holloway for his support.

I've enthusiastically told all of my friends about the wonderful place you have. Some of us are hoping to organize a group retreat. Rest assured that you'll see me again. Going to Dunston will become a yearly event for me.

Sincerely,

Doris Patterson

To create this home page, you'll use nested tables to organize the page design elements.

To create the Dunston Retreat Center Home Page:

1. In your text editor, open the **DRCtext.htm** file in the Cases subfolder of the Tutorial.04 folder on your Data Disk, and then save the file as Dunston.htm in the same folder.

2. Create a table that has three columns and one row. The width of the first column should be 200 pixels, the second column 5 pixels, and the third column 395 pixels.

3. Above the first column, insert the comment "Welcoming Message"; above the second column, insert the comment "Gutter"; and, above the third column, insert the comment "Nested Table."

4. Specify that any text within the three cells should be vertically aligned with the top of the cell.

5. Insert the contents (but not the <BODY> tags or information within the <HEAD> tags) of the **Welcome.htm** file (from the Cases folder) into the first cell of the table. Format the background of this cell using the same background color found in the Welcome.htm file.

Explore ➤

6. Within the third cell, insert a nested table with the following dimensions: four rows by three columns. Both the first and second rows of the nested table should contain a single cell that spans three columns. The third row of the nested table should have a single nonspanning cell with a width of 210 pixels, followed by a cell that spans two rows and is 5 pixels wide, and then a third cell that is 180 pixels wide and also spans two rows. The fourth row of the nested table should contain a single cell 210 pixels in width—making a total of six cells in the nested table.

7. Insert comments into the nested table. Label the first cell "Dunston Logo," the second cell "Dunston Photo," the third cell "Midwest Marriage Encounter," the fourth cell "Nested Table Gutter," the fifth cell "Letter," and the sixth cell "List of upcoming events."

8. Vertically align the contents of the nested table cells with the cell top.

9. Insert the inline image **DLogo.jpg** (from the Cases folder) into the first cell of the nested table. Specify that the dimensions of the image should be 390 pixels wide by 75 pixels high.

10. Insert the inline image **Dunston.jpg** (from the Cases folder) into the second cell of the nested table. Enter a dimension of 390 pixels by 170 pixels for the image's width and height.

11. Insert the body contents of the **Nextweek.htm** file (from the Cases folder) into the third cell of the nested table.

12. Insert a blank space into the fourth cell of the table to ensure that the gutter will appear.

13. Insert the body contents of the **Letter.htm** file (from the Cases folder) into the fifth cell of the table.

14. Insert the body contents of the **Upcoming.htm** file (from the Cases folder) into the sixth cell of the table.

15. Save your changes to the Dunston.htm file.

16. Print the HTML code and the resulting Web page.

17. Close your Web browser and your text editor.

Case 4. Creating the TravelWeb E-Zine   Magazines on the Web, sometimes called e-zines, provide useful material to subscribers online. You have joined the staff of an e-zine called TravelWeb, which publishes travel information and tips. You've been asked to work on the layout for the e-zine's home page. You've been given files that you should use in creating the page. Figure 4-65 lists and describes these files.

Figure 4-65

FILE	DESCRIPTION
LuxAir.htm	Article about LuxAir reducing airfares to Europe
Photo.htm	Article about the Photo of the Week
PPoint.jpg	Image file of the Photo of the Week (320 × 228)
PPoint2.jpg	Small version of the Photo of the Week image (180 × 128)
Toronto.htm	Article about traveling to Toronto
TWLinks.htm	Links to other TravelWeb pages (list version)
TWLinks2.htm	Links to other TravelWeb pages (table version)
TWLogo.jpg	Image file of the TravelWeb logo (425 × 105)
Yosemite.htm	Article about limiting access to Yosemite National Park
Yosemite.jpg	Image file of Yosemite National Park (112 × 158)

To create the TravelWeb e-zine front page:

1. Use the files listed in Figure 4-65 to create a newspaper-style page. All of these files are stored in the Cases folder of the Tutorial.04 folder on your Data Disk. The page should include several columns, but the number, size, and layout of the columns are up to you.

2. Use all of the files on the page, with the following exceptions: use only one of the two files TWLinks.htm and TWLinks2.htm, and use only one of the two image files PPoint.jpg and PPoint2.jpg. (*Note*: Not all of the links on this page point to existing files.)

3. Use background colors and spot color to give your page an attractive and interesting appearance.

4. Include comment tags to describe the different parts of your page layout.

5. Save your page as TW.htm in the Cases folder of the Tutorial.04 folder on your Data Disk.

6. Print a copy of the page and the HTML code.

7. Close your Web browser and your text editor.

QUICK CHECK ANSWERS

Session 4.1

1. Text tables and graphical tables. The text table is supported by all browsers and is easier to create. The graphical table is more difficult to create but provides the user with a wealth of formatting options. Graphical tables are also more flexible and attractive since the text tables have to be created in a fixed width font.

2. A proportional font assigns different widths to each character based on the character's shape. A fixed-width font assigns the same width to each character regardless of shape.

3. the <PRE> tag

4. The <TABLE> tag identifies the beginning of a table. The <TR> tag identifies the beginnning of a table row. The <TD> tag identifies individual table cells, and the <TH> tag identifies table cells that will act as table headers.

5. The number of rows in a table is determined by the number of <TR> tags. The number of columns is equal to the largest number of <TD> and <TH> tags within a single table row.

6. Text within the <TH> tag is automatically bolded and centered within the table cell.

7. <CAPTION ALIGN=BOTTOM>Product Catalog</CAPTION>

   Place this tag anywhere between the <TABLE> and </TABLE> tags.

Session 4.2

1. <TABLE BORDER=5 CELLSPACING=3 CELLPADDING=4>

2. <TD VALIGN=TOP>

   or

   <TH VALIGN=TOP>

3. <TR ALIGN=CENTER>

4. In pixels or as a percentage of the display area. Use pixels if you want to exactly control the size of the table. Use percentages if you want your table to adapt itself to the user's monitor resolution.

5. <TABLE WIDTH="50%">

6. <TD WIDTH=60>

   or

   <TH WIDTH=60>

   This will not keep the cell from exceeding 60 pixels in width. The only way to do that is to set the width of *all* cells in that table column to 60 pixels.

7. <TABLE BGCOLOR=YELLOW>

   This property is not supported by earlier browsers.

8. <TD ROWSPAN=3 COLSPAN=2>

   or

   <TH ROWSPAN=3 COLSPAN=2>

Session 4.3

1. ```
<TABLE>
   <TR>
        <TD>
        <TABLE><TR><TD></TD><TD></TD></TR>
              <TR><TD></TD><TD></TD></TR>
        </TABLE>
        </TD>
        <TD></TD>
   </TR>
   <TR>
        <TD></TD>
        <TD></TD>
   </TR>
</TABLE>
```

2. <! Nested table starts here>

3. <TABLE BORDERCOLOR=YELLOW>

4. <TABLE BORDERCOLORDARK=BLUE BORDERCOLORLIGHT=RED>

5. <TABLE FRAME=ABOVE>

6. <TABLE RULES=COLS>

7. It works for browsers that support HTML 4.0. It may not work for older browsers that support the earlier HTML specifications.
```

OBJECTIVES

In this tutorial you will:

- Create frames for a Web site

- Control the appearance and placement of frames

- Control the behavior of hyperlinks on a page with frames

- Use magic target names to specify the target for a hypertext link

- Create a page that is viewable both by browsers that support frames and by those that do not

- Work with extensions that change the appearance of frames

USING FRAMES IN A WEB SITE

Creating a Web Site Containing Multiple Frames

CASE

Advertising for The Colorado Experience

One of the most popular climbing schools and back-country touring agencies in Colorado is The Colorado Experience. Located in Vale Park, outside Rocky Mountain National Park, The Colorado Experience specializes in teaching beginning and advanced climbing techniques. The school also sponsors several tours, leading individuals to some of the most exciting, challenging, and picturesque climbs in the Vale Park area. The school has been in existence for 15 years and, in that time, it has helped thousands of people experience the mountains in ways they never thought possible.

The Colorado Experience has stiff competition in the area from other climbing schools and touring groups. The owner, Debbie Chen, is always looking for ways to improve the visibility of the school. Early on, she decided to use the Internet and the World Wide Web as a means of advertising the school's services. She has already created an extensive number of Web pages to highlight the company's offerings.

Debbie has seen other Web sites that use frames, which are windows that allow the browser to display several HTML files on the screen at one time. She feels that this would be a good way of showcasing her business in an easy-to-use one-page design. She asks you to help her modify the company's Web presentation to take advantage of frames.

SESSION 5.1

In this session you will create a Web site that contains frames. You will learn about the HTML tags that control the placement and appearance of frames. You'll also learn how to specify a source document for each frame, and how to nest one set of frames inside another.

Introducing Frames

When Web sites contain several pages, each page is usually dedicated to a particular subject or set of topics. One page might contain a list of hypertext links, another page might display contact information for the company or school, and another page might describe the company's history and philosophy. As more pages are created, you might start wishing that there were some way in which the user could view information from two or more pages simultaneously. One solution would be to repeat the information on several pages, but such a solution presents problems as well. For example, it would require a great deal of time and effort to type (or copy and paste) the same information over and over again. Also, each time you wanted to change the information on one page, you would need to change the same information on all other pages in the presentation—something that is hard to do accurately.

Such considerations led to the creation of frames. **Frames** are windows that appear within the browser's display area, each capable of displaying the contents of a different HTML file. An example of a page with two frames is shown in Figure 5-1. In this example, a page consisting of hypertext links appears in a frame on the left, while the Products Home Page appears in a frame on the right.

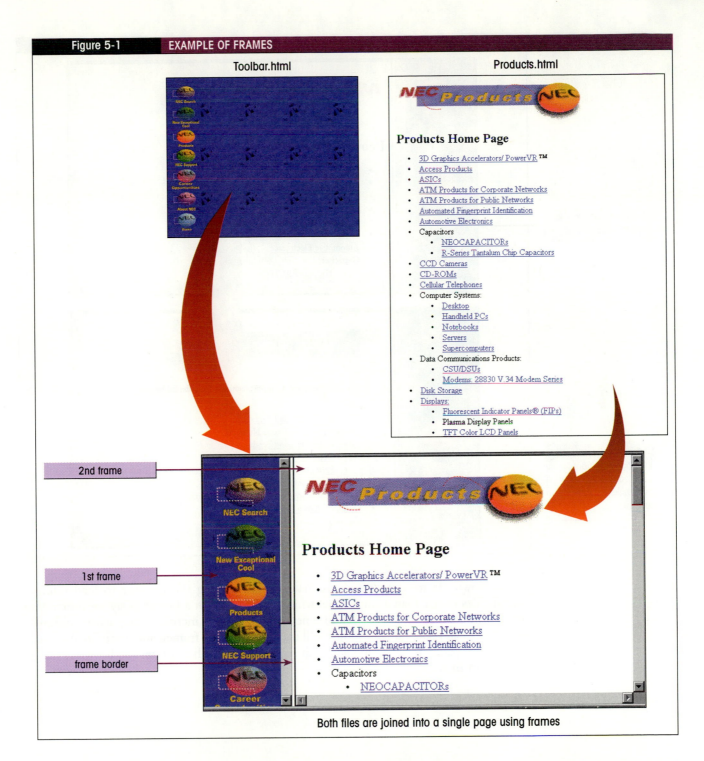

Figure 5-1   EXAMPLE OF FRAMES

Toolbar.html

Products.html

2nd frame

1st frame

frame border

Both files are joined into a single page using frames

Frames can be set up to be permanent, allowing users to move through the contents of the Web presentation while always being able to see an overall table of contents in a frame that doesn't change or disappear. Figure 5-2 illustrates how the list of hyperlinks remains on the screen while the contents of the frame on the right change, depending on which hyperlink is clicked.

Figure 5-2	ACTIVATING A HYPERLINK WITH FRAMES

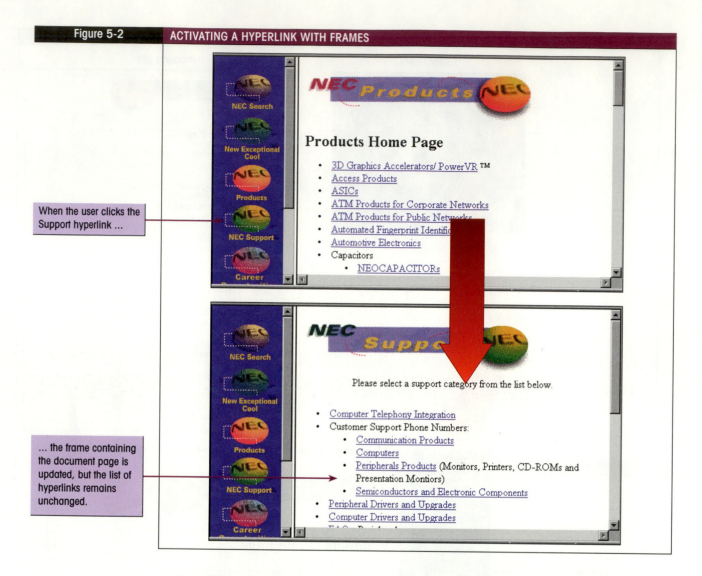

One downside to using frames is that you are causing the browser to load multiple HTML files rather than a single one, which could result in a longer delay for users. Also, not all browsers are able to display a framed page. With the increasing popularity of frames, this is less of an issue, but you should still try to create both framed and nonframed versions of your Web pages, to accommodate both users who do not like frames and browsers that do not support them.

Planning **Your Frames**

Before you start creating your frames, you should first plan their appearance and use. There are several issues to consider:

- What information will be displayed in each of the frames?
- How do you want the frames placed on the Web page? What is the size of each frame?
- Which frames will be static—that is, always showing the same content?
- Which frames will change in response to hyperlinks being clicked?
- What Web pages will users see first when they access the site?
- Do you want to allow users to resize the frames and change the layout of the page?

As you proceed in designing the Web site for The Colorado Experience, you'll consider each of these questions. Debbie has already thought about what information should be displayed on some of the pages in The Colorado Experience's Web site. Figure 5-3 lists the files for these pages.

Figure 5-3	SOME OF THE FILES AT THE COLORADO EXPERIENCE'S WEB SITE	
TOPIC	**FILENAME**	**CONTENT**
Biographies	Staff.htm	Links to biographical pages of The Colorado Experience staff
Home page	TCE.htm	The Colorado Experience home page
Lessons	Lessons.htm	Climbing lessons offered by The Colorado Experience
Logo	Head.htm	A page containing the company logo
Philosophy	Philosph.htm	Statement of The Colorado Experience's business philosophy
Table of contents	Links.htm	Links to The Colorado Experience Web pages
Tours	Diamond.htm	Description of the Diamond climbing tour
Tours	Eldorado.htm	Description of the Eldorado Canyon climbing tour
Tours	Grepon.htm	Description of the Petit Grepon climbing tour
Tours	Kieners.htm	Description of the Kiener's Route climbing tour
Tours	Lumpy.htm	Description of the Lumpy Ridge climbing tour
Tours	Nface.htm	Description of the North Face climbing tour

The files are organized into various topic areas such as pages devoted to tour descriptions, climbing lessons, and company philosophy. Two of the files, Links.htm and Staff.htm, do not cover topics, but rather contain hyperlinks to other Colorado Experience Web pages. How should this kind of material be organized on the Web site, and what should the user see first?

Debbie has considered these questions and has sketched a layout detailing how she would like the frames organized on the company's Web site (Figure 5-4).

Figure 5-4   FRAMES FOR THE COLORADO EXPERIENCE WEB SITE

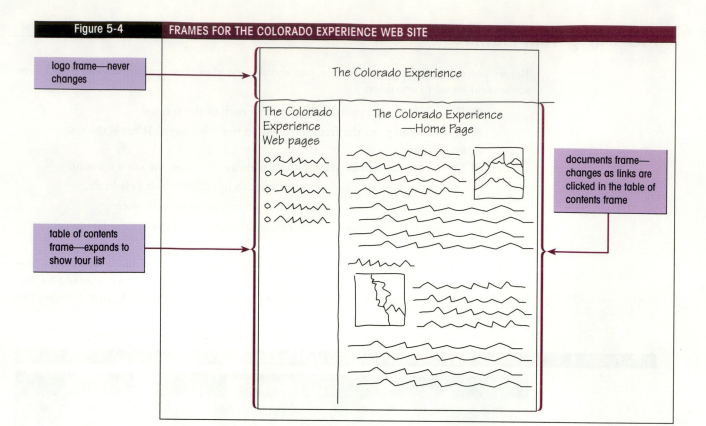

logo frame—never changes

table of contents frame—expands to show tour list

documents frame—changes as links are clicked in the table of contents frame

Debbie would like to have three frames in the presentation. The top frame will display the company logo and will always be visible to the user (that is, it will be static). She has already created this logo in the Head.htm file, listed in Figure 5-3. The frame on the left will display the table of contents page, Links.htm, with each item in the list acting as a hyperlink to a specific page. This frame, too, should always be visible, but users should be able to expand it. Finally, the frame on the right will display different Colorado Experience documents, depending on which hyperlink the user clicks in the table of contents frame. The Colorado Experience home page should be the first page that the user sees in this frame. This is a standard layout and a typical use of frames.

Your first task will be to insert the HTML code that creates the type of layout Debbie has in mind.

Creating a Frame Layout

Frame layout is defined using the <FRAMESET> tag. The general syntax for the <FRAMESET> tag in your HTML file is:

```
<HTML>
<HEAD>
<TITLE>Page Title</TITLE>
</HEAD>
<FRAMESET>
     Frame Definitions
</FRAMESET>
</HTML>
```

Notice that this code does not include the <BODY> tags. When you use the <FRAMESET> tag, you omit the <BODY> tag. The reason for this should be clear: a page with frames displays the content of other pages. There is no page body to speak of. There is one situation in which you'll use the <BODY> tag in a page with frames—when you are creating a page that can be displayed whether the browser supports frames or not. This situation is discussed later in the tutorial. You can use more than one <FRAMESET> tag in your file if you place one inside another—a technique you'll apply later in this tutorial.

Specifying Frame Size and Orientation

The <FRAMESET> tag has two properties: ROWS and COLS. You use the ROWS property when you want to create frames that are laid out in rows, and you use the COLS property to lay the frames out in columns. See Figure 5-5. You must choose only one layout for a single <FRAMESET> tag, either rows or columns. You cannot use both properties at once inside a single <FRAMESET> tag.

Figure 5-5	FRAMES DEFINED IN EITHER ROWS OR COLUMNS

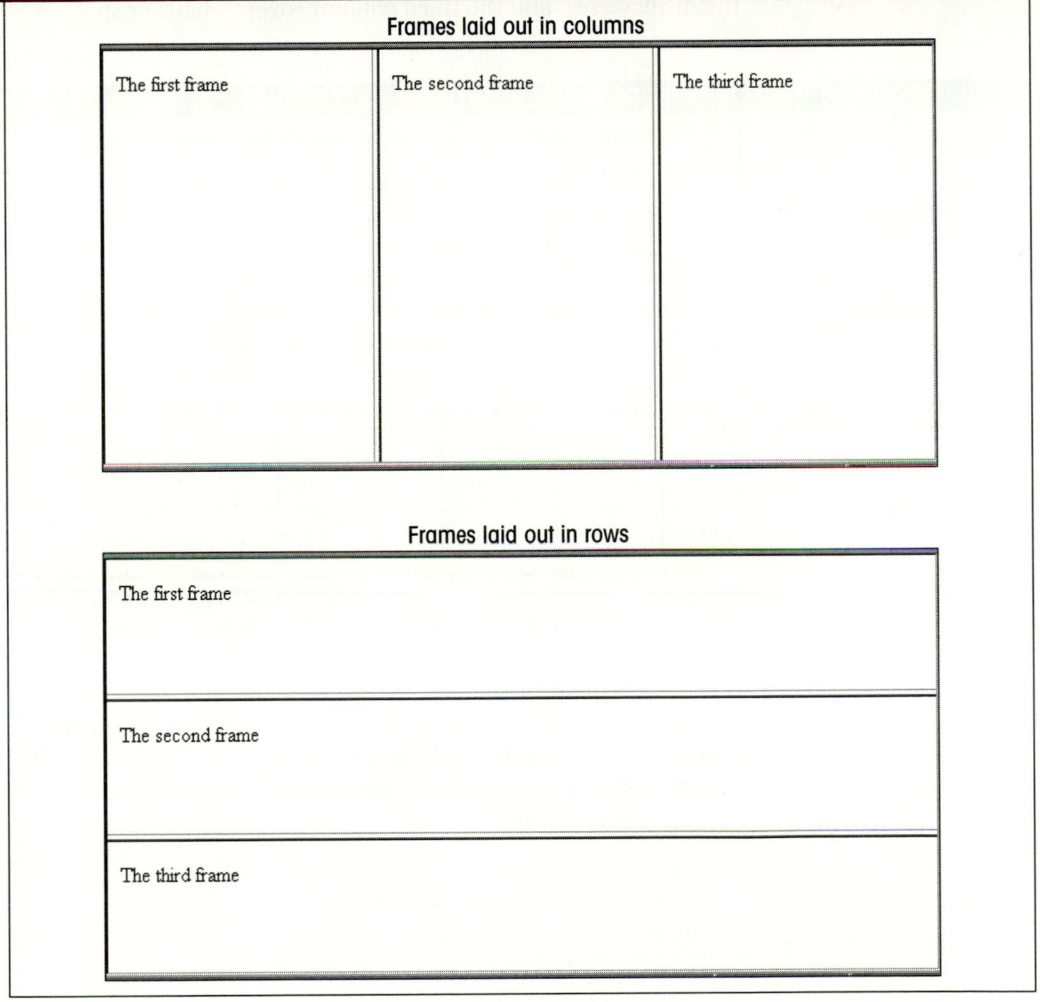

Frames laid out in columns

The first frame	The second frame	The third frame

Frames laid out in rows

The first frame

The second frame

The third frame

The syntax for specifying the row or column layout for the <FRAMESET> tag is:

`<FRAMESET ROWS="row height 1, row height 2, row height 3, . . .">`

or

`<FRAMESET COLS="column width 1, column width 2, column width 3, . . .">`

where *row height* is the height of each row, and *column width* is the width of each column. There is no limit to the number of rows or columns you can specify for a frameset.

Row and column sizes are specified in three ways: in pixels, as a percentage of the total size of the frameset, or by an asterisk (*). The asterisk tells the browser to allocate any unclaimed space in the frameset to the particular row or column. For example, the tag <FRAMESET ROWS="160,*"> creates two rows of frames. The first row has a height of 160 pixels, and the height of the second row is equal to whatever space remains in the display area. For a display area that is 400 pixels high, this would be 240 pixels.

You can use all three ways of specifying row or column size in a single <FRAMESET> tag. The tag <FRAMESET COLS="160,25%,*"> creates the series of columns shown in Figure 5-6. The first column is 160 pixels wide, the second column is 25% of the width of the display area, and the third column covers whatever space is left.

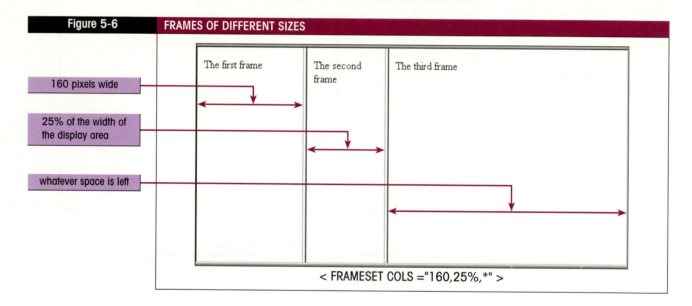

Figure 5-6 — **FRAMES OF DIFFERENT SIZES**

The first frame

The second frame

The third frame

160 pixels wide

25% of the width of the display area

whatever space is left

< FRAMESET COLS ="160,25%,*" >

At least one of the rows or columns of your <FRAMESET> tag should be specified with an asterisk to guarantee that the frames fill up the screen regardless of the user's monitor resolution. You can also include multiple asterisks, where each size is allocated to each frame with the asterisk. For example, the tag <FRAMESET ROWS="*,*,*"> creates three rows of frames with equal heights.

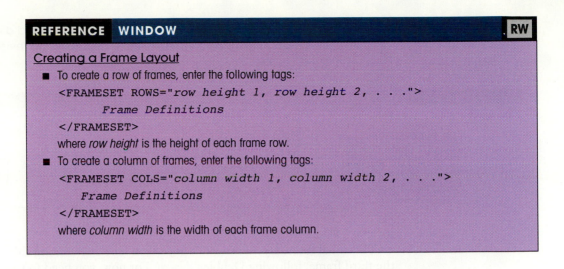

An initial file for use in setting up the frames for the Colorado Experience Web page has been created for you and saved as COLtext.htm in the Tutorial.05 folder of your Data Disk. You'll open that file now and save it with a new name.

To open the COLtext.htm file and save it with a new name:

1. Start your text editor.

2. Open the file **COLtext.htm** from the **Tutorial.05** folder on your Data Disk, and then save the file in the same folder as **Colorado.htm**.

The first set of frames you'll create for the Colorado Experience page will have two rows. The top row will be used for the company logo (saved in the Head.htm file), and the second row will be used for the rest of the page's content. A frame that is 60 pixels high should be tall enough to display the logo. The rest of the browser's display area will be taken up by the second row.

To create the first set of frames:

1. Create a new blank line directly below the </HEAD> tag in the Colorado.htm file.

2. Insert the following code:

```
<FRAMESET ROWS="60,*">
</FRAMESET>
```

This code specifies a height of 60 pixels for the top row and allocates the remaining space to the second row. Figure 5-7 shows the revised Colorado.htm file.

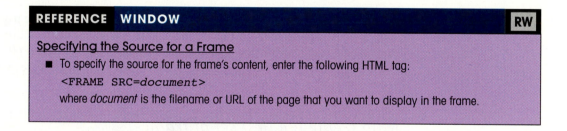

Figure 5-7 — **CREATING TWO ROWS OF FRAMES**

tag creates two rows of frames: the first 60 pixels high and the second occupying the remaining display area

```
<HTML>
<HEAD>
<TITLE>The Colorado Experience</TITLE>
</HEAD>
<FRAMESET ROWS="60,*">
</FRAMESET>
</HTML>
```

The initial frame layout is now defined. You'll be augmenting this layout later to include the third frame, following Debbie's design. For now, you need to specify the source for the two frame rows.

Specifying a Frame Source

The tag used to specify the page that will be inserted into a frame is the <FRAME> tag. The syntax for this tag is:

    <FRAME SRC=*document*>

where *document* is the URL or filename of the page that you want to load. You must insert the <FRAME> tag between the <FRAMESET> and </FRAMESET> tags.

REFERENCE WINDOW   **RW**

Specifying the Source for a Frame
- To specify the source for the frame's content, enter the following HTML tag:
      <FRAME SRC=*document*>
  where *document* is the filename or URL of the page that you want to display in the frame.

The top frame should display the Head.htm file, which contains the company logo. Figure 5-8 previews the contents of this file and its placement on the page.

Figure 5-8   **HEAD.HTM FILE CONTAINING THE COLORADO EXPERIENCE LOGO**

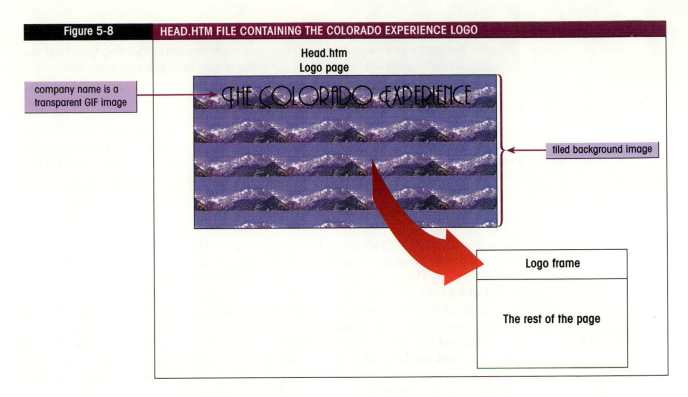

Note that the logo consists of the company name, formatted as a transparent GIF image and then placed on a tiled background of mountain images. Using a tiled background is a common technique for frames that display company logos. In this case, the advantage of this approach is that it guarantees that the mountain images will fill the frame under any monitor resolution.

To insert the Head.htm frame source:

1. Go to the end of the opening <FRAMESET> tag line, and then press the **Enter** key.

2. Type the following comment and frame source code (indent the code three spaces to make the code easier to read):

```
<!--- Company Logo --->
<FRAME SRC="Head.htm">
```

Figure 5-9 shows the inserted code.

Figure 5-9   **SPECIFYING THE SOURCE FOR THE FIRST FRAME ROW**

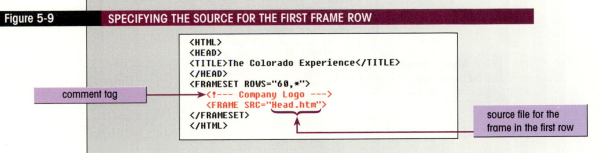

```
<HTML>
<HEAD>
<TITLE>The Colorado Experience</TITLE>
</HEAD>
<FRAMESET ROWS="60,*">
   <!--- Company Logo --->
   <FRAME SRC="Head.htm">
</FRAMESET>
</HTML>
```

comment tag

source file for the frame in the first row

> Because this is the first <FRAME> tag, the browser will display the Head.htm file in the first frame row. Note that using the comment tag and indenting the <FRAME> tag a few spaces will help make your code easier to follow and interpret.

You've specified the source for the first row of the layout, but what about the second row? Looking back at Debbie's sketch in Figure 5-4, you notice that this row will contain two additional frames. So rather than specify a source for the second row, you have to create another set of frames. To do this, you have to nest a second set of <FRAMESET> tags within the first.

Nesting <FRAMESET> Tags

Because a <FRAMESET> tag can include either a ROWS property or a COLS property, but not both, you have to nest <FRAMESET> tags if you want to create a grid of frames on your Web page. When you do this, the meaning of the ROWS or COLS property for the nested <FRAMESET> tag changes slightly. For example, a row height of 25% does not mean 25% of the display area, but rather 25% of the height of the frame into which that row has been inserted (or nested).

The second row of your current frame layout should consist of two columns. The first column should display a table of contents, and the second column should display various Colorado Experience documents. You'll specify a width of 140 pixels for the first column, and whatever remains in the display area will be allotted to the second column.

To create the second set of frames:

1. Go to the end of the <FRAME> tag line that you just inserted, and then press the **Enter** key to create a blank line below it.

2. Type the following code (indent the text three spaces to make the code easier to follow):

```
<!--- Nested frames --->
<FRAMESET COLS="140,*">
</FRAMESET>
```

Your file should appear as shown in Figure 5-10.

| Figure 5-10 | CREATING A NESTED SET OF FRAMES IN THE SECOND FRAME ROW |

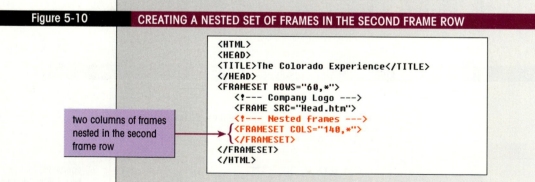

two columns of frames nested in the second frame row

```
<HTML>
<HEAD>
<TITLE>The Colorado Experience</TITLE>
</HEAD>
<FRAMESET ROWS="60,*">
   <!--- Company Logo --->
   <FRAME SRC="Head.htm">
   <!--- Nested frames --->
   <FRAMESET COLS="140,*">
   </FRAMESET>
</FRAMESET>
</HTML>
```

Next you'll specify the sources for the two frames in this row. The frame in the first column should display the contents of the Links.htm file. The Colorado Experience home page, stored in the TCE.htm file, should appear in the second frame. Figure 5-11 shows the content of these two pages and their placement on the Web page.

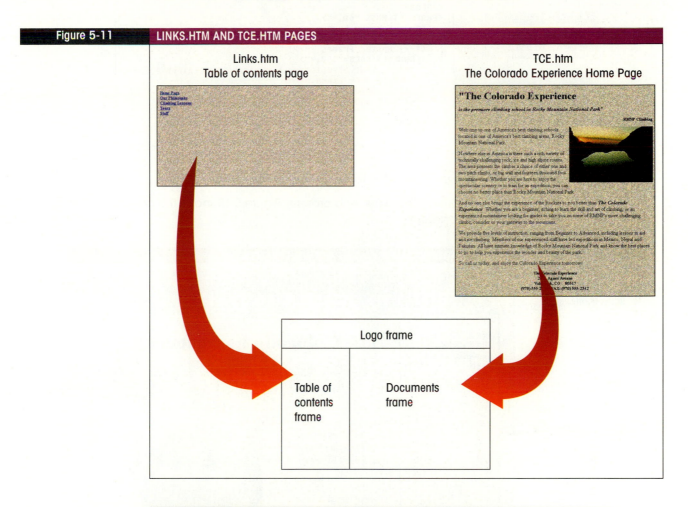

Figure 5-11   **LINKS.HTM AND TCE.HTM PAGES**

To insert the sources for the two frames:

1. Insert a blank line below the nested <FRAMESET> tag you just created.

2. Type the following code, indented six spaces (to make the code easier to read):

```
<!--- List of Colorado Experience hyperlinks --->
<FRAME SRC="Links.htm">
<!--- Colorado Experience Web pages --->
<FRAME SRC="TCE.htm">
```

Figure 5-12 shows the code for the two new frames.

Figure 5-12   SOURCES FOR THE TWO FRAMES IN THE SECOND ROW

table of contents will appear in first column of the nested frame

the Colorado Experience home page will appear in second column of the nested frame

```
<HTML>
<HEAD>
<TITLE>The Colorado Experience</TITLE>
</HEAD>
<FRAMESET ROWS="60,*">
    <!--- Company Logo --->
    <FRAME SRC="Head.htm">
    <!--- Nested frames --->
    <FRAMESET COLS="140,*">
        <!--- List of Colorado Experience hyperlinks --->
        <FRAME SRC="Links.htm">
        <!--- Colorado Experience Web pages --->
        <FRAME SRC="TCE.htm">
    </FRAMESET>
</FRAMESET>
</HTML>
```

3. Save your changes to the Colorado.htm file.

4. Open the file in your Web browser. Figure 5-13 shows the page's current appearance.

Figure 5-13   COLORADO EXPERIENCE WEB PAGE WITH FRAMES

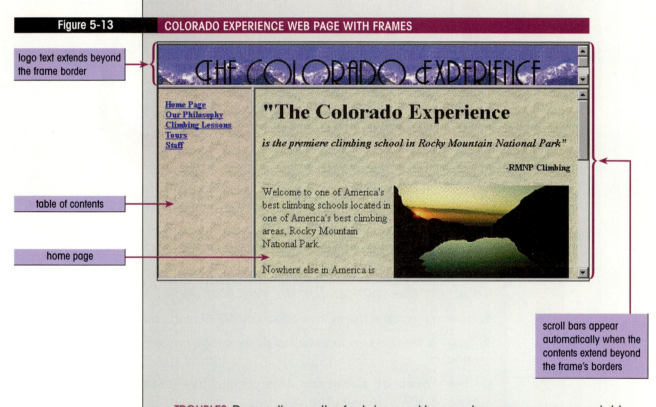

logo text extends beyond the frame border

table of contents

home page

scroll bars appear automatically when the contents extend beyond the frame's borders

TROUBLE? Depending on the font size used by your browser, your page might look slightly different.

The page shows the three HTML files that Debbie wants on the page. However, the page's appearance needs some improvement. The company name is cut off in the logo frame, which also causes a scroll bar to appear. Scroll bars appear whenever the contents of a page overflow the size of the frame. For example, scroll bars do not appear in the links frame, because the entire list of links is visible, but they do appear in the home page frame, because its contents are not completely visible. You can use the scroll bars to see the rest of the home page, but do not click any hypertext links yet. You will be working with hyperlinks in frames in the next session. For now, your task is to control how each frame appears on the page.

Controlling the Appearance of Your Frames

You can control three properties of a frame's appearance: the frame's scroll bars, the size of the margin between the source document and the frame border, and whether or not the user is allowed to change the frame's width or height.

REFERENCE WINDOW	RW

Changing the Appearance of Frames

- To control the appearance of a frame's scroll bars, add the SCROLLING property to the FRAME tag as follows:

  `<FRAME SRC=document SCROLLING=value>`

  where *value* can be either YES (to display scroll bars) or NO (to remove scroll bars). If you do not specify the SCROLLING property, scroll bars will appear only when the content of the frame source cannot fit within the frame's boundaries.

- To control the amount of space between the frame source and the frame boundary, add the MARGINWIDTH and/or the MARGINHEIGHT properties to the FRAME tag:

  `<FRAME SRC=document MARGINWIDTH=value MARGINHEIGHT=value>`

  where the width and height *value* is expressed in pixels. The margin width is the space to the left and right of the frame source. The margin height is the space above and below the frame source. If you do not specify a margin height or width, the browser will assign dimensions based on the content of the frame source.

- To keep users from resizing frames, add the NORESIZE property to the FRAME tag:

  `<FRAME SRC=document NORESIZE>`

The first property you'll work with is the property for controlling scroll bars.

Controlling the Appearance of Scroll Bars

By default, scroll bars appear whenever the content of the source page cannot fit within the frame. You can override this setting by using the SCROLLING property. The syntax for this property is:

`<FRAME SRC=document SCROLLING=value>`

where *value* can either be YES (to always display scroll bars) or NO (to never display scroll bars). If you don't specify a setting for the SCROLLING property, the browser will display scroll bars whenever it needs to.

Because the logo is not centered vertically within its frame and, therefore, not entirely visible, scroll bars appear on the right side of the logo frame. Debbie feels that scroll bars are inappropriate for the logo frame, and wants to make sure that it never displays them. Therefore, you need to add the SCROLLING=NO property to the logo <FRAME> tag. However, Debbie does want scroll bars to appear for the other two frames, as needed, so you won't specify this property for their <FRAME> tags.

Note that when you are making changes to a framed Web page with Netscape Navigator, you will have to reopen the file to view the changes. If you simply click the Reload button, you will not see the results of your modifications. This is not the case with Internet Explorer 3.0 and above, in which you can view changes to the page by clicking the Refresh button.

To remove the scroll bars from the logo frame:

1. Return to the Colorado.htm file in your text editor.

2. Within the <FRAME> tag for the logo frame, enter the property **SCROLLING=NO**, as shown in Figure 5-14.

Figure 5-14	REMOVING THE SCROLL BARS FROM THE LOGO FRAME

set SCROLLING equal to NO to remove scroll bars from the logo frame

```
<FRAMESET ROWS="60,*">
   <!--- Company Logo --->
   <FRAME SRC="Head.htm" SCROLLING=NO>
   <!--- Nested frames --->
   <FRAMESET COLS="140,*">
      <!--- List of Colorado Experience hyperlinks --->
      <FRAME SRC="Links.htm">
      <!--- Colorado Experience Web pages --->
      <FRAME SRC="TCE.htm">
   </FRAMESET>
</FRAMESET>
```

3. Save your changes, and then view the file in your Web browser. You might have to reopen (rather than just reload) the Colorado.htm file to see the effects of your code changes.

Note that although the scroll bars for the logo frame have been removed, the logo itself is still not centered vertically within the frame. You'll correct this problem next by setting the frame margins.

When designing your Web pages, keep in mind that you should remove scroll bars from a frame only when you are convinced that all the contents of the frame source will be displayed in the frame. To do this, you should view your page using several different monitor resolutions. A particular frame's contents might be displayed correctly in 800×600 resolution or higher, but this might not be the case with a resolution of 640×480. Few things are more irritating to users than to discover that some content is missing from a frame with no scroll bars available to display the missing content.

With that in mind, your next task is to solve the problem of the off-centered logo. To do so, you have to modify the internal margins of the frame.

Controlling Frame Margins

When your browser retrieves a Web page to display inside a frame, it automatically determines the amount of space between the page's content and the frame border. Sometimes the browser makes the margin between the border and the content too large. Generally you want the margin to be big enough to keep the source's text or images from running into the frame's borders; however, you do not want the margin to take up too much space, because you usually want to display as much of the source as possible.

You've already noted that the margin height for the logo frame is too large and has caused part of the logo's text to be pushed down beyond the frame's border. To fix this problem, you need to specify a smaller margin for the frame. This should cause the logo to move up in the frame and allow the entire text to be displayed.

The syntax for specifying the frame's margin is:

`<FRAME SRC=`*`document`*` MARGINHEIGHT=`*`value`*` MARGINWIDTH=`*`value`*`>`

Here, MARGINHEIGHT is the amount of space (in pixels) that appears above and below the content of the page in the frame, and MARGNWIDTH is the amount of space that appears to the page's left and right. You do not have to specify both the margin height and width; however, if you specify only one, the browser will assume that you want to use the same value for both. In general you will want to have margin sizes of 0 or 1 pixels for frames that display only an inline image (like the logo frame), and 5 to 10 pixels for frames that display text (such as the frame that is displaying the Colorado Experience home page). Setting margin values is a process of trial and error, as you try to determine what combination of margin sizes looks best.

To correct the problem with the logo frame, you'll decrease its margin size to 0 pixels. This setting should allow the complete logo to be displayed within the frame. Also, to keep the home page text from running into the frame borders, you'll specify a margin width of 10 pixels for its frame. However, since Debbie would like users to be able to view more of the home page without scrolling, she asks you to decrease the margin height for the home page frame to 0 pixels. The links frame margin does not require any changes.

To set the margin sizes for the frames:

1. Return to the Colorado.htm file in your text editor.

2. Within the <FRAME> tag for the logo frame, enter the property **MARGINHEIGHT=0**. This will, by default, set both the margin height and the margin width to 0.

3. Within the <FRAME> tag for the home page frame, enter the properties **MARGINHEIGHT=0 MARGINWIDTH=10**.

   Figure 5-15 shows the revised HTML code in the Colorado.htm file.

Figure 5-15   SPECIFYING THE MARGIN SIZES FOR THE FRAMES

```
<FRAMESET ROWS="60,*">
   <!--- Company Logo --->
   <FRAME SRC="Head.htm" SCROLLING=NO MARGINHEIGHT=0>
   <!--- Nested frames --->
   <FRAMESET COLS="140,*">
      <!--- List of Colorado Experience hyperlinks --->
      <FRAME SRC="Links.htm">
      <!--- Colorado Experience Web pages --->
      <FRAME SRC="TCE.htm" MARGINHEIGHT=0 MARGINWIDTH=10>
   </FRAMESET>
</FRAMESET>
```

height of the margin for the logo frame will be 0 pixels

height of the margin for the home page frame will be 0 pixels, and the width will be 10 pixels

4. Save your changes, and then reload the file in your Web browser. (Netscape Navigator users might have to reopen the file to see the changes.) The revised appearance of the Colorado Experience page is shown in Figure 5-16.

Figure 5-16

COLORADO EXPERIENCE PAGE WITH RESIZED FRAME MARGINS

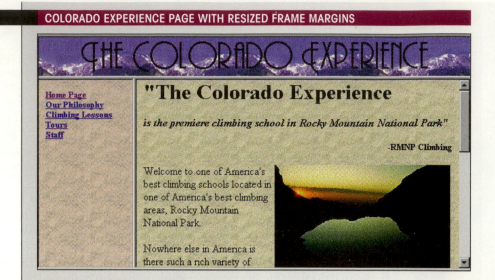

Debbie is satisfied with the changes to the page's appearance. Your next task is to "lock in" the sizes and margins for each frame on the page, to prevent users from moving the borders.

Controlling Frame Resizing

By default, users can resize frame borders in the browser by dragging a frame border. This allows them to see more of a frame's content without scrolling. However, some Web authors prefer to freeze the size of the frames, so that users cannot drag the frame borders. To do this for the Colorado Experience page, you have to specify that the frame borders cannot be resized. The syntax for controlling frame resizing is:

```
<FRAME SRC=document NORESIZE>
```

The NORESIZE property takes no value—you simply include it within the <FRAME> tag to prevent users from modifying the size of your frames. You'll add this property now to all the frames in the Colorado.htm file.

To prevent the frames from being resized:

1. Return to your text editor and the Colorado.htm file.

2. Add the property **NORESIZE** within each of the three <FRAME> tags in the file.

3. Save your changes, and then reload the file in your Web browser. Verify that you cannot resize any of the frames.

You've completed your work with the frame layout and appearance for the Web presentation for The Colorado Experience. Debbie is pleased with the progress you've made. The page is not yet finished, however. You still must specify how the hyperlinks interact between one frame and another. You'll do this in the next session.

Session 5.1 QUICK CHECK

1. What are frames, and why are they useful in displaying a Web presentation?

2. Why is the <BODY> tag unnecessary for pages that contain frames?

3. What code would you enter to create three rows of frames with the height of the first row set to 200 pixels, the height of the second row set to 50% of the display area, and the height of the third row set to the space that is left?

4. What code would you enter to use the Home.htm file as a source for a frame?

5. What code would you enter to remove the scroll bars from the frame for the Home.htm file?

6. What code would you enter to set the size of the margin above and below the Home.htm frame to 3 pixels?

7. What is the size of the margin to the right and left of the frame in Quick Check 6?

8. What code would you enter to keep users from moving the frame borders for the Home.htm file?

SESSION 5.2

In this session you will learn how hyperlinks work within frames. You will control which frame displays the source of an activated hyperlink. You'll also learn how to create a Web page that can be used both by browsers that support frames and browsers that do not. Finally, you'll examine some extensions to the <FRAME> and <FRAMESET> tags, and you'll learn how to create internal frames, using the <IFRAME> tag.

Working with Frames and Hypertext Links

Now that you've created the necessary frames for the Colorado Experience Web page, you're ready to work on the hypertext links on the page. The table of contents frame contains five hyperlinks: Home Page, Our Philosophy, Climbing Lessons, Tours, and Staff. Figure 5-17 shows the files to which each of these hyperlinks points. The Home Page link points to the TCE.htm file; the Our Philosophy link points to Philosph.htm; Climbing Lessons points to Lessons.htm; Tours points to Tours.htm; Staff points to the Staff.htm file.

Figure 5-17   **HYPERLINKS FROM THE TABLE OF CONTENTS FRAME**

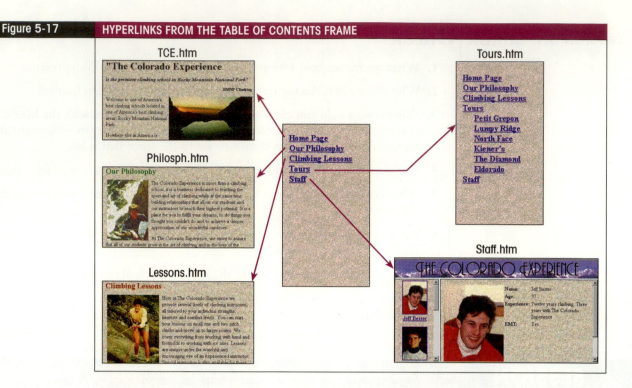

By default, clicking a hyperlink within a frame will open the linked file inside the same frame. However, this is not the way Debbie wants each of the hyperlinks to work. She wants the Home Page, Our Philosophy, and Climbing Lessons pages to open in the frame currently occupied by the home page. She wants the Tours page to replace the current table of contents, and, finally, she wants the Staff page to replace the entire frame structure.

When you want to control the behavior of hyperlinks in a framed page, you have to do two things: give each frame on the page a name and then point each hyperlink to one of those named frames.

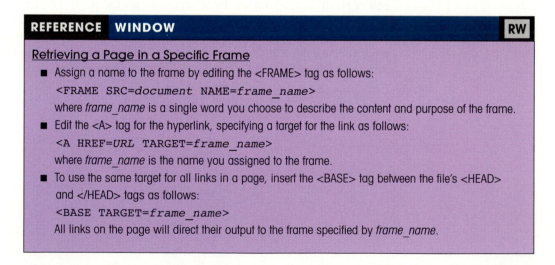

REFERENCE WINDOW   **RW**

Retrieving a Page in a Specific Frame

- Assign a name to the frame by editing the <FRAME> tag as follows:

  `<FRAME SRC=document NAME=frame_name>`

  where *frame_name* is a single word you choose to describe the content and purpose of the frame.

- Edit the <A> tag for the hyperlink, specifying a target for the link as follows:

  `<A HREF=URL TARGET=frame_name>`

  where *frame_name* is the name you assigned to the frame.

- To use the same target for all links in a page, insert the <BASE> tag between the file's <HEAD> and </HEAD> tags as follows:

  `<BASE TARGET=frame_name>`

  All links on the page will direct their output to the frame specified by *frame_name*.

Assigning a Name to a Frame

To assign a name to a frame, you add the NAME property to the FRAME tag. The syntax for this property is:

```
<FRAME SRC=document NAME=frame_name>
```

where *frame_name* is any single word you want to assign to the frame. Case is important in assigning names. A frame named "information" is different from one named "INFORMATION."

You'll name the three frames in the Colorado Experience page "Logo," "Links," and "Documents."

To assign names to the frames:

1. If you took a break after the previous session, start your text editor and open the **Colorado.htm** file.

2. Within the tag for the logo frame, enter the property **NAME=Logo**.

3. Within the tag for the links frame, enter the property **NAME=Links**.

4. Within the tag for the home page frame, enter the property **NAME=Documents**. Figure 5-18 shows the revised code for the Colorado.htm file.

Figure 5-18   ASSIGNING A NAME TO EACH FRAME

```
<!--- Company Logo --->
<FRAME SRC="Head.htm" SCROLLING=NO MARGINHEIGHT=0 NORESIZE NAME=Logo>
<!--- Nested frames --->
<FRAMESET COLS="140,*">
    <!--- List of Colorado Experience hyperlinks --->
    <FRAME SRC="Links.htm" NORESIZE NAME=Links>
    <!--- Colorado Experience Web pages --->
    <FRAME SRC="TCE.htm" MARGINHEIGHT=0 MARGINWIDTH=10 NORESIZE NAME=Documents>
</FRAMESET>
```

5. Save your changes to the Colorado.htm file.

Now that you've named the frames, your next task is to specify the Documents frame as the target for the Home Page, Our Philosophy, and Climbing Lessons hyperlinks, so that clicking each of these links will open the corresponding file in the home page frame.

Specifying a Link Target

To display a page within a specific frame of another page, you add the TARGET property to the <A> tag of the hyperlink. Recall that the <A> tag is used to specify a hyperlink. The syntax for this property is:

```
<A HREF=URL TARGET=frame_name>
```

where *frame_name* is the name you've assigned to a frame on your page. In this case the target name for the frame you need to specify is "Documents." To change the targets for the links, you have to edit the <A> tags in the Links.htm file. You'll start by editing only the <A> tags pointing to the Home Page, Our Philosophy, and Climbing Lessons pages—the ones you want displayed in the Documents frame of the Colorado.htm file. You'll work with the other hyperlinks later.

To specify the targets for the hypertext links:

1. In your text editor, open the **Links.htm** file from the **Tutorial.05** folder on your Data Disk.

2. Within the <A> tag for the Home Page, Our Philosophy, and Climbing Lessons hyperlinks, enter the property **TARGET=Documents**. The revised code is shown in Figure 5-19.

Figure 5-19	ASSIGNING A TARGET TO A HYPERLINK

the Web page will appear within the Documents frame

```
<A HREF="TCE.htm" TARGET=Documents>Home Page</A><BR>
<A HREF="Philosph.htm" TARGET=Documents>Our Philosophy</A><BR>
<A HREF="Lessons.htm" TARGET=Documents>Climbing Lessons</A><BR>
<A HREF="Tours.htm">Tours</A><BR>
<A HREF="Staff.htm">Staff</A>
```

3. Save the modified file.

    TROUBLE? If you need to return to the original version of the file, you can use the Linktext.htm file also found in the Tutorial.05 folder of your Data Disk.

    Now test the first three hyperlinks in the list.

4. Open the **Colorado.htm** file in your Web browser.

5. Click the **Our Philosophy** link in the Links frame. The Our Philosophy Web page appears in the Documents frame. See Figure 5-20.

Figure 5-20	THE OUR PHILOSOPHY PAGE IN THE DOCUMENTS FRAME

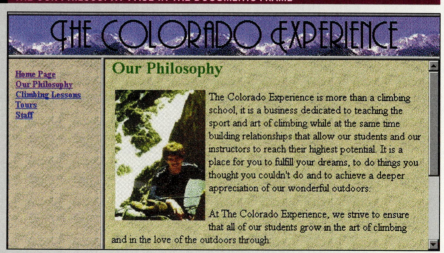

TROUBLE? If the Our Philosophy page appears in the left frame, you either have to reload or reopen the Colorado.htm file.

6. Click the **Home Page** and **Climbing Lessons** links to verify that the links are working properly and the pages are appearing in the Documents frame.

Sometimes a table of contents frame will contain many hyperlinks that the Web author wants to open in the same frame. It would be tedious to type TARGET properties for each link. Fortunately, HTML gives you a way to specify a target for all the hyperlinks in a single file.

Using the <BASE> Tag

The <BASE> tag appears within the <HEAD> tags of your HTML file and is used to specify global options for the page. One of the properties of the <BASE> tag is the TARGET property, which identifies a default target for all of the page's hyperlinks. The syntax for this property is:

```
<BASE TARGET=frame_name>
```

where *frame_name* is the name of the target frame. The <BASE> tag is useful when your page contains a lot of hypertext links that all point to the same target. Rather than adding the TARGET property to each <A> tag, you can enter the information only once with the <BASE> tag.

You can use the <BASE> tag even if your file contains a few links that you do not want pointing to the target in the <BASE> tag. You can specify a different target for any links that should open in a different location. When the <BASE> tag points to one target, and an individual <A> tag points to a different target, the target in the <A> tag takes precedence for that link.

To see how the <BASE> tag works, you'll use it to specify the Documents frame as the default target for all hyperlinks in the Links.htm file. In the process you'll remove the TARGET properties you've just entered.

To specify a default target with the <BASE> tag:

1. Return to the Links.htm file in your text editor.

2. Delete from the three <A> tags the TARGET=Documents properties you entered previously.

3. Insert the line **<BASE TARGET=Documents>** directly above the </HEAD> tag, as shown in Figure 5-21.

Figure 5-21	SPECIFYING A DEFAULT TARGET FOR ALL HYPERLINKS

```
<HTML>
<HEAD>
<TITLE>The Colorado Experience Hypertext Links</TITLE>
<BASE TARGET=Documents>
</HEAD>
<BODY BACKGROUND="Wall2.jpg">
<FONT SIZE=2><B>
<A HREF="TCE.htm">Home Page</A><BR>
<A HREF="Philosph.htm">Our Philosophy</A><BR>
<A HREF="Lessons.htm">Climbing Lessons</A><BR>
<A HREF="Tours.htm">Tours</A><BR>
<A HREF="Staff.htm">Staff</A>
</B></FONT>
</BODY>
</HTML>
```

by default, all pages will appear in the Documents frame

4. Save your changes, and then reload the Colorado.htm file in your Web browser. You might have to reopen the file to see the changes.

5. Test the **Home Page**, **Our Philosophy**, and **Climbing Lessons** hypertext links to verify that the pages still appear within the Documents frame. Do not test the other hyperlinks yet.

TROUBLE? If any hyperlinks do not work correctly, check the frame name and target name to verify that they match exactly, both in spelling and use of uppercase and lowercase letters.

You've so far worked with only the first three hyperlinks in the list. The remaining two links require different methods, since Debbie wants them to appear in different frames.

Using Magic Target Names

The last two tags in the list of hypertext links point to a list of the tours offered by The Colorado Experience and to a staff information page, respectively. The Tours hypertext link points to the Tours.htm file. The Tours.htm file does not contain any information about individual tours; instead, it is an expanded table of contents of Colorado Experience Web pages, some of which are devoted to individual tours. Each tour has its own Web page, as shown in Figure 5-22.

Figure 5-22	TOURS PAGE WITH HYPERLINKS TO EACH TOUR

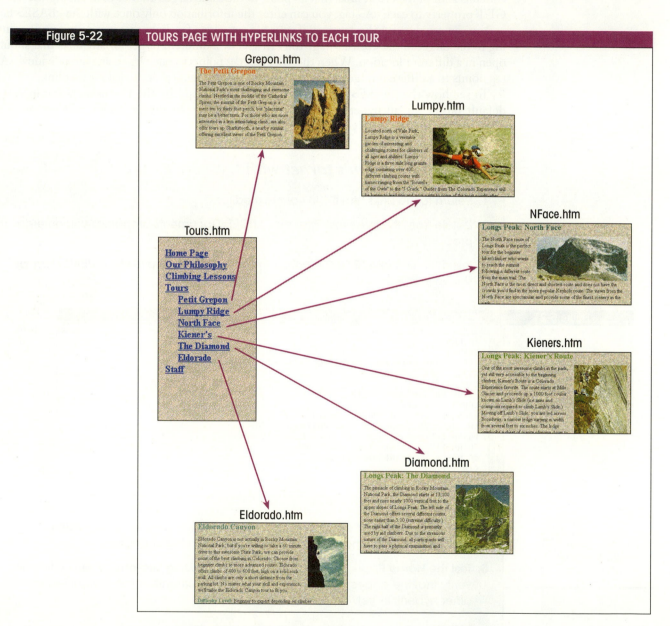

Debbie wants the Tours.htm file to appear in the Links frame. This will give the effect of expanding the table of contents whenever a user clicks the Tours hypertext link. Because the Tours.htm page will appear in the Links frame, you could specify Links (the name of the frame) as its target. However, there is another way to do this with magic target names.

Magic target names are special names that can be used in place of a frame name as a target for a hypertext link. Magic target names are useful in situations where you want the page to appear in a new window or to replace the current frame layout. Figure 5-23 lists and describes the magic target names.

Figure 5-23	MAGIC TARGET NAMES

MAGIC TARGET NAME	DESCRIPTION
_blank	Loads the document into a new browser window
_self	Loads the document into the same frame or window that contains the hyperlink tag
_parent	In a layout of nested frames, loads the document into the frame that contains the frame with the hyperlink tag
_top	Loads the document into the full display area, replacing the current frame layout

All magic target names begin with the underscore character (_) to distinguish them from other target names. Note that magic target names are case-sensitive, so you must enter them in lowercase.

Because Debbie wants the contents of the Tours.htm file to appear in the Links frame, you can use the _self magic target name, which will take precedence over the <BASE> tag and directs the browser to open the page in the same frame that contains the hypertext link.

To use the magic target name to specify the target for the Tours link:

1. Return to the Links.htm file in your text editor.

2. Within the <A> tag for the Tours hypertext link, enter the property **TARGET=_self**. See Figure 5-24.

Figure 5-24	USING THE _SELF MAGIC TARGET NAME IN THE LINKS.HTM FILE

```
<HTML>
<HEAD>
<TITLE>The Colorado Experience Hypertext Links</TITLE>
<BASE TARGET=Documents>
</HEAD>
<BODY BACKGROUND="Wall2.jpg">
<FONT SIZE=2><B>
<A HREF="TCE.htm">Home Page</A><BR>
<A HREF="Philosph.htm">Our Philosophy</A><BR>
<A HREF="Lessons.htm">Climbing Lessons</A><BR>
<A HREF="Tours.htm" TARGET=_self>Tours</A><BR>
<A HREF="Staff.htm">Staff</A>
</B></FONT>
</BODY>
</HTML>
```

page will appear in the frame containing the hyperlink

3. Save your changes to the Links.htm file.

The Tours.htm file is an expanded table of contents for Web pages containing information about specific tours; Debbie wants each of these pages to appear in the Documents frame. To do this, you need to specify the Documents frame as the default hyperlink target in the Tours.htm file. The Tours.htm file also contains a hyperlink that takes the user back to the Links.htm file. You should specify _self as the target for this hyperlink.

To modify the Tours.htm file as you did the Links.htm file:

1. In your text editor, open the **Tours.htm** file from the **Tutorial.05** folder on your Data Disk.

2. Insert the tag **<BASE TARGET=Documents>** directly above the </HEAD> tag. This will make the individual tour pages appear in the Documents frame when a user clicks any of the tour hyperlinks.

3. Within the <A> tag that points to the Links.htm file, enter the property **TARGET=_self**. This will redisplay the Links.htm file, containing the original table of contents, in the Links frame. See Figure 5-25.

Figure 5-25	REVISED TOURS.HTM FILE

the default hyperlink target is the Documents frame

clicking this link displays the Links.htm file

```
<HTML>
<HEAD>
<TITLE>The Colorado Experience Hypertext Links</TITLE>
<BASE TARGET=Documents>
</HEAD>
<BODY BACKGROUND="Wall2.jpg">
<FONT SIZE=2 COLOR=BLUE><B>
<A HREF="TCE.htm">Home Page</A><BR>
<A HREF="Philosph.htm">Our Philosophy</A><BR>
<A HREF="Lessons.htm">Climbing Lessons</A><BR>
<A HREF="Links.htm" TARGET=_self>Tours</A><BR>
      <A HREF="Grepon.htm">Petit Grepon</A><BR>
      <A HREF="Lumpy.htm">Lumpy Ridge</A><BR>
      <A HREF="NFace.htm">North Face</A><BR>
      <A HREF="Kieners.htm">Kiener's</A><BR>
      <A HREF="Diamond.htm">The Diamond</A><BR>
      <A HREF="Eldorado.htm">Eldorado</A><BR>
<A HREF="Staff.htm">Staff</A>
</B></FONT>
</BODY>
</HTML>
```

4. Save your changes to the Tours.htm file.

   TROUBLE? The original version of the Tours.htm file is stored in the Tutorial.05 folder of your Data Disk as Tourtext.htm, in case you need to return to the original version for some reason.

5. Return to your Web browser and refresh the Colorado.htm file. (You might have reopen the page if you're using the Netscape browser.)

6. Click the **Tours** link and verify that the tours list appears to alternately expand and contract as you click it. Also click the individual tour pages and verify that they appear in the Documents frame. See Figure 5-26.

Figure 5-26	VIEWING A TOUR PAGE

tour list

currently selected tour

The technique employed here is one commonly used for tables of contents that double as hypertext links. Clicking the Tours hyperlink gives the effect that the list is expanding and contracting, but what is actually happening is that one table of contents file is being replaced by another. You'll see this technique used on other pages on the Web.

The last link in the list points to a page of staff biographies, stored in the Staff.htm file. Debbie asked another employee to produce the contents of this page. The results are shown in Figure 5-27.

Figure 5-27	STAFF WEB PAGE

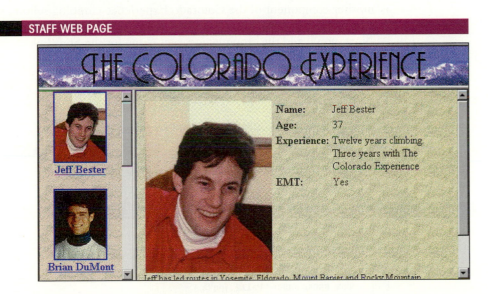

As you can see, this page also uses frames. How should this page be displayed within your frame layout? If you use the Documents frame as the target, you'll end up with the series of nested frame images shown in Figure 5-28.

Figure 5-28   ONE SET OF FRAMES APPEARING INSIDE ANOTHER

This is not what Debbie wants. She wants the Staff page to load into the full display area, replacing the frame layout with its own layout. To target a link to the full display area, you use the _top magic target name. The _top target is often used when one framed page is accessed from another. It's also used when you are linking to pages that lie outside your Web presentation, such as to pages on the World Wide Web. For example, a link to the Colorado Tourism Board Web site should not appear within a frame on the Colorado Experience page for two reasons. First, once you go outside your Web presentation, you lose control of the frame layout, and you could easily end up with nested frame images. The second reason is that such a setup could confuse users, making it appear as if the Colorado Tourism Board is another component of the Colorado Experience climbing school, which would create an inaccurate impression.

Next, you'll add the _top magic target name for the Staff link to the link's <A> tag.

To use the _top magic target name to specify the target for the Staff link:

1. Open the **Links.htm** file in your text editor.

2. Within the <A> tag for the Staff link, enter the property **TARGET=_top**. See Figure 5-29.

Figure 5-29   REVISED LINKS.HTM FILE USING THE _TOP MAGIC TARGET NAME

```
<HTML>
<HEAD>
<TITLE>The Colorado Experience Hypertext Links</TITLE>
<BASE TARGET=Documents>
</HEAD>
<BODY BACKGROUND="Wall2.jpg">
<FONT SIZE=2><B>
<A HREF="TCE.htm">Home Page</A><BR>
<A HREF="Philosph.htm">Our Philosophy</A><BR>
<A HREF="Lessons.htm">Climbing Lessons</A><BR>
<A HREF="Tours.htm" TARGET=_self>Tours</A><BR>
<A HREF="Staff.htm" TARGET=_top>Staff</A>
</B></FONT>
</BODY>
</HTML>
```

target is the _top magic name, superceding the current frame layout

3. Save your changes to the Links.htm file.

Because the Tours.htm file also acts as a table of contents (with the added references to the tour pages), you should also edit the hyperlink to the Staff page in that file. In this way, a user can click the Staff hyperlink from both the table of contents with the expanded list of tours and the original table of contents.

To edit the Tours.htm file:

1. Open the **Tours.htm** file in your text editor.

2. Within the <A> tag for the Staff link, enter the property **TARGET=_top**.

3. Save your changes to the Tours.htm file.

4. Reopen the Colorado Experience page in your Web browser and verify that the Staff link now opens the Staff page and replaces the existing frame layout with its own. Be sure to test the Staff link from both the original table of contents and the table of contents with the expanded list of tours.

   TROUBLE? If the Staff link does not work properly, verify that you used lowercase letters for the magic target name.

Debbie has viewed all the hypertext links on the Colorado Experience page and is satisfied with the results. However, she wonders what would happen if a user with an older browser encountered the page. Is there some way to accommodate browsers that don't support frames? Yes, by using the <NOFRAMES> tag.

Using the <NOFRAMES> Tag

If you want your page to be viewable by browsers that do not support frames, as well as by those that do, you need to use the <NOFRAMES> tags, which identify a section of your HTML file that contains code to be read by frame-blind browsers. The general syntax for the <NOFRAMES> tag is:

```
<HTML>
<HEAD>
<TITLE>Page Title</TITLE>
</HEAD>
<FRAMESET>
      Frame Definitions
</FRAMESET>
<NOFRAMES>
<BODY>
      Page Layout
</BODY>
</NOFRAMES>
</HTML>
```

If a browser that supports frames retrieves this code, it knows that it should ignore everything within the <NOFRAMES> tags and concentrate solely on the code within the <FRAMESET> tags. If a browser that doesn't support frames retrieves this code, it doesn't know what to do with the <FRAMESET> and <NOFRAMES> tags, so it just ignores them. However it does know that it's supposed to render whatever appears within the <BODY> tags on the page. In this way, both types of browsers are supported within a single HTML file. Note that when you use the <NOFRAMES> tag, you need to include <BODY> tags to indicate to frame-blind browsers what to display on the page.

The Colorado Experience has been using a nonframed version of its home page for some time now. This page is shown in Figure 5-30.

Figure 5-30   NONFRAMED VERSION OF THE COLORADO EXPERIENCE WEB PAGE

If you want this page to appear for frame-blind browsers but still use your framed Colorado.htm file, you need to copy the HTML code, including the <BODY> tags, from the source code of the nonframed file and place it within a pair of <NOFRAMES> tags in your Colorado.htm file.

To insert support for frame-blind browsers:

1. Open the **Colorado.htm** file in your text editor.

2. Insert a blank line above the </HTML> tag.

3. Enter the following HTML code:

```
<!- - - Frameless version of this page - - ->
<NOFRAMES>
</NOFRAMES>
```

4. Save your changes to the Colorado.htm file.

   Next you'll copy the code from the nonframed page into the Colorado.htm file.

5. In your text editor, open the **Noframes.htm** file from the **Tutorial.05** folder on your Data Disk.

6. Copy the HTML code, beginning with the <BODY> tag and going down to the </BODY> tag. Be sure to include both the opening and closing <BODY> tags in your selection.

7. Reopen the Colorado.htm file in the text editor (or simply return to the file if you have multiple versions of your text editor running).

8. Insert a blank line below the <NOFRAMES> tag.

9. Paste the text you copied from the Noframes.htm file in the blank line below the <NOFRAMES> tag. Figure 5-31 shows the beginning and end of the revised code.

| Figure 5-31 | INSERTING THE NOFRAMES CODE INTO THE COLORADO.HTM FILE |

```
<NOFRAMES>
<BODY BACKGROUND="Wall.gif">
<TABLE WIDTH=610>
<TR>
    <!--- Company Logo --->
    <TD ALIGN=CENTER COLSPAN=2>
        <IMG SRC="Logo.jpg" WIDTH=550 HEIGHT=60 ALT="The Colorado Experience">
    </TD>
</TR>
<TR>
```

```
        2411 Agnes Avenue<BR>
        Vale Park, CO     80517<BR>
        (970) 555-2341 &#183 FAX: (970) 555-2342
        </B></FONT></CENTER>
    </TD>
</TR>
</TABLE>

</BODY>
</NOFRAMES>
```

10. Save the file in your text editor.

To test your page, you should try to locate a browser that does not support frames (you can retrieve early versions of Netscape Navigator and Internet Explorer from their Web sites). Note that the table structure of the frameless page closely matches the frame layout you created. In this case, the first row is a single cell that spans two columns and displays the company logo, and the second row contains the list of links in the first cell and the home page text in the second cell.

Another way of supporting browsers that do not display frames is to create a Web page that contains links to the framed and nonframed versions of your Web site. A user with an older browser can therefore avoid the frames. This technique has the added advantage that users who don't like working with frames can avoid the frame version and go directly to the nonframed version.

DESIGN	WINDOW	DW

Tips for Using Frames

- Create framed and nonframed versions of your Web page to accommodate all browsers, and provide links to both versions.
- Do not turn off vertical or horizontal scrolling unless you are certain that all the content will appear within the frame borders.
- Assign names to all of your frames to make your HTML code easier to interpret.
- Simplify your HTML code by using the <BASE> tag when most of the hyperlinks in your framed page point to the same target.
- Never display pages that lie outside your Web presentation (such as pages created by other authors on the World Wide Web) within a frame.

You're finished working with the Colorado Experience page. There are some additional features you can add to this page, which are not supported by all browsers. You'll investigate them next.

Using Frame Extensions

Netscape Navigator and Internet Explorer both support extensions to the <FRAME> tag that allow you to change border size and appearance. For example, you can remove borders from your frames to free up more space for text and images, or you can change the color of the frame border so that it matches your color scheme more closely. As with other extensions, you should use care when implementing these extensions, because they might not be supported by all browsers or all versions of Netscape and Internet Explorer.

Using EXTENSIONS to the <FRAME> and <FRAMESET> Tags

- To define a color for your frame borders, add the BORDERCOLOR property to either the <FRAME-SET> or <FRAME> tag:

  `<FRAMESET BORDERCOLOR=color>`

  or

  `<FRAME BORDERCOLOR=color>`

  where *color* is either the color name or color value. Enter the BORDERCOLOR property in the <FRAMESET> tag to change all of the frame border colors in a set of frames. In Internet Explorer, enter the property in the <FRAME> tag to change the color of a single frame border (*Note*: In Netscape, using the BORDERCOLOR property in a single <FRAME> tag applies the color to *all* of the frames.)

- To change the width of your frame borders, apply the BORDER property to the <FRAMESET> tag:

  `<FRAMESET BORDER=value>`

  where *value* is the width of the border in pixels. You cannot change the width of individual frame borders (*Note*: You can also change border width in Internet Explorer, using the FRAMESPACING property; however this property is *not* supported by Netscape Navigator.)

Setting the Border Color

One of the extensions supported by Netscape Navigator and Internet Explorer is the ability to change the color of a frame's border. The BORDERCOLOR property can be applied either to an entire set of frames (within the <FRAMESET> tag) or to individual frames (within the <FRAME> tag). The syntax for this property is:

`<FRAMESET BORDERCOLOR=color>`

or

`<FRAME BORDERCOLOR=color>`

where *color* is either a color name or a color value. Applying the BORDERCOLOR property to a set of frames colors all of the frames and nested frames within the set. If you apply the BORDERCOLOR property to a single <FRAME> tag, that color of that frame's border will change in Internet Explorer, but in Netscape Navigator, *all* of the frame borders will change. The bottom line is that when you apply these types of tags and properties to your Web page, you should always view the page in a variety of browsers and, if possible, browser versions. The results can be unpredictable.

Debbie asks you to test the BORDERCOLOR property on the Colorado Experience page by changing the color of the frame borders to blue.

To change the frame border color:

1. Return to the Colorado.htm file in your text editor.

2. Within the initial <FRAMESET> tag, enter the property, **BORDERCOLOR=BLUE**.

3. Save your changes to the file, and then reopen the file in your browser. Figure 5-32 shows the frames with a blue border.

| Figure 5-32 | WEB SITE WITH BLUE FRAME BORDERS |

TROUBLE? Depending on your browser or browser version, the effect of this tag on the Web site may vary.

Another way of modifying frame borders is to change their widths.

Setting the Border Width

Netscape Navigator and Internet Explorer also support the BORDER property, an extension that allows you to specify the width of the frame borders. Unlike the BORDERCOLOR property, this property can be used only in the <FRAMESET> tag, and not in individual <FRAME> tags. The syntax for the BORDER property is:

```
<FRAMESET BORDER=value>
```

where *value* is the width of the frame borders in pixels.

To see how this property affects the appearance of your page, Debbie asks you to use it to remove the frame borders by setting the width to 0 pixels. Once again, this change may not appear in all browsers, including early versions of Netscape Navigator and Internet Explorer.

To change the size of the frame borders:

1. Return to the Colorado.htm file in your text editor.

2. Delete the BORDERCOLOR property that you entered in the previous set of steps. You don't need this property because you're going to remove the frame borders entirely.

3. Within the first <FRAMESET> tag, enter the property **BORDER=0**. See Figure 5-33.

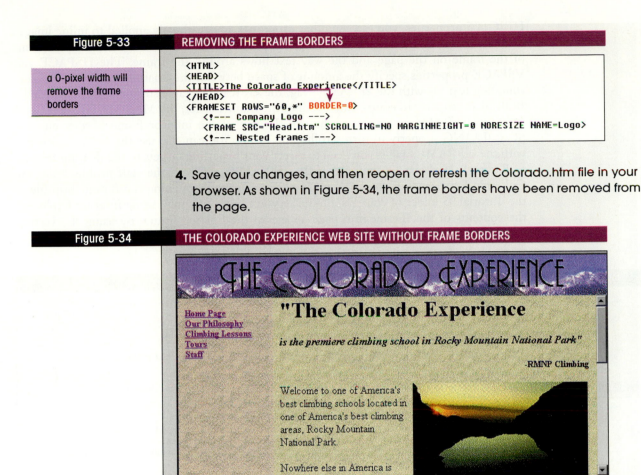

Figure 5-33   REMOVING THE FRAME BORDERS

a 0-pixel width will remove the frame borders

```
<HTML>
<HEAD>
<TITLE>The Colorado Experience</TITLE>
</HEAD>
<FRAMESET ROWS="60,*" BORDER=0>
    <!--- Company Logo --->
    <FRAME SRC="Head.htm" SCROLLING=NO MARGINHEIGHT=0 NORESIZE NAME=Logo>
    <!--- Nested frames --->
```

4. Save your changes, and then reopen or refresh the Colorado.htm file in your browser. As shown in Figure 5-34, the frame borders have been removed from the page.

Figure 5-34   THE COLORADO EXPERIENCE WEB SITE WITHOUT FRAME BORDERS

By removing the borders, you created more space for the text and images in each of the pages. You've also created the impression of a "seamless" Web page. Some Web authors prefer to eliminate frame borders, in order to give the illusion of having a single Web page rather than three separate ones. Other Web authors point out that hiding the frame borders confuses some users.

You can create a similar effect by using the FRAMEBORDER property. This is another property that is supported by both Netscape Navigator and Internet Explorer. Specifying FRAMEBORDER=NO in a <FRAMESET> tag removes the borders from the frames in your page. Internet Explorer also supports the FRAMESPACING property, which has the same effect as the BORDER property. Note that Netscape does not support this property.

Creating Floating Frames

Another way of inserting frames into your Web site is to use floating frames. Introduced by Internet Explorer 3.0 and added to the HTML 4.0 specifications (but not currently supported by Netscape), a **floating frame** or **internal frame** appears as a separate box or window within a Web page rather than on one side or the top or bottom. A floating frame can be placed within a Web page in the same way that an inline image is placed within a page. To create a floating frame, you use the <IFRAME> tag. The syntax for a floating frame is:

```
<IFRAME WIDTH=value HEIGHT=value SRC=URL >
</IFRAME>
```

where the width and height values are the width and height of the floating frame in pixels, and *URL* is the document that appears within the frame. In addition to the WIDTH and

HEIGHT properties, you can use other properties you've already applied to inline images via the <IMG> tag. For example, the ALIGN property allows you to control the placement of the frame on the page and the way text flows around the frame. The HSPACE and VSPACE properties specify the amount of space between the floating frame and the surrounding text. As with the <FRAME> tag, the <IFRAME> tag also supports the FRAMEBORDER property to control the width of the frame border, the MARGINHEIGHT and MARGINWIDTH properties to control the size of the interior frame border, and the SCROLLING property to turn scrolling on or off. You can also use the NAME property with the <IFRAME> tag if you need to direct your hyperlink targets to the floating frame.

Figure 5-35 shows an example of the <IFRAME> tag with the staff profiles from the Colorado Experience Web site. You can view this page by opening the IFrame.htm file in the Tutorial.05 folder of your Data Disk. As you can see (if you're using Internet Explorer), the contents of the IFrame.htm page appear in the floating frame. By using the vertical scroll bars, you can view the entire document of staff biographies.

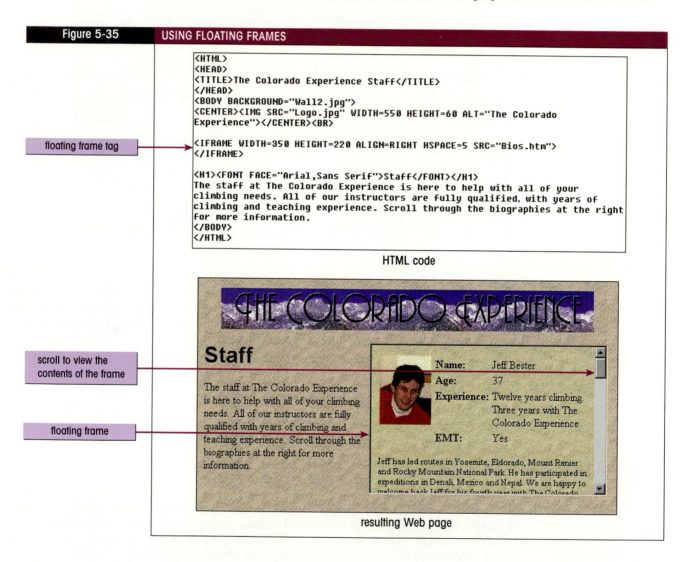

Figure 5-35   USING FLOATING FRAMES

```
<HTML>
<HEAD>
<TITLE>The Colorado Experience Staff</TITLE>
</HEAD>
<BODY BACKGROUND="Wall2.jpg">
<CENTER><IMG SRC="Logo.jpg" WIDTH=550 HEIGHT=60 ALT="The Colorado
Experience"></CENTER><BR>

<IFRAME WIDTH=350 HEIGHT=220 ALIGN=RIGHT HSPACE=5 SRC="Bios.htm">
</IFRAME>

<H1><FONT FACE="Arial,Sans Serif">Staff</FONT></H1>
The staff at The Colorado Experience is here to help with all of your
climbing needs. All of our instructors are fully qualified, with years of
climbing and teaching experience. Scroll through the biographies at the right
for more information.
</BODY>
</HTML>
```

floating frame tag

HTML code

scroll to view the contents of the frame

floating frame

resulting Web page

If you want to use floating frames in your Web page, you must make sure that your users are running Internet Explorer 3.0 or higher. Users of other browsers might not be able to see the floating frame at all.

You've completed your work with the Web page for The Colorado Experience. Using frames, you created an interesting presentation that is easy to navigate and attractive to the eye. Debbie looks over your work and will get back to you with any changes.

Session 5.2 QUICK CHECK

1. When you click a hyperlink inside a frame, in what frame will the page appear by default?

2. What code would you enter to assign the name "Address" to a frame with the document source Address.htm?

3. What code would you enter to direct a hyperlink to a frame named "News"?

4. What code would you enter to point a hyperlink to the document "Sales.htm" with the result that the Sales.htm file is retrieved into the entire display area, overwriting any frames in the process?

5. What tag would you enter to direct all hyperlinks in a document to the "News" target?

6. Describe what you would do to make your page readable both by browsers that support frames and those that do not.

7. What tag would you enter to set the frame border color of every frame on the page to red?

8. What tag would you enter to set the frame border width to 5 pixels?

9. What is the limitation of the tags you created in Quick Checks 7 and 8?

REVIEW ASSIGNMENTS

Debbie has some suggestions for modifications to the Web presentation for The Colorado Experience. Recall that the Staff page already uses frames. Debbie would like you to make a few changes to the design of this page. Specifically, she wants you to:

■ Create a new frame containing a hyperlink pointing back to the Colorado.htm file.
■ Remove any scroll bars from the frame and keep it from being resized by the user.
■ Remove the frame borders.
■ Insert HTML code to support users with frame-blind browsers.

To implement Debbie's suggestions:

1. Start your text editor and open the **Stafftxt.htm** file in the Review folder of the **Tutorial.05** folder on your Data Disk, and then save the file as Staff.htm in the same folder.

Explore ➤ 2. Replace the <FRAME> tag (the frame that displays the "Photos.htm" file) and the corresponding comment tag in the first column of the second row with a <FRAMESET> tag, to create two rows of nested frames. The height of the first row should be 25 pixels. The height of the second row should be whatever space is left.

3. Specify the file Return.htm as the source for the frame in the first row. Do not allow users to resize this frame, and remove any scroll bars. Set the width of the frame margins to 1 pixel. Name the frame "Return."

4. Specify the file Photos.htm as the source for the frame in the second row. Turn off frame resizing, but allow the browser to display scroll bars when needed. Set the margin height of this frame to 1 pixel, and set the margin width to 10 pixels. Name the frame "Photos."

5. Close off the two <FRAME> tags with a </FRAMESET> tag.

6. Insert an opening and closing <NOFRAME> tag below the last </FRAMESET> tag.

7. Copy the HTML code from the StaffNF.htm file (in the Review folder), including the <BODY> tags, and paste the code between the <NOFRAMES> tags in the Staff.htm file.

8. Change the border width of the frames in the Staff.htm file to 0 pixels.

9. Insert comment tags that document the different frames you created in the file.

10. Save your changes to the Staff.htm file.

11. Open the Retrntxt.htm file in the Review folder of the Tutorial.05 folder on your Data Disk, and then save the file as Return.htm in the same folder.

12. Change the text "Go to home page" to a hyperlink pointing to the **Colorado.htm** file. Set up the hyperlink so that it loads Colorado.htm into the full display window when clicked.

13. Save your changes to the Return.htm file.

Explore ▷ 14. Open the Links.htm and Tours.htm files in your text editor and change the hyperlinks to the staff page so that the staff page is opened in a new browser window when the linked is clicked. (*Note*: If you have to go back to original versions of these files, they are stored in the Linkstxt.htm and Tourstxt.htm files, respectively.)

15. Open the Staff.htm file from the Review folder in your Web browser and verify that the frames appear correctly and that all hyperlinks are working properly. Figure 5-36 shows the finished appearance of the page.

Figure 5-36

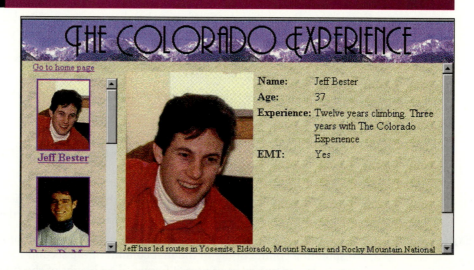

16. Print your Web page and the corresponding HTML code for the Staff.htm, Return.htm, Links.htm, and Tours.htm files.

17. Close your Web browser and your text editor.

Case 1. Creating a Sales Report for Doc-Centric Copiers   Doc-Centric Copiers, located in Salt Lake City, is one of the nation's leading manufacturers of personal and business copiers. The annual shareholders' convention in Chicago is approaching, and the general manager, David Edgars, wants you to create an online report for the convention participants. The report will run off a computer located in the convention hall and will be accessible to everyone. David feels that creating a Web presentation to run locally on the computer is the best way of presenting the sales data. Using hyperlinks between various reports will enable Doc-Centric Copiers to make a wealth of information available to shareholders in an easy-to-use format. Most of the Web pages have already been created for you. Your job is to combine the information into a single page, using frames. A preview of the page you'll create is shown in Figure 5-37.

Figure 5-37

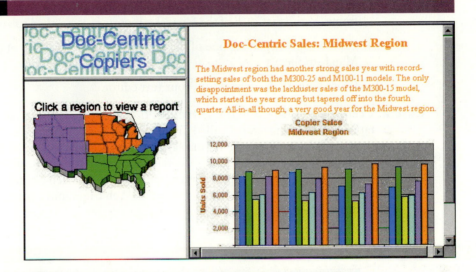

To create the Doc-Centric Copiers sales report page:

1. Open the file DCCtxt.htm in the Cases folder of the Tutorial.05 folder on your Data Disk, and then save the file as DCC.htm in the same folder.

2. Create a frame layout. The layout should consist initially of two columns. The left column should be 240 pixels wide, and the right column should fill up the rest of the display area.

3. Within the first frame column, insert two rows of nested frames. The frame in the first row should be 75 pixels high, and the second row should fill up the remaining space. The source for the first frame row is the Head.htm file (in the Cases folder), which contains the company logo. The source for the second frame row is the Map.htm file (in the Cases folder), which contains a map showing the different sales regions for the company. Name the first frame "Logo" and the second frame "USMap."

4. The source for the frame in the second column is the file Report.htm. This frame will contain the various sales reports that David wants displayed. Name the frame "Reports."

5. Complete the tags required for the frame layout and add comment tags describing each frame. Save your changes.

6. Open the file Maptxt.htm in the Cases folder of the Tutorial.05 folder on your Data Disk, and then save the file as Map.htm in the same folder.

Explore

7. The Map.htm file contains an image map of the different sales regions. For each hyperlink in the Map.htm file, direct the link to the Reports target, so that the pages appear in the Reports frame. Save your changes.

8. View the DCC.htm file in your Web browser. What improvements could be made to the page? What things should be removed?

9. Return to the DCC.htm file in your text editor and reduce the margin for the Logo frame to 1 pixel. Reduce the margin width for the USMap frame to 1 pixel, and change the margin height to 30 pixels.

10. Remove scroll bars from both the Logo and USMap frames.

11. View the page again to verify that the problems you identified in Step 8 have been resolved.

12. Return to the DCC.htm file and lock the size of the frames to prevent users from inadvertently changing the frame sizes.

13. Reopen the Doc-Centric Copiers sales report page and test the image map in the USMap frame. Verify that each of the four sales reports is correctly displayed in the Reports frame.

14. Print a page displaying one of the sales reports. Print a copy of both the DCC.htm and Map.htm files.

15. Close your Web browser and your text editor.

Case 2. Creating a Tour Page for Travel Scotland! You've been asked to create a Web presentation for a touring agency called Travel Scotland!, which organizes tours to Scotland and the British Isles. The page will display an itinerary and photo for four popular tours: the Lake District tour, the Castles of Scotland tour, a tour of the Scottish Highlands, and, finally, a tour of the Hebrides. A page with a frame layout has been created for each tour. Your task is to create a page that ties the four separate Web pages into a single presentation. A preview of the completed Web page is shown in Figure 5-38.

Figure 5-38

To create the Travel Scotland! page:

1. Open the file Scottxt.htm in the Cases folder of the Tutorial.05 folder on your Data Disk, and then save the file as Scotland.htm in the same folder.

2. Create a frame layout for the Scotland.htm page that consists of three rows of frames. The size of the first row should be 45 pixels, the third row should be 75 pixels, and the middle row should occupy whatever space is left.

3. Specify the file TSLogo.htm (in the Cases folder)—a file containing the company logo—as the source for the first frame. The source for the second frame is Laketour.htm (in the Cases folder), a file describing the Lake District tour. Finally, the source for the third frame is TSList.htm (in the Cases folder), a page containing a graphic with the four tour names.

4. Assign the following names to the frames: Logo, Tours, and TourList, respectively.

5. Save your changes to the Scotland.htm file.

6. The TourList frame refers to a file that contains an inline image with titles for the four main tours offered by Travel Scotland! Change this graphic to an image map:

   a. Open the file TSLtxt.htm in the Cases folder of the Tutorial.05 folder on your Data Disk, and then save the file as TSList.htm in the same folder.

   b. Assign an image map named "TourList" to the inline image, with the following hotspots (all files are in the Cases folder):

      ■ A rectangular hotspot at (17,0) (158,59) that points to Laketour.htm

      ■ A rectangular hotspot at (159,0) (306,59) that points to Casttour.htm

      ■ A rectangular hotspot at (307,0) (454,59) that points to Hightour.htm

      ■ A rectangular hotspot at (455,0) (593,59) that points to Hebdtour.htm

   c. For each hotspot in the graphic, specify the Tours frame as the target.
   d. Save your changes to TSList.htm.

7. Open the Scotland.htm file in your Web browser. What problems do you see? Reopen Scotland.htm in your text editor and fix the problems.

8. Reopen Scotland.htm in your browser. Is the problem fixed? If so, return to the file in your text editor and lock the size and position of the frame borders to prevent users from resizing the frames. Reopen the page in the browser.

Explore ▶ 9. Test the hyperlinks in the image map. Note that when you click a hyperlink, two frames are updated in the page. This is because the source for the frame in the middle row is itself a framed page. This is one way you can have two frames updated with a single click of a hyperlink.

10. Print the Travel Scotland! Web page and the source code in the Scotland.htm and TSList.htm files.

Explore ▶ 11. Trace the code for the series of hyperlinks and framed pages in this case problem and create a diagram showing how all of the files are connected.

12. Close your Web browser and your text editor.

Case 3. Creating a Sonnets Page for English 220 Professor Sherry Lake is teaching a course on 16th and 17th century poetry. She's asked you to help her create a Web presentation of a section of her course dealing with sonnets. She has collected 10 sonnets written by John Donne, William Shakespeare, and Edmund Spenser that she wants the students to learn and has placed them in HTML files. She has also created a page that shows the title of the course and a list of the 10 sonnets. She wants you to organize this material, using frames. A preview of the page you'll create is shown in Figure 5-39.

Figure 5-39

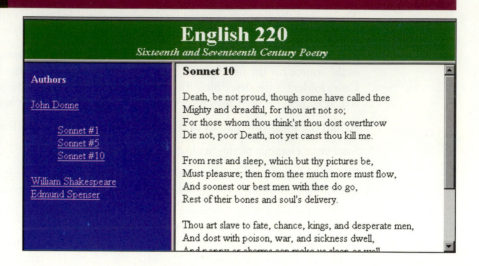

The table of contents for this page appears in the leftmost frame. Sherry wants the links in the table of contents frame to work as follows:

- If a user clicks the name of an author, a list of sonnets by that author alternately expands and contracts in the table of contents frame.
- If a user clicks the name of a sonnet, the sonnet appears in the rightmost frame.

Sherry doesn't want the layout of the page to be locked in; that is, she wants to give students the ability to resize the frames when they're viewing the page.

To create the sonnets page:

1. Open the file Sontxt.htm in the Cases folder of the Tutorial.05 folder on your Data Disk, and then save the file as Sonnet.htm in the same folder.

2. Create a frame layout in which the first frame row is 60 pixels high, and the height of the second frame row is whatever space remains on the page.

3. Within the second frame row, create a nested frame layout of two columns. The first column should be 220 pixels wide, and the second column should cover the rest of the page.

4. The source for the first frame is Eng220.htm. The source for the second frame is SonTOC.htm, and the source for the third frame is Blank.htm. All of these files are in the Cases folder.

5. Name the first frame "Head," the second frame "List," and the third frame "Sonnet."

6. Set the margin height for the Head and Sonnet frames to 1 pixel. Set the margin width for the Sonnet frame to 10 pixels.

7. Save your changes to Sonnet.htm, and then close the file.

8. Open the SnTOCtxt.htm file in the Cases folder of the Tutorial.05 folder on your Data Disk, and then save the file as SonTOC.htm in the same folder.

9. Set the base target for all hyperlinks in this file to the magic target name that loads the document into the same frame that contains the hyperlink tag.

10. Convert the names of the three authors to hypertext links: "John Donne" should point to the SonnetJD.htm file, "William Shakespeare" to SonnetWS.htm, and "Edmund Spenser" to SonnetES.htm (you'll be creating these files in a moment). Save your changes to SonTOC.htm, and then close the file.

11. Open the John Donne file, JDtxt.htm, in the Cases folder of the Tutorial.05 folder on your Data Disk, and then save the file as SonnetJD.htm in the same folder.

12. Convert the author names and sonnet names to hypertext links. The sonnets should point to the files SonJD1.htm, SonJD5.htm, and SonJD10.htm, respectively. The author name "John Donne" should point back to the SonTOC.htm file, and the author names "William Shakespeare" and "Edmund Spenser" should point to the files SonnetWS.htm and SonnetES.htm, respectively.

13. Set the Sonnet frame as the base target for hyperlinks in this document. Set the target for each author name to the magic target name that loads the document into the same frame that contains the hyperlink tag. Save your changes.

14. Repeat Steps 11 through 13 for the William Shakespeare file, WStxt.htm, in the Cases folder. Save the file as SonnetWS.htm. Create hyperlinks to the sonnet files SonWS12.htm, SonWS18.htm, SonWS116.htm, and SonWS130.htm. The author name "William Shakespeare" should point back to the SonTOC.htm file, and the author names "John Donne" and "Edmund Spenser" should point back to SonnetJD.htm and SonnetES.htm, respectively. Save your changes.

15. Repeat Steps 11 through 13 for the Edmund Spenser file, EStxt.htm, in the Cases folder. Save the file as SonnetES.htm. Create hyperlinks to the sonnet files SonES54.htm, SonES64.htm, and SonES79.htm. The author name "Edmund Spenser" should point back to the SonTOC.htm file, and the author names "John Donne" and "William Shakespeare" should point back to SonnetJD.htm and SonnetWS.htm, respectively. Save your changes.

16. Open Sonnet.htm in your Web browser. Verify that by clicking the names of the authors, the list of sonnets is alternately expanded and contracted, and that when the names of the sonnets are clicked, the text of the sonnet appears in the rightmost frame.

17. Print a copy of the Web page and the code for the following files: Sonnet.htm, SonTOC.htm, SonnetJD.htm, SonnetWS.htm, and SonnetES.htm.

18. Close your Web browser and your text editor.

Case 4. Creating a Web Presentation for Warner Peripherals   Warner Peripherals, a company located in Tucson, makes high-quality peripherals for computers. The company leads the industry in disk drives and tape drives. Its most popular products include the SureSave line of tape drives and the SureRite line of disk drives. You've been asked to consolidate several Web pages describing these products into a single Web presentation that uses frames. The files shown in Figure 5-40 are available for your use.

Figure 5-40

FILE	CONTENTS
Drive15L.htm	Description of the 15L SureRite hard drive
Drive20M.htm	Description of the 20M SureRite hard drive
Drive33M.htm	Description of the 33M SureRite hard drive
Drive60S.htm	Description of the 60S SureRite hard drive
Tape800.htm	Description of the 800 SureSave tape backup drive
Tape3200.htm	Description of the 3200 SureSave tape backup drive
Tape9600.htm	Description of the 9600 SureSave tape backup drive
WLogo.htm	Web page containing the Warner Peripherals logo

To create the Warner Peripherals Web presentation:

1. Create a table of contents page that includes hyperlinks to the files listed in Figure 5-40. The layout and appearance of this page are up to you. Save this page as WTOC.htm in the Cases folder of the Tutorial.05 folder on your Data Disk.

2. Create a file named Warner.htm that consolidates the logo page, table of contents page, and product description pages into a single page, using frames. The layout of the frames is up to you. Include comment tags in the file describing each element of the page. Save the Warner.htm file in the Cases folder of the Tutorial.05 folder on your Student Disk.

3. Test your page and verify that each link works properly and appears in the correct frame.

4. Print a copy of the page and the HTML code.

5. Close your Web browser and your text editor.

QUICK CHECK ANSWERS

Session 5.1

1. Frames are windows appearing within the browser's display area, each capable of displaying the contents of a different HTML file.
2. Because there is no page body. Instead the browser displays the <BODY> tags from other pages.
3. <FRAMESET ROWS="2,50%,*">
4. <FRAME SRC="Home.htm">
5. <FRAME SRC="Home.htm" SCROLLING=NO>
6. <FRAME SRC="Home.htm" MARGINHEIGHT=3>
7. 3 pixels
8. <FRAME SRC="Home.htm" NORESIZE>

Session 5.2

1. the frame containing the hyperlink
2. <FRAME SRC="Address.htm" NAME=Address>
3. <A HREF=URL TARGET=News>
4. <A HREF="Sales.htm" TARGET=_top>
5. Place the tag, <BASE TARGET=News>, in the <HEAD> section of the HTML file
6. Create a section starting with the <NOFRAMES> tag. After the <NOFRAMES> tag enter a <BODY> tag to identify the text and images you want frame-blind browser to display. Complete this section with a </BODY> tag followed by a </NOFRAMES> tag.
7. <FRAMESET BORDERCOLOR=RED>
8. <FRAMESET BORDERWIDTH=5>
9. They cannot be used by all browsers and all browser versions.

LEVEL III

New Perspectives on

CREATING WEB PAGES WITH HTML

2ⁿᵈ Edition

Read This Before You Begin

To the Student

Data Disks

To complete the Level III tutorials, Review Assignments, and Case Problems in this book, you need seven Data Disks. Your instructor will either provide you with Data Disks or ask you to make your own.

If you are making your own Data Disks, you will need seven blank, formatted, high-density disks. You will need to copy onto your disks a set of folders from a file server, or stand-alone computer, or the Web. Your instructor will tell you which computer, drive letter, and folders contain the files you need. You could also download the files by going to www.course.com, and following the directions on the screen.

The following shows you which folders go on your disks, so that you will have enough disk space to complete all the tutorials, Review Assignments, and Case Problems:

Data Disk 1
Write this on the disk label
Data Disk 1: Level III Tutorials 6 and 7
Put these folders on the disk
Tutorial.06 and Tutorial.07

Data Disk 2
Write this on the disk label
Data Disk 2: Level III Tutorials 8 and 9
Put these folders on the disk
Tutorial.08 and Tutorial.09

Data Disk 3
Write this on the disk label
Data Disk 3: Level III Tutorial 10
Put these folders on the disk
Tutorial.10 (don't include any of the Case folders)

Data Disk 4
Write this on the disk label
Data Disk 4: Level III Tutorial 10 (Case Problem 1)
Put this folder on the disk
Case1 folder of the Tutorial.10 folder

Data Disk 5
Write this on the disk label
Data Disk 5: Level III Tutorial 10 (Case Problem 2)
Put this folder on the disk
Case2 folder of the Tutorial.10 folder

Data Disk 6
Write this on the disk label
Data Disk 6: Level III Tutorial 10 (Case Problem 3)
Put this folder on the disk
Case3 folder of the Tutorial.10 folder

Data Disk 7
Write this on the disk label
Data Disk 7: Level III Additional Cases
Put these folders on the disk
Case1, Case2, Case3 folder of the Tutorial.add folder

When you begin each tutorial, be sure you are using the correct Data Disk. See the inside back cover of this book for more information on Data Disk files, or ask your instructor or technical support person for assistance.

Course Labs

Tutorial 10 and the Additional Cases feature interactive Course Labs. Refer to the Lab Assignments at the end of those tutorials for instructions on starting the Labs.

Additional Resource: CD in the back of this book

Take advantage of this special feature of *New Perspectives on Creating Web Pages with HTML—Comprehensive, 2nd Edition*. By using the CD in the back of this book, you can access Java applets, an HTML Tag Reference, additional coverage, and other multimedia elements. Use any or all of these items to enhance your learning process.

Using Your Own Computer

If you are going to work through this book using your own computer, you need:

- **Computer System** A text editor (such as Notepad or Word) and a Web browser (preferably Netscape Navigator 4.7 or Internet Explorer 5.0) must be installed on your computer. If you are using a non-standard browser, it must support frames and HTML 3.2 or above.

- **Data Disks** You will not be able to complete the tutorials or exercises in this book using your own computer until you have Data Disks. The Data Disk Files may be downloaded from the Internet. See the inside front cover for more details.

Visit Our World Wide Web Site

Additional materials designed especially for you are available on the World Wide Web. Go to http://www.course.com. For example, see our Student Online Companion, which contains additional coverage of selected topics in the text. These topics are indicated in the text by an Online Companion icon located in the left margin.

To the Instructor

The Data Disk Files are available on the Instructor's Resource Kit for this title. Follow the instructions in the Help file on the CD-ROM to install the programs to your network or standalone computer. For information on creating Data Disks, see the "To the Student" section above.

You are granted a license to copy the Data Disk Files to any computer or computer network used by students who have purchased this book.

OBJECTIVES

In this tutorial you will:

- Learn about CGI scripts

- Review the various parts of an online form

- Create form elements

- Create a hidden field on a form

- Work with form properties

- Learn how to send data from a form to a CGI script

- Learn how to send form information without using CGI scripts

- Learn about enhancements to the HTML form elements

CREATING WEB PAGE FORMS

Designing a Product Registration Form

CASE

Creating a Registration Form for Jackson Electronics

Jackson Electronics, located in Seattle, is one of the leading manufacturers of imaging equipment such as printers, copiers, and flatbed scanners. The company has already established a presence on the World Wide Web with pages that describe the company's products and its corporate philosophy. Now, Jackson Electronics would like to improve that presence by creating interactive pages that will allow customers to give feedback about the company's products online.

Lisa Clemente, the director of customer support for Jackson Electronics, would like to have a page for customer registration. She's aware that fewer than 10% of the registration cards included with the product packaging are ever returned to the company, and she feels that this low response could be improved if product registration could be accomplished on the Web. Customers could fill out the registration form online and then send the information via e-mail to one of Lisa's assistants, who would enter the information into the company's database.

Lisa has asked you to help her create such a registration page. To do so, you'll have to learn how to create HTML forms and how to use those forms to record information for the company.

In this session you will learn some of the fundamentals of creating forms with HTML. You'll learn how forms interact with CGI scripts to transfer information from the Web browser to the Web server. You'll also create your first form element, an input box.

Working with CGI Scripts

Lisa has been considering how she wants the product registration form to appear, keeping in mind that the company plans to use the form to record customer information. Lisa decides to model the form on the registration cards already packaged with Jackson Electronics' products. Because a long form would discourage customers from completing it, Lisa wants the form kept brief and focused on the information the company is most interested in. She sketches out the form she would like you to create (Figure 6-1).

Figure 6-1	LISA'S PROPOSED REGISTRATION FORM

First Name: [   ]   Last Name: [   ]

Address #1: [   ]

Address #2: [   ]

City: [   ]   State: [   ]   Zip: [   ]

Country: [   ]

Product: [▼]

Date Purchased: [   ]

Used for:
○ Home
○ Business
○ Government
○ Education
○ Other

System (check all that apply):
☐ Windows
☐ Macintosh
☐ UNIX
☐ Other

Comments? [   ]

[Send Registration]   [Cancel]

The form collects contact information for each customer, information on which product the customer purchased, what operating system the customer uses, and how the customer will use the product. There is also a place for customers to enter comments about the product or Jackson Electronics. With this registration form, Lisa hopes to collect information that will help Jackson Electronics better understand its customers and their needs.

Before you begin to create the form, you need to understand how such forms are interpreted and processed on the Web. Although HTML supports tags that allow you to create forms like the one shown in Figure 6-1, it does not have the ability to process that information. One way of processing information is to send it to a program running on the Web server, called a CGI script. A **CGI (Common Gateway Interface) script** is any program or set of commands running on the Web server that receives data from the Web page and then acts on that data to perform a certain task. Figure 6-2 illustrates how a Web page form interacts with a CGI script.

Figure 6-2   **THE INTERACTION BETWEEN A WEB PAGE FORM AND A CGI SCRIPT**

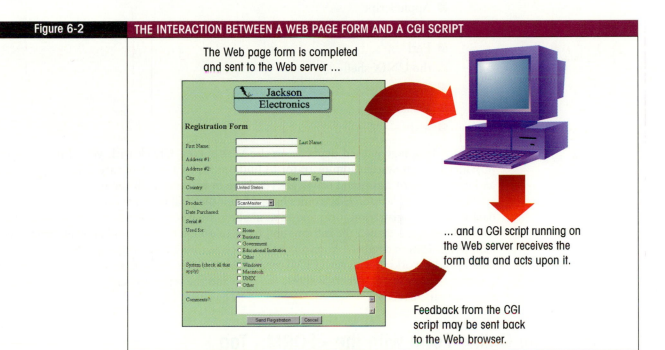

The introduction of CGI scripts represented a dramatic change in how the Web was perceived and used. By giving users access to programs that react to user input, the Web became a dynamic environment in which companies could interact with customers and vice versa, instead of customers simply reading static Web documents. CGI scripts made it possible for Web authors to:

- maintain online databases containing customer information
- publish catalogues for ordering and purchasing items online
- publish databases containing product support information
- determine the number of times a Web page has been accessed
- create server-side image maps
- create message boards for online discussion forums
- manage e-mail for discussion groups

Because CGI scripts run on the Web server, you, as a Web page author, might not have the ability to create or edit them. In some cases, another programmer will create the scripts offered by the Web server and provide you with their specifications, indicating what input the scripts expect and what output they create.

Internet service providers and universities often provide CGI scripts that their customers and students can access from their Web pages, but which they cannot directly access or modify.

There are several good reasons to restrict direct access to a CGI script. The main reason is that when you run a CGI script, you are actually running a program directly on the server. Mindful of the dangers that computer hackers can present and the drain on system resources caused by large numbers of programs running simultaneously, system administrators are understandably anxious to control access to their servers.

CGI scripts can be written in a variety of different computer languages. The most commonly used languages are:

- AppleScript
- C/C++
- Perl
- the UNIX shell
- TCL
- Visual Basic
- ASP

Which language is used depends on the Web server. Check with your Internet service provider or your system administrator to find out how CGI scripts are used on your server and what kinds of rights and privileges you have in working with them.

The servers at Jackson Electronics have a script that will perform the task of retrieving the data from the registration form and then mailing the results to one of Lisa's assistants. The assistant will then extract the information from an e-mail message and enter it into the company's registration database. You will not have access to the CGI scripts on the Web server, so you'll just be working with the HTML end of this process. After Lisa uploads the page to the company's Web server, others will test the page and the script to verify that the information is passed on correctly.

Starting an Online Form with the <FORM> Tag

Now that you're familiar with how CGI scripts interact with Web page forms, you can begin to work on the registration form that Lisa wants you to create. As shown in Figure 6-3, the form contains the following elements, which are commonly used in Web page forms:

- **input boxes** for text and numerical entries
- **radio buttons**, also called **option buttons**, to select a single option from a predefined list
- **selection lists** for long lists of options, usually in a **drop-down list box**
- **check boxes** to specify an item as being either present or absent
- **text areas** for extended entries that might include several lines of text
- **submit** and **reset buttons** to either submit the form to the CGI script or reset the form to its original state

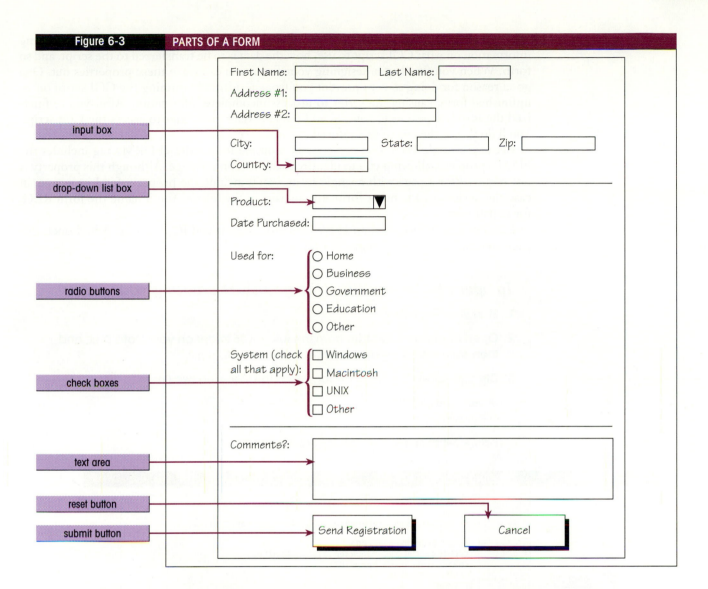

Figure 6-3   PARTS OF A FORM

Each element in which the user can enter information is called a **field**. Information entered into a field is called the **field value**, or simply the **value**. In some fields, users are free to enter anything they choose. Other fields, such as selection lists, confine their values to a predefined list of possible options.

Before you can create any fields, you must first indicate to the browser that the page will contain fields. You do this using the <FORM> tag. The <FORM> tag identifies the beginning and end of a form, in the same way that the <TABLE> tag defines the beginning and end of a graphical table. A single page can include several different forms, one after another, but you cannot nest one form inside another, as you can with tables. The general syntax of the <FORM> tag is:

```
<FORM Properties>
     Form elements and layout tags
</FORM>
```

Between the <FORM> and </FORM> tags, you place the various tags for each of the fields in the form. You can also specify the form's appearance using standard HTML tags. For example, you can place a selection list within a table or insert an input box within an italicized <H2> heading.

The <FORM> tag includes properties that control how the form is processed, including information on what CGI script to use, how the data is to be transferred to the script, and so forth. When you first begin designing your form, you can leave these properties out. One good reason for doing so is to prevent you from accidentally running the CGI script on an unfinished form, causing the script to process incomplete information. After you've finalized the form's appearance, you can add the necessary properties to access the CGI script. You'll do that at the end of this tutorial.

Because a single Web page can contain multiple forms, the <FORM> tag includes the NAME property, allowing you to identify each form on the page. Although this property is not required for a page with a single form, you'll include the property for Lisa's page, in case she decides to add other forms to the page in the future. You'll name the form REG, for registration.

Lisa has already prepared an HTML file for you, named Regtext.htm. You'll open this page and start to create the registration form.

To open the Regtext.htm file and start creating your form:

1. Start your text editor.

2. Open the file **Regtext.htm** from the Tutorial.06 folder on your Data Disk, and then save the file as **Register.htm** in the same folder.

3. Directly above the </BODY> tag, insert the following two lines:

   ```
   <FORM NAME=REG>
   </FORM>
   ```

   Figure 6-4 shows the updated Register.htm file.

Figure 6-4   ADDING <FORM> TAGS

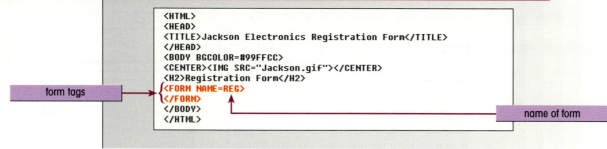

```
<HTML>
<HEAD>
<TITLE>Jackson Electronics Registration Form</TITLE>
</HEAD>
<BODY BGCOLOR=#99FFCC>
<CENTER><IMG SRC="Jackson.gif"></CENTER>
<H2>Registration Form</H2>
<FORM NAME=REG>
</FORM>
</BODY>
</HTML>
```

form tags

name of form

With the <FORM> tags in place, you can start creating the form layout. Look again at Lisa's plan for the form, shown in Figure 6-3. Notice that input boxes and other form elements are aligned on the page. This makes the form easier to read than if the elements were scattered across the width of the form. Although you don't need to use tables to create forms, they do help you control the layout of form objects. Figure 6-5 shows the simple two-column table that you'll use to create the form. Notice that some table cells in the second column contain more than one form field.

| Figure 6-5 | PLACING A FORM WITHIN A TABLE |

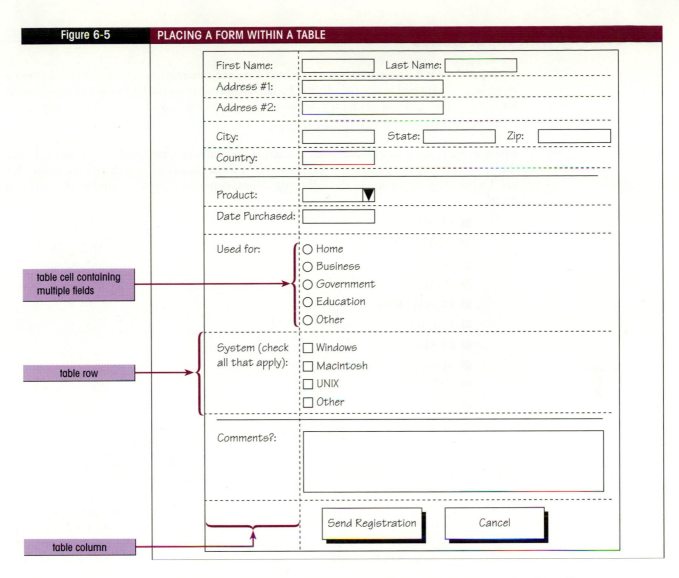

Next, you'll add the tags for the two-column table to the Register.htm file.

To insert the table tags:

1. Go to the <FORM> tag in the Register.htm file.

2. Insert the following two lines between the <FORM> and </FORM> tags:

   ```
   <TABLE>
   </TABLE>
   ```

3. Save your changes to the Register.htm file.

With the <FORM> and <TABLE> tags in place, you can now start to insert tags for each field in the form. You'll begin by learning how to create input boxes. Remember that you will be creating table rows and columns as you go.

Working with Input Boxes

An **input box** is a single-line box into which the user can enter text or numbers. To create input boxes, you need to use the <INPUT> tag. However, the <INPUT> tag can also be used for several other types of fields on your form. The general syntax of the <INPUT> tag is:

```
<INPUT TYPE=option NAME=text>
```

where *option* is the type of input field, and *text* is the name assigned to the input field. To use the <INPUT> tag for the many different kinds of form elements, you change the values for the TYPE property to one of the following values, depending on what kind of element you want:

- BUTTON
- CHECKBOX
- HIDDEN
- IMAGE
- PASSWORD
- RADIO
- RESET
- SUBMIT
- TEXT
- TEXTAREA

You'll learn about all these types as you progress with Lisa's registration form. The field you want to create now is an input box, which you create using TEXT as the value for the TYPE property. In fact, TEXT is the TYPE property's default value, so in most cases Web authors simply leave out the TYPE property when they want to create an input box.

The NAME property is required with the <INPUT> tag. When information from the form is sent to the CGI script, field names are used to identify what values have been entered in each field. As shown in Figure 6-6, when the form data is sent, the CGI script receives the name of each field in the form paired with whatever value the user entered into the field. The script will then process the information according to each name/value pair.

Figure 6-6	NAME/VALUE PAIRS SENT FROM THE WEB FORM TO THE CGI SCRIPT

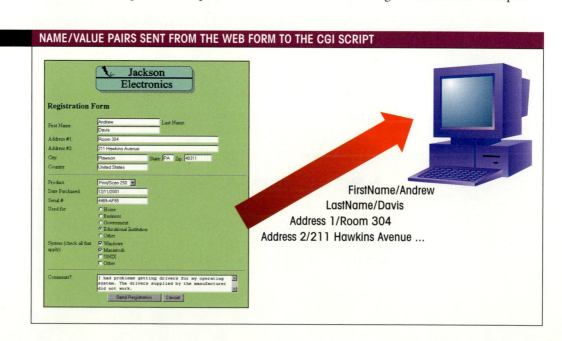

FirstName/Andrew
LastName/Davis
Address 1/Room 304
Address 2/211 Hawkins Avenue ...

Note that the value you enter for the NAME property is not necessarily the "name" you see next to a form element. For example, in Figure 6-6, the value for the NAME property of the first address line is "Address1," but the "name" of the input box is "Address #1." The latter is what the user sees, and the former is sent to the CGI script. The two can be the same, but they don't have to be.

Some CGI scripts will require that each form contain a particular field. For example, a CGI script whose purpose is to mail the form results to another user might require a field named "email" that contains the e-mail address of the recipient. Before using a CGI script, you should check with your Internet service provider or system administrator to see whether there are any such required fields.

Finally, be aware that case is important in field names. A field named "email" might not be interpreted by the CGI script in the same way as a field named "EMAIL."

REFERENCE   WINDOW   **RW**

Creating an Input Box

■ To create an input box, use the following tag:

`<INPUT NAME=text VALUE=value SIZE=value MAXLENGTH=value>`

where the NAME property sets the field name, the VALUE property assigns a default value to the input box, the SIZE property defines the width of the input box in number of characters, and the MAXLENGTH property defines the maximum number of characters allowed in the field.

The first part of the registration form deals with contact information for the customer. Each of the fields in this section is an input box. Because input boxes are blank boxes without any accompanying text, you have to insert a text description (such as "First Name") next to each box so that the user knows what to enter. In Lisa's form you are also using a table to control the form's layout, so you'll have to add the appropriate row and cell tags as well.

To insert the input boxes on the form:

1. Between the <TABLE> and </TABLE> tags in the Register.htm file, enter the following lines (make your code easier to follow by indenting the lines as shown):

```
<TR>
        <TD WIDTH=100>First Name:</TD>
        <TD><INPUT NAME=FirstName>
                Last Name: <INPUT NAME=LastName></TD>
</TR>
<TR>
        <TD>Address #1:</TD>
        <TD><INPUT NAME=Address1></TD>
</TR>
<TR>
        <TD>Address #2:</TD>
        <TD><INPUT NAME=Address2></TD>
</TR>
<TR>
```

```
          <TD>City:</TD>
          <TD><INPUT NAME=City> State: <INPUT NAME=State>
                 Zip: <INPUT NAME=ZIP></TD>
     </TR>
     <TR>

          <TD>Country:</TD>
          <TD><INPUT NAME=Country></TD>
     </TR>
```

2. Save your changes to the **Register.htm** file.

3. Open the **Register.htm** file in your browser, as shown in Figure 6-7. Note that by using a table, you've caused the leftmost input boxes in each row to be vertically aligned, giving a uniform appearance to the registration form.

| Figure 6-7 | CONTACT FIELDS IN THE REGISTRATION FORM |

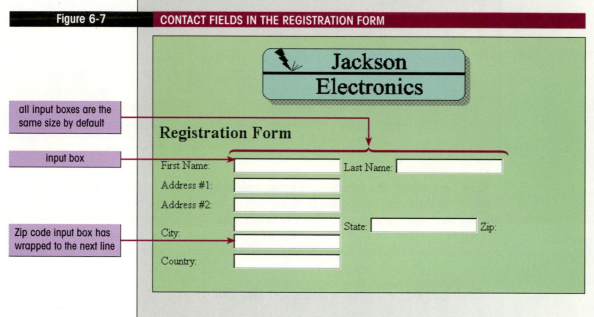

all input boxes are the same size by default

input box

Zip code input box has wrapped to the next line

TROUBLE? Depending on your browser and browser version, your Web page may look slightly different from the one shown in Figure 6-7.

One of the problems with the registration form is the fact that the input box for the Zip code field has been wrapped to the next line on some browsers. This is because there is not enough space to display the input box and corresponding text on a single line. You'll fix that problem next.

Controlling the Size of an Input Box

By default, the browser made all of the input boxes in the registration form the same size—20 characters wide. You can specify a different size. The syntax for changing the size of an input box is:

```
<INPUT SIZE=value>
```

where *value* is the size of the input box in number of characters.

After looking over the form, Lisa decides that the size of both the First Name field and the Last Name field should be increased to 25 characters, to allow for longer names. Similarly, the Address #1 and Address #2 fields should be increased to about 50 characters each, to allow for street numbers and street names. The State field can be reduced to a size of three characters for state abbreviations, and the size of the Zip field should be reduced to 10 characters. The City and Country fields can remain unchanged, with the default width of 20 characters each.

To specify the size of the input boxes:

1. Return to the Register.htm file in your text editor.

2. For the FirstName and LastName <INPUT> tags, insert the property **SIZE=25**.

3. For the Address1 and Address2 <INPUT> tags, insert the property **SIZE=50**.

4. For the State <INPUT> tag, insert the property **SIZE=3**.

5. For the Zip <INPUT> tag, insert the property **SIZE=10**.

   Figure 6-8 shows the revised Register.htm file.

Figure 6-8   CHANGING THE SIZE OF THE INPUT BOXES

```
<TR>
    <TD WIDTH=100>First Name:</TD>
    <TD><INPUT NAME=FirstName SIZE=25>
       Last Name: <INPUT NAME=LastName SIZE=25></TD>
</TR>
<TR>
    <TD>Address #1:</TD>
    <TD><INPUT NAME=Address1 SIZE=50></TD>
</TR>
<TR>
    <TD>Address #2:</TD>
    <TD><INPUT NAME=Address2 SIZE=50></TD>
</TR>
<TR>
    <TD>City:</TD>
    <TD><INPUT NAME=City> State: <INPUT NAME=State SIZE=3>
       Zip: <INPUT NAME=ZIP SIZE=10></TD>
</TR>
<TR>
    <TD>Country:</TD>
    <TD><INPUT NAME=Country></TD>
</TR>
```

6. Save your changes and then reload the file in your Web browser. Figure 6-9 shows the revised form.

   TROUBLE? Users of the Netscape Navigator browser might have to reopen the file in the browser rather than simply click the Reload button to see the changes in the Web form.

Figure 6-9

REGISTRATION FORM WITH RESIZED INPUT BOXES

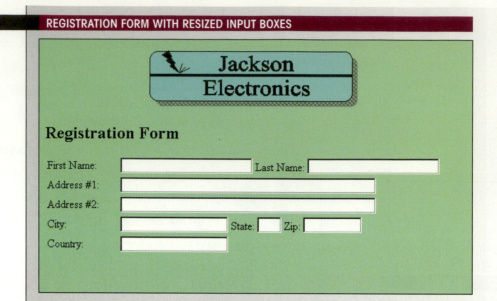

Setting the Maximum Length for Text Input

By setting the size of an input box, you are not putting limitations on the text that can be entered into that field. If a user tries to enter text longer than the input box, the text will automatically scroll to the left. The user will not be able to see all of the text at once, but all of the text will be sent to the CGI script.

Sometimes you might want to limit the number of characters the user enters, as a check to verify that the input is valid. For example, if you have a Social Security Number field, you know in advance that only nine characters are needed. You can keep users from erroneously entering a 10-character value by setting the maximum length of the field to 9. The syntax for setting the maximum length of the input is:

```
<INPUT MAXLENGTH=value>
```

To apply this to the registration form, revise the field for the Zip code to restrict input values to no more than five characters.

To specify the maximum length for the Zip code field:

1. Return to the Register.htm file in your text editor.

2. With the <INPUT> tag for the Zip field, enter the property **MAXLENGTH=5**, as shown in Figure 6-10.

Figure 6-10

SETTING THE MAXIMUM LENGTH FOR THE ZIP INPUT BOX

no more than five characters are allowed for this field

```
<TR>
    <TD>City:</TD>
    <TD><INPUT NAME=City> State: <INPUT NAME=State SIZE=3>
         Zip: <INPUT NAME=ZIP SIZE=10 MAXLENGTH=5></TD>
</TR>
```

3. Save your changes to the file and then reload the Register.htm file in your browser.

4. Click the **Zip** input box and try to type more than five characters into the box. Note that symbols beyond the fifth character are ignored by the browser.

Setting a Default Value for an Input Box

Another property you can use with the <INPUT> tag is the VALUE property. The VALUE property sets the default value of the field and is also the value that appears in the input box when the form is initially displayed. If most people will enter the same value into a certain input box, it saves time and increases accuracy if the value appears for them. The syntax for the VALUE property is:

```
<INPUT VALUE="value">
```

where *value* is the default text or number that will appear in the field. Note that you must enclose the default value in quotation marks if it is a text string consisting of several words.

Lisa wants the Country field on the registration form to have a default value of "United States" because domestic sales account for over 80% of Jackson Electronics' income, and she wants to save the majority of her users the task of typing this information.

To set the default value for the Country field:

1. Return to the Register.htm file in your text editor.

2. Type **VALUE="United States"** in the Country <INPUT> tag, as shown in Figure 6-11.

Figure 6-11	SETTING THE DEFAULT VALUE FOR THE COUNTRY FIELD

```
<TR>
    <TD>Country:</TD>
    <TD><INPUT NAME=Country VALUE="United States"></TD>
</TR>
</TABLE>
```

default value

3. Save your changes and then reopen or refresh the file in your browser. Verify that "United States" now appears in the Country field.

If customers from countries outside of the United States use this Web form, they can remove the default value by selecting the text and pressing the Delete key.

Creating a Password Field

In some instances users will not want information that they enter into an input box to appear on the screen. For example, one part of your form might prompt the user for a credit card number. If so, you would like to prevent the card number from being displayed on the computer monitor, as a security measure. You can accomplish this with a Password field. A **Password field** is identical to an input box, except that the characters typed by the user are displayed as bullets or asterisks. The syntax for creating a Password field is:

```
<INPUT TYPE=PASSWORD>
```

As with input boxes, you can specify a size, maximum length, and name for your password. Using a Password field should not be confused with having a secure connection between the Web client and the Web server. The password itself is not encrypted, so it is still possible for someone to intercept the information as it is being sent from your Web browser to the CGI script, if the connection is not secure. The Password field only acts as a mask for the field entry as it is displayed on the computer screen. Lisa does not need you to specify any Password fields for the registration form.

You've completed the first part of the registration form. Because the first few fields you've entered so far deal solely with collecting contact information, Lisa suggests that you set them off with a horizontal line located below the Country field. Many Web page designers recommend this visual separation of different topics.

To add a horizontal line to your form:

1. Return to the Register.htm file in your text editor.

2. Directly above the </TABLE> tag, insert the following lines:

```
<TR>
        <TD COLSPAN=2><HR></TD>
</TR>
```

Note that the COLSPAN property will cause the horizontal line to span the two columns in the table.

3. Save your changes to **Register.htm**, and then reload the file in your browser. There should now be a horizontal line below the Country field.

Before going on to other tasks, you'll test the registration form by entering some test values in it. To move from one input box to the next, you press the Tab key. To move to the previous input box, press the Tab key while holding down the Shift key. Pressing the Enter key usually submits the form, but because you have not created a submit button for the form yet, pressing the Enter key will do nothing at this point.

To test your form:

1. Click the input box for the First Name field, type **Wayne**, press the **Tab** key to move to the Last Name field, and then type **Hollins**.

2. Continue entering the text shown in Figure 6-12, pressing **Tab** to move from one input box to the next.

Figure 6-12   **SAMPLE DATA FOR THE REGISTRATION FORM**

Jackson
Electronics

Registration Form

First Name:	Wayne	Last Name:	Hollins
Address #1:	Apt. 58		
Address #2:	120 Thorpe Avenue		
City:	Oak Creek	State: WI Zip:	53154
Country:	United States		

You might want to try other test values for the registration form. Try inserting extra text in an input box, and notice that the text automatically scrolls to the left when it exceeds the width of the box. This feature allows you to enter more text than can be displayed in the form.

You've finished working on the first part of the registration form. You've learned how forms and CGI scripts work together to allow Web authors to collect information from users. You've also seen how to create simple text input boxes using the <INPUT> tag. In the next session, you'll learn other uses for the <INPUT> tag by adding new fields to the form, including a selection list, radio buttons, and check boxes.

Session 6.1 QUICK CHECK

1. What is a CGI script?

2. What is the purpose of the <FORM> tag?

3. What tag would you enter to create a text input box with the name "Phone"?

4. What property would you enter to create a Phone input box that is 10 characters wide?

5. What property would you enter to limit entry to the Phone input box to no more than 10 characters?

6. What tag would you enter to create an input box named "Subscribe" with a default value of "yes"?

7. How would you prevent the contents of an input box from being displayed on the user's computer screen?

SESSION 6.2

In this session you will learn how to create selection lists to allow users to select single or multiple options from a drop-down list box. You'll also create radio buttons for selecting single option values, and you'll create check boxes for selecting one or more items in a list. Finally, you'll create text areas, also known as text boxes, for entering extended comments and memos.

Creating a Selection List

The next section of the registration form is dedicated to collecting information about the product that the customer has purchased and about how the customer intends to use it. The first field you'll create in this section records the product name. There are six Jackson Electronics products that the registration form covers:

- ScanMaster
- ScanMaster II
- LaserPrint 1000
- LaserPrint 5000
- Print/Scan 150
- Print/Scan 250

Because the products constitute a predefined list of values for the product name, Lisa wants this information displayed with a selection list. A **selection list** is a list box from which the user selects a particular value or set of values, usually by clicking an arrow to open the list and then clicking the item or items. It's a good idea to use selection lists rather than input boxes when you have a fixed set of possible responses. By using a selection list, you can guard against spelling mistakes and erroneous entries.

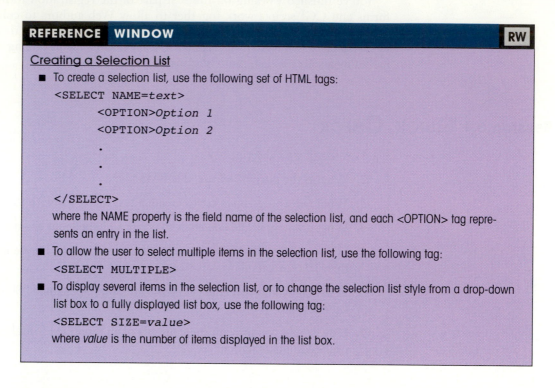

REFERENCE WINDOW   **RW**

Creating a Selection List

■ To create a selection list, use the following set of HTML tags:

```
<SELECT NAME=text>
        <OPTION>Option 1
        <OPTION>Option 2
            .
            .
            .
</SELECT>
```

where the NAME property is the field name of the selection list, and each <OPTION> tag represents an entry in the list.

■ To allow the user to select multiple items in the selection list, use the following tag:

```
<SELECT MULTIPLE>
```

■ To display several items in the selection list, or to change the selection list style from a drop-down list box to a fully displayed list box, use the following tag:

```
<SELECT SIZE=value>
```

where *value* is the number of items displayed in the list box.

Using the <SELECT> and <OPTION> Tags

You create a selection list using the <SELECT> tag, and you specify individual selection items with the <OPTION> tag. The general syntax for the <SELECT> and <OPTION> tags is:

```
<SELECT NAME=text>
        <OPTION>Option 1
        <OPTION>Option 2
            .
            .
            .
</SELECT>
```

where *text* is the name you've assigned to the selection field, and *Option 1*, *Option 2*, and so forth are the possible values displayed in the selection list. The structure of the <SELECT> and <OPTION> tags is similar to that of the unordered list tags, <UL> and <LI>. Recall that the syntax of an unordered list is:

```
<UL>
        <LI>Item 1
        <LI>Item 2
            .
            .
            .
</UL>
```

Note that the values for each option are entered to the right of the <OPTION> tag rather than inside the tag, just as with the <LI> tag.

Your next task is to add the product selection list to the registration form.

To add the selection list to the form:

1. If you took a break after the previous session, start your text editor and reopen the **Register.htm** file from the Tutorial.06 folder of your Data Disk.

2. Directly above the </TABLE> tag, insert the following lines:

```
<TR>
<TD>Product:</TD>
<TD><SELECT NAME=Product>
    <OPTION>ScanMaster
    <OPTION>ScanMaster II
    <OPTION>LaserPrint 1000
    <OPTION>LaserPrint 5000
    <OPTION>Print/Scan 150
    <OPTION>Print/Scan 250
    </SELECT></TD>
</TR>
```

Figure 6-13 shows the revised HTML code.

Figure 6-13	CREATING A SELECTION LIST

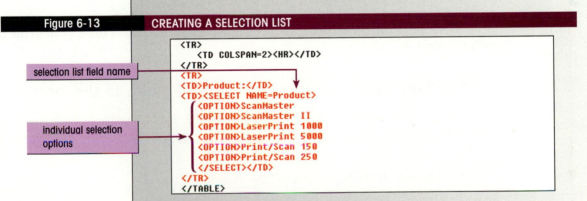

selection list field name

individual selection options

3. Save your changes to the file, and then load the file in your Web browser. The form now contains the selection list. Note that the first item in the list, ScanMaster, is displayed in the selection list box.

4. Click the **Product** drop-down list arrow and verify that the six products you entered with the <OPTION> tag are displayed. See Figure 6-14.

Figure 6-14   **USING THE PRODUCT SELECTION LIST**

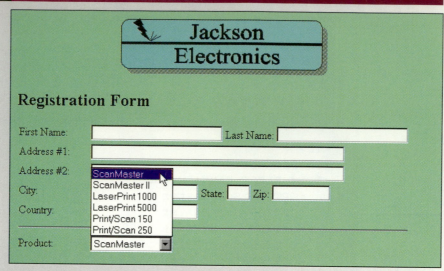

TROUBLE? Your selection list might look slightly different in some versions of the Netscape Navigator browser.

There are two additional input boxes associated with the product information: the product serial number and the date the product was purchased. You'll add these fields to the registration form now.

To add the Date Purchased and Serial # fields to the form:

1. Return to the Register.htm file in your text editor.

2. Directly above the </TABLE> tag, insert the following lines:

```
<TR>
   <TD>Date Purchased:</TD>
   <TD><INPUT NAME=Date></TD>
</TR>
<TR>
   <TD>Serial #:</TD>
   <TD><INPUT NAME=Serial></TD>
</TR>
```

The revised HTML code is shown in Figure 6-15.

Figure 6-15	ADDING TWO MORE INPUT BOXES TO THE REGISTRATION FORM

```
<TR>
<TD>Product:</TD>
<TD><SELECT NAME=Product>
    <OPTION>ScanMaster
    <OPTION>ScanMaster II
    <OPTION>LaserPrint 1000
    <OPTION>LaserPrint 5000
    <OPTION>Print/Scan 150
    <OPTION>Print/Scan 250
    </SELECT></TD>
</TR>
<TR>
    <TD>Date Purchased:</TD>
    <TD><INPUT NAME=Date></TD>
</TR>
<TR>
    <TD>Serial #:</TD>
    <TD><INPUT NAME=Serial></TD>
</TR>
</TABLE>
```

3. Save your changes to **Register.htm**, and then reload the file in your Web browser. Figure 6-16 shows the registration form with the two new input boxes.

Figure 6-16	DATE PURCHASED AND SERIAL # INPUT BOXES

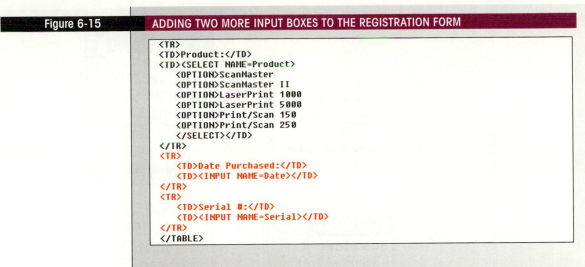

new input boxes

Modifying the Appearance of a Selection List

HTML provides several properties to modify the appearance and behavior of selection lists and selection options. By default, the <SELECT> tag displays only one option from the selection list, along with a drop-down list arrow that you click to view other selection options. You can change the number of options displayed by modifying the SIZE property. The syntax of the SIZE property is:

```
<SELECT SIZE=value>
```

where *value* is the number of items that the selection list will display in the form. By specifying a SIZE value greater than 1, you change the selection list from a drop-down list box to a list box with a scroll bar that allows the user to scroll through the various options. If you set the SIZE property to be equal to the number of options in the selection list, the scroll bar is either not displayed or is dimmed. See Figure 6-17.

Figure 6-17   SELECTION LISTS WITH DIFFERENT SIZE VALUES

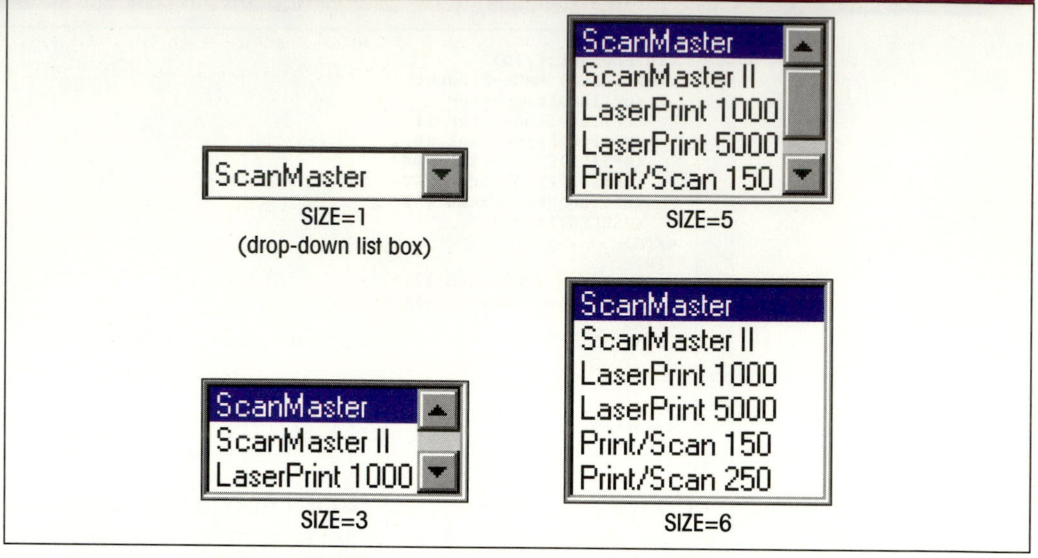

Lisa likes the product selection list as it is, so you don't have to specify a different value for the SIZE property.

Making Multiple Selections

The user is not limited to making only a single selection from a selection list. You can modify your list to allow multiple selections, by adding the MULTIPLE property to the <SELECT> tag. The syntax for this property is:

```
<SELECT MULTIPLE>
```

The most common way to make multiple selections from a selection list is to hold down a specific key while you click the selected items. With the Windows interface, you can make multiple selections in the following ways:

- For a noncontiguous selection, hold down the Ctrl key and click each item you want to choose in the selection list.
- For a contiguous selection, click the first item in the range of items you want to select, hold down the Shift key, and click the last item in the range of items. The two items you clicked, plus any items between them, will be selected.

If you decide to use a multiple selection list in one of your forms, you should be aware that the form will send a name/value pair to the CGI script for each option the user selects from the list. This means that the CGI script needs to be able to handle a single field with multiple values. You should check and verify that your CGI scripts are set up to handle this before using a multiple selection list.

Working with Option Values

By default, your form will send to the CGI script the values that appear in the selection list. In your form, for example, the values ScanMaster II, LaserPrint 5000, and so on will be sent to the CGI script. Sometimes you will want to send the CGI script a different text string from the text displayed in the selection list. This occurs when you display long descriptive text for each option in the selection list, in order to help the user make an informed choice, but you need only an abbreviated version of the user's selection for your records. You can specify the value that is sent to the CGI script with the VALUE property. For example, the following HTML code sends the value "1" to the CGI script if the ScanMaster is selected, "2" if the ScanMaster II is selected, and so forth:

```
<SELECT NAME=Product>
      <OPTION VALUE=1>ScanMaster
      <OPTION VALUE=2>ScanMaster II
      <OPTION VALUE=3>LaserPrint 1000
      <OPTION VALUE=4>LaserPrint 5000
      <OPTION VALUE=5>Print/Scan 150
      <OPTION VALUE=6>Print/Scan 250
</SELECT>
```

You can also specify which option in the selection list is initially selected (highlighted) when the form is displayed. By default, the first option in the list is selected; however, using the SELECTED property, you can specify a different value. For example, in the following HTML code, the LaserPrint 1000 will be the option that is initially selected when the user first encounters the Product field on the form:

```
<SELECT NAME=Product>
      <OPTION>ScanMaster
      <OPTION>ScanMaster II
      <OPTION SELECTED>LaserPrint 1000
      <OPTION>LaserPrint 5000
      <OPTION>Print/Scan 150
      <OPTION>Print/Scan 250
</SELECT>
```

You don't have to make any changes to the selection list at this point, because Lisa wants to follow the default settings, which send the text associated with each selection option to the CGI script, and select the first option in the selection list by default. Having finished your work with selection lists on the registration form, you'll next turn to creating fields using radio buttons.

Working with Radio Buttons

Radio buttons are similar to selection lists in that they display a list of choices from which the user makes a selection. Unlike the items in a selection list, only one radio button can be selected, and the act of selecting one option automatically deselects any previously selected option.

Radio buttons use the same <INPUT> tag as input boxes, except that the TYPE property is set to RADIO. The syntax for an individual radio button is:

```
<INPUT TYPE=RADIO NAME=text VALUE=value>
```

where *text* is the name assigned to the field containing the radio button, and *value* is the value of the radio button, which will be sent to the CGI script if that option is selected. The NAME property is important because it groups distinct radio buttons together, so that selecting one radio button in the group automatically deselects all of the other radio buttons in that group. Note that, like the text input boxes you created earlier, the <INPUT> tag does not create any text for the radio button. In order for users to understand the purpose of the radio button, you must insert descriptive text next to the <INPUT> tag, as you did with the input boxes. The value of the radio button does not have to match the accompanying text. Figure 6-18 shows an example of HTML code that creates radio buttons for party affiliations.

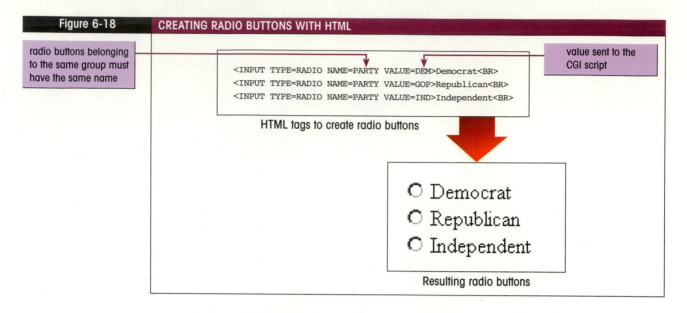

| Figure 6-18 | CREATING RADIO BUTTONS WITH HTML |

radio buttons belonging to the same group must have the same name

```
<INPUT TYPE=RADIO NAME=PARTY VALUE=DEM>Democrat<BR>
<INPUT TYPE=RADIO NAME=PARTY VALUE=GOP>Republican<BR>
<INPUT TYPE=RADIO NAME=PARTY VALUE=IND>Independent<BR>
```

value sent to the CGI script

HTML tags to create radio buttons

○ Democrat
○ Republican
○ Independent

Resulting radio buttons

Note that in this sample code, the value sent to the CGI script does not match the text displayed with the radio button. If the user selects the Republican radio button, the value "GOP" is sent to the CGI script paired with the field name "PARTY".

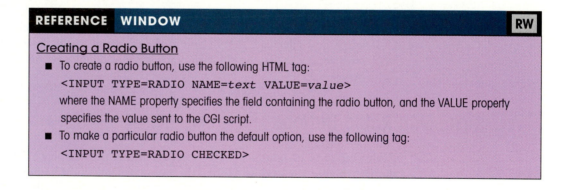

| REFERENCE | WINDOW | RW |

Creating a Radio Button

■ To create a radio button, use the following HTML tag:

```
<INPUT TYPE=RADIO NAME=text VALUE=value>
```

where the NAME property specifies the field containing the radio button, and the VALUE property specifies the value sent to the CGI script.

■ To make a particular radio button the default option, use the following tag:

```
<INPUT TYPE=RADIO CHECKED>
```

Lisa has indicated that she would like you to create radio buttons for product usage on the registration form. The name of the field that will contain the radio buttons is USE. There are five possible choices: Home, Business, Government, Educational Institution, and Other. You can enter the HTML code for this field now.

To add the USE field and radio buttons to the form:

1. Return to the Register.htm file in your text editor.

2. Directly above the </TABLE> tag, insert the following lines:

```
<TR>
<TD VALIGN=TOP>Used for:</TD>
<TD><INPUT TYPE=RADIO NAME=USE VALUE=HOME>Home<BR>
    <INPUT TYPE=RADIO NAME=USE VALUE=BUS>Business<BR>
    <INPUT TYPE=RADIO NAME=USE VALUE=GOV>Government<BR>
    <INPUT TYPE=RADIO NAME=USE VALUE=ED>Educational
    Institution<BR>
    <INPUT TYPE=RADIO NAME=USE VALUE=OTHER>Other</TD>
</TR>
```

Note that you use the <BR> tag in this code to start each radio button on a new line within the table cell. Your HTML code should appear as shown in Figure 6-19.

Figure 6-19	ADDING RADIO BUTTONS TO THE REGISTRATION FORM

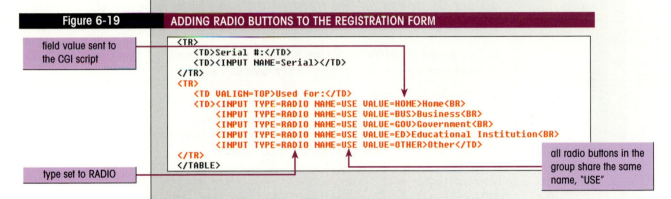

field value sent to the CGI script

type set to RADIO

all radio buttons in the group share the same name, "USE"

3. Save your changes to Register.htm, and then reload the file in your Web browser. Figure 6-20 shows the new registration form with the radio buttons for various product usage options. Note that the VALIGN=TOP property causes the table cell containing the text "Used for:" to be aligned with the top of the cell containing the radio buttons.

Figure 6-20	THE "USED FOR" RADIO BUTTONS

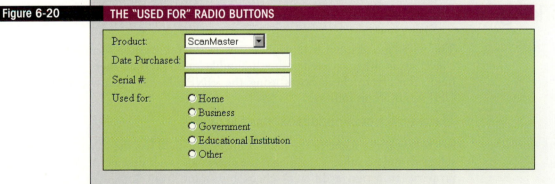

4. Practice clicking each of the radio buttons. Verify that clicking one of the radio buttons deselects any other selected button in the list.

> **TROUBLE?** If clicking one radio button fails to deselect another, check the names you've assigned to each button and verify that they are identical and that the cases (uppercase and lowercase) match.

Notice that when you first open the registration form, none of the radio buttons is selected. In some cases you might want to designate one of the radio buttons as the default and have it already selected when the form opens. You can do this by adding the CHECKED property to the <INPUT> tag for that particular radio button. For example, to set the Business radio button as the default option in the registration form, you would enter the following tag:

```
<INPUT TYPE=RADIO NAME=USE VALUE=BUS CHECKED>Business
```

Lisa informs you that most Jackson Electronics products are used by businesses, and she would like to see this option set as the default in the Web page form.

To set Business as the default option in the USE field:

1. Return to the Register.htm file in your text editor.

2. Locate the **<INPUT>** tag for the Business radio button, and then type **CHECKED** within the tag, following the syntax previously shown.

3. Save your changes.

4. Return to your Web browser and reload the Web page. Verify that the Business radio button is selected automatically when the form opens in the browser and that you can still select the other radio buttons.

When should you use radio buttons, and when should you use a selection list? Generally, if you have a very long list of options that would be difficult or cumbersome to display within your form, you should use a selection list. If you want to allow users to select more than one option, you should use a selection list with the MULTIPLE property turned on. If you have a short list of possible options with only one option allowed at a time, you should use radio buttons.

Working with Check Boxes

The next type of input field you'll create in the registration form is the check box field. A check box is either selected or not, but unlike radio buttons, there is only one check box per field. You create check boxes using the <INPUT> tag with the TYPE property set to CHECKBOX, as follows:

```
<INPUT TYPE=CHECKBOX NAME=text>
```

where *text* is the name of the field. A check box field has the value "on" if the check box is selected, and no value is assigned if the check box is left deselected. You can use the VALUE property to assign a different check box value from "on." For example, the following HTML code assigns the value "YES" to the DEMOCRAT field if the check box is selected:

```
<INPUT TYPE=CHECKBOX NAME=DEMOCRAT VALUE=YES>
```

As with text input boxes and radio buttons, the <INPUT> tag for the check box does not display any text. You must add text next to the <INPUT> tag to describe the purpose of the check box.

By default, check boxes are deselected when the form opens. As with radio buttons, you can use the CHECKED property to automatically select a check box. The appropriate HTML code is:

```
<INPUT TYPE=CHECKBOX NAME=DEMOCRAT VALUE=YES CHECKED>
```

In this example, the DEMOCRAT check box field will be selected when the browser opens the form.

REFERENCE   WINDOW   **RW**

Creating a Check Box

■ To create a check box, use the following HTML tag:

```
<INPUT TYPE=CHECKBOX NAME=text VALUE=value>
```

where the NAME property specifies the field containing the check box, and the VALUE property specifies the value sent to the CGI script if the check box is selected.

■ To make a check box selected by default, use the following tag:

```
<INPUT TYPE=CHECKBOX CHECKED>
```

Lisa has specified four check boxes for the registration form. Each one identifies a type of operating system, and customers can select one or more to indicate which systems they are using the product with. Even though you'll arrange these check boxes together on the form, each one is associated with a different field (unlike the radio buttons you just created, which are all associated with the USE field).

To add the check boxes to your form:

1. Return to your text editor and the Register.htm file.

2. Directly above the </TABLE> tag, insert the following lines:

```
<TR>
   <TD VALIGN=TOP>System (check all that apply):</TD>
   <TD><INPUT TYPE=CHECKBOX NAME=WINDOWS>Windows<BR>
       <INPUT TYPE=CHECKBOX NAME=MAC>Macintosh<BR>
       <INPUT TYPE=CHECKBOX NAME=UNIX>UNIX<BR>
       <INPUT TYPE=CHECKBOX NAME=OTHER_SYSTEM>Other</TD>
</TR>
```

Your HTML code should appear as shown in Figure 6-21.

Figure 6-21   ADDING CHECK BOXES TO THE REGISTRATION FORM

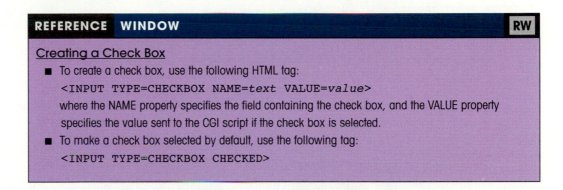

field name

You've completed the fields on the form that deal with the product the customer purchased and how the customer plans to use it. As you did earlier with the contact information, you'll separate these fields from others on the form with a horizontal line.

To add a second horizontal line to your form:

1. Directly above the </TABLE> tag, insert the following tags:

```
<TR>
    <TD COLSPAN=2><HR></TD>
</TR>
```

2. Save your changes to **Register.htm**.

Next, view the registration form in your Web browser to confirm that the check boxes work properly.

To test your form:

1. Return to your Web browser and reload the Register.htm file. Figure 6-22 shows the appearance of the check boxes in the form. Notice the horizontal line that appears below the check boxes.

Figure 6-22 | **OPERATING SYSTEM CHECK BOXES**

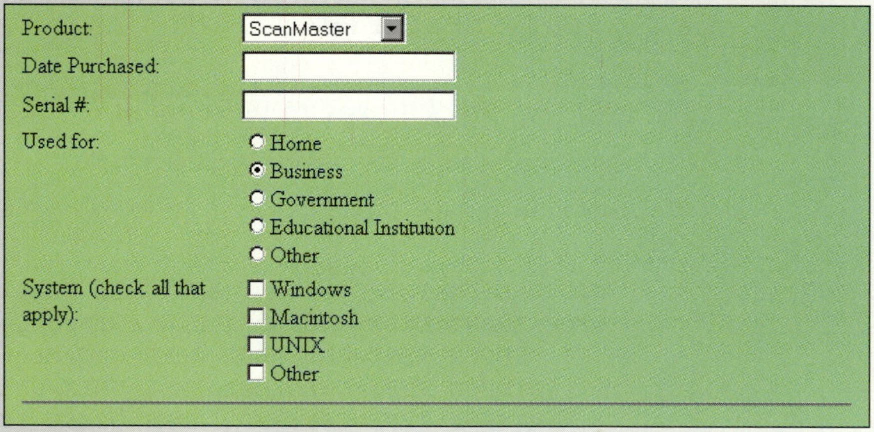

2. Click each of the check boxes you just created and verify that clicking them will alternately select and deselect them, but that clicking one does not deselect the others.

Creating a Text Area

The next section of the registration form allows users to enter comments about the products they purchased. Because these comments will probably consist of long text strings and sentences, an input box might be too small to display them. Instead you need to use the <TEXTAREA> tag. The <TEXTAREA> tag creates a text box, like the one shown in Figure 6-23, in which the user enters extended comments.

Figure 6-23   **A SAMPLE TEXT BOX**

Enter comments here:
The Print/Scan 150 is a great addition to our small business. We've managed to increase productivity with this printer/scanner combination.

The syntax of the <TEXTAREA> tag is:

```
<TEXTAREA ROWS=value COLS=value NAME=text>default
text</TEXTAREA>
```

where the ROWS and COLS properties define the number of rows and columns in the text box. ROWS and COLS do not refer to the rows and columns of a table; rather, ROWS is the number of lines (though some earlier versions of browsers will show more lines than indicated by the ROWS property), and COLUMNS is the number of characters allowed in each line. *Default text* is the text that appears in the text box when the form opens. Although it is not required, you could use default text to provide additional instructions to the user about what to enter in the text box, as in the following example:

```
<TEXTAREA ROWS=3 NAME=COMMENTS>Enter comments here</TEXTAREA>
```

When the form is displayed by the browser, the text "Enter comments here" is automatically entered into the text box. Note that unlike the other field tags, <TEXTAREA> is a two-sided tag, which means that it has an opening tag, <TEXTAREA>, and a closing tag, </TEXTAREA>. You need to include the </TEXTAREA> tag even if you don't specify any default text.

The text you enter into a text box does not automatically wrap to the next row in the box. Instead, a text box acts like an input box, in which the text is automatically scrolled to the left as additional text is typed. You can override this default setting using the WRAP property. The values for the WRAP property are shown in Figure 6-24.

Figure 6-24   **VALUES OF THE <TEXTAREA> WRAP PROPERTY**

VALUE	DESCRIPTION
OFF	All the text is displayed on a single line, scrolling to the left if the text extends past the width of the box. Text goes to the next row in the box only if the Enter key is pressed. The text is sent to the CGI script in a single line.
SOFT (or VIRTUAL)	Text wraps automatically to the next row when it extends beyond the width of the text box. The text is still sent to the CGI script in a single line without any information about how the text was wrapped within the text box.
HARD (or PHYSICAL)	Text wraps automatically to the next row when it extends beyond the width of the text box. When the text is sent to the CGI script, the line-wrapping information is included, allowing the CGI script to work with the text exactly as it appears in the text box.

You will usually want to set the value of the WRAP property to either VIRTUAL or PHYSICAL, to allow the text to automatically wrap within the text box. The difference between these two options lies in how the text is sent to the CGI script. Setting the WRAP property to PHYSICAL preserves any line wrapping that takes place in the text box; the VIRTUAL option does not. You should check the documentation of the CGI script to see whether one method is preferred over the other.

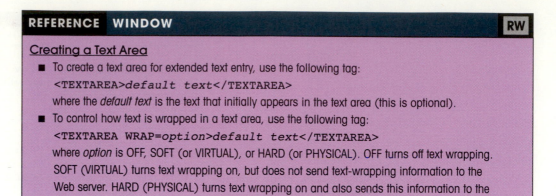

REFERENCE   WINDOW   RW

Creating a Text Area
- To create a text area for extended text entry, use the following tag:

  `<TEXTAREA>default text</TEXTAREA>`

  where the *default text* is the text that initially appears in the text area (this is optional).
- To control how text is wrapped in a text area, use the following tag:

  `<TEXTAREA WRAP=option>default text</TEXTAREA>`

  where *option* is OFF, SOFT (or VIRTUAL), or HARD (or PHYSICAL). OFF turns off text wrapping.
  SOFT (VIRTUAL) turns text wrapping on, but does not send text-wrapping information to the
  Web server. HARD (PHYSICAL) turns text wrapping on and also sends this information to the
  Web server.

For the Comments field, you'll use the <TEXTAREA> tag with the WRAP property set to VIRTUAL so that the user's comments wrap automatically to the next line in the box. The size of the text area will be 4 lines high and 50 characters wide, which Lisa thinks should be enough for the typed comments. You won't specify any default text for the Comments field.

To add a text box to the registration form:

1. Return to your text editor and the Register.htm file.

2. Directly above the </TABLE> tag, insert the following lines:

```
<TR>
    <TD VALIGN=TOP>Comments?:</TD>
    <TD>
    <TEXTAREA ROWS=4 COLS=50 NAME=Comments WRAP=VIRTUAL>
</TEXTAREA>
    </TD>
</TR>
```

3. Save your changes to **Register.htm**, and then reload the page in your Web browser.

4. Test the line-wrapping feature of the text box by typing the following text in the Comments field:

   I'm very pleased with my purchase of the ScanMaster II. Is there equipment that would allow me to scan photo negatives and transparencies?

   The text should wrap automatically, as shown in Figure 6-25.

Figure 6-25	ENTERING COMMENTS INTO THE COMMENTS TEXT AREA BOX

text wraps automatically

Note that the text box includes a vertical scroll bar so that if the user enters more text than can be displayed within the area of the text box, the user can scroll to see the hidden text.

TROUBLE? If you are using some earlier versions of Netscape Navigator or Internet Explorer, your Comments text box will look slightly different from the one shown in Figure 6-25. Netscape and Internet Explorer also use slightly different fonts in the text box.

You've created the last input field for the registration form. Using HTML you've added input boxes, a selection list, radio buttons, check boxes, and a text area to your form. In the next session, you'll learn how to set up your form to work with a CGI script.

Session 6.2 QUICK CHECK

1. What tag would you enter to create a selection list with a field named State and with the options California, Nevada, Oregon, and Washington?

2. How would you modify the tag in Quick Check 1 to allow more than one state to be selected from the list?

3. What tag would make Oregon the default selection in Quick Check 1?

4. What tag would you enter to create a series of radio buttons for a field named State with the options California, Nevada, Oregon, and Washington?

5. How would you modify the tag in Quick Check 4 to send the number 1 to the CGI script if the user selects California, 2 for Nevada, 3 for Oregon, and 4 for Washington?

6. What tag would you enter to create a check box field named California? If you don't specify otherwise, what value is sent to the CGI script if the check box is selected?

7. What tag would you enter to create a text box field named Memo that is 5 rows high and 30 columns wide, and has the default text "Enter notes here."?

8. What property would you add to the tag in Quick Check 7 to cause the Memo text to automatically wrap to the next row and to send that text-wrapping information to the CGI script?

In this session you will learn how to create submit and reset buttons to either send your form to a CGI script or reset it to its initial state. You'll learn how to create image fields. You'll also work with form properties to control how your form is submitted to the CGI script. You'll learn about one way to process form data without using a CGI script. Finally, the session ends with an introduction to some of the new form tags and properties.

Creating Form Buttons

Up to now, all of your form elements have been input fields of one kind or another. Another type of form field is one that performs an action when activated—as a button does when the user clicks it. Buttons can be used to run programs, submit forms, or reset the form to its original state.

REFERENCE WINDOW   **RW**

Creating Form Buttons

- To create a button to submit the form to the CGI script, enter the following tag:
  ```
  <INPUT TYPE=SUBMIT VALUE="text">
  ```
  where the VALUE property defines the text that appears on the button and specifies the value that is sent to the CGI script to indicate which button on the form has been clicked.
- To create a button to cancel or reset the appearance of your form, use the TYPE property shown in the following tag:
  ```
  <INPUT TYPE=RESET>
  ```
- To create a button to perform an action within the Web page by running a program or script, use the following tag:
  ```
  <INPUT TYPE=BUTTON>
  ```

Creating Buttons that Perform Actions

If you want to include a button on your form that performs an action, such as calculating a value or validating the user's input on the form, you can create a button using the TYPE=BUTTON property. For example, the following tag creates a button with the label "Click to calculate total order":

```
<INPUT TYPE=BUTTON VALUE="Click to calculate total order">
```

You can insert programs into your Web page that will respond when this button is clicked and run the described calculations. You'll learn how to write and attach programs to your Web page in later tutorials.

Creating Submit and Reset Buttons

When the user finishes entering information into the form, that information can be submitted to the CGI script, or, if the user made a mistake, the form can be reset to its original default values without submitting anything to the CGI script. Both actions can be accomplished by clicking a button on the form. You create Submit and Reset buttons using the same <INPUT> tag you've used for other form elements. The TYPE property is set to either SUBMIT or RESET. The syntax for the two buttons is:

```
<INPUT TYPE=SUBMIT>
<INPUT TYPE=RESET>
```

You can also specify NAME and VALUE properties for Submit and Reset buttons, although these properties are not required. You would use these properties when you have more than one Submit button and the CGI script performs different actions when different buttons are clicked. For example, a Web page advertising a shareware program might include three buttons: one used to download the program from the company's Web site, another used to retrieve additional information about the product, and the third used to cancel the form submission. The HTML tags for such buttons might appear as shown in Figure 6-26.

Figure 6-26	CREATING FORM BUTTONS WITH HTML

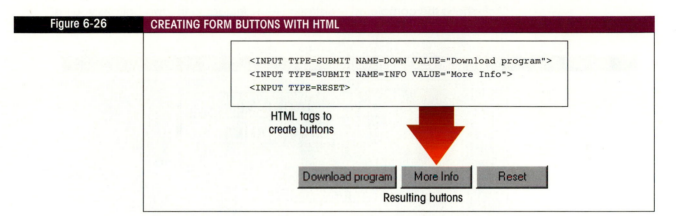

As shown in the figure, the VALUE property also changes the text that appears on the button, from either "Submit" or "Reset" to whatever you choose; Submit buttons don't have to be labeled "Submit," and Reset buttons don't have to be labeled "Reset."

Lisa wants the registration form to include two buttons: a Submit button and a Reset button. The Submit button, which she wants labeled "Send Registration," will send the form information to the CGI script. The Reset button, to be labeled "Cancel," will cancel the form, resetting all the fields to their default values. You'll place these buttons at the bottom of the form, centered within the table.

To add the Submit and Reset buttons to the registration form:

1. If you took a break after the previous session, start your text editor and reopen the **Register.htm** file from the Tutorial.06 folder of your Data Disk.

2. Directly above the </TABLE> tag, insert the following tags:

```
<TR>
    <TD COLSPAN=2 ALIGN=CENTER>
    <INPUT TYPE=SUBMIT VALUE="Send Registration">
    <INPUT TYPE=RESET VALUE="Cancel">
    </TD>
</TR>
```

Figure 6-27 shows the current code in the Register.htm file.

Figure 6-27   ADDING SUBMIT AND RESET BUTTONS TO THE REGISTRATION FORM

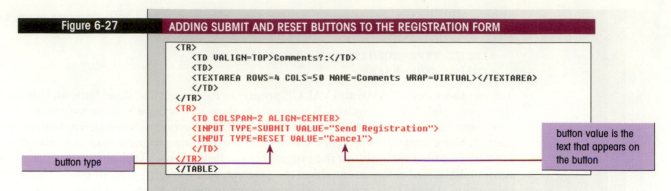

```
<TR>
   <TD VALIGN=TOP>Comments?:</TD>
   <TD>
   <TEXTAREA ROWS=4 COLS=50 NAME=Comments WRAP=VIRTUAL></TEXTAREA>
   </TD>
</TR>
<TR>
   <TD COLSPAN=2 ALIGN=CENTER>
   <INPUT TYPE=SUBMIT VALUE="Send Registration">
   <INPUT TYPE=RESET VALUE="Cancel">
   </TD>
</TR>
</TABLE>
```

button type

button value is the text that appears on the button

3. Save your changes and then reload the file in your Web browser. Figure 6-28 shows the completed registration form, including the two buttons you just created.

Figure 6-28   THE COMPLETED REGISTRATION FORM

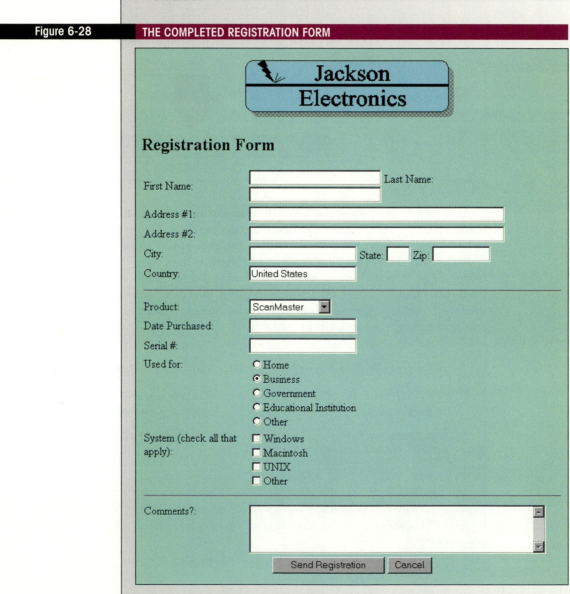

TROUBLE? Your registration form might look slightly different from the one shown in Figure 6-28, depending on which browser you are using.

4. Test the Cancel button by entering test values into the form and then clicking the **Cancel** button. The form should be returned to its initial state.

TROUBLE? If the Cancel button doesn't work, check the HTML code for the button and verify that you've entered the code correctly. The Send Registration button will not do anything yet, because you have not identified the CGI script to receive the form data.

Creating **Image Fields**

Another form element that you can use in your Web pages is the inline image. Inline images can act like Submit buttons so that when the user clicks the image, the form is submitted. Image fields differ from Submit buttons in what kind of information is sent to the CGI script. You create inline images using the <INPUT> tag, but with the TYPE property set to IMAGE. The syntax for this type of form element is:

```
<INPUT TYPE=IMAGE SRC=URL NAME=text VALUE=text>
```

where *URL* is the filename or URL of the inline image, the NAME property assigns a name to the field, and the VALUE property assigns a value to the image. When the form is submitted to the CGI script, the coordinates corresponding to where the user clicked inside the image are attached to the image's name and value in the format: *NAME.x_coordinate, VALUE.y_coordinate*. For example, suppose your Web page contains the following inline image form element:

```
<INPUT TYPE=IMAGE SRC="USAMAP.gif" NAME=USA VALUE="STATE">
```

Assume that a user loads your page and clicks the inline image at the coordinates (15,30). In this case, the Web page will send the field name and *x* coordinate, USA.15, paired with the field value and *y* coordinate, STATE.30, to the script. Once the CGI script receives this information, the action it performs will depend on where the user clicked within the image. See Figure 6-29.

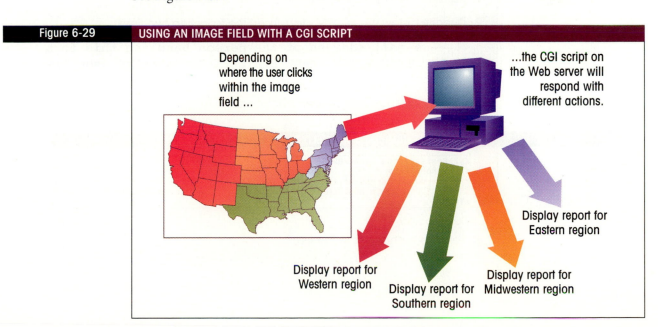

Figure 6-29   USING AN IMAGE FIELD WITH A CGI SCRIPT

Depending on where the user clicks within the image field ...

...the CGI script on the Web server will respond with different actions.

Display report for Eastern region

Display report for Western region

Display report for Southern region

Display report for Midwestern region

You do not have to include any inline image fields in your Web page form.

Working with Hidden Fields

Lisa is pleased with the final appearance of the registration form. She shows the code for the form to Warren Kaughman, one of the programmers at Jackson Electronics and the person responsible for the CGI script that you'll be using. Warren notices only one thing missing from the code—the e-mail address of Lisa's assistant, who will receive the registration forms through e-mail. Warren's CGI script requires that the form include a field named EMAIL containing the recipient's e-mail address—otherwise the CGI script won't know what to do with the form when a user clicks the Submit button (labeled Send Registration). You need to add an e-mail field to the form.

Unlike the other fields you've created, the e-mail field has a predefined value (the e-mail address of Lisa's assistant), which customers should not be able to change. In fact, the customers shouldn't even see the e-mail address of Lisa's assistant displayed on the form. You need a **hidden field**, one that is part of the form but not displayed on the Web page, to prevent the customers from seeing the address.

You create a hidden field using the <INPUT> tag with the TYPE property set to HIDDEN. The syntax for this tag is:

```
<INPUT TYPE=HIDDEN NAME=text VALUE=value>
```

You've already learned from Warren that the name of the e-mail field should be EMAIL, and you learn from Lisa that the e-mail address of her assistant is "adavis@Jkson_Electronics.com" (note that this is a fictional address used for the purposes of this tutorial). Now that you know both the field name and the field value, you can add the hidden field to the registration form.

Because the field is hidden, you can place it anywhere between the opening and closing <FORM> tags. A standard practice is to place all hidden fields in one location, usually at the beginning of the form, to make it easier to interpret your HTML code. You should also include a comment describing the purpose of the field.

To add the hidden field to the registration form:

1. Return to the Register.htm file in your text editor.

2. Directly below the <FORM> tag, insert the following two lines:

```
<!--- e-mail address of the person handling this form --->
<INPUT TYPE=HIDDEN NAME=EMAIL VALUE="adavis@Jkson_Electron
ics.com">
```

Figure 6-30 shows the revised HTML code.

Figure 6-30 | ADDING THE HIDDEN E-MAIL FIELD TO THE REGISTRATION PAGE

```
<H2>Registration Form</H2>
<FORM NAME=REG>
<!--- e-mail address of the person handling this form --->
<INPUT TYPE=HIDDEN NAME=EMAIL VALUE="adavis@Jkson_Electronics.com">
<TABLE>
```

3. Save your changes to the file.

With the recipient field now placed in the registration form, you'll return to the first tag you entered into this document, the <FORM> tag, and insert the properties needed for it to interact with the Jackson Electronics CGI script.

Working with Form Properties

You've added all the elements needed for the form. Your final task is to specify where to send the form data and how to send it. To do this, you must modify the properties of the <FORM> tag. There are three properties you'll work with: ACTION, METHOD, and ENCTYPE.

The **ACTION property** identifies the CGI script that will process your form. The syntax for this property is:

```
<FORM ACTION=URL>
```

where *URL* is the URL of the CGI script. Your Internet service provider or the person who wrote the CGI script will provide this information for you. Warren, the programmer responsible for the CGI script at Jackson Electronics, tells you that the CGI script used for e-mailing form information is located at the following URL:

http://www.Jkson_electronics.com/cgi/mailer

(Remember that this is a fictional URL and that you cannot actually connect to a CGI script at this address.)

Now that you know where to send the form information, you next have to determine how to send that information. The **METHOD property** controls how your Web browser sends data to the Web server running the CGI script. The syntax for the METHOD property is:

```
<FORM METHOD=type>
```

where *type* is either GET or POST. The distinction between the GET and POST methods is technical and extends beyond the scope of this book. In brief, the **GET method**, which is the default, packages the form data by appending it to the end of the URL specified in the ACTION property. The Web server then retrieves the modified URL and stores it in a text string for processing by the CGI script. The **POST method** sends form information in a separate data stream, allowing the Web server to receive the data through what is called "standard input." Because it is more flexible, the POST method is considered the preferred way of sending data to the Web server. It is also safer, because some Web servers limit the amount of data sent via the GET method and will truncate the URL, cutting off valuable information. Don't be concerned if you don't completely understand the difference between using GET and POST. Your Internet service provider will usually provide the necessary information about which of the two methods you should use in your <FORM> tag. If you start writing your own CGI scripts, this issue becomes more important. Warren informs you that his e-mail program uses the POST method to retrieve form data.

Another form property you might have to be concerned with is the ENCTYPE property. The **ENCTYPE property** specifies the format of the data when it is transferred from your Web page to the CGI script. The syntax of this property is:

```
<FORM ENCTYPE=text>
```

where *text* is the data format. Once again, this is a complex technical issue that goes beyond the scope of this book. The default ENCTYPE value is "application/x-www-form-urlencoded," so if you do not specify an encoding value, this is the one the Web server will assume is used for your data. Another ENCTYPE value that is often used is "multipart/form-data," which allows the form to send files to the Web server along with any form data. Your Internet service provider will indicate any special values that you need to include with the ENCTYPE property. Warren's CGI script uses the default encoding value, so you do not have to enter it into the <FORM> tag.

A final possible property you might use with the <FORM> tag is the TARGET property. If your form is part of a framed Web site, you use the **TARGET property** to specify which frame receives output from the CGI script. If your page is not using frames, you do not need to be concerned with this property.

Now that you've been introduced to the issues involved in sending form data to a CGI script, you are ready to make some final modifications to the Register.htm file. You need to enter the ACTION property to specify what CGI script will receive the form data, and the METHOD property to specify that the POST method will be used for processing the form data.

To add the properties to the <FORM> tag:

1. Insert the following properties within the <FORM> tag:

```
ACTION="http://www.Jkson_Electronics.com/cgi/mailer"
METHOD=POST
```

The revised file should appear as shown in Figure 6-31.

Figure 6-31   SPECIFYING WHERE AND HOW TO SEND THE FORM DATA

```
<H2>Registration Form</H2>
<FORM NAME=REG ACTION="http://www.Jkson_Electronics.com/cgi/mailer" METHOD=POST>
<!--- e-mail address of the person handling this form --->
<INPUT TYPE=HIDDEN NAME=EMAIL VALUE="adavis@Jkson_Electronics.com">
<TABLE>
```

location of the CGI script

how the form data will be sent to the CGI script

2. Save your changes.

3. Close the file and your text editor.

You've finished the registration form. Warren will take the Register.htm file and transfer it to a folder on the company's Web server. From there it can be fully tested to verify that the CGI script and the form work properly, and that the form data is mailed to Lisa's assistant.

To allow you to see how this form would work in practice (once it's installed on a Web server along with the appropriate CGI script), a modified version of it has been placed on the Web at the URL:

http://www.careys.com/Jkson_Electronics/Register.htm

If you have a connection to the Web, you can open this page and test the form and the CGI script.

To test the registration form:

1. Open the URL **http://www.careys.com/Jkson_Electronics/Register.htm** in your Web browser.

A modified version of the page that you created in this tutorial is displayed.

TROUBLE? If the page does not appear, carefully check the URL you entered. You must match not only the spelling, but also the case (upper or lower) of all of the letters in the address.

2. Type (*your e-mail address*) in the E-mail input box in the first field of the form.

Note that unlike the form you created, this form will mail the form data to the e-mail address you enter.

3. Enter contact information for yourself in the appropriate fields.

4. Complete the rest of the form, using test entries of your own choosing.

5. Click the **Click to register** button. Your Web browser presents a page, an example of which is shown in Figure 6-32, displaying the name of each field in the form and the value you've assigned to it. At the same time, the CGI script will be formatting a mail message to be sent to the address you entered in Step 2.

Figure 6-32	RESPONSE TO THE ONLINE REGISTRATION FORM

Thank You For Filling Out This Form

Below is what you submitted to adavis@Jkson_Electronics.com on Thursday, February 17, 19100 at 14:59:47

Serial: 3221-42164

Product: LaserPrint 5000

State: WI

ZIP: 53701

Country: United States

LastName: Davis

Comments: Can the LaserPrint 5000 printer cartridge be recycled?

Address1: Room 634

Address2: 211 Hawkins Avenue

FirstName: Andrew

City: Lawrence

WINDOWS: on

USE: BUS

Date: 8/1/2001

You should soon receive a message in your mail box that looks like the page shown in Figure 6-32.

TROUBLE? If you don't receive an e-mail message within a few hours, either there is a problem with your mail server, causing a delay in the posting of the message, or you might have mistyped your e-mail address on the registration form. You should try again, carefully checking your e-mail address in the form.

Using the MAILTO Action

So far in working with Lisa's registration file, you have built a form to use Warren's e-mail CGI script. There is a way to send form information through e-mail without using a script. Starting with version 3.0, Netscape Navigator began supporting an ACTION property called MAILTO. This action accesses the user's own mail program and uses it to mail form information to a specified e-mail address, bypassing the need for using CGI scripts on a Web server. The syntax of the MAILTO action is:

```
<FORM ACTION="mailto:e-mail_address" METHOD=POST>
```

where *e-mail_address* is the e-mail address of the recipient of the form information. Because the MAILTO action does not require a CGI script, you can avoid some of the problems associated with coordinating your page with a program running on the Web server. One disadvantage of this action is that not all browsers support it. For example, versions of Internet Explorer earlier than 4.0 and Netscape Navigator 3.0 will not support it. Another concern is that messages sent via the MAILTO access are not encrypted for privacy. This means that, for example, the contact information that Jackson Electronics customers enter could be intercepted by hackers. Also, the recipient's e-mail address will be revealed to the user (so, for example, Lisa's assistant's e-mail address would be revealed to Jackson Electronics customers). Both of these issues make some Web page authors leery of using the MAILTO action.

When you click the Submit button on a form that uses the MAILTO action, the operating system on your computer accesses your mail program and receives the content for the mail message from your Web browser. Depending on how your system is configured, either you will have a chance to edit the mail message further, or it will be sent automatically to the e-mail address the form's creator specified, without allowing you to intervene.

An e-mail message generated by the MAILTO action is full of special characters that must be interpreted either by the recipient (such as Lisa's assistant) or by a special translation program, before the message can be read. Figure 6-33 shows the e-mail message that the MAILTO action generated for the registration form you completed in this tutorial (filled in with some sample data).

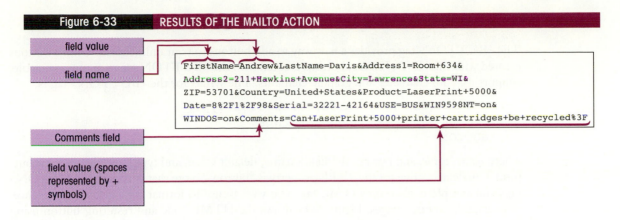

| Figure 6-33 | RESULTS OF THE MAILTO ACTION |

field value

field name

```
FirstName=Andrew&LastName=Davis&Address1=Room+634&
Address2=211+Hawkins+Avenue&City=Lawrence&State=WI&
ZIP=53701&Country=United+States&Product=LaserPrint+5000&
Date=8%2F1%2F98&Serial=32221-42164&USE=BUS&WIN9598NT=on&
WINDOS=on&Comments=Can+LaserPrint+5000+printer+cartridges+be+recycled%3F
```

Comments field

field value (spaces
represented by +
symbols)

The mail message shows each field name and field value pair. The field name is first, followed by an equals sign and then the field value. The next field name/field value pair is indicated by an ampersand (&). Because the mail message is one long continuous text string, no spaces are allowed. Spaces are replaced with plus symbols. Some of the other symbols used in messages generated by the MAILTO action are listed in Figure 6-34.

| Figure 6-34 | SPECIAL CHARACTERS USED BY THE MAILTO ACTION |

MAILTO CHARACTER	REPRESENTS
+	Space
&	Line break or new field
%25	%
%2B	+
%2F	/
%5C	\
%7E	~

If you want to use a program to translate messages created by the MAILTO action into easily readable files, you can use the WebForms program located at *http://www.q-d.com/wf.htm*.

If you use the MAILTO action, keep in mind that some users might be working with browsers that do not support it. As this action becomes a more standard way of retrieving and sending form information, this should change. Because some browsers do not support the MAILTO action and she is concerned about the lack of encryption, Lisa decides not to use it in the registration form at this time and, instead, to continue using Warren's CGI script.

Additional Form Elements

The specifications for HTML forms are constantly being modified and updated. In HTML 4.0, several new enhancements have been proposed that will make online forms more flexible and easier to create. Not all of these features are supported by all of the major browsers, so you need to use care when including them in your Web page. As always, you should test any form you create on a variety of browsers and browser versions. All of the following tags and properties should work with versions of Internet Explorer 4.0 and higher. They have not been supported by any version of Netscape Communicator as of this writing.

Creating Buttons with the <BUTTON> Tag

The <BUTTON> tag provides a new way to add buttons to your online form. Unlike buttons created with the <INPUT> tag, buttons created with the <BUTTON> tag are more versatile, supporting both character and graphic elements. The syntax for the <BUTTON> tag is:

```
<BUTTON NAME=name VALUE=value TYPE=type>
     button text and HTML tags
</BUTTON>
```

where *name*, *value*, and *type* are the field's name, default value, and type (submit, reset, or button.) The default value for the TYPE property is "button." Note that within the <BUTTON> tags you can place whatever HTML tags you wish to use to format the button's appearance. This includes inline images. Figure 6-35 shows the HTML code and resulting button using this tag.

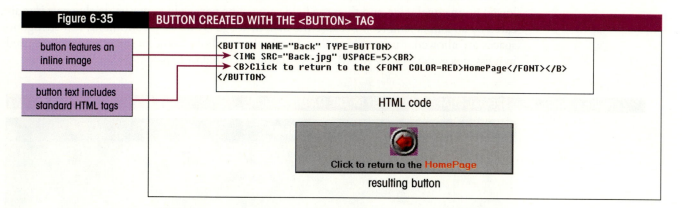

Figure 6-35	BUTTON CREATED WITH THE <BUTTON> TAG

button features an inline image

button text includes standard HTML tags

```
<BUTTON NAME="Back" TYPE=BUTTON>
   <IMG SRC="Back.jpg" VSPACE=5><BR>
   <B>Click to return to the <FONT COLOR=RED>HomePage</FONT></B>
</BUTTON>
```

HTML code

Click to return to the HomePage

resulting button

Assigning Labels to Fields

In creating the Jackson Electronics form, you had to enter the text for each input field alongside the field itself. HTML 4.0 introduces the <LABEL> tag by which you can assign labels to each field. A label can be associated with a field in one of two ways: either the field is placed within a pair of <LABEL> tags, or the <LABEL> tag is assigned to a specific field using the FOR property. Here is the general syntax for placing an input field within a <LABEL> tag:

```
<LABEL>label text
     input field tag and properties
</LABEL>
```

Here, *label text* is the text that you'll associate with the field. To assign a label to a specific field, use the syntax:

```
<LABEL FOR=field_name>label text</LABEL>
input field tag and properties
```

In this approach, *label text* is the text associated with the input field, and *field_name* is the name that you've assigned to the field. This approach allows you to place the label in one part of the document and the input field in another. This could occur if you were placing the label text in one table cell and the input field in another. For example, you could have created a label for the Windows check box in the registration form as follows:

```
<TR>
   <TD><LABEL FOR=WINDOWS>Windows:</LABEL></TD>
   <TD><INPUT TYPE=CHECKBOX NAME=WINDOWS>
</TR>
```

One advantage of using the <LABEL> tag with radio buttons and check boxes is that the user can click either the label or the field itself to select or deselect the radio button or check box.

The <LABEL> tag also includes the ACCESSKEY property. An **access key**, or **accelerator key**, is a keyboard character that can be pressed, usually along with the CTRL, ALT, or OPTION key, in order to jump to or select a field. The syntax for creating an access key is:

```
<LABEL ACCESSKEY="key_letter">
```

For example, the following code:

```
LABEL FOR=WINDOWS ACCESSKEY="W"><U>W</U>indows:
   <INPUT TYPE=CHECKBOX NAME=WINDOWS>
</LABEL>
```

will create an access key, "w" for the Windows checkbox. If the user presses, ALT+w (in Windows) or OPTION+w (on a Macintosh), this particular check box will be selected. Note that the "W" in Windows has been formatted with the underline tag, <U>. While this is not necessary, a standard convention in software packages has been to underline the letter associated with the access or accelerator key.

Creating Group Boxes

Sometimes you will want to group together fields on your form that share a common theme or appearance. Often a **group box** will be placed around these fields to visually show the grouping. In HTML 4.0, you can create such a group box using the <FIELDSET> tag. The syntax for the <FIELDSET> tag is:

```
<FIELDSET>
     collection of input fields and text
</FIELDSET>
```

In this syntax, a box will be placed around the input fields and text located within the <FIELDSET> tags. You can also add a legend to that group box with the <LEGEND> tag, that is:

```
<FIELDSET>
<LEGEND ALIGN=align>legend text</LEGEND>
      collection of input fields and text
</FIELDSET>
```

where *legend text* is the text of the group box legend, and the ALIGN property specifies how the legend text will be aligned on the group box. The possible ALIGN values are: TOP (the default), BOTTOM, LEFT, and RIGHT. For example, if you were to redesign the registration form using the <FIELDSET> and <LEGEND> tags, you could submit the following code for the product usage radio buttons:

```
<FIELDSET>
<LEGEND ALIGN=TOP>Used for:</LEGEND>
  <INPUT TYPE=RADIO NAME=USE VALUE=HOME>Home<BR>
  <INPUT TYPE=RADIO NAME=USE VALUE=BUS>Business<BR>
  <INPUT TYPE=RADIO NAME=USE VALUE=GOV>Government<BR>
  <INPUT TYPE=RADIO NAME=USE VALUE=ED>Educational Institution
<BR>
  <INPUT TYPE=RADIO NAME=USE VALUE=OTHER>Other</TD>
</FIELDSET>
```

The resulting group box would appear as shown in Figure 6-36.

If a browser that does not support the <FIELDSET> and <LEGEND> tags encounters them, it will ignore the <FIELDSET> tag completely, and display the legend text as simple text within the Web page form.

Specifying the Tab Order

Users usually move through a Web form with the tab key. The default order is to move from one field to another in the order that the field tags have been entered into the HTML file. This means that you have to carefully place the field tags within the file if you want your users to encounter the fields in the correct order.

Another option is to specify the tab order with the TABINDEX property. The TABINDEX property can be added to any field tag in your form. Each field is assigned a tab index number. The fields are then tabbed to in order of their tab index numbers—from the lowest positive number to the highest. For example, to assign the tab index number 1 to the FirstName field from the registration form, you would enter the code:

```
<INPUT NAME=FirstName TABINDEX=1>
```

If you assign a tab index number of 0 to a field, that field will be tabbed to in the order that it's encountered in the file (just as if you had never used a tab index). Fields with negative tab indexes are left out of the tabbing order entirely. If a user wanted to enter information into one of these fields, he or she would have to select it with the mouse.

Web page authors can use tab index numbers in their forms without worrying about older browsers that do not support this new standard. Older browsers will simply ignore the TABINDEX property and continue to tab to the fields in the order that you've entered them into the HTML file.

You're now finished working with forms and form properties. The page you created for Lisa has been stored on the company's Web server. She is reviewing the page with her assistant and will inform you of any additional modifications required.

Session 6.3 QUICK CHECK

1. What tag would you enter to create a Submit button with the label "Send Form"?

2. What tag would you enter to create a Reset button with the label "Cancel Form"?

3. What tag would you enter to create an image field named Sites for the graphic image Sites.gif with the VALUE property GotoPage?

4. What tag would you enter to create a hidden field named Subject with the field value Form Responses?

5. You need to have your form work with a CGI script located at *http://www.j_davis.com/cgi-bin/post-query*. The method the Web server uses is the GET method. What should the <FORM> tag be, to correctly access this CGI script?

6. You want to use the MAILTO action to send your form to the e-mail address walker@j_davis.com. What is the appropriate <FORM> tag to enter? What are some limitations of this Web page that you should be concerned about?

7. Show two ways to assign the label "First Name" to the input box named FirstName. Assign the access key N to the FirstName field.

8. What code would you enter to create a group box around the check boxes in the Jackson Electronics registration form, containing the text "Check all that apply"?

REVIEW ASSIGNMENTS

Lisa and her assistant have worked with your registration form and have decided on some changes they would like you to make to the form. Specifically, they want you to:

- remove the Address1 and Address2 fields and replace them with a single text area field
- add the following items to the product list: PrintMaster 300, PrintMaster 600, and ColorPrinter Plus
- change the selection list from a drop-down list box to a list box displaying four items
- add Linux to the list of possible operating systems
- include a question asking whether the customer wants to be on the Jackson Electronics mailing list. Specify "Yes" as the default response to this question.
- add an input field for the customer's e-mail address

Warren also has some changes he'd like you to make to the form:

- Add a hidden field to the form with the field name SUBJECT and the value "Registration form response." Warren's CGI script will insert this information in the subject line of the mail message sent to Lisa's assistant.
- Modify the form so that it uses a new CGI script located at *http://www.Jkson_Electronics.com/cgi/formmail*, using the POST method.

When finished, the modified form should appear as shown in Figure 6-37.

Figure 6-37

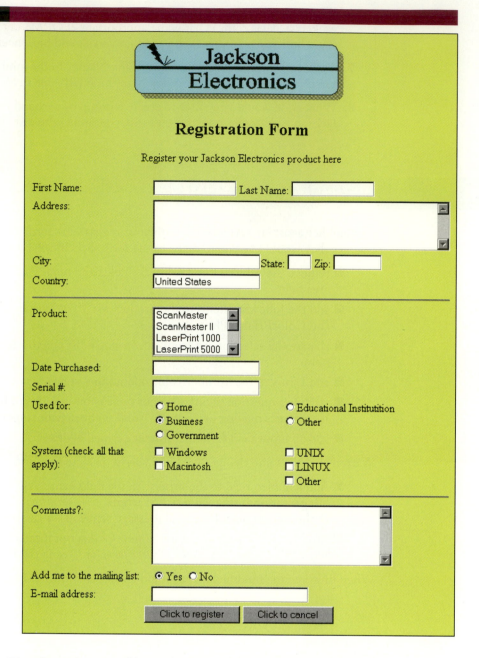

Lisa gives you a new file in which you'll make the suggested changes.

To implement the changes to the registration form:

1. Start your text editor and open the **Regtext.htm** file in the Review subfolder of the Tutorial.06 folder on your Data Disk, and then save the file as Register.htm in the same folder.

2. Insert a hidden field tag after the <FORM> tag, with a field name of SUBJECT and a value of "Registration form response."

3. Remove the two rows from the table that contain the Address1 and Address2 fields. Insert a single row in their place with the following properties:

   ■ The first cell in the row should contain the text "Address:" vertically aligned with the top of the cell.

■ The second cell in the row should span two columns and contain a text area box. The size of the text area should be 4 rows by 50 columns. Assign the text area the field name "Address". Do not insert any default text into the text area.

4. Go to the selection list for the product field. Add options to the end of the list for PrintMaster 300, PrintMaster 600, and ColorPrinter Plus.

Explore ▶

5. Increase the size of the selection list to 4.

6. Vertically align the text "Product:" located in the first cell of the row containing the selection list with the top of the cell.

7. Go to the table row containing check boxes for the various operating systems. Add a new check box for the LINUX operating system in the same table cell that contains the UNIX check box field. Name the new field LINUX.

8. Below the Comments text area field, insert a new row in the table with the following specifications:

■ In the first cell, insert the text "Add me to the mailing list:".

■ In the second cell, add a pair of radio buttons with the common field name, MLIST. Assign the radio buttons the values "Yes" and "No." Insert the text "Yes" directly to the right of the Yes button, and the text "No" directly to the right of the No button. Make the "Yes" radio button selected by default.

9. Below the row containing the mailing list radio buttons, insert another row with the following specifications:

■ In the first cell of the row, insert the text "E-mail address:".

■ The second cell of the row should span two columns and contain an input box with the field name MAILADDRESS.

10. Modify the properties of the form so that it accesses the CGI script located at *http://www.Jkson_Electronics.com/cgi/formmail*, using the POST method.

11. Save your changes to the Register.htm file, and then view it in your Web browser.

12. Print a copy of your form and the HTML code.

13. Close your Web browser and text editor.

CASE PROBLEMS

Case 1. Creating a Search Form for Gordon Media Gordon Media owns several newspapers in the Midwest. Recently Gordon Media has been moving toward online publishing. One of the company's ventures is to place classified ads from Gordon Media's many papers online and to give customers the ability to search the classified listings.

Tim Steward, the managing editor of the online publishing group, has contacted you about creating the search form for the classified ads page. The search form will allow customers to search in several different classified ad sections, to specify the newspapers they want to examine, and to indicate the time period they want to search in. Once this search form is completed, the form information will be sent to a CGI script for processing. The users will also have the option of viewing a helpful Web page containing search tips. A preview of the page you'll create is shown in Figure 6-38.

Figure 6-38

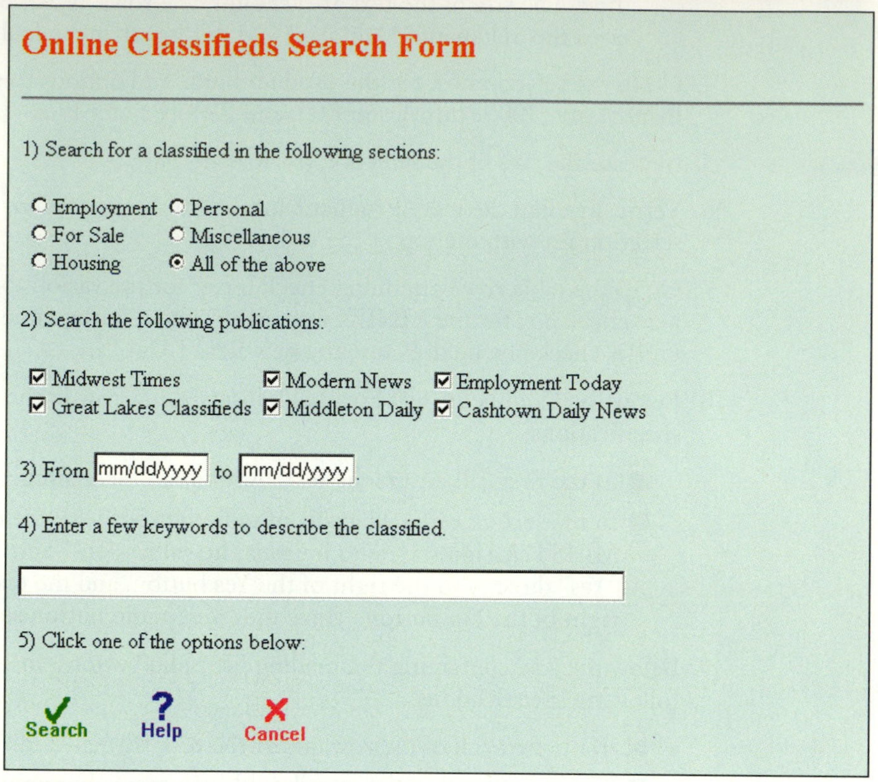

Online Classifieds Search Form

1) Search for a classified in the following sections:

- ○ Employment   ○ Personal
- ○ For Sale   ○ Miscellaneous
- ○ Housing   ⊙ All of the above

2) Search the following publications:

- ☑ Midwest Times   ☑ Modern News   ☑ Employment Today
- ☑ Great Lakes Classifieds ☑ Middleton Daily ☑ Cashtown Daily News

3) From [mm/dd/yyyy] to [mm/dd/yyyy].

4) Enter a few keywords to describe the classified.

[   ]

5) Click one of the options below:

✓   ?   ✗
Search   Help   Cancel

To create the Online Classifieds Search Form:

1. Start your text editor and open the file **Adstext.htm** in the Cases subfolder of the Tutorial.06 folder on your Data Disk, and then save the file as Ads.htm in the same folder.

2. Add an opening and closing <FORM> tag to the body of the page. Name the form "Ads."

3. Below the first entry in the form, insert a table with one row and two columns. In the first table cell, insert on separate lines within the cell (using the
 tag) the following radio buttons and button descriptions (use the fieldname ADTYPE for each radio button, and place the radio buttons before the text descriptions):

   - Employment (set the field value to EMP)
   - For Sale (set the field value to FORSALE)
   - Housing (set the field value to HOUSE)

4. In the second cell of the table, insert the following radio buttons and button descriptions, using the ADTYPE field name for each radio button. As before, place each radio button on a separate line within the table cell.

   - Personal (set the field value to PERSON)
   - Miscellaneous (set the field value to MISC)
   - All of the above (set the field value to ALL)

5. Make "All of the above" the default radio button.

6. Below the second entry, insert a table with one row and three columns. In the first table cell, insert the following check boxes (place the check boxes on separate lines within the cell, and put the text descriptions after the check boxes):

- Midwest Times (field name=MWT)
- Great Lakes Classifieds (field name=GLC)

7. In the second cell, create the following check boxes, on separate lines:

- Modern News (field name=MN)
- Middleton Daily (field name=MD)

8. In the third cell, add these two check boxes on separate lines:

- Employment Today (field name=ET)
- Cashtown Daily News (field name=CD)

9. Format all the check boxes so that they are selected by default.

10. Add two input boxes to the third form question, as shown in Figure 6-38. Make each input box 10 characters in width, and give each input box the default value of "mm/dd/yyyy." Name the first input box START and the second input box END.

11. Insert an input box after the fourth search form question. Set the width of the input box to 60 characters. Assign the input box the field name KEYWORDS.

Explore ▶ 12. Add three inline image fields at the bottom of the form. Use the file **Search.gif** to create the Search image, the file **Help.gif** to create the Help image, and the file **Cancel.gif** to create the Cancel image. Separate each inline image by two nonbreaking spaces.

13. Set the form to access a CGI script located at *http://www.gordonmed.com/cgi/fsearch.cgi*, using the POST method.

14. Save your changes to the Ads.htm file.

15. View the file in your Web browser. Print a copy of the completed page and the corresponding HTML code.

16. Close your Web browser and text editor.

Case 2. Creating a Travel Expense Form for DeLong Enterprises   DeLong Enterprises, a manufacturer of computer components, is setting up a corporate intranet to put news and information online for company employees. One item that Dolores Crandall, a payroll manager, would like to put online is travel expense forms. Company employees fill out these forms after they attend conferences or business meetings. Dolores has contacted the company's computer service division for help, and they have assigned you the task of creating the travel expense form.

The travel expense form requires the employee to provide information about the business trip and to itemize various travel deductions. A preview of the form you'll create is shown in Figure 6-39.

Figure 6-39

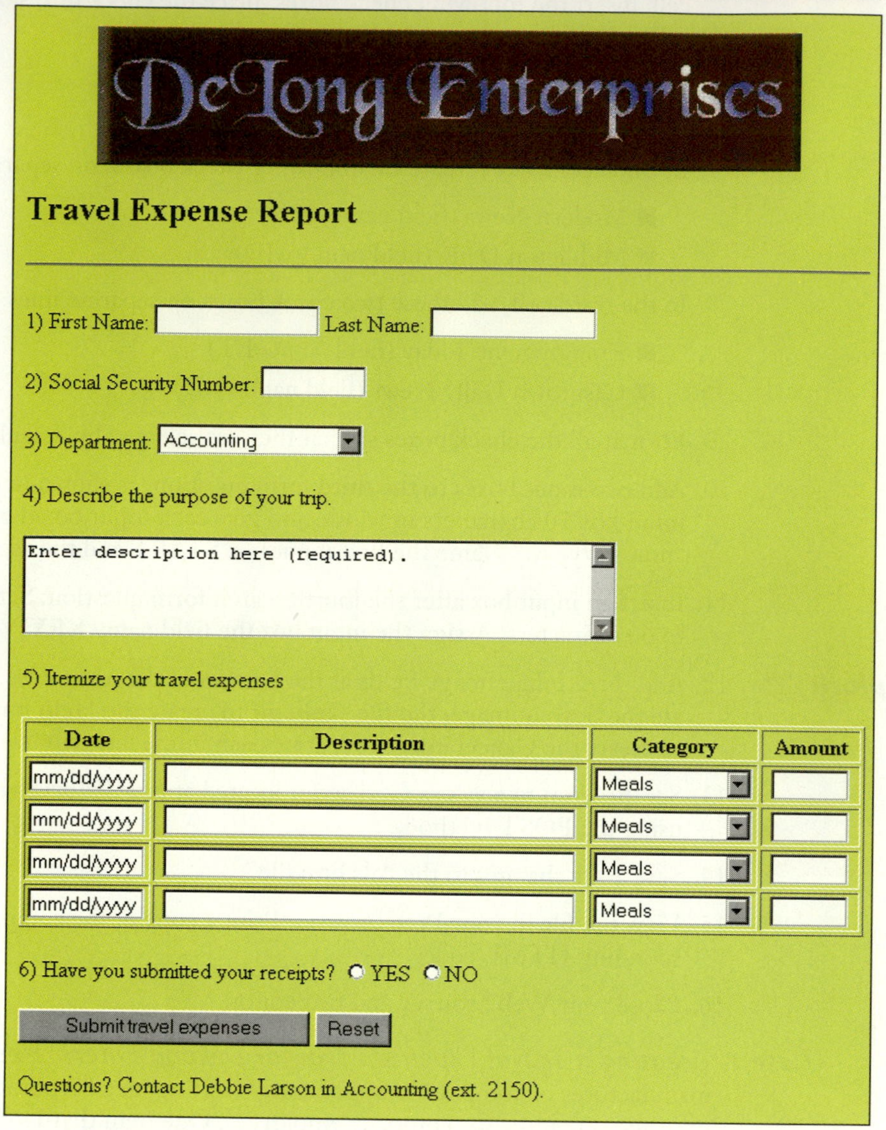

To create the travel expense form:

1. Start your text editor, open the file **Travltxt.htm** in the Cases subfolder of the Tutorial.06 folder on your Data Disk, and then save the file as Travel.htm in the same folder.

2. Add an opening and closing <FORM> tag to the body of the page. Name the form "Travel."

3. Insert input boxes for the employee's first name and last name in item #1 of the form. Assign these fields the names FIRST and LAST. Set the size of both input boxes to 15 characters.

Explore

4. Create a password input box for the Social Security number in item #2 of the form. Set the width and maximum length of the input box to 9 characters.

5. Create a drop-down list box for the list of departments in item #3. Insert the following options into the drop-down list box: Accounting, Advertising, Consumer Relations, Sales, Management, Payroll, Quality Control, and R & D. Set DEPT as the field name for the list box.

6. Create a text area field for the trip description in item #4. The text area field should be 4 rows high and 50 columns wide. Set DESC as the field name. Specify "Enter description here (required)." as the default text. .

7. For each row (except the header row) of the expense itemization table (item #5), do the following:

Explore ▶

- In the first column, insert an input box with the field name DATE and a size of 10 characters. Specify "mm/dd/yyyy" as the default text.
- In the second column, insert an input box that is 40 characters long and has the field name DESCRIPTION.
- In the third column, insert a selection list with the field name CATEGORY, and include the following options in the list: Meals, Miscellaneous, Registration, and Transportation.
- In the fourth column, insert an input box named AMOUNT that is 6 characters wide.

Explore ▶

8. Create a pair of radio buttons for item #6, regarding submitting a receipt. Name both fields RECEIPT. Assign the first radio button the value YES and the second button the value NO. Insert the text "YES" next to the first radio button and the text "NO" next to the second button.

9. Below item #6 insert two form buttons. The first button should be a Submit button with the value "Submit travel expenses." The second button should be a Reset button with the default value, "Reset".

10. Set the form to access the CGI script at the URL *http://www.DeLongEnt.com/cgi/Trvl.cg,* using the POST method.

11. Save your changes to the Travel.htm file.

12. View the file in your Web browser. Print a copy of the completed page and the corresponding HTML code.

13. Close your Web browser and text editor.

Case 3. Registering Patients at St. Mary's of Northland Pines   St. Mary's of Northland Pines is creating a system to register patients online, using Web pages. You've been asked by Dr. Louise Mayer to create a registration form for newborn infants. The form should contain the infant's name, the name of the parents, the infant's medical record number, date of birth, birth weight, and 5-minute APGAR score. Dr. Mayer also wants you to include information about which physicians were involved in the birth. She has a list of seven physicians, and she wants the form to allow users to select multiple physicians in cases where more than one doctor was involved.

A preview of the form you'll create is shown in Figure 6-40.

Figure 6-40

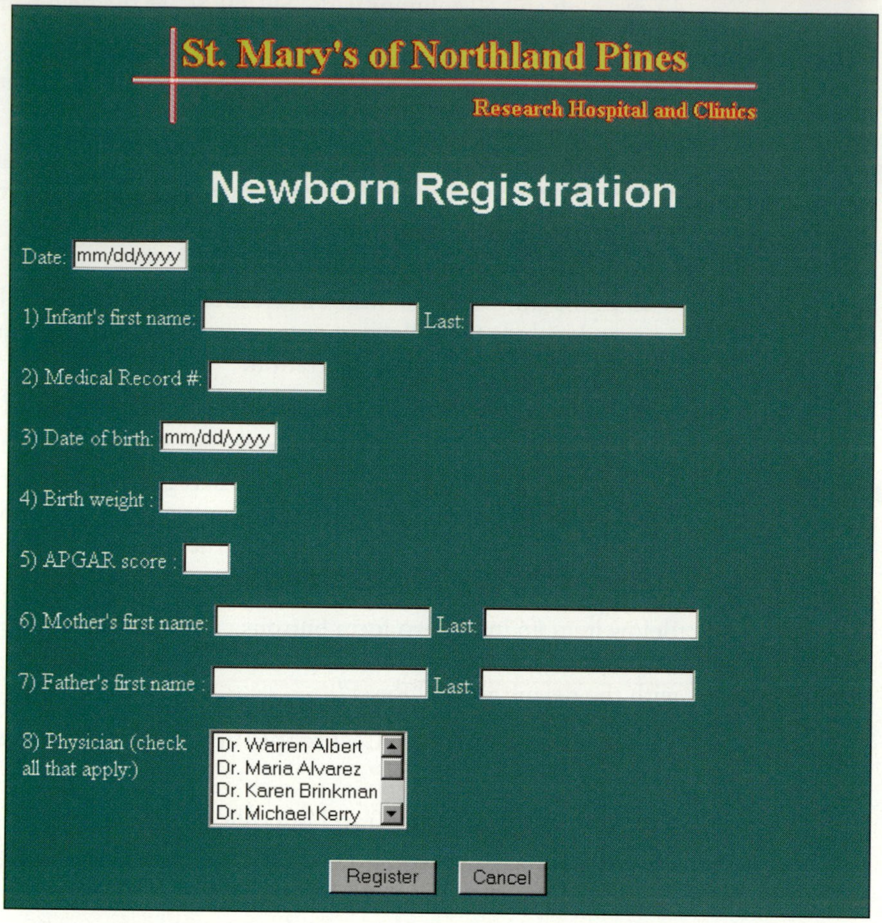

Dr. Mayer wants all results of the form mailed to Robert Brockton, whose e-mail address is brockton@StMarysNP.com. All browsers in the hospital can support the MAILTO action, so she wants you to use the MAILTO action in your form.

To create the newborn registration form:

1. Start your text editor and open the file **NBtext.htm** in the Cases subfolder of the Tutorial.06 folder on your Data Disk, and then save the file as Newborn.htm in the same folder.

Explore

2. Add an opening and closing <FORM> tag to the body of the page. Name the form "Newborn." Insert the MAILTO action in the <FORM> tag with the email address brockton@StMarysNP.com (your instructor might ask you to insert a different e-mail address here). Use the POST method.

3. Insert an input box for the Date line at the top of the form. Set the size and maximum length of text in the input box to 10 characters, and set the default text to "mm/dd/yyyy." Assign the Date field the name FORMDATE.

4. Insert input boxes for the infant's first and last name. Use the field names FIRST and LAST.

5. Insert an input box for the medical record number. Use the field name MEDRECNO. Set the size and maximum length of data in this field to 10 characters.

6. Insert an input box for the infant's birth date named DOB. Set the size and maximum length of this input box to 10 characters. Set the default text to "mm/dd/yyyy."

7. Insert input boxes for the birth weight and APGAR score with the field names BWGT and APGAR. Set the size of the input boxes to 6 and 3 characters, respectively.

8. Create input boxes for the first and last name of the mother. Name the fields MFIRST and MLAST.

9. Create input boxes for the first and last name of the father. Name the fields FFIRST and FLAST.

Explore ▶ 10. Item #8 of the form should contain a selection box with the names of possible physicians. Assign the field name, DOCTOR, to the selection list. A table has already been created for you, and you should insert the selection box into the second cell of the table. The selection box should have the following options (the value for each option is shown in parentheses):

■ Dr. Warren Albert (1)   ■ Dr. Chad Nichols (5)

■ Dr. Maria Alvarez (2)   ■ Dr. Karen Paulson (6)

■ Dr. Karen Brinkman (3)   ■ Dr. Tai Webb (7)

■ Dr. Michael Kerry (4)   ■ Other (99)

Set up the selection box so that four options are shown within the box, and allow for multiple selections on the part of the user.

11. Insert a Submit button labeled "Register" and a Reset button labeled "Cancel," centered at the bottom of the form. Insert two non-breaking spaces between the buttons.

12. Save your changes to the Newborn.htm file.

13. View the file in your Web browser. Print a copy of the completed page and the corresponding HTML code.

Explore ▶ 14. If you used an e-mail address supplied by your instructor for the MAILTO action, complete the form in your Web browser with test data and mail the form to the address specified.

15. Close your Web browser and text editor.

Case 4. Order Form for Millennium Computers You work at Millennium Computers, a discount

Explore ▶ mail-order company specializing in computers and computer components. You've been asked by your supervisor, Sandy Walton, to create an order form Web page for customers who want to purchase products online. Your order form will be for computer purchases only. There are several different options available to customers purchasing computers from Millennium; these are:

■ Processor speed: 150 MHz, 200 MHz, 300 MHz, 400 MHz

■ Memory: 16 meg, 32 meg, 64 meg, and 128 meg

■ Drive size: 5 gigabyte, 10 gigabyte, 20 gigabyte

■ Monitor size: 15-inch, 17-inch, 19-inch, 21-inch

■ CD-ROM: 12x24x, 16x32x, 48x

Create Sandy's order form using the following guidelines (the layout and appearance of the page are up to you):

1. Create input boxes for the customer's first and last name, phone number, and credit card number and expiration date. Make sure the credit card information that the user enters is not displayed on the screen.

2. Using selection boxes or radio buttons, create fields in the form for the different component options listed previously.

3. Insert a check box asking whether the customer wants to be placed on the Millennium Computers mailing list.

4. Place three buttons on the form: a Submit button to send the order, a Reset button to reset the page, and a second Submit button to request that a Millennium Computers representative call the customer to process the order. Use the values "Send", "Cancel", and "Call Me" for the three buttons.

5. Assign the <FORM> tag the NAME property C_ORDER. Use the POST method and set up the form to use the CGI script located at *http://www.mill_computers.com* (a fictional URL).

6. Save your file as Computer.htm in the Cases folder of the Tutorial.06 folder on your Student Disk. Print a copy of your HTML code and the page as it appears in the Web browser.

7. Close your Web browser and text editor.

QUICK | CHECK ANSWERS

Session 6.1

1. A CGI script is any program or set of commands running on the Web server that receives data from the Web page and then acts upon that data to perform a certain task.
2. The <FORM> tag identifies the beginning and end of a form.
3. <INPUT NAME=Phone>
4. <INPUT NAME=Phone SIZE=10>
5. <INPUT NAME=Phone SIZE=10 MAXLENGTH=10>
6. <INPUT NAME=Subscribe VALUE="Yes">
7. Set the value of the TYPE property to PASSWORD.

Session 6.2

1.
```
<SELECT NAME=States>
     <OPTION>California
     <OPTION>Nevada
     <OPTION>Oregon
     <OPTION>Washington
</SELECT>
```
2. Change the <SELECT> tag to <SELECT MULTIPLE>
3. <OPTION SELECTED>Oregon
4.
```
<INPUT TYPE=RADIO NAME=State VALUE=California>California
<INPUT TYPE=RADIO NAME=State VALUE=Nevada>Nevada
<INPUT TYPE=RADIO NAME=State VALUE=Oregon>Oregon
<INPUT TYPE=RADIO NAME=State VALUE=Washington>Washington
```
5.
```
<INPUT TYPE=RADIO NAME=State VALUE=1>California
<INPUT TYPE=RADIO NAME=State VALUE=2>Nevada
<INPUT TYPE=RADIO NAME=State VALUE=3>Oregon
<INPUT TYPE=RADIO NAME=State VALUE=4>Washington
```
6. <INPUT TYPE=CHECKBOX>California

   A value of "on" is sent to the CGI script.
7. <TEXTAREA ROWS=5 COLS=30 NAME=Memo>Enter notes here.</TEXTAREA>
8. WRAP=PHYSICAL or WRAP=HARD

Session 6.3

1. <INPUT TYPE=SUBMIT VALUE="Send Form">
2. <INPUT TYPE=RESET VALUE="Cancel Form">
3. <INPUT TYPE=IMG NAME=Sites SRC="Sites.gif" VALUE="GotoPage">
4. <INPUT TYPE=HIDDEN NAME=Subject VALUE="Form Responses">
5. <FORM METHOD=GET ACTION="http://www.j_davis.com/cgi-bin/post-query">
6. <FORM ACTION="mailto:walker@j_davis.com">

   This action might not be supported by all browsers.
7. <LABEL>First Name <INPUT NAME="FirstName"> </LABEL>

   or

   <LABEL FOR="FirstName">First Name</LABEL> <INPUT NAME="FirstName">
8.
```
<FIELDSET>
<LEGEND>Check all that apply</LEGEND>
     <INPUT TYPE=CHECKBOX NAME=WINDOWS>Windows<BR>
     <INPUT TYPE=CHECKBOX NAME=MAC>Macintosh<BR>
     <INPUT TYPE=CHECKBOX NAME=UNIX>UNIX<BR>
     <INPUT TYPE=CHECKBOX NAME=OTHER_SYSTEM>Other
</FIELDSET>
```

OBJECTIVES

In this tutorial you will:

- Learn about the history and theory of cascading style sheets

- Create inline styles, embedded styles, and style sheets

- Understand style precedence and style inheritance

- Use cascading style sheets to format the appearance of paragraphs, lists, and headers

- Design a style for hypertext links in their four conditions

- Define document content with the CLASS and ID properties and create styles for them

- Mark document content with the <DIV> and <SPAN> tags and create styles for them

- Use cascading styles to control page layout

WORKING WITH CASCADING STYLE SHEETS

Designing a Style for a Web Site at Maxwell Scientific

CASE

Maxwell Scientific

Maxwell Scientific is a mail-order firm that sells science kits and science education products to schools and educators. The company's marketing team plans to put portions of its catalog on its Web site and give people the ability to purchase items online. Part of the Web site will include product information, comments, and science articles for various science disciplines.

Chris Todd, the head of the Web site development team, has asked you to assist her in the design of the Web pages. You'll start by designing the pages that describe some of Maxwell Scientific's products. However, because the company's Web site will eventually contain a large number of pages, she wants your work to be easily adapted to the larger site. She wants a design should be easy to apply and easy to change. Chris does not want a situation in which a simple design change means editing every single page in the site.

To make this task easier, Chris suggests that you use cascading style sheets. Chris has seen other Web sites use styles sheets as a design tool, making their Web sites more flexible, easier to maintain, and more aesthetically interesting.

SESSION 7.1

In this session you'll learn about the history and theory of style sheets. You'll see how to create inline styles, embedded styles, and external style sheets. You'll study how styles are applied to a wide range of tags in your Web site and how the styles are cascaded through the structure of nested tags on your Web pages.

Introduction to Cascading Style Sheets

At Maxwell Scientific, they have a Web page devoted to every scientific discipline. To make things easier, you're going to limit yourself to only two of those Web pages: a page devoted to the company astronomy products and a page of chemistry materials.

Chris asks you to open the Astronomy page so that you can become familiar with the basic structure of these documents.

To open the Astronomy page:

1. Start your text editor and then locate and open the **Astrotxt.htm** file in the Tutorial.07 folder of your Data Disk.

2. Save the file as **Astro.htm**.

Figure 7-1 shows the current form of the page. Chris explains that this page displays many of the common elements you'll see in many of the product pages:

- A logo along with a list of links to other product pages
- An H1 header identifying the science discipline for that Web page
- A short introductory paragraph
- A science column by one of Maxwell Scientific's science writers
- A bulleted list of products, along with a few monthly specials
- A few selected quotes from satisfied customers
- Contact information for Maxwell Scientific

Figure 7-1   **MAXWELL SCIENTIFIC'S ASTRONOMY PAGE**

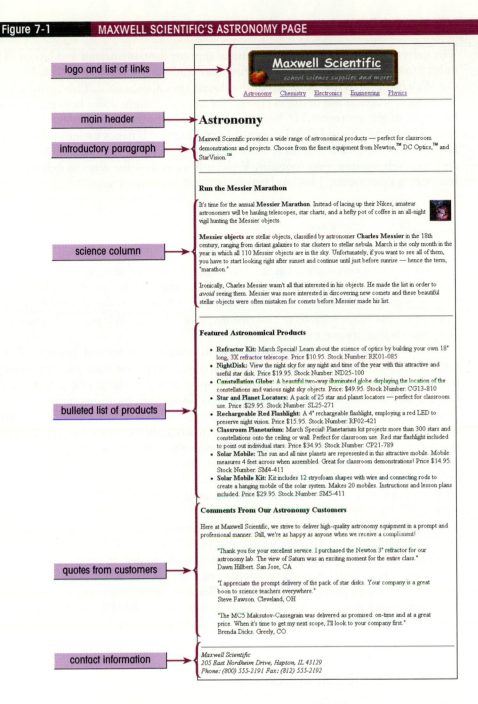

logo and list of links

main header

introductory paragraph

science column

bulleted list of products

quotes from customers

contact information

Since the content of the Maxwell Scientific Web pages will change from day to day, any design you create for their Web pages should focus more on these common elements than on the specific content of each page. Ideally the style you create for the astronomy page should be easily applied to any of the other pages in the site so there is a consistent look and feel across the Web site. The design should also be easy to modify. How can you accomplish this with HTML?

HTML and Page Layout

The early versions of HTML had minimal support for page design and layout. The philosophy, after all, was to have basic text files that could be quickly downloaded, and to rely on the Web browser to format much of the document's appearance. This approach meant that the exact representation of the <H1> tag, for example, might differ between browsers. Some browsers might represent H1 headers with a 20-point font, others might use a 24-point font. The simplicity of HTML tags made creating Web pages easier and made pages load faster, but it also meant that there was little control over the page layout. As HTML evolved and the Web became more popular, Web authors looked for ways to deliver more visually interesting documents. This has been done chiefly in three ways:

- Using HTML tag extensions
- Converting text to images
- Controlling page layout with tables

Each of these approaches has its drawbacks. As you've seen, extensions to HTML can provide the Web author with more choices in layout and design. Some, like the <FONT> tag, became part of future HTML standards. Of course, the downside is that not all browsers support the various tag extensions, which leaves Web page authors with powerful design tools that are not entirely useful.

The second approach, converting text to images, has several benefits. For example, rather than worry whether a browser will support a particular font, you can convert the text to an inline image and have the browser display that. Similarly, one can create text boxes using inline images, which can then be placed in specific locations on the Web page. The problem with this approach is that you are limited in the number of inline images you can use and still have the page downloaded in a timely fashion. Moreover, it's difficult to make quick changes to the page's content if you have to edit the inline graphics first.

Tables are not a completely satisfactory solution either. When tables were introduced, no one thought of them as a layout tool; however, table tags have proven to be the most popular way of defining page layout. Yet, this comes at the expense of making HTML files more complicated to write and to interpret.

Part of the problem is that the way HTML works is at odds with the fundamental concepts of design theory. In designing any sort of document, one wants to separate, as much as possible, the content from the design. One should be able to create the design and then *apply* the design elements to the content. For example, what if you want to display all H1 headers in a red, 24 point, bold, Arial font? Because the tags that specify these attributes are intertwined with the content in HTML, you must locate *all* of the occurrences of the <H1> tag and modify each one individually. For a Web site containing dozens of pages, this is a daunting task to say the least.

History and Support of CSS

The limitations of HTML led to the creation of style sheets. A **style** is a rule that defines the appearance of an element in the document. For example, instead of relying on Web browsers to determine the appearance of the <H1> tag, a style explicitly defines this for the browser. When the browser retrieves the file from the Web server, it receives the element and also the rules for displaying that element. The collection of styles for a Web page or Web site is known as a **style sheet**.

Like HTML, style sheets must use a common language and follow common rules. This language is known as **Cascading Style Sheets**, or more simply, **CSS**. CSS has been developed by the World Wide Web Consortium, the same organization that develops standards for HTML. The first CSS standard, **CSS1**, was released in 1996. The most recent specification,

CSS2, was released in 1998. CSS is designed to augment HTML, not replace it; but learning CSS is like learning a whole new way of formatting your Web pages. As you'll see, CSS provides several tools not available with standard HTML.

Browser support for CSS has proven to be uneven. Internet Explorer led the way, introducing style sheets in version 3.0 and providing support for the CSS1 standard with version 4.0. Of all the major browsers, Internet Explorer 5.0 may provide the best support for CSS1, though there are still bugs in the implementation of Internet Explorer. Netscape's support for CSS1 has been spotty. This was due in part to Netscape's decision to push its own style sheet language over CSS. Even through version 4.7, Netscape is not considered CSS1-compliant (though this will presumably change with Netscape 5.0.) No browsers are fully CSS2-compliant at this point in time, so when using cascading style sheets, one must be careful to test the Web page on a variety of browsers and browser versions, especially if styles use some features of CSS2.

The uneven support for CSS is a shame, since this approach holds the promise of giving Web page authors more control over the appearance of their Web pages and more options for creating dynamic and interesting documents. For more information about the compliance of various browsers with CSS1 and CSS2, and for information about the standards themselves, you can access the Web sites shown in Figure 7-2.

| Figure 7-2 | WEB SITES WITH INFORMATION ON CASCADING STYLE SHEETS |

WEB SITE	URL
The World Wide Web Consortium	http://www.w3c.org
The Web Standards Project	http://www.webstandards.org/css/
CSS Bugs and Workarounds	http://css.nu/pointers/bugs.html
Little Shop of CSS Horrors	http://haughey.com/csshorrors/

Style Types

There are three ways of employing CSS in your Web pages:

- **Inline styles**: In this approach, you add styles to each individual tag within the HTML file. The style affects that particular tag, but does not affect other tags in the document.
- **Embedded or global styles**: With embedded or global styles, a style is applied to the entire HTML file, allowing the Web author to modify the appearance of any tag in the document.
- **Linked** or **external style sheets**: A linked or external style sheet is a text file containing the style declaration. The Web author can create styles for any tag in the Web site whose HTML file is linked to the style sheet.

Which approach you choose depends on your style needs. If you need to format just a single section in your Web page, you'd probably use an inline style. If you need to modify all instances of particular element (say, all H1 headers) in a Web page, you'd use an embedded or global style. Finally, if you need to control the style for an entire Web site, you'll use a linked style sheet. In designing the Maxwell Scientific site, you'll use each approach.

Using Inline Styles

To create an inline style, you add the STYLE property to the HTML tag using the following syntax:

```
<tag STYLE="style declarations">
```

where *tag* is the name of the tag (H1, P, etc.) and *style declarations* are the styles you'll define for that particular tag. Note that the style declaration must be enclosed within double quotation marks for inline styles.

A style declaration consists of attribute names that control such features as the font size, color, and font type, followed by a colon and then the attribute's value. Multiple attributes can be used as long as you separate each one by a semicolon. The general syntax for the style declaration is therefore:

```
attribute1:value1; attribute2:value2; …
```

One common mistake is to forget the semicolon separating the attributes. If this semicolon is missing, then your browser might not display any of your style changes.

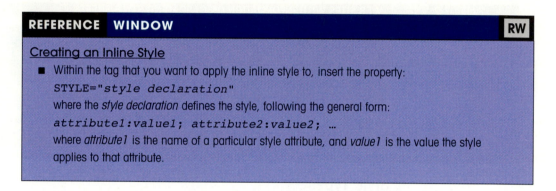

REFERENCE WINDOW   RW

Creating an Inline Style
■ Within the tag that you want to apply the inline style to, insert the property:
STYLE="*style declaration*"
where the *style declaration* defines the style, following the general form:
attribute1:value1; attribute2:value2; …
where *attribute1* is the name of a particular style attribute, and *value1* is the value the style applies to that attribute.

Chris would like to see the first H1 header in the Astro.htm file appear in a gold sans-serif font. This is done with the following code (you'll learn where these attribute names and values come from later):

```
<H1 STYLE="color:gold; font-family:sans-serif">
```

Add this code to the Astro.htm file now.

To change the style for the first <H1> tag:

1. Scroll down the Astro.htm text file until you locate the initial <H1> tag.

2. Within the <H1> tag type **STYLE="color:gold; font-family:sans-serif"**. See Figure 7-3.

| Figure 7-3 | INSERTING AN INLINE STYLE |

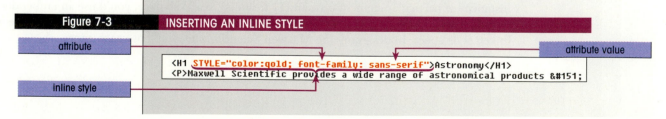

```
<H1 STYLE="color:gold; font-family: sans-serif">Astronomy</H1>
<P>Maxwell Scientific provides a wide range of astronomical products &#151;
```

attribute   attribute value

inline style

3. Save your changes to the file.

4. Open **Astro.htm** in your Web browser. Note that the initial header is now visible in a sans-serif font and in the color gold. See Figure 7-4.

| Figure 7-4 | ASTRONOMY HEADER WITH NEW STYLE |

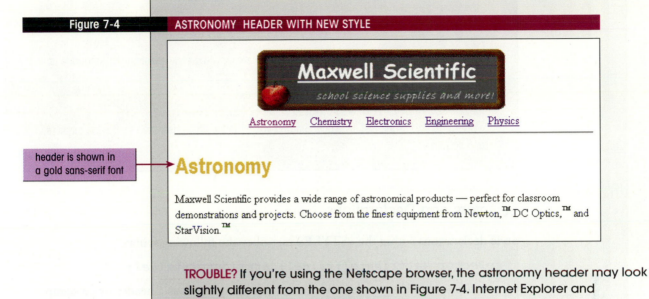

header is shown in a gold sans-serif font

TROUBLE? If you're using the Netscape browser, the astronomy header may look slightly different from the one shown in Figure 7-4. Internet Explorer and Netscape display fonts differently.

Creating an Embedded Style

Chris would like to see the style you used for the astronomy header applied to other H1 headers. To do that you could insert inline styles into other <H1> tags that already exist and into new ones as they're created, but a much better way is to create an embedded style for all H1 headers. To do that, you insert a <STYLE> tag within the head section of your HTML file. Within the <STYLE> tag, you enclose the style declarations you need for the entire Web page. The syntax of an embedded style is:

```
<STYLE TYPE="style sheet language">
      style declarations
</STYLE>
```

Here, *style sheet language* identifies the type of style language used in the document. There are several style languages available, but the most common language (and the default) is "text/css" for use with CSS.

Creating an Embedded Style

- Within the Head section of your HTML file, insert the following HTML code:

```
<STYLE TYPE="style sheet language">
    style declarations
</STYLE>
```

where *style sheet language* is the language of your cascading style sheets. If no language is specified, the default value, "text/css" is used.

- To enter a *style declaration*, use the following syntax:

```
selector {attribute1:value1; attribute2:value2; …}
```

where *attribute1* is the first style attribute and *value1* is the value assigned to the first attribute, and so forth.

Selectors and Declarations

Style declarations within the <STYLE> tags obey the following syntax:

```
selector {attribute1:value1; attribute2;value2; …}
```

where *selector* identifies an element in your document (such as a header or paragraph), and the attributes and values within the curly braces indicate the styles applied to all the occurrences of that element. This collection of attributes and values is also referred to as the **declaration** of the selector. For example, to display *all* H1 headers in the HTML document using a gold sans-serif font, you could use the following embedded style:

```
<STYLE>
      H1 {color: gold; font-family: sans-serif}
</STYLE>
```

In this example, "H1" is the selector and the text in the braces is the declaration. Note that the TYPE property was not included within the <STYLE> tag. This is because "text/css" is the default style language, and unless you specify a different style language, you don't need to enter the TYPE property. Also, since you are using the <STYLE> tags, you don't need to include double quotes around the attributes and attribute values as you did for inline styles.

Try adding this embedded style to the Astro.htm file now.

To insert an embedded style:

1. Return to the **Astro.htm** file in your text editor.

2. Delete the inline style you created for the initial <H1> tag.

3. Move back to the top of the file, and above the </HEAD> tag enter the following text:

```
<STYLE>
    H1 {color:gold; font-family:sans-serif}
</STYLE>
```

4. Figure 7-5 shows the revised file.

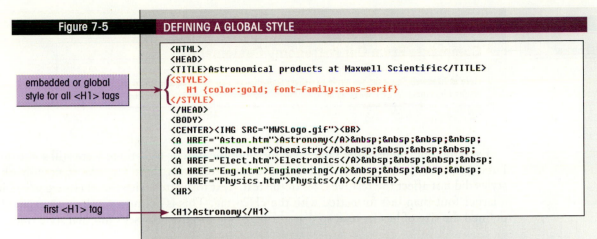

Figure 7-5   **DEFINING A GLOBAL STYLE**

embedded or global style for all <H1> tags

first <H1> tag

```
<HTML>
<HEAD>
<TITLE>Astronomical products at Maxwell Scientific</TITLE>
<STYLE>
    H1 {color:gold; font-family:sans-serif}
</STYLE>
</HEAD>
<BODY>
<CENTER><IMG SRC="MWSLogo.gif"><BR>
<A HREF="Aston.htm">Astronomy</A>    
<A HREF="Chem.htm">Chemistry</A>    
<A HREF="Elect.htm">Electronics</A>    
<A HREF="Eng.htm">Engineering</A>    
<A HREF="Physics.htm">Physics</A></CENTER>
<HR>

<H1>Astronomy</H1>
```

5. Save the file and reload Astro.htm in your Web browser. The "Astronomy" heading should still appear in a gold sans-serif font even though you deleted the inline style, because you applied a global style to all the H1 text.

   TROUBLE? If the main header is not shown in the gold sans-serif font, check the syntax of the style declaration you entered in the Astro.htm file.

Grouping Selectors

You can apply the same declaration to a group of selectors by including all of the selector names separated by commas. Chris would like to see all headers formatted in a gold sans-serif font. You can do this in the following style declaration:

```
<STYLE>
    H1, H2, H3, H4, H5, H6 {color:gold; font-family:sans-serif}
</STYLE>
```

Modify the Astro.htm file so that all header tags use the same color and font family.

To apply a declaration to a group of selectors:

1. Return to **Astro.htm** in your text editor.

2. Modify the style declaration for the H1 tag, changing the selector to **H1, H2, H3, H4, H5, H6** as shown in Figure 7-6.

Figure 7-6   **APPLYING A DECLARATION TO A GROUP OF SELECTORS**

this style will apply to the H1–H6 headers

```
<STYLE>
    H1, H2, H3, H4, H5, H6 {color:gold; font-family:sans-serif}
</STYLE>
```

3. Save your changes and reload the file in your Web browser.

   Figure 7-7 shows a portion of the revised Web page. Note that all header text now appears in a gold sans-serif font.

Figure 7-7   **STYLE APPLIED TO AN H2 HEADER**

H2 header → **Comments From Our Astronomy Customers**

Here at Maxwell Scientific, we strive to deliver high-quality astronomy equipment in a prompt and professional manner. Still, we're as happy as anyone when we receive a compliment!

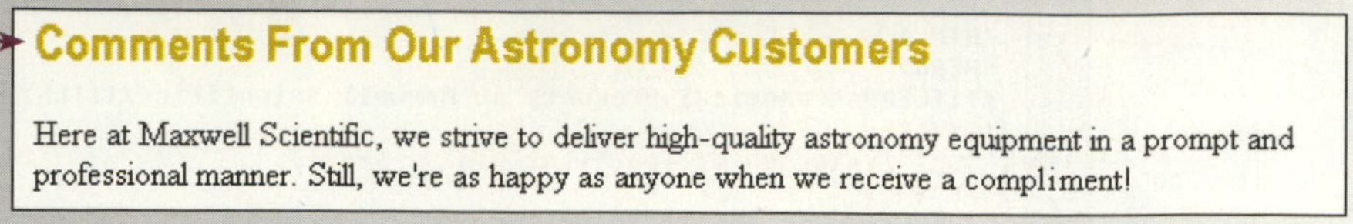

Even though you used the same style for all of the header tags, there were still some differences in how the browser displayed text formatted with these tags. Most notably, the styles did not affect the relative sizes of the text. Text formatted with the <H1> tag is still in a larger font than text formatted with the <H2> tag. This is because you haven't explicitly defined the size of header text, so that attribute is left to the browser's internal style rules.

Using an External Style Sheet

The final task that Chris wants you to do is to create styles that apply to an entire Web site. Chris wants all headers on the Web site to be formatted in a gold sans-serif font. To do this you'll first create a text file containing your style declarations, and then you'll create a link to that file in each page of the Web site.

To create an external style sheet:

1. Open a new blank document in your text editor.

2. Type the following line in the new file:

```
H1, H2, H3, H4, H5, H6 {color:gold; font-family: sans-
serif}
```

3. Save your document as **MWS.css** in the Tutorial.07 folder of your Data Disk.

   Most style sheets have the extension ".css," though this is not a requirement. Also note that within a style sheet, you don't need <STYLE> tags, just the style declarations.

The simple file you have created is a style sheet, even though you have just one line in yours. Most style sheets, of course, have many selectors and declarations.

REFERENCE WINDOW   **RW**

Creating a Linked Style Sheet
- Create a text file containing the style definitions that you want to apply to the pages on the Web site.
- For each Web page that you want to apply the styles to, insert the following tag in the head section of the HTML file:
  `<LINK HREF=URL REL="relation_type" TYPE="link_type">`
  where *URL* is the URL or filename of the style sheet, *relation_type* equals "stylesheet," and *link_type* equals "text/css" (or whatever language you are using for your styles).

Linking to Style Sheets with the <LINK> Tag

Now that you have a style sheet, you have to link your Web page (or pages) to it. This is accomplished by adding a <LINK> tag to the HEAD section of your HTML file. The general syntax for using the <LINK> tag is as follows:

```
<LINK HREF=URL REL="relation_type" TYPE="link_type">
```

where *URL* is the URL of the linked document, *relation_type* establishes the relationship between the linked document and the Web page, and *link_type* indicates the language used in the linked document. In order to link to a style sheet, the value of the REL property should be "stylesheet" and the value of the TYPE property should be "text/css". Thus, to link to a style sheet named "MWS.css", the <LINK> tag would be:

```
<LINK HREF="MWS.css" REL="stylesheet" TYPE="text/css">
```

Add this tag to the Astro.htm file.

To link to the MWS.css style sheet:

1. Reopen the **Astro.htm** file in your text editor.

2. Since you don't need it anymore, delete the style declaration between the <STYLE> and </STYLE> tags (but keep both the <STYLE> and </STYLE> tags, since you'll be using them later).

3. Above the embedded <STYLE> tag, insert the single line:

   ```
   <LINK HREF="MWS.css" REL="stylesheet" TYPE="text/css">
   ```

4. Save your changes and reload the file in your Web browser to verify that the headers still appear in a gold sans-serif font.

To apply this style sheet to other pages in the Web site, you need only add the <LINK> tag to each HTML file. Try this with the Chemistry page.

To add the MWS style sheet to the Chemistry page:

1. In your text editor, open the **Chemtxt.htm** file in the Tutorial.07 folder of your Data Disk.

2. Before the </HEAD> tag enter the new line (you can copy and paste this line from the Astro.htm file to this file if you prefer):

   ```
   <LINK HREF="MWS.css" REL="stylesheet" TYPE="text/css">
   ```

3. Save the file as **Chem.htm**.

4. Open the **Chem.htm** file in your Web browser. As shown in Figure 7-8, the page now employs the same H1 style used by the Astronomy page.

Figure 7-8   **THE CHEMISTRY PAGE**

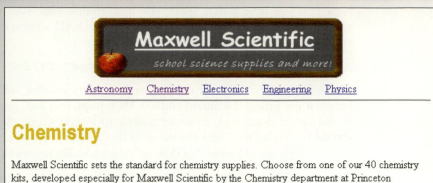

Chris points out that once you have a final form for the external style sheet, you can quickly modify the design of any of the pages in the Maxwell Scientific Web site, by simply adding a <LINK> tag pointing to the MWS.css style sheet.

Linking to Style Sheets with @import

Another way to link to a style sheet is to use the @import command, which accesses the style sheet definitions from another file. To use @import with your styles, you enclose the @import command within the embedded <STYLE> tags as follows:

```
<STYLE>
    @import url(stylesheet.css);
    style declarations
</STYLE>
```

where *stylesheet.css* is the URL of the style sheet file. If you want to access a style sheet from within another style sheet, you simply add the @import command to your style sheet file:

```
@import url(stylesheet.css);
styles
```

The advantage of this approach is that it allows you to easily combine different style sheets. For example, Maxwell Scientific could create a style sheet named "Basic.css" for all of its Web pages. You, as the designer of the products pages, could create a style sheet named "Products.css" that adds a few new styles applicable only to your pages. The contents of the Products.css file would then read:

```
@import url(Basic.css);
styles specific to the product pages …
```

and the resulting collection of styles would contain the basic style definitions plus your additional styles.

The @import command provides greater flexibility than the <LINK> tag in working with multiple style sheets, but at present only Internet Explorer supports it—Netscape (through version 4.7) does not. Thus, if you plan to use @import you need to verify that it'll work with all of your users' browsers. Unless you have a compelling need to use @import, you are probably better off using the <LINK> tag at present.

Resolving Style Precedence

You've now used three different methods of creating and applying styles to your Web site. What if you were to use all three in the same Web page and you mistakenly used different formatting for the same content? How does your Web browser determine how to apply the various styles? In cases where the styles conflict, precedence is determined in the following order:

1. An inline style has precedence over any embedded style and over any external style sheet.

2. An embedded style has precedence over an external style sheet.

3. An external style sheet has precedence over the internal style rules set by the Web browser.

4. Any style attributes left undefined by an inline style, an embedded style, or an external style sheet are left to the Web browser.

For example, if you set the H1 header, "Astronomy" in the Astro.htm file to appear in a blue sans-serif font, this style definition would override any conflicting style declaration for H1 headers in the embedded style or the external style sheet.

Note that precedence only becomes an issue when the styles are in conflict (using gold sans-serif versus blue sans-serif, for example.) If the styles *don't* conflict, then your browser merges the various styles.

To see how this works, Chris suggests that you modify the external style sheet so that all headers appear in a sans-serif font, but font color is determined by the embedded styles within each page. She would like to see headers in the Astronomy page appear in gold type as before, but she would like the headers in the Chemistry page to appear in red type.

To modify the styles for the Web site:

1. Reopen the **MWS.css** file in your text editor and edit the style definition line, deleting the color attribute so that it reads:

   ```
   H1, H2, H3, H4, H5, H6 {font-family:sans-serif}
   ```

2. Save your changes to the file.

3. Reopen the **Astro.htm** file in your text editor, and between the <STYLE> and </STYLE> tags enter the line:

   ```
   H1, H2, H3, H4, H5, H6 {color: gold}
   ```

4. Save your changes to Astro.htm.

5. Reopen the **Chem.htm** file in your text editor and after the <LINK> tag insert the following lines:

   ```
   <STYLE>
       H1, H2, H3, H4, H5, H6 {color: red}
   </STYLE>
   ```

6. Save your changes to Chem.htm.

7. Reload the **Chem.htm** file in your Web browser. Figure 7-9 shows the current state of this page.

Figure 7-9   **THE CHEMISTRY PAGE WITH EMBEDDED STYLES AND AN EXTERNAL STYLE SHEET**

Maxwell Scientific
school science supplies and more!

Astronomy   Chemistry   Electronics   Engineering   Physics

Chemistry

Maxwell Scientific sets the standard for chemistry supplies. Choose from one of our 40 chemistry kits, developed especially for Maxwell Scientific by the Chemistry department at Princeton University. All kits have been safety-tested. Chemicals are enlosed in protected bottles, using Maxwell Scientific's patented spillproof system.

Featured Chemistry Products

headers appear in a red sans-serif font

The Chemistry page now displays headers in a red sans-serif font, where the red style is taken from the embedded style in the Chem.htm file and the sans-serif style is taken from the MWS.css style sheet.

As a change is made to a style at one level, the changes are *cascaded* through to the other levels (hence the term, *cascading style sheets*). If you were to change the font from sans-serif to Times Roman in the MWS.css style sheet, the change will be cascaded through the embedded and inline styles, changing the font to Times Roman in every case where a different font has not already been specified.

As you define more styles for your Web site, you need to keep track of the inline, embedded, and external style sheets to correctly predict the impact that style changes have on the appearance of each page.

Working with Style Inheritance

Web pages will invariably have elements placed within other elements. For example, a Web page might have a bold tag, <B>, placed within a paragraph tag, <P>, to create boldface text within the paragraph. The paragraph tag is likewise placed within the <BODY> tag. You can display this relationship using a tree diagram like the one shown in Figure 7-10.

Figure 7-10   **SAMPLE TREE STRUCTURE OF HTML ELEMENTS**

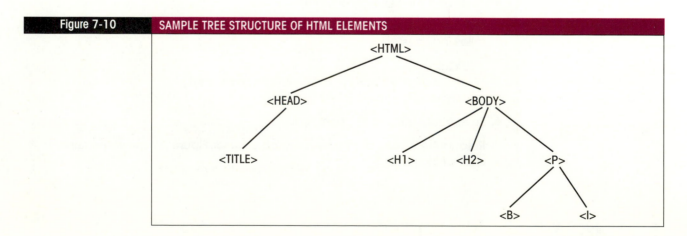

Parent and Descendant Elements

An element that lies within another element is called a **descendant** or **descendant element**. An element that contains another element is called the **parent** or **parent element**. The <BODY> tag is the ultimate parent, since it contains all of the other tags that you'll use in formatting the content of your page.

Using the principle of **inheritance**, styles defined for each parent tag are transferred to that tag's descendants. If Figure 7-10 represents all of the elements and their relationships in a particular HTML file, you could change the font color of every element in the Web page using the following style definition:

```
H1, H2, P {color: blue}
```

and all of the H1, H2, and paragraph text will appear in a blue font. Note that any boldface or italic text using the <B> and <I> tags within a paragraph tag will also inherit this blue color. However, as you add more tags to your Web page, the tree structure becomes more complicated and the style declarations would become long and unwieldy. A much simpler approach is to define a style for the <BODY> tag. You could set all font color to blue using the style definition:

```
BODY {color: blue}
```

Since all elements are descendants of the body element, all the text in the page will be shown in a blue-colored font.

You can override this inheritance by specifying a different style for the element's descendants. For example, look at the following style definitions:

```
BODY {color: blue}
H1, H2 {color: green}
```

These definitions will cause all text in the Web page to be displayed in a blue font *except* the H1 and H2 text (and any descendants of the H1 and H2 elements), which will be displayed in green. Note that the order in which you enter these style definitions does not matter; the Web browser will resolve the style definitions according to the underlying tree structure. Still, it is considered good practice to enter your style definitions in an order that follows the tree hierarchy.

Chris suggests that you change the default font color in the Maxwell Scientific pages to green, but leave the current header text color (gold) alone. This will render all of the headers in gold and the rest of the text in green.

To specify a default font color for the Maxwell Scientific Web site:

1. Reopen the **MWS.css** file in your text editor.

2. Before the style definitions for the H1—H6 tags, enter the new line:

   ```
   BODY {color:green}
   ```

3. Figure 7-11 shows the revised file.

Figure 7-11   **CHANGING THE BODY TEXT COLOR TO GREEN**

```
BODY {color:green}
H1, H2, H3, H4, H5, H6 {font-family: sans-serif}
```

4. Save your changes to MWS.css.

5. Return to your Web browser and reload the **Astro.htm** file. Figure 7-12 shows the new version of the Web page with a green font color except for the headers, which are displayed in gold.

Figure 7-12 REVISED FONT COLOR IN THE ASTRONOMY PAGE

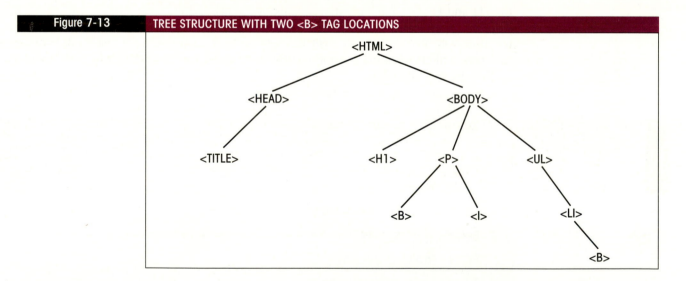

Contextual Selectors

You can use the tree structure concept to better control how your styles are applied to your Web page. Consider the structure of the tags shown in Figure 7-13.

Figure 7-13 TREE STRUCTURE WITH TWO <B> TAG LOCATIONS

```
                          <HTML>
                         /      \
                  <HEAD>          <BODY>
                    |            /   |    \
                 <TITLE>     <H1>  <P>    <UL>
                                  /  \      \
                               <B>   <I>    <LI>
                                              \
                                              <B>
```

A <B> tag appears in two locations: within the <P> tag and within the <LI> tag. You want to display the boldface text that appears within the <LI> tag in a blue font, but you want the rest of the bold text to remain green. If you use the following style declaration:

```
B {color: blue}
```

all boldface text will be displayed in blue, including text that does not lie within <LI> tags. To restrict the application of this style, you use a **contextual selector**, indicating the context in which the style is to be applied. For example, the declaration:

```
LI B {color: blue}
```

indicates that you should apply the blue color to any boldface text that lies within the <LI> tag. Any boldface text located elsewhere in Web page will not be affected by this style. You'll have a chance to work with a contextual selector in the next session.

You've completed your work with the various methods of applying styles to the Maxwell Scientific Web site. In the next session, you'll learn about more attributes that you can control with styles.

Session 7.1 QUICK CHECK

1. What do the acronyms CSS1 and CSS2 refer to?

2. What are inline styles, embedded styles, and linked style sheets? Which would you use to create a set of styles for an entire Web site?

3. What style would you use to change the color of all text found within the paragraph tag, <P>, to blue?

4. What style would you use to change the color of both the H1 and H2 headers to yellow?

5. What style would you use to change the color of boldface text within your paragraphs to red? Will boldface text located elsewhere be affected by your style?

6. What tag would you enter to link to the external style sheet, "BasicStyle.css"? Where should this tag be placed in your HTML file?

7. If a style sheet sets the color of H1 headers to blue, and an embedded style in the Web page sets the H1 color to green, what color will be displayed in the Web browser and why?

SESSION 7.2

In this session you'll learn more about the CSS language. You'll learn about specific attributes that you can use with styles to modify the appearance of fonts, including font size and alignment. You'll learn how to use styles to work with colors and background images. Finally, you'll use style attributes to create and format lists.

Setting Font and Text Attributes

In the last session you learned how to apply styles to the Maxwell Scientific Web site. To keep things simple, you worked with only two attributes: font color and font family. Now you're ready to learn more about the style language of CSS and how to create other styles. You will start by examining more closely the font-family attribute.

Using Font Families

The font-family attribute allows you to choose a font face for use in your Web page. CSS works with two types of font faces: specific and generic. A **specific font** is a font such as Arial, Garamond, or Times New Roman, that is actually installed on a user's computer. A

generic font is a general description of a font type. CSS supports five generic font types: serif, sans-serif, monospace, cursive, and fantasy. Figure 7-14 shows examples of each of these generic types. Note that for each generic font, there can be a wide range of designs.

Figure 7-14   GENERIC FONTS

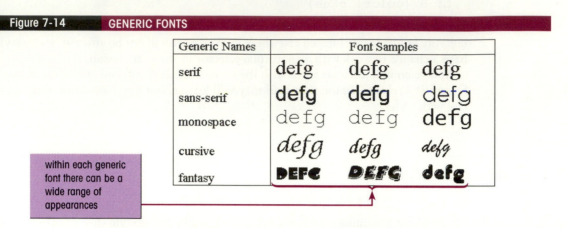

within each generic font there can be a wide range of appearances

---

REFERENCE WINDOW   RW

Choosing a Font Family

- To choose a font family for a Web page element, use the style:

  ```
  font-family:font_name1, font_name2 …
  ```
  where *font_name1*, *font_name2*, and so forth are either specific or generic font names. Generic font names must be either serif, sans-serif, monospace, cursive, or fantasy.

A typical Web design will use serif fonts for the body text and sans-serif for all headers. You would use a cursive or fantasy font where you needed to have special effects. If you need a typewriter-style font, you would use the monospace font name, which has the same effect as using the <PRE> tag on your text.

The problem with generic fonts is that you cannot be sure which specific font the Web browser will ultimately use to display your text, as shown in Figure 7-14. It is usually better to use a specific font whenever possible. To do this effectively, you should give the Web browser several fonts to choose from—that way browsers that don't have access to the font you specified as your first choice will have your second or third choices available. You list specific font names first, and you end the list with a generic font name, which the browser will use only as a "last resort" if none of the specific fonts can be found. A comma should separate one font name from another. For example, look at the following style declaration:

```
BODY {font-family: Times Roman, Century Schoolbook, serif}
```

This declaration will cause the browser to display body text in a Times Roman font. If that font is not on a user's machine, the browser will look for Century Schoolbook, and if that font is also missing, the browser will use whatever serif font is available.

In your earlier work, you specified only the generic sans-serif font for header text. Now that you've seen how to better use the font-family attribute, Chris suggests that you augment your earlier style, allowing the browser to first search for the Arial font and then for Helvetica before resorting to the generic font.

To modify the font-family attribute for the header text:

1. Open (or return to) the **MWS.css** style sheet file in your text editor.

2. Change the style for the H1–H6 tags to:

```
H1, H2, H3, H4, H5, H6 {font-family: Arial, Helvetica,
sans-serif}
```

3. Save your changes to MWS.css.

4. Reload the **Astro.htm** and **Chem.htm** files in your Web browser. Depending on the fonts installed on your computer, you may or may not notice a slight change in the appearance of the header text.

Managing Font Size

Chris has other suggestions to improve the design of the Web page. At the bottom of each page is address information formatted with the <ADDRESS> tag. By default, text formatted with this tag is displayed in normal-sized type, italicized, and aligned with the left edge of the page. Chris doesn't like this style and has several changes to propose. First of all, she wants the address information to take up less space on the Web page and would like you to reduce the font size for the <ADDRESS> tag.

The standard way of controlling font sizes with HTML is by using the SIZE property of the <FONT> tag. While useful for simple formatting, the SIZE property limits you to only seven font sizes (1 through 7), and the Web browser determines what these varying sizes actually are. Two browsers might display a size 7 font quite differently, depending on how the browsers are configured.

REFERENCE WINDOW	RW

Specifying a Font Size

■ To specify a font size for an element, use the style:

```
font-size: size
```

where *size* can either be a unit of length (specified as mm, cm, in, pt, pc, em, or ex), a keyword (xx-small, x-small, small, medium, large, x-large, xx-large), a percentage of the font size of the parent element, or a keyword describing the size relative to the parent element (larger or smaller).

In CSS, you use the font-size attribute to manage font sizes. There are four ways of expressing the value of this attribute:

■ As a unit of length

■ Using a keyword description

■ As a percentage of the parent element

■ Using a keyword expressing the size relative to the parent element

If you choose to express size as a unit of length, you can use absolute units or relative units. Because absolute and relative units come up a lot in CSS, it's worthwhile to spend some time understanding them.

Absolute units define the font size based on a standard unit of measurement. Size values can be whole numbers (0, 1, 2 …) or fractions (0.5, 1.6, 3.9 …). You can use the following units: mm (millimeter), cm (centimeter), in (inch), pt (point), and pc (pica.) For comparison, there are 72 points in an inch and 12 points in a pica (or 6 picas in an inch.) If you want your H1 headers to be ½ inch in size, you can use any of the following styles (note that you should not insert a space between the size value and the unit abbreviation):

```
H1 {font-size: 0.5in}
H1 {font-size: 36pt}
H1 {font-size: 3pc}
```

These measurement units are useful if you intend to have users print the Web page on standard 8½ x 11 sheets of paper. They don't work as well in the browser window, where the size of the user's monitor and resolution is unknown. The appearance that a ½-inch header has on a 14-inch monitor has a very different impact from the same size header on a 21-inch monitor.

To overcome this problem, use a **relative unit**, one that expresses the font size relative to a size of a standard character. There are two standard typesetting characters, referred to as "em" and "ex." The **em unit** is equal to the width of the capital letter "M." in the default font used by the browser. The **ex unit** is equal to the height of a small "x" in the default font (see Figure 7-15.)

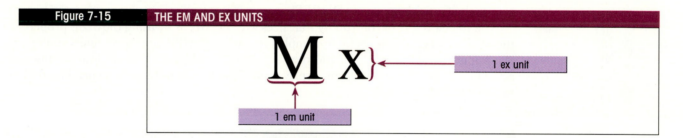

| Figure 7-15 | THE EM AND EX UNITS |

Of these two units, the em unit is more useful for page design, because 1 em is exactly equal to the browser's default font size for body text. This is true no matter what font is being used (unlike the ex unit, whose size changes based on the font face being used). For example, if the Web browser displays body text in a 12-point font, the following style:

```
H1 {font-size: 2em}
```

will cause all H1 headers to displayed at twice the default font size, or 24 points. As with absolute units, you can specify fractional values for the em and ex units. Unlike the absolute units, em and ex units are **scalable** in that they can be used under any monitor size or resolution and retain their relative proportions.

The final unit of measurement is the **pixel**, entered with the unit abbreviation "px". A pixel is smallest display element on your computer monitor. To set the size of your H1 headers to 20 pixels, use the style:

```
H1 {font-size: 20px}
```

Pixels give you the finest control over size (since you are working with the smallest display element recognized by the monitor), but they should be used with some caution. Text that is 10 pixels high may be perfectly readable at a monitor resolution of 640 x 480, but it can become unreadable if your user's monitor is set to 1024 x 768.

If you don't want to deal with units of length, you can use one of the seven descriptive keywords: xx-small, x-small, small, medium, large, x-large, or xx-large. These keywords match the seven values of the SIZE property in the <FONT> tag. For example, to format an H1 header with the largest font size, you can use either the HTML command:

```
<H1><FONT SIZE=7>Your Header Text</FONT></H1>
```

or the style:

```
H1 {font-size: xx-large}
```

If you want the size of certain text to be expressed relative to the size of the text's parent element, you can do so using percentage values. In the following set of style definitions, the size of boldface type has been increased to 150% of the size of its parent element. Since the body text is 12 points, boldface body text will be rendered in 18-point type.

```
BODY {font-size:12pt}
B {font-size:150%}
```

Figure 7-16 shows the impact of such a style definition on boldface text in a Web page. Note that such a style would have the same impact within a header, since in that case the header would be the parent element, and the boldface text would be increased to 150% of the surrounding header text.

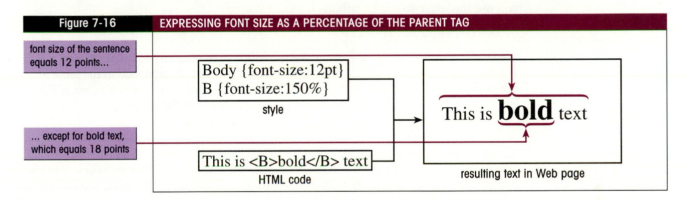

| Figure 7-16 | EXPRESSING FONT SIZE AS A PERCENTAGE OF THE PARENT TAG |

font size of the sentence equals 12 points...

Body {font-size:12pt}
B {font-size:150%}
style

This is **bold** text

... except for bold text, which equals 18 points

This is <B>bold</B> text
HTML code

resulting text in Web page

The final way to express a font size is with the two keywords: "larger" and "smaller," which make the font one size larger or smaller than the size of the parent element. To make the H2 header one size larger than the body text, you could use the following style:

```
BODY {font-size: medium}
H2 {font-size: larger}
```

Note that you could have achieved the same effect by using the keyword, "large" for the H2 style.

Armed with an almost-dizzying array of possible font size values, you're ready to apply your knowledge to the <ADDRESS> tag in the Astronomy page. Recall that Chris wanted this font to be smaller. You decide to reduce to the font to 0.6 em, or 60% of the size of normal body text.

To decrease the font-size of the <ADDRESS> tag:

1. Return to the **MWS.css** style sheet in your text editor.

2. Insert a new line at the bottom of the file reading,

```
ADDRESS {font-size:0.6em}
```

3. Save your changes to the file.

4. Reload the **Astro.htm** and **Chem.htm** files in your Web browser and scroll to the bottom of each page. As shown in Figure 7-17, the address information has been reduced in size.

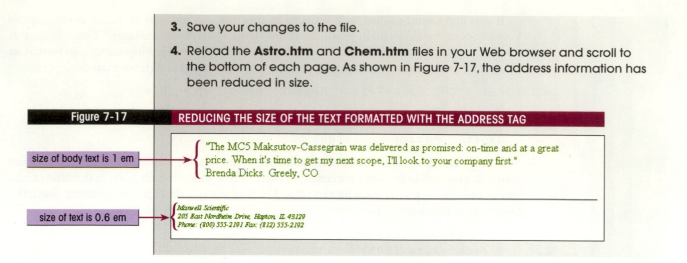

Figure 7-17   REDUCING THE SIZE OF THE TEXT FORMATTED WITH THE ADDRESS TAG

size of body text is 1 em

"The MC5 Maksutov-Cassegrain was delivered as promised: on-time and at a great price. When it's time to get my next scope, I'll look to your company first."
Brenda Dicks. Greely, CO

size of text is 0.6 em

Maxwell Scientific
205 East Nordheim Drive, Hopton, IL 43129
Phone: (800) 555-2191 Fax: (812) 555-2192

Specifying Word, Letter, and Line Spacing

Beyond the size of the font, you can also use CSS font attributes to control the size of the space between letters, words, and lines of text. To set the space between individual letters, you use the letter-spacing attribute, with the syntax:

```
letter-spacing: size
```

where either *size* can have the value "normal", which allows the browser to determine the letter spacing based on the font being used, or a value can be entered, expressed in the same measuring units used to describe font size (inches, millimeters, centimeters, em units, etc.). To set the letter spacing for text in a paragraph to 0.5 em, you would use the style:

```
P {letter-spacing: 0.5em}
```

Using the letter-spacing attribute to stretch a word over an E X T E N D E D space is one way of adding flair and impact to your page design. Another technique is to change the spacing between individual words. This is achieved with the word-spacing attribute:

```
word-spacing: size
```

where once again, *size* is either equal to "normal", to allow the browser to set the word spacing, or to a specific length in the usual system of measurements. Modifying the space between words is not usually done, but you can do it with CSS if you need to.

Finally, you can use the line-height attribute to modify the vertical space between lines of text. The line-height attribute specifies the minimum distance between the baseline of adjacent lines. Figure 7-18 shows how the line height relates to the font size. Notice that the line height is usually larger than the font size to leave additional space between adjacent text lines.

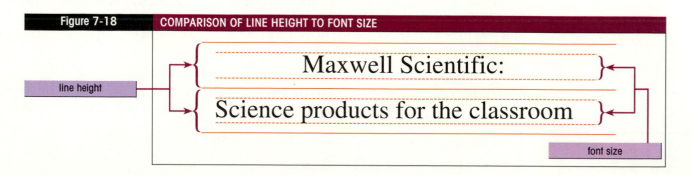

Figure 7-18   COMPARISON OF LINE HEIGHT TO FONT SIZE

line height

Maxwell Scientific:

Science products for the classroom

font size

To set the line height, use the style:

```
line-height:size
```

where *size* is either a specific length, a percentage of the font size, or a number representing the ratio of the line height to the font size. The standard ratio is 1.2, which means that the line height is 1.2 times the font size. If you wanted your paragraphs to be double-spaced, you would enter the style definition:

```
P {line-height:2}
```

In modern advertising it's not uncommon to see titles with large fonts and small line heights. Figure 7-19 shows an example in which the line height is actually smaller than the font size. This causes the lines to be bunched up and gives the title a greater impact than it would have with more space between the two lines.

| Figure 7-19 | A TITLE WITH A LARGE FONT SIZE AND SMALL LINE HEIGHT |

Maxwell Scientific
Science Products for the Classroom
large font, normal line height

Maxwell Scientific
Science Products for the Classroom
large font, line height < font size

REFERENCE WINDOW RW

Controlling Letter, Word, and Line Spacing
- To define the space between individual letters, use the style:

  ```
  letter-spacing:size
  ```

  where *size* is the amount of space between letters.
- To define the space between individual words, use the style:

  ```
  word-spacing:size
  ```

  where *size* is the space between individual words.
- To define the vertical space between lines of text, use the style:

  ```
  line-height:size
  ```

  where *size* is either the specific length between the baseline of the lines, a percentage of the font size of the text in the lines, or a number representing the ratio of the line height to the font size.

Setting Font Styles and Weights

Chris feels that the address information with the smaller font size is difficult to read. Perhaps it would help if the text weren't in italics (recall that the <ADDRESS> tag uses italics by default). Font styles are controlled by the font-style attribute, which has three possible values: normal, italic, or oblique.

REFERENCE WINDOW

Controlling Font Appearance and Weight

- To specify the appearance for your font, use the style:

  `font-style:style_type`

  where *style_type* is either normal, italic, or oblique.

- To control the weight of your fonts, use the style:

  `font-weight:weight`

  where *weight* is either a value ranging from 100 (lightest) to 900 (heaviest) in intervals of 100, a keyword describing the weight of the font (normal or bold), or a keyword that describes the weight relative to the weight of the parent element (lighter or bolder).

The italic and oblique styles are extremely similar; both display text slanted to the right, though there can be small differences for some fonts. Netscape does not support the oblique attribute value.

Since you want to remove the italics from the address information, you can add the font-style:normal attribute to your style sheet. This will override the default italic setting in the <ADDRESS> tag.

To remove italics from the <ADDRESS> tag:

1. Return to the **MWS.css** style sheet in your text editor.

2. Insert the code **; font-style:normal** in the style declaration for the <ADDRESS> tag, as shown in Figure 7-20.

Figure 7-20   **SETTING THE FONT STYLE OF THE ADDRESS ELEMENT TO NORMAL TEXT**

```
BODY {color:green}
H1, H2, H3, H4, H5, H6 {font-family: Arial, Helvetica, sans-serif}
ADDRESS {font-size:0.6em; font-style:normal}
```

3. Save your changes and reload the **Astro.htm** and **Chem.htm** files in your Web browser. Verify that the italics are removed from the address information for both pages.

   TROUBLE? If there has been no change in the text, return to your style sheet. You might have forgotten to place a semicolon between the attributes.

You may be wondering why "bold" was not included as one of the font-style values. This is because CSS considers "bold" to be an aspect of the font's weight, or line thickness. Font weights can be expressed as an absolute number ranging in intervals of 100, going from 100 (the lightest) up to 900 (the heaviest or "most bold"). While this is good in theory, most fonts do not support nine different font weights. For most fonts, you can assume that a weight of 400 corresponds to normal text, a weight of 700 can be used for bold text, and 900 for "extra" bold text. For light text, you can try a weight of 100, but for many fonts you won't see a difference between the 100 and 400 weight.

You can also use the keywords "normal" and "bold" in place of a weight value, or you can express the font weight relative to the parent tag by using the keywords, "bolder" or "lighter." For example, in HTML all text in headers is already in boldface, so the <B> tag has no effect within an <H2> tag. This is not true with CSS, where you can use the bolder attribute to get even more bold text, as shown below:

```
H2 {font-weight:700}
B {font-weight:bolder}
```

If these style definitions are applied to a Web page, H2 text formatted with <B> tag will be "bolder" (that is, the line will be thicker) in appearance than the surrounding header text. How noticeable this difference will be depends on the Web browser and the type of font used.

Aligning Text Horizontally and Vertically

In looking over the current design of the Astronomy page, you decide that the address information would look better centered on the bottom of the page. To do this with CSS, you use the text-align attribute:

```
text-align:alignment
```

where *alignment* can be left, center, right, or justify. Setting the text-align value to "justify" stretches the text, extending it from the left to the right margin, but in actual practice not all browsers interpret the "justify" value in this way. Some browsers will ignore this attribute value altogether.

To center the address information:

1. Return to the **MWS.css** style sheet in your text editor.

2. Add the following attribute to the ADDRESS tag style, **; text-align: center**, as shown in Figure 7-21.

Figure 7-21   **CENTERING TEXT FORMATTED WITH THE <ADDRESS> TAG**

```
BODY {color:green}
H1, H2, H3, H4, H5, H6 {font-family: Arial, Helvetica, sans-serif}
ADDRESS {font-size:0.6em; font-style:normal; text-align:center}
```

3. Save your changes and then reload the **Astro.htm** and **Chem.htm** files in your browser. The address text should now be centered at the bottom of both pages.

REFERENCE WINDOW

Controlling Text Alignment
- To specify the horizontal alignment of your text, use the style:
  ```
  text-align:alignment
  ```
  where *alignment* is either left, center, right, or justify.
- To control the vertical alignment of text and images relative to the baseline of the parent element, use the style:
  ```
  vertical-align:alignment
  ```
  where *alignment* equals one of the following keywords: baseline, bottom, middle, sub, super, text-bottom, text-top, or top, or is expressed as a distance or percentage that the element is raised or lowered relative to the height of the parent element.

CSS also provides the ability to vertically align elements such as text and images relative to the surrounding text. The syntax for setting the vertical alignment is:

```
vertical-align:alignment
```

where *alignment* has one of the keyword values shown in Figure 7-22.

Figure 7-22	VALUES OF THE VERTICAL ALIGNMENT ATTRIBUTE

ATTRIBUTE VALUE	DESCRIPTION
baseline	Aligns the element with the baseline
bottom	Aligns the bottom of the element with the bottom of the lowest element (text or graphic) in the line
middle	Aligns the element in the middle of the text
sub	Aligns the element as a subscript
super	Aligns the element as a superscript
text-bottom	Aligns the element with the font's bottom
text-top	Aligns the element with the top of the tallest letter
top	Aligns the element with the top of the tallest element (text or graphic) in the line

Figure 7-23 shows an example of each vertical-align value on a sample of text. The default value for vertical alignment is baseline.

Figure 7-23	EXAMPLES OF THE VERTICAL ALIGNMENT VALUES

Maxwell Scientific *teaches science!*
vertical-align:baseline

Maxwell Scientific *teaches science!*
vertical-align:bottom

Maxwell Scientific *teaches science!*
vertical-align:middle

Maxwell Scientific *teaches science!*
vertical-align:sub

Maxwell Scientific *teaches science!*
vertical-align:super

Maxwell Scientific *teaches science!*
vertical-align:text-top

Maxwell Scientific *teaches science!*
vertical-align:text-bottom

Maxwell Scientific *teaches science!*
vertical-align:top

In place of the keywords, you can also enter a distance or percentage that the element will be raised relative to the surrounding text. A positive value or percentage raises the element above the surrounding text, and a negative value or percentage lowers the element. For example, the style:

```
vertical-align:50%
```

raises the element by half of the line height of the surrounding text, while the style

    `vertical-align:-50%`

lowers the element by half.

Indenting Text

CSS allows you to indent the first line of a paragraph. The syntax for creating an indentation is:

    `text-indent:`*indentation*

where *indentation* is either the length (in either absolute or relative units) of the indentation or a percentage of the width of the paragraph. For example, an indentation value of 5% indents the first line by 5% of the width of the paragraph, while an indentation value of 2em indents the first line by 2 em units. The length and percentage values also can be negative, which extends the first line out by the value or percentage indicated, and then indents the rest of the lines in the paragraph. This particular effect, called a **hanging indent**, works sporadically on many browsers, so you should be sure to test your style sheet thoroughly if you intend to create a hanging indent in your Web page.

Special Text Attributes

CSS provides three attributes for special text effects: text-decoration, text-transform, and font-variant. As shown in Figure 7-24, the text-decoration attribute can be used to underline your text, or place a line over or through your text. You can also make your text blink on and off using the text-decoration:blink attribute.

| Figure 7-24 | VALUES OF THE TEXT-DECORATION ATTRIBUTE |

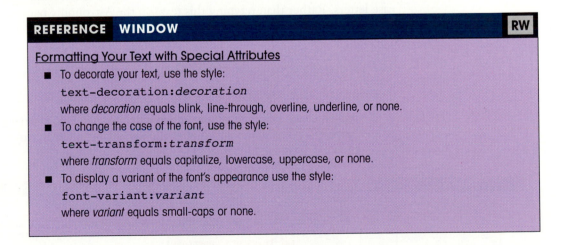

| REFERENCE | WINDOW | RW |

Formatting Your Text with Special Attributes

- To decorate your text, use the style:
  `text-decoration:`*decoration*
  where *decoration* equals blink, line-through, overline, underline, or none.
- To change the case of the font, use the style:
  `text-transform:`*transform*
  where *transform* equals capitalize, lowercase, uppercase, or none.
- To display a variant of the font's appearance use the style:
  `font-variant:`*variant*
  where *variant* equals small-caps or none.

The text-transform attribute can be used to capitalize the first letter of each word in a paragraph, display the text in all capital letters, or display the text in all lowercase letters. Figure 7-25 shows the effect of the various text-transform values.

Figure 7-25   **VALUES OF THE TEXT-TRANSFORM ATTRIBUTE**

Maxwell Scientific teaches science
text-transform:none

Maxwell Scientific Teaches Science
text-transform:capitalize

MAXWELL SCIENTIFIC TEACHES SCIENCE
text-transform:uppercase

maxwell scientific teaches science
text-transform:lowercase

Finally, you can use the font-variant command to create small caps. Small caps are capital letters that are the same size as lowercase letters. Figure 7-26 shows the interesting effect that can be achieved by using the style

```
font-variant:small-caps
```

on your text. Netscape does not support the font-variant attribute through version 4.7.

Figure 7-26   **VALUES OF THE FONT-VARIANT ATTRIBUTE**

Maxwell Scientific teaches science
font-variant:normal

MAXWELL SCIENTIFIC teaches science
font-variant:small-caps

Chris wants to examine whether the address information would look better in all uppercase letters. Rather than retyping this text (on the Astronomy page and every other page in the Web site!), you'll apply the text-transform:uppercase style to the <ADDRESS> tag.

To change the address information to uppercase:

1. Return to the **MWS.css** style sheet in your text editor.

2. Insert the text, ; **text-transform:uppercase** to the style definition of the ADDRESS element. You may want to place this new style definition on a separate line as shown in Figure 7-27.

Figure 7-27   **ADDING THE TEXT-TRANSFORM ATTRIBUTE TO THE STYLE FOR THE ADDRESS ELEMENT**

```
BODY {color:green}
H1, H2, H3, H4, H5, H6 {font-family: Arial, Helvetica, sans-serif}
ADDRESS {font-size:0.6em; font-style:normal; text-align:center;
         text-transform:uppercase}
```

3. Save your changes.

4. Reload the **Astro.htm** and **Chem.htm** files in your Web browser. Figure 7-28 shows the revised appearance of the contact information.

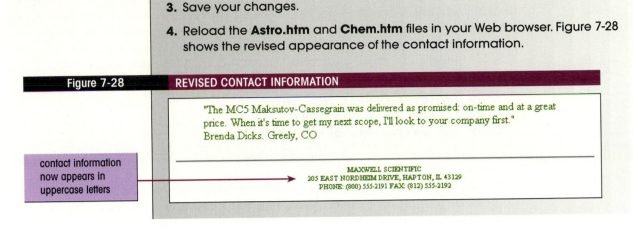

| Figure 7-28 | REVISED CONTACT INFORMATION |

"The MC5 Maksutov-Cassegrain was delivered as promised: on-time and at a great price. When it's time to get my next scope, I'll look to your company first."
Brenda Dicks. Greely, CO

contact information now appears in uppercase letters

MAXWELL SCIENTIFIC
205 EAST NORDHEIM DRIVE, HAPTON, IL 43129
PHONE: (800) 555-2191 FAX: (812) 555-2192

Chris examines the address text and is happy with the final style you choose for the ADDRESS tag element. You won't have to make any more changes to the address information.

The Font Attribute

You can pool many of the individual text and font attributes you've learned about into one single attribute, called the font attribute. The syntax for the font attribute is:

```
font:font-style; font-variant; font-weight; font-size/
line-height; font-family
```

where *font-style*, *font-variant*, and so forth are the values for font and text attributes you've learned about. The font attribute provides a compact way of expressing these multiple attributes. For example, the following two style forms are equivalent:

```
H2 {font-style:italic; font-variant: small-caps;
font-weight:bold;
     font-size:3em; line-height:0.8em;
     font-family:Times Roman, serif }
```

```
H2 {font: italic small-caps bold 3em/0.8em Times Roman, serif}
```

The font attribute requires that you specify the font size and font family—the other font attributes are optional. If you don't include a font attribute, your browser will assign the normal or standard value for the element.

Working with Color and Background

You now want to turn your attention to the color and background choices you'll make for the Maxwell Scientific Web site. In Session 1, you worked with color names by changing the body text to green and the header text to gold, but that was kept simple to introduce the concept of styles. Now you can further examine the syntax of the color attribute.

The Color Attribute

There are many ways of defining color with CSS. As you saw in Session 1, you can use color names to specify color; CSS works with most of the color names supported by HTML.

Another way to specify color in CSS is to use the RGB color values. You can enter the hexadecimal form of the color value just as you did with HTML, but you can also enter the color values directly (yeah, no more hexadecimals!) or as a percentage of the RGB values. For example, to format the body text in the color Teal, which has a RGB color value of (0, 128, 128)—008080 in hexadecimal—you can use any of the following styles:

```
body {color:teal}
body {color:#008080}
body {color:rgb(0,128,128)
body {color:rgb(0%, 50%, 50%}
```

Remember that hexadecimal color values range from 0 to 255, so specifying a color percentage of 50% for green and blue is close to a color value of 128.

You decide that the gold color value used for the headers in the Astro.htm file is too light. In reviewing possible color choices, you decide that a brownish gold with a color value corresponding to rgb(153,102,6) would be more appealing. Since this is an embedded style, you'll make your changes to Astro.htm file.

To revise the color of headers in the Astronomy page:

1. Re-open the **Astro.htm** file in your text editor.
2. Change the color of the H1-H6 headers from gold to **rgb(153,102,6)** as shown in Figure 7-29.

Figure 7-29 CHANGING THE EMBEDDED COLOR STYLE OF THE H1–H6 HEADERS

new color value

```
<HTML>
<HEAD>
<TITLE>Astronomical products at Maxwell Scientific</TITLE>
<LINK HREF="MWS.css" REL="stylesheet" TYPE="text/css">
<STYLE>
   H1, H2, H3, H4, H5, H6 {color:rgb(153,102,6)}
</STYLE>
</HEAD>
```

3. Save your changes and reload the file in your Web browser. The headers in the page should now be a brownish-gold color, as shown in Figure 7-30.

Figure 7-30 NEW COLOR IN THE ASTRONOMY HEADER

color value has changed

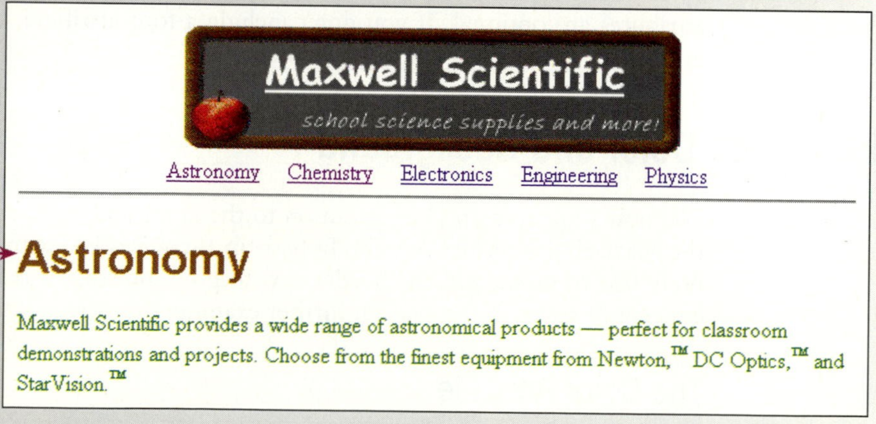
Maxwell Scientific
school science supplies and more!
Astronomy Chemistry Electronics Engineering Physics
Astronomy
Maxwell Scientific provides a wide range of astronomical products — perfect for classroom demonstrations and projects. Choose from the finest equipment from Newton,™ DC Optics,™ and StarVision.™

Working with Background Color

If you want to change the background color, you use the background-color attribute. However, contrary to what you might expect, you can apply background color to almost any element in your Web page, not just to the page itself.

Chris wants you try this approach with the customer comments that appear on the product pages. Each comment has been formatted with the <BLOCKQUOTE> tag, which is used to indent blocks of text. Chris suggests that you apply a silver background to all of the quotes in your Web site, so you'll make the change in your style sheet.

To change the background color of the customer quotes:

1. Reopen the **MWS.css** style sheet in your text editor.

2. Add the following style declaration to the bottom of the file (see Figure 7-31):

   ```
   BLOCKQUOTE {background-color:silver}
   ```

Figure 7-31	APPLYING THE BACKGROUND-COLOR ATTRIBUTE TO THE BLOCKQUOTE ELEMENT

```
BODY {color:green}
H1, H2, H3, H4, H5, H6 {font-family: Arial, Helvetica, sans-serif}
ADDRESS {font-size:0.6em; font-style:normal; text-align:center;
         text-transform:uppercase}
BLOCKQUOTE {background-color: silver}
```

3. Save your changes to the file.

4. Reload the **Astro.htm** and **Chem.htm** files in your Web browser. As shown in Figure 7-32, both pages should now display the customer comments with a silver background.

   TROUBLE? If you're using Netscape, the background color covers only the text in the blockquote. In Internet Explorer, the background color is applied to the entire block of text.

Figure 7-32	BACKGROUND COLOR APPLIED ONLY TO THE CUSTOMER COMMENTS

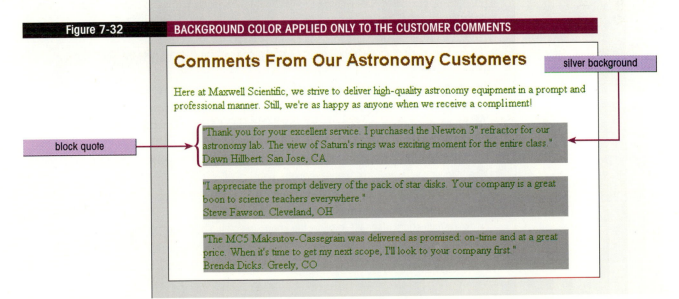

Comments From Our Astronomy Customers   silver background

Here at Maxwell Scientific, we strive to deliver high-quality astronomy equipment in a prompt and professional manner. Still, we're as happy as anyone when we receive a compliment!

block quote

"Thank you for your excellent service. I purchased the Newton 3" refractor for our astronomy lab. The view of Saturn's rings was exciting moment for the entire class."
Dawn Hillbert, San Jose, CA

"I appreciate the prompt delivery of the pack of star disks. Your company is a great boon to science teachers everywhere."
Steve Fawson, Cleveland, OH

"The MC5 Maksutov-Cassegrain was delivered as promised: on-time and at a great price. When it's time to get my next scope, I'll look to your company first."
Brenda Dicks, Greely, CO

Working with Background Images

Like background color, background images can be applied to an entire page or to any element on a page. There are four attributes of the background you control: the image file used, how the image is repeated in the background, where the image is placed on the background, and whether the image scrolls with the display window.

To specify which file you want to use for a background, use the syntax:

```
background-image:url(image)
```

where *image* is the URL or filename of the image file. You can create background images for almost any element on your page. Figure 7-33 demonstrates how you can apply this attribute to the <B> tag to make an interesting design for your boldface text.

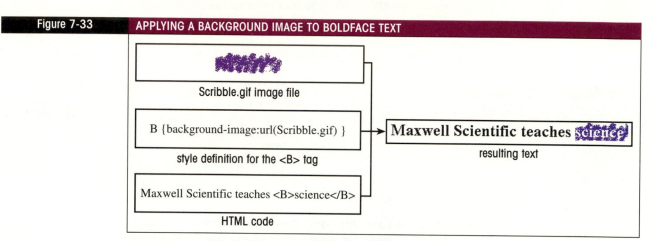

Figure 7-33   **APPLYING A BACKGROUND IMAGE TO BOLDFACE TEXT**

Scribble.gif image file

B {background-image:url(Scribble.gif) }

style definition for the <B> tag

Maxwell Scientific teaches <B>science</B>

HTML code

Maxwell Scientific teaches science

resulting text

REFERENCE   WINDOW   **RW**

Controlling the Background Image

- To specify an image for an element's background, use the style:
  ```
  background-image: url(image)
  ```
  where *image* is the URL or filename of the graphic file.
- To control how the image is tiled over the background of the element, use the style:
  ```
  background-repeat: repeat_value
  ```
  where *repeat_value* is either repeat, repeat-x, repeat-y, or none.
- To place the image in a specific position on the background, use the style:
  ```
  background-position: horizontal_position vertical_position
  ```
  where *horizontal_position* and *vertical_position* can be expressed as the horizontal and vertical distance from the upper-left corner of the background, using either length, percentages, or one of the following keywords: top, center, bottom, right, or left.
- To specify whether the image scrolls with the element, use the style:
  ```
  background-attachment: attach
  ```
  where *attach* equals "scroll," to allow the image to scroll along with the background, or "fixed," to prevent the image from scrolling.

HTML tiles background images both horizontally and vertically across the page until the entire display area is filled up. CSS does the same thing, except that you can use the background-repeat attribute to control how the imaged is tiled. The background-repeat attribute has four values, discussed in Figure 7-34. Examples of each attribute value are shown in Figure 7-35.

Figure 7-34   **VALUES OF THE BACKGROUND-REPEAT ATTRIBUTE**

BACKGROUND-REPEAT	DESCRIPTION
repeat	The image is tiled both horizontally and vertically until the entire background of the element is covered.
repeat-x	The image is tiled only horizontally across the width of the element.
repeat-y	The image is tiled only vertically across the height of the element.
no-repeat	The image is not repeated at all.

Figure 7-35   **EXAMPLES OF THE BACKGROUND-REPEAT VALUES**

background image

background-image:repeat

background-image:repeat-x

background-image:repeat-y

background-image:no-repeat

By default, every background image is placed in the upper-left corner of the element, and then tiling (if it's being used) proceeds from there. You can specify a different position with the background-position attribute. You enter two attribute values. The first attribute value indicates the horizontal distance from the left edge of the display area; the second value indicates the vertical distance from the top edge. These values can be expressed as a percentage of the display area, in units of length, or using keywords.

For example, the style:

```
P {background-image:url(logo.gif); background-position:10% 20%}
```

places the image file, logo.gif, at point 10% to right and 20% down from the upper-left corner of the paragraph. Similarly, the style:

```
P {background-image:url(logo.gif); background-position:2cm 5cm}
```

places the same image file 2 centimeters to the right and 5 centimeters down from the upper-left corner of the paragraph. If you enter only one attribute value, the browser will apply that value to the horizontal position and then vertically center the image.

For a more general description of image position, you can use a combination of the six keywords: left, center, right (for the horizontal position), and top, center, bottom (for the vertical position). Figure 7-36 shows how these keywords relate to the percentage values. Unlike percentages and units of length, you do not need to place the keywords in any particular order. The browser will interpret the background position (top, right) the same way it interprets (right,top). Note that Netscape does not support the background-position property through version 4.7.

| Figure 7-36 | BACKGROUND-POSITION KEYWORDS AND PERCENTAGES |

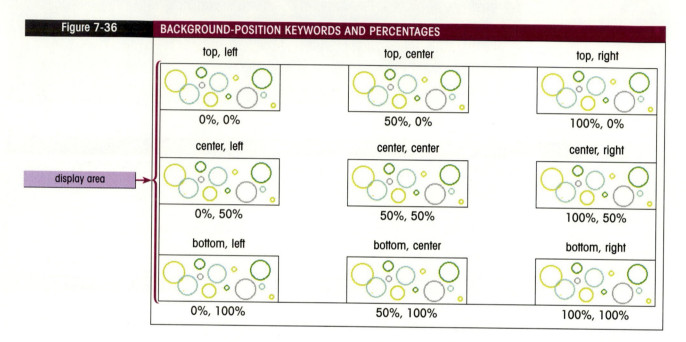

By default, all background images will move along with the page's background as the user scrolls through the Web page. You can change this with the background-attachment attribute. The syntax of this style is:

```
background-attachment:attach
```

where attach is either "scroll," to scroll the image along with the element, or "fixed, which places the image in a fixed place in the browser's display window, preventing it from moving even if the user scrolls down through the Web page. The background-attachment attribute is not currently supported by Netscape through version 4.7.

Fixed background images are often used to create the impression of a **watermark**, a typesetting term that refers to a translucent graphic impressed onto the very fabric of the paper, and used for specialized stationery and corporate reports.

If you use a background image that employs a transparent color, you can combine the background-color and background-image attributes to create a new image. For example, the style:

```
BODY {background-color:yellow; background-
image:url(logo.gif) }
```

will display the image file, "logo.gif" on the background, and anywhere that a transparent color appears in the logo the background color, "yellow" will shine through.

The Background Attribute

Like the font attribute discussed earlier, you can combine all of the various attributes for backgrounds into one attribute, called the background attribute. The syntax for the background attribute is:

```
background:background-color background-image background-repeat
           background-attachment background-position
```

Where *background-color*, *background-image*, etc., are the values for the various background attributes. For example, to center the nonrepeating image file "logo.gif" as a fixed image in the body of your Web page along with a yellow background color, you would use the style definition:

```
BODY {background:yellow url(logo.gif) no-repeat fixed
center center}
```

You do not have to enter all of the attribute values for the background attribute, but the ones you do specify should follow the order indicated by the syntax. Failure to do this can lead to unpredictable results in some browsers.

At Maxwell Scientific, Web authors are asked to place a watermark with the word "DRAFT" on every Web page that is in the process of being designed. This watermark has been stored in the file Draft.jpg. Because this is a watermark, you'll want to fix the graphic, centered in the display area.

To insert the DRAFT watermark to the pages' background:

1. Return to the **MWS.css** style sheet in your text editor.

2. Add the following attribute to the BODY style (see Figure 7-37):

```
; background: white url(Draft.jpg) no-repeat fixed center
center
```

Figure 7-37	USING THE BACKGROUND ATTRIBUTE

attributes of the background image for the Web pages' body

```
BODY {color:green;
      background: white url(Draft.jpg) no-repeat fixed center center}
H1, H2, H3, H4, H5, H6 {font-family: Arial, Helvetica, sans-serif}
ADDRESS {font-size:0.6em; font-style:normal; text-align:center;
         text-transform:uppercase}
BLOCKQUOTE {background-color: silver}
```

Note that with these attributes, the Draft.jpg graphic will be placed in the center of the display window, it will not be tiled, and it will not scroll.

3. Save your changes to the MWS.css file.

4. Reload the **Astro.htm** and **Chem.htm** files in your Web browser. As shown in Figure 7-38, the DRAFT watermark has been added. As you scroll through the display window, the watermark stays in the center of the browser window.

Figure 7-38   VIEWING THE DRAFT WATERMARK

DRAFT watermark, centered and fixed on the Web page

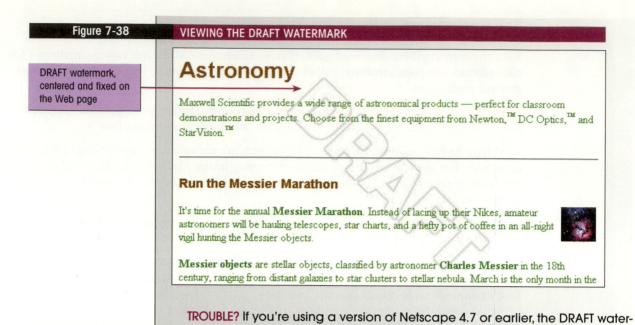

TROUBLE? If you're using a version of Netscape 4.7 or earlier, the DRAFT watermark will not appear in the center of the display window, and it will scroll.

Working with List Styles

CSS gives you more control than does HTML over the appearance and behavior of ordered, unordered, and definition lists. For example, you can control the type of labels to attach to the list items and how to position the labels with respect to the label text.

Choosing a List Style Type

The list-style-type attribute allows you to choose the type of label to display alongside text formatted with the <UL>, <OL>, or <LI> tags. Figure 7-39 shows the values you can use with the list-style-type attribute.

Figure 7-39   VALUES OF THE LIST-STYLE-TYPE ATTRIBUTE

ATTRIBUTE VALUE	THE WEB BROWSER DISPLAYS
disc (the default)	•
circle	o
square	☐
decimal	1, 2, 3, …
decimal-leading-zero	01, 02, 03, …
lower-roman	i, ii, iii, …
upper-roman	I, II, III, …
lower-alpha	a, b, c, …
upper-alpha	A, B, C, …

Recall from the first session that you can use a contextual selector to create a style for one element nested inside another element. You also can use contextual selectors to create an outline style for several levels of nested lists. In Figure 7-40 a set of contextual selectors is used to create an outline style for many different outline levels.

| Figure 7-40 | USING CONTEXTUAL SELECTORS TO CREATE A NESTED OUTLINE STYLE |

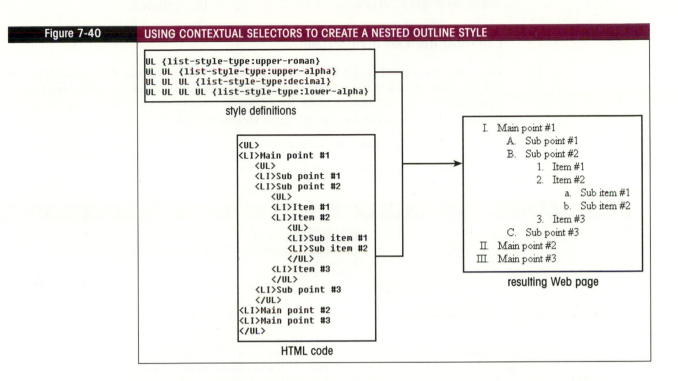

```
UL {list-style-type:upper-roman}
UL UL {list-style-type:upper-alpha}
UL UL UL {list-style-type:decimal}
UL UL UL UL {list-style-type:lower-alpha}
```
style definitions

```
<UL>
<LI>Main point #1
   <UL>
   <LI>Sub point #1
   <LI>Sub point #2
      <UL>
      <LI>Item #1
      <LI>Item #2
         <UL>
         <LI>Sub item #1
         <LI>Sub item #2
         </UL>
      <LI>Item #3
      </UL>
   <LI>Sub point #3
   </UL>
<LI>Main point #2
<LI>Main point #3
</UL>
```
HTML code

```
 I.  Main point #1
      A.  Sub point #1
      B.  Sub point #2
            1.  Item #1
            2.  Item #2
                  a.  Sub item #1
                  b.  Sub item #2
            3.  Item #3
      C.  Sub point #3
 II.  Main point #2
III.  Main point #3
```
resulting Web page

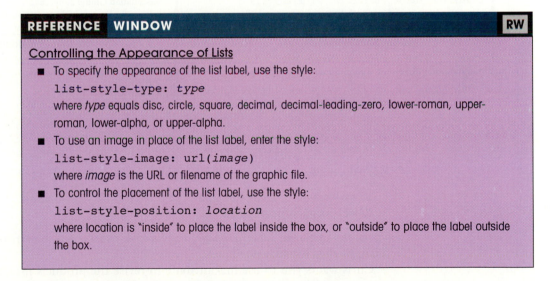

Using a List Style Image

If you want to use a label not included in the list-style-type values, you can create your own with an image file and the list-style-image attribute. The syntax for applying this attribute is:

```
list-style-image: url(image)
```

where *image* is the URL of the filename of the graphic file. This attribute is not supported by Netscape version 4.7 or earlier. Because of this, it's a good idea to include the list-style-type attribute along with the list-style-image attribute. Then, if a viewer's browser doesn't support this attribute (or if for some reason the graphic file is not available), the browser will display whatever label is indicated by the list-style-type attribute.

Defining the List Style Position

List items are treated by CSS as if they have an invisible box around them (actually, other HTML elements have this property too – you'll learn more about that in the next session). The labels for the list items can be either placed outside this box or within this box (see Figure 7-41). The syntax for specifying the location of the list item label is:

```
list-style-position: location
```

where *location* is either "inside," or the default value, "outside."

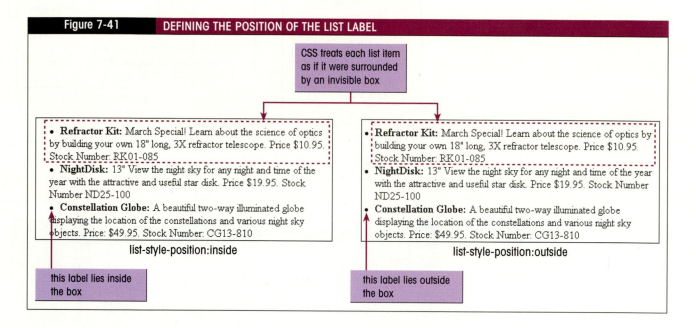

Figure 7-41   DEFINING THE POSITION OF THE LIST LABEL

The List-Style Attribute

You can combine all of these attributes into the list-style attribute. The syntax for this style is:

```
list-style: list-style-type list-style-image
list-style-position
```

where *list-style-type*, *list-style-image*, and *list-style-position* are the attribute values for each of the individual list style attributes.

Chris wants you to use this attribute to revise the products list. In place of bullets, she wants you to display the Apple.jpg graphic, placed outside the box. Since some versions of Netscape do not support the use of graphic images, you'll also specify a list style type, replacing the bullet with an open circle for Netscape users.

To define a style for the product list:

1. Return to the **MWS.css** style sheet in your text editor.

2. Insert the following style definition at the bottom of the file (see Figure 7-42).

   ```
   UL {list-style: circle url(Apple.jpg) outside}
   ```

Figure 7-42	DEFINING THE APPEARANCE OF THE LIST LABEL

```
BODY {color:green;
      background: white url(Draft.jpg) no-repeat fixed center center}
H1, H2, H3, H4, H5, H6 {font-family: Arial, Helvetica, sans-serif}
ADDRESS {font-size:0.6em; font-style:normal; text-align:center;
         text-transform:uppercase}
BLOCKQUOTE {background-color: silver}
UL {list-style: circle url(Apple.jpg) outside}
```

label will appear as a circle unless the browser supports the use of graphic images

labels will be placed outside the rectangular box

3. Save your changes to the file.

4. Reload the **Astro.htm** and **Chem.htm** files in your Web browser. The list bullets have been replaced with a graphic of an apple, as shown in Figure 7-43.

Figure 7-43	REPLACING THE LIST LABEL WITH A GRAPHIC

Featured Astronomical Products

Refractor Kit: March Special! Learn about the science of optics by building your own 18" long, 3X refractor telescope. Price $10.95. Stock Number: RK01-085

NightDisk: View the night sky for any night and time of the year with this attractive and useful star disk. Price $19.95. Stock Number: ND25-100

Constellation Globe: A beautiful two-way illuminated globe displaying the location of the constellations and various night sky objects. Price: $49.95. Stock Number: CG13-810

Apple.jpg graphic

TROUBLE? If you are using Netscape version 4.7 or earlier, your labels will appear as open circles.

Chris likes the look of the new style. She has one suggestion. She wants the name of each product shown in dark red. Currently the product name is in boldface type. You can use the color attribute to change the boldface type to a dark red, but you don't want to change boldface type everywhere on the Web page. This means that you have to use a contextual selector for text formatted with the <B> tag nested within the <UL> tag.

To display the product names in dark red:

1. Return to the **MWS.css** style sheet in your text editor.

2. Insert the following new line at the bottom of the file:

   ```
   UL B {color:rgb(155,0,0)}
   ```

3. Save your changes to the file.

4. Reload the **Astro.htm** and **Chem.htm** files in your Web browser. As shown in Figure 7-44, the product names are a dark red color that matches the color of the apple.

Figure 7-44   CHANGING THE COLOR OF THE BOLDFACE TEXT WITHIN EACH LIST ITEM

Featured Astronomical Products

●**Refractor Kit:** March Special! Learn about the science of optics by building your own 18" long, 3X refractor telescope. Price $10.95. Stock Number: RK01-085

boldface text —

●**NightDisk:** View the night sky for any night and time of the year with this attractive and useful star disk. Price $19.95. Stock Number: ND25-100

●**Constellation Globe:** A beautiful two-way illuminated globe displaying the location of the constellations and various night sky objects. Price: $49.95. Stock Number: CG13-810

You've added a lot changes to the style sheet for Maxwell Scientific. In the next session, you'll use CSS to format hyperlinks and to work with the layout of your Web pages.

Session 7.2 QUICK CHECK

1. What style would you use to change the font of a block quote to Times Roman, or if Times Roman is not available, to change to a serif font?

2. What style would you use to set the size of paragraph text to 12-point type?

3. What is the difference between an absolute unit and a relative unit? What are the two relative units supported by CSS?

4. What style would you use to underline all your headers, and display the header text in uppercase letters?

5. What style would you use to center your paragraph text and to display it in boldface italics?

6. What style would you enter to display your unordered lists with the Lists.gif background image, centered in the background?

7. What style would you use to display your ordered lists with an integer label?

SESSION 7.3

In this session you'll format the appearance of hyperlinks on your Web page, and you'll learn how to create a "rollover" effect for them. You'll work with CSS classes and pseudo-classes, and you'll see how to use the <DIV> and <SPAN> tags to create containers for blocks of text. Finally, you'll learn how to format block-level elements in order to format the layout of your page.

Formatting Hypertext Links

The next area Chris wants you to focus on is the hypertext links located at the top of each product page. In the future, you'll be adding a few more product categories, and she wants you to reduce the size of the hypertext font so that the additional text will still fit on a single line. She also wants you to format the hyperlinks so that when a user's mouse passes over the hyperlinks, they change appearance—indicating to the user that the text is a hyperlink.

First, you'll change the text formatted with the <A> tag to green, with a font size of 0.65 em.

To modify the font size of the hypertext links:

1. Open (or return to) the **MWS.css** file in your text editor.

2. At the bottom of the file, insert the following new line:

   ```
   A {font-size: 0.65em; color:green}
   ```

3. Save your changes to the file.

4. Reload the **Astro.htm** and **Chem.htm** files in your browser, and verify that the font size has been reduced and the font color changed.

You can use all of the CSS attributes that you learned in the last session on hypertext. Some Web designs do away with the popular style of underlining hypertext. Instead, these designs display hypertext links in a different color from normal text but with no underline. The following style is one way of accomplishing this:

```
A {text-decoration:none}
```

Remember that setting value of the text-decoration attribute to none removes the underlining. Hypertext also has an additional property that normal text doesn't have—the condition of the hyperlink itself. The hyperlink can be in one of four states:

- The link's target has already been visited.
- The link's target has never been visited.
- The link is currently being clicked.
- The mouse pointer is hovering over the link.

Web browsers usually provide a visual clue for each of these states, such as a different color for visited links, and a different shape for the pointer when it hovers over a link. CSS provides a different selector for each condition. The general syntax is:

```
A:visited {styles for previously visited targets}
A:link {styles for targets that have never been visited}
A:active {styles for links that are currently being clicked}
A:hover {styles when the mouse cursor is hovering over the
link}
```

You use the variety of CSS attributes to create a different style for each condition. For example, to change the color of previously visited targets to red, and that of targets that have never been visited to green, use the styles:

```
A:visited {color:red}
A:link {color:green}
```

Chris wants you to make it so that when a user's pointer passes over a hyperlink, the link will change appearance, indicating that the text is a link. This is called the **rollover effect**. Try this now by adding the A:hover selector to your style sheet and creating a style that uses bold, red text in all uppercase letters.

To create the rollover effect:

1. Return to your text editor and the **MWS.css** style sheet.

2. Insert the following line at the bottom of the file (see Figure 7-45):

   ```
   A:hover {color:red; text-transform:uppercase; font-
   weight:bold}
   ```

Figure 7-45	CREATING A "ROLLOVER" EFFECT

```
BODY {color: green;
      background: white url(Draft.jpg) no-repeat fixed center center}
H1, H2, H3, H4, H5, H6 {font-family: Arial, Helvetica, sans-serif}
ADDRESS {font-size: 0.6em; font-style:normal; text-align:center;
         text-transform:uppercase}
BLOCKQUOTE {background-color:silver}
UL {list-style: circle url(Apple.jpg) outside}
UL B {color: rgb(155,0,0)}
A {font-size:0.65em; color:green}
A:hover {color:red; text-transform:uppercase; font-weight:bold}
```

style for hyperlinks when the pointer hovers over the link

3. Save your changes.

4. Reload the **Astro.htm** and **Chem.htm** files in your Web browser. Verify that as you pass your pointer over the hyperlinks, the text changes color, case, and weight (see Figure 7-46).

Figure 7-46	THE ROLLOVER EFFECT

text changes color, case, and weight (from normal to boldface)

TROUBLE? If you are running Netscape version 4.7 or earlier, you will not be able to see the rollover effect.

Note that Internet Explorer supports all four of the conditions for hypertext; Netscape (through version 4.7) does not support the hover condition.

Working with IDs and Classes

The preceding example of adding the rollover effect demonstrates a feature of CSS called a pseudo-class. A **pseudo-class** is a classification of an element based on its status or its use. In this case the status was the condition of the hypertext link. The element itself, a hyperlink with the pointer hovering over it, is called a **pseudo-element**. In CSS2, other pseudo-classes have been introduced, including the first-line pseudo-class and the first-letter pseudo-class, which are used for formatting the first line and first letter of a block of text, respectively. For example, if you wish to display the first line of your paragraphs in uppercase, you could create the following style definition:

```
P:first-line {text-transform: uppercase}
```

Similarly, you can increase the size of the first letter of your paragraphs by using this pseudo-class style:

```
P:first-letter {font-size: 200%}
```

After applying these two styles, your paragraphs would look like the one shown in Figure 7-47.

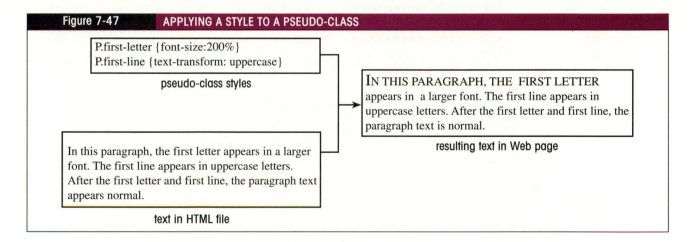

Figure 7-47   APPLYING A STYLE TO A PSEUDO-CLASS

P.first-letter {font-size:200%}
P.first-line {text-transform: uppercase}

pseudo-class styles

IN THIS PARAGRAPH, THE FIRST LETTER appears in a larger font. The first line appears in uppercase letters. After the first letter and first line, the paragraph text is normal.

In this paragraph, the first letter appears in a larger font. The first line appears in uppercase letters. After the first letter and first line, the paragraph text appears normal.

resulting text in Web page

text in HTML file

The Class Property

At present the only pseudo-classes that are supported by most browsers are the four conditions applied to hyperlinks. Many browsers do not yet support the first-letter and first-line pseudo-classes. However, you can create your own classes in your HTML tags with the CLASS property. The syntax for creating a class is:

```
<tag CLASS=class_name>
```

where *tag* is the HTML tag and *class_name* is the name of the class. For example, to create a class named "FirstHeader" for the first H1 header in the Astronomy page, you would use the following tag in your HTML file:

```
<H1 CLASS=FirstHeader>Astronomy</H1>
```

Once a class has been created, you can apply a style specific to that class with the declaration:

```
tag.class_name {style attributes and values}
```

where once again, *tag* is the HTML tag and *class_name* is the name of the class you created. Figure 7-48 demonstrates this approach by creating an underline style for the H1 header with the class name "FirstHeader." This technique is useful when you have multiple Web pages in which you want the first header in each page to be formatted the same.

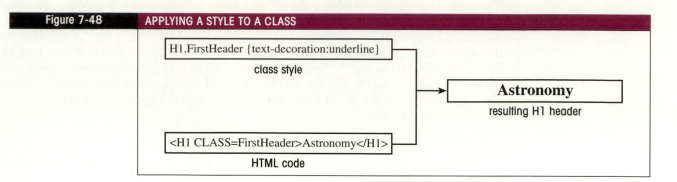

Figure 7-48   APPLYING A STYLE TO A CLASS

H1.FirstHeader {text-decoration:underline}

class style

Astronomy

resulting H1 header

<H1 CLASS=FirstHeader>Astronomy</H1>

HTML code

If the same class name is used for several different types of tags, you would omit the tag name from the style declaration, following the syntax:

`.class_name {style attributes and values}`

For example, the two following headers both use the same class name:
`<H1 CLASS=NewHeader>Astronomical Products</H1>`
`<H2 CLASS=NewHeader>Comments</H2>`

If you want to display both of these headers in italics, you could apply the style to the class, using the statement:

`.NewHeader {font-style:italic}`

and this style would apply to any tag with the CLASS=NewHeader property.

Class names must be single words, although you can use digits and dashes. Class names are also case-sensitive. The class name, "FirstHeader" is different from the class name "firstheader."

The ID Property

You can achieve a similar effect using HTML's ID property. Here the syntax is:

`<tag ID=ID_name>`

where *tag* is the HTML tag and *ID_name* is an ID name assigned to the tag. To apply a style to an ID, you use the style declaration:

`#id_name {style attributes and values}`

The difference between the CLASS property and the ID property is that the value of the ID property must be unique. You can't have more than one tag with the same ID value. On the other hand, you can apply the same CLASS value to multiple document tags.

The CLASS and ID properties are useful features of HTML that you can use with CSS to define styles for specific content in your Web page without having to use inline styles.

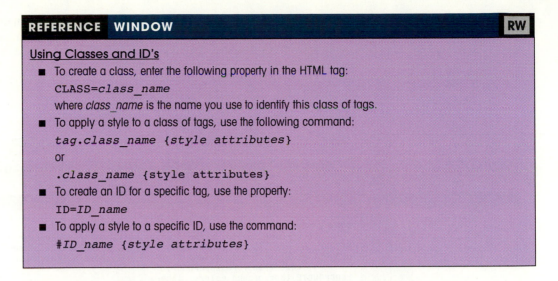

Using Classes and ID's
- To create a class, enter the following property in the HTML tag:

  CLASS=*class_name*

  where *class_name* is the name you use to identify this class of tags.
- To apply a style to a class of tags, use the following command:

  tag.class_name {style attributes}

  or

  .class_name {style attributes}
- To create an ID for a specific tag, use the property:

  ID=*ID_name*
- To apply a style to a specific ID, use the command:

  #ID_name {style attributes}

Each month, Maxwell Scientific offers special deals on selected merchandise. Chris would like to see these products displayed in a different color in the product list. You can do this quickly and easily by creating a class named "Special" for those particular products. There are two such specials in the Astronomy page (there are no specials listed in the Chemistry page).

To create a class of special products:

1. Open the **Astro.htm** file in your text editor.

2. Scroll down and locate the first list item, "Refractor Kit."

3. Within the <LI> tag, enter the property **CLASS=Special**.

4. Locate the <LI> tag for the "Classroom Planetarium" and enter the property **CLASS=Special** into that tag. See Figure 7-49.

5. Save your changes.

| Figure 7-49 | CREATING A CLASS FOR MONTHLY SPECIALS |

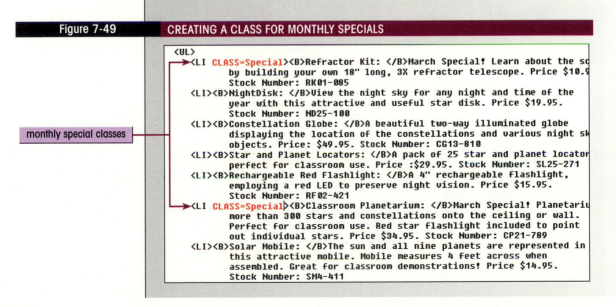

```
<UL>
<LI CLASS=Special><B>Refractor Kit: </B>March Special! Learn about the sc
        by building your own 18" long, 3X refractor telescope. Price $10.9
        Stock Number: RK01-085
<LI><B>NightDisk: </B>View the night sky for any night and time of the
        year with this attractive and useful star disk. Price $19.95.
        Stock Number: ND25-100
<LI><B>Constellation Globe: </B>A beautiful two-way illuminated globe
        displaying the location of the constellations and various night sk
        objects. Price: $49.95. Stock Number: CG13-810
<LI><B>Star and Planet Locators: </B>A pack of 25 star and planet locator
        perfect for classroom use. Price :$29.95. Stock Number: SL25-271
<LI><B>Rechargeable Red Flashlight: </B>A 4" rechargeable flashlight,
        employing a red LED to preserve night vision. Price $15.95.
        Stock Number: RF02-421
<LI CLASS=Special><B>Classroom Planetarium: </B>March Special! Planetariu
        more than 300 stars and constellations onto the ceiling or wall.
        Perfect for classroom use. Red star flashlight included to point
        out individual stars. Price $34.95. Stock Number: CP21-789
<LI><B>Solar Mobile: </B>The sun and all nine planets are represented in
        this attractive mobile. Mobile measures 4 feet across when
        assembled. Great for classroom demonstrations! Price $14.95.
        Stock Number: SM4-411
```

monthly special classes

Now that you've created the class, you can define a style for it in your style sheet. You decide to display the monthly specials in a boldface font with the same brown color that you used for the astronomy headers. The color has the RGB value (153, 102, 6).

To define the special products style:

1. Reopen the **MWS.css** style sheet in your text editor.

2. At the bottom of the file, insert the new style (see Figure 7-50):

```
LI.Special {color: rgb(153,102,6); font-weight:bold}
```

Figure 7-50   DEFINING THE MONTHLY SPECIAL STYLE

```
BODY {color:green;
      background: white url(Draft.jpg) no-repeat fixed center center}
H1, H2, H3, H4, H5, H6 {font-family: Arial, Helvetica, sans-serif}
ADDRESS {font-size:0.6em; font-style:normal; text-align:center;
         text-transform:uppercase}
BLOCKQUOTE {background-color: silver}
UL {list-style: circle url(Apple.jpg) outside}
UL B {color:rgb(155,0,0)}
A {font-size:0.65em}
A:hover {color:red; text-transform:uppercase; font-weight:bold}
LI.Special {color: rgb(153, 102, 6); font-weight:bold}
```

3. Save your changes.

4. Reload **Astro.htm** in your Web browser. Figure 7-51 shows the revised appearance of the products on special.

Figure 7-51   MONTHLY SPECIALS IN THE PRODUCTS LIST

Featured Astronomical Products

monthly specials

- **Refractor Kit: March Special!** Learn about the science of optics by building your own 18" long, 3X refractor telescope. Price $10.95. Stock Number: RK01-085
- **NightDisk:** View the night sky for any night and time of the year with this attractive and useful star disk. Price $19.95. Stock Number: ND25-100
- **Constellation Globe:** A beautiful two-way illuminated globe displaying the location of the constellations and various night sky objects. Price: $49.95. Stock Number: CG13-810
- **Star and Planet Locators:** A pack of 25 star and planet locators — perfect for classroom use. Price :$29.95. Stock Number: SL25-271
- **Rechargeable Red Flashlight:** A 4" rechargeable flashlight, employing a red LED to preserve night vision. Price $15.95. Stock Number: RF02-421
- **Classroom Planetarium: March Special!** Planetarium kit projects more than 300 stars and constellations onto the ceiling or wall. Perfect for classroom use. Red star flashlight included to point out individual stars. Price $34.95. Stock Number: CP21-789
- **Solar Mobile:** The sun and all nine planets are represented in this attractive mobile. Mobile measures 4 feet across when assembled. Great for classroom demonstrations! Price $14.95. Stock Number: SM4-411

TROUBLE? If you are using Netscape, the monthly special text will not be changed by the Special style, but the open circle in the bulleted list will change color to match the color of the headers. You'll deal with this problem shortly.

Working with <DIV> and <SPAN>

You show the current Astronomy page to Chris, who views the page in both the Internet Explorer and Netscape browsers. She immediately notices the discrepancy in the way that the product list is displayed, as shown in Figure 7-52.

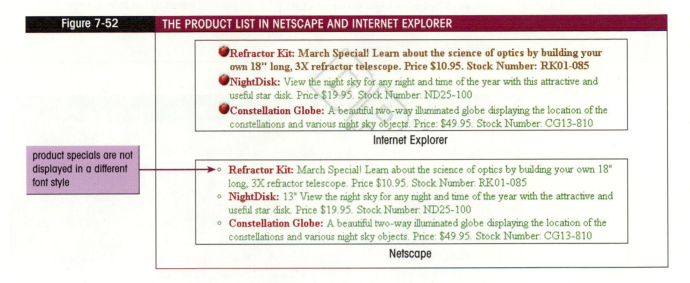

Figure 7-52	THE PRODUCT LIST IN NETSCAPE AND INTERNET EXPLORER

product specials are not displayed in a different font style

Part of the problem is that Netscape, version 4.7 and below, is not fully compliant with the CSS1 specification. It also doesn't apply styles to the LI elements in the same way that Internet Explorer does. Chris is willing to live with minor differences, such as the absence of the apple graphic in the product list. On the other hand, she feels that it's very important for the monthly specials to be highlighted somehow, and they're not in Netscape.

One way to deal with this problem is to create an inline style for each <LI> tag that brackets a monthly special; both Netscape and Internet Explorer would then display the correct style. Chris doesn't like this approach, however, because making the change each month in the Web page for each science discipline would be tedious and prone to errors. What Chris wants is a tag that will "mark" the monthly special text.

The <DIV> Tag

HTML supports such a tag, called the <DIV> tag. Unlike other tags in HTML, the <DIV> tag does not format content. Instead, used with the CLASS or ID property, the <DIV> tag assigns a name to whatever document content it contains. The syntax of the <DIV> tag is:

```
<DIV CLASS=class_name> Document content </DIV>
```

Note that you can also use the ID property in place of the CLASS property.

Figure 7-53 shows the <DIV> tag in action. In this example, a statement about the company slogan has been enclosed within opening and closing <DIV> tags and given the class name, "Slogan." A style (in this case, bold) can then be applied to whatever content has been enclosed by the <DIV> tag.

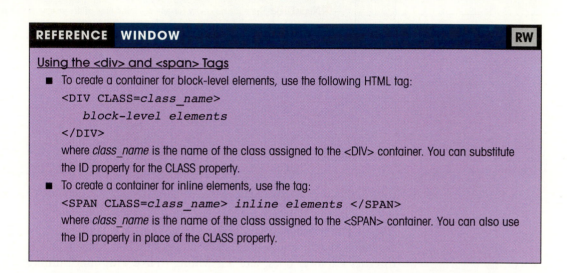

Figure 7-53   THE <DIV> TAG

DIV.Slogan {font-weight: bold}

style

Maxwell Scientific's new slogan is: "We teach science"

resulting text in Web page

<DIV CLASS=Slogan>Maxwell Scientific's new slogan is:
 "We teach science" </DIV>

HTML code

REFERENCE   WINDOW   RW

Using the <div> and <span> Tags

■ To create a container for block-level elements, use the following HTML tag:

```
<DIV CLASS=class_name>
    block-level elements
</DIV>
```

where *class_name* is the name of the class assigned to the <DIV> container. You can substitute the ID property for the CLASS property.

■ To create a container for inline elements, use the tag:

```
<SPAN CLASS=class_name> inline elements </SPAN>
```

where *class_name* is the name of the class assigned to the <SPAN> container. You can also use the ID property in place of the CLASS property.

The <SPAN> Tag

The <DIV> tag is used for blocks of text, such as paragraphs, block quotes, headers, or lists. Collectively, these text blocks are known as **block-level elements**. Block-level elements contain **inline elements**, such as individual letters, words, or phrases. Some of the HTML tags that apply to inline elements are the <B> and <I> tags (for displaying text in italics and boldface). It's considered bad style to mark inline elements with the <DIV> tag; instead, you should use the <SPAN> tag. The syntax for the <SPAN> tag is:

```
<SPAN CLASS=class_name> Inline elements </SPAN>
```

Figure 7-54 shows the application of the <SPAN> tag to a phrase that lies within the block of text. You could have created the same effect using the <I> tag, but then you also would not be able to quickly change the style (especially on multiple pages) at a later date if you chose to do so.

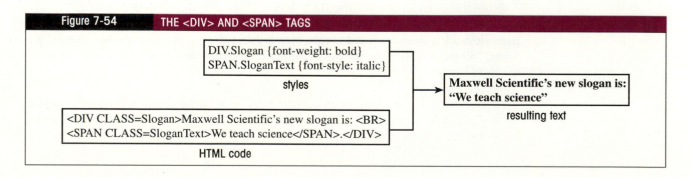

Figure 7-54   THE <DIV> AND <SPAN> TAGS

DIV.Slogan {font-weight: bold}
SPAN.SloganText {font-style: italic}

styles

Maxwell Scientific's new slogan is: "We teach science"

resulting text

<DIV CLASS=Slogan>Maxwell Scientific's new slogan is:
 <SPAN CLASS=SloganText>We teach science</SPAN>.</DIV>

HTML code

Chris suggests that you use the <DIV> tag to mark the products on special. You can then apply the same style definition you used earlier, with only a minor modification to the style sheet.

To use the <DIV> tag in the Astronomy page:

1. Open the **Astro.htm** file in your text editor.

2. Locate the first <LI> tag in the products list. Insert the tag **<DIV CLASS=Special>** in a blank line above it.

3. Append the closing **</DIV>** tag in a new line directly after the stock number for the Refractor Kit, "RK01-085."

4. Locate the <LI> tag for the classroom planetarium. Insert the tag **<DIV CLASS=Special>** in a blank line above it.

5. Append the closing **</DIV>** tag in a new line after the stock number, "CP21-789."

   Figure 7-55 shows the revised HTML code.

Figure 7-55   ADDING <DIV> TAGS TO THE MONTHLY SPECIALS

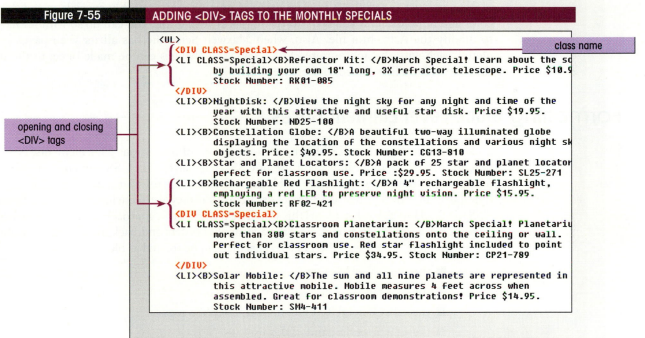

6. Save your changes to the file.

7. Reopen the **MWS.css** style sheet in your text editor.

8. Change the style selector "LI.Special" to **.Special** by removing the selector "LI".

   Since you are using this class with both the <LI> and <DIV> tag, you should specify only the class name, not the tag and class name. This style will then be applied wherever the CLASS=Special property is used.

9. Save your changes.

10. Reload the **Astro.htm** file in your Web browser. Netscape users should now see the product list shown in Figure 7-56. The product list for Internet Explorer users should be unchanged.

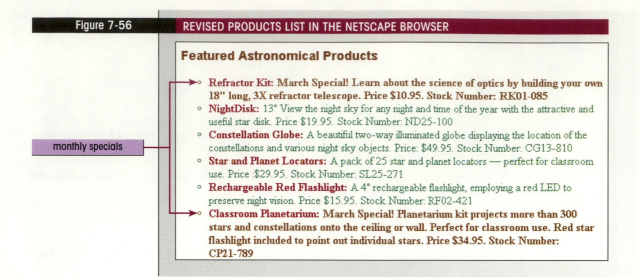

Figure 7-56   REVISED PRODUCTS LIST IN THE NETSCAPE BROWSER

Featured Astronomical Products

- **Refractor Kit: March Special! Learn about the science of optics by building your own 18" long, 3X refractor telescope. Price $10.95. Stock Number: RK01-085**
- **NightDisk:** 13" View the night sky for any night and time of the year with the attractive and useful star disk. Price $19.95. Stock Number: ND25-100
- **Constellation Globe:** A beautiful two-way illuminated globe displaying the location of the constellations and various night sky objects. Price: $49.95. Stock Number: CG13-810
- **Star and Planet Locators:** A pack of 25 star and planet locators — perfect for classroom use. Price :$29.95. Stock Number: SL25-271
- **Rechargeable Red Flashlight:** A 4" rechargeable flashlight, employing a red LED to preserve night vision. Price $15.95. Stock Number: RF02-421
- **Classroom Planetarium: March Special! Planetarium kit projects more than 300 stars and constellations onto the ceiling or wall. Perfect for classroom use. Red star flashlight included to point out individual stars. Price $34.95. Stock Number: CP21-789**

monthly specials

The product list in the Netscape browser now displays monthly specials in a different color and in boldface. If you want to revise this style later on, you can do so without having to modify the Astro.htm file. Also, when Maxwell Scientific has all its Web pages completed, each with the appropriate <DIV> tags, any changes can be made once, in the style sheet, for all the files linked to the style sheet.

Formatting Block-Level Element Boxes

So far, all of your work in CSS has been in the design of the various page elements. Now it's time to turn to the other important use of CSS—page layout. In CSS you control layout by manipulating the size and location of block-level elements. You learned earlier with the list-style-position attribute that CSS treats list items as if they were enclosed in a box. Actually, CSS treats all block-level elements this way. The power of this approach is that you can format these boxes: move them around on the page, apply borders and background colors to them, and so on. Here are a few of the HTML tags that can be treated as block-level elements:

- the <H1> – <H6> tags
- the <P> tag
- the <BLOCKQUOTE> and <ADDRESS> tags
- the <UL>, <OL>, and <DL> list tags
- individual list items using the <LI>, <DT> or <DD> tags
- the <DIV> tag
- the <BODY> tag
- the <HR> tag
- the <IMG> tag

CSS2 introduces many new features for manipulating these boxes. Unfortunately, most browsers haven't implemented all of these features yet, so you'll focus your attention on the features that are commonly supported.

Parts of the Block-Level Element Box

Figure 7-57 shows a diagram of a block-level element (in this case, a paragraph) with the key features of the box that surrounds it. There are three elements:

- the **margin** between the box and the parent element
- the **border** of the box
- the **padding**, which is the space between the box around the block-level element and the border

CSS provides attributes to control the appearance and behavior of each of these elements.

Figure 7-57	FEATURES OF THE BOX AROUND A BLOCK-LEVEL ELEMENT

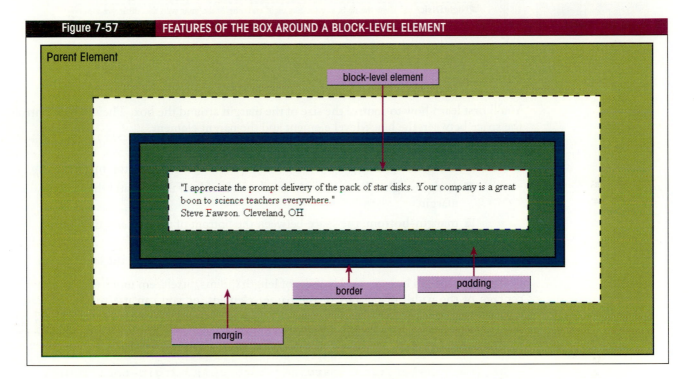

Your entire Web page can be thought of as a series of nested boxes. For example, list items created with the <LI> tag are block-level elements, each with its own box. Each of these boxes exists inside the box created by its parent element—either the <UL> or <OL> tag. The list itself lies within a box defined for its parent—the entire Web page. Figure 7-58 shows some of the boxes in the Astronomy page.

Figure 7-58   SOME OF THE BOXES IN THE ASTRONOMY PAGE

part of the box for
the entire page

Ironically, Charles Messier wasn't all that interested in his objects. He made the list in order to *avoid* seeing them. Messier was more interested in discovering new comets and these beautiful stellar objects were often mistaken for comets before Messier made his list.

Featured Astronomical Products

parent box of the boxes
for the list items

Refractor Kit: March Special! Learn about the science of optics by building your own 18" long, 3X refractor telescope. Price $10.95. Stock Number: RK01-085

box nested inside
other boxes

NightDisk: 13" View the night sky for any night and time of the year with the attractive and useful star disk. Price $19.95. Stock Number ND25-100

Controlling the Margins

You'll first learn how to control the size of the margin around the box. The margin controls the space between the block-level element and the parent element.

The four attributes that control the size of the margin are:

- **margin-top**: the space between the top of the box and the top margin
- **margin-right**: the space between the right side of the box and the right margin
- **margin-bottom**: the space between the bottom of the box and the bottom margin
- **margin-left**: the space between the left side of the box and the left margin.

Margin sizes can be expressed in units of length (points, pixels, em units, etc.) or as a percentage of the width of the box of the parent element, or you can use the "auto" value, which leaves it to the browser to determine the margin size. To create a margin of 2 em units on each side, and 1 em unit above and below each of your list items, you could enter the following style:

```
LI {margin-left:2em; margin-right: 2em; margin-top: 1em;
margin-bottom: 1 em}
```

If you want the size of the margins of the Web page body to be 5% of the display window (the parent element of the <BODY> tag), enter this style definition:

```
BODY {margin-left:5%; margin-right: 5%; margin-top: 5%;
margin-bottom: 5%}
```

A margin size also can be negative, although this can lead to unpredictable results in some browsers. Web page designers use negative margins to place one block-line element on top of another, creating an "overlay" effect like the one shown in Figure 7-59.

Figure 7-59   CREATING AN OVERLAY WITH THE MARGIN-TOP ATTRIBUTE

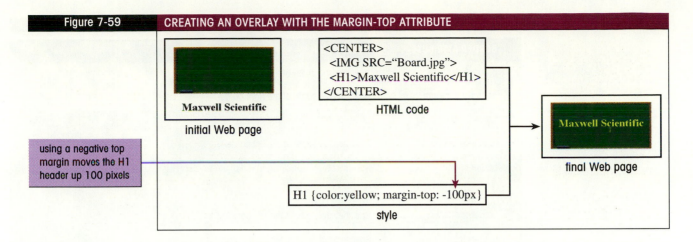

Using the margin attribute you can set the size of all four margins at once. You can insert any or all of the margin values. The values are applied according to the following rules:

- If all four values are entered, they are applied to the margins, in the following order: top, right, bottom, left.
- If three values are entered, they are applied in the order: top, right, bottom, and then the left margin is set to equal the right margin.
- If two values are entered, they are applied to the top and right margins, the bottom margin is set to equal the top margin, and the left margin is set to equal the right margin.
- If only one margin value is entered, this value is applied to all the margins.

You can apply these same rules in the box attributes that follow.

Setting the Padding Size

Padding is useful for relieving the crowding around your elements. The technique for dealing with the amount of padding is the same as for margins. Four attributes control the size of the padding space:

- padding-top
- padding-right
- padding-bottom
- padding-left

A fifth attribute, padding, allows you to control the padding size in much the same way that the margin attribute does for margin sizes. One difference is that if padding is expressed as a percentage, it indicates the size of the padding as a percentage of the width of the block-level element rather than the parent element (as is the case for margins.)

Formatting the Border

CSS provides a wide variety of attributes for managing the box border—not all of which are supported by the major browsers. With these attributes you can control the border width, color, and style. These attributes can be applied to all four borders at once, or you can work with individual borders. Figure 7-60 summarizes the various border attributes.

Figure 7-60   **VALUES OF THE BORDER ATTRIBUTES**

BORDER ATTRIBUTE	DESCRIPTION
border-top-width	Specifies the width of the top border
border-right-width	Specifies the width of the right border
border-bottom-width	Specifies the width of the bottom border
border-left-width	Specifies the width of the left border
border-width	Specifies the width of any or all of the borders
border-top-color	Specifies the color of the top border
border-right-color	Specifies the color of the right border
border-bottom-color	Specifies the color of the bottom border
border-left-color	Specifies the color of the left border
border-color	Specifies the color of any or all of the borders
border-top-style	Specifies the line style of the top border
border-right-style	Specifies the line style of the right border
border-bottom-style	Specifies the line style of the bottom border
border-left-style	Specifies the line style of the left border
border-style	Specifies the line style of any or all of the borders

Border widths can be expressed using units of length or with the keywords: thin, medium, or thick. There are nine different styles you can apply to any or all of the borders. Figure 7-61 shows each of these border styles.

Figure 7-61   **EXAMPLES OF THE BORDER VALUES**

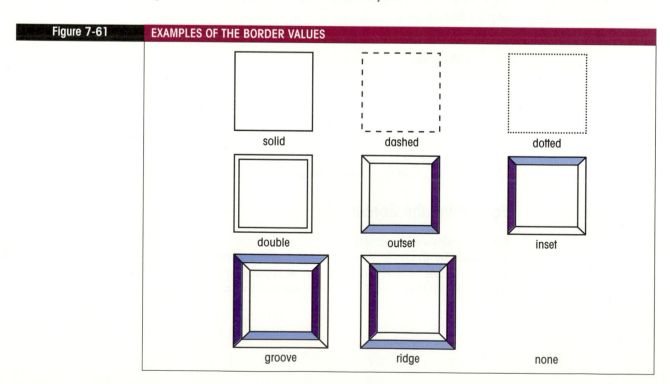

solid   dashed   dotted

double   outset   inset

groove   ridge   none

Chris wants you to create and format a box around the science article on the Messier marathon, found in the Astronomy page. To do this, you'll first have to enclose the entire article within a <DIV> tag. You'll give the article the class name, "Article."

To create a container for the science article:

1. Reopen the **Astro.htm** file in your text editor.

2. Scroll down the file and locate the <HR> tag found directly before the <H3> tag for the "Run the Messier Marathon" header.

3. Replace the <HR> tag with:

   <DIV CLASS=Article>

4. Scroll down the file again until you locate the next <HR> tag, located above the <H3> tag for the "Feature Astronomical Products" header.

5. Replace the <HR> tag with a **</DIV>** tag and then save your changes. See Figure 7-62.

| Figure 7-62 | CREATING A CONTAINER FOR THE SCIENCE ARTICLE |

the entire article is contained within the <DIV> tag with the class name, "Article"

```
<DIV CLASS=Article>
<H3>Run the Messier Marathon</H3>
<P><IMG SRC="M20.jpg" ALIGN=RIGHT HEIGHT=49 WIDTH=50 VSPACE=2>
It's time for the annual <B>Messier Marathon</B>. Instead of lacing up their
Nikes, amateur astronomers will be hauling telescopes, star charts, and a
hefty pot of coffee in an all-night vigil hunting the Messier objects.</P>

<P><B>Messier objects</B> are stellar objects, classified by astronomer
<B>Charles Messier</B> in the 18th century, ranging from distant galaxies to
star clusters to stellar nebula. March is the only month in the year in whic
all 110 Messier objects are in the sky. Unfortunately, if you want to see al
of them, you have to start looking right after sunset and continue until jus
before sunrise &#151; hence the term, "marathon."</P>

<P>Ironically, Charles Messier wasn't all that interested in his objects. He
made the list in order to <I>avoid</I> seeing them. Messier was more
interested in discovering new comets and these beautiful stellar objects
were often mistaken for comets before Messier made his list.</P>
</DIV>
```

Now that you've created a container for the article, your next step is to create a style for it. Chris wants the box to have the following attributes:

■ The padding around the article text should be 0.5 em on each side.

■ The border should be a solid line, 2 pixels in width.

■ The color of the article's background should be the color value (252, 221, 163).

To create the style for the science article:

1. Reopen the **MWS.css** style sheet in your text editor.

2. At the bottom of the file, insert the following style declaration (see Figure 7-63):

   DIV.Article {padding: 0.5em; border-style: solid;
   border-width: 2px; background-color: rgb(252, 221, 163) }

Figure 7-63   CREATING A STYLE FOR THE SCIENCE ARTICLE

```
BODY {color:green;
      background: white url(Draft.jpg) no-repeat fixed center center}
H1, H2, H3, H4, H5, H6 {font-family: Arial, Helvetica, sans-serif}
ADDRESS {font-size:0.6em; font-style:normal; text-align:center;
         text-transform:uppercase}
BLOCKQUOTE {background-color: silver}
UL {list-style: circle url(Apple.jpg) outside}
UL B {color:rgb(155,0,0)}
A {font-size:0.65em; color:green}
A:hover {color:red; text-transform:uppercase; font-weight:bold}
.Special {color: rgb(153, 102, 6); font-weight:bold}
DIV.Article {padding: 0.5em; border-style: solid; border-width: 2px;
             background-color: rgb(252, 221, 163)}
```

style for the
science article

3. Save your changes to the style sheet.

4. Reload the **Astronomy** page in your Web browser. The science article is now
   displayed in a box as shown in Figure 7-64.

Figure 7-64   THE REVISED SCIENCE ARTICLE

Astronomy

Maxwell Scientific provides a wide range of astronomical products — perfect for classroom
demonstrations and projects. Choose from the finest equipment from Newton,™ DC Optics,™ and
StarVision.™

Run the Messier Marathon

It's time for the annual **Messier Marathon**. Instead of lacing up their Nikes, amateur
astronomers will be hauling telescopes, star charts, and a hefty pot of coffee in an all-
night vigil hunting the Messier objects.

Messier objects are stellar objects, classified by astronomer **Charles Messier** in the 18th
century, ranging from distant galaxies to star clusters to stellar nebula. March is the only month in
the year in which all 110 Messier objects are in the sky. Unfortunately, if you want to see all of
them, you have to start looking right after sunset and continue until just before sunrise — hence
the term, "marathon."

Ironically, Charles Messier wasn't all that interested in his objects. He made the list in order to
avoid seeing them. Messier was more interested in discovering new comets and these beautiful
stellar objects were often mistaken for comets before Messier made his list.

TROUBLE? If you're using Netscape, the color of both the article text and the
border will be black.

Resizing and Moving Block-Level Boxes

Chris likes the new text box for the science article. She wonders whether the width of the
box can be reduced and then moved to the right margin to act as a sidebar. You tell her that
you'll make the necessary changes.

Formatting the Width and Height of Box-Level Boxes

To change the width of a box, you use the width attribute. You can express widths in terms of absolute or relative units of length, or as a percentage of the width of the parent element. For example, the style:

```
BODY {width: 75%}
```

reduces the width of the Web page body to 75% of the width of the browser's display area. The width attribute is seldom used except for text boxes, like the science article, and inline images. The problem is that for other elements, the results can be unpredictable with some browsers. Also note that the width value you set is not the width of the document content. The actual width is what is left after you subtract the element's margin, border, and padding.

REFERENCE WINDOW **RW**

Sizing the Width and Height of a Block-level Element

- To set the width of a block-level element, use the style declaration:

  width:*value*

  where *value* is the width of the element in absolute or relative units, or a percentage of width of the parent element.
- To set the height of a block-level element, use the style declaration:

  height:*value*

  where *value* is the height of the element in absolute or relative units.

The height property sets the height of the element. Heights are set in absolute or relative lengths, but not percentages. Usually you won't set the height of any block-level element. Problems can easily arise when the amount of text required exceeds the height allowed. If that happens, the browser might introduce a scrollbar or other device to allow you to view the hidden text. More often, the browser will ignore the style, or worse, the browser will truncate the extra text. For these reasons, the height property is usually applied to inline images and little else.

Using the Float Attribute

When your browser retrieves a Web page, it lays out all of the block-level elements one after another on the page, with the exact positions determined by the element's width, margin, and padding. All of this is done by the browser "under the hood." With CSS you can override the browser and place each block-level in a specific location on the page. This is good in theory, but in actual practice the results haven't always been positive. The Web designer's worst nightmare is to see a finely crafted Web page rendered like the one in Figure 7-65.

Figure 7-65   A LESS-THAN-SUCCESSFUL LAYOUT

REFERENCE WINDOW   **RW**

Floating a Block-level Element

■ To float a block-level element, use the style declaration:

`float:margin`

where *margin* indicates the margin of the parent element that the floating element will be aligned with. Possible values of *margin* are "right" and "left."

■ To prevent a floating element from appearing alongside a block-level element, insert the following style declaration into the nonfloating element:

`clear:margin`

where *margin* can be "right," "left," or "both," to leave the right, left, or both margins clear.

There are so many attributes and techniques for managing page layout that the topic deserves a chapter all to itself. However, you'll concentrate on one of the simpler tools: the float attribute. The float attribute works like the ALIGN=LEFT or ALIGN=RIGHT properties used with the <IMG> tags. It places the block-level element on the left or right margin of the parent element. As shown in Figure 7-66, when the browser encounters the float attribute, it moves the element over to whatever margin the Web author has indicated, and then brings the next block-level element up. The text in that element is then wrapped around the floating element.

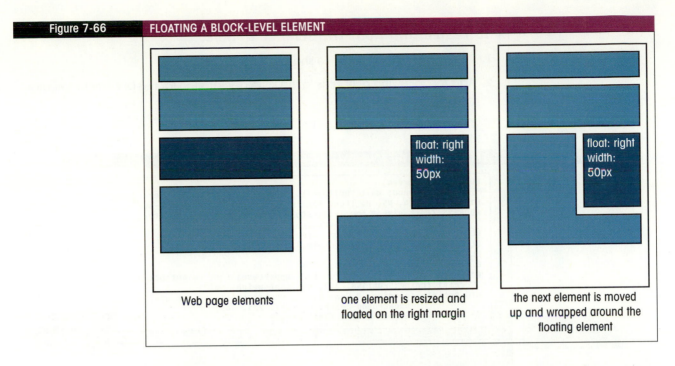

Figure 7-66 **FLOATING A BLOCK-LEVEL ELEMENT**

Web page elements

one element is resized and floated on the right margin

the next element is moved up and wrapped around the floating element

float: right width: 50px

You can prevent other elements from wrapping around the floating element by adding the clear attribute to the element below the floating element. By setting the value of the clear attribute to "right," the browser will display the element on the page at the point where the right margin is clear. See Figure 7-67. Other possible values for the clear attribute are "left" and "both" (for both margins).

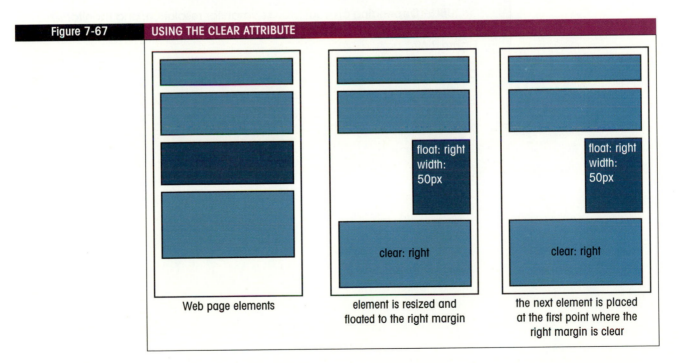

Figure 7-67 **USING THE CLEAR ATTRIBUTE**

Web page elements

element is resized and floated to the right margin

the next element is placed at the first point where the right margin is clear

float: right width: 50px

clear: right

You decide to resize the science article, setting the width to 250 pixels. You'll also float the article against the right margin, but you'll allow the remaining block-level elements to wrap around the article.

To resize and float the science article:

1. Return to the **MWS.css** style sheet in your text editor.

2. Add the following attributes to the style declaration for the DIV.Article selector (see Figure 7-68):

```
; width: 250px; float: right
```

Figure 7-68   FINAL FORM OF THE MWS STYLE SHEET

```
BODY {color:green;
      background: white url(Draft.jpg) no-repeat fixed center center}
H1, H2, H3, H4, H5, H6 {font-family: Arial, Helvetica, sans-serif}
ADDRESS {font-size:0.6em; font-style:normal; text-align:center;
         text-transform:uppercase}
BLOCKQUOTE {background-color: silver}
UL {list-style: circle url(Apple.jpg) outside}
UL B {color:rgb(155,0,0)}
A {font-size:0.65em; color:green}
A:hover {color:red; text-transform:uppercase; font-weight:bold}
.Special {color: rgb(153, 102, 6); font-weight:bold}
DIV.Article {padding: 0.5em; border-style: solid; border-width: 2px;
             background-color: rgb(252, 221, 163);
             width: 250px; float:right}
```

width of the science article

the science article will float alongside the right margin of the Web page

3. Save your changes and close the text editor. You've completed your work on the style sheet.

4. Reload the **Astro.htm** file in your browser. Figure 7-69 shows the completed version of the Astronomy Web page.

   TROUBLE? Depending on your browser, monitor resolution, and monitor size, the position and size of the science article may differ from the one shown in Figure 7-69.

5. Close your Web browser.

Figure 7-69   FINAL ASTRONOMY PAGE

As shown in Figure 7-69, the science article now floats on the right margin and the rest of the page wraps around it. With the style sheet you created, you can easily re-create this effect on other Web pages by enclosing any block of text within a set of <DIV> tags with the Article class name, and then linking the HTML file to your style sheet.

Chris is pleased with the current design. She'll show the two pages you designed to other people in the Web site group and get back to you with any changes.

Session 7.3 QUICK CHECK

1. What style would you use to change your hypertext to white text on a red background whenever the pointer hovers over the link?

2. What HTML code would you enter to assign a block of text the class name "Report"?

3. What HTML code would you use to assign a single word the ID name "Author"?

4. What is a block-level element? What is an inline element? Give examples of each.

5. What style declaration would you use to change the margin around your block quote elements to 10 pixels?

6. What style declaration would you use to create a dashed border around your block quotes?

7. What style declaration would you use to float your block quotes against the left margin of the Web page?

REVIEW ASSIGNMENTS

Chris has received feedback on your pages from the other members of the Web site team at Maxwell Scientific. They like the way you've used style sheets to create an overall design, but there are some style changes they'd like you to make.

Also, the physics, engineering, and electronics pages have been written, so your first task will be to apply the style sheet to those pages. Chris also would like you to continue giving each products page a distinct header color. Finally, she wants you to insert the watermark graphic, "Review.jpg" on each page to indicate that these Web pages will be going back to the Web site team for final review once you're finished.

To make the design changes to the Web site:

1. In your text editor, open the files, Physicstxt.htm, Engtxt.htm, and Electtxt.htm located in the Review subfolder of the Tutorial.07 folder on your Data Disk. Save the three files as Physics.htm, Eng.htm, and Elect.htm, respectively, in the Review folder.

2. In your text editor, open the file MWSPtxt.css located in the Tutorial.07/Review folder on your Data Disk, and save it as MWSP.css.

3. Change the font color for headers in the Engineering page to blue, in the Electronics page to teal, and in the Physics pages to the rgb color value (158, 160, 224).

4. Replace the horizontal lines surrounding the science articles in the Electronics and Physics pages with a <DIV> container that has the class name "SciArticle."

5. Locate the product specials in the Engineering, Electronics, and Physics pages and add the property CLASS=Special to the appropriate <LI> tags. Also, to make the page work for Netscape users, enclose the monthly specials within <DIV> tags.

6. Link the three pages to the MWSP style sheet.

7. Add, for all three pages, a new background—white in color, with the Review.jpg graphic fixed (no scrolling) horizontally and vertically in the center of the display window, and with no tiling of the graphic.

8. For every page, reduce the font size of the customer comments to 0.8 em, and display the comment text, customer name, and customer location in italics.

9. Change the current style of hyperlinks. Display all hyperlinks with a background color value of (128, 128, 128), in a white font, with no underlining. Also, the size of the text should be 1 em unit, and the font choices should be first Arial, then Helvetica, and then any other generic sans-serif font. If a pointer is hovering over the link, the font color should change to yellow. (Remember that this effect will not work in Netscapeversions 4.7 and below.)

Explore
10. Create the illusion of a 3-D box around all the science articles by changing the width of the top and left borders to 1 pixel, and the width of the right and bottom borders to 4 pixels.

Explore
11. Create a new class named "SciTitle" for the title of all science articles. Display the science article titles centered within a white box with a solid black border one pixel wide.
12. Save your changes to all of the files.
13. Print your style sheet and the HTML code for the five Web pages.
14. Open each of the five pages in your Web browser and print each one.

CASE PROBLEMS

Case 1. Creating an opening page for The Stuff Shop   You've been asked to create an opening page for The Stuff Shop, an online store for buying, selling, and trading of used merchandise, antiques, and rare collectibles. Sandy Baxter, the head of the Web development team, wants a crisp and bold style for the opening screen. Figure 7-70 shows a preview of the page you'll create for her. Since she'll want a different style for the rest of the pages in the Web site, you won't have to work with an external style sheet. All styles should be either inline or embedded.

Figure 7-70

To create the opening page for The Stuff Shop:
1. In your text editor, open the file Stufftxt.htm located in the Tutorial.07/Cases folder of your Data Disk, and save the file as Stuff.htm in the same folder.
2. Using an embedded style, change the background color of the page to black, the font color to white, and the font family to Arial, Helvetica, or, if those fonts are missing, sans-serif.
3. Enclose the list of product categories at the beginning of the document in a container, using the <DIV> tag. Give the container the class name, "LEFTBOX."
4. Format the style of the LEFTBOX so that it floats against the left margin of the page. The width of the left box should be 30% of the width of the display area.
5. Each product category is formatted as an H5 header. Change the style so that each H5 header has a background color of red, and the amount of padding to the left of the heading is equal to 5 pixels.
6. The text for each product category acts as a hyperlink. Modify the style of hypertext links in the document so that the links are displayed in a white font, with a size of 20 pixels. Remove the underlining from the hypertext links. If a pointer is hovering over the hyperlink, the font color should change to yellow.

Explore

7. Using an inline style and the <SPAN> tag, change the color of the first letter of each product category. The color of the first letters should be as follows:
   - Antique = black
   - Books = blue
   - Clothes = teal
   - Electronics = lime
   - Furniture = maroon
   - Jewelry = aqua
   - Music and Videos = silver
   - Sporting Goods = navy

8. Use the <DIV> tag to enclose the title "The Stuff Shop" within another container. Name the container "RIGHTBOX."

9. Center the contents of the RIGHTBOX. Give the text a font weight of 900. Change the font size to 60 pixels and the line height to 40 pixels.

10. Below the RIGHTBOX, change the style of the block quote. Center the contents of the block quote and change the font size to 12 pixels.

11. Save your changes to the Stuff.htm file.

12. Open the file in your browser to verify the changes. (*Note to users of Netscape 4.7 or earlier:* The red boxes you create will not all be the same width. Also, the color of the hypertext link will not change when you pass the pointer over the link.)

13. Print out your HTML file and the resulting Web page.

Case 2. Creating a Web page for Master Lee's Tae Kwon Do   Master Lee, owner and head instructor of Master Lee's Tae Kwon Do, has asked you to create a Web page for his school. The Web page contains contact information and some information about the school and its goals. He wants a design that's simple, yet eye-catching. A preview of the page you'll create is shown in Figure 7-71.

Figure 7-71

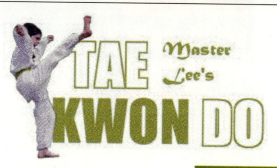

Sign up today for classes at **Master Lee's Tae Kwon Do**. We offer a wide variety of classes for all age levels and physical conditions. Tae Kwon Do trains your mind and body, relieves stress, and improves your flexibility and coordination.

- 30 Years of Experience
- Day and Evening Classes
- Group and Private Lessons
- Family Rates and Classes
- Children's Courses
- Cardio Kick Boxing

We are proud to offer special classes for children, starting as young as 5 years old. Tae Kwon Do teaches our youth confidence, discipline and self-control. Children's classes start every day at 3 p.m. After school pick-up is available.

MASTER LEE'S TAE KWON DO
211 OAKVIEW LANE   GREENDALE, IL 68011   (414) 555-2891

To create Master Lee's Web page:

1. In your text editor, open the file Leetxt.htm located in the Tutorial.07/Cases folder of your Data Disk, and then save the files as Lee.htm in the same folder.
2. Create an inline style for the page's body, where the background color is white, and the left and right margins are 25 pixels wide.
3. Float the unordered list of bulleted points on the right margin of the page.
4. Change the font of the bulleted list to have the browser display Arial, Helvetica, or a sans-serif font. Decrease the font size to 0.75 em, change the font weight to bold, and the font color to white.
5. Change the color of the background of the bulleted list to the color value (174, 167, 66).
6. Change the width of the bulleted list to 200 pixels, and change the width of the padding around the bulleted list to 0.75 em on the bottom, and 0.25 em elsewhere.

Explore ▶ 7. Add a 1 em indent to the paragraph text.

8. Change the color of boldface text to the value (168, 160, 0).
9. Change the address font to have the browser use Arial, Helvetica, or sans-serif. Decrease the font size to 0.7 em and remove the italics.
10. Center the address information on the page and change the text to uppercase letters.
11. Display a 2-pixel-wide solid border above the address information. The color of the border should be the value (168, 160, 0). Increase the top margin of the address to 5 pixels.

Explore ▶ 12. Prevent the address information from being displayed by the browser unless the right margin is clear.

13. Save your changes to Lee.htm, and open the Web page in your browser to verify that the style has been changed. (*Note to users of Netscape 4.7 or earlier*: The color of the border above the address information will be black in your browser, and the address information will not be centered.)
14. Print your Web page and the HTML code.

Case 3. Creating Web pages for the Willet Creek Golf Course You've been asked to create a Web site for the Willet Creek golf course. Part of the Web site will be a preview of each of the 18 holes with hole statistics and shot recommendations. The current Web pages have been stored in 18 files named H01txt.htm through H18txt.htm. You decide to create an external style sheet so that you can easily edit the appearance of these 18 Web pages. A preview of one of the pages you'll create is shown in Figure 7-72.

Figure 7-72

To create course information for the Willet Creek Web site:

1. In your text editor, open the files H01txt.htm through H18txt.htm located in the Tutorial.07/Cases folder of your Data Disk. Save these files as H01.htm through H18.htm in the same folder.

2. Within each of the 18 Web pages, make the following changes:
   - Enclose the list of hyperlinks at the top of the file within a set of <DIV> tags with the class name "HOLELIST."
   - Enclose the information on the hole's par value, distance, and handicap for men and women within a set of <DIV> tags with the class name "HOLESTATS."
   - Replace the pair of <CENTER> tags that enclose the hyperlinks at the bottom of the file with a set of <DIV> tags with the class name "FLAGS."

3. Open your text editor and create an external style sheet named Willet.css. Link each of the 18 Web pages to the style sheet (you may want to use copy and paste to save typing and reduce the possibility of errors).

4. Change the body style for the Web site by setting the size of the left and right margins to 18 pixels.

5. Use the fonts Arial, Helvetica, or, if those are missing, any sans-serif font for the body text.

6. Set the background color of the page body to white.

7. Display all paragraph text using a Times Roman or serif font. Set the width of the top margin of your paragraphs to 0 pixels.

8. Display all H1 headers right-aligned, in an italic Times Roman, or serif font. Set the margin around your H1 headers to 0 pixels.

9. Display all hyperlinks on the Web pages without an underline.

10. Set the width of the HOLELIST box to 100% of the display area. The margin width should be 1 pixel on top and 0 pixels everywhere else. The size of the border should be 1 pixel. The background color and the border color should both be set to the color value (53, 43, 48). The text in the HOLELIST box should be centered.

11. Display all hyperlinks within the HOLELIST box in a white boldface font, 1.25 em units in size. If the pointer is hovering over one of these hyperlinks, the background color should change to yellow and the font color to black.

12. Set to the width of the HOLESTATS box to 150 pixels. Set the size of the right margin to 10 pixels. Set the bottom padding to 25 pixels and set the padding to 10 pixels elsewhere. Set the box's background color to the value (53, 43, 48). Display all text within the box in a white font, 0.7 em units in size.

13. All boldface text within the HOLESTATS box should be displayed in a yellow font with a normal font weight.

14. Float the HOLESTATS box on the left margin of the display window.

15. Display the FLAGS box only when the left margin is clear, and center any text or images within the box.

16. Save your changes to the Willet.css style sheet.

17. Open the H01.htm file in your Web browser and verify that your changes match Figure 7-72. Use the hyperlinks to move through the rest of the Web site (either by clicking hole numbers at the top of the page, or by clicking the forward and backward flags located at the bottom). Verify that a rollover effect is seen when you move the pointer over the list of hole numbers (*Note to users of Netscape 4.7 or earlier*: There will be a vertical gap between the HOLELIST and HOLESTATS box. There also will be a white border around your list of hyperlinks, and there will be no rollover effect when you pass the pointer over the hole numbers.)

18. Print the contents of the Willet.css style sheet. Print the HTML code for the first hole of the Willet Web site. Print all 18 Web pages from your Web browser.

Explore 19. Print the H01txt Web page in your Web browser. Compare this printout with the printout for the H01 Web page that takes advantage of the Willet style sheet you created.

How could you have created the same kind of Web page without using style sheets? How easy would it have been to do this for all 18 Web pages? What are some effects you could not have created without the style sheet?

Case 4. Creating an Opera Composers Web site   You've been hired by the music department at MidWest University to create some Web pages for an opera course. The instructor, Faye Dawson, has given you information on five different composers: Mozart, Verdi, Puccini, Bizet, and Wagner. She would like to have a separate Web page for each composer. There should be a common style for all five pages, but you can apply minor variations of the main style on each page. Professor Dawson has given you the following:

- a graphic file of each composer
- a list of each composer's operas
- a short biography of each composer

The opera list and biography are in text files on your Data Disk. For example, the list of Mozart's operas is stored in the file MozartList.txt. The Mozart biography is in the file MozartBio.txt. Mozart's image is Mozart.jpg. Other composer's files are similarly named. Feel free to use any additional material that is available to you.

Using this information, create a Web site consisting of five different pages. The actual design of the site is up to you, but it must contain each of the following features.

- Each page must have at least one example of an embedded style.
- Each page must be linked to a style sheet named "Opera.css" that contains styles applied to the entire site.
- You must have at least one example of a style modifying the body element of your pages.
- You must have at least one example of a style that defines a font family and font size.
- You must use the <DIV> or <SPAN> tags at least once in your Web site, with styles defined for either a class or ID name.
- You must show at least one example of a floating box, with a value defined for the margin, the border, and the padding.
- You must place hyperlinks to the other pages on each page, and you must define a style for your hypertext links, including a special style for the link when the pointer is hovering over the link.

Explore
- If possible, test your page in both Internet Explorer and Netscape. What kinds of discrepancies do you notice? How could you resolve them?
- When you're finished, print your HTML code and the resulting Web pages.

QUICK | CHECK ANSWERS

Session 7.1

1. CSS1 and CSS2 are the first and second standards developed for the application of cascading style sheets.
2. Inline styles are styles that are added to a specific tag within an HTML file. An embedded style is a style defined for a group of tags within the HTML file. A linked style sheet is a separate text file containing the styles used for one or more Web pages.
3. P {color: blue}
4. H1, H2, {color: yellow}

5. P B {color :red}

   This style will affect only boldface text located within a <P> tag.

6. <LINK HREF="BasicStyle.css" REL="stylesheet" TYPE="text/css">

   This tag should be placed within the HEAD section of the HTML file.

7. Green, because embedded styles have precedence over linked style sheets when there is a conflict in the style declarations.

Session 7.2

1. BLOCKQUOTE {font-family: Times Roman, serif}

2. P {font-size: 12pt}

3. Absolute units, such as inches, centimeters, and millimeters, retain their sizes for any monitor resolutions. Relative units are scalable, and will change size based on the monitor resolution. There are two relative units: em and ex.

4. H1, H2, H3, H4, H5, H6 {text-decoration: underline; text-transform: uppercase}

5. P {text-align: center; font-weight: bold; font-style: italic}

6. UL {background-image: url(List.gif); background-position: center center}

   or

   UL {background: url(List.gif) center center}

7. OL {list-style-type: decimal}

   OL {list-style-type: decimal-leading-zero}

Session 7.3

1. A:hover {color:white; background-color:red}

2. <DIV CLASS=Report>*text block* </DIV>

3. <SPAN ID=Author>*single word*</SPAN>

4. Block-level elements are elements that enclose blocks of text, such as paragraphs, block quotes, headers, or lists. Individual letters, words, or phrases that appear within block-level elements are known as inline elements.

5. margin: 10px

6. border-style: dashed

7. float: left

OBJECTIVES

In this tutorial you will:

- Learn about the features of JavaScript

- Send output to a Web page

- Work with variables and data

- Work with expressions and operators

- Create a JavaScript function

- Work with arrays and conditional statements

- Learn about program loops

PROGRAMMING WITH JAVASCRIPT

Creating a Programmable Web Page for North Pole Novelties

Calculating Shopping Days for North Pole Novelties

North Pole Novelties, located in Seton Grove, Minnesota, is a gift shop specializing in toys, decorations, and other items for the Christmas season. Founded in 1968 by David Watkins, the company is one of the largest Christmas stores in the country, with over 300 employees serving customers from around the world.

Because December 25th is the "red letter" day for North Pole Novelties, and 85% of its business occurs during the Christmas season, the company is always aware of the number of shopping days remaining until Christmas and wants its customers to be aware of this, too.

With this in mind, Andrew Savatini, the director of marketing, wants the company's home page to include a reminder of the number of days remaining until Christmas. The Web page will have to be updated daily to reflect the correct number of days left. Although the company could assign someone the task of manually changing the Web page every morning, it would be much better if this task could be performed automatically by a program running on the Web page itself.

Andrew has asked you to create such a program. To do this, you'll have to learn how to write and run programs in **JavaScript**, a programming language designed for Web pages.

SESSION 8.1

In this session you will learn about the development and features of JavaScript. You'll learn how to insert a JavaScript program into an HTML file and how to hide that program from older browsers that don't support JavaScript. Finally, you'll write a simple JavaScript program to send customized output to a Web page.

Introduction to JavaScript

In your work with HTML so far, you've created only static Web pages, whose content and layout do not change. Beginning with this tutorial, you'll learn how to create Web pages whose content and layout can be modified using built-in programs.

Server-side and Client-side Programs

In Tutorial 6, you learned about accessing programs involving forms and CGI scripts. In that example, the program was stored on and run off the Web server. There are some disadvantages to this approach: users have to be connected to the Web server to run the CGI script; only the programmer of the script can alter the script itself; the system administrator of the Web server can place limitations on how users access the script, and so on. Such an approach also poses problems for the system administrator, who has to be concerned about users continually accessing the server, slowing it down, and potentially overloading the system. With the Web increasing in popularity, the prospect of even *more* users accessing the server could mean costly machine upgrades to handle the increased usage.

Issues like these led to the development of programs, or scripts, that could be run from the Web browser on the user's own computer (the client), as illustrated in Figure 8-1.

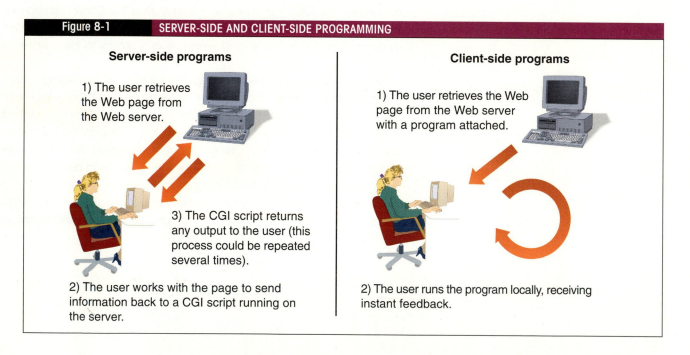

Figure 8-1 **SERVER-SIDE AND CLIENT-SIDE PROGRAMMING**

Server-side programs

1) The user retrieves the Web page from the Web server.

3) The CGI script returns any output to the user (this process could be repeated several times).

2) The user works with the page to send information back to a CGI script running on the server.

Client-side programs

1) The user retrieves the Web page from the Web server with a program attached.

2) The user runs the program locally, receiving instant feedback.

Client-side programs solve many of the problems associated with CGI scripts. Computing is distributed over the Web so that no one server is overloaded with handling programming requests. Web pages containing client-side scripts can be tested locally without first uploading them to the Web server. The client-side program is likely to be more responsive to the user, because the user does not have to wait for data to be sent over the Internet to the Web server. However, client-side programs can never completely replace CGI scripts. For example, if you need to run a search form or process a purchase order, that type of job must be run from a central server, because the server will most likely contain the database needed to complete those operations.

The Development of Java and JavaScript

As with many innovations in the history of computing, client-side programming came from unexpected sources. In the early 1990s, before the World Wide Web became hugely popular, programmers at Sun Microsystems foresaw a day when even common consumer devices, such as refrigerators, toasters, and garage door openers, would all be networked and capable of being controlled by a single operating system. The programmers began to develop such an operating system and based it on a language called **Oak**. Oak was designed to be extremely reliable and flexible. Unfortunately the project did not succeed, but Oak worked so well that Sun Microsystems realized that it could be used on the Internet. Oak was modified in 1995 and renamed **Java**.

Sun Microsystems also released a product called **HotJava**, which could run programs written in the Java language. HotJava acted as a **Java interpreter**, which means that it was able to interpret a Java program and run it for the user. The idea was that Java programs would run inside Java interpreters, and because Java interpreters could be created for different operating systems, users could run Java in any environment, including the UNIX, Windows, DOS, and Macintosh operating systems. Just as Web pages are designed to be platform-independent, so was Java.

The advantages of Java were immediately apparent, and Netscape incorporated a Java interpreter into Netscape Navigator version 2.0, making HotJava unnecessary for Navigator users. The Microsoft Internet Explorer browser followed suit, beginning with version 3.0.

With Java, the user downloads a program, called an **applet**, along with the Web page. The browser, with the built-in Java interpreter, is able to run the applet from the user's own machine, freeing up the Web server for other purposes (Figure 8-2).

| Figure 8-2 | APPLETS AND JAVA INTERPRETERS |

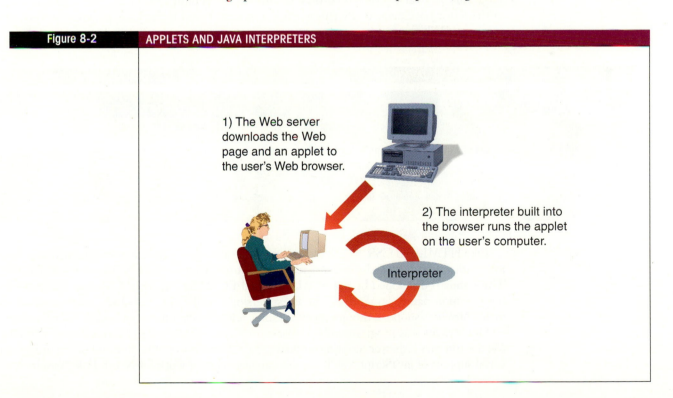

1) The Web server downloads the Web page and an applet to the user's Web browser.

2) The interpreter built into the browser runs the applet on the user's computer.

Interpreter

One problem with Java was that nonprogrammers found it difficult to learn and use. Users also needed access to the JDK (Java Developer's Kit) first to create the programs and then to compile them (**compiling** is the process by which a program is converted from a readable text file into an executable file). To simplify the process, a team of developers from Netscape and Sun Microsystems created JavaScript. **JavaScript** is a subset of Java with several differences. Users don't need to work with a developer's kit or to compile a JavaScript program, and JavaScript commands can be inserted directly into an HTML file rather than being placed in a separate applet. This saves the Web browser from having to download a separate file when the page is accessed, which speeds up the process. JavaScript is not as powerful a computing language as Java, but it is simpler to use, and it meets the needs of most users who want to create programmable Web pages.

Figure 8-3 highlights some of the differences between Java and JavaScript.

Figure 8-3	COMPARISON OF JAVA AND JAVASCRIPT	
JAVA		**JAVASCRIPT**
Complicated		Easy to learn and use
Requires the JDK (Java Developer's Kit) to create applets		No developer's kit required
Programs must be saved as separate files and compiled before they can be run		Scripts are written directly into the HTML file and require no compiling
Powerful; used for complex tasks		Used for relatively simple tasks

Several versions of JavaScript have been developed, the most recent being version 1.3. Figure 8-4 lists the different versions and describes how Netscape and Internet Explorer support them. Internet Explorer actually uses a variation of JavaScript called **JScript**. For all practical purposes, JScript is identical to JavaScript, but some JavaScript commands are not supported in JScript, and vice versa. You should, as always, test your JavaScript programs on a variety of Web browsers. Although it is tempting to use commands available in the latest JavaScript or JScript version, doing so could make your page uninterpretable for many Web users.

Figure 8-4	VERSIONS OF JAVASCRIPT
VERSION NUMBER	**DESCRIPTION**
JavaScript 1.0	The first version of JavaScript, used in Netscape 2.0 and supported by Internet Explorer 3.0
JavaScript 1.1	Introduced in Netscape 3.0; parts, but not all, implemented in Internet Explorer 3.0
JavaScript 1.2	Used in Netscape 4.0 and supported by Internet Explorer 4.0
JavaScript 1.3	Introduced in Netscape 4.06, featuring corrections to JavaScript's date feature. Supported by Internet Explorer 4.0 and above.

Like HTML and CSS, the development of a JavaScript standard has been turned over to an international body, called the **European Computer Manufacturers Association (ECMA)**. The standard developed by the ECMA is called ECMAScript, though browsers will still use the common name, JavaScript. The latest version is called **ECMA-262**, which most of the major browsers support, though there are still a few areas that have not been implemented.

Other client-side programming languages are also available to the Web page author. You can use the Internet Explorer scripting language, VBScript, for example. Because of the nearly universal support of JavaScript, you'll use this language in your work for North Pole Novelties.

Running JavaScript

Your task is to use JavaScript to create a page that calculates the remaining days until Christmas for North Pole Novelties. Andrew wants this information to appear on the company's home page, shown in Figure 8-5, so that customers know how long they have to make their holiday purchases.

Figure 8-5	NORTH POLE NOVELTIES HOME PAGE

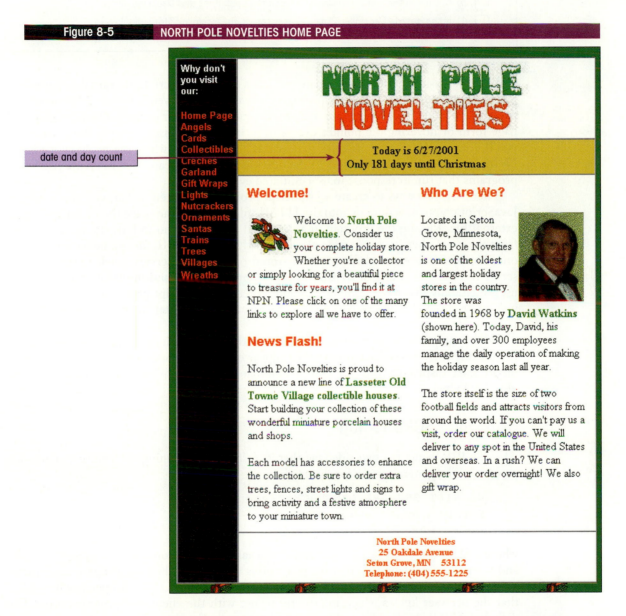

The home page shows the number of days remaining until Christmas, but this information has been explicitly entered into the HTML file and, therefore, works only if the date is June 27th, 2001. Andrew wants this information to be calculated automatically for the current date, whatever that might be. Furthermore, if the current date is between December 25th and December 31st, he wants the page to display the text "Happy Holidays from North Pole Novelties" instead of the day count.

Before you start to write a program, it's a good idea to outline the main tasks you have to perform. In this case, the tasks are as follows:

> ◯ 1) Learn how to display text on a Web page using JavaScript
> ◯ 2) Display date values on a Web page
> ◯ 3) Calculate the number of days between the test date and December 25th
> ◯ 4) If the date is December 25th or later (through December 31st), display a greeting message; otherwise, display the number of days remaining until Christmas

Your first task, therefore, is to create and run a simple JavaScript program that sends output to your Web page. A JavaScript program is run by the Web browser either when the page is first loaded, or in response to an event, such as the user clicking a button on a Web page form or hovering the pointer over a hyperlink. In the case of North Pole Novelties, you'll create a JavaScript program that is run automatically when the browser loads the North Pole Novelties home page. In the next tutorial, you'll learn how to create JavaScript programs that run in response to user-initiated events.

There are two ways to create a JavaScript program. As noted earlier, you can place the JavaScript commands directly into the HTML file. You also can place the commands in an external file. Placing the program in an external file allows you to hide the program code from the user, whereas source code placed directly in the HTML file can be viewed by anyone. However, an external file must be stored on the Web server, which means that the server has the added task of transferring both the Web page and the JavaScript file to the user. Generally, the more complicated and larger the JavaScript program, the more likely you are to place it in an external file. In this tutorial you'll enter the code directly into the HTML file.

When you place JavaScript code directly into the HTML file, you need some way of distinguishing it from text that you want to appear on the Web page; otherwise your browser might start displaying your JavaScript commands on your page. You do this with the <SCRIPT> tag.

Using the <SCRIPT> Tag

The <SCRIPT> tag is a two-sided tag that identifies the beginning and end of a client-side program. The general syntax for this tag is:

```
<SCRIPT SRC=URL LANGUAGE="language">
Script commands and comments
</SCRIPT>
```

where URL is the URL or filename of an external document containing the program code, and language is the language that the program is written in. The SRC property is required only if you place your program in a separate file. The LANGUAGE property is needed so that the browser knows which interpreter to use with the client-side program code. The default LANGUAGE value is "JavaScript." (Internet Explorer interprets "JavaScript" as being identical to "JScript.") If you omit the LANGUAGE property, the browser will assume that the program is written in JavaScript.

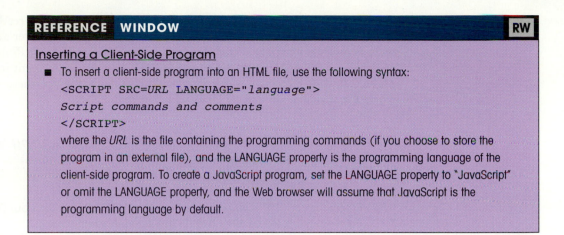

Your program can be placed anywhere within the HTML file, either within the <HEAD> tags or the <BODY> tags. Many programmers favor placing their programs between <HEAD> tags in order to separate the programming code from the page's content and layout. Others favor placing their programs within the page's body, at the location where output from the program is generated and displayed. In this tutorial, you'll do a little of both.

Hiding Your Script from Older Browsers

Older browsers that do not support JavaScript present a problem. If such browsers encounter JavaScript commands, they will attempt to display them on the page, treating the script as part of the page's content. To avoid this problem, you can hide the script using comment tags.

You've already used comment tags in your HTML files to explain the purpose of your various HTML tags. JavaScript supports similar comment tags, using a set of double slashes (//) at the beginning of a line to tell the browser to ignore the line and not interpret it as a JavaScript command.

By combining the HTML comment tag and JavaScript comment symbols, you can hide your JavaScript program from browsers that don't support the <SCRIPT> tag. The syntax for doing this is as follows:

```
<SCRIPT LANGUAGE="JavaScript">
<!-- Hide this script from browsers that don't support
JavaScript
      JavaScript commands
// Stop hiding from other browsers -->
</SCRIPT>
```

When a browser that doesn't support scripts encounters this code, it first ignores the <SCRIPT> tag, as it does any tag it doesn't recognize. The next line it sees is the start of the HTML comment tag, which doesn't close until the > symbol in the second-to-last line. So, everything in the JavaScript program is ignored. The final </SCRIPT> tag is similarly ignored by the older browser.

A browser that supports JavaScript recognizes the <SCRIPT> tag and will ignore any HTML tags found between the <SCRIPT> and </SCRIPT> tags. So it passes the comment tag in the second line and processes the JavaScript program as written. The JavaScript comment (starting with the // symbol) in the second-to-last line is there to help other users understand and interpret your code.

Having seen the basic structure of a JavaScript program, you're ready to insert the necessary lines of code into the North Pole Novelties home page in order to hide the script from older browsers. The page is stored on your Data Disk in the file NPNtext.htm, which you'll rename as NPN.htm. You'll delete the HTML tags already present in the file that has the 6/27/2001 date information, because you'll eventually replace these with a program that works for any date.

To open the NPNtext.htm file and start creating your programmable Web page:

1. Start your text editor.

2. Open the file **NPNtext.htm** from the Tutorial.08 folder on your Data Disk, and then save the file as **NPN.htm** in the same folder.

3. Scroll down the file until you locate the HTML comment tag, "<--- Days until Christmas --->".

4. Delete the lines of code that read:

   ```
   Today is 6/27/2001<BR>
   Only 181 days until Christmas
   ```

   but the leave the opening and closing <SPAN> tags that were surrounding this text. These tags will be used to format the appearance of the date information.

5. In place of the deleted lines, insert the following lines (indented to make your code easier to interpret):

   ```
   <SCRIPT LANGUAGE="JavaScript">
      <!-- Hide from non-JavaScript browsers
      // Stop hiding -->
   </SCRIPT>
   ```

   Your file should appear as shown in Figure 8-6. At this point, no date information would appear on the page if you opened the file in your browser.

| Figure 8-6 | INSERTING A JAVASCRIPT PROGRAM INTO AN HTML FILE |

comment tag to hide code from older browsers

beginning and closing of the script

script language

```
<!--- Days until Christmas --->
<TD VALIGN=TOP ALIGN=CENTER BGCOLOR=GOLD>
   <SPAN STYLE="font-size:small; font-weight:bold">
   <SCRIPT LANGUAGE="JavaScript">
      <!--- Hide from non-JavaScript browsers
      // Stop hiding --->
   </SCRIPT>
   </SPAN>
</TD>
</TR>
<TR>

<!--- Articles about the company --->
<TD>
```

6. Save your changes to the file.

With the <SCRIPT> tags and comments in place, your next task is to write a JavaScript program that sends output to the Web page. Because you haven't yet learned how to either determine the current date or calculate the number of days until Christmas, this program will display a simple text string.

Sending Output to a Web Page

JavaScript provides two methods to display text on a Web page: the document.write() and document.writeln() method. The syntax for these commands is:

```
document.write("text");
document.writeln("text");
```

where *text* is a string of characters that you want to appear on the Web page. For example, the following method will display the text *Only 45 days until Christmas* in the Web page:

```
document.write("Only 45 days until Christmas");
```

The document.write() and document.writeln() methods reflect the object-oriented nature of the JavaScript language. Here, "document" is an object (the page that your Web browser is accessing), and "write" or "writeln" are actions that can be applied to the document. You'll learn more about objects and methods in the next tutorial. For now, when the term "method" is used, understand that it means an action applied to something existing on your Web page or in your Web browser.

Most of the time you'll use the document.write() method rather than document.writeln(). The document.writeln() method differs from the document.write() method in that it attaches a carriage return to the end of each text string sent to the Web page. This becomes relevant only when the text string is preformatted with the <PRE> tag for which the browser recognizes the existence of carriage returns.

REFERENCE WINDOW **RW**

Sending Output to a Web Page

■ To display text on your Web page, use the following JavaScript commands:

```
document.write("text");
```
or
```
document.writeln("text");
```
where *text* is the text and HTML tags that you want to send to your Web page. The document.write() and document.writeln() methods are identical, except that the document.writeln() method attaches a carriage return to the text. This is important only if you are using preformatted text, which uses carriage returns.

A text string created with the document.write() method is enclosed within double or single quotation marks. This allows you to include single or double quotation marks as part of your text string. Consider the following JavaScript command:

```
document.write("Come meet David 'Bud' Davis");
```

This command will display the text Come meet David 'Bud' Davis (including the single quotation marks) on the Web page. Similarly, you can display double quotation marks by enclosing your text string within single quotation marks.

You're not limited to displaying only text; you also can include HTML tags in the text string to format the text and to insert images. For example, the following command displays the text News Flash! formatted with the <H3> header tag:

```
document.write("<H3>News Flash!</H3>");
```

As when working with HTML, there are some syntax issues you should be aware of in JavaScript. Most JavaScript commands and names are case-sensitive. Your Web browser will understand "document.write()" and apply the method correctly, but your browser will not recognize the method "Document.Write()" and will give you an error message.

Also note that each JavaScript command line ends with a semicolon to distinguish it from the next command line in the program. In some situations, the semicolon is optional, but you should still use it to make your code easier to follow.

Now that you've learned a little about the document.write() method, you'll add it to the JavaScript program you just created in the NPN.htm file. Because this is your first JavaScript program, you'll create a simple program to display the number of days until Christmas, assuming that the current date is December 15, 2001.

To display text on your Web page with JavaScript:

1. Below the line "<!--- Hide from non-JavaScript browsers," insert the following two commands:

```
document.write("Today is 12/15/2001<BR>");
document.write("Only 10 days until Christmas");
```

Note that the text you're sending to the Web page includes the <BR> tag to create a line break between the date and the number of days until Christmas. Figure 8-7 shows the revised file.

Figure 8-7   USING JAVASCRIPT TO DISPLAY TEXT ON THE WEB PAGE

HTML code that is sent to the Web browser for displaying text on the page

```
<!--- Days until Christmas --->
<TD VALIGN=TOP ALIGN=CENTER BGCOLOR=GOLD>
   <SPAN STYLE="font-size:small; font-weight:bold">
   <SCRIPT LANGUAGE="JavaScript">
   <!--- Hide from non-JavaScript browsers
   document.write("Today is 12/15/2001<BR>");
   document.write("Only 10 days until Christmas");
   // Stop hiding --->
   </SCRIPT>
   </SPAN>
</TD>
</TR>
<TR>
```

[handwritten note: hides code in web site source code]

2. Save your changes to the file, and then open the **NPN.htm** file in your Web browser. The browser should display the date and days information you inserted into your JavaScript program.

TROUBLE? If you receive a JavaScript error message, close the Error Message dialog box and return to your text editor. Check the code you entered against the code shown in the steps. Minor errors, such as omitting a quotation mark, can cause your program to fail.

DESIGN   WINDOW   DW

Tips for Writing a JavaScript Program

- Use comments extensively to document your program and its features. Comments will help you and others better understand the program.
- Use indented text where appropriate to make your code easier to read and follow.
- Watch the use of uppercase and lowercase letters. Most JavaScript commands and names are case-sensitive.
- Enclose your JavaScript commands within the HTML comment tag to hide your JavaScript code from older browsers that do not support JavaScript.
- Test your JavaScript program under a variety of browsers and browser versions. Some browsers might not support the commands you have written.

You've completed your first JavaScript program! True, the program does nothing more than display text you could have entered directly with HTML, but it's a program you'll build upon in the next sessions to perform the more sophisticated tasks required to meet Andrew's goals for the North Pole Novelties Web page.

Session 8.1 QUICK CHECK

1. What is a client-side program? What is a server-side program?

2. Describe two differences between Java and JavaScript.

3. What are the two ways JavaScript can be run from a Web page?

4. What HTML tags do you enter to indicate the beginning and end of a JavaScript program?

5. Why should you place your JavaScript commands within an HTML comment tag?

6. What JavaScript command would you enter to place the text "Avalon Books", formatted with the <H1> heading style, into your Web page?

SESSION 8.2

In this session you will learn some of the fundamentals of the JavaScript language. You'll learn how to create variables and how to work with different data types. You'll also learn about expressions and operators and how to use them to change the variable values. Finally, you'll create your own JavaScript function and use it in a program.

Working with Variables and Data

In the previous session you learned how to insert text onto your Web page using the document.write() method. You had to specify the text explicitly; therefore, the program did no more than what you could have accomplished by placing the text directly in the HTML file. The next task on your list for the North Pole Novelties home page is to have your program determine the current date and then display that information on the page.

To do this, you have to create a JavaScript variable. A **variable** is a named element in a program, used to store and retrieve information. Variables are useful because they can store information created in one part of your program and use that information in another part. For example, you could create a variable named "Year" to store the value of the current year, and then use the Year variable at different locations in your program.

To assign the value 2001 to the variable "Year," you would enter the following JavaScript command:

```
Year=2001;
```

With the Year variable assigned a value, you can use the document.write() method to display this value on the Web page, as follows:

```
document.write(Year);
```

This code would cause the text "2001" to appear on the Web page. You also can combine text with the variable value by using a plus symbol (+), as in the following example:

```
document.write("The year is " + Year);
```

This command will display the text *The year is 2001* on the Web page.

In the program you're creating for Andrew, you won't explicitly enter the date information. Instead, your program will determine the current date and year for you and store that information in a variable so that you can use the date from the variable later in the program. For now, though, you'll learn about variables by entering a fixed value.

The following restrictions apply to your variable names:

■ The first character must be either a letter or an underscore (_).

■ The rest of the characters can be letters, numbers, or underscores.

■ Variable names cannot contain spaces.

■ You cannot use words that JavaScript has reserved for other purposes. For example, you cannot name a variable "document.write."

Variable names are case-sensitive. A variable named "Year" is considered different from a variable named "YEAR". If your JavaScript program isn't working properly, it might be because you did not match the uppercase and lowercase letters.

Types of Variables

JavaScript supports four different types of variables:

■ numeric variables

■ string variables

■ Boolean variables

■ null variables

A **numeric variable** can be any number, such as 13, 22.5, or -3.14159. Numbers also can be expressed in scientific notation: for example, 5.1E2 for the value 5.1×10^2, or 510. A **string**

variable is any group of characters, such as "Hello" or "Happy Holidays!" Strings must be enclosed within either double or single quotation marks, but you must be consistent. The string value 'Hello' is acceptable, but the string value "Hello' is not. **Boolean variables** are variables that can take only one of two values, either true or false. You use Boolean variables in situations in which you want the program to act in a particular way, depending on whether a condition, represented by the Boolean variable, is true or false. A **null variable** is a variable that has no value at all. This will happen when you have created a variable in the program, but have not assigned it a value yet. Once a value has been given to a variable, it will fall into one of the other three data types.

Declaring a Variable

Before you can use a variable in your program, you have to create it. This is also known as **declaring a variable**. You declare a variable in JavaScript using the **var** command or by assigning the variable a value. For example, any of the following commands will create a variable named "Month":

```
var Month;
var Month = "December";
Month = "December";
```

The first command creates the variable without assigning it a value, while the second and third commands both create the variable and assign it a value.

It's considered good programming style to include the var command whenever you create your variables. Doing so helps you keep track of the variables the program will use. It also makes it easier for others to interpret your code. Many programmers place all of their variable declarations at the beginning of the program along with comments describing each variable's purpose in the program.

REFERENCE WINDOW   RW

Declaring a JavaScript Variable

You can create (declare) variables with any of the following three JavaScript commands:

```
var variable;
var variable = value;
variable = value;
```

where *variable* is the name of the variable, and value is the initial value of the variable. The first command creates the variable without assigning it a value; the second and third commands both create the variable and assign it a value.

Before going further, you will create some variables for your JavaScript program. You need the following variables:

- **Today**, which will contain information about the current date and time
- **ThisDay**, which will store the current day of the month
- **ThisMonth**, which will store a number indicating the current month
- **ThisYear**, which will store a number indicating the current year
- **DaysLeft**, which will store the number of days until Christmas

To add variables to the JavaScript program:

1. Reopen the **NPN.htm** file in your text editor.

2. Below the "<!--- Hide from non-JavaScript browsers" line, enter the following JavaScript code (see Figure 8-8):

```
var Today;
var ThisDay;
var ThisMonth;
var ThisYear;
var DaysLeft;
```

Figure 8-8 | **DECLARING JAVASCRIPT VARIABLES**

variable declarations

```
<SCRIPT LANGUAGE="JavaScript">
   <!--- Hide from non-JavaScript browsers
   var Today;
   var ThisDay;
   var ThisMonth;
   var ThisYear;
   var DaysLeft;
   document.write("Today is 12/15/2001<BR>");
   document.write("Only 10 days until Christmas");
   // Stop hiding --->
</SCRIPT>
```

Now that you've declared the variables, you need to use the JavaScript date methods to calculate the variable values.

Working with Dates

In your program for North Pole Novelties, you'll be working with dates as you try to calculate the number of days remaining until December 25th. JavaScript does not provide a date data type as some other programming languages do; however, it allows you to create a **date object**, which is an object that contains date information. The date object can then be saved as a variable in your JavaScript program. There are two ways to save a date as a variable:

```
variable = new Date("month, day, year, hours:minutes:seconds")
```

or

```
variable = new Date(year, month, day, hours, minutes, seconds)
```

where *variable* is the name of the variable that will contain the date information, and *month*, *day*, *year*, *hours*, *minutes*, and *seconds* indicate the date and time. The keyword **new** in the above example indicates that you're creating a new object. Note that in the first command form you specify the date using a text string, and in the second command form you use values. For example, each of the following commands will create a variable named "SomeDay" corresponding to a date of June 15th, 2001, and a time of 2:35 p.m.:

```
SomeDay = new Date("June, 15, 2001, 14:35:00");
```

or

```
SomeDay = new Date(2001, 5, 15, 14, 35, 0);
```

In this example, you might have noticed a couple of quirks in how JavaScript handles dates. First, when you specify the month with values rather than a text string, you must subtract 1 from the month number. This is because JavaScript numbers the months starting with 0 for January up through 11 for December. So, in the second command, the date for June 15 is expressed as (2001, 5, 15 ...) and not as (2001, 6, 15 ...). Also note that hours are expressed in military (24-hour) time (14:35 rather than 2:35 p.m.).

If you omit the hours, minutes, and seconds values, JavaScript assumes that the time is 0 hours, 0 minutes, and 0 seconds. If you omit both the date and time information, JavaScript returns the current date and time, which it gets from the system clock on the user's computer. For example, the following command creates a variable named "Today" that contains information about the current date and time:

```
Today = new Date();
```

This command is exactly what you will eventually want for your program.

REFERENCE   WINDOW   **RW**

__Creating a Date and Time Variable__
- To create a date and time variable, use the following JavaScript command:
  variable = new Date("*month, day, year, hours:minutes:seconds*")
  or
  variable = new Date(*year, month, day, hours, minutes, seconds*)
  For example, the following two commands create a date and time variable named DayVariable, representing the same date and time:
  ```
  DayVariable = new Date("April, 4, 2001, 16:40:00");
  DayVariable = new Date(2001, 3, 4, 16, 40, 0);
  ```
- Use the following command to return the current date and time:
  variable = new Date();

Now that you've seen how to store date and time information in a variable, you can add that feature to the JavaScript program. Eventually, you'll want to set the Today variable to whatever the current date is. For now you will use a specific date, October 15, 2001, so that a single date is discussed throughout the course of this tutorial.

To enter a value for the Today variable:

1. In the NPN.htm file, change the line that declares the Today variable from "var Today;" to:

```
var Today=new Date("October 15, 2001");
```

2. Save your changes.

Retrieving the Day Value

The Today variable now has all the date and time information that you need, but unfortunately, it's not in a form that will be very useful to you. The problem is that JavaScript stores date and time information as a numeric value—the number of milliseconds since January 1, 1970. All of the JavaScript date and time functions are numerical calculations of these hidden numbers. Fortunately, you don't have to do the calculations that translate those numbers into dates. Instead you can use some of the built-in JavaScript date methods to do it for you. For each part of the date that you want visible in your Web page (or used in a calculation), you need a date method to retrieve just its value.

For example, the second variable on your list is the ThisDay variable, which will contain the day of the month. To get just that information, you apply the **getDate()** method to your date variable. The general syntax of this method is:

```
DayValue = DateObject.getDate()
```

where *DayValue* is the name of a variable that will contain the day of the month, and *DateObject* is a date object or a date variable that contains the complete date and time information.

REFERENCE WINDOW   **RW**

Retrieving Date and Time Values

- To retrieve the year value from a date and time variable named DateVariable, use the command:

  ```
  Year = DateVariable.getYear();
  ```

- To retrieve the month value from a date and time variable named *DateVariable*, use the command:

  ```
  Month = DateVariable.getMonth();
  ```

- To retrieve the day of the month value from a date and time variable named *DateVariable*, use the command:

  ```
  Day = DateVariable.getDate();
  ```

- To retrieve the day of the week value from a date and time variable named *DateVariable*, use the command:

  ```
  DayofWeek = DateVariable.getDay();
  ```

For example, to retrieve the day of the month from the Today variable, you would use the command:

```
ThisDay = Today.getDate();
```

Retrieving the Month Value

A similar method exists for extracting the value of the current month. This method is named **getMonth()**. There is one important point about this method: because JavaScript starts counting the months with 0 for January, you need to add 1 to the month number JavaScript produces. The following JavaScript code extracts the current month number, increases it by 1, and stores it in a variable named ThisMonth:

```
ThisMonth = Today.getMonth()+1;
```

If the current date is June 28th in this example, the value of the ThisMonth variable will be 6.

Retrieving the Year Value

The final date method you'll be using in your program is the getFullYear () method. As the name implies, the **getFullYear()** method extracts the year value from the date variable. The following code shows how you would store the value of the current year in a variable you name ThisYear:

```
ThisYear = Today.getFullYear();
```

If the date stored in the Today variable is October 15, 2001, the value of the getFullYear variable will be 2001.

Why is the method name getFullYear(), and not simply, getYear()? There is a getYear() method. The problem with this date method is that it returns the only the last two digits of the year for years prior to 2000. For example, instead of 1999, a date of 99 would be returned. However, as shown in Figure 8-9, you run into difficulty once you get past 1999.

Figure 8-9	VALUES OF THE GETYEAR() METHOD FOR THE YEARS 1998 TO 2001

YEAR	GETYEAR() VALUE
1998	98
1999	99
2000	2000
2001	2001

The getYear() date method returns a value of 2000 for year 2000, so if you use it to calculate the number of years between 1998 and 2000, you would come up with an answer of 1902 years! This is a classic example of a Y2K bug that caused so much concern in the late 1990s. The getFullYear() date method was introduced in JavaScript 1.3 to correct this problem, and it is supported by Netscape 4.5 and Internet Explorer 4.0 or above. So even though there is a getYear() date method, you should not use it if your program will be calculating a difference in dates before and after the year 2000. In this program, we'll use the getFullYear() date method.

Most of the date methods you can use with JavaScript are shown in Figure 8-10.

Figure 8-10	DATE METHODS	

METHOD	DESCRIPTION	EXAMPLE
getSeconds()	Returns the seconds	For the date object: Date ("April, 8, 2002, 12:25:28");
getMinutes()	Returns the minute	
getHours()	Returns the hour in military time	
getDate()	Returns the day of the month	getSeconds() = 28
getDay()	Returns the day of the week (0 = Sunday, 1 = Monday, 2 = Tuesday, 3 = Wednesday, 4 = Thursday, 5 = Friday, 6 = Saturday)	getMinutes() = 25 getHours() = 12 getDate() = 8 getDay() =1 (Monday)
getMonth()	Returns the number of the month (0 = January, 1 = February,...)	getMonth = 3 (April) getFullYear = 2002
getFullYear()	Returns the year number	getTime() = 1,018,286,728,000
getTime()	Returns the time value, expressed as the number of milliseconds since January 1, 1970	

Now that you've learned how to extract date information, you are ready to modify your JavaScript program to work with the Today variable. Remember, eventually you'll set up the program to use whatever the current date is; for now, however, you'll use a specific date, October 15, 2001, to test the program.

To calculate the day, month, and year values:

1. Return to the **NPN.htm** file in your text editor.

2. Modify the variable declarations for the ThisDay, ThisMonth, and ThisYear variables, so that they read:

```
var ThisDay=Today.getDate();
var ThisMonth=Today.getMonth()+1;
var ThisYear=Today.getFullYear();
```

To display this date information in your Web page, use the command:

```
document.write("Today is
"+ThisMonth+"/"+ThisDay+"/"+ThisYear);
```

So if the current date is October 15, 2001, JavaScript will display the text:

```
Today is 10/15/2001
```

You haven't calculated the value of the DaysLeft variable yet. At this point, you'll set this value equal to 999. You'll learn how to calculate the true value shortly.

To display the day, month, and year values:

1. Modify the variable declaration for the DaysLeft variable to read:

```
var DaysLeft=999;
```

2. Replace the first document.write() command with the following:

```
document.write("Today is
"+ThisMonth+"/"+ThisDay+"/"+ThisYear+"<BR>");
```

3. Replace the second document.write command with:

```
document.write("Only "+DaysLeft+" days until Christmas");
```

When entering this code, be sure to carefully note the placement of the double quotation marks and uppercase and lowercase letters. Your complete code should appear as shown in Figure 8-11.

| Figure 8-11 | RETRIEVING DATE INFORMATION WITH JAVASCRIPT |

day of the month

month number

year number

days until Christmas
(test value)

```
<SCRIPT LANGUAGE="JavaScript">
   <!--- Hide from non-JavaScript browsers
   var Today=new Date("October, 15, 2001");
   var ThisDay=Today.getDate();
   var ThisMonth=Today.getMonth()+1;
   var ThisYear=Today.getFullYear();
   var DaysLeft=999;
   document.write("Today is "+ThisMonth+"/"+ThisDay+"/"+ThisYear+"<BR>");
   document.write("Only "+DaysLeft+" days until Christmas");
   // Stop hiding --->
</SCRIPT>
```

test date

4. Save your changes to the file.

5. Open the **NPN.htm** file in your Web browser. The revised page should appear as shown in Figure 8-12.

| Figure 8-12 | DISPLAYING THE DATE VALUES |

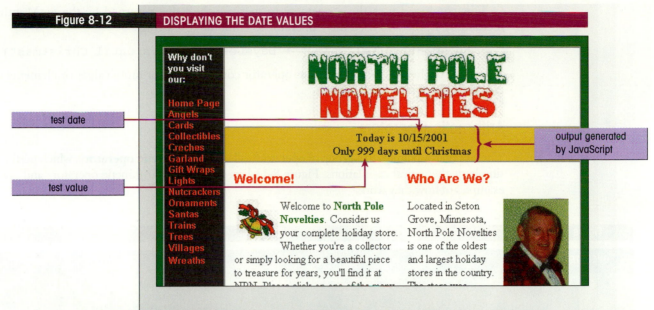

TROUBLE? If you receive an error message when you try to open this page, or if the page looks incorrect, you might not have inserted all of the double quotation marks required in the code. Go back to your text editor and compare your lines of code with those shown in Figure 8-11. Make any necessary corrections, save your file, and then reload it in your Web browser.

You've completed the second item on your task list by displaying date information on the Web page.

1) Learn how to display text on a Web page using JavaScript ●
2) Display date values on a Web page ●
3) Calculate the number of days between the test date and December 25th ○
4) If the date is December 25th or later (through December 31st), display a greeting message; otherwise, display the number of days remaining until Christmas ○

Your next step is to take those date values and use them to calculate the days remaining until December 25. To do this, you have to learn how to work with expressions, operators, and functions.

Working with Expressions and Operators

Expressions are JavaScript commands that assign values to your variables. You've already worked with several expressions in your JavaScript program. For example, you used DaysLeft=999 to assign the value 999 to the DaysLeft variable. Expressions will always use some sort of assignment operator, such as the = sign, but they also can contain a variety of other **operators**, which are elements that perform actions within the expression. A simple example is the **+ operator**, which performs the action of adding or combining two elements. You used the plus operator in your program with the following command:

```
var ThisMonth = Today.getMonth()+1;
```

This command uses the + operator to increase the value returned by the getMonth() method by 1. You also used the + operator to combine text strings:

```
document.write("Only " + DaysLeft + " days until Christmas");
```

In both of these examples, the plus operator combines two or more values or elements to create a single value or element.

Arithmetic Operators

The + operator belongs to a group of operators called the **arithmetic operators**, which perform simple mathematical calculations. Figure 8-13 lists some of the arithmetic operators and gives examples of how they work.

Figure 8-13	ARITHMETIC OPERATORS	
OPERATOR	**DESCRIPTION**	**EXAMPLE**

+	Adds two values together	var Men = 20;
		var Women = 25;
		var TotalPeople = Men + Women;

−	Subtracts one value from another	var Price = 1000;
		var Expense = 750;
		var Profit = Price - Expense;

*	Multiplies two values together	var Width = 50;
		var Length = 25;
		var Area = Width*Length;

/	Divides one value by another	var People = 50;
		var TotalCost = 200;
		var CostperPerson = TotalCost/People;

%	Shows the remainder after dividing one value by another	var TotalEggs = 64;
		var CartonSize = 12;
		var EggsLeft = TotalEggs % CartonSize;

++	Increases a value by 1 (unary operator)	var Eggs = 12; var BakersDozen = Eggs++;
- -	Decreases a value by 1 (unary operator)	var Eggs = 12; var EggsIfOneIsBroken = Eggs- -;
−	Changes the sign of a value (unary operator)	var MyGain = 50; var YourLoss = − MyGain;

Some of the arithmetic operators in Figure 8-13 are also known as **binary operators** because they work on two elements in an expression. There are also **unary operators**, which work on only one variable. These include the increment (++), decrement (--), and negation (-) operators. The **increment operator** can be used to increase the value of a variable by 1. In the following code, the value of the x variable is 100, and the value of the y variable is 101:

```
x = 100;
y = x++;
```

The decrement operator has the opposite effect, reducing the value of a variable by 1. The following JavaScript code assigns the value 100 to the x variable and 99 to the y variable:

```
x = 100;
y = x--;
```

Finally, the negation operator simply changes the sign of a variable, as in the following example:

```
x = -100;
y = -x;
```

In this example, the value of the x variable is -100, and the value of the y variable is opposite that, or 100.

Assignment Operators

Expressions assign values using **assignment operators**. You've already seen one example of an assignment operator, the equals (=) sign. JavaScript provides other assignment operators that manipulate elements in an expression and assign values within a single operation. One of these is the += operator. In JavaScript, the following two expressions create the same result:

```
x = x + y;
x += y
```

In both expressions, the value of the x variable is added to the value of the y variable and stored in x.

An assignment operator also can be used with numbers to increase a variable by a specific amount. For example, to increase the value of the x variable by 2, you can use either of the following two expressions:

```
x = x + 2;
x += 2
```

Other assignment operators are shown in Figure 8-14.

Figure 8-14	ASSIGNMENT OPERATORS
OPERATOR	**DESCRIPTION**
=	Assigns the value of the variable on the right to the variable on the left (x = y)
+=	Adds the two variables and assigns the result to the variable on the left (equivalent to x = x + y)
-=	Subtracts the variable on the right from the variable on the left and assigns the result to the variable on the left (equivalent to x = x – y)
*=	Multiplies the two variables together and assigns the result to the variable on the left (equivalent to x = x*y)
/=	Divides the variable on the left by the variable on the right and assigns the result to the variable on the left (equivalent to x = x/y)
%=	Divides the variable on the left by the variable on the right and assigns the remainder to the variable on the left (equivalent to x = x % y)

As you can see, once you master the syntax, assignment operators allow you to create expressions that are both efficient and compact. As you start learning JavaScript, you might prefer using the longer form for such expressions. However, if you study the code of other JavaScript programmers, you will certainly encounter programs that make substantial use of assignment operators to reduce program size.

The Math Object and Math Methods

Another way of performing a calculation is to use one of the JavaScript built-in Math methods. These methods are applied to an object called the **Math object**. The syntax for applying a Math method is:

```
value = Math.method(variable);
```

where *method* is the method you'll apply to a variable, and *value* is the resulting value. For example, to calculate the absolute value of a variable named NumVar, you use the "abs" method as follows:

```
AbsValue = Math.abs(NumVar);
```

and the value of the AbsValue variable is set to the absolute value of the NumVar variable. Figure 8-15 lists some of the other math methods supported by JavaScript.

Figure 8-15	MATH METHODS

MATH METHOD	DESCRIPTION
Math.abs(*number*)	Returns the absolute value of *number*
Math.sin(*number*)	Calculates the sine of *number*, where *number* is an angle expressed in radians
Math.cos(*number*)	Calculates the cosine of *number*, where *number* is an angle expressed in radians
Math.round(*number*)	Rounds *number* to the closet integer
Math.ceil(*number*)	Rounds *number* up to the next highest integer
Math.floor(*number*)	Rounds *number* down to the next lowest integer
Math.random()	Returns a random number between 0 and 1

As usual, case is important with Javascript commands. You must type "Math" (with an uppercase M) instead of "math" when using these commands.

Creating JavaScript Functions

You can use all of the JavaScript different expressions and operators to create your own customized functions. A **function** is a series of commands that either performs an action or calculates a value. A function consists of the **function name**, which identifies it; **parameters**, which are values used by the function; and a set of commands that are run when the function is used. Not all functions require parameters. The general syntax of a JavaScript function is:

```
function function_name(parameters){
        JavaScript commands
}
```

where *function_name* is the name of the function, *parameters* are the values sent to the function, and *JavaScript commands* are the actual commands and expressions used by the function. Note that curly braces { } are used to mark the beginning and end of the commands in the function. The group of commands set off by the curly braces is called a **command block** and, as you'll see, command blocks exist for other JavaScript structures in addition to functions.

Function names, like variable names, are case-sensitive. XMASDAYS and XmasDays are considered different function names. The function name must begin with a letter or underscore (_) and cannot contain any spaces.

You are not limited in the number of function parameters a function contains. The parameters must be placed within parentheses (following the function name), and each parameter must be separated from the others with a comma.

REFERENCE WINDOW   **RW**

Creating and Using a JavaScript Function

■ To create a user-defined function, use the following syntax:

```
function function_name(parameters){
        JavaScript commands

}
```

where *function_name* is the name of the function, *parameters* are the parameters of the function (a list of variable names separated by commas), and the opening and closing braces enclose the JavaScript commands used by the function.

■ To run (or call) a user-defined function, use the following command:

```
function_name(values);
```

where *function_name* is the name of the function, and *values* are the values substituted for each of the function parameters.

Performing an Action with a Function

To see how a function works, consider the following function, which displays a message with the current date:

```
function ShowDate(date) {
        document.write("Today is " + date + "<BR>");
}
```

In this example, the function name is ShowDate, and it has one parameter, date. There is one line in the function's command block, which displays the current date along with a text string. To run a function, you insert a JavaScript command containing the function name and any parameters it requires. This process is known as **calling** a function. To call the ShowDate function, you could enter the following commands:

```
var Today = "3/25/2001";
ShowDate(Today);
```

In this example, the first command creates a variable named "Today" and assigns it the text string, "3/25/2001". The second command runs the ShowDate function, using the value of the Today variable as a parameter. The result of calling the ShowDate function is that the following sentence appears on the Web page:

Today is 3/25/2001

Returning a Value from a Function

You can also use a function to calculate a value. This process is also known **as returning a value**, and is achieved by placing a **return** command along with a variable or value, at the end of the function's command block. Consider the following Area function:

```
function Area(Width, Length) {
        var Size = Width*Length;
        return Size;
}
```

Here, the Area function calculates the area of a rectangular region, given its width and length, and places the value in a variable named "Size". The value of the Size variable is then returned by the function. A simple JavaScript program that uses this function might appear as follows:

```
var x = 8;
var y = 6;
var z = Area(x,y);
```

The first two commands assign the values 8 and 6 to the x and y variables, respectively. The values of both of these variables are then sent to the Area function, corresponding to the Width and Length parameters. The Area function uses these values to calculate the area, which it then returns, assigning that value to the z variable. The result of these commands is that 48 is assigned to the value of the z variable.

Placing a Function in an HTML File

Where you place a function in the HTML file is important. The function definition must be placed before the command that calls the function. If you try to call a function before it is defined, you might receive an error message from the browser. Although not a requirement, one programming convention is to place all of the function definitions used in the Web page between the <HEAD> and </HEAD> tags. This ensures that each function definition has been read and interpreted before being called by the JavaScript commands in the body of the Web page. When the browser loads the HTML file containing a function, the browser passes over the function and does not execute it. The function will be executed only when called by another JavaScript command.

Create the XmasDays Function

You now have all of the information you need to create your own function, the XmasDays function. The function will have only one parameter, CurrentDay, which is the current date. The function will return one value, the number of days between the current date and December 25 of the current year. The function will have three variables:

- **XYear**: The current year
- **XDay**: The date of Christmas. The initial value of this variable will be the date "December 25, 2001."
- **DayCount**: The number of days between current date and December 25. This is the value that will be returned by the function.

Thus the initial structure of the XmasDays function will look like this:

```
function XmasDays(CurrentDay) {
   var XYear=CurrentDay.getFullYear();
   var XDay=new Date("December, 25, 2001");
   var DayCount;
return DayCount;
}
```

Your first task is to set XDay to December 25 of the current year. After all, it might not be 2001! You do this using the JavaScript **setFullYear()** method. The command would look as follows:

```
XDay.setFullYear(XYear);
```

If the current year is actually 2002, the date stored in the XDay variable changes from "December 25, 2001" to "December 25, 2002". Next you calculate the difference between December 25 and the current date. This would be:

```
DayCount=XDay — CurrentDay;
```

There's a problem. Remember that JavaScript stores date information in terms of milliseconds. Taking the difference between these two dates calculates the number of milliseconds before Christmas. This is hardly the information you want in the Web page (unless the Christmas shopper is *especially* frantic). So you have to convert this value by dividing the difference by the number of milliseconds in one day. This would then be:

```
DayCount=(XDay — CurrentDay)/(1000*60*60*24);
```

because there are 1000 milliseconds in a second, 60 seconds in a minute, 60 minutes in an hour, and 24 hours in one day.

There is one more issue. When the user opens the Web page, it's unlikely that it will be *exactly* a certain number of days before Christmas. It's more likely that it will be a certain number of days, plus a fraction of a day. Andrew doesn't want that fractional part displayed. You'll remove the fractional part by rounding the value of DayCount to the nearest day using the round Math method. The command would be:

```
DayCount = Math.round(DayCount);
```

The complete XmasDays function would then look as follows:

— pass today's date in this parameter

```
function XmasDays(CurrentDay) {
    var XYear=CurrentDay.getFullYear();
    var XDay=new Date("December, 25, 2001");
    XDay.setFullYear(XYear);
    var DayCount=(XDay-CurrentDay)/(1000*60*60*24);
    DayCount=Math.round(DayCount);
return DayCount;   — returns how many days left.
}
```

Now that you see what the XmasDays function looks like, you'll insert it into the NPN.htm file. Following standard practice, you'll place the code for this function between the <HEAD> and </HEAD> tags. Once again, you must place this JavaScript code within a set of <SCRIPT> tags.

To insert the XmasDays function into the NPN.htm file:

1. Return to your text editor and the **NPN.htm** file.

2. Below the <TITLE> tag at the beginning of the HTML file, insert the following lines:

```
<SCRIPT LANGUAGE="JavaScript">
<!--- Hide from non-JavaScript browsers
function XmasDays(CurrentDay) {
    var XYear=CurrentDay.getFullYear();
    var XDay=new Date("December, 25, 2001");
    XDay.setFullYear(XYear);
    var DayCount=(XDay-CurrentDay)/(1000*60*60*24);
    DayCount=Math.round(DayCount);
return DayCount;
}
// Stop hiding --->
</SCRIPT>
```

Figure 8-16 shows the revised HEAD section of the NPN.htm file.

Figure 8-16   THE XMASDAYS FUNCTION

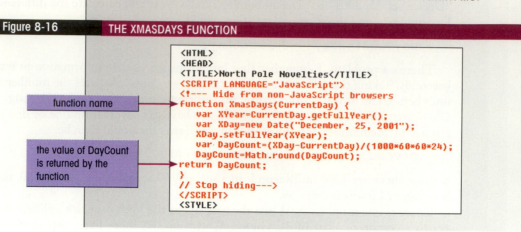

```
<HTML>
<HEAD>
<TITLE>North Pole Novelties</TITLE>
<SCRIPT LANGUAGE="JavaScript">
<!--- Hide from non-JavaScript browsers
Function XmasDays(CurrentDay) {
    var XYear=CurrentDay.getFullYear();
    var XDay=new Date("December, 25, 2001");
    XDay.setFullYear(XYear);
    var DayCount=(XDay-CurrentDay)/(1000*60*60*24);
    DayCount=Math.round(DayCount);
return DayCount;
}
// Stop hiding--->
</SCRIPT>
<STYLE>
```

function name

the value of DayCount is returned by the function

Next you have to insert a command into the NPN.htm file to call the function. Recall that you previously set the value of the DaysLeft variable to 999. You'll replace that command with one that calls the XmasDay function using the Today variable. The DaysLeft variable will then be set to whatever value is returned by the XmasDays function.

To call the XmasDays function:

1. Scroll down the NPN.htm file to the line "var DaysLeft = 999;" and replace this line with:

```
var DaysLeft=XmasDays(Today);
```

Figure 8-17 shows the revised code.

Figure 8-17   CALLING THE XMASDAYS FUNCTION

```
<SCRIPT LANGUAGE="JavaScript">
    <!--- Hide from non-JavaScript browsers
    var Today=new Date("October, 15, 2001");
    var ThisDay=Today.getDate();
    var ThisMonth=Today.getMonth()+1;
    var ThisYear=Today.getFullYear();
    var DaysLeft=XmasDays(Today);
    document.write("Today is "+ThisMonth+"/"+ThisDay+"/"+ThisYear+"<BR>");
    document.write("Only "+DaysLeft+" days until Christmas");
    // Stop hiding --->
</SCRIPT>
```

DaysLeft is set to the value returned by the XmasDays function

2. Save your changes to the file.

3. Reload the Web page in your browser. As shown in Figure 8-18, the Web page now shows that there are 71 days between the test date of October 15 and December 25.

Figure 8-18	DAYS UNTIL CHRISTMAS IN THE NPN WEB PAGE

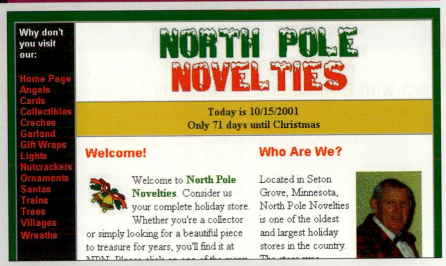

TROUBLE? If you receive an error message or if your Web page shows an incorrect value, check your use of uppercase and lowercase letters, and verify that each JavaScript command ends with a semicolon.

You've completed the XmasDays function. Andrew will test the page you've created and get back to you with any changes.

Session 8.2 QUICK CHECK

1. What are the four data types supported by JavaScript?

2. What command would you use to store the current date into a variable named Now?

3. What command would you use to extract the current day of the month from the Now variable and store it in a variable called Tdate?

4. If the current month is September, what value would be returned by the getMonth() method?

5. Define the following terms:

   Expression
   Operator
   Binary operator
   Unary operator

6. Give two commands you could use to take the variable x, increase its value by 1, and store the result in a variable named y.

7. Provide the general syntax of a JavaScript function.

SESSION 8.3

In this session you'll learn how to add decision-making capabilities to your JavaScript program through the use of conditional statements. You'll learn how to create and use arrays. Finally, you'll be introduced to program loops in order to run a command block repeatedly.

Working with Conditional Statements

Now that you've created a function that calculates the number of days until Christmas using a test date, you and Andrew look at how far you've gotten in the task list.

- ● 1) Learn how to display text on a Web page using JavaScript
- ● 2) Display date values on a Web page
- ● 3) Calculate the number of days between the test date and December 25th
- ○ 4) If the date is December 25th or later (through December 31st), display a
        greeting message; otherwise, display the number of days remaining until Christmas

The only task remaining is to have the Web page display a greeting message in place of the day count from December 25 through December 31. To do this, you need to create a conditional statement.

A **conditional statement** is one that runs only under certain conditions. There are many types of conditional statements, the one most often used is the If statement. An If statement has the following general syntax:

```
if(condition){
        JavaScript Commands
}
```

where *condition* is an expression that is either true or false. If the condition is true, then the *JavaScript Commands* in command block are executed. If the condition is not true, then no action is taken.

Comparison and Logical Operators

To create a condition in JavaScript, you need to use two types of operators: comparison operators and logical operators. A **comparison operator** compares the value of one element with that of another, creating a **Boolean expression** that is either true or false. Here are two examples of Boolean expressions:

```
x < 100;
y == 20;
```

In the first example, if x is less than 100, this expression returns the value *true*, however, if x is 100 or greater, the expression is *false*. In the second example, the y variable must have an exact value of 20 for the expression to be true. Note that this comparison operator uses a double equal sign (==) rather than a single one. The single equal sign is an assignment operator and is not used for making comparisons. Figure 8-19 lists some of the other comparison operators used in JavaScript.

Figure 8-19	COMPARISON OPERATORS

OPERATOR	DESCRIPTION
==	Returns true if variables are equal (x = y)
!=	Returns true if variables are not equal (x != y)
>	Returns true if the variable on the left is greater than the variable on the right (x > y)
<	Returns true if the variable on the left is less than the variable on the right (x < y)
>=	Returns true if the variable on the left is greater than or equal to the variable on the right (x >= y)
<=	Returns true if the variable on the left is less than or equal to the variable on the right (x <= y)

A **logical operator** connects two or more Boolean expressions. One such operator is the && operator, which returns a value of *true* only if all of the Boolean expressions are true. For example, the following expression will be true only if x is less than 100 and y is equal to 20:

```
(x < 100) && (y == 20);
```

Figure 8-20 lists some of the logical operators used by JavaScript.

Figure 8-20	LOGICAL OPERATORS	

OPERATOR	DESCRIPTION	EXAMPLE
&&	Returns true only when both expressions are true	Var x = 20; Var y = 25;
||	Returns true when either expression is true	(x == 20) && (y == 25) returns true (x == 20) && (y == 20) returns false (x == 20) || (y == 20) returns true (x == 25) || (y == 20) returns false ! (x == 20) returns false
!	Returns true if the expression is false, and false if the expression is true	! (x == 25) returns true

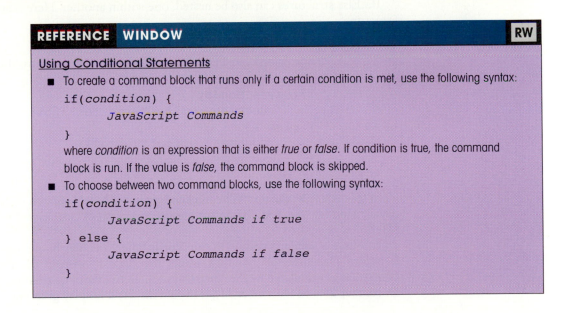

REFERENCE WINDOW   **RW**

Using Conditional Statements

- To create a command block that runs only if a certain condition is met, use the following syntax:

```
if(condition) {
        JavaScript Commands
}
```

where *condition* is an expression that is either *true* or *false*. If condition is true, the command block is run. If the value is *false,* the command block is skipped.

- To choose between two command blocks, use the following syntax:

```
if(condition) {
        JavaScript Commands if true
} else {
        JavaScript Commands if false
}
```

Using an If Statement

Now you will see how these comparison and logical operators work in an If statement. The following is an example of an If statement that controls what text is sent to the Web page:

```
if(Day=="Friday"){
        document.write("The weekend is almost here!");
}
```

In this example, if the Day variable is equal to "Friday," the text string "The weekend is almost here!" is sent to the Web page. If Day is *not* equal to "Friday," then no action is taken.

Using an If...Else Statement

The If statement runs a set of commands if the condition is true, but does nothing if the condition is false. Sometimes you want the If statement to run one set of commands if the condition is true and another set of commands if the condition is false. An If...Else statement allows you to do this. The syntax for this statement is:

```
if(condition){
        JavaScript Commands if true
} else {
        JavaScript Commands if false
}
```

where *condition* is an expression that is either true or false, and one set of commands is run if the expression is true, and another is run if the expression is false. The following is an example of an If...Else statement:

```
if(Day=="Friday"){
document.write("The weekend is almost here!");
} else {
document.write("Hello!").;
}
```

In this example, the text "The weekend is almost here!" is generated if Day equals "Friday;" otherwise, the text "Hello!" appears.

If...Else structures can also be nested, one within another. Here is an example of a nested structure:

```
if(Day=="Friday"){
        document.write("The weekend is almost here!");
} else {
        if(Day=="Monday") {
                document.write("Time for another work week");
        } else {
                document.write("Hello");
        }
}
```

In this example, the text "The weekend is almost here!" appears if the day is Friday. If the day is Monday, the text "Time for another work week" appears. On other days the text "Hello" is generated.

You have a similar situation in the North Pole Novelties home page. If the current date is before December 25, Andrew wants the page to display the number of days until Christmas as calculated by the XmasDays function; otherwise (that is, if the date is between December 25 and December 31), it should display a holiday greeting.

You can distinguish between the two situations by creating an If...Else statement that looks at the value returned by the XmasDays function. If that value is positive, then the current date is before December 25, and the page should display the number of days left in the holiday season. On the other hand, if the value is 0 or negative, then the current date is December 25 or later in the year, and a holiday message should be generated. The code to perform this is as follows:

```
if(DaysLeft > 0) {
        document.write("Only " + DaysLeft + " days until
        Christmas");
} else {
        document.write("Happy Holidays from North Pole Novelties");
}
```

You need to insert these statements into the NPN.htm file, replacing the previous document.write() method you used to display the number of days until Christmas.

1. Reopen the **NPN.htm** file in your text editor.

2. Replace the line 'document.write("Only " + DaysLeft + " days until Christmas");' with:

```
if(DaysLeft > 0) {                    <= XMAS DAY
    document.write("Only "+DaysLeft+" days
    until Christmas");
} else {
document.write("Happy Holidays from North Pole Novelties");
}
```

Indent the various lines of your program to make it easier to read. The revised code should appear as shown in Figure 8-21.

Figure 8-21	USING AN IF...ELSE CONDITIONAL STATEMENT

```
<SCRIPT LANGUAGE="JavaScript">
    <!--- Hide from non-JavaScript browsers
    var Today=new Date("October, 15, 2001");
    var ThisDay=Today.getDate();
    var ThisMonth=Today.getMonth()+1;
    var ThisYear=Today.getFullYear();
    var DaysLeft=XmasDays(Today);
    document.write("Today is "+ThisMonth+"/"+ThisDay+"/"+ThisYear+"<BR>");
    if(DaysLeft > 0) {
        document.write("Only "+DaysLeft+" days until Christmas");
    } else {
        document.write("Happy Holidays from North Pole Novelties");
    }
    // Stop hiding --->
</SCRIPT>
```

command that is run for dates prior to December 25

command that is run from December 26 through December 31

3. Save your changes and then reopen **NPN.htm** in your Web browser. The page should still display the text "Only 71 days until Christmas" because the date specified in the Today variable is still October 15, 2001.

4. Return to your text editor and the NPN.htm file.

5. Change the date of the Today variable to "December, 28, 2001".

6. Save your changes, and then reload the file in your Web browser. As shown in Figure 8-22, the page should now display the Happy Holidays greeting.

Figure 8-22   DISPLAYING A SPECIAL HOLIDAY GREETING

You've completed all of the tasks on your list. Now you have to deal with some of the things Andrew wants you to change.

1) Learn how to display text on a Web page using JavaScript

2) Display date values on a Web page

3) Calculate the number of days between the test date and December 25th

4) If the date is December 25th or later (through December 31st), display a greeting message; otherwise, display the number of days remaining until Christmas

Using Arrays

Andrew has gotten some feedback on your Web page. While everyone likes the Christmas days feature, many feel that the date format looks dry and uninviting. Instead of displaying:

Today is 10/15/2001

they would much rather see:

Today is October 15

Unfortunately, there are no built-in JavaScript methods to display dates in this format, so you'll have to create your own. One approach would be to create a series of conditional statements based on the value of the ThisMonth variable, and then display a different text string for each month. That would require 12 nested If ...Else statements—not a very cheery prospect. You can do it more simply by using arrays.

Creating and Populating an Array
- To create an array variable, use the command:
  ```
  var variable = new Array();
  ```
  where *variable* is the name of the array variable.
- To populate the array with values, use the command:
  ```
  variable[i]=value;
  ```
  where *variable* is the name of the array variable, *i* is the *i*th element of the array, and *value* is the value of the *i*th element.

An **array** is an ordered collection of values referenced by a single variable name. The syntax for creating an array variable is:

```
var variable = new Array(size);
```

where *variable* is the name of the array variable, and *size* is the number of **elements**, or distinct values, in the array. Specifying a size for your array is optional. If you don't specify a size, JavaScript will automatically increase the size of the array as you add more elements. The code for creating an array named "Month" would be:

```
var Month = new Array();
```

Once the array is created, you create values for each individual element in the array. To create values for the Month array, you would use the following commands:

```
Month[1] = "January";
Month[2] = "February";
Month[3] = "March";
Month[4] = "April"
Month[5] = "May";
Month[6] = "June";
Month[7] = "July";
Month[8] = "August";
Month[9] = "September"
Month[10] = "October";
Month[11] = "November";
Month[12] = "December";
```

These commands create 12 new elements in the Month array. Each element is identified by its **index**, which is an integer that appears between the brackets. For example, the element "August" has an index value of 8 in the Month array. The first element in any array has an index value of 0, the second item has an index value of 1, and so forth. In the Month array, there are actually thirteen total elements. The first element, Month[0], is not shown and has a null value. This is because you want the index number to match the month number. It seems counterintuitive to assign December an index value of 11, though one could write a program that way if one chose.

You can also use variables in place of index values. For example, if the variable "IndexNumber" has the value 5, then:

```
Month[IndexNumber]
```

would be equal to the value of Month[5] which is "May."

You can use arrays to create a function named "MonthTxt". The function has one parameter, "MonthNumber" which is the number of a month, and the function returns the name of that month. Here's the code for the function:

```
function MonthTxt (MonthNumber) {
    var Month = new Array();
    Month[1]="January";
    Month[2]="February";
    Month[3]="March";
    Month[4]="April"
    Month[5]="May";
    Month[6]="June";
    Month[7]="July";
    Month[8]="August";
    Month[9]="September"
    Month[10]="October";
    Month[11]="November";
    Month[12]="December";
    return Month[MonthNumber];
}
```

For example, the command MonthTxt(10), will return the text "October". This is the function you should add to the HEAD section of the NPN.htm file so that the name of the month, rather than the number, will be shown on the Web page.

To add the MonthTxt function:

1. Return to the **NPN.htm** file in your text editor.

2. After the XmasDays function, insert the code for the new function, MonthTxt (see Figure 8-23):

```
function MonthTxt (MonthNumber) {
    var Month = new Array();
    Month[1]="January";
    Month[2]="February";
    Month[3]="March";
    Month[4]="April"
    Month[5]="May";
    Month[6]="June";
    Month[7]="July";
    Month[8]="August";
    Month[9]="September"
    Month[10]="October";
    Month[11]="November";
    Month[12]="December";
    return Month[MonthNumber];
}
```

Figure 8-23   CREATING THE MONTHTXT FUNCTION

```
    return DayCount;
}
function MonthTxt (MonthNumber) {
    var Month=new Array();
    Month[1]="January";
    Month[2]="February";
    Month[3]="March";
    Month[4]="April";
    Month[5]="May";
    Month[6]="June";
    Month[7]="July";
    Month[8]="August";
    Month[9]="September";
    Month[10]="October";
    Month[11]="November";
    Month[12]="December";
return Month[MonthNumber];
}

// Stop hiding--->
</SCRIPT>
```

Next you'll use the value of the ThisMonth variable to call this function and then store the results in a new variable named "MonthName." You'll then display the name of the month in the Web page, along with the day of the month.

To call the MonthTxt function and display the results:

1. Return to the **NPN.htm** file in your text editor.

2. Locate the document.write() command that displays the current date, in the main body of the HTML file.

3. Above that command, insert the new commands:

   ```
   var MonthName=MonthTxt(ThisMonth);
   document.write("Today is "+MonthName+" "+ThisDay+"<BR>");
   ```

   Note that you insert a blank space between the MonthName variable and the ThisDay variable. This is to keep the name of the month from running into the day of the month.

4. Delete the document.write() command that displayed the current date in the old style. Your code should resemble Figure 8-24.

Figure 8-24   CREATING THE MONTHTXT FUNCTION

```
<SCRIPT LANGUAGE="JavaScript">
    <!--- Hide from non-JavaScript browsers
    var Today=new Date("December, 28, 2001");
    var ThisDay=Today.getDate();
    var ThisMonth=Today.getMonth()+1;
    var ThisYear=Today.getFullYear();
    var DaysLeft=XmasDays(Today);
    var MonthName=MonthTxt(ThisMonth);
    document.write("Today is "+MonthName+" "+ThisDay+"<BR>");
    if(DaysLeft > 0) {
        document.write("Only "+DaysLeft+" days until Christmas");
    } else {
        document.write("Happy Holidays from North Pole Novelties");
    }
    // Stop hiding --->
</SCRIPT>
```

determine the name of the current month

display the name of the month and the day of the month in the Web page

5. Save your changes.

6. Reopen **NPN.htm** in your Web browser. As shown in Figure 8-25, the new date style should appear in the Web page.

Figure 8-25   DATE DISPLAYED IN THE NEW STYLE

new style for the date

Before showing the Web page to Andrew for his final approval, you need to remove the test date and allow the page to use the current date (whatever that might be). Recall that if you don't specify a date value, the current date and time are automatically used. You'll make this change to the NPN.htm file now.

To use the current date in the North Pole Novelties Web page:

1. Return to your text editor.

2. Change the line 'var Today=new Date("December, 28, 2001")' to:

```
var Today=new Date();
```

3. Save your changes to the file and close your text editor.

4. Open the file in your Web browser and verify that the correct date and days until Christmas are shown.

You've completed your work with the JavaScript program. Figure 8-26 shows the code for the main portion of your program.

| Figure 8-26 | FINAL JAVASCRIPT COMMANDS TO DISPLAY THE DATE AND DAYS UNTIL CHRISTMAS |

```
<SCRIPT LANGUAGE="JavaScript">
   <!--- Hide from non-JavaScript browsers
   var Today=new Date();
   var ThisDay=Today.getDate();
   var ThisMonth=Today.getMonth()+1;
   var ThisYear=Today.getFullYear();
   var DaysLeft=XmasDays(Today);
   var MonthName=MonthTxt(ThisMonth);
   document.write("Today is "+MonthName+" "+ThisDay+"<BR>");
   if(DaysLeft > 0) {
      document.write("Only "+DaysLeft+" days until Christmas");
   } else {
      document.write("Happy Holidays from North Pole Novelties");
   }
   // Stop hiding --->
</SCRIPT>
```

5. Close your Web browser.

Working with Loops

In the future, Andrew may have other JavaScript programs he wants you to run. He suggests that you learn about some of the other types of programs you can create. He notes that the JavaScript code you created for North Pole Novelties was designed to run once every time the Web is either opened by or refreshed by the browser. However, programming often involves creating code that does not run just once, but is repeated an indefinite number of times.

To provide the program with this capability, you must use a program loop. A **program loop** is a set of instructions that is executed repeatedly. There are two types of loops: loops that repeat a set number of times before quitting, and loops that repeat until a certain condition is met. You create the first type of loop using a For statement.

REFERENCE WINDOW   **RW**

Creating Program Loops

- To create a For loop, use the following syntax:

  ```
  for(start; condition; update) {
        JavaScript Commands
  }
  ```

  where *start* is an expression defining the starting value of the For loop's counter, *condition* is a Boolean expression that must be true for the loop to continue, and *update* is an expression defining how the counter changes as the For loop progresses.

- To create a While loop, use the following syntax:

  ```
  while(condition) {
        JavaScript Commands
  }
  ```

  where *condition* is a Boolean expression that halts the while loop when its value becomes false.

The For Loop

The **For loop** allows you to create a group of commands that will be executed a set number of times through the use of a **counter**, which tracks the number of times the command block has been run. You set an initial value for the counter, and each time the command block is executed, the counter changes in value. When the counter reaches a value above or below a certain stopping value, the loop ends. The general syntax of the For loop is:

```
for(start; condition; update) {
        JavaScript Commands
}
```

where *start* is the starting value of the counter, *condition* is a Boolean expression that must be true for the loop to continue, and *update* specifies how the counter changes in value each time the command block is executed. Like a function, the command block in the For loop is set off by curly braces { }. The following is an example of a For loop that displays several lines of text:

```
for(Num=1; Num<4; Num++) {
        document.write("The value of Num is " + Num + "<BR>");
}
```

The counter in this example is the variable Num, which starts with an initial value of 1. As long as the value of Num is less than 4, the condition for running the loop is met. When the value of Num reaches 4, the loop stops. Finally, the expression, "Num++" indicates that each time the command block is run, the value of Num increases by 1. As you learned earlier in the discussion of arithmetic operators, this is an example of an increment operator. When this For loop is run, the following lines will be generated on the Web page:

```
The value of Num is 1
The value of Num is 2
The value of Num is 3
```

and then the loop will end.

The For loop is not limited to incrementing the value of the counter by 1. You can specify one of several different counting methods. Here are some other possible For loops:

```
for(i=10; i>0; i--)
for(i=0; i<=360; i+=15)
for(i=2; i<64; i*=2)
```

In the first example, the counter i starts with the value 10 and is decreased by 1 as long as it remains greater than 0. This update expression uses the decrement operator to decrease the value of the counter. In the second example, the counter starts at 0 and increases in value as long as it's less than or equal to 360. Note that the update expression for this example uses an assignment operator, which is equivalent to the expression i = i + 15, and so has the effect of increasing the value of the i counter by 15 each time the command block is run. In the third example, the counter starts with a value of 2 and is doubled in value as long it remains less than 64. Once again, an assignment operator, i*=2, which is equivalent to i = i*2, accomplishes the task of incrementing the counter.

The While Loop

Similar to the For loop is the While loop, which also runs a command group as long as a specific condition is met, but does not employ any counters. The general syntax of the While loop is:

```
while(condition) {
        JavaScript Commands
}
```

where *condition* is a Boolean expression that can be either true or false. As long as the condition is true, the group of statements will be executed by JavaScript. The following is an example of a While loop:

```
var Num=1;
while(Num<4) {
        document.write("The value of Num is " + Num);
        Num++;
}
```

Note that this While loop produces the same results as the sample For loop discussed earlier. The Num variable starts with a value of 1 and is increased by 1 each time the command group is run. The loop ends when the condition that Num should be less than 4 is no longer true. For loops and While loops are similar, but you use them in different situations. You would use a While loop instead of a For loop in situations in which there is no counter variable, and you want more flexibility in halting the program loop.

You've completed your study of JavaScript. Andrew has received the final version of your page and the JavaScript programs you wrote. He has viewed the page on his Web browser and is happy that it works so well. He'll review the page with his colleagues and get back to you with any final modifications they suggest.

Session 8.3 QUICK CHECK

1. What code would you enter to display the text "Welcome back to school!" if the value of the MonthName variable is "September"?

2. What code would you enter to display the text "Welcome back to school!" if MonthName equals "September," or the text "Today's Headlines" if the month is not September?

3. What code would you enter to display the text "Welcome back to school!" if MonthName equals September; "Summer's here!" if the MonthName equals June; or "Today's headlines" for other months?

4. What is an array? What command would you use to create an array named Colors?

5. The Colors array should contain five values: Red, Green, Blue, Black, and White. What commands would you enter to insert these values into the array? How many elements are in this array?

6. What is a program loop? Name the two types of program loops supported by JavaScript.

7. What code would you enter to run the command document.write("News Flash!
"); five times?

8. What values will the counter variable i take in the following For loop?

```
for(i=5; i<=25; i+=5)
```

REVIEW ASSIGNMENTS

Andrew has worked with your Web page and shown it to other employees at North Pole Novelties. They would like you to make two changes to the page:

- Include the day of the week in the date information. In other words, instead of displaying, "Today is October 15", display "Today is Monday, October 15".

■ Change the message for December 24 so that it reads "Last day for Christmas shopping." Keep the other messages the same.

To make these changes:

1. Start your text editor and open the NPNtext2.htm file in the Review subfolder of the Tutorial.08 folder on your Data Disk, and then save the file as NPN2.htm in the same folder.

2. After the MonthTxt function (but before the "// Stop hiding -->" comment within the <SCRIPT> tags), create a new function named WeekDayTxt. The function will have one parameter named WeekDayNumber.

3. Within the WeekDayTxt function, create an array named WeekDay. Populate the elements of the WeekDay array with the names of each day of the week; that is, WeekDay[1]="Sunday" and so on.

4. Use the value of the WeekDayNumber parameter as the index and have WeekDayTxt function return the value of WeekDay[WeekDayNumber].

Explore ▶ 5. Go to the section in the NPN2.htm file that displays the current date and holiday message. Create a new variable named "ThisWeekDay" that calculates the day of the week for the Now variable. Add one to this value so that if the day of the week is Sunday, ThisWeekDay will have a value of 1, and so forth.

Explore ▶ 6. Call the WeekDayTxt function using the value of ThisWeekDay and determine the day of the week. Store this value in a new variable named "WeekDayName".

7. Revise the document.write() method so that it displays the day of the week followed by a comma, and then the month name and the day of the month.

Explore ▶ 8. Delete the current If...Else statement and replace it with a set of nested If...Else statements that display text using the following conditions:

■ If DayCount < 0, then display "Happy Holidays from North Pole Novelties"
■ Else if DayCount equals 1, display "Last day for Christmas shopping" (*Hint*: Be sure to use == and not = as your comparison operator.)
■ Else, display the number of days until Christmas.

9. View your page with the following test dates and print a copy of each test.

August 12, 2001
December 24, 2001
December 31, 2001

10. Print a copy of your JavaScript code for both the WeekDayTxt function and the revised script to display the daily messages.

11. Close your Web browser and your text editor.

CASE PROBLEMS

Case 1. *Displaying the Daily Dinner Specials at Kelsey's Diner* Kelsey's Diner has made its dinner menu available on the World Wide Web. The only item missing from the menu is the chef's nightly special. Each day of the week, there is a different special. Rather than having to update the page every day, or include a cumbersome list of all the specials, the manager would like you to use JavaScript to display the special that is available on the current day. The daily specials (shown in italics) and their descriptions are:

- Sunday: *Chicken Burrito Amigo*. Chicken with mushrooms, onions, and Monterey Jack in flour tortilla. 9.95
- Monday: *Chicken Tajine*. Chicken baked with garlic, olives, capers, and prunes. 8.95
- Tuesday: *Pizza Bella*. Large pizza with pesto, goat cheese, onions, and mozzarella. 8.95
- Wednesday: *Salmon Filet*. Grilled salmon with spicy curry sauce and baked potato. 9.95
- Thursday: *Greek-style Shrimp*. Shrimp, feta cheese, and tomatoes simmered in basil and garlic. 9.95
- Friday: *All you can eat fish*. Deep-fried cod with baked potato and roll. 9.95
- Saturday: *Prime Rib*. 12-oz cut with baked potato, rolls, and dinner salad. 12.95

You'll write a program that will create a variable with the current date, and extract from the date the day of the week, using the getDay() method. Using the day of the week value, you'll create two functions, DishName and DishDesc, which will return the name of the nightly special and a description of the nightly special, respectively. You'll place these text strings in the appropriate places on the Web page. Your finished Web page should look like Figure 8-27 for Sunday's menu.

Figure 8-27

To create the nightly dinner menu:

1. Start your text editor and open the file Menutext.htm in the Cases subfolder of the Tutorial.08 folder on your Data Disk, and then save the file as Menu.htm in the same folder.

2. In the HEAD section of the HTML file, insert <SCRIPT> tags for the functions that you'll be creating. Add an HTML comment tag and a JavaScript comment line to hide the script from older browsers.

3. Within the <SCRIPT> tags create a new function named DishName with a single parameter, Day.

4. Within the DishName function, create an array variable named DName. Populate the array with the names of the nightly dish specials (that is, for Sunday let DName[0]="Chicken Burrito Amigo" and so on).

5. Using the value of the Day parameter as the index variable, have the DishName function return the value of DName[Day].

6. Below the DishName function, create another function named DishDesc that contains a single parameter, Day.

7. Within the DishDesc function create an array variable named DDesc. Populate the array with the descriptions of the nightly dish specials. Use the same index numbering that you used for the DishName function (that is, for Sunday let DDesc[0]="Chicken with mushrooms, onions, and Monterey Jack in flour tortilla. 9.95" and so on). Using the value of the Day parameter as the index variable, have the DishDesc function return the value of DDesc[Day].

8. Go to the <Script> tags already entered in the body of the document. Within the first set of <SCRIPT> tags enter a command line to retrieve the current date information and save it to a variable named Today.

9. Using the getDay() method, extract the day of the week number from the Today variable and save it as a variable named WeekDay.

10. Use the document.write() method to display the value of DishName(WeekDay) on your Web page.

11. Go to the second <SCRIPT> tag in the body of the Web page and enter another command line to retrieve the current date information and save it to a variable named Today. As before, extract the day of the week number from this variable and save it in the WeekDay variable.

12. Use the document.write() method to display the value of DishDesc(WeekDay) on your Web page.

13. Test your JavaScript program for the dates September 16, 2001, through September 22, 2001.

14. Print the resulting Web page for each test date.

15. Restore your Web page so that it uses the current date.

16. Save and print a copy of the Menu.htm file.

17. Close your Web browser and your text editor.

Case 2. Displaying Random Quotes from Mark Twain Professor Stewart Templeton of the Humanities Department at Madison State College has created a Web site devoted to the works of Mark Twain. One of the pages in the site is dedicated to Mark Twain's quotations. Stewart would like you to help him with the Web page by creating a JavaScript program to display random Twain quotes. He has given you the Web page and a list of five quotes. You have to use these to create a function, MQuote, which will display one of these quotes on the page.

JavaScript includes a Math method for generating random numbers, but it only creates a random number between 0 and 1. You can convert the random number it generates to an integer between 0 and n (where n is the upper range of the integers) using the JavaScript command:

```
Rnum = Math.round(Math.random()*n)
```

In this function, the random number is multiplied by n and then, using the Math.round method, that value is rounded to the nearest integer. Rnum will therefore be restricted to integer values between 0 and n.

You'll use this command with n set to 5, to select which one of the five quotes to be shown. The five Mark Twain quotes Stewart wants you to use are:

- "I smoke in moderation, only one cigar at a time."
- "Be careful of reading health books, you might die of a misprint."
- "Man is the only animal that blushes—or needs to."
- "Clothes make the man. Naked people have little or no influence on society."
- "One of the most striking differences between a cat and a lie is that a cat has only nine lives."

A preview of the page you'll create is shown in Figure 8-28.

Figure 8-28

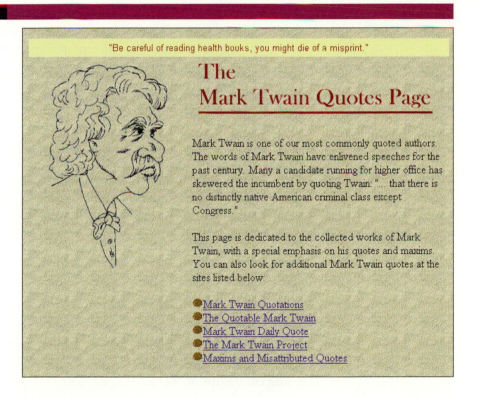

To create the Mark Twain random quotes function:

1. Start your text editor and open the file Twaintxt.htm in the Cases subfolder of the Tutorial.08 folder on your Data Disk, and then save the file as Twain.htm in the same folder.

2. Go to the <SCRIPT> tags located in the HEAD section of the document. Create a function named MQuote containing a single parameter, Qnum.

Explore

3. Within the MQuote function create an array named Quotes that contains five elements. The first element Quotes[0] should contain the text "'I smoke in moderation, only one cigar at a time.'" (Note that the double quotation marks of the statement are enclosed within single quotation marks. This allows the double quotation marks to be part of the text that appears on the page.) Set the next four elements in the array equal to the remaining quotes in Stewart's list.

4. Using the value of the Qnum parameter as the index variable, have the MQuote function return the value of Quotes[Qnum].

Explore

5. Directly below the MQuote function (but still within the <SCRIPT> tags), create a second function named RandInt. The function should have one parameter, Size, and one variable Rnum. Set Rnum equal to a random integer between 0 and Size. Return the value of Rnum.

6. Scroll down the Twain.htm document until you locate the <SCRIPT> tags to insert a random Mark Twain quote into the Web page. Within the <SCRIPT> tags, create a variable named RandValue and set the value of the variable by calling the RandInt function with a value of 4. What are the possible values of the RandValue variable?

7. Create a variable named QuoteText and set its value by calling the MQuote function using the RandValue variable as a parameter.

8. Using the document.write() method, display the value of QuoteText on your Web page.

9. Save your changes to the Twain.htm file.

10. Open Twain.htm in your Web browser. Reload the page several times and verify that doing so allows you to eventually see five different quotations from Mark Twain.

11. Print a copy of the Twain.htm file as it appears in your Web browser.

12. Print a copy of the source code for the MQuote and Rand5 functions you created.

13. Close your Web browser and your text editor.

Case 3. *Displaying a Table of Trigonometric Functions* Professor Karen Franklin of the Mathematics Department at Southern Missouri State University is creating a Web site for her trigonometry students. One of the Web pages in her site will deal with geometry and trigonometric functions. She would like to have a page that displays the sine and cosine values for various angles from 0 degrees up to 360 degrees. Karen would like to avoid typing this information and would like you to write a program that automatically generates this table. Because JavaScript calculates sines and cosines in radians, and not degrees, you will have to convert the degree value to radians using the following command:

```
var Radian = Math.PI/180*d;
```

where *d* is the angle expressed in degrees. Once you have the angle expressed in radians, you can calculate the sine and cosine values, using the following two JavaScript commands:

```
var SineValue = Math.sin(Radian);
var CosineValue = Math.cos(Radian);
```

Using these three commands along with a For loop, you'll create a table of sine and cosine values from 0 to 360 degrees in increments of 15 degrees. A preview of part of the page you'll create is shown in Figure 8-29. Some of the page has already been created for you. Your job is to finish the JavaScript program.

Figure 8-29

Table of Sines and Cosines

Degrees	Sin(d)	Cos(d)
0	0	1
15	0.25881904510252074	0.9659258262890683
30	0.49999999999999994	0.8660254037844387
45	0.7071067811865475	0.7071067811865476
60	0.8660254037844386	0.5000000000000001
75	0.9659258262890683	0.25881904510252074
90	1	6.123031769111886e-17
105	0.9659258262890683	-0.25881904510252085
120	0.8660254037844387	-0.4999999999999998

To create the table of trigonometric functions:

1. Start your text editor and open the file Trigtext.htm in the Cases subfolder of the Tutorial.08 folder on your Data Disk, and then save the file as Trig.htm in the same folder.

2. Within the <SCRIPT> tags create a For loop. The loop should use a counter variable named d, which starts with a value of 0 and increases by 15 as long as it is less than or equal to 360. The variable d will contain the degree value.

3. Within the For loop's command block, use the document.write() method to send a <TR> tag to the Web page. This will start a new row in your trigonometry table.

4. Below the <TR> tag, insert a document.write() method that will display the value of d between <TD> and </TD> tags. This will cause the degree values to be displayed in the first column of your trigonometry table.

Explore   5. Convert d to radians and store the value in a variable named Radian.

Explore   6. Calculate the value of sin(Radian) and store it in a variable named SineValue.

7. Display the value of the SineValue variable in the second column of your table by using the document.write() method. (Remember that you must enclose the SineValue variable within <TD> and </TD> tags.) The sine values will go in the second column of your table.

Explore   8. Calculate the value of cos(Radian) and store it in a variable named CosineValue.

9. Display the value of the CosineValue variable in the third column of the trigonometry table.

10. Finish the For loop's command block with a document.write() method to send a </TR> tag to the Web page. This will end the row in your table.

11. Open Trig.htm in your Web browser. Verify that the page displays a list of sines and cosines from 0 degrees up to 360 degrees in increments of 15 degrees.

Explore   12. The cos(90) should be equal to 0, but what value appears in your table? What would you tell Karen about the reliability of using JavaScript in calculating trigonometric functions?

13. Print a copy of the Trig.htm file as it appears in your Web browser.

14. Print a copy of the JavaScript program you wrote to create the trigonometry table.

15. Close your Web browser and your text editor.

Case 4. Creating a List of Daily Events at Avalon Books The Avalon Books bookstore sponsors several special events each month. You've been asked by store manager Liu Davis to create a Web page that will display a calendar of the current month's activities as well as a list of any events occurring that day. The following is a list of the special events for the upcoming month of November:

- Every Monday: Storytime with Susan Sheridan. 12 noon.
- Every Friday: Storytime with Doug Evans. 12 noon.
- First Saturday of the month: A Novel Idea: Discussion Group. 7-9p.m.
- November 4th: Young Authors' Workshop. 1-4 p.m.
- November 14th: Meet author Jeff Farley. 7-8 p.m.
- November 24th: Meet author Karen Charnas. 7-8 p.m.

Figure 8-30 shows an example of a page you could create. The final layout and design of the page are up to you, however.

Figure 8-30

November Events at Avalon Books

Today's Events: 11/4/2001
Young Author's Workshop. 1-4 p.m.

Events in November, 2001						
Sunday	**Monday**	**Tuesday**	**Wednesday**	**Thursday**	**Friday**	**Saturday**
				1)	2)	3) A Novel Idea: Discussion Group. 7-9 p.m.
4) Young Authors' Workshop. 1-4 p.m.	5) 12:00 pm. Story time with Susan Sheridan	6)	7)	8)	9) 12:00 pm. Story time with Doug Evans	10)
11)	12) 12:00 pm. Story time with Susan Sheridan	13)	14) Meet author Jeff Farley. 7-8 p.m.	15)	16) 12:00 pm. Story time with Doug Evans	17)
18)	19) 12:00 pm. Story time with Susan Sheridan	20)	21)	22)	23) 12:00 pm. Story time with Doug Evans	24) Meet author Karen Charnas. 7-8 p.m.
25)	26) 12:00 pm. Story time with Susan Sheridan	27)	28)	29)	30) 12:00 pm. Story time with Doug Evans	

To create the daily events schedule for Avalon Books:

1. Create a file named Avalon.htm in the Cases subfolder of the Tutorial.08 folder on your Data Disk.

2. Copy the tags used to create the November Events calendar from the November.htm file (located in the Cases subfolder of the Tutorial.08 folder) and paste them into Avalon.htm.

3. Add title tags and descriptive text to Avalon.htm.

4. Use JavaScript to send the following output to your Web page:

   - Display the current date in the mm/dd/yy format.
   - If it is Monday, display the Susan Sheridan storytime event.
   - If it is Friday, display the Doug Evans storytime event.
   - If it is Saturday and the day of the month is less than or equal to 7, display the Novel Idea Discussion Group event.
   - If it is the 4th day of the month, display the Young Authors' Workshop event.
   - If it is the 14th day of the month, display the Meet Jeff Farley event.
   - If it is the 24th day of the month, display the Meet Karen Charnas event.

5. Use the following test dates to test Avalon.htm: 11/3/2001, 11/4/2001, 11/12/2001, 11/14/2001, 11/24/2001, and 11/30/2001.

6. Open Avalon.htm in your Web browser for each of the six test dates and confirm that the proper daily event appears on the page.

7. Print a copy of your Web page for the test date 11/30/2001.

8. Print a copy of the HTML tags and JavaScript commands you used to create this Web page.

9. Close your Web browser and your text editor.

QUICK | CHECK ANSWERS

Session 8.1

1. A client-side program is a program that is run on the user's own computer, usually within the user's Web browser. A server-side program is run off of the Web server.

2. Java can be more difficult to learn than JavaScript. Java requires a development kit to create executable applets; JavaScript does not. Java programs must be compiled; JavaScript programs are scripts that can be run without compiling. Java is the more powerful of the two languages.

3. A JavaScript program is run by the Web browser either in the process of rendering the HTML file or in response to an event, such as the user clicking a Submit button or positioning the pointer on a hyperlink.

4. <SCRIPT> and </SCRIPT>

5. To prevent older browsers, which do not support JavaScript, from displaying the JavaScript commands on the Web page.

6. document.write("<H1>Avalon Books</H1>")

Session 8.2

1. numbers, strings, Boolean, and null values

2. var Now = new Date();

3. var Tdate = Now.getDate();

4. 8

5. Expressions are JavaScript commands that assign values to your variables. Operators are elements that perform actions within an expression. Binary operators work on two elements in an expression. Unary operators work on only a single expression element.

6. Y = X + 1;
   Y = X++;

7. ```
   function function_name(parameters){
        JavaScript commands
   }
   ```

Session 8.3

1. ```
   if(Month=="September") {
        document.write("Welcome back to school!");
   }
   ```

2. ```
   if(Month=="September") {
        document.write("Welcome back to school!");
   } else {
        document.write("Today's headlines");
   }
   ```

3. ```
   if(Month=="September") {
        document.write("Welcome back to school!");
   } else {
        if(Month="June") {
             document.write("Summer's here!")
        } else {
             document.write("Today's headlines");
        }
   }
   ```

4. An array is an ordered collection of values referenced by a single variable name.
   ```
   var Colors = new Array();
   ```

5. Colors[1]="Red";
   Colors[2]="Green";
   Colors[3]="Blue";
   Colors[4]="Black";
   Colors[5]="White";

6. A loop is a set of instructions that is executed repeatedly. There are two types of loops: loops that repeat a set number of times before quitting (For loops), and loops that repeat until a certain condition is met (While loops.)

7. ```
   for(i=1; i<=5; i++) {
        document.write("News Flash!<BR>");
   }
   ```

8. 5, 10, 15, 20, 25
   ```

OBJECTIVES

In this tutorial you will:

- Learn about form validation

- Study the object-based nature of the JavaScript language

- Work with objects, properties, methods, and events

- Create programs that run in response to user actions

- Create dialog boxes that prompt the user for input

- Create message boxes that alert the user to problems

WORKING

WITH JAVASCRIPT OBJECTS AND EVENTS

Enhancing Your Forms with JavaScript

CASE

Validating User Input in the Neonatal Feeding Study

St. Mary's hospital, located in the city of Northland Pines, is a large complex serving the needs of the community and neighboring towns. St. Mary's is also a research hospital, which means that it is the home of several research institutions, including the Midwest Clinical Cancer Center and General Clinical Research Center.

One of the tasks involved in clinical research is enrolling patients in various studies. Each patient in a study must go through a registration process, including the completion of a registration form used to determine whether the patient is eligible to participate.

In past years, these forms were paper records, filled out by hand by the attending nurse or physician. Recently, however, the hospital has developed an intranet—a network similar to the World Wide Web, but limited to the employees of the hospital. Some researchers want to place registration forms on the hospital intranet, allowing them to be filled out online and automatically sent to a database for storage.

You've been asked to help develop one of the first online registration forms, for a study run by Dr. Karen Paulson on the effects of different feeding methods on newborn infants. The form will have to be interactive in that it will have to calculate key items as well as check the user's entries for mistakes. To create this Web page form, you'll have to use JavaScript to control how users access and enter data into the form.

SESSION 9.1

In this session you will learn about the principle of form validation. You'll see how validation applies to the objects found on a Web page form. You'll learn about the object-based nature of the JavaScript language and explore the principles of objects, properties, and methods.

Understanding Form Validation

You meet with Dr. Paulson to discuss the online form she wants you to create for her clinical study. She brings with her a copy of the current paper registration form, which she already saved in HTML format as Studytxt.htm. This is the form that she wants you to modify. Although you won't be working with this form right away (you have to learn more about JavaScript first), you'll open the Studytxt.htm file now, save it with a different name, and view it in your Web browser.

To open Dr. Paulson's Web page form:

1. Start your text editor.

2. Open the file **Studytxt.htm** from the Tutorial.09 folder on your Data Disk, and then save the file as **Study.htm** in the same folder.

3. Close your text editor, and then open the **Study.htm** file in your Web browser. Figure 9-1 shows the current state of the Web page form.

Figure 9-1   **DR PAULSON'S REGISTRATION FORM**

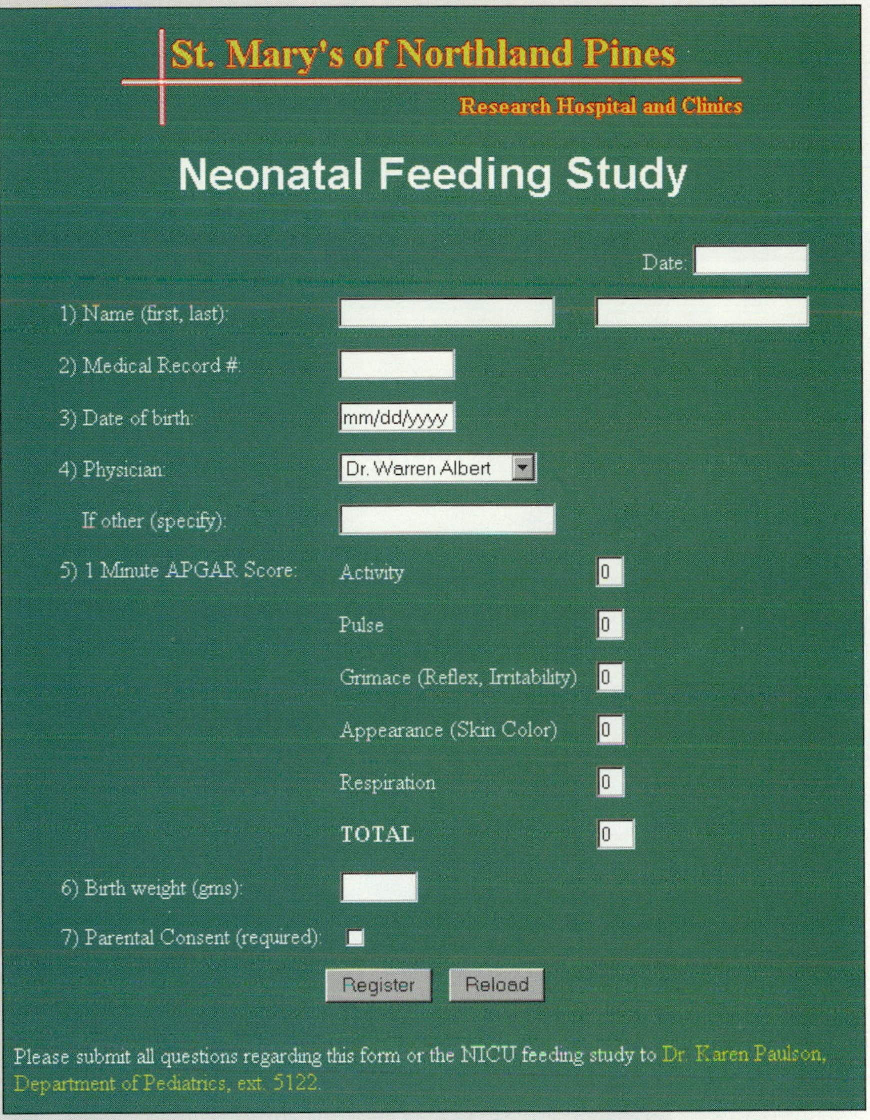

TROUBLE? If you're using the Netscape browser, your form will look slightly different from the form in the figure.

4. Scroll through the form and review its structure. Enter some test data to help you become familiar with the form's layout and content.

As you examine Dr. Paulson's form, notice that it collects basic information on newborns. The first field is used to record the date that the form was filled out. The next fields record the baby's name and medical record number (to easily tie in with the hospital database) and date of birth.

A selection list follows, containing the names of the physicians in the pediatric ward who might be participating in the study. The selection list also includes an option labeled "Other" for situations in which none of the seven primary physicians is involved in the birth. In such a case, the input field below the selection list should contain that physician's name.

Next, a series of boxes calculates the infant's 1-minute APGAR score, a measure of a new-born baby's health summed up from the evaluation of five criteria (activity, pulse, grimace, appearance, and respiration). Doctors assign a value of 0, 1, or 2 to each of the five scores.

The form concludes with a record of the newborn's birth weight and whether or not a parental consent form has been filled out, allowing the baby to be enrolled in Dr. Paulson's study. Figure 9-2 shows the names of each field in the registration form. The name of the form itself is "REG." Take time to review these field names now; you'll use them extensively later on when you modify Dr. Paulson's form.

Figure 9-2   FIELD NAMES IN THE REGISTRATION FORM

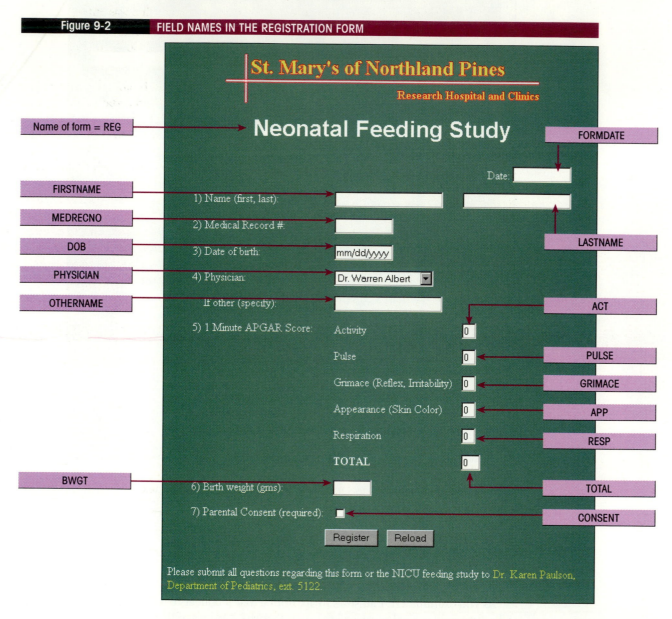

As the form is currently designed, almost any value could be entered into any of the input fields. This concerns Dr. Paulson, and to address her concerns, she explains what she would like the online form to do automatically for the user:

- The Date field should be completed automatically for the user, to avoid the possibility of an incorrect date being entered. The user should still be able to change the date if necessary.

■ If "Other" is selected from the Physician selection list, the user should be prompted to enter the physician's name in the "If other" input box. Otherwise, the insertion point should jump directly to the APGAR scores when the user presses the Tab key.

■ The 1-minute total APGAR score should be calculated automatically based on the value of its five component parts.

■ The value of each component of the APGAR score (activity, pulse, grimace, appearance, and respiration) can be only 0, 1, or 2. The form should reject all other values and alert the user that an improper value was entered.

■ No registration form should be submitted unless a parental consent form has been filled out, as indicated by a check in the Parental Consent check box on the registration form.

To meet Dr. Paulson's requirements, your Web page form must be able to react in different ways, depending on the user's input. The form must be able to skip certain fields if the user selects a certain item, but not if the user selects a different item. The form must also check the APGAR values that the user enters and either calculate a total score or, if necessary, inform the user that a mistake has been made.

Dr. Paulson's criteria are examples of **form validation**, a process by which the server or the browser checks form entries and, where possible, errors are eliminated. On the Web, form validation can occur on either the client side or the server side. As shown in Figure 9-3, in **server-side validation**, the form is sent to the Web server, which then checks the values. If a mistake is found, the user is notified and asked to resubmit the form. In **client-side validation**, the form is checked as the user enters the information, and immediate feedback is provided if the user makes a mistake. Dr. Paulson wants this type of validation for her form. Form validation is a critical aspect of data entry. A properly designed form will reduce the possibility of the user entering faulty data.

Figure 9-3	SERVER-SIDE AND CLIENT-SIDE VALIDATION

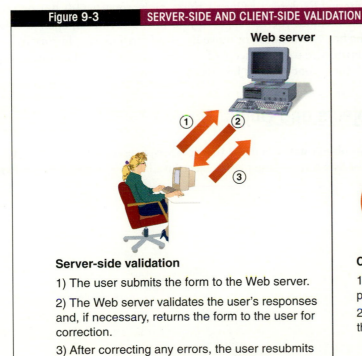

Web server   **Web server**

Server-side validation

1) The user submits the form to the Web server.

2) The Web server validates the user's responses and, if necessary, returns the form to the user for correction.

3) After correcting any errors, the user resubmits the form to the Web server for another validation.

Client-side validation

1) The user submits the form, and validation is performed on the user's computer.

2) After correcting any errors, the user submits the form to the Web server.

One powerful use of JavaScript is to provide this kind of client-side validation. With a script built into the Web page form, you can give immediate feedback to users as they enter data, which also reduces the amount of network traffic between users and the Web server. Before you can do this for Dr. Paulson's form, however, you must first learn how JavaScript can be used to manipulate elements on your Web page, not just when the page is initially loaded, but also in response to events initiated by the user. The first step in accomplishing this is to understand the object-based nature of the JavaScript language and how it can be used to control the behavior of the Web page, the form on the page, and even the Web browser itself.

Working with an Object-based Language

JavaScript is an **object-based language**, which means that the language is based on manipulating objects by either modifying their properties or applying methods to them. That definition might sound daunting, but the concept is simple. **Objects** are items that exist in a defined space on a Web page. Each object has **properties** that describe its appearance, purpose, or behavior. Furthermore, an object can have **methods**, which are actions that can be performed with it or to it.

Consider the example of an oven in your kitchen. The oven is an object. It has certain properties, such as its model name, age, size, and color. There are certain methods you can perform with the oven object, such as turning on the grill or the self-cleaner. Some of these methods change the properties of the oven, such as the oven's current temperature. You modify the oven's temperature property through the method of turning the stove on or off.

Similarly, your Web browser has its own set of objects, properties, and methods. The Web browser itself is an object, and the page you're viewing is an object. If the page contains frames, each frame is an object, and if the page contains forms, each field on the form (as well as the form itself) is an object. These objects have properties. The browser object has the type property (Netscape, Internet Explorer, or Opera), the version property (3.0, 4.0, or 5.0), and so forth. There are some methods you can apply to your browser: you can open it, close it, reload the contents of the browser window, or move back and forth in your history list.

Now that you've been introduced to the concept of objects, properties, and methods, you can learn how to work with these concepts in a JavaScript program.

Understanding JavaScript Objects and Object Names

An object is identified by its **object name**, a name that JavaScript reserves for referring to a particular object. Figure 9-4 lists some of the many objects available in JavaScript and their corresponding object names.

Figure 9-4   **SOME JAVASCRIPT OBJECTS AND THEIR OBJECT NAMES**

OBJECT	JAVASCRIPT OBJECT NAME
The browser window	window
A frame within the browser window	frame
The history list containing the Web pages the user has already visited in the current session	history
The Web browser being run by the user	navigator
The URL of the current Web page	location
The Web page currently shown in the browser window	document
A hyperlink on the current Web page	link
A target or anchor on the current Web page	anchor
A form on the current Web page	form

When you want to use JavaScript to manipulate the current window, for example, you have to use the object name "window." Operations that affect the current Web page use the "document" object name.

An object can also use a name that you've assigned to it. You've seen many HTML tags that include the NAME property, such as the <FORM>, <FRAME>, and <INPUT> tags. You can refer to objects created from those tags with the values specified in the NAME property. For example, in Dr. Paulson's registration form, the following tag starts the form:

```
<FORM NAME=REG>
```

You refer to this form using the object name, REG, in your JavaScript program.

It is helpful to visualize the object names shown in Figure 9-4 as part of a hierarchy of objects. Figure 9-5 shows the layout of this hierarchy.

Figure 9-5 | **JAVASCRIPT OBJECT HIERARCHY**

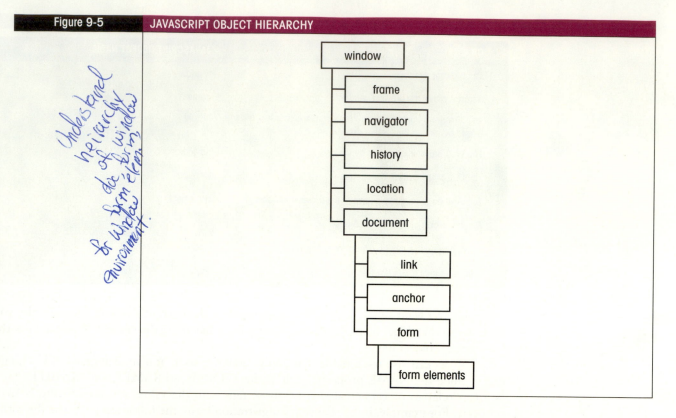

Understand hierarchy of window doc form elem for window environment.

The topmost object in the hierarchy is the window object. The window object contains the other objects in the list, such as the current frame, history list, or document. The document contains its own set of objects, including links, anchors, forms, and within each form, form elements such as input boxes.

In some situations, you will need to specify this hierarchy when referring to an object. You can do that by separating each object by a period and including the objects in the object name, starting at the top of the hierarchy and moving down. For example, in Dr. Paulson's form, the MEDRECNO input box lies within the REG form, which lies within the application window. The complete object reference for the input box, including the other objects in the hierarchy, is:

```
window.document.REG.MEDRECNO
```

Notice that you have to type REG and MEDRECNO in uppercase letters, since the names given to these objects are also in uppercase. In most cases, you can omit the window object name from the hierarchy, and JavaScript will assume that it is there. In other words, JavaScript treats the above object reference in the same way as the following reference:

```
document.REG.MEDRECNO
```

When working with objects on Web page forms, such as the form you'll be developing for Dr. Paulson, you should include the entire hierarchy of object names (except for the window object). Some browsers cannot interpret the object names without the complete hierarchy.

Figure 9-6 illustrates how the hierarchy applies to other objects on Dr. Paulson's Web registration form. Study this information and compare the object names in Figure 9-6 with the form names shown earlier in Figure 9-2. You'll need to use this information later when you start to work on the form.

Figure 9-6   OBJECT REFERENCES IN THE REGISTRATION FORM

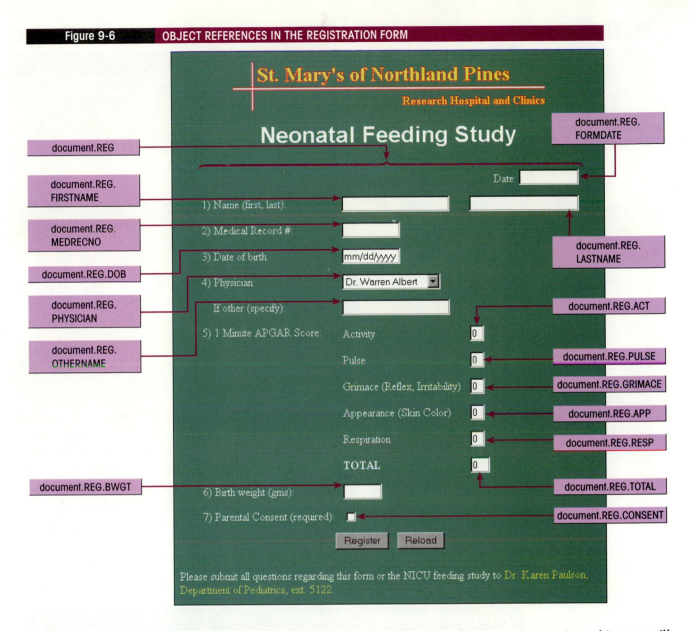

Now that you understand how JavaScript assigns object names to various objects, you'll next look at how JavaScript works with objects and their properties.

Working with Object Properties

Each object in JavaScript has properties associated with it. The number of properties varies depending on the particular object. Some objects have only a few properties, whereas others have dozens. As with object names, there are certain keywords that identify these properties. A partial list of objects and their properties is shown in Figure 9-7.

Figure 9-7 | JAVASCRIPT OBJECTS AND THEIR PROPERTIES

OBJECT NAME	PROPERTY NAME	DESCRIPTION
window	DefaultStatus	The default message displayed in the window's status bar
	frames	An array of all the frames in the window
	length	The number of frames in the window
	name	The target name of the window
	status	A priority or temporary message in the window's status bar
frame	document	The document displayed within the frame
	length	The number of frames within the frame
	name	The target name of the frame
history	length	The number of entries in the history list
navigator	appCodeName	The code name of the browser
	appName	The name of the browser
	appVersion	The version of the browser
location	href	The URL of the location
	protocol	The protocol (HTTP, FTP, etc.) used by the location
document	bgColor	The page's background color
	fgColor	The color of text on the page
	lastModified	The date the document was last modified
	linkColor	The color of hyperlinks on the page
	title	The title of the page
link	href	The URL of the hyperlink
	target	The target window of the hyperlink (if specified)
anchor	name	The name of the anchor
form	action	The ACTION property of the <FORM> tag
	length	The number of elements in the form
	method	The METHOD property of the <FORM> tag
	name	The name of the form

There are several ways of working with properties. You can change the value of a property, store the property's value in a variable, or test whether the property equals a specified value in an If...Then expression.

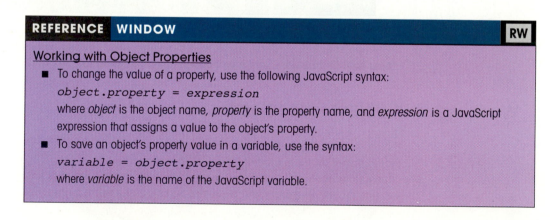

REFERENCE WINDOW | **RW**

Working with Object Properties

- To change the value of a property, use the following JavaScript syntax:

  `object.property = expression`

  where *object* is the object name, *property* is the property name, and *expression* is a JavaScript expression that assigns a value to the object's property.

- To save an object's property value in a variable, use the syntax:

  `variable = object.property`

  where *variable* is the name of the JavaScript variable.

Modifying a Property's Value

The syntax for changing the value of a property is:

```
object.property = expression
```

where *object* is the JavaScript name of the object you want to manipulate, *property* is a property of that object, and *expression* is a JavaScript expression that assigns a value to the property. Figure 9-8 shows how you could use objects and properties to modify your Web page and Web browser.

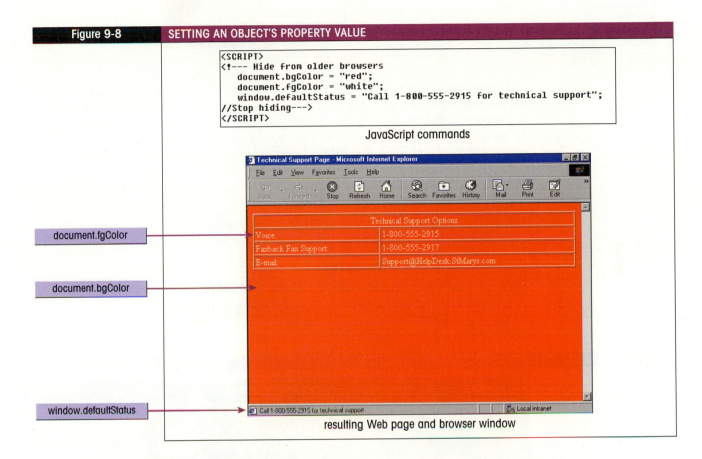

Figure 9-8   SETTING AN OBJECT'S PROPERTY VALUE

```
<SCRIPT>
<!--- Hide from older browsers
    document.bgColor = "red";
    document.fgColor = "white";
    window.defaultStatus = "Call 1-800-555-2915 for technical support";
//Stop hiding--->
</SCRIPT>
```

JavaScript commands

resulting Web page and browser window

In this example, the first JavaScript command, document.bgColor="red", modifies the current Web page, changing the background color to red. Note that this will override the browser's default background color. Similarly, the second command, document.fgColor="white", changes the foreground color, the text color, to white. The final command uses the window.defaultStatus property to display the text "Call 1-800-555-2915 for technical support" in the window's status bar. This is the default status bar text, but it might be replaced by other text (such as the URL of a Web page when the user passes the mouse over a hyperlink) at certain times.

Not all properties can be changed. Some properties are **read-only**, which means that you can read the property value, but you can't modify it. One such property is the appVersion property of the navigator object, which identifies the version number of your Web browser. Although it would be nice to upgrade the version of your browser by using a simple JavaScript command, you're not allowed to change this value. Figure 9-9 shows how you would use JavaScript to display other read-only information about your browser.

Figure 9-9   DISPLAYING SOME READ-ONLY BROWSER PROPERTIES

```
<HTML>
<HEAD>
<TITLE>Browser Information</TITLE>
</HEAD>

<BODY>
<SCRIPT>
<!--- Hide from older browsers
    document.write(navigator.appCodeName+"<BR>");
    document.write(navigator.appName+"<BR>");
    document.write(navigator.appVersion+"<BR>");
//Stop hiding--->
</SCRIPT>
</BODY>

</HTML>
```

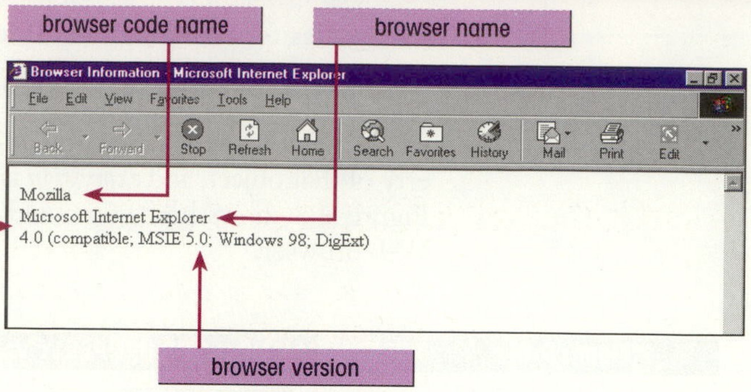

browser code name   browser name

Browser Information - Microsoft Internet Explorer

File Edit View Favorites Tools Help

Back   Forward   Stop   Refresh   Home   Search   Favorites   History   Mail   Print   Edit

Mozilla
Microsoft Internet Explorer
4.0 (compatible; MSIE 5.0; Windows 98; DigExt)

browser version

In this example, the values of the appCodeName, appName, and appVersion properties are used to display the browser code name, browser name, and version on the Web page. You might use this information when creating pages that involve HTML extensions supported by specific browsers or browser versions. Your JavaScript program could first test to see whether the user is running one of those browsers before inserting the tags into the Web page.

Assigning a Property to a Variable

Although you cannot change the value of read-only properties, you can assign that value to a variable in your JavaScript program. The syntax for assigning a property to a variable is:

```
variable = object.property
```

where *variable* is the variable name, *object* is the name of the object, and *property* is the name of its property. Figure 9-10 shows three examples of property values being assigned to JavaScript variables:

Figure 9-10   ASSIGNING PROPERTY VALUES TO VARIABLES

COMMAND	DESCRIPTION
PageColor=document.bgColor;	Assign the background color of the page to the PageColor variable.
FrameNumber=window.length;	Store the number of frames in the window in the variable FrameNumber.
BrowserName=navigator.appName;	Save the name of the browser in the variable BrowserName.

Using Properties in Conditional Expressions

A final situation in which you might need to work with properties is a conditional statement that changes how the page behaves based on the value of an object property. You'll use this technique later when adding form validation to Dr. Paulson's registration form. The following JavaScript code shows how you could incorporate object properties into a simple conditional expression:

```
if(document.bgColor=="black") {
      document.fgColor="white";
} else {
      document.fgColor="black";
}
```

In this example, JavaScript first checks the background color of the Web page. If the background color is black, then JavaScript changes the color of the text on the page to white (using the fgColor property of the page). On the other hand, if the background color is not black, then the text color is changed to black. As you can see, using objects, properties, and conditional statements gives you a great deal of control over the appearance of your Web page.

Working with Object Methods

Another way of controlling your Web page is to use methods. Recall that **methods** are actions that objects can perform or actions that you can apply to objects.

REFERENCE WINDOW   **RW**

Working with Object Methods

■ To apply a method to an object, use the syntax:

`object.method(parameters)`

where *object* is the object name, *method* is the name of a JavaScript method that applies to the object, and *parameters* are any values that are used in applying the method to the object. If you are using multiple parameters, separate each parameter value with a comma.

The syntax for applying a method to an object is:

`object.method(parameters);`

where *object* is the name of the object, *method* is the method to be applied, and *parameters* are any values used in applying the method to the object. If you are using multiple parameters, you should separate each value with a comma. One of the most commonly used methods is the write() method applied to the document object, which sends text to the Web page document. Figure 9-11 shows three examples of objects and methods:

Figure 9-11   **EXAMPLES OF JAVASCRIPT OBJECTS AND METHODS**

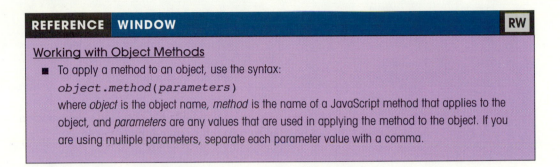

COMMAND	DESCRIPTION
history.back();	Make the browser go back to the previously viewed page in the browser's history list.
form.submit();	Submit the form to the CGI script.
document.write("Thank you");	Write the text "Thank you" in the document.

Figure 9-12 lists other JavaScript objects and some of the methods associated with them. A more complete list of objects, properties, and methods is included in Appendix D. For now, you have a sufficient understanding of the JavaScript object-based design to see how useful it can be in manipulating your Web pages and controlling your Web browser.

Figure 9-12	JAVASCRIPT OBJECTS AND THEIR METHODS	
OBJECT NAME	**METHOD NAME**	**DESCRIPTION**
window	alert(*message*) close() prompt(*message, default_text*) scroll(*x, y*)	Displays a dialog box with a message in the window Closes the window Displays a dialog box prompting the user for information Scrolls to the (x,y) coordinate in the window
frame	alert(*message*) close() prompt(*message, default_text*)	Displays a dialog box with a message in the frame Closes the frame Displays a dialog box prompting the user for information
history	back() forward()	Returns to the previous page in the history list Goes to the next page in the history list
location	reload()	Reloads the current page
document	write(*string*) writeln(*string*)	Writes text and HTML tags to the current document Writes text and HTML tags to the current document on a new line
form	reset() submit()	Resets the form Submits the form

In the next session, as you modify Dr. Paulson's registration form, you'll learn how JavaScript can be used to respond to user-initiated events.

Session 9.1 QUICK CHECK

1. What is the difference between server-side validation and client-side validation?

2. Define the following terms: object, property, and method.

3. What object reference would you use for a check box named JOIN located in a form named ENROLL?

4. What command would change the text color on a Web page to blue?

5. What command would assign the value of the page's text color to a variable named tcolor?

6. What command would you use to reset a form named ENROLL?

SESSION 9.2

In this session you will learn about events in JavaScript and how to run JavaScript programs in response to specific events. You'll also learn how to initiate these events from within a program. Then using what you've learned about objects, properties, methods, and events, you'll validate a Web page form. You'll see how to prompt the user for information and how to alert the users when mistakes have been made.

Managing Events

The following is a checklist of changes Dr. Paulson wants you to make to her form.

◯ 1) Automatically enter the current date in the FORMDATE field and move the cursor to the next field in the form.

◯ 2) If "Other" is selected from the Physician selection list box, prompt the user for the name of the physician; otherwise go to the APGAR component fields.

◯ 3) Automatically calculate the total APGAR score.

◯ 4) Check that valid APGAR component scores have been entered.

◯ 5) Check that parental consent has been obtained before submitting the form.

Your first task is to set up the form so that the current date is entered automatically into the FORMDATE field whenever the browser opens the page. The action of the user opening the form is an example of an event. An **event** is a specific action that triggers the browser to run a block of JavaScript commands. Up to now, your JavaScript programs have run exclusively when the Web page is loaded by the browser. But in Dr. Paulson's form, some of the programs must run in response to what the user is doing to the form.

JavaScript supports several different kinds of events, many of which are associated with forms and form fields. Each event has a unique name. A list of these events is shown in Figure 9-13.

Figure 9-13	JAVASCRIPT EVENTS

EVENT	DESCRIPTION
Abort	Occurs when the user cancels the loading of an image
Blur	Occurs when the user leaves a form field (either by clicking outside the field or pressing the Tab key)
Click	Occurs when the user clicks a field or a hyperlink
Change	Occurs when the value of a form field is changed by the user
Error	Occurs when the browser encounters an error in running a JavaScript program
Focus	Occurs when a window or form field is made active (usually by moving the cursor into the field or by clicking the object)

Events can take place in rapid succession. Consider the example shown in Figure 9-14. A user presses the Tab key to enter text into an input field, changes the field's value, and leaves the field by pressing the Tab key. The first event that the browser recognizes in this scenario is the **Focus event** as the input field becomes the active field in the form. After the user changes the value in the field and leaves the field, the **Change event** is triggered as the browser notes that the value of the field has been changed. Finally, the **Blur event** occurs as the focus leaves the field and goes to a different field on the form.

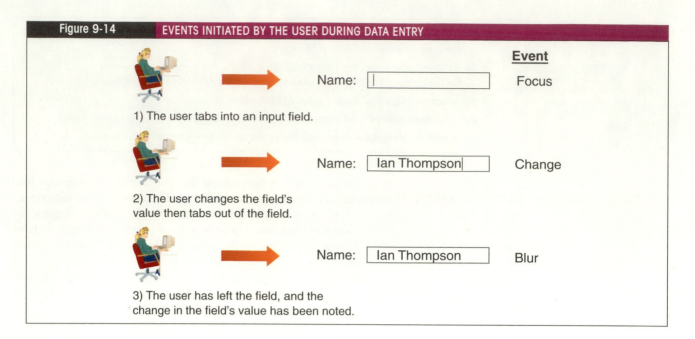

Figure 9-14   EVENTS INITIATED BY THE USER DURING DATA ENTRY

Event

Name: [   ]   Focus

1) The user tabs into an input field.

Name: [Ian Thompson|]   Change

2) The user changes the field's
value then tabs out of the field.

Name: [Ian Thompson]   Blur

3) The user has left the field, and the
change in the field's value has been noted.

With so many different events associated with your Web objects, you need some way of telling the browser how to run a set of commands whenever a specific event occurs. This is where an event handler becomes important.

Using Event Handlers

An **event handler** is code added to an HTML tag that is run whenever a particular event occurs within that tag. The syntax for invoking an event handler is:

```
< tag event_handler ="JavaScript commands;">
```

where *tag* is the name of the HTML tag where the even occurs, *event_handler* is the name of an event handler, and *JavaScript commands* are the set of commands, or more often a single command, that calls a JavaScript function to be run when the event occurs.

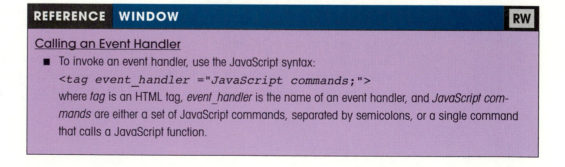

REFERENCE   WINDOW   **RW**

Calling an Event Handler
- To invoke an event handler, use the JavaScript syntax:
  ```
  <tag event_handler ="JavaScript commands;">
  ```
  where *tag* is an HTML tag, *event_handler* is the name of an event handler, and *JavaScript com-mands* are either a set of JavaScript commands, separated by semicolons, or a single command that calls a JavaScript function.

Different HTML tags have different event handlers. Figure 9-15 lists some of the names of event handlers available in JavaScript and the objects with which they are associated.

Figure 9-15	RESPONDING TO EVENTS WITH EVENT HANDLERS

OBJECT	NAMES OF EVENT HANDLERS
button	onClick
check box	onClick
document	onLoad, onUnload, onError
form	onSubmit, onReset
frames	onBlur, onFocus
hyperlink	onClick, onMouseOver, onMouseOut
image	onLoad, onError, onAbort
image map hotspot	onMouseOver, onMouseOut
input box	onBlur, onChange, onFocus, onSelect
radio button	onClick
reset button	onClick
selection list	onBlur, onChange, onFocus
submit button	onClick
text area box	onBlur, onChange, onFocus, onSelect
window	onLoad, onUnload, onBlur, onFocus

In the example shown in Figure 9-16, the onClick event handler is used with radio buttons to change the page's background color to red, blue, or green in response to the user clicking one of the three options. Note that the JavaScript commands invoked in this way do not require <SCRIPT> tags, but they do have to be placed within a pair of single or double quotation marks in the tag. You can enter several commands in this way, separating one command line from another with a semicolon; however, when you have several JavaScript commands to run, the standard practice is to place them in a function, which can then be called using a single command line.

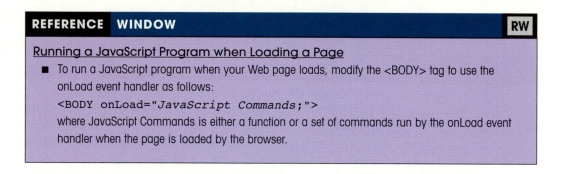

Figure 9-16   USING THE ONCLICK EVENT HANDLER

```
<HTML>
<HEAD>
</HEAD>
<BODY TEXT=WHITE BGCOLOR=TEAL>
<FORM>
<P>Change background color to:</P>
<INPUT TYPE=RADIO NAME=COLORS onClick="document.bgColor='red';">Red <BR>
<INPUT TYPE=RADIO NAME=COLORS onClick="document.bgColor='blue';">Blue<BR>
<INPUT TYPE=RADIO NAME=COLORS onClick="document.bgColor='green';">Green
</FORM>
</BODY>
</HTML>
```

HTML code

initial Web page

user clicks the red button

user clicks the blue button

user clicks the green button

Using the onLoad Event Handler

Now that you've learned about objects, properties, methods, and events, you are ready to start modifying Dr. Paulson's form.

REFERENCE WINDOW   **RW**

Running a JavaScript Program when Loading a Page

■ To run a JavaScript program when your Web page loads, modify the <BODY> tag to use the onLoad event handler as follows:

    `<BODY onLoad="`*JavaScript Commands;*`">`

where JavaScript Commands is either a function or a set of commands run by the onLoad event handler when the page is loaded by the browser.

The event handler for the opening of a Web page is called **onLoad**. Because this handler is associated with the document object, you must place it in the <BODY> tag of the HTML file. The event handler should run the function StartForm(). StartForm() is a user-defined function that you'll create shortly.

To add the onLoad event handler to Dr. Paulson's form:

1. Start your text editor and open the **Study.htm** file from the Tutorial.09 folder on your Data Disk.

2. Type **onLoad="StartForm();"** in the <BODY> tag of the HTML file. See Figure 9-17.

Figure 9-17   **INSERTING THE ONLOAD EVENT HANDLER**

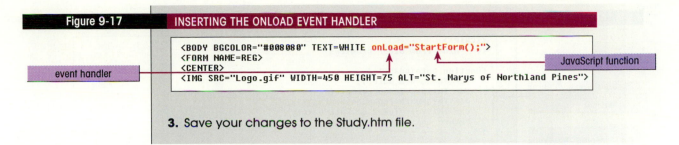

```
<BODY BGCOLOR="#008080" TEXT=WHITE onLoad="StartForm();">
<FORM NAME=REG>
<CENTER>
<IMG SRC="Logo.gif" WIDTH=450 HEIGHT=75 ALT="St. Marys of Northland Pines">
```

event handler

JavaScript function

3. Save your changes to the Study.htm file.

Now you have to create the StartForm() function. This function will have two purposes: first it will enter the current date into the Date field, and then it will move the cursor to the next field in the form.

JavaScript functions are usually collected together between a set of <SCRIPT> tags located in the HEAD section of the file. The StartForm() function relies on another JavaScript function named DateToday(), which has already been created for you in the Study.htm file. The code for the DateToday() function is as follows:

```
function DateToday() {
        var Today=new Date();
        var ThisDay=Today.getDate();
        var ThisMonth=Today.getMonth()+1;
        var ThisYear=Today.getFullYear();
return ThisMonth+"/"+ThisDay+"/"+ThisYear;
}
```

This function contains JavaScript commands that you should be familiar with. It uses the date object and extracts the current day, month, and year, and then combines those values in a text string, which it then returns to the user. StartForm() will call the DateToday() function to retrieve a text string containing the current date, and then it will place that text in the Date field in the registration form. The code for the StartForm() function is as follows:

```
function StartForm() {
        document.REG.FORMDATE.value=DateToday();
}
```

Before you enter this function into the Study.htm file, take a moment to examine the code. The program calls the DateToday() function which creates a text string displaying the current date. The value of the FORMDATE field of the REG form in the current document is then made equal to this text string. In other words, the current date is displayed in the FORMDATE field, which is what Dr. Paulson wants.

To add the StartForm() function to the Study.htm file:

1. Go to the <SCRIPT> tag in the Study.htm file.

2. Below the closing bracket of the DateToday() function, enter the following commands:

```
function StartForm() {
        document.REG.FORMDATE.value=DateToday();    PS 9.09
}                                                      Date
```

Your file should look like Figure 9-18.

Figure 9-18   CREATING THE STARTFORM() FUNCTION

the DateToday()
function

the StartForm() function
gets the current date
from the DateToday()
function and places the
date in the FORMDATE
field of the REG form

```
<SCRIPT>
<!-- Hide from older browsers

function DateToday() {
   var Today=new Date();
   var ThisDay=Today.getDate();
   var ThisMonth=Today.getMonth()+1;
   var ThisYear=Today.getFullYear();
   return ThisMonth+"/"+ThisDay+"/"+ThisYear;
}

function StartForm() {
   document.REG.FORMDATE.value=DateToday();
}
//Stop hiding -->
</SCRIPT>
</HEAD>

<BODY BGCOLOR="#008080" TEXT=WHITE onload="StartForm();">
<FORM NAME=REG>
<CENTER>
```

the StartForm() function
is run when the page
is loaded

3. Save your changes to the file and then reload Study.htm in your Web browser. Your Web page should now show the current date in the Date field. See Figure 9-19.

Figure 9-19   CURRENT DATE INSERTED INTO THE REGISTRATION FORM

current date

St. Mary's of Northland Pines

Research Hospital and Clinics

Neonatal Feeding Study

Date: 10/22/2001

1) Name (first, last):

2) Medical Record #:

3) Date of birth: mm/dd/yyyy

4) Physician: Dr. Warren Albert

TROUBLE? Your date will be different from the one shown in the figure. If your browser displays an error message, return to your text editor and verify that you have entered the new code exactly as shown in the steps.

A field's "value" property is only one of many properties you can associate with input boxes such as the FORMDATE field. Other properties and methods associated with fields are shown in Figure 9-20.

Figure 9-20   PROPERTIES AND METHODS OF INPUT BOXES

PROPERTY	DESCRIPTION
defaultValue	The default value of the input box
name	The name of the input box
type	The type of the input box
value	The current value of the input box

METHOD	DESCRIPTION
focus()	Makes the input box active
blur()	Leaves the input box
select()	Selects the text in the input box

The function does one of the two jobs it needs to; it displays the date in the Date field. Dr. Paulson also wants the function to move the cursor to the next field in the form. To accomplish this, you have to learn how to make JavaScript not only respond to an event, but also initiate one.

Emulating Events

When you use JavaScript to **emulate** an event, you are causing the Web page to perform an action for the user, such as having the cursor move to the next field. To emulate an event, you apply an event method to an object on your Web page.

Figure 9-21 shows three examples of JavaScript commands that emulate events. The examples are based on a Web page that contains a form named ORDERS and an input box named PRODUCT.

Figure 9-21   EMULATING AN EVENT WITH JAVASCRIPT

COMMAND	DESCRIPTION
document.ORDERS.PRODUCT.focus();	Move the cursor to the PRODUCT field, by giving it the focus.
document.ORDERS.PRODUCT.blur();	Remove the focus from the PRODUCT field, moving the cursor to the next field in the form.
document.ORDERS.submit();	Submit the ORDERS form to a CGI script.

Other events that you can emulate in your forms are shown in Figure 9-22.

Figure 9-22   EMULATING AN EVENT WITH EVENT METHODS

OBJECT	EVENT METHODS
button	click()
check box	click()
document	clear()
form	reset(), submit()
frames	blur(), close(), focus()
input box	focus(), blur(), select()
radio button	click()
reset button	click()
submit button	click()
text area box	focus(), blur(), select()
window	blur(), close(), focus()

REFERENCE   WINDOW   **RW**

Moving Between Input Fields

- To have the cursor move to a different field on your Web page form, use the JavaScript command:

  `document.FORM.FIELD.focus();`

  where *FORM* is the name of the Web page form, and *FIELD* is the name of the field that the cursor will move to.

- To have the cursor move out of a field on your Web page form, use the JavaScript command:

  `document.FORM.FIELD.blur();`

  where the blur() method removes the cursor from the specified input field.

You need to add a command to the StartForm() function that places the cursor in the next field in the REG form, which in this case is the FIRSTNAME field. The command to move the cursor to the FIRSTNAME field is:

`document.REG.FIRSTNAME.focus();`

To revise the StartForm() function:

1. Return to the **Study.htm** file in your text editor.

2. Locate the StartForm() function at the beginning of the file, and then add the following command to the end of the command block:

   `document.REG.FIRSTNAME.focus();`

   See Figure 9-23.

| Figure 9-23 | MOVING THE FOCUS TO THE FIRSTNAME FIELD |

the FIRSTNAME field receives the focus of the cursor after the current date is entered in the FORMDATE field

```
function StartForm() {
    document.REG.FORMDATE.value=DateToday();
    document.REG.FIRSTNAME.focus();
}
```

3. Save your changes to the Study.htm file, and then reload the file in your Web browser.

TROUBLE? If you're using Netscape Navigator or Netscape Communicator, you might have to reopen the file. Simply clicking the Reload button might not invoke the changes you've made to the JavaScript program.

When the page is reopened, the FIRSTNAME field should be selected. You can verify this by noticing whether the cursor is blinking in the field or by typing some text. The characters should appear in this field and nowhere else.

You've completed the first task on your list for Dr. Paulson.

1) Automatically enter the current date in the FORMDATE field and move the cursor to the next field in the form.

2) If "Other" is selected from the Physician selection list box, prompt the user for the name of the physician; otherwise go to the APGAR component fields.

3) Automatically calculate the total APGAR score.

4) Check that valid APGAR component scores have been entered.

5) Check that parental consent has been obtained before submitting the form.

The next few fields in the form don't require any modifications. However, Dr. Paulson does want you to change the behavior of the Physician selection list.

Working with a Selection Object

Dr. Paulson wants the form to control how the user selects a physician from the selection list. If the user selects one of the seven physicians in the list, the cursor should immediately go to the field for the APGAR Activity score, skipping over the If other field. On the other hand, if the user selects "Other" from the list of physicians, the form should prompt the user to enter that physician's name before continuing.

You need to create another function to handle this task. The function, which you'll name CheckOther(), should run whenever the cursor leaves the Physician selection list. This action of leaving a field is managed by the onBlur() event handler. You'll now add this event handler to the <SELECT> tag for the Physician selection list.

To add the onBlur() event handler to the tag:

1. Return to your text editor and the Study.htm file.

2. Locate the <SELECT> tag for the Physician selection list, and then insert the following code into the tag:

```
onBlur="CheckOther();"
```

See Figure 9-24.

Figure 9-24   **ADDING THE ONBLUR EVENT HANDLER TO THE <SELECT> TAG**

```
<TD>
    <SELECT NAME=PHYSICIAN onBlur="CheckOther();">
    <OPTION VALUE="Albert">Dr. Warren Albert
    <OPTION VALUE="Alvarez">Dr. Maria Alvarez
    <OPTION VALUE="Brinkman">Dr. Karen Brinkman
    <OPTION VALUE="Kerry">Dr. Michael Kerry
    <OPTION VALUE="Nichols">Dr. Chad Nichols
    <OPTION VALUE="Paulson">Dr. Karen Paulson
    <OPTION VALUE="Webb">Dr. Tai Webb
    <OPTION VALUE="Other">Other
    </SELECT>
</TD>
```

onBlur event handler

the CheckOther() function will be run when the cursor leaves the selection box

Now you need to create the CheckOther() function. To do so, you need to learn a little about how JavaScript works with selection lists and their options. JavaScript treats a selection list as an array of option values. In the case of Dr. Paulson's form, the tags that define the Physician selection list are:

```
<SELECT NAME=PHYSICIAN>
        <OPTION VALUE="Albert">Dr. Warren Albert
        <OPTION VALUE="Alvarez">Dr. Maria Alvarez
        <OPTION VALUE="Brinkman">Dr. Karen Brinkman
        <OPTION VALUE="Kerry">Dr. Michael Kerry
        <OPTION VALUE="Nichols">Dr. Chad Nichols
        <OPTION VALUE="Paulson">Dr. Karen Paulson
        <OPTION VALUE="Webb">Dr. Tai Webb
        <OPTION VALUE="Other">Other
</SELECT>
```

Each option in the selection list has a value property that corresponds to the VALUE property entered into the <OPTION> tag. For the Physician selection list, the following are the JavaScript objects and properties for each option value:

```
document.REG.PHYSICIAN.options[0].value="Albert"
document.REG.PHYSICIAN.options[1].value="Alvarez"
document.REG.PHYSICIAN.options[2].value="Brinkman"
document.REG.PHYSICIAN.options[3].value="Kerry"
document.REG.PHYSICIAN.options[4].value="Nichols"
document.REG.PHYSICIAN.options[5].value="Paulson"
document.REG.PHYSICIAN.options[6].value="Webb"
document.REG.PHYSICIAN.options[7].value="Other"
```

Each option in the selection list belongs to a hierarchy of object names. In this case, the hierarchy starts with the document object, goes to the REG form within the document, then goes to the PHYSICIAN field within the form, and finally goes to each individual option within the selection list. Note that the array of selection options starts with an index value of 0, not 1.

Similarly, the text that actually appears in the selection list is specified by the text property. For options in the Physician selection list, this results in the following objects and properties:

```
document.REG.PHYSICIAN.options[0].text="Dr. Warren Albert"
document.REG.PHYSICIAN.options[1].text="Dr. Maria Alvarez"
document.REG.PHYSICIAN.options[2].text="Dr. Karen Brinkman"
document.REG.PHYSICIAN.options[3].text="Dr. Michael Kerry"
document.REG.PHYSICIAN.options[4].text="Dr. Chad Nichols"
document.REG.PHYSICIAN.options[5].text="Dr. Karen Paulson"
document.REG.PHYSICIAN.options[6].text="Dr. Tai Webb"
document.REG.PHYSICIAN.options[7].text="Other"
```

Figure 9-25 shows some of the other properties and methods associated with selection lists and selection options.

Figure 9-25	PROPERTIES AND METHODS OF SELECTION LISTS

PROPERTIES OF SELECTION LISTS	DESCRIPTION
length	The number of options in the list
name	The name of the selection list
selectedIndex	The index value of the currently selected option in the list

PROPERTIES OF OPTIONS IN THE LIST	DESCRIPTION
defaultSelected	A Boolean value indicating whether the option is selected by default
index	The index value of the option
selected	A Boolean value indicating whether the option is currently selected
text	The text associated with the option displayed in the browser
value	The value of the option

METHODS OF SELECTION LISTS	DESCRIPTION
focus()	Makes the selection list active
blur()	Leaves the selection list

Referring to Values in a Selection List

■ To refer to the value of an option in a selection list, use the object and property:

```
document.FORM.FIELD.options[index].value
```

where *FORM* is the name of the Web page form, *FIELD* is the name of the selection field, and *index* is the index number of the option.

■ To refer to the text of an option (the text that is shown to the user) in a selection list, use the object and property:

```
document.FORM.FIELD.options[index].text
```

■ To determine the index number of the currently selected option, use the JavaScript command:

```
IndexVariable = document.FORM.FIELD.selectedIndex;
```

where *IndexVariable* is a variable that will contain the value of the currently selected index.

The first task the CheckOther() function should perform is to determine whether the user has chosen the option "Other" from the Physician selection list. The option the user selects is stored in the selectedIndex property of the selection list. The full reference for the physician selection list is:

```
document.REG.PHYSICIAN.selectedIndex
```

For example, if the user selects "Other" from the selection list, the selectedIndex property has a value of 7, because Other is the seventh item in the array of physician options.

If the user selects "Other" from the list of physicians, you want the CheckOther() function to prompt the user for the physician's name before going on to the next field in the form (the ACT field). However, if the user selects one of the physicians in the list, then the form should proceed to the ACT field without prompting. The code for the CheckOther() function, therefore, is an If/Else statement, as follows:

```
function CheckOther() {
    if(document.REG.PHYSICIAN.selectedIndex==7) {
        //Prompt for the name of the physician
    }
    document.REG.ACT.focus();
}
```

The first line of the command block checks whether the Other option (index value 7) is selected. The second line of the command block, which is only a comment right now, will prompt the user to enter the name of the doctor in the Other field. You don't know how to prompt the user for information yet—that topic will be covered shortly. The last line of the command block, the Else statement, causes the cursor to move to the Activity field if the index value of 7 was not selected.

To add the CheckOther() function to the Study.htm file:

1. Go to the <SCRIPT> tag in the Study.htm file.

2. Below the StartForm() function, enter the following commands:

```
function CheckOther() {
    if(document.REG.PHYSICIAN.selectedIndex==7) {
        //Prompt for the name of the physician
    }
    document.REG.ACT.focus();
}
```

Your file should look like Figure 9-26.

| Figure 9-26 | INSERTING THE CHECKOTHER() FUNCTION |

```
function StartForm() {
    document.REG.FORMDATE.value=DateToday();
    document.REG.FIRSTNAME.focus();
}
function CheckOther() {
    if(document.REG.PHYSICIAN.selectedIndex==7) {
        //Prompt for the name of the physician
    }
    document.REG.ACT.focus();
}

//Stop hiding -->
</SCRIPT>
```

check whether the user has selected Other from the list of physicians

3. Save your changes to the file.

4. Reload the **Study.htm** file in your Web browser.

5. Click the **Physician** selection list on the form and select one of the physician names.

6. Press the **Tab** key on your keyboard.

Note that after pressing the tab key, the cursor does not move to the next field in the list, the OTHER field; instead, the cursor moves to the ACT field—the field you specified with the onBlur event handler.

Prompting the User for Input

To prompt the user for input, you use the prompt() method. The **prompt() method** creates a dialog box containing a message you create, and an input field into which the user can type a value or text string. The syntax for the prompt() method is:

```
prompt("Message", "Default_text");
```

where *Message* is the message that you want to appear in the dialog box, and *Default_text* is the default text that you want to appear in the dialog box's input field. Figure 9-27 shows an example of the JavaScript prompt() method.

Figure 9-27   **THE PROMPT METHOD**

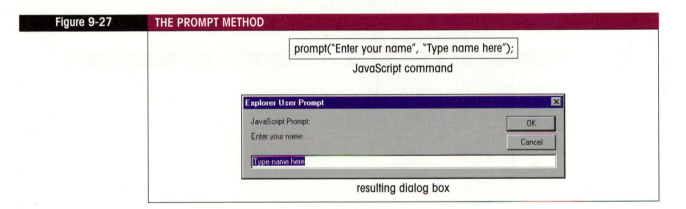

Note that different browsers will display their dialog boxes slightly differently; however all dialog boxes will share the common features of a title bar, default value, OK button, and Cancel button.

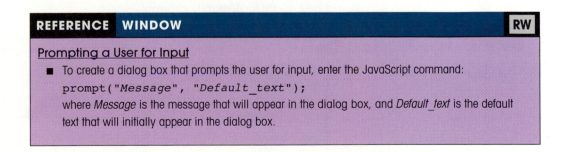

REFERENCE WINDOW   **RW**

Prompting a User for Input
- To create a dialog box that prompts the user for input, enter the JavaScript command:
  ```
  prompt("Message", "Default_text");
  ```
  where *Message* is the message that will appear in the dialog box, and *Default_text* is the default text that will initially appear in the dialog box.

The prompt() method also returns a result that can be stored in a variable or placed in an object. For example, the following JavaScript command will place whatever text the user enters in the dialog box into the UserName variable:

```
UserName=prompt("Enter your name","Type name here");
```

You can use the prompt() method in the CheckOther() function to prompt the user for the name of the physician, and then to insert the response into the OTHERNAME field. The command to do this is:

```
document.REG.OTHERNAME.value=prompt("Enter name of
physician","Name");
```

You'll replace the comment in the CheckOther() function with this command now.

To add the prompt() method to the CheckOther() function:

1. Return to your text editor and locate the CheckOther() function in the Study.htm file.

2. Replace the comment, "//Prompt for the name of the physician", in the function with the following line (make sure to type this text all on one line—it's okay if it wraps, but don't press the Enter key):

```
document.REG.OTHERNAME.value=prompt("Enter name of
physician","Name");
```

Figure 9-28 shows the revised code for the CheckOther() function.

Figure 9-28   CREATING A PROMPT DIALOG BOX

```
function CheckOther() {
    if(document.REG.PHYSICIAN.selectedIndex==7) {
        document.REG.OTHERNAME.value=prompt("Enter name of physician", "Name");
    }
    document.REG.ACT.focus();
}
```

prompt message

default text in the
dialog box

3. Save your changes to the file.

   Now check the behavior of the form in your Web browser.

4. Reload the **Study.htm** file in your Web browser.

5. Select **Other** from the Physician selection list, and then press the **(Tab)** key.

6. Enter the name **Dr. Carol White** in the dialog box, as shown in Figure 9-29 (your dialog box might look slightly different).

Figure 9-29   ENTERING A PHYSICIAN NAME IN THE DIALOG BOX

7. Click the **OK** button. The form should now display the text "Dr. Carol White" in the OTHERNAME field, and the cursor should be blinking in the Activity input box. See Figure 9-30.

Figure 9-30 | PHYSICIAN'S NAME AUTOMATICALLY ENTERED INTO THE OTHERNAME FIELD

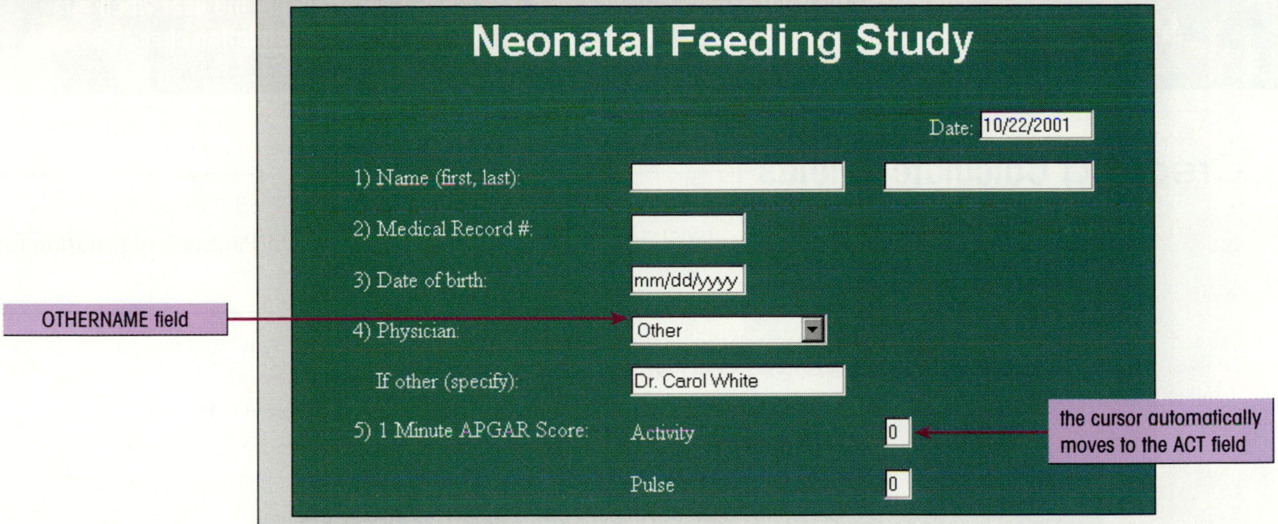

Neonatal Feeding Study

Date: 10/22/2001

1) Name (first, last):

2) Medical Record #:

3) Date of birth: mm/dd/yyyy

OTHERNAME field → 4) Physician: Other

If other (specify): Dr. Carol White

5) 1 Minute APGAR Score: Activity 0 ← the cursor automatically moves to the ACT field

Pulse 0

You've learned how to work with events and event handlers, and you've used JavaScript to insert text automatically into a form field and to control the movement of the cursor in Dr. Paulson's form. In the next session you'll learn how to create a calculated field and how to alert users when they enter unacceptable values into the form.

Session 9.2 QUICK CHECK

1. Define the following terms: event, event handler, and event method.

2. How would you modify your HTML file to run the function Welcome() whenever the page is loaded into the browser?

3. How would you modify the following tag so that it runs the CheckCredit()function whenever the user exits the input field?

```
<INPUT NAME=CreditNumber>
```

Use the following HTML tags to answer Quick Checks 4 through 6:

```
<FORM NAME=PRODUCT>
    <SELECT NAME=MODEL>
        <OPTION VALUE="P220">Pentium 220
        <OPTION VALUE="P300">Pentium 300
        <OPTION VALUE="P500">Pentium 500
    </SELECT>
</FORM>
```

4. What JavaScript command would you enter to change the value of the first option in the selection list to "P250"?

5. What JavaScript command would you enter to change the text of the first option in the selection list to "Pentium 250"?

6. What JavaScript command would you enter to store the index of the option the user selected in a variable named ModelNumber?

7. What JavaScript command creates an input box prompting the user with the message "Enter a new model"?

SESSION 9.3

In this session you will learn how to create a calculated field and how to perform validation checks on values that the user enters. You'll learn how to notify the user when mistakes have been made. You'll also learn how to perform a final validation check when the form is submitted.

Creating Calculated Fields

At this point you've completed the first two tasks on your list for Dr. Paulson's registration form.

1) Automatically enter the current date in the FORMDATE field and move the cursor to the next field in the form.

2) If "Other" is selected from the Physician selection list box, prompt the user for the name of the physician; otherwise go to the APGAR component fields.

3) Automatically calculate the total APGAR score.

4) Check that valid APGAR component scores have been entered.

5) Check that parental consent has been obtained before submitting the form.

Your next task is to calculate the total APGAR score automatically and store this value in the TOTAL field. The APGAR score is a measure of the general health of a newborn baby and has five components: activity, pulse, grimace, appearance, and respiration. Each component is given a score of 0, 1, or 2, and the formula for the total APGAR score is simply the sum of all five components:

TOTAL = ACTIVITY + PULSE + GRIMACE + APPEARANCE + RESPIRATION

Dr. Paulson wants the form to recalculate the total APGAR value every time the user enters a value in one of the APGAR fields. The first thing you'll do then, is add the onBlur() event handler to each of the five APGAR fields in the form. Every time the user tabs out of one of these fields, the Web browser will call a function (which you'll create shortly) that calculates the current APGAR total. The total value will then be stored in the TOTAL field on the form.

To add the onBlur() event handler to the five APGAR fields:

1. If you took a break after the previous session, start your text editor and reopen the **Study.htm** file from the Tutorial.09 folder of your Data Disk.

2. Go to the <INPUT> tag for the Activity field and insert within the tag the following onBlur event handler (see Figure 9-31):

```
onBlur="APGAR();"
```

APGAR() is the name of the JavaScript function that you'll create to calculate the total APGAR score and then store the result in the TOTAL field.

Figure 9-31   **USING THE ONBLUR EVENT TO CALL THE APGAR() FUNCTION**

```
<!--- Activity component of the APGAR score --->
<TR>
   <TD ROWSPAN=6 VALIGN=TOP>
      5) 1 Minute APGAR Score:
   </TD>
   <TD>
      Activity
   </TD>
   <TD>
      <INPUT NAME=ACT VALUE=0 SIZE=1 MAXLENGTH=1 onBlur="APGAR();">
   </TD>
</TR>
```

3. Add this same line of code to the <INPUT> tags of the other four component fields (but not to the TOTAL field). You might want to use the Copy and Paste functions of your text editor.

4. Save your changes to the Study.htm file.

Next, you need to create the APGAR() function. This function should add up the values entered into each of the component fields; however, JavaScript has a quirk you have to account for.

JavaScript treats values entered into input boxes as text strings, so you must first convert them from the text format to the number format. Otherwise the APGAR() function will produce an error. You can change text to numbers with the eval() function.

REFERENCE   WINDOW

Converting a Text Value to a Number Value
- To change a text value into a numeric value, use the eval() function as follows:

  NumberVariable = eval(*TextValue*);

  where *NumberVariable* is a variable that will contain the number value, and *TextValue* is a text string or text variable. For example, Age=eval("55") produces the numeric value 55 and stores it in a variable named "Age."

One feature of the **eval()** function is that it takes a number that is represented as a text string and converts it to a number. For example, the following command takes the text string "10," converts it to the number 10, and stores that value in the variable TOTAL:

```
TOTAL = eval("10");
```

Converting the text values to numbers is important; otherwise, JavaScript will simply append one text string to the other. For example, consider the following command:

```
"10" + "5"
```

This command produces the text string "105" because you're adding two text strings together, rather than the values the text strings represent. However, the following command results in the numeric value 15:

```
eval("10") + eval("5")
```

Using the eval() function, you would create the APGAR() function as follows:

```
function APGAR() {
        var A = eval(document.REG.ACT.value);
        var P = eval(document.REG.PULSE.value);
        var G = eval(document.REG.GRIMACE.value);
        var AP = eval(document.REG.APP.value);
        var R = eval(document.REG.RESP.value);
        document.REG.TOTAL.value = A + P + G + AP + R;
}
```

This function takes the values from each of the five component fields, stores them in numeric variables, and then adds the variables together. The result is placed into the TOTAL field. Try adding the APGAR() function to the Study.htm file.

To create the APGAR() function:

1. Locate the CheckOther() function at the top of the Study.htm file and insert the following lines of code below it.

```
function APGAR() {
        var A = eval(document.REG.ACT.value);
        var P = eval(document.REG.PULSE.value);
        var G = eval(document.REG.GRIMACE.value);
        var AP = eval(document.REG.APP.value);
        var R = eval(document.REG.RESP.value);
        document.REG.TOTAL.value=A+P+G+AP+R;
}
```

Figure 9-32 shows the revised file.

Figure 9-32	INSERTING THE APGAR() FUNCTION

```
function CheckOther() {
    if(document.REG.PHYSICIAN.selectedIndex==7) {
        document.REG.OTHERNAME.value=prompt("Enter name of physician", "Name")
    }
    document.REG.ACT.focus();
}

function APGAR() {
    var A=eval(document.REG.ACT.value);
    var P=eval(document.REG.PULSE.value);
    var G=eval(document.REG.GRIMACE.value);
    var AP=eval(document.REG.APP.value);
    var R=eval(document.REG.RESP.value);
    document.REG.TOTAL.value=A+P+G+AP+R;
}

//Stop hiding -->
</SCRIPT>
```

2. Save your changes to the Study.htm file, and then reload the file in your Web browser. Notice that each APGAR component field has a default value of 0.

Next, you'll check the function by entering some test values.

3. Enter the following APGAR component values (press the **Tab** key to move between the fields):

2 in the Activity field

0 in the Pulse field

1 in the Grimace field

2 in the Appearance field

2 in the Respiration field

Each time you enter a component value and press the Tab key to leave the field, the onBlur() event handler is triggered and the APGAR() function is run, updating the value in the TOTAL field. Figure 9-33 shows the final result after you tab out of the Respiration field.

Figure 9-33	CALCULATING THE TOTAL APGAR SCORE

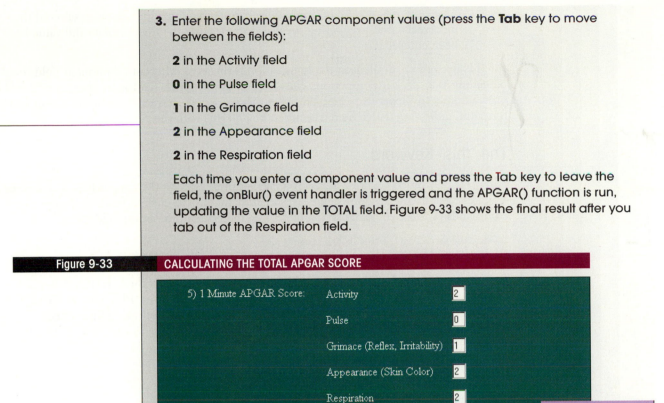

By using the onBlur() event handler and the APGAR() function, you've created a field that is automatically calculated for the user. In its current form, the APGAR() function will accept any value for each of the components; however, as indicated on your task list, the function must also make sure that only valid APGAR component scores are entered. You'll make this change next.

1) Automatically enter the current date in the FORMDATE field and move the cursor to the next field in the form.
2) If "Other" is selected from the Physician selection list box, prompt the user for the name of the physician; otherwise go to the APGAR component fields.
3) Automatically calculate the total APGAR score.
4) Check that valid APGAR component scores have been entered.
5) Check that parental consent has been obtained before submitting the form.

Validating User Input

Dr. Paulson wants the form to allow only the values 0, 1, and 2 to be entered into the APGAR component fields; these are the only values physicians assign when performing an examination of a newborn. Therefore, you have to include some way of checking the user's entries in these fields to make sure that they are valid. If the user enters an incorrect value in one of the component fields, two things must happen:

1. The browser should display a dialog box informing the user of the mistake.

2. The cursor should be positioned back in the field in which the user entered the incorrect value, preventing the user from leaving the field until a valid value has been entered.

This presents a problem in the registration form. Five different component fields could be calling the APGAR() function. How do you know which field is the one in which the user entered an incorrect value? To make this work, you have to pass information to the function, indicating which field is using it. You do this with the "this" keyword.

The "this" Keyword

The **this** keyword is a word reserved by JavaScript to refer to the currently selected object, whatever that might be. For example, if the Pulse field is the current field, the following two commands produce the same action (changing the value of the Pulse field to 2.)

```
document.REG.PULSE.value = 2;
this.value = 2;
```

You can also use the "this" keyword to pass information about the currently selected field to a function. For example, assume that you have two input boxes, PULSE and RESP, both of which will use the same function, SetVal(), as shown in the following lines of code:

```
<SCRIPT>
        function SetVal(field) {
                field.value = 0;
        }
</SCRIPT>

<INPUT NAME = PULSE onFocus="SetVal(this);">
<INPUT NAME = RESP onFocus="SetVal(this);">
```

+ 4 more inls

When the PULSE input box receives the focus, it calls the SetVal() function, including the "this" keyword, as a parameter value. The SetVal() function is then applied to the currently selected object. When the PULSE field is the currently selected object, the SetVal() function changes the PULSE value to zero. When the RESP field is the currently selected object, its value is similarly set to zero.

In the same way, you can modify the APGAR() function to include information, through the "this" keyword, to indicate which field is calling the function. You can test then whether the value of the field violates the rules that Dr. Paulson has set up for APGAR scores.

> ### To add the "this" keyword to the onBlur() event handlers:
>
> **1.** Return to the **Study.htm** file in your text editor and go to the <INPUT> tag for the Activity field.
>
> **2.** In the code onBlur="APGAR();" type the word **this** within the parentheses, so that the code now reads, **onBlur="APGAR(this);"**.
>
> **3.** Repeat Step 2 for the remaining four components of the APGAR score.
>
> **4.** Save your changes.

Now that you've added the "this" keyword to the event handler that calls the APGAR() function, you need to make several changes to the function itself. First, the function must store the value of the active field in a variable. Then it needs to test whether or not the value of that variable is equal to 0, 1, or 2. If it is, the function can calculate the total APGAR score as before; if not, the function should alert the user that a mistake has been made and return the cursor to the appropriate field so that the user can enter the correct value. The revised APGAR() function should be as follows:

```
function APGAR(field) {
if(field.value==0 || field.value==1 || field.value==2) {
        var A = eval(document.REG.ACT.value);
        var P = eval(document.REG.PULSE.value);
        var G = eval(document.REG.GRIMACE.value);
        var AP = eval(document.REG.APP.value);
        var R = eval(document.REG.RESP.value);
        document.REG.TOTAL.value = A + P + G + AP + R;
} else {
        //alert the user
        field.focus();
}
}
```

Figure 9-34 illustrates how this function works.

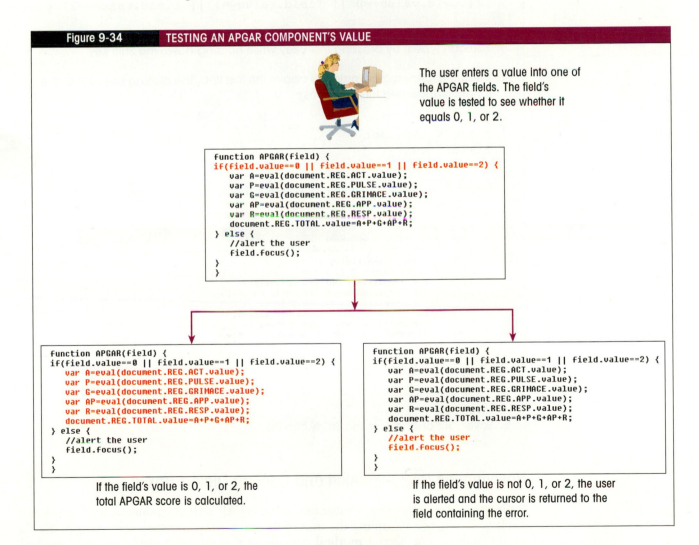

Figure 9-34   **TESTING AN APGAR COMPONENT'S VALUE**

The user enters a value into one of the APGAR fields. The field's value is tested to see whether it equals 0, 1, or 2.

```
function APGAR(field) {
if(field.value==0 || field.value==1 || field.value==2) {
    var A=eval(document.REG.ACT.value);
    var P=eval(document.REG.PULSE.value);
    var G=eval(document.REG.GRIMACE.value);
    var AP=eval(document.REG.APP.value);
    var R=eval(document.REG.RESP.value);
    document.REG.TOTAL.value=A+P+G+AP+R;
} else {
    //alert the user
    field.focus();
}
}
```

```
function APGAR(field) {
if(field.value==0 || field.value==1 || field.value==2) {
    var A=eval(document.REG.ACT.value);
    var P=eval(document.REG.PULSE.value);
    var G=eval(document.REG.GRIMACE.value);
    var AP=eval(document.REG.APP.value);
    var R=eval(document.REG.RESP.value);
    document.REG.TOTAL.value=A+P+G+AP+R;
} else {
    //alert the user
    field.focus();
}
}
```

If the field's value is 0, 1, or 2, the total APGAR score is calculated.

```
function APGAR(field) {
if(field.value==0 || field.value==1 || field.value==2) {
    var A=eval(document.REG.ACT.value);
    var P=eval(document.REG.PULSE.value);
    var G=eval(document.REG.GRIMACE.value);
    var AP=eval(document.REG.APP.value);
    var R=eval(document.REG.RESP.value);
    document.REG.TOTAL.value=A+P+G+AP+R;
} else {
    //alert the user
    field.focus();
}
}
```

If the field's value is not 0, 1, or 2, the user is alerted and the cursor is returned to the field containing the error.

The new version of the APGAR() function has a single parameter, "field," which records which field called the function. Then the function tests whether the field value equals 0, 1, or 2 (remember that the || symbols represent the "or" logical operator). If this is the case, the function calculates the total APGAR score as before, and the user continues to the next field in the form. However, if the field's value is other than 0, 1, or 2, the function should alert the user that a mistake has been made and return the user to the field using the focus() method. The command for alerting the user is inserted as a comment at this point. In the next section, you'll learn how to create a dialog box that alerts the user to an error.

Now you need to revise the APGAR() function to include the new commands.

To revise the APGAR() function:

1. Locate the APGAR() function at the top of the Study.htm file.

2. Change the function line "function APGAR() {" to **function APGAR(field) {**.

3. Add the following two lines below the function statement as indicated in Figure 9-35 (indented three spaces to make the code easier to follow):

```
if(field.value==0 || field.value==1 || field.value==2) {
```

TROUBLE? The | symbol is often located above the \\ symbol on your keyboard. You can type it by pressing the \ key while holding down the Shift key.

4. Insert the following commands above the last line (the closing brace }) of the function (indented three spaces):

```
} else {
//alert the user
field.focus();
}
```

Figure 9-35 shows the entire function as it should appear in your text editor.

Figure 9-35 | THE REVISED APGAR() FUNCTION

```
function APGAR(field) {
if(field.value==0 || field.value==1 || field.value==2) {
   var A=eval(document.REG.ACT.value);
   var P=eval(document.REG.PULSE.value);
   var G=eval(document.REG.GRIMACE.value);
   var AP=eval(document.REG.APP.value);
   var R=eval(document.REG.RESP.value);
   document.REG.TOTAL.value=A+P+G+AP+R;
} else {
   //alert the user
   field.focus();
}
}
```

5. Save your changes to the Study.htm file.

Notifying the User with Alert and Confirm Dialog Boxes

If the user enters an incorrect value for one of the APGAR components, the form should display a dialog box informing the user of the error. To accomplish this, you can use the alert() method. The **alert() method** operates in the same way as the prompt() method, except that it does not provide an input box in which the user can type a response. Instead, it simply displays a dialog box containing a message. The syntax for the alert() method is:

```
alert("Message");
```

where *Message* is the message that will appear in the dialog box. An example of an alert dialog box is shown in Figure 9-36. Different browsers display slightly different dialog boxes.

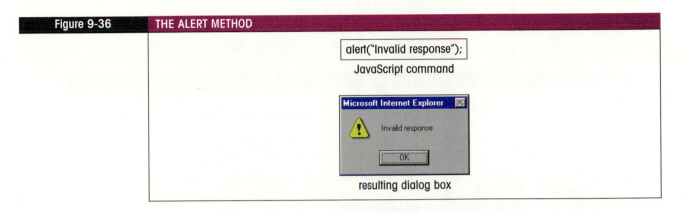

Figure 9-36   THE ALERT METHOD

JavaScript provides another method called the confirm() method, which works in the same way as the prompt() and alert() methods. The **confirm() method** displays a message in a dialog box that is similar to the alert dialog box, except that it includes both an OK button and a Cancel button. If the user clicks the OK button, the value "true" is returned. If the user clicks the Cancel button, the value "false" is returned. Figure 9-37 shows an example of using the confirm() method to create a dialog box. You would use the confirm() method in situations that require a simple "yes" (OK) or "no" (Cancel) response from the user.

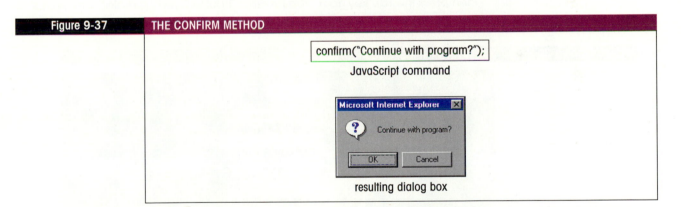

Figure 9-37   THE CONFIRM METHOD

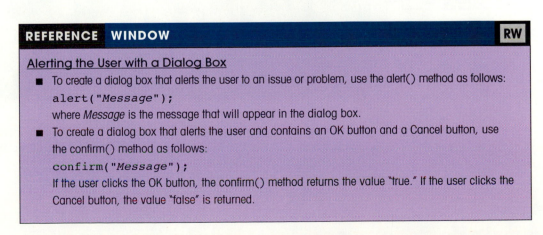

REFERENCE WINDOW   **RW**

Alerting the User with a Dialog Box
- To create a dialog box that alerts the user to an issue or problem, use the alert() method as follows:
  ```
  alert("Message");
  ```
  where *Message* is the message that will appear in the dialog box.
- To create a dialog box that alerts the user and contains an OK button and a Cancel button, use the confirm() method as follows:
  ```
  confirm("Message");
  ```
  If the user clicks the OK button, the confirm() method returns the value "true." If the user clicks the Cancel button, the value "false" is returned.

In your program, you need to use the alert() method. You'll replace the comment line in the APGAR() function with a command to alert the user that only values of 0, 1, and 2 are allowed.

To add the alert() method to the APGAR() function:

1. In the APGAR() function, replace the comment "//alert the user" with the following line of code:

   ```
   alert("You must enter a 0, 1, or 2");
   ```

   Figure 9-38 shows the final version of the APGAR() function.

Figure 9-38   **FINAL APGAR() FUNCTION**

```
function APGAR(field) {
if(field.value==0 || field.value==1 || field.value==2) {
    var A=eval(document.REG.ACT.value);
    var P=eval(document.REG.PULSE.value);
    var G=eval(document.REG.GRIMACE.value);
    var AP=eval(document.REG.APP.value);
    var R=eval(document.REG.RESP.value);
    document.REG.TOTAL.value=A+P+G+AP+R;
} else {
    alert("You must enter a 0, 1, or 2");
    field.focus();
}
}
```

alert the user that a mistake has been made →

2. Save your changes, and then reload the file in your Web browser.

   To test the revised APGAR() function, you'll enter an incorrect value in the Activity field.

3. Select the **Activity** input box, change its value from the default of 0 to **3**, and then press the **Tab** key. Your Web browser should display a dialog box similar to the one shown in Figure 9-39.

Figure 9-39   **ALERTING THE USER TO AN INVALID ENTRY**

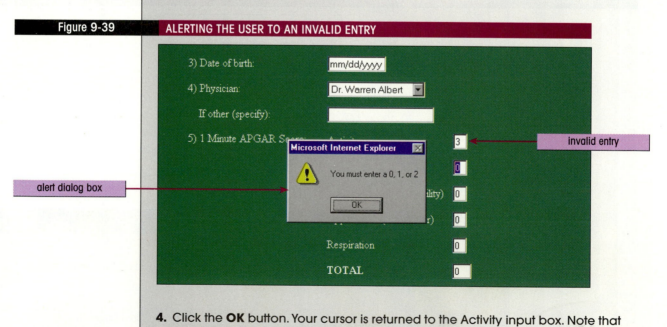

4. Click the **OK** button. Your cursor is returned to the Activity input box. Note that you cannot tab out of this box or click outside it without receiving the error message.

5. Change the value in the Activity input box to **2**, and then press the **Tab** key. The cursor advances to the Pulse input box.

6. Attempt to enter values greater than 2 in the other component input boxes, and verify that the alert dialog box opens when you do so.

You've finished modifying the necessary fields on the registration form. The next task on your list is to provide one final validity check before the form is submitted to a CGI script running on the hospital's Web server.

● 1) Automatically enter the current date in the FORMDATE field and move the cursor to the next field in the form.

● 2) If "Other" is selected from the Physician selection list box, prompt the user for the name of the physician; otherwise go to the APGAR component fields.

● 3) Automatically calculate the total APGAR score.

● 4) Check that valid APGAR component scores have been entered.

○ 5) Check that parental consent has been obtained before submitting the form.

Controlling Form Submission

Dr. Paulson wants the registration form to perform a validity check to determine whether or not a parental consent form has been filled out. This is indicated on the registration form by the Parental Consent check box. If the box is checked, then it is assumed that the consent form has been filled out. This validity check must be performed when the user tries to submit the form.

When a user completes a form and then clicks the Submit button, a Submit event is initiated. JavaScript provides the **onSubmit** event handler to allow you to run a program in response to this action. Because the Submit event is associated with the form object, you must place the event handler in the <FORM> tag, as shown in the following example:

```
<SCRIPT>
      function goodbye() {
      alert("Thank you for your time");
      }
</SCRIPT>

<FORM onSubmit="goodbye();">
```

In this example, the goodbye() function is run automatically when the user clicks the Submit button located elsewhere in the HTML file, and a dialog box with the message "Thank you for your time" appears. This is a simple example in which the function does not actually perform any validation; it just displays a message. When you need to validate the form or a particular field in it, the situation is a bit different.

The syntax for validating your form before submitting it, is:

```
<FORM onSubmit="return Function_Name();">
```

where *Function_Name* is the name of the function that is used to validate your form. The function must return a value of either "true" or "false." If the function's value is "true," the form will be submitted to the CGI script. If the value is "false," submission is canceled, and the user is returned to the form (presumably to correct the problem). Note the inclusion of the keyword "return" in this command. The **return** keyword forces the browser to apply the results of the validation function. If you do not include the return keyword, the browser will submit the form whether or not it passes the validation test.

For example, if you create a function named Check_Data() to validate your form, the correct version of the onSubmit event handler will be:

```
<FORM onSubmit="return Check_Data();">
```

and *not*:

```
<FORM onSubmit="Check_Data();">
```

With this in mind, you'll next add the onSubmit event handler to the <FORM> tag, using the function name Check_Data(). You haven't created this function yet, but you will do so in the next set of steps.

To add the Check_Data() function to the onSubmit event handler:

1. Return to the **Study.htm** file in your text editor and go to the <FORM> tag (located below the list of functions).

2. Within the <FORM> tag, insert the following command (see Figure 9-40):

```
onSubmit="return Check_Data();"
```

Figure 9-40	USING THE ONSUBMIT EVENT HANDLER

command runs when the form is submitted to the browser

```
<BODY BGCOLOR="#008080" TEXT=WHITE onload="StartForm();">
<FORM NAME=REG onSubmit="return Check_Data();">
<CENTER>
<IMG SRC="Logo.gif" WIDTH=450 HEIGHT=75 ALT="St. Marys of Northland Pines">
```

3. Save your changes to the file.

Now you need to create the Check_Data() function. The purpose of this function is to simply determine whether or not the Parental Consent check box has been checked. Some of the properties and methods associated with check boxes are shown in Figure 9-41.

Figure 9-41	PROPERTIES AND METHODS OF CHECK BOXES	
PROPERTY	**DESCRIPTION**	
checked	A Boolean value indicating whether or not the check box has been checked	
defaultChecked	A Boolean value indicating whether or not the check box is checked by default	
name	The name of the check box	
value	The value associated with the check box when it is checked	
METHOD	**DESCRIPTION**	
click()	Clicks the check box	
focus()	Makes the check box active	

You can tell whether a check box object has been checked by using the "checked" property. This property is a Boolean value: it will be either true or false. In Dr. Paulson's form, the Parental Consent check box has the field name CONSENT. So if,

```
document.REG.CONSENT.checked
```

equals "true," then the check box has been checked. If the property value is "false," the check box has been left unchecked and the form should not be submitted because no parental consent has been given.

The Check_Data() function will test which of these two conditions has occurred. If the check box has been selected, the function will alert the user that the form has been completed successfully and will return a value of "true." If the check box has not been selected, the function will alert the user of the problem and return a value of "false." The Check_Data() function appears as follows:

```
function Check_Data() {
    if(document.REG.CONSENT.checked==true) {
        alert("Form completed successfully");
        return true;
    } else {
        alert("You still need parental consent");
        return false;
    }
}
```

You'll add this function to the Study.htm file now.

To create the Check_Data() function:

1. Below the APGAR() function at the top of the Study.htm file, insert the following lines:

```
function Check_Data() {
    if(document.REG.CONSENT.checked==true) {
        alert("Form completed successfully");
        return true;
    } else {
        alert("You still need parental consent");
        return false;
    }
}
```

Figure 9-42 shows the new function as it appears in your file.

Figure 9-42 **CREATING THE CHECK_DATA() FUNCTION**

```
function Check_Data() {
    if(document.REG.CONSENT.checked==true) {
        alert("Form completed successfully");
        return true;
    } else {
        alert("You still need parental consent");
        return false;
    }
}


//Stop hiding -->
</SCRIPT>
</HEAD>

<BODY BGCOLOR="#008080" TEXT=WHITE onload="StartForm();">
<FORM NAME=REG onSubmit="return Check_Data();">
<CENTER>
<IMG SRC="Logo.gif" WIDTH=450 HEIGHT=75 ALT="St. Marys of Northland Pines">
```

2. Save your changes to Study.htm, and then reload the file in your Web browser.

Now you can test the Check_Data() function by trying to submit the form without first checking the Parental Consent check box.

3. Click the **Register** button on the form. Your browser displays the dialog box shown in Figure 9-43, indicating that you still need to get parental consent.

Figure 9-43 **A FORM IS REJECTED BECAUSE OF LACK OF PARENTAL CONSENT**

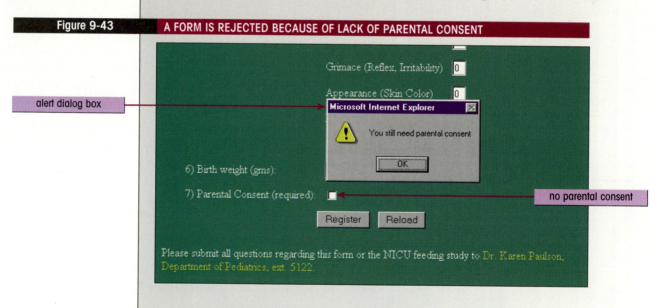

4. Click the **OK** button to return to the form.

5. Click the **Parental Consent** check box, and then click the **Register** button again.

Your browser displays a dialog box indicating that the form has been successfully completed. See Figure 9-44.

Figure 9-44   **A VALID FORM IS SUBMITTED**

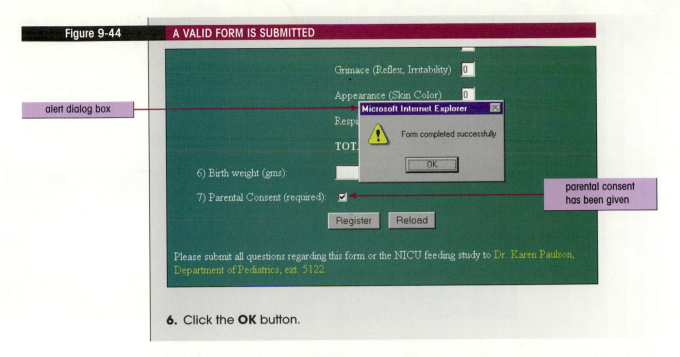

6. Click the OK button.

In a more advanced version of this page, you might add other validation criteria to the Check_Data() function. For example, you might check whether or not a name and medical record number have been entered for the patient. You might double-check the values of each APGAR component to verify that they are still valid, and so forth. In that case, the Check_Data() function would include several If…Else conditions. However, this example gives you an idea of how a final validation check would work. You've completed the tasks on your list for Dr. Paulson's registration form.

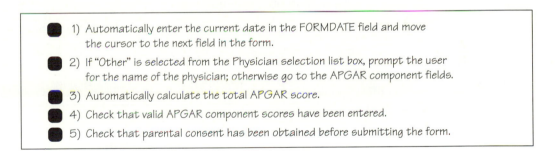

1) Automatically enter the current date in the FORMDATE field and move the cursor to the next field in the form.

2) If "Other" is selected from the Physician selection list box, prompt the user for the name of the physician; otherwise go to the APGAR component fields.

3) Automatically calculate the total APGAR score.

4) Check that valid APGAR component scores have been entered.

5) Check that parental consent has been obtained before submitting the form.

Reloading a Page with the Location Object

There is one more issue to consider with the registration form. A user who wants to reset the form can press the Reload button located next to the Register button. The Reload button resets all of the all fields in the form to their default values. Is this what Dr. Paulson wants? Not exactly; recall that the first action this form takes is to insert the current date into the FORMDATE field. This action runs whenever the page is loaded. Unfortunately, resetting a form is not the same as reloading the page. The date value would not be entered automatically if you simply reset the form. Instead, your form should actually be reloaded, an action which includes the onLoad event, which runs the StartForm() function, which in turn inserts the current date in the form.

To reload a page, you use the location object. The **location object** indicates the location of the page in the browser. To reload the page, use the reload() method:

```
location.reload();
```

You also can use JavaScript to access a page in a different location. The following command:

```
location=URL
```

will cause the browser to load a Web page with the address, *URL*.

REFERENCE WINDOW   **RW**

Loading a Web Page

- To load a Web page in your browser, use the JavaScript command:
  ```
  location = URL
  ```
  where *URL* is the address of the Web page you want to load.
- To reload the current page in your Web browser, use the command:
  ```
  location = location.reload();
  ```

Because the command for reloading a page is a single-line command, you can enter it directly into the <INPUT> tag for the Reload button. The command should be activated whenever the button is clicked, so you'll use the onClick event handler in the tag.

To insert the command to reload the page:

1. Return to the Study.htm file in your text editor, and go to the <INPUT> tag for the Reload button at the bottom of the form. This tag is located in the section "Form registration and reset buttons."

2. Insert the following command into the <INPUT> tag (see Figure 9-45):

```
onClick="location.reload();"
```

Figure 9-45   **RELOADING THE PAGE WITH THE LOCATION OBJECT**

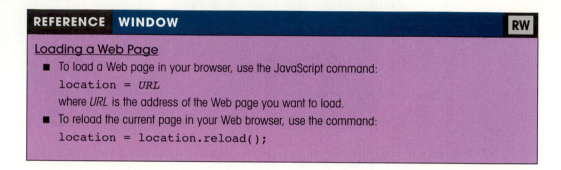

```
<!--- Form registration and reset buttons --->
<TR>
   <TD COLSPAN=3 ALIGN=CENTER>
      <INPUT TYPE=SUBMIT VALUE="Register">  
      <INPUT TYPE=RESET VALUE="Reload" onClick="location.reload();">
   </TD>
</TR>
</TABLE>
</CENTER>
```

page is reloaded when the Reload button is clicked

3. Save your changes to the Study.htm file, and then reopen the file in your Web browser.

4. Enter some text in the form, and then click the **Reload** button at the bottom of the form. Verify that the page reloads properly: all the fields should be reset to their default values, the current date should be inserted into the FORMDATE field, and the cursor should be in the First Name input box.

5. Close your Web browser and your text editor.

DESIGN	WINDOW	DW

Form Validation Tips

- Include informative labels for your input fields so that users know ahead of time what values are appropriate to enter in each field.
- Use check boxes, selection lists, and radio buttons as often as possible, rather than text input boxes, to control which values the users are allowed to enter.
- Create JavaScript functions that test values entered into your input boxes. If a value should be entered only within a defined range, create a function that rejects values outside that range.
- Make sure that any alert or prompt dialog boxes you create are clear and precise, informing the user exactly of the error that was made and what should be done to fix it.
- Perform a second validation at the time the form is submitted to confirm that appropriate data values have been entered in all fields.

You give the Study.htm file to Dr. Paulson for her evaluation. She will take the Web page you created and place it on the hospital's Web server. Before making it available to her clinical study, she'll test it to verify that the form validation commands you inserted work properly and that the form correctly places data into the hospital database via a CGI script running on the Web server. Dr. Paulson will get back to you with any changes she would like you to make.

Session 9.3 QUICK CHECK

1. Why must you use the eval() function when adding input box values together?

2. If the input field WEIGHT in the STUDY form contains the value 50, and the WEIGHT2 input field contains the value 25, what text will be returned by the following expression?

   ```
   document.STUDY.WEIGHT.value + document.STUDY.WEIGHT2.value;
   ```

3. What is the "this" keyword used for?

4. What command will create a dialog box containing the message "Weight Invalid" and an OK button?

5. What command will create a dialog box containing the message "Accept weight value?" along with an OK button and a Cancel button?

6. What should you add to the following tag so that it runs the form validation function CheckIt() when the user clicks the Submit button?

   ```
   <FORM NAME=STUDY>
   ```

7. In Quick Check 6, what must the CheckIt() function return for it to prohibit invalid forms from being submitted to a CGI script?

8. What JavaScript command would you use to load the Web page "http://www.StMarysNP.com"?

REVIEW ASSIGNMENTS

After reviewing your form, Dr. Paulson made a few changes to it. She also has some additional modifications she wants you to make. The following is the list of changes and additions Dr. Paulson would like you to complete:

- Revise the APGAR function so that if the current field is the Respiration input box, the function will jump past the APGAR TOTAL input box to the Birth Weight input box. This will help prevent users from inadvertently entering data into the APGAR TOTAL input box, thereby undoing the calculation performed by the APGAR() function you created.

- Dr. Paulson does not want to include newborns whose birth weight is less than 1200 grams. The form should alert users of this whenever a birth weight of less than 1200 grams is entered in the BWGT field.

- Revise the form so that it prohibits the user from submitting the form if parental consent has not been given or if an infant has a birth weight of less than 1200 grams.

To revise Dr. Paulson's form:

1. Start your text editor and open the Studtxt2.htm file in the Review subfolder of the Tutorial.09 folder on your Data Disk, and then save the file as Study2.htm in the same folder.

Explore 2. Go to the APGAR() function. Below the line that calculates the total APGAR score, insert an If command block that tests whether or not the name of the current field is equal to RESP. If so, it should set the focus to the BWGT field. (*Hint*: Use the name property of the field.)

3. Revise the BWGT field so that the CheckWgt() function is run whenever the cursor leaves the field.

4. Create the CheckWgt() function, inserting it between the APGAR() and CheckData() functions in the HEAD section of the document.

5. In the CheckWgt() function, create a variable named "wgt" that stores the value of the BWGT field. If the wgt variable is less than 1200, display an alert dialog box with the message "Patients with birth weights less than 1200 grams are ineligible for participation in this study."

6. Go to the <FORM> tag and insert an event handler that will return the value of the CheckData() function when the form is submitted.

Explore 7. Go to the CheckData() function. Using what you know about JavaScript commands, provide a line-by-line interpretation of the function, indicating on a separate piece of paper what each command does and what the overall result of the function is.

8. Save your changes to the file.

9. Load Study2.htm in your Web browser. Verify that pressing the Tab key in the Respiration field jumps you past the APGAR TOTAL field.

10. Try to submit the form under the following conditions:
    - birth weight = 1000 grams/parental consent
    - birth weight = 1800 grams/no parental consent
    - birth weight = 1200 grams/parental consent

What happens under each condition? Write your answers on the same paper you used for Question 7.

11. Print a copy of your HTML and JavaScript code.

12. Close your Web browser and your text editor.

CASE PROBLEMS

Case 1. Creating an Online Order Form for UB Computing UB Computing is one of the leading manufacturers of PCs in the United States. Originally a mail-order company, UB Computing has recently created a Web site where customers can purchase its products. Dale Crawford, the supervisor of Web sales, has asked you to work on a Web page order form for the PS500 computer, a PC marketed to small businesses.

Customers can select different options for processor speed, memory, hard disk size, and monitor size. They also can add additional components such as modems and network cards. Because of this, the order form has to calculate the total cost of the PS500 under each possible configuration. The configuration options and their costs are shown in Figure 9-46.

Figure 9-46

Base Price of PS500 system = $2300
Initial configuration: 500 MHz CPU, 12 GB hard drive, 64 MB memory, 15" monitor

Other Configurations

CPU	650 MHz (add $400)
Hard drive	21 GB (add $300)
Memory	32 MB (subtract $50); 96 MB (add $100); 128 MB (add $150)
Monitor	17" (add $300); 19" (add $400); 21" (add $700)
Modem	add $75
Network card	add $75

Dale gives you a Web page with the order form already created, as shown in Figure 9-47. Your job is to create a JavaScript function named TotalCost() that will calculate the total cost based on what the user has selected in the order form. The function will run whenever the user clicks the Calculate Total button at the bottom of the order form.

Figure 9-47

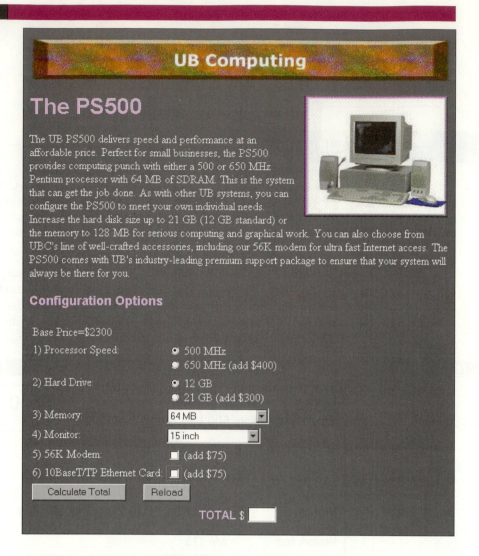

To create the UB Computing order form:

1. Start your text editor and open the file PSText.htm in the Cases subfolder of the Tutorial.09 folder on your Data Disk, and then save the file as PS500.htm in the same folder.

2. Within the <SCRIPT> tags at the top of the PS500.htm file, create the function TotalCost() (no parameters are needed).

   Within the TotalCost() function, write JavaScript commands to perform the actions listed in Steps 3 through 11.

3. Declare the following variables with the indicated initial values:

   - CPUCost (the initial cost of the CPU) set to 0 *— if not selected initialized to 0*
   - HDCost (the initial cost of the hard drive) set to 0
   - MEMCost (the initial cost of the computer memory) set to 0
   - MONCost (the initial cost of the monitor) set to 0
   - MODEMCost (the initial cost of the modem) set to 0
   - ECARDCost (the initial cost of the Ethernet card) set to 0
   - BASE (the base price of the system) set to 2300

Explore

4. Individual radio buttons in the CPU field of the ORDER form are referred to using the following object property references:

   - document.ORDER.CPU[0] for the first radio button (500 MHz CPU)
   - document.ORDER.CPU[1] for the second radio button (650 MHz CPU)

   Use an If statement to determine whether the second radio button has been checked. (*Hint*: Use the checked property.) If the second radio button has been checked, change the value of CPUCost to 400.

Explore

5. Determine which Hard Drive radio button the user has selected in the form, usng the same techniques you used in Step 4. If the user has selected the second button (corresponding to a 21 GB hard drive), increase the value of the HDCost variable to 300.

6. Create a variable named MEMIndex that contains the index value of the selected option from the Memory selection list.

7. Set the value of the MEMCost variable to the value of the selected option. (*Hint*: The value of the selected option is equal to:

   eval(document.ORDER.MEM.options[MEMIndex].value)

8. Create a variable named MONIndex that contains the index value of the option selected from the Monitor selection list, and then use the same techniques you employed in Step 7 to set the value of the MONCost variable to the value of the selected option.

9. Determine whether or not the Modem check box has been selected; if so, change the value of the MODEMCost variable to 75.

10. Determine whether or not the Ethernet Card check box has been selected; if so, change the value of the ECARDCost variable to 75.

11. Set the value of the Total input box to the sum of each of the six configuration variables (CPUCost, HDCost, MemCost, MonCost, MODEMCost, ECARDCost) plus the value of the BASE variable.

12. Add an event handler to the Calculate Total button so that it runs the TotalCost() function when clicked.

13. Add an event handler to the Reload button so that it reloads the Web page when clicked.

14. Save and print the PS500.htm file.

15. Load the page in your Web browser and print the Web page for each of the following configurations:

    - CPU = 650 MHz, hard drive = 21 GB, memory = 64 MB, monitor = 15", 56K modem
    - CPU = 500 MHz, hard drive = 12 GB, memory = 96 MB, monitor = 19", 56K modem, Ethernet card
    - CPU = 650 MHz, hard drive = 21 GB, memory = 128 MB, monitor = 21", Ethernet card

16. Close your Web browser and your text editor.

Case 2. Creating a Hyperlink Selection List for the Monroe Public Library The Monroe Public Library has added Web access for its patrons. To make it easier for new users to access particular pages, the library has employed you to create custom Web pages for different topics. One of these pages contains links to various government Web sites.

Because there are so many hyperlinks, your supervisor, Denise Kruschev, thinks the best approach is for the list of hyperlinks to be contained within selection list boxes. Denise envisions users clicking a site within a selection list, which would then open up the Web page automatically.

Denise has already created the Web page shown in Figure 9-48. Now you have to use JavaScript to open up the Web pages indicated by the options in the selection lists.

Figure 9-48

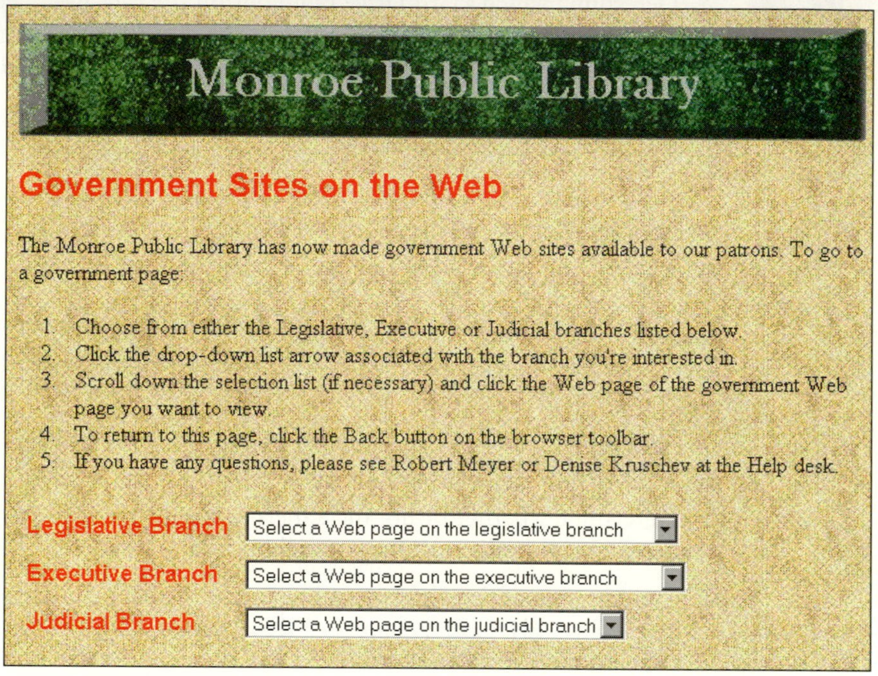

To finish the Monroe Public Library government Web page:

1. Start your text editor and open the file **MPLtext.htm** in the Cases subfolder of the Tutorial.09 folder on your Data Disk, and then save the file as MPL.htm in the same folder.

2. Scroll through the MPL.htm file. Note that the values of the selection options are all URLs, and that the text in the selection list consists of descriptions of the Web pages.

Explore ▶ 3. In the <SELECT> tag for each of the three selection lists, insert an event handler that will run the function JumpToLink(this) whenever the value of the selection list changes.

4. Within the HEAD section of the MPL.htm file, create a JavaScript function named JumpToLink(WebList).

5. Create a variable in the JumpToLink function named URLNumber, and then set the variable equal to the value of the selectedIndex property of the WebList parameter. This variable will contain the index number of the selected option from the WebList field.

Explore ▶ 6. Set the location object equal to the value of the selected option in WebList field. (*Hint*: The selected option has the object name, WebList.options[URLNumber].)

7. Save and print the MPL.htm file.

8. Open the MPL.htm file in your Web browser. Click the "Department of Education" option in the Executive Branch selection list, and verify that the appropriate Web page is loaded in your browser.

9. Close your Web browser and your text editor.

Case 3. Creating a Color Picker for WebWorld Graphics You work as a Web author at WebWorld Graphics. You want to create a simple Web page that will allow you to compare various color values for text and background colors. You decide to use JavaScript to create a Color Picker Web page. Assume that you've already created the form for the page, as shown in Figure 9-49. The form includes input boxes in which you'll place the hexadecimal color values for the red, green, and blue components for the background and foreground colors.

Figure 9-49

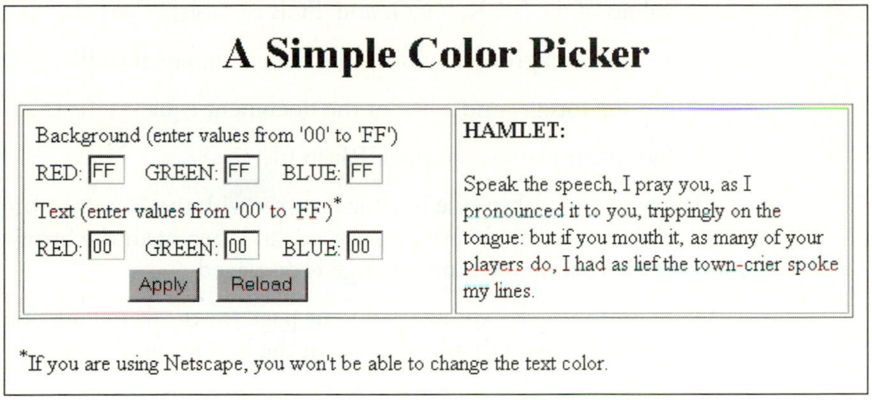

Your task is to create a JavaScript function that takes those values, combines them, and applies them to the page's background and foreground (text) colors. Remember that you cannot use Netscape to change the text colors of a page already loaded by the browser, so you should also add a JavaScript function to test what kind of browser is using the page. If the browser is Netscape, the browser should display a warning message.

To create the Color Picker Web page:

1. Start your text editor and open the file CPtext.htm in the Cases subfolder of the Tutorial.09 folder on your Data Disk, and then save the file as CP.htm in the same folder.

2. Add to the <BODY> tag an onLoad event handler that runs the test_browser() function when the page is first loaded by the browser.

Explore

3. Create the test_browser() function in the HEAD section of the file (remember to include the <SCRIPT> tags). Have the function test whether the browser is Netscape. If it is, display an alert dialog box with the message, "Netscape users can change only the background color." (*Hint*: Use the navigator.appName property to determine the browser type.)

4. Go to the tag for the Apply button at the bottom of the form and insert an event handler that will run the ApplyColor() function when this button is clicked.

5. Insert an event handler in the tag for the Reload button that will reload the Web page when this button is clicked.

6. Create the function ApplyColor() in the HEAD section of the CP.htm file. Do not include any parameters for the function.

Apply the instructions in Steps 7 through 11 to the ApplyColor() function.

7. Create the following variables with the following values:

   - BCR equal to the value of the BackRed input box
   - BCG equal to the value of the BackGreen input box
   - BCB equal to the value of the BackBlue input box
   - TCR equal to the value of the TextRed input box
   - TCG equal to the value of the TextGreen input box
   - TCB equal to the value of the TextBlue input box

8. Create a variable named BackColor equal to the pound symbol (#) combined with the values of the BCR, BCG, and BCB variables.

9. Create a variable named TextColor equal to the pound symbol (#) combined with the values of the TCR, TCG, and TCB variables.

10. Set the background color of the document equal to BackColor.

11. Set the foreground color of the document equal to TextColor.

12. Save your changes to the CP.htm file.

13. Open the CP.htm file in your browser with the Netscape browser (if available) and verify that the warning message is issued, and then open the browser in Internet Explorer and verify that no warning message is displayed.

14. With Internet Explorer test your page for the following color combinations (Netscape users can test only the changes in the background color).

    - Background = "#CC33CC" Text="#FFFFFF"
    - Background = "#3300CC" Text ="#FFCCCC"
    - Background = "#333300" Text = "#FFFFCC"

15. Click the Reload button and verify that it reloads your Web page and resets the colors to your browser's default values.

16. Print your HTML code, and then close your Web browser and your text editor.

Case 4. Creating a Mortgage Calculator for Frontier Savings and Loan The mortgage finance officers at Frontier Savings and Loan have asked you to create a mortgage calculator that customers can use to estimate monthly payments for various mortgage amounts. Your manager, Lisa Drummond, explains that the page should contain a form in which the customer enters the loan amount, the number of monthly payments, and the yearly interest rate, and then clicks a button to see what the monthly payment and total payments for the loan would be. You need JavaScript to accomplish this task. A function named Monthly(), which is used to calculate the monthly payment, is shown below:

```
function Monthly(I, N, S) {
      // I = yearly interest rate;
      // N = number of monthly payments;
      // S = loan amount;
return (S*I/12*Math.pow(I/12+1,N))/(Math.pow(I/12+1,N)-1);
}
```

The Monthly() function takes three parameter values: the yearly interest rate (I), the total number of monthly payments (N), and the amount of the loan (S). With these parameters the function returns the value of the monthly payment needed to pay off the loan.

Note that this function uses the Math.pow() method, which calculates the value of a base value raised to an exponent; for example:

```
Math.pow(a, n) = a^n
```

Once you know the value of the monthly payment, the total amount paid is simply the monthly payment multiplied by the total number of payments. Using the Monthly() function, you'll complete the rest of the Web page for Frontier Savings and Loan.

To create the mortgage calculator Web page:

1. Start your text editor and create a file named Mortgage.htm in the Cases subfolder of the Tutorial.09 folder on your Data Disk.

2. Create a form that contains the following fields (the layout of the form is up to you):

   - Five input fields used for the loan amount, yearly interest rate, number of payments, monthly payment amount, and total payment.
   - Two buttons: one labeled Calculate (used to calculate the monthly and total payments) and the other labeled Reset (used to reset the form).

3. Within the HEAD section of the Mortgage.htm file, insert the Monthly() function shown earlier.

4. Create a function named ShowVal() that extracts the values in the interest rate, number of payments, and loan amount fields and calls the Monthly() function with those values to determine the monthly payment. (*Hint*: Don't forget to use the "eval" function when extracting field values.) Use the results of the Monthly() function to determine the total amount of payments to the bank. Place the results of your two calculations in the appropriate fields on your form.

5. Add an event handler to the Calculate button that runs the ShowVal() function when this button is clicked.

6. The Monthly() function requires that the interest rate be a number between 0 and 1. Create a function named CheckInterest() that checks to see if the interest rate is greater than 0 and less than 1. If it is not, the CheckInterest() function should display a message to the user and return the user to the interest rate field.

7. Add an event handler to the interest rate field that calls the CheckInterest() function whenever the user leaves the field.

8. At the top of the Web page, before the calculator, insert the <H2> heading "Mortgage Calculator" along with a paragraph describing the purpose of the Web page and how to use the calculator you created.

9. Save your changes to Mortgage.htm, and then print the HTML code and JavaScript commands you created.

10. Open the Mortgage.htm file in your Web browser. Test your mortgage calculator with the following values, and print the resulting Web pages:

    - loan = 100000, interest rate = 0.085, number of payments = 300
    - loan = 100000, interest rate = 0.10, number of payments = 300
    - loan = 100000, interest rate = 0.085, number of payments = 360

11. Close your Web browser and your text editor.

QUICK CHECK ANSWERS

Session 9.1

1. In server-side validation, the user input is checked on the Web server, usually via a cgi script. In client-side validation, user input is checked within the Web browser on the user's computer.

2. Objects are items that exist in a defined space such as the Web page, Web browser, form, or table. Properties describe an object's appearance, purpose, or behavior. Methods are actions that can be performed with an object or to an object.

3. `document.ENROLL.JOIN;`

4. `document.fgColor="blue";`

5. `document.fgColor=tcolor;`

6. `document.ENROLL.reset();`

Session 9.2

1. An event is a specific action that triggers the browser to run a block of JavaScript commands. An event handler is code added to an HTML tag that is run whenever a particular event occurs. An event method is a method applied to a JavaScript object that emulates the occurrence of an event.

2. Edit the <BODY> tag to read: `<BODY onLoad="Welcome();">`

3. `<INPUT NAME=CreditNumber onBlur="CheckCredit();">`

4. `document.PRODUCT.MODEL.options[0].value=P250;`

5. `document.PRODUCT.MODEL.options[0].text="Pentium 250";`

6. `var ModelNumber = document.PRODUCT.MODEL.selectedIndex;`

7. `prompt("Enter a new model");`

Session 9.3

1. Input box values are stored as text strings; you must use the eval function to convert the text string into a number.

2. 5025

3. To refer to the currently selected object

4. `alert("Weight Invalid");`

5. `confirm("Accept weight value?");`

6. `<FORM NAME=STUDY onSubmit="return CheckIt();">`

7. A Boolean value, either true or false

8. `location="http://www.StMarysNP.com";`

OBJECTIVES

In this tutorial you will:

- Work with external and embedded multimedia files

- Learn about the principles of sound and video clips

- Work with the <EMBED> tag to enhance a Web page with sound and video

- Provide tags for browsers that do not support embedded objects

- Learn how to create a background sound with Internet Explorer

- Use the <APPLET> tag to add a Java applet to a Web page

- Create a scrolling marquee with the <MARQUEE> tag

LAB

Multimedia

CREATING A MULTIMEDIA WEB PAGE

Enhancing a Page with Sound, Video, and Java Applets

CASE

The Mount Rainier Newsletter

Mount Rainier dominates the skyline of the state of Washington, and Mount Rainier National Park is a popular vacation spot for travelers to the Northwest. The park publishes a monthly newsletter, *Mount Rainier News*, which is handed out to visitors at each entrance gate. The newsletter contains information on upcoming events, tips on park trails and enjoying nature, and information on campsites and lodging. In recent years, the newsletter has also been published on the World Wide Web so travelers can receive park news before they arrive. The Web page contains all the information available in the printed version, as well as links to other sites on the Web about Mount Rainier and the surrounding communities of Sunrise, Longmire, and Paradise.

Tom Bennett, the supervisor of *Mount Rainier News*, has been looking at other newsletter sites on the Web and has noticed how multimedia elements like sound, video, and animation, have been used to add interest and information to those pages. Tom has asked you to add these elements to the *Mount Rainier News* Web page to make it more appealing. The current page features stories on an upcoming folk festival and a new attraction at the Paradise visitors' center. Tom would like you to locate sound and video clips that can be used to enhance those stories.

SESSION 10.1

In this session after you learn about the properties of external and embedded media, you'll learn how to add sounds to a Web page. You'll examine how sound waves can be saved in a sound file, and you'll learn how to reduce the size of a sound file. You'll create a hyperlink to a sound clip and also embed the sound clip within a Web page. Finally, you'll see how Internet Explorer allows you to specify a background sound for your Web page.

Working with Multimedia

One of the most popular and useful features of the World Wide Web is the ability to transfer information through the use of sound and video. In creating Web pages that feature these elements, you have to consider several factors, not the least of which is the issue of bandwidth. **Bandwidth** is a measure of the amount of data that can be sent through a communications circuit each second. Bandwidth values range from slow connections—such as phone lines, which transfer data at a rate of 58.6 kbps—to high-speed direct network connections capable of transferring data at several megabytes per second. Large sound and video files cause the most trouble for users with low-bandwidth connections. One of the goals when using multimedia is to create media clips that are compact in size without sacrificing quality.

As shown in Figure 10-1, multimedia can be added to a Web page in one of two ways: as external media or inline media. With **external media**, the sound or video file is accessed through a hyperlink. **Inline media** clips are placed into the Web page itself as embedded objects. The advantage of using an external file is that the users can retrieve the multimedia clip only if they want to. This is useful in situations in which the user has a low-bandwidth connection and wants the choice of whether or not to take the time to download a large multimedia file. An embedded media clip works like an inline image and can be played within the Web page itself. Because the clip appears within the Web page, you can supplement it with other material on the page. For example, descriptive text can appear alongside an embedded video clip. The downside of inline media is that the user is forced to wait for the clip to be retrieved by the browser. If the user has a low-bandwidth connection, this could be a long wait.

| Figure 10-1 | INLINE AND EXTERNAL MEDIA |

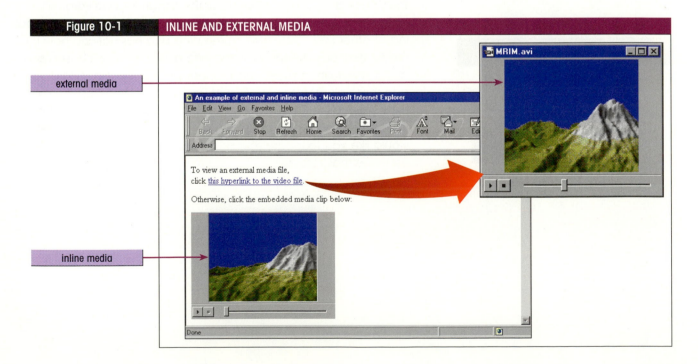

You ask Tom whether he wants to use inline or external media with the *Mount Rainier News* Web page. Tom tells you to create two versions of the page, one using each method. One page, which you'll name Rainier.htm, will use external media and will be posted on the Web server for users with low-bandwidth Internet connections, such as phone lines. The second page, Rainier2.htm, will be made available to users at the park headquarters; since this page will be accessed directly with a high-speed connection, it will use inline media.

The version of the newsletter that you'll be working with is shown in Figure 10-2. In addition to a table of links to other Web sites, the page contains three news articles. One is the current weather forecast, located at the top of the page. The second is an article about the upcoming folk festival at Sunrise. The third article describes MRIM, the Mount Rainier Interactive Map, recently installed at the Paradise visitors' center.

Figure 10-2   THE *MOUNT RAINIER NEWS* WEB PAGE

CLICK TO VIEW TODAY'S WEATHER FORECAST
TODAY...Partly sunny.
TONIGHT...Partly cloudy. Showers with snow level lowering to 4000.

Autumn Folk Festival

From September 10th - 12th, come to Sunrise for the annual autumn folk festival. The Sunrise Festival is quickly becoming one of the Northwest's top folk events, with its intimate performances from world-famous troubadours. Camping spots are still available at Sunrise campground, but they're going fast.

In addition to the intimate song sharing in the campground every evening during the festival, there'll be workshops, great food and craft vendors. Call Maria Thompson at 555-9011 for camping information. Call Ted Cashman (555-8122) to sign up for one of the workshops.

Folk singers, Joan Adams and Shannon Davis

Other Web Pages

About Mount Rainier

Mt. Rainier Natn'l Park
Mt. Rainier Associates
Visitor Centers
Campgrounds
Picnic Areas
Food & Lodging
Climbing Information
Winter Recreation

Visiting the Park

Longmire
Paradise
Ohanapecosh
Sunrise
Mowich Lake

Current News

Weather Forecast
Road Conditions
Trail Conditions

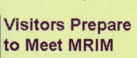

Visitors Prepare to Meet MRIM

Want to see what it's like to hover over Columbia Crest at 14,400 feet, or ski down the Ingraham Glacier without fear of falling? Then visit **MRIM**, the Mount Rainier Interactive Map now available at the Paradise visitors' center.

MRIM uses state-of-the-art computer animation combined with data from geological satellites to help you explore places you might never visit on foot. The results of your journey are displayed on a large screen monitor - perfect for group presentations or individual explorations. Contact Doug LeCourt at Paradise for more information.

Your first task is to add a sound clip to the article on the Sunrise Folk Festival. Before doing that, you need to learn a little more about sound files.

Understanding Sound Files

In order to work with sound clips, it is helpful to understand some of the issues involved in converting a sound from an analog form to a digital form suitable for saving as a sound file. Consider the simple sound wave shown in Figure 10-3. There are two components to the sound wave: amplitude and frequency. The **amplitude** is the height of the sound wave, and it relates to the loudness of the sound—the higher the amplitude, the louder the sound. The **frequency** is the speed at which the sound wave moves, and it relates to the sound pitch. Sounds with high frequency have higher pitches.

Figure 10-3	A SIMPLE SOUND WAVE

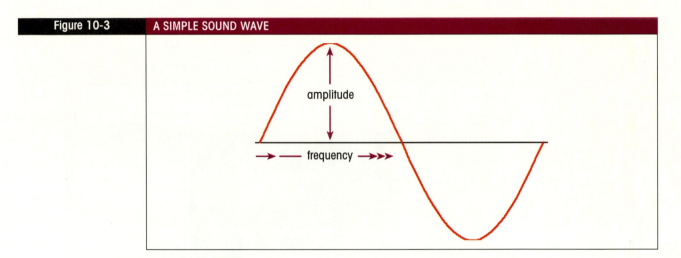

Sampling Rate and Sample Resolution

A sound wave is a continuous function. To convert it to a form that can be stored in a sound file, your computer must record measurements of the sound at discrete moments in time. Each measurement is called a **sample**. The number of samples taken per second is called the **sampling rate**. Sampling rate is measured in kilohertz (KHz). The most commonly used sampling rates are 11 KHz, 22 KHz, and 44 KHz. A higher sampling rate means that more samples are taken per second, resulting in a sound that more closely matches the original sound wave. See Figure 10-4. The tradeoff in increasing the sampling rate is that it increases the size of the sound file.

Figure 10-4   **APPROXIMATING A SOUND WAVE WITH DIFFERENT SAMPLING RATES**

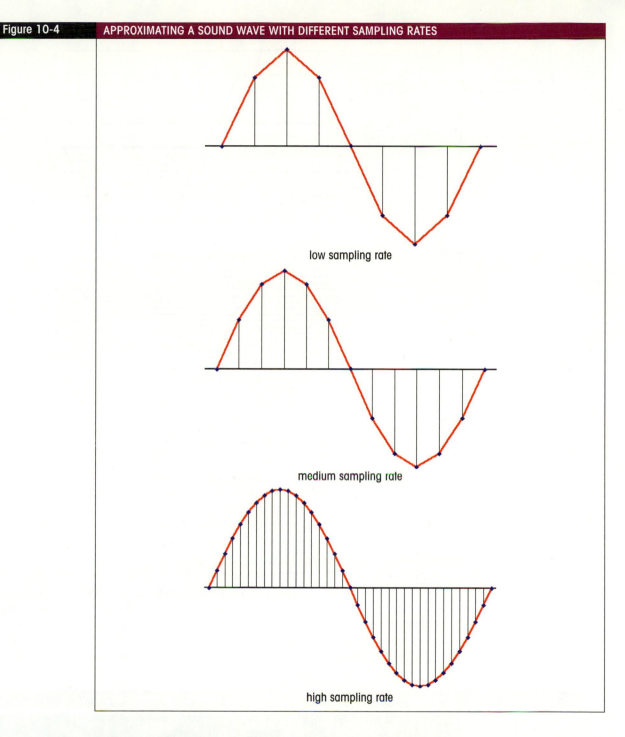

low sampling rate

medium sampling rate

high sampling rate

A second factor in converting a sound to digital form is the sample resolution. **Sample resolution** indicates the precision in measuring the sound within each sample. There are two sample resolution values, 8-bit and 16-bit. As shown in Figure 10-5, increasing the resolution creates a sound file that represents the sound wave in greater detail. However, a 16-bit sound file is twice the size of an 8-bit sound file. Generally, you should save your files at the 16-bit resolution because the improved sound quality is worth the increased file size.

Figure 10-5 | **APPROXIMATING A SOUND WAVE AT DIFFERENT SAMPLE RESOLUTIONS**

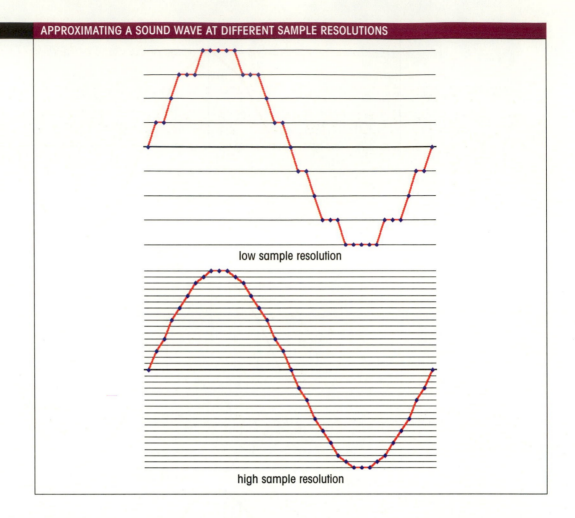

low sample resolution

high sample resolution

A final choice you'll have to make with your sound files is determining the number of channels to use. The choice is typically between using stereo or monaural (mono) sound, although in some situations you may want to add extra channels. Stereo provides a richer sound, but at the expense of approximately doubling the size of the sound file over mono.

Figure 10-6 shows how sampling rate, sample resolution, and channel size relate to sound quality in terms of everyday objects. Your telephone provides the poorest sound quality, and this is a reflection of the low sampling rate and sample resolution as well as the monaural sound. A CD player provides much higher sound quality at a higher sampling rate and sample resolution. The CD player also supports stereo sound (and in some cases additional sound channels).

Figure 10-6 | **SAMPLING RATE AND SAMPLE RESOLUTION AS RELATED TO SOUND QUALITY**

SAMPLING RATE AND SAMPLE RESOLUTION	SOUND QUALITY
8 KHz, 8-bit, mono	Telephone
22 KHz, 16-bit, stereo	Radio
44 KHz, 16-bit, stereo	CD

If you want to create a sound file, you will need a computer with a sound card, speakers, a microphone, and sound-editing software. There are several sound editors available on the Web.

In addition to modifying the sampling rate, sample resolution, and number of channels, these sound editors also allow you to add special sound effects, remove noise, and copy and paste sounds between files. Figure 10-7 lists some of the sound editors you can access on the Web.

Figure 10-7	SOUND EDITING SOFTWARE ON THE WEB	
TITLE	**URL**	**DESCRIPTION**
CoolEdit	http://www.syntrillium.com	Sound editing software for Windows
Shareware Music Machine	http://www.hitsquad.com/smm/	Links to audio software on the Web
Sonic Control	http://www.soniccontrol.com/	Links to audio software on the Web
The Sonic Spot	http://www.sonicspot.com	Links to audio software on the Web

Sound File Formats

Several different competing sound formats are in use on the Web. The various formats are used by different operating systems and provide varying levels of sound quality and **sound compression** (the ability to reduce the size of the sound file). Figure 10-8 lists some of the common sound file formats that might be used for the Sunrise Folk Festival sound clip.

Figure 10-8	SOUND FILE FORMATS
FORMAT	**DESCRIPTION**
AIFF/AIFC	Audio Interchange File Format. Sound files with this format usually have an .aiff or .aif filename extension. AIFF was developed by Apple for use on the Macintosh operating system. AIFF sound files can be either 8 bit or 16 bit, can be mono or stereo, and can be recorded at several different sampling rates.
AU	Also called μlaw (mu-law) format. Sound files with this format usually have an .au filename extension. One of the oldest sound formats, it is primarily used on UNIX workstations. AU sound files have 8-bit sample resolutions, use a sampling rate of 8 KHz, and are recorded in mono.
MIDI	Musical Digital Interface. MIDI files cannot be used for general sound recording like other sound formats, but are limited to synthesizers and music files. The MIDI format represents sound by recording each note's pitch, length, and volume. MIDI files tend to be much smaller in size than other sound formats.
MPEG	Moving Pictures Expert Group. A format primarily used for video clips, though occasionally MPEGS are used for audio files. MPEG files are usually small due to the MPEG file compression algorithm. Because of their small size, MPEGs are most often used for transferring whole music recordings. The most recent MPEG standard is MP3.
RealAudio	Another popular sound format on the Web, RealAudio files are designed for real-time playing over low- to high-bandwidth connections. RealAudio files tend to be much smaller than AU or VAV files, but the sound quality is usually not as good.
SND	The SND format is used primarily on the Macintosh operating system for creating system sounds. This format is not widely supported on the Web.
WAV	WAV sound files were developed for the Windows operating system and are one of the most common sound formats on the Web. WAV files can be recorded in 8-bit or 16-bit sample resolutions, in stereo or mono, and under a wide range of sampling rates. WAV sound files usually have the .wav filename extension.

WAV files are the most commonly used formats on the Web because of the dominance of the Windows operating system and the fact that support for WAV files is built into Windows. If your users primarily work on Macintosh systems, you should consider AIFF or SND files. Web sites designed primarily for UNIX workstations should use the AU sound format.

For larger sound files, such as recordings of complete songs or even concerts, MPEG is the preferred sound format because of its ability to greatly compress the size of the sound file. The latest version of the MPEG format is **MP3**. Some recording companies already distribute their products over the Internet as MP3s. Unfortunately, because it is so easy to create a MP3 file, the Web is awash with sites in which illegally recorded records or concerts are available as MP3 files.

WAV, AIFF, SND, AU, and MPEG sound files must be completely downloaded by the user before playing them. If the file is large, this can result in unacceptable delays. In response to the desire to immediately hear what is being downloaded, the RealAudio format was developed. **RealAudio** sound files employ **streaming media** technology, which allows data (such as sound) to be processed in a steady and continuous stream as it is being downloaded. Rather than waiting for the entire file, users of RealAudio files can begin listening to the sound clip almost immediately. This makes RealAudio ideal for broadcasting up-to-the-minute news and sporting events. The success of streaming media depends in part on the speed and quality of the connection. A low-bandwidth connection can often result in a sound recording that has frequent breaks, because the connection cannot keep up with the speed of the sound clip. To play RealAudio files, your browser must have the RealAudio player installed. You can find out more about RealAudio and the RealAudio player at *http://www.real.com*.

Another popular sound format is the MIDI format. **MIDI** (**Musical Instrument Digital Interface**) is a standard adopted for synthesizers and sound cards. The MIDI format reduces sound to a series of values that describe the pitch, length, and volume of each note. Because MIDI is a supported standard, sounds created on one synthesizer can be played and manipulated on another synthesizer, and sound-editing software can manipulate the MIDI files to create new sounds and sound effects. An additional advantage of MIDI files is that they are much smaller in size than other sound formats. One could write a MIDI composition that lasts several minutes and is less than 20 KB in size. A similar file in WAV format would be several megabytes in size. However, the MIDI format is limited to music. You cannot use MIDI for general sounds, such as speech.

If you don't want to create your own sound clips, many sites on the Web maintain an archive of sound clips that you can download. A few of these sites are listed in Figure 10-9. Be aware that some sound clips have copyright restrictions.

Figure 10-9	SOUND ARCHIVES ON THE WEB	
TITLE	**URL**	**DESCRIPTION**
Broadcast.com	http://www.broadcast.com	A collection of live and archived recordings that use streaming media
Historic sound clips	http://www.webcorp.com/sounds/	Sound clips from historical figures and events in history
Index of sounds	http://www.sunsite.sut.ac.jp/multimed/sounds/	An archive of sound clips broken down into categories
MP3.com	http://www.mp3.com	Resource for news and information about MP3s, including links to MP3 archives
MSU Voice Library	http://www.lib.msu.edu/vincent/	Selections from the G. Robert Vincent Voice library at Michigan State University
Sound America	http://www.soundamerica.com	An archive of almost 30,000 sound clips broken down into categories

Because of the popularity of the WAV format, Tom saved the Folk Festival sound clip as a WAV file. He has already used a sound editor to experiment with different values for the sampling rate, sample resolution, and stereo versus monaural sound. As shown in Figure 10-10, the size of Tom's various sound files ranged from 105 KB to more than 3 MB.

Figure 10-10   **FILE SIZES OF THE SUNRISE FESTIVAL SOUND CLIP**

	SAMPLE RESOLUTION			
	MONAURAL		STEREO	
SAMPLING RATE	8-BIT	16-BIT	8-BIT	16-BIT
6KHz	105 KB	211 KB	211 KB	422 KB
8KHz	142 KB	285 KB	285 KB	570 KB
11KHz	190 KB	380 KB	380 KB	740 KB
22KHz	391 KB	782 KB	782 KB	1564 KB
44KHz	752 KB	1505 KB	1505 KB	3010 KB

Tom doesn't want to overwhelm users with a huge sound file; but he also doesn't want a sound file that poorly represents the Folk Festival. After listening to the sound clip under each combination, you and Tom decide on a monaural recording with a 16-bit sample resolution and a sampling rate of 6 KHz. The size of this file is only 211 kilobytes, and you're both satisfied with the sound quality. Tom saves the sound file for you under the filename AF2000.wav. The file is on your Data Disk.

Linking to a Sound File

Now that you've decided on the format for the sound clip and saved the clip in a file, you're ready to create the Rainier.htm file and insert a hyperlink to the AF2000.wav file. Recall that Rainier.htm is the page that will be accessed by users with low-bandwidth connections and will use hyperlinks to external media files. Because media clips tend to be large, it's a good idea to include information about their size in your Web page. This will give users some idea of how long it will take to retrieve the clip before initiating the download. Create the Rainier.htm file and add a hyperlink to the sound clip now.

To create a link to the AF2000.wav sound file:

1. Start your text editor.

2. Open the file **Raintext.htm** from the Tutorial.10 folder on your Data Disk, and then save the file as **Rainier.htm** in the same folder.

3. Locate the last paragraph of the article on the Sunrise Folk Festival.

4. Directly below, insert the following text (indented to make your code easier to read):

```
<P>Click below to listen to the sounds of <I>Adams &
Davis</I>from the 2000 festival:</P>
<BLOCKQUOTE>
   <A HREF="AF2000.wav">Wild Mountain Thyme (211K — WAV
format)</A>
</BLOCKQUOTE>
```

TROUBLE? In case your browser or operating system does not support the WAV format, the file AF2000.au has also been placed on your Data disk. You can use that file in these steps. If you use this file, change the hyperlink text to indicate that the sound format is AU.

Figure 10-11 displays the revised text of the Rainier.htm file.

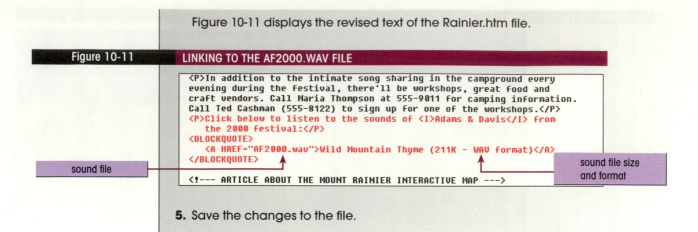

Figure 10-11   **LINKING TO THE AF2000.WAV FILE**

```
<P>In addition to the intimate song sharing in the campground every
evening during the festival, there'll be workshops, great food and
craft vendors. Call Maria Thompson at 555-9011 for camping information.
Call Ted Cashman (555-8122) to sign up for one of the workshops.</P>
<P>Click below to listen to the sounds of <I>Adams & Davis</I> from
    the 2000 festival:</P>
<BLOCKQUOTE>
    <A HREF="AF2000.wav">Wild Mountain Thyme (211K - WAV format)</A>
</BLOCKQUOTE>

<!--- ARTICLE ABOUT THE MOUNT RAINIER INTERACTIVE MAP --->
```

sound file

sound file size and format

5. Save the changes to the file.

Now that you've inserted a hyperlink to the sound clip, you're ready to test the link. What happens when you do so depends on how your system and browser have been configured. When your browser encounters a link to an external file, like a sound file, it checks to see if there is any program installed on your system designed to handle those types of files. Such programs are called **helper applications** because they help the browser to interpret and present the file. Different users will have different helper applications installed on their systems. As you saw earlier, there are many different brands of sound editors and, similarly, there are many different kinds of sound players. If the browser does not find a helper application on the system that will play the sound file, the browser might display an error message and prompt you to download one from the browser's Web site.

In the following steps you'll test your newly created hyperlink. These steps assume that you have the Microsoft Media Player installed on your system and that it is set up to handle WAV files. However, you might have a completely different helper application installed on your system. If so, you should use that instead. If necessary, check with your instructor or technical support person to determine which player is installed on your system. If no player has been installed, you will have to download a player and install it if you want to hear the sound clip.

To test the hyperlink to the AF2000.wav file:

1. Open the file **Rainier.htm** in your Web browser.

2. Click the hyperlink **Wild Mountain Thyme (211K - WAV format)** located on the page. As shown in Figure 10-12, the browser should access a helper application. You might have to click a play button to start playing the sound clip.

   TROUBLE? If you are asked to choose whether to open the file or save it, choose to open the sound file.

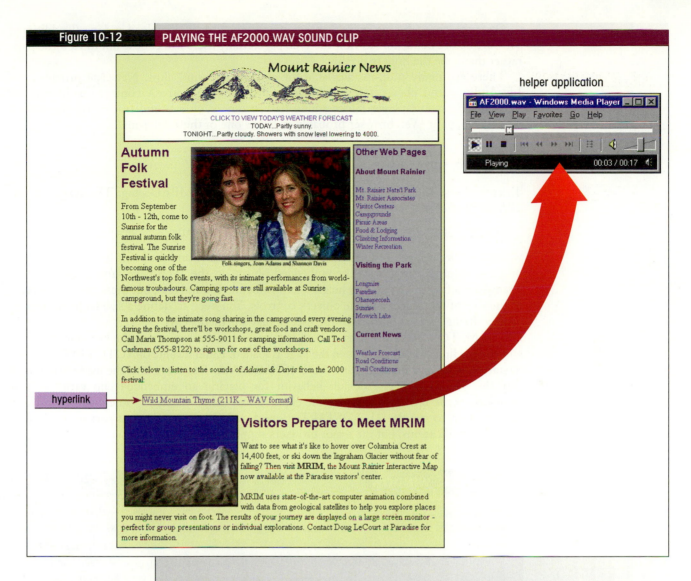

Figure 10-12   PLAYING THE AF2000.WAV SOUND CLIP

3. After listening to the sound file, close your helper application.

Now that you've created a hyperlink to the AF2000 sound clip, you'll repeat this process to create the second version of the page. But this time, instead of creating a hyperlink to the sound file, you'll embed the clip in the Web page.

Embedding a Sound File

A sound clip placed directly into a Web page is one example of an embedded object. An **embedded object** is any media clip, file, program, or other object that can be run or viewed from within the Web page. To use embedded objects, the browser must support them and it must have access to software called plug-ins. **Plug-ins**, also called **add-ons**, are programs that enable the browser to work with an embedded object. When the browser encounters an embedded object, it will load the appropriate plug-in plus any controls needed to manipulate the object. For example, a sound file plug-in might place controls on the Web page that enable the user to play the sound clip, pause it, rewind it, or change the volume. Because the object is embedded, these controls appear as part of the Web page.

One problem with plug-ins is that they require the user to download and install additional software before being able to view the Web page. Many users will choose not to view the page rather than take the time to do this.

There are many plug-ins available for embedded sound clips. Netscape provides the LiveAudio sound player. Internet Explorer provides the ActiveX controls, including the ActiveMovie media player. Since sound has become such a useful feature on the World Wide Web, your Web browser probably supports one of these plug-ins.

Using the <EMBED> Tag

To embed a sound clip into a Web page, you use the <EMBED> tag. The syntax of the <EMBED> tag is:

```
<EMBED SRC=URL WIDTH=value HEIGHT=value AUTOSTART="startvalue">
```

where *URL* is the URL or filename of the embedded object, and the HEIGHT and WIDTH properties define the size of the embedded object on the Web page. You might think it strange to define the width and height of an embedded sound clip, but these properties refer to the size of the object and the object's controls. You need to define a size large enough to display the necessary controls for the user to play the media clip.

The AUTOSTART property is used to determine whether or not the browser starts the embedded clip automatically when the page is loaded. Enter a value of AUTOSTART="true" to start the clip automatically, and AUTOSTART="false" to leave it to the user to manually play the sound clip. The default behavior for playing an embedded clip varies among browsers. Some browsers will play the clip automatically by default, others will not. To be sure, it's best to use the AUTOSTART property. AUTOSTART is not part of the official HTML specifications, but the major browsers support it.

REFERENCE WINDOW   **RW**

Embedding a Media Clip
- To embed a sound or video clip on your Web page, use the following HTML tags:
  ```
  <EMBED SRC=URL WIDTH=value HEIGHT=value AUTOSTART="startvalue">
  ```
  where *URL* is the name of the sound or video file that is to be embedded, and the WIDTH and HEIGHT properties are used to define the size of the embedded object on your Web page. Set AUTOSTART to "true" to play the clip automatically when the browser loads the page. Set AUTOSTART to "false" to leave it to the user to play the clip.

Having learned how to create an embedded object, you'll now create the Rainier2.htm file and then embed the Sunrise Festival sound clip. Once again, you'll use the AF2000.wav file from your Data Disk. (If you used the AF2000.au file in the previous set of steps, use that file again here.) Remember that the Rainier2 page is the page that will be installed at the visitor center and accessed directly by the user through a high-speed connection.

To embed the AF2000.wav sound file:

1. Return to your text editor and reopen the **Raintext.htm** file from the Tutorial.10 folder on your Data Disk. Save the file as **Rainier2.htm** in the same folder.

2. After the article on the Sunrise Folk Festival, insert the following text (substitute the AF2000.au file if your system supports that format):

```
<P>Listen to the sounds of <I>Adams & Davis</I> from
the 2000 festival:</P>
<BLOCKQUOTE>
        <EMBED SRC="AF2000.wav" WIDTH=145 HEIGHT=60
        AUTOSTART="false">
</BLOCKQUOTE>
```

See Figure 10-13.

| Figure 10-13 | INSERTING AN EMBEDDED SOUND CLIP |

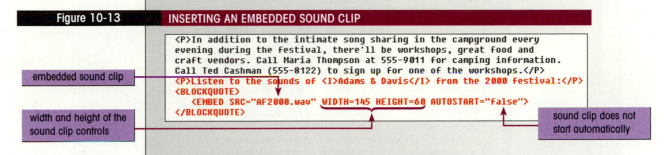

Note that in inserting the embedded sound clip you did not need to specify the clip's size, as you did earlier with the hyperlink. This is because the sound clip will be downloaded automatically to the user's browser, whether the user wants it or not. The height and width values were determined for you. When you embed your own media clips in the future, you'll probably have to test various height and width values to find a size that looks right. Also, you set the AUTOSTART value to "false" to allow the users to play the clip manually.

3. Save your changes to the file and then close your text editor.

4. Open the **Rainier2.htm** file in your Web browser. As shown in Figure 10-14, the page loads with the controls for the embedded sound clip shown on the page.

Figure 10-14   USING AN EMBEDDED SOUND CLIP

Mount Rainier News

CLICK TO VIEW TODAY'S WEATHER FORECAST
TODAY...Partly sunny.
TONIGHT...Partly cloudy. Showers with snow level lowering to 4000.

Autumn Folk Festival

Folk singers, Joan Adams and Shannon Davis

From September 10th - 12th, come to Sunrise for the annual autumn folk festival. The Sunrise Festival is quickly becoming one of the Northwest's top folk events, with its intimate performances from world-famous troubadours. Camping spots are still available at Sunrise campground, but they're going fast.

In addition to the intimate song sharing in the campground every evening during the festival, there'll be workshops, great food and craft vendors. Call Maria Thompson at 555-9011 for camping information. Call Ted Cashman (555-8122) to sign up for one of the workshops.

Listen to the sounds of *Adams & Davis* from the 2000 festival:

embedded sound clip with controls (your controls may differ) →

Other Web Pages

About Mount Rainier

Mt. Rainier Natn'l Park
Mt. Rainier Associates
Visitor Centers
Campgrounds
Picnic Areas
Food & Lodging
Climbing Information
Winter Recreation

Visiting the Park

Longmire
Paradise
Ohanapecosh
Sunrise
Mowich Lake

Current News

Weather Forecast
Road Conditions
Trail Conditions

Visitors Prepare to Meet MRIM

Want to see what it's like to hover over Columbia Crest at 14,400 feet, or ski down the Ingraham Glacier without fear of falling? Then visit **MRIM**, the Mount Rainier Interactive Map now available at the Paradise visitors' center.

MRIM uses state-of-the-art computer animation combined with data from geological satellites to help you explore places you might never visit on foot. The results of your journey are displayed on a large screen monitor - perfect for group presentations or individual explorations. Contact Doug LeCourt at Paradise for more information.

TROUBLE? If you do not see controls for the sound clip on your Web page, it could be because your browser does not support embedded objects. Or, you might have mistyped the name of the sound file. Return to your text editor and verify that your code matches the code shown in Figure 10-13.

5. If necessary, click the **play** button on the embedded object to start playing the sound clip.

TROUBLE? If necessary, consult the documentation for your browser or plug-in to learn how to work with the sound clip, or ask your instructor or technical support person for assistance.

Using the <BGSOUND> Tag

In version 3.0, Internet Explorer introduced a tag for playing background sounds on your Web page. The syntax of the <BGSOUND> tag is:

```
<BGSOUND SRC=URL LOOP=value>
```

where *URL* is the URL or location of the sound file, and the LOOP property defines how many times the sound clip will be played in the background. LOOP can be either an integer (1, 2, 3, ...), or INFINITE if you want the sound clip to be played continuously. The default LOOP value is 1. For example, to set the AF2000.wav file to play once in the background when the Rainier2.htm page is loaded, you could add the following tag anywhere in the file:

```
<BGSOUND SRC="AF2000.wav" LOOP=1>
```

Because this is a background sound, no control or object appears on the Web page; therefore, the user cannot stop the sound from playing, pause it, or rewind it. Because the user has little control over the sound, you should use the <BGSOUND> tag with caution. You should also set the LOOP value to 1 or a small number. Having a sound clip played over and over again can be extremely irritating to users.

REFERENCE WINDOW   **RW**

Creating a Background Sound
- To create a background sound, use the following tag for Internet Explorer browsers:
  ```
  <BGSOUND SRC=URL LOOP=value>
  ```
  where *URL* is the filename or location of the sound file, and the LOOP parameter determines how many times the sound file should be played. LOOP can be either a digit or INFINITE.
- To create a background sound with the <EMBED> tag, use the HTML tag:
  ```
  <EMBED SRC=URL WIDTH=0 HEIGHT=0 AUTOSTART="true">
  ```

The <BGSOUND> tag is not supported by Netscape and will be ignored by that browser. You should keep this in mind when deciding whether or not to use the <BGSOUND> tag on your Web page. You can create an effect similar to that produced by the <BGSOUND> tag by inserting an embedded sound clip on your Web page, setting it's width and height properties to 0, and having the clip start automatically when loaded. For example, to insert a background sound clip with Netscape, use the following HTML tag:

```
<EMBED SRC="AF2000.wav" WIDTH=0 HEIGHT=0 AUTOSTART="true">
```

The sound clip will start automatically, but because its size is 0, it will not appear on the Web page.

You've finished adding sound to the Mount Rainier newsletter page. You show your work to Tom and he approves of both files you've created. In the next session you'll learn about various video file formats and how to insert them into your Web pages.

Session 10.1 QUICK CHECK

1. Describe two ways of adding sound to your Web page.

2. Define the following terms: bandwidth, sampling rate, and sample resolution.

3. What sound file formats would you use on an intranet composed exclusively of Macintosh computers?

4. What tag would you enter to allow users to access the sound file Music.wav as an external sound clip?

5. What is an embedded object? What two things must a browser have to use an embedded object?

6. What tag would you enter to allow users to access the sound file Music.wav as an embedded object?

7. What tag would you enter to have the Music.wav file played once in the background when the page is loaded by Internet Explorer? How about Netscape?

SESSION 10.2

In this session you'll work with an external and inline video. You'll learn about different video formats and how to use them to control the size of your video clips. You'll also work with the <EMBED> tag to embed a video clip in the Rainier2.htm page. Finally, you'll learn about an extension to the <IMG> tag that allows you to create inline images that also work as inline video clips.

Working with Video Files

Tom's next task for you is to add a video clip to the Web page taken from the Mount Rainier Interactive Map, which was recently installed at the Paradise visitors' center. This video clip shows a simulated flyby of Mount Rainier.

Displaying video is one of the most popular uses of the Web. Video files can be exciting and provide lots of information. At the same time, video files can be very large and difficult to work with. Depending on the format, a single video clip, no more than 30 seconds in length, can be as large as 10 MB.

You can create video files with a video capture board installed on your computer to record images from a camcorder, television, or VCR. You can also create video clips using computer animation software. In either case, creating a video file can be a time-consuming process as you try to balance the desire to create an interesting and visually attractive clip against the need to create a file that is compact in size. To create and work with video files, you can install some of the video editors listed in Figure 10-15.

Figure 10-15   **VIDEO-EDITING SOFTWARE AVAILABLE ON THE WEB**

TITLE	URL	OPERATING SYSTEM
Main Actor	http://www.mainconcept.com/	Windows
MMStudio	http://www.lerstad.com/	Windows
Quick Editor	http://www.shareware.com	Macintosh
VideoFramer	http://www.flickerfree.com/	Windows
VideoStudio	http://www.ulead.com/	Windows

Frame Rates and Codecs

A video file is composed of frames, where each **frame** is an individual image. When the video file is played, each frame is shown in sequence, giving the illusion of motion. The number of frames shown in each unit of time is called the **frame rate** and is expressed in frames per second (fps). Working with the frame rate is one way you can control the size and quality of your video file. A video file with a high frame rate will have a smooth playback, but at the expense of taking up a lot of space on your hard drive. For comparison, a VCR renders video at the speed of 30 fps. Video files that try to match this speed are usually quite large in size. You can reduce the frame rate to reduce the size of the file. When you do so, you're not slowing down the video; instead, you're reducing the number of frames shown each second and thereby reducing the total number of frames in the file. For example, instead of using 30 frames in one second of video, you might be using only 15. The overall duration of the video clip remains the same, but the size of the file will be reduced. The downside of reducing the frame rate is that the video playback might appear ragged.

Another way of controlling the size of the video file is by compressing each individual frame. The image is compressed when stored in the file. Then, as the video clip is played, the image is decompressed and shown. The technique of compressing and decompressing video frames is a called a **codec** (for compression/decompression). There are many different types of codecs, each with its own advantages and disadvantages. Your video editor will usually allow you to choose the codec for your video file. You'll have to experiment to determine which codec provides the best file compression without sacrificing video quality. Different codecs perform better on different files.

You can also reduce the size of your video files by simply reducing the size of the video frames. A frame size of 160 pixels wide by 120 pixels high is considered standard on the Web, but you can reduce this size if you find that your video file is too large. Changing the video from color to grayscale can also reduce the size of the file. If your video clip contains a sound track, you can reduce the sampling rate, sample resolution, or the number of channels to further reduce the size of the video file. Each of these techniques should be available to you in your video-editing software.

Video File Formats

Video on the Web typically appears in one of five formats: ASF, AVI, MPEG, QuickTime, or RealVideo. Figure 10-16 describes each of these formats.

Figure 10-16   **VIDEO FILE FORMATS**

FORMAT	DESCRIPTION
ASF	Advanced Streaming Format. Developed by Microsoft to eventually replace the AVI video format, ASF employs streaming media technology to provide live video over low- and high-bandwidth connections.
AVI	Audio Video Interleave. AVI is the standard video format for Windows. AVI files can have a resolution no larger than 320 × 240 pixels with a frame rate no faster than 30 fps, which means that AVI files cannot be used for full-screen, full-motion video. However, AVI files require no special hardware, making AVI one of the standard video formats for the Web.
MPEG	Moving Pictures Group. The MPEG format allows for high compression of the video file, resulting in smaller files sizes. There are two MPEG formats: MPEG-1 and MPEG-2. MPEG-1 files have a maximum resolution of 352 × 240 pixels at 30 fps. MPEG-2 files can be displayed at a maximum resolution of 1280 × 720 pixels with a frame rate of 60 fps, making MPEG-2 files appropriate for full-screen, full-motion video. Special software is required to create and play MPEG files.
QuickTime	Developed by Apple Computer for the Macintosh, QuickTime movies can also be played in Windows if the user has installed the proper software and drivers (available free from *http://www.quicktime.apple.com*.) Because of its popular support, QuickTime is also a Web standard for video files.
RealVideo	Developed by RealNetworks, RealVideo uses streaming media technology to provide live video over low- and high-bandwidth connections. Video quality is usually poorer than what can be achieved using nonstreaming video.

Which format should you use for your Web page? The answer depends in part on who you think your audience will be. The QuickTime format was developed for the Macintosh, but QuickTime players exist for other operating systems (such as QuickTime for Windows); therefore, QuickTime might be the format with the most cross-platform support. On the other hand, support for AVI is built into Windows, and cross-platform support might not be that important, given that the Windows platform controls 80% of the computer market. Video players for MPEG files are also available for all operating systems, but MPEG files are not as prevalent as AVI or QuickTime videos. If you want to use streaming technology to allow your users to view the video file in real time, you should use either the ASF or RealVideo format, though the quality of the video will not be as high as with any of the other three formats. Given the current situation, many developers advise Web authors to provide both QuickTime and AVI video clips to their users if they want to provide maximum coverage. You'll follow that recommendation in your work on the *Mount Rainier News* Web page.

Tom has an excerpt from the Mount Rainier Interactive Map—a three-second video clip simulating a flyby of the summit at 14,000 feet. Using video editing software, you and Tom save the video clip in AVI format under a variety of sizes and frame rate settings, shown in Figure 10-17.

Figure 10-17   **FILE SIZES OF THE MRIM VIDEO CLIP U**

	FRAME SIZE (IN PIXELS)	
FRAME RATE	**200 X 167**	**400 X 334**
5 fps	187 KB	595 KB
10 fps	371 KB	719 KB
15 fps	671 KB	745 KB
20 fps	890 KB	974 KB
25 fps	917 KB	969 KB

The size of this video clip ranges from just under 1 MB down to 187 KB. As you can see from the figure, there is no easy way of predicting what the size of the video clip will be under varying conditions. Reducing the frame rate from 25 fps to 20 fps even increased the file size for the 400 × 334 video clip. You must experiment to find the best setting for your needs. After viewing the different clips, you and Tom decide to use the smallest video clip (187 KB in size). Tom saves the clip under the filename "MRIM.avi." Tom also uses his video editor to convert this file to QuickTime format and saves the file as "MRIM.mov." The size of this file is 215 KB. Tom gives you both of these clips (which are on your Data Disk) and asks you to add hyperlinks to the Rainier.htm file that point to these files.

Linking to a Video File

You follow the same procedure to link to a video clip as you did to link to a sound clip. Once again you should include information about the size of each video file so that users can determine whether or not they want to retrieve the clip. You'll place the hyperlinks to the video clip files at the bottom of the Rainier.htm file.

To create hyperlinks to the MRIM.avi and MRIM.mov files:

1. In your text editor, open the **Rainier.htm** file from the Tutorial.10 folder of your Data Disk.

2. Locate the last paragraph of the article on the Mount Rainier Interactive Map.

3. Below the paragraph, insert the following code:

```
<P>Preview a clip from the Mount Rainier Interactive
Map.</P>
<BLOCKQUOTE>
        <A HREF="MRIM.avi">Summit Flyby (187K - AVI
        format)</A><BR>
        <A HREF="MRIM.mov">Summit Flyby (215K - QuickTime
        format)</A>
</BLOCKQUOTE>
```

The revised code is shown in Figure 10-18.

Figure 10-18   INSERTING HYPERLINKS TO THE MRIM VIDEO FILES

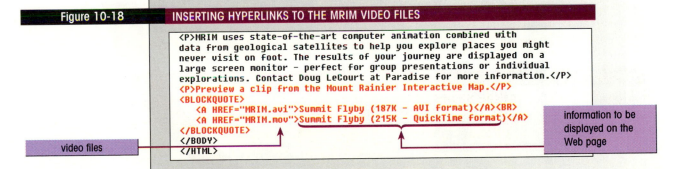

4. Save the changes to the file.

As you discovered earlier with sound files, different browsers will respond in different ways to hyperlinks to video clips. Both Internet Explorer and Netscape are capable of displaying AVI and MOV files directly within the browser without the use of plug-ins. In this case, when a user clicks a hyperlink for a video file, the clip is shown in its own Web page. The user can start the clip either by clicking a control that appears with the clip or by clicking the image if no controls appear. If no controls appear, the user can also right-click the image to view a shortcut list of commands, such as Pause, Stop, and Rewind.

On other browsers, a plug-in will be activated when the user clicks the hyperlink, making the video clip play in a separate window. With this in mind, you'll test the hyperlinks you just created to learn if your browser supports video files, and if so, how.

To test your video file hyperlinks:

1. Open the **Rainier.htm** file in your browser.

2. Click the hyperlinks to the AVI and MOV files you just created. Depending on their configurations, your computer and browser might be able to display only one of the video files. If so, verify that that video clip works. Figure 10-19 shows a sample of how one user might access the MRIM.avi video clip.

| Figure 10-19 | PLAYING THE MRIM VIDEO CLIP |

> **TROUBLE?** It's possible that your browser has not been set up to handle video. If so, you may see a dialog box informing you of this fact when you click the AVI or MOV hyperlink. The dialog box may also give you the option of downloading the necessary software from the Internet. If you are working on a computer on a campus network, you should talk to your instructor or technical resource person before installing any software.
>
> **TROUBLE?** If you are asked to choose whether to open the file or save it, choose to open the video file.
>
> **3.** After viewing the video, close your helper application.

Now that you've created a hyperlink to the video clips, your next task is to modify the Rainier2 Web page by placing the video clip within the page itself.

Embedding a Video File

To embed a video file, you can use the <EMBED> tag, just as you did to embed the sound file in the previous session. As before, you must specify a source for the embedded video clip with the SRC property and a size for the clip using the HEIGHT and WIDTH properties. The object's height and width should be large enough to display any controls needed to operate the clip. You usually have to decide the size by trial and error. In addition to these properties, you can also specify whether or not you want the clip to start automatically when the page is loaded by entering AUTOSTART="true" within the <EMBED> tag.

In this example, you'll embed the MRIM.avi video clip in the Rainier2.htm file. (If your browser supports only QuickTime files, you can substitute the MRIM.mov file.) The size of this clip is 200 pixels wide by 167 pixels high. You'll increase the value of the HEIGHT property to 200 to accommodate the embedded object's video clip controls. Also, Tom does not want the clip to start automatically, so you'll set the value of the AUTOSTART property to "false."

> ### To embed the MRIM video clip:
>
> **1.** Return to your text editor and open the **Rainer2.htm** file.
>
> **2.** Insert the following code at the end of the article on the Mount Rainier Interactive Map (use MRIM.mov instead of MRIM.avi if your browser supports only QuickTime videos):
>
> ```
> <P>Click the image below for a preview of the Mount Rainier
> Interactive Map.</P>
> <EMBED SRC="MRIM.avi" WIDTH=200 HEIGHT=200 AUTOSTART="false">
> ```
>
> Figure 10-20 shows the revised code.

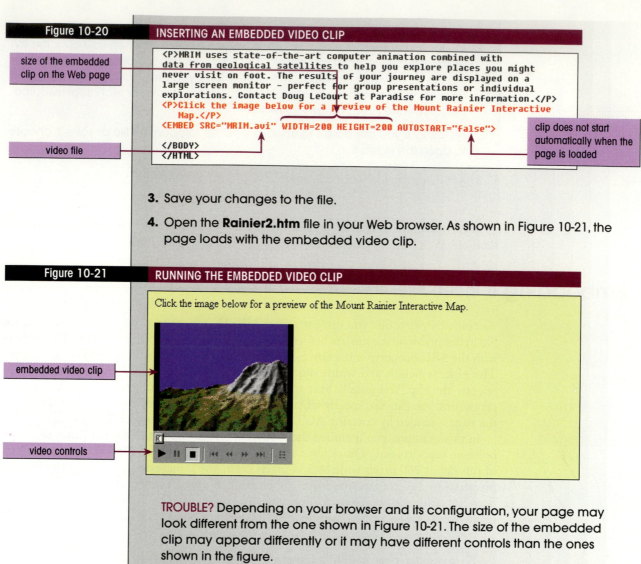

Figure 10-20   INSERTING AN EMBEDDED VIDEO CLIP

size of the embedded
clip on the Web page

```
<P>MRIM uses state-of-the-art computer animation combined with
data from geological satellites to help you explore places you might
never visit on foot. The results of your journey are displayed on a
large screen monitor – perfect for group presentations or individual
explorations. Contact Doug LeCourt at Paradise for more information.</P>
<P>Click the image below for a preview of the Mount Rainier Interactive
    Map.</P>
<EMBED SRC="MRIM.avi" WIDTH=200 HEIGHT=200 AUTOSTART="false">

</BODY>
</HTML>
```

video file

clip does not start
automatically when the
page is loaded

3. Save your changes to the file.

4. Open the **Rainier2.htm** file in your Web browser. As shown in Figure 10-21, the page loads with the embedded video clip.

Figure 10-21   RUNNING THE EMBEDDED VIDEO CLIP

Click the image below for a preview of the Mount Rainier Interactive Map.

embedded video clip

video controls

TROUBLE? Depending on your browser and its configuration, your page may look different from the one shown in Figure 10-21. The size of the embedded clip may appear differently or it may have different controls than the ones shown in the figure.

5. Start the video clip by either clicking the **play** button or clicking the **video clip** itself. See the documentation for your plug-in or browser for more details on how to start the clip.

Using the <NOEMBED> Tag

Older browsers don't support embedded objects such as the MRIM video clip. If you still want to support those older browsers, you can use the <NOEMBED> tag.

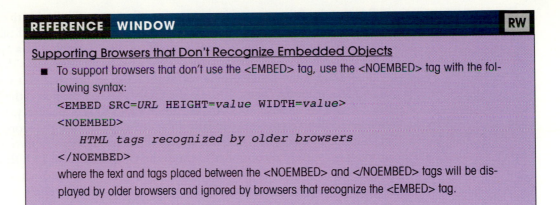

The <NOEMBED> tag works like the <NOFRAME> tag for framed presentations. It provides a way of supporting older browsers that don't recognize the <EMBED> tag. The general syntax of the <NOEMBED> tag is:

```
<EMBED SRC=URL HEIGHT=value WIDTH=value>
<NOEMBED>
    HTML tags recognized by older browsers
</NOEMBED>
```

A browser that recognizes the <EMBED> tag will embed the object on the Web page listed in the first line of code. It will also recognize the <NOEMBED> tags and will ignore any text that lies within them. An older browser, on the other hand, will ignore the <EMBED> and <NOEMBED> tags because it doesn't recognize them, but it will run whatever tags are entered between the <NOEMBED> tags.

For example, if you wanted to provide support for both new and older browsers with the MRIM.avi movie clip, you could enter the following HTML code:

```
<P>Preview a clip from the Mount Rainier Interactive Map</P>
<EMBED SRC="MRIM.avi" WIDTH=200 HEIGHT=200>
<NOEMBED>
    <A HREF="MRIM.avi">Summit Flyby (187K - AVI format)</A>
</NOEMBED>
```

In this case, new browsers would see only the embedded video clip, while older browsers would see only the hyperlink to the video file.

Using the DYNSRC Property

If your users have Internet Explorer version 3.0 and above, you can take advantage of some additional properties for the <IMG> tag. One of these is the DYNSRC property, which stands for "dynamic source." This property allows you to specify a video clip that is associated with an inline image. For example, the MRIM article contains an inline image that was inserted using the following <IMG> tag:

```
<IMG SRC="MRIM.jpg" ALIGN=RIGHT HSPACE=5 VSPACE=1>
```

You could replace this tag with the following:

```
<IMG DYNSRC="MRIM.avi" SRC="MRIM.jpg" ALIGN=RIGHT HSPACE=5
VSPACE=1>
```

The result of the new tag is that Internet Explorer will display the MRIM.jpg graphic as an inline image, but if the user clicks the image, the browser will play the MRIM.avi file. Using this tag allows you to display a GIF or JPEG graphic as a "preview" of the inline video clip, but to play the video clip itself whenever the user clicks the image.

There are some other properties of the <IMG> tag that you can use along with the DYNSRC property. These include the CONTROLS property, the LOOP property, and the START property. You can use the CONTROLS property to specify whether to include VCR-like controls beneath the video clip, include the word CONTROLS in the <IMG> tag to insert the controls, and omit this property to remove them. Use the LOOP property to specify the number of times the video is played; LOOP can be either an integer or the word INFINITE (to allow the clip to be played without stopping). Use the START property to control how the video clip is started; (enter START=FILEOPEN in the <IMG> tag to start the clip automatically when the browser opens the file, enter START=MOUSEOVER to start the clip when the user moves the mouse over the image, and omit the START property to start the clip when the image is clicked by the user.

Because the DYNSRC property and its associated properties are supported only by Internet Explorer, if you use these properties you will probably have to supplement your HTML code with the <EMBED> tag to allow other browsers to use the embedded video clip.

One way of doing this is to create a JavaScript program to test whether the user is running Internet Explorer and, if so, you can have JavaScript insert an <IMG> tag with the DYNSRC property. If the user is not running Internet Explorer, JavaScript would insert an <EMBED> tag. Sample code for doing this is shown below:

```
<SCRIPT>
<!--- Hide from non-JavaScript browsers
      var btype = navigator.appName;
      if (btype == "Microsoft Internet Explorer") {
            document.write('<IMG SRC="MRIM.jpg"
            DYNSRC="MRIM.avi">');
      } else {
            document.write('<EMBED SRC="MRIM.avi">');
      }
//Stop hiding --->
</SCRIPT>
```

Note that this code uses the navigator object, which refers to the current browser, and the appName property, which contains the name of the current browser. You could supplement this code by adding the HEIGHT, WIDTH, and other properties to the tags created by the document.write() methods.

DESIGN   WINDOW   **DW**

Tips for Using Multimedia in Your Web Page

■ Avoid embedding large files on your Web page if the page will accessed by users with slow Internet connections. Use hyperlinks instead.

■ Always indicate the size of the media clip when creating a hyperlink to it, so that your users know how large the file is before committing to retrieving it.

■ Provide different media formats to your users. Provide both WAV and AU versions of your audio files. Provide both AVI and QuickTime versions of your video files.

■ Test your media clips on different browsers and browser versions.

This concludes your work with external and embedded video clips. In the next session you'll supplement the Rainier2 page by adding a Java applet to display a scrolling window of current news and reports.

Session 10.2 QUICK CHECK

1. Define the following terms: frame, frame rate, and codec.

2. Name three ways of reducing the size of a video file.

3. What are the three nonstreaming video file formats used on the Web? Which would you use in a network primarily composed of computers running Windows?

4. What tag would you enter to allow users to access the Movie.mov video clip as an external video clip?

5. What tag would you enter to allow users to access the Movie.mov video clip as an embedded object?

6. What HTML tag would you enter to run the tag you created in Quick Check 4 for older browsers, and the tag you created in Quick Check 5 for new browsers?

7. If your users are running Internet Explorer, how would you modify the tag <IMG SRC="Movie.jpg"> to allow it to run the video file "Movie.mov" whenever the user places the mouse over the inline image?

8. What are the limitations of the tag you created in Quick Check 7?

SESSION 10.3

In this session you'll work with Java applets to create a scrolling marquee. You'll learn how Java applets are stored in .class files and how to access those files from your Web page. You'll also control your Java applet by specifying parameter values for it. Finally, you'll learn how to create a scrolling marquee using one of the HTML extensions supported by Internet Explorer, and you'll learn about the <OBJECT> tag, which can be used to create another type of embedded object.

Introducing Java Applets

Tom has reviewed your work with sound and video and has only one more task for you. The top of the *Mount Rainier News* Web page contains a table that shows the current weather forecast. Tom would like to expand the forecast to include two-day predictions. Doing so presents a problem, however. Including more text in the box will push the articles further down the page. Tom would like to avoid this because he wants users to see as much of the newsletter as possible without scrolling. The best solution would be to retain the current box size, but have the text automatically scroll, as it does in theatre marquees. Tom has seen scrolling text in other Web pages and knows that it requires the use of a Java applet.

Understanding Applets and .class Files

As you learned earlier in Tutorial 8, the Java computing language was developed to allow users to run programs from within their Web browsers rather than on the Web server. Each Java program is called an **applet**. You can find Java applets for stock market tickers, games, animations and other utilities. Unlike JavaScript, a Java applet is not inserted into your HTML file; rather it is an external file that is downloaded and executed by your browser. The applet itself usually appears as an embedded object on your Web page in an area called an **applet window**. You can specify the size and position of the applet window as it appears on your Web page. Some applets however, might appear outside of your browser, as separate program windows that can be resized, minimized, and placed on the desktop.

Many prewritten Java applets are available on the Web. Figure 10-22 lists a few of the more popular sources for applets.

Figure 10-22	JAVA APPLET ARCHIVES ON THE WEB	
TITLE	**URL**	
Applets from Sun	http://java.sun.com/applets/	
Gamelan	http://www.gamelan.com/	
Java Boutique	http://www.javaboutique.com/	
Java Rating Service	http://www.jars.com/	
Yahool's list of Java applets	http://www.yahoo.com/Computers_and_Internet/Programming_Languages/Java/Applets/	

To create a Java applet, you need a Java Developer's Kit (JDK). You can download a free copy of the Java Developer's Kit at the Sun Microsystems Java page located at *http://www.java.sun.com*. Commercial JDKs also exist that provide easy-to-use graphical tools and menus to help you create your Java applets quickly and easily. Once you have the JDK, be prepared to hit the books to learn the Java computing language. It is somewhat similar to JavaScript, but it is a more complicated (and powerful) language.

After you write the code for a Java program using one of the JDKs, you save the source code as a file with the four-letter extension *.java*. This file is then changed into an executable file (that is, a file that runs by itself without requiring additional software) in a process called **compiling**. The executable file has the filename extension *.class* and is called a **.class file**. A single Java applet may require more than one class file to work properly. Class files are different from the other program files you have on your computer. Unlike an .exe or .com file, which are run by your operating system, a class file can be run only from within a Java Interpreter. In most cases, the Java Interpreter is your Web browser. This feature is what allows the same Java applet to be run under Windows or on a Macintosh, as long as the browser supports Java.

Working with the <APPLET> and <PARAM> Tags

Once you've either located a Java applet to use or written one of your own, you use the <APPLET> tag to insert it in your Web page. The <APPLET> tag identifies the .class file used by the applet and allows you to specify any parameters needed by the .class file to run. The general syntax of the <APPLET> tag is:

```
<APPLET CODE=file.class WIDTH=value HEIGHT=value>
    <PARAM>
    <PARAM>
  . . .
    <PARAM>
</APPLET>
```

where *file.class* is the filename of the .class file, and WIDTH and HEIGHT specify the size of the applet window in pixels. The <PARAM> tags, used for special parameters required by the applet, are optional. Documentation is usually supplied with the applet to specify which parameters, if any, are required. The syntax of the <PARAM> tag is:

```
<PARAM NAME=text VALUE=value>
```

where *text* is a text string identifying the name of the parameter (as specified in the documentation for the applet), and *value* is the parameter value.

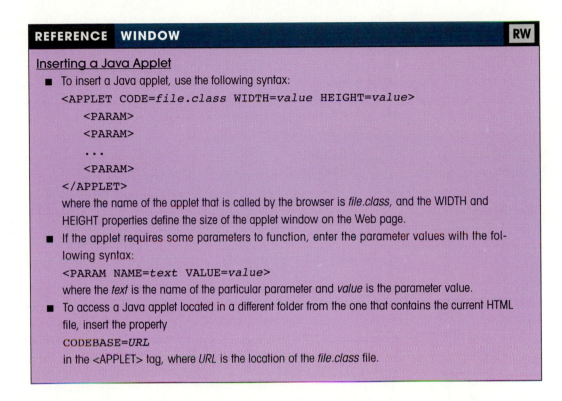

REFERENCE WINDOW RW

Inserting a Java Applet
- To insert a Java applet, use the following syntax:
  ```
  <APPLET CODE=file.class WIDTH=value HEIGHT=value>
      <PARAM>
      <PARAM>
      . . .
      <PARAM>
  </APPLET>
  ```
  where the name of the applet that is called by the browser is *file.class*, and the WIDTH and HEIGHT properties define the size of the applet window on the Web page.
- If the applet requires some parameters to function, enter the parameter values with the following syntax:
  ```
  <PARAM NAME=text VALUE=value>
  ```
  where the *text* is the name of the particular parameter and *value* is the parameter value.
- To access a Java applet located in a different folder from the one that contains the current HTML file, insert the property
  ```
  CODEBASE=URL
  ```
  in the <APPLET> tag, where *URL* is the location of the *file.class* file.

Some of the other properties supported by the <APPLET> tag are shown in Figure 10-23.

Figure 10-23	ADDITIONAL PROPERTIES OF THE <APPLET> TAG
PROPERTY	**DESCRIPTION**
ALT=*text*	A text string that is displayed in place of the applet before the browser has finished loading the applet
CODEBASE=*URL*	The location of the .class file, if different from the Web page
CODE=*filename*.class	The filename of the .class file
HEIGHT=*value*	The height of the embedded applet in pixels
HSPACE=*value*	The horizontal space between the embedded applet and the surrounding text, in pixels
NAME=*text*	The name of applet
VSPACE=*value*	The vertical space between the embedded applet and the surrounding text, in pixels
WIDTH=*value*	The width of the embedded applet in pixels

The CODEBASE property enables you to run an applet placed in a different location than your Web page. This allows you to maintain only one copy of your applet, which you can then access from many different Web pages located in different folders. Web authors often place all of their applets in a single folder so that they can better manage them. Another aspect of the CODEBASE property is that it allows you to run *someone else's* Java applet off that person's Web server. However, this practice is discouraged and, in some cases, is a violation of a copyright. If you want to use someone else's Java applet in your own Web page, you should first obtain permission, retrieve the .class file, and place it on your own Web server.

Notice that Java applets require an opening, <APPLET>, and closing, </APPLET>, tag. In addition to inserting <PARAM> tags between them, you can also insert other HTML tags and text. You would do this for older browsers that don't support Java applets. These older browsers will ignore the <APPLET> and <PARAM> tags and will instead display the text you specify. New browsers that support Java applets will ignore that text. So if you use the following structure in your HTML file:

```
<APPLET CODE=file.class>
    <PARAM>
    <PARAM>
    ...
    <H3>To fully enjoy this page, upgrade your browser to
    support Java</H3>
</APPLET>
```

the browser will display the applet, or if it's an older browser, the message to upgrade.

Inserting a Java Applet into a Web Page

Tom has located a Java applet for you to use in the Rainer2.htm file. The applet allows you to specify several lines of text that can be scrolled vertically through a window, like movie credits. The name of the .class file is CreditRoll.class, and it is located on your Data Disk. Tom read through the documentation that came with the applet, and determined that the CreditRoll.class file uses the parameters shown in Figure 10-24.

Figure 10-24	PARAMETERS OF THE CREDITROLL APPLET
PARAMETER NAME	**DESCRIPTION**
BGCOLOR	The background color of the applet window, expressed as a color value
FADEZONE	The text in the applet window will fade in and out as it scrolls. This parameter sets the size of the area in which the text fades (in pixels).
TEXTCOLOR	The color value of the text in the applet window
FONT	The font used for the scrolling text in the applet window
TEXTx	Each line of text in the applet window requires a separate TEXTx parameter, where x is the line number. For example, the parameter TEXT1 sets the text for the first line in the applet window, TEXT2 sets the text for the second line in the applet window, and so forth.
URL	If the applet window is clicked, it will open the Web page specified in this URL parameter.
REPEAT	Specifies whether the text in the applet window is repeated. Setting this parameter's value to "yes" causes the text to scroll continuously.
SPEED	The speed at which the text scrolls, expressed in pixels per 1/100 of a second
VSPACE	The space between each line of text, in pixels
FONTSIZE	The point size of the text in the applet window

After considering how he wants the weather information to appear, Tom asks you to use the parameter values shown in Figure 10-25. These values will create a marquee box with dark purple text on a white background. The box will include eight lines of text (including two blank lines) forecasting the weather for the next two days. The text will be set to scroll continuously. The size of the applet window will be 400 pixels wide by 60 pixels high.

Figure 10-25   **VALUES FOR THE CREDITROLL APPLET**

PARAMETER NAME	PARAMETER VALUE
BGCOLOR	FFFFFF (white)
FADEZONE	20
TEXTCOLOR	663366 (dark purple)
FONT	ARIAL
TEXTx	TODAY'S WEATHER FORECAST TODAY...Partly sunny. TONIGHT...Partly cloudy. Showers with sleet. TUESDAY...Rain heavy at times. Snow likely. WEDNESDAY...Clearing. Click to view the Weather Page.
URL	http://www.nps.gov/mora/weather.htm
REPEAT	yes
SPEED	100
VSPACE	3
FONTSIZE	12

Now that you know the value of the parameters, you are ready to replace the box containing the weather information with a window containing the CreditRoll applet. Because there is a lot of text involved in inserting this applet, a text file with the parameter values has been prepared for you and saved in the CRoll.txt file.

To insert the CreditRoll applet:

1. In your text editor, open the **CRoll.txt** file in the Tutorial.10 folder of your Data Disk.

2. Copy all of the text in the file and close the file.

3. Open the **Rainier2.htm** file in your text editor.

4. Locate the <DIV CLASS=WEATHER> tag located midway through the file.

5. Delete all of the text between (but not including) the <DIV CLASS=WEATHER> and </DIV> tags.

6. Paste the text you copied from the CRoll.txt file between the <DIV> and </DIV> tags.

   The revised code in the Rainier2.htm file should appear as shown in Figure 10-26. Take some time to study the HTML code you just inserted. Note that blank lines are indicated in the values for the TEXT2 and TEXT7 parameters by the empty space allotted to those values.

Figure 10-26   INSERTING THE CREDITROLL APPLET AND APPLET PARAMETERS

.class file

parameter values

dimensions of the applet window

```
<!---WEATHER REPORT -->
<DIV CLASS=WEATHER>
<APPLET CODE="CreditRoll.class" WIDTH=400 HEIGHT=60>
    <PARAM NAME=BGCOLOR VALUE="FFFFFF">
    <PARAM NAME=TEXTCOLOR VALUE="663366">
    <PARAM NAME=FADEZONE VALUE=20>
    <PARAM NAME=FONT VALUE="ARIAL">
    <PARAM NAME=TEXT1 VALUE="TODAY'S WEATHER FORECAST">
    <PARAM NAME=TEXT2 VALUE=" ">
    <PARAM NAME=TEXT3 VALUE="TODAY...Partly sunny.">
    <PARAM NAME=TEXT4 VALUE="TONIGHT...Partly cloudy. Showers with sleet.">
    <PARAM NAME=TEXT5 VALUE="TUESDAY...Rain heavy at times. Snow likely.">
    <PARAM NAME=TEXT6 VALUE="WEDNESDAY...Clearing.">
    <PARAM NAME=TEXT7 VALUE=" ">
    <PARAM NAME=TEXT8 VALUE="Click to view the Weather Page.">
    <PARAM NAME=URL VALUE="http://www.nps.gov/mora/weather.htm">
    <PARAM NAME=REPEAT VALUE="yes">
    <PARAM NAME=SPEED VALUE=100>
    <PARAM NAME=VSPACE VALUE=3>
    <PARAM NAME=FONTSIZE VALUE=12>
</APPLET>
</DIV>
<!---END OF REPORT --->
```

7. Save your changes to Rainier2.htm.

8. Open the **Rainier2.htm** file in your Web browser. Because of the large number of embedded objects and the Java applet, the page will take longer to load. After the page loads, you should see the weather forecast scrolling in the window at the top of the Web page. Figure 10-27 shows the CreditRoll applet as it appears on the Web page.

Figure 10-27   THE CREDIT APPLET IN ACTION

text fades as it exits the applet window

text scrolls vertically

TROUBLE? If your browser has trouble accessing the CreditRoll applet, check the <APPLET> and <PARAM> tags for any errors or misspellings. If you are running Netscape, you may have to close your browser and then reopen the Rainier2.htm file to have the applet run properly.

Using the Internet Explorer <MARQUEE> Tag

If you don't want to use an applet to create a box with scrolling text, and you know that users accessing your Web page will be using Internet Explorer 3.0 or above, you can take advantage of the Internet Explorer <MARQUEE> tag to create a theatre-style marquee. The general syntax of the <MARQUEE> tag is:

```
<MARQUEE>Marquee Text</MARQUEE>
```

where *Marquee Text* is the text that will appear in the marquee box. Browsers that do not support the <MARQUEE> tag, such as Netscape Navigator or Communicator, will simply display the entire marquee text without any scrolling.

Modifying the Marquee's Appearance

By default, the marquee will be placed within a box that is a single line high, extending the entire width of the Web page (or in the case of tables, the entire width of the table cell). The box's background color is transparent by default, displaying whatever color or background image you've selected for the page. You can modify the appearance of the marquee using the BGCOLOR, HEIGHT, and WIDTH properties. The syntax for these properties is:

```
<MARQUEE WIDTH=value HEIGHT=value BGCOLOR=value>
```

where WIDTH and HEIGHT are the box's width and height expressed in pixels, and BGCOLOR is the box's background color, expressed either as a color value or color name. Figure 10-28 shows a sample <MARQUEE> tag and its appearance in Internet Explorer.

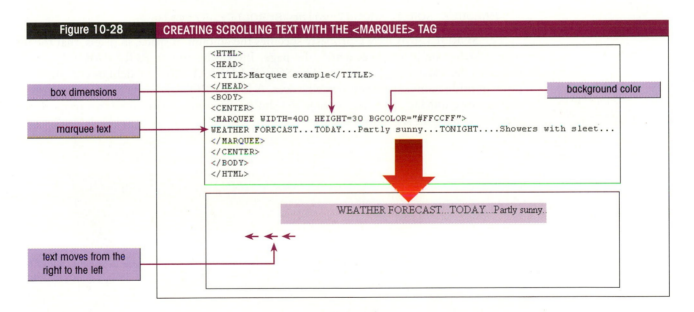

Figure 10-28 CREATING SCROLLING TEXT WITH THE <MARQUEE> TAG

```
<HTML>
<HEAD>
<TITLE>Marquee example</TITLE>
</HEAD>
<BODY>
<CENTER>
<MARQUEE WIDTH=400 HEIGHT=30 BGCOLOR="#FFCCFF">
WEATHER FORECAST...TODAY...Partly sunny...TONIGHT....Showers with sleet...
</MARQUEE>
</CENTER>
</BODY>
</HTML>
```

box dimensions

background color

marquee text

WEATHER FORECAST...TODAY...Partly sunny...

text moves from the right to the left

Because the marquee appears within a box, Internet Explorer provides properties similar to those used with inline images to control the placement of the box with the surrounding text. The syntax for controlling the layout of the marquee is:

```
<MARQUEE HSPACE=value VSPACE=value ALIGN=alignment>
```

where the HSPACE and VSPACE properties are used to specify the amount of horizontal and vertical space, in pixels, around the marquee box. The ALIGN property controls how the surrounding text is aligned with the box. The ALIGN property can have the TOP, MIDDLE, or

BOTTOM value, which aligns the surrounding text with the top, middle, or bottom of the marquee box, respectively. You cannot control the alignment of the text within the box. That text is always aligned with the top of the box.

Modifying the Marquee's Behavior

Text within the marquee scrolls continuously at a predefined rate from the right side of the box to the left. The <MARQUEE> tag provides properties to allow you to alter the direction of the scrolling, the speed of the scrolling, and the number of times the text scrolls. The syntax for changing the marquee's behavior is:

```
<MARQUEE BEHAVIOR=item DIRECTION=item LOOP=value>
```

where the BEHAVIOR property controls how the text moves across the box, the DIRECTION property controls the direction of the text, and the LOOP property defines the number of times the text scrolls by. The BEHAVIOR property has three possible values: SCROLL, SLIDE, or ALTERNATE. The default value is SCROLL, which causes the text to scroll across the box. Specifying a value of SLIDE for the BEHAVIOR property will cause the text to slide from the box's right edge to the left and then stop there. The ALTERNATE value will cause the text to bounce back and forth between the left and right edges of the box.

The DIRECTION property has two values: LEFT or RIGHT. The default value is RIGHT, which causes the text to start from the right edge of the box. LEFT causes the text to start from the box's left edge. The LOOP parameter can have either an integer value or the value INFINITE (the default) for continuous scrolling.

Two other properties, SCROLLAMOUNT and SCROLLDELAY, control the speed at which the text moves across the marquee. The syntax for these properties is:

```
<MARQUEE SCROLLAMOUNT=value SCROLLDELAY=value>
```

The SCROLLAMOUNT property specifies the amount of space, in pixels, that the text moves each time it advances across the page. Increasing the SCROLLAMOUNT value increases the speed of the marquee. The SCROLLDELAY property defines the amount of time, in milliseconds, between text advances. A low SCROLLDELAY value will cause the text to move quickly across the screen. You should experiment with these two properties to arrive at a marquee speed that you like.

REFERENCE   WINDOW   **RW**

Creating a Marquee with Internet Explorer

- To create a marquee (a box of scrolling text) for Internet Explorer browsers, use the following HTML tag:

  `<MARQUEE>`*`Marquee Text`*`</MARQUEE>`

  where *Marquee Text* is the text that will scroll from right to left across the box.

- To control the appearance and size of the marquee, insert the following properties into the `<MARQUEE>` tag:

  `BGCOLOR=`*`color`* `WIDTH=`*`value`* `HEIGHT=`*`value`*

  where the BGCOLOR property controls the background color of the marquee box, and the WIDTH and HEIGHT properties define the box's dimensions.

- To control the placement of the marquee with the surrounding text, use the properties:

  `HSPACE=`*`value`* `VSPACE=`*`value`* `ALIGN=`*`alignment`*

  where the HSPACE and VSPACE properties define the amount of horizontal and vertical space around the box (in pixels) and the ALIGN property determines the alignment of the box with the surrounding text (see the `<IMG>` tag for information on ALIGN values).

- To control the behavior of text within the marquee, use the properties:

  `BEHAVIOR=`*`item`* `DIRECTION=`*`item`* `LOOP=`*`value`*

  where BEHAVIOR is either SCROLL (to continuously scroll the text across the box), SLIDE (to slide the text across the box and stop) or ALTERNATE (to bounce the text back and forth across the box.) The DIRECTION property is either LEFT or RIGHT, defining in which direction the text moves (the `<MARQUEE>` tag cannot be used for vertical scrolling). The LOOP value determines how often the text moves across the box and is either an integer or INFINITE.

- To control the speed of the text within the marquee, use the properties:

  `SCROLLAMOUNT=`*`value`* `SCROLLDELAY=`*`value`*

  where SCROLLAMOUNT is the amount of space, in pixels, that the text moves each time it advances across the page, and SCROLLDELAY is the amount of time, in milliseconds, between text advances.

You should show restraint in using the `<MARQUEE>` tag. Like animated GIFs, marquees can distract your users from other elements on your Web page. Also, a continuous marquee can quickly become a nuisance.

Because the `<MARQUEE>` tag is supported only by Internet Explorer, you decide against using it in the Rainier2.htm file.

Tom would like you to learn about one final tag, the `<OBJECT>` tag, before concluding your work with multimedia Web pages. Again, because the `<OBJECT>` tag is supported only by Internet Explorer, you'll learn about it without implementing it in your newsletter for Tom. Therefore, you can close your text editor and your browser.

To close your work:

1. Close your Web browser.

2. Return to your text editor, and then close the Rainier2.htm file.

Using the <OBJECT> Tag

In general, there are four types of embedded objects that can exist on your Web page: images, sound clips, video clips, and applets. In order to deal with these objects in a uniform way, HTML 4.0 has introduced the <OBJECT> tag, which should be used for any embedded object. The <OBJECT> tag will entirely replace the <IMG>, <EMBED>, and <APPLET> tags in the future, but for now you may still need to use those tags to remain compatible with older browsers. Netscape, in particular, does not support the <OBJECT> tag through version 4.7

The general syntax for the <OBJECT> tag is:

```
<OBJECT DATA=URL TYPE="ContentType" CLASSID=URL CODEBASE=URL>
    <PARAM parameter names and values>
    <PARAM parameter names and values>
    ...
    Text and tags that are displayed by browsers that don't
    support the <OBJECT> tag
</OBJECT>
```

where the DATA property is used to indicate the source of the data for the embedded object (similar to the SRC property in the <EMBED> tag), the TYPE property indicates the type of data to be embedded (enclosed in quotes) the CLASSID property identifies the class of object being embedded, and the CODEBASE property indicates the location of the source data, if it differs from the location of the Web page (similar to the CODEBASE property of the <APPLET> tag). Some of the other properties associated with the <OBJECT> tag are shown in Figure 10-29.

Figure 10-29	ADDITIONAL PROPERTIES OF THE <OBJECT> TAG
PROPERTY	**DESCRIPTION**
ALIGN=alignment	The alignment of the embedded object with respect to the surrounding text
BORDER=value	The thickness of the border around the object, in pixels
HEIGHT=value	The height of the object, in pixels
HSPACE=value	The horizontal space between the object and the surrounding text, in pixels
NAME=text	The name of the object
STANDBY=text	Text to display while the browser is loading the object into the page
USEMAP=map_name	The name of an image map associated with the object (used for inline images only)
VSPACE=value	The vertical space between the object and the surrounding text, in pixels
WIDTH=value	The width of the object, in pixels

Specifying the TYPE Value

Some of the properties of the <OBJECT> tag require further explanation. Let's start with the TYPE property. You express the TYPE property in terms of the MIME data type. The **MIME (Multipurpose Internet Mail Extension)** data type was developed to allow e-mail messages to include nontext objects such as sound and video files. Later, MIME was adapted for use on the World Wide Web. Each MIME data type has a name associated with it. Figure 10-30 lists the MIME names for some of the objects you'll embed in your Web pages.

Figure 10-30	SOME MIME DATA TYPES				
IMAGE		**AUDIO**		**VIDEOS**	
TYPE	MIME NAME	TYPE	MIME NAME	TYPE	MIME NAME
GIF	image/gif	AIFF	audio/aiff	ASF	video/x-ms-af
JPG	image/jpeg	AU	audio/basic	AVI	video/m-msvideo
		MIDI	audio/mid	MPEG	video/mpeg
		MP3	audio/mpeg	QuickTime	video/quicktime
		WAV	audio/wav		

If you don't specify a value for TYPE property, the Web browser may have difficulty rendering the Web page. If the browser doesn't support the MIME data type, it will not try to download the object from the Web server. In the case of large object files, this can save valuable time.

For example, to embed the MRIM.avi file using the <OBJECT> tag rather than the <EMBED> tag, you could use the following code:

```
<OBJECT DATA="MRIM.avi" TYPE="video/x-msvideo"HEIGHT=200
WIDTH=200 AUTOSTART="false"></OBJECT>
```

Note that in this example, the TYPE property value is "video/x-msvideo," which is the MIME data type for AVI files. Similarly, you can replace this <IMG> tag:

```
<IMG SRC="Logo.gif" ALT="Mount Rainier News">
```

with the following <OBJECT> tag:

```
<OBJECT DATA="Logo.gif" TYPE="image/gif">
        Mount Rainier News
</OBJECT>
```

Note that by treating the inline image as an embedded object, you specify alternate text between the <OBJECT> and </OBJECT> tags.

Specifying the CLASSID Value

The CLASSID property provides information to the browser on how the object is to be implemented on the Web page. For inline images, sound files, and video files, you won't have to specify a value for the CLASSID property. However, for Java applets, the CLASSID property takes the place of the DATA property. The syntax for embedding a Java applet within the <OBJECT> tag is:

```
<OBJECT CLASSID="java:class_filename">
        <PARAM>
        <PARAM>
        . . .
</OBJECT>
```

To insert the CreditRoll applet with the <OBJECT> tag, you would use the following code:

```
<OBJECT CLASSID="java:CreditRoll.class" WIDTH=400 HEIGHT=60>
     <PARAM>
     <PARAM>
     ...
</OBJECT>
```

using all of the <PARAM> tags as you did for the <APPLET> tag.

ActiveX controls also require the CLASSID property along with the <OBJECT> tag to use them in your Web pages. ActiveX controls can be inserted into your document with the following CLASSID property value:

```
<OBJECT CLASSID="CLSID:class_identifier">
     <PARAM>
     <PARAM>
     ...
</OBJECT>
```

where *class_identifier* is a complex text string that identifies the ActiveX control for the browser. For example, the class identifier for the ActiveX control that displays a label is:

99B42120-6EC7-11CF-A6C7-00AA00A47DD2

ActiveX controls can add a lot to your Web page, and Microsoft supports a large library of controls. To help you work with them (and to determine their class ID strings!) you can use the Microsoft Control Pad tool, located at *http://msdn.microsoft.com/workshop/misc/cpad/*.

Nesting <OBJECT> Tags

One final advantage of the <OBJECT> tag is that you can nest one <OBJECT> inside another. This is useful in situations in which you want to give the browser alternatives for displaying an embedded object. For example, if you have multiple versions of the MRIM video file, the following code will give the browser four options in displaying the video clip:

```
<OBJECT DATA="MRIM.mpg" TYPE="video/mpeg">
     <OBJECT DATA="MRIM.mov" TYPE="video/quicktime">
          <OBJECT DATA="MRIM.avi" TYPE="video/x-msvideo">
               <IMG SRC="MRIM.jpg">
          </OBJECT>
     </OBJECT>
</OBJECT>
```

In this example, the browser will first try to display the MPEG version. If it can't support that video format, it will try the QuickTime version, and then the AVI format. If the browser can't display *any* of these video formats, it will display an inline image. To do the same thing with the <EMBED> tag would require writing a special JavaScript program.

The <OBJECT> tag shows great promise for expanding the capability of HTML in dealing with embedded objects. You should wait, however, for browser support to catch up with the <OBJECT> tag's potential before using it in Web pages that will be viewed by users with a variety of browsers.

Satisfied with the condition of both the Rainier.htm and Rainer2.htm pages, you present them to Tom for his approval. He is impressed by the use of sound and video in the newsletter and is happy with how the CreditRoll applet allows him to enter an almost unlimited amount of weather information without altering the layout of the page. He wants to examine the pages a little more closely and will contact you later with his changes.

Session 10.3 QUICK CHECK

1. What is compiling?

2. How does a .class file differ from other executable files you might find on your computer?

3. What tag would you enter to insert the Java applet StockTicker.class in your Web page?

4. What tag would you enter to remotely access the applet StockTicker.class, if it is located at the URL *http://www.wstreet.com*?

5. The StockTicker.class applet has two parameters. The URL parameter identifies the URL of a Web resource containing stock data, and the TIME parameter specifies the time lag, in seconds, between stock market updates. If URL="http://www.stockinfo.com" and TIME=60, what HTML tags would you add to use these values?

6. In Internet Explorer, what tag would you enter to create a scrolling marquee containing the text "Stock Information" in white letters on a black background?

7. What property or properties would you add to the tag in Quick Check 6 to cause the text to scroll once from the left side of the marquee to the right and then stop?

8. What <OBJECT> tag would you enter to insert a video file named "Rainier.mov" with a width of 150 pixels and a height of 100 pixels, into your Web page? What is a limitation of embedding the video file in this way?

REVIEW ASSIGNMENTS

Tom has returned with some additional multimedia clips he would like you to add to the *Mount Rainier News* Web page. One is a sound clip containing some more music from the previous year's Sunrise Folk Festival. The sound file has been saved in both the WAV format (as AF2000b.wav) and the AU format (as AF2000b.au). The other clip is a video clip with some more excerpts from the Mount Rainier Interactive Map. You have two video files—MRIM2.avi and MRIM2.mov. You'll modify both of the pages you created in the tutorial, creating two versions of the newsletter: one with hyperlinks to external files and the other with embedded media clips. Tom also wants you to add a background sound to the Web page with embedded media clips. The background sound is based on a short sound file that welcomes users to Mount Rainier.

Tom would also like you to modify the behavior of the CreditRoll applet. He wants you to add an additional line to the applet with the long-range forecast. He also thinks that the text scrolls a little too slowly and would like you to speed up the scrolling. He wants the fade-zone area set to 1 and would like to have the text of the applet window changed to black.

To make Tom's changes to the *Mount Rainier News* Web page:

1. Open the Raintxt3.htm file in the Review subfolder of the Tutorial.10 folder on your Data Disk, and then save the file as Rainier3.htm in the same folder.

2. Below the hyperlink for the *Wild Mountain Thyme* sound file, insert a hyperlink to the AF2000b sound file (either the WAV file or the AU file, depending on your operating system). In the hyperlink include the name of the piece, *À la Claire Fontaine*, and the size of the sound file.

3. Below the hyperlink for the MRIM video file, insert a second hyperlink to the MRIM2 video (both the AVI and MOV files). Include information on the size of each video clip and the description "Mount Rainier Flyby - East Ridge."

4. Save your changes to the Rainier3.htm file.

5. Open the Rainier3.htm file in your browser and verify that all of the hyperlinks work correctly.

6. Print a copy of the Rainier3.htm in your browser and text editor.

7. Open the Raintext4.htm file from the Review subfolder of the Tutorial.10 folder on your Data Disk, and then save the file as Rainier4.htm in the same folder.

8. Below the embedded sound clip for the AF2000.wav (or AF2000.au) file, insert an embedded sound clip for the AF2000b sound file (either WAV or AU format). Set the size of the embedded object to 145 by 60. Set the AUTOSTART value to "false."

9. Below the embedded MRIM video clip, insert a video clip for the MRIM2 video file. Use either the AVI or QuickTime version, depending on the configuration of your operating system and browser. Set the size of the embedded video clip to 200 by 200. Set the AUTOSTART value to "false."

10. At the bottom of the document, embed the audio file Welcome.wav (or Welcome.au if that is the sound format your system supports) with a width and height of 0 pixels. Set the AUTOSTART value to "true."

Explore ▶ 11. Locate the CreditRoll applet tag and make the following changes:

- Insert a new TEXT parameter after TEXT6 (name it TEXT7) with the forecast: "LONGTERM...Warmer and drier." Revise the numbers of the succeeding TEXT parameters accordingly.
- Increase the value of the SPEED parameter to 120.
- Set the FADEZONE value to 1.
- Change the TEXTCOLOR parameter to black. (*Hint*: The applet's specifications require you to use black's hexadecimal color value, not its color name.)

12. Save your changes to the Rainier4.htm file.

13. Open the Rainier4.htm file in your browser and verify that the embedded links and Java applet work correctly. If you are using Internet Explorer, verify that the background sound file plays correctly.

14. Print a copy of the Rainier4.htm file from both the browser window and your text editor.

15. Close your browser and your text editor.

CASE PROBLEMS

Case 1. Adding Multimedia to the Lincoln Museum Web Page Maria Kalski is the Director of Public Relations for the Lincoln Museum of Natural History located in Lincoln, Iowa. Maria wants to overcome the idea that museums are boring, stuffy places, so she has asked you to help liven up the museum's Web page. You've done this by adding some fun graphics and text fonts. Maria likes the revised page, but she would also like you to add some video and sound clips. She gives you a couple of files that she wants added to the Web site. She wants you to create a hyperlink to the video file (a clip of a dinosaur coming to life in a museum), and she wants the sound file to be added to the page's background, to be played once whenever the page is loaded by the browser. The final version of your Web page is shown in Figure 10-31.

Figure 10-31

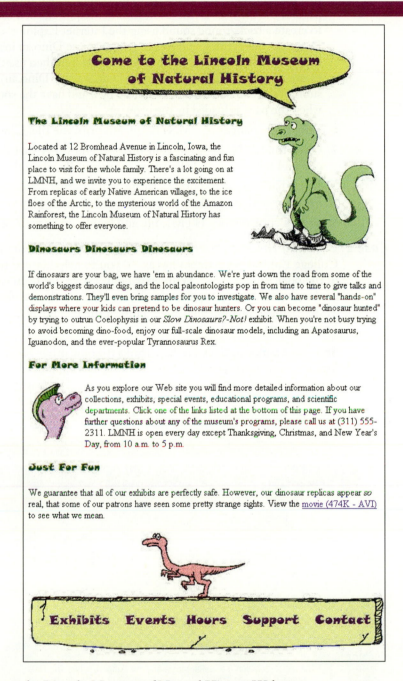

To create the Lincoln Museum of Natural History Web page:

1. Open the file LMNHtext.htm in the Cases subfolder of the Tutorial.10 folder on your Data Disk, and then save the file as LMNH.htm in the same folder.
2. Locate the word "movie" in the final paragraph of the page. Change this text to a hyperlink pointing to either the Dino.avi or Dino.mov file (depending on which video format your system supports).
3. Include (in the hyperlink tag) text that will appear on the Web page and note the type of video format you choose in Step 2, as well as the size of the video file.

4. Go to the bottom of the file and directly after the image map, insert <SCRIPT> tags for a JavaScript program.

Explore

5. Using the JavaScript program presented earlier in the tutorial as a model, write a program that uses the appName property to determine which browser is displaying the LMNH page. If the browser is Microsoft Internet Explorer, then use the document.write() method to create a background sound using the Internet Explorer <BGSOUND> tag. Use the Dino.wav file as the sound source (you may use Dino.au instead, if that is what your system supports). If the browser is *not* Internet Explorer, then use the document.write() method to create an embedded sound clip with Dino.wav (or Dino.au) as the source. Set the dimensions of the embedded sound clip to 0 by 0 and have the sound clip played automatically when the page is loaded by the browser.

6. Save your changes to LMNH.htm and print the file. Close your text editor.

7. Open the LMNH page in your browser and verify that the hyperlink displays the video clip and that the sound clip plays automatically when the page loads.

Explore

8. If you have access to both Netscape and Internet Explorer, open the page in both browsers and verify that the background sound is played each time.

9. Print a copy of your HTML file and hand it in to your instructor.

Case 2. Creating the Robert Frost Web Page   Professor Debra Li of the Madison State College English department has asked you to help her create a page devoted to the works of the poet Robert Frost. With your help, a page has been created with a short biography of the poet and the complete text of two of his works. Professor Li would like to add interest to the page by inserting sound clips of the two poems, so that her students can listen to Frost's poetry as well as read it.

She also wants you to create hyperlinks to some other Frost pages on the Web. She's located a Java applet that creates a set of graphical buttons which act as hyperlinks. Professor Li thinks this applet would also make her page more interesting. The Java applet uses the button.class file and has the following parameters (parameter names are in lowercase and should be enclosed in double quotes):

Figure 10-32

PARAMETER NAME	DESCRIPTION
"buttons"	The number of buttons in the set
"color"	The color of all the buttons in the set
"direction"	The orientation of the set of buttons (0=vertical orientation, 1=horizontal orientation)
"border width"	The width of the borders of the buttons, in pixels
"f_size"	The point size of the text labels on each button
"f_color"	The color value of the button labels
"f_color2"	The color value of the button labels when the mouse passes over the button or when the button is clicked
"f_offset"	The space between the button labels and the button borders, in pixels
"font"	The font face of the button labels; can be either TimesRoman, Helvetica, or Courier
"label x"	The label for each button; use the "label 0" parameter for the first button's label, "label 1" for the second button's label, and so forth
"link x"	The URL that each button links to; use the "link 0" parameter for the first button's hyperlink, "link 1" for the second button's hyperlink, and so forth

A preview of the page you'll create for Professor Li is shown in Figure 10-33.

Figure 10-33

To create the Robert Frost Web page:

1. Open the file RFtext.htm in the Cases subfolder of the Tutorial.10 folder on your Data Disk, and then save the file as RF.htm in the same folder.

2. Locate the title of the *Fire and Ice* poem in the table at the bottom of the page.

3. After the title insert the inline graphic, Sound.gif. Align the graphic with the bottom of the surrounding text, set the horizontal space to 3 pixels, and the image border to 0 pixels.

4. Change the Sound graphic to a hyperlink that points to the FireIce.wav file (or FireIce.au if your browser does not support the WAV format).

5. Repeat Steps 3 and 4 for the *Devotion* poem located in the first row and second column of the table. Have the Sound graphic point to the Devotion.wav (or Devotion.au) file.

6. Indicate the size of the two sound files at the end of the last paragraph before the table.

7. At the bottom of the RF.htm file, within the <P ALIGN=CENTER> and </P> tags, insert the Java applet that calls the button.class file. Set the size of the applet to 600 by 26.

Explore

8. Use the following parameter values in the applet:

   ■ There should be 3 buttons.
   ■ The color value of the buttons should be "C0C0C0."
   ■ The buttons should be oriented horizontally on the page.
   ■ The button border width should be 3 pixels.
   ■ The font size of the button labels should be 13.
   ■ The color of the button labels should be "000000" ("FFFFFF" when clicked).
   ■ There should be 4 pixels between the button labels and the button borders.
   ■ The font face should be Helvetica.
   ■ The label of the first button should be "Frost at MP3Lit" and it should point to *http://www.mp3lit.com/poetry/frost.html*.
   ■ The second button label should be "Robert Frost on the Web" and it should point to *http://www.amherstcommon.com/walking_tour/frost.html*.
   ■ The third button label should be "A Frost Bouquet" and it should point to *http://www.lib.virginia.edu/exhibits/frost/home.html*.

9. Print the HTML tags for the Java applet, and save and close the RF.htm file.

10. View the page in your Web browser and test the three links to the other Frost pages as well as the links to the two sound clips.

11. Print a copy of the Web page.

Case 3. Creating a Page About Fractals   Fractals are geometric objects discovered by mathematicians, and that closely model the sometimes-chaotic world of nature. Mr. Doug Hefstadt, a mathematics teacher at Franklin High School in Monroe, Illinois, has just begun a unit on fractals for his senior math class. He's used the topic to construct a Web page that will be placed on the school network, and he needs your help to complete the page. He has a video clip of a fractal that he wants placed on the page, as well as a Java applet that allows students to interactively explore the Mandelbrot set (a type of fractal object). He wants your assistance in putting these two objects on his Web page. A preview of the page you'll create is shown in Figure 10-34.

Figure 10-34

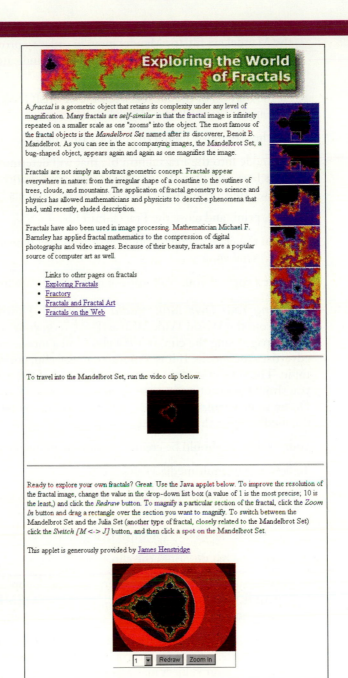

To create the Fractal page:

1. Open the file Fractext.htm in the Cases subfolder of the Tutorial.10 folder on your Data Disk, and then save the file as Fractal.htm in the same folder.

2. After the paragraph inviting the user to run the video clip, insert an embedded video clip between the <P ALIGN=CENTER> and </P> tags. The source of the video clip is Mandel.avi (you may substitute Mandel.mov if your system requires it).

3. Set the size of the embedded object to 104 by 120, and set the browser to *not* start the movie clip automatically.

Explore   4. Beneath the embedded video clip, use the <NOEMBED> tags to insert a hyperlink to the Mandel.avi file (or Mandel.mov) in order to provide support for older browsers that cannot display embedded objects. Be sure to indicate the size of the video file alongside the hyperlink.

5. At the bottom of the file, between the <P ALIGN=CENTER> and </P> tags, insert a Java applet that calls the Mandel.class file.

6. Set the size of the applet to 250 by 210 pixels.

Explore   7. Add code into the Fractal.htm file that will determine whether a user's browser recognizes Java, and then if the browser does not support it, have your code display the statement, "Your browser does not support Java applets."

8. Save, print, and close the Fractal.htm file.

9. Open the page in your Web browser and play the video clip to verify that it works. Test the Fractal applet.

10. Print a copy of your Web page and close the Web browser.

Case 4. Creating Your Own Multimedia Web Page   Download a media file (sound or video or both) from the World Wide Web and save it on your computer or your Data Disk. Create a Web page using the clip. If it is a clip from a movie, create a Web page that describes and advertises the movie. If it is a sports or music clip, create a Web page that describes that topic. The subject matter, content, and layout of the page are totally up to you. Note that you should use caution in posting your Web page on the World Wide Web for public use. Doing so may violate the copyright privileges of the person or organization that created the media clip in the first place.

Your Web page should be created within the following guidelines:

To create your multimedia Web page:

1. Create a file named "MyMedia.htm" in the Cases subfolder of the Tutorial.10 folder of your Data Disk.

2. Embed the media clip (or clips) that you have chosen on the Web page.

3. Insert text that describes the clip.

4. Provide support for older browsers that don't support embedded objects by including a hyperlink to your multimedia file. Use the <NOEMBED> tag so that the hyperlink appears only in older browsers.

5. Use the CreditRoll.class applet located in the Cases subfolder of the Tutorial.10 folder to add a scrolling window to your page. The window can contain information about the media clip, your subject matter, or yourself.

6. Open your Web page in your browser and verify that the layout and behavior of the page is as your code specifies.

7. Print a copy of the HTML code and the page itself.

LAB ASSIGNMENTS

Multimedia

Multimedia brings together text, graphics, sound, animation, video, and photo images. In this Lab you will learn how to apply multimedia and then have the chance to see what it might be like to design some aspects of multimedia projects.

1. Click the Steps button to learn about multimedia development. As you proceed through the Steps, answer the Quick Check questions. After you complete the Steps, you will see a Quick Check Report. Follow the instructions on the screen to print this report.

2. In Explore, browse through the STS-79 Multimedia Mission Log. How many videos are included in the Multimedia Mission Log? The image on the Mission Profile page is a vector drawing, what happens when you enlarge it?

3. Listen to the sound track on Day 3. Is this a WAV file or a MIDI file? Why do you think so? Is this a synthesized sound or a digitized sound? Listen to the sound track on page 8. Can you tell if this is a WAV file or a MIDI file?

4. Suppose you were hired as a multimedia designer for a multimedia series on targeting fourth- and fifth-grade students. Describe the changes you would make to the Multimedia Mission Log so it would be suitable for these students. Also, include a sketch showing a screen from your revised design.

5. When you view the Mission Log on your computer, do you see palette flash? Why or why not? If you see palette flash, list the images that flash.

6. Multimedia can be effectively applied to projects such as Encyclopedias, atlases, and animated storybooks; to computer-based training for foreign languages, first aid, or software applications; for games and sports simulations; for business presentations; for personal albums, scrapbooks, and baby books; for product catalogs and Web pages. Suppose you were hired to create one of these projects. Write a one-paragraph description of the project you would be creating. Describe some of the multimedia elements you would include. For each of the elements indicate its source and whether you would need to obtain permission for its use. Finally, sketch a screen or two showing your completed project.

QUICK CHECK ANSWERS

Session 10.1

1. You can add sound by either embedding a sound clip into the Web page or providing a hyperlink to a sound file.

2. Bandwidth is a measure of the amount of data that can be sent through a communications circuit each second. The number of samples taken per second from a sound source is called the sampling rate. Sample resolution indicates the precision in measuring the sound within each sample.

3. AIFF, AIFC, or SND

4. <A HREF="Music.wav">

5. An embedded object is any media clip, file, program, or other object that can be run or viewed from within the Web page. First of all, the browser must be able to support the <EMBED> tag, and then it must have a plug-in or add-on installed to work with the object.

6. <EMBED SRC="Music.wav">

7. `<BGSOUND SRC="Music.wav" LOOP=1>`
In Netscape, you can use the tag:

`<EMBED SRC="MUSIC.wav" WIDTH=0 HEIGHT=0 AUTOSTART="true">`

Session 10.2

1. A frame is an individual image in a video file. The number of frames displayed in each unit of time is called the frame rate. The technique of compressing and decompressing video frames is a called a codec (for compression/decompression).

2. Reducing the size of each frame, reducing the frame rate, compressing the file via the codec, reducing the size of the sound track by changing the sample size or sampling rate, or reducing the color depth of the images in the video file

3. AVI, MPEG, and QuickTime. You would use AVI files on a Windows network.

4. `<A HREF="Movie.mov">`

5. `<EMBED SRC="Movie.mov">`

6. `<EMBED SRC="Movie.mov">`
`<NOEMBED>`
    `<A HREF="Movie.mov">`
`</NOEMBED>`

7. `<IMG SRC="Movie.jpg" DYNSRC="Movie.mov" START=MOUSEOVER>`

8. It might not be supported by browsers other than Internet Explorer.

Session 10.3

1. Compiling is a process that changes a file into an executable file (that is, a file that runs by itself without requiring additional software).

2. It must be run within a Java interpreter, such as your Web browser.

3. `<APPLET CODE="StockTicker.class">`

4. `<APPLET CODE="StockTicker.class"`
`CODEBASE="http://www.wstreet.com">`

5. `<PARAM NAME=URL VALUE="http://www.stockinfo.com">`
`<PARAM NAME=TIME VALUE=60>`

6. `<FONT COLOR="#FFFFFF">`
`<MARQUEE BGCOLOR="#000000">Stock Information</MARQUEE>`
`</FONT>`

7. `DIRECTION=LEFT BEHAVIOR=SLIDE`

8. `<OBJECT DATA="Rainier.mov" HEIGHT=100 WIDTH=150`
`TYPE="video/quicktime">`

This tag will not be supported by some browsers.

OBJECTIVES

In this case you will:

- Paste text into a Web page formatted with tables

- Create hyperlink anchors and link to anchors on other Web pages

- Insert a registered trademark symbol, using a special character code

- Create form elements for a product order form

- Create a JavaScript program to calculate the total cost of an order

CREATING A COMPANY WEB SITE

CASE

FrostiWear Winter Clothes

FrostiWear is a retail mail-order company that specializes in winter clothing and gear. Recently, the company created a Web site to advertise its wares on the World Wide Web. Part of the Web site will allow customers to order products online.

Susan Crawford, the director of the company's Internet Advertising Division, has asked you to create three Web pages for the company's line of gloves and mittens. She's given you a list of four popular products that she would like you to add to the company's Web site. Later on, after she approves your work, she'll ask you to add the complete company line (over 35 styles of gloves and mittens).

Susan wants the pages you create to match the established style of the company's Web site. She gives you a file, Frosti.txt, containing one of the standard page layouts. You'll use this layout as a guide for two of the pages she wants you to create. These are:

- **Gloves.htm**: a page containing an overview of FrostiWear's glove and mitten products
- **GProduct.htm**: a page with specific information on the four products that Susan wants you to add to the site

Susan also wants you to create a third page, GOrder.htm, which contains an order form for the company's glove and mitten products. This page should be based on the company's standard form, which is saved in the Order.txt file. Your form should automatically calculate the total cost of the order. In addition, FrostiWear provides a 5% discount (rounded to the nearest dollar) for customers who have a FrostiWear Club card. Your form should take the discount into account when calculating the total. If the customer is not a FrostiWear Club member, the form should display a message inviting the customer to join.

To complete these pages, Susan gives you graphic files of the glove products, graphic files for the logo and a background, and text files containing product specifications and descriptions. Figure AC1-1 and Figure AC1-2 list the files you'll be working with.

Figure AC1-1   TEXT FILES FOR THE FROSTIWEAR WEB SITE

FILENAME	DESCRIPTION
Arctic.txt	Description of the ArcticBlast glove
FLG.txt	Description of the Fingerless Glove
Frosti.css	Stylesheet for the FrostiWear Web site
Frosti.htm	FrostiWear home page
Frosti.txt	Basic layout of all FrostiWear Web pages
Gloves.txt	Overview of the line of FrostiWear gloves and mittens
GMitt.txt	Description of the Glomitt glove/mitt combination product
Order.txt	Standard layout for FrostiWear's online order forms
PFM.txt	Description of the PolyFleece mitt

Figure AC1-2   GRAPHIC FILES FOR THE FROSTIWEAR WEB SITE

FILENAME	DESCRIPTION
ArcticB.jpg	Graphic of the ArcticBlast glove
Blueline.jpg	Background image, to be used on all Web pages except the online order form page
FLess.jpg	Graphic of the Fingerless Glove
FLogo.jpg	FrostiWear company logo, to be included on all Web pages
Glomitt.jpg	Graphic of the Glomitt glove/mitt combination product
Gloves.jpg	Graphic to be used in the Glove Overview Web page
PolyFlce.jpg	Graphic of the PolyFleece mitt
Sweaters.jpg	Graphic displayed on the FrostiWear home page

To create Web pages for the FrostiWear Web site:

1. Start your text editor and open the file Frosti.txt in the Case1 subfolder of the Tutorial.add folder on your Data Disk, and then save the file as Gloves.htm in the same folder.
2. Change the title of the Web page to "FrostiWear Gloves."
3. Within the second table cell, after the "Enter Page text here" comment, insert the Gloves.jpg inline image, aligned with the right cell margin.

4. Below the inline image, but within the table cell, insert the contents of the Gloves.txt file (you might want to use the copy and paste features of your text editor to do this). Format the paragraph title as a H1 header. Separate one paragraph from another using paragraph marks.

Explore

5. After the first occurrence of each of the three words PolyFleece, ArcticBlast, and Gore-Tex, insert the registered trademark symbol ® as a superscript.

6. Change the following text to hypertext (each item, except the last, appears in the second paragraph; the last item appears in the third paragraph):

- ◼ "Fingerless Gloves" linked to the FLess anchor in the GProduct.htm file
- ◼ "PolyFleece mitts" linked to the PolyF anchor in the GProduct.htm file
- ◼ "Glomitt" linked to the Glomitt anchor in the GProduct.htm file
- ◼ "ArcticBlast Gore-Tex mitts" linked to the ArcticBlast anchor in the GProduct.htm file
- ◼ "online order form" linked to the GOrder.htm file

7. Save the Gloves.htm file and preview it in your Web browser. Your page should appear similar to the one shown in Figure AC1-3 (your browser might render the page slightly differently). Print your Web page.

Figure AC1-3   **THE GLOVES AND MITTS PAGE**

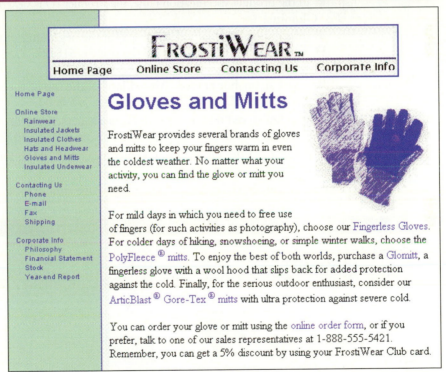

8. Reopen the Frosti.txt template file in your text editor and save it as GProduct.htm.

9. Change the Web page title to "FrostiWear Glove Products."

10. In the second table cell below the "Enter page text here" comment, insert the FLess.jpg graphic, aligned with the right cell margin.

11. Below the graphic, insert the contents of the FLG.txt file, which describes the Fingerless Glove.

12. Format the text you inserted by displaying the title as an H1 heading header, and insert an anchor named "FLess" at the beginning of the H1 header. Place paragraph tags around the paragraph describing the fingerless glove.

13. Below the paragraph, insert the product specification table shown in Figure AC1-4. Create a row of table headers and set the width of the first table column to 150 pixels, and the second column's width to 300 pixels. Set the border width of the table to 2 pixels.

Figure AC1-4	TABLE OF FINGERLESS GLOVES PRODUCT SPECIFICATIONS

SPECIFICATION	DESCRIPTION
Product ID	G725
Color	Burgundy, Red, Black, Gray
Size	Small, Medium, Large, XLarge
Price	$28.00

14. Below the table, enter additional text from the files for the three remaining products. Use the files PFM.txt, GMitt.txt, and Arctic.txt. Format those sections in the same way you formatted the Fingerless Gloves section, and include the appropriate inline image and product information table for each item. Make the following changes to each section:

For PolyFleece mitts:
- Insert an anchor named "PolyF" at the beginning of the section.
- In the product specification table, the Product ID is G726, and the price is $38.00.

For Glomitts:
- Insert an anchor named "Glomitt" at the beginning of the section.
- The Product ID is G727, and the price is $18.00.

For ArcticBlast mitts:
- Insert an anchor named "ArcticBlast" at the top of the section.
- The Product ID is G728, and the price is $98.00.

Explore
15. Insert the registered trademark symbol as a superscript after the first occurrence (other than in headers) of the words: PolyFleece, ArcticBlast, and Gore-Tex on the page.

16. Link the text "Order online." to GOrder.htm (each of the four times this text occurs on the page).

17. Open the page in your Web browser. Your page should look similar to the one shown in Figure AC1-5.

Figure AC1-5	THE GLOVE PRODUCTS PAGE

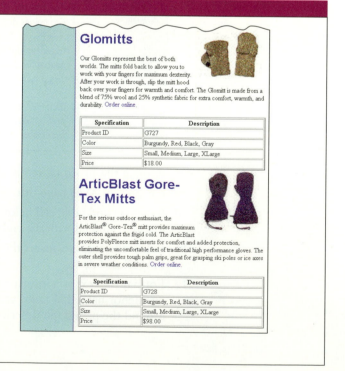

18. Verify that each of the four product hyperlinks you created in the Gloves.htm file jumps to the appropriate location in the GProduct.htm page. Print a copy of your page as it appears in your Web browser.

19. Open the Order.txt file and save it as GOrder.htm.

20. Change the text "Product Order Form" in the page's title and heading to "Gloves and Mitts Order Form." Change the text "Product page" in the initial paragraph to "Gloves and Mitts page," and link it to the Gloves.htm file.

21. Within the Order form, change the Brand selection list so that it displays the names of the four glove brands along with their prices. Set the value of each of the four options in the selection list to the price of the glove or mitt.

22. Enter options for the Size and Color selection lists, based on the table entries in the GProduct.htm page.

Explore ➤ 23. Within the HEAD section of the GOrder.htm file, create a JavaScript function named "Calculate()." The Calculate() function should do the following:
   - ■ Determine the value (price) of the selected brand (*Hint*: First determine the selected index in the Brand selection list, and then use this information to determine the value of the option corresponding to that index).
   - ■ Multiply the brand's price by the quantity ordered. Store this value in a variable named "Subtotal."
   - ■ Determine the customer discount and store it in a variable named "Discount." The discount should be either 0 or, if the customer is a FrostiWear card holder, it should be equal to Math.round(0.05*Subtotal).
   - ■ Subtract Discount from Subtotal and store the result in a variable named "Total."
   - ■ Store the Subtotal value in the SUBTOTAL input box, the Discount value in the DISCOUNT input box, and the Total value in the TOTAL input box.

24. Modify the Calculate Total button so that it runs the Calculate() function when clicked.

Explore ➤ 25. Modify the form so that if the customer is not a FrostiWear Club member, an alert box appears with the text "You can enjoy additional savings with a FrostiWear Club card" when the customer submits the order.

26. Go to your Web browser and open the GOrder.htm page. Your page should appear similarly to the one shown in Figure AC1-6.

Figure AC1-6   **THE GLOVES AND MITTS ORDER FORM**

FrostiWear ™

Home Page   Online Store   Contacting Us   Corporate Info

Gloves and Mitts Order Form

Go to the Gloves and Mitts page to learn more about our products and styles.

1) I am a FrostiWear Club Member* ☐   Club ID: FC-#####

2) Brand: Fingerless Gloves ($28)

3) Gender: Male

4) Size: Small

5) Color: Burgundy

6) Quantity: 0

Subtotal: 0

Discount: 0

Total: 0

[Calculate Total]   [Add to Shopping Cart]   [Reset Form]

*FrostiWear Club members receive a 5% discount on all merchandise (rounded to the nearest dollar amount).

27. Print a copy of the Web page showing the total order cost for the following values:

- FrostiWear Club Member = yes, Brand = Glomitt, Quantity = 3
- FrostiWear Club Member = no, Brand = Fingerless Gloves, Quantity = 4
- FrostiWear Club Member = yes, Brand = ArcticBlast, Quantity = 1
- FrostiWear Club Member = no, Brand = PolyFleece Mitts, Quantity = 3

28. Open the Gloves.htm page and verify that all of the hyperlinks you created between the three pages work properly. (Links to Web pages other than the FrostiWear home page will not work.) Close your Web browser.

29. Print a copy of the HTML code for all the pages you created.

In this case you will:

- Use embedded styles and a linked style sheet to create styles for a Web site

- Insert an animated GIF to display a slide show

- Create and use an image map involving polygonal hotspots

- Insert an embedded video clip

- Provide support for older browsers that do not support inline media

CREATING A STYLE FOR A WEB SITE

CASE

Mayer Photography

Mayer Photography is a family-owned photography studio founded by Ted and Jane Mayer in 1972. They've managed to create a successful business in Elmridge, New Hampshire, and the neighboring communities. Ted Mayer recently approached you to create a Web site for his service.

Ted envisions four Web pages for his Web site: a home page that describes the company and provides contact information for customers, a page describing the company's wedding services, a page devoted to the company's portrait services, and a final page that will describe monthly specials offered by the company. You'll name these pages Mayer.htm, Weddings.htm, Portraits.htm, and Specials.htm, respectively.

Ted has also collected four recommendations from Mayer Photography customers. He would like to include these comments on each of the four Web pages. He has provided text files containing these comments as well as the general text that he wants you to place on his Web site. He also has given you graphic files containing samples of his company's work. Because Mayer Photography has lately been involved in providing video services for weddings, he has also provided a video clip (in AVI and QuickTime format) that he would like you to add to the Web page describing the company's wedding services. Figure AC2-1 shows the files you'll place on each Web page.

Figure AC2-1　　**FILES FOR THE MAYER PHOTOGRAPHY WEB SITE**

WEB PAGE	FILES	FILE DESCRIPTIONS
Mayer.htm		
	MLogo.jpg	The company logo and list of Web pages
	Slides.gif	Animated graphic
	Mayer.txt	Description of Mayer Photography's services
	Guitar.jpg	Photo to be placed next to the description of the company's services
	Comment1.txt	Comments from a satisfied customer
	Comment1.jpg	Photo of the satisfied customer
Weddings.htm		
	MLogo.jpg	The company logo and list of Web pages
	Slides.gif	Animated graphic
	Weddings.txt	Description of Mayer Photography's wedding services
	Wedding.jpg	Photo to accompany the wedding services article
	Comment2.txt	Comments from a satisfied wedding customer
	Comment2.jpg	Photo of the wedding customer
	Wedding.avi	Wedding video (AVI format)
	Wedding.mov	Wedding video (QuickTime format)
Portraits.htm		
	MLogo.jpg	The company logo and list of Web pages
	Slides.gif	Animated graphic
	Portraits.txt	Description of Mayer Photography's portrait services
	Family.jpg	Photo to accompany the portrait services article
	Baby.jpg	Second photo to accompany the portrait services article
	Comment3.txt	Comments from a satisfied portrait customer
	Comment3.jpg	Photo of the portrait customer
Specials.htm		
	MLogo.jpg	The company logo and list of Web pages
	Slides.gif	Animated graphic
	Specials.txt	Description of Mayer Photography's specials and special services
	Couple.jpg	Photo to accompany the special services article
	Comment4.txt	Comments from a satisfied customer
	Comment4.jpg	Photo of the satisfied customer

A preview of the first page you'll create, Mayer.htm, is shown in Figure AC2-2 (Netscape users: the top of the initial header will not be aligned with the top of the comment box.)

Figure AC2-2   THE MAYER PHOTOGRAPHY HOME PAGE

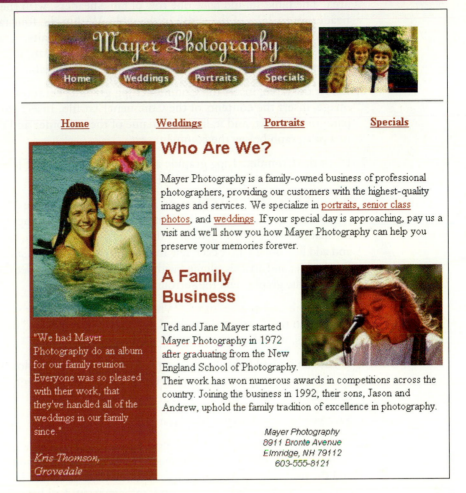

Figure AC2-2   THE MAYER PHOTOGRAPHY HOME PAGE

To create Web pages for the Mayer Photography Web site:

1. Create a file named Mayer.htm in the Case2 subfolder of the Tutorial.add folder on your Data Disk. Specify the title "Mayer Photography: Home Page" for the Web page.

2. At the top of the page, insert the MLogo.jpg file. Set the border width to 0 pixels and specify "Mayer Photography" as the alternate text. Create an image map for the logo with the following polygonal hotspot coordinates:

   - (3,83)(20,69)(40,66)(60,69)(81,83)(60,97)(40,100)(20,97) pointing to the Mayer.htm file
   - (103,83)(120,69)(140,66)(160,69)(181,83)(160,97)(140,100)(120,97) pointing to the Weddings.htm file (you'll create this file, along with Portraits.htm and Specials.htm, in a moment)
   - (203,83)(220,69)(240,66)(260,69)(281,83)(260,97)(240,100)(220,97) pointing to the Portraits.htm file
   - (303,83)(320,69)(340,66)(360,69)(381,83)(360,97)(340,100)(320,97) pointing to the Specials.htm file

3. Directly to the right of the logo, insert the animated GIF, Slides.gif.

4. Insert a horizontal line below the logo and animated GIF, and then center these three elements on the Web page (as shown in Figure AC2-2).

5. Below the horizontal line, create a centered table with a width of 100% of the display area. The table should have one row of table headers, with the width of each table header set to 25% of the width of the table. Within the four table headers, insert the following centered text: "Home," "Weddings," "Portraits," and "Specials," and link the appropriate word to the files: Mayer.htm, Weddings.htm, Portraits.htm, and Specials.htm, respectively. Set the cell padding of the table to 10 pixels.

6. Below the table, insert the Comment1.jpg graphic, centered horizontally. Below the image, insert the contents of the Comment1.txt file. Insert paragraph tags around the paragraph in text, and italicize the name of the customer and the customer's home town in a paragraph below the comment text.

7. Place the Comment1.jpg graphic and the Comment1.txt file within a pair of <DIV> tags with the class name, COMMENTS.

8. Below the COMMENTS element, insert the contents of the Mayer.txt file. Add paragraph tags around each paragraph and format the titles of each paragraph as an H2 heading. Format the address information at the bottom of the column, using the <ADDRESS> tag, and add line breaks after each line in the address. Insert the Guitar.jpg graphic between the first and second articles, aligned with the right cell margin. Set the horizontal distance between the graphic and the surrounding text to 5 pixels.

9. Within the first article (titled "Who Are We?"), link the text "portraits, senior class photos" to the Portraits.htm file. Link the text "weddings" in the same sentence to the Weddings.htm file.

10. Create an embedded style for the page, setting the text color of hyperlinks and all headers to brown, and the background color of the class element, COMMENTS, to brown as well.

11. Save your changes to the Mayer.htm file.

12. Create a style sheet named Mayer.css in the Case2 subfolder of the Tutorial.add folder on your Data Disk. In the style sheet, set the background color of the page body to white and the font color to black. Also set the font face of all headers to Arial, Helvetica, and sans-serif. Reduce the size of the top margin around all headers to 0 pixels. Set the font size of any text in an Address element to 0.75em, center the address text, and set the font face to Arial, Helvetica, and sans-serif.

13. Within the Mayer.css style sheet, create a style for the class element COMMENTS, such that the COMMENT element is a box floating on the left, with a width of 175 pixels, a margin of 5 pixels, and a padding of 5 pixels. Set the font color of text in the COMMENTS element to white.

14. Save your changes to the Mayer.css style sheet and print a copy of the sheet.

15. Reopen the Mayer.htm file in your text editor and link it to the Mayer.css style sheet.

16. Save your changes to Mayer.htm. Print a copy of the HTML code, and then open the page in your Web browser and print a copy of the page as it appears in the browser.

17. Create the Weddings.htm page with your text editor, using the same layout you applied to the Mayer.htm page and linking it to the Mayer.css style sheet. Once again, the COMMENTS box should contain a graphic and a recommendation from a satisfied customer, and the right column should contain information on how Mayer Photography handles weddings. Use the Comment2.txt file along with the Comment2.jpg graphic for the recommendation. Use the Weddings.txt file along with the Wedding.jpg graphic for the column containing wedding information. The Wedding.jpg image should be aligned with the right margin, alongside the text of the first paragraph of wedding information.

18. Use a different color style for the Weddings.htm page. Instead of brown, use the rgb color values (153, 102, 255) to create a lavender color for the text links, headers, and the background of the COMMENTS box.

19. Italicize the words "Draybeck Video Services" in the paragraph on wedding videos.

20. Directly below the wedding videos paragraph, insert a centered embedded video clip using either the Wedding.avi or Wedding.mov file (depending on which video format your computer supports). Set the width and height of the embedded clip to 120 pixels, and set the AUTOSTART value to "false."

Explore ▶ 21. If the customer's browser does not support inline video, have the Weddings.htm page display hyperlinks to the Wedding.avi and Wedding.mov files instead. Include information on the size and format of each video clip along with the linked text.

22. Save the Weddings.htm file. Your page should appear as shown in Figure AC2-3. Print a copy of the HTML code you used to create your page, and print your page as it appears in the Web browser.

Figure AC2-3 **THE MAYER PHOTOGRAPHY WEDDINGS PAGE**

23. Create the Portraits.htm page shown in Figure AC2-4. Apply the same layout and style choices you used in the two other pages. Use the Comment3.txt file for the Greer family recommendation, along with the Comment3.jpg graphic. Use the Portraits.txt file for

the information on Mayer Photography portraits, along with the Family.jpg and Baby.jpg graphics. The color value of the COMMENTS box background, text links, and paragraph headings should be rgb(0,102,153). Print a copy of the HTML code for this file, along with the page as it appears in your Web browser.

Figure AC2-4   **THE MAYER PHOTOGRAPHY PORTRAITS PAGE**

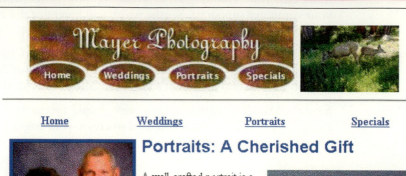

Home   Weddings   Portraits   Specials

Portraits: A Cherished Gift

A well-crafted portrait is a gift you'll cherish forever. At Mayer Photography, we understand this and we strive to create portraits of unsurpassed quality. We work with you to create the portrait you deserve. You can choose between a formal studio setting or, if the mood strikes you, we can go to locations that highlight your personality and interests.

"Mayer Photography has done numerous portraits for our family. We've always been very pleased with their work and professionalism."

Paul & Sue Greer, Idaville

For Any Occasion

Whether you're interested in large group photos, family portraits, or Senior class pictures, Mayer Photography is the place to go for portraits. We offer competitive group rate pricing for organizations, businesses and students. Our highly-trained and experienced staff is ready to serve you.

24. Create the Specials.htm page shown in Figure AC2-5. Use the Comment4.txt file for the recommendation from Barbara Lee, along with the Comment4.jpg graphic. Insert the text from the Specials.txt file into the right column, along with the Couple.jpg graphic. The color value of the COMMENTS box background, text links, and paragraph headings should be rgb(0,102,0).

25. Center the e-mail address and change the e-mail address itself into hypertext pointing to the specified address.

26. Print both the Web page and the corresponding HTML code you created.

27. Test the hyperlinks you created for this Web site, both at the bottom of the page and within the Mayer Photography logo. Verify that the links allow you to open each of the four pages you created.

28. Close your Web browser and your text editor.

OBJECTIVES

In this case you will:

- Design and create an online newsletter incorporating several Web pages

- Format your newsletter using tables, styles, special fonts, and other layout features

- Create an image map containing hotspots to each page in the Web site

- Create a JavaScript program that displays the current date

- Insert a scrolling banner Java applet that displays a list of events

- Create an online survey form containing several form elements

CREATING AN ONLINE NEWSLETTER

CASE

Twin Life Magazine*

Twin Life is a magazine created for parents of twins, triplets, and other multiple-birth children. Recently the company has decided to go online and publish parts of its monthly magazine on the World Wide Web. Elise Howard, the magazine's editor, has asked you to create a Web site for the contents of Twin Life. You've been handed a disk containing text files of the articles she wants you to add and graphics files of the images she wants to have placed on the site.

Elise envisions a total of five Web pages for the site: a front page, a news page, a monthly features page, a page of special articles, and a customer survey page. Figure AC3-1 lists the files that you should use for each page of the Web site.

*Please note: All of Additional Case 3 is an Exploration Exercise.

The actual layout of the pages in the Web site is up to you, but it should incorporate the following features:

- Each Web page should have a title, and you need to specify a style for the colors of the pages' background, text, and linked text.

- The front page should display a message with the current date, for example, "Today is 11/4/2001."

- The site should show at least one example of a font that uses the Arial, Helvetica, or Sans Serif font family and that is a different color from the surrounding text.

- The magazine's logo (TwinLogo.gif) should include an image map linking to the five Web pages in the Web site. (You will have to determine the coordinates for each hotspot using either your graphics software or an image map editor.) In addition, each page in the site should have text links to all five pages, in order to provide support for browsers that cannot display client-side image maps.

- The pages should use tables or styles to format the layout of the different articles in the newsletter. There should be at least one example of an article that has a different background color from the rest.

- The list of upcoming events (found in the Calendar.txt file) should be displayed in a scrolling window, using the CreditRoll.class Java applet. You need to determine the values of each parameter in the applet, aside from the TEXTx parameters.

- Any text in one article that refers to the contents of another article should be changed to a hyperlink pointing to that article.

- A Submit button and a Reset button should be included with the online survey form.

To create Web pages for the Twin Life Web site:

1. Using your text editor, create HTML files named TwinLife.htm, News.htm, Feature.htm, Articles.htm, and Survey.htm.

2. Using the list of files shown in Figure AC3-1, insert the appropriate text and graphics into each of these Web pages (you can copy the text using the copy and paste functions of your text editor). Format the pages with an attractive layout.

Figure AC3-1   **FILES FOR THE *TWIN LIFE* WEB SITE**

WEB PAGE	FILES	FILE DESCRIPTIONS
Front page		
	TwinLogo.gif	The magazine logo
	Twins.jpg	A photo of twins to be used on the front page
	Editor.txt	A message from the editor
	Howard.jpg	A photo of the editor
	Staff.txt	A list of the magazine's staff
	Calendar.txt	A list of upcoming events (to be displayed as scrolling text via a Java applet)
News		
	Chicago.txt	An article on a convention in Chicago of mothers of multiple births
	Lasker.jpg	A photo of the author of the Chicago article
	Rates.txt	An article on twin birth rates
	MBirths.txt	An article on the increase in multiple-birth pregnancies
Features		
	TwinTips.txt	Twin Tips question and answer forum
	Lawson.jpg	A photo of the author of Twin Tips
	Deliver.jpg	Photo of the month
	Deliver.txt	Text to accompany the photo of the month
	Recipe.txt	The recipe of the month
Articles		
	Roles.txt	An article on the roles that twins play
	Kerkman.jpg	A photo of the author of the Roles article
	Talk.txt	An article on how twins acquire speech
	Kuhlman.jpg	A photo of the author of the Talk article
Survey	Survey.txt	The text of the online survey form

3. Open the TwinLife.htm file in your Web browser and test each of the hyperlinks you created. When satisfied with the behavior and appearance of the Web site, print a copy of each Web page as it appears in your Web browser.

4. Return to your text editor and print the HTML code for each of the five Web pages.

5. Close your Web browser and your text editor.

Web Pages & HTML

LAB ASSIGNMENTS

Web Pages & HTML It's easy to create your own Web pages. There are many software tools to help you become a Web author. In this Lab you'll experiment with a Web authoring wizard that automates the process of creating a Web page. You'll also try your hand at working directly with HTML code.

1. Click the Steps button to activate the Web authoring wizard and learn how to create a basic Web page. As you proceed through the Steps, answer all of the Quick Check questions. After you complete the Steps, you will see a Quick Check summary Report. Follow the instructions on the screen to print this report.

2. In Explore, click the File menu, and then click New to start working on a new Web page. Use the wizard to create a Home page for a veterinarian who offers dog day-care and boarding services. After you create the page, save it on drive A or C, and print the HTML code. Your site must have the following characteristics:

   a. Title: Dr. Dave's Dog Domain
   b. Background color: Gold
   c. Graphic: Dog.jpg
   d. Body text: Your dog will have the best care day and night at Dr. Dave's Dog Domain. Fine accommodations, good food, playtime, and snacks are all provided. You can board your pet by the day or week. Grooming services also available.
   e. Text link: "Reasonable rates" links to *www.cciw.com/np3/rates.htm*
   f. E-mail link: "For more information:" links to daveassist@drdave.com

3. In Explore, use the File menu to open the HTML document called Politics.htm. After you use the HTML window (not the wizard) to make the following changes, save the revised page on drive A or C, and print the HTML code. Refer to the HTML Tag Reference at the end of this book for a list of HTML tags you can use.

   a. Change the title to Politics 2000.
   b. Center the page heading.
   c. Change the background color to FFE7C6 and the text color to 000000.
   d. Add a line break before the sentence "What's next?"
   e. Add a bold tag to "Additional links on this topic:".
   f. Add one more link to the "Additional links" list. The link should go to the site *http://www.elections.ca* and the clickable link should read "Elections Canada."
   g. Change the last graphic to display the image "next.gif."

4. In Explore use the Web authoring wizard and the HTML window to create a home page about yourself. You should include at least a screenful of text, a graphic, an external link, and an e-mail link. Save the page on drive A, then print the HTML code. Turn in your disk and printout.

New Perspectives on

CREATING WEB PAGES WITH DYNAMIC HTML

Read This Before You Begin

To the Student

Data Disks

To complete the tutorials, Review Assignments, and Case Problems in this book, you need five Data Disks. Your instructor will either provide you with Data Disks or ask you to make your own.

If you are making your own Data Disks, you will need five blank, formatted, high-density disks. You will need to copy onto your disks a set of folders from a file server, or stand-alone computer, or the Web. Your instructor will tell you which computer, drive letter, and folders contain the files you need. You could also download the files by going to www.course.com, and following the directions on the screen.

The following shows you which folders go on your disks, so that you will have enough disk space to complete all the tutorials, Review Assignments, and Case Problems:

Data Disk 1

Write this on the disk label
Data Disk 1: Tutorial 1
Put this folder on the disk
Tutorial.01D

Data Disk 2

Write this on the disk label
Data Disk 2: Tutorial 2
Put this folder on the disk
Tutorial.02D

Data Disk 3

Write this on the disk label
Data Disk 3: Tutorial 3
Put this folder on the disk
Tutorial.03D

Data Disk 4

Write this on the disk label
Data Disk 4: Tutorial 4
Put this folder on the disk
Tutorial.04D

Data Disk 5

Write this on the disk label
Data Disk 5: Tutorial 5
Put this folder on the disk
Tutorial.05D

When you begin each tutorial, be sure you are using the correct Data Disk. See the inside back cover of this book for more information on Data Disk files, or ask your instructor or technical support person for assistance.

Additional Resource: CD in the back of this book

Take advantage of this special feature of *New Perspectives on Creating Web Pages with DHTML—Introductory*. By using the CD in the back of this book, you can access Java applets, an HTML Tag Reference, additional coverage, and other multimedia elements. Use any or all of these items to enhance your learning process.

Using Your Own Computer

If you are going to work through this book using your own computer, you need:

- ■ **Computer System** A text editor (such as Notepad or Word) and a Web browser (preferably Netscape Navigator 4.7 or Internet Explorer 5.0) must be installed on your computer. If you are using a non-standard browser, it must support frames and HTML 3.2 or above.

- ■ **Data Disks** You will not be able to complete the tutorials or exercises in this book using your own computer until you have Data Disks. The Data Disk files may be downloaded from the Internet. See the inside front cover for more details.

Visit Our World Wide Web Site

Additional materials designed especially for you are available on the World Wide Web. Go to http://www.course.com. For example, see our Student Online Companion, which contains additional coverage of selected topics in the text. These topics are indicated in the text by an Online Companion icon located in the left margin.

To the Instructor

The Data Disk files are available on the Instructor's Resource Kit for this title. Follow the instructions in the Help file on the CD-ROM to install the programs to your network or standalone computer. For information on creating Data Disks, see the "To the Student" section above.

You are granted a license to copy the Data Disk files to any computer or computer network used by students who have purchased this book.

OBJECTIVES

In this tutorial you will:

- Arrange objects using CSS positioning attributes

- Learn about the history and theory of DHTML

- Learn how DHTML is implemented on different browsers

- Work with cross-browser DHTML pages

- Create and link to an API of customized JavaScript functions

- Arrange objects using JavaScript

- Create an animation using JavaScript

Read Carefully

WORKING WITH DYNAMIC PAGE LAYOUT

Creating an Opening Screen for Avalon Books

CASE

Avalon Books

Avalon Books is a popular bookstore chain, with several stores scattered throughout the western United States and in parts of Canada. In recent years, Avalon Books has begun to make its products available online. You've been hired as part of the Web site development team.

Your supervisor, Terry Schuler, wants you to create the opening screen for the company's Web site. The page should be visually interesting, with eye-catching motion and graphics. Some of this can be done with animated GIFs and Java applets, but Terry doesn't want too many of these kinds of elements because they tend to take a long time to load. If the page takes a long time to load, potential customers will be unlikely to wait, and will do their shopping elsewhere. Terry doesn't want the total size of the page and associated elements to be more than 40 KB in size.

One way of adding animation to a page, without the overhead of extra applets or large graphics, is to use **dynamic HTML**, or **DHTML**. Terry suggests that you explore the features of DHTML to see how it can be used to create an interesting opening screen for the company.

SESSION 1.1

In this session you'll be introduced to the theory and history of DHTML. You'll learn how to control the placement of objects on your Web page with CSS. You'll learn about style sheet attributes that control the appearance of your objects. Finally, you'll apply your knowledge to design the layout of an opening page for Avalon Books.

Introduction to DHTML

Early in the development of HTML, Web page authors were limited to creating completely static Web pages. As the World Wide Web became a more important vehicle for the sharing of information, Web page authors and Web browser developers began to look for ways to create more dynamic presentations, whose content and design could be changed after the page had been loaded by the browser. Some of the early attempts to do this involved the use of applets, small programs that the Web browser would retrieve and install along with the Web page.

Starting with the 4.0 versions of Netscape and Internet Explorer, a new approach was offered, in which the HTML code itself supported dynamic elements. Unlike applets, no additional software was needed to create and display dynamic Web pages. These enhancements are known collectively as **dynamic HTML**, or **DHTML**. DHTML involves the interaction of three elements:

- The HTML code of the page
- Cascading style sheets to define the appearance of the page
- A scripting language, usually either JavaScript or VBScript, to control the behavior of elements on the page

By working with these elements, the Web page author can create documents that dynamically interact with the user. Some uses for DHTML that you may have seen include:

- Animated text that moves and changes in response to user action
- Pop-up menus that provide users with quick access to other pages in the Web site without devoting valuable screen space to a long, complicated list of links
- Web pages that retrieve their content from external data sources, giving Web page authors more freedom in the type of material they can display in their pages

Terry wants you to create an opening Web page for Avalon Books that contains animated text and graphics. Terry has sketched out the general appearance and content she wants for the opening screen, which is shown in Figure 1-1. The screen will have five elements:

- An image of Avalon Books' best-selling fiction book
- An image of Avalon Books' best-selling nonfiction book
- An image of a person reading a book, which contains a link to the rest of Avalon Book's Web site
- The text string "Avalon"
- The text string "Books"

THE LAYOUT OF AVALON BOOKS' OPENING PAGE

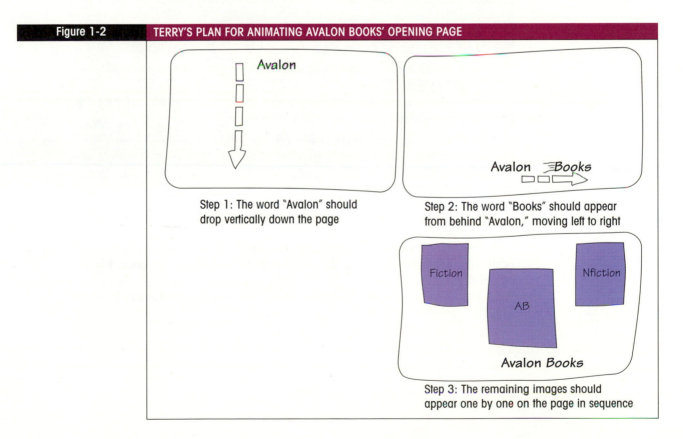

Terry wants to have the single word "Avalon" appear near the top of the page and then drop vertically down the page. At a certain point, "Avalon" should stop dropping, and the word "Books" should appear, moving to the right from behind "Avalon". After that, the three other images should appear on the screen in sequence (see Figure 1-2).

TERRY'S PLAN FOR ANIMATING AVALON BOOKS' OPENING PAGE

Step 1: The word "Avalon" should drop vertically down the page

Step 2: The word "Books" should appear from behind "Avalon," moving left to right

Step 3: The remaining images should appear one by one on the page in sequence

To create this page, you first need to know how to place objects at specific coordinates on the page; then, you need to know how to move those objects. Placing objects on the page can be done by using the style attributes of the Cascading Style Sheets language.

Positioning Objects with CSS

Cascading style sheets were originally used to control the appearance of content on a Web page. An extension to the CSS1 specifications, called **CSS-Positioning**, or **CSS-P**, added the ability to control the layout of the page. CSS-P eventually became part of the CSS2 specification, though you will still occasionally see the term "CSS-P" used to refer specifically to those style attributes that deal with layout and object positioning.

With CSS, you can define the position of any element that is enclosed within a two-sided HTML tag. The style attributes for positioning an object on your Web page are:

```
position:position_type; left:value; top:value;
```

where the position_type attribute indicates the type of positioning used with the object, the left attribute indicates the location of the left edge of the object, and the top attribute indicates the location of the object's top edge. The left and top values can be defined in absolute coordinates (pixels, inches, centimeters, and so forth) or as a percentage of the width of the parent object. The default unit is pixels.

REFERENCE WINDOW	RW

Positioning Elements with CSS
- To control the positioning type, use the style declaration:
  ```
  position:type
  ```
  where *type* is absolute, relative, fixed, or static.
- To control the position of the left edge of the object, use the style:
  ```
  left:value
  ```
  where *value* is the coordinate of the left edge in absolute or relative units, or is a percentage of the height of the parent element. The default unit is pixels.
- To control the position of the top edge of the object, use the style:
  ```
  top:value
  ```

There are four possible values for the position attribute: absolute, relative, fixed, and static. Let's consider each of these in turn.

An **absolute position** places the object at a defined coordinate in the document, regardless of the object's initial location or the location of other objects on the page. Figure 1-3 shows an object that has been placed at the (30, 100) coordinate on the page, that is, 30 pixels to the right and 100 pixels down from the upper-left corner of the display window.

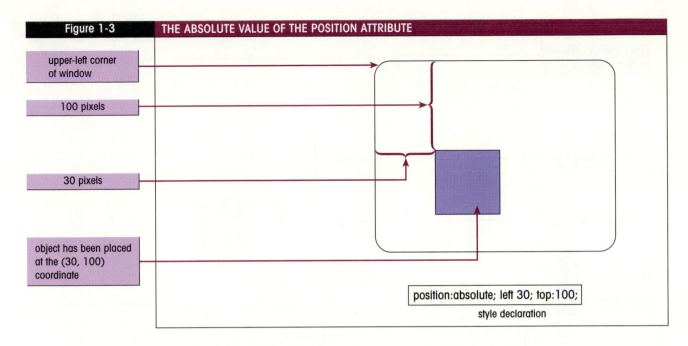

The absolute position is always determined relative to the upper-left corner of the parent object. A positive top value places the object down from the top edge; a negative value places the object above the top edge. Similarly, a positive left value places the object to the right of the left edge and a negative value places the object to the left of the left edge.

In most cases, the parent object will be the browser's display window, but as shown in Figure 1-4, the object also can be positioned within another element on the page. In this example, the object has been placed 30 pixels to the right and 100 pixels down from the upper-left corner of its parent element.

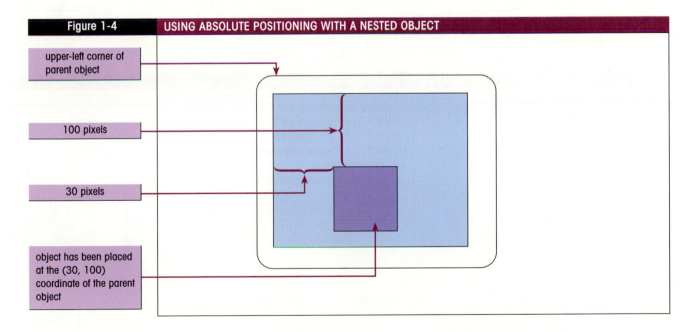

A **relative position** places the object at a point relative to its location in the natural flow of the document. The object shown in Figure 1-5 is moved 30 pixels to the left and 100 pixels down from where the browser would have originally placed the object.

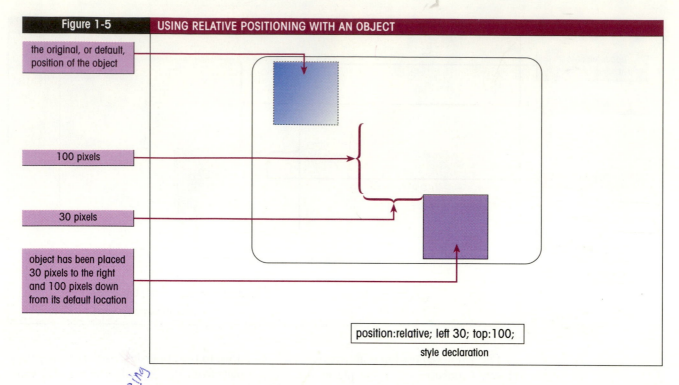

Figure 1-5 — USING RELATIVE POSITIONING WITH AN OBJECT

the original, or default, position of the object

100 pixels

30 pixels

object has been placed 30 pixels to the right and 100 pixels down from its default location

position:relative; left 30; top:100;

style declaration

Placing @ B.S.

Placing an object by using relative positioning can be an exercise in frustration, because how will you know the default location of the object unless you first render the page in your browser? And even then, the default location may change from one browser to another, as well as under different monitor resolutions. Placing an object 50 pixels to the left may result in an attractive layout at the 640 × 480 resolution, but could be a real mess at 800 × 600. A general rule of thumb is that you should use absolute positioning whenever you have objects that are seemingly independent of each other, and use relative positioning for objects that appear to be related. Figure 1-6 shows how relative positioning can be used to achieve an interesting visual effect with words within a sentence.

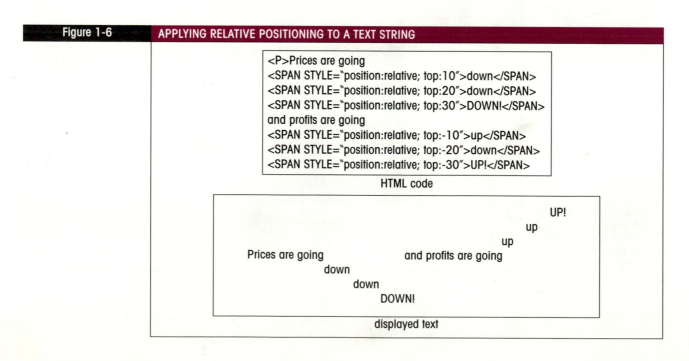

Figure 1-6 — APPLYING RELATIVE POSITIONING TO A TEXT STRING

```
<P>Prices are going
<SPAN STYLE="position:relative; top:10">down</SPAN>
<SPAN STYLE="position:relative; top:20">down</SPAN>
<SPAN STYLE="position:relative; top:30">DOWN!</SPAN>
and profits are going
<SPAN STYLE="position:relative; top:-10">up</SPAN>
<SPAN STYLE="position:relative; top:-20">down</SPAN>
<SPAN STYLE="position:relative; top:-30">UP!</SPAN>
```

HTML code

UP!
up
up
Prices are going   and profits are going
down
down
DOWN!

displayed text

The **fixed** position value places the object at a fixed location in the display window. The object will remain at that fixed position and will not scroll with other elements in the Web page. Currently the major browsers do not support the fixed attribute value.

Finally, the **static** position value places the object in its natural position in the flow of the document, as determined by the Web browser. In this case, you are letting the browser handle the layout of the object for you. If you use static positioning, you cannot define values for the top and left attributes.

Layering Objects

Frequently, positioned objects overlap. When this happens you need to specify which object is placed on top of the others. By default, objects that appear later in the HTML file are placed on top of earlier elements. To specify your own stacking order, use the z-index style attribute, which has the syntax:

```
z-index: value;
```

where *value* is a positive or negative integer, or the value "auto."

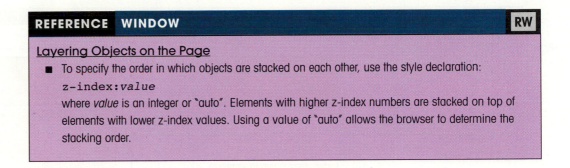

REFERENCE WINDOW   RW

Layering Objects on the Page
- To specify the order in which objects are stacked on each other, use the style declaration:
  `z-index:value`
  where *value* is an integer or "auto". Elements with higher z-index numbers are stacked on top of elements with lower z-index values. Using a value of "auto" allows the browser to determine the stacking order.

Objects with a higher z-index value are placed on top of objects with lower z-indexes. Figure 1-7 shows the effect of the z-index attribute on the layering of several different objects.

Figure 1-7   APPLYING THE Z-INDEX ATTRIBUTE

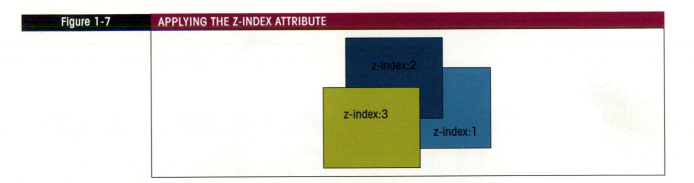

If two objects have the same z-index value, the object that is defined later in the HTML file will be shown on top. A z-index value of 0, or "auto" causes the object to be placed in its default layer, just as if no z-index value was defined in the first place. Note that the z-index attribute has no effect for objects from within different parent elements. The z-index value can only be used to layer objects within the same parent element.

Controlling Object Visibility

Usually the only reason for hiding an object is that you're going to "unhide it" later using a script. You can do this by using the visibility attribute with the syntax:

```
visibility: visibility_type;
```

where *visibility_type* is visible, inherit, or hidden. The visible value makes the object visible on the page. Setting the visibility attribute to inherit (the default) causes the object to inherit the visibility property of its parent element. Setting the visibility property to hidden causes the browser to hide the object, but the object still takes up space on the Web page, and your Web browser will have to flow other document objects around it. If you want to hide the object *and* have it take up no space on the page, use the display attribute with the value "none," as follows:

```
display: none;
```

Figure 1-8 shows the difference between the visibility:hidden attribute and the display:none attribute.

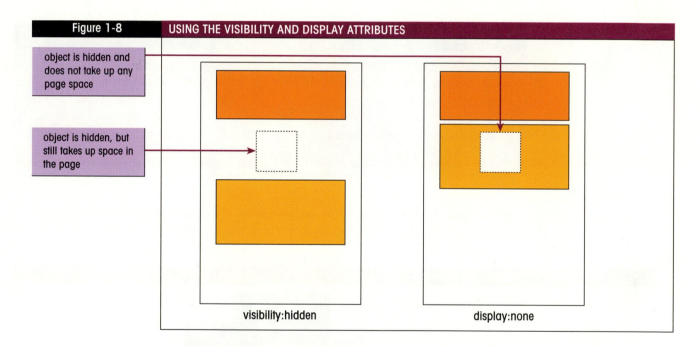

| Figure 1-8 | USING THE VISIBILITY AND DISPLAY ATTRIBUTES |

object is hidden and does not take up any page space

object is hidden, but still takes up space in the page

visibility:hidden   display:none

REFERENCE WINDOW   **RW**

Hiding and Unhiding an Object with CSS

■ To hide or unhide an object, use the style:

```
visibility: type
```

where **type** is either inherit, hidden, or visible. Specifying "inherit" (the default) causes the element to inherit the visibility attribute of its parent. Specifying a value of "hidden" hides the object on the page. The "visible" value unhides the object.

Only Internet Explorer allows you to change the display attribute after the browser has loaded the page.

Working with Overflow and Clipping

Other attributes that you will have to consider when using CSS for layout are the dimensions of your object. You can define the width and height of each object on your page by using the width and height attributes, as follows:

```
width: value; height: value;
```

where *value* is the width and height values as measured in absolute or relative units, or as a percentage of the width or height of the parent element. If you do not define the height and width values, the browser will choose one for you based on the content of the object.

If the content of the object is greater than the dimensions you've allowed for it, you can control how the browser handles the extra content. The syntax is:

```
overflow: overflow_type;
```

where *overflow_type* is: visible, hidden, scroll, or auto. Setting the overflow value to visible causes the browser to increase the size to fit the extra content (the default). In the case of text, the browser will usually only increase the object's height, leaving the width at the specified value. Using an overflow value of hidden keeps the object at the specified size and hides the extra content. If you set the overflow attribute to scroll, your browser keeps the object at the specified size and adds scroll bars for viewing the extra content. Finally, setting overflow to auto will display scroll bars only as needed. Figure 1-9 shows the effect of various overflow values on a block of text.

Figure 1-9	OVERFLOW VALUES

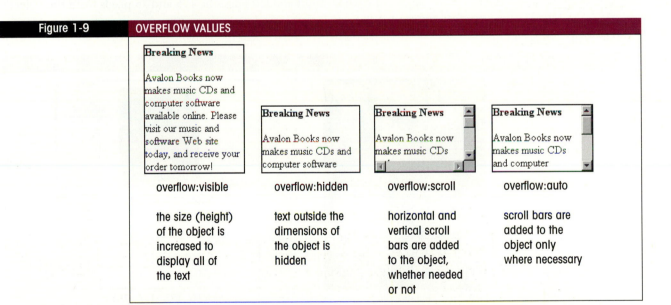

Netscape through version 4.7 supports only the hidden and visible values for the overflow attribute. Internet Explorer supports all four attribute values.

Controlling Overflow and Clipping with CSS

■ To specify how the browser should handle extra content, use the style declaration:

  overflow: *type*

  where *type* is either visible (to enlarge the object to fit the extra content), hidden (to hide the extra content), scroll (to display scroll bars to view the extra content, whether the scroll bars are needed or not), or auto (to display scroll bars only when needed).

■ To control the size of the clipping rectangle around the element, use the style declaration:

  clip: rect(*top*, *right*, *bottom*, *left*)

  where *top*, *right*, *bottom*, and *left* are the coordinates of the top, right, bottom, and left edges of the clipping rectangle.

Closely related to the overflow attribute is the clip attribute. The clip attribute allows you to define a rectangular region through which the object's content can be viewed. Anything that lies outside the boundary of the rectangle is hidden. Clipping can be used to hide certain portions of the page's content until needed.

The syntax for using the clip attribute is:

clip: rect(*top*, *right*, *bottom*, *left*);

where *top*, *right*, *bottom*, and *left* define the coordinates of the rectangle. The coordinates are all relative to the top and left edges of the object. For example, a clip value of rect(10, 175, 125, 75) defines a rectangle whose top and bottom edges lie 10 and 125 pixels from the top edge of the object, and whose right and left edges lie 175 and 75 pixels from the object's left edge (see Figure 1-10).

Figure 1-10   **CLIPPING AN OBJECT**

full graphic   clip: rect(10, 175, 125, 75)

The *top*, *right*, *bottom*, and *left* values can also be set to "auto," which moves the clipping region to the top, right, bottom, and left edges of the object. For example, a clip value of rect(10, auto, 125 75) creates a clipping rectangle whose right edge matches the right edge of the object, while the rest of the edges are clipped.

The clip attribute can be used only with absolute positioning.

Creating an Opening Screen for Avalon Books

Now that you've learned about the CSS attributes that control the placement and appearance of objects on your Web page, you're ready to create an opening screen for Avalon Books. Much of the HTML file has already been created for you and saved in the file ABtext.htm. Your first task will be to position the items on the page using the various CSS positioning attributes.

To open the ABtext.htm file:

1. Start your text editor and then locate and open the **ABtext.htm** file in the Tutorial.01D folder of your Data Disk.

2. Save the file as **Avalon.htm**.

3. Take some time to study the HTML code in the file.

Each object in the page (including the words "Avalon" and "Books") has been placed in a separate <DIV> container tag. While it's not necessary at this point to put the two words in separate containers, it will prove useful later on, when you apply animation to the Web page.

Also note that each object has a different ID value. The script you'll write will use these ID values as a reference for each object.

To position these objects on the Web page, you'll use absolute positioning. By trial and error, you arrive at the following coordinates for each object:

- Place the word "Avalon" at the coordinate (175, 260)—that is 175 pixels from the left edge of the display window and 260 pixels down from the window's top edge.
- Place the word "Books" at the coordinate (320, 260).
- Place the AB.jpg image at the coordinate (230, 40).
- Place the Fiction.jpg image at the coordinate (5, 5).
- Place the NFiction.jpg image at the coordinate (475, 5).

When you use absolute positioning, it's important to make sure that your coordinates work for different monitor resolutions. For example, if you place an object at the coordinate (750, 500), it will be off the screen for users with 640×480 monitors!

Now that you know the coordinates, you can modify each object's style to include this information.

To enter the coordinates for each object:

1. Scroll down the Avalon.htm file and locate the style for the avalon object.

2. At the end of the style declaration (after the word "bold" and before the closing quotation mark), insert a semicolon and then type the following:

```
position:absolute; left:175; top:260
```

Note: Make sure that each style attribute is separated from the others with a semicolon and that the *entire* style declaration is enclosed within double quotation marks.

3. Add a semicolon and the following style to the books object:

```
position:absolute; left:320; top:260
```

4. Add a semicolon and the following style to the AB object:

```
position:absolute; left:230; top:40
```

5. Add a semicolon and the following style to the Fiction object:

```
position:absolute; left:5; top:5
```

6. Finally, add a semicolon and the following style to the NFiction object:

```
position:absolute; left:475; top:5
```

Your completed code should appear as shown in Figure 1-11.

| Figure 1-11 | SETTING THE COORDINATES FOR THE OBJECTS IN THE AVALON BOOKS PAGE |

```
<DIV ID="avalon"
    STYLE="background-color:black; font-size:24pt; font-weight:bold;
        position:absolute; left:175; top:260">
    AVALON
</DIV>

<DIV ID="books"
    STYLE="color:red; font-style:italic; font-size:24pt; font-weight:bold;
        position:absolute; left:320; top:260">
    BOOKS
</DIV>

<DIV ID="AB"
    STYLE="width:150; height:225;
        position:absolute; left:230; top:40">
    <A HREF="ABStore.htm"><IMG SRC="AB.jpg" BORDER=0></A>
</DIV>

<DIV ID="Fiction"
    STYLE="font-family:Arial,Helvetica,sans-serif;font-size:x-small;
        width:120; position:absolute; left:5; top:5">
    <CENTER><IMG SRC="Fiction.jpg"><BR>
    <B>AB Sales Rank: #1<BR>
    Fiction</B><BR>
    <I>Before the Fall</I><BR>Jeffrey Unwin</CENTER>
</DIV>

<DIV ID="NFiction"
    STYLE="font-family:Arial,Helvetica,sans-serif; font-size:x-small;
        width:120; position:absolute; left:475; top:5">
    <CENTER><IMG SRC="NFiction.jpg"><BR>
    <B>AB Sales Rank: #1<BR>
    Nonfiction</B><BR>
    <I>Vietnam Memoirs</I><BR>Gen. John Hartford</CENTER>
</DIV>
```

7. Save your changes to the Avalon.htm file.

8. Open the **Avalon.htm** file in your Web browser. Figure 1-12 shows the layout of the page along with the coordinates for each of the five objects.

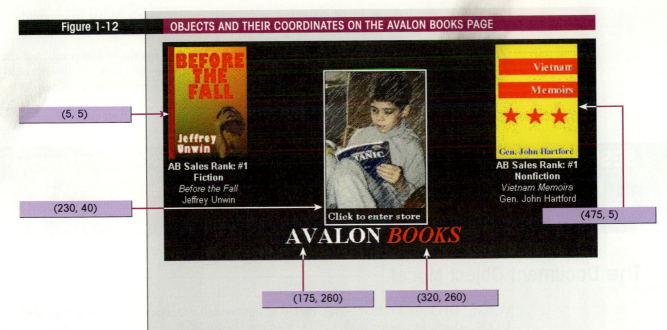

Figure 1-12 OBJECTS AND THEIR COORDINATES ON THE AVALON BOOKS PAGE

TROUBLE? The page shown in Figure 1-12 has a resolution of 640 × 480. If your monitor is set to a different resolution, your page will look slightly different.

TROUBLE? If your objects are not set to appropriate positions on the page, check your style declarations. Verify that each style attribute is separated from the others by a semicolon, and that the entire inline style is enclosed in double quotation marks. Check your spelling against the styles shown in Figure 1-11.

You show the layout of the Avalon.htm page to Terry, and she gives you the go ahead to add animation to this page. You'll start that process in the next session by learning how to use style attributes in your JavaScript programs.

Session 1.1 QUICK CHECK

1. What style would you enter to fix an object on the Web page, and prevent it from scrolling in the document window?

2. What style would you enter to place an object 3 centimeters down and 5 centimeters to the right of the upper-left corner of the browser window?

3. What HTML code would you use to offset the words "Avalon Books" 25 pixels up from their normal position in the document?

4. Describe the z-index attribute. Where is the object with the lowest z-index value placed?

5. What is the difference between display:none and visibility:hidden?

6. An object has a width of 200 pixels and a height of 150 pixels. What style would you use to create a clipping region that clips 10 pixels off each side of the object?

7. An object's content requires a width of 150 pixels and a height of 200 pixels, but the dimensions given are only 150 pixels by 150 pixels. What two style attributes could you use to make scroll bars available for the hidden content? What is a potential problem with these two attributes?

SESSION 1.2

In this session you'll learn how DHTML is implemented in Netscape and Internet Explorer. You'll see how to detect the type of browser your user is running and how to create code that works for both of the major browsers. You'll learn how to create an API, an external file of customized commands and functions. Finally, you'll see how to write JavaScript programs to modify the style attributes of your objects.

The Document Object Model

Writing DHTML code requires that you understand the **document object model**, or **DOM**, which, in theory, makes every element on the Web page available to the scripting language. We say, "in theory," because in actual practice most browsers and browser versions do not offer a complete DOM, though versions 4.0 and 5.0 of Internet Explorer come very close. By accessing the document object model through DHTML, the Web page author can write scripts that control almost every element that appears on the Web page. This means that the document is no longer a static entity, but instead becomes an application that can be manipulated in response to actions by the user or programs written by the Web page developer. The document object model can be thought of as a hierarchy of elements, with the window object at the top of the tree. Figure 1-13 shows a sample DOM hierarchy.

Figure 1-13	THE DOM HIERARCHY

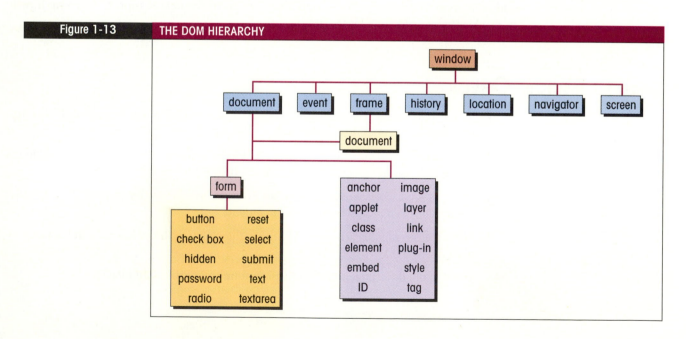

Element Collections

In JavaScript you translate this hierarchy of elements into **reference names**, which indicate the location of the element in the DOM hierarchy. Elements can be grouped into **element collections**, which are arrays of all of the elements of a particular type within the Web document. The syntax for an element collection is:

```
document.collection[i].property;
```

where *collection* is the name of the collection, *i* is either an index number or the ID name of the collection object, and *property* is a JavaScript property of the object. The first object in the collection has an index number of 0. You can also use the ID names of individual elements in place of the index number. The syntax of this type of reference name is either:

```
document.collection["id"]
```

or

```
document.collection.id
```

where *id* is the ID name of the element.

Figure 1-14 describes the different element collections and their browser support. Note that not all element collections are supported by both Netscape and Internet Explorer.

Figure 1-14	JAVASCRIPT OBJECT COLLECTIONS		
ARRAY	**DESCRIPTION**	**BROWSER SUPPORT**	
		NETSCAPE	**IE**
document.all	All HTML elements in the document		4.0
document.anchors	All anchor objects in the document	2.0	3.0
document.applets	All Java applets in the document. The applet must be started and running before being recognized as part of the DOM	2.0	3.0
document.classes	All classes defined for the document	4.0	
document.embeds	All embedded objects (created with the <EMBED>tag) in the document		4.0
document.forms	All forms in the document	2.0	3.0
document.frames	All internal frames (created with the <IFRAME> tag) in the document		4.0
document.ids	All IDs defined for the document	4.0	
document.images	All inline images (created with the <IMG> tag) in the document	2.0	3.0
document.layers	All block-level elements defined with either the <LAYER> tag or the <DIV> tag	4.0	
document.links	All linked items in the document (elements created with the <A> tag and the HREF property, or <AREA> tag)	2.0	3.0
document.plugins	All plug-ins in the document (created with the <EMBED> tag)		4.0
document.scripts	All script objects (created with the <SCRIPT> tag)		4.0
document.styleSheets	All style sheet objects (created with the <STYLE> tag)		4.0
document.tags	All tags defined in the document	4.0	

For example, the object reference to the first linked item, named Home, can be expressed using any of the following reference names:

```
document.links[0]
document.links["Home"]
document.links.Home
```

Referencing <DIV> Containers

For Avalon Books, you'll need to create reference names for the various <DIV> elements located on the opening page. Netscape and Internet Explorer use different references for <DIV> tags. Netscape refers to objects formatted with the <DIV> tag as layers and places them in the layers collection.

```
document.layers["id"]
document.layers.id
document.id
```

where *id* is the ID name given to the <DIV> tag. The reason that Netscape uses the layers collection is that there is a Netscape-supported tag called the <LAYER> tag, which is similar to the <DIV> tag. You'll learn more about the <LAYER> tag in the next tutorial.

In Internet Explorer, the reference syntax for the same object can be any of the following:

```
document.all["id"]
document.all.id
id
```

For example, if in your document, you have created the following tag:

```
<DIV ID="Greetings">Welcome to Avalon Books</DIV>
```

You can refer to this object in Netscape by using any of the following reference names:

```
document.layers.Greetings
document.layers["Greetings"]
document.Greetings
```

while in Internet Explorer, you would probably use one of these references:

```
document.all.Greetings
document.all["Greetings"]
Greetings
```

Referencing Styles

The syntax rules for changing one of the style attributes of an element also differ between the two browsers. In Netscape, the syntax for referencing a style attribute is:

```
object.attribute
```

where *object* is the reference name of the element, and *attribute* is the name of the style attribute. In Internet Explorer, this same reference would be:

```
object.style.attribute
```

REFERENCE WINDOW   **RW**

Referencing a Style Attribute
- To reference a style attribute in Netscape, use:
  ```
  object.attribute
  ```
- To reference a style attribute in Internet Explorer, use:
  ```
  object.style.attribute
  ```
  where *object* is the object reference of the element, and *attribute* is the name of the style attribute.

As you'll see later, not only do the browsers differ in how they reference style attributes, but the names and values of the style attributes can also vary greatly between browsers. You'll learn more about JavaScript style attributes later in this tutorial.

Referencing Nested Objects

Netscape and Internet Explorer also differ in how they handle nested objects. In Netscape you use the reference syntax:

```
document.id1.document.id2.document.id3
```

where *id1* is an object at the top of the hierarchy, *id2* is nested inside *id1*, *id3* is nested inside *id2*, and so forth. If you have a lot of nested objects, this reference name can become quite long and complicated.

With Internet Explorer you don't have to worry about the various levels of nested objects. As long as you've given a unique ID name to the object, you can reference it directly, regardless of its location in the hierarchy. So to reference *id3*, you would simply use the reference name:

```
id3
```

For example, to reference the Title object in the following HTML code:

```
<DIV ID="Greetings">Welcome to <SPAN ID="Title">Avalon
Books</SPAN></DIV>
```

Netscape uses the reference name:

```
document.Greetings.document.Title
```

because the Title object is nested inside the Greetings object. However, in Internet Explorer you would just use the ID name:

```
Title
```

because you don't need to worry about where it is in the object hierarchy.

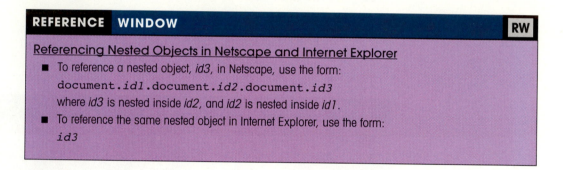

Any HTML code that you write needs to take into account all of these differences in reference name syntax.

Implementing the DOM

The two browsers also have some major differences in how they implement the document object model. In the Netscape version of the DOM, you can't make fundamental changes to the structure of the Web page after the page has been loaded by the browser. You are also limited in how you can change the form and content of the document.

Starting with version 4.0, the Internet Explorer implementation of the DOM is much more flexible and robust. Your scripts can dynamically alter the property of any object in the document, even after the page has been loaded. The Internet Explorer DOM even allows the Web page author to change tag associations. For example, text formatted with an H1 header can be turned into an H3 header "on the fly." Internet Explorer also provides additional features such as filters that allow you to change the appearance of document content by adding drop shadows or other special effects. The Internet Explorer DOM also provides the ability to retrieve information from databases, allowing greater flexibility in document content. As useful as these features are, they must always be implemented with the knowledge that not all browsers support them, and that workarounds must be provided.

Why do Internet Explorer and Netscape express the DOM so differently? The problem is that the two browsers developed DHTML separately. It is only in recent years that attempts have been made to create a standard DOM with standard object references. In most cases, the Internet Explorer approach has been adopted as the accepted standard, but you still have to deal with both approaches until both browsers adopt a common standard, and even then it will be several years before older browser versions have been filtered out of the marketplace.

Creating a Cross-Browser Web Site

Clearly, the animation you develop for the Avalon Books pages needs to accommodate both Netscape and Internet Explorer. To do this, you need to have some way of determining what type of browser the user is running, and then to have the browser run the correct set of commands for that browser. There are two ways of detecting this information: browser detection and object detection.

Using Browser Detection

With **browser detection** you determine the type of browser and version that the user is running and then apply a script designed for that browser version. This assumes that you've done your homework and have mapped out the capabilities of each browser and browser version: no easy task!

The browser type can be retrieved from the appName property of the navigator object. To store the name of the browser in a variable named "bName" you would use the command:

```
var bName=navigator.appName;
```

For Netscape, bName will have the value "Netscape." For Internet Explorer, the value of bName would be "Microsoft Internet Explorer." That's easy enough. However, detecting the browser version is more complicated.

To determine the browser version, you use the appVersion property of the navigator object. Unfortunately, this property includes both the version number and additional text that describes features of the version. Usually you won't need this extra information. You can extract the version number from the appVersion property by using either the parseInt() or parseFloat() methods . The parseInt() method extracts an integer value from a text string, while the parseFloat() method extracts a whole number (integer plus decimal). For example, the value of the navigator.appVersion property for Netscape 4.7 is:

4.7 [en]C-CCK-MCD NSCPCD47 (Win98;I)

To extract the major version number use:

```
var bVer=parseInt(navigator.appVersion);
```

and the value of bVer will be 4. If you want to store the full version number in the bVer variable, use the command:

```
var bVer=parseFloat(navigator.appVersion);
```

which stores the value, 4.7 in bVer. Most of the time you will need only the major version number, not the full version number, since the major version number is used to signify big changes in the software.

These commands also work for all versions of Internet Explorer, *except* for Internet Explorer 5.0, which stores a value of 4.0 in the bVer variable! As long as your page doesn't contain features that are unique to Internet Explorer 5.0, this should not be a problem. If it is important to distinguish Internet Explorer 4.0 from Internet Explorer 5.0, you will have to write a more complicated script. You discuss this issue with Terry Schuler, and she decides that as long as you don't use features that require Internet Explorer 5.0, this shouldn't be a problem and you can make your page compatible with Internet Explorer 4.0.

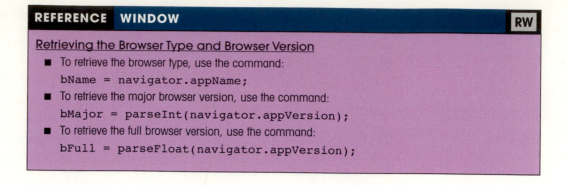

Once you know the browser type and browser version, you can combine these values in a new variable, which you could name "browser," and save them in one compact text string. The code could appear as follows:

```
var browser;
var bName = navigator.appName;
var bVer = parseInt(navigator.appVersion);
if (bName == "Netscape" && bVer == 4) browser="ns4";
if (bName == "Netscape" && bVer == 3) browser="ns3";
if (bname == "Netscape" && bVer == 2) browser="ns2";
if (bName == "Microsoft Internet Explorer" && bVer == 4)
browser="ie4";
if (bName == "Microsoft Internet Explorer" && bVer == 3)
browser="ie3";
if (bName == "Microsoft Internet Explorer" && bVer == 2)
browser="ie2";
```

For example, if the user is running Netscape version 3.0, the value of the browser variable will be ns3. If the user is running Internet Explorer 4.0 or 5.0, the browser variable will have a value of ie4.

Using Object Detection

Many Web page developers recommend bypassing browser detection entirely, and instead rely on object detection. With **object detection**, you check which types of DOM reference names are supported by the browser (if any) and write your code to fit the reference name syntax rather than the browser type. You can use the fact that Netscape supports the document.layers reference name for <DIV> elements, and Internet Explorer uses document.all to distinguish between the two reference syntaxes. The JavaScript code to do this could look as follows:

```
var isNS = false;
var isIE = false;
if (document.layers) isNS=true;
if (document.all) isIE=true;
```

The variables, isNS and isIE, are Boolean variables that indicate whether the object reference syntax follows the Netscape or Internet Explorer convention. If the browser recognizes the term "document.layers," it will change the value of the isNS variable to true, indicating that the browser is using Netscape's reference syntax; if the browser recognizes the term "document.all," it will change the value of isIE to true for the Internet Explorer approach.

This method has the advantage that if, at a future date, Netscape begins supporting the Internet Explorer reference syntax, Web authors won't have to revise their code to take advantage of this change. The other advantage of object detection is that it works for browsers (besides the big two) such as Opera which also support DHTML. The only problem with object detection is that you can't distinguish between browser versions, so if a feature on your Web site is supported by one browser version but not by another, you still will have to test for version number.

Employing Cross-Browser Strategies

Once you've determined the capabilities of the browser (by either browser or object detection), your next task is to choose a cross-browser strategy for your Web site. One strategy, called **page branching**, creates separate pages for each browser (and if you need to get really detailed, for each browser version) along with an initial page. When the user opens the initial page, a script determines the capability of the user's browser and automatically loads the appropriate page (see Figure 1-15). The initial page itself can be used for browsers that don't support a scripting language.

Figure 1-15	PAGE BRANCHING

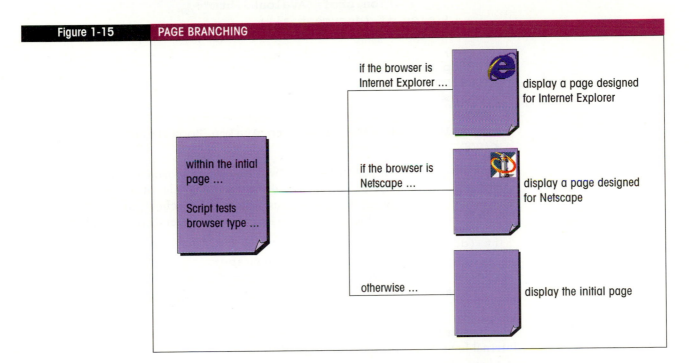

To automatically load a page into the browser based on the type of browser detected, use the command:

```
location=URL;
```

where *URL* is the URL of the new page to be loaded. The page branching commands should be placed in the header section of the HTML file to ensure that the script is run *before* the initial page is loaded.

The following is code for a page that will load the AvalonNS.htm page if the user's browser recognizes the Netscape reference name syntax. Failing that, it will load AvalonIE.htm if it encounters a browser that supports Internet Explorer's reference names. Presumably you will insert into those two pages DHTML code that is appropriate for the browser detected. If the browser does not support either reference syntax (or it doesn't support the scripting language at all), it will finish loading the page, displaying the text "Welcome to Avalon Books" as a centered H1 header.

```
<HTML>
HEAD>
<TITLE>Avalon Books</TITLE>
<SCRIPT>
<!--- Hide from non-JavaScript browsers
      if (document.layers) {
          location.href="AvalonNS.htm";
      } else if (document.all) {
          location.href="AvalonIE.htm";
      }
// Stop hiding --->
</SCRIPT>
</HEAD>
<BODY>
<H1 ALIGN="CENTER">Welcome to Avalon Books!</H1>
</BODY>
```

Page branching requires you to maintain two versions of the same page. In a Web site with several pages that may have to be updated daily, this means a lot of extra work.

A second cross-browser strategy is to use **internal branching**, in which each piece of DHTML code is enclosed in an If...Else statement. The general syntax would be:

```
if (document.layers) {
   JavaScript commands for Netscape;
} else if (document.all) {
   JavaScript commands for Internet Explorer;
}
```

This construction would have to be repeated every time you run a set of DHTML commands. Internal branching works well for pages that do not employ a lot of DHTML code. Pages that have a lot of DHTML code will quickly become unwieldy and prone to errors if you use internal branching.

Many Web developers apply a third cross-browser strategy: they create an application programming interface. An **application programming interface** or **API** is an external text file that contains custom JavaScript commands and functions. These customized functions are written to resolve any cross-browser differences. When you create a Web page, you link it to the API and use commands from the API file in your Web page (see Figure 1-16) rather than placing the code within the HTML file on your page.

Figure 1-16	USING AN API FILE

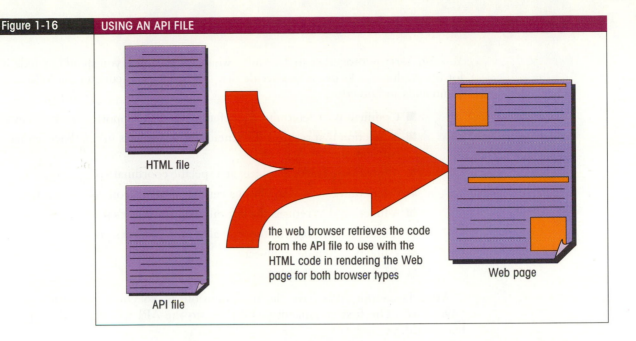

For example, you'll soon learn that Netscape and Internet Explorer have different commands to hide objects on the page. Rather than creating two separate Web pages or using internal branching every time you want to run a command to hide an object, a custom function called "hideIt(object)" can be added to the API. The general form of the function would be as follows:

```
function hideIt(object) {
   if (document.layers) {
      Commands to hide the object in Netscape;
   } else if (document.all) {
      Commands to hide the object in Internet Explorer;
   }
}
```

Once you link your Web page to the API file, the hideIt() command can then be accessed and run from within the page. If the developer wants to hide a particular object when the page is loaded, the following command can be added to the <BODY> tag:

```
<BODY onLoad="hideIt(object)">
```

where *object* is the reference to the object that needs to be hidden. Since the API is in an external file, the functions it contains can be used over and over again from different pages in the Web site, and the author does not have to go through the process of reentering the code, nor does the developer have to create a browser test for each page, since this can be accomplished from within the API. This speeds up development time and greatly simplifies the structure of the Web document.

If you do create an API file for your Web page, you cannot place it in the root directory of your hard drive. Doing so causes Internet Explorer to report a security error when accessing the file.

You discuss the various approaches to creating a cross-browser Web site with Terry. Since the Avalon Books Web site contains many Web pages, you both agree that creating a custom API is the best solution.

Creating an API for Avalon Books

You and Terry get together to determine what sort of things you should include in the API for the Avalon Books page. You decide that the API should contain the following types of commands and functions:

- Commands to determine the reference syntax supported by the browser
- A function that resolves the syntactical differences in reference names between the two browsers
- A function to place an object at a specific coordinate on the page
- A function to move an object a certain distance from its current location
- A function that returns the left value of the object's position
- A function that returns the top value of the object's position
- A function to hide an object
- A function to unhide an object

Most JavaScript APIs have the file extension .js, so you'll name this particular API "Avalon.js". The first commands you'll put into the API will detect the type of browser being used.

To start creating the Avalon.js API:

1. Open your text editor and a new, blank text file.

2. Type the following commands into the text file:

```
var isNS=false;
var isIE=false;
if (document.layers) isNS=true;
if (document.all) isIE=true;
```

3. Save the file as **Avalon.js** in the Tutorial.01D folder on your Data Disk.

This set of commands in the API created two variables, isNS and isIE, that determine the reference syntax supported by the browser. By placing these commands outside a function command block, both isNS and isIE will be **global variables**, and their values will be accessible from any function in the API or in the Web page. Thus, you will not have to perform the browser test more than once.

Next, you need a function that resolves the differences in how objects are referenced by the two browsers. For this case, we're only going to work with the style attributes of the <DIV> objects on the page. The syntax for Netscape browsers is:

```
document.id.attribute
```

and Internet Explorer uses the syntax:

```
id.style.attribute
```

where id is the ID name of the <DIV> tag, and *attribute* is the style attribute. Thus if you know the object's ID name, you can create the reference name for Netscape browsers by inserting the text string "document." before the ID name. Similarly, the Internet Explorer reference name can be created by appending the text string ".style" to the object's ID name. You could then apply the style attribute to the tail end of both reference names.

If the ID of the object is stored in the variable "id," the following commands will store the correct object reference for both browsers in a variable named obj:

```
if (isNS) obj="document."+id;
if (isIE) obj=id+".style";
```

Note that the obj variable is a text string; it's not an object on the Web page. To create an object from this text string, you use the eval() function. The eval() function will evaluate the text string and create an object based on the reference name. The entire function will look as follows:

```
function getObject(id) {
    if (isNS) obj="document."+id;
    if (isIE) obj=id+".style";
    var object=eval(obj);
    return object;
}
```

What the getObject() function will then do is take the object's ID name and return a variable that points to the object itself—and it will do this correctly for both Netscape and Internet Explorer. For example, to reference the following element in the Web page:

```
<DIV ID="avalon">Avalon Books</DIV>
```

you would use the command:

```
getObject("avalon");
```

Note that the getObject() function works only for objects at the top of the hierarchy. You would need a more complicated function for nested objects, since Netscape refers to nested objects differently from Internet Explorer. Since you won't need to manipulate nested objects for the Avalon Books Web page, this will not be a problem.

To add the getObject() function to the Avalon.js file:

1. Below the commands you just entered, type the following function:

```
function getObject(id) {
    if (isNS) obj="document."+id;
    if (isIE) obj=id+".style";
    var object=eval(obj);
    return object;
}
```

Compare your file to the code shown in Figure 1-17. It is crucial that you enter this function correctly.

| Figure 1-17 | THE AVALON.JS FILE |

determines the reference syntax in use

converts the ID name to a variable pointing to the object

```
var isNS = false;
var isIE = false;
if (document.layers) isNS=true;
if (document.all) isIE=true;

function getObject(id) {
    if (isNS) obj="document."+id;
    if (isIE) obj=id+".style";
    var object=eval(obj);
    return object;
}
```

2. Save your changes to the file.

Positioning Objects with JavaScript

Move obs.

You've entered the building blocks for the API file by resolving both the browser question and the reference name issue. Now, you'll begin creating some JavaScript functions that will position and move the objects for the Avalon home page correctly. JavaScript's positioning properties work much the same way as the CSS positioning attributes, though by now you probably won't be surprised to learn that there are differences in how Netscape and Internet Explorer express those properties.

The first property to consider is the positioning type. The syntax for defining this in Netscape is:

```
id.position=value;
```

while in Internet Explorer, the syntax is:

```
id.style.position=value;
```

where *id* is the ID name of the object to be positioned, and *value* is the type of position (either absolute, relative, or static). It's very rare that you would change the position type in a script. In most situations you will set the position type in the HTML file via the style sheet. Also note that you cannot change the position type *after* the page is loaded with Netscape, but you can with Internet Explorer.

Both Internet Explorer and Netscape provide several different properties for defining the coordinate of the object. Figure 1-18 summarizes some of these properties.

Figure 1-18	POSITION ATTRIBUTES FOR INTERNET EXPLORER AND NETSCAPE		
	INTERNET EXPLORER		**NETSCAPE**
left	A text string displaying the value of the CSS left attribute	left	The horizontal position of the objects's left edge relative to the object's parent in pixels
pixelLeft	The horizontal position of the object's left edge, in pixels	pageX	The horizontal position of the object's left edge of the page in pixels
posLeft	The horizontal position of the object's left edge in whatever units are used by the CSS left attribute		
top	A text string displaying the value of the CSS top attribute	top	The vertical position of the object's top edge relative to the object's parent in pixels
pixelTop	The vertical position of the object's top edge, in pixels	pageY	The vertical position of the object's top edge on the page in pixels
posTop	The vertical position of the object's top edge in whatever units are used by the CSS top attribute		

In Netscape, you have two choices: you can define the object position relative to the object's parent element using the left and top properties, or relative to the page using the pageX and pageY properties. In Internet Explorer, the location of the object is always relative to the parent element (which in most cases is the page). Internet Explorer's top and left properties return a text string indicating both the position and the measuring unit. If you need the actual values (perhaps for mathematical calculations), you should use the pixelTop/pixelLeft or posTop/posLeft properties. The only difference between these two sets of properties is that pixelTop/pixelLeft returns the coordinates in pixels, and posTop/posLeft returns the coordinates in whatever unit is indicated in the style sheet.

As long as you use pixels as the unit, the following sets of commands are equivalent in Netscape and Internet Explorer.

In Netscape:

```
document.id.left=100;
document.id.top=50;
```

In Internet Explorer:

```
id.style.pixelLeft=100;
id.style.pixelTop=50;
```

(handwritten margin note: if Netscape code, if Int Explores code)

Layering Objects

You can also use JavaScript to control overlapping objects. JavaScript uses the zIndex property, which works the same way as the z-index style attribute. In the following example, for Netscape browsers, the zIndex values for the Avalon and Books objects are switched. This will display the object listed later in the code in front of the upper object.

```
var Za=document.Avalon.zIndex;
var Zb=document.Books.zIndex;
document.Avalon.zIndex=Zb;
document.Books.zIndex=Za;
```

the equivalent code for Internet Explorer would be:

```
var Za=Avalon.style.zIndex;
var Zb=Books.style.zIndex;
Avalon.style.zIndex=Zb;
Books.style.zIndex=Za;
```

In addition to the zIndex property, Netscape supports two additional properties, above and below, which indicate the object placed above and below the current object. For example, if the Avalon object is stacked on top of the Books object, then

```
document.Avalon.below
```

refers to the Books object, and

```
document.Books.above
```

refers to the Avalon object. No similar property is available with Internet Explorer.

Controlling Object Visibility

Both browsers use the visibility property to show or hide objects. Unfortunately, while the browsers use the same property name, they use different property values. Netscape uses the values "show" and "hide" as follows:

```
document.id.visibility="show";
document.id.visibility="hide";
```

while in Internet Explorer the values are:

```
id.style.visibility="visible";
id.style.visibility="hidden";
```

When you hide or unhide objects with JavaScript, you'll need to take these differences into account.

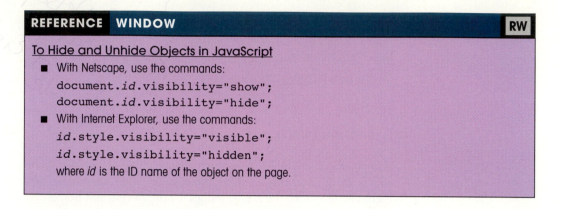

REFERENCE	WINDOW	RW

To Hide and Unhide Objects in JavaScript
- With Netscape, use the commands:
  ```
  document.id.visibility="show";
  document.id.visibility="hide";
  ```
- With Internet Explorer, use the commands:
  ```
  id.style.visibility="visible";
  id.style.visibility="hidden";
  ```
  where *id* is the ID name of the object on the page.

Working with Overflow and Clipping

You can control the height and width of an object by using JavaScript's height and width properties. These properties operate the same for Netscape and Internet Explorer.

If the document content is greater than the object's dimension, Internet Explorer supports the use of the overflow property, which works like the overflow style attribute. Thus, to change the overflow an object in Internet Explorer, use the syntax:

```
id.style.overflow=overflow_type;
```

where *overflow_type* can be "visible," "hidden," "scroll," or "auto." Netscape does not currently support the overflow property.

The two browsers differ in how they handle the clipping rectangle. Figure 1-19 shows the various Netscape properties for controlling the clipping region of an object.

Figure 1-19   NETSCAPE CLIPPING PROPERTIES

PROPERTY	DESCRIPTION
clip.top	The position of the top edge of the clipping rectangle in pixels
clip.right	The position of the right edge of the clipping rectangle in pixels
clip.bottom	The position of the bottom edge of the clipping rectangle in pixels
clip.left	The position of the left edge of the clipping rectangle in pixels
clip.width	The width of the clipping rectangle in pixels
clip.height	The height of the clipping rectangle in pixels

REFERENCE   WINDOW   **RW**

Defining a Clipping Region in JavaScript
- With Netscape, use the commands:
  ```
  document.id.clip.top=top;
  document.id.clip.right=right;
  document.id.clip.bottom=bottom;
  document.id.clip.left=left;
  ```
- With Internet Explorer, use the commands:
  ```
  id.style.clip="rect("+top+" "+right+" "+bottom+" "+left+")";
  ```
  where *top, right, bottom,* and *left* are the coordinates of the top, right, bottom, and left edges of the clipping rectangle.

To change the clipping region for an object using Netscape, you would use the following syntax:

```
document.id.clip.top=top;
document.id.clip.right=right;
document.id.clip.bottom=bottom;
document.id.clip.left=left;
```

where *top*, *right*, *bottom*, and *left* are the coordinates of the top, right, bottom, and left edges of the clipping rectangle. Note that you can also use the clip.width and clip.height properties to set the width and height of the clipping rectangle without specifying the exact coordinate values.

Internet Explorer does not support separate properties for each edge of the clipping rectangle. Instead you set the value of the clip property to a text string, as follows:

```
id.style.clip="rect(10, 150, 100, 20)";
```

If you need to use variables for the clipping values, you have to combine the variable values with the text string. The syntax would be:

```
id.style.clip="rect("+top+" "+right+" "+bottom+" "+left+")";
```

where once again *top*, *right*, *bottom*, and *left* are the coordinates of the edges of the clipping rectangle. Note that each coordinate value has to be separated from the others by either a space (as shown above) or by a comma.

Netscape Layer Methods

In addition to properties, Netscape also supports methods to give you even greater control over the position and size of your objects. Figure 1-20 describes some of these methods.

Figure 1-20	NETSCAPE LAYER METHODS	
METHOD	**DESCRIPTION**	
load(*url, width*)	Changes the source of the layer to the URL specified by *url*, and changes the width of the layer to *width*	
moveAbove(*layer*)	Moves the layer above the *layer* object	
moveBelow(*layer*)	Moves the layer below the *layer* object	
moveBy(*dx, dy*)	Moves the layer *dx* pixels to the right and *dy* pixels down	
moveTo(*x, y*)	Moves the layer to the (*x, y*) coordinate within the parent object	
moveToAbsolute(*x, y*)	Moves the layer to the (*x, y*) coordinate on the Web page	
resizeBy(*dx, dy*)	Resizes the layer by *dx* pixels horizontally and *dy* pixels vertically	
resizeTo(*width, height*)	Resizes the layer to *width* pixels by *height* pixels	

For example, the following tag:

```
<DIV ID="Avalon" STYLE="position:absolute; left:50; top:100">
   Avalon
</DIV>
```

can be moved to the (100,150) coordinate with the JavaScript command:

```
document.Avalon.moveTo(100,150);
```

To achieve the same effect in Internet Explorer, you have to create a custom function that modifies the value of the pixelLeft and pixelTop properties. For example:

```
Avalon.pixelLeft=100;
Avalon.pixelTop=150;
```

Adding Positioning Functions to the API

Now that you've reviewed some of the issues associated with positioning objects with JavaScript, you're ready to add some new functions to the API. The first function you'll create will place an object at a specified (x, y) coordinate. You'll use this function later to place objects on the Avalon Web page. The function will appear as follows:

```
function placeIt(id, x, y) {
   var object=getObject(id);
   if (isNS) {
      object.moveTo(x, y);
   } else if (isIE) {
      object.pixelLeft=x;
      object.pixelTop=y;
   }
}
```

The placeIt() function first takes the ID name of an object and uses the getObject() function to create a variable that refers to the object. If the browser is Netscape, the object is moved to the (x, y) coordinate using the moveTo() method. If the browser is Internet Explorer, the object is moved by modifying the values of the pixelLeft and pixelTop coordinates (you could have also used the posLeft/posTop properties).

To add the placeIt() function to the API:

1. Below the getObject() function in the Avalon.js file, enter the following function:

```
function placeIt(id, x, y) {
    var object=getObject(id);
    if (isNS) {
        object.moveTo(x, y);
    } else if (isIE) {
        object.pixelLeft=x;
        object.pixelTop=y;
    }
}
```

2. Save your changes to the file.

The next function you'll add to the API shifts an object *dx* pixels to the right and *dy* pixels down from its current location. You'll use this function later on to move objects on the Avalon Books Web page. The function, shiftIt(), is:

```
function shiftIt(id, dx, dy) {
    var object=getObject(id);
    if (isNS) {
        object.moveBy(dx, dy);
    } else if (isIE) {
        object.pixelLeft=object.pixelLeft+dx;
        object.pixelTop=object.pixelTop+dy;
    }
}
```

In this function we use the moveBy() method for Netscape browsers, and for Internet Explorer, we add the value of *dx* and *dy* to the object's current coordinates and then store the new coordinate values. All coordinates are expressed in pixels by default.

To add the shiftIt() function to the API:

1. Below the placeIt() function, insert the following commands:

```
function shiftIt(id, dx, dy) {
    var object=getObject(id);
    if (isNS) {
        object.moveBy(dx, dy);
    } else if (isIE) {
        object.pixelLeft=object.pixelLeft+dx;
        object.pixelTop=object.pixelTop+dy;
    }
}
```

2. Save your changes to the file.

The next two functions you'll add to the API will return the values of the left and top attributes of the object's position. You'll use these two functions later on to determine the current location of objects on the Avalon Books Web page. The functions are:

```
function xCoord(id) {
    var object=getObject(id);
    if (isNS) xc=object.left;
    if (isIE) xc=object.pixelLeft;
    return xc;
}

function yCoord(id) {
    var object=getObject(id);
    if (isNS) yc=object.top;
    if (isIE) yc=object.pixelTop;
    return yc;
}
```

The xCoord() function calculates the value of the left or pixelLeft property for the object and stores this value in the xc variable. That value is then returned by the function. The yCoord() function does the same thing with the top or pixelTop property.

To add the xCoord() and yCoord() functions:

1. Below the shiftIt() function, enter the following code:

```
function xCoord(id) {
    var object=getObject(id);
    if (isNS) xc=object.left;
    if (isIE) xc=object.pixelLeft;
    return xc;
}

function yCoord(id) {
    var object=getObject(id);
    if (isNS) yc=object.top;
    if (isIE) yc=object.pixelTop;
    return yc;
}
```

2. Save your changes to the Avalon.js file.

hideIt(id) *showIt(id)*

The last two functions you'll add to the API will be used to hide and unhide an object. The functions are:

```
function hideIt(id) {
    var object=getObject(id);
    if (isNS) object.visibility="hide";
    if (isIE) object.visibility="hidden";
}

function showIt(id) {
    var object=getObject(id);
    if (isNS) object.visibility="show";
    if (isIE) object.visibility="visible";
}
```

To add the hideIt() and showIt() functions to the Avalon.js file:

1. Below the yCoord() function, add the following commands:

```
function hideIt(id) {
    var object=getObject(id);
    if (isNS) object.visibility="hide";
    if (isIE) object.visibility="hidden";
}

function showIt(id) {
    var object=getObject(id);
    if (isNS) object.visibility="show";
    if (isIE) object.visibility="visible";
}
```

2. Figure 1-21 shows the completed functions for the API. You should check the code you entered against this figure. Make sure that the text matches exactly, including the use of uppercase and lowercase letters.

Figure 1-21 | FUNCTIONS ADDED TO THE API

```
function placeIt(id, x, y) {
    var object=getObject(id);
    if (isNS) {
        object.moveTo(x, y);
    } else if (isIE) {
        object.pixelLeft=x;
        object.pixelTop=y;
    }
}

function shiftIt(id, dx, dy) {
    var object=getObject(id);
    if (isNS) {
        object.moveBy(dx, dy);
    } else if (isIE) {
        object.pixelLeft=object.pixelLeft+dx;
        object.pixelTop=object.pixelTop+dy;
    }
}

function xCoord(id) {
    var object=getObject(id);
    if (isNS) xc=object.left;
    if (isIE) xc=object.pixelLeft;
    return xc;
}

function yCoord(id) {
    var object=getObject(id);
    if (isNS) yc=object.top;
    if (isIE) yc=object.pixelTop;
    return yc;
}

function hideIt(id) {
    var object=getObject(id);
    if (isNS) object.visibility="hide";
    if (isIE) object.visibility="hidden";
}

function showIt(id) {
    var object=getObject(id);
    if (isNS) object.visibility="show";
    if (isIE) object.visibility="visible";
}
```

3. Save your changes to the file.

You should take some time to study these custom functions, comparing them to the syntax that each browser requires for modifying these properties. The nice thing about an API file is that once the custom function works, you won't have to worry about the cross-browser differences again.

You've completed the API for the Avalon Books Web page. In the next session, you'll create a link to this file and use the custom functions you created to animate your Web page.

Session 1.2 QUICK CHECK

1. Your Web page contains the following object:

<DIV ID="Logo">Avalon Books</DIV>

Assuming that this object is not nested within another object, give an object reference to the Logo object for both Netscape and Internet Explorer.

2. For the object shown in Question 1, what is the object reference for the Logo object's style property for both Netscape and Internet Explorer?

3. Give the Netscape and Internet Explorer reference names for the Title object in the following tag:

    <DIV ID="Logo"><DIV ID="Title">Avalon</DIV> Books</DIV>

4. What JavaScript command would you use to extract the full version number of the browser viewing your Web page?

5. Describe the three strategies for creating a cross-browser Web site.

    For the following questions, provide both the Netscape and Internet Explorer versions of the JavaScript command.

6. What command would you use to increase the z-index value of the Logo object by 1?

7. What command would you use to move the Logo object to the coordinate (150, 350)?

8. What command would you use to hide the Logo object?

9. What command would you use to set the size of the clipping rectangle to (10, 210, 150, 10)?

SESSION 1.3

In this session you'll link your Web page to the API file you created in the last session and use the API to control the placement and movement of objects in the Avalon Books Web page. You'll learn how to create an animated sequence, and how to control the timing of that sequence. You'll also learn how to adapt your Web page for different monitor resolutions.

Linking to an API File

You've put a lot of work into creating the API file, but the purpose of the API file is to remove from the Web page much of the complexity involved with designing a page for two types of browsers. Now that the API is written, you can use the placeIt(), shiftIt(), and the other functions you created as if they were native to HTML, without worrying about the cross-browser problems.

Before you can use the commands from the API file in your Web page file, you have to link the files. Linking to an external file of JavaScript commands (such as the Avalon.js file you created) involves simply placing a SRC property in a <SCRIPT> tag, located in the head section of the HTML file (Avalon.htm). You need both an opening and closing <SCRIPT> tag. When the browser encounters the SRC property, it will run any commands from the Avalon.js file. Thereafter, if your Web page code calls any of the functions from the API, the browser will be able to retrieve the functions and return the results.

Because of how Netscape handles JavaScript, you need to place the link to the API file *after* any <SCRIPT> tags placed in the HTML document.

To link to the Avalon.js API:

1. Open the **Avalon.htm** file from the Tutorial.01D folder on your Data Disk.

2. In the head section of the file, after the </STYLE> tag, enter the following tags (see Figure 1-22):

```
<SCRIPT SRC="Avalon.js"></SCRIPT>
```

Figure 1-22	LINKING TO THE AVALON.JS FILE

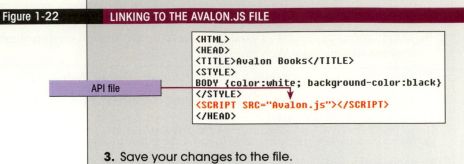

API file

```
<HTML>
<HEAD>
<TITLE>Avalon Books</TITLE>
<STYLE>
BODY {color:white; background-color:black}
</STYLE>
<SCRIPT SRC="Avalon.js"></SCRIPT>
</HEAD>
```

3. Save your changes to the file.

Designing the Opening Screen

Recall from Figure 1-2 that Terry wants to have the single word "Avalon" appear near the top of the page and then drop vertically down the page. At a certain point, "Avalon" should stop dropping, and the word, "Books" should appear, moving to the right from behind the word Avalon. After that, the three other images should appear on the screen in sequence.

To make this animation work, you'll place the words "Avalon" and "Books" near the top of the page, with "Avalon" stacked on top of "Books" to hide it (this is why you were instructed to place these words in different container tags back in the first session). You will also place the three images in their current locations on the page, but hidden. While some of these tasks (such as placing the objects on the page) can be performed with CSS style attributes, you'll use this opportunity to test the API file you created. First you should remove some of the old style attributes you entered, replacing them with new ones.

To modify the style attributes:

1. Delete the left and top attributes for all five objects on the page, but leave the position:absolute style attribute. (Be sure to leave the closing quotation mark at the end of each style.)

2. Insert **z-index:2** in the style attribute for the avalon object.

3. Insert **z-index:1** in the style attribute for the books object.

This will give the effect of hiding the books object as long as it is behind the avalon object.

4. Insert **visibility:hidden** in the style attributes for the AB, Fiction, and NFiction objects.

Figure 1-23 shows the revised style attributes for the five objects on the page.

Figure 1-23 **THE REVISED STYLE ATTRIBUTES**

```
<DIV ID="avalon"
   STYLE="background-color:black; font-size:24pt; font-weight:bold;
         position:absolute; z-index:2">
   AVALON
</DIV>

<DIV ID="books"
   STYLE="color:red; font-style:italic; font-size:24pt; font-weight:bold;
         position:absolute; z-index:1">
   BOOKS
</DIV>

<DIV ID="AB"
   STYLE="width:150; height:225;
         position:absolute; visibility:hidden">
   <A HREF="ABStore.htm"><IMG SRC="AB.jpg" BORDER=0></A>
</DIV>

<DIV ID="Fiction"
   STYLE="font-family:Arial,Helvetica,sans-serif;font-size:x-small;
         width:120; position:absolute; visibility:hidden">
   <CENTER><IMG SRC="Fiction.jpg"><BR>
   <B>AB Sales Rank: #1<BR>
   Fiction</B><BR>
   <I>Before the Fall</I><BR>Jeffrey Unwin</CENTER>
</DIV>

<DIV ID="NFiction"
   STYLE="font-family:Arial,Helvetica,sans-serif; font-size:x-small;
         width:120; position:absolute; visibility:hidden">
   <CENTER><IMG SRC="NFiction.jpg"><BR>
   <B>AB Sales Rank: #1<BR>
   Nonfiction</B><BR>
   <I>Vietnam Memoirs</I><BR>Gen. John Hartford</CENTER>
</DIV>
```

Now you'll set the initial places for the five objects. The coordinates for the AB, Fiction, and NFiction objects should remain unchanged, but the avalon and books objects should be placed at new coordinates: 175 pixels to the left and 10 pixels down from the upper-left corner of the window. The coordinates for the five objects are therefore:

- ■ "avalon": (175, 10)
- ■ "books": (175, 10)
- ■ "AB": (230, 40)—as before
- ■ "Fiction": (5, 5)—as before
- ■ "NFiction": (475, 5)—as before

Because these are the coordinates you want when the page is loaded, but not necessarily at other times, you'll set these coordinates within a function called placeObjects, which you'll run when the page is loaded by the browser. The placeObjects() function appears as follows:

```
function placeObjects() {
   placeIt("avalon", 175, 10);
   placeIt("books", 175, 10);
   placeIt("AB", 230, 40);
   placeIt("Fiction", 5, 5);
   placeIt("NFiction", 475, 5);
}
```

Note that since we're using the placeIt() function from the API for this task, we need to specify only the ID name of the objects (as a text string). The API will handle the whole cross-browser issue behind the scenes.

To add the placeObjects() function to the Web page:

1. Scroll up the HTML file to the </SCRIPT> tag.

2. Above the <SCRIPT> tag insert the following code (see Figure 1-24):

```
<SCRIPT>
function placeObjects() {
    placeIt("avalon", 175, 10);
    placeIt("books", 175, 10);
    placeIt("AB", 230, 40);
    placeIt("Fiction", 5, 5);
    placeIt("NFiction", 475, 5);
}
</SCRIPT>
```

Figure 1-24	THE ABSOLUTE VALUE OF THE POSITION ATTRIBUTE

```
<HTML>
<HEAD>
<TITLE>Avalon Books</TITLE>
<STYLE>
BODY {color:white; background-color:black}
</STYLE>
<SCRIPT SRC="Avalon.js"></SCRIPT>
<SCRIPT>
    function placeObjects() {
        placeIt("avalon", 175, 10);
        placeIt("books", 175, 10);
        placeIt("AB", 230, 40);
        placeIt("Fiction", 5, 5);
        placeIt("NFiction", 475, 5);
    }
</SCRIPT>
</HEAD>

<BODY>
```

the "NFiction" object will be placed at the coordinates (475,5)

3. Save your changes.

The placeObjects() function should be run when the page loads, so add this function to the onLoad event handler for the <BODY> tag.

To run the placeObjects() function when the page loads:

1. Locate the <BODY> tag.

2. Insert **onLoad="placeObjects();"** within the <BODY> tag (see Figure 1-25).

Figure 1-25 | **RUNNING THE PLACEOBJECTS() FUNCTION WHEN THE PAGE IS LOADED**

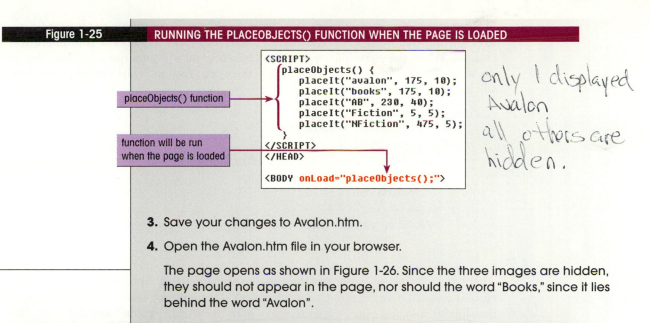

placeObjects() function

function will be run when the page is loaded

```
<SCRIPT>
  placeObjects() {
      placeIt("avalon", 175, 10);
      placeIt("books", 175, 10);
      placeIt("AB", 230, 40);
      placeIt("Fiction", 5, 5);
      placeIt("NFiction", 475, 5);
  }
</SCRIPT>
</HEAD>

<BODY onLoad="placeObjects();">
```

only I displayed Avalon all others are hidden.

3. Save your changes to Avalon.htm.

4. Open the Avalon.htm file in your browser.

The page opens as shown in Figure 1-26. Since the three images are hidden, they should not appear in the page, nor should the word "Books," since it lies behind the word "Avalon".

Figure 1-26 | **THE INITIAL SCREEN FOR THE AVALON.HTM PAGE**

the word "Books" is hidden behind "Avalon"

all other objects are hidden on the page

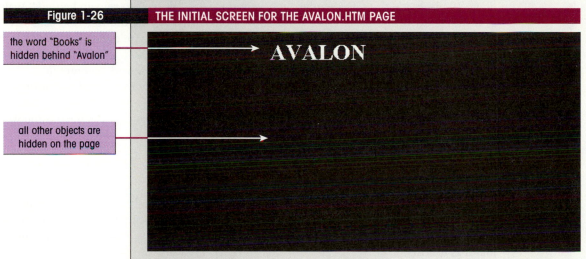

AVALON

TROUBLE? If you receive an error message when loading the page, check the code in the Avalon.js file. Some common programming errors include: mismatching uppercase and lowercase letters, misspellings of variable names, forgetting to close up double-quote-marked text, and forgetting to enclose command blocks and functions within curly braces.

Animating an Object

Moving an object in small increments over a specified interval of time creates the illusion of animation. The first piece of animation you'll add to the Avalon Web page will be the word "Avalon" dropping down the page. The initial position of the word is at the coordinate (175, 10). Terry suggests dropping it down to the (175, 260) coordinate, which is the same coordinate you used earlier when placing your objects using the style attributes.

This means that as you move the object, you'll need to retrieve the y-coordinate, and stop moving the word when the value exceeds 260 (note that the x-coordinate will not change). When the y-coordinate value exceeds 260, you will then run a function that moves the word "Books" to the right from behind the word "Avalon." The moveAvalon() function will appear as follows:

```
function moveAvalon() {
    var y=yCoord("avalon");
    if (y <= 260) {
        shiftIt("avalon", 0, 10);
        shiftIt("books", 0, 10);
        moveAvalon();
    } else {
        // run moveBooks function;
    }
}
```

There are a couple of important things to notice about this function. First, it retrieves the current y-coordinate from the yCoord() function you entered into the API. Second, it uses the shiftIt() function you created to move both the word "Avalon" and the word "Books" down 10 pixels at a time. Remember, you want the word "Books" to remain behind "Avalon" as it moves down the page. Once it has moved those two words, the function calls itself to start the moving process all over again. Finally, if the y-coordinate exceeds 260, it will then run the moveBooks function—a function you haven't written yet—to begin moving the word "Books" out from behind "Avalon". For now we'll mark that spot with a comment.

The only other thing missing from the function is some way to control the timing. The Web browser will process these commands in milliseconds, so from the viewpoint of the user, the word "Avalon" will jump down the page in a blink of an eye. We need some way to slow down this process a bit.

Creating a Time-Delayed Command

JavaScript does not provide a pause command to temporarily halt the execution of program code, like some other programming languages. Instead, you can have JavaScript execute a command after a specified time delay. The method for doing this uses the setTimeout command as follows:

```
setTimeout("command", delay);
```

where *command* is a JavaScript command or expression, and *delay* is the delay time in milliseconds. Note that the command must be placed within quotes. For example, to set a 5 millisecond delay before the moveAvalon() function is run, use the command:

```
setTimeout("moveAvalon()", 5);
```

You can have several time-delayed commands running simultaneously. If that's the case, you need to have a way of separating one time-delayed command from another. This is done by assigning each command an id variable. The syntax is:

```
id_variable = setTimeout("command", delay);
```

To assign the moveAvalon() command its own ID, you could enter:

```
MAdelay = setTimeout("moveAvalon()", 5);
```

Setting Timed Commands

- To run a command after a specified delay and to assign the delay an ID, use the command:

  `id_variable = setTimeout("command", delay);`

  where *command* is a JavaScript command or expression, and *delay* is the delay time in milliseconds. The *id_variable* is optional and can be used to identify the command if you want to cancel it before it runs or run another delay command.
- To cancel a time-delayed command use:

  `clearTimeout(id_variable);`

  where *id_variable* is the ID of the time-delayed command.
- To run a command every *interval* in milliseconds, use:

  `id_variable=setInterval("command", interval);`

  where *id_variable* is an optional ID for the command, *command* is the JavaScript command that will be repeatedly run, and *interval* is the interval, in milliseconds, between each running of the command.
- To cancel a time interval command use:

  `clearInterval(id_variable);`

  where *id_variable* is the ID of the time-delayed command.

Clearing a Time-Delayed Command

The id variable becomes important when your script needs to control the behavior of a time-delayed command. If you had several time-delayed commands running, and you wanted to cancel one, you would need an ID to indicate which command to cancel. Canceling a time-delayed command is done by using the clearTimeout() method as follows:

`clearTimeout(id_variable);`

where *id_variable* is the ID of the time-delayed command. So to cancel the MAdelay command before it's run, enter:

`clearTimeout(MAdelay);`

If you have a single time-delayed command, you don't need the ID; you can cancel it using the command:

`clearTimeout();`

Running Commands at Specified Intervals

In some scripts, you'll want to repeat the same command at specified intervals. For example, you may write a script displaying the current time on your page, which needs to be run every second. To run a command at specified intervals, rather than after a specified time delay, JavaScript provides the setInterval() method. The syntax for applying this method is:

`id_variable=setInterval("command", interval);`

where *id_variable* is an ID for the command, *command* is the JavaScript command that will be run repeatedly, and *interval* is the interval, in milliseconds, between each running of the command. The id variable is not necessary unless you need to cancel the command at some point in time. If you don't need the ID, or you only have one time-interval command running, use the simpler form:

```
setInterval("command", interval);
```

To cancel the command, use the clearInterval() method with the syntax:

```
clearInterval(id_variable);
```

or, if you have only a single time-interval command, with no id variable needed:

```
clearInterval();
```

An important point to remember about the setTimeout() and setInterval() methods is that after the browser processes the command, it proceeds to the next command in the script and does not wait for the delay or the interval time to pass. For example, if you try to use the following structure to run three functions at 50 millisecond intervals:

```
setTimeout("function1()", 50);
setTimeout("function2()", 50);
setTimeout("function3()", 50);
```

your browser will run all three functions almost simultaneously after a single 50 millisecond delay. To run them with a separation of about 50 milliseconds between them, you need to use three different delay times, as follows:

```
setTimeout("function1()", 50);
setTimeout("function2()", 100);
setTimeout("function3()", 150);
```

Animating the Avalon Books Text

Using the knowledge you gained about controlling the timing of your commands, you can add this feature to the moveAvalon() function. The function should now read:

```
function moveAvalon() {
    var y=yCoord("avalon");
    if (y <= 260) {
        shiftIt("avalon", 0, 10);
        shiftIt("books", 0, 10);
        setTimeout("moveAvalon()", 5);
    } else {
        // run moveBooks function;
    }
}
```

Now the function will move the words, "Avalon" and "Books" down 10 pixels, and then wait 5 milliseconds before moving them down another 10 pixels. Generally, when you do animation, you have to experiment with several different movement and time delay values before you arrive at a combination that creates a smooth motion.

To insert the moveAvalon() function:

1. Return to the Avalon.htm file in your text editor.

2. After the placeObjects() function, insert the function:

```
function moveAvalon() {
    var y=yCoord("avalon");
    if (y <= 260) {
        shiftIt("avalon", 0, 10);
        shiftIt("books", 0, 10);
        setTimeout("moveAvalon()", 5);
    } else {
        // run moveBooks function;
    }
}
```

You'll call the moveAvalon() function from within the placeObjects() function.

3. At the end of the placeObjects() function, directly after the command to place the NFiction object, insert the command:

```
moveAvalon();
```

Your script should resemble the code shown in Figure 1-27.

| Figure 1-27 | THE MOVEAVALON() FUNCTION |

```
function placeObjects() {
    placeIt("avalon", 175, 10);
    placeIt("books", 175, 10);
    placeIt("AB", 230, 40);
    placeIt("Fiction", 5, 5);
    placeIt("NFiction", 475, 5);
    moveAvalon();
}

function moveAvalon() {
    var y=yCoord("avalon");
    if (y <= 260) {
        shiftIt("avalon", 0, 10);
        shiftIt("books", 0, 10);
        setTimeout("moveAvalon()", 5);
    } else {
        // run moveBooks function;
    }
}
```

run moveAvalon() after placing the objects

4. Save your changes and reopen or refresh the Avalon.htm file in your Web browser.

The text "Avalon" should now move down the page once, and "Books" should move with it, behind it and hidden.

Next, your script needs to move the books object out from behind the avalon object. The moveBooks() function will resemble the moveAvalon() function except that it moves only the books object and it moves it from the left to the right. Terry used trial and error to determine that you should move "books" from the (175, 260) coordinate to the (320, 260) spot. Once the text is in location, the script should then unhide the remaining figures. The moveBooks() function appears as follows:

```
function moveBooks() {
    var x=xCoord("avalon");
    if (x <= 320) {
        shiftIt("books", 10, 0);
        setTimeout("moveBooks()", 5);
    } else {
    // display the hidden images;
    }
}
```

Note that instead of using the yCoord() function from the API, moveBooks() uses the xCoord() function to move the object in the horizontal direction. Also, the parameters of the shiftIt() function are now switched so that the books object moves 10 pixels to the right every 5 milliseconds.

To add the moveBooks() function:

1. Return to Avalon.htm in your text editor.

2. After the moveAvalon() function insert:

```
function moveBooks() {
    var x=xCoord("avalon");
    if (x <= 320) {
        shiftIt("books", 10, 0);
        setTimeout("moveBooks()", 5);
    } else {
    // display the hidden images;
    }
}
```

Revise the moveAvalon() function so that it calls moveBooks() when it finishes.

3. Scroll up to the moveAvalon() function and change the text, "// run moveBooks function;" to:

```
moveBooks();
```

Figure 1-28 shows the revised text.

| Figure 1-28 | THE MOVEBOOKS() FUNCTION |

```
function moveAvalon() {
    var y=yCoord("avalon");
    if (y <= 260) {
        shiftIt("avalon", 0, 10);
        shiftIt("books", 0, 10);
        setTimeout("moveAvalon()", 5);
    } else {
        moveBooks();
    }
}

function moveBooks() {
    var x=xCoord("books");
    if (x <= 320) {
        shiftIt("books", 10, 0);
        setTimeout("moveBooks()", 5);
    } else {
        // display the hidden images;
    }
}
```

run moveBooks() after moving the Avalon text

4. Save your changes to Avalon.htm.

5. Reload or refresh Avalon.htm in your Web browser.

The text "Avalon" should move down the page, and then after stopping, the text "Books" should move from behind it.

The last step in the animation is to unhide the three images: AB, Fiction, and NFiction. You'll do this in a function calling the showIt() function from the Avalon.js API. You decide to unhide each image at half-second intervals. The function appears as:

```
function showObjects() {
    setTimeout("showIt('AB')',500);
    setTimeout("showIt('Fiction')", 1000);
    setTimeout("showIt('NFiction')", 1500);
}
```

Notice you have to insert the object names in single quotes rather than double quotes, since you have to enclose the entire command in double quotes.

To insert the showObjects() function:

1. Return to Avalon.htm in your text editor.

2. After the moveBooks() function insert:

```
function showObjects() {
    setTimeout("showIt('AB')",500);
    setTimeout("showIt('Fiction')", 1000);
    setTimeout("showIt('NFiction')", 1500);
}
```

3. Replace the comment in the moveBooks() function with:

```
showObjects();
```

Figure 1-29 shows the revised code.

Figure 1-29   THE SHOWOBJECTS() FUNCTION

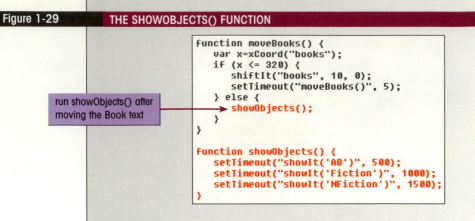

run showObjects() after
moving the Book text

```
function moveBooks() {
   var x=xCoord("books");
   if (x <= 320) {
      shiftIt("books", 10, 0);
      setTimeout("moveBooks()", 5);
   } else {
      showObjects();
   }
}

function showObjects() {
   setTimeout("showIt('AB')", 500);
   setTimeout("showIt('Fiction')", 1000);
   setTimeout("showIt('NFiction')", 1500);
}
```

4. Save your changes to Avalon.htm and refresh or reload the page in your Web browser.

The complete animation should appear, ending with the three images being shown in sequence.

You may have noticed that in creating this animation, each function called the next one in sequence after it was finished (see Figure 1-30). This is a common technique when doing animation in DHTML. By calling the next function only after the current function is finished, you ensure that your effects are presented in the proper order.

Figure 1-30   RUNNING FUNCTIONS IN SEQUENCE

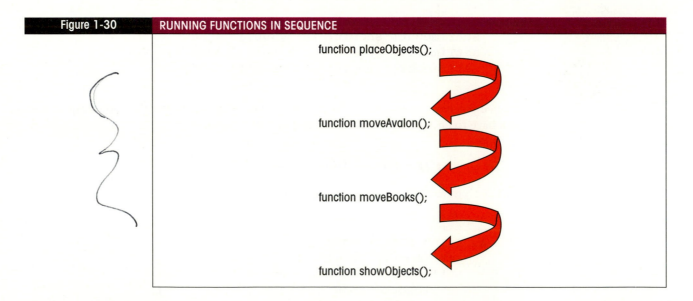

function placeObjects();

function moveAvalon();

function moveBooks();

function showObjects();

Controlling Layout for Different Monitor Resolutions

Terry is pleased with the opening screen you've designed. She notices, however, that you've created the page based on a monitor resolution of 640 × 480 pixels. What happens, she wonders, when users view the page under other resolutions? After experimenting, she shows you your page viewed under three different, but commonly used, resolutions (see Figure 1-31).

| Figure 1-31 | THE AVALON BOOKS PAGE UNDER DIFFERENT MONITOR RESOLUTIONS |

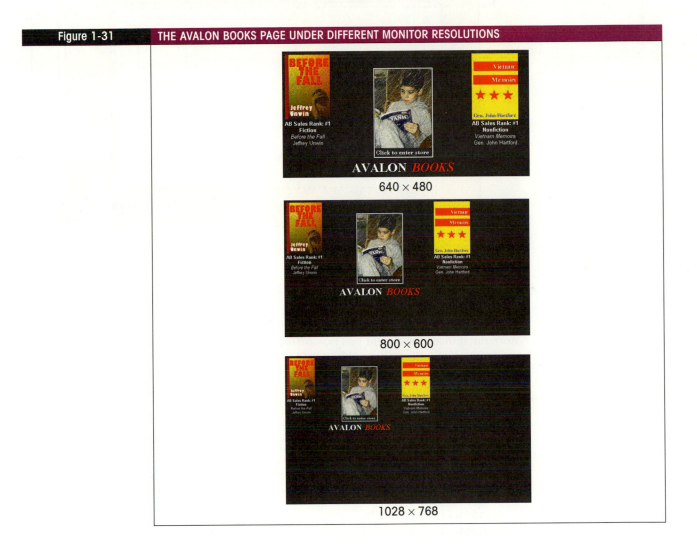

At sizes larger than 640 × 480, the images and text move progressively toward the upper-left corner of the display window. Terry would like to see the images remain in the center of the display window, both horizontally and vertically. Rather than create a different page for each monitor resolution, Terry suggests that you think of the objects as existing on a canvas that is 620 pixels wide by 300 pixels high. Every object would then be offset from the left and top edges of the window by a distance equal to the size of the border around this imaginary canvas. For example, if the dimensions of the display window are 760 × 560 pixels, the border width would be (760 - 620)/2 or 70 pixels, and the border height would be (560 - 300)/2 or 80 pixels (see Figure 1-32).

Figure 1-32   PLACING AN IMAGINARY CANVAS INSIDE THE DISPLAY WINDOW

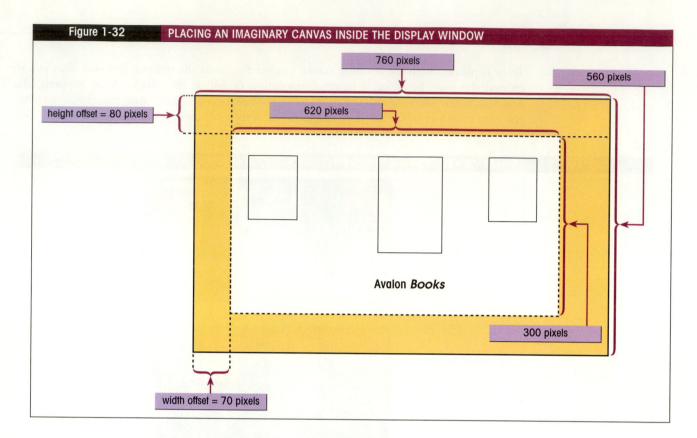

Under Terry's proposal, if the width of the display window is W, then the offset in the horizontal direction would be (W - 620)/2. If the height of the window is H, the offset in the vertical direction will be (H -300)/2. By adding the offsets to the current coordinates of each object, the display could be centered for any monitor resolution. However, in order to use this calculation, you need to be able to determine the width (W) and height (H) of each user's display window.

Calculating the Size of the Display Window

Netscape and Internet Explorer use different techniques to calculate the width and height of the display window. In Netscape, these values are properties of the window object, where:

```
window.innerWidth
window.innerHeight
```

store the width and height of the display window within the browser, excluding any tool-bars, menus, or status bars. To include those elements in the calculation, use the properties:

```
window.outerWidth
window.outerHeight
```

Internet Explorer does not support these properties. Instead, you have to measure the width and height of the body of the document. The syntax is:

```
document.body.clientWidth
document.body.clientHeight
```

Because of how Internet Explorer processes this property, it can only be used *after* the entire HTML file has been processed. If you try to evaluate these commands within the header section of the document, an error message will result.

REFERENCE WINDOW   **RW**

Calculating the Size of the Display Window
- In Netscape, use the properties:
  ```
  window.outerWidth
  window.outerHeight
  ```
- In Internet Explorer, use:
  ```
  document.body.clientWidth
  document.body.clientHeight
  ```

To calculate the W and H offsets for the Avalon Books page, you'll add the following commands to the placeObjects() function:

```
if (isNS) {
    W=(window.innerWidth-620)/2;
    H=(window.innerHeight-300)/2;
}
if (isIE) {
    W=(document.body.clientWidth-620)/2;
    H=(document.body.clientHeight-300)/2;
}
```

Note that you don't have to recalculate the values of the isNS and isIE variables, since this has already been done for you in the API.

To modify the placeObjects() function:

1. Return to the Avalon.htm file in your text editor.

2. In the placeObjects() function, just above the command to place the avalon object, insert the lines (see Figure 1-33):

```
if (isNS) {
    W=(window.innerWidth-620)/2;
    H=(window.innerHeight-300)/2;
}
if (isIE) {
    W=(document.body.clientWidth-620)/2;
    H=(document.body.clientHeight-300)/2;
}
```

Figure 1-33	INSERTING COMMANDS IN THE PLACEOBJECTS() FUNCTION

```
function placeObjects() {
    if (isNS) {
        W=(window.innerWidth-620)/2;
        H=(window.innerHeight-300)/2;
    }
    if (isIE) {
        W=(document.body.clientWidth-620)/2;
        H=(document.body.clientHeight-300)/2;
    }
    placeIt("avalon", 175, 10);
    placeIt("books", 175, 10);
    placeIt("AB", 230, 40);
    placeIt("Fiction", 5, 5);
    placeIt("NFiction", 475, 5);
    moveAvalon();
}
```

Now you to have to add the W and H values to each coordinate in the placeObjects() function so that objects are placed in appropriate locations for all display windows.

To modify the coordinate values:

1. For the avalon and books objects, change the coordinates from (175, 10) to **(W+175, H+10)**.

2. Change the coordinates for the AB object to **(W+230, H+40)**.

3. Change the coordinates for the Fiction object to **(W+5, H+5)**.

4. Change the coordinates for the NFiction object to **(W+475, H+5)**.

Figure 1-34 shows the revised placeObjects() function.

Figure 1-34	SETTING THE OFFSETS FOR THE OBJECT COORDINATES

```
function placeObjects() {
    if (isNS) {
        W=(window.innerWidth-620)/2;
        H=(window.innerHeight-300)/2;
    }
    if (isIE) {
        W=(document.body.clientWidth-620)/2;
        H=(document.body.clientHeight-300)/2;
    }
    placeIt("avalon", W+175, H+10);
    placeIt("books", W+175, H+10);
    placeIt("AB", W+230, H+40);
    placeIt("Fiction", W+5, H+5);
    placeIt("NFiction", W+475, H+5);
    moveAvalon();
}
```

You also need to change the value of the coordinates used to determine where to stop moving the Avalon and Books text.

To modify the moveAvalon() and moveBooks() functions:

1. Scroll down to the moveAvalon() function.

2. Change the text, "y <= 260" to **y <= H+260**.

3. Scroll down the moveBooks() function.

4. Change the text, "x <= 320" to **x <= W+320**.

   Figure 1-35 shows the revised form of these functions.

Figure 1-35   **CHANGING THE COORDINATE VALUES**

```
function moveAvalon() {
    var y=yCoord("avalon");
    if (y <= H+260) {
        shiftIt("avalon", 0, 10);
        shiftIt("books", 0, 10);
        setTimeout("moveAvalon()", 5);
    } else {
        moveBooks();
    }
}

function moveBooks() {
    var x=xCoord("books");
    if (x <= W+320) {
        shiftIt("books", 10, 0);
        setTimeout("moveBooks()", 5);
    } else {
        showObjects();
    }
}
```

5. Save your changes to the file.

6. Reload or refresh the Avalon.htm file in your Web browser and verify that the animation still works correctly.

7. If you have the capability of changing the resolution of your monitor, view the page under different screen sizes and verify that the page objects appear approximately in the center of the page each time (see Figure 1-36).

Figure 1-36	THE AVALON BOOKS PAGE REMAINS CENTERED UNDER DIFFERENT MONITOR RESOLUTIONS

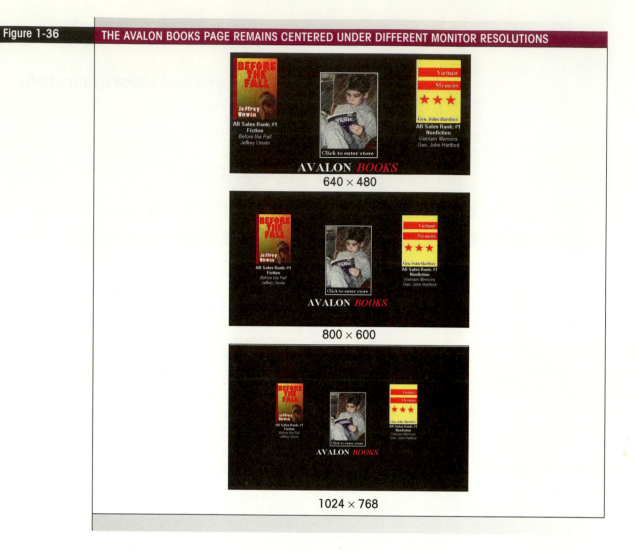

640 × 480

800 × 600

1024 × 768

Terry reviews the page and approves of the design under different monitor resolutions.

Determining Screen Properties

For more general information about the user's monitor settings in future projects, you can use the screen object. Figure 1-37 describes some of the properties associated with this object.

Figure 1-37	PROPERTIES OF THE SCREEN OBJECT

SCREEN PROPERTIES	DESCRIPTION
Screen.availHeight	The height of the screen after subtracting any operating system elements such as the Windows taskbar or Macintosh menu bar
screen.availWidth	The width of the screen after subtracting any operating system elements such as the Windows taskbar or Macintosh menu bar
screen.colorDepth	The number of bits per pixel used to display video color
screen.height	The height of the screen in pixels
screen.width	The width of the screen in pixels

Both Internet Explorer and Netscape support all of these properties.

Using **Path Animation**

The animation you did for the Avalon Books page is an example of **linear animation** because the animation takes place over a straight line, going from one point to the next (either down or to the right). Another type of animation is **path animation**, in which each coordinate in the path is entered into an array and the animation moves from point to point. The path can be any shape, as shown in Figure 1-38.

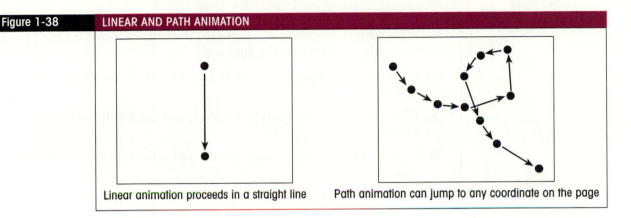

Figure 1-38	LINEAR AND PATH ANIMATION

Linear animation proceeds in a straight line   Path animation can jump to any coordinate on the page

To use path animation, you store the x and y coordinate values in arrays. This means you have to go through the work of calculating all of the coordinate positions in your path. Once you have the values entered into two arrays, you retrieve the coordinates from the arrays, one coordinate at a time, until the entire arrays have been read. Sample code appears below:

```
x = new Array(0, 40, 80, 120, 200, 300, 400, 300, 150);
y = new Array(0, 20, 40, 120, 120, 80, 60, 30, 0);
index = 0;

function moveObject() {
   if (index <= x.length-1) {
      shiftIt("path_object", x[index], y[index]);
      index++;
      setTimeout("moveObject()", 10);
   }
}
```

In this example, an object named "path_object" is moved from point to point following the x and y coordinate values previously entered into the x and y arrays. Note that the index value is initially set to 0, to point to the first item in the array. Each time the path object moves to a new location, the index value is increased by one, using the increment operator (++). When the value of the index exceeds the length of the array minus one, as indicated by the property x.length-1, the path animation stops.

Why use the length of the array minus one, rather than the length of the array? Recall that the first array element has an index value of zero; therefore the last array element has the array value *n*-1, if the length of the array is *n*.

For more interesting path animations, you can add a third array containing the delay times between each movement, rather than always using the same delay time.

You've completed your work on the Avalon Books opening Web page. Terry is going to have some other people in the design team review your work. She'll get back to you with any changes she wants you to make, or with other projects. You can close your text editor and Web browser now.

Session 1.3 QUICK CHECK

1. What tag would you enter to link an HTML file to a API file named Scripts.js?

2. What command would you enter to run the function moveGraphic() after a tenth-of-a-second delay?

3. What command would you enter to run the function moveGraphic() every tenth-of a-second and give it the ID name "mg"?

4. What command would you enter to stop running the function you created in Question 3?

5. What command would you enter to determine the width and height of your users' screens?

6. What command would you enter to determine the available width and height of your users' screens?

7. What is the difference between linear animation and path animation?

REVIEW ASSIGNMENTS

Terry has reviewed your page and recommended the following changes:

- There should be a page, index.htm, that supports older browsers. If a browser that doesn't support DHTML is detected, this page should be automatically loaded.
- On the DHTML page, the title "Avalon Books" should move from the left edge of the page to the center when the page opens. Also the text "Books" should appear in a red italic font below and overlapping the text "Avalon."
- After moving the title, the three image files Kids.jpg, Fiction.jpg, and NFiction.jpg should appear below the title. The images should be stacked on top of each other, and every two seconds the top image in the stack should be moved to the bottom, and the other images should be moved up in the stack.

Figure 1-39 shows a preview of the page you'll create for Terry.

Figure 1-39

To create this opening screen for Avalon Books:

1. Open the **indextxt.htm** file from the Tutorial.01D/Review folder on your Data Disk in your text editor, and save it as **index.htm**.

Explore
2. Within the <SCRIPT> tags in the header (between the two tags that hide the script command from older browsers), insert a command that tests whether the browser recognizes either the document.layers or the document.all reference name. If it does, have the browser load the Avalon2.htm file, using the location object.

3. Save your changes and close the file.

4. Open **ABJStext.js** from the Tutorial.01D/Review folder on Data Disk in your text editor, and save it as **Avalon2.js**.

Explore
5. Create a new function named swapIt(). The function should have three parameters: id1, id2, and id3. Within the function, convert the three id variables from text strings to objects: object1, object2, and object3, using the getObject() function found in the API file. Create three variables: z1, z2, and z3, which are equal to the z-index values of object1, object2, and object3, respectively. Change the z-index value of object1 to z3. Change the z-index value of object2 to z1. Change the z-index value of object3 to z2.

6. Save your changes to the Avalon2.js file and close it.

7. Open the **AB2text.htm** file, and save it as **Avalon2.htm**.

8. Using inline styles, set the position attribute for the Kids, Fiction, NFiction, and Avalon objects to absolute.

9. Using an inline style, set the position attribute for the Books object to relative. Set the position of the Books object to 10 pixels down and 60 pixels to the left. (*Hint*: To move an object to the left, you must use a negative value.)

10. Using inline styles, hide the Kids, Fiction, and NFiction objects. Set the z-index values of these three objects to 3, 2, and 1, respectively.

11. Create a JavaScript function in the head section of the file called "init()." The first task of the init() function should be to create a variable named "W" that is equal to half of the width of the document window. Use the values of the isNS and isIE variables from the API to create the correct JavaScript syntax for the browser. After calculating the value of W, have the function call the moveAvalon() function.

12. Below the init() function, insert the moveAvalon() function. Set a variable named "x" to the value of the x-coordinate of the Avalon object. (*Hint*: Use the xCoord() function from the API file.) If x is less than or equal to the value of W minus 125, have the moveAvalon() function do the following:

- call the shiftIt() function from the API to move the Avalon object 10 pixels to the right.
- Call the moveAvalon() function again after a delay of 50 milliseconds

If x is greater than W - 125, call the swapImages() function.

13. Below the moveAvalon() function, insert the swapImages() function. First have this function use the placeIt() function from the API to place the Kids, Fiction, and NFiction objects at the coordinates (W - 75, 100), where W is the variable you created earlier. Then have the swapImages() function use the showIt() function to unhide the Kids, Fiction, and NFiction objects.

Explore

Finally, have the swapImages() function call the swapIt() function from the API to swap the z-index values of the Kids, Fiction, NFiction objects, and set the swapIt() function to run every 2 seconds.

14. Link the Avalon2.htm file to the Avalon2.js API file.

15. Within the <BODY> tag, use the onLoad event handler to run the init() function when the page is loaded.

16. Save your changes to Avalon2.htm.

17. Load the index.htm file in your Web browser. Verify that the following occurs:

- The page automatically loads the Avalon2.htm file.
- The Avalon2.htm file starts with the text "Avalon Books" on the left edge of the page.
- The text "Avalon Books" moves to the center of the page.
- After "Avalon Books" reaches the center, the image file Kids.jpg appears along with its caption.
- Every two seconds thereafter, the image file is swapped with the next image file in the stack.

18. If you can, test the layout of your page at various monitor resolutions. Verify that the content appears horizontally centered in each resolution.

19. Print a copy of the Avalon2.htm file in your Web browser. Print a copy of the code you used for the index.htm, Avalon2.htm, and Avalon2.js files.

CASE PROBLEMS

Case 1. Using Path Animation in an Opening Screen for The Golf Page Mark Reim, the owner of an online golf store called The Golf Page has asked you to create an animated opening screen for his Web site. Mark envisions a ball flying through the air, bouncing once, and then landing in the middle of the company name, taking the place of the letter "o" in "Golf." Mark suggests that you do this with a Java applet, but you assure him that you can do the same thing using DHTML and path animation.

Mark also wants the text "Your Online Source of Golf Equipment" to appear after the ball has landed. The text should appear in black with a white drop shadow. Figure 1-40 shows a preview of the page you'll create for Mark.

Figure 1-40

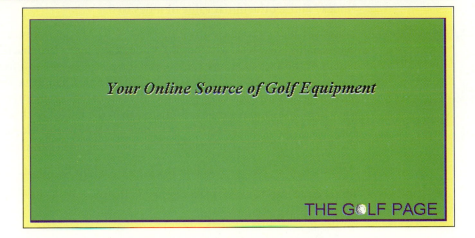

The page you'll create will link to an API named Golf.js. The Golf.js file has a function named placeIt() that places an object at a specified coordinate, and a function named showIt()that unhides a hidden object. The API also uses object detection, creating a Boolean variable named isNS, which is true if the browser supports the document.layers reference name, and isIE, which is true if the browser supports the document.all reference.

Another text file available to you is the BallPath.txt file, which contains the coordinates of the flying ball, relative to its final location on the page.

To create the page for The Golf Page:

1. In your text editor, open the **Golftext.htm** file from the Tutorial.01D/Cases folder on your Data Disk. Save the file as **GolfPage.htm**.

2. Scroll down the page and locate the inline image that is surrounded by the <SPAN> tag with the ID name Ball. Add an inline style to this <SPAN> tag, setting the value of the position attribute to relative, and setting the coordinates of the image within the <SPAN> tag to (0, 0).

3. Locate the "Slogan" object below the <SPAN> tag. Add an inline style to the <DIV> tag for this object, which places the object at the coordinates (120, 100) with absolute positioning. Set the z-index value of the object to 2, and hide the object on the page.

4. Create a drop shadow for the Slogan text. To do this, create a copy of the Slogan object (including the opening <DIV> and closing </DIV> tags), paste the new tags below the tags for the Slogan object. Change the ID of this object from Slogan to Slogan2. Change the color of the Slogan2 text from black to white. Change the coordinates of the object from (120, 100) to (121, 101). Finally, change the z-index of the Slogan2 object from 2 to 1.

5. Within the head section of the HTML file, insert a new set of <SCRIPT> tags. Within the new set of <SCRIPT> tags, paste the code found in the **BallPath.txt** file. The x array contains the x-coordinates of the flying ball. The y array contains the y-coordinates.

6. Below the array declaration, but within the <SCRIPT> tags, declare a variable named "index" and set the initial value of index to 0.

Explore

7. Below the index variable but within the <SCRIPT> tags, insert a function named "moveBall()" that tests whether the value of the index variable is less than or equal to the length of the x array minus 1. If so, call the placeIt() function from the API, placing the Ball object at the coordinates, (x[index], y[index]). Then, have the value of the index variable increased by 1, and call the moveBall() function again after a 5 millisecond delay. If the value of the index variable is greater than the length of the x array minus 1, call the showIt() function from the API to unhide the Slogan and Slogan2 objects. (*Hint*: Review the material presented in this tutorial on creating path animations using arrays.)

8. Below the </SCRIPT> tag, link the GolfPage.htm file to the Golf.js file.

9. Insert code into the <BODY> tag to run the moveBall() function when the page loads.

10. Save your changes to the file.

11. Open the GolfPage.htm file in your Web browser and verify that the ball flies across the page, landing in the appropriate location in the page. Also check that the Slogan and Slogan2 objects are made visible, and that Slogan2 appears as a white drop shadow for the Slogan object.

12. Print a copy of your page and a copy of the code the GolfPage.htm file.

Case 2. Creating a Marquee for the Carson Civic Center   Laura Bromquist, the director of the Carson Civic Center in Carson, Nebraska, has asked you to design a page listing the upcoming events at the center. Laura would like to have the page display a marquee, in which the event names are automatically scrolled up for the user. She would also like to give the user the ability to start and stop the marquee.

A preview of the page you'll create is shown in Figure 1-41.

Figure 1-41

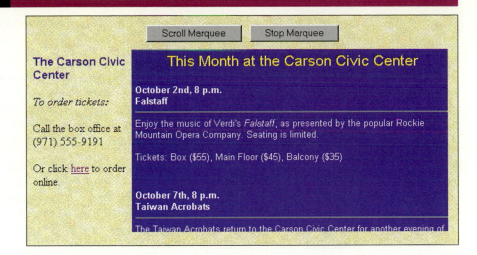

Much of the work in setting up the page has already been done for you. Your remaining task is to program the movements of the marquee.

To create the scrolling marquee:

1. In your text editor, open the file **CCCtext.htm**, located in the Tutorial.01D/Cases folder of your Data Disk, and save the file as **CCC.htm**.

2. Locate the <DIV> tag for the BOX element on the page. Using the inline style, set the positioning attribute of this element to absolute, and place the element at the (150, 50) coordinate on the page. Set the element to hide any overflowed content.

3. Locate the <DIV> tags for the Text1–Text6 elements. Each of these objects represents either a title line or text describing an upcoming event at the center. These are the objects you'll want to move vertically up the box. For each object, add an inline style to set the initial object position with absolute positioning. Use the following coordinates for the six objects:

   - Text1: (5, 5)
   - Text2: (5, 50)
   - Text3: (5, 200)
   - Text4: (5, 350)
   - Text5: (5, 500)
   - Text6: (5, 650)

4. Save your changes to the file.

5. Open the **CCCtext.js** file in your text editor and then save it as **CCC.js**.

Explore

6. In the CSS.htm Web page, the Text1–Text6 objects are nested inside the BOX object. Revise the getObject() function in the CCC.js API, so that for Netscape browsers, the command:

   getObject("Text1")

will correctly reference the Text1 object in the CCC.htm page.

7. Save your change to the CCC.js file and close it.

8. Reopen the **CCC.htm** file (if necessary) in your text editor and add a link to the CCC.js API file.

9. Above the link, insert a second set of <SCRIPT> tags. Within the <SCRIPT> tags, create a function named "moveIt(id)" that has a single parameter variable, "id." Using the YCoord() function from the API, store the y-coordinate of the id object in a variable named "y". If the value of y-coordinate is less than -100, use the placeIt() function from the API to move the id object to coordinate (5, 750); otherwise use the API's moveIt() function to move the object up 5 pixels.

Explore ▶ 10. Above the moveIt(id) function, insert a function named "Marquee()." This function will be used to start the marquee text moving. Have the Marquee() function call the moveIt(id) function every 130 milliseconds, using the text string Text1 as a parameter value, in order to move the Text1 object in the box. (*Hint*: Use the setInterval function, and enclose the name of the moveIt() command in single quotes, and the name of the parameter value in double quotes.) Save the id value of this time interval command in a variable named "t1." Repeat this command for the remaining objects, Text2–Text6, in the box. Store the id values of those five other time interval commands in variables named t2–t6.

Explore ▶ 11. Below the Marquee() function, insert a function named Stop(). This function will be used to halt the marquee text. Have the Stop() function clear the time interval commands for ids t1–t6.

12. Locate the button labeled Scroll Marquee and add an onClick event handler to run the Marquee() function when the button is clicked.

13. Locate the button labeled Stop Marquee and add an onClick event handler to run the Stop() function when it's clicked.

14. Save your changes to the file and open the page in your Web browser. Verify that when you click the Scroll Marquee button, the marquee starts scrolling vertically from bottom to top, and when you click the Stop Marquee button, the movement stops.

15. Print a copy of the Web page as it appears in your browser. Print a copy of the CCC.htm and CCC.js files.

Case 3. Adding Animation to the AJA Web page The American Juggling Association is planning their annual convention. Lisa Blanchard is in charge of getting the Web page ready and has asked you for help. She has already designed much of the page, but would like to put a "fun" element on the page. She's seen how some people use DHTML to create animated effects for their Web sites, and she wonders if you can create a juggling animation for her page. You tell her that you would be happy to help.

Figure 1-42 shows a preview of the page that you'll create. In your Web page, the three juggling balls shown in the photo of Tony Gaton will travel back and forth between the juggler's hands.

Figure 1-42

Welcome

Welcome to the AJA Convention Web site. This year's convention will take place from March 22-26 at the University of Wisconsin campus in Madison, Wisconsin. This Web site will provide you with the latest convention information, links to hotels in the Madison area, a convention schedule, and much more.

Workshops

Of course with every convention, there are convention workshops! This year we'll have our largest selection of convention workshops. Some of the best jugglers in the United States will be on hand to teach their techniques. *Tony Gaton* has generously provided his time to show off his 5 ball routines. Seating is limited, so be sure to register early.

Tony Gaton

The coordinates of the ball path have already been calculated for you and stored in the TossPath.txt text file. An image of a juggling ball has been stored in the JBall.gif file. Also an API file, AJAC.js, has been provided with commands for placing an object at a specified coordinate on the page.

To create the juggling animation:

1. In your text editor, open the file **AJACtext.htm** from the Tutorial.01D/Cases folder on your Data Disk. Save the file as **AJAC.htm**.

2. Below the <BODY> tag insert an inline image using the **JBall.gif** file. Enclose the inline image within a pair of <DIV> tags. Give the <DIV> an ID name of "Ball." Using an inline style, place the ball at the coordinate (63, 382) on the Web page, using absolute positioning.

3. Repeat Step 2 two more times, creating two more images of juggling balls on the Web page. Give the second ball the ID name "Ball2" and place it at the coordinate (129, 337) with absolute positioning. Give the third ball the ID name "Ball3" and place it at the (111, 288) coordinate with absolute positioning.

4. Insert a pair of <SCRIPT> tags within the head section of the AJAC.htm file.

5. The **TossPath.txt** text file contains the coordinates of the path the juggling ball will follow in the photo. Copy the coordinates from the text file and place them within the <SCRIPT> tags you created in the previous step.

6. Below the coordinates you just inserted, create three variables named "index", "index2", and "index3". These index values will point to the initial coordinates of the three balls. Give the index variable an initial value of 0; assign index2 a value of 34; give index3 a value of 60.

7. Create a function named "juggle()" that calls three other functions: moveBall(), moveBall2(), and moveBall3().

Explore

8. Below the juggle() function, create the moveBall() function. Use the technique of path animation and the coordinates of the ball path stored in the x and y array variables to move the Ball object along the path. Increase the value of the index variable as the Ball object moves along the path. Set the delay time between points on the path to 10 milliseconds. When you reach the end of the path, set the value of the index variable back to 0, and then repeat the path.

9. Create the moveBall2() and moveBall3() functions to move the Ball2 and Ball3 objects along the ball path. The function should follow the same structure that you used for the moveBall() function, except that you should use the index2 and index3 variables to track the path coordinates.

10. Below the </SCRIPT> tag, insert a link to the AJAC.js API file that contains functions you'll need to use in the Web page.

11. Set the file to run the juggle() function when the page is loaded by the browser.

12. Save your changes to the file and open the page in your Web browser. Verify that the three balls move in succession from one hand to the other.

13. Print a copy of the page from your browser. Also print a copy of your AJAC.htm file.

Case 4. Creating an Animation for The Exterminators   The Exterminators is a pest control company that specializes in the removal of insects, rodents, and small animals from urban homes and offices. Bruce Feinman has asked you to create a Web site for his company. He would like to have an opening screen in which a small bug flies around the page, only to be squashed. After the opening animation, he would like to have information about the company appear on the page. Bruce provides you with the following files:

- Bug.jpg — a clip art image of a bug
- BugDead.jpg — a clip art image of a squashed bug
- Shoe.jpg — a clip art image of a giant shoe print
- Bugs.txt — A text file describing Bruce's company

You may use additional material if it is available to you. The final design of the Web site is up to you, but it must have the following features:

1. An index.htm file that contains a Web page for customers whose browsers do not support DHTML.

2. If the customer's browser supports DHTML, use page branching to send the user from the index.htm file to an animated page, named Bug.htm.

3. Within the Bug.htm file, show at least one example of each of the following techniques:

- Positioning with CSS
- Positioning with JavaScript
- Linear animation
- Path animation
- Unhiding objects
- The setTimeout or the setInterval method

4. Your Web page must work for both Internet Explorer and Netscape.

5. When completed, print a copy of all the code you used in constructing your Web site. Also display the animation used in the page to your instructor.

QUICK | CHECK ANSWERS

Session 1.1

1. position: fixed

2. position: absolute; top: 3cm; left: 5cm

3. <DIV STYLE="position: relative; top: -25">Avalon Books</DIV>

   or

   <SPAN STYLE="position: relative; top: -25">Avalon Books</DIV>

4. The z-index attribute determines the stacking order of overlapping objects. The object with the lowest z-index value is placed on the bottom of the stack.

5. The display:none attribute hides the object, removing it from the page. The visibility:hidden attribute hides the object, but it still takes up space on the page.

6. clip: rect(10, 190, 140, 10);

7. overflow:scroll or overflow:auto. Netscape does not support either of these style attributes.

Session 1.2

1. Netscape: document.Logo

   Internet Explorer: Logo

2. Netscape: document.Logo.*attribute*

   Internet Explorer: Logo.style.*attribute*

3. Netscape: document.Logo.document.Title

   Internet Explorer: Title

4. parseFloat(navigator.appVersion);

5. The three ways to create a cross-browser Web site are: 1) page branching, in which you create separate pages for the browsers; 2) internal branching, in which every piece of code in the Web page uses an If . . . Else construct to determine the browser type and run the correct command; and 3) linking to an API, which contains custom functions and commands that resolve all the cross-browser problems.

6. Netscape: document.Logo.zIndex = document.Logo.zIndex+1;

   Internet Explorer: Logo.style.zIndex = Logo.style.zIndex+1;

7. Netscape: document.Logo.moveTo(150, 350);

   Internet Explorer: Logo.pixelLeft = 150; Logo.pixelTop = 350;

8. Netscape: document.Logo.visibility = hide;

   Internet Explorer: Logo.style.visibility = hidden;

9. Netscape: document.Logo.clip.top = 10; document.Logo.clip.right = 210; document.Logo.clip.bottom = 150; document.Logo.clip.left = 10;

   Internet Explorer: Logo.style.clip = rect(10 210 150 10);

Session 1.3

1. <SCRIPT SRC="Scripts.js"></SCRIPT>

2. setTimeout("moveGraphic()", 100);

3. mg = setInterval("moveGraphic()", 100);

4. clearInterval(mg);

5. screen.width and screen.height

6. screen.availWidth and screen.availHeight

7. In linear animation, you add or subtract a fixed value to change the coordinates of the object. In path animation, the coordinates are retrieved from an array of coordinate values.

OBJECTIVES

In this tutorial you will:

- Replace the content of your Web pages with new, dynamic content

- Learn about Netscape's <LAYER> tag

- Display the contents of an external file in a Netscape layer or Internet Explorer inline frame

- Work with dynamic styles in Internet Explorer

- Create an expandable outline in Netscape and Internet Explorer

- Use Netscape's JASS language to create dynamic styles

WORKING
WITH DYNAMIC CONTENT AND STYLES

Creating a Product Information Web Site

CASE

Pixal Digital Products

Pixal Digital Products manufactures digital imaging equipment, including scanners, digital tablets, and digital cameras. Sandy Bernstein is one of the supervisors in Pixal's Web site team. You've been recently hired to assist her in developing the pages for Pixal's line of digital cameras.

Sandy would like the pages to have dynamic content, so that the text and images on the page change in response to customer actions. Rather than have separate pages for each digital camera model, Sandy wants you to create a page in which the customer selects one of the camera models, and the page is then reformatted to display information on that model.

Sandy is also aware that a Web page with too much text can overwhelm a customer. She would like you to create pages in which the user chooses how much of the content to view at any one time.

To do these tasks, you'll have to employ DHTML to control the type and amount of content that is presented to the customer.

SESSION 2.1

In this session you'll learn how Internet Explorer and Netscape allow you to create and insert new content in your Web pages. You'll explore how to use the Internet Explorer innerText and innerHTML properties, and you'll see how to work with Netscape's <LAYER> tag. Finally, you'll learn how to display the contents of external HTML files using Internet Explorer internal frames and Netscape's layers.

Working with Dynamic Content

Dynamic content is material on a Web page that is added or altered, usually after the page has already been loaded and shown by the Web browser and usually in response to actions or requests by the user.

Internet Explorer and Netscape require very different approaches to creating dynamic content. Internet Explorer makes almost all of the content on the page accessible to JavaScript, making it a relatively simple matter to change the content or appearance of a paragraph, even down to the level of a single word or phrase. Netscape does not provide this level of control. Instead, you must run JavaScript commands that rewrite sections of the page, and then redisplay those sections to the user. Because Sandy wants the Pixal Web site to be cross-browser-compatible, you'll need to work with both of these methods.

Sandy shows you a sample of the first page you'll help create. The page as she's hoping it will look, shown in Figure 2-1, is designed to provide a general overview of three of Pixal's digital cameras (she'll add the full line after you finalize the code.) The three are:

- The DC100 sold for $399
- The DC250 sold for $599
- The DC500 sold for $749

Figure 2-1	ADDING DYNAMIC CONTENT TO THE PIXAL WEB PAGE

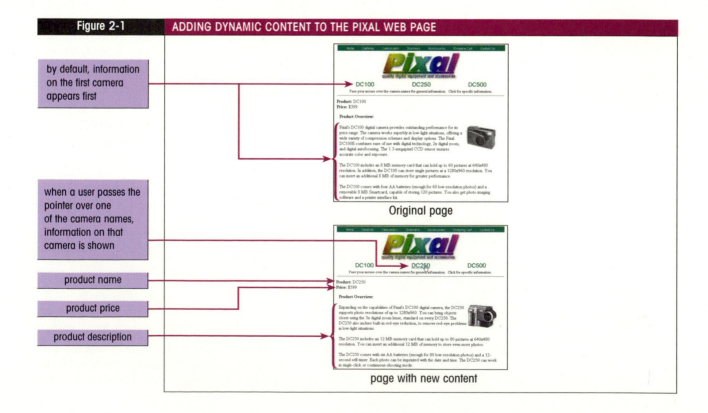

The page that Sandy shows you lists the three camera models on a single line at the top of the page. Sandy envisions the page content being automatically updated to provide information about whichever camera model the pointer is currently over. If the user actually clicks one of the camera names, the browser will load a page with more detailed technical information on the selected camera.

Sandy explains that there are three items on the page that need to be changed in response to the user's action:

- The name of the digital camera
- The price of the camera
- Paragraphs describing the properties of the digital camera

The basic structure of this page has already been created for you. Your job will be to insert the code to create the dynamic content.

To open the digital camera page:

1. In your text editor, open the file **Pixaltxt.htm** located in the Tutorial.02D folder of your Data Disk.

2. Save the file as **Pixal.htm**.

3. Open **Pixal.htm** in your Web browser (shown in Figure 2-2).

| Figure 2-2 | THE INITIAL PIXAL.HTM PAGE |

Take some time to study the HTML code for this file. Note that there is already some JavaScript code entered into the page to identify the type of browser being used by the customer. If the customer is using a Netscape browser, the Boolean variable isNS will be set to "true." If the user is running Internet Explorer, the variable isIE will be set to "true."

The page opens with the product name "DC100" and the price "$399" appearing below the list of the three cameras. Your first task will be to write a JavaScript program to turn this into dynamic text. You'll start with a solution for Netscape browsers.

Using the <LAYER> Tag in Netscape

To create dynamic content with Netscape, you must use Netscape's <LAYER> tag. Introduced in version 4.0, the <LAYER> tag encloses document content in a container (what Netscape calls a "layer"), much as the <DIV> tag is used to create block-level elements in standard

HTML. The syntax of the <LAYER> tag is:

```
<LAYER ID=id properties>
    document content
</LAYER>
```

where *id* is the ID name of the layer, *properties* are the properties that define the appearance and location of the layer, and *document content* is the content that will be placed within the layer.

This content can include text, inline images, font formatting tags, and so forth. For example, you can insert an H1 header within a layer using the tag:

```
<LAYER ID=Header><H1>Pixal Products</H1></LAYER>
```

Note that you could also have used the <DIV> tag for this example, but as you'll see, Netscape's <LAYER> tag is more flexible than the <DIV> tag.

REFERENCE WINDOW   **RW**

<u>Creating a Netscape Layer</u>
- To create a layer in Netscape, enter the <LAYER> tag as follows:
  ```
  <LAYER ID=id properties>
    document content
  </LAYER>
  ```
  where *id* is the ID name of the layer, *properties* are the properties that define the appearance and location of the layer, and *document content* is the content that will be placed within the layer.

<LAYER> Properties

Figure 2-3 summarizes some of the important properties of the <LAYER> tag (more are included in the appendix).

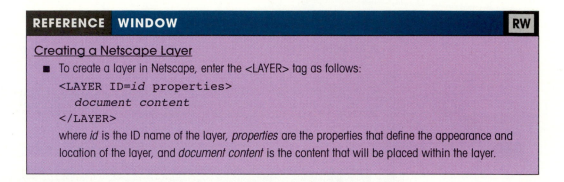

Figure 2-3	PROPERTIES OF THE <LAYER> TAG
PROPERTY	**DESCRIPTION**
CLIP=*top_x, left_y, bottom_x, right_y*	Specifies the coordinates of the viewable region of the layer
HEIGHT=*Value*	The height of the layer, in pixels
LEFT=*Value*	Specifies the horizontal offset of the layer, in pixels
PAGEX=*Value*	Specifies the horizontal position of the layer
PAGEY=*Value*	Specifies the vertical position of the layer
SRC=*URL*	Specifies the URL of the document displayed in the layer
TOP=*Value*	Specifies the vertical offset of the layer, in pixels
VISIBILITY=*Option* (HIDE | INHERIT | SHOW)	Specifies whether the layer is hidden, shown, or inherits its visibility from the layer that contains it
WIDTH=*Value*	The width of the layer, in pixels
Z-INDEX=*Value*	Specifies the stacking order of the layer, relative to the other layers

For example, the tag:

```
<LAYER ID=Header WIDTH=200 HEIGHT=150>Pixal Products</LAYER>
```

places the text "Pixal Products" in a layer that is 200 pixels wide by 150 pixels high.

In actual practice, if there is more content than can be fitted into the specified width and height, Netscape will increase the height of the layer to compensate.

If you need to keep the size of the layer constant despite whatever the content of the layer is, you can use the CLIP property of the <LAYER> tag. The syntax is:

```
<LAYER ID=id CLIP=top_x, left_y, bottom_x, right_y>
```

where *top_x*, *left_y*, *bottom_x*, and *right_y* are the coordinates for the clipping region around the layer. For example, to fix a layer at a width of 300 pixels and a height of 100 pixels, you could use the following tag:

```
<LAYER WIDTH=300 HEIGHT=100 CLIP=0,0,300,100>
```

Note that if the content exceeds the dimensions of the layer, Netscape will truncate the excess content; so use this technique only if you are sure that the layer can display all of your text and images.

REFERENCE   WINDOW   **RW**

Setting the Size of a Netscape Layer
- To set the size of a Netscape layer, use the tag:
  ```
  <LAYER WIDTH=width HEIGHT=height></LAYER>
  ```
  where *width* and *height* are the width and height values of the layer, in pixels.
- To clip a portion of the layer, use the tag:
  ```
  <LAYER ID=id CLIP=top_x, left_y, bottom_x, right_y>
  ```
  where *top_x, left_y, bottom_x,* and *right_y* are the coordinates for the clipping region around the layer.

Linking a Layer to an HTML File

If you have a large block of text, it is often more efficient to link the layer to an HTML file containing the text and images you want to appear. In this way, a layer can act as an inline window, showing the content of other files. The syntax for linking to an external file is:

```
<LAYER ID=id SRC=URL></LAYER>
```

where *URL* is the filename or URL of the external file. For example, to link to the Pixal.htm file, you would use the <LAYER> tag:

```
<LAYER SRC="Pixal.htm"></LAYER>
```

You can use the WIDTH and HEIGHT properties to specify the space reserved for the external file. Once again, if the content of the external file exceeds the dimensions of the layer, Netscape will increase the layer's height to compensate.

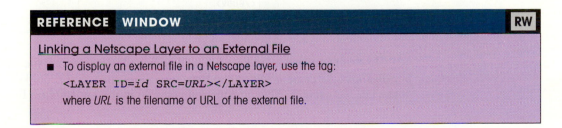

REFERENCE   WINDOW   **RW**

Linking a Netscape Layer to an External File
- To display an external file in a Netscape layer, use the tag:
  ```
  <LAYER ID=id SRC=URL></LAYER>
  ```
  where *URL* is the filename or URL of the external file.

The <ILAYER> and <NOLAYER> Tags

Content that is enclosed within a <LAYER> tag uses absolute positioning on the Web page. If you want to use relative positioning, so that the contents of the layer flow alongside other content in your Web page, you must use the <ILAYER> tag (where ILAYER stands for "inflow layer.")

The properties for the <ILAYER> tag are similar to the <LAYER> tag. However, Netscape does not provide the same level of JavaScript support for ilayer objects. For example, the <LAYER> tag supports the onMouseOver and onMouseOut event handlers, but the <ILAYER> tag does not. So you may find the <ILAYER> tag less useful, especially if you need to manipulate the properties or contents of the layer via JavaScript.

If you want to make your page available to browsers that do not support the <LAYER> and <ILAYER> tags, you can do so with the <NOLAYER> tag. Any tags placed inside the <NOLAYER> tag will be ignored by Netscape, but will be available to other browsers. For example, the following code:

```
<LAYER SRC="Pixal.htm" WIDTH=200 HEIGHT=150></LAYER>
<NOLAYER>
    <H1>Pixal Products</H1>
</NOLAYER>
```

will display the content of the Pixal.htm file for Netscape users, but for users of browsers that do not support layers, the H1 header "Pixal Products" will be shown.

Netscape has pledged to follow the HTML 4.0 standards, so it is unlikely to further develop the <LAYER> tag in the future.

Using Layers in the Pixal Page

Now that you've seen how to work with Netscape's <LAYER> tag, you'll use it to write dynamic content to the Pixal page. You'll create layers for the camera name and price, and then you'll create a third layer containing a summary of the camera's properties. The ID names of the first two layers will be "NameNS," and "PriceNS."

To create the NameNS and PriceNS layers:

1. Return to the **Pixal.htm** file in your text editor.

2. Scroll to the bottom of the text file and enclose the text "DC100" within a set of **<LAYER>** tags with the property **ID=NameNS**, as shown in Figure 2-4.

3. Enclose the text "$399" within a set of **<LAYER>** tags with the property **ID=PriceNS**. Your HTML file should look like Figure 2-4.

Figure 2-4	CREATING THE NAMENS AND PRICENS LAYERS

```
<B>Product: </B>
<LAYER ID=NameNS>DC100</LAYER>
<BR>
<B>Price: </B>
<LAYER ID=PriceNS>$399</LAYER>
<BR>

</BODY>
</HTML>
```

The third layer, named PageNS, will be linked to an external file with summary information about the camera. When the Pixal.htm file is opened, it should display the summary for the DC100 camera. This information is stored in the DC100.htm file.

To create the PageNS layer:

1. Above the </BODY> tag, insert the text:

```
<LAYER ID=PageNS SRC="DC100.htm" WIDTH=600></LAYER>
```

As shown in Figure 2-5, the width of this layer will be 600 pixels. Netscape will set the layer height to match the content of the DC100.htm file.

Figure 2-5   CREATING THE PAGENS LAYER

```
<B>Product: </B>
<LAYER ID=NameNS>DC100</LAYER>
<BR>
<B>Price: </B>
<LAYER ID=PriceNS>$399</LAYER>
<BR>
<LAYER ID=PageNS SRC="DC100.htm" WIDTH=600></LAYER>
</BODY>
</HTML>
```

2. Save your changes to Pixal.htm.

3. Reload the file in your Netscape browser. Figure 2-6 shows the current state of the page.

Figure 2-6   DISPLAYING INFORMATION ABOUT THE DC100 CAMERA IN NETSCAPE

Home   Cameras   Camcorders   Scanners   Accessories   Shopping Cart   Contact Us

quality digital equipment and accessories

DC100   DC250   DC500

Pass your mouse over the camera names for general information.   Click for specific information.

Product: DC100
Price: $399
Product Overview:

Information about the DC100 camera

Pixal's DC100 digital camera provides outstanding performance for its price range. The camera works superbly in low-light situations, offering a wide variety of compression schemes and display options. The Pixal DC100E combines ease of use with digital technology, 2x digital zoom, and digital autofocusing. The 1.3-megapixel CCD sensor ensures accurate color and exposure.

The DC100 includes an 8 MB memory card that can hold up to 60 pictures at 640x480 resolution. In addition, the DC100 can store single pictures at a 1280x960 resolution. You can insert an additional 8 MB of memory for greater performance.

The DC100 comes with four AA batteries (enough for 60 low-resolution photos) and a removable 8 MB Smartcard, capable of storing 120 pictures. You also get photo imaging software and a printer interface kit.

Working with Layer Objects

The page displays information for the DC100 camera, but Sandy wants this content to change in response to actions by the user. To do this, you'll write JavaScript functions to alter the properties and content of the three layers you created.

Writing Content to a Layer

To insert content in a layer, you use the write() method. The syntax is:

```
document.id.document.write(dynamic content);
```

where *id* is the name of the layer, and *dynamic content* is the new content of the layer. For example, if the initial content of a layer is:

```
<LAYER ID=Intro>Digital Equipment</LAYER>
```

you can change the content to "Quality Digital Equipment and Accessories" using the command:

```
document.Intro.document.write("Quality Digital Equipment and
Accessories");
```

If you need to change the format of the layer as well as the text, you must insert specific formatting tags as part of the new content. For example, to create boldface text, you would use the <B> tag as follows:

```
document.Intro.document.write("<B>Quality Digital Equipment
and Accessories</B>");
```

The Intro layer would now display the new text in a boldface font.

When you use the document.write() method in this fashion, it opens an "input stream" to the layer. The first document.write() command will replace whatever content was previously in the layer. Succeeding document.write() commands will append their content to the layer.

Whenever you open an input stream via the document.write() command, you must close it before your script finishes running. If you don't close the input stream, your changes will not appear in the browser window. The command to close the input stream is:

```
document.id.document.close();
```

where *id* is once again the ID name of the layer. For example, the following command block:

```
document.Intro.document.write("<H2>Pixal Products</H2>");
document.Intro.document.write("Quality Digital Equipment");
document.Intro.document.close();
```

inserts two lines into the Intro layer. First, it inserts the H2 header "Pixal Products", then the line "Quality Digital Equipment." The close() method then closes the input stream to the layer.

Writing Dynamic Content to the Pixal Page

Since Sandy wants the content in these layers to change in response to the mouseover event for the three product names located on the top of the page, you need to add event handlers to each of those names. As the user passes a mouse over each name, the browser will run a function called "showText()." You haven't created the showText() function yet, but its purpose will be to write new content to the two layers. The function will have one parameter, the name of the camera.

To create the event handler for the three camera names:

1. Scroll up the document to the <A> tags for the DC100–DC500 cameras.

2. Within the <A> tag for the DC100 camera, insert the property **onMouseOver='showText("DC100")'** as shown in Figure 2-7.

3. Within the DC250 <A> tag, insert **onMouseOver='showText("DC250")'**.

4. Within the DC500 <A> tag, insert **onMouseOver='showText("DC500")'**.

   Figure 2-7 shows the revised HTML code.

Figure 2-7   ADDING EVENT HANDLERS

```
<TR>
   <TD ALIGN=CENTER WIDTH=33%>
      <A CLASS=Prod HREF=# onMouseOver='showText("DC100")'>DC100</A>
   </TD>
   <TD ALIGN=CENTER WIDTH=33%>
      <A CLASS=Prod HREF=# onMouseOver='showText("DC250")'>DC250</A>
   </TD>
   <TD ALIGN=CENTER WIDTH=33%>
      <A CLASS=Prod HREF=# onMouseOver='showText("DC500")'>DC500</A>
   </TD>
</TR>
```

Note that while these camera names are enclosed within <A> tags, they're not actually linked to anything yet. The HREF property has the value, "#," which points back to the Pixal.htm file. We're enclosing the camera names within <A> tags because the <A> tag is one of the few tags for which Netscape recognizes the onMouseOver event handler.

Next you need to create the showText() function, which you just called with the onMouseOver event handler. The function will have two variables: "Pname," which stores the name of the camera, and "Price," which stores the camera price. The PName and Price values are then written to the NameNS and PriceNS layers. The complete code for the showText() function is:

```
function showText(PName) {
    if (PName=="DC100') Price="$399";
    if (PName=="DC250") Price="$599";
    if (PName=="DC500") Price="$749";

    if (isNS) {
        document.NameNS.document.write(PName);
        document.NameNS.document.close();
        document.PriceNS.document.write(Price);
        document.PriceNS.document.close();
    } else {
    }
}
```

Note that the function uses the isNS variable to determine the type of browser being used by the customer. The commands to write new content to the NameNS and PriceNS layers will be run only if the browser is Netscape. You'll write the code for Internet Explorer users in a moment.

To add the showText() function to the Pixal.htm file:

1. Scroll up the document to the </SCRIPT> tag.

2. Above the </SCRIPT> tag, insert the following JavaScript code (see Figure 2-8):

```
function showText(PName) {
    if (PName=="DC100") Price="$399";
    if (PName=="DC250") Price="$599";
    if (PName=="DC500") Price="$749";

    if (isNS) {
        document.NameNS.document.write(PName);
        document.NameNS.document.close();
        document.PriceNS.document.write(Price);
        document.PriceNS.document.close();
    } else {
    }
}
```

Figure 2-8	INSERTING THE SHOWTEXT() FUNCTION

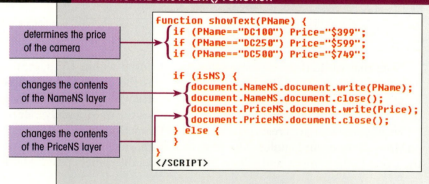

determines the price of the camera

changes the contents of the NameNS layer

changes the contents of the PriceNS layer

```
function showText(PName) {
    if (PName=="DC100") Price="$399";
    if (PName=="DC250") Price="$599";
    if (PName=="DC500") Price="$749";

    if (isNS) {
        document.NameNS.document.write(PName);
        document.NameNS.document.close();
        document.PriceNS.document.write(Price);
        document.PriceNS.document.close();
    } else {
    }
}
</SCRIPT>
```

3. Save your changes to the file.

4. Open **Pixal.htm** in a Netscape browser, version 4.0 or later.

   TROUBLE? If you don't have access to Netscape, you won't be able to check the changes, but you should leave the code in to make your page cross-browser-compatible.

5. Verify that as you pass your pointer over the three camera names, the product name and price are automatically changed.

Changing the Source of a Layer Object

The showText() function also needs to change the source for the PageNS layer. To change the source of a layer, the JavaScript syntax is:

```
document.id.src=URL;
```

where *id* is the ID name of the <LAYER> tag, and *URL* is the URL of the new source for the layer.

REFERENCE WINDOW   **RW**

Changing the Source of a Netscape Layer
- To change the source file of a Netscape layer, use the JavaScript command:
  ```
  document.id.src=URL;
  ```
  where *id* is the ID name of the <LAYER> tag, and *URL* is the URL of the new source for the layer.

Sandy has already created three HTML files for the three cameras. The files are named DC100.htm, DC250.htm, and DC500.htm. Since the PName variable already contains the names of the three cameras, you can use it to specify the names of the different HTML files. The command you'll add to the showText() function is:

```
document.PageNS.src=PName+".htm";
```

Add this command now.

To modify the showText() function:

1. Return to the **Pixal.htm** file in your text editor.

2. Locate the showText() function, and below the line "document.PriceNS.document.close();" insert the new line:

   ```
   document.PageNS.src=PName+".htm";
   ```

   The revised code for the showText() function appears in Figure 2-9.

Figure 2-9 | **CHANGING THE SOURCE OF THE PAGENS LAYER**

```
function showText(PName) {
    if (PName=="DC100") Price="$399";
    if (PName=="DC250") Price="$599";
    if (PName=="DC500") Price="$749";

    if (isNS) {
        document.NameNS.document.write(PName);
        document.NameNS.document.close();
        document.PriceNS.document.write(Price);
        document.PriceNS.document.close();
        document.PageNS.src=PName+".htm";
    } else {
    }
}
</SCRIPT>
```

3. Save your changes to the file.

4. Reload the **Pixal.htm** page in your Netscape browser.

5. Verify that as you pass the mouse over the three camera names, the product information text changes to match each one.

Resizing the Layer Object

As you write additional content to a layer, or change the layer's source, you need to be sure that the layer is large enough to display the content. When the page is initially loaded, the height of the layer will increase to accommodate the additional text, but after the page is loaded, the layer's dimensions can only be modified through a JavaScript command. To change the width and height of a layer, use the commands:

```
document.id.clip.width=width;
document.id.clip.height=height;
```

where *id* is the name of the layer object, and *width* and *height* are the new width and height of the layer in pixels.

Note that you cannot change the width or height of the layer so as to exceed the initial dimensions of the Web page. For example, if Netscape displays the page with a height of 500 pixels, and you need to increase the height of a layer within the page by 100 pixels, Netscape will not increase the overall height of the page to compensate. This means that the last 100 pixels of the new page will be truncated. To get around this problem, you should set the initial height of the layer large enough to accommodate any additional text you plan to add later via JavaScript.

Working with the <LAYER> tag and properties of the document layers is the extent of what you can do with dynamic content in Netscape. By combining the technique of writing content directly into the layer and changing the source and properties of the layer, you can do most of the tasks needed for creating dynamic content on your page.

Dynamic Content in Internet Explorer

Internet Explorer handles dynamic content with greater flexibility and power than Netscape. Unlike Netscape, which can use dynamic content only with the <LAYER> tag, the content of almost any tag can be modified in Internet Explorer.

Working with Inner and Outer Properties

Internet Explorer treats each two-sided tag as having an "inner" and "outer" part. The inner portion is any content that lies between the opening and closing tag. The outer portion includes both the inner content and the two-sided tags themselves (along with any properties of the tags). For example, in the following HTML code:

```
<P><SPAN>Pixal Products</SPAN></P>
```

The inner part of the paragraph tag is:

```
<SPAN>Pixal Products</SPAN>
```

and the outer portion includes the inner part and the <P> tags themselves:

```
<P><SPAN>Pixal Products</SPAN></P>
```

Internet Explorer allows you to specify either text or HTML code for the inner and outer parts of the tag. To specify text for the inner part, the general syntax is:

```
object.innerText = "text";
```

where *object* is a two-sided tag on the Web page, and *text* is the text of the inner part of the tag. For example, if the Web page has the following paragraph tag:

```
<DIV ID=Intro>Digital Equipment</DIV>
```

you can change the text to "Quality Digital Equipment and Accessories" by using the JavaScript command:

```
Intro.innerText="Quality Digital Equipment and Accessories";
```

Note that if you try to use HTML tags with the innerText property, Internet Explorer will treat the HTML tags as text and not code. The following JavaScript command:

```
Intro.innerText="<B>Quality Digital Equipment and
Accessories</B>";
```

will result in the following text being shown on the Web page:

```
<B>Quality Digital Equipment and Accessories</B>
```

If you want to write this text in boldface, you must use the innerHTML property, which interprets any HTML code and applies it to the document content. The syntax of the innerHTML property is:

```
object.innerHTML="text and HTML code";
```

If your JavaScript command is:

```
Intro.innerHTML="<B>Quality Digital Equipment and
Accessories</B>";
```

the text will be written in boldface font.

In the same way, the outerText and outerHTML properties can be used to modify the text or HTML code of the contents of the tag, as well as the tag itself. For example, the following H1 header:

```
<H1 ID=Title>Pixal Products</H1>
```

can be turned into an H2 header by using the JavaScript command:

```
Title.outerHTML="<H2 ID=Title>Pixal Products</H2>";
```

Changing the outer properties also changes the enclosing tags. This can occasionally result in error messages. For example, the following set of JavaScript commands when applied to the tag <H1 ID=Title>Pixal Products</H1> will result in an error message:

```
Title.outerHTML="<H2>Pixal Products</H2>";
Title.innerHTML="<I>Pixal Products</I>";
```

The error occurs because the first JavaScript command replaces the "<H1 ID=Title>" tag with an "<H2>" tag, but since no ID property is included in this new content, the Title object disappears from the Internet Explorer object hierarchy. The second command, which tries to reference the now-defunct Title object, results in an error message. Thus you should use caution whenever you apply the outer properties to change the content of an object on your page.

REFERENCE WINDOW   **RW**

Changing the Content of a Tag in Internet Explorer

- To change the text within a two-sided tag, use the JavaScript command:
  `object.innerText = "text";`
  where *object* is a two-sided tag on the Web page, and *text* is the text of the inner part of the tag.
- To change the HTML code within a two-sided tag, use the JavaScript command:
  `object.innerHTML="text and HTML code";`
- To change the text within the two-sided tag and the text of the two-sided tag itself, use the command:
  `object.outerText = "text";`
- To change the HTML code within the two-sided tag and the HTML code of the tag itself, use the command:
  `object.outerHTML="text and HTML code";`

Inserting Content into a Tag

You can also use the insertAdjacentText() and insertAdjacentHTML() methods to create dynamic content in Internet Explorer. The syntax of these methods is:

```
object.insertAdjacentText("position", text);
object.insertAdjacentHTML("position", text);
```

where *object* is the object on the page, and *position* is the position within the tag where the new *text* should be inserted. Note that the position value must be placed in quotation marks. The *position* parameter has four possible values:

- BeforeBegin   To insert text directly before the object's opening tag
- AfterBegin   To insert text directly after the object's opening tag
- BeforeEnd   To insert text directly before the object's closing tag
- AfterEnd   To insert text directly after the object's closing tag

For example, if the tag in the HTML file is:

```
<H1 ID=Title>Pixal Cameras</H1>
```

the JavaScript command,

```
Title.insertAdjacentText("BeforeEnd", "and Accessories");
```

will change the text of the H1 header to "Pixal Cameras and Accessories." Now if you run a second JavaScript command:

```
Title.insertAdjacentText("AfterBegin", "<I>Introducing
    </I>");
```

the browser will display the header as:

Introducing Pixal Products and Accessories

where the first italicized word, "Introducing", is inserted via the JavaScript command.

REFERENCE WINDOW   **RW**

Inserting Text into a Tag in Internet Explorer

- To insert new text into a two-sided tag, use the command:

  object.insertAdjacentText("*position*", *text*);

  where *object* is the object on the page, and *position* is the position within the tag where the new *text* should be inserted. Position can have the value "BeforeBegin", "AfterBegin", "BeforeEnd", or "AfterEnd". Note that the position value must be placed in quotation marks.

- To insert new HTML code into a two-sided tag, use the command:

  object.insertAdjacentHTML("*position*", *text*);

Adding Dynamic Content to the Pixal Page

To insert dynamic content into the Pixal page for Internet Explorer users, you'll use the innerText property. However, before you do that, you must place the product name and product price within a set of <SPAN> tags in order to "mark" them on the page (Internet Explorer does not recognize the <LAYER> tag). You'll assign these two sets of <SPAN> tags the ID names NameIE and PriceIE.

To add <SPAN> tags to the Pixal page:

1. Return to the **Pixal.htm** file in your text editor.

2. Locate the <LAYER> tag for the product name located near the bottom of the file.

3. Before "<LAYER ID=NameNS>," insert the tag **<SPAN ID=NameIE>**.

4. After the closing </LAYER> tag, insert a closing **</SPAN>** tag.

5. Enclose the <LAYER> tags for the product price within a similar set of <SPAN> tags with the ID value "PriceIE." Figure 2-10 shows the revised HTML code.

| Figure 2-10 | INSERTING <SPAN> TAGS INTO THE PIXAL.HTM FILE |

```
<B>Product: </B>
<SPAN ID=NameIE><LAYER ID=NameNS>DC100</LAYER></SPAN>
<BR>
<B>Price: </B>
<SPAN ID=PriceIE><LAYER ID=PriceNS>$399</LAYER></SPAN>
<BR>
<LAYER ID=PageNS SRC="DC100.htm" WIDTH=600></LAYER>
</BODY>
</HTML>
```

To change the content of these two <SPAN> tags, you'll add the following commands to the showText() function:

```
NameIE.innerText=PName;
PriceIE.innerText=Price;
```

where PName is the product name variable in the showText() function, and Price contains the price of the product.

To revise the showText() function:

1. Scroll up to the showText() function at the top of the Pixal.htm file.

2. After the line "} else {", insert the commands:

```
NameIE.innerText=PName;
PriceIE.innerText=Price;
```

   Figure 2-11 shows the revised function. Note that these two commands will not be run for Netscape browsers.

Figure 2-11   CHANGING THE TEXT OF THE <SPAN> ELEMENTS

```
function showText(PName) {
    if (PName=="DC100") Price="$399";
    if (PName=="DC250") Price="$599";
    if (PName=="DC500") Price="$749";

    if (isNS) {
        document.NameNS.document.write(PName);
        document.NameNS.document.close();
        document.PriceNS.document.write(Price);
        document.PriceNS.document.close();
        document.PageNS.src=PName+".htm";
    } else {
        NameIE.innerText=PName;
        PriceIE.innerText=Price;
    }
}
</SCRIPT>
```

3. Save your changes to the file.

4. Reload the **Pixal.htm** file in your Internet Explorer browser (version 4.0 or later).

5. Verify that as you pass the mouse over the three camera names, the product name and price change to reflect your actions.

   TROUBLE? If you do not have the Internet Explorer browser, you will not be able to test these commands.

Linking to an HTML File

Netscape's <LAYER> tag allows you to display the contents of other HTML files in your Web page. You can do the same thing with the Internet Explorer <IFRAME> tag, which places an internal frame on the page. The syntax for the <IFRAME> tag is:

```
<IFRAME SRC=URL WIDTH=value HEIGHT=value>
```

Unlike the <LAYER> tag, the size of the internal frame is fixed at the specified width and height values. If the content of the frame exceeds the frame size, Internet Explorer will automatically display vertical and horizontal scroll bars to allow users to scroll to the hidden content in the frame. The internal frame automatically displays the HTML file surrounded by a frame border. You can remove the frame border by using the property:

```
FRAMEBORDER=NO
```

Sandy would like you to place an internal frame on the page for Internet Explorer browsers. She does not want a frame border to appear, because she wants the text to integrate seamlessly with the rest of the page. For the same reason, she does not want scrollbars to appear, so you should set the width and height of the frame large enough to accommodate the amount of text in the external HTML files. After some and trial and error to determine the proper frame dimension, you settle on the following frame properties:

```
<IFRAME ID=PageIE SRC="DC100.htm" WIDTH=600 HEIGHT=400
FRAMEBORDER=NO>
```

Note that the ID of this frame is "PageIE"–similar to the ID name PageNS given to Netscape's page <LAYER>, added earlier.

To add an internal frame to the Pixal.htm file:

1. Return to the **Pixal.htm** file in your text editor.

2. Above the </BODY> tag, insert the following tag (see Figure 2-12):

```
<IFRAME ID=PageIE SRC="DC100.htm" WIDTH=600 HEIGHT=400
FRAMEBORDER=NO>
```

Figure 2-12	INSERTING AN INTERNAL FRAME

```
<BR>
<LAYER ID=PageNS SRC="DC100.htm" WIDTH=600></LAYER>
<IFRAME ID=PageIE SRC="DC100.htm" WIDTH=600 HEIGHT=400 FRAMEBORDER=NO>
</BODY>
</HTML>
```

3. Save your changes.

4. Reload the **Pixal.htm** file in your Internet Explorer browser and verify that the contents of the DC100.htm file now appear on the page (see Figure 2-13).

   TROUBLE? On some browsers, a vertical scroll bar will still appear next to the contents of the DC100.htm file.

Figure 2-13   DISPLAYING THE DC100.HTM PAGE IN INTERNET EXPLORER

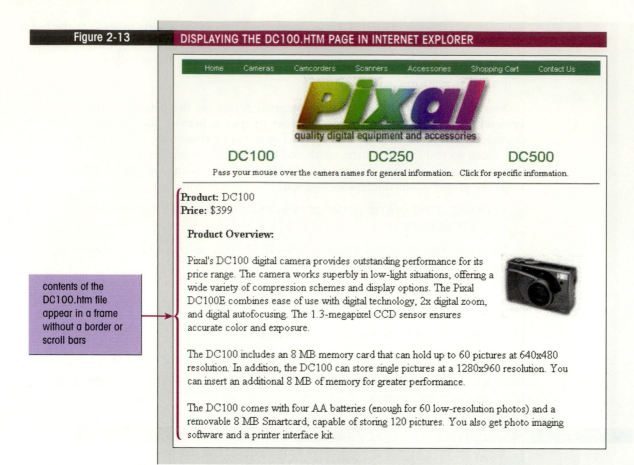

contents of the DC100.htm file appear in a frame without a border or scroll bars

Next you have to change the source of this frame in response to the user's actions. The syntax to change the source of an internal frame is:

```
document.all.frame.src=URL;
```

where *frame* is the ID of the internal frame, and *URL* is the URL of the new source for the frame. Note that you must include the "all" keyword since frames fall below "all" in the Internet Explorer document object model.

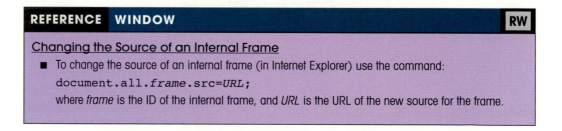

REFERENCE   WINDOW   RW

Changing the Source of an Internal Frame
- To change the source of an internal frame (in Internet Explorer) use the command:
  ```
  document.all.frame.src=URL;
  ```
  where *frame* is the ID of the internal frame, and *URL* is the URL of the new source for the frame.

You'll modify the showText() function to display the correct HTML file for each selected camera. For Internet Explorer browsers, the command is:

```
document.all.PageIE.src=PName+".htm";
```

Note the similarity of this command to the one you wrote earlier to change the source of the Netscape layer.

To add this command to the showText() function:

1. Return to the **Pixal.htm** file in your text editor and locate the showText() function.

2. Insert the command

   ```
   document.all.PageIE.src=PName+".htm";
   ```

   as shown in Figure 2-14.

| Figure 2-14 | CHANGING THE SOURCE OF THE INTERNAL FRAME |

```
function showText(PName) {
   if (PName=="DC100") Price="$399";
   if (PName=="DC250") Price="$599";
   if (PName=="DC500") Price="$749";

   if (isNS) {
      document.NameNS.document.write(PName);
      document.NameNS.document.close();
      document.PriceNS.document.write(Price);
      document.PriceNS.document.close();
      document.PageNS.src=PName+".htm";
   } else {
      NameIE.innerText=PName;
      PriceIE.innerText=Price;
      document.all.PageIE.src=PName+".htm";
   }
}
</SCRIPT>
```

3. Save your changes.

4. Reload the **Pixal.htm** file in your Internet Explorer browser.

5. Verify that as you move the pointer over each of the three camera names, the content of the Web page changes in response.

Page Branching to Separate HTML Files

You've completed your work creating dynamic content for the Pixal page. The next page that Sandy wants you to work on is a page for the DC100 digital camera that contains more detailed and technical information. This page will also contain some dynamic content, which you'll learn about in the next session; however, because of the differences between the two browsers, it'll be easier to create two separate HTML files: one for Internet Explorer and one for Netscape. You'll name the Netscape page DC100_NS.htm, and the Internet Explorer page DC100_IE.htm.

When the user clicks the name "DC100" in the list of camera names at the top of the Pixal page, Sandy wants the browser to display the page with detailed information about the DC100 camera. However, since you'll have different pages for Netscape and Internet Explorer users, you cannot simply link the text to the page. Instead, you need to add an onMouseDown event handler to the <A> tag for the DC100 camera name, so that when the user presses the mouse button, the browser loads the correct page.

To add the onMouseDown event handler:

1. Return to the **Pixal.htm** file in your text editor.

2. Locate the <A> tag for the DC100 digital camera, and insert the property, **onMouseDwn='showFile("DC100")'** as shown in Figure 2-15.

Figure 2-15   **CREATING AN ONMOUSEDOWN EVENT HANDLER**

```
<TR>
   <TD ALIGN=CENTER WIDTH=33%>
      <A CLASS=Prod HREF=# onMouseDown='showFile("DC100")'
       onMouseOver='showText("DC100")'>DC100</A>
   </TD>
   <TD ALIGN=CENTER WIDTH=33%>
      <A CLASS=Prod HREF=# onMouseOver='showText("DC250")'>DC250</A>
   </TD>
   <TD ALIGN=CENTER WIDTH=33%>
      <A CLASS=Prod HREF=# onMouseOver='showText("DC500")'>DC500</A>
   </TD>
</TR>
```

Now you need to add the showFile() function to determine which file to display for the user. The function you'll write will look as follows:

```
function showFile(PName) {
    if (isNS) {
        location=PName+"_NS.htm";
    } else {
        location=PName+"_IE.htm";
    }
}
```

So if the browser is Netscape, the page is changed to DC100_NS.htm, and if the browser is Internet Explorer, the DC100_IE.htm page is loaded.

To add the showFile() function to the file:

1. Above the </SCRIPT> tag, insert the following function:

```
function showFile(PName) {
    if (isNS) {
        location=PName+"_NS.htm";
    } else {
        location=PName+"_IE.htm";
    }
}
```

2. Save your changes to Pixal.htm and close your text editor.

You haven't created these two pages yet, so you can't test the showFile() function. You'll do that in the next session, when you create the DC100_IE.htm file for Internet Explorer browsers. In the third session, you'll create the DC100_NS.htm file for Netscape browsers.

Session 2.1 QUICK CHECK

1. What is dynamic content?

2. Describe the fundamental difference between how Netscape and Internet Explorer implement dynamic content.

3. What JavaScript command would you enter to change the text of the Netscape layer "Intro" to "Pixal Digital Products"?

4. What JavaScript command would you enter to change the text of the <H1> tag with the ID name "Title" to "Pixal Digital Products" for Internet Explorer users? What command would you enter to change the text to "Pixal Digital Products" *and* change the format to an H2 header?

5. What JavaScript command would you enter to change the source of the Memo layer to "Memo2.html"?

6. Describe the difference between the innerText and outerText properties.

7. What JavaScript command would you enter to change the source of the Memo internal frame to "Memo2.html"?

SESSION 2.2

In this session you'll learn how to create dynamic styles with Internet Explorer. You'll work with style definitions for individual objects, tags, and classes of objects. You'll also see how to work with style sheets, and you'll learn how to switch between style sheets within a single page. Finally, you'll create dynamic content that expands and contracts in response to the actions of the user.

Expanding and Collapsing an Outline

You sit down with Sandy to discuss the Web page for the DC100 digital camera. A preview of the page is shown in Figure 2-16.

Figure 2-16 | THE FULL DC100 PAGE

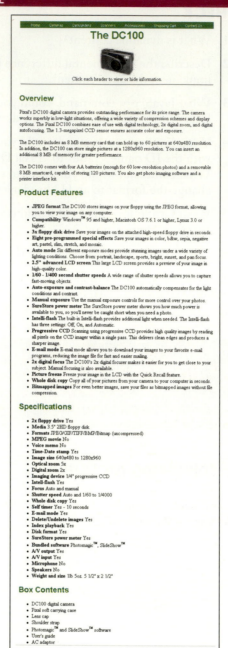

The page contains detailed information for interested users, but Sandy is concerned about the length of the page. She worries that there is so much text, it'll overwhelm the customer and make it difficult for the user to find useful information. She suggests that only the four main headers—Overview, Features, Specifications, and Box Content—should be displayed initially to the user. Then, when the user clicks on one of the headers, the contents of that header will be "expanded" and shown to the user. Clicking the header again will "contract" the content, hiding it from the user (see Figure 2-17). This way the user can view the content that he or she is most interested in, without being distracted by other details.

Figure 2-17	EXPANDING AN OUTLINE

Overview

Product Features

Specifications

Box Contents

clicking a header ...

Overview

Pixal's DC100 digital camera provides outstanding performance for its price range. The camera works superbly in low-light situations, offering a wide variety of compression schemes and display options. The Pixal DC100 combines ease of use with digital technology, 2x digital zoom, and digital autofocusing. The 1.3-megapixel CCD sensor ensures accurate color and exposure.

The DC100 includes an 8 MB memory card that can hold up to 60 pictures at 640x480 resolution. In addition, the DC100 can store single pictures at a 1280x960 resolution. You can insert an additional 8 MB of memory for greater performance.

The DC100 comes with four AA batteries (enough for 60 low-resolution photos) and a removable 8 MB Smartcard, capable of storing 120 pictures. You also get photo imaging software and a printer interface kit.

Product Features

Specifications

Box Contents

... "expands" the contents of the header

Netscape and Internet Explorer use fundamentally different approaches to creating this page, which is why you'll create two different versions of the DC100 page. With Netscape you'll create content that expands and contracts by editing the positions and sizes of different layers on the page. With Internet Explorer you'll work with the style attributes of different page objects to expand and contract the content.

You'll start by learning how to manage styles with Internet Explorer.

Changing Style Attributes

As you saw in the previous session, it's easy to change the content of an HTML tag "on the fly" with Internet Explorer. You can do the same thing with the style of your document content. The general syntax is:

```
object.style.styleAttribute=value;
```

where *object* is the ID of an object on the Web page, *styleAttribute* is one of the CSS style attributes, and *value* is the value you want to assign to the attribute.

In most cases, CSS attributes are converted to JavaScript properties by removing the dash from the attribute name and capitalizing any words following the dash. For example, the CSS attribute:

```
background-image
```

becomes

```
backgroundImage
```

in JavaScript.

Figure 2-18 lists some of the JavaScript properties that Internet Explorer uses to modify the appearance of document content. Compare these JavaScript properties with their CSS equivalents listed in Appendix F, "Cascading Style Sheets."

Figure 2-18	JAVASCRIPT STYLE PROPERTIES FOR USE WITH INTERNET EXPLORER
ATTRIBUTE TYPE	**JAVASCRIPT PROPERTIES**
Background	background, backgroundAttachment, backgroundColor, backgroundImage, backgroundPosition, backgroundPositionX, backgroundPositionY, backgroundRepeat
Border	border, borderBottom, borderBottomColor, borderBottomStyle, borderBottomWidth, borderCollapse, borderLeft, borderLeftColor, borderLeftStyle, borderLeftWidth, borderRight, borderRightColor, borderRightStyle, borderRightWidth, borderStyle, borderTop, borderTopColor, borderTopStyle, borderTopWidth, borderWidth
Color	color
Font	font, fontFamily, fontSize, fontStyle, fontVariant, fontWeight
List	listStyle, listStyleImage, listStylePosition, listStyleType
Margin	margin, marginBottom, marginLeft, marginRight, marginTop
Padding	padding, paddingBottom, paddingLeft, paddingRight, paddingTop
Size	width, height
Text	letterSpacing, lineHeight, textAlign, textDecoration, textIndent, textTransform, verticalAlign, wordSpacing

For example, to change the font size of a paragraph with the ID name "Quote" to 16 points, you would use the JavaScript command:

```
Quote.style.fontSize="16pt";
```

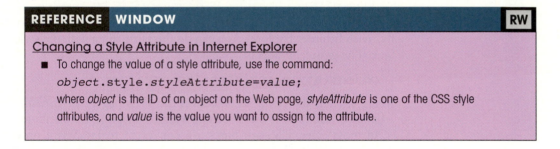

REFERENCE WINDOW   RW

Changing a Style Attribute in Internet Explorer
- To change the value of a style attribute, use the command:
  object.style.*styleAttribute=value;*
  where *object* is the ID of an object on the Web page, *styleAttribute* is one of the CSS style attributes, and *value* is the value you want to assign to the attribute.

To see how it easy it is to change the style of the text on your Web page, a demo page has been created for Internet Explorer users. Open it now.

To run the Style Attributes demo:

1. Open the file **StylesIE.htm** in your Internet Explorer browser (version 4.0 or higher).

2. Select the style attributes from the drop-down list boxes on the Web page.

   As you change the style attributes, a JavaScript program applies the new style attribute values to the paragraph describing the DC100 camera. Since Internet Explorer allows style values to be changed "on the fly," the paragraph's appearance instantly changes to match your selection (see Figure 2-19).

Figure 2-19	CHANGING STYLES DYNAMICALLY WITH INTERNET EXPLORER

Dynamic Styles with Internet Explorer

Select a style attribute value from the selection lists below. Internet Explorer will automatically apply the style to the paragraph that follows.

select the style attributes from the drop-down list boxes

color: [red ▼]   backgroundColor: [black ▼]   fontStyle: [italic ▼]   textDecoration: [sans-serif ▼]   fontSize: [12pt ▼]

the format of the paragraph is automatically updated as users select attributes from the list boxes

Pixal's DC100 digital camera provides outstanding performance for its price range. The camera works superbly in low-light situations, offering a wide variety of compression schemes and display options. The Pixal DC100 combines ease of use with digital technology, 2x digital zoom, and digital autofocusing. The 1.3-megapixel CCD sensor ensures accurate color and exposure.

3. Open the **StylesIE.htm** file in your text editor and take some time to study the underlying JavaScript code. Close the file when you're finished studying it.

The only style attributes that cannot be changed via JavaScript are the position property, which determines whether an object is positioned absolutely or relatively on the page, and the float property, used to create floating text boxes on the page. Both of these properties are read-only, which means that you can view the values of the properties in your scripts, but you cannot modify them.

Changing Multiple Style Attributes and Classes

To change several style attributes at once, you can enter a text string of the style attributes with the cssText property. The syntax is:

```
object.style.cssText=styles;
```

where *object* is the ID name of the object on the page, and *styles* is a text string containing the style attributes. For example, to change the color and font size of the Quote object on the page, you could enter the following command:

```
Quote.style.cssText="color:red font-size:16pt";
```

Another way of doing is this to create a different class for each set of style attributes. You would then change the class of the object to change the object's appearance. The syntax for setting the class name of an object is:

```
object.className=class;
```

where *object* is the ID name of the tag, and *class* is the name of a class previously defined in a global style sheet or in an external style sheet. For example, to change The Quote object to the "casual" class, you would enter the JavaScript command:

```
Quote.className="casual";
```

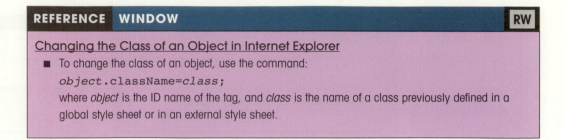

REFERENCE WINDOW **RW**

Changing the Class of an Object in Internet Explorer
- To change the class of an object, use the command:
  `object.className=class;`
  where *object* is the ID name of the tag, and *class* is the name of a class previously defined in a global style sheet or in an external style sheet.

To see how dynamic classes can be used in your Web page, a demo page named ClassIE.htm has been prepared for you. Open this file now.

To run the class demo:

1. Open the file **ClassIE.htm** in your Internet Explorer browser.

2. Click each radio button and observe how the appearance of the text changes on the page (see Figure 2-20).

   As you click each radio button, a JavaScript program changes the class name of the bottom paragraph to match. The paragraph's appearance is then updated to reflect the style attributes for the selected class.

| Figure 2-20 | CHANGING CLASSES DYNAMICALLY WITH INTERNET EXPLORER |

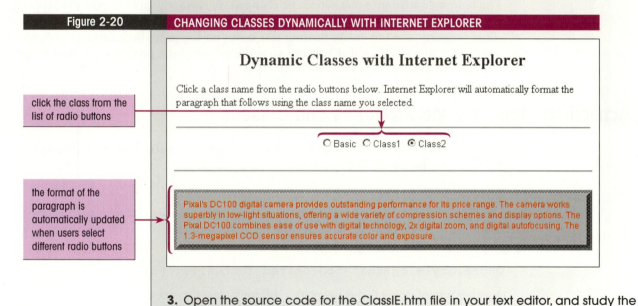

click the class from the list of radio buttons

the format of the paragraph is automatically updated when users select different radio buttons

3. Open the source code for the ClassIE.htm file in your text editor, and study the source code involved. Close the file when you're finished.

Changing Style Sheets

So far you've learned how to change the style of a single object on your page. By changing the style sheet used by the page, you can simultaneously affect the style for *all* of the elements on your Web page. To do this you have to create multiple global style sheets for your page, and then disable those sheets that are not in use.

Referencing and Disabling Style Sheets

You must first have a way of uniquely identifying each set of styles. The syntax for doing this is:

```
<STYLE ID=id_name>
    style declarations
</STYLE>
```

where *id_name* is the style sheet's ID name. For example, the following tags provide two ways of formatting the size of H1 headers on the Web page:

```
<STYLE ID="Large_Txt">
   H1 {font-size:24pt}
   H2 {font-size:20pt}
</STYLE>
<STYLE ID="Small_Txt">
   H1 {font-size:12pt}
   H2 {font-size:10pt}
</STYLE>
```

When you switch from the Large_Txt to the Small_Txt style sheet, the size of the H1 and H2 headers is automatically reduced from 24 and 20 points to 12 and 10 points.

When you have multiple style sheets, you have to be careful that the style attributes are not in conflict. In the previous code, the style attributes for the two headers conflict, which means that the browser will only use the latest style declaration. In this case, that means that the two headers will appear in 12- and 10-point type.

To get around this problem, you have to disable all of the style sheets, except the one you want to display in your document. The syntax for disabling a style sheet is:

```
<STYLE ID=id_name DISABLED>
```

In the following code:

```
<STYLE ID="Large_Txt">
   H1 {font-size:24pt}
   H2 {font-size:20pt}
</STYLE>
<STYLE ID="Small_Txt" DISABLED>
   H1 {font-size:12pt}
   H2 {font-size:10pt}
</STYLE>
```

only the Large_Txt style sheet is active, so the H1 and H2 headers will appear in a 24- and 20-point type.

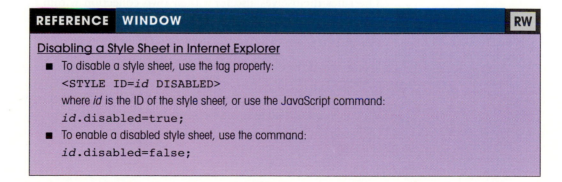

REFERENCE WINDOW   **RW**

Disabling a Style Sheet in Internet Explorer
- To disable a style sheet, use the tag property:
  ```
  <STYLE ID=id DISABLED>
  ```
  where *id* is the ID of the style sheet, or use the JavaScript command:
  ```
  id.disabled=true;
  ```
- To enable a disabled style sheet, use the command:
  ```
  id.disabled=false;
  ```

Working with Style Sheet Objects

Internet Explorer treats each style sheet available to the Web page as an object. The style sheet can be one that was created using the <STYLE> tag, or imported using either the <LINK> tag or the @import statement. Style sheets are referenced by using their ID name or as part of the styleSheets collection. For example, if the first style sheet in the collection has the ID name Large_Txt, Internet Explorer allows you to use either of these reference names in your JavaScript code:

```
Large_Txt
styleSheets(0)
```

There are several different properties and methods for the styleSheet object. Some of these are described in Figure 2-21.

Figure 2-21	PROPERTIES AND METHODS OF THE STYLE SHEET OBJECT
PROPERTY OR METHOD	**DESCRIPTION**
disabled	Sets whether the style sheet is disabled or enabled
href=URL	Sets the URL of an external style sheet linked to the page
readOnly	Indicates whether the contents of the style sheet can be modified; external style sheets cannot be changed
type	Sets the type of the style sheet; Internet Explorer supports only the "text/css" type
addImport(URL)	Imports an external style sheet with the indicated URL, and adds it to the style sheet
addRule(selector, style)	Adds a new rule to the style sheet for the specified selector with the specified style declaration

For example, to disable a style with the ID name, Small_Txt, you would use the JavaScript command:

```
Small_Txt.disabled=true;
```

To enable the style sheet, set the disabled property to false:

```
Small_Txt.disabled=false;
```

You can also work with individual style declarations or **rules** within the style sheet. To add a new rule for H3 headers to the Large_Txt style sheet, for example, use the addRule() method to specify the selector and the style declaration for the style:

```
Large_Txt.addRule("H2", "font-size:16pt");
```

In this case, a new rule has been added to set the size of the H3 header to 16 points.

The rules themselves also form their own collection within the style sheet object. The first style rule or declaration for the Large_Txt style sheet would have the reference name:

```
Large_Txt.rules(0);
```

By using the rules collection, you can modify individual style declarations within each style sheet.

Having learned how Internet Explorer handles style sheets, you can view a demo in which you swap one style sheet for another.

To open the style sheets demo:

1. Open the file **SheetsIE.htm** in your Internet Explorer browser.

2. Click the radio buttons to switch between the Basic, Sheet1, and Sheet2 style sheets (see Figure 2-22).

Figure 2-22

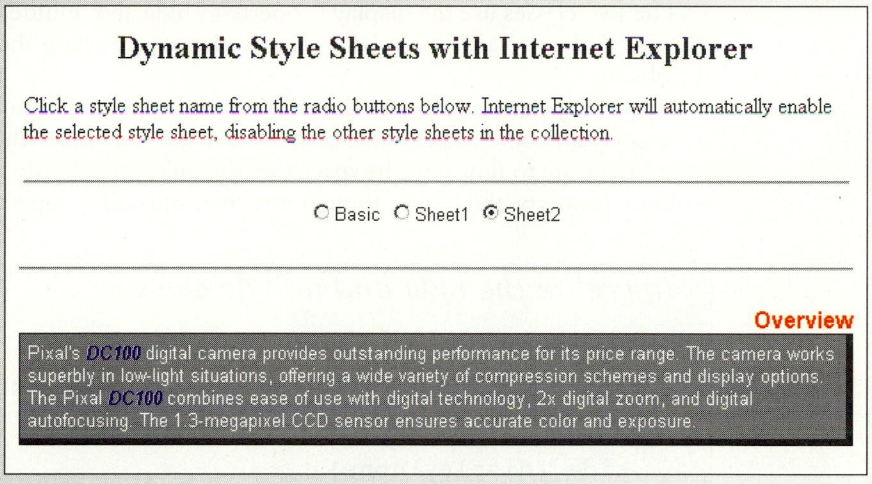

As you click each radio button, a JavaScript program enables the selected style sheet, disabling the other style sheets in the collection. Note that the styles for the header, paragraph, and boldface text are affected by the change.

3. Open the source code for the Web page in your text editor and spend some time studying the JavaScript code. Close the file when you're finished.

Creating an Expandable Outline in Internet Explorer

Now that you've seen the great control that Internet Explorer gives you over the styles used in your page content, you're ready to create the expandable/collapsible content for the DC100 Web page. The text you'll work with is stored in the DC100txt.htm file. Recall that for Internet Explorer, this file has to be saved with the filename, DC100_IE.htm.

To create the DC100 page in Internet Explorer:

1. Open the **DC100txt.htm** file in your text editor.

2. Save the file as **DC100_IE.htm**.

    Recall that in the last session, you created an onMouseDown event handler in the Pixal.htm file, which would open the DC100_IE.htm file when you pressed the mouse button down on the DC100 camera name. Verify that this file can now be opened from the Pixal page.

3. Open the **Pixal.htm** file in your Internet Explorer browser.

4. Click **DC100** in the list of the digital cameras at the top of the page.

    The DC100_IE.htm file should appear in your browser.

The DC100 page opens, showing all of the details about the digital camera. To allow the user to hide and unhide this content, you'll first create two style classes: "hide" and "unhide." The styles of these two classes are:

```
<STYLE>
.hide {display:none}
.unhide {display: ""}
</STYLE>
```

The two classes use the display property to hide and unhide objects. When display is set to "none," the object will not be shown on the page. Setting the display value to "" unhides the object.

Note that you could also use the visibility attribute to hide/unhide your objects. However, the display attribute has the advantage that it not only hides the object, but also causes the rest of the page to flow into the space that the object previously occupied. When you use the visibility property, the object, though invisible, will still occupy space on the page.

To create the hide and unhide classes:

1. Return to the **DC100_IE.htm** file in your text editor.

2. Above the </STYLE> tag at the top of the page, insert the following styles (see Figure 2-23):

   ```
   .hide {display:none}
   .unhide {display:""}
   ```

Figure 2-23	CREATING THE HIDE AND UNHIDE CLASSES

```
<STYLE>
   BODY {margin-top:0px; font-size:12pt}
   H1, H2 {font-family: Arial, Helvetica, sans-serif; color:teal}
   H1 {font-size:24pt}
   H2 {font-size:18pt}
   A.Links {font-family: Arial, Helvetica, sans-serif; font-size:8pt;
            text-decoration:none; color:white}
   A:hover.Links {text-decoration:underline}
   .hide {display:none}
   .unhide {display:""}
</STYLE>
```

Now that you've created the two classes, you'll apply the hide class to the four sections of the page–Overview, Product Features, Specifications, and Box Content. To do this you must enclose those four blocks of text within <DIV> tags, assigning the value "hide" to the CLASS property of each <DIV> tag. When Internet Explorer initially opens the page, the text within the <DIV> tags will be hidden from the user.

To create <DIV> tags:

1. Below the <H2> tag for the Overview section, insert the following <DIV> tag
   `<DIV ID=Overview CLASS=hide>`

2. Insert a **</DIV>** tag after the third paragraph of the product overview (see Figure 2-24).

Figure 2-24   **INSERTING A <DIV> TAG FOR THE OVERVIEW SECTION**

```
<H2>Overview</H2>
<DIV ID=Overview CLASS=hide>
Pixal's DC100 digital camera provides outstanding performance for its
price range. The camera works superbly in low-light situations, offering
a wide variety of compression schemes and display options. The Pixal
DC100 combines ease of use with digital technology, 2x digital zoom,
and digital autofocusing. The 1.3-megapixel CCD sensor ensures accurate
color and exposure.</P>
<P>The DC100 includes an 8 MB memory card that can hold up to 60 pictures
at 640x480 resolution. In addition, the DC100 can store single pictures
at a 1280x960 resolution. You can insert an additional 8 MB of memory
for greater performance.</P>
<P>The DC100 comes with four AA batteries (enough for 60 low-resolution
photos) and a removable 8 MB Smartcard, capable of storing 120 pictures.
You also get photo imaging software and a printer interface kit.</P>
</DIV>
```

3. Below the <H2> tag for the Product Features section, insert the tag:

   <DIV ID=Features CLASS=hide>

4. Below the </UL> tag for this section, insert the tag **</DIV>**.

5. Below the <H2> tag for the Specifications section, insert:

   <DIV ID=Specs CLASS=hide>

6. Below the </UL> tag for the Specifications section, insert the tag **</DIV>**.

7. In the same way, enclose the Box Contents section within a set of <DIV> tags with the ID name "Box" and the class name "hide."

8. Save your changes to the DC100_IE.htm file.

9. Refresh the **DC100_IE.htm** page in your Internet Explorer browser. Only the four main headers should be visible (see Figure 2-25).

Figure 2-25   **THE DC100_IE PAGE WITH THE COLLAPSED OUTLINE**

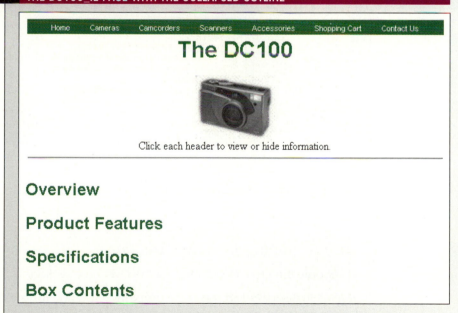

To unhide or hide a block of text, you'll add the following function to the DC100_IE.htm file:

```
function toggleView(Text) {
    if (Text.className=="hide") {
        Text.className="unhide"
    } else {
        Text.className="hide"
    }
}
```

The toggleView() function has one parameter, Text, which represents one of the four sections on the DC100 Web page. If the class name of Text is "hide" (that is, it's hidden on the page), the function switches the class name to "unhide" (making the section visible again). Similarly, if the class name is "unhide," the toggleView() function changes the class name to "hide" and hides the object.

To insert the toggleView() function:

1. Return to the DC100_IE.htm file in your text editor.

2. Above the </HEAD> tag, insert the following lines (see Figure 2-26):

```
<SCRIPT>
    function toggleView(Text) {
        if (Text.className=="hide") {
            Text.className="unhide"
        } else {
            Text.className="hide"
        }
    }
<SCRIPT>
```

Figure 2-26   THE TOGGLEVIEW() FUNCTION

```
</STYLE>
<SCRIPT>
    function toggleView(Text) {
        if (Text.className=="hide") {
            Text.className="unhide";
        } else {
            Text.className="hide";
        }
    }
</SCRIPT>
</HEAD>
```

The toggleView() function should be run when the user clicks one of the four headers on the page.

To run the toggleView() function:

1. Locate the <H2> header tag for the Overview section.

2. Within the <H2> tag, insert the property **onClick="toggleView(Overview)"** as shown in Figure 2-27.

Figure 2-27   **CALLING THE TOGGLE VIEW() FUNCTION**

```
<H2 onClick="toggleView(Overview)">Overview</H2>
<DIV ID=Overview CLASS=hide>
Pixal's DC100 digital camera provides outstanding performance for its
price range. The camera works superbly in low-light situations, offering
a wide variety of compression schemes and display options. The Pixal
DC100 combines ease of use with digital technology, 2x digital zoom,
and digital autofocusing. The 1.3-megapixel CCD sensor ensures accurate
color and exposure.</P>
```

Note that if the Overview section has the class name "hide," clicking the header will switch the class name to "unhide," thus displaying the section.

3. Within the <H2> tag for the Product Features section, insert the property **onClick="toggleView(Features)"**.

4. Within the Specifications <H2> header, insert the property **onClick="toggleView(Specs)"**.

5. Within the Box Contents <H2> header, insert the property **onClick="toggleView(Box)"**.

6. Save your changes to the DC100_IE.htm file and close the file in your text editor.

7. Reload the file in your Internet Explorer browser.

8. Verify that as you click each of the four headers, the contents below the header are alternately hidden and unhidden.

You've completed your work on the Internet Explorer version of this page. Sandy is pleased with the page and awaits your work on the Netscape version.

Session 2.2 QUICK CHECK

1. What JavaScript command would you enter to change the font size of an object with the ID "Title" to 14-point type?

2. What single JavaScript command would you enter to change the Title object to 14-point red type?

3. What JavaScript command would you enter to change the class of the Title object to the "Large_Red" class?

4. How would you change the tag <STYLE ID=Formal> to disable it? What JavaScript command would accomplish the same thing?

5. What JavaScript command would you enter to add the style declaration "H3 {color:red; font-size:14pt}" to the Formal style sheet?

6. What is the difference between the display property and the visibility property?

SESSION 2.3

In this session you'll learn about JASS, the language used by Netscape to create dynamic styles. You'll learn how to create styles for individual tags, classes, specificIDs, and contextual selectors. You'll work with a demo that creates random styles for a page shown by a Netscape browser. Finally, you'll create content for the DC100 page that expands and contracts in Netscape.

Managing Styles with JASS

You're now ready to turn to the task of creating the DC100 page for Netscape users. Netscape provides its own language for creating dynamic styles, called **JavaScript Accessible Style Sheets**, or **JASS**. Can JASS be used to create the expandable/collapsible outline for the DC100 page in the same way that the Internet Explorer style objects were used? You decide to explore the properties of the language for Sandy.

JASS has many similarities to the way Internet Explorer uses the style object—with one critical exception: JASS cannot change style attributes *after* the page has been loaded. However, if you need to create a Web page whose style attributes are determined as the page is initially rendered by the browser, you can use JASS for that task.

Because of its limitations, JASS cannot be used to create an expandable/collapsible outline for the DC100 page. Still, Sandy would like you to learn more about JASS for future projects, where you may be able to take advantage of its features.

The syntax of JASS closely matches the style names and attributes of CSS. However, since Netscape through version 4.7 is not completely CSS-compliant, you'll find that some CSS style attributes are not recognized in JASS. A good rule of thumb is that if Netscape supports the CSS style attribute, it also supports the equivalent attribute in JASS.

JASS styles are applied within a set of <STYLE> tags with the TYPE property set to "text/javascript," rather than to "text/css" for cascading style sheets. The syntax is:

```
<STYLE TYPE="text/javascript">
    JASS commands;
</STYLE>
```

The JASS commands all follow the *object.property* form used for JavaScript commands. JASS supports styles for four different types of elements: tags, classes, IDs, and contextual selectors.

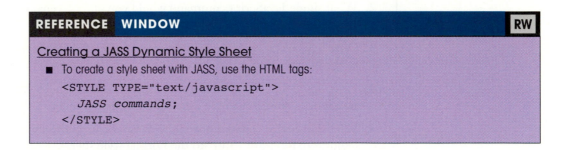

REFERENCE WINDOW   **RW**

Creating a JASS Dynamic Style Sheet
- To create a style sheet with JASS, use the HTML tags:
```
<STYLE TYPE="text/javascript">
  JASS commands;
</STYLE>
```

Working with Tag Styles

To define a style for a tag in JASS, you use the command syntax:

```
tags.tagName.attribute="value";
```

where *tagName* is the name of the tag, *attribute* is the name of the style attribute, and *value* is the value assigned to the attribute. Note that the value is placed within double quotation marks. This is necessary to distinguish between values and variable names.

For example, the following CSS style declaration:

```
H1 {color:red}
```

is expressed in JASS as:

```
tags.H1.color="red";
```

REFERENCE WINDOW   **RW**

Defining a Tag Style in JASS

■ To define a style for a tag in JASS, use the command:

```
tags.tagName.attribute="value";
```

where *tagName* is the name of the tag, *attribute* is the name of the style attribute, and *value* is the value assigned to the attribute.

Attribute names follow the same convention employed by the Internet Explorer style objects. JASS removes the central dash from the style attribute and capitalizes all internal words. The CSS style attribute background-color is backgroundColor in JASS.

If you need to set several style attributes at once, you can use the "with" keyword to group the attributes together. The syntax is:

```
with (tags.tagName) {
    attribute1 = "value1"
    attribute2 = "value2"
    . . .
}
```

To set both the color and font size of the H1 header, for example, you would enter the following command:

```
with (tags.H1) {
    color="red"
    fontSize="14pt"
}
```

Working with Class Styles

If you need to apply a style to a whole class of elements on the Web page, JASS uses the form:

```
classes.className.element.attribute = "value";
```

where *className* is the name of the class, *element* is the name of the element, and *attribute* and *value* are the style attribute and value. For example, to change the color of all paragraphs with the class name "Quotes" to green, you would use the JASS command:

```
classes.Quotes.P.color="green";
```

Defining a Class Style in JASS
- To define a style for a class of objects, use the JASS command:

  ```
  classes.className.element.attribute = "value";
  ```
  where *className* is the name of the class, *element* is the name of the element, and *attribute* and *value* are the style attribute and value. To set the style for all objects of a particular class, set the value of *element* to "all".

If you want to apply the style to all classes with the name, *className*, regardless of the element type, you replace the element type with the keyword "all." Thus, to change the font color of all classes with the name "Quotes," use the JASS command:

```
class.Quotes.all.color="green";
```

Working with ID Styles

To change the style of a single element on the Web page, use the form:

```
ids.idName.attribute = "value";
```

where *idName* is the ID name of the element. If the CSS style is:

```
#Intro {color:red}
```

the equivalent JASS command would be:

```
ids.Intro.color="red";
```

Defining an ID Style in JASS
- To define a style for a particular ID in JASS, use the command:

  ```
  ids.idName.attribute = "value";
  ```
  where *idName* is the ID name of the element.

Working with Contextual Selectors

The final way a style can be defined with JASS is with a contextual selector. For example, to create a style for boldface text nested within a paragraph, the CSS style declaration is:

```
P B {color: "red"}
```

In JASS, contextual selectors follow the syntax:

```
contextual(selector1, selector2, ...).attribute="value";
```

where *selector1*, *selector2*, . . . represent the selectors whose *attribute* is changed to the indicated *value*. If you had written the previous CSS style declaration in JASS, the command would be:

```
contextual(tags.P, tags.B).color="red";
```

To see how JASS can be used to create dynamic styles in Netscape, a demo page, StylesNS.htm, has been prepared for you. The page prompts the user to enter one of three possible style values. JASS is then used to load the correct group of styles

To test the JASS demo:

1. Open the **StylesNS.htm** file in your Netscape browser.

2. In response to the JavaScript prompt, enter the value **1**.

3. The page is loaded using the first set of style rules.

4. Click the **Reload** button two more times, entering a value of **2**, and then **3**. Each time, Netscape runs JASS commands to open the page with a different set of style rules (see Figure 2-28).

Figure 2-28	LOADING A SET OF STYLES IN NETSCAPE

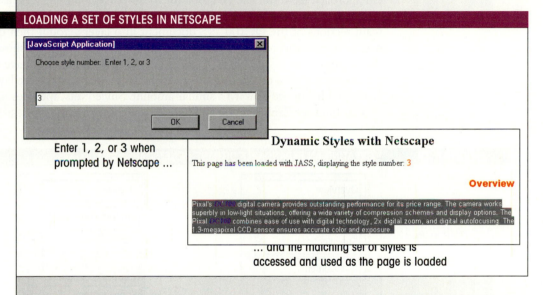

Enter 1, 2, or 3 when prompted by Netscape …

… and the matching set of styles is accessed and used as the page is loaded

5. Open the **StylesNS.htm** file in your text editor and study the source code. When you are finished, close the file.

You've finished your work studying JASS. You can now work on modifying the DC100 page for the Netscape browser.

Creating an Expandable Outline in Netscape

To create the DC100 page for Netscape, you'll start with the basic text stored in the DC100txt.htm file, the same file you started with when you created the page for Internet Explorer. For Netscape browsers, this file has to be saved with the filename DC100_NS.htm.

To create the DC100 page in Netscape:

1. Open the **DC100txt.htm** file in your text editor.

2. Save the file as **DC100_NS.htm**.

Verify that this file can be opened from the Pixal page.

3. Open the **Pixal.htm** file in your Netscape browser.

4. Click **DC100** in the list of the digital cameras at the top of the page.

The DC100_NS.htm file should appear in your browser with all of the details showing.

TROUBLE? If you don't have the Netscape browser installed, you will not be able to see the results of your work, but you should still enter the code to ensure that the page works for the two browser types.

Creating content that expands and contracts in Netscape requires a fundamentally different approach from the one you took for Internet Explorer since Netscape does not automatically rearrange document elements when they change size. What you'll do is place the four main sections of the DC100_NS document into layers. You'll then decrease or increase the height of the layers to hide or unhide the content of each layer. As shown in Figure 2-29, when the height of one of the layers is increased, the other layers will have to be moved down into the correct location on the page to compensate. If the height of the layer is reduced, the other layers will be moved upward a similar amount. Since Netscape does not do this automatically as does Internet Explorer, you will have to write the functions to resize and move the layers.

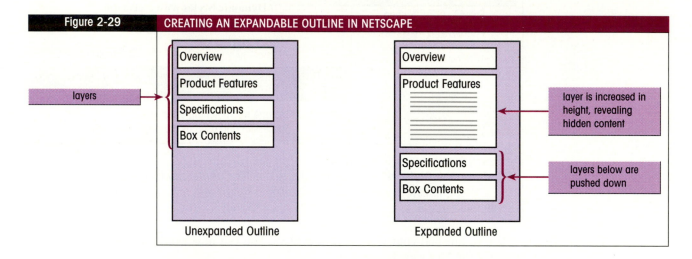

Figure 2-29 — **CREATING AN EXPANDABLE OUTLINE IN NETSCAPE**

Your first task will be to create <LAYER> tags for the four sections of the document.

To insert <LAYER> tags for each section:

1. Return to the **DC100_NS.htm** file in your text editor.

2. Before the <H2> tag for the Overview section, insert the tag:

```
<LAYER ID=Overview>
```

3. Insert a **</LAYER>** tag after the third paragraph of this section as shown in Figure 2-30.

Figure 2-30 | **MAKING THE OVERVIEW SECTION A LAYER**

```
<LAYER ID=Overview>
<H2>Overview</H2>
Pixal's DC100 digital camera provides outstanding performance for its
price range. The camera works superbly in low-light situations, offering
a wide variety of compression schemes and display options. The Pixal
DC100 combines ease of use with digital technology, 2x digital zoom,
and digital autofocusing. The 1.3-megapixel CCD sensor ensures accurate
color and exposure.</P>
<P>The DC100 includes an 8 MB memory card that can hold up to 60 pictures
at 640x480 resolution. In addition, the DC100 can store single pictures
at a 1280x960 resolution. You can insert an additional 8 MB of memory
for greater performance.</P>
<P>The DC100 comes with four AA batteries (enough for 60 low-resolution
photos) and a removable 8 MB Smartcard, capable of storing 120 pictures.
You also get photo imaging software and a printer interface kit.</P>
</LAYER>
```

4. Before the <H2> tag for the Product Features section, insert the tag:

   <LAYER ID=Features>

5. Insert a **</LAYER>** tag after the </UL> tag for the section.

6. Above the <H2> tag for the Specifications section, insert:

   <LAYER ID=Specs>

7. After the </UL> tag for the Specifications section, insert the tag **</LAYER>**.

8. In the same way, enclose the Box Contents section within a set of <LAYER> tags with the ID name "Box."

9. Save your changes to the DC100_NS.htm file.

10. Reload the **DC100_NS.htm** file in your Netscape browser. The resulting page is shown in Figure 2-31.

Figure 2-31 **THE DC100_NS PAGE WITH OVERLAPPING LAYERS**

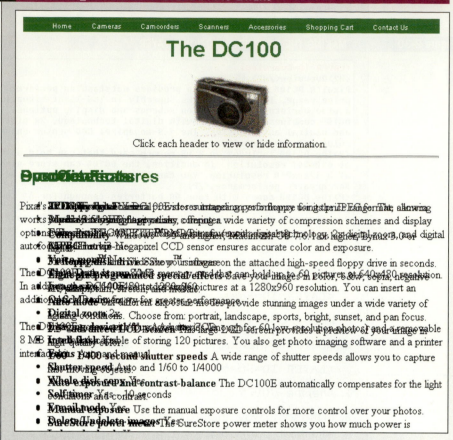

What happened? When Netscape encounters the four layers you just created, it treats each layer as a separate document and places them in the same location in the document flow, right after the graphic image of the DC100 digital camera.

You can use the <ILAYER> tag instead of the <LAYER> tag to create the layers. Since the <ILAYER> tag places content within the natural flow of the document, the layers will not overlap. However, there are some bugs associated with the <ILAYER> tag that makes it difficult to complete this task properly. So you'll stick with the <LAYER> tag.

Another approach is to realize that if you knew the height of each of the layers, you could stack them accordingly. For example, if the height of the Overhead section is 300 pixels, the Product Features section will be located 300 pixels below the top of the Overhead section. Similarly, the Specifications section will be located 300 pixels plus the height of the Features sections below the Overhead section. The code for stacking the four layers is:

```
var OverHgt=document.Overview.clip.height;
var FeatHgt=document.Features.clip.height;
var SpecsHgt=document.Specs.clip.height;
var BoxHgt=document.Box.clip.height;

StartPos=document.Overview.top;
```

```
document.Features.top=StartPos+OverHgt;
document.Specs.top=StartPos+OverHgt+FeatHgt;
document.Box.top=StartPos+OverHgt+FeatHgt+SpecsHgt;
```

The code uses the clip.height property of the layer object to record the heights of the four layers and stores them in four variables: OverHgt, FeatHt, SpecsHgt, and BoxHgt. An additional variable, StartPos, uses the top property to record the starting position of the Overview section. From these five variables, the location of each section is determined by adding the heights of the sections above it to the starting position.

You have to add these commands to the end of the **DC100_NS.htm** file, because Netscape will not be able to determine the height of the various layers until after it has encountered the layers within the HTML file.

To stack the layers:

1. Return to the **DC100_NS.htm** file in your text editor.

2. Before the </BODY> tag at the end of the file, insert the following code:

```
<SCRIPT>
    var OverHgt=document.Overview.clip.height;
    var FeatHgt=document.Features.clip.height;
    var SpecsHgt=document.Specs.clip.height;
    var BoxHgt=document.Box.clip.height;

    var StartPos=document.Overview.top;

    document.Features.top=StartPos+OverHgt;
    document.Specs.top=StartPos+OverHgt+FeatHgt;
    document.Box.top=StartPos+OverHgt+FeatHgt+SpecsHgt;
</SCRIPT>
```

3. Save your changes.

4. Reload the file in your Netscape browser, and verify that the four sections are now stacked on top of each other.

With the four layers in place, you next have to create the effect of expanding and contracting the layers. To contract a layer, you'll clip the layer's height so that only the header is showing—this is a height of about 40 pixels. To expand the layer, you have to change the clipping height back to the original height of the layer, which you've already stored in the OverHgt, FeatHgt, SpecsHgt, and BoxHgt variables.

You'll store the current height of the layer in four variables named OverClip, FeatClip, SpecsClip, and BoxClip. Each of these variables will have an initial value of 40.

To create the four clipping variables:

1. Return to the **DC100_NS.htm** file in your text editor.

2. Above the </SCRIPT> tag at the bottom of the file, insert the following line of code (see Figure 2-32):

```
var OverClip=40; var FeatClip=40; var SpecsClip=40; var
BoxClip=40;
```

Figure 2-32 CREATING THE CLIP HEIGHT VARIABLES

```
<SCRIPT>
   var OverHgt=document.Overview.clip.height;
   var FeatHgt=document.Features.clip.height;
   var SpecsHgt=document.Specs.clip.height;
   var BoxHgt=document.Box.clip.height;

   var StartPos=document.Overview.top;

   document.Features.top=StartPos+OverHgt;
   document.Specs.top=StartPos+OverHgt+FeatHgt;
   document.Box.top=StartPos+OverHgt+FeatHgt+SpecsHgt;

   var OverClip=40; var FeatClip=40; var SpecsClip=40; var BoxClip=40;
</SCRIPT>
</BODY>
</HTML>
```

Whenever the height of one of the layers is changed, all of the layers on the page must be moved on the page to compensate for the new clip height. To do this, you'll create a new function named "setPage()" that changes the height of each layer to the size of the OverClip, FeatClip, SpecsClip, and BoxClip variables, and then restacks the layers. The code for the function follows the same pattern that you used to stack the initial position of the layers.

```
function setPage() {
   document.Overview.clip.height=OverClip;
   document.Features.clip.height=FeatClip;
   document.Specs.clip.height=SpecsClip;
   document.Box.clip.height=BoxClip;

   document.Features.top=StartPos+OverClip;
   document.Specs.top=StartPos+OverClip+FeatClip;
   document.Box.top=StartPos+OverClip+FeatClip+SpecsClip;
}
```

Sandy wants the page to open with the height of the four sections set to 40 pixels, so that only the headers are showing. Therefore you should run the setPage() function when the page initially loads with the initial values of the OverClip, FeatClip, SpecsClip, and BoxClip variables.

To insert and run the setPage() function:

1. Before the </SCRIPT> insert the code:

```
function setPage() {
   document.Overview.clip.height=OverClip;
   document.Features.clip.height=FeatClip;
   document.Specs.clip.height=SpecsClip;
   document.Box.clip.height=BoxClip;

   document.Features.top=StartPos+OverClip;
   document.Specs.top=StartPos+OverClip+FeatClip;
   document.Box.top=StartPos+OverClip+FeatClip+SpecsClip;
}
```

2. Scroll to the top of the document.

3. Within the <BODY> tag, insert the property **onLoad= "setPage()"** (see Figure 2-33).

Figure 2-33   RUNNING THE SETPAGE() FUNCTION WHEN THE PAGE LOADS

```
<BODY onLoad="setPage()">
```

4. Save your changes.

5. Reload the **DC100_NS.htm** file in your Netscape browser.

6. As shown in Figure 2-34, the page now displays only the four main headers.

Figure 2-34   THE DC100_NS PAGE IN NETSCAPE, SHOWING ONLY THE HEADERS

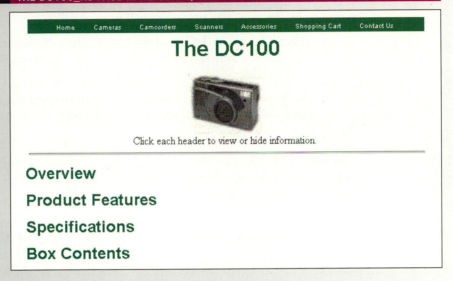

The final function you need to create toggles the value of the OverClip, FeatClip, SpecsClip, and BoxClip variables between 40 pixels and the full height of the layer. The toggle() function appears as:

```
function toggle(Clip, Hgt) {
    if (Clip==40) {
        Clip=Hgt;
    } else {
        Clip=40;
    }
    return Clip;
}
```

The toggle() function has two parameters: Clip and Hgt. The Clip parameter represents the current height of the layer. The Hgt parameter represents the maximum height of the layer. If the current height is 40 pixels, the toggle() function will set the value to the maximum height (expanding the layer); otherwise the height is reduced to 40 pixels (collapsing the layer.)

To create the toggle() function:

1. Return to the **DC100_NS.htm** file in your text editor.

2. Above the </SCRIPT> tag at the bottom of the file, insert:

```
function toggle(Clip, Hgt) {
    if (Clip==40) {
        return Hgt;
    } else {
        return 40;
    }
}
```

You now have all of the pieces to create an outline that expands and contracts in response to actions by the user. The procedure will work as follows:

1. When the user clicks one of the four headers, Netscape runs the toggle() function and switches the height of the layer between 40 pixels and the full layer height.

2. Netscape then runs the setPage() function to apply the new layer height to the page and restacks the other layers on the page to compensate.

Because Netscape does not support the onClick() event handler for headers, you enclose each of the <H2> tags within a set of <A> tags with the HREF property set to "#," which points to the same page.

To create <A> tags for the four sections of the document:

1. Scroll up to the <H2> tag for the Overview section.

2. Before the <H2> tag, insert the following tag:

```
<A HREF=# onClick="OverClip=toggle(OverClip,OverHgt);
setPage()">
```

3. After the <H2> tag, insert an **</A>** tag as shown in Figure 2-35.

Figure 2-35 | ADDING THE ONCLICK() EVENT HANDLER TO AN <H2> TAG

```
<LAYER ID=Overview>
<A HREF=# onClick="OverClip=toggle(OverClip, OverHgt); setPage()">
<H2>Overview</H2>
</A>
Pixal's DC100 digital camera provides outstanding performance for its
price range. The camera works superbly in low-light situations, offering
a wide variety of compression schemes and display options. The Pixal
DC100 combines ease of use with digital technology, 2x digital zoom,
and digital autofocusing. The 1.3-megapixel CCD sensor ensures accurate
color and exposure.</P>
```

When the user clicks the header for Overview section, Netscape toggles the value of the OverClip variable, and then restacks the layers, using the setPage() function.

4. Before the <H2> tag for the Product Features section, insert:

```
<A HREF=# onClick="FeatClip=toggle(FeatClip,FeatHgt);
setPage()">
```

5. After the <H2> tag insert the closing **</A>** tag.

6. Enclose the <H2> tag for the Specifications header within an <A> tag with the following properties:

```
<A HREF=#
onClick="SpecsClip=toggle(SpecsClip,SpecsHgt);
setPage()">
```

7. Enclose the <H2> tag for the Box Contents section within an <A> tag with the properties:

```
<A HREF=# onClick="BoxClip=toggle(BoxClip,BoxHgt);
setPage()">
```

8. Save your changes to the file.

9. Reload the **DC100_NS.htm** file in your Netscape browser.

10. Verify that as you click each of the four headers, the content beneath that header expands and contracts, and that the other sections are properly positioned on the page (see Figure 2-36).

| Figure 2-36 | EXPANDING CONTENT IN NETSCAPE |

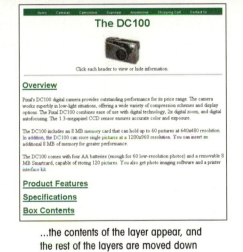

When a user clicks the Overview header...

...the contents of the layer appear, and the rest of the layers are moved down on the page.

Sandy would like you to remove the underlining from the headers. Since you've formatted these headers using <A> tags, Netscape treats them as linked text. To keep the text from being underlined, you have to define a style for an H2 header nested inside an <A> tag. The CSS style declaration is:

```
A H2 {text-decoration:none}
```

To remove the underlining from the H2 headers:

1. Return to the **DC100_NS.htm** file in your text editor.

2. Above the </STYLE> tag, insert the style:

   `A H2 {text-decoration:none}`

3. Save your changes and close the file.

4. Reload the page in your Netscape browser and verify that the underlining has been removed, and that the outline still expands and collapses when you click the section headers.

You've completed your work on the Netscape version of the DC100 details page. By properly placing and moving the various layers on the page, you've managed to create the effect of an outline that alternately expands and contracts. Sandy has tested your work for the two browsers and is pleased with the results.

She takes your completed Web pages and gives them to her Web team for further study. She'll get back to you with any modifications or additions they suggest.

Session 2.3 QUICK CHECK

1. What is JASS? How do you apply JASS commands in your Web page?

2. What JASS command would you enter to change the size of H1 headers on your page to 12-point type?

3. What JASS command would you enter to change the font family of all H1 headers with the class name "Title" to the Arial font?

4. What JASS command would you enter to change the font of all elements with the class name "Title" to Arial?

5. What JASS command would you enter to change the color of an H1 header with the ID name "Intro" to teal?

6. What JASS command would you enter to remove underlining from any H2 header nested within an <A> tag?

7. Discuss how to create an expandable/collapsible outline in Netscape, as compared to Internet Explorer.

REVIEW ASSIGNMENTS

Sandy has asked you to create a new version of the page describing the specifications of the DC100 digital camera. She would like to have a page in which users select information about their interests by clicking check boxes on a form. Then, by clicking a button on the form, a report is generated containing the selected information. A preview of this page is shown in Figure 2-37.

Figure 2-37

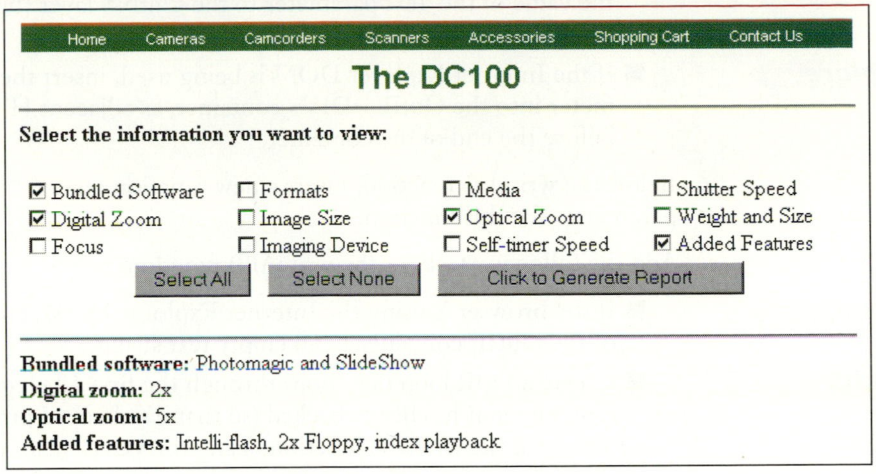

The layout of the page and part of the JavaScript code have already been created for you. Two variables, isNS and isIE, have been created to determine the DOM in use by the browser. An additional variable, SText, contains an array of possible text strings that could be inserted into the report.

Your job will be to write the code that inserts the appropriate text into the page in response to the user's selections. To do this you'll create two functions: writeIt() and writeAll(). The writeIt() function will write a single line of text to the report.

The writeAll() function will first erase any previous information from the report. It will then loop through the collection of check boxes on the page. If the check box has been selected, the writeAll() function will call the writeIt() function to write the selected information into the report.

To create the writeAll() function, you'll work with the elements() collection of the form object. Each element on the form, whether it is an input box, button, check box, or other object, is part of the elements collection. To reference an element on the form, the syntax is:

```
document.form.elements[i]
```

where *form* is the name of the form, and *i* is the index number. As with other object collections, the first element has index number of 1, the second element has an index number of 2, and so forth.

To create the report for Sandy:

1. Open the **Specstxt.htm** file from the Tutorial.02D/Review folder on your Data Disk in your text editor, and save it as Specs.htm.

2. At the bottom of the file, above the </BODY> tag, insert a two-sided <DIV> tag with the ID name "OutIE." There should be no content between the opening and closing tags.

3. Below the </DIV> tag, insert a two-sided <LAYER> tag with the ID name "OutNS." There should be no content in the layer.

4. Set the clipping coordinates of the OutNS layer to (0, 0, 600, 250).

5. Above the <SCRIPT> tag at the top of the file, create a function named "writeIt()" that has a single parameter variable named "Text."

   Add the following two commands to the writeIt() function:

- If the browser supports the Netscape DOM, have the writeIt() function write the value of the Text parameter to the OutNS layer (but do *not* close the layer after writing).

Explore

- If the Internet Explorer DOM is being used, insert the value of the Text parameter into the OutIE <DIV> container, as adjacent HTML code, placing it before the end of the container.

6. Below the writeIt() function, insert a new function named "writeAll()". There are no parameters for this function.

Add the following tasks to the writeAll() function:

Explore

- If the browser is using the Internet Explorer DOM, change the inner HTML of the OutIE container to an empty text string.

Explore

- Create a FOR loop that loops through the first 12 elements of the Specs form. If an element has been checked (so that it's checked property has a value of *true*), call the writeIt() function, using the values from the SText array as your parameter values. The first SText array value corresponds to the first check box, the second array value corresponds to the second check box and so forth. (*Hint:* Examine the code for the showAll() and hideAll() functions earlier in the file, to see how to loop through the elements in the Specs form.)

- After the FOR loop has been completed, close the input stream for the OutNS document layer if the user is running a Netscape browser.

7. Add an onClick event hander to the "Generate Report" button to run the writeAll() function when the button is clicked.

8. Print a copy of your HTML file, and then close the file, saving your changes.

9. Open the file in your Web browser. Verify that when you select certain items from the form and then click the Generate Report button, information about the selected items appears on the page.

10. Print a copy of your page from your browser, showing information for all items in the form (Internet Explorer users only).

CASE PROBLEMS

Case 1. Translating French Phrases for French 101   Professor Eve Granger teaches French 101 at MidWest University. She is working on creating a Web site containing French phrases that she wants her students to review for their weekly quizzes. She wants you to create a page containing a list of 10 French phrases. If a student passes a pointer over one of the phrases, she wants the English translation of that phrase to appear. When the student moves the pointer off the phrase, the French version should return. Figure 2-38 shows a preview of the page you'll create for Professor Granger.

Figure 2-38

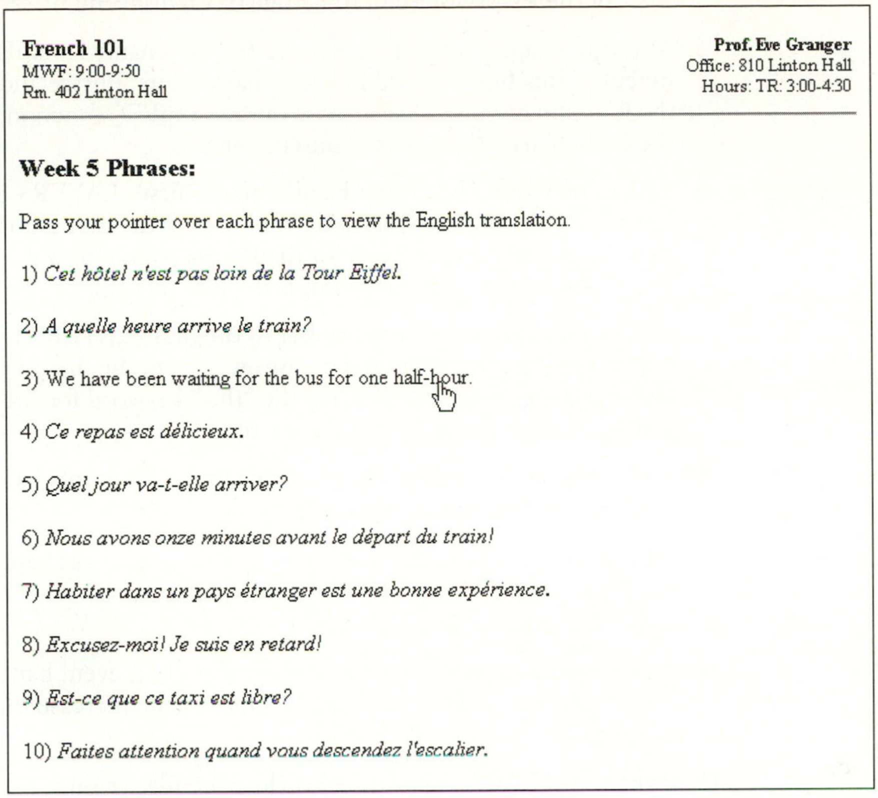

French 101   **Prof. Eve Granger**
MWF: 9:00-9:50   Office: 810 Linton Hall
Rm. 402 Linton Hall   Hours: TR: 3:00-4:30

Week 5 Phrases:

Pass your pointer over each phrase to view the English translation.

1) *Cet hôtel n'est pas loin de la Tour Eiffel.*

2) *A quelle heure arrive le train?*

3) We have been waiting for the bus for one half-hour.

4) *Ce repas est délicieux.*

5) *Quel jour va-t-elle arriver?*

6) *Nous avons onze minutes avant le départ du train!*

7) *Habiter dans un pays étranger est une bonne expérience.*

8) *Excusez-moi! Je suis en retard!*

9) *Est-ce que ce taxi est libre?*

10) *Faites attention quand vous descendez l'escalier.*

The layout and some of the JavaScript code have already been created for you. The isNS and isIE variables have already been created to determine the type of browser DOM in use. Also, the French phrases and their English translations have been stored in two arrays named French and English.

To create the French Phrases page:

1. In your text editor, open the **Frtxt.htm** file from the Tutorial.02D/Cases folder on your Data Disk. Save the file as French.htm.

2. Enclose each of the 10 French phrases within <LAYER> tags (include the opening and closing <P> tags within each layer).

Explore

3. Set the PAGEY property of the first phrase to 170 in order to place the layer 170 pixels down from the top of the page. Place the second layer 30 pixels lower, or 200 pixels from the top. Place each succeeding layer 30 pixels below the one that precedes it.

4. Before the </SCRIPT> tag, insert a function named "swapFE()" to swap the French phrase with the English translation. The swapFE() function should have two parameters, named Phrase and Pnum. The Phrase parameter will represent an object on the Web page containing one of the 10 phrases, and the Pnum parameter will contain the phrase number.

Insert the following tasks into the swapFE() function:

■ If the browser is using the Netscape DOM, insert the value of English[Pnum] into the Phrase object: (*Hint:* Use the object method, Phrase.document.write(), to change the text of the phrase.) Close the input stream to the Phrase object after changing its content.

■ If the browser is using the Internet Explorer DOM, change the inner HTML of the Phrase object to the value of English[Pnum].

5. After the swapFE() function, insert a function named swapEF(). As with the swapFE() function, this function will have two parameters, Phrase and Pnum. The commands of the function are the same as those of the swapFE() function, except that the contents of the French array are inserted into the phrase.

Explore

6. Add an onMouseOver event handler to the first <LAYER> tag to run the swapFE() function when the user passes the mouse over the first phrase. Use the keyword "this" (to refer to the current layer) for the Phrase parameter value, and the value 1 for the Pnum parameter value (since this is the first phrase).

7. Add an onMouseOut event handler to the first <LAYER> tag to run the swapEF() function when the user moves the mouse away from the first phrase. As with the onMouseOver event handler, use the "this" keyword for the Phrase parameter value, and the value 1 for the Pnum parameter.

8. Add these same onMouseOver and onMouseOut events handlers to the <P> tag that encloses the first phrase in the list.

9. Add these same onMouseOver and onMouseOut event handlers to the remaining nine <LAYER> tags. For each <LAYER> tag, increase the value of the Pnum parameter to match the number of the phrase.

10. Add these same onMouseOver and onMouseOut event handlers to the <P> tags that enclose the remaining nine phrases. Once again, increase the value of the Pnum parameter to match the phrase number.

11. Print your HTML code, and then close the file, saving your changes.

12. Open the **French.htm** file in your Web browser. Verify that as you pass your pointer over each of the 10 phrases, the browser swaps the French phrase with the English translation. Check that when you move the pointer off the translation, the original French phrase returns.

13. Print a copy of the page from your browser (Internet Explorer users only).

Case 2. **Creating an Online Quiz for European History**   Professor Anthony Li of the History Department has asked you to help him put together an online quiz for his course on European history. Professor Li envisions a separate Web page for each question on the quiz. The questions are multiple choice. If the student clicks the correct answer, the Web page should notify the student of this, and direct the student to the next question in the exam. If the student clicks the incorrect answer, the page should tell the student that the answer was wrong, and then present additional material on the topic for the student to review. You'll create a simple prototype of a single question for Professor Li to review. A preview of the page is shown in Figure 2-39.

Figure 2-39

European History: 1905-1938, Online Quiz

Previous Question	**Events of the First World War**	Next Question

3) Early in WWI, where did the Allies halt the German advance?   ◉ The Rhine river   ○ The Marne river
　　　　　　　　　　　　　　　　　　　　　　　○ Verdun   ○ The Maginot Line

Your answer is: <u>Incorrect!</u> Please review the material below.

The Battle of the Marne

Date: September 6 - September 12, 1914

The **Battle of the Marne** was *the* crucial battle during the early months of the World War I.

To create the history quiz page:

1. In your text editor, open the **HQuiztxt.htm** file from the Tutorial.02D/Cases folder on your Data Disk. Save the file as HQuiz.htm.

2. At the bottom of the HTML file, insert an opening and closing <SPAN> tag after the line "Your answer is:" Give the <SPAN> tag the ID name "IE_Ans."

3. Within the <SPAN> tags you just entered, insert a two-sided <LAYER> tag with the ID name "NS_Ans."

4. Above the </BODY> tag, insert an inline frame. Set the width and height of the frame to 600 pixels. Remove the frame border. Assign the inline frame the ID name IE_File.

5. Below the inline frame, insert a two-sided <LAYER> tag. Set the width and height of the layer to 600 pixels, and assign it the ID name NS_File.

6. Above the </SCRIPT> tag, insert a function named Correct(). The Correct() function should do the following tasks:

   ■ Create a variable named "Response," whose value is equal to the text string "<U>Correct!</U> It was the Marne river. Please go to the next question."

   ■ Write the value of the Response variable to the IE_Ans object for Internet Explorer users, and to the NS_Ans object for Netscape users.

   ■ Display the contents of the blank.htm file in the IE_File inline frame for Internet Explorer users, and in the NS_File layer for Netscape users.

7. Below the Correct() function, insert the Incorrect() function, which should perform the following tasks:

   ■ Create a variable named "Response," whose value is equal to the text string "<U>Incorrect!</U> Please review the material below."

   ■ Write the value of the Response variable to the IE_Ans object for Internet Explorer users, and to the NS_Ans object for Netscape users.

   ■ Display the contents of the Marne.htm file in the IE_File inline frame for Internet Explorer users, and in the NS_File layer for Netscape users.

8. Add an onClick event handler to the radio buttons for the first, second, and fourth answers to run the Incorrect() function when those radio buttons are clicked.

9. Add an onClick event handler to the third answer ("The Marne river") to run the Correct() function when that answer is clicked.

10. Print your HTML code, and close the file saving your changes.

11. Open the HQuiz.htm file in your Web browser, and verify that the quiz responds correctly to your actions.

12. Print a copy of the page from your browser (Internet Explorer users only).

Case 3. Creating a Newspaper Table of Contents (Internet Explorer Users Only) The *Ridgewood Herald Tribune* has been delivering the news for the midsized community of Ridgewood for over 70 years. In the last year, the paper has started to put its stories on the Web. The editor of the online edition, Stewart Wilkes, has asked you to help develop the site.

One of your tasks is to create a navigation bar. The bar should contain links to all of the main sections of the online paper. Stewart would like to have the sections arranged into expandable and collapsible menus. For example, he would like to have all of the sports-related links placed within a sports menu. Users who wish to view the list of sports links would click the word "Sports" to expand the menu and view their options. A preview of the page you'll create is shown in Figure 2-40.

Figure 2-40

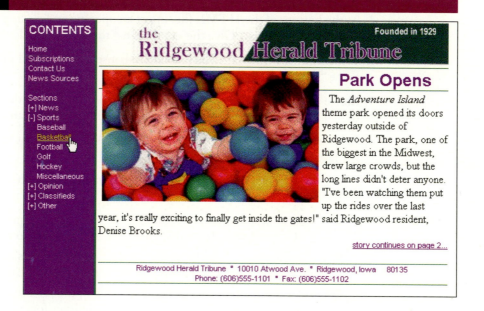

Much of the layout and design has been done for you. Your job will be to program the expandable and collapsible table of contents. Because of the difficulty in working with Netscape layers to accomplish this task, you need only create a solution for the Internet Explorer browser.

To create the table of contents:

1. In your text editor, open the **TOCtxt.htm** file from the Tutorial.02D/Cases folder on your Data Disk. Save the file as TOC.htm.

2. Put <SPAN> tags around the five TOC section titles: News, Sports, Opinion, Classifieds, and Other.

3. Beneath each of the section titles, enclose the pages for that section within <DIV> container tags. Give the five <DIV> tags the ID names News, Sports, Opinion, Classifieds, and Other.

4. Above the </SCRIPT> tag, insert a function named "setContents()" that sets the class name of the five sections you created in Step 3 to "hide" if the user is running the Internet Explorer browser.

5. Create a style for the "hide" class in which the display attribute is set to the value "none."

6. Create a second style for the "unhide" class in which the display attribute is the value "".

Explore

7. Below the setContents() function create a function named "toggleHide()", which has two parameters named "SectionTitle" and "Section." The SectionTitle parameter will contain a text string of the name of the section to hide (or unhide). The Section parameter will point to one of the five section titles that you created earlier with the <SPAN> tags. The toggleHide() function should do the following:

   ■ Create a variable named "SectionObject" that points to the object in the document with the value of the SectionTitle variable. (*Hint:* Use the eval() function on the SectionTitle parameter to create the SectionObject variable.)

   ■ If the class name of the SectionObject variable is "hide," set the class name to "unhide." Also, change the inner text of the Section object to "[-] "+SectionTitle.

   ■ If the class name of the SectionObject variable is "unhide," set the class name to "hide." Also, change the inner text of the Section object to "[+] "+SectionTitle.

8. Within the <SPAN> tag you created for the title of the News section, create an event handler for the onClick event. When the user clicks anywhere within this tag, run the toggleHide() function with the text string "News" as the value for the SectionTitle parameter, and the keyword "this," as the value for the Section parameter.

9. Add onClick event handlers for the other four sections of the table of contents, using the name of the section for the SectionTitle parameter.

10. Add an event handler to run the setContents() function when the page is loaded by the browser.

11. Print the HTML file, and close it, saving your changes.

12. Open the TOC.htm file in your Web browser and verify that the table of contents menu opens and closes when you click each section title.

13. Print a copy of the page from your browser.

Case 4. Creating Dynamic Styles for *A Midsummer Night's Dream*   Professor Andrew Kennedy of the English Department at TriState College is creating an online catalog of classical plays. He's asking your assistance in creating the Web site. Professor Kennedy is not sure what kind of styles he would like to use in his Web pages. He would like you to create styles for a sample page from Shakespeare's *A Midsummer Night's Dream*. Rather than creating separate pages for each style sheet, Professor Kennedy would like to be able to switch between styles "on the fly." Your job will be to create four different dynamic styles for his sample Web page.

Each of the four style sheets you create should display the following attributes:

   ■ A style for stage directions, such as the entrance and exit of key players.

   ■ A style for the name of the character speaking the lines.

   ■ A style for the lines spoken by the character.

   ■ A style for the page title and page background.

The appearance of these styles is up to you. You should create two versions of your page: one for Internet Explorer users and one for Netscape users. The Internet Explorer page should enable Professor Kennedy to switch from one style to another by using a drop-down list box located at the top of the page. The Netscape page should prompt Professor Kennedy to enter the name of the style he wants to apply, when the browser is initially loading the file. Based on which style Professor Kennedy chooses, the Netscape browser should then use JASS to apply the correct style to the page. You can use the demo pages from this tutorial to guide you in writing your code.

To complete Professor Kennedy's Web pages:

1. Open the **Dream.htm** file located in the Tutorial.02D/Cases folder of your Data Disk.

2. Create the Internet Explorer version of the page as Dream_IE.htm.

3. Create the Netscape version of the page as Dream_NS.htm.

4. Hand in printouts of your HTML code for both pages, as well as printouts of each of the four styles as viewed within the Web browser.

QUICK | CHECK ANSWERS

Session 2.1

1. Dynamic content is content on a Web page that is added or altered, usually after the Web browser loads and displays the page, and usually in response to actions or requests by the user.

2. Internet Explorer can change the content and style of any object on the Web page after the page has been loaded by the browser. Netscape can change content only by writing to a <LAYER> tag on the page. Netscape cannot modify the layout of the page after the browser has loaded it.

3. `document.Intro.document.write("Pixal Digital Products");`
   `document.Intro.document.close();`

4. `Title.innerText="Pixal Digital Products";`
   `Title.outerHTML="<H2>Pixal Digital Products</H2>';`

5. `document.Memo.src="Memo2.html";`

6. The innerText property refers to any text within a two-sided tag. The outerText property references both the text within the two-sided tag and the two-sided tags themselves.

7. `document.all.Memo.src="Memo2.html";`

Session 2.2

1. `Title.style.fontSize="14pt";`

2. `Title.style.cssText="color:red; font-size:16pt';`

3. `Title.className="Large_Red";`

4. `<STYLE ID=Formal DISABLED>`
   `Formal.disabled=true;`

5. `Formal.addRule("H3", "color:red; font-size:14pt");`

6. The display property will hide objects and then reflow the document content to fill in the hidden space. The hide property hides the object, but does not allow any other object to occupy that space.

QUICK CHECK ANSWERS

Session 2.3

1. JASS is the style language that Netscape employs for creating dynamic styles.

2. `tags.H1.fontSize="12pt";`

3. `classes.Title.H1.fontFamily="Arial";`

4. `class.Title.all.fontFamily="Arial";`

5. `ids.Intro.color="teal";`

6. `contextual(tags.A, tags.H2).textDecoration="none";`

7. With Netscape, you must create separate layers for each element that must be expanded or collapsed within the outline. To collapse or expand a layer, you must change the clip.height property of the layer, and then move any layers below it up or down on the page to compensate. With Internet Explorer, you only have to change the display property of the element, and Internet Explorer will automatically reflow the page.

OBJECTIVES

In this tutorial you will:

- Create and work with image objects

- Create image rollovers

- Learn about text rollovers

- Learn about and create pop-up and pull-down menus

- Work with Internet Explorer's filters and transitions

- Create interpage transitions

WORKING WITH SPECIAL EFFECTS

Creating Rollovers, Menus, Filters, and Transitions

CASE

The William Shakespeare Web Site

Clare Daynes is a professor of English literature at MidWest University. One of Clare's areas of research is the writings of William Shakespeare. To this end, Clare is creating a site on the World Wide Web containing the complete works of Shakespeare. The site will have several tools of interest to researchers, such as a search engine to locate particular words or phrases from Shakespeare's plays.

Clare has asked for your help in designing the Web site. She wants the site to have a user-friendly interface, and also some visual impact. She's seen sites on the Web that employ special effects such as rollovers and pop-up menus to aid in navigation. She would like to see these elements added to her site. She also wonders whether there are other special effects that can be added to her site.

Clare wants the page to remain compact in size, so she doesn't want any large multimedia files or applets attached to the site. She hopes you can create an interesting site using only DHTML.

SESSION 3.1

In this session you'll create and work with image objects. You'll learn about image object properties and event handlers, and you'll see how to create image rollovers. Finally, you'll explore how to create text rollovers, and you'll learn about some of the cross-browser challenges in using text rollovers.

Working with Image Objects

You and Clare sit down to discuss the current state of her Web page. She shows you the opening screen of her Web site, shown in Figure 3-1. The opening screen contains graphical links to five different pages, covering the following topics: Shakespeare's plays, his sonnets, his biography, the Globe Theatre, and the town of Stratford-on-Avon.

Figure 3-1   THE SHAKESPEARE PAGE

graphic images, which are links to other pages →

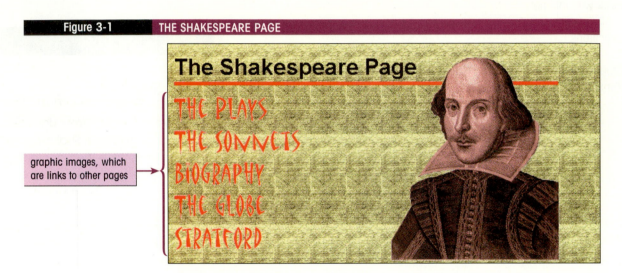

Clare would like you to create a rollover effect, so that when the user moves the pointer over each of these five links, the graphic image changes. Clare suggests that you add a drop shadow to each graphic image as the pointer moves over the link (see Figure 3-2). She feels that the addition of the drop shadow will give the page visual interest, as well as give users an additional visual clue as to which link their pointers are currently over.

Figure 3-2   USING A ROLLOVER EFFECT

as the pointer moves over a link, the graphic image is changed to one containing a drop shadow →

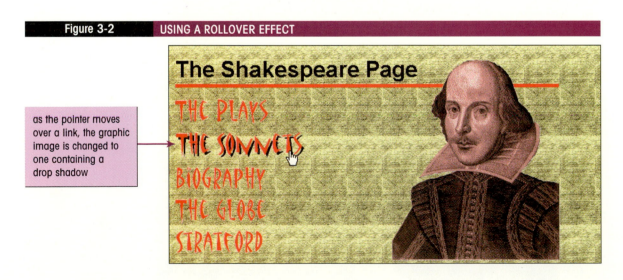

To create a rollover effect for Clare's page, you first have to study how DHTML creates and manages image objects.

Referencing an Image Object

Both Netscape and Internet Explorer use the same reference syntax for their image objects, making it much easier to create cross-browser Web pages. The only exception is when the inline image is nested within other objects on the page, in which case you have to take into account the different ways in which Netscape and Internet Explorer reference nested objects.

For an inline image that has the NAME property with the value, *ImageName*, both browsers use the JavaScript reference:

```
document.ImageName
```

For example, the tag:

```
<IMG NAME=Image1 SRC="Logo.jpg">
```

has the JavaScript reference name:

```
document.Image1
```

Another way of referencing an image on the page is to use the **images collection**. The images collection is the array of all of the inline images on a single page. A single image can be referenced using the syntax:

```
document.images[i]
```

where *i* is the index number of the inline image in the array. The first inline image in the HTML file has the index value 0; the second inline image has an index value of 1, and so forth. For example, if your HTML file contains the following two <IMG> tags:

```
<IMG NAME="Image1" SRC="Logo.jpg">
<IMG NAME="Image2" SRC="Profile.jpg">
```

you can reference these elements either as:

```
document.Image1
document.Image2
```

or

```
document.images[0]
document.images[1]
```

An advantage of using the images collection is that it is easier to create a single script that can be applied to several inline images on the page. For example, you can create a function named "ChangeImage()" in which you need only to specify the index value of the image.

```
function ChangeImage(i) {
    JavaScript commands to modify document.images[i]
}
```

By changing the value of the *i* parameter, this function can be easily applied to any inline image in the page.

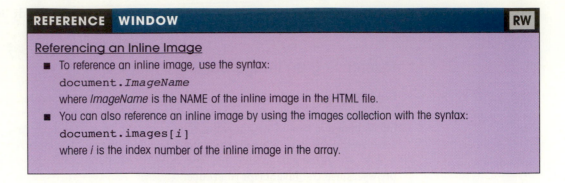

REFERENCE WINDOW — **RW**

Referencing an Inline Image

- To reference an inline image, use the syntax:
  `document.ImageName`
  where *ImageName* is the NAME of the inline image in the HTML file.
- You can also reference an inline image by using the images collection with the syntax:
  `document.images[i]`
  where *i* is the index number of the inline image in the array.

Figure 3-3 shows the reference names for the inline images for the Shakespeare page. You'll be using an images collection to refer to individual images when you create the image rollovers later on, so you'll need to keep this information in mind.

Figure 3-3   IMAGES IN THE SHAKESPEARE PAGE

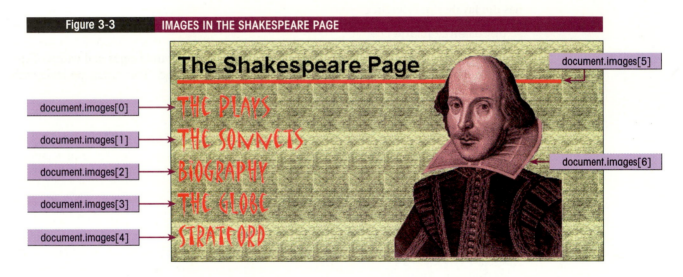

Image Properties

To manipulate the appearance of an inline image, you modify the image's properties. Figure 3-4 describes some of the properties of the image object.

Figure 3-4   IMAGE PROPERTIES

PROPERTY	DESCRIPTION	EXAMPLE	IE	NETSCAPE
alt	Text displayed by nongraphical browsers in place of the inline image	document.Logo.alt="Avalon Books";	4.0	
border	The size of the border around in the image, in pixels	document.Logo.border=2;	4.0	3.0
complete	A Boolean variable indicating whether the browser has finished loading the image	if (document.Logo.complete) ...	4.0	3.0
height	The height of the image, in pixels	document.Logo.height=75;	4.0	3.0
hspace	The horizontal space around the image, in pixels	document.Logo.hspace=5;	4.0	3.0

Figure 3-4	IMAGE PROPERTIES (CONTINUED)			
PROPERTY	**DESCRIPTION**	**EXAMPLE**	**IE**	**NETSCAPE**
lowsrc	The URL of a low-resolution version of the image to be displayed while the high-resolution version is being downloaded	document.Logo.lowsrc="Logo2.jpg";	4.0	3.0
name	The name of the inline image	document.images[3].name="Logo";	3.0	2.0
src	The URL of the inline image	document.Logo.src="Logo.jpg";	3.0	2.0
vspace	The vertical space around the image, in pixels	document.Logo.vspace=5;	4.0	3.0
width	The width of the image, in pixels	document.Logo.width=100;	4.0	3.0

Because of how Netscape implements its document object model, you cannot modify the appearance of an inline image once your browser has loaded it. For example, you cannot change the dimensions of the image by modifying the height and width properties. Netscape allows you to do this only *before* the page has been loaded. Internet Explorer on the other hand, makes all of the properties of the inline image available to you to modify "on the fly." You could create a function like the one below, which increases the height and width of the Grow.jpg image by 5 pixels every time the user clicks the image. This is not possible with Netscape through version 4.7.

```
<SCRIPT>
    function Enlarge() {
        document.GrowImage.width += 5;
        document.GrowImage.height += 5;
    }
</SCRIPT>
<IMG SRC="Grow.jpg" NAME="GrowImage" onClick="Enlarge();">
```

It is rare that you'll need to resize an inline image, so this difference in the browsers shouldn't be a problem in the Shakespeare page. The property most often used with inline images is the src property, which indicates the graphic file used for the image. It is the src property that you'll modify to create the rollover effect that Clare wants.

Image Event Handlers

A rollover occurs when the mouse moves over the image and then off it. One of the easiest way to create a rollover effect is to change the src property of the inline image in response to the onMouseOver and onMouseOut events:

```
<IMG NAME=Swap SRC="Out.jpg" onMouseOver="this.src='Over.jpg'"
onMouseOut="this.src='Out.jpg'">
```

In this tag, the default source for the inline image is the Out.jpg graphic file. If the user moves the mouse pointer over the image, the onMouseOver event is triggered and the browser changes the src property of the image to "Over.jpg". This causes the browser to retrieve (and display) the Over.jpg file. When the mouse pointer moves out from the inline image, the onMouseOut event is triggered and the Out.jpg file is again displayed on the page. Note that the keyword "this" is used to refer to the current inline image.

However, the example above doesn't work with the Netscape browser, because Netscape doesn't support the onMouseOver and onMouseOut event handlers for the <IMG> tag. It does support them for the <A> tag, though, as long as the <A> tag includes the HREF property. To create a rollover effect for both Netscape and Internet Explorer, you have to place the <IMG> tag within a pair of <A> tags as follows:

```
<A HREF=# onMouseOver="document.Swap.src='Over.jpg'"
onMouseOut="document.Swap.src='Out.jpg'">


<IMG NAME=Swap SRC="Out.jpg" BORDER=0>


</A>
```

Note that the HREF property has been set to "#" to cause the link to point back to the current page. Thus, if the user does click the inline image, he or she will not jump out of the page. In many cases, rollover effects are used for images that act as hyperlinks anyway, so you would replace the # symbol with the URL of the linked page.

Preloading Images

Performance is an important consideration when creating a rollover effect. You do not want the user to have to wait while the browser downloads the new image. To avoid this problem, you can preload all of the image files that the user may need, storing the images in the browser's cache. When the browser invokes the rollover effect, the new image file is then quickly retrieved from a local computer rather than from a remote Web server.

To preload an image, you first create an image object in the head section of the HTML file. The image object will store the image in the computer's memory, even though it won't necessarily display the image on the Web page. An image object is created using the syntax:

```
ImageVariable = new Image(width, height);
```

where *ImageVariable* is the variable name you give the image object, and *width* and *height* are the width and height of the image in pixels. The width and height values are optional. If you don't specify a width and height, the image object will be sized to match the dimensions of the graphic file. There is no parameter for specifying the source of the image object. To provide this information you treat the image object as you would an inline image in the Web page and enter a value for the src property. For example, the code:

```
var OutImage = new Image();
OutImage.src = "Out.jpg";
var OverImage = new Image();
OverImage.src = "Over.jpg";
```

creates two new image objects named OutImage and OverImage. The sources for these two image objects are "Out.jpg" and "Over.jpg," respectively. If you want to use these two image objects in the Web page, you could use the HTML code that follows:

```
<A HREF=# onMouseOver="document.Swap.src=OverImage.src"
onMouseOut="document.Swap.src=OutImage.src">


<IMG NAME=Swap SRC="Out.jpg" BORDER=0>


</A>
```

Here, the browser retrieves the OutImage and OverImage objects in response to the onMouseOver and onMouseOut events, and along with those objects it retrieves the graphic files specified in the src property.

In many cases, you will apply rollover effects to several images on your page. If that is the situation, it is often more efficient to store all of your image objects in their own arrays. The following is a typical example:

```
var ImgOver = new Array();
ImgOver[0] = new Image();
ImgOver[1] = new Image();
ImgOver[2] = new Image();
ImgOver[0].src = "Over1.jpg";
ImgOver[1].src = "Over2.jpg";
ImgOver[2].src = "Over3.jpg";
```

These arrays can then be matched with the collection of image objects on the page. For example, the command:

```
document.images[0].src = ImgOver[0].src
```

replaces the first inline image on the page with the first image object in the ImgOver array. A more general function to do this would be:

```
function RollOver(i) {
    document.images[i].src = ImgOver[i].src;
}
```

where the *i* parameter indicates which inline image on the page to use.

Object Detection

Not all versions of Internet Explorer and Netscape support image objects. To avoid errors on your page, you should use object detection to determine whether the browser supports the code you're entering. If the browser supports image objects, it will recognize the document.images reference name. Therefore, you can use the following structure to test the user's browser:

```
if (document.images) {
    JavaScript commands to create and modify image objects
}
```

If the user is running an older browser, the value of document.images will be FALSE, and the JavaScript command block that follows will be skipped. Such users will still be able to use the Web site, but they won't see the image rollovers. Browsers that do support the document.images object will run the command block.

Creating an Image Rollover

You now have enough information to create an image rollover for the Shakespeare page.

The source for Clare's Shakespeare Web page is saved in the file, WStext.htm. Open this file now.

To open the Shakespeare Web page:

1. Start your text editor and open the **WStext.htm** file located in the Tutorial.03D folder on your Data Disk.

2. Save the file as **WS.htm** in the same folder.

Clare shows you a collection of images and alternate images to be used in the Web page, shown in Figure 3-5. When the user hovers the mouse pointer over the images in the left column of Figure 3-5, the browser should load the images from Figure 3-5's right column. When the mouse pointer moves off the image, the images from the left column in Figure 3-5 should be redisplayed.

Figure 3-5   IMAGES AND ALTERNATE IMAGES

Image	Rollover Image
THE PLAYS PlaysOut.gif	THE PLAYS PlaysOver.gif
THE SONNETS SonOut.gif	THE SONNETS SonOver.gif
BIOGRAPHY BioOut.gif	BIOGRAPHY BioOver.gif
THE GLOBE GlobeOut.gif	THE GLOBE GlobeOver.gif
STRATFORD StratOut.gif	STRATFORD StratOver.gif

Your first step will be to store these images in two image object arrays: ImgOver and ImgOut. The ImgOver array will contain the images to be displayed when the mouse pointer moves over the graphic links. The ImgOut array will contain the images that are displayed when the mouse moves off the links.

To create the ImgOver and ImgOut image arrays:

1. After the </STYLE> tag in the WS.htm file, insert the following code (see Figure 3-6):

```
<SCRIPT>
    if (document.images) {
        var ImgOver=new Array();
        ImgOver[0]=new Image();
        ImgOver[1]=new Image();
        ImgOver[2]=new Image();
        ImgOver[3]=new Image();
```

```
        ImgOver[4]=new Image();
        var ImgOut=new Array();
        ImgOut[0]=new Image();
        ImgOut[1]=new Image();
        ImgOut[2]=new Image();
        ImgOut[3]=new Image();
        ImgOut[4]=new Image();
    }
</SCRIPT>
```

Figure 3-6	CREATING THE IMGOVER AND IMGOUT ARRAYS

```
<SCRIPT>
    if (document.images) {
        var ImgOver=new Array();
        ImgOver[0]=new Image();
        ImgOver[1]=new Image();
        ImgOver[2]=new Image();
        ImgOver[3]=new Image();
        ImgOver[4]=new Image();
        var ImgOut=new Array();
        ImgOut[0]=new Image();
        ImgOut[1]=new Image();
        ImgOut[2]=new Image();
        ImgOut[3]=new Image();
        ImgOut[4]=new Image();
    }
</SCRIPT>
```

2. Save your changes to the file.

Next you have to populate these arrays with the graphic files displayed in Figure 3-5. You'll do this by specifying a value for the src property of each image object in the two arrays.

To populate the ImgOver and ImgOut arrays:

1. Before the command to create the ImgOut array, insert the following commands to specify the source for the ImgOver objects:

```
ImgOver[0].src="PlaysOver.gif";
ImgOver[1].src="SonOver.gif";
ImgOver[2].src="BioOver.gif";
ImgOver[3].src="GlobeOver.gif";
ImgOver[4].src="StratOver.gif";
```

2. Before the closing curly brace, insert the source for the ImgOut objects (you may want to use the copy and paste features of your editor to reduce the amount of typing required).

```
ImgOut[0].src="PlaysOut.gif";
ImgOut[1].src="SonOut.gif";
ImgOut[2].src="BioOut.gif";
ImgOut[3].src="GlobeOut.gif";
ImgOut[4].src="StratOut.gif";
```

Figure 3-7 shows the revised WS.htm file.

Figure 3-7   SPECIFYING THE SOURCE FOR THE IMAGE OBJECTS

```
<SCRIPT>
    if (document.images) {
        var ImgOver=new Array();
        ImgOver[0]=new Image();
        ImgOver[1]=new Image();
        ImgOver[2]=new Image();
        ImgOver[3]=new Image();
        ImgOver[4]=new Image();
        ImgOver[0].src="PlaysOver.gif";
        ImgOver[1].src="SonOver.gif";
        ImgOver[2].src="BioOver.gif";
        ImgOver[3].src="GlobeOver.gif";
        ImgOver[4].src="StratOver.gif";
        var ImgOut=new Array();
        ImgOut[0]=new Image();
        ImgOut[1]=new Image();
        ImgOut[2]=new Image();
        ImgOut[3]=new Image();
        ImgOut[4]=new Image();
        ImgOut[0].src="PlaysOut.gif";
        ImgOut[1].src="SonOut.gif";
        ImgOut[2].src="BioOut.gif";
        ImgOut[3].src="GlobeOut.gif";
        ImgOut[4].src="StratOut.gif";
    }
</SCRIPT>
```

Next you need to create two functions: RollOver() and RollOut(). The RollOver() function replaces an inline image in the Web page with an image object from the ImgOver array. The RollOut() function does the same thing, but with image objects from the ImgOut array. The commands for the two functions are:

```
function RollOver(i) {
    if (document.images) {
        document.images[i].src=ImgOver[i].src;
    }
}


function RollOut(i) {
    if (document.images) {
        document.images[i].src=ImgOut[i].src;
    }
}
```

Note that, to avoid error messages from an older browser, we need to test whether the browser supports the document.images reference name before attempting to replace image files.

To add the RollOver() and RollOut() functions to the file:

1. Before the closing </SCRIPT> tag, enter the following commands:

```
function RollOver(i) {
    if (document.images) {
        document.images[i].src=ImgOver[i].src;
    }
}
```

```
      function RollOut(i) {
         if (document.images) {
            document.images[i].src=ImgOut[i].src;
         }
      }
```

2. Save your changes to WS.htm.

Now you need to call the RollOver() and RollOut() functions in response to actions from the user. When the pointer moves onto a graphic image, the RollOver() function should be called with a parameter value equal to the index value of the inline image (refer to Figure 3-3 for the index numbers). When the mouse pointer moves off the inline image, the RollOut() function should be called.

To call the RollOver() and RollOut() functions:

1. Scroll down the file until you locate the <A> tag that links to the Plays.htm file.

2. Within the <A> tag, insert the following commands (see Figure 3-8):

```
onMouseOver="RollOver(0)" onMouseOut="RollOut(0)"
```

Note that a index value of 0 is used for the RollOver() and RollOut() functions since this is the first image in the collection of inline images on the page.

Figure 3-8	ADDING THE MOUSEOVER AND MOUSEOUT EVENT HANDLERS TO THE PLAYS.HTM LINK

```
<DIV STYLE="float:left">
<A HREF="Plays.htm" onMouseOver="RollOver(0)" onMouseOut="RollOut(0)">
   <IMG SRC="PlaysOut.gif" BORDER=0>
</A><BR>
```

run the RollOver( ) function when the mouse moves over the <A> tag

run the RollOut( ) function when the mouse moves out from the <A> tag

Now add the onMouseOver andonMouseOut commands for the rest of the <A> tags (you may want to use the copy and paste features of your browser).

3. Locate the <A> tag that links to the Sonnets.htm page and insert within the tag:

```
onMouseOver="RollOver(1)" onMouseOut="RollOut(1)"
```

4. Insert within the <A> tag for the Bio.htm page:

```
onMouseOver="RollOver(2)" onMouseOut="RollOut(2)"
```

5. Insert within the <A> tag for the Globe.htm page:

```
onMouseOver="RollOver(3)" onMouseOut="RollOut(3)"
```

6. Finally, locate the <A> tag for the Stratford.htm page and insert:

```
onMouseOver="RollOver(4)" onMouseOut="RollOut(4)"
```

7. The <A> tags for the WS.htm file should appear as shown in Figure 3-9.

Figure 3-9 | **ADDING EVENT HANDLERS TO THE REMAINING LINKS IN THE SHAKESPEARE PAGE**

```
<DIV STYLE="float:left">
<A HREF="Plays.htm" onMouseOver="RollOver(0)" onMouseOut="RollOut(0)">
    <IMG SRC="PlaysOut.gif" BORDER=0>
</A><BR>

<A HREF="Sonnets.htm" onMouseOver="RollOver(1)" onMouseOut="RollOut(1)">
    <IMG SRC="SonOut.gif" BORDER=0>
</A><BR>

<A HREF="Bio.htm" onMouseOver="RollOver(2)" onMouseOut="RollOut(2)">
    <IMG SRC="BioOut.gif" BORDER=0>
</A><BR>

<A HREF="Globe.htm" onMouseOver="RollOver(3)" onMouseOut="RollOut(3)">
    <IMG SRC="GlobeOut.gif" BORDER=0>
</A><BR>

<A HREF="Stratford.htm" onMouseOver="RollOver(4)" onMouseOut="RollOut(4)">
    <IMG SRC="StratOut.gif" BORDER=0>
</A>
</DIV>
```

Now you can test the page to see the effect of the rollover functions.

To test the rollovers:

1. Save your changes to the WS.htm file and close your text editor.

2. Open the **WS.htm** file in your Web browser.

3. Move your mouse cursor over each of the five linked images and verify that a drop shadow appears as a rollover image is swapped with the original image. (Note that Clare hasn't created the other five Web pages yet, so if you test the links you will get an error message from your browser.)

4. Close your Web browser.

Text Rollovers

The Shakespeare page employs only rollovers of graphical images. The rollover effect can also be applied directly to text, but due to some cross-browser problems, this is not often done. If you are supporting only Internet Explorer users (as might occur within a company's Intranet), you have a wider range of possible approaches than with Netscape.

Using the Hover Pseudo-Class

If you are creating a rollover effect for linked text, the simplest approach is to use a style declaration for the <A> tag that employs the hover pseudo-class. The general syntax is:

```
A:hover {style when the mouse is hovering over the link}
```

For example, to change your hyperlinks to a bold red font when the mouse pointer is hovering over them, use the style:

```
A:hover {color:red; font-weight:bold}
```

Netscape to version 4.7 does not support the hover pseudo-class, nor does Internet Explorer prior to version 5.0. If the browser supports it, however, this approach does allow you to create your rollover effect without writing JavaScript code.

Text Rollovers with Internet Explorer

A more general approach in Internet Explorer version 4.0 or above is to modify the style properties of the element in response to a rollover. The following code shows how you would change the appearance of a bulleted list item.

```
<UL>
    <LI onMouseOver="this.style.color='red'"
     onMouseOut="this.style.color='black'">
        The Globe
    </LI>
</UL>
```

As the mouse pointer passes over the list item, the font color changes to red, and then changes to black when the pointer moves away from the item. To control more attributes than just the font color, you can create a new style class, and then change the class name of the element.

```
<STYLE>
    .RollOver {color: red; font-weight: bold}
</STYLE>

<P onMouseOver="this.className='RollOver'"
    onMouseOut="this.className=''">
    The Globe
</P>
```

When the mouse pointer moves over the paragraph, the browser changes the class name to "RollOver." This results in the style attributes of RollOver class being applied to the element, changing the text to a bold red font. When the mouse pointer moves off the element, the class name is removed (by changing the value of the className property to '') and the paragraph returns to its default appearance. Remember that Netscape does not support this approach.

Text Rollovers with Netscape

To create a text rollover in Netscape, you have to enclose the text between a set of <LAYER> tags and then use the document.write() command to rewrite the content of the layer. The following code is one such example.

```
<HEAD>
<SCRIPT>
    function Over() {
        document.Globe.document.write("<FONT COLOR=RED><B>The
Globe</B></FONT>");
        document.Globe.document.close();
    }

    function Out() {
        document.Globe.document.write("The Globe");
        document.Globe.document.close();
    }
</SCRIPT>
</HEAD>
<BODY>
```

```
<LAYER NAME="Globe" onMouseOver="Over()" onMouseOut="Out()">
   The Globe
</LAYER>
</BODY>
```

In this example, "The Globe" has been placed within a set of <LAYER> tags named "Globe." When the user moves the mouse pointer over the Globe layer, the Over() function is called, and new content is written into the layer in a bold red font. Note that this is achieved by using both the <FONT> and <B> tags, and the entire content of the Globe layer has to be rewritten. When the mouse pointer moves off the layer, the Out() function is called. Once again, the content of the layer is rewritten, but this time without the <FONT> and <B> tags.

Imagine having to do this for a large block of text, or for a page full of text rollovers, and you can see the difficulty of the Netscape approach. The problem is only magnified if you are trying to create a page that is compatible with both Netscape and Internet Explorer. For that reason, most Web page authors convert text to a graphic image, since graphical rollovers are relatively straightforward, and text rollovers can be more complicated.

You've completed your work with rollovers for Clare. She's going to examine your work and get back to you with other effects to add to the Web site.

Session 3.1 QUICK CHECK

1. The second inline image on your Web page has the name "Links." What are two ways of referencing this image in JavaScript?

2. What code would you enter to change the dimensions of an inline image named "Links" to 150 pixels wide by 200 pixels high?

3. What code would you enter the change the source of the Links image to "Links2.jpg"?

4. What code would you use to create an image object named "LinksOver" that is 75 pixels wide and 100 pixels high?

5. The following tags are found in your HTML file:

```
<A HREF="Links.htm">
   <IMG NAME=LINK SRC="Links.jpg">
</A>
```

   Revise these tags so that the browser displays the Links2.jpg file when the mouse pointer moves over the image, and then displays the Links.jpg file again when the pointer moves off the image.

6. What code would you enter to create an array of image objects named LinksArray, containing image objects pointing to graphic files Img1.src, Img2.src, and Img3.src?

7. What IF condition must you use to determine whether the browser supports image objects?

In this session you'll learn about pop-up and pull-down menus. You'll explore various techniques for creating these menus. Using a rollover effect, you'll create a pull-down menu for Clare's Web site that is compatible with both Internet Explorer and Netscape.

Working with Menus

Clare is pleased with the opening screen you created. Now she wants you to work on a page that contains links to all of Shakespeare's plays. Shakespeare wrote almost forty plays, and Clare is concerned that a page with so many links will be cumbersome to work with. Ideally, she would like to have the contents of the page fit within the space of a single screen.

Clare wonders whether you can create a menu containing links to each of the plays. She envisions four menus, one for each of the four types of Shakespeare's plays: comedies, histories, tragedies, and romances. Clare sketches out her idea for you, as shown in Figure 3-10.

| Figure 3-10 | MENUS FOR THE PAGE ON SHAKESPEARE'S PLAYS |

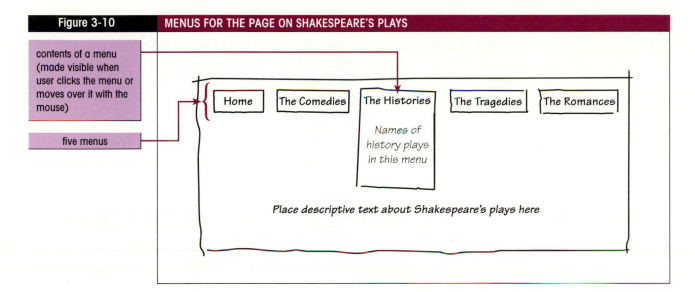

What Clare would like to see is five boxes at the top of the page, for the four types of plays, and a fifth box that is linked back to the opening screen. When the user moves the mouse over a play type, a menu should appear, listing all of Shakespeare's plays of that type. The user can then click one of the plays from the list to go to a Web page containing the text of that play. If the user moves the mouse pointer off the list, the menu should disappear.

Creating a Pop-Up Menu

Menus fall into two general classes: pop-ups and pull-downs. In a **pop-up menu**, the user clicks an object on the page and the menu appears, perhaps elsewhere on the page. To close the pop-up menu, the user either clicks the menu itself, or another item on the page.

The most common way to create a pop-up menu for the Web is to place the menu contents within a set of <DIV> container tags, hidden on the page by using the visibility style attribute. When the user clicks an object on the page, a JavaScript program is run that unhides the menu (see Figure 3-11). To rehide the menu, a second JavaScript program is run that changes the menu's visibility property back to hidden.

Figure 3-11   A POP-UP MENU

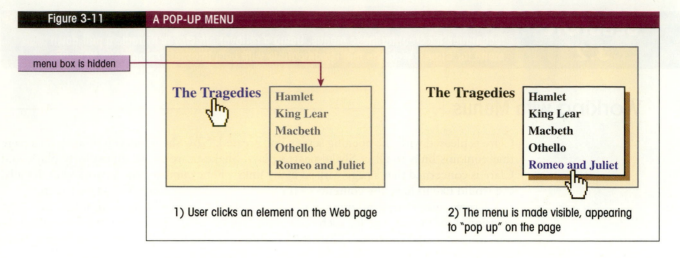

menu box is hidden

1) User clicks an element on the Web page

2) The menu is made visible, appearing to "pop up" on the page

Creating a Pull-Down Menu

In a **pull-down menu**, part of the menu is visible. When the user either clicks the visible part (or moves a mouse pointer over it) the rest of the menu is revealed. This creates the illusion that the rest of the menu is being "pulled down" from the visible part.

To create a pull-down menu, you place the contents within a set of <DIV> tags, and use the clip style attribute to "cut off" part of the menu. The part of the menu that is still visible will usually contain a title describing the menu's contents. When the user either clicks the title, or moves the mouse pointer over the title, a JavaScript command is run that displays the hidden section (see Figure 3-12). Clicking another menu on the page pulls the menu back up.

Figure 3-12   A PULL-DOWN MENU

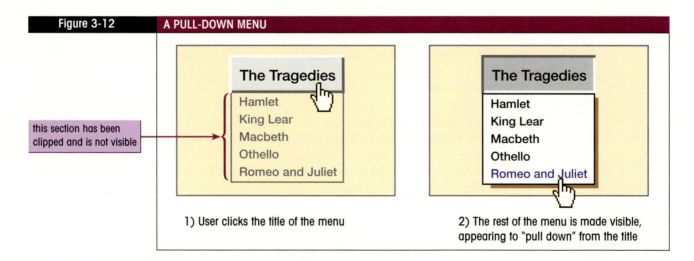

this section has been clipped and is not visible

1) User clicks the title of the menu

2) The rest of the menu is made visible, appearing to "pull down" from the title

Clare decides to go with a pull-down rather than a pop-up menu. Most of the work in setting up the content of the menus, and their position on the page, has already been done for you. The Plays page in its current state has been stored in the Playstxt.htm file. Open this file now.

To open the Playstxt.htm file:

1. In your text editor, open the **Playstxt.htm** file located in the Tutorial.03D folder of your Data Disk.

2. Save the file as **Plays.htm**.

3. Open **Plays.htm** in your Web browser.

   Figure 3-13 shows the current appearance of the page in Internet Explorer.

   TROUBLE? Netscape displays the menus with a rose-colored top border. This will not affect the operation of the pull-down menus you'll be creating.

Figure 3-13   THE MENUS FOR THE PLAYS WEB PAGE

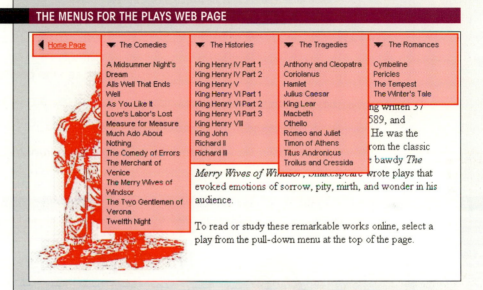

The menu contains five menu elements, created using <DIV> tags and given the ID values "Home," "Comedy," "History," "Tragedy," and "Romance." An additional <DIV> tag, labeled "Summary," is placed around the text describing Shakespeare's page and the inline image on the page's left edge. The width of each menu box is 130 pixels, and the height varies depending on the number of menu entries. Within each menu is a list of plays for that genre, linked to individual pages for each play.

The menus hide most of the page content, so to view the rest of the page you have to clip the menus. After experimenting with various sizes, you decide to clip each menu box to a width of 130 pixels, and a height of 30 pixels.

To clip the menus:

1. Return to Plays.htm in your text editor.

2. Locate the styles attributes for the #Home – #Romance selectors at the top of the file.

3. Insert the style attribute, **clip: rect(0, 130, 30, 0)**, as shown in Figure 3-14 (be sure to separate the clip attribute from the previous attributes, using a semicolon).

Figure 3-14	CLIPPING THE MENUS

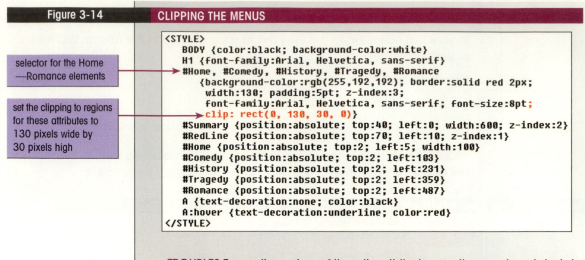

selector for the Home
—Romance elements

set the clipping to regions
for these attributes to
130 pixels wide by
30 pixels high

```
<STYLE>
    BODY {color:black; background-color:white}
    H1 {font-family:Arial, Helvetica, sans-serif}
    #Home, #Comedy, #History, #Tragedy, #Romance
        {background-color:rgb(255,192,192); border:solid red 2px;
        width:130; padding:5pt; z-index:3;
        font-family:Arial, Helvetica, sans-serif; font-size:8pt;
        clip: rect(0, 130, 30, 0)}
    #Summary {position:absolute; top:40; left:0; width:600; z-index:2}
    #RedLine {position:absolute; top:70; left:10; z-index:1}
    #Home {position:absolute; top:2; left:5; width:100}
    #Comedy {position:absolute; top:2; left:103}
    #History {position:absolute; top:2; left:231}
    #Tragedy {position:absolute; top:2; left:359}
    #Romance {position:absolute; top:2; left:487}
    A {text-decoration:none; color:black}
    A:hover {text-decoration:underline; color:red}
</STYLE>
```

TROUBLE? For a discussion of the clip attribute, see the previous tutorial.

4. Save your changes to the file.

5. Reload the page in your Web browser.

   As shown in Figure 3-15, the menus should now be truncated, leaving only the menu titles visible.

Figure 3-15	MENUS AFTER BEING CLIPPED

each menu is now
30 pixels high (the extra
text is hidden)

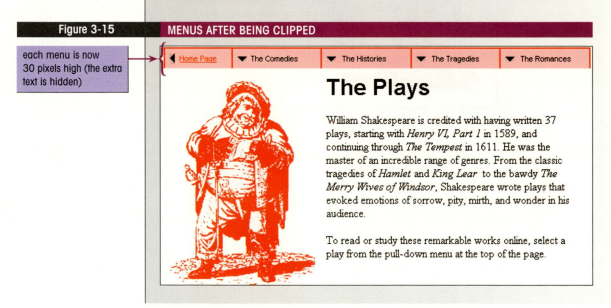

Creating a Clip Function

Before going further, you need to create a function that will clip an element on the Web page to a specified dimension. Unfortunately, Netscape and Internet Explorer use different syntax to accomplish this. As discussed in an earlier tutorial, you set the dimension of the clipping region in Netscape, with the following syntax:

```
document.object.clip.top=top;
document.object.clip.right=right;
document.object.clip.bottom=bottom;
document.object.clip.left=left;
```

where *top*, *right*, *bottom*, and *left* are the coordinates of the top, right, bottom, and left edges. To do the same in Internet Explorer, the syntax is:

```
object.style.clip="rect("+top+" "+right+" "+bottom+"
"+left+")";
```

Note that blank spaces must be inserted between the values of the *top*, *right*, *bottom*, and *left* parameters.

In order to keep the code in the Plays.htm file as simple as possible, you'll insert the clipping function in an external API file, which you'll link to in a moment. The first part of the file already exists for you. Your job will be to create the clipping function.

To open the API file:

1. In your text editor, open **APItext.js**, located in the Tutorial.03D folder on your Data Disk.

2. Save the file as **API.js**.

The file already includes a function named getObject that takes the ID name of an element on the page and returns the variable for the object itself (after correcting for the differences between Netscape and Internet Explorer in assigning object reference names). It also includes two Boolean variables: isNS, which is true if the browser supports the document.layers reference syntax (for Netscape browsers), and isIE, which is true if the document.all reference syntax is supported (for Internet Explorer).

To this API file, you'll add the following function:

```
function clipIt(o, t, r, b, l) {
    var object=getObject(o);
    if (isNS) {
        object.clip.top=t;
        object.clip.right=r;
        object.clip.bottom=b;
        object.clip.left=l;
    }
    if (isIE) {
        object.clip="rect("+t+" "+r+" "+b+" "+l+")";
    }
}
```

In this function, the o parameter is the ID name of the element, and the t through l parameters represent the coordinates of the top, right, bottom, and left edges. To change the clipping region of the Romance element on the Web page to (0, 130, 30, 0), you would add this command to the API file:

```
clipIt("Romance", 0, 130, 30, 0);
```

This command will work for both the Netscape and Internet Explorer browsers. Take some time to study this function, and once you understand the syntax involved, enter it into the API file.

To insert the clipIt() function:

1. At the bottom of the API.js file, insert the following code:

```
function clipIt(o, t, r, b, l) {
    var object=getObject(o);
    if (isNS) {
        object.clip.top=t;
        object.clip.right=r;
        object.clip.bottom=b;
        object.clip.left=l;
    }
    if (isIE) {
        object.clip="rect("+t+" "+r+" "+b+" "+l+")";
    }
}
```

2. Save your changes to the API.js file and close the file.

3. Reopen the **Plays.htm** file in your text editor, if necessary.

4. Below the closing </STYLE> tag, insert the following tags to link to the API.js file (see Figure 3-16):

```
<SCRIPT SRC="API.js"></SCRIPT>
```

Figure 3-16	LINKING TO THE API.JS FILE

```
</STYLE>
<SCRIPT SRC="API.js"></SCRIPT>
</HEAD>
```

Now you can use the clipIt() function in the Plays Web page to change the clipping dimensions of the menus.

Creating Functions for the Pull-Down Menu

You discuss with Clare exactly how she wants the menus to work. Clare outlines the following behaviors:

- The contents of only one pull-down menu should be displayed at any time.
- If the mouse pointer moves over a menu title, the contents of that menu should be displayed, and any other active menu should be clipped.
- If the mouse pointer moves over the page content, below the menus, any active menu should be clipped.

To write code for these behaviors, you need some way of tracking which, if any, menu is currently active. You'll do this by creating a variable named "ActiveMenu," which will store the ID name of the active menu. The possible values of the ActiveMenu variable are: "Comedy," "History," "Tragedy," and "Romance," corresponding to the ID labels of the four <DIV> tags that contain the four pull-down menus (the Home <DIV> element is not a pull-down menu, since it only has one entry). You'll set the initial value of ActiveMenu to be empty, since no menu contents are displayed when the page is first opened.

To create the ActiveMenu variable:

1. Above the <SCRIPT> tag you just entered to link to the API.js file, insert the following code (see Figure 3-17):

```
<SCRIPT>
    var ActiveMenu="";
</SCRIPT>
```

2. Save your changes to the file.

Figure 3-17   **CREATING THE ACTIVEMENU VARIABLE**

```
</STYLE>
<SCRIPT>
    var ActiveMenu="";
</SCRIPT>
<SCRIPT SRC="API.js"></SCRIPT>
</HEAD>
```

Displaying Menu Contents

Next you need to create two functions: one will display the contents of a menu, and the other will hide the contents. Both functions will call the clipIt() function from the API file. You'll first create a function named PullMenu() to display a menu. This function will have three purposes:

1. Hide the active menu.

2. Display the menu chosen by the user.

3. Make this menu the new active menu.

The code for this function appears as follows:

```
function PullMenu(M) {
    HideMenu();
    clipIt(M, 0, 130, 600, 0);
    ActiveMenu=M;
}
```

The PullMenu function has one parameter, M, which is the ID name of the menu that will be displayed on the page.

The first line of the function calls the HideMenu() function to hide the active menu (you'll create this function shortly). The second line calls the clipIt() function from the API file and sets the width of the menu to 130 pixels and the height to 600 pixels.

Why was a height of 600 pixels chosen? The value used for the height doesn't matter, provided that it's large enough to display the content of every menu on the page. The browser will ignore any excess space in the clipping region. In this page, every menu is less than 600 pixels in height, but if more entries are later added to the menus, this value may have to be increased.

Finally, the third line changes the value of the ActiveMenu variable to the ID name of the menu that is now displayed on the page, since that is the new active menu.

For example, to display the contents of the History menu, you would use the command:

```
PullMenu("History");
```

and the browser would hide the active menu (if one exists), and then display the History menu, making it the new active menu. Add the PullMenu() function to the Plays.htm file now.

To add the PullMenu() function to the file:

1. Above the </SCRIPT> tag, insert the following code, as shown in Figure 3-18.

```
function PullMenu(M) {
    HideMenu();
    clipIt(M, 0, 130, 600, 0);
    ActiveMenu=M;
}
```

Figure 3-18   THE PULLMENU() FUNCTION

2. Save your changes to the file.

Hiding the Active Menu

The HideMenu() function will have the task of hiding the active menu, if one exists. It does this by reducing the clipping height of the active menu back to 30 pixels, hiding the menu content except for the menu title. The code for the HideMenu() function is:

```
function HideMenu() {
    if (ActiveMenu !=="") {
        clipIt(ActiveMenu, 0, 130, 30, 0);
        ActiveMenu="";
    }
}
```

The function first has to test whether there is an active menu to hide (to avoid generating an error message if there is not). It does this by testing the value of the ActiveMenu variable. If the variable is not empty, the function clips the active menu back to the (0, 130, 30, 0) dimension, and resets the value of the ActiveMenu variable.

To add the HideMenu() function to the file:

1. Insert the following code (as shown in Figure 3-19):

```
function HideMenu() {
    if (ActiveMenu !=="") {
        clipIt(ActiveMenu, 0, 130, 30, 0);
        ActiveMenu="";
    }
}
```

Figure 3-19   THE HIDEMENU() FUNCTION

```
<SCRIPT>
   var ActiveMenu="";
   function PullMenu(M) {
       HideMenu();
       clipIt(M, 0, 130, 600, 0);
       ActiveMenu=M;
   }

   function HideMenu() {
       if (ActiveMenu !=="") {
          clipIt(ActiveMenu, 0, 130, 30, 0);
          ActiveMenu="";
       }
   }
</SCRIPT>
```

test whether a menu is active

if so, clip it, displaying only the menu title

indicate that no menu is currently active

2. Save your changes to the file.

Calling the Menu Functions

To run these functions, you need to add the onMouseOver event handler to the tags for each of the menus. However, like image rollovers, you need a workaround for the Netscape browser, since it does not support the onMouseOver event handler with the <DIV> tag. To get around this problem, you'll place the menu titles within a set of <A> tags (as you did for image rollovers) and add the onMouseOver event handler to that tag. Start with the Comedy menu.

To modify the Comedy menu:

1. Scroll down the file to the <DIV> tag for the Comedy menu.

2. After the <DIV> tag insert the tag:

```
<A Class=Over HREF=# onMouseOver='PullMenu("Comedy")'>
```

3. Before the pair of <BR> tags, two lines below, insert a closing **</A>** tag. See Figure 3-20.

Figure 3-20   INSERTING AN EVENT HANDLER FOR THE COMEDY MENU

when the mouse pointer passes over the menu title, display the Comedy menu

```
<DIV ID="Comedy">
   <A Class=Over HREF=# onMouseOver='PullMenu("Comedy")'>
   <IMG SRC="Down.jpg" VALIGN=TOP BORDER=0>
    The Comedies</A><BR><BR>
   <A HREF="AMND.htm">A Midsummer Night's Dream</A><BR>
   <A HREF="AWTEW.htm">Alls Well That Ends Well</A><BR>
   <A HREF="AYLI.htm">As You Like It</A><BR>
   <A HREF="LLL.htm">Love's Labor's Lost</A><BR>
   <A HREF="MFM.htm">Measure for Measure</A><BR>
   <A HREF="MAAN.htm">Much Ado About Nothing</A><BR>
   <A HREF="TCOE.htm">The Comedy of Errors</A><BR>
   <A HREF="TMOV.htm">The Merchant of Venice</A><BR>
   <A HREF="TMWOW.htm">The Merry Wives of Windsor</A><BR>
   <A HREF="TTGOV.htm">The Two Gentlemen of Verona</A><BR>
   <A HREF="TN.htm">Twelfth Night</A>
</DIV>
```

Link file (handwritten)

text displayed (handwritten)

As with the image rollovers from the previous session, you have to insert the HREF=# property in order for Netscape to recognize the onMouseOver event handler. Also, the <A> tag you inserted contains a CLASS value. You'll be using that information later on. For now, repeat this process for the remaining three menus.

To add event handlers for the remaining menus:

1. Scroll down to the <DIV> tag for the History menu.

2. After the <DIV> tag, insert:

   ```
   <A Class=Over HREF=# onMouseOver='PullMenu("History")'>
   ```

3. Before the pair of <BR> tags located two lines later, insert an **</A>** tag.

4. After the <DIV> tag for the Tragedy menu, insert:

   ```
   <A Class=Over HREF=# onMouseOver='PullMenu("Tragedy")'>
   ```

5. Insert an **</A>** tag before the

 tags two lines below.

6. After the <DIV> tag for the Romance menu, insert:

   ```
   <A Class=Over HREF=# onMouseOver='PullMenu("Romance")'>
   ```

7. Place an **</A>** tag before the

 tags.

8. Save your changes to the file.

9. Reload the **Plays.htm** file in your Web browser. Verify that, as you move the mouse pointer over the menu titles, the menu contents pull down.

You show Clare the page. Clare notices that when her mouse pointer passes over the menu title, the title changes color and becomes underlined. This is a result of using a hover pseudo-element in the style attributes for linked text on the page. The effect is only noticeable in Internet Explorer, but Clare would much rather have the menu titles stay in black with no underlining. Since you've given all of the menu titles the class name "Over," you can modify the hover style for them.

To change the style for the menu titles:

1. Return to the Plays.htm file in your text editor.

2. Above the </STYLE> tag near the top of the page, insert the style declaration:

   ```
   A.Over:hover {text-decoration: none; color:black}
   ```

3. Save your changes to the file.

4. Reload the page in your Web browser, and verify that the menu titles do not change color or style when the mouse pointer hovers over them (Internet Explorer users only).

A second concern for Clare is that there should be way of hiding the menus after you open one of them. One of the behaviors that Clare wanted to see in this page, was that if the user passes the mouse pointer over the main page content, any active menu will be closed.

To program this, you'll need to enclose the rest of the page within a set of <A> tags in the same way that you did for the menu titles. Then, you'll need to add an event handler that runs the HideMenu() function whenever the user passes the mouse pointer over the main part of the page. This will have the effect of closing whatever menu happens to be active.

To add an event handler for the main part of the page:

1. Return to the Plays.htm file in your text editor.

2. Scroll down the to "Summary" <DIV> tag at the bottom of the page.

3. After the <DIV> tag, insert the line:

```
<A Class=Over HREF=# onMouseOver="HideMenu()">
```

4. Before the closing </DIV> tag, insert an **</A>** tag, as shown in Figure 3-21.

Figure 3-21	INSERTING AN EVENT HANDLER FOR THE MAIN PAGE CONTENT

when the mouse pointer passes over the main page content, hide whatever menu is active

```
<DIV ID=Summary>
<A Class=Over HREF=# onMouseOver="HideMenu()">
    <IMG SRC="Falstaff.jpg" ALIGN=LEFT BORDER=0>
    <H1>The Plays</H1>
    <P>William Shakespeare is credited with having written 37 plays,
    starting with <I>Henry VI, Part 1</I> in 1589, and continuing through
    <I>The Tempest</I> in 1611. He was the master of an incredible range of
    genres. From the classic tragedies of <I>Hamlet</I> and <I>King Lear</I>,
    to the bawdy <I>The Merry Wives of Windsor</I>, Shakespeare wrote plays
    that evoked emotions of sorrow, pity, mirth, and wonder in his audience.
    <P>To read or study these remarkable works online, select a play
    from the pull-down menu at the top of the page.</P>
</A>
</DIV>
```

5. Save your changes to the file, and close the text editor.

6. Return to your Web browser and reload the Web page. The pull-down menus should now disappear whenever you move the mouse pointer over the main part of the page (see Figure 3-22).

Figure 3-22   THE PULL-DOWN MENU FOR THE PLAYS WEB PAGE

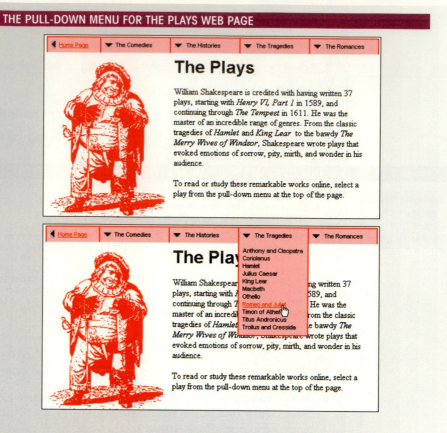

TROUBLE? At this point, the Web pages for the individual plays have not been created, so you will receive an error message if you click the links in the pull-down menus.

7. After you are finished viewing the Web page, you can close your Web browser.

Clare is pleased with the Web page. She feels that the pull-down menu you created will give her users quick access to the rest of her Web site, and the page is still simple and easy to use.

However, the menu does have limitations. For example, you cannot easily insert a hyperlink on the main part of the page, since all of that content is already embedded within a set of <A> tags (you can't nest one <A> tag within another). As you continue to learn DHTML, you'll explore other ways of creating pull-down and pop-up menus, each with its own advantages and disadvantages. There is no one right way of creating menus, and the approach you use will depend on the structure of your page, the needs of your users, and your sense of aesthetics.

Session 3.2 QUICK CHECK

1. What is a pop-up menu?

2. What is a pull-down menu?

3. What limitation does Netscape have in creating rollovers for <DIV> tags?

4. What is one way of overcoming the limitation noted in question #3?

5. What JavaScript command would you use to set the clipping region of the Menu object to (10, 100, 150, 20) in Internet Explorer?

6. How would you set the clipping region noted in question #5 using Netscape?

SESSION 3.3

In this session, you'll learn about the Internet Explorer filters. You'll see how to modify the appearance of objects on your Web pages by using a filter. You'll learn how to employ JavaScript to create a dynamic filter whose effect varies over time. You'll also learn about how Internet Explorer supports transitions. You'll see how to use transition effects for objects within a page, and also when switching between pages.

Working with Filters in Internet Explorer

For Clare's Web site, you've employed two special effects: an image rollover and a pull-down menu. Internet Explorer (but not Netscape) supports another kind of special effect, called a filter. A **filter** is an effect that is applied to an object or page to change its appearance. With the Internet Explorer filters, you can make your text or images appear partially transparent, add a drop shadow, or make an object appear to glow. Figure 3-23 shows examples of the filters supported by Internet Explorer.

Figure 3-23   **INTERNET EXPLORER FILTERS**

Filters cannot be applied to every element on the page. You can apply filters only to elements created with the following tags:

- <DIV> and <SPAN> (with a defined height, width, or absolute position)
- <IMG> and <MARQUEE>
- <BUTTON>, <INPUT>, and <TEXTAREA>
- <TABLE>, <TR>, <TH>, <TD>, <THEAD>, and <TFOOT>

Note that if you want to use the <DIV> or <SPAN> tags, you must define either an absolute position for the element, set the height, or set the width; otherwise, Internet Explorer will generate an error message.

To apply a filter, you either create a filter style with CSS, or you use a JavaScript program to define the properties of the filter.

Applying Filters by Using Styles

The syntax for applying a filter by using CSS is:

```
filter: filter_name(parameters)
```

where *filter_name* is the name of one of the Internet Explorer filters, and *parameters* are the parameter values (if any) that apply to the filter. Figure 3-24 describes the filter names and parameters supported by Internet Explorer.

Figure 3-24   **FILTER NAMES AND PARAMETERS**

FILTER NAME	PARAMETERS	DESCRIPTION
Alpha	Opacity = 1–100	Applies a transparent filter, where the Opacity parameter varies from 1 (transparent) to 100 (opaque)
Blur	Direction = 0 – 360 Strength = 1 – 100	Applies a blurring effect, where the Direction parameter determines the angle of the blur, and the Strength parameter controls the amount of blurring
Chroma	Color = #RRGGBB	Makes a specific color on the element transparent

DropShadow	Color = #RRGGBB
	OffX = # of pixels
	OffY = # of pixels
		Creates a drop shadow of length OffX in the x-direction and OffY in the y-direction; the Color parameter determines the color of the shadow

FlipH	None	Flips the element horizontally
FlipV	None	Flips the element vertically

Glow	Color = #RRGGBB
	Strength = 1 – 255
		Applies a glowing border around the element, with the amount of glow determined by the Strength parameter; the Color parameter determines the color of the glow

Gray	None	Displays in the element in grayscale
Invert	None	Reverses the hue, saturation, and brightness values of the object
Light	Multiple parameters	Projects a light source (defined by multiple parameters) onto the element
Mask	Color=#RRGGBB	Changes the element into a transparent mask. The Color parameter determines the color of the mask
Shadow	Direction = 0 – 360	Applies a simple drop shadow to the element, with the angle of the shadow determined by the Direction parameter.
Wave	Multiple parameters	Applies a sine-wave distortion to the element; the shape and direction of the wave is determined by multiple parameters
Xray	None	Changes the color depth of the object, making it appear like a black and white x-ray

Code for changing image

For example, applying the following style:

```
<IMG SRC="Falstaff.jpg" STYLE="filter: Alpha(Opacity = 30)">
```

will create the slightly transparent image shown in Figure 3-25.

can be others too, to change appearance

Figure 3-25   **CREATING A TRANSPARENT FIGURE WITH THE ALPHA FILTER**

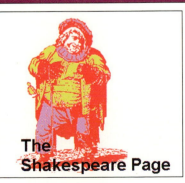

original image

filtered image created with the tag filter: Alpha(Opacity = 30)

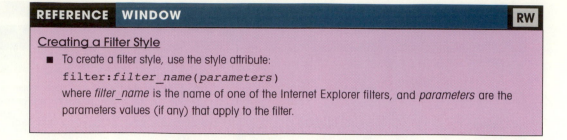

REFERENCE **WINDOW** RW

Creating a Filter Style
- To create a filter style, use the style attribute:

  `filter:filter_name(parameters)`

  where *filter_name* is the name of one of the Internet Explorer filters, and *parameters* are the parameters values (if any) that apply to the filter.

Some filters, such as light and wave, employ several parameters, and are more complicated, but they can create interesting effects. If you're interested, you can learn more about these filters and their parameter values at the Microsoft Online Web Workshop at *http://msdn.microsoft.com/workshop/*.

Filters can also be combined to create interesting visual effects. The effects are added in the order in which they are entered into the style declaration. To combine the alpha filter with a drop shadow, you could enter the following style:

`filter: Shadow Alpha(Opacity=30)`

which applies a shadow to the object and then changes the opacity value to 30. If you switch the order of the filters, the drop shadow will be added after the object is made transparent, which means that the shadow itself will not be made transparent (see Figure 3-26).

| Figure 3-26 | COMBINING FILTERS |

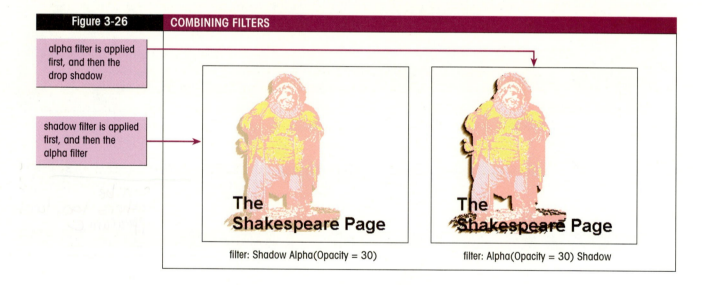

alpha filter is applied first, and then the drop shadow

shadow filter is applied first, and then the alpha filter

filter: Shadow Alpha(Opacity = 30)   filter: Alpha(Opacity = 30) Shadow

You can also apply the same filter several times. This style

`filter: Shadow Shadow`

creates two sets of drop shadows for the same object.

Netscape browsers do not display the results of your filters. In fact, if your style includes other attributes in addition to the filter attribute, the inclusion of the filter will cause Netscape to ignore *all* style attributes for the object. This problem occurs because Netscape internally converts CSS style attributes into JASS. If Netscape encounters an unknown attribute, such as the filter attribute, it can cause the conversion to fail completely.

To get around this problem, you can create the filters with JavaScript.

Applying Filters Using JavaScript

There are two ways of applying a filter in a JavaScript program. One way is to use a text string containing the filter values. The syntax for this approach is:

```
object.style.filter = "filter string";
```

where *object* is the name of the object on the page, and *filter string* is the filter name (or names) and the filter parameters. For example, to apply the Alpha filter to an inline image named Falstaff, you would use the following command:

```
Falstaff.style.filter = "Alpha(Opacity = 30)";
```

If you want to combine several filters, you have to separate their values by a semicolon as follows (note that you do not have to do this with CSS):

```
Falstaff.style.filter = "Shadow; Alpha(Opacity = 30)";
```

A different approach is to treat the filter as part of the document object model, allowing the parameters to be treated as properties of the filter object. The general syntax is:

```
object.filters.filter_name.filter_parameter = value;
```

where *object* is the name of the object on the page, *filter_name* is the name of a filter applied to the object, and *filter_parameter* is one of the parameters of the filter. For example, if the following tag has been added to the HTML file:

```
<DIV ID=Logo STYLE="filter: DropShadow(Color=#FF0000 Offx=5
Offy=5)">
```

you can change the color of the drop shadow to blue by using the JavaScript command:

```
Logo.filters.DropShadow.Color=#0000FF;
```

Note that you must have already defined the filter as part of the object's style to use this approach. If you don't, JavaScript will return an error because it will not have encountered the filter as part of its document object model.

REFERENCE   WINDOW   **RW**

<u>Working with Filters in Javascript</u>
- To apply a filter to an object, use the JavaScript command:
  ```
  object.style.filter = "filter string";
  ```
  where *object* is the name of the object on the page, and *filter string* is the filter name (or names) and the filter parameters.
- To modify the value of one of a filter's properties, use the syntax:
  ```
  object.filters.filter_name.filter_parameter = value;
  ```
  where *object* is the name of the object on the page, *filter_name* is the name of a filter applied to the object, and *filter_parameter* is one of the parameters of the filter.

As you've seen, a single object can contain multiple filters. The keyword "filters" in the previous commands applies to the collection of filters for a single object. As with the images collection for inline images, you may want to refer to a filter using the filters collection. For the Logo filter shown above, any of the following reference names is appropriate.

```
Logo.filters.DropShadow
Logo.filters["DropShadow"]
Logo.filters[0]
```

Using JavaScript, you can write scripts that apply filters to objects on your Web page, but avoid the problem of Netscape browsers not recognizing the filter attribute. You only need to create a Boolean variable to determine the type of browser in use. For example, the following set of commands:

```
if (isIE) {
    Falstaff.style.filter = "Alpha(Opacity = 30)";
}
```

applies the Alpha filter, but only for Internet Explorer browsers (the "isIE" variable is a Boolean variable that determines whether Internet Explorer is being used).

Using the Light Filter

Interesting effects can be achieved by using the Light filter. The Light filter presents the illusion of light falling on an object. You can have up to 10 light sources defined for an object. Each light source is identified by a unique number. The first defined light source has the number zero, the second source has a value of two, and so forth. There are many methods to control the behavior of the light. Two useful methods are the addPoint() method and the MoveLight() method. The addPoint property adds a light source, illuminating an object on your page. The syntax of the addPoint() method is:

```
object.filters.Light.addPoint(x, y, z, R, G, B, strength)
```

where *object* is the name of the object, *x*, *y*, and *z* are the (x, y, z) coordinates of the light source (in pixels), *R*, *G*, and *B* are the RGB color values of the light, and *strength* is the strength of the light source.

The MoveLight() method moves the light source. The syntax is:

```
object.filters.Light.MoveLight(light, x, y, z, absolute)
```

where *light* is the light source number, *x*, *y*, and *z* are the new coordinates of the light source, and *absolute* is a Boolean variable that has the value "true" when the new coordinates are expressed in absolute terms, and has the value "false" when the coordinates are expressed relative to the present coordinates of the light source. You'll have a chance to work with these two methods in the third Case problem at the end of the tutorial.

Creating a Rollover Effect with Filters

Filters can greatly simplify the creation of image rollovers. Earlier, you swapped images in order to create a drop shadow effect for the Shakespeare page. You can create the same effect by using filters applied to a single graphic file. The tag to do this could look as follows:

```
<IMG SRC="Plays.gif" onMouseOver='this.style.filter="Shadow"
' onMouseOut='this.style.filter="" '>
```

When the mouse pointer hovers over the Plays.gif graphic image, the Shadow filter is applied, creating a drop shadow effect. When the mouse pointer moves out, no filter is applied to the image (see Figure 3-27). The great benefit here is that you don't have to load multiple versions of the same image.

Figure 3-27   CREATING A ROLLOVER EFFECT WITH FILTERS

the original image   a filter applied to the
                          image in response to
                          an onMouseOver event

However, the filter approach only works for Internet Explorer. If your Web site needs to support the Netscape browser, you will still have to use the image-swapping technique shown earlier in this tutorial.

Adding a Filter Effect to the Plays Page

You discuss the Internet Explorer filters capability with Clare. She's intrigued by the idea and suggests that you add a filter to the Plays page. Clare's idea is to have the main part of the page become slightly transparent whenever one of the pull-down menus is accessed. A preview of Clare's suggestion is shown in Figure 3-28.

Figure 3-28   APPLYING THE ALPHA FILTER TO THE MAIN PAGE CONTENT

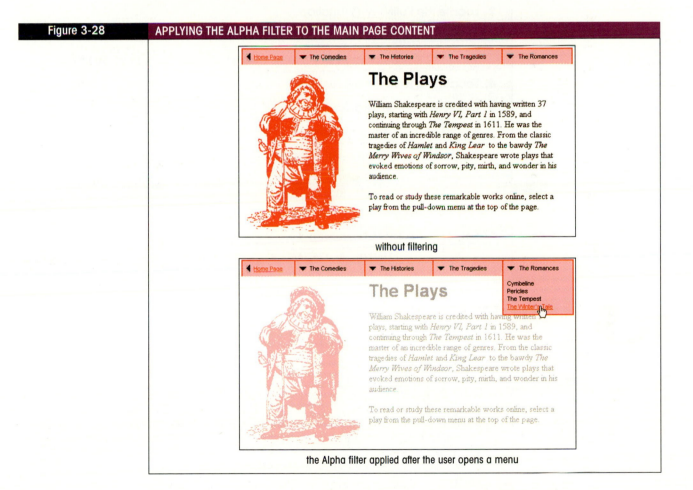

To create this effect, you'll add an additional command to the PullMenu() and HideMenu() functions. Recall that the main page content has been placed within a set of <DIV> tags with the ID name "Summary." When a menu is accessed in the PullMenu() function, you want to make the page content slightly transparent, so you'll add this command:

```
if (isIE) Summary.style.filter = "Alpha(Opacity = 30)";
```

which sets the opacity level of the main page content to 30 points. Note that since this syntax is not supported by Netscape, an IF structure has been used that runs the command only if the browser is Internet Explorer. The Boolean variable isIE has already been calculated in the API file the page is linked to.

When the pointer moves back to the main page content, you need a command that removes the Alpha filter. You can do that by adding the following command to the HideMenu() function:

```
if (isIE) Summary.style.filter = "";
```

where setting the filter style to empty removes any filter applied to the Summary object.

To add the Alpha filter to the Web page:

1. Open the **Plays.htm** file in your text editor.

2. Locate the PullMenu() function.

3. Before the command, ActiveMenu=M, insert the command:

   ```
   if (isIE) Summary.style.filter="Alpha(Opacity=30)";
   ```

4. Locate the HideMenu() function.

5. Before the command, ActiveMenu="", insert the command:

   ```
   if (isIE) Summary.style.filter = "";
   ```

   Figure 3-29 shows the revised functions.

Figure 3-29	INSERTING THE ALPHA FILTER INTO THE PLAYS.HTM FILE

```
<SCRIPT>
    var ActiveMenu="";
    function PullMenu(M) {
        HideMenu();
        clipIt(M, 0, 130, 600, 0);
        if (isIE) Summary.style.filter="Alpha(Opacity=30)";
        ActiveMenu=M;
    }

    function HideMenu() {
        if (ActiveMenu !=="") {
            clipIt(ActiveMenu, 0, 130, 30, 0);
            if (isIE) Summary.style.filter = "";
            ActiveMenu="";
        }
    }
</SCRIPT>
```

make the main page content slightly transparent

remove the Alpha filter

6. Save your changes and open **Plays.htm** in your Web browser, and verify that the main page content becomes slightly transparent whenever a pull-down menu is selected.

   TROUBLE? If you're running the Netscape browser, you will not see any transparent effect, but the page should still be rendered correctly.

Creating Dynamic Filters

The effect you created for the Plays Web page is an example of a **dynamic filter**, in which the parameter values of the filter change either in response to a user's action or over an interval of time (as opposed to **static filters**, which do not change). One popular dynamic filter is a "fade-in" effect created by slowly increasing the opacity value of the Alpha filter over time. Here is sample code that can be used to create a fade-in effect for the first image in a Web page.

```
var OpLevel = 0;
setInterval("FadeIn(document.images[0])", 100);

function FadeIn(Object) {
   if (OpLevel <= 100) {
      Object.filters.Alpha.Opacity = OpLevel;
      OpLevel += 5;
   } else {
      clearInterval();
   }
}
```

In this sample code, the opacity value is stored in a variable named "OpLevel." Every 100 milliseconds the FadeIn() function is run, changing the opacity of the image object to the value of the OpLevel variable, which is immediately increased by 5 points. The FadeIn() function runs continually until the value of the OpLevel variable exceeds 100 points, at which time the clearInterval() command halts the process. The effect for the user is that the image object slowly becomes visible on the Web page.

Working with Transitions in Internet Explorer

A **transition** is a visual effect applied to an object over an interval of time—the concept is much like that of dynamic filters. Transitions are often used to create an interesting visual effect as one object is gradually replaced by another. Transitions can be used to create slide shows with visually interesting effects. They can also be used when switching from one page to another in the browser. As with filters, only Internet Explorer supports transitions. Netscape will not display the results of the transition, and if you include the transition in a CSS style sheet, Netscape will ignore *all* of the style attributes for the object.

Blend and Reveal Transitions

Like filters, transitions can be defined by using styles or as part of a JavaScript program. Internet Explorer supports two kinds of transitions: blend and reveal.

A **blend transition** fades an object in and out of view (much like the FadeIn() function described above). The syntax for defining a blend transition within a style sheet is:

```
filter: blendTrans(Duration = value)
```

where *value* is the amount of time, in seconds, for the fade-in or fade-out process to take place.

A **reveal transition** allows you to specify not only the duration of the transition, but also an effect for the transition. The syntax for the reveal transition is:

```
filter: revealTrans(Duration = value, Transition = type)
```

where *type* is a number of from 0 to 23, specifying the transition effect. The various transition effects and their numeric values are listed in Figure 3-30.

Figure 3-30 | REVEAL TRANSITION TYPES

TRANSITION	NUMERIC CODE	TRANSITION	NUMERIC CODE
Box In	0	Random Dissolve	12
Box Out	1	Split Vertical In	13
Circle In	2	Split Vertical Out	14
Circle Out	3	Split Horizontal In	15
Wipe Up	4	Split Horizontal Out	16
Wipe Down	5	Strips Left Down	17
Wipe Right	6	Strips Left Up	18
Wipe Left	7	Strips Right Down	19
Vertical Blinds	8	Strips Right Up	20
Horizontal Blinds	9	Random Bars Horizontal	21
Checkerboard Across	10	Random Bars Vertical	22
Checkerboard Down	11	Random	23

See the TransTour.htm Web page on your Data Disk for examples of these transitions

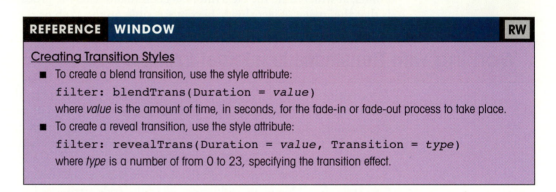

REFERENCE | WINDOW | RW

Creating Transition Styles
- To create a blend transition, use the style attribute:
  ```
  filter: blendTrans(Duration = value)
  ```
  where *value* is the amount of time, in seconds, for the fade-in or fade-out process to take place.
- To create a reveal transition, use the style attribute:
  ```
  filter: revealTrans(Duration = value, Transition = type)
  ```
  where *type* is a number of from 0 to 23, specifying the transition effect.

To better understand the transition effects, a page of sample transitions has been prepared for you. Open it now.

To open the transitions tour page:

1. Open the **TransTour.htm** file (located in the Tutorial.03D folder on your Data Disk) in your Web browser.

2. Select a transition type from the **Transition Type** drop-down list box.

   The image on the right displays the effects of the transition type, as shown in Figure 3-31.

| Figure 3-31 | USING THE TRANSTOUR.HTM WEB PAGE TO VIEW DIFFERENT TRANSITION TYPES |

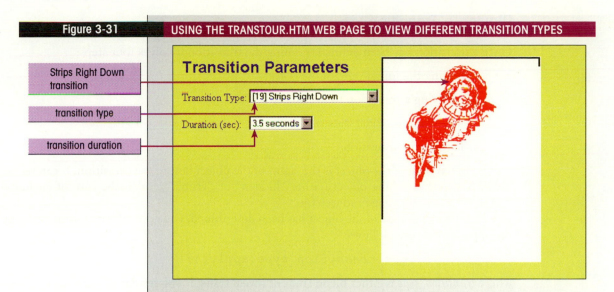

Strips Right Down transition

transition type

transition duration

TROUBLE? If you're running Netscape, you will not be able to see these transition effects.

3. Continue going through the list of transition effects.

4. To change the duration, select a duration time from the Duration drop-down list box.

5. Close the Web page when you're finished.

Scripting Transitions

The syntax for referring to transitions is the same as for filters. To set the duration value for a blend transition you can either specify a text string as follows:

```
object.style.filter = "blendTrans(Duration = 2)";
```

or use the filters collection:

```
object.filters.blendTrans.Duration = 2;
```

where *object* is the name of the object to which you want to apply the transition.

Similarly, the JavaScript commands for working with reveal transitions can be of the form:

```
object.style.filter = "revealTrans(Duration = 2,
Transition = 5)";
```

or

```
object.filters.revealTrans.Duration = 2;
object.filters.revealTrans.Transition = 5;
```

Once again, if you use a filters collection, you must define the filter style in the style sheet for the object.

Playing a Transition

Once a transition has been defined, running the transition involves four steps:

1. Setting the initial state of the object

2. Applying a transition to the object

3. Specifying the final state of the object

4. Playing the transition

The initial state of the object is the status of the object before the transition. It can be the visibility property of the object (either "hidden" or "visible"), or in the case of an inline image, it can be the image's source file.

Once the initial state of the object has been determined, you apply the transition by using the apply() method as follows:

```
object.filters.transition_type.apply();
```

where *transition_type* is either blendTrans or revealTrans. If you have multiple filters defined for the object, it may be easier to use the filters collection syntax:

```
object.filters[i].apply();
```

where *i* is the index number of the filter.

Applying the transition does not actually run the transition, because the final state of the object has not been indicated yet. If the transition causes an object to move from a visible to a hidden state (or vice versa), the final state will be object's visibility. If the transition is being used to swap one image with another, the final state will be the new source of the image file.

After you've defined the final state of the object, you use the play() method to run the transition effect. The syntax is:

```
object.filters.transition_type.play();
```

or equivalently:

```
object.filters[i].play();
```

The following code demonstrates how to create a transition between two sources for an inline image.

```
<STYLE>
    #Img1 {filter: revealTrans(Duration = 2, Transition = 6)}
</STYLE>
<SCRIPT>
    function SwapIt() {
        Img1.filters.revealTrans.apply();
        Img1.src = "Image2.jpg";
        Img1.filters.revealTrans.play();
    }
</SCRIPT>

<IMG NAME=Img1 SRC="Image1.jpg" onClick = "SwapIt()">
```

The object in this case is the inline image named "Img1." Initially, the image uses the Image1.jpg source file. When the user clicks the inline image, the SwapIt() function is called. The browser then applies a transition, replacing the source of the image with the Image2.jpg graphic file (see Figure 3-32).

Figure 3-32   **CREATING A TRANSITION BETWEEN TWO IMAGE FILES**

image1.jpg	playing the Wipe Right transition	image2.jpg

To create a fade-in or fade-out transition, you would use the same basic structure, except that the initial and final states are based on the object's visibility. The following is an example of a transition that is applied to some text on the page.

```
<STYLE>
   #Hamlet {position: absolute; visibility: visible;
           filter: blendTrans(Duration=2)}
</STYLE>
<SCRIPT>
function FadeOut() {
   Hamlet.filters.blendTrans.apply();
   Hamlet.style.visibility="hidden";
   Hamlet.filters.blendTrans.play();
}
</SCRIPT>
<DIV ID=Hamlet onClick="FadeOut()">
   <H1>The Rest is Silence</H1>
</DIV>
```

In this example, the text string "The Rest is Silence" will fade out when the user clicks on it, changing its state from visible to hidden. Note that because this is a <DIV> tag, we have to define an absolute position before the transition can be applied. The <SPAN> tag has a similar requirement.

REFERENCE   WINDOW   **RW**

Playing a Transition

- To play a transition, first set the initial state of the object (either its visibility property, or, in the case of an image object, the source of the image.
- Then apply the transition effect to the object, using the syntax:

  `object.filters.transition_type.apply();`

  where *transition_type* is either blendTrans or revealTrans.
- Then specify the final state in which the object will be after the transition.
- Finally, play the transition, using the syntax:

  `object.filters.transition_type.play();`

Adding a Transition to the Plays Page

You discuss the use of transitional effects in Internet Explorer with Clare. Clare wonders whether you can use the Wipe Down transition when the user selects a menu from the page. Clare's idea is that when the menu is displayed, the Wipe Down transition will be activated, giving the illusion of a menu unwrapping. Figure 3-33 demonstrates Clare's idea. Remember that Netscape users won't be able to see this effect, but they will still be able to use the menus as before.

Figure 3-33 | **APPLYING THE WIPE DOWN TRANSITION TO A MENU**

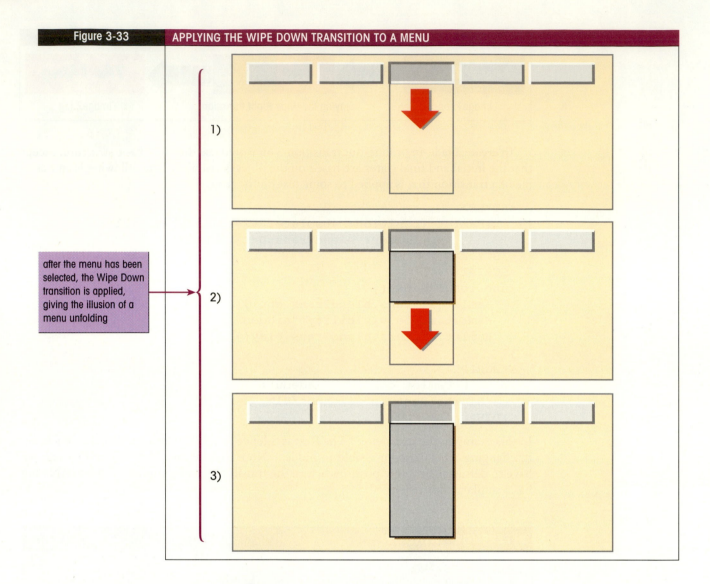

after the menu has been selected, the Wipe Down transition is applied, giving the illusion of a menu unfolding

The Wipe Down transition has a numeric value of 5 on the list of Internet Explorer transitions. You decide to allow one second for the transition.

To add this effect, you need to create a function named WipeMenu() that will apply the Wipe Down transition effect to a menu. To create the illusion, the menu will be initially hidden, and as the transition is applied, more and more of the menu will become visible. The WipeMenu() command will look as follows:

```
function WipeMenu(M) {
    var Menu=eval(M);
    Menu.style.filter="revealTrans(Duration = 1.0, Transition
= 5)";
    Menu.style.visibility = "hidden";
    Menu.filters.revealTrans.Apply();
    Menu.style.visibility = "visible";
    Menu.filters.revealTrans.Play();
}
```

The WipeMenu() function has only one parameter, M, which is the ID of the menu. Since this is a text string, you have to use the eval() function to create an object variable named "Menu," which points to the selected menu. The next line in the function applies the revealTrans transition to the menu. The function then sets the initial state of the menu; in this case it is hiding it. The third line of the function applies the Wipe Down transition, changing the state of the menu from hidden to visible. The final line of the function plays the transition effect.

To insert the WipeMenu() function:

1. Return to the Plays.htm file in your text editor.

2. Before the first </SCRIPT> tag, insert the following command lines (see Figure 3-34):

```
function WipeMenu(M) {
var Menu=eval(M);
Menu.style.filter="revealTrans(Duration = 1.0,
Transition = 5)";
Menu.style.visibility = "hidden";
Menu.filters.revealTrans.Apply();
Menu.style.visibility = "visible";
Menu.filters.revealTrans.Play();
}
```

Figure 3-34   CREATING THE WIPEMENU() FUNCTION

```
function WipeMenu(M) {
    var Menu=eval(M);
    Menu.style.filter="revealTrans(Duration = 1.0, Transition = 5)";
    Menu.style.visibility = "hidden";
    Menu.filters.revealTrans.Apply();
    Menu.style.visibility = "visible";
    Menu.filters.revealTrans.Play();
}
</SCRIPT>
<SCRIPT SRC="API.js"></SCRIPT>
```

3. Save your changes to the file.

To run the WipeMenu() function, you add a command to the PullMenu() function you created in the last session. The idea is to have the PullMenu() function open the menu, and *then* apply the transition effect. Since transitions work only with Internet Explorer, you need to include an IF statement that tests whether the browser being used is Internet Explorer.

To call the WipeMenu() function:

1. Locate the PullMenu() function in the file.

2. Before the command applying the Alpha filter to the Summary object, insert the following command (see Figure 3-35):

```
if (isIE) WipeMenu(M);
```

Figure 3-35   CALLING THE WIPEMENU() FUNCTION

run the Wipe Down transition with the newly opened menu

```
function PullMenu(M) {
    HideMenu();
    clipIt(M, 0, 130, 600, 0);
    if (isIE) WipeMenu(M);
    if (isIE) Summary.style.filter="Alpha(Opacity=30)";
    ActiveMenu=M;
}
```

3. Save your changes.

4. Open the **Plays.htm** file in your Web browser. Verify that, as you pass your mouse pointer over the menu titles, the menu opens, simulating a pull-down effect.

5. Close the **Plays.htm** file in your text editor.

   TROUBLE? If you are using Netscape, you will not see any pull-down effect in the menus.

Using Interpage Transitions

You can also create transitions between one Web page and another. These **interpage transitions** involve effects applied to the page when the browser either enters or exits the page. Interpage transitions are created by using the <META> tag within the head section of the HTML file. The <META> tag specifies the type of transition, the duration, and whether it's applied on entering or exiting the page.

The syntax for creating an interpage transition is:

```
<META http-equiv = "Page-Enter" CONTENT = "transition_type">
<META http-equiv = "Page-Exit" CONTENT = "transition_type">
```

where *transition_type* is one of the transitions supported by Internet Explorer. The syntax for the transition type is the same for interpage transition as it is for an object within a page. Note that these transitions appear only when you go from one page to another. You will not see the Page-Enter transition if the page is the first file you open when starting your Web browser.

REFERENCE WINDOW   **RW**

Creating an Interpage Transition
- To create an interpage transition when either entering or exiting a Web page, use the HTML tags:
  ```
  <META http-equiv = "Page-Enter" CONTENT = "transition_type">
  <META http-equiv = "Page-Exit" CONTENT = "transition_type">
  ```
  where *transition_type* is one of the transitions supported by Internet Explorer.

To display a Box Out transition with a duration of 3 seconds when the user enters the page, insert the following <META> tag in the head section of the HTML file:

```
<META http-equiv = "Page-Enter" CONTENT =
"revealTrans(Transition = 1, Duration = 3)">
```

To use a 3-second blend transition upon exiting the page, use the <META> tag:

```
<META http-equiv = "Page-Exit" CONTENT
= "blendTrans(Duration = 3)">
```

Clare suggests that you modify the WS.htm file, so that it runs a 3-second Wipe Up transition whenever the user exits the page.

To insert the Wipe Up interpage transition:

1. Open the **WS.htm** file in your text editor.

2. After the <HEAD> tag, insert the following <META> tag, as shown in Figure 3-36:

```
<META http-equiv = "Page-Exit"
 CONTENT = "revealTrans(Duration = 3, Transition = 4)">
```

Figure 3-36 CREATING AN INTERPAGE TRANSITION

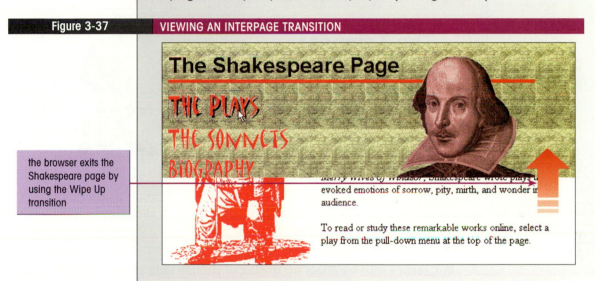

run the transition when the browser exits the page

use a duration of 3 seconds

use the Wipe Up transition

3. Save your changes to the WS.htm file.

4. Open **WS.htm** in your Web browser.

5. Click **The Plays** hyperlink and verify that as the browser exits the Shakespeare page, the Wipe Up transition is played (see Figure 3-37).

Figure 3-37 VIEWING AN INTERPAGE TRANSITION

the browser exits the Shakespeare page by using the Wipe Up transition

You've completed your work on Clare's Web site, for now. Clare is pleased with the special effects that you've created for her. She feels that they add a lot of visual interest to the page. As she adds more pages to her Web site, she'll get back to you for more assistance.

Session 3.3 QUICK CHECK

1. What style declaration would you enter to flip an inline image in the vertical direction?

2. What JavaScript command would you enter to apply the Blur filter to an object named "Logo"?

3. What JavaScript command would you enter to store the opacity level of an object named "Logo" in a variable named "OpLevel"?

4. Name and describe the two types of transitions supported by Internet Explorer.

5. What effect would the transition revealTrans(Duration = 3 , Transition = 2) have on an object? How long would the transition effect last?

6. What JavaScript command would you use to store the duration of the Logo object's first filter in a variable named DLevel?

7. What HTML tag would you enter to create a random transition effect lasting 2 seconds, whenever the HTML file is opened by the browser?

REVIEW ASSIGNMENTS

Clare is pleased with the work you did on the two Shakespeare pages. She now wants you to work on the design for the opening screen for a page on Shakespeare's play *The Tempest*. In this page, you'll employ some of the features you used in the WS.htm and Plays.htm files.

A preview of the page you'll create is shown in Figure 3-38.

Figure 3-38

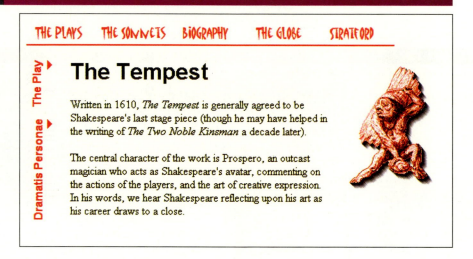

Your job will include the following tasks:

- Create a rollover effect for the list of graphic links at the top of the page, so that when a user passes the mouse pointer over one of the five links, a drop shadow appears.

- Add a drop shadow to the graphic image of Caliban, located on the right edge of the page.

- Create a pop-up menu that appears when a user clicks the graphic images, "The Play", or "Dramatis Personae". Have the pop-up menu disappear when the user clicks anywhere within the description of the play.

- Add the Wipe Right transition effect to the pop-up menu.

- Add the Box Out interpage transition, to be run when the user initially enters the page.

Much of the work in setting up the page has been done for you. The two pop-up menus have been stored within <DIV> tags with the ID names ThePlay and Dramatis. You'll use these ID names to identify which pop-up menu to display.

The HTML file also contains a link to an API file, named API.js. The API file creates two variables, isNS and isIE, that determine the type of browser in use. The file also contains two functions, hideIt() and showIt(), which can be used to hide and show the pop-up menus.

To create the Web page for *The Tempest*:

1. Open the **Temptxt.htm** file from the Tutorial.03D/Review folder on your Data Disk in your text editor and save it as **Tempest.htm**.

2. Create two image arrays named ImgOver and ImgOut. Populate the ImgOver array with the following images: **PlaysOver.gif**, **SonOver.gif**, **BioOver.gif**, **GlobeOver.gif**, and **StratOver.gif**. Populate the ImgOut array with the image files: **PlaysOut.gif**, **SonOut.gif**, **BioOut.gif**, **GlobeOut.gif**, and **StratOut.gif**. Use the arrays created in the first session of this tutorial as your model.

3. Create a function named RollOver() with a single parameter named "i." Have the function test whether the user's browser supports the document.images() collection, and if so, swap the ith image from the document.images() collection with the ith image from ImgOver array. Create a similar function named RollOut(), that swaps the ith image from the document.images() collection with the ith image from ImgOut array.

4. Add onMouseOver and onMouseOut event handlers to the <A> tags for the **PlaysOut.gif**, **SonOut.gif**, **BioOut.gif**, **GlobeOut.gif**, and **StratOut.gif** inline images. When the user passes the mouse over these images, run the RollOver() function, using the image's index number from the document.images() collection. Similarly, run the RollOut() function with the appropriate index number, when the user passes the mouse out from each image.

5. The two pop-up menus belong to the Links class. Add a style attribute to the Links class, setting the visibility attribute to "hidden."

6. Create a variable named ActiveMenu that will contain the name of the active pop-up menu. Set the initial value of ActiveMenu to "".

7. Create a function named HideMenu(), whose purpose is to hide the active menu. Have the function test whether the value of the ActiveMenu variable is not equal to "". If that is the case, hide the active menu (using the hideIt() function from the API file), and set the value of the ActiveMenu variable to "". (*Hint:* Use the HideMenu() function from this tutorial as a model for your function.)

8. Create a function named TransMenu() with a single parameter, M—the name of one of the two pop-up menus on the page. The TransMenu function should run a revealTrans transition, moving the visibility property of the pop-up menu from hidden to visible over the space of 5 seconds. Use a Wipe Right transition filter. (*Hint:* Refer to the TransMenu() function described in the tutorial.)

Explore ▶ 9. Create a function named PopMenu() with a single parameter variable, M. The M parameter will contain the name of a pop-up menu to be displayed. Have the PopMenu() function first hide the active menu by calling the HideMenu() function you just created. Then, if the user is running the Netscape browser call the showIt() function from the API file, using M as the parameter value; otherwise, call the TransMenu() function with the M parameter value. Finally change the value of the ActiveMenu variable to the value of the M parameter. (*Hint:* Use the PullMenu() function from this tutorial as a model for the PopMenu() function.)

10. Add event handlers to the **Links1.gif** and **Links2.gif** inline images, running the PopMenu() function when the user presses the mouse button down on the images. For the **Links1.gif** image, use the parameter value "ThePlay" in place of the M parameter. For the **Links2.gif** image, use the parameter value "Dramatis."

11. For the <A> tag that surrounds the description of the play, insert an event handler that runs the HideMenu() function when the user presses the mouse button down on the play summary.

Explore ▶ 12. Add a drop shadow filter to the **Caliban.gif** graphic. Set the direction of the shadow to 145 degrees.

Explore ▶ 13. Add an interpage transition to the file, running the Box Out transition over an interval of 1 second whenever a user enters the page.

14. Print the HTML code of the Tempest.htm file.

15. Open **Tempest.htm** in your Web browser. Verify that as you pass the mouse pointer over the list of links at the top of the top of the page, a drop shadow appears behind the link names. Also test that as you click the graphic images "The Play" and "Dramatis," menus pop up with links for the individual scenes and characters from the play. Verify that these pop-up menus disappear whenever you click the description of the play.

16. If you are running Internet Explorer, verify that a drop shadow appears behind the inline image of Caliban, located at the right edge of the page. Test whether the Wipe Right transition is run when you open the pop-up menus. Finally, enter the Tempest.htm page from another page and test whether the Box Out transition is run.

CASE PROBLEMS

Case 1. Creating a Slide Show for Prospect Realty Connie Peres of Prospect Realty in Vale Park, Colorado, has asked you to help her with the design of Web pages detailing the company's listings. Each listing will have its own page with a brief introductory paragraph, a table of specific information, and a collection of photos of the property.

Connie would like to see the photos organized in a slide show. Potential buyers would click buttons to move forward and backward through the slide show. If you could add some transitional effects to the slide show to increase the visual impact, Connie thinks that would be great. A preview of the page you'll create is shown in Figure 3-39.

Figure 3-39

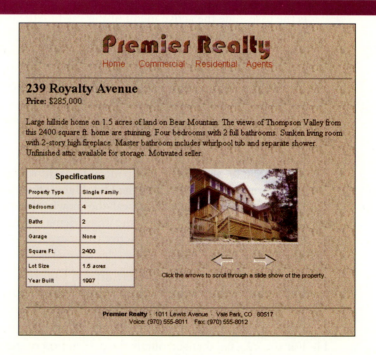

Much of the initial layout of the page has already been done for you. A few JavaScript commands have been inserted, creating two variables, isNS and isIE, that will allow you to distinguish between the Netscape and Internet Explorer browsers.

The photos for the slide show have been stored in 12 JPEG files, named in consecutive order, starting with **Slide00.jpg** and finishing with **Slide11.jpg**. The initial photo displayed in the page is Slide00.jpg. The name of the inline image in the HTML file is "Slide."

In addition, graphic images for the left and right arrow buttons have been provided. The graphic files, **LDown.gif** and **LUp.gif**, display the left arrow button when it is pressed down and released back up. Similarly, the down and up positions of the right arrow button are stored in the **RDown.gif** and **RUp.gif** files. The names of these two inline images in the HTML file are LeftArrow and RightArrow.

When a user clicks the left arrow in the slide show, the page should display the previous graphic image in the list. For example, if the user is viewing Slide05.jpg, clicking the left arrow should retrieve Slide04.jpg. Clicking the right arrow moves the user up in the list of images. When the beginning of the list is reached, the slide show should jump to the end of the list. Similarly, when the user reaches the end of the slide show, they should jump back to the beginning.

When Internet Explorer users click the left arrow button, the Wipe Right transition should be played as the page swaps the image files. When Internet Explorer users click the right arrow button, the Wipe Left transition should be used. Netscape users will not see these transition effects.

To create the Slide show:

1. In your text editor, open the **Housetxt.htm** file from the Tutorial.03D/Cases folder on your Data Disk. Save the file as **House.htm** in the same folder.

2. Within the <SCRIPT> tags at the top of the page, create four image objects named RUp, RDown, LUp, and LDown. Set the source of these four image objects as **RUp.gif**, **RDown.gif**, **LUp.gif**, and **LDown.gif**.

3. Create four functions named LIn(), LOut(), RIn(), and ROut(). Have the LIn() function set the source of the LeftArrow inline image to the source of the LDown image object. In the LOut() function, set the source of the LeftArrow inline image to the source of the LUp image object. Add similar code to the RIn() and ROut() functions, except modifying the source of the RightArrow inline image.

4. Add event handlers to the <A> tag that surrounds the LeftArrow inline image. Run the LIn() function when the user presses the mouse button down. Run the LOut() function when the user releases the mouse button. Make similar changes to the <A> tag that surrounds the RightArrow inline image.

5. Save your changes to the file, and open the page in your browser. Verify that the left and right arrows change appearance when you press them with your mouse button and then release it.

6. Return to the House.htm file in your text editor. Within the <SCRIPT> tag, create an image array named "Slides" that contains image objects for each of the 12 slide graphic files. Start your array with an index value of 0, and continue up through an index value of 11.

7. Create a variable named SlideNum that will store the index number of the currently displayed slide. Set the initial value of SlideNum to 0.

8. Create a function named Back(). In the Back() function, test whether the value of SlideNum equals zero. If so, set the value of SlideNum to 11, otherwise reduce the value of SlideNum by 1. If the user is running a Netscape browser, set the source of the Slide inline image to the source of the Slides image array object whose index value is equal to SlideNum; otherwise, have the browser run a function named "TransLeft()."

9. Create a function named Forward(). In the Forward function, test whether the value of SlideNum equals 11. If so, set the value of SlideNum back to zero, otherwise increase the value of SlideNum by 1. If the user is running a Netscape browser, set the source of the Slide inline image to the source of the Slides image array object with an index value of SlideNum; otherwise, have the browser run a function named "TransRight()."

10. At the top of the file, insert a global style attribute for the Slide inline image and create a revealTrans filter with a duration of 1 second. Do not specify any transition type.

Explore

11. Within the <SCRIPT> tags at the top of the HTML file, create a function named TransLeft(). The TransLeft() function should apply and play a Wipe Right transition to the Slide inline image, changing the source of the Slide inline image to the source of the Slides image array object whose index value is equal to SlideNum.

12. Create a similar function named TransRight, expect that this function should apply the Wipe Left transition to the Slide inline image.

13. Return to the onMouseDown event handler, and run the Back() function in addition to the LIn() function when the user presses the mouse button down on the left arrow.

14. Modify the onMouseDown event handler for the right arrow so that the browser runs the Forward() function in addition to the RIn() function when the user presses the mouse button down.

15. Save your changes to the House.htm file, and print your HTML code.

16. Open the **House.htm** file in your Web browser, and verify that when you press the left arrow button under the house image, the browser scrolls back through the slide show. Also test that when you press the right arrow button, the browser moves forward through the slide show.

17. If you are running Internet Explorer, verify that when you move forward through the slide show, a Wipe Left transition is used, and when you move backward through the slide show, the browser applies a Wipe Right transition.

Case 2. Creating a Concentration Game for Games Etc. Games Etc. is a company that specializes in games and puzzles. Part of the company's Web site includes online games for customers to enjoy while shopping around. Pete Burdette, the supervisor of the Web Site development team, has asked you to help create a Concentration game. In Concentration, images are turned over on a table, and the object is to turn over matched pairs of images, until all of the images have been turned over. Pete has set up a board with eight pairs of images laid out in a four by four grid. The eight images for the game have been stored in JPEG files with the names **Image1.jpg** through **Image8.jpg**. An additional image file, **Tile.jpg**, represents the tile when the image is turned over. A preview of this page is shown in Figure 3-40.

Figure 3-40

Pete wants you to program part of this page. Some of the programming has already been done for you and is stored in the file, **Tiles.js**. The Tiles.js file creates an array named Tiles, containing 16 image objects, representing the 16 possible tile images. The first image object is Tiles[0] and represents the tile located in the first row and first column of the game board. The last image object is Tiles[15] and represents the tile in the last row and column. The source for each of the 16 image objects is randomly assigned, and will change each time the page is reopened.

Your job will be to program the action of the game. The rules are as follows:

- A tile is turned over by clicking the tile image with the mouse.
- If the player turns over two tiles with the same image, the tiles remain face up on the board.
- If the player turns over tiles with different images, the tiles are flipped over after ³⁄₁₀ of a second.
- A player can view the complete solution to the puzzle by clicking the Show All button on the page.
- A player can reload the page, and thus scramble the order of the tiles, by clicking the Reload Tiles button.

To program this page, you'll need three variables named FlipCount, Tile1, and Tile2. The FlipCount variable counts the number of tiles that have been flipped within a single turn (either 0, 1, or 2). The Tile1 variable will record the index number of the first tile the player flips over. The Tile2 variable will record the index number of the second tile flipped over.

To create the Slide show:

1. In your text editor, open the **Tilestxt.htm** file from the Tutorial.03D/Cases folder on your Data Disk. Save the file as **Tiles.htm** in the same folder.

2. Within the Head section of the HTML file, create a link to the **Tiles.js** API file.

3. Below the link, insert another set of <SCRIPT> tags, and create three variables named FlipCount, Tile1, and Tile2. Set the initial value of the FlipCount variable to zero.

Explore ▶ 4. Create a function named Flip() with a single parameter, i. The purpose of the Flip() function will be to swap the source of an inline image on the game board with an image from the Tiles image object array. The Flip() function will be run whenever a player clicks a tile on the board. Add the following commands to the Flip() function:

- Replace the source of the ith object in the document.images collection with the ith object in the Tiles array.
- Increase the value of the FlipCount variable by 1.
- If the value of the FlipCount variable is 1, store the value of i in the Tile1 variable.
- If the value of the FlipCount variable is 2, store the value of i in the Tile2 variable. Then, test whether the source of the image for the first tile turned over is equal to the source of the image for the second tile turned over (*Hint:* Use the document.images collection to determine the source of the two images.) If the sources are not the same, run a function named "FlipBack()," after ³⁄₁₀ of a second. Finally, set the value of the FlipCount variable back to zero.

5. Create a function named FlipBack(). Use the values of the Tile1 and Tile2 variables to change the image source for those two tiles back to **Tile.jpg**.

Explore ▶ 6. Create a function named ShowAll(). The purpose of ShowAll() is to loop through the first 16 image objects on the page, and for each ith inline image, display the ith image object from the Tiles array.

7. Locate the 16 inline images for the Concentration board. For each <A> tag surrounding those inline images, add an event handler to run the Flip() function whenever the user clicks the mouse button down on a tile. The Flip() function should have one parameter value — the index number of the inline image in the document.images collection.

8. Locate the Reload Tiles button at the bottom of the HTML file. When this button is clicked, have the browser reload the page.

9. Locate the Show Tiles button. When this button is clicked, have the browser run the ShowAll() function.

10. Save your changes to the Tiles.htm file and print the file.

11. Open **Tiles.htm** in your Web browser. Play the game and test whether pairs of unlike tiles are automatically flipped over after a brief interval. Verify that pairs of like tiles remain face up. Click the Show Tiles button and confirm that it displays the location of all of the tiles. Click the Reload Tiles button and verify that it randomizes the order of the tiles on the game board.

Case 3. Creating a Splash Screen for Scavenger Scavenger is a Web site that provides users with state-of-the-art search tools and utilities. By logging on to Scavenger, users can search phone directories, yellow pages, Web sites, and even maps. Lori Vandzandt, who works on the Web site development team, has approached you about designing an opening splash screen for the site. She envisions a red light moving across the page, "searching" for the company's logo. The light eventually illuminates the entire logo. When the user clicks on the logo, Scavenger's home page is then displayed (Lori tells you that this page is still under construction). Lori would like you to apply a blend interpage transition when a user moves from the opening page to the home page. Figure 3-41 shows a preview of the opening page in action.

Figure 3-41

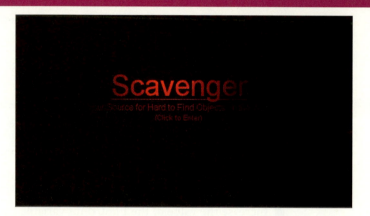

To display this effect, you need to create a dynamic filter with the Internet Explorer Light filter, employing both the addPoint() and MoveLight() methods. You'll start by defining a light source using the addPoint() method and then move the light to the right, left, and finally up (in the z-direction) above the page.

To create the Scavenger opening page:

1. In your text editor, open the **Scavtxt.htm** file from the Tutorial.03D/Cases folder on your Data Disk. Save the file as **Scav.htm** in the same folder.

2. Add the style attribute filter:Light() to the style for the Logo object. Do not specify any parameters for this filter.

3. Above the </BODY> tag, insert a two-sided <SCRIPT> tag.

Explore   4. Using the addPoint() method, add a light source to the Logo object centered at the (x, y) coordinate, (35, 0), and lying 30 pixels above the page in the z-direction. Use an RGB value of (255,0,0) for the light source. Set the strength of the light source to 350.

5. Create a variable name "Count" and set its initial value to 0.

Explore

6. Create a function named "MoveRight()," which you'll use to move the light source to the right. The MoveRight() function should perform the following tasks:

   ■ Using the MoveLight() method, move the light source a distance of 10 pixels in the y-direction (*Hint:* Use a value of zero for the light source number, and "false" for the value of the absolute parameter).

   ■ Increase the value of the Count variable by 1.

   ■ If the value of the Count variable is less than or equal to 40, call the MoveRight() function again after a delay of 125 milliseconds, otherwise call the MoveLeft() function.

7. Create a function named "MoveLeft()," which you'll use to move the light source to the left. The MoveLeft() function should perform the following:

   ■ Move the light source a distance of 10 pixels in the left direction (*Hint:* Use a value of -10 for the y parameter of the MoveLight() method.

   ■ Reduce the value of the Count variable by 1.

   ■ If the value of Count variable is greater than or equal to 25, call the MoveLeft() function again after a delay of 125 milliseconds, otherwise set the value of the Count variable to 0, and call the moveUp() function.

8. Create the moveUp() function, whose purpose is to create the illusion of the light source moving higher above the page. The moveUp() function should do the following:

   ■ Move the light source up 10 pixels in the z-direction.

   ■ Increase the value of the Count variable by 1.

   ■ If the value of the Count variable is less than or equal to 30, call the MoveUp() function again after a delay of 125 milliseconds; otherwise, end the function.

9. At the top of the page, insert an interpage blend transition that runs for a duration of 2 seconds.

10. Print a copy of the Scav.htm file and close your text editor.

11. Open **Scav.htm** in your Internet Explorer Web browser, and verify that a red light source appears to move right and then left and then high above the page.

12. Click the link to the Start.htm file and verify that the browser performs a blend transition over a duration of 2 seconds.

Case 4. Creating Product Pages for Jackson Electronics You work for Paul Reichtman of Jackson Electronics, a company specializing in printers and scanners. Paul has asked you to update some Web pages that describe three of the company's products: the ScanMaster, the LaserPrint 5000, and the Print/Scan 150. Information on these three products can be found in the files, **Scantxt.htm**, **Printtxt.htm**, and **PS150txt.htm**, respectively.

Paul would like you insert graphical links between these three pages. He's supplied you with three graphic files named **SM1.gif**, **LP1.gif**, and **PS1.gif**. He's also supplied "rollover" versions of these files, named **SM2.gif**, **LP2.gif**, and **PS2.gif**.

To create the Web site for Jackson Electronics:

1. Create three files named **Scanner.htm**, **Printer.htm**, and **PS150.htm**, containing the information on the ScanMaster, the LaserPrint 5000, and the Print/Scan 150.

2. Each page should have graphical links to the other files, with rollover effects. The layout of the pages is up to you.

3. Add an interpage transition effect to each page; display a random transition whenever the user exits these pages.

4. Print copies of the HTML files for each of the three pages you create.

5. Print copies of the three pages as they appear in your Web browser.

QUICK CHECK ANSWERS

Session 3.1

1. ```
document.Links
document.images[1]
```

2. ```
document.Links.width=150;
document.Links.height=200;
```

3. ```
document.Links.src="Links2.jpg";
```

4. ```
var LinksOver = new Image(75, 100);
```

5. ```
<A HREF="Links.htm"
    onMouseOver='document.LINK.src="Links2.jpg"'
    onMouseOut='document.LINK.src="Links.jpg"'
    <IMG NAME=LINK SRC="Links.jpg">
</A>
```

6. ```
var LinksArray = new Array();
LinksArray[0] = new Image();
LinksArray[1] = new Image();
LinksArray[2] = new Image();
LinksArray[0].src = Img1.src;
LinksArray[1].src = Img2.src;
LinksArray[2].src = Img2.src;
```

7. ```
if (document.images)
```

### Session 3.2

1. In a pop-up menu, the user clicks an object on the page and the menu appears, perhaps elsewhere on the page.

2. In a pull-down menu, part of the menu is visible. When the user either clicks the visible part, or moves a mouse pointer over it, the rest of the menu is revealed.

3. It does not support the onMouseOver or onMouseOut events.

4. Enclosing the <DIV> tag within a set of <A> tags.

5. ```
Menu.style.clip="rect(10,100,150,20)";
```

6. ```
document.Menu.clip.top=10;
document.Menu.clip.right=100;
document.Menu.clip.bottom=150;
document.Menu.clip.left=20;
```

### Session 3.3

1. filter: FlipV();

2. ```
document.Logo.style.filter = "Blur()";
```

3. ```
OpLevel = Logo.filters.Alpha.Opacity;
```

4. A blend transition fades an object in and out of view. A reveal transition allows you to specify a transition effect as one object is replaced with another.

5. This would create a Circle In transition lasting 3 seconds.

6. ```
DLevel = Logo.filters[0].blendTrans.Duration;
```

7. ```
<META http-equiv = "Page-Enter" CONTENT =
"revealTrans(Transition=23, Duration=2)">
```
```

In this tutorial you will:

- Investigate ways of running event handlers

- Learn about the Netscape and Internet Explorer event models

- Learn how to respond to mouse actions

- Learn how to create drag-and-drop objects on your Web page

- Learn how to respond to keyboard actions

WORKING WITH THE EVENT MODEL

Creating a Drag-and-Drop Shopping Cart for Games Etc.

CASE

Games Etc.

Games Etc. is a company that sells puzzles and games. Recently, they've decided to put their merchandise online. You've been hired to help in the effort. Your supervisor, Pete Burdette, has asked you to create a Web page for the monthly specials offered by Games Etc. The page should allow users to select which of the specials they want to purchase from a list of items.

Because of the nature of the company, Pete wants to have an interface that incorporates various elements of board games. For example, rather than clicking a check box to select an item, Pete would like to see users click and drag the items into a shopping cart area—much as games pieces are moved on a game board. Thus the elements on the page won't be fixed in one place; rather, the user will be able to move them around.

To add this feature to the Games Etc. Web page, you have to work with the event models of Netscape and Internet Explorer, and learn how to make the Web page respond to mouse and keyboard actions that are initiated by the user.

SESSION 4.1

In this session you'll learn about event handlers and the three different ways that you can run an event handler. You'll learn about event models, and you'll examine how Netscape and Internet Explorer implement event models in their Web browsers. You'll also examine the differences between the two models in order to create a cross-browser Web page that supports both event models.

Setting Up the Games Etc. Web Page

Pete and you sit down to discuss the page you'll be working on for Games Etc. The basic layout of the page has already been created for you. Pete asks you to open the file to view its current layout.

To open the Games Etc. Web page:

1. In your text editor, open the **Gamestxt.htm** file located in the Tutorial.04D folder of your Data Disk.

2. Save the file as **Games.htm**.

3. Open the page in your Web browser (see Figure 4-1).

Figure 4-1   THE GAMES ETC. PAGE PETE CREATED

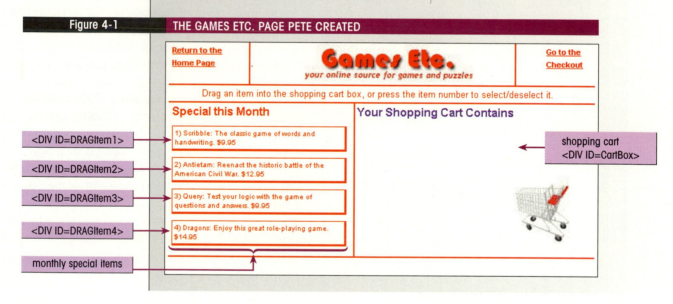

The Games Etc. page has two boxes displayed side by side. The box on the left shows the four specials for the current month. The box on the right will be used to display the items the user has decided to purchase. This box will act as a "shopping cart" for the prospective customer.

Many of the objects on the page have been placed within separate <DIV> container tags and placed on the page using absolute positioning. In particular, each of the four monthly specials is stored within a different <DIV> tag. Figure 4-1 indicates the ID names for these four items. Take some time to study the HTML code in this file to become familiar with the ID names and positions of the various page elements.

As shown in Figure 4-2, Pete would like you to modify the page so that each of the monthly special items in the left box can be dragged and dropped into the shopping cart box. Then, when the user clicks the "Go to the Checkout" hyperlink, a CGI script can be run that totals the cost of the selected items and prompts the user for additional purchase information. Your task is to program the drag-and-drop aspect of this page. Someone else will create the CGI script.

Figure 4-2   **HOW DRAG AND DROP WILL LOOK IN THE GAMES ETC. WEB PAGE**

To assist you in programming this page, Pete has supplied an API file that contains several customized functions that handle various cross-browser issues. Figure 4-3 describes the different functions available in the API. You'll be adding some additional functions to this API file as you work on the Games Etc. page.

Figure 4-3   **CUSTOM FUNCTIONS IN THE GAMESAPI.JS FILE**

FUNCTION	DESCRIPTION
getObject(o)	Converts the object ID string, "o," into an object reference
placeIt(object, x, y)	Places the object the page coordinate (x, y)
getXCoord(object)	Returns the x-coordinate of the object on the page
getYCoord(object)	Returns the y-coordinate of the object on the page
withinIt(x, y, object)	Returns "true" if the (x, y) coordinates lie within the boundaries of the object; returns "false" if the (x, y) coordinates lie outside the boundaries of the object
setZ(object, z)	Returns the z-index value of the object
colorIt(object, c)	Changes the text and border color of the object to "c"

In addition, the API file creates two Boolean variables that you can use in your Web page: isNS, a variable that indicates whether the browser supports the Netscape DOM, and isIE, a variable that indicates whether the browser supports the Internet Explorer DOM. Open the API file now to familiarize yourself with its contents.

To open the API file:

1. Return to your text editor and open the **Gamestxt.js** file located in the Tutorial.04D folder of your Data Disk.

2. Save the file as **GamesAPI.js**.

Review the functions in the API file. Most of these functions have been discussed in previous tutorials and should be familiar to you. One function you haven't seen before is the withinIt() function. This function has three parameters: the first two parameters represent the (x, y) coordinates of a point on the Web page, and the third parameter represents an object on the page. The withinIt() function determines whether the specified (x, y) coordinates lie within the boundary of the object. If so, the function returns a value of "true." Otherwise the function returns a value of "false." Figure 4-4 shows the code for this function.

Figure 4-4 | **THE WITHINIT FUNCTION IN THE GAMESAPI.JS FILE**

```
function withinIt(x, y, object) {
   within=false;
   if (isNS) {
      otop=object.top;
      obottom=object.top+object.clip.height;
      oleft=object.left;
      oright=object.left+object.clip.width;
   } else {
      otop=object.style.pixelTop;
      obottom=object.style.pixelTop+parseInt(object.style.height);
      oleft=object.style.pixelLeft;
      oright=object.style.pixelLeft+parseInt(object.style.width);
   }
   if ((y>otop && y<obottom) && (x>oleft && x<oright)) within=true;
   return within;
}
```

You'll have a chance to use the withinIt() function later in the tutorial. Before doing that, you'll need an overview of how Web browsers work with actions and events.

Working with Events

Pete would like the online users at Games Etc. to be able to do the following:

- Click an object on the Web page with the mouse to "grab" it
- Move the mouse pointer across the page, dragging the object along with it
- Release the mouse button, "dropping" the object into its new location on the page

In each of these tasks you need to relate the layout of the page to the actions of the mouse. You do that by working with events. Events are actions that can be initiated by the user, by the browser, or by another software program. In this case, the user, through the actions of the mouse, initiates all of the events. As you've seen in other tutorials, one of the most common ways to work with events is through an **event handler**, which specifies what response the browser has to the occurrence of an event. Event handlers can be created within an object's HTML tag, as property of an object in a JavaScript program, or within the <SCRIPT> for a collection of JavaScript code.

Event Handlers as Tag Properties

The most common and oldest way of creating an event handler is by adding an event handler property to the object's HTML tag. For example, in the following tag:

 handler

```
<INPUT TYPE=Button NAME=CALC VALUE="Calculate Total"
onClick="calc()">
```

the calc() function is run when the user clicks the button. Event handlers invoked in this way have the following characteristics:

- The event handlers are case insensitive. The browser treats event handlers named "onclick," "onClick," and "OnClick" the same.
- The event handlers are applied to specific tags on the Web page and have no influence outside that tag.
- This technique is supported by version 3.0 or above of Netscape and Internet Explorer.

Event handlers have been created for a wide variety of events. Most of these are described in Figures 4-5 through 4-9.

Figure 4-5 BROWSER EVENT HANDLERS

EVENT HANDLER	DESCRIPTION	NETSCAPE	INTERNET EXPLORER
onAbort	The transfer of an image has been aborted.	3.0	4.0
onDragDrop	A desktop icon has been dropped into the browser window or frame.	4.0	
onError	An error has occurred in the JavaScript program.	3.0	4.0
onHelp	The user has pressed the F1 key for help.		4.0
onLoad	The browser has completed loading the document.	2.0	3.0
onMove	The user has moved the browser window.	4.0	3.0
onResize	The user has resized the browser window.	4.0	4.0
onScroll	The user has moved the scrollbar.		4.0
onUnload	The browser has completed unloading the document.	2.0	3.0

Figure 4-6 FORM EVENT HANDLERS

EVENT HANDLER	DESCRIPTION	NETSCAPE	INTERNET EXPLORER
onBlur	The user has exited an input field.	2.0	3.0
onChange	The content of an input field has changed.	2.0	3.0
onFocus	The user has entered an input field.	2.0	3.0
onReset	The user has clicked the Reset button.	3.0	4.0
onSelect	The user has selected text in an input or textarea field.	2.0	3.0
onSubmit	A form has been submitted.	2.0	3.0

Figure 4-7	KEYBOARD EVENT HANDLERS		
EVENT HANDLER	**DESCRIPTION**	**NETSCAPE**	**INTERNET EXPLORER**
onKeyDown	The user has begun pressing a key.	4.0	4.0
onKeyPress	The user has pressed and released a key.	4.0	4.0
onKeyUp	The user has released a key.	4.0	4.0

Figure 4-8	MOUSE EVENT HANDLERS		
EVENT HANDLER	**DESCRIPTION**	**NETSCAPE**	**INTERNET EXPLORER**
onClick	The user has clicked the mouse button.	2.0	3.0
onDblClick	The user has double-clicked the mouse button.	4.0	4.0
onDragStart	The user has selected content by dragging the mouse pointer over it.		4.0
onMouseDown	The user has begun pressing the mouse button.	4.0	4.0
onMouseMove	The user has moved the mouse pointer.	4.0	4.0
onMouseOut	The user has moved the mouse out from an element.	3.0	4.0
onMouseOver	The user has moved the mouse over an element.	2.0	3.0
onMouseUp	The user has released the mouse button.	4.0	4.0
onSelectStart	The user is beginning to select an element.		4.0

Figure 4-9	MARQUEE EVENT HANDLERS		
EVENT HANDLER	**DESCRIPTION**	**NETSCAPE**	**INTERNET EXPLORER**
onBounce	The content of the marquee has reached the edge of the marquee.		4.0
onFinish	A marquee has finished looping.		4.0
onStart	A marquee element has begun looping.		4.0

Internet Explorer can apply these event handlers to most of the tags in your HTML file. Netscape's event handlers apply to only a few specific tags. If you're working with keyboard or mouse events, only those tags shown in Figure 4-10 can support event handlers for your actions. Thus, if you're trying to create a cross-browser Web page with support for mouse and keyboard events, you have to take into account Netscape's limitations when you apply your event handlers.

Figure 4-10 **NETSCAPE TAGS THAT SUPPORT MOUSE AND KEYBOARD EVENT HANDLERS**

EVENT HANDLER	HTML TAGS
onClick	<A>, <AREA>, <INPUT (TYPE=CHECKBOX, RADIO, RESET, SUBMIT)>
onDblClick	<A>
onKeyDown	<INPUT (TYPE=PASSWORD, TEXT)>, <TEXTAREA>
onKeyPress	<INPUT (TYPE=PASSWORD, TEXT)>, <TEXTAREA>
onKeyUp	<INPUT (TYPE=PASSWORD, TEXT)>, <TEXTAREA>
onMouseDown	<A>, <INPUT (TYPE=CHECKBOX, RADIO, RESET, SUBMIT)>
onMouseOut	<A>, <AREA>, <LAYER>
onMouseOver	<A>, <AREA>, <LAYER>
onMouseUp	<A>, <INPUT (TYPE=CHECKBOX, RADIO, RESET, SUBMIT)>, <LAYER>

One way to get around this problem is to place your page content within <A> tags with the HREF property set to #. For example, in Internet Explorer, you could run the Banner() function by using the following code:

```
<P onClick="Banner()">Display banner window</P>
```

while in Netscape, you would have to use <A> tags:

```
<P><A onClick="Banner()" HREF=#>Display banner window</A></P>
```

When you use this technique, you should change the style of the <A> tags that you are using with event handlers so that the browser does not underline the text. This hides the fact that the text is formatted as a hyperlink.

Event Handlers with <SCRIPT> Tags

Internet Explorer supports another way of invoking event handlers: through the <SCRIPT> tag. The general syntax is:

```
<SCRIPT FOR=ID EVENT=event_handler>
```

where *ID* is the ID of an element in the Web page, and *event_handler* is the event that causes the commands within the script to run. For example, the following tag:

```
<SCRIPT FOR=MouseText EVENT=onmouseover>
```

will cause the JavaScript commands entered after the <SCRIPT> tag to run when the user passes the mouse over the object on the Web page with the ID name "MouseText."
Event handlers that are created in this way have the following characteristics:

- The event handlers must be in lowercase. For example, EVENT=onmouseover is correct, while EVENT=onMouseOver isn't.
- The event handlers are applied to specific IDs on the Web page.
- The <SCRIPT> technique is supported only by versions 4.0 or above of Internet Explorer.

Because most event handlers are placed with the HTML tag for the object (to make them cross-browser-compatible), you won't usually see event handlers used in this way.

Event Handlers as Object Properties

The most flexible and powerful way to work with event handlers is as object properties. Supported by both Netscape and Internet Explorer (versions 4.0 and above), the syntax for this technique is:

```
object.event_handler=function
```

where *object* is the object that the event applies to, *event_handler* is the event, and *function* is the name of the JavaScript function that is run in response to the event. For example, to run the function StartPage when the window loads, you could run the following JavaScript command:

```
window.onload=StartPage;
```

Note that we use the name of the function. We don't call the function. It would *not* be the correct syntax to use this construction:

```
window.onload=StartPage();
```

One of the main disadvantages of handling events as object properties is that you cannot pass parameters to the function. This limits your flexibility in creating and running programs in response to events. Other characteristics of the object property method are:

■ The event handler must be in lowercase. The property onmouseover is correct, while onMouseOver isn't.

■ The event handler is applied to objects on the Web page.

■ The object property technique is supported only by version 4.0 or above of Internet Explorer and Netscape.

Another important consideration in using the object property method is that you must insert the JavaScript command *after* the HTML tag for the object. If the browser attempts to run the JavaScript command before it has loaded the object into the Web page an error will result.

REFERENCE WINDOW | **RW**

Running Event Handlers

There are three ways to run an event handler.

■ Add an event handler property to an HTML tag as follows:

```
<tag event_handler="function()">
```

■ where *tag* is the HTML tag name, *event_handler* is the name of the event handler, and *function()* is the name of the function to run in response to the event.

■ Create a <SCRIPT> tag for the event and object that receives the event (Internet Explorer only). The syntax is:

```
<SCRIPT FOR=ID EVENT=event_handler>
```

where *ID* is the ID of an element in the Web page, and *event_handler* is the event that causes the commands within the script to run.

■ Write a JavaScript command to assign an event handler to an object. The syntax is:

```
object.event_handler=function;
```

where *object* is the object that the event applies to, *event_handler* is the event, and *function* is the name of the JavaScript function that is run in response to the event.

For the task that Pete wants you to accomplish, you'll use the object property method of handling events. The reason for this is that you need to control the movements of the mouse as applied to several different objects on the Web page. It would be more cumbersome to write a separate event handlers for each object on the page. Using the object property method gives you more flexibility in writing your script. However, Netscape and Internet Explorer have different ways of defining and controlling events, and the script that you'll write will have to take these differences into account. Pete asks that you start by exploring the Netscape event model.

The Netscape **Event Model**

An **event model** specifies how the Web browser processes events. The Netscape browser handles events by beginning with the object at the top of the object hierarchy and moving down to the individual target elements. For example, the action of moving the mouse is first "noticed" by the browser window, next by the document window, and then by an object within the document. If you want your Web browser to take an action in response to an event, you must capture the event as it moves down the object hierarchy.

Capturing an Event

In Netscape, event capturing is done with either the window, document, or layer object. Capturing an event doesn't do anything except signal to the Netscape browser that an event has occurred. To capture an event, you use the JavaScript method:

```
object.captureEvents(Event.EVENT_TYPE)
```

where *object* is the object in which the event is captured, and *EVENT_TYPE* is the type of event. Note that the name of the event must be in all capital letters. You will usually capture events for the browser window or for the document. Figure 4-11 lists the various events that can be captured with Netscape.

Figure 4-11	WINDOW, DOCUMENT, AND LAYER EVENTS THAT CAN BE CAPTURED BY NETSCAPE		
	Event.ABORT	Event.KEYDOWN	Event.MOUSEUP
	Event.BLUR	Event.KEYPRESS	Event.MOVE
	Event.CHANGE	Event.KEYUP	Event.RESET
	Event.CLICK	Event.LOAD	Event.RESIZE
	Event.DBLCLICK	Event.MOUSEDOWN	Event.SCROLL
	Event.DRAGDROP	Event.MOUSEMOVE	Event.SELECT
	Event.ERROR	Event.MOUSEOUT	Event.SUBMIT
	Event.FOCUS	Event.MOUSEOVER	Event.UNLOAD

REFERENCE	WINDOW	RW

Capturing Events in Netscape

■ To capture an event in Netscape, use the JavaScript command:

```
object.captureEvents(Event.EVENT_TYPE)
```

where *object* is the object in which the event is captured (either the window, document, or a document layer), and *EVENT_TYPE* is the type of event. *EVENT_TYPE* must be in all uppercase letters.

For example, to capture the event when the user double-clicks the mouse anywhere within the browser window, you enter the command:

```
window.captureEvents(Event.DBLCLICK);
```

Here, window is the object, and DBLCLICK is the event type. If you wanted to capture only the double-clicks within the first <LAYER> tag, you would capture the event at a different level in the object hierarchy:

```
window.layers[0].captureEvents(Event.DBLCLICK);
```

Any double-clicks that occur outside this layer would be ignored by this command.

In the Games Etc. page, one of the events you'll want to capture is the action of the pointer as it moves across the document. The JavaScript command to do this is:

```
document.captureEvents(Event.MOUSEMOVE)
```

You can capture several types of events at once by separating the events with the OR operator (represented by the | symbol). The following JavaScript command captures the mousedown, mousemove, and mouseup events within the Web page document:

```
document.captureEvents(Event.MOUSEDOWN | Event.MOUSEMOVE |
Event.MOUSEUP)
```

Assigning a Function to an Event

To have the Web page respond to a captured event, you must apply a function to that event by using the object property technique discussed above. For example, to run a function named "grabIt()" when the user presses the pointer down, you first capture the mousedown event and then use the object property method to assign the grabIt() function to the event. The JavaScript code would look as follows:

```
document.captureEvents(Event.MOUSEDOWN);
document.onmousedown=grabIt;
```

Whenever the user presses the mouse button down anywhere within the document window, Netscape will run the grabIt() function in response.

Releasing an Event

You can turn off event capturing in Netscape by using the releaseEvents() method. For example, if you want the browser to initially capture the mousemove event, but then at a later point in your script, you do not need to capture that event anymore, you can turn off the capture by using the command:

```
document.releaseEvents(Event.MOUSEMOVE);
```

Events can be released and then recaptured multiple times within your program code.

Routing Events to Their Targets

You may want to run event functions for some objects and not for others. If you don't want Netscape to capture the event, but instead want to allow the event to continue to propagate down the object hierarchy without interference, you can use the routeEvents() method. For example, to route the mousemove event down the object hierarchy you could use the command:

```
document.routeEvents(Event.MOUSEMOVE);
```

Redirecting Events

The final method in Netscape that you can apply to events is the handleEvent() method. While the routeEvent() method passes events to the intended target, you can use the handleEvent() method to pass the event to a different target. For example, if you want to have a hyperlink activated no matter *where* the user clicks on the Web page, you can redirect all click events in the document to that hyperlink by using the command:

```
document.links[0].handleEvent(Event.CLICK);
```

where document.links[0] is the object reference for the first hyperlink on the page.

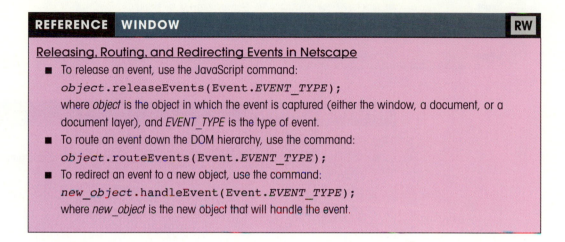

Netscape's Event Object

Every time you apply a function to an event, Netscape creates an **event object** that contains information about the event. The event object exists as a parameter in the function called when the event occurs. You can give the event object any parameter name, but the standard practice is to name the parameter "e" or "evt." For example, if you wanted to run the grabIt() function when the user presses the mouse button down, you would insert the JavaScript commands this way:

```
function grabIt(e) {
     JavaScript command block
}

document.captureEvents(Event.MOUSEDOWN);
document.onmousedown=grabIt;
```

The "e" parameter in the grabIt() function represents the mousedown event, and contains information describing that event. The properties that describe the event are shown in Figure 4-12.

Figure 4-12	PROPERTIES OF THE NETSCAPE EVENT OBJECT
PROPERTY	**DESCRIPTION**
data	The URL resulting from the dragdrop event in which a desktop item is dropped into the browser window
layerX, layerY	The coordinates of the event, relative to the layer containing the object
modifiers	An integer representing the modifier key pressed at the time of the event
pageX, pageY	The coordinates of the event, relative to the page
screenX, screenY	The coordinates of the event, relative to the screen
target	An object reference pointing to the intended target of the event
type	The string representation of the event (for example, "click")
which	An integer representing the mouse button pressed or the ASCII code of the key pressed

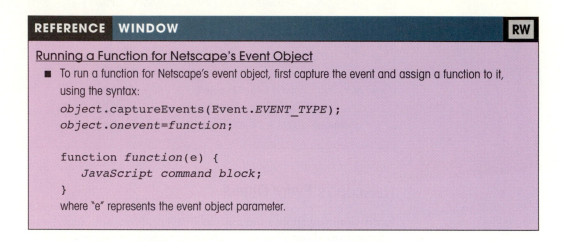

REFERENCE WINDOW   **RW**

Running a Function for Netscape's Event Object

■ To run a function for Netscape's event object, first capture the event and assign a function to it, using the syntax:

```
object.captureEvents(Event.EVENT_TYPE);
object.onevent=function;


function function(e) {
    JavaScript command block;
}
```
where "e" represents the event object parameter.

In the Games Etc. page, you'll be using the mouse to drag objects across the page. To do that, you'll need to know the location of the mouse pointer as it moves around. The following code is an example of how you can track that information, displaying it in Netscape's status bar.

```
function EventPosition(e) {
    XPosition = e.pageX;
    YPosition = e.pageY;
    window.status=XPosition+","+YPosition;
}

document.captureEvents(Event.MOUSEMOVE);
document.onmousemove=EventPosition;
```

In this example, "e" is the Netscape event object that represents the action of pressing the mouse button down, and the XPosition and YPosition variables indicate the (x, y) coordinates on the page where this event occurred. These coordinate values are then displayed in the browser's status bar.

If you have a Netscape browser, you can see this function in action by opening the CursorN.htm file.

To view the coordinates of your pointer in Netscape:

1. In your Netscape browser, open the file **CursorN.htm** (located in the Tutorial.04D folder on your Data Disk).

2. Move the pointer over the display window and observe the coordinates of the pointer as displayed in the status bar (see Figure 4-13).

| Figure 4-13 | TRACKING THE MOUSE POINTER IN NETSCAPE |

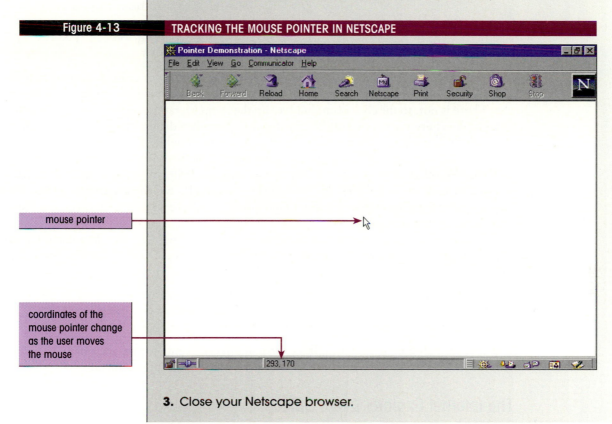

mouse pointer

coordinates of the
mouse pointer change
as the user moves
the mouse

3. Close your Netscape browser.

As you create the drag-and-drop effect for the Games Etc. page, you'll work extensively with the page coordinates of the pointer. Before doing that however, you need to examine the Internet Explorer event model so your page works under both browsers.

The Internet Explorer Event Model

While Netscape handles events from the top of the object hierarchy going down, in Internet Explorer it is just the opposite. Internet Explorer starts with events at the bottom of the object hierarchy and then works its way to the top. One result of this approach is that you can control events within individual tags in your HTML document, even down to individual letters and phrases. This level of specificity provides more flexibility for handing events and is much more difficult to achieve with the Netscape event model.

Event Bubbling

The process by which Internet Explorer tracks events is called **event bubbling**. To understand how event bubbling works, consider the following HTML code:

```
<BODY onClick='alert("You clicked the document")'>
    <P onClick='alert("You clicked a paragraph")'>
        Click to display <B> two alert dialog boxes.</B>
    </P>
    <P>This paragraph only displays one dialog box.</P>
</BODY>
```

When the user clicks the boldface text in the first paragraph, Internet Explorer checks to see if there is any event handler for the <B> tag, because that is the lowest object in the hierarchy. There is not, so the click event bubbles up the event hierarchy to the <P> tag of the first paragraph. There is an event handler for this tag, so an alert dialog box is displayed with the message "You clicked a paragraph." The click event then bubbles up to the next object in the hierarchy—the <BODY> tag. At that point another alert dialog box is displayed with the message "You clicked the document." Note that if the user clicks the text in the second paragraph, the click event bubbles up through the second <P> tag (because there is no event handler for it) and up to the <BODY> tag (which does have an event handler), displaying only one alert box instead of two.

Without event bubbling, you would have to create a separate event handler for every object that is nested within the parent element. For example, the previous tags would have to be written as:

```
<P onClick='alert("You clicked a paragraph")'>
    Click to display <B onClick='alert("You clicked a
paragraph")'>two alert dialog boxes.</B></P>
```

Thus, event bubbling greatly simplifies the handling of events within the object hierarchy. It is much more difficult to do this with Netscape's top-down approach.

The Internet Explorer Event Object

Unlike Netscape, with Internet Explorer you don't have to capture an event in order to assign a function to it. Instead, Internet Explorer supports an event object similar to the one provided by Netscape. The Internet Explorer event object provides information about each action as it occurs in the Web browser. The syntax for retrieving the properties of an event is:

```
window.event.property
```

or more simply:

```
event.property
```

where *property* is one of the Internet Explorer event properties. A list of event properties is shown in Figure 4-14.

Figure 4-14	PROPERTIES OF THE INTERNET EXPLORER EVENT OBJECTS
PROPERTY	**DESCRIPTION**
altKey, ctrlKey, shiftKey	A Boolean value indicating whether the Alt, Ctrl, and/or Shift key have been pressed
button	An integer specifying the mouse button pressed by the user
cancelBubble	A Boolean value indicating if event bubbling should be continued up the object hierarchy
clientX, clientY	The coordinates of the event, relative to the page
fromElement	The object that the mouse pointer is moving away from during a mouseover or mouseout event
keyCode	An integer specifying the Unicode key code for the key pressed by the user
offsetX, offsetY	The coordinates of the event, relative to the parent element containing the event
returnValue	A Boolean value specifying the return value from the event handler; setting the value to *false* cancels the default action of the event
screenX, screenY	The coordinates of the event, relative to the screen
srcElement	The object that initiated the event
srcFilter	The filter object that initiated the event
toElement	The object that the mouse is moving toward during a mouseover or mouseout event
type	The string representation of the event (for example, "click")

REFERENCE   WINDOW   **RW**

Retrieving an Event Property in Internet Explorer
■ To retrieve the property of an event, use the JavaScript command:
   `event.property;`
   where *property* is the event property.

For example, to display the page position of the mouse as it moves across the page in Internet Explorer, you would use the following code:

```
function EventPosition() {
    XPosition = event.clientX;
    YPosition = event.clientY;
    window.status=XPosition+","+YPosition;
}

document.onmousemove=EventPosition;
```

In this code, Internet Explorer runs the EventPosition() function whenever the pointer moves across the document window. The function records the current position of the mouse and displays that coordinate in the browser window's status bar. To see how this works in Internet Explorer, open the CursorIE.htm file.

To view the coordinates of your pointer in Internet Explorer:

1. In your Internet Explorer browser, open the file **CursorIE.htm** (located in the Tutorial.04D folder on your Data Disk).

2. Move the pointer over the display window and observe the coordinates of the pointer as displayed in the status bar (see Figure 4-15).

Figure 4-15	TRACKING THE MOUSE POINTER IN INTERNET EXPLORER

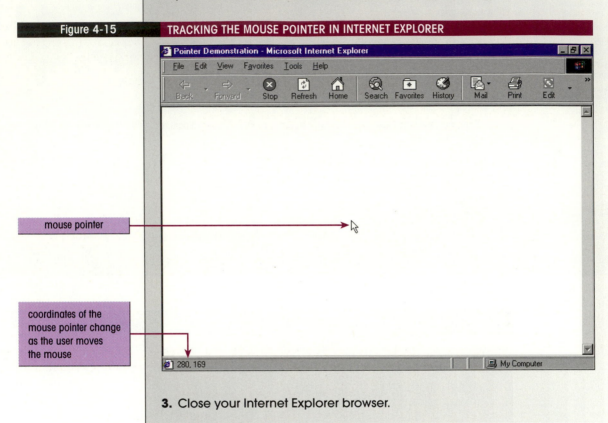

mouse pointer

coordinates of the mouse pointer change as the user moves the mouse

3. Close your Internet Explorer browser.

Internet Explorer doesn't need to use Netscape's captureEvents() method to capture events, and it also doesn't use Netscape's releaseEvents() method to stop capturing events. To turn off event capturing in Internet Explorer, you have to remove the event function by using the null keyword. For example, to run the grabIt() function when the user clicks the mouse button, you use the command:

```
document.onClick=grabIt;
```

To disable the grabIt() function, use the command:

```
document.onClick=null;
```

You can use this technique in Netscape as well.

Canceling Event Actions

Most events have default actions associated with them. If you click a hyperlink, the browser will load the link's target. If you drag your mouse pointer over text on the page, the text will be selected. The Internet Explorer event model allows you to cancel these default actions. This is done by modifying the event's **returnValue** property, a Boolean value that can be set to either true or false. If the returnValue is set to true, the default action associated with the event occurs. If property is set to false, the default action does not occur.

In the following sample code, the returnValue property of the onclick event is set to false. This overrides the action normally associated with clicking the hyperlink (displaying the Home.html page); the browser will do nothing in response to the mouse click.

```
<A ID=Link HREF="Home.html">View home page</A>

<SCRIPT>
   Link.onclick=DisableLink;

   function DisableLink() {
      event.returnValue=false;
   }
</SCRIPT>
```

To restore the link in the example, you would have to run the JavaScript command:

```
event.returnValue=true;
```

for the event of clicking the hyperlink.

Canceling Event Bubbling

Besides overriding the default actions of an event, you can also override event bubbling by using the cancelBubble property. By setting the cancelBubble property to true as follows:

```
event.cancelBubble=true;
```

the event bubbling stops at the current object. For example, with the following code:

```
<P onClick='alert("Normal text")'>
This is normal text and this is
<B onClick='alert("Bold-faced text");
event.cancelBubble=true'> boldfaced text.</B>
</P>
```

clicking the text "boldfaced text" displays a dialog box with the message, "Boldfaced text," and since the cancelBubble property is set to "true," this click event is *not* bubbled up to the <P> tag. Clicking elsewhere in the paragraph causes the alert message "Normal text" to appear (see Figure 4-16). If the event bubbling were not canceled, clicking the boldfaced text would cause Internet Explorer to display both dialog boxes, since both the <B> tag and the <P> tag have event handlers that respond to the click event.

Figure 4-16 | **CANCELING EVENT BUBBLING**

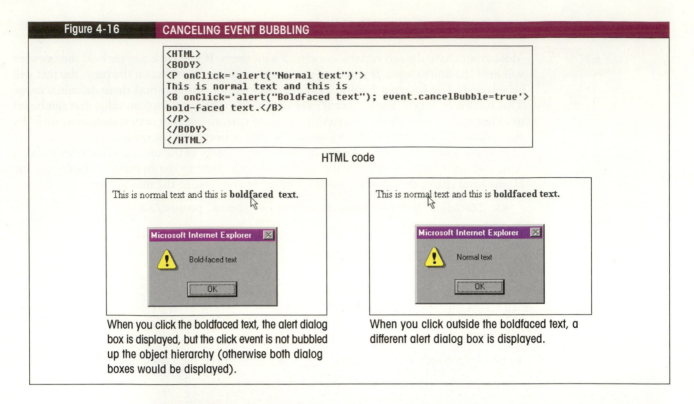

```
<HTML>
<BODY>
<P onClick='alert("Normal text")'>
This is normal text and this is
<B onClick='alert("Boldfaced text"); event.cancelBubble=true'>
bold-faced text.</B>
</P>
</BODY>
</HTML>
```

HTML code

When you click the boldfaced text, the alert dialog box is displayed, but the click event is not bubbled up the object hierarchy (otherwise both dialog boxes would be displayed).

When you click outside the boldfaced text, a different alert dialog box is displayed.

REFERENCE WINDOW | **RW**

Canceling Event Actions and Event Bubbling in Internet Explorer
- To cancel the default action of an event, use the command:
  ```
  event.returnValue=false;
  ```
- To cancel event bubbling, use the command:
  ```
  event.cancelBubble=true;
  ```

Comparing the Netscape and Internet Explorer Event Models

Netscape and Internet Explorer support many of the same event properties, through often with different terminology. Figure 4-17 compares the event properties for the two browsers.

Figure 4-17 | **EQUIVALENT PROPERTIES OF EVENT OBJECTS IN NETSCAPE AND INTERNET EXPLORER**

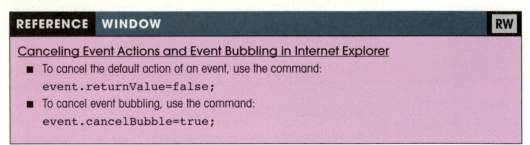

INTERNET EXPLORER	TYPE	NETSCAPE	TYPE
altKey, ctrlKey, shiftKey	Boolean	modifiers	Event object properties
clientX, clientY	Integer	pageX, pageY	Integer
screenX, screenY	Integer	screenX, screenY	Integer
srcElement	Object	target	Object
type	Character string	type	Character string
button, keyCode	Integer	which	Integer

In some cases there are slight differences between the Netscape and Internet Explorer interpretations of the properties shown in Figure 4-17. For example, the Netscape pageX and pageY properties and the Internet Explorer clientX and clientY properties both purport to identify the page coordinates of an event. However, Netscape includes segments of the page that have been scrolled out of the document window. On the other hand, Internet Explorer does not include parts of the page that are not displayed in the document window. If you need to record the exact location of the event with respect to the coordinates of the page, you need to modify the values of the clientX and clientY properties by adding the amount of the page that has been scrolled out of the document window. The proper equations are:

```
pageX = clientX + document.body.scrollLeft;
pageY = clientY + document.body.scrollTop;
```

Now that you've learned about the event models for both browsers, in the next session you'll create the grabIt, moveIt, and dropIt functions that add drag-and-drop capability to the Web page. In the third session, you'll learn how to control the appearance of your mouse pointer, and you'll learn how to work with keyboard events.

You can close any open files now.

Session 4.1 QUICK CHECK

1. Describe the three ways to run an event handler.

2. For Netscape, what JavaScript command would you enter to capture the keypress event in the browser window?

3. What JavaScript command would you enter to run the function CalcTotal() when the user presses a key?

4. Describe the difference between how Netscape and Internet Explorer handle events.

5. What is event bubbling?

6. What commands would you enter to determine the screen coordinates of the mouse as it moves across the computer screen in Netscape and Internet Explorer?

SESSION 4.2

In this session you'll create a drag-and-drop effect for the Games Etc. Web page. You'll learn how to determine the current location of the mouse as it moves across the page. You'll learn how to drag an object to follow the motions of the mouse, and you'll see how to determine the location of an object with respect to the shopping cart.

Capturing Events for Games Etc.

You are now ready to start creating the drag-and-drop shopping cart for Games Etc. There are three events you'll want to track. These are:

- onmousedown: When the user clicks one of the sales items
- onmousemove: When the user moves the pointer and drags the item across the page
- onmouseup: When the user releases the mouse button, dropping the item in a new location

For Netscape users, you need to capture these events before you can write functions for them. Once captured, you'll assign these three events to the following three functions: grabIt, moveIt, and dropIt. The JavaScript code is:

```
if (isNS) document.captureEvents(Event.MOUSEDOWN|
Event.MOUSEMOVE|Event.MOUSEUP);
document.onmousedown=grabIt;
document.onmousemove=moveIt;
document.onmouseup=dropIt;
```

This code uses the "isNS" Boolean variable from the GamesAPI.js file, to determine whether the user is running the Netscape browser before trying to capture the events. After capturing, each of the three events is assigned a function reference. Add this code to the Games.htm file.

To capture events in the Games.htm file:

1. Open the **Games.htm** file in your text editor.

2. At the bottom of the page before the </BODY> tag, insert the following code (see Figure 4-18):

```
<SCRIPT>
if (isNS)
document.captureEvents(Event.MOUSEDOWN|Event.MOUSEMOVE|
Event.MOUSEUP);
document.onmousedown=grabIt;
document.onmousemove=moveIt;
document.onmouseup=dropIt;
</SCRIPT>
```

Figure 4-18	ASSIGNING FUNCTIONS TO THE MOUSEDOWN, MOUSEMOVE, AND MOUSEUP EVENTS

capture the mousedown, mousemove and mousedrop events (for Netscape users only)

assign functions to the three mouse events

```
<SCRIPT>
if (isNS) document.captureEvents(Event.MOUSEDOWN|Event.MOUSEMOVE|Event.MOUSEUP);
document.onmousedown=grabIt;
document.onmousemove=moveIt;
document.onmouseup=dropIt;
</SCRIPT>
</BODY>
</HTML>
```

3. Save the changes and close your file.

Creating the grabIt Function

The first function you'll add to the Games Etc. Web page is the grabIt function. This function should run whenever the user presses the mouse button while the mouse pointer resides inside the document window. The grabIt() function will perform the following tasks:

1. Determine the page coordinates of the pointer at the moment the user presses the mouse button down.

2. Identify the object that lies beneath the pointer.

3. Calculate the difference between the coordinates of the pointer and the coordinates of the object.

You'll start by writing the code to determine the location of the mouse pointer when the user presses the mouse button.

Determining the Event Position

To determine the position of an event, such as pressing the mouse button, you need to add two new functions to the GamesAPI.js file: EventPositionX() and EventPositionY(). The code for the two functions is:

```
function EventPositionX(e) {
    if (isNS) return e.pageX;
    if (isIE) return event.clientX+document.body.scrollLeft;
}

function EventPositionY(e) {
    if (isNS) return e.pageY;
    if (isIE) return event.clientY+document.body.scrollTop;
}
```

In both of these functions, the browser calculates the (x, y) page coordinates of the event. If the event is the mousedown action, these functions will indicate where the pointer is in the document window when the mousedown occurs. If the event is the mousemove action, these functions will indicate the coordinates of the mouse as it begins to move.

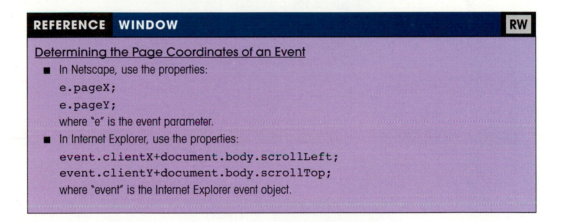

REFERENCE WINDOW   RW

Determining the Page Coordinates of an Event
- In Netscape, use the properties:
  e.pageX;
  e.pageY;
  where "e" is the event parameter.
- In Internet Explorer, use the properties:
  event.clientX+document.body.scrollLeft;
  event.clientY+document.body.scrollTop;
  where "event" is the Internet Explorer event object.

Note that in these functions we use a parameter named "e" to represent the event for the Netscape browser, and for Internet Explorer, we use the "event" object. Also note that we have to add the amount of the hidden page space to the clientX and clientY values for the Internet Explorer browser.

To add these functions to the GamesAPI.js file:

1. Reopen the **GamesAPI.js** file in your text editor.

2. At the bottom of the file, enter the following code:

```
function EventPositionX(e) {
    if (isNS) return e.pageX;
    if (isIE) return event.clientX+document.body.scrollLeft;
}

function EventPositionY(e) {
    if (isNS) return e.pageY;
    if (isIE) return event.clientY+document.body.scrollTop;
}
```

3. Save the changes to your file.

Now you can return to the Games.htm file and start using these functions in your Web page. A link has already been created to the GamesAPI.js file, so you don't have to add that to the HTML file.

To call the EventPosition functions:

1. Reopen the **Games.htm** file in your text editor.

2. Above the </SCRIPT> tag at the bottom of the file, insert the following code (see Figure 4-19):

```
function grabIt(e) {
  MouseX=EventPositionX(e);
    MouseY=EventPositionY(e);
}
```

3. Save the changes to your file.

Figure 4-19   **DETERMINING THE COORDINATES OF THE MOUSEDOWN ACTION**

```
function grabIt(e) {
    MouseX=EventPositionX(e);
    MouseY=EventPositionY(e);
}
</SCRIPT>
</BODY>
</HTML>
```

The grabIt function stores the (x, y) coordinates of the mousedown action in two variables: MouseX and MouseY. This will tell us where on the page the mousedown action occurred, but we won't know which element is located there, and hence which element to "grab." You'll determine that next.

Identifying the Element to Grab

Pete suggests that first you create an object variable for grabbed items, called "dragItem." Since no object is grabbed when the page opens, this variable will have an initial value of "null."

To create the dragItem variable:

1. Before the grabIt() function, insert the following command (see Figure 4-20):

```
var dragItem=null;
```

Figure 4-20	DECLARING THE DRAGITEM VARIABLE

```
document.onmouseup=dropIt;
var dragItem=null;

function grabIt(e) {
    MouseX=EventPositionX(e);
    MouseY=EventPositionY(e);
}
</SCRIPT>
</BODY>
</HTML>
```

2. Save the changes to your file.

Whatever object is under the pointer when the user presses the mouse button down should be stored in the dragItem variable. How do we determine which object on the page this is? If the user is running Internet Explorer, we can use the srcElement property as follows:

```
dragItem = event.srcElement;
```

and the dragItem variable will point to the object that initiated the action—the object that is under the mouse when the user presses the mouse button down.

REFERENCE WINDOW	RW

Identifying the Object that Received the Event
- In Netscape, you must loop through all the objects in the Web page and locate the object that contains the coordinates of the event.
- In Internet Explorer, use the JavaScript command:
  ```
  event.srcElement;
  ```

The solution is more complicated with Netscape. Because of Netscape's top-down event model, there is no way to directly determine which of the many elements on the page received the mouse action. Instead, we'll compare the coordinates of the mousedown action (as stored in the MouseX and MouseY variables) to the location of various objects on the page. When we find the object that encloses the mouse coordinates, we'll know that we've found the object that initiated the action.

Recall that the withinIt() function from the GamesAPI.js file can be used to determine whether a given set of coordinates lies within the boundary of an object. If the coordinates lie within the object, the withinIt() function returns the Boolean value true, otherwise it returns the value false. We can use it here to determine whether the mouse down action occurred within a given object. The code to do this is as follows:

```
inside=false;
for (i=0; i<document.layers.length; i++) {
    inside=withinIt(MouseX, MouseY, document.layers[i]);
    if (inside) dragItem=document.layers[i];
}
```

This code uses a Boolean variable named "inside", which will have the value true if the mouse coordinates lie within the object's boundaries, and false otherwise. The initial value of the inside variable is set to false. After that, we create a FOR loop that loops through the layers collection, using "i" to represent the index number of each layer. The total number of layers on the page is equal to document.layers.length.

For each layer, we call the withinIt() function, use MouseX and MouseY as the coordinates and document.layers[i] as the object, and store the value returned by the function in the "inside" variable. If this value is "true", we set the dragItem variable equal to the selected object.

The complete code for both browsers is then:

```
if (isNS) {
    inside=false;
    for (i=0; i<document.layers.length; i++) {
        inside=withinIt(MouseX, MouseY, document.layers[i]);
        if (inside) dragItem=document.layers[i];
    }
} else {
    dragItem=event.srcElement;
}
```

After this command block is run, the dragItem variable will either point to the object that lies underneath the mouse cursor, or if there is no object under the mouse cursor, it will retain the value null.

Add this code to the grabIt() function.

To determine the object of the dragItem variable:

1. After the command "MouseY=EventPositionY(e)," insert the following command block, as shown in Figure 4-21:

```
if (isNS) {
    inside=false;
    for (i=0; i<document.layers.length; i++) {
        inside=withinIt(MouseX, MouseY, document.layers[i]);
        if (inside) dragItem=document.layers[i];
    }
} else {
    dragItem=event.srcElement;
}
```

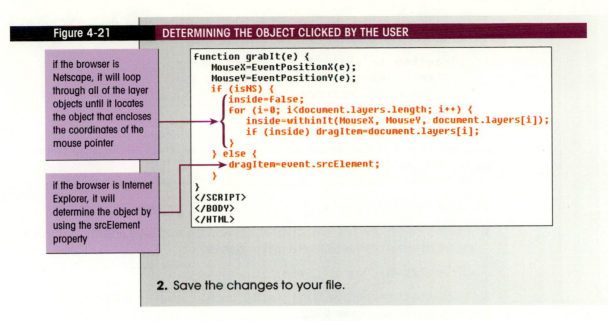

Figure 4-21   DETERMINING THE OBJECT CLICKED BY THE USER

if the browser is Netscape, it will loop through all of the layer objects until it locates the object that encloses the coordinates of the mouse pointer

if the browser is Internet Explorer, it will determine the object by using the srcElement property

```
function grabIt(e) {
    MouseX=EventPositionX(e);
    MouseY=EventPositionY(e);
    if (isNS) {
        inside=false;
        for (i=0; i<document.layers.length; i++) {
            inside=withinIt(MouseX, MouseY, document.layers[i]);
            if (inside) dragItem=document.layers[i];
        }
    } else {
        dragItem=event.srcElement;
    }
}
</SCRIPT>
</BODY>
</HTML>
```

2. Save the changes to your file.

The grabIt function now can calculate the position of the mouse at the occurrence of the mousedown action, and it can determine the object the user was pointing to when the mouse button was pressed. Next you need to calculate the difference between the coordinates of the dragItem and the initial coordinates of the mouse.

Calculating the Distance from the Pointer

The coordinates of an object are always expressed in relation to the location of the upper-left corner of the object. This means that you need to calculate the two variables diffX and diffY, which represent the horizontal and vertical distances between the pointer and the object's upper-left corner (see Figure 4-22).

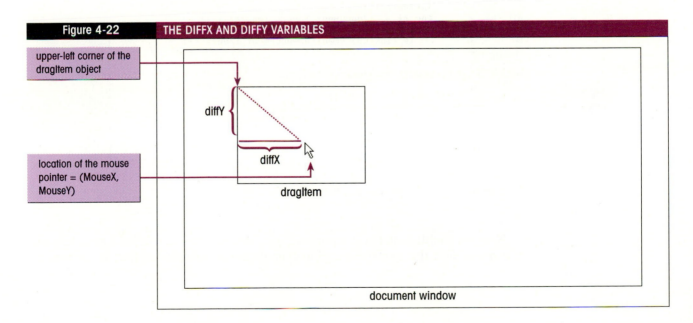

Figure 4-22   THE DIFFX AND DIFFY VARIABLES

upper-left corner of the dragItem object

location of the mouse pointer = (MouseX, MouseY)

diffY

diffX

dragItem

document window

The coordinates of the dragItem can be determined by using the getXCoord() and getYCoord() functions from the API file. Thus, the values of diffX and diffY are:

```
if (dragItem != null) {
    diffX=MouseX-getXCoord(dragItem);
    diffY=MouseY-getYCoord(dragItem);
}
```

Note that to avoid getting an error message, we need to ensure that the dragItem is not equal to null (that is, that a user actually has "grabbed" an object on the page) before calculating the diffX and diffY values.

To add the diffX and diffY values to the grabIt() function:

1. After the command "var dragItem=null;" insert the following commands to set the initial values of the diffX and diffY variables:

   ```
   var diffX=0; var diffY=0;
   ```

2. Before the closing brace of the grabIt() function, insert the following command block (see Figure 4-23):

   ```
   if (dragItem != null) {
       diffX=MouseX-getXCoord(dragItem);
       diffY=MouseY-getYCoord(dragItem);
   }
   ```

Figure 4-23	CALCULATING THE VALUES OF THE DIFFX AND DIFFY VARIABLES

sets the initial values →

determines values of variables by using functions in the API file →

```
var dragItem=null;
var diffX=0; var diffY=0;

function grabIt(e) {
    MouseX=EventPositionX(e);
    MouseY=EventPositionY(e);
    if (isNS) {
        inside=false;
        for (i=0; i<document.layers.length; i++) {
            inside=withinIt(MouseX, MouseY, document.layers[i]);
            if (inside) dragItem=document.layers[i];
        }
    } else {
        dragItem=event.srcElement;
    }
    if (dragItem != null) {
        diffX=MouseX-getXCoord(dragItem);
        diffY=MouseY-getYCoord(dragItem);
    }
}
</SCRIPT>
```

3. Save the changes to your file.

Now the grabIt function is complete. Your next task is to create the moveIt function, which will allow the user to move an item on the page from one location to another.

Creating the moveIt Function

The moveIt() function is run whenever the mousemove action occurs. The purpose of the moveIt() function is to move the grabbed item in conjunction with the moving mouse pointer. The moveIt function needs to do the following tasks:

1. Test whether an object has been grabbed on the page.

2. If so, calculate the new coordinates of the mouse pointer and keep the grabbed object a constant distance of (diffX, diffY) pixels from the mouse pointer (see Figure 4-24).

Figure 4-24	KEEPING THE DRAGITEM OBJECT A CONSTANT DISTANCE FROM THE MOUSE POINTER

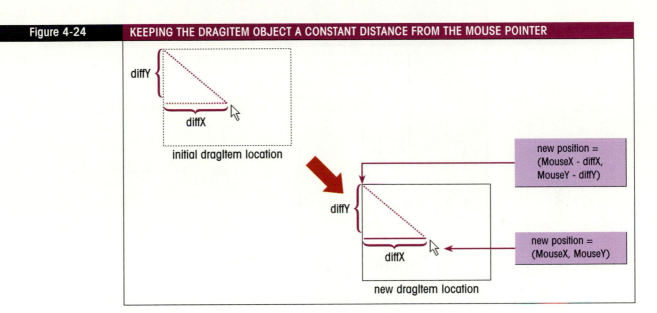

To place the grabbed object at the new location, you need to use the placeIt command from the GamesAPI.js file. The moveIt() function will look as follows:

```
function moveIt(e) {
    if (dragItem != null) {
        MouseX=EventPositionX(e);
        MouseY=EventPositionY(e);
        placeIt(dragItem, MouseX-diffX, MouseY-diffY);
    }
}
```

Note that you first have to verify that dragItem is not equal to null before trying to place the dragItem object. One of the important uses of the dragItem variable is to determine whether the user has grabbed an item or not. Remember that the mouse will be constantly moving across the Web page, and not every instance of a mousemove action means that we're dragging a sales item. So if dragItem has a null value, the browser will know not to run any commands to move objects on the page.

To create the moveIt() function:

1. Below the closing brace of the grabIt() function, insert the following JavaScript commands (see Figure 4-25):

```
function moveIt(e) {
   if (dragItem != null) {
      MouseX=EventPositionX(e);
      MouseY=EventPositionY(e);
      placeIt(dragItem, MouseX-diffX, MouseY-diffY);
   }
}
```

Figure 4-25	CREATING THE MOVEIT() FUNCTION

```
function moveIt(e) {
   if (dragItem != null) {
      MouseX=EventPositionX(e);
      MouseY=EventPositionY(e);
      placeIt(dragItem, MouseX-diffX, MouseY-diffY);
   }
}
</SCRIPT>
</BODY>
</HTML>
```

2. Save the changes to your file.

Creating **the dropIt Function**

The final function to create for the Games Etc. drag-and-drop effect is the dropIt() function. The dropIt() function should be run when the user releases the mouse button. The function should do the following tasks:

1. Test whether there is a grabbed object that needs to be dropped on the page

2. If so, release the mousemove event, and set the value of the dragItem object back to null

The code for the dropIt() function is:

```
function dropIt(e) {
   if (dragItem != null) {
      if (isNS) releaseEvents(Event.MOUSEMOVE);
      dragItem=null;
   }
}
```

Note that only Netscape users need to use the releaseEvents() method. Also, by setting the dragItem variable back to null, we ensure that additional mouse movements on the page won't be dragging any objects, unless we grab them first by pressing the mouse button down.

To create the dropIt() function:

1. Below the moveIt() function, insert the following commands (see Figure 4-26):

```
function dropIt(e) {
   if (dragItem != null) {
      if (isNS) releaseEvents(Event.MOUSEMOVE);
      dragItem=null;
   }
}
```

Figure 4-26	CREATING THE DROPIT() FUNCTION

```
function dropIt(e) {
   if (dragItem != null) {
      if (isNS) releaseEvents(Event.MOUSEMOVE);
      dragItem=null;
   }
}
</SCRIPT>
</BODY>
</HTML>
```

2. Save the changes to your file.

Now that you've created all three functions, you're ready to test the drag-and-drop capability of the Games Etc. page.

To view the page:

1. Open the **Games.htm** file in your Web browser.

2. Position the pointer over the box describing the Scribble game in the list of specials, and then hold down the pointer and drag the Scribble game into the Shopping Cart box, as shown in Figure 4-27.

Figure 4-27	DRAGGING THE SCRIBBLE GAME

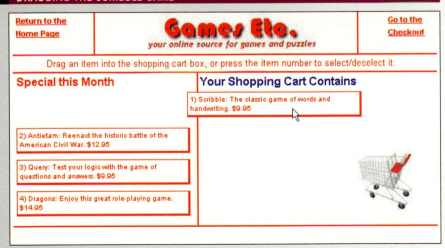

3. Release the mouse button, dropping the game into the Shopping Cart box.

4. Continue experimenting, moving the four different monthly specials between the two boxes on the Web page.

TROUBLE? If you receive an error message, return to the Games.htm file in your text editor. Check the code in your file against the figures and instructions in this book.

Refining **the Drag-and-Drop Feature**

You show the Games.htm page to Pete. As Pete works with the page, he immediately notices a problem. The page allows him to drag not only the monthly special items, but also almost *any* item on the page. In Figure 4-28, Pete demonstrates that someone can drag the link to the home page across the screen—something that will certainly confuse customers!.

Figure 4-28	DRAGGING THE HOME PAGE HYPERLINK BY MISTAKE

Pete suggests that you modify the page so that only the four sale items can be dragged and dropped on the page.

Identifying Movable Objects

To determine whether the grabbed item is movable, one could create an IF...THEN statement that tests whether the ID of the grabbed item matches one of the four monthly special IDs. Pete doesn't like that approach because he may want to use this drag-and-drop technique on other pages. Imagine how difficult it would be to create an IF...THEN statement for 100 different movable items on the page, rather than for just four.

Instead, he suggests that you use the ID names of the four sale objects to identify them as movable objects. The four movable items (see Figure 4-1) are named DRAGItem1, DRAGItem2, DRAGItem3, and DRAGItem4. No other object on the page has an ID name that includes the word "DRAG".

Therefore, to determine whether the grabbed item is movable, your program needs only to determine whether the ID name of the item contains the characters "DRAG." You can do this by using JavaScript's indexOf() text string method, which determines whether a string of characters can be found within a larger string. If the character string is found, the location of the character string is returned; however, if the character string is not found, a value of –1 is returned.

For example, the following code:

```
"Games Etc.".indexOf("Etc");
```

returns a value of 7 (the first character in the string has a location value of 0). On the other hand, the code:

```
"Games Etc.".indexOf("Puzzles");
```

returns a value of –1, since the text string "Puzzles" cannot be found within "Games Etc."

If the grabbed item is not movable (in other words, if you do not find the text "DRAG" within the object's ID name), you should set the object reference of the dragItem variable back to null. This will indicate that the user has not selected a movable item. The command would look as follows:

```
if (dragItem.id.indexOf("DRAG") == -1) dragItem=null;
```

The revised grabIt() function will now do the following:

1. Locate the position of the pointer when the user clicks on the page

2. Identify the object underneath the pointer, and determine whether the object is movable

3. Determine the distance between the object and pointer

To modify the grabIt() function:

1. Return to the **Games.htm** file in your text editor.

2. Scroll to the grabIt() function at the bottom of the file.

3. Insert the following command, as shown in Figure 4-29:

```
if (dragItem.id.indexOf("DRAG") == -1) dragItem=null;
```

Figure 4-29	THE REVISED GRABIT() FUNCTION

```
function grabIt(e) {
    MouseX=EventPositionX(e);          ← determines the mouse position
    MouseY=EventPositionY(e);
    if (isNS) {
        inside=false;
        for (i=0; i<document.layers.length; i++) {
            inside=withinIt(MouseX, MouseY, document.layers[i]);
            if (inside) dragItem=document.layers[i];     ← indentifies the dragItem item
        }
    } else {
        dragItem=event.srcElement;
    }
    if (dragItem.id.indexOf("DRAG") == -1) dragItem=null;   ← determines whether the dragItem is movable

    if (dragItem != null) {
        diffX=MouseX-getXCoord(dragItem);                    ← calculates the distance from the mouse pointer
        diffY=MouseY-getYCoord(dragItem);
    }
}
```

4. Save the changes to your file.

5. Refresh or reload the **Games.htm** file in your Web browser, and verify that the only movable objects are the four monthly special boxes.

   TROUBLE? If you can still move other objects, change the code for the indexOf() method. Verify that your uppercase and lowercase letters match those in Figure 4-29.

Using this approach requires judicious use of ID names. If you're creating a drag-and-drop page for only Internet Explorer users, you can use a simpler approach. Internet Explorer supports the creation of customized properties in HTML tags. For example, you can create a property named "Drag," which can be set to "true" for movable objects and "false" for static objects. In the following HTML code, Object1 and Object2 have different Drag values.

```
<DIV ID=Object1 Drag="true"></DIV>
<DIV ID=Object2 Drag="false"></DIV>
```

To test whether an object is movable in this approach, you use the getAttribute() method as follows:

```
if (dragItem.getAttribute("Drag")=="false") dragItem=null;
```

This approach will not work for Netscape browsers, since Netscape does not support customized properties and the getAttribute method.

Keeping Dragged Items on Top

In returning to the Games.htm page, Pete now notices that in some instances, the object that is being moved "disappears" behind other objects as it is being dragged across the page, as shown in see Figure 4-30. He'd like you to make sure the dragged item is always on top.

Figure 4-30   **A DRAGGED OBJECT HIDDEN BEHIND ANOTHER OBJECT ON THE PAGE**

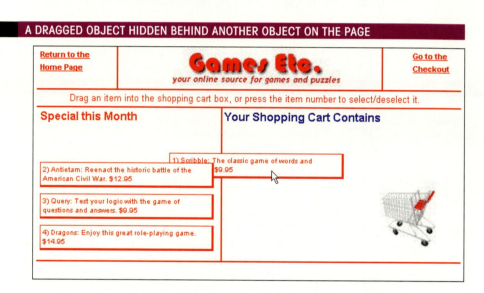

To do this, you'll create a variable named "maxZ", which is equal to the maximum z-index on the page. Each time you grab an item, the value of maxZ is increased by 1, and the z-index of the grabbed item is set to the maxZ value. Thus, when the grabbed item is dragged across the page, it will have the highest z-index of any object on the page and will always appear on top. The initial value of maxZ is 1. To set the value of the grabbed item to the maxZ value, you'll use the setZ() function found in the GamesAPI.js file.

To create the maxZ variable:

1. Return to the **Games.htm** file in your text editor.

2. Below the command "var diffX=0; var diffY=0;" insert the following command:

   `var maxZ=1;`

3. Scroll down to the grabIt() function.

4. Insert the following commands, as shown in Figure 4-31:

```
maxZ++;
setZ(dragItem, maxZ);
```

Figure 4-31   **MAKING SURE THE DRAGGED ITEM STAYS ON TOP**

sets the initial value of the maximum z-index →

increases the maximum z-index by 1 →

sets the z-index of dragItem to the maximum →

```
var dragItem=null;
var diffX=0; var diffY=0;
var maxZ=1;

function grabIt(e) {
    MouseX=EventPositionX(e);
    MouseY=EventPositionY(e);
    if (isNS) {
        inside=false;
        for (i=0; i<document.layers.length; i++) {
            inside=withinIt(MouseX, MouseY, document.layers[i]);
            if (inside) dragItem=document.layers[i];
        }
    } else {
        dragItem=event.srcElement;
    }
    if (dragItem.id.indexOf("DRAG") == -1) dragItem=null;

    if (dragItem != null) {
        maxZ++;
        setZ(dragItem, maxZ);
        diffX=MouseX-getXCoord(dragItem);
        diffY=MouseY-getYCoord(dragItem);
    }
}
```

5. Save the changes to your file.

6. Reload or refresh the **Games.htm** page in your Web browser.

7. Verify that each item you drag remains on top of the other objects on the page.

Returning Dragged Items to Their Starting Point

The final problem Pete notices is that users can drag an item from the list of specials and drop it anywhere on the page—not just in the shopping cart. The monthly specials should be either within the shopping cart box or back at their starting point on the page. When a user drops one of the monthly specials on the page outside the shopping cart, Pete wants the dropIt() function to do the following:

1. Determine whether the item lies within the boundaries of the shopping cart

2. If the item does fall within the shopping cart's boundaries, leave it there

3. If the item lies outside the cart's boundaries, it should "snap back" to its original location on the page.

To determine whether dragItem falls within the boundaries of the shopping cart, Pete suggests you use the same withinIt() function that you used earlier. You'll add the following command block to the dropIt() function:

```
dragPosX=getXCoord(dragItem);
dragPosY=getYCoord(dragItem);
Cart=getObject("CartBox");
if (!withinIt(dragPosX, dragPosY, Cart)) {
    snapBack();
}
```

Here dragPosX and dragPosY represent the (x, y) coordinates of the item as it is dropped onto the page. The Cart variable points to the Cart object (with the ID name "CartBox") on the page (see Figure 4-1).

Note that the "!" symbol is a negation operator and has the effect of switching the value of a Boolean variable. In this case it switches the value of the withinIt() function from false to true, and vice versa. So if the expression !withinIt(dragPosX, dragPosY, Cart) is true (in other words, if the coordinates are *not* inside the Cart object), then the snapBack() function is run.

You'll create the snapBack() function shortly. For now, add the command block to the dropIt() function that will determine whether an object is dropped in the shopping cart or not.

To determine whether a dropped item is in the shopping cart:

1. Return to the **Games.htm** file in your text editor.

2. Locate the dropIt() function.

3. Insert the following command block, as shown in Figure 4-32:

```
dragPosX=getXCoord(dragItem);
dragPosY=getYCoord(dragItem);
Cart=getObject("CartBox");
if (!withinIt(dragPosX, dragPosY, Cart)) {
    snapBack();
}
```

Figure 4-32 SENDING DRAGGED ITEMS BACK TO THEIR ORIGINAL LOCATIONS

```
function dropIt(e) {
    if (dragItem != null) {
        dragPosX=getXCoord(dragItem);
        dragPosY=getYCoord(dragItem);
        Cart=getObject("CartBox");
        if (!withinIt(dragPosX, dragPosY, Cart)) {
            snapBack();
        }
        if (isNS) releaseEvents(Event.MOUSEMOVE);
        dragItem=null;
    }
}
```

Now you need to create the snapBack() function, which should return the dragItem item to its original location. From the <DIV> tags in the Games.htm file, we know that the original coordinates for the four monthly specials are:

- DRAGItem1 (Scribble): (10, 120)
- DRAGItem2 (Antietam): (10, 165)
- DRAGItem3 (Query): (10, 210)
- DRAGItem4 (Dragons): (10, 255)

The snapBack() function should therefore appears as follows:

```
function snapBack() {
    if (dragItem.id=="DRAGItem1") placeIt(dragItem, 10, 120);
    if (dragItem.id=="DRAGItem2") placeIt(dragItem, 10, 165);
    if (dragItem.id=="DRAGItem3") placeIt(dragItem, 10, 210);
    if (dragItem.id=="DRAGItem4") placeIt(dragItem, 10, 255);
}
```

Add this function to the Games.htm file.

To create the snapBack() function:

1. Below the dropIt() function, insert the following set of commands, as shown in Figure 4-33:

```
function snapBack() {
    if (dragItem.id=="DRAGItem1") placeIt(dragItem, 10, 120);
    if (dragItem.id=="DRAGItem2") placeIt(dragItem, 10, 165);
    if (dragItem.id=="DRAGItem3") placeIt(dragItem, 10, 210);
    if (dragItem.id=="DRAGItem4") placeIt(dragItem, 10, 255);
}
```

Figure 4-33	CREATING THE SNAPBACK() FUNCTION

```
function snapBack() {
    if (dragItem.id=="DRAGItem1") placeIt(dragItem, 10, 120);
    if (dragItem.id=="DRAGItem2") placeIt(dragItem, 10, 165);
    if (dragItem.id=="DRAGItem3") placeIt(dragItem, 10, 210);
    if (dragItem.id=="DRAGItem4") placeIt(dragItem, 10, 255);
}
</SCRIPT>
</BODY>
</HTML>
```

2. Save the changes to your file.

3. Reload or refresh the **Games.htm** page in your Web browser.

4. Verify that if you attempt to drop any of the monthly specials anywhere but within the shopping cart box, the special will jump back to its original location on the page.

TROUBLE? If the monthly specials all jump to the fourth spot in the list, check the code for the snapBack() function and verify that you used double equal signs in the IF...THEN statement, rather than a single "=" sign.

You've completed your work on enhancing the drag-and-drop features of the Games Etc. page. Pete has a few more things he wants you to add to the page, including keyboard support. You'll look at those issues in the next session.

Session 4.2 QUICK CHECK

1. What JavaScript code would you enter to determine the page coordinates of an event, using Netscape?

2. What JavaScript code would you enter to determine the same page coordinates using Internet Explorer?

3. In Internet Explorer, what command would store the object that received a mouseover event in a variable named "ImgObject"?

4. Describe how to determine the object reference in the previous question when using Netscape.

5. If a text string does *not* contain the characters "DRAG," what value is returned by the method indexOf("DRAG")?

6. What technique can you use to ensure that a dragged item will always be on top as it moves across the Web page?

SESSION 4.3

In this session you'll learn how to control the appearance of the pointer. You'll learn how to capture keyboard events, and how to determine which key the user has pressed on the keyboard. Finally, you'll learn how to work with the Alt, Ctrl, and Shift modifier keys.

Working with Mouse Pointers

Pete has looked over your Web page and would like to have the page provide the user with more visual feedback. For example, when the user hovers the pointer over one of the movable objects, Pete would like to have the pointer change shape to a ⬌ to indicate that the object is movable.

Internet Explorer provides support for changing the shape of the pointer through its cursor property. The syntax of the cursor property is:

```
object.style.cursor="cursor_type";
```

where *object* is the page object, and *cursor_type* is a text string that identifies the type of pointer to be displayed. You can also define the pointer style in a style declaration by using the syntax:

```
cursor: "cursor_type"
```

Note that this style is supported by Internet Explorer but not by Netscape.

Figure 4-34 shows the different types of pointers you can display with either the JavaScript object property command or a style sheet declaration. In addition to the types listed in the figure, you can also specify a pointer type of "auto," which allows the browser to determine the appearance of the pointer for you.

Figure 4-34   **CURSOR TYPES**

CURSOR	CURSOR TYPE	CURSOR	CURSOR TYPE
↖	"default"	⇒	"e-resize"
⬌	"move"	⇓	"s-resize"
👆	"hand"	↖	"nw-resize"
+	"crosshair"	↗	"ne-resize"
⌛	"wait"	↘	"se-resize"
↖?	"help"	↙	"sw-resize"
⇐	"w-resize"	I	"text"
⇑	"n-resize"		

REFERENCE WINDOW   **RW**

Controlling the Appearance of the Mouse Pointer

There are two ways of controlling the appearance of the mouse pointer (Internet Explorer only):

■ In a style sheet, use the syntax:
```
object.style.cursor="cursor_type";
```
where *cursor_type* is the type of mouse pointer to be displayed.

■ In JavaScript, use the command:
```
cursor: "cursor_type"
```

Pete wants the move pointer, ✛, to appear whenever the mouse hovers over a movable item. To do this, you have to insert an event handler for the mouseover event, and run a function when the event occurs.

To create an event handler for the mouseover event:

1. If necessary, reopen the **Games.htm** file in your text editor.

2. Scroll down the file.

3. After the command "document.onmouseup=dropIt;" insert the command:

```
document.onmouseover=showCursor;
```

See Figure 4-35.

4. Save the changes to your file.

Figure 4-35	CREATING AN EVENT HANDLER FOR THE MOUSEOVER EVENT

```
document.onmousedown=grabIt;
document.onmousemove=moveIt;
document.onmouseup=dropIt;
document.onmouseover=showCursor;
var dragItem=null;
var diffX=0; var diffY=0;
var maxZ=1;
```

Now you need to write the showCursor function. Pete wants it to do the following tasks:

1. Determine whether browser is Internet Explorer (because only Internet Explorer supports the cursor property).

2. Identify the object on the page that the mouse is hovering over.

3. Determine whether that object is moveable and if so, change the pointer to the "move" cursor type, ✛.

The showCursor() function should appear as follows:

```
function showCursor() {
   if (isIE) {
      hoverItem=event.srcElement;
      if (hoverItem.id.indexOf("DRAG")!=-1)
hoverItem.style.cursor="move";
   }
}
```

Because this function will be run by only Internet Explorer browsers, we can use the srcElement property to determine the object that receives the mouseover action. We'll store the object reference in a variable named "hoverItem." Then we'll once again use the fact that all the movable items in this page have the text string "DRAG" in their ID names to determine whether hoverItem is movable. As long as the indexOf("DRAG") method is *not* equal to –1, hoverItem will be movable and the cursor style will be changed to "move", ✛.

To add the showCursor() function to the Web page:

1. Scroll to the bottom of the document.

2. Above the </SCRIPT> tag, insert the command block:

```
function showCursor() {
   if (isIE) {
       hoverItem=event.srcElement;
       if (hoverItem.id.indexOf("DRAG")!=-1)
hoverItem.style.cursor="move";
   }
}
```

See Figure 4-36.

Figure 4-36	CREATING THE SHOWCURSOR FUNCTION TO CHANGE THE CURSOR STYLE

check whether the user is running the Internet Explorer browser

determine the object that receives the mouseover event

if the object is movable, change the cursor style to

```
function showCursor() {
  if (isIE) {
    hoverItem=event.srcElement;
    if (hoverItem.id.indexOf("DRAG")!=-1) hoverItem.style.cursor="move";
  }
}
</SCRIPT>
</BODY>
</HTML>
```

3. Save your changes to the file.

4. Open the **Games.htm** file in your Internet Explorer browser.

5. Move the pointer over the monthly special items. The pointer should change shape, as shown in Figure 4-37.

Figure 4-37	CHANGING THE POINTER FOR MOVABLE ITEMS

when the pointer hovers over a movable item, the pointer changes shape

TROUBLE? If you are using Netscape, you will not see a change in the mouse pointer.

Changing the Color of Dragged Items

The second enhancement that Pete wants you to make is to change the color of items once they've been placed into the shopping cart. Pete would like all items in the shopping cart to appear in blue, while outside the cart they should appear in red. As with changing the pointer, you'll only do this with Internet Explorer. To do this with the Netscape browser, you would have to enclose the shopping items within <LAYER> tags and then rewrite the entire content of the layer using a different font color.

One of the functions in the GamesAPI.js file is the colorIt() function, which allows you to specify the text and border color of an object (see Figure 4-3). To change the color of the dragItem object to blue, you would use the command:

```
colorIt(dragItem, "blue");
```

You'll insert the following command block into the moveIt() function so that whenever the user moves an item into the shopping cart box, it will change color (for Internet Explorer users only).

```
if (isIE) {
    Cart=getObject("CartBox");
    if (withinIt(MouseX-diffX, MouseY-diffY, Cart)) {
        colorIt(dragItem, "blue");
    } else {
        colorIt(dragItem, "red");
    }
}
```

Once again, you'll use the withinIt() function to determine whether the coordinates of the upper-left corner of the object fall within the shopping cart boundaries. Note that these coordinates are (MouseX-diffX, MouseY-diffY).

To add this command block to the moveIt() function:

1. Return to the **Games.htm** file in your text editor.

2. Locate the moveIt() function.

3. Below the command "placeIt(dragItem, MouseX-diffX, MouseY-diffY)," insert the command block (see Figure 4-38):

```
if (isIE) {
    Cart=getObject("CartBox");
    if (withinIt(MouseX-diffX, MouseY-diffY, Cart)) {
        colorIt(dragItem, "blue");
    } else {
        colorIt(dragItem, "red");
    }
}
```

Figure 4-38 THE REVISED MOVEIT() FUNCTION

```
function moveIt(e) {
   if (dragItem != null) {
      MouseX=EventPositionX(e);
      MouseY=EventPositionY(e);
      placeIt(dragItem, MouseX-diffX, MouseY-diffY);
      if (isIE) {
         Cart=getObject("CartBox");
         if (withinIt(MouseX-diffX, MouseY-diffY, Cart)) {
            colorIt(dragItem, "blue");
         } else {
            colorIt(dragItem, "red");
         }
      }
   }
}
```

4. Save your changes to the file.

5. Open **Games.htm** in your Web browser.

6. Drag one of the monthly special items into the shopping cart box and observe that it changes color (see Figure 4-39).

Figure 4-39 CHANGING THE COLOR OF THE DRAGGED ITEM

item changes color as it is dragged into the shopping cart box

Controlling Keyboard Events

Pete is aware that some customers have problems manipulating the mouse, and others simply prefer to use the keyboard. Each of the four sale items has a number in front of it. Pete wants to make it possible for users to select items by pressing the item number on their computer keyboard. Pete foresees the browser handling the following keyboard events (see Figure 4-40):

1. If the user presses 1, 2, 3, or 4 on the keyboard, the product with that item number should be moved into the shopping cart.

2. If the item is in the shopping cart already, it should be moved back to the list of specials when the corresponding key is pressed.

3. If any other key is pressed, nothing should happen.

| Figure 4-40 | USING THE KEYBOARD TO MOVE ITEMS ON THE PAGE |

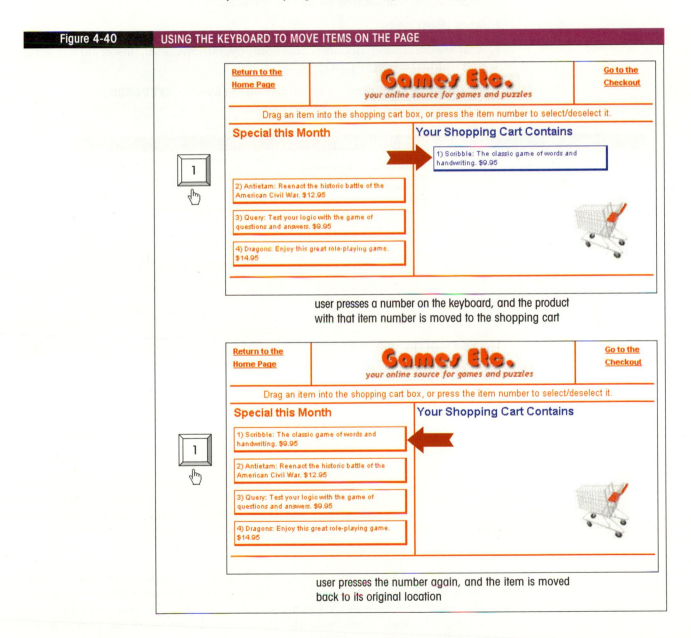

Capturing a Keyboard Event

Netscape and Internet Explorer support three keyboard events:

- keydown: The user has begun pressing a key.
- keypress: The user has pressed and released a key.
- keyup: The user has released a key.

As with the mouse events, keyboard events must be captured before they can be used by Netscape. For this page, you'll capture the keypress event. Once the user presses the key, the browser should run the function, keyDrag().

To capture the keypress event:

1. Return to the **Games.htm** file in your text editor.

2. Scroll down the file.

3. After the command "document.onmouseover=showCursor;" insert the following commands (see Figure 4-41):

```
if (isNS) document.captureEvents(Event.KEYPRESS);
document.onkeypress=keyDrag;
```

Figure 4-41	CAPTURING A KEYBOARD EVENT

captures the keypress event in the document (for Netscape browsers)

asigns the keypress event to the keyDrag() function

```
document.onmousedown=grabIt;
document.onmousemove=moveIt;
document.onmouseup=dropIt;
document.onmouseover=showCursor;
if (isNS) document.captureEvents(Event.KEYPRESS);
document.onkeypress=keyDrag;
var dragItem=null;
var diffX=0; var diffY=0;
var maxZ=1;
```

4. Save the changes to your file.

The keyDrag() function will have two main features. First it will have to identify which key was pressed. Then, using that information, it will move the appropriate item on the Web page.

Examining Key Codes

Internet Explorer and Netscape use different methods to determine which key is being pressed. In Netscape the syntax is:

```
key = e.which;
```

where "e" is the Netscape event object, and *key* is the variable that stores the key that was pressed. Keys are identified by their **ASCII** numbers—a standard numbering system for keyboard characters. The corresponding command in Internet Explorer is:

```
key = event.keyCode;
```

where *key* stores the Unicode number of the key. **Unicode** is an extended numbering system for characters that allows for more characters—especially foreign symbols—than ASCII does. The first 128 Unicode and ASCII numbers represent the same characters. Figure 4-42 lists the ASCII/Unicode numbers for the 10 numeric digits and for the 26 letters of the alphabet (in both uppercase and lowercase).

Figure 4-42 | **ASCII/UNICODE KEY NUMBERS**

CHARACTERS	ASCII/UNICODE NUMBERS
0–9	48–57
A–Z	65–90
a–z	97–122

For example, if the user presses the 1 key, the browser stores the ASCII/Unicode value 49. The 2 key is equal to the ASCII/Unicode value 50, 3 has an ASCII/Unicode value of 51, and the 4 key has a value of 52.

Note that the ASCII/Unicode numbers are equal to the symbol numbers that HTML uses for displaying special characters. Appendix B includes a fuller list of ASCII/Unicode numbers and the symbols they represent.

To convert the ASCII or Unicode numbers back into the character, use the String.fromCharCode() method as follows:

```
character = String.fromCharCode(key);
```

where *character* is the text character represented by the *key* number. For example, the command:

```
String.fromCharCode(65);
```

returns the character "A." Note that this method only returns correct characters when used with the keypress event. It gives incorrect results when used with the keydown event.

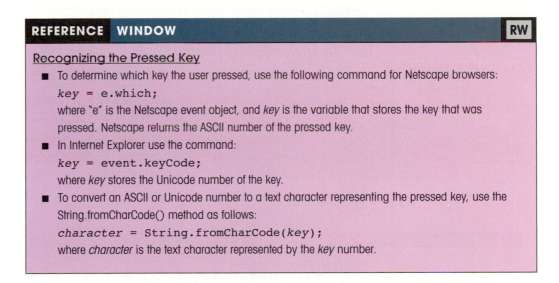

REFERENCE WINDOW | **RW**

Recognizing the Pressed Key

- To determine which key the user pressed, use the following command for Netscape browsers:

  `key = e.which;`

  where "e" is the Netscape event object, and *key* is the variable that stores the key that was pressed. Netscape returns the ASCII number of the pressed key.

- In Internet Explorer use the command:

  `key = event.keyCode;`

  where *key* stores the Unicode number of the key.

- To convert an ASCII or Unicode number to a text character representing the pressed key, use the String.fromCharCode() method as follows:

  `character = String.fromCharCode(key);`

  where *character* is the text character represented by the *key* number.

To resolve the different syntaxes between the two browsers, you'll add a new function to the GamesAPI.js file called getKey(). The getKey() function will return the ASCII/Unicode number for the pressed key, no matter which browser is being used. The code for the function is:

```
function getKey(e) {
    if (isNS) return e.which;
    if (isIE) return event.keyCode;
}
```

To create the getKey() function:

1. Open the **GamesAPI.js** file in your text editor.

2. At the bottom of the file, insert the function:

```
function getKey(e) {
    if (isNS) return e.which;
    if (isIE) return event.keyCode;
}
```

3. Save your changes and close the GamesAPI.js file.

Creating the keyDrag() Function

Before writing the keyDrag() function, you need to create one additional function. In the last session, you created the snapBack() function, which moves items to their original locations. Now you'll create a similar function, snapIn(), whose purpose will be to place items inside the shopping cart. The code for the snapIn() function is:

```
function snapIn() {
    if (dragItem.id=="DRAGItem1") placeIt(dragItem, 300, 120);
    if (dragItem.id=="DRAGItem2") placeIt(dragItem, 300, 165);
    if (dragItem.id=="DRAGItem3") placeIt(dragItem, 300, 210);
    if (dragItem.id=="DRAGItem4") placeIt(dragItem, 300, 255);
}
```

The function places each of the four movable objects in a different location in the shopping cart.

To add the snapIn() function:

1. Reopen (if necessary) the **Games.htm** file in your text editor.

2. Below the snapBack() function, insert the following function (see Figure 4-43):

```
function snapIn() {
    if (dragItem.id=="DRAGItem1") placeIt(dragItem, 300, 120);
    if (dragItem.id=="DRAGItem2") placeIt(dragItem, 300, 165);
    if (dragItem.id=="DRAGItem3") placeIt(dragItem, 300, 210);
    if (dragItem.id=="DRAGItem4") placeIt(dragItem, 300, 255);
}
```

Figure 4-43	INSERTING THE SNAPIN() FUNCTION

```
function snapBack() {
    if (dragItem.id=="DRAGItem1") placeIt(dragItem, 10, 120);
    if (dragItem.id=="DRAGItem2") placeIt(dragItem, 10, 165);
    if (dragItem.id=="DRAGItem3") placeIt(dragItem, 10, 210);
    if (dragItem.id=="DRAGItem4") placeIt(dragItem, 10, 255);
}

function snapIn() {
    if (dragItem.id=="DRAGItem1") placeIt(dragItem, 300, 120);
    if (dragItem.id=="DRAGItem2") placeIt(dragItem, 300, 165);
    if (dragItem.id=="DRAGItem3") placeIt(dragItem, 300, 210);
    if (dragItem.id=="DRAGItem4") placeIt(dragItem, 300, 255);
}
```

3. Save the changes to your file.

With all of the other functions in place, you can now write the keyDrag() function. The keyDrag() function should perform the following tasks:

1. Determine the ASCII/Unicode value of the pressed key

2. Use that information to "grab" the numbered item on the page and store it in the dragItem variable

3. Determine whether the grabbed item lies inside or outside the shopping cart box

4. If the grabbed item is outside the shopping cart, move it inside the shopping cart, and change the color to blue

5. If item is inside the shopping cart, move it back to its original location on the page, and change the color to red

6. Set the object reference of the dragItem variable back to null after moving it

Let's break down these tasks into separate command blocks.

To determine the ASCII/Unicode of the pressed key, the function will call the getKey() function from the API file and store the value in a variable named "key". The code is:

```
key=getKey(e);
```

If key equals 49, the user pressed "1" on the keyboard. If key equals 50, the user pressed "2," and so forth. Based on which number the user pressed, the keyDrag() function will point the dragItem variable to that sales item. If the user doesn't press 1, 2, 3, or 4, the value of dragItem remains null. The code is:

```
if (key==49) dragItem=getObject("DRAGItem1");
if (key==50) dragItem=getObject("DRAGItem2");
if (key==51) dragItem=getObject("DRAGItem3");
if (key==52) dragItem=getObject("DRAGItem4");
```

To determine whether dragItem lies inside or outside the shopping cart, use the getXCoord() and getYCoord() functions to determine the location of the sales item, and then use the withinIt() function, to determine if the item lies inside or outside the shopping cart.

If the object lies within the shopping cart, snap it back to its original position and color it red. If the object lies outside the shopping cart, snap it into the cart, and color it red. After moving the object, reset dragItem to a null value. The commands to do this are:

```
if (dragItem !=null) {
   dragPosX=getXCoord(dragItem);
   dragPosY=getYCoord(dragItem);
   Cart=getObject("CartBox");
   if (withinIt(dragPosX, dragPosY, Cart)) {
      snapBack();
      colorIt(dragItem, "red");
   } else {
      snapIn();
      colorIt(dragItem, "blue");
   }
   dragItem=null;
}
```

The complete code for the keyDrag() function is therefore:

```
function keyDrag(e) {
   key=getKey(e);
   if (key==49) dragItem=getObject("DRAGItem1");
   if (key==50) dragItem=getObject("DRAGItem2");
   if (key==51) dragItem=getObject("DRAGItem3");
   if (key==52) dragItem=getObject("DRAGItem4");
   if (dragItem !=null) {
      dragPosX=getXCoord(dragItem);
      dragPosY=getYCoord(dragItem);
      Cart=getObject("CartBox");
      if (withinIt(dragPosX, dragPosY, Cart)) {
         snapBack();
         colorIt(dragItem, "red");
      } else {
         snapIn();
         colorIt(dragItem, "blue");
      }
      dragItem=null;
   }
}
```

To insert the keyDrag() function:

1. Above the </SCRIPT> tag at the bottom of the page, insert the following code, as shown in Figure 4-44:

```
function keyDrag(e) {
   key=getKey(e);
   if (key==49) dragItem=getObject("DRAGItem1");
   if (key==50) dragItem=getObject("DRAGItem2");
   if (key==51) dragItem=getObject("DRAGItem3");
   if (key==52) dragItem=getObject("DRAGItem4");
   if (dragItem !=null) {
      dragPosX=getXCoord(dragItem);
      dragPosY=getYCoord(dragItem);
      Cart=getObject("CartBox");
      if (withinIt(dragPosX, dragPosY, Cart)) {
         snapBack();
         colorIt(dragItem, "red");
      } else {
         snapIn();
         colorIt(dragItem, "blue");
      }
      dragItem=null;
   }
}
```

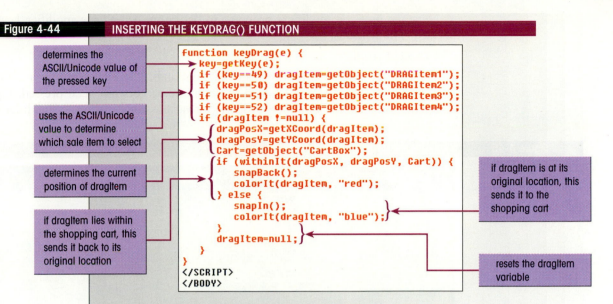

Figure 4-44   **INSERTING THE KEYDRAG() FUNCTION**

determines the ASCII/Unicode value of the pressed key

uses the ASCII/Unicode value to determine which sale item to select

determines the current position of dragItem

if dragItem lies within the shopping cart, this sends it back to its original location

```
function keyDrag(e) {
  key=getKey(e);
  if (key==49) dragItem=getObject("DRAGItem1");
  if (key==50) dragItem=getObject("DRAGItem2");
  if (key==51) dragItem=getObject("DRAGItem3");
  if (key==52) dragItem=getObject("DRAGItem4");
  if (dragItem !=null) {
    dragPosX=getXCoord(dragItem);
    dragPosY=getYCoord(dragItem);
    Cart=getObject("CartBox");
    if (withinIt(dragPosX, dragPosY, Cart)) {
        snapBack();
        colorIt(dragItem, "red");
    } else {
        snapIn();
        colorIt(dragItem, "blue");
    }
    dragItem=null;
  }
}
</SCRIPT>
</BODY>
```

if dragItem is at its original location, this sends it to the shopping cart

resets the dragItem variable

2. Save your changes to Games.htm and close the file.

3. Reload or refresh the **Games.htm** page in your Web browser.

4. Verify that as you press the numbers 1 through 4 on your keyboard, the sales items 1–4 are alternately selected and removed from the shopping cart.

   TROUBLE? Netscape users: The color of the shopping item will not change as it is moved to and from the shopping cart.

Modifier Keys

In addition to keyboard characters, keyboards contain **modifier keys**, which are the Ctrl, Alt, and Shift keys. Modifier keys, pressed along with letter keys, are often used as keyboard shortcuts to menu commands. For example, holding down the Ctrl key while pressing the "P" runs the browser's Print command. You can create your own key combinations to run customized functions from the keyboard, but in doing so you must be careful not to interfere with the key combinations already reserved by the browser. In case of a conflict, the browser might ignore your customized keyboard shortcut.

Internet Explorer and Netscape use different methods to determine whether a modifier key is being held down. Internet Explorer uses the following object properties:

```
event.altKey;
event.ctrlKey;
event.shiftKey;
```

to determine the state of the Alt, Ctrl, and Shift keys. If the value of any of these properties is true, the corresponding key is being held down. If the value of the property is false, the modifier key is not being pressed.

Netscape uses the modifiers property to determine whether a modifier key has been pressed. The syntax is:

```
e.modifiers;
```

where "e" is the parameter representing the event object. The value of the e.modifiers property can be used to determine which of the modifier keys has been pressed. Figure 4-45 shows the value of the e.modifiers property for various combinations of modifier keys.

Figure 4-45   **VALUES OF NETSCAPE'S E.MODIFIERS PROPERTY**

E.MODIFIERS VALUE	MODIFIER KEY(S) BEING PRESSED
0	None
1	Alt
2	Ctrl
3	Alt+Ctrl
4	Shift
5	Alt+Shift
6	Ctrl+Shift
7	Alt+Ctrl+Shift

Another approach in Netscape is to combine the e.modifiers object with built-in Netscape constants to determine whether the modifier key is being pressed. The general syntax is:

```
e.modifiers & Event.MODIFIER_MASK
```

where *MODIFIER_MASK* can be the constant ALT_MASK, CONTROL_MASK, or SHIFT_MASK for the Alt, Ctrl, and Shift keys, respectively. This expression will be true if the modifier key is being pressed. For example, the Netscape expression:

```
e.modifiers & Event.CONTROL_MASK
```

is equivalent to the Internet Explorer expression:

```
event.ctrlKey
```

Both expressions will be true if the Ctrl key is being held down, false if otherwise. At this point you don't need to use any modifier keys for the Games Etc. page.

REFERENCE WINDOW

Determining Whether a Modifier Key Is Being Pressed
- In Netscape, if the following expressions return the value true, the Alt, Ctrl, and Shift keys are being pressed:
  ```
  e.modifiers & Event.ALT_MASK
  e.modifiers & Event.CONTROL_MASK
  e.modifiers & Event.SHIFT_MASK
  ```
  where "e" is Netscape's event object parameter.
- In Internet Explorer, if the following expressions return the value true, the Alt, Ctrl, and Shift keys are being pressed:
  ```
  event.altKey;
  event.ctrlKey;
  event.shiftKey;
  ```

Having completed your work on the Web page, Pete will look over your work and get back to you with any further ideas or projects. You can close any open files in your text editor or browser.

Session 4.3 QUICK CHECK

1. What style declaration would you use to display an hourglass as the pointer? What is the equivalent JavaScript command to do this?

2. What is the ASCII/Unicode number for the letter "b" (lowercase)?

3. What JavaScript command would you enter to determine which key the user pressed in a Netscape browser? What is the equivalent command for Internet Explorer browsers?

4. What are modifier keys? How are modifier keys typically used?

5. What JavaScript command would you enter to determine whether the Alt key is being pressed in the Netscape browser? What is the equivalent command in Internet Explorer?

REVIEW ASSIGNMENTS

Pete has approved your design of the Shopping Cart page for the company's Web site. He now wants you to finish a Web page displaying a sliding block puzzle. In a sliding block puzzle, the puzzle pieces are laid out in a grid with one blank space. The object of the puzzle is to move the pieces around in the puzzle until the puzzle image is restored. A preview of the page is shown in Figure 4-46. The puzzle is divided into a 5×5 grid, with each piece in the grid 60 pixels wide by 60 pixels high. Each piece is formatted as a separate <DIV> tag. Starting from the upper-right grid and moving right and then down, the <DIV> tags have the ID names, Piece01, Piece02, and so forth. The blank space in the grid has the ID name "Blank."

Figure 4-46

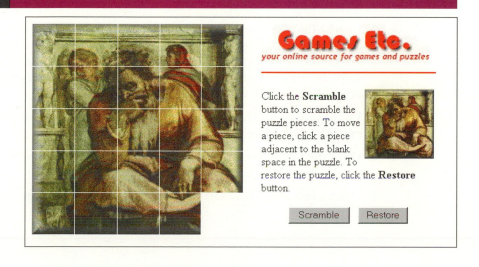

Games Etc.
your online source for games and puzzles

Click the **Scramble** button to scramble the puzzle pieces. To move a piece, click a piece adjacent to the blank space in the puzzle. To restore the puzzle, click the **Restore** button.

Scramble   Restore

The part of the page that displays and scrambles the pieces has already been done; your job will be to program the part that moves the pieces in response to actions by the user.

To help you, two API files are available. The file Random.js contains a function named "Scramble()" that scrambles the order of the tiles on the page. The Random.js file also creates the isNS and isIE variables to determine the browser type. The file Puzzletxt.js contains the functions described in Figure 4-47.

Figure 4-47

FUNCTION NAME	DESCRIPTION
placeIt(*object, x, y*)	Places the *object* at the page coordinates (x, y)
getXCoord(*object*)	Returns the x-coordinate of an object on the page
getYCoord(*object*)	Returns the y-coordinate of an object on the page
withinIt(*x, y, object*)	Returns "true" if the page coordinates (x, y) lie within the boundaries of the *object*, and "false" if otherwise
getDIV(*x, y*)	Returns an object created with the <DIV> tag, that contains the page coordinates (x, y)

Pete wants the puzzle to work as follows:

■ If a user clicks a piece adjacent to the blank space (diagonals don't count) the piece and the blank space should swap positions.

■ If the user clicks a piece that is not adjacent to the blank space, no action should be taken.

Neither Internet Explorer or the Netscape DOM recognizes the action of clicking on an inline image within a <DIV> tag. However, they do recognize the mouseup event. So you'll need to write your code to respond to the mouseup event, not to the click event.

To create the sliding block puzzle:

1. Open the **Puzzletxt.js** API file from the Tutorial.04D/Review folder on your Data Disk in your text editor, and save it as PuzzleAPI.js.

2. Insert a function named "EventX()" which calculates the x page coordinate of an event.

3. Insert a function named "EventY()" which calculates the y page coordinate of an event.

4. Insert a function named "swapPiece()", which has two parameters, named "Object1" and "Object2." The purpose of this function will be to switch the coordinates of the two objects. Have the function first determine the (x, y) page coordinates of each object and store the values in variables named x1, y1, x2, and y2, and then place each object at the other object's coordinates.

5. Print the code for the three new functions you created and close the PuzzleAPI.js file, saving your changes.

6. Open the **Puzzletxt.htm** file from the Tutorial.04D/Review folder on your Data Disk in your text editor, and save it as Puzzle.htm.

7. Insert a link to the PuzzleAPI.js file at the bottom of the page, before the </BODY> tag.

8. Insert a new set of <SCRIPT> tags before the </BODY> tag. Within the <SCRIPT> tags, create two variables named "Piece" and "BlankPiece", but do not give these variables any values. Piece and BlankPiece will be object variables that point to the selected puzzle piece and the blank space in the puzzle, respectively.

9. Capture the mouseup event and run a function named grabPiece(), which you'll create later, in response to the event.

Explore 10. Create a function named "findBlank()" that has two parameters named "x" and "y," which represent the (x, y) coordinates of the mouseup event. The purpose of the findBlank() function will be to determine whether the user has clicked a puzzle piece that is adjacent to the blank space, and if so, to store the location of the blank space in the BlankPiece variable. Insert the following commands into the findBlank() function:

   ■ Create a variable named "PieceLeft" and using the getDIV() function from the API file, set the PieceLeft variable equal to the piece located at the (x-61, y) page coordinate.

   ■ Create a variable named "PieceRight", and set the variable equal to the piece located at the (x+61, y) page coordinate.

   ■ Create a variable name "PieceUp", which points to the piece located at the (x, y-61) page coordinate.

   ■ Create a variable named "PieceDown", which points to the puzzle piece located at the (x, y+61) coordinate.

   ■ If PieceLeft is not equal to null, test whether the ID name of PieceLeft is equal to "Blank". If so, have the findBlank() function return the PieceLeft object variable.

   ■ If PieceRight is not equal to null, test whether its ID name is equal to "Blank", and if so, return the PieceRight variable.

   ■ In the same way, test whether the PieceUp and PieceDown variables are equal to null, and if so, further test whether their ID names are equal to "Blank". Return the PieceUp or PieceDown variables if they point to the blank space in the puzzle.

Explore 11. Insert the grabPiece() function, and within the function insert the following commands:

   ■ Set the initial values of Piece and BlankPiece to null.

   ■ Determine the (x, y) page coordinate of the mouseup event and store the coordinate values in two variables named mouseX and mouseY.

   ■ Call the getDIV() function from the PuzzleAPI.js file to determine which piece in the puzzle was clicked, and store the result in the Piece variable.

   ■ Call the findBlank() function with mouseX and mouseY as the parameter values, and store the result in the BlankPiece variable.

   ■ If Piece is not equal to null, test whether the ID name of the Piece object contains the text string "Piece", and whether BlankPiece is not equal to null. If both of these conditions are true, swap the coordinates of the Piece and BlankPiece. (*Hint*: Use the swapPiece() function you created in the PuzzleAPI.js file.)

12. Print the JavaScript code you inserted into the Puzzle.htm file. Close the file, saving your changes.

13. Open **Puzzle.htm** in your Web browser. Click the Scramble button to scramble the order of the puzzle pieces. Verify that when you click a puzzle piece adjacent to the blank space in the grid, the piece switches places with the blank space. If you like, try to solve the puzzle (but it's not necessary to complete the assignment).

CASE PROBLEMS

Case 1. Creating a Quiz for Opera 101   Faye Dawson teaches Opera 101 at MidWest University. She has asked you to help her put some of her quiz questions online for her students to study. Some of the quiz questions involve matching the name of a composer to an operatic work. She wants students to be able to perform the matching by typing a number for the composer, followed by a letter representing the musical piece. The page would then provide visual feedback to the student by moving the composer's image next to the selected work. Figure 4-48 shows a preview of the page you'll create for Faye.

Figure 4-48

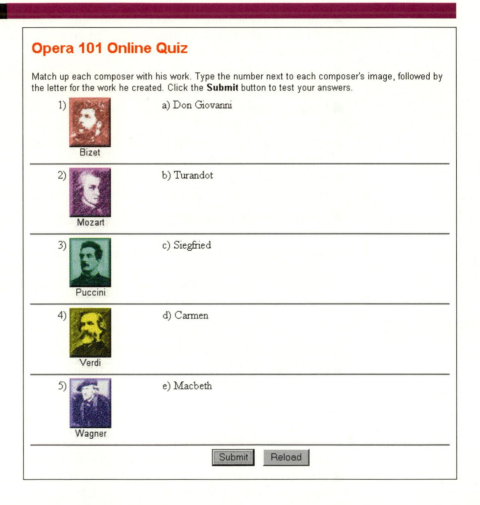

The layout of the page has been created for you. Also, an API file has been created that creates the isNS and isIE variables for determining the browser type. In addition, the API file contains the following functions:

- getObject(*o*)   Which returns an object variable pointing to an object with the ID name *o*
- placeIt(*object, x, y*)   Which places an *object* at the page coordinates (*x, y*)
- getXCoord(*object*)   Which returns the x page coordinate of an *object*
- getYCoord(*object*)   Which returns the y page coordinate of an *object*

Your task is to program the part of the page that responds to the student's keystrokes. For example, if the student presses the "1" key, followed by "e", the image of Bizet should move down to the right of the text string "Carmen" on the page.

After the student has matched the composers and works, he or she can check the score by clicking the Submit button on the Web page. The answer to the quiz is: 1-d, 2-a, 3-b, 4-e, and 5-c.

To create the Opera 101 quiz page:

1. Open the **Operatxt.js** API file from the Tutorial.04D/Cases folder on your Data Disk in your text editor, and save it as OperaAPI.js.

2. Insert a new function at the end of the API file named "useKey()" that returns the ASCII/Unicode number of the key pressed by the student.

3. Print the new function you entered into the file. Close the OperaAPI.js file, saving your changes.

4. Open the **Operatxt.htm** API file from the Tutorial.04D/Cases folder on your Data Disk in your text editor, and save it as **Opera.htm**.

5. Above the </BODY> tag, insert a link to the OperaAPI.js file.

6. Below the link you just created, insert a set of <SCRIPT> tags. Within the <SCRIPT> tags, create two new variables: Composer and Work. The Composer variable will indicate which composer the student selected. The Work variable will indicate which work was selected. Set the initial values of these variables to null.

7. Capture the keypress event, and have the browser run the function Match() in response to the event.

Explore

8. Create the Match() function, with the following commands:

   - Determine the ASCII/Unicode number of the key pressed by the user, and store the value in a variable named "key".
   - If the user pressed the "1" key, point the Composer variable to the "Bizet" object. (*Hint*: Use the getObject() function from the API file.)
   - If the user pressed one of the numbers "2" through "5", point the Composer variable to the appropriate composer object as indicated on the Web page.
   - If the user pressed either an "a" or an "A", point the Work variable to the "Giovanni" object on the page.
   - If the user pressed one of the letters "b" through "e" (in either uppercase or lowercase), point the Work variable to the appropriate work object on the page.
   - If Composer is not equal to null and Work is not equal to null, then: 1) create a variable named "x" that is equal to the x-coordinate of the Work object plus 150; 2) create a variable named "y" that is equal to the y-coordinate of the Work object; 3) place the Composer object at the (x, y) page coordinates; and 4) reset the values of the Composer and Work objects to null.

9. Create a function named Score(), containing the following commands:

   - Create a variable named "Correct" with an initial value of 0.
   - If the y-coordinate of the "Bizet" object is 400, increase the value of Correct by 1.
   - If the y-coordinate of the "Mozart" object is 100, increase Correct by 1.
   - If the y-coordinate of the "Puccini" object is 200, increase Correct by 1.

- If the y-coordinate of the "Verdi" object is 500, increase Correct by 1.
- If the y-coordinate of the "Wagner" object is 300, increase Correct by 1.
- Display an alert dialog box with the message: "You got *Correct* out of 5 correct." where *Correct* is the value of the Correct variable.

10. Modify the Submit button, so that it runs the Score() function when clicked.

11. Print the new JavaScript code you entered for the Opera.htm file. Close the file, saving your changes.

12. Open Opera.htm in your Web browser, and verify that, as you press the number of the composer, followed by the letter of the work, the composer images shift on the page.

13. Click the Submit button, and verify that it reports the correct number of matches.

Case 2. Creating a Preference List for Consumer Surveys Derek Mahnaz organizes the Online Consumer Survey, a Web site that reports consumer preferences and opinions. Derek has asked you to create a Web page in which consumers can list their preferences for department stores. Derek envisions the Web page listing the stores in separate boxes. Users would then be able to drag and drop the boxes in the order of store preference, with the stores they frequent most often at the top, and those least often visited at the bottom. A CGI script can then be run to tally the results. Figure 4-49 shows a preview of Derek's page.

Figure 4-49

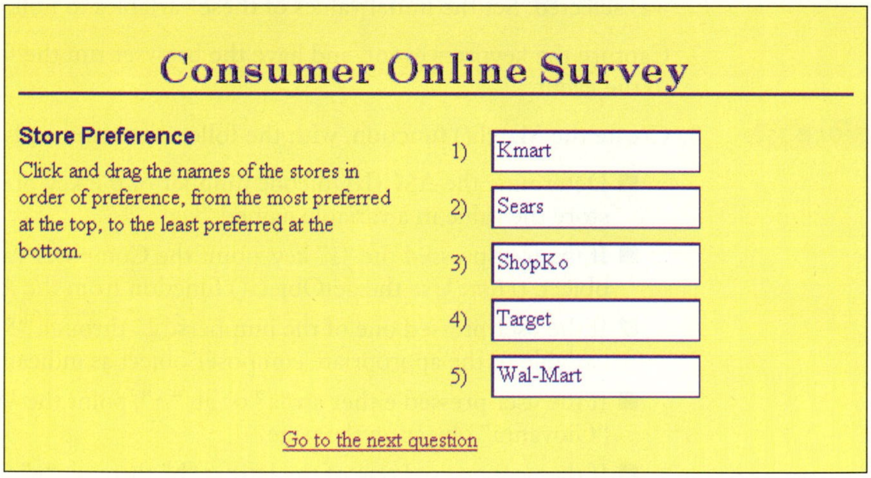

To complete this project, you need to add drag-and-drop capability to the Web page. This feature will work as follows:

- The user grabs a store by clicking on it. The store is moved across the page as long as the mouse is in the down position.
- When the store is being moved across the page, it should appear on top of all other stores.
- When the user drops the store on top of another, the stores swap positions.
- If the user drops the store anywhere else on the page, it snaps back to its original position.

The API file Survey.js contains many of the functions you'll need to create the drag-and-drop effect (most of these functions should be familiar to you by now.) Each store on the page is placed within separate <DIV> tags, and given an ID name from Store1 through Store5.

To create the Online Consumer Survey page:

1. Open the **Surveytxt.htm** file from the Tutorial.04D/Cases folder on your Data Disk in your text editor, and save it as Survey.htm.

2. Above the </HEAD> tag, insert a link to the Survey.js file.

3. Above the </BODY> tag, insert a pair of <SCRIPT> tags.

4. Capture the following events: mousedown, mousemove, and mouseup, and assign them to the following functions (respectively): selectStore, moveStore, and dropStore.

5. Create the following variables:

   ■ Store: An object variable that points to the currently selected store. Set its initial value to null.

   ■ startX and startY: The initial page coordinates of Store. Do not specify an initial value.

   ■ diffX and diffY: The difference between the initial page coordinates of Store and the coordinates of the mouse button when pressed down. Do not specify an initial value.

   ■ maxZ: The maximum z-index on the page. Set its initial value to 1.

6. To allow the users to "grab" a store from the page, create the selectStore() function to do the following:

   ■ Determine the location of the mousedown event, and store the (x, y) page coordinates in two variables named mouseX, and mouseY.

   ■ Determine what page object lies underneath the (mouseX, mouseY) page coordinates, and save that information in the Store object.

   ■ If the ID name of the Store object does not contain the text string "Store", set Store to null.

   ■ If Store is not equal to null, 1) increase the value of maxZ by 1, and assign Store the highest z-index value on the page; 2) determine its (x, y) page coordinates and save the values in the startX and startY variables; and 3) calculate the difference between the (mouseX, mouseY) and (startX, startY) coordinates, saving the values in the diffX and diffY variables.

7. To move the store across the page, perform the following in the moveStore() function:

   ■ If Store is not equal to null, determine the current location of the mouse pointer, and store the page coordinates in the mouseX and mouseY variables.

   ■ Place Store at the page coordinates, (mouseX – diffX, mouseY – diffY).

8. To drop the store on the page, use the dropStore() function; first test that Store is not equal to null, and then perform the following tasks:

   ■ Save the current page coordinates of Store, in the variables StoreX and StoreY.

   ■ Determine if the user has dropped Store on top of another store name on the page by calling the getDIV() function from the API file, using the StoreX and StoreY variables as parameter values. Save the object returned by this function as "SwapStore."

   ■ If SwapStore is equal to null, place the Store object that the user originally selected with the mousedown action back at its start location, as indicated by the startX and startY variables.

- If SwapStore is not equal to null, test whether the ID name of SwapStore contains the text string "Store." If it doesn't, place the Store object back at its starting location. If it does (which means that the user dropped the selected Store on top of another store in the list), save the page coordinates of SwapStore in the variables SwapX and SwapY. Then, swap the location of Store and SwapStore, placing Store at the page coordinates (SwapX, SwapY), and SwapStore at the coordinates (startX, startY).

- Release the mousemove event, and set the value of Store back to null.

9. Assign the mouseover event to the showCursor() function.

10. Create the showCursor function to do the following:

- Test whether the user is running an Internet Explorer browser.

- If so, change the cursor style of the mouse pointer to "move" whenever the user hovers the mouse over an object with the text string "Store" in its ID name.

11. Print your JavaScript code, and close the Survey.htm file, saving your changes.

12. Open Survey.htm in your Web browser. Confirm that you can drag-and-drop the store names on the Web page. Verify that as you move one store name on top of another, the two names swap places in the list, and further verify that when you drop the store name anywhere else on the page, it snaps back to its original location.

Case 3. Creating an HTML demonstration page (Internet Explorer only) You are a teaching assistant for Professor Diane Wheaton of the Computer Science Department at Reardon College. Professor Wheaton is preparing an introduction to HTML tags, and she would like you to create a demonstration page. The page will have two boxes: an input box into which she'll type HTML code, and an output box that shows the results of that code. When she hovers the mouse pointer over the input box, she wants the characters she types from the keyboard to be captured and displayed within the box. This is where she plans to type HTML code. Then, when she moves the mouse pointer over the output box, she wants the code she enters into the input box to be rendered in the output box. Figure 4-50 shows a preview of the page.

Figure 4-50

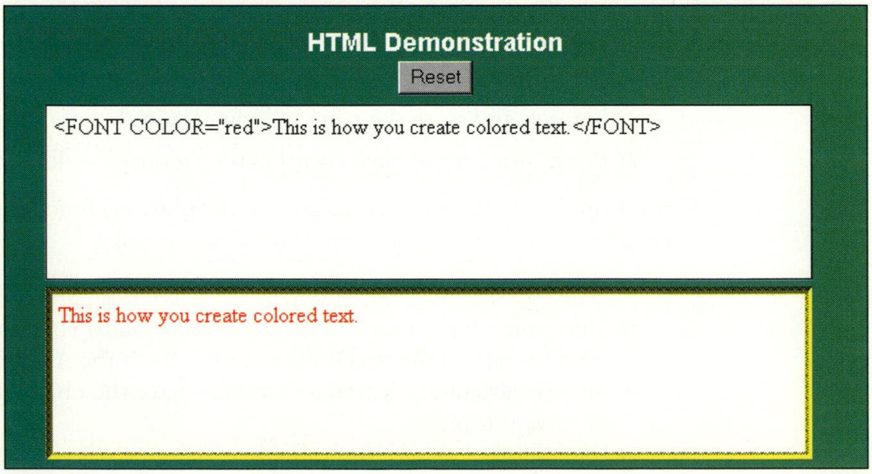

HTML Demonstration

Reset

<FONT COLOR="red">This is how you create colored text.</FONT>

This is how you create colored text.

To create the HTML demonstration page:

1. Open the **Demotxt.htm** file from the Tutorial.04D/Cases folder on your Data Disk in your text editor, and save it as Demo.htm.

Explore

2. Add the cursor style to the inline style for the input box, changing the mouse pointer to the "text" pointer.

3. Above the </BODY> tag insert a pair of <SCRIPT> tags.

4. Create a variable named "InputString" that will be used to store the characters that Professor Wheaton types into the input box. Set the initial value of InputString to "".

5. When the user passes the mouse pointer over objects in the document, run the function highlightBorder().

6. When user passes the mouse pointer out from objects in the document, run the function normalBorder().

7. When the user passes the mouse pointer over the input box, run the function startInput().

8. When the user passes the mouse pointer over the output box, run the function, showOutPut().

9. Create the highlightBorder() function. In this function, do the following:

   ■ Create an object variable named "Box" and set it equal to the source of the mouseover event.

   ■ If Box points to either the input or output box, change the border color of the box to yellow, the border width to 5, and the border style to "inset."

10. Create the normalBorder() function to perform the following tasks:

    ■ Create an object variable named "Box" and set it equal to the source of the mouseover event.

    ■ If Box points to either the input or output box, change the border color of the box to black, the border width to 1, and the border style to "solid."

11. Create the startInput() function. The function should have one task: to run the insertCode() function when the user presses a keyboard key.

Explore

12. Create the insertCode() function. The function should do the following:

    ■ Save the key code that was pressed by the user in a variable named "key."

    ■ Convert key to a text character. (*Hint*: Use the fromCharCode() method.) Store the results in a variable named "Letter."

    ■ Add Letter to the InputString variable.

    ■ Insert Letter as adjacent text before the end of the input box.

13. Create the showOutput() function. The function should do the following:

    ■ Release the key press event by setting it to null.

    ■ Change the inner HTML code of the output box to InputString.

14. Print your JavaScript code, and close Demo.htm, saving your changes.

15. Open Demo.htm in your Internet Explorer browser. Verify that as you pass the mouse pointer over the input and output boxes, the appearance of the border changes. Check that when the mouse pointer is over the input box, HTML code that you type from the keyboard appears in the box; then, move the mouse pointer over the output box and verify that the code you entered in the input box is rendered there. (*Note*: You will not be able to use the backspace key to correct typing mistakes, nor will you be able to move the insertion point for new text. If you make a typing mistake, click the Reset button.)

Case 4. Creating a Shopping Cart for Produce World Produce World, a local grocery store, is making some of its products available on the World Wide Web. Customers will be able to visit the Web site and select items for purchase. Their selections will be then sent to the store, where they will be gathered and packaged for pickup by the customer.

Steve Adronski, a manager at Produce World, has asked for your help in creating a Web page that will feature a drag-and-drop shopping cart. The page will display the following items for purchase:

- Bananas at $1.60/bunch
- Red Delicious Apples at $2.80/bag
- Georgia Peaches at $1.90/bag
- Blueberries at $1.49/carton
- Strawberries at $2.49/carton
- Cantaloupe at $0.29/piece
- Red Seedless Grapes at $1.59/bag
- Green Seedless Grapes at $1.59/bag

The design of the shopping cart is up to you. You can add inline graphics for each of the produce items, if you can locate the appropriate clip art. You may also want to create a distinctive logo for Produce World.

1. Create a file named **Produce.htm** that contains the layout and content of your Web page.

2. Create an API file named **Produce.js** that contains any specialized JavaScript functions you need for your task.

3. Add drag-and-drop capability to the produce items in the Produce.htm file.

4. Display a helpful mouse cursor symbol when the user selects produce to drag (Internet Explorer only).

5. If a customer fails to drop a selected produce item in the shopping cart, have the item snap back to its original spot on the page.

Explore

6. Create a button named "Total" on the page that tallies up the total number of items selected and the total cost, and then displays that information in an alert dialog box when clicked.

7. Print copies of the HTML code you entered to complete this task.

8. Print a copy of the Produce.htm file as it appears in your browser.

QUICK CHECK ANSWERS

Session 4.1

1. As a property within a tag, with a <SCRIPT> tag (Internet Explorer only), and as a property of an object

2. `window.captureEvents(Event.KEYPRESS);`

3. `document.onkeypress=CalcTotal;`

4. Netscape must capture events before assigning functions to them. Netscape handles events from the top of the document object model hierarchy and moves down. Internet Explorer applies events from the bottom of the hierarchy and bubbles the events up.

5. Event bubbling is the process in Internet Explorer by which events start at the bottom of the object hierarchy and move up.

6. In Netscape:

   The x-coordinate of the mouse position = e.pageX, where "e" is the event object parameter, and the y-coordinate of the mouse position = e.pageY

   In Internet Explorer:

   The x-coordinate of the mouse position = event.clientX, where "event" is the Internet Explorer event object, and the y-coordinate of the mouse position = event.clientY

Session 4.2

1. `e.pageX;`
   `e.pageY;`

2. `event.clientX+document.body.scrollLeft;`
   `event.clientY+document.body.scrollTop;`

3. `ImgObject=event.srcElement;`

4. You will have to loop through all of the objects in the Web page and determine which object contains the page coordinates of the event.

5. –1

6. Keep track of the maximum z-index value on the Web page, and set the z-index value of the dragged item to one value higher than that.

Session 4.3

1. `cursor: "wait"`
   `object.style.cursor="wait";`

2. 98

3. In Netscape:

   `key = e.which;`

   In Internet Explorer:

   `key = event.keyCode;`

4. Modifier keys are pressed along with letter keys, and are often used as keyboard shortcuts to menu commands. There are three modifier keys: Ctrl, Alt, and Shift.

5. In Netscape, if the following command is true:

   `e.modifiers & Event.ALT_MASK;`

   the ALT key is being pressed.

   In Internet Explorer, if the following command is true:

   `event.ctrlKey;`

   the ALT key is being pressed.

OBJECTIVES

In this tutorial you will:

- Modify the appearance and behavior of browser windows

- Create messages that appear in the browser's status bar

- Automatically redirect your Web browser to new Web pages

- Create pop-up windows and modify their contents

- Work with the appearance, content, and behavior of frames and framesets

WORKING WITH WINDOWS AND FRAMES

Enhancing a Web Site with Interactive Windows

CASE

Enhancing an Interactive Online Course for iMusicHistory

Teresa Jenner, a professional musician and college instructor, started a music history Web site two years ago to supplement the university courses she teaches. Since she and her students found it to be so helpful, Teresa decided to expand the site further, create a new name for it, and market it as an online course. Last month Teresa bought a new domain name for the Web site, iMusicHistory, so that she can take it off her university's server. Teresa has hired you to add interactive features to her online music history course Web site.

Because this is a new site, she needs you to create scripts to automatically redirect users to the new URL from the old university one. Beyond that, Teresa wants to have more control over the interaction between the browser and her Web site. For example, she would like to create her own customized status bar messages. She would also like to add pop-up windows to her Web site for use in an online quiz, and add a glossary of musical terms.

Finally, part of her Web site uses frames. She would like you to write some scripts to control the appearance and behavior of her frames. Teresa hopes that any solutions you create will be cross-browser compatible.

SESSION 5.1

In this session you'll be introduced to the window, history, and location objects, their properties and methods, and the necessary security precautions associated with these objects. You'll learn how to use the window object's properties and methods to add messages to the browser window's status bar and how to use the history and location objects to redirect the user to a new window or to allow the user to go forward or backward in the browser's history list.

Working with the Window Object

At your first meeting with Teresa, she shows you the current status of her Web site, and you discuss the changes she wants you to make. Figure 5-1 displays the current home page of the Web site.

Figure 5-1   THE IMUSICHISTORY HOME PAGE

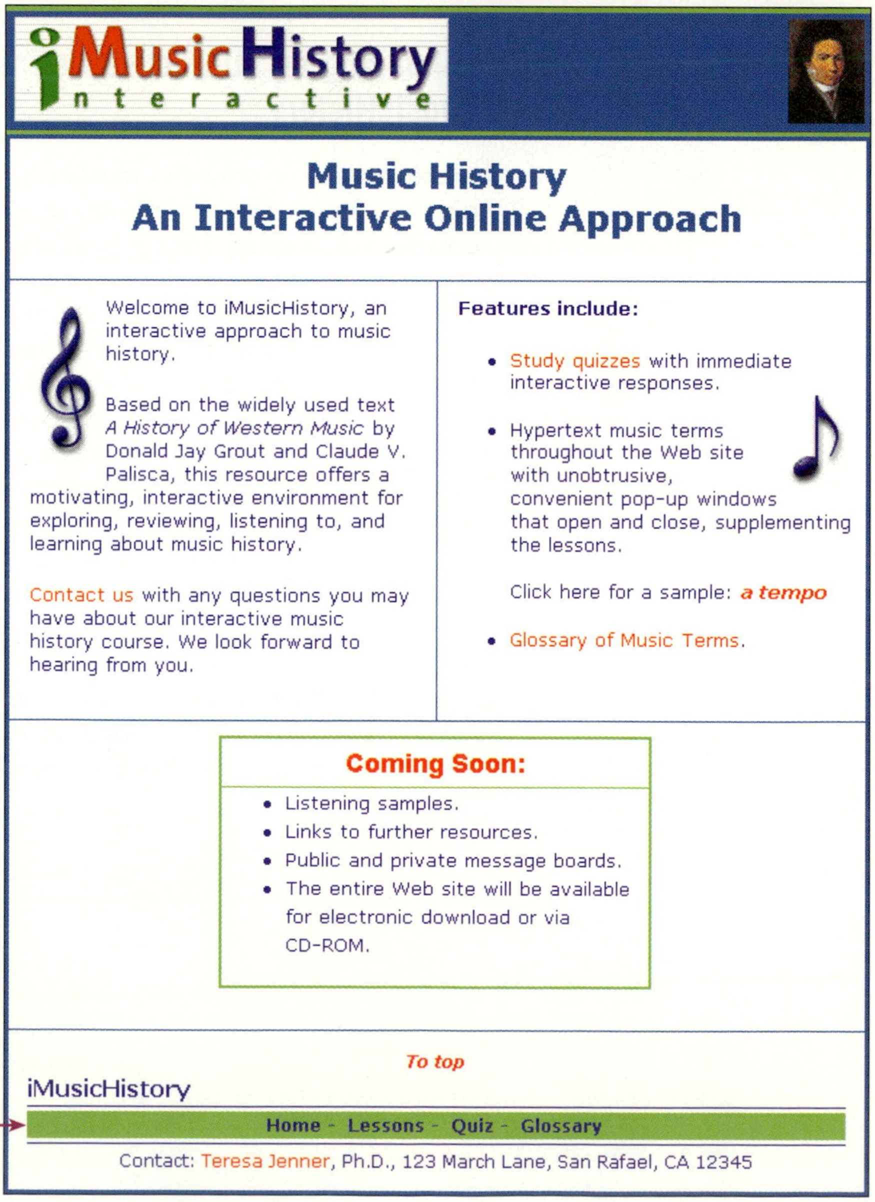

iMusic History
i n t e r a c t i v e

Music History
An Interactive Online Approach

Welcome to iMusicHistory, an interactive approach to music history.

Based on the widely used text *A History of Western Music* by Donald Jay Grout and Claude V. Palisca, this resource offers a motivating, interactive environment for exploring, reviewing, listening to, and learning about music history.

Contact us with any questions you may have about our interactive music history course. We look forward to hearing from you.

Features include:

- Study quizzes with immediate interactive responses.

- Hypertext music terms throughout the Web site with unobtrusive, convenient pop-up windows that open and close, supplementing the lessons.

  Click here for a sample: *a tempo*

- Glossary of Music Terms.

Coming Soon:
- Listening samples.
- Links to further resources.
- Public and private message boards.
- The entire Web site will be available for electronic download or via CD-ROM.

To top

iMusicHistory

text navigation hyperlinks for Web site →

Home - Lessons - Quiz - Glossary

Contact: Teresa Jenner, Ph.D., 123 March Lane, San Rafael, CA 12345

As you can see from the links on the home page, the iMusicHistory Web site has four main pages:

- A home page, describing the purpose and features of the site
- A Lessons page, containing an interactive lesson on music history
- A Quiz page, containing an online quiz for students to review
- A Glossary page, containing definitions of musical terms

The first changes that Teresa wants you to make to her Web site involve the text that appears in the Web browser's status bar. Teresa would like a status bar message welcoming visitors to the site to appear as soon as the home page of the Web site loads. She would also like a description of each navigational link to appear in the status bar whenever someone moves the mouse pointer over a navigation link.

Later, Teresa would like you to make modifications to other pages in the Web site. The home page of the site is stored in the Defaulttxt.htm file. Open this file now.

To open the iMusicHistory home page:

1. In your text editor, open the **Defaulttxt.htm** file located in the Tutorial.05D folder of your Data Disk.

2. Save the file as **Default.htm** in the same folder.

3. Open the **Default.htm** page in your Web browser (see Figure 5-1).

4. Review the overall design and layout of the page, keeping in mind the code and corresponding style sheet and their impact on the Web page in the browser.

TROUBLE? Some of the links in the Web page will not work yet, since you haven't created the required files.

To create the messages in the status bar that Teresa wants, you'll need to manipulate the window object. Recall that the objects in JavaScript are organized in a hierarchy, with the **window object** at the top. Figure 5-2 describes some of the properties of the window object and how they are supported by the two major browsers.

Figure 5-2	PROPERTIES OF THE WINDOW OBJECT			
PROPERTY	**DESCRIPTION**	**VALUE**	**NETSCAPE**	**IE**
closed	Indicates whether the window is closed	Boolean	2.0	3.0
defaultStatus	The default message in the window's status bar	Text	2.0	3.0
innerHeight	The height of the window, excluding all toolbars, scroll bars, and other features	Integer	4.0	
innerWidth	The width of the window, excluding all toolbars, scroll bars, and other features	Integer	4.0	
location	The URL of the document currently loaded in the window	URL	2.0	3.0
name	The name of the window	Text	2.0	3.0
outerHeight	The height of the window, including all toolbars, scroll bars, and other features	Integer	4.0	
outerWidth	The width of the window, including all toolbars, scroll bars, and other features	Integer	4.0	
status	The current message in the window's status bar	Text	2.0	3.0

Modifying the Status Bar Message

The two different kinds of status bar messages that Teresa has asked you to add (a welcome message when the page loads and description messages for navigation links) require two different methods. To change the welcome message, you'll modify the status property of the window object.

Creating a Status Bar Welcome Message for iMusicHistory

You've probably seen a variety of status bar messages in different Web pages, including static messages and moving text. While some Web users enjoy moving text, many do not like continuous scrolling messages in the status bar. Not only are such messages distracting, but they can also crash earlier browser versions, in particular Netscape version 2.0. Additionally, some users prefer to see the URL of the current page in the status bar. Therefore, Teresa has recommended that you create a workable compromise: include the URL with a static welcome message rather than create a scrolling message.

Two window properties reference the status bar: the defaultStatus property and the status property. The **defaultStatus property** specifies the status bar default; its message appears when there is no message specified by the status property. If no message is specified by either property, the default is a blank status bar. The syntax for changing the value of the defaultStatus property is:

```
window.defaultStatus="message";
```

where "*message*" is the message that will appear by default in the browser window's status bar. Note that it is generally recommended that you not use the defaultStatus property, since it directly competes with the browser's ability to report such things as the progress of downloading.

The **status property** will display a transient message in the status bar, for example, when the user loads the page or moves the mouse pointer over a link. As soon as the mouse pointer moves away from a link, the status bar returns to its default setting (which may be blank). This is far less intrusive and more cross-browser compatible than the defaultStatus property. The syntax changing the message in the status bar when using the status property is:

```
window.status="message";
return true;
```

Note that this approach requires that you include the "return true;" command after changing the status message.

To change the message in the status bar, you'll add the following function to the Default.htm file:

```
function showStatus(msg) {
      window.status = msg
      return true
}
```

The showStatus() function has one parameter—msg, which is the message you want to appear in the browser window's status bar. Since Teresa has asked that the welcome message in the status bar appear when the page loads, you'll call this function by using the onLoad event handler in the <BODY> tag.

To run the showStatus ( ) function when the iMusicHistory Web page loads:

1. Return to the **Default.htm** file in your text editor.

2. Above the </HEAD> tag, insert the following code:

```
<SCRIPT>
function showStatus(msg) {
      window.status = msg
      return true
}
</SCRIPT>
```

3. Insert the following code within the <BODY> tag:

```
onLoad='showStatus("Welcome to iMusicHistory
(www.imusichistory.com)")'
```

4. Press the **Enter** key after BGCOLOR=WHITE" to force the message within the double quotes onto its own line. If the message isn't all on the same line, an error may result.

Your revised file should appear as shown in Figure 5-3.

| Figure 5-3 | ADDING THE SHOWSTATUS() FUNCTION TO THE ONLOAD EVENT HANDLER |

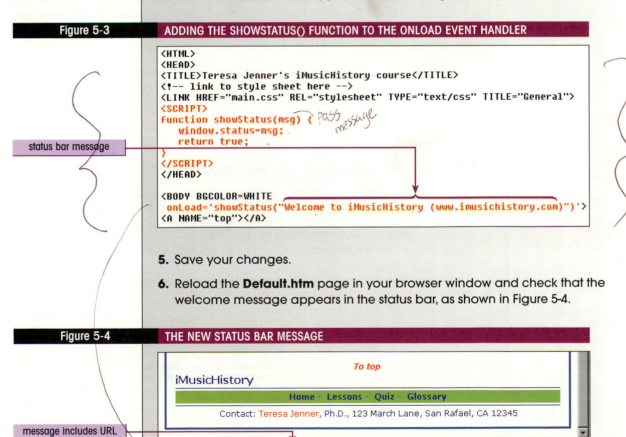

status bar message

message includes URL

| Figure 5-4 | THE NEW STATUS BAR MESSAGE |

5. Save your changes.

6. Reload the **Default.htm** page in your browser window and check that the welcome message appears in the status bar, as shown in Figure 5-4.

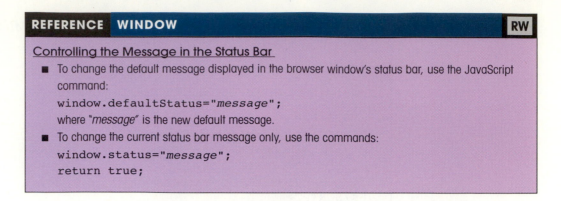

Creating Status Bar Messages for the iMusicHistory Hyperlinks

By default, most browsers display the URL of a hyperlink in the status bar when the user passes the pointer over the link. However, Teresa would like the following message to appear in the status bar when the user passes the pointer over the Home page hyperlink: "Go to the iMusicHistory home page." When the user moves the pointer off the hyperlink, the status bar should become blank. To accomplish this, you'll once again call the showStatus() function, but this time in response to the onMouseOver and onMouseOut events for hyperlinks on the page. However, because browsers have a default message for the status bar for hyperlinks, you need to include the command "return" before calling the showStatus() function. The HTML code you'll enter is therefore:

```
onMouseOver='return showStatus("Go to the iMusicHistory home
page")'
onMouseOut='return showStatus("")'
```

To add the status bar message to the Home hyperlink:

1. Return to the **Default.htm** file in your text editor and scroll to the bottom of the file.

2. Within the <A> tag for the Home hyperlink, insert the following code, as shown in Figure 5-5:

```
onMouseOver='return showStatus("Go to the iMusicHistory
home page")' onMouseOut='return showStatus("")'
```

Figure 5-5	CHANGING THE STATUS BAR MESSAGE ACTIVATED BY A HYPERLINK

include the return keyword before calling the showStatus function

make sure message appears on one line

```
<!-- Begin navigation text cell -->
<TR>
<TD VALIGN=MIDDLE BGCOLOR="#99CC99" ALIGN=CENTER CLASS="nav">
<A CLASS="nav" HREF="Default.htm"
 onMouseOver='return showStatus("Go to the iMusicHistory home page")'
 onMouseOut='return showStatus("")'>Home</A> - 
<A CLASS="nav" HREF="Lesson3.htm">Lessons</A> - 
<A CLASS="nav" HREF="Quiz.htm">Quiz</A> - 
<A CLASS="nav" HREF="Terms.htm">Glossary</A><BR>
<IMG SRC="dotclear.gif" BORDER=0></TD>
</TR>
```

3. Press the **Enter** key before "onMouseOver" so that the text within the double quotes is entered on the same line (otherwise an error message may result).

4. Save your changes.

5. Reload the page in your browser.

6. Pass the pointer over the Home page link at the bottom of the page; the message shown in Figure 5-6 should appear.

Figure 5-6 **THE NEW STATUS BAR MESSAGE FOR THE HOME HYPERLINK**

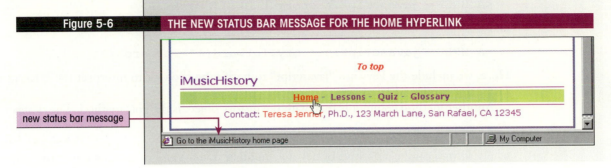

new status bar message

You've completed your work for now on the status bar messages. There are other links and pages in the Web site, and you'll have to apply the techniques you just learned in those places. For now, however, Teresa wants you to work more with the main browser window.

Working with the History and Location Objects

Previously, the iMusicHistory Web site was stored on the servers at Teresa's university and the home page was located in a file named index.htm (rather than Default.htm). Teresa still wants the index.htm page in her site since some users will still have links or bookmarks that point to it; but that page should now alert users about the changes and provide a link to Default.htm. Teresa would also like to have a link on the old home page that, when clicked, takes the user back to the previous page they visited. This way users can notify the authors of pages that have links to the iMusicHistory Web site that the link should be updated. Finally, if the user does nothing, Teresa would like the browser to automatically load the new site after a brief interval.

The browser maintains a lot of information about where you've been and the page you're currently visiting. The browser stores information about pages that have been previously visited in the **history object**. The **location property** contains information about the Web page that's currently open in the browser. You'll be working with both of these objects as you create the redirect page. First you'll learn about the history object to create links to pages previously visited by the user.

Moving Forward and Backward in the History List

The history object has evolved quite a bit since its inclusion in the document object model. In Netscape versions 2 and 3 and Internet Explorer 3 and 4, the history list applied to the entire browser window, whether or not the window included frames. Beginning with Netscape version 4.0, however, each frame has its own history list.

Two popular uses of the history object are the back() and forward() methods, which perform actions similar to the Back and Forward buttons on the Web browser's toolbar. The syntax of these two methods is:

```
history.back();
history.forward();
```

The back() method causes the browser to load the page prior to the current page in the history list; in other words, it jumps the browser back to the page the user was previously viewing. If you're at the beginning of the history list, there will be no page to go back to, and the current page will not be replaced. The forward() method loads the next page in the history list after the current page. If you're at the end of the history list, there will be no page to go to, and the current page will remain in the browser.

A common way to implement the back() and forward() methods is as hyperlinks with the following structure:

```
<A HREF="javascript:history.back()">Back</A>
```

and

```
<A HREF="javascript:history.forward()">Forward</A>
```

Here, we include the keyword "javascript" to notify the browser to interpret the URL as a Javascript command.

Another method commonly used with the history object is the go() method. The syntax is:

```
history.go(integer)
```

where *integer* can be a positive or negative number or zero and represents how many pages the browser should move through in the history list. For example, the command history.go(-1) moves the user back one page in the history list. The command, history.go(1) moves the user to the next page in the list, and the command, history.go(0) keeps the user at the current page. The only exception to this occurs with Internet Explorer 3.0. In that browser version, all invocations of the go() method with a non-zero value are executed assuming a value of -1. For this reason, the go() method should be used with some caution if you are worried about interacting with older browsers.

Netscape 4.0 also includes the window.back() and window.forward() methods to move backward and forward through the history list, and while they are similar to the history.back() and history.forward() methods, they are not supported by Internet Explorer.

Much of the content of the revised index.htm page has been created for you and is stored as "indextxt.htm." Your first task will be to create a hyperlink on the index.htm page that points to the page previously visited by the user.

To link to the previously visited page:

1. Return to your text editor and open **indextxt.htm** from the Tutorial.05D file on your Data Disk.

2. Save the file as **index.htm**.

3. Locate the word "return" two lines above the </CENTER> tag.

4. Enclose "return" within a pair of <A> tags, with the URL: **javascript:history.back()**, as shown in Figure 5-7.

Figure 5-7	CREATING A LINK TO A PREVIOUSLY VISITED PAGE

link to the previously visited Web page

```
<P>You will automatically be transported there<BR> in 8 seconds or less.</P>
<P>If your browser doesn't recognize the command,<BR> please click
<A HREF="Default.htm">iMusicHistory.com</A> to move to the new page.</P>
<P>If a link has led you erroneously to this page, <BR>please click
<A HREF="javascript:history.back()">return</A> to go back to the previous
page,<BR> and notify the page's author of the outdated link.</P>
```

window obj.
function

5. Save your changes to the file.

6. Return to your Web browser.

7. Open the **index.htm** page.

8. Verify that when you click **return** on the index.htm page, the previous page you opened (in this case, Default.htm) is loaded by the browser. See Figure 5-8.

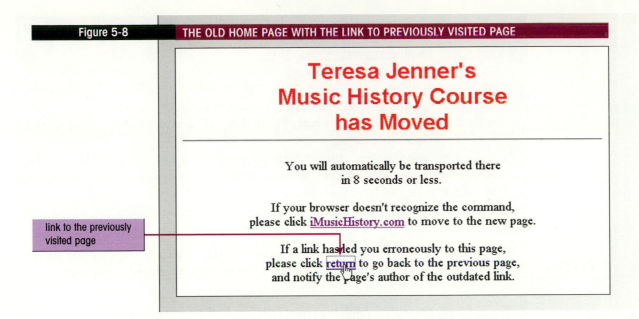

Figure 5-8 **THE OLD HOME PAGE WITH THE LINK TO PREVIOUSLY VISITED PAGE**

link to the previously visited page

With the link to the previous page taken care of, your next task will be to automatically redirect the browser to the new Web site.

Automatic Page Navigation

There are two ways to automatically redirect the user to another Web page. One way is to add a command to the <META> tag located in the Head section of the HTML file. The other is to create a JavaScript program that runs when the page is loaded and jumps the user to the new page. Since some browser versions do not support JavaScript, you'll employ both methods in the index.htm file.

The syntax for redirecting a page by using the <META> tag is:

```
<META HTTP-EQUIV="Refresh" CONTENT="sec;URL=URL">
```

where *sec* is the amount of time in seconds that will elapse before opening the new page, and the *URL* is the new page to be loaded. For example, to automatically load the Default.htm page after 8 seconds, you would add the following tag to the index.htm file:

```
<META HTTP-EQUIV="Refresh" CONTENT="8;URL=Default.htm">
```

Setting the time value to zero causes the redirection to occur almost instantaneously, so that often the user is not even aware that a redirection has taken place. However, in this case, you want the user to have time to read the text notifying users that their links to iMusicHistory need to be updated.

The other approach, using JavaScript, employs the following syntax:

```
window.location.href = "URL";
```

where *URL* is the new page to be loaded. To redirect the browser to the Default.htm page, you would add the following JavaScript command to the index.htm file:

```
window.location.href="Default.htm";
```

To add a delay, you can run this command with the setTimeout method(), setting a delay time of 8000 milliseconds (8 seconds):

```
function redirect() {
        setTimeout('window.location.href="Default.htm"',8000);
}
```

REFERENCE   WINDOW   RW

Automatically Redirecting Web Pages

- To automatically redirect visitors from one page to another (for example, for a Web page or Web site that has moved to a new location), use a <META> tag in the Head section of the HTML file, as follows:

  `<META HTTP-EQUIV="Refresh" CONTENT="`*sec*`;URL=`*URL*`">`

  where *sec* is the amount of time in seconds that will lapse before opening the new page, and the *URL* is the new page to be loaded.

- Or, to create the same effect using Javascript, run the following command when the page initially loads:

  `setTimeout('window.location.href="`*URL*`"', `*msec*`);`

  where *msec* is the delay time in milliseconds.

Teresa would like you to add these commands to the index.htm page so that the new iMusicHistory home page automatically loads when users go to the old home page.

To add automatic redirection to the index.htm page:

1. Return to the **index.htm** file in your text editor.

2. Below the <HEAD> tag, insert the following tag:

   `<META HTTP-EQUIV="Refresh" CONTENT="8;URL=Default.htm">`

3. Below the </STYLE> tag, insert:

   ```
   <SCRIPT>
   function redirect() {
         setTimeout('window.location.href="Default.htm"',8000);
   }
   </SCRIPT>
   ```

4. Within the <BODY> insert the event handler **onLoad="redirect()"** so that the redirect() function runs when the browser loads the page. Figure 5-9 shows the revised index.htm file.

Figure 5-9   ADDING AUTOMATIC REDIRECTION TO THE INDEX.HTM PAGE

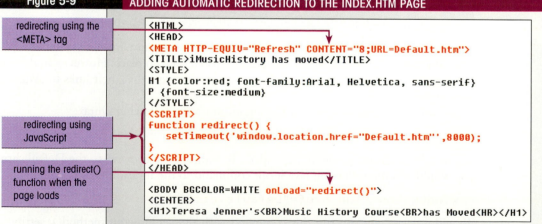

5. Save your changes to the file.

6. Reopen the **index.htm** file in your Web browser. Verify that, after about 8 seconds, your browser opens the Default.htm file.

Visitors to the old iMusicHistory Web site will now be redirected to the new Default.htm page. If the redirection fails, they can still click the link to the old page to get to the new one.

Security Issues

In Netscape, the history object also supports three properties, current, next, and previous, which contain the URLs of the previous, current, and next page in the user's history list. However, use of these properties is restricted to prevent Web page authors from creating scripts to record what sites their users have been visiting. Most people would consider such tracking an invasion of privacy.

Netscape (version 4 and above) uses **signed scripts** to request permission to access restricted information such as the current, next, and previous properties. Signed scripts are not available in Internet Explorer, however, and prior to Netscape version 4, these properties were not available at all from a script.

Another way of retrieving this information is through Netscape's document.referrer property, which records the URL of the page from which the current page was accessed. The following code could be helpful, for example, in tracking Web site referrals, including visitors finding your Web site from search engines and other Web sites:

```
<SCRIPT>
if (document.referrer != '') {
    document.write('You came from: ' + document.referrer);
}
</SCRIPT>
```

This script doesn't work with Internet Explorer 3, though, so this should be kept in mind when tracking statistics. As with the current, next, and previous properties, using this property requires a signed script. For more information on the way Netscape handles such security issues, visit Netscape's DevEdge Online section, Netscape Object Signing, at http://developer.netscape.com/docs/manuals/signedobj/trust/index.htm.

What does all of this mean for a Web designer who wants to use the back() or forward() methods in a Web page? Since no information is being recorded about the user, signed scripts are not required.

Teresa has finished examining your work and is pleased with the messages you created for the status bar, and with your solution to redirecting visitors from her old domain to her new one. In the next session you'll work on her online music history glossary terms, which will require creating new windows with JavaScript.

Session 5.1 QUICK CHECK

1. Explain the difference between the defaultStatus and showStatus properties and how each is used.

2. What single JavaScript command would you enter to move the user two places backward in the history list?

3. What JavaScript command(s) would you enter to change the status bar message to "View News page"?

4. Describe at least two methods (a JavaScript method and a non-JavaScript method) of redirecting visitors from a Web site or Web page to its new location.

5. What is the document.referrer property used for? What are two limitations of this property?

SESSION 5.2

In this session you'll learn how to open a new browser window. You'll see how to control the content and features of the window. You'll also learn how to write new content into the window. Finally, you'll learn how to create modal and modeless dialog windows using Internet Explorer.

Creating New Browser Windows

The iMusicHistory Web site contains a glossary of musical terms. When the user clicks a highlighted term, he or she is jumped to the appropriate place in the glossary page. See Figure 5-10.

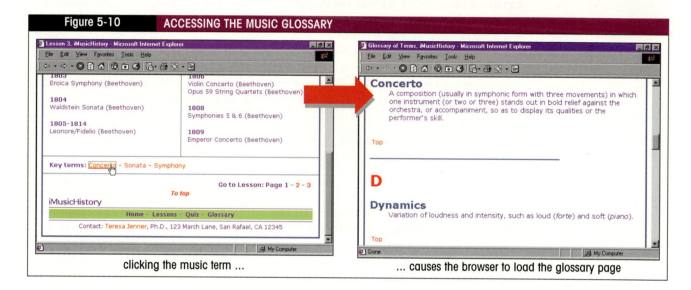

Figure 5-10   ACCESSING THE MUSIC GLOSSARY

clicking the music term ...

... causes the browser to load the glossary page

Teresa is concerned that jumping from one page to another to view definitions is inconvenient and distracting. As a user goes back and forth between the two windows, it's easy to get lost. She would much rather see a smaller window appearing alongside the main window. The user can then quickly read the definition without losing contact with the main window. Figure 5-11 shows a preview of the system she would like you to create.

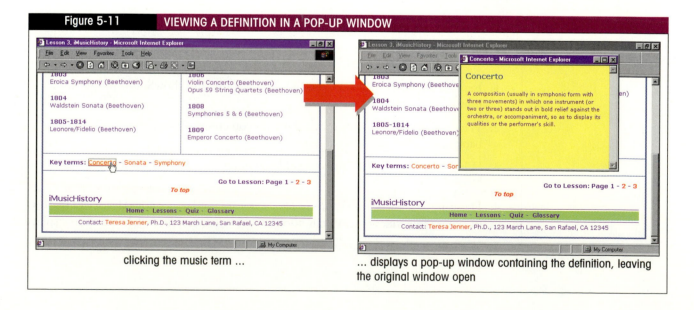

Figure 5-11   VIEWING A DEFINITION IN A POP-UP WINDOW

clicking the music term ...

... displays a pop-up window containing the definition, leaving the original window open

Windows that open in addition to the main browser window are called **secondary** or **pop-up windows**. Teresa wants you to add pop-up windows to her Web site.

Opening New Windows with HTML

By default, each Web page you open appears in the main browser window. As you move from one page to another, the contents of the browser window change accordingly. If you want a page to open in a new window, you specify the window name in the hyperlink's TARGET property. The general syntax is:

```
<A HREF="URL" TARGET="WindowName">Text for hyperlink</A>
```

where *URL* is the URL of the page to be loaded into a new browser window, and *WindowName* is a name of the secondary window. The value of *"WindowName"* doesn't affect the appearance or content of the new window. In fact, you only need to keep track of the value of *"WindowName"* if you intend to use the same window for other hyperlinks. For example, Teresa's Web site could contain a secondary window that displays biographies of the great composers. The HTML tag for links to that window could appear as follows:

```
<A HREF="Wagner.htm" TARGET="Composer">View Wagner's
biography</A><BR>
<A HREF="Mozart.htm" TARGET="Composer">View Mozart's
biography</A>
```

Clicking either link would open a secondary window with the target name "Composer." If the Composer window were already open, its contents would be replaced with the new page.

You can give your new window any name, except one that is reserved by HTML for other purposes. For example, if your Web page contains frames, you can't give the new window the same name assigned to one of your frames, because the page will appear in the frame rather than in a separate window.

If you don't want to specify a window name, you can use the _blank keyword as follows:

```
<A HREF="URL" TARGET=_blank>Text for Hyperlink</A>
```

Note that when you use the _blank keyword, you won't have a target name that you can use as a reference for other links in your document.

Opening New Windows with JavaScript

Why use JavaScript, then, to create new windows? There is far more control and there are many more options available with JavaScript. For example, you can control the contents of the window you create; the window size (height and width properties); the position on the browser screen; and whether or not the new window will have toolbars (and which ones), a menu bar, and a status bar. In contrast, any new windows created using the TARGET property will draw their appearance (toolbars, menu bars, scroll bars, etc.) from the appearance of the main browser window.

To create a new window with JavaScript, use the command:

```
window.open("URL","WindowName","FeatureList")
```

where *URL* is the URL of the page to be displayed in the window, and *WindowName* is the target name assigned to the window. The *FeatureList* is a list of features that control the appearance and behavior of the window. This can include the size and width of the window, as well as whether the window's scroll bar, toolbar, status bar, and menu bar are to be displayed.

The new window can be stored as an object in your JavaScript program. This is useful if your script will be modifying the appearance or content of the window later on. In that case, you would use the syntax:

```
WindowObject = window.open("URL","WindowName","FeatureList")
```

where *WindowObject* is a window object that points to the new window.

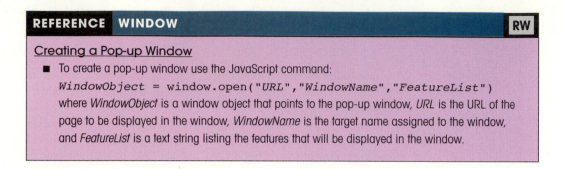

REFERENCE   WINDOW   RW

Creating a Pop-up Window
■ To create a pop-up window use the JavaScript command:
```
WindowObject = window.open("URL","WindowName","FeatureList")
```
where *WindowObject* is a window object that points to the pop-up window, *URL* is the URL of the page to be displayed in the window, *WindowName* is the target name assigned to the window, and *FeatureList* is a text string listing the features that will be displayed in the window.

Before actually creating a window, let's examine the feature list in more detail.

Working with Window Features

Recall that all of the features of the browser window that lie outside the document window are known collectively as a window's **chrome**. Figure 5-12 identifies many of the elements of the chrome that you can work with.

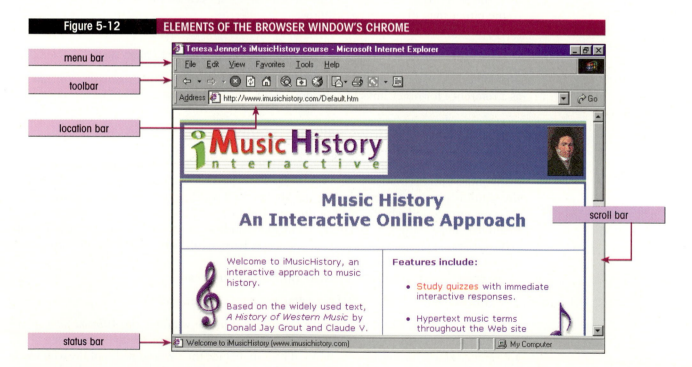

Figure 5-12   ELEMENTS OF THE BROWSER WINDOW'S CHROME

You control which features your window will use by entering values into the features list. The syntax for the feature list is:

```
"Feature1=value1,Feature2=value2,...FeatureN=valueN"
```

where *Feature1*, *Feature2*, . . . are the names of the different window features, and *value1*, *value2*, . . . are the values associated with those features. Figure 5-13 lists some of these window features and their browser support.

Figure 5-13	FEATURES AVAILABLE IN THE WINDOW.OPEN() METHOD			
FEATURE	**DESCRIPTION**	**VALUES**	**NETSCAPE**	**IE**
alwaysLowered	Displays the window behind all other windows; signed script required	yes/no	4.0	
alwaysRaised	Displays the window on top of all other windows; signed script required	yes/no	4.0	
dependent	Window closes when the parent window closes	yes/no	4.0	
directories	Displays directory buttons	yes/no	2.0	3.0
fullscreen	Displays the window in fullscreen mode	yes/no		3.0
height	Sets the height of the window in pixels	integer	2.0	3.0
hotkeys	Disables menu keyboard shortcuts	yes/no	4.0	
innerheight	Sets the height of the page in the document window, excluding the chrome; signed script required for small values	integer	4.0	
innerwidth	Sets the width of the page in the document window, excluding the chrome; signed script required for small values	integer	4.0	
left	Sets the left edge, in pixels, of the window relative to the left edge of the screen	integer	4.0	3.0
location	Displays the location box	yes/no	2.0	3.0
menubar	Displays the window's menu bar	yes/no	2.0	3.0
outerheight	Sets the height of the window, including the chrome; signed script required for small values	integer	4.0	
outerwidth	Sets the width of the window, including the chrome; signed script required for small values	integer	4.0	
resizable	Allows the user to resize the window (always available on a Macintosh)	yes/no	2.0	3.0
screenX	Sets the left edge, in pixels, of the window relative to the left edge of the screen; signed script required to move window offscreen	integer	4.0	
screenY	Sets the top edge, in pixels, of the window relative to the top edge of the screen; signed script required to move window offscreen	integer	4.0	
scrollbars	Displays scroll bars in the window	yes/no	2.0	3.0
status	Displays the window's status bar	yes/no	2.0	3.0
titlebar*	Specifies if the title bar is visible on the new window; signed script required	yes/no	4.0	
toolbar	Displays the window's toolbar	yes/no	2.0	3.0
top	Sets the top edge, in pixels, of the window relative to the top edge of the screen	integer	4.0	3.0
width	Sets the width of the window in pixels	integer	2.0	3.0
z-lock*	Fixes the window below other browser windows; signed script required	yes/no	4.0	

For example, to make your window resizable, but to remove the menu bar, location box, and tool bar, you would use the following features list:

```
"resizable=yes,menubar=no,location=no,toolbar=no"
```

Note that there are no spaces following the commas within the windowFeatures string. One of the common scripting errors is incorrect spacing (whether added or omitted), so this is an important formatting detail to check. Also, you can substitute the number "1" for "yes", and "0" for "no" in your feature list. For example, you can also enter the above feature list as:

```
"resizable=1,menubar=0,location=0,toolbar=0"
```

If you don't specify a feature list, the new window will adopt whatever size and chrome is being applied to the browser window. However, once you start applying a feature list, the new window follows these rules:

- If you don't specify a width or height, the width or height of the browser window is used.
- If you don't include a chrome feature in the list, that feature will not appear in the window.

For example, if the feature list appears as:

```
"width=300,height=200,resizable=yes"
```

the new window will have a width of 300 pixels, a height of 200 pixels, and will be resizable; however, none of the other features of the window (toolbars, status bar, scroll bars, etc.) will appear.

Besides controlling the appearance of the window, you can also control where it appears on your screen. Internet Explorer and Netscape use different features for this. Internet Explorer uses features named left and top, while Netscape uses screenX and screenY (Netscape 4.0 also supports the left and top feature names). By default, the pop-up window will appear near the upper-left corner of the browser window; however, if you want to place the window at the screen coordinates (200, 250), which is 200 pixels from the left edge and 250 pixels down, you would specify the features as follows:

```
"left=200,top=250,screenX=200,screenY=250"
```

To see how JavaScript can be used to define the properties of the pop-up window, a demo page has been prepared for you.

To open the demo page:

1. In your Web browser, open the file **PopupDemo.htm** located in the Tutorial.05 folder of your Data Disk.

2. In the Web page form, enter **400** in the Left Edge box.

3. Enter **10** in the Top Edge box.

4. Set the width and height values to **200** and **150**, respectively.

5. Click the **Display Status Bar** check box to select it.

6. Click the **Show Pop-up Window** button on the form.

   Your browser displays a pop-up window (see Figure 5-14).

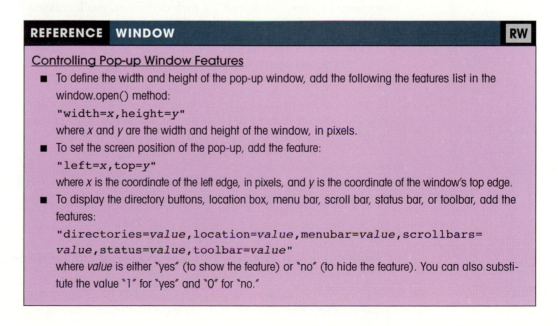

Figure 5-14   DISPLAYING A POP-UP WINDOW

properties of the pop-up window

TROUBLE? If you are running Netscape, your browser window will look slightly different.

7. Close the pop-up window.

8. Continue generating pop-up windows with different features.

9. When you're finished, you may wish to study the underlying code to learn more about generating pop-up windows (open **PopupDemo.htm** in your text editor).

REFERENCE   WINDOW   **RW**

Controlling Pop-up Window Features

- To define the width and height of the pop-up window, add the following the features list in the window.open() method:

  `"width=x,height=y"`

  where *x* and *y* are the width and height of the window, in pixels.
- To set the screen position of the pop-up, add the feature:

  `"left=x,top=y"`

  where *x* is the coordinate of the left edge, in pixels, and *y* is the coordinate of the window's top edge.
- To display the directory buttons, location box, menu bar, scroll bar, status bar, or toolbar, add the features:

  `"directories=value,location=value,menubar=value,scrollbars=`
  `value,status=value,toolbar=value"`

  where *value* is either "yes" (to show the feature) or "no" (to hide the feature). You can also substitute the value "1" for "yes" and "0" for "no."

Now that you've worked with the pop-up window demo, you are ready to create a small pop-up window for the music definitions in Teresa's Web site.

Adding a Pop-up Window to the iMusicHistory Site

Teresa has begun the process of copying the musical definitions into their own separate HTML files for use as pop-up windows. She has already created three HTML files for the musical terms concerto, sonata, and symphony. Since you'll be modifying the contents of these files later on, open and save them under different names now.

To open the definition files:

1. In your text editor, open **Concertotxt.htm** in the Tutorial.05D folder of your Data Disk, save the file as **Concerto.htm**, and then close it.

2. Open **Sonatatxt.htm** from the Tutorial.05 folder, save it as **Sonata.htm**, and then close it .

3. Open **Symphonytxt.htm** from the same folder, save it as **Symphony.htm**, and then close it.

You'll open these files from hyperlinks on the Lesson3 page. Currently this is saved as Lesson3txt.htm on your Data Disk.

To open the Lesson3 page:

1. In your text editor, open **Lesson3txt.htm** from the Tutorial.05D folder of your Data Disk, and then save the file as **Lesson3.htm**.

Teresa would like the pop-up window for the definitions to be fairly small, perhaps with a hyperlink or button to close it, and without any chrome besides a scroll bar. To avoid retyping the same commands for each definition, you'll create a function named to display the Web page as a pop-up window. The function appears as follows:

```
function PopWin(url) {
    window.open(url,"pop","width=330,height=220,scrollbar=yes")
}
```

In this function, the parameter *url* contains the URL of the Web page to be displayed. Note that only the scroll bar will be displayed. Since the other chrome features are not included in the list, they will not be applied to the pop-up window.

To add pop-up definitions to the Lesson3 page:

1. Before the </HEAD> tag at the top of the file, insert:

```
<SCRIPT>
function PopWin(url) {
    window.open(url,"pop","width=330,height=220,
    scrollbar=yes")
}
</SCRIPT>
```

To call this function, you have to replace the targets of the hyperlinks for the three music definitions with the following:

```
HREF="javascript:PopWin('url')
```

where *url* is the name of one of the definition pages (Concerto.htm, Sonata.htm, or Symphony.htm).

To link to the PopWin() function:

1. Scroll to the Key Term section of the Lesson3.htm file (located near the midpoint of the file).

2. Replace the target for the Concerto definition ("Terms_noframes.htm#concerto") with **"javascript:PopWin('Concerto.htm')"**.

3. Set the target for the Sonata term to **"javascript:PopWin('Sonata.htm')"**.

4. Set the target for the Symphony term to **"javascript:PopWin('Symphony.htm')"**. Figure 5-15 shows the revised file.

Figure 5-15	ADDING THE POPWIN() FUNCTION AS A HYPERLINK

HTML file to be displayed in the pop-up window

```
<!--- Key Terms --->
<TR>
<TD COLSPAN=2 BGCOLOR=WHITE CLASS="body">
<P><B>Key terms:</B>
<A HREF="javascript:PopWin('Concerto.htm')">Concerto</A> -
<A HREF="javascript:PopWin('Sonata.htm')">Sonata</A> -
<A HREF="javascript:PopWin('Symphony.htm')">Symphony</A><BR>
</P>
</TD>
</TR>
```

5. Save your changes to **Lesson3.htm** and then open it in your Web browser.

6. Verify that when you click the key term **Concerto**, located near the bottom of the page, the Concerto pop-up window appears (see Figure 5-16.)

Figure 5-16	RUNNING THE POPWIN() FUNCTION AS A HYPERLINK

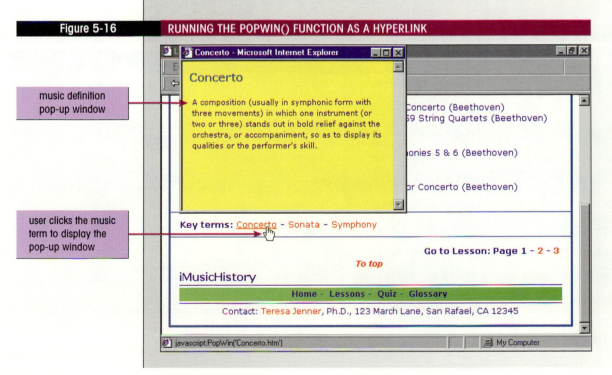

music definition pop-up window

user clicks the music term to display the pop-up window

7. Close the Concerto pop-up window.

8. Verify that when you click the two other definitions, the Sonata and Symphony pop-up windows appear.

Window Security Issues

There are some security issues involved when a browser can open new windows on the user's computer. For this reason, some of the window features cannot be implemented unless a signed script is used. For example, you cannot create a new window with a width and height less than 100 pixels. This restriction is designed as a precaution to prevent the creation of windows that might be invisible or almost invisible to the visitor.

Working with Multiple Windows

Teresa likes the work you've done on the pop-up definitions, but she is concerned that users will not like to have extra windows cluttering up their desktops. She wonders if there is a way in which the pop-up window can be automatically closed once the user is done looking at it—perhaps when the user returns to the Lesson3 page.

JavaScript can be used to control the interaction between your various browser windows. You can specify which browser window has the focus (is active) on your desktop. You can remove the focus from one window and give it to another. You can allow users to move the windows to different locations on the screen and resize them, and finally, you can automatically close windows that are no longer needed. Most of these features are controlled by the methods applied to the window object.

Window Methods

Figure 5-17 describes some of the methods you can use to manipulate your windows once they're created.

Figure 5-17	WINDOW METHODS		
METHOD	**DESCRIPTION**	**NETSCAPE**	**IE**
blur()	Removes the focus from the window	3.0	4.0
close()	Closes the window	2.0	3.0
focus()	Gives the window the focus	3.0	4.0
moveBy(dx, dy)	Moves the window dx pixels to the right, and dy pixels down	4.0	4.0
moveTo(x, y)	Moves the window to the screen coordinates (x, y)	4.0	4.0
print()	Prints the contents of the window	4.0	5.0
resizeBy(dx, dy)	Resizes the window by dx pixels to the right, and dy pixels down	4.0	4.0
resizeTo(x, y)	Resizes the window to x pixels wide by y pixels high	4.0	4.0
scrollBy(dx, dy)	Scrolls the document in the window by dx pixels to the right, and dy pixels down	4.0	4.0
scrollTo(x, y)	Scrolls the document in the window to the page cooordinates (x, y)	4.0	4.0

Most of the time your scripts will be used to open and close the browser windows, or add or remove the focus from each window. For example, you can create a window object named "PopWin" by using the following command:

```
PopWin=window.open("Pop.htm", "Demo', "width=200,height=150")
```

If at a certain point in your script, you want to give PopWin the focus, you would use the JavaScript command:

```
PopWin.focus();
```

and PopWin would become the active window on your desktop. To remove the focus from PopWin, use the command:

```
PopWin.blur();
```

Finally, if you want to close the window, run the JavaScript command:

```
PopWin.close();
```

You can also use the resizeBy() and resizeTo() methods to change the dimensions of your browser windows, and the moveBy() and moveTo() methods to move the window across your screen.

REFERENCE **WINDOW**   **RW**

Applying Methods to Pop-up Windows

- To give the focus to a window, use the command:

    `WindowObject.focus();`

    where *WindowObject* is the window to receive the focus.
- To remove the focus from a window, use the command:

    `WindowObject.blur();`
- To close a window, use the command:

    `WindowObject.close();`
- To move the window, use either:

    `WindowObject.moveBy(dx, dy);`

    or

    `WindowObject.moveTo(x, y);`

    where *dx* and *dy* are the distance in pixels to shift the window to the right and down, respectively, and *x* and *y* are coordinates on the screen.
- To resize the window, use either:

    `WindowObject.resizeBy(dx, dy);`

    or

    `WindowObject.resizeTo(x, y);`

    where *dx* and *dy* are the amount of space to increase the width and height of the window, respectively, in pixels, and *x* and *y* are the width and height of the window in pixels.

To see how these methods can be used in your Web page, a demo page has been prepared in which you use JavaScript to open a pop-up window on your desktop, move it and resize it, and then close it.

To run the pop-up demo page:

1. In your Web browser, open **PopupDemo2.htm** from the Tutorial.05D folder on your Data Disk.

2. Click the **Show Pop-up Window** button to display the pop-up window.

3. Click the moving buttons to move the pop-up window around your screen.

4. Click the resizing buttons to expand and contract the width and height of the pop-up window (see Figure 5-18).

Figure 5-18 | CONTROLLING A POP-UP WINDOW WITH JAVASCRIPT

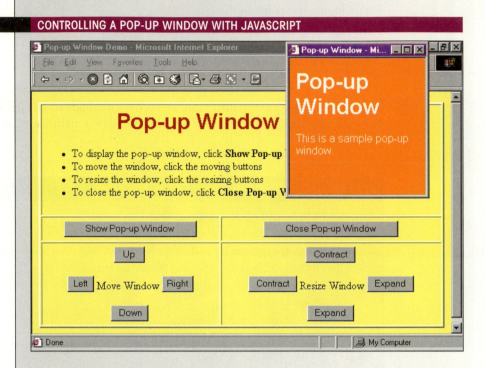

TROUBLE? You cannot reduce the width or height of the pop-up window to below 100 pixels.

TROUBLE? As the focus shifts between the main browser window and the pop-up window, you may notice a bit of sluggishness in moving the window around your desktop.

5. Click the **Close Pop-up Window** button to close the pop-up window.

6. Close the **PopupDemo2.htm** page.

7. Open the **PopupDemo2.htm** file in your text editor, and take some time to study the underlying code to see how the various window methods have been applied to allow you to control the pop-up window.

8. Close the file when you have finished examining the code.

The Self and Opener Windows

If your script opens several windows, it can be confusing for the user to keep track of the various window objects. There are several ways of identifying the different windows. One way is with the object name you assign to each window as you create it, as in the PopWin example above. JavaScript also provides two keywords: self and opener.

The **self** keyword refers to the currently active window. The self keyword is synonymous with the window keyword, but you may see it used to improve clarity when the script refers to many different windows and frames. This means to close the current window, you can use either the command:

```
self.close();
```

or

```
window.close();
```

The **opener** keyword refers to the window or frame that used the window.open() method to open the current window. For example, you want to create a script in which the browser window opens a secondary window, after which the first window should be automatically closed. You can do this by running the command:

```
opener.close();
```

from within the secondary window.

Automatically Closing the Definition Window

You now have the information to make the change to the pop-up window that Teresa requested. Recall that Teresa wants the pop-up window to close whenever it loses the focus. You can do this by adding the following onBlur event handler to the <BODY> tag of each pop-up definition window:

```
onBlur="self.close()"
```

You have to make this change to all three of the definition windows.

To modify the pop-up definitions:

1. Open **Concerto.htm** in your text editor.

2. Insert the following text into the <BODY> tag, as shown in Figure 5-19.

   ```
   onBlur="self.close()"
   ```

| Figure 5-19 | CLOSING THE ACTIVE WINDOW AT THE ONBLUR EVENT |

```
<HTML>
<HEAD>
<TITLE>Concerto</TITLE>
<LINK HREF="main.css" REL="stylesheet" TYPE="text/css" TITLE="General">
<STYLE>
  body {background-color:rgb(255,255,128)}  H2 {font-size:12pt}
  P {font-size:8pt}
</STYLE>
</HEAD>

<BODY onBlur="self.close()">
<H2>Concerto</H2>
<P>A composition (usually in symphonic form with three movements) in which
one instrument (or two or three) stands out in bold relief against the
orchestra, or accompaniment, so as to display its qualities or the
performer's skill.
</P>
</BODY>

</HTML>
```

close the window when it loses focus

3. Save your changes to the file and close it.

4. Open the **Sonata.htm** file in your text editor.

5. Insert **onBlur="self.close()"** into the <BODY> tag.

6. Close the file, saving your changes.

7. Add the same onBlur event handler to the <BODY> tag of the **Symphony.htm** file.

8. Return to your Web browser and open the **Lesson3.htm** file.

9. Click each of the definitions, and verify that when you click back anywhere on the Lesson3 page, the pop-up window closes automatically.

Now that you have completed pop-up windows for some of the definitions, you can turn your attention to the changes Teresa wants you to make to her online quiz.

Writing **Window Content for the iMusicHistory Quiz**

Another part of the iMusicHistory Web site is an online quiz about music history. Currently, the page consists of a series of multiple choice questions in a Web page form. The Quiz page is stored in the Quiztxt.htm file.

To open the Quiz page:

1. In your text editor open **Quiztxt.htm** from the Tutorial.05D folder of your Data Disk, and then save the file as **Quiz.htm**.

2. Open **Quiz.htm** in your Web browser.

3. Select answers for each of the four questions. Note that in response to each selection, the browser displays an alert box indicating whether or not the answer is correct (Figure 5-20).

| Figure 5-20 | ALERT BOX WITH MESSAGE TO USER TAKING STUDY QUIZ |

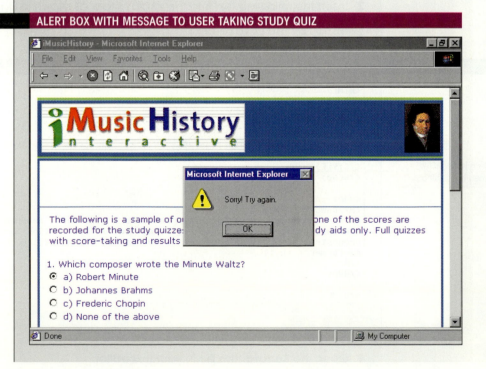

To create the alert box in this Quiz page, two functions are called. If the user selects the correct answer, the Correct() function is called:

```
function Correct(ans) {
    alert("Congratulations! That's correct!");
}
```

where *ans* is a parameter that identifies which radio button in the form was clicked. Currently you don't need this information, but you will shortly. If the user selects the incorrect answer, the Incorrect() function is called:

```
function Incorrect(ans) {
    alert("Sorry! Try again.");
}
```

The correct answers in the quiz are: 1–a, 2–c, 3–c, and 4–b.

An alert box is an example of a **modal window**, which prevents the user from doing anything else in the browser until a button is clicked on the dialog box to close it. Because this could be potentially disruptive to users, modal dialog windows must be used judiciously. Other examples of modal dialog windows include those created with the Confirm() method and the Prompt() method. A window that stays open and allows the user to perform other actions is called a **modeless window**.

Teresa wonders if it's possible to remove the exclamation points on the alert boxes and replace them with something more related to music. Also she would like to include the text of the user's response in the dialog box (see Figure 5-21).

Figure 5-21	TERESA'S SUGGESTION FOR REPLACING THE ALERT BOX WITH A POP-UP WINDOW

While it is not possible to do this with the alert(), method, you can do this by creating a customized pop-up window. In order to change the message for each response, you either need to create a separate file for each possible response, or—more simply—write HTML code into the pop-up window that changes for different answers.

Using the document.write() Method

To write content to a window, you use the document.write() method, specifying the window that will receive the new content. The syntax is:

```
WindowObject.document.write("Content");
WindowObject.document.close();
```

where *WindowObject* is the name of the window object that is to receive the new content, and *Content* is a text string containing the HTML code that will be placed in the window. Since you are writing the entire HTML code in the window, you will usually want to break up the *Content* text string into smaller text strings. You can do this by using multiple write commands as follows:

```
WindowObject.document.write("Content 1");
WindowObject.document.write("Content 2");
. . .
WindowObject.document.write("Content N");
```

or you can create one variable containing the text string, and then use an assignment operator to add additional text strings to it.

```
Content  = "String 1";
Content += "String 2";
Content += "String 3";
...
Content += "String N";
```

Here *Content* is a variable that contains all of the text contained in the text strings, "*String 1*" to "*String N*". Which approach you take is a matter of personal preference.

REFERENCE WINDOW **RW**

Writing Window Content
- To insert HTML code into a pop-up window, use the command block:

  `WindowObject.document.write("Content");`

  `WindowObject.document.close();`

  where *WindowObject* is the name of the window object to receive the new content, and *Content* is a text string containing the HTML code that will be placed in the window.

Now you're ready to replace the alert boxes with the customized pop-up windows that Teresa wanted.

Creating the Quiz Pop-Up Window

Here is the HTML code that you'll use to create the pop-up window:

```
<HTML>
<HEAD>
<TITLE>Answer</TITLE>
<LINK REL="STYLESHEET" TYPE="text/css" HREF="main.css">
</HEAD>
<BODY CLASS="dialogw" BGCOLOR=WHITE>
<IMG SRC="treble2.gif" BORDER=0 ALIGN=LEFT HSPACE=10 VSPACE=0>
Message
</BODY>
</HTML>
```

where *Message* is the message in the pop-up window. The message will differ for each question and will change depending on whether or not the user answered the question correctly.

To insert this content into the pop-up window, you'll add the following function to the Quiz.htm file:

```
function writePop(Message) {
PopWin=window.open("","Pop","width=300,height=100");
Content ='<HTML>';
Content+='<HEAD>';
Content+='<TITLE>Answer</TITLE>';
Content+='<LINK REL="STYLESHEET" TYPE="text/css" HREF="main.css">';
Content+='</HEAD>';
Content+='<BODY CLASS="dialogw" BGCOLOR=WHITE>';
Content+='<IMG SRC="treble2.gif" ALIGN=LEFT HSPACE=10>';
Content+=Message;
Content+='</BODY>';
Content+='</HTML>';
PopWin.document.write(Content);
PopWin.document.close();
}
```

The writePop() function first creates a pop-up window named PopWin that is 300 pixels wide and 100 pixels high. Note that no URL is specified for the window since we will be writing the HTML code directly into the window. The HTML code will be stored as a text string in the Content variable. Finally, the Content variable will be written to the PopWin pop-up window. The document.close() command will then close the input stream to the window.

To create the writePop() function:

1. Return to the **Quiz.htm** file in your text editor.

2. Above the </SCRIPT> tag, insert:

```
function writePop(Message) {
PopWin=window.open("","Pop","width=300,height=100");
Content ='<HTML>';
Content+='<HEAD>';
Content+='<TITLE>Answer</TITLE>';
Content+='<LINK REL="STYLESHEET" TYPE="text/css" HREF="main.css">';
Content+='</HEAD>';
Content+='<BODY CLASS="dialogw" BGCOLOR=WHITE>';
Content+='<IMG SRC="treble2.gif" ALIGN=LEFT HSPACE=10>';
Content+=Message;
Content+='</BODY>';
Content+='</HTML>';
PopWin.document.write(Content);
PopWin.document.close();
}
```

To run the writePop() function, you'll revise the Correct() and Incorrect() functions already present in the Quiz.htm file. If the user answers the question correctly, the Correct() function will be:

```
function Correct(ans) {
   Message='<B><FONT COLOR=GREEN>'+ans.value+'</FONT> is
correct!';
   Message+='<BR><BR>Congratulations.</B>';
   writePop(Message);
}
```

In this function, ans.value contains the text string of the answer the user selected. The answer will be displayed in a green font. The entire message will be displayed in boldface type.

In case the user answers the question incorrectly, the Incorrect() function is revised as follows:

```
function Incorrect(ans) {
   Message='<B><FONT COLOR=RED>'+ans.value+'</FONT> is
incorrect.';
   Message+='<BR><BR>Try again.</B>';
   writePop(Message);
}
```

If the user answers the question incorrectly, the answer will be displayed in a red font, along with the message to try again.

To revise the Correct() and Incorrect() functions:

1. In the Quiz.htm file, go to the Correct() function near the top, and replace the Correct() function with:

```
function Correct(ans) {
   Message='<B><FONT COLOR=GREEN>'+ans.value+'</FONT> is
correct!';
   Message+='<BR><BR>Congratulations.</B>';
   writePop(Message);
}
```

2. Replace the Incorrect() function with:

```
function Incorrect(ans) {
   Message='<B><FONT COLOR=RED>'+ans.value+'</FONT> is
incorrect.';
   Message+='<BR><BR>Try again.</B>';
   writePop(Message);
}
```

Figure 5-22 shows the revised JavaScript code for the Quiz.htm file.

Figure 5-22	REVISING THE CORRECT() AND INCORRECT() FUNCTIONS

```
function Correct(ans) {
   Message='<B><FONT COLOR=GREEN>'+ans.value+'</FONT> is correct!';
   Message+='<BR><BR>Congratulations.</B>';
   writePop(Message);
}

function Incorrect(ans) {
   Message='<B><FONT COLOR=RED>'+ans.value+'</FONT> is incorrect.';
   Message+='<BR><BR>Try again.</B>';
   writePop(Message);
}
```

3. Save your changes to the file and then reload the **Quiz.htm** file in your Web browser.

4. Click **a) Robert Minute** as the answer for the first question.

   The browser displays the pop-up window shown in Figure 5-23.

Figure 5-23	DISPLAYING THE INCORRECT POP-UP WINDOW

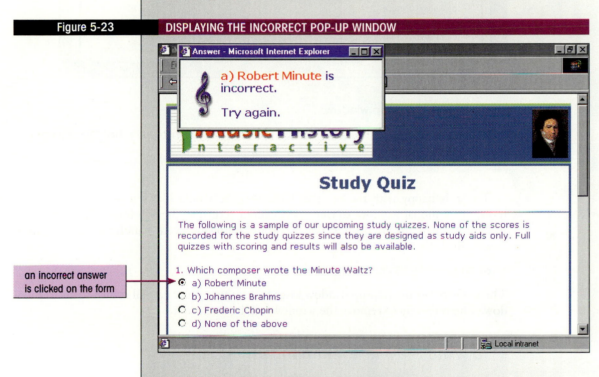

an incorrect answer is clicked on the form

5. Close the pop-up window.

6. Click **c) Frederic Chopin** on the Quiz page.

   As shown in Figure 5-24, the browser displays a pop-up window indicating that the answer is correct.

Figure 5-24   DISPLAYING THE CORRECT POP-UP WINDOW

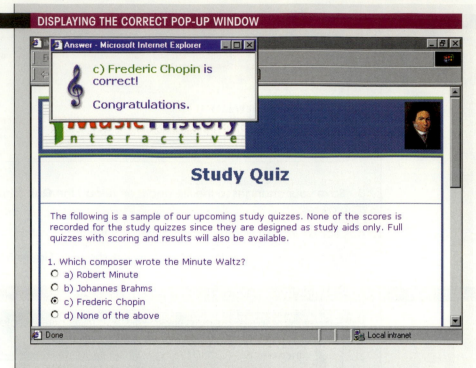

7. Close the pop-up window.

8. Check the rest of the questions on the Quiz page and verify that the appropriate pop-up window appears each time.

Teresa is happy with the change. However, she would like the pop-up window to act more like a modal window, so that users cannot return to the window without first closing the pop-up window. To do this, you'll add the following event handler to the pop-up window's <BODY> tag:

```
onBlur="self.focus()"
```

Thus, whenever the pop-up window loses focus, this command will return focus to the window. The only way to remove the window will be to close it.

To write the blur event handler:

1. Return to **Quiz.htm** in your text editor.

2. Revise the writePop() function by adding the event handler **onBlur="self.focus();"** as shown in Figure 5-25.

Figure 5-25	DISPLAYING THE CORRECT DIALOG BOX

the onBlur event handler forces the focus back to the window

```
function writePop(Message) {
    PopWin=window.open("","Pop","width=300,height=100");
    Content='<HTML>'
    Content+='<HEAD>';
    Content+='<TITLE>Answer</TITLE>';
    Content+='<LINK REL="STYLESHEET" TYPE="text/css" HREF="main.css">';
    Content+='</HEAD>';
    Content+='<BODY CLASS="dialogw" BGCOLOR=WHITE onBlur="self.focus();">';
    Content+='<IMG SRC="treble2.gif" BORDER=0 ALIGN=LEFT HSPACE=10 VSPACE=0>'
    Content+=Message;
    Content+='</BODY>';
    Content+='</HTML>';
    PopWin.document.write(Content);
    PopWin.document.close();
}
```

3. Save your changes to **Quiz.htm** and close the file.

4. Reload or refresh **Quiz.htm** in your Web browser.

5. Verify that you cannot click outside the pop-up window to make it lose focus.

TROUBLE? If you are running Netscape, you may have to close Netscape and reopen it for this change to take effect.

Modal and Modeless Windows with Internet Explorer

Internet Explorer 4.0 and 5.0 each introduced new methods to allow JavaScript to create secondary windows. Internet Explorer 4 introduced the showModalDialog() method to create modal windows, and Internet Explorer 5 added the showModelessDialog() method for modeless windows. The syntax of the showModalDialog() method is:

```
ReturnValue = window.showModalDialog("URL", "Arguments",
"FeatureList");
```

where *URL* is the URL of the file to display in the modal window, and *Arguments* is an optional text string that specifies the arguments to use when displaying the document. The *Arguments* parameter can include data in the form of a text string, numbers, or an array of values. Finally, the *FeatureList* is a list of the features of the window. The *ReturnValue* property stores the value returned by the modal window. For example, if the window includes a Web form in which the user can enter a text string or value, this information can be stored and returned to the browser window that called the modal window.

The syntax of the showModelessDialog() method is similar:

```
ReturnValue = window.showModelessDialog("URL", "Arguments",
"FeatureList");
```

The main difference between the two methods is that the showModalDialog() method creates a window that retains the focus until the user closes it. With the modeless dialog box, the user can still work with the browser window, leaving the dialog box open.

Dialog boxes created with these two methods cannot interact with the browser window that opens them. You cannot, for example, use the write() method to update the content of the window. All values necessary for displaying the content must be included either in the HTML file specified in the *URL* parameter, or as a value in the *Arguments* parameter.

Working with the Features List

Both methods allow you to control the appearance of the window through the *FeatureList* parameter. The syntax of the features list is:

```
Feature1:Value1,Feature2:Value2,...FeatureN:ValueN
```

Where *Feature* is one of the features of the window, and *Value* is the value of the feature. Figure 5-26 describes the features and feature values available to you.

Figure 5-26		FEATURES OF THE SHOWMODALDIALOG() AND SHOWMODELESS DIALOG() METHODS
FEATURE	**VALUE**	**DESCRIPTION**
dialogHeight	Numeric	Sets the height of the dialog window; the default unit of measurement is "em" in Internet Explorer 4.0, and pixels in Internet Explorer 5.0
dialogLeft	Numeric	Specifies the screen coordinates of the left edge of the dialog box, in pixels
dialogTop	Numeric	Specifies the screen coordinates of the top edge of the dialog box, in pixels
dialogWidth	Numeric	Sets the width of the dialog window; the default unit of measurement is "em" in Internet Explorer 4.0, and pixels in Internet Explorer 5.0
center	yes, no	Specifies whether to center the dialog box on the desktop
dialogHide	yes, no	Specifies whether to hide the dialog box when printing or using print preview
edge	sunken, raised	Specifies the edge style of the window; the default is raised
help	yes, no	Specifies whether the window displays the context-sensitive Help icon in the title bar
resizable	yes, no	Specifies whether the window is resizable
scroll	yes, no	Specifies whether the window displays scroll bars
status	yes, no	Specifies whether the window displays a status bar
unadorned	yes, no	Specifies whether the window displays the browser chrome

For example, you could create a modal window with the following features list:

```
Name = window.showModalDialog("Name.htm","dialogHeight:150,
dialogWidth:300,edge:sunken,resizable:yes,scroll:yes,
status:no,unadorned:no");
```

In this case, the Name.htm file is displayed in the modal window. The window will be 150 pixels high and 300 pixels wide. It will have sunken edges and scroll bars, but will not have a status bar or any of the browser window chrome. The user will be able to resize the window, however. Note that no *Arguments* parameter has been used in creating this window.

Working with the Arguments List

If your code does include the *Arguments* parameter, how does the window read and store that information? You can retrieve this information by running the following command from a script within the window:

```
Variable = window.dialogArguments;
```

where *Variable* is a JavaScript variable that stores the value of the *Arguments* parameter. For example, the following command:

```
Data = window.dialogArguments;
```

stores the value of the *Arguments* parameter in a variable called "Data." You can then use the Data variable in any script running within the window.

Working with the Return Value

Your dialog window may need to return a value to the main browser window. To specify which value to return, run the following command in the dialog window:

```
window.returnValue = ReturnValue;
```

where *ReturnValue* is the value that will be returned to the main window.

Netscape does not currently support the showModalDialog() or showModelessDialog() methods, so you can only use them for Internet Explorer browsers. You and Teresa decide against using these methods for the iMusicHistory Web site.

You've now completed your work on creating a variety of new windows, closing windows, and writing to a window via script-generated HTML. In the next session, you'll learn how to enhance the Glossary section of Teresa's iMusicHistory Web site with interactive frames.

Session 5.2 QUICK CHECK

1. What HTML tag would you enter to open the file "Home.htm" as a new window with the target name "HomePage"?

2. What JavaScript command would you run to open the file "Home.htm" as a pop-up window that is 300 pixels wide and 150 pixels high?

3. What JavaScript command would you enter to include scroll bars and a status bar in the pop-up window described in the previous question?

4. What is a modal window?

5. What is a modeless window?

6. What JavaScript command would you enter to write the HTML tag "<BODY BGCOLOR=YELLOW>" to a window object named "Home"?

7. What JavaScript command would you enter to display the file "Home.htm" as a modal dialog window that is 300 pixels wide and 150 pixels high?

8. What JavaScript command would you enter to display the file "Home.htm" as a modeless dialog window that is 300 pixels wide and 150 pixels high?

SESSION 5.3

In this session you'll learn how to control the behavior and content of frames. You'll learn about the various frame objects supported by Netscape and Internet Explorer. You'll see how to modify the appearance of your frames and how to collapse a frame. You'll also learn how to keep your pages from appearing within someone else's frameset, and you'll see how to keep your own frames fixed within their framesets.

Using Frames for iMusicHistory

Frames are considered one of the most powerful features of HTML. They enable the division of the browser window into multiple panes, with each frame displaying a separate document. With JavaScript you can add even greater flexibility and scope to your frames.

Recall that frames are organized into **framesets**, using the following HTML tag structure:

```
<FRAMESET ID=Frameset>
    <FRAME ID="Frame1" NAME="Frame1" SRC="URL1">
    <FRAME ID="Frame2" NAME="Frame2" SRC="URL2">
...
    <FRAME ID="FrameN" NAME="FrameN" SRC="URLN">
</FRAMESET>
```

where each frame displays a separate *URL*. A single window can contain multiple framesets, and framesets can be nested inside each other. Note that each <FRAME> tag in this example contains both an ID value and a NAME value. The NAME property is used when creating links whose targets are designed to appear in specific frames. The syntax for linking to a specific frame is:

```
<A HREF=URL TARGET=Frame_Name>
```

In this case, the target *URL* will appear in the frame named *Frame_Name*. However, JavaScript uses the ID property rather than the NAME property to reference specific frames. To keep things simple, you can assign the same value to both properties, as in the following example:

```
<FRAME ID=Top NAME=Top SRC="Home.htm">
```

Teresa would like to use frames in iMusicHistory's Glossary page. Figure 5-27 shows a preview of how she would like this page to look. There will be three frames in the Glossary frameset. The Top frame will provide an alphabetic list of links to the glossary terms, the Main frame will display the glossary of musical terms, and the Bottom frame will display a navigation bar with links to the other pages of the iMusicHistory Web site.

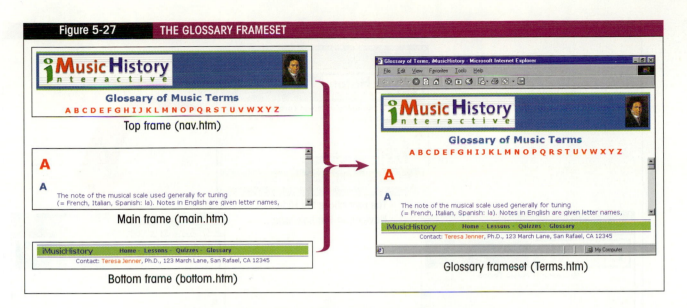

Figure 5-27   THE GLOSSARY FRAMESET

Top frame (nav.htm)

Main frame (main.htm)

Bottom frame (bottom.htm)

Glossary frameset (Terms.htm)

The following is the HTML code for the Glossary frameset:

```
<FRAMESET ROWS="160,*'64" ID=Glossary FRAMEBORDER=0 BORDER=0>
    <FRAME NAME=Top ID=Top SRC="nav.htm" SCROLLING=NO NORESIZE>
    <FRAME NAME=Main ID=Main SRC="main.htm" NORESIZE>
    <FRAME NAME=Bottom ID=Bottom SRC="bottom.htm" SCROLLING=NO
NORESIZE>
</FRAMESET>
```

One problem some people point out about frames is that they can take up valuable screen space. Teresa would like to give users the ability to give more screen space to the music glossary. As described in Figure 5-28, she would like hyperlinks labeled "Hide Navigation Bar" and "Display Navigation Bar" added to the Top frame. When users click the Hide Navigation Bar hyperlink, Teresa wants the browser to collapse the Bottom frame, giving extra space to the Main frame. If a user clicks "Display Navigation Bar," the Bottom frame should reappear.

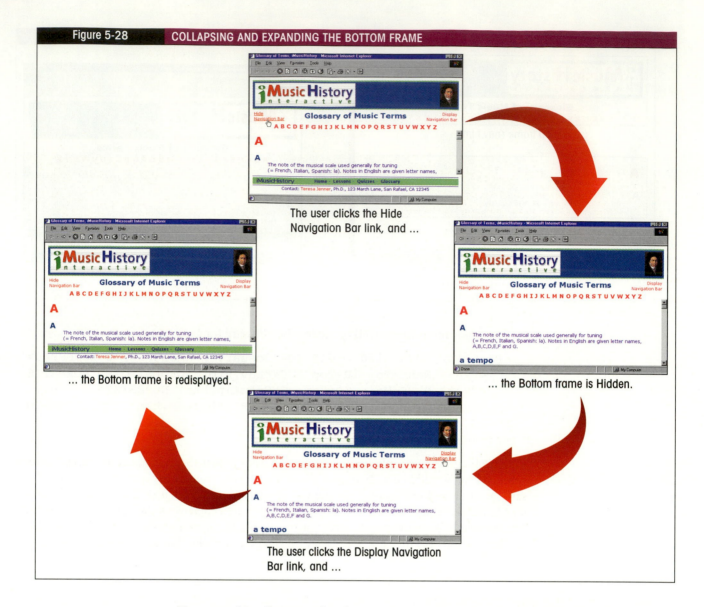

Figure 5-28   COLLAPSING AND EXPANDING THE BOTTOM FRAME

The user clicks the Hide Navigation Bar link, and …

… the Bottom frame is Hidden.

… the Bottom frame is redisplayed.

The user clicks the Display Navigation Bar link, and …

To create this effect, you first have to learn how JavaScript handles frames.

Working with the Frame Object

In the document object model, each frame is part of the **frames collection**—an array of all of the frames within the browser window. The frames collection uses the following reference syntax:

```
WindowObject.frames[i]
```

where *WindowObject* is the name of a window object, and *i* is the index number of the frame. The first frame in the collection has an index value of 0, the second has an index of 1, and so forth. If you include an ID name in the <FRAME> tag, you can use the ID value in place of the index number as follows:

```
WindowObject.frames["id"]
```

or

```
WindowObject.id
```

where *id* is the ID name of the frame. For example, in the Glossary frameset, the first frame is the Top frame. You can reference that frame in your JavaScript program by using any of the following reference names:

```
WindowObject.frames[0]
WindowObject.frames["Top"]
WindowObject.Top
```

REFERENCE WINDOW   **RW**

Referencing Frame and Frameset Objects

- To reference a frame, use any of the following forms:

  WindowObject.frames[*i*]

  WindowObject.frames["*id*"]

  WindowObject.*id*

  where *id* is the value of the ID property in the <FRAME> tag.

- In addition, you can reference an individual frame in Internet Explorer by using the form:

  WindowObject.document.all.*id*;

- To reference a frameset containing a collection of frames in Internet Explorer, use the syntax:

  WindowObject.document.all.*id*

  where *id* is the value of the ID property for the <FRAMESET> tag.

The Top and Parent Windows

WindowObject represents the window that contains the frameset. If you're running a script within the HTML file that creates the frameset, you can use the keywords "window" or "self" in place of *WindowObject*. In most cases, however, the script will be running from an HTML document displayed in one of the frames. Figure 5-29 shows a schematic diagram of the Glossary frameset. If you wanted to run a script in the nav.htm file that changes the layout or content of the Glossary frameset, you would need to go "up" the hierarchy of windows and objects.

Figure 5-29   **FRAME HIERARCHY OF THE GLOSSARY FRAMESET**

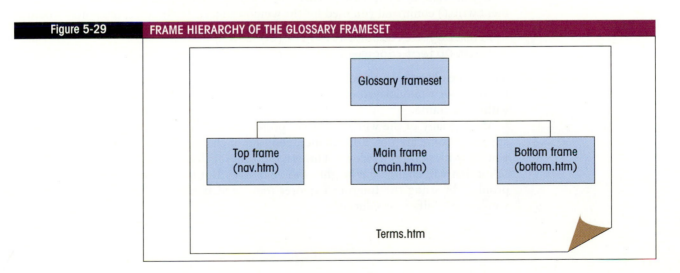

JavaScript provides two keywords to do this: parent and top. The **parent** keyword refers to any object that is placed immediately above another object in the document object model. In this case, the Term.htm window is the parent object, and the three files nav.htm, main.htm, and bottom.htm are child objects since they're "contained" within the glossary page. To reference the first frame in the Glossary frameset from a script running in the nav.htm file, for example, you could use any of the following references:

```
parent.frames[0]
parent.frames["Top"]
parent.Top
```

If you have several levels of nested objects, you can stack parent references. The reference name:

```
parent.parent.parent.object
```

refers to an object that lies three levels up.

If you want to go directly to the top of the hierarchy, you can use the **top** keyword. In the case of frames, the top keyword refers to the topmost browser window, which contains all of the frames and nested framesets. When there are only two levels to the hierarchy (as is the case with the Glossary frameset) you can use either the parent or top keyword.

Working with Frames as Windows

Because both Netscape and Internet Explorer allow you treat frames as "windows within windows," you can apply many of the properties and events you've associated with the window objects to your frames. For example, when you want to change the document source of a window, you use the JavaScript command:

```
WindowObject.location.href=url;
```

where *url* is the URL of the new window source. The syntax to change the source for a frame is similar:

```
FrameObject.location.href=url;
```

where *FrameObject* is frame's object reference.

If you want to write new HTML code into a frame, you would use the same document.write() command you used for the window object. In this case, the syntax would be:

```
FrameObject.document.write(Content);
FrameObject.document.close();
```

The frame object also supports such window methods as the setInterval() and setTimeout() methods for time-delayed commands, and the alert() method for displaying an alert box within the frame.

While many of the window object's properties and features are supported through this approach, some are not. For instance, you cannot change the width or height of a frame as you can with pop-up windows. This is a problem for Teresa, since she wants you to write a script that will change the height of the glossary's Bottom frame. You can get around this problem by using the Internet Explorer frame and frameset objects. For Netscape users, you'll need a different solution.

Changing the Content of a Frame

- To change the frame's source document, use the command:

  `FrameObject.location.href=url;`

  where *FrameObject* is frame's object reference.
- To write new HTML code into a frame, use the command:

  `FrameObject.document.write(Content);`

  `FrameObject.document.close();`

  where *Content* is a text string of the HTML code you want to place in the frame.

The Internet Explorer Frame Object

The Internet Explorer document object model includes both the frame and frameset object. The syntax for accessing an individual frame is:

`WindowObject.document.all.id;`

where *id* is the frame's ID. The value of this approach (for Internet Explorer users) is that it opens more of the frame properties to your JavaScript program. For example, you can write scripts to change the border color, frame margins, or frame source. You can add or remove scroll bars from the frame, and control whether the user is allowed to resize the frame. These properties are not available when treating frames as "windows." Figure 5-30 describes some of these frame properties in more detail.

Figure 5-30	PROPERTIES OF THE FRAME OBJECT			
PROPERTY	**DESCRIPTION**	**VALUE**	**NETSCAPE**	**IE**
borderColor	Sets the color of the frame border	hexadecimal color value or color name		4.0
frameborder	Specifies whether to display the frame border	yes, no		4.0
height	Specifies the height of the frame, in pixels	Integer		4.0
marginHeight	The height of the interior margin of the frame, in pixels	Integer		4.0
marginWidth	Specifies the width of the interior margin of the frame, in pixels	Integer		4.0
name	The name of the frame	Text		4.0
noResize	Specifies whether the user can resize the frame	true, false		4.0
scrolling	Specifies whether scroll bars will appear in the frame	auto, no, yes		4.0
src	Specifies the URL of the frame source	URL		4.0

For example, to change the border color of the Top frame to "red," use the JavaScript command:

`WindowObject.Top.borderColor="red";`

Unfortunately, Netscape doesn't support the frame object or these frame properties. There is no way of modifying the appearance of the frame with Netscape once the frame has been rendered in the browser window.

The Internet Explorer Frameset Object

If you want to control the behavior of the entire frameset, you can use The Internet Explorer frameset object. The reference name of the frameset object follows the syntax:

`WindowObject.document.all.id`

where *id* is the value of the ID property for the <FRAMESET> tag. The reference name for the Glossary frameset described above would be:

`WindowObject.document.all.Glossary`

Working with the frameset object, you can make global changes to all of the frames within the window. Among these is the ability to change the height or width of the rows or columns of the frameset—and thereby change the height or width of the frames themselves. Figure 5-31 describes the properties of the frameset object.

Figure 5-31	PROPERTIES OF THE FRAMESET OBJECT			
PROPERTY	**DESCRIPTION**	**VALUE**	**NETSCAPE**	**IE**
border	Sets the thickness of the spaces between the frames, in pixels	Integer		4.0
borderColor	Sets the border color of frames within the frameset	hexadecimal color value or color name		4.0
cols	Specifies the width of the columns (frames) in the frameset, in pixels	Text		4.0
frameBorder	Specifies whether to display borders between frames in the frameset	yes, no		4.0
frameSpacing	Specifies the amount of spacing, in pixels, between frames within the frameset	Integer		4.0
rows	Specifies the height of the rows (frames) in the frameset, in pixels	Text		4.0

For example, to set the border color of all the frames in the Glossary frameset, you would use the command:

`WindowObject.document.all.Glossary.borderColor="red";`

Like the frame object, the frameset object and properties are not supported by Netscape.

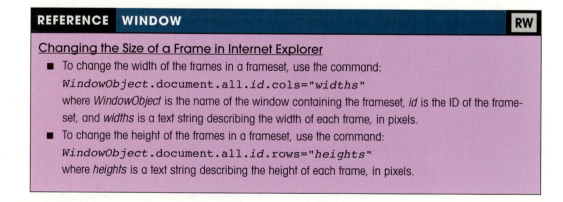

REFERENCE WINDOW | RW

Changing the Size of a Frame in Internet Explorer
- To change the width of the frames in a frameset, use the command:
  `WindowObject.document.all.id.cols="widths"`
  where *WindowObject* is the name of the window containing the frameset, *id* is the ID of the frameset, and *widths* is a text string describing the width of each frame, in pixels.
- To change the height of the frames in a frameset, use the command:
  `WindowObject.document.all.id.rows="heights"`
  where *heights* is a text string describing the height of each frame, in pixels.

Creating a Collapsible Frame for iMusicHistory.com

You now have the information you need to create functions to collapse and expand the glossary's Bottom frame. The functions named Collapse() and Expand() will be run from hyperlinks in the nav.htm file. The functions will run a different set of commands, depending on whether the user is running Netscape or Internet Explorer.

To open the nav.htm file:

1. In your text editor, open **navtxt.htm** located in the Tutorial.05D folder on your Data Disk, and then save the file as **nav.htm**.

2. Locate the <A> tag for the text "Hide Navigation Bar" (located about halfway down the file).

3. Insert within the <A> tag the property **HREF="javascript:Collapse()"** as shown in Figure 5-32.

4. Within the <A> tag for the text "Display Navigation Bar," insert the property **HREF="javascript:Expand()"**.

Figure 5-32 **LINKING TO THE COLLAPSE() AND EXPAND() FUNCTIONS**

```
<!--- Place Display/Hide Navigation Bars Here -->
<TR>
<TD WIDTH=100 ALIGN=LEFT>
<P CLASS="gloss">
<A HREF="javascript:Collapse()">Hide Navigation Bar</A></P>
</TD>

<TD BGCOLOR=WHITE CLASS="body" VALIGN=TOP ALIGN=CENTER>
<A CLASS="gloss" NAME="glossary">Glossary of Music Terms</A></TD>

<TD WIDTH=100 ALIGN=RIGHT>
<P ALIGN=RIGHT CLASS="gloss">
<A HREF="javascript:Expand()">Display Navigation Bar</A></P>
</TD>
</TR>
<!--- End of Navigation Bars --->
```

If the user is running Internet Explorer, the Collapse() function will change the size of the frames. Recall that the Glossary frameset defines the heights of the three frames in the ROWS property as follows:

```
ROWS="160,*,64"
```

so that the Top frame is 160 pixels high, the Bottom frame is 64 pixels high, and the height of the Main frame occupies whatever space remains in the browser window. To collapse the Bottom frame, you can set its height to 0 pixels, using the rows property of the frame object:

```
parent.document.all.Glossary.rows="160,*,0"
```

Netscape does not support the rows property. For Netscape browsers, you need to load a new file in the browser window, in which the Bottom frame is not displayed. This file has been stored on your Data Disk as Terms2.htm. This file contains only the Top and Main frames, arranged with row heights of:

```
ROWS="160,*"
```

To change the file displayed by the browser window, enter the command:

```
parent.location.href="Terms2.htm"
```

The complete Collapse() function will then be:

```
function Collapse() {
   if (document.all) {
      parent.document.all.Glossary.rows="160,*,0";
   } else {
      parent.location.href="Terms2.htm";
   }
}
```

Note that this function uses object detection to determine whether Internet Explorer or Netscape is being used.

The Expand() function is similar, except that it expands the height of the Bottom frame to 64 pixels for Internet Explorer browsers, and retrieves the original Terms.htm file for Netscape browsers. The Expand() function appears as:

```
function Expand() {
   if (document.all) {
      parent.document.all.Glossary.rows="160,*,64";
   } else {
      parent.location.href="Terms.htm";
   }
}
```

To insert the Collapse() and Expand() functions:

1. Above the </HEAD> tag at the top of the nav.htm file, insert the following code:

```
<SCRIPT>
function Collapse() {
   if (document.all) {
      parent.document.all.Glossary.rows="160,*,0";
   } else {
      parent.location.href="Terms2.htm";
   }
}

function Expand() {
   if (document.all) {
      parent.document.all.Glossary.rows="160,*,64";
   } else {
      parent.location.href="Terms.htm";
   }
}
</SCRIPT>
```

2. Save your changes to the file and then open **Terms.htm** in your Web browser.

3. Click the **Hide Navigation Bar** hyperlink in the Top frame. Verify that the Bottom frame disappears from the document window.

4. Click the **Display Navigation Bar** hyperlink and verify that the Bottom frame is restored.

   TROUBLE? If you are using Netscape, you may notice a slight delay as the browser swaps between the Terms.htm and Terms2.htm files.

Next, Teresa would like you to control the interaction between the pages in her Web site and other sites on the Web. She's particularly concerned about the behavior of frames.

Controlling Frame Behavior

There are many people who do not like framed Web sites for a variety of reasons. For example, some Web site designers either aren't aware of or don't add code to prevent external Web pages from being caught inside their frames. Additionally, a page that is designed to be viewed only within a frame might be mistakenly opened outside the frameset. Without the context of the rest of the frames, such a page can be meaningless and irritating to the casual Web surfer.

Both problems have happened to the iMusicHistory Web site on a number of occasions. Teresa has complained to you that sometimes her Web site gets stuck inside another Web site's frames, and that search engines often bring visitors to the iMusicHistory site via one of the frames in the Glossary frameset. She would like you to control the behavior of frames with respect to her Web site.

Blocking Unwanted Frames

When one of Teresa's Web pages gets stuck within another Web site's frames, her page becomes a child frame to the other Web site's parent window. You can see the effect this has on the Default.htm file you worked on in the first session, by opening the BlockDemo.htm file.

To view the BlockDemo.htm file:

1. In your browser, open **BlockDemo.htm** located in the Tutorial.05D folder on your Data Disk.

2. Click **Default.htm** in the left frame.

   Figure 5-33 displays the Default.htm file stuck within the frameset of the BlockDemo page.

Figure 5-33	THE DEFAULT.HTM FILE STUCK WITHIN A FRAMESET OF A DIFFERENT WEB SITE

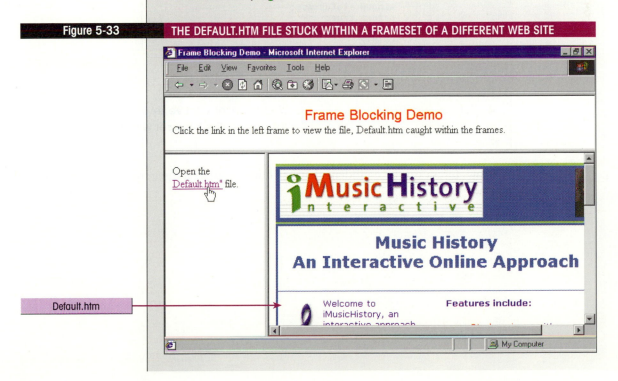

When this happens to one of Teresa's pages, she would like the page to "jump" out of the frame and occupy the browser window. To do this, you need to run a command testing whether the page is at the top of the window hierarchy when the browser loads the page. The commands to do this are:

```
if (top.location.href != self.location.href) {
    top.location.href = self.location.href;
}
```

In this code, JavaScript compares the URL of the topmost window to the currently active window. If they're different, JavaScript changes the location of the topmost window to the current window's location. The result will be that the page cannot be forced into someone else's frame. It will always "jump" up to the top of the hierarchy, replacing the frameset. Nothing will occur if the page is already at the top of the hierarchy. Try this now by adding frame-blocking to the Default.htm file.

To add frame-blocking to the iMusicHistory home page:

1. In your text editor open the **Default.htm** page located in the Tutorial.05 folder on your Data Disk.

2. Below the <SCRIPT> tag insert the following JavaScript code, as shown in Figure 5-34:

```
if (top.location.href != self.location.href) {
    top.location.href = self.location.href;
}
```

Figure 5-34	MOVING A FILE OUT OF A FRAME

if the topmost window is not the active window, ...

... replace the topmost window with the active window

```
<SCRIPT>
if (top.location.href != self.location.href) {
    top.location.href = self.location.href;
}
function showStatus(msg) {
    window.status=msg;
    return true;
}
</SCRIPT>
```

3. Save your changes and close the file.

4. Reload **BlockDemo.htm** in your Web browser, and verify that the Default.htm file "jumps" out of its frame to occupy the entire browser window.

Now Teresa can be confident that her home page won't get stuck within the frames of another Web site.

REFERENCE WINDOW   RW

<u>Blocking and Forcing Frames</u>

- To keep a page from being displayed in a frame, run the following commands when the page is loaded by the browser:

```
if (top.location.href != self.location.href) {
    top.location.href = self.location.href;
}
```

- To keep a frame fixed within its frameset, run the following commands when the source file of the frame is loaded by the browser:

```
if (top.location.href == self.location) {
    top.location.href = "URL";
}
```

where *URL* is the URL of the frame file.

Now Teresa would like you to ensure that her pages don't become separated from one another.

Forcing Pages into a Frameset

Teresa's second task involves the opposite problem: instead of jumping a page out of a frameset, she wants to ensure that the three files that compose the Glossary frameset (nav.htm, main.htm, and bottom.htm) are *always* displayed within their frames. This prevents visitors from inadvertently accessing one of those pages outside the context of the iMusicHistory Glossary.

Although the problem is different, the solution is similar. It involves verifying that whenever nav.htm, main.htm, or bottom.htm is opened, the URL of the topmost window is Terms.htm. The code is:

```
if (top.location.href == self.location) {
    top.location.href = "Terms.htm";
}
```

Here, JavaScript checks whether the URL of the topmost window is the same as that of the active window. If it is, the Terms.htm file is displayed in the topmost window. The result will be that a file such as nav.htm will not be displayed outside its frame.

For now you'll apply this technique only to the nav.htm file.

To modify the nav.htm file:

1. Open **nav.htm** in your text editor.

2. Below the <SCRIPT> tag, insert the following commands (see Figure 5-35):

```
if (top.location.href == self.location) {
    top.location.href = "Terms.htm";
}
```

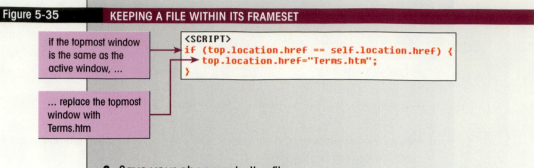

Figure 5-35   KEEPING A FILE WITHIN ITS FRAMESET

if the topmost window is the same as the active window, ...

... replace the topmost window with Terms.htm

```
<SCRIPT>
if (top.location.href == self.location.href) {
    top.location.href="Terms.htm";
}
```

3. Save your changes to the file.

4. Open **nav.htm** in your Web browser, and verify that your browser opens the entire Glossary frameset.

The Glossary section is now finished. Teresa is excited about the progress you've made with her Web site. Later, she wants you to incorporate the work you've done on these pages into the rest of the iMusicHistory Web site.

Session 5.3 QUICK CHECK

1. What reference name would you use to access a frame named "Logo" located in the topmost window of the browser window hierarchy?

2. What command would you use to change the source of the Logo frame to "Logo.html"?

3. What command would you use to write the text string "<HTML></HTML>" to the Logo frame?

4. What command would you use to prevent the Logo frame from being resized by the user? Can this command be used in a Netscape browser?

5. Assume that the Logo frame is part of a frameset with the ID name "Home." What command would you use to change the column widths of the frames in the Home frameset to "150,150,*"? Can this command be used by Netscape?

6. The Home frameset is saved in an HTML file named "Home.htm." What JavaScript command(s) would you add to the Logo.html file so that it always appears within the Home.htm page?

REVIEW ASSIGNMENTS

Teresa has reviewed your work on the iMusicHistory Web site. She's happy with the work you've done and wants you to apply the changes you've made so far to the rest of the Web site. She's also added a new quiz page to the site and she wants you to add pop-up windows to it.

To revise the iMusicHistory Web site:

1. Go to the Tutorial.05D/Review folder on your Data disk, and open the files, **Defaulttxt.htm, atempotxt.htm, Quiztxt.htm, Quiz2txt.htm, maintxt.htm,** and **bottomtxt.htm** in your text editor, and save them as Default.htm, atempo.htm, Quiz.htm, Quiz2.htm, main.htm, and bottom.htm, respectively.

2. Within the Default.htm file do the following:

- Add an onMouseOver event handler to the hyperlink for the Lesson3.htm file to display "Go to the Lessons page" in the status bar. Add an onMouseOut event handler to the Lesson3.htm hyperlink to display a blank space in the status bar.

- Change the status bar message for the two Quiz.htm hyperlinks to "Go to the First Online Quiz."

- Change the status bar message for the two Terms.htm hyperlinks to "View the Music Glossary."

- Change the status bar message for the #top hyperlink to "Go to the top of the page."

- Create a function named showDef() that has a single parameter named "source" that opens a file with the URL "source" in a window that is 200 pixels wide and 100 pixels high, located 100 pixels down and to the right of the upper-left corner of your screen.

- Run the showDef() function when the user clicks the "a tempo" hyperlink.

- Change the status bar message for the "a tempo" hyperlink to "Open a pop-up window."

3. Within the atempo.htm file, modify the file so that it automatically closes when the page loses the focus.

4. Within the Quiz2.htm file, do the following:

- Create a function named writePop() that has a single parameter named "Message" that opens a pop-up window 300 pixels wide and 130 pixels high, located 100 pixels down and to the right of the upper-left corner of the screen. The writePop() function should write the following code into the window:

```
<HTML>
<HEAD>
<TITLE>Answer</TITLE>
<LINK REL="STYLESHEET" TYPE="text/css" HREF="main.css">
</HEAD>
<BODY CLASS="dialogw">
<IMG SRC="treble.gif" BORDER=0 ALIGN=LEFT HSPACE=10
VSPACE=0>
Message
</BODY>
```

- Create a function named Correct() that has a single parameter named "answer," where "answer.value" contains the answer that the user clicked in the Quiz2 page. The Correct() function should store the following text string in a variable named "Message:"

```
<B><FONT COLOR=GREEN><I>
answer.value
</I></FONT> is correct!
```

and then call the writePop() function, using the Message variable as the parameter value.

- Create a function named Incorrect() that also uses the "answer" parameter you used for the Correct() function. The Incorrect() function should store the following text string in the Message variable:

```
<B><FONT COLOR=RED><I>
answer.value
</I></FONT> is incorrect.
```

Call the writePop() function, using the Message variable as the parameter value.

■ Modify the pop-up window created by the writePop() function so that it always retains the focus unless closed by the user.

■ Modify the Quiz2.htm file so that it cannot be opened within a frameset.

5. Modify the Quiz.htm file so that it cannot be opened within a frameset.

6. Modify the bottom.htm and main.htm files so that they are forced into the Glossary frameset when opened.

7. Save all changes to your files and print the revised code.

CASE PROBLEMS

Case 1. Creating a Pop-up Window for The Civil War Journal Terrence Whyte is the editor of the online version of *The Civil War Journal*, a magazine for people interested in the Civil War. Terrence would like to have a small pop-up window appear when users open the home page of the online edition. The window will advertise the print version of the magazine and provide a link to a subscription form. Also, Terrence would like to have the status bar display informative text for hyperlinks on the page. Figure 5-36 shows a preview of the windows you'll create.

Figure 5-36

To create the pop-up windows:

1. Open **CWJtxt.htm** from the Tutorial.05D/Cases folder on your Data Disk in your text editor. Save the file as CWJ.htm.

2. Create a new function named Subscribe() that opens a file named "Cover.htm" in a target window named "PopWin." Set the width and height of the pop-up window to 125 pixels by 240 pixels. Open the window 10 pixels down and to the right of the upper-left corner of the screen.

3. Add an event handler to run the Subscribe() function when the page loads.

4. Create a function name writeStatus() that has one parameter variable named Message, which contains the text you want to write to the browser window's status bar.

5. Call the writeStatus() function from the onMouseOver and onMouseOut event handlers to change the status bar message for each of the five hyperlinks at the top of the page to the following (when the user moves the mouse pointer off a hyperlink, no status bar message should be displayed):

- Home Page: "Go to the Home Page"
- News: "View Current Events"
- Features: "Go to Feature Articles"
- Forum: "Go to the Civil War Forum"
- Subscriptions: "Subscribe Today!"

6. Print the revised code, and save your changes to the CWJ.htm file.

7. In your text editor, open the **Covertxt.htm** file from the Tutorial.05D Cases folder on your Data Disk, and save it as Cover.htm.

Explore ▶ 8. Create a function named showForm() that does the following:

- Opens the file, Form.htm" in the window from which the Cover.htm file was opened
- Closes the current window

9. Change the HREF value of the <A> tag in the file to run the showForm() function.

10. Print the revised code and save your changes to the Cover.htm file.

11. Open CWJ.htm in your Web browser. Verify that the status bar messages change in response to the onMouseOver actions. Also, verify that the Cover.htm pop-up window is automatically opened by the browser.

12. Click the hyperlink for the pop-up window. Verify that the subscription form appears in the main browser window.

Case 2. Writing to a pop-up window for Anatomy 101   Jacob Terrell teaches Anatomy 101 at Thomas More College. He's asked your help in creating a Web page on the brain. The page displays an inline image showing different parts of the human brain. As students move their mouse pointers over a section, he would like to have a pop-up window appear on the desktop containing a description of that part of the brain. Figure 5-37 shows a preview of the page he wants you to create for him.

Figure 5-37

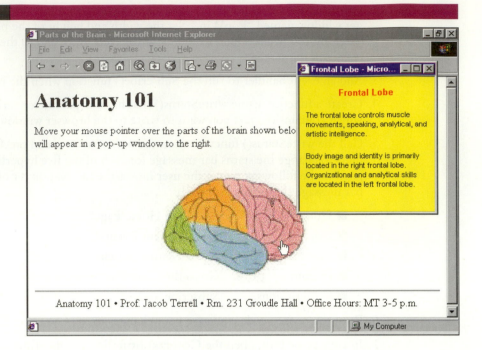

The text of the pop-up window has already been entered for you and stored in two arrays. The Head array stores the names of four different brain lobes. The Summary array contains a brief description of each lobe. Your job will be to insert the content of these arrays into the pop-up window.

To create Professor Terrell's Web page:

1. Start your text editor, and open **Braintxt.htm** from the Tutorial.05D/Cases folder on your Data Disk.

2. Save the file as Brain.htm.

3. Create a function named writeWin() that contains a single parameter named "i." The i parameter stores the index number of the entry from the Head and Summary arrays that should appear in the pop-up window. The writeWin() function should perform the following actions:

   - Create a pop-up window that is 200 pixels wide and 200 pixels high. Place the window 400 pixels to the right and 50 pixels down from the upper-left corner of the screen. Store the pop-up window as a window object named "PopWin."
   - Apply the focus to PopWin
   - Write the following HTML code to PopWin:

   ```
   <HTML>
   <HEAD>
   <TITLE>
   Head
   </TITLE>
   <LINK REL="STYLESHEET" TYPE="text/css" HREF="Brain.css">
   </HEAD>
   <BODY>
   <H2>
   Head
   ```

```
</H2>
Summary
</BODY>
</HTML>
```

where *Head* is the value of the Head array with index number "i," and *Summary* is the value of the Summary array with index number "i."

Explore

4. Add the onMouseOver event handler to the Frontal lobe <AREA> tag that runs the writeWin() function, with a parameter value of 1.

Explore

5. Add the onMouseOut event handler to the frontal lobe <AREA> tag that runs the writeWin() function, with a parameter value of 0.

6. Repeat Steps 4 and 5 for the remaining <AREA> tags. Use a parameter value of 2 for the parietal Lobe, 3 for the occipital lobe, and 4 for the temporal lobe. Use a parameter value of 0 for all of the onMouseOut events.

7. Print the code for the Brain.htm file and close the file, saving your changes.

8. Open Brain.htm in your Web browser. Verify that as you pass your mouse pointer over the various parts of the brain, a pop-up window appears with a brief description of the lobe selected.

Case 3. Writing HTML code into a frame Keri Liddle is teaching a course on HTML, and she wants your help in creating an HTML demo page. The page should have two frames. In the upper frame, she will have students enter HTML code into a text area box. Then the students will click a button on the Web page to render that HTML code in the bottom frame. She also wants a button to expand and contract the size of the upper frame to give students more screen space for the code they enter (Internet Explorer users only). A preview of the page you'll create is shown in Figure 5-38.

Figure 5-38

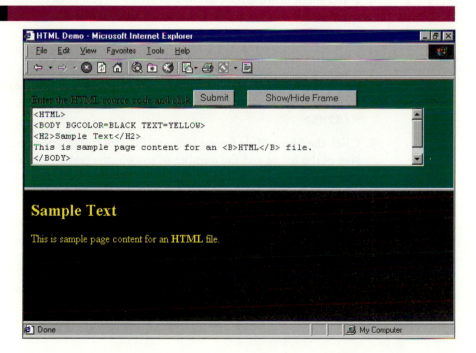

The frame page contains one frameset with the ID name Demo. The top frame is named Source. The bottom frame is named Output.

To create the HTML demo page:

1. Open your text editor and open the file **Sourcetxt.htm** from the Tutorial.05D/Cases folder on your Data Disk. Save the file as Source.htm.

Explore

2. Create a function named "renderCode()", which takes whatever code has been entered into the Code text area box on the Web page form, and writes it to the Output frame in the Demo.htm file. (*Hint*: The text entered into the Source text can be found by using the document.HTMLForm.Code.value property.)

3. Run the function when the user clicks the Submit button on the Web page form.

4. Create a function named showHideF(), which does the following:

   ■ If the user is running Internet Explorer (use object detection to determine this), test whether the size of the frame rows in the Demo frameset is equal to "160,*". If so, change the height of the rows to "*,0" and change the number of rows in the Code text area to 15. (*Hint*: Use the document.HTMLForm.Code.rows property.) If the height of the frame rows is *not* equal to "160,*" change the height to "160,*" and change the number of rows in the Code text area to 5.

   ■ If the user is running Netscape, display an alert box with the message "Drag the bottom of the frame border to enlarge or reduce the height of the top frame."

5. Run the showHideF() function when the user clicks the Show/Hide Frame button on the form.

6. Print the revised code, and close the file, saving your changes.

7. Open **Source.htm** in your Web browser.

8. Enter the following code in the text area box, and click the Submit button. Verify that the browser renders the code in the bottom window.

```
<HTML>
<BODY BGCOLOR=BLACK TEXT=WHITE>
<H2>Sample Text</H2>
This is sample page content for an <B>HTML</B> file.
</BODY>
</HTML>
```

9. Click the Show/Hide Frame button. If you're running Internet Explorer, verify that the size of the frame and the number of rows in the text area box change in response to clicking the button. If you're running Netscape, verify that an alert box is displayed.

10. Hand in your printouts and files to your instructor.

Case 4. Creating an information window for UB Computing

Dale Crawford of UB Computing, a leading manufacturer of PCs in the United States, has asked you to work on an information page for one of the company's computers—the PS300. The page should contain an image of the computer with hotspots created with the <AREA> tag. As the customer moves the mouse over each of the hotspots, information about that feature of the computer should appear in a pop-up window.

The graphic file and hotspot coordinates have already been provided for you in the PS300.jpg and UBtxt.htm files. The company logo has been saved in the UBLogo.jpg file. Finally, information on the computer features has been saved in the Features.txt file.

To create the information page:

1. Create a file named "UB.htm" in the Tutorial.05D/Cases folder that contains the inline image and the code required for displaying the pop-up window.

2. As the mouse pointer moves over the hotspot, display the pop-up window and the descriptive text in the main browser window's status bar.

3. The pop-up window can either be an external HTML file, or the HTML code can be written directly into the window.

4. The design of the page and the pop-up window is up to you.

5. All solutions must be cross-browser-compatible.

6. Hand in your solution file and all necessary printouts to your instructor.

QUICK | CHECK ANSWERS

Session 5.1

1. The defaultStatus property is the default message in the status bar. The showStatus property is the current status bar message.

2. `history.go(-2);`

3. `window.status="View News page"`
   `return true;`

4. One ways is with the <META> tag, using the following syntax:

   `<META HTTP-EQUIV="Refresh" CONTENT="sec;URL=URL">`

   where *sec* is the amount of time in seconds that will elapse before opening the new page, and the *URL* is the new page to be loaded.

   Another way is to use the window.location.href property along with the setTimeout method.

5. The document.referrer property records the URL of the page from which the current page was accessed. However, this property is not supported by Internet Explorer, and for Netscape it requires the use of a signed script.

Session 5.2

1. `<A HREF="Home.htm" TARGET="HomePage">`

2. `window.open("Home.htm","width=300,height=150");`

3. `window.open("Home.htm","width=300,height=150,`
   `scrollbars=yes,status=yes");`

4. a window that prevents the user from doing anything outside the window, until it is closed

5. a window that allows the user to work in other windows while it's open

6. `Home.document.write("<BODY BGCOLOR=YELLOW">);`

7. `window.showModalDialog("Home.htm","width:300,height:150");`

8. `window.showModelessDialog("Home.htm","width:300,`
   `height:150");`

Session 5.3

1. `Top.Logo`

2. `Top.Logo.location.href="Logo.html";`

3. `Top.Logo.document.write("<HTML></HTML>");`

4. `Top.Logo.resize="no";`

   This command can be run only in Internet Explorer.

5. `Top.Home.cols="150,150,*";`

   This command can be run only in Internet Explorer.

6. ```
   if (top.location.href == self.location) {
        top.location.href = "Home.htm";
   }
   ```
   ```

HTML Extended Color Names

The following is a list of extended color names and their corresponding hexadecimal triplets supported by most Web browsers. To view these colors, you must have a video card and monitor capable of displaying up to 256 colors. As with other aspects of Web page design, you should test these color names on a variety of browsers before committing to their use. Different browsers may render these colors differently, or not at all.

Extended Color Names

COLOR NAME	HEXADECIMAL VALUE	PREVIEW	COLOR NAME	HEXADECIMAL VALUE	PREVIEW
ALICEBLUE	#F0F8FE		DARKPURPLE	#871F78	
ANTIQUEWHITE	#FAEBD7		DARKSALMON	#E9967A	
AQUA	#00FFFF		DARKSLATEBLUE	#6B238E	
AQUAMARINE	#70DB93		DARKSLATEGRAY	#2F4F4F	
AZURE	#F0FFFF		DARKTAN	#97694F	
BEIGE	#F5F5DC		DARKTURQUOISE	#7093DB	
BLACK	#000000		DARKVIOLET	#9400D3	
BLUE	#0000FF		DARKWOOD	#855E42	
BLUEVIOLET	#9F5F9F		DIMGRAY	#545454	
BRASS	#B5A642		DUSTYROSE	#856363	
BRIGHTGOLD	#D9D919		FELDSPAR	#D19275	
BRONZE	#8C7853		FIREBRICK	#8E2323	
BROWN	#A52A2A		FORESTGREEN	#238E23	
CADETBLUE	#5F9F9F		GOLD	#CD7F32	
CHOCOLATE	#D2691E		GOLDENROD	#DBDB70	
COOLCOPPER	#D98719		GRAY	#C0C0C0	
COPPER	#B87333		GREEN	#00FF00	
CORAL	#FF7F50		GREENCOPPER	#527F76	
CRIMSON	#DC143C		GREENYELLOW	#93DB70	
CYAN	#00FFFF		HOTPINK	#FF69B4	
DARKBLUE	#00008B		HUNTERGREEN	#215E21	
DARKBROWN	#5C4033		INDIANRED	#4E2F2F	
DARKCYAN	#008B8B		INDIGO	#4B0082	
DARKGOLDENROD	#B8860B		IVORY	#FFFFF0	
DARKGRAY	#A9A9A9		KHAKI	#9F9F5F	
DARKGREEN	#006400		LAVENDER	#E6E6FA	
DARKKHAKI	#BDB76B		LIGHTBLUE	#C0D9D9	
DARKMAGENTA	#8B008B		LIGHTCORAL	#F08080	
DARKOLIVEGREEN	#4F4F2F		LIGHTCYAN	#E0FFFF	
DARKORANGE	#FF8C00		LIGHTGRAY	#A8A8A8	
DARKORCHID	#9932CD		LIGHTGREEN	#90EE90	

COLOR NAME	HEXADECIMAL VALUE	PREVIEW
LIGHTPINK	#FFB6C1	
LIGHTSTEELBLUE	#8F8FBD	
LIGHTWOOD	#E9C2A6	
LIME	#00FF00	
LIMEGREEN	#32CD32	
MAGENTA	#FF00FF	
MANDARINORANGE	#E47833	
MAROON	#8E236B	
MEDIUMAQUAMARINE	#32CD99	
MEDIUMBLUE	#3232CD	
MEDIUMFORESTGREEN	#6B8E23	
MEDIUMGOLDENROD	#EAEAAE	
MEDIUMORCHID	#9370DB	
MEDIUMSEAGREEN	#426F42	
MEDIUMSLATEBLUE	#7F00FF	
MEDIUMSPRINGGREEN	#7FFF00	
MEDIUMTURQUOISE	#70DBDB	
MEDIUMVIOLETRED	#DB7093	
MEDIUMWOOD	#A68064	
MIDNIGHTBLUE	#2F2F4F	
MINTCREAM	#F5FFFA	
MISTYROSE	#FFE4E1	
NAVYBLUE	#23238E	
NEONBLUE	#4D4DFF	
NEONPINK	#FF6EC7	
NEWMIDNIGHTBLUE	#00009C	
NEWTAN	#EBC79E	
OLDGOLD	#CFB53B	
OLIVE	#808000	
ORANGE	#FF7F00	
ORANGERED	#FF2400	
ORCHID	#DB70DB	
PALEGOLDENROD	#EEE8AA	
PALEGREEN	#8FBC8F	
PALETURQUOISE	#AFEEEE	

COLOR NAME	HEXADECIMAL VALUE	PREVIEW
PINK	#BC8F8F	
PLUM	#EAADEA	
POWDERBLUE	#B0E0E6	
PURPLE	#800080	
QUARTZ	#D9D9F3	
RED	#FF0000	
RICHBLUE	#5959AB	
ROYALBLUE	#4169E1	
SADDLEBROWN	#8B4513	
SALMON	#6F4242	
SANDYBROWN	#F4A460	
SCARLET	#8C1717	
SEAGREEN	#238E68	
SIENNA	#8E6B23	
SILVER	#E6E8FA	
SKYBLUE	#3299CC	
SLATEBLUE	#007FFF	
SNOW	#FFFAFA	
SPICYPINK	#FF1CAE	
SPRINGGREEN	#00FF7F	
STEELBLUE	#236B8E	
SUMMERSKY	#38B0DE	
TAN	#DB9370	
TEAL	#008080	
THISTLE	#D8BFD8	
TOMATO	#FF6347	
TURQUOISE	#ADEAEA	
VERYDARKBROWN	#5C4033	
VERYDARKGRAY	#CDCDCD	
VIOLET	#4F2F4F	
VIOLETRED	#CC3299	
WHEAT	#D8D8BF	
WHITE	#FFFFFF	
YELLOW	#FFFF00	
YELLOWGREEN	#99CC32	

HTML Special Characters

The following table lists the extended character set for HTML, also known as the ISO Latin-1 Character set. Characters in this table can be entered either by code number or code name. For example, to insert the registered trademark symbol, ®, you would use either &reg or &#174.

Not all code names are recognized by all browsers. Some older browsers that support only the HTML 2.0 standard will not recognize the code name &times, for instance. Code names that may not be recognized by older browsers are marked with an asterisk. If you are planning to use these symbols in your document, you may want to use the code number instead of the code name.

CHARACTER	CODE	CODE NAME	DESCRIPTION
	&#00 - &#08		Unused
	&#09		Tab
	&#10		Line feed
	&#11 - &#31		Unused
	&#32		Space
!	&#33		Exclamation mark
"	&#34	&quot	Double quotation mark
#	&#35		Pound sign
$	&#36		Dollar sign
%	&#37		Percent sign
&	&#38	&amp	Ampersand
'	&#39		Apostrophe
(	&#40		Left parenthesis
)	&#41		Right parenthesis
*	&#42		Asterisk
+	&#43		Plus sign
,	&#44		Comma
-	&#45		Hyphen
.	&#46		Period
/	&#47		Forward slash
0 - 9	&#48 - &#57		Numbers 0 - 9
:	&#58		Colon
;	&#59		Semicolon
<	&#60	&lt	Less than sign
=	&#61		Equals sign
>	&#62	&gt	Greater than sign
?	&#63		Question mark
@	&#64		Commercial at
A - Z	&#65 - &#90		Letters A - Z
[	&#91		Left square bracket

CHARACTER	CODE	CODE NAME	DESCRIPTION
\	&#92		Back slash
]	&#93		Right square bracket
^	&#94		Caret
_	&#95		Horizontal bar
`	&#96		Grave accent
a - z	&#97 - &#122		Letters a - z
{	&#123		Left curly brace
|	&#124		Vertical bar
}	&#125		Right curly brace
~	&#126		Tilde
	&#127 - &#129		Unused
‚	&#130		Low single comma quotation mark
ƒ	&#131		Function sign
„	&#132		Low double comma quotation mark
…	&#133		Ellipses
†	&#134		Dagger
‡	&#135		Double dagger
ˆ	&#136		Caret
‰	&#137		Per mile sign
Š	&#138		Capital S with hacek
<	&#139		Less than sign
Œ	&#140		Capital OE ligature
	&#141 - &#144		Unused
`	&#145		Single beginning quotation mark
'	&#146		Single ending quotation mark
"	&#147		Double beginning quotation mark
"	&#148		Double ending quotation mark
•	&#149		Middle dot
–	&#150		En dash
—	&#151		Em dash
~	&#152		Tilde
™	&#153	&trade*	Trademark symbol
š	&#154		Small s with hacek
›	&#155		Greater than sign
œ	&#156		Small oe ligature
	&#157 - &#158		Unused
Ÿ	&#159		Capital Y with umlaut

CHARACTER	CODE	CODE NAME	DESCRIPTION
		*	Non-breaking space
¡	&#161	&iexcl*	Inverted exclamation point
¢	&#162	&cent*	Cent symbol
£	&#163	&pound*	Pound sterling
¤	&#164	&curren*	General currency symbol
¥	&#165	&yen*	Yen sign
¦	&#166	&brvbar*	Broken vertical bar
§	&#167	&sect*	Section sign
¨	&#168	&uml*	Umlaut
©	&#169	&copy*	Copyright symbol
ª	&#170	&ordf*	Feminine ordinal
«	&#171	&laquo*	Left angle quotation mark
¬	&#172	&not*	Not sign
	&#173	&shy*	Soft hyphen
®	&#174	&reg*	Registered trademark
¯	&#175	&macr*	Macron
°	&#176	&deg*	Degree sign
±	&#177	&plusmn*	Plus/minus symbol
²	&#178	&sup2*	Superscript 2
³	&#179	&sup3*	Superscript 3
´	&#180	&acute*	Acute accent
µ	&#181	&micro*	Micro symbol
¶	&#182	&para*	Paragraph sign
·	&#183	&middot*	Middle dot
¸	&#184	&cedil*	Cedilla
¹	&#185	&sup1*	Superscript 1
º	&#186	&ordm*	Masculine ordinal
»	&#187	&raquo*	Right angle quotation mark
¼	&#188	&frac14*	Fraction one-quarter
½	&#189	&frac12*	Fraction one-half
¾	&#190	&frac34*	Fraction three-quarters
¿	&#191	&iquest*	Inverted question mark
À	&#192	&Agrave	Capital A, grave accent
Á	&#193	&Aacute	Capital A, acute accent
Â	&#194	&Acirc	Capital A, circumflex accent
Ã	&#195	&Atilde	Capital A, tilde
Ä	&#196	&Auml	Capital A, umlaut

CHARACTER	CODE	CODE NAME	DESCRIPTION
Å	&#197	&Aring	Capital A, ring
Æ	&#198	&Aelig	Capital AE ligature
Ç	&#199	&Ccedil	Capital C, cedilla
È	&#200	&Egrave	Capital E, grave accent
É	&#201	&Eacute	Capital E, acute accent
Ê	&#202	&Ecirc	Capital E, circumflex accent
Ë	&#203	&Euml	Capital E, umlaut
Ì	&#204	&Igrave	Capital I, grave accent
Í	&#205	&Iacute	Capital I, acute accent
Î	&#206	&Icirc	Capital I, circumflex accent
Ï	&#207	&Iuml	Capital I, umlaut
Ð	&#208	&ETH*	Capital ETH, Icelandic
Ñ	&#209	&Ntilde	Capital N, tilde
Ò	&#210	&Ograve	Capital O, grave accent
Ó	&#211	&Oacute	Capital O, acute accent
Ô	&#212	&Ocirc	Capital O, circumflex accent
Õ	&#213	&Otilde	Capital O, tilde
Ö	&#214	&Ouml	Capital O, umlaut
×	&#215	&times*	Multiplication sign
Ø	&#216	&Oslash	Capital O slash
Ù	&#217	&Ugrave	Capital U, grave accent
Ú	&#218	&Uacute	Capital U, acute accent
Û	&#219	&Ucirc	Capital U, circumflex accent
Ü	&#220	&Uuml	Capital U, umlaut
Ý	&#221	&Yacute	Capital Y, acute accent
þ	&#222	&THORN	Capital THORN, Icelandic
ß	&#223	&szlig	Small sz ligature
à	&#224	&agrave	Small a, grave accent
á	&#225	&aacute	Small a, acute accent
â	&#226	&acirc	Small a, circumflex accent
ã	&#227	&atilde	Small a, tilde
ä	&#228	&auml	Small a, umlaut
å	&#229	&aring	Small a, ring
œ	&#230	&aelig	Small AE ligature
ç	&#231	&ccedil	Small C, cedilla
è	&#232	&egrave	Small e, grave accent
é	&#233	&eacute	Small e, acute accent

CHARACTER	CODE	CODE NAME	DESCRIPTION
ê	&#234	&ecirc	Small e, circumflex accent
ë	&#235	&euml	Small e, umlaut
ì	&#236	&igrave	Small i, grave accent
í	&#237	&iacute	Small i, acute accent
î	&#238	&icirc	Small i, circumflex accent
ï	&#239	&iuml	Small i, umlaut
ð	&#240	&eth	Small ETH, Icelandic
ñ	&#241	&ntilde	Small N, tilde
ò	&#242	&ograve	Small o, grave accent
ó	&#243	&oacute	Small o, acute accent
ô	&#244	&ocirc	Small o, circumflex accent
õ	&#245	&otilde	Small o, tilde
ö	&#246	&ouml	Small o, umlaut
÷	&#247	&divide*	Division sign
ø	&#248	&oslash	Small o slash
ù	&#249	&ugrave	Small u, grave accent
ú	&#250	&uacute	Small u, acute accent
û	&#251	&ucirc	Small u, circumflex accent
ü	&#252	&uuml	Small u, umlaut
ý	&#253	&yacute	Small y, acute accent
þ	&#254	&thorn	Small thorn, Icelandic
ÿ	&#255	&yuml	Small y, umlaut

Putting a Document on the World Wide Web

Once you've completed your work on your HTML file, you're probably ready to place it on the World Wide Web for others to see. To make a file available to the World Wide Web, you have to transfer it to a computer connected to the Web called a **Web server**.

Your **Internet Service Provider (ISP)**—the company or institution through which you have Internet access—usually has a Web server available for your use. Because each Internet Service Provider has a different procedure for storing Web pages, you should contact your ISP to learn its policies and procedures. Generally you should be prepared to do the following:

- Extensively test your files under a variety of browsers and under different display conditions. Weed out any errors and design problems before you place the page on the Web.

- If your HTML documents have a three-letter "HTM" extension, rename those files with the four-letter extension "HTML." Some Web servers will require the four-letter extension for all Web pages.

- Check the hyperlinks and inline objects in each of your documents to verify that they point to the correct filenames. Verify the filenames with respect to upper and lower cases. Some Web servers will distinguish between a file named "Image.gif" and one named "image.gif." To be safe, match the uppercase and lowercase letters.

- If your hyperlinks use absolute pathnames, change them to relative pathnames.

- Find out from your ISP the name of the folder into which you'll be placing your HTML documents. You may also need a special user name and password to access this folder.

- Use **FTP**, a program used on the Internet that transfers files, or e-mail to place your pages in the appropriate folder on your Internet Service Provider's Web server. Some Web browsers, like Internet Explorer and Netscape Navigator, have this capability built in, allowing you to transfer your files with a click of a toolbar button.

- Decide on a name for your site on the World Wide Web (such as "http://www.jackson_electronics.com"). Choose a name that will be easy for customers and interested parties to remember and return to.

- If you select a special name for your Web site, you may have to register it. Registration information can be found at http://www.internic.net. This is a service your ISP may also provide for a fee. Registration is necessary to ensure that any name you give to your site is unique and not already in use by another party. Usually you will have to pay a yearly fee to keep control of a special name for your Web site.

- Add your site to the indexes of search pages on the World Wide Web. This is not required, but it will make it easier for people to find your site. Each search facility has different policies regarding adding information about Web sites to its index. Be aware that some will charge a fee to include your Web site in their list.

Once you've completed these steps, your work will be available on the World Wide Web in a form that is easy for users to find and access.

JavaScript Objects, Properties, Methods, and Event Handlers

The following are some of the more important JavaScript objects, properties, and methods. The two columns at the right indicate the earliest Netscape and Internet Explorer versions that support these JavaScript commands. For example, a version number of "4.0" for Internet Explorer indicates that versions of Internet Explorer 4.0 and above support the tag or attribute.

Many objects within the Web document should be referred to by their names. For example, to apply the click( ) method to a button named "RUN," use the JavaScript command:

RUN.click( );

JAVASCRIPT ELEMENTS	DESCRIPTION	IE	NETSCAPE
Anchor	**An anchor in the document (use the anchor's name)**	4.0	4.0
Properties			
name	The name of the anchor	4.0	4.0
text	The anchor text	4.0	
Applet	**A Java applet in the document (use the applet's name)**	4.0	3.0
Properties			
name	The name of the applet		3.0
Area	**An area defined in an image map (use the area's name)**	3.0	3.0
Properties			
hash	The anchor name from the URL	3.0	3.0
host	The host and domain name from the URL	3.0	3.0
hostname	The hostname from the URL	3.0	3.0
href	The entire URL	3.0	3.0
pathname	The pathname from the URL	3.0	3.0
port	The port number from the URL	3.0	3.0
protocol	The protocol from the URL	3.0	3.0
search	The query portion from the URL	3.0	3.0
target	The TARGET attribute of the <AREA> tag	3.0	3.0
Methods			
getSelection()	Returns the value of the current selection		3.0
Event Handlers			
onDblClick()	Runs when the area is double-clicked	4.0	4.0
onMouseOut()	Runs when the mouse leaves the area	3.0	3.0
onMouseOver()	Runs when the mouse enters the area	3.0	3.0

JAVASCRIPT ELEMENTS	DESCRIPTION	IE	NETSCAPE
Array	**An array object**	3.0	3.0
Properties			
length	The number of elements in the array	3.0	3.0
prototype	A mechanism to add properties to an array object	3.0	3.0
Methods			
concat(*array*)	Combines two arrays, storing the results in a third array named *array*	4.0	4.0
join(*string*)	Stores each element, separated by commas, in a text string named *string*	3.0	3.0
reverse()	Reverses the order of the array	3.0	3.0
pop()	"Pops" the last element off the array and reduces the length of the array by 1		4.0
push(*arg1*, *arg2*, ...)	"Pushes" the elements in the list to the end of the array		4.0
slice(*array*, *begin*,*end*)	Extracts a portion of the array starting at the index number *begin*, and ending at the index number *end*; the elements are then stored in *array*	4.0	4.0
sort(*function*)	Sorts the array based on the function named *function*; if *function* is omitted, the sort applies dictionary order to the array	3.0	3.0
Button	**A push button in an HTML form (use the button's name)**	3.0	3.0
Properties			
enabled	Indicates whether the button has been enabled	3.0	4.0
form	The name of the form containing the button	3.0	4.0
name	The name of the button element	3.0	2.0
type	The value of the TYPE attribute for the <BUTTON> tag	4.0	3.0
value	The value of the button element	3.0	2.0
Methods			
blur()	Removes focus from the button	3.0	3.0
click()	Emulates the action of clicking on the button	3.0	2.0
focus()	Gives focus to the button	4.0	4.0
Event Handlers			
onBlur	Runs when the button loses the focus	3.0	3.0
onClick	Runs when the button is clicked	3.0	2.0
onFocus	Runs when the button receives the focus	4.0	4.0

JAVASCRIPT ELEMENTS	DESCRIPTION	IE	NETSCAPE
onMouseDown	Runs when the mouse button is pressed down	3.0	2.0
onMouseUp	Runs when the mouse button is released	3.0	2.0
Checkbox	**A check box in an HTML form (use the check box's name)**	3.0	2.0
Properties			
checked	Indicates whether the check box is checked	3.0	2.0
defaultChecked	Indicates whether the check box is selected by default	3.0	2.0
enabled	Indicates whether the check box is enabled	3.0	4.0
form	The name of the form containing the check box	3.0	4.0
name	The name of the check box element	3.0	2.0
type	The value of the TYPE attribute for the <INPUT> tag	4.0	3.0
value	The value of the check box element	3.0	2.0
Methods			
blur()	Removes the focus from the check box	3.0	3.0
click()	Emulates the action of clicking on the check box	3.0	2.0
focus()	Gives focus to the check box	4.0	4.0
Event Handlers			
onBlur	Runs when the check box loses the focus	4.0	3.0
onClick	Runs when the check box is clicked		
onFocus	Runs when the check box receives the focus	4.0	4.0
Date	**An object containing information about a specific date or the current date. Dates are expressed either in local time or in UTC (Universal Time Coordinates), otherwise known as Greenwich Mean Time**	3.0	2.0
Methods			
getDate()	Returns the day of the month, from 1 to 31	3.0	2.0
getDay()	Returns the day of the week from 0 to 6 (Sunday = 0, Monday = 1, ...)	3.0	2.0
getFullYear()	Returns the year portion of the date in four-digit format	4.0	4.0
getHours()	Returns the hour in military time from 0 to 23	3.0	2.0
getMilliseconds()	Returns the number of milliseconds	4.0	4.0
getMinutes()	Returns the minute from 0 to 59	3.0	2.0
getMonth()	Returns the value of the month from 0 to 11 (January = 0, February = 1, ...)	3.0	2.0

JAVASCRIPT ELEMENTS	DESCRIPTION	IE	NETSCAPE
getSeconds()	Returns the seconds	3.0	2.0
getTime()	Returns the date as an integer representing the number of milliseconds since January 1st, 1990, at 00:00:00	3.0	2.0
getTimezoneOffset()	Returns the difference between the local time and Greenwich Mean Time in minutes	3.0	2.0
getYear()	Returns the number of years since 1990 (in other words, 1996 is represented by '96'—this value method is inconsistently applied past the year 1999)	3.0	2.0
getUTCDate()	Returns the UTC getDate() value	4.0	4.0
getUTCDay()	Returns the UTC getDay() value	4.0	4.0
getUTCFullYear()	Returns the UTC getFullYear() value	4.0	4.0
getUTCHours()	Returns the UTC getHours() value	4.0	4.0
getUTCMilliseconds()	Returns the UTC getMilliseconds() value	4.0	4.0
getUTCMinutes()	Returns the UTC getMinutes() value	4.0	4.0
getUTCMonth()	Returns the UTC getMonth() value	4.0	4.0
getUTCSeconds()	Returns the UTC getSeconds() value	4.0	4.0
getUTCTime()	Returns the UTC getTime() value	4.0	4.0
getUTCYear()	Returns the UTC getYear() value	4.0	4.0
setDate(*date*)	Sets the day of the month to the value specified in *date*	3.0	2.0
setFullYear(*year*)	Set the year to the four digit value specified in *year*	4.0	4.0
setHours(*hour*)	Sets the hour to the value specified in *hour*	3.0	2.0
setMilliseconds(*milliseconds*)	Sets the millisecond value to *milliseconds*	4.0	4.0
setMinutes(*minutes*)	Sets the minute to the value specified in *minutes*	3.0	2.0
setMonth(*month*)	Sets the month to the value specified in *month*	3.0	2.0
setSeconds(*seconds*)	Sets the second to the value specified in *seconds*	3.0	2.0
setTime(*time*)	Sets the time using the value specified in *time*, where *time* is a variable containing the number of milliseconds since January 1st, 1990, at 00:00:00	3.0	2.0
setYear(*year*)	Sets the year to the value specified in *year*	3.0	2.0
toGMTString()	Converts the current date to a text string in Greenwich Mean Time	3.0	2.0
toLocaleString()	Converts a date object's date to a text string, using the date format the Web browser is set up to use	3.0	2.0
UTC(*date*)	Returns *date* in the form of the number of milliseconds since January 1st, 1970, 00:00:00 for Universal Coordinated Time	3.0	2.0

JAVASCRIPT ELEMENTS	DESCRIPTION	IE	NETSCAPE
setUTCDate(*date*)	Applies the setDate() method in UTC time	4.0	4.0
setUTCFullYear(*year*)	Applies the setFullYear() method in UTC time	4.0	4.0
setUTCHours(*hour*)	Applies the setHours() method in UTC time	4.0	4.0
setUTCMilliseconds(*milliseconds*)	Applies the setMilliseconds() method in UTC time	4.0	4.0
setUTCMinutes(*minutes*)	Applies the setMinutes() method in UTC time	4.0	4.0
setUTCMonth(*month*)	Applies the setMonth() method in UTC time	4.0	4.0
setUTCSeconds(*seconds*)	Applies the setSeconds() method in UTC time	4.0	4.0
setUTCTime(*time*)	Applies the setTime() method in UTC time	4.0	4.0
setUTCYear(*year*)	Applies the setYear() method in UTC time	4.0	4.0
document	**An HTML document**	3.0	2.0
Properties			
alinkColor	The color of active hyperlinks in the document	3.0	2.0
all	An array of each of the HTML tags in the document	4.0	
anchors	An array of the anchors in the document		3.0
applets	An array of the applets in the document	3.0	3.0
bgColor	The background color used in the document	3.0	2.0
classes.*class.tag.style*	The *style* associated with the element in the document with the class name *class* and the tag name *tag*		4.0
cookie	A text string containing the document's cookie values	3.0	2.0
domain	The domain of the document	4.0	3.0
embeds	An array of the embedded objects in the document	4.0	3.0
fgColor	The text color used in the document	3.0	2.0
form	A form within the document (the form itself is also an object)	3.0	2.0
forms	An array of the forms in the document	3.0	2.0
ids.*id.tag.style*	The *style* associated with the element in the document with the id name *id* and the tag name *tag*		4.0
lastModified	The date the document was last modified	3.0	2.0
layers	An array of LAYER objects		4.0
linkColor	The color of hyperlinks in the document	3.0	2.0
links	An array of the links within the document.	3.0	2.0
location	The URL of the document	3.0	2.0
referrer	The URL of the document containing the link that the user accessed to get to the current document	3.0	2.0

JAVASCRIPT ELEMENTS	DESCRIPTION	IE	NETSCAPE
tags.*tag.style*	The *style* associated with the tag name *tag*		4.0
title	The title of the document	3.0	2.0
URL	The URL of the document	3.0	2.0
vlinkColor	The color of followed hyperlinks	3.0	2.0
Methods			
clear()	Clears the contents of the document window	3.0	2.0
close()	Closes the document stream	3.0	2.0
getSelection()	Returns the selected text from the document		4.0
open()	Opens the document stream	3.0	2.0
write()	Writes to the document window	3.0	2.0
writeln()	Writes to the document window on a single line (used only with preformatted text)	3.0	2.0
Event Handlers			
onClick	Runs when the document is clicked	3.0	2.0
onDblClick	Runs when the document is double-clicked	3.0	2.0
onKeyDown	Runs when a key is pressed down	3.0	2.0
onKeyPress	Runs when a key is initially pressed	3.0	2.0
onKeyUp	Runs when a key is released	3.0	2.0
onLoad	Runs when the document is initially loaded	3.0	2.0
onMouseDown	Runs when the mouse button is pressed down	3.0	2.0
onMouseUp	Runs when the mouse button is released	3.0	2.0
onUnLoad	Runs when the document is unloaded	3.0	2.0
FileUpload	**A file upload element in an HTML form (use the FileUpload box's name)**	3.0	2.0
Properties			
form	The form object containing the FileUpload box	3.0	2.0
name	The name of the FileUpload box	3.0	2.0
type	The TYPE attribute of the FileUpload box	3.0	2.0
value	The pathname of the selected file in the FileUpload box	3.0	2.0
Methods			
blur()	Removes the focus from the FileUpload box	4.0	3.0
focus()	Gives the focus to the FileUpload box	4.0	3.0
handleEvent(*event*)	Invokes the event handler for the specified *event*	4.0	3.0
select()	Selects the input area of the FileUpload box	3.0	2.0

JAVASCRIPT ELEMENTS	DESCRIPTION	IE	NETSCAPE
Event Handlers			
onBlur	Runs when the focus leaves the FileUpload box	4.0	3.0
onChange	Runs when the value in the FileUpload box is changed	4.0	3.0
onFocus	Runs when the focus is given to the FileUpload box	4.0	3.0
Form	**An HTML form (use the form's name)**	3.0	2.0
Properties			
action	The location of the CGI script that receives the form values	3.0	2.0
elements	An array of elements within the form	3.0	2.0
encoding	The type of encoding used in the form	3.0	2.0
length	The number of elements in the form	3.0	2.0
method	The type of method used when submitting the form	3.0	2.0
name	The name of the form	3.0	2.0
target	The name of window into which CGI output should be directed	3.0	2.0
Methods			
handleEvent(*event*)	Invokes the event handler for the specified *event*	4.0	3.0
reset()	Resets the form	3.0	2.0
submit()	Submits the form to the CGI script	3.0	2.0
Event Handlers			
onReset	Runs when the form is reset	4.0	3.0
onSubmit	Runs when the form is submitted	3.0	2.0
Frame	**A frame window (use the frame's name)**	3.0	2.0
Properties			
document	The current document in the frame window	3.0	2.0
frames	An array of frames within the frame window	3.0	2.0
length	The length of the frames array	3.0	2.0
name	The name of the frame	3.0	2.0
parent	The name of the window that contains the frame	3.0	2.0
self	The name of the current frame window	3.0	2.0
top	The name of the topmost window in the hierarchy of frame windows	3.0	2.0
window	The name of the current frame window	3.0	2.0

JAVASCRIPT ELEMENTS	DESCRIPTION	IE	NETSCAPE
Methods			
alert(*message*)	Displays an Alert box with the text string *message*	3.0	2.0
blur()	Removes the focus from the frame	4.0	3.0
clearInterval(*ID*)	Cancels the repeated execution *ID*	4.0	4.0
clearTimeout(*ID*)	Cancels the delayed execution *ID*	4.0	4.0
confirm(*message*)	Displays a Confirm box with the text string *message*	3.0	2.0
open(*URL, name, features*)	Opens a URL in the frame with the name *name* and a feature list indicated by *features*	3.0	2.0
print()	Displays the Print dialog box	4.0	4.0
prompt(*message, response*)	Displays a Prompt dialog box with the text string *message* and the default value *response*	3.0	2.0
setInterval(*expression, time*)	Runs an *expression* after *time* milliseconds	4.0	4.0
setTimeout(*expression, time*)	Runs an *expression* every *time* milliseconds	4.0	4.0
Event Handlers			
onBlur	Runs when the focus is removed from the frame	4.0	4.0
onFocus	Runs when the frame receives the focus	4.0	4.0
onMove	Runs when the frame is moved	4.0	4.0
onResize	Runs when the frame is resized	4.0	4.0
Hidden	**A hidden field on an HTML form (use the name of the hidden field)**	3.0	2.0
Properties			
form	The name of the form containing the hidden field	3.0	2.0
name	The name of the hidden field	3.0	2.0
type	The type of the hidden field	4.0	3.0
value	The value of the hidden field	3.0	2.0
history	**An object containing information about the Web browser's history list**	3.0	2.0
Properties			
current	The current URL in the history list	4.0	3.0
length	The number of items in the history list	3.0	2.0
next	The next item in the history list	4.0	3.0
previous	The previous item in the history list	3.0	2.0
Methods			
back()	Goes back to the previous item in the history list	3.0	2.0
forward()	Goes forward to the next item in the history list	3.0	2.0

JAVASCRIPT ELEMENTS	DESCRIPTION	IE	NETSCAPE
go(*location*)	Goes to the item in the history list specified by the value of *location*. The *location* variable can be either an integer or the name of the Web page	3.0	2.0
Image	**An inline image (use the name assigned to the image)**	4.0	3.0
Properties			
border	Width of the image border, in pixels	4.0	3.0
complete	A Boolean value that indicates whether the image has been completely loaded by the browser	4.0	3.0
height	The height of the image, in pixels	4.0	3.0
hspace	The horizontal space around in the image, in pixels	4.0	3.0
lowsrc	The value of the LOWSRC property of the <IMG> tag	4.0	3.0
name	The name of the image	4.0	3.0
src	The URL of the image	4.0	3.0
vspace	The vertical space around an image, in pixels	4.0	3.0
width	The width of the image, in pixels	4.0	3.0
Methods			
handleEvent(*event*)	Invokes the event handler for the specified *event*	4.0	4.0
Event Handlers			
onAbort	Runs when the image load is aborted	4.0	3.0
onError	Runs when an error occurs while loading the image	4.0	3.0
onKeyDown	Runs when a key is pressed down	4.0	3.0
onKeyPress	Runs when a key is pressed	4.0	4.0
onKeyUp	Runs when a key is released	4.0	4.0
onLoad	Runs when the image is loaded	4.0	3.0
Layer	**A document layer (use the name of the layer)**		4.0
Properties			
above	The layer above the current layer		4.0
background	The background image of the layer		4.0
below	The layer below the current layer		4.0
bgColor	The background color of the layer		4.0
clip.bottom, clip.height, clip.left, clip.right, clip.top, clip.width	The size and position of the layer's clipping area		4.0
document	The document containing the layer		4.0

JAVASCRIPT ELEMENTS	DESCRIPTION	IE	NETSCAPE
left	The x-coordinate of the layer		4.0
name	The name of the layer		4.0
pageX	The x-coordinate relative to the document		4.0
pageY	The y-coordinate relative to the document		4.0
parentLayer	The containing layer		4.0
siblingAbove	The layer above in the zIndex		4.0
siblingBelow	The layer below in the zIndex		4.0
src	The URL of the layer document		4.0
top	The y-coordinate of the layer		4.0
visibility	The state of the layer's visibility		4.0
zIndex	The zIndex value of the layer		4.0
Methods			
handleEvent(*event*)	Invokes the event handler for the specified *event*		4.0
load(*source, width*)	Loads a new URL into the layer from *source* with the specified *width*		4.0
moveAbove(*layer*)	Moves the layer above *layer*		4.0
moveBelow(*layer*)	Moves the layer below *layer*		4.0
moveBy(*x, y*)	Moves the *x* pixels in the x-direction, and *y* pixels in the y-direction		4.0
moveTo(*x, y*)	Moves the upper-left corner of the layer to the specified (*x, y*) coordinate		4.0
moveToAbsolute(*x, y*)	Moves the layer to the specified coordinate (*x, y*) within the page		4.0
resizeBy(*width, height*)	Resizes the layer by the specified *width* and *height*		4.0
resizeTo(*width, height*)	Resizes the layer to the specified *height* and *width*		4.0
Event Handlers			
onBlur	Runs when the focus leaves the layer		4.0
onFocus	Runs when the layer receives the focus		4.0
onLoad	Runs when the layer is loaded		4.0
onMouseOut	Runs when the mouse leaves the layer		4.0
onMouseOver	Runs when the mouse hovers over the layer		4.0
Link	**A link within an HTML document (use the name of the link)**	**3.0**	**2.0**
Properties			
hash	The anchor name from the link's URL	3.0	2.0

JAVASCRIPT ELEMENTS	DESCRIPTION	IE	NETSCAPE
host	The host from the link's URL	3.0	2.0
hostname	The hostname from the link's URL	3.0	2.0
href	The link's URL	3.0	2.0
pathname	The path portion of the link's URL	3.0	2.0
port	The port number of the link's URL	3.0	2.0
protocol	The protocol used with the link's URL	3.0	2.0
search	The search portion of the link's URL	3.0	2.0
target	The target window of the hyperlinks	3.0	2.0
text	The text used to create the link	4.0	4.0
Methods			
handleEvent(*event*)	Invokes the event handler for the specified *event*	4.0	4.0
Event Handlers			
onClick	Runs when the link is clicked	3.0	2.0
onDblClick	Runs when the link is double-clicked	4.0	4.0
onKeyDown	Runs when a key is pressed down	4.0	4.0
onKeyPress	Runs when a key is initially pressed	4.0	4.0
onKeyUp	Runs when a key is released	4.0	4.0
onMouseDown	Runs when the mouse button is pressed down on the link	4.0	4.0
onMouseOut	Runs when mouse moves away from the link	4.0	4.0
onMouseOver	Runs when the mouse hovers over the link	4.0	4.0
onMouseUp	Runs when the mouse button is released	4.0	4.0
location	**The location of the document**	3.0	2.0
Properties			
hash	The location's anchor name	3.0	2.0
host	The location's hostname and port number	3.0	2.0
href	The location's URL	3.0	2.0
pathname	The path portion of the location's URL	3.0	2.0
port	The port number of the location's URL	3.0	2.0
protocol	The protocol used with the location's URL	3.0	2.0
Methods			
reload()	Reloads the location	4.0	3.0
replace(*URL*)	Loads a new location with the address *URL*	4.0	3.0

JAVASCRIPT ELEMENTS	DESCRIPTION	IE	NETSCAPE
Math	**An object used for advanced mathematical calculations**	3.0	2.0
Properties			
E	The value of the base of natural logarithms (2.7182...)	3.0	2.0
LN10	The value of the natural logarithm of 10	3.0	2.0
LN2	The value of the natural logarithm of 2	3.0	2.0
LOG10E	The base 10 logarithm of E	3.0	2.0
LOG2E	The base 2 logarithm of E	3.0	2.0
PI	The value of pi (3.1416...)	3.0	2.0
SQRT1_2	The square root of ½	3.0	2.0
SQRT2	The square root of 2	3.0	2.0
Methods			
abs(*number*)	Returns the absolute value of *number*	3.0	2.0
acos(*number*)	Returns the arc cosine of *number* in radians	3.0	2.0
asin(*number*)	Returns the arc sine of *number* in radians	3.0	2.0
atan(*number*)	Returns the arc tangent of *number* in radians	3.0	2.0
ceil(*number*)	Rounds *number* up to the next highest integer	3.0	2.0
cos(*number*)	Returns the cosine of *number*, where *number* is an angle expressed in radians	3.0	2.0
exp(*number*)	Raises the value of E (2.7182...) to the value of *number*	3.0	2.0
floor(*number*)	Rounds *number* down to the next lowest integer	3.0	2.0
log(*number*)	Returns the natural logarithm of *number*	3.0	2.0
max(*number1, number2*)	Returns the greater of *number1* and *number2*	3.0	2.0
min(*number1, number2*)	Returns the lesser of *number1* and *number2*	3.0	2.0
pow(*number1, number2*)	Returns the value of *number1* raised to the power of *number2*	3.0	2.0
random()	Returns a random number between 0 and 1	3.0	2.0
round(*number*)	Rounds *number* to the closest integer	3.0	2.0
sin(*number*)	Returns the sine of *number*, where *number* is an angle expressed in radians	3.0	2.0
tan(*number*)	Returns the tangent of *number*, where *number* is an angle expressed in radians	3.0	2.0
toString(*number*)	Converts *number* to a text string	3.0	2.0

JAVASCRIPT ELEMENTS	DESCRIPTION	IE	NETSCAPE
navigator	**An object representing the browser currently in use**	3.0	2.0
Properties			
appCodeName	The code name of the browser	3.0	2.0
appName	The name of the browser	3.0	2.0
appVersion	The version of the browser	3.0	2.0
language	The language of the browser	4.0	4.0
mimeTypes	An array of the MIME types supported by the browser	4.0	4.0
platform	The platform on which the browser is running	4.0	4.0
plugins	An array of the plug-ins installed on the browser	4.0	3.0
userAgent	The user-agent text string sent from the client to the Web server	3.0	2.0
Methods			
javaEnabled()	Indicates whether the browser supports Java	4.0	3.0
plugins.refresh()	Checks for newly installed plug-ins	4.0	3.0
Option	**An option from a selection list (use the name of option or the index value from the options array)**	3.0	2.0
Properties			
defaultSelected	A Boolean value indicating whether the option is selected by default	4.0	3.0
index	The index value of the option	3.0	2.0
selected	A Boolean value indicating whether the option is currently selected	3.0	2.0
text	The text of the option as it appears on the Web page	3.0	2.0
value	The value of the option	3.0	2.0
Password	**A password field in an HTML form (use the name of the password field)**	3.0	2.0
Properties			
defaultValue	The default value of the password	3.0	2.0
name	The name of the password field	3.0	2.0
type	The type value of the password field	3.0	2.0
value	The value of the password field	3.0	2.0
Methods			
focus()	Gives the password field the focus	3.0	2.0
blur()	Leaves the password field	3.0	2.0
select()	Selects the password field	3.0	2.0

JAVASCRIPT ELEMENTS	DESCRIPTION	IE	NETSCAPE
Event Handlers			
onBlur	Runs when the focus leaves the password field	3.0	2.0
onFocus	Runs when the password field receives the focus	3.0	2.0
plugin	**A plug-in object in the Web page**	4.0	3.0
Properties			
description	The description of the plug-in	4.0	3.0
filename	The plug-in filename	4.0	3.0
length	The number of MIME types supported by the plug-in	4.0	3.0
name	The name of the plug-in	4.0	3.0
Radio	**A radio button in an HTML form (use the radio button's name)**	3.0	2.0
Properties			
checked	A Boolean value indicating whether a specific radio button has been checked	3.0	2.0
defaultChecked	A Boolean value indicating whether a specific radio button is checked by default	3.0	2.0
form	The name of the form containing the radio button	3.0	2.0
name	The name of the radio button	3.0	2.0
type	The type value of the radio button	4.0	3.0
value	The value of the radio button	3.0	2.0
Methods			
blur()	Gives the radio button the focus	3.0	2.0
click()	Clicks the radio button	3.0	2.0
focus()	Gives focus to the radio button	3.0	2.0
handleEvent(*event*)	Invokes the event handler for the specified *event*	4.0	4.0
Event Handlers			
onBlur	Runs when the focus leaves the radio button	3.0	2.0
onClick	Runs when the radio button is clicked	3.0	2.0
onFocus	Runs when the radio button receives the focus	3.0	2.0
RegExp	**An object used for searching regular expressions**	4.0	4.0
Properties			
global	Specifies whether to use a global pattern match	4.0	4.0
ignoreCase	Specifies whether to ignore case in the search string	4.0	4.0
input	The search string	4.0	4.0

JAVASCRIPT ELEMENTS	DESCRIPTION	IE	NETSCAPE
lastIndex	Specifies the index at which to start matching the next string	4.0	4.0
lastMatch	The last matched characters	4.0	4.0
lastParen	The last parenthesized substring match	4.0	4.0
leftContext	The substring preceding the most recent match	4.0	4.0
multiline	Specifies whether to search on multiple lines	4.0	4.0
rightContext	The substring following the most recent match	4.0	4.0
source	The string pattern	4.0	4.0
Methods			
compile()	Compiles a regular search expression	4.0	4.0
exec(*string*)	Executes the search for a match to *string*	4.0	4.0
test(*string*)	Tests for a match to *string*	4.0	4.0
Reset	**A reset button in an HTML form (use the name of the reset button)**	3.0	2.0
Properties			
form	The name of the form containing the reset button	3.0	2.0
name	The name of the reset button	3.0	2.0
type	The type value of the reset button	4.0	3.0
value	The value of the reset button	3.0	2.0
Methods			
blur()	Removes the focus from the reset button	3.0	2.0
click()	Clicks the reset button	3.0	2.0
focus()	Gives the focus to the reset button	3.0	2.0
handleEvent(*event*)	Invokes the event handler for the specified *event*	4.0	4.0
Event Handlers			
onBlur	Runs when the focus leaves the reset button	3.0	2.0
onClick	Runs when the reset button is clicked	3.0	2.0
onFocus	Runs when the reset button receives the focus	3.0	2.0
screen	**An object representing the user's screen**	4.0	4.0
Properties			
availHeight	The height of the screen, minus toolbars or any other permanent object	4.0	4.0
availWidth	The width of the screen, minus toolbars or any other permanent object	4.0	4.0

JAVASCRIPT ELEMENTS	DESCRIPTION	IE	NETSCAPE
colorDepth	The number of possible colors in the screen	4.0	4.0
height	The height of the screen	4.0	4.0
pixelDepth	The number of bits (per pixel) in the screen	5.0	4.0
width	The width of the screen	4.0	4.0
Select	**A selection list in an HTML form (use the name of the selection list)**	**3.0**	**2.0**
Properties			
form	The name of the form containing the selection list	3.0	2.0
length	The number of options in the selection list	3.0	2.0
name	The name of the selection list	3.0	2.0
options	An array of options within the selection list. See the options object for more information on working with individual selection list options	3.0	2.0
selectedIndex	The index value of the selected option from the selection list	3.0	2.0
type	The type value of the selection list	4.0	3.0
Methods			
blur()	Removes the focus from the selection list	3.0	2.0
focus()	Gives the focus to the selection list	3.0	2.0
handleEvent(*event*)	Invokes the event handler for the specified *event*	4.0	4.0
Event Handlers			
onBlur	Runs when the focus leaves the selection list	3.0	2.0
onChange	Runs when focus leaves the selection list and the value of the selection list is changed	3.0	2.0
onFocus	Runs when the selection list receives the focus	3.0	2.0
String	**An object representing a text string**	**3.0**	**2.0**
Properties			
length	The number of characters in the string	3.0	2.0
Methods			
anchor(*name*)	Converts the string into a hyperlink anchor with the name *name*	3.0	2.0
big()	Displays the string using the <BIG> tag	3.0	2.0
blink()	Displays the string using the <BLINK> tag	3.0	2.0
bold()	Displays the string using the <B> tag	3.0	2.0

JAVASCRIPT ELEMENTS	DESCRIPTION	IE	NETSCAPE
charAt(*index*)	Returns the character in the string at the location specified by *index*	3.0	2.0
concat(*string2*)	Concatenates the string with the second text string *string2*	4.0	4.0
fixed()	Displays the string using the \<TT\> tag	3.0	2.0
fontColor(*color*)	Sets the COLOR attribute of the string	3.0	2.0
fontSize(*value*)	Sets the SIZE attribute of the string	3.0	2.0
indexOf(*string, start*)	Searches the string, beginning at the *start* character, and returns the index value of the first occurrence of the string *string*	3.0	2.0
italics()	Displays the string using the \<I\> tag	3.0	2.0
lastIndexOf(*string, start*)	Searches the string, beginning at the *start* character, and locates the index value of the last occurrence of the string *string*	3.0	2.0
link(*href*)	Converts the string into a hyperlink pointing to the URL *href*	3.0	2.0
match(*expression*)	Returns an array containing the matches based on the regular expression *expression*	4.0	4.0
replace(*expression, new*)	Performs a search and replace based on the regular expression *expression*, and replaces the text with *new*	4.0	4.0
search(*expression*)	Performs a search based on the regular expression *expression*, and returns the index number	4.0	4.0
slice(*begin, end*)	Returns a substring between the *begin* and *end* index values; the *end* index value is optional	4.0	4.0
small()	Displays the string using the \<SMALL\> tag	3.0	2.0
split(*separator*)	Splits the string into an array of strings at every occurrence of the *separator* character	4.0	4.0
strike()	Displays the string using the \<STRIKE\> tag	3.0	2.0
sub()	Displays the string using the \<SUB\> tag	3.0	2.0
substr(*begin, length*)	Returns a substring starting at the *begin* index value and continuing for *length* characters; the *length* parameter is optional	4.0	4.0
substring(*begin, end*)	Returns a substring between the *begin* and *end* index values; the *end* index value is optional	3.0	2.0
sup()	Displays the string using the \<SUP\> tag	3.0	2.0
toLowerCase()	Converts the string to lowercase	3.0	2.0
toUpperCase()	Converts the string to uppercase	3.0	2.0

JAVASCRIPT ELEMENTS	DESCRIPTION	IE	NETSCAPE
Submit	**A submit button in an HTML form (use the name of the submit button)**	3.0	2.0
Properties			
form	The name of the form containing the submit button	3.0	2.0
name	The name of the submit button	3.0	2.0
type	The type value of the submit button	4.0	3.0
value	The value of the submit button	3.0	2.0
Methods			
blur()	Removes the focus from the submit button	3.0	2.0
click()	Clicks the submit button	3.0	2.0
focus()	Gives the focus to the submit button	3.0	2.0
handleEvent(*event*)	Invokes the event handler for the specified *event*	4.0	4.0
Event Handlers			
onBlur	Runs when the focus leaves the submit button	3.0	2.0
onClick	Runs when the submit button is clicked	3.0	2.0
onFocus	Runs when the submit button receives the focus	3.0	2.0
Text	**An input box from a HTML form (use the name of the input box)**	3.0	2.0
Properties			
defaultValue	The default value of the input box	3.0	2.0
form	The form containing the input box	3.0	2.0
name	The name of the input box	3.0	2.0
type	The type value of the input box	4.0	3.0
value	The value of the input box	3.0	2.0
Methods			
blur()	Removes the focus from the input box	3.0	2.0
focus()	Gives the focus to the input box	3.0	2.0
handleEvent(*event*)	Invokes the event handler for the specified *event*	4.0	4.0
select()	Selects the input box	3.0	2.0
Event Handlers			
onBlur	Runs when the focus leaves the input box	3.0	2.0
onChange	Runs when the focus leaves the input box and the input box value changes	3.0	2.0

JAVASCRIPT ELEMENTS	DESCRIPTION	IE	NETSCAPE
onFocus	Runs when the input box receives the focus	3.0	2.0
onSelect	Runs when some of the text in the input box is selected	3.0	2.0
Textarea	**A text area box in an HTML form (use the name of the text area box)**	3.0	2.0
Properties			
defaultValue	The default value of the text area box	3.0	2.0
form	The form containing the text area box	3.0	2.0
name	The name of the text area box	3.0	2.0
type	The type value of the text area box	4.0	3.0
value	The value of the text area box	3.0	2.0
Methods			
blur()	Removes the focus from the text area box	3.0	2.0
focus()	Gives the focus to the text area box	3.0	2.0
handleEvent(*event*)	Invokes the event handler for the specified *event*	4.0	4.0
select()	Selects the text area box	3.0	2.0
Event Handlers			
onBlur	Runs when the focus leaves the text area box	3.0	2.0
onChange	Runs when the focus leaves the text area box and the text area box value changes	3.0	2.0
onFocus	Runs when the text area box receives the focus	3.0	2.0
onKeyDown	Runs when a key is pressed down	4.0	4.0
onKeyPress	Runs when a key is pressed	4.0	4.0
onKeyUp	Runs when a key is released	4.0	4.0
onSelect	Runs when some of the text in the text area box is selected	3.0	2.0
window	**The document window**	3.0	2.0
Properties			
defaultStatus	The default message shown in the window's status bar	3.0	2.0
document	The document that appears in the window	3.0	2.0
frames	An array of frames within the window (see the frames object for properties and methods applied to individual frames)	3.0	2.0
history	The history list of visited URLs	4.0	3.0
innerHeight	The height of the window's display area	4.0	4.0

JAVASCRIPT ELEMENTS	DESCRIPTION	IE	NETSCAPE
innerWidth	The width of the widow's display area	4.0	4.0
length	The number of frames in the window	3.0	2.0
location	The URL loaded into the window	3.0	2.0
locationbar.visible	A Boolean value indicating the visibility of the window's location bar	4.0	4.0
menubar.visible	A Boolean value indicating the visibility of the window's menu bar	4.0	4.0
name	The name of the window	3.0	2.0
opener	The name of the window that opened the current window	4.0	3.0
outerHeight	The height of the outer area of the window	4.0	4.0
outerWidth	The width of the outer area of the window	4.0	4.0
pageXOffset	The x-coordinate of the window	4.0	4.0
pageYOffset	The y-coordinate of the window	4.0	4.0
parent	The name of the window containing this particular window	3.0	2.0
personalbar.visible	A Boolean value indicating the visibility of the window's personal bar	4.0	4.0
scrollbars.visible	A Boolean value indicating the visibility of the window's scroll bars	4.0	4.0
self	The current window	3.0	2.0
status	The message shown in the window's status bar	3.0	2.0
statusbar.visible	A Boolean value indicating the visibility of the window's status bar	4.0	4.0
toolbar.visible	A Boolean value indicating the visibility of the window's toolbar	4.0	4.0
top	The name of the topmost window in a hierarchy of windows	3.0	2.0
window	The current window	3.0	2.0

Methods

alert(*message*)	Displays the text contained in *message* in a dialog box	3.0	2.0
back()	Loads the previous page in the window	4.0	4.0
blur()	Removes the focus from the window	4.0	3.0
captureEvents()	Sets the window to capture all events of a specified type	4.0	4.0
clearInterval(*ID*)	Clears the interval for *ID*, set with the SetInterval method	4.0	4.0

JAVASCRIPT ELEMENTS	DESCRIPTION	IE	NETSCAPE
clearTimeout()	Clears the timeout, set with the setTimeout method	3.0	2.0
close()	Closes the window	3.0	2.0
confirm(*message*)	Displays a confirmation dialog box with the text *message*	3.0	2.0
disableExternalCapture	Disables external event capturing	4.0	4.0
enableExternalCapture	Enables external event capturing	4.0	4.0
find(*string, case, direction*)	Displays a Find dialog box, where *string* is the text to find in the window, *case* is a Boolean value indicating whether the find is case-sensitive, and *direction* is a Boolean value indicating whether the find goes in the backward direction (all of the parameters are optional)	4.0	4.0
focus()	Gives focus to the window	4.0	3.0
forward()	Loads the next page in the window	4.0	4.0
handleEvent(*event*)	Invokes the event handler for the specified *event*	4.0	4.0
moveBy(*horizontal, vertical*)	Moves the window by the specified amount in the *horizontal* and *vertical* direction	4.0	4.0
moveTo(*x, y*)	Moves the window to the *x* and *y* coordinates	4.0	4.0
open()	Opens the window	3.0	2.0
print()	Displays the Print dialog box	4.0	4.0
prompt(*message, default_text*)	Displays a Prompt dialog box with the text *message* (the default message is: *default_text*)	3.0	2.0
releaseEvents(*event*)	Releases the captured events of a specified *event*	4.0	4.0
resizeBy(*horizontal, vertical*)	Resizes the window by the amount in the *horizontal* and *vertical* direction	4.0	4.0
resizeTo(*width, height*)	Resizes the window to the specified *width* and *height*	4.0	4.0
routeEvent(*event*)	Passes the *event* to be handled natively	4.0	4.0
scroll(*x, y*)	Scrolls the window to the *x, y* coordinate	4.0	3.0
scrollBy(*x, y*)	Scrolls the window by *x* pixels in the *x*-direction, and *y* pixels in the *y*-direction	4.0	4.0
scrollTo(*x, y*)	Scrolls the window to the *x, y* coordinate	4.0	4.0
setInterval(*expression, time*)	Evaluates the *expression* every *time* milliseconds have passed	4.0	4.0
setTimeout(*expression, time*)	Evaluates the *expression* after *time* milliseconds have passed	3.0	2.0
stop()	Stops the windows from loading	4.0	4.0

JAVASCRIPT ELEMENTS	DESCRIPTION	IE	NETSCAPE
Event Handlers			
onBlur	Runs when the window loses the focus	4.0	3.0
onDragDrop	Runs when the user drops an object on or within the window	4.0	4.0
onError	Runs when an error occurs while loading the page	4.0	3.0
onFocus	Runs when the window receives the focus	4.0	3.0
onLoad	Runs when the window finishes loading	3.0	2.0
onMove	Runs when the window is moved	4.0	4.0
onResize	Runs when the window is resized	4.0	4.0
onUnload	Runs when the window is unloaded	3.0	2.0

JavaScript Operators, Syntactical Elements, and Keywords

OPERATORS	DESCRIPTION	IE	NETSCAPE
Assignment	**Operators used to assign values to variables**		
=	Assigns the value of the variable on the right to the variable on the left (x = y)	3.0	2.0
+=	Adds the two variables and assigns the result to the variable on the left (x += y is equivalent to x = x + y)	3.0	2.0
-=	Subtracts the variable on the right from the variable on the left and assigns the result to the variable on the left (x-=y is equivalent to x = x - y)	3.0	2.0
*=	Multiplies the two variables together and assigns the result to the variable on the left (x* = y is equivalent to x = x * y)	3.0	2.0
/=	Divides the variable on the left by the variable on the right and assigns the result to the variable on the left (x/ = y is equivalent to x = x / y)	3.0	2.0
&=	Combines two expressions into a single expression (x& = y is equivalent to x = x & y)	3.0	2.0
%=	Divides the variable on the left by the variable on the right and assigns the remainder to the variable on the left (x% = y is equivalent to x = x % y)	3.0	2.0
Arithmetic	**Operators used for arithmetic functions**		
+	Adds two variables together (x + y)	3.0	2.0
-	Subtracts the variable on the right from the variable on the left (x - y)	3.0	2.0
*	Multiplies two variables together (x * y)	3.0	2.0
/	Divides the variable the left by the variable on the right (x / y)		
%	Calculates the remainder after dividing the variable on the left by the variable on the right (x % y)	3.0	2.0
++	Increases the value of a variable by 1 (x + + is equivalent to x = x + 1)	3.0	2.0
&	Combines two expressions (x & y)	3.0	2.0
--	Decreases the value of variable by 1 (x -- is equivalent to x = x - 1)	3.0	2.0
-	Changes the sign of a variable (- x)	3.0	2.0
Comparison	**Operators used for comparing expressions**		
==	Returns true when the two expressions are equal (x == y)	3.0	2.0
!=	Returns true when the two expressions are not equal (x != y)	3.0	2.0
!==	Returns true when the values of the two expressions are equal (x !== y)	5.0	5.0

OPERATORS	DESCRIPTION	IE	NETSCAPE
>	Returns true when the expression on the left is greater than the expression on the right (x > y)	3.0	2.0
<	Returns true when the expression on the left is less than the expression on the right (x < y)	3.0	2.0
>=	Returns true when the expression on the left is greater than or equal to the expression on the right (x >= y)	3.0	2.0
<=	Returns true when the expression on the left is less than or equal to the expression on the right (x <= y)	3.0	2.0
Conditional	**Operators used to determine values based on conditions that are either true or false**		
(condition) ? value1 : value2	If condition is true, then this expression equals value1, otherwise it equals value2		
Keywords	**JavaScript keywords are reserved by JavaScript**		
infinity	Represents positive infinity (often used with comparison operators)	5.0	4.0
this	Refers to the current object	3.0	2.0
var	Declares a variable	3.0	2.0
with	Allows the declaration of all the properties for an object without directly referencing the object each time	3.0	2.0
Logical	**Operators used for evaluating true and false expressions**		
!	Reverses the Boolean value of the expression	3.0	2.0
&&	Returns true only if both expressions are true (also known as an AND operator)		
||	Returns true when either expression is true (also known as an OR operator)	3.0	2.0
.|	Returns true if the expression is false, and false if the expression is true (also known as a NEGATION operator)	3.0	2.0
Syntax	**Syntactical elements**		
;	Indicates the end of a command line	3.0	2.0
/* comments*/	Used for inserting comments within a JavaScript command line	3.0	2.0
// comments	Used to create a line of comments	3.0	2.0

Cascading Style Sheets

The following information tells you about the selectors, units, and attributes supported by CSS and the two major browsers. Additional information about CSS and browser support for current CSS standards can be found at these Web sites:

http://www.w3c.org

http://www.webreview.com

http://builder.cnet.com

Because the World Wide Web changes constantly, you should test this information against your current browser.

Selectors

The general form of a style declaration is:

selector {attribute1:value1; attribute2:value2; ...}

Selectors indicate which element or elements in the document are affected by the style declaration. Selectors can take many different forms. The following table shows some of the different forms that a selector can take.

SELECTORS	DESCRIPTION	CSS	IE	NETSCAPE
*	All elements in the document	2.0		
E	An element, E, in the document	1.0	3.0	4.0
E1, E2, E3, ...	A group of elements, E1, E2, E3, ... in the document	1.0	3.0	4.0
E1 E2	An element, E2, that is contained within the parent element E1	1.0	3.0	4.0
E1 > E2	An element, E2, that is the direct descendant (child) of a parent element	2.0		
E1+E2	An element, E2, that directly follows the element, E1	2.0		
#id	An element with the ID name id	1.0	3.0	4.0
E.class	An element, E, with the class name class	1.0	3.0	4.0
.class	Any element with the class name class	1.0	3.0	4.0
E [attribute]	An element, E, that contains a specified attribute	2.0		
E [attribute=value]	An element, E, that contains a specified attribute with a specified value	2.0		
E [attribute~=value]	An element, E, that contains a specified attribute, with part of a specified value	2.0		

Units

Many attribute values have units of measurements. These units can be used to indicate width, height, or color. The following are the types of measuring units used in cascading style sheets.

UNITS	DESCRIPTION	CSS	IE	NETSCAPE
Color	**Units of Color**			
name	A color name. There are 16 base color names recognized by all browsers: aqua, black, blue, fuchsia, gray, green, lime, maroon, navy, olive, purple, red, silver, teal, white, and yellow. Additional color names are available, and are roughly equivalent to the extended HTML color names.	1.0	3.0	4.0
#rrggbb	The hexadecimal color value where *rr* is the red value, *gg* is the green value, and *bb* is the blue value	1.0	3.0	3.0
#rgb	A compressed hexadecimal value where the *r*, *g*, and *b* values are doubled, so that, for example, #A2F = #AA22FF	1.0	3.0	3.0
rgb*(red, green, blue)*	The decimal color value, where *red* is the red value, *green* is the green value, and *blue* is the blue value	1.0	3.0	3.0
rgb*(red%, green%, blue%)*	The color value percentage, where *red%* is the percent of maximum red, *green%* is the percent of maximum green, and *blue%* is the percent of maximum blue	1.0	3.0	3.0
Length	**Units of width or height**			
em	A relative unit indicating the width and height of the capital "M" character in the browser's default font	1.0	4.0	4.0
ex	A relative unit indicating the height of the small "x" character in the browser's default font	1.0	4.0	
px	A pixel, indicating the smallest element on the monitor	1.0	3.0	3.0
in	An inch	1.0	3.0	3.0
cm	A centimeter	1.0	3.0	3.0
mm	A millimeter	1.0	3.0	3.0
pt	A point, approximately $\frac{1}{72}$ of an inch	1.0	3.0	3.0
pc	A pica, approximately $\frac{1}{12}$ of an inch	1.0	3.0	3.0
p%	The percent, *p*, of the size of the parent element	1.0	3.0	3.0
p%	The percent, *p*, of the size of the parent element	1.0	3.0	3.0
xx-small	Keyword corresponding to the SIZE=1 attribute of the <FONT> tag	1.0	3.0	3.0
x-small	Keyword corresponding to the SIZE=2 attribute of the <FONT> tag	1.0	3.0	3.0
small	Keyword corresponding to the SIZE=3 attribute of the <FONT> tag	1.0	3.0	3.0
medium	Keyword corresponding to the SIZE=4 attribute of the <FONT> tag	1.0	3.0	3.0
large	Keyword corresponding to the SIZE=5 attribute of the <FONT> tag	1.0	3.0	3.0
x-large	Keyword corresponding to the SIZE=6 attribute of the <FONT> tag	1.0	3.0	3.0
xx-large	Keyword corresponding to the SIZE=7 attribute of the <FONT> tag	1.0	3.0	3.0

Attributes and Values

The following are the attributes and values for different types of elements. Note that in some cases, browser support is incomplete or unreliable, even if the browser version supports the style declaration. The only way to verify the support of a browser for a particular style is to test it.

ATTRIBUTES AND VALUES	DESCRIPTION	CSS	IE	NET-SCAPE
Boxes	**Styles applied to block-level boxes**			
border	The border attribute applies width, style, and color attributes to all four borders at once using the syntax {border: *border-width border-style border-color*}.	1.0	4.0	
border-bottom	The border-bottom attribute is a shorthand application of the various border-bottom attributes using the syntax {border-bottom: *border-bottom-width border-style border-bottom-color*}.	1.0	4.0	
border-left	The border-left attribute is a shorthand application of the various border-left attributes using the syntax {border-left: *border-left-width border-style border-left-color*}.	1.0	4.0	
border-right	The border-right attribute is a shorthand application of the various border-right attributes using the syntax {border-right: *border-right-width border-style border-right-color*}.	1.0	4.0	
border-top	The border-top attribute is a shorthand application of the various border-top attributes using the syntax {border-top: *border-top-width border-style border-top-color*}.	1.0	4.0	
border-color	The border-color attribute is a shorthand application of the various border-color attributes using the syntax {border-color: *border-top-color border-right-color border-bottom-color border-left-color*}.	1.0	4.0	4.0
border-bottom-color	The border-bottom-color attribute controls the color of the bottom border.	1.0	4.0	
color	Sets the *color* of the bottom border using a color name or color value	1.0	4.0	
border-left-color	The border-left-color attribute controls the color of the left border.	1.0	4.0	
color	Sets the *color* of the left border using a color name or color value	1.0	4.0	
border-right-color	The border-right-color attribute controls the color of the right border.	1.0	4.0	
color	Sets the *color* of the right border using a color name or color value	1.0	4.0	
border-top-color	The border-top-color attribute controls the color of the top border.	1.0	4.0	
color	Sets the *color* of the top border using a color name or color value	1.0	4.0	

ATTRIBUTES AND VALUES	DESCRIPTION	CSS	IE	NET-SCAPE
Boxes	**Styles applied to block-level boxes**			
border-style	The border-style attribute defines the style of border to be used around the block-level box.	1.0	4.0	4.0
dashed	Displays a dashed line	1.0		
dotted	Displays a dotted line	1.0		
double	Displays a double line	1.0	4.0	4.0
groove	Displays a grooved line	1.0	4.0	4.0
inset	Displays an inset line	1.0	4.0	4.0
none	Displays no line	1.0	4.0	4.0
outset	Displays an outset line	1.0	4.0	4.0
ridge	Displays a ridged line	1.0	4.0	4.0
solid	Displays a solid line	1.0	4.0	4.0
border-width	The border-width attribute is a shorthand application of the various border-width attributes using the syntax {border-width: *border-top-width border-right-width border-bottom-width border-left-width*}.	1.0	4.0	4.0
border-bottom-width	The border-bottom-width attribute controls the width of the bottom border.	1.0	4.0	4.0
length	Sets the *length* of the bottom border, in absolute or relative units	1.0	4.0	4.0
thin, medium, thick	Sets the length using one of the width keywords	1.0	4.0	4.0
border-left-width	The border-left-width attribute controls the width of the left border.	1.0	4.0	4.0
length	Sets the *length* of the left border, in absolute or relative units	1.0	4.0	4.0
thin, medium, thick	Sets the length using one of the width keywords	1.0	4.0	4.0
border-right-width	The border-right-width attribute controls the width of the right border.	1.0	4.0	4.0
length	Sets the *length* of the right border, in absolute or relative units	1.0	4.0	4.0
thin, medium, thick	Sets the length using one of the width keywords	1.0	4.0	4.0
border-top-width	The border-top-width attribute controls the width of the top border.	1.0	4.0	4.0
length	Sets the *length* of the top border, in absolute or relative units	1.0	4.0	4.0
thin, medium, thick	Sets the length using one of the width keywords	1.0	4.0	4.0
margin	The margin attribute is a shorthand application of the various margin attributes using the syntax {margin: *margin-top margin-right margin-bottom margin-left*}.	1.0	3.0	
margin-bottom	The margin-bottom attribute controls the space below the box.	1.0	3.0	
length	Sets the *length* of the bottom margin, in absolute units, relative units, or as a percentage of the width of the containing box	1.0	3.0	
auto	Allows the browser to control the size of the bottom margin	1.0	3.0	
margin-left	The margin-top attribute controls the space to the left of the box.	1.0	3.0	4.0
length	Sets the *length* of the left margin, in absolute units, relative units, or as a percentage of the width of the containing box	1.0	3.0	4.0
auto	Allows the browser to control the size of the left margin	1.0	3.0	4.0

ATTRIBUTES AND VALUES	DESCRIPTION	CSS	IE	NET-SCAPE
Boxes	**Styles applied to block-level boxes**			
margin-right	The margin-top attribute controls the space to the right of the box.	1.0	3.0	4.0
length	Sets the *length* of the right margin, in absolute units, relative units, or as a percentage of the width of the containing box	1.0	3.0	4.0
auto	Allows the browser to control the size of the right margin	1.0	3.0	4.0
margin-top	The margin-top attribute controls the space above the box.	1.0	3.0	4.0
length	Sets the *length* of the top margin, in absolute units, relative units, or as a percentage of the width of the containing box	1.0	3.0	4.0
auto	Allows the browser to control the size of the top margin	1.0	3.0	4.0
padding	The padding attribute is a shorthand application of the various padding attributes using the syntax {margin: *padding-top padding-right padding-bottom padding-left*}.	1.0	4.0	4.0
padding-bottom	The padding-bottom attribute controls the space between the bottom of the content and the bottom border.	1.0	4.0	4.0
length	Sets the *length* of the bottom padding, in absolute units, relative units, or as a percentage of the width of the block-level box	1.0	4.0	4.0
padding-left	The padding-top attribute controls the space between the left of the content and the left border.	1.0	4.0	4.0
length	Sets the *length* of the left padding, in absolute units, relative units, or as a percentage of the width of the block-level box	1.0	4.0	4.0
padding-right	The padding-top attribute controls the space between the right of the content and the right border.	1.0	4.0	4.0
length	Sets the *length* of the right padding, in absolute units, relative units, or as a percentage of the width of the block-level box	1.0	4.0	4.0
padding-top	The padding-top attribute controls the space between the top of the content and the top border.	1.0	4.0	4.0
length	Sets the *length* of the top padding, in absolute units, relative units, or as a percentage of the width of the block-level box	1.0	4.0	4.0
height	The height attribute sets the height of the block-level box.	1.0	5.0	
length	Sets the *length* of the box in absolute units, relative units, or as a percentage of the height of the parent box	1.0	5.0	
auto	Allows the browser to control the height of the box	1.0	5.0	
width	The width attribute sets the width of the block-level box.	1.0	5.0	4.0
length	Sets the *length* of the box in absolute units, relative units, or as a percentage of the width of the parent box	1.0	5.0	4.0
auto	Allows the browser to control the width of the box	1.0	5.0	4.0

ATTRIBUTES AND VALUES	DESCRIPTION	CSS	IE	NET- SCAPE
Classification	**Styles that affect the display of elements**			
display	The display attribute specifies the element's display type.	1.0	4.0	4.0
block	Treats the element as a block-level element	1.0	5.0	
inline	Treats the element as an inline element	1.0	5.0	
list-item	Treats the element as a list item	1.0		
none	Does not display the element	1.0	4.0	4.0
white-space	The white-space attribute controls how spaces, tabs, and newline characters are handled.	1.0		4.0
normal	Removes extra blank spaces and automatically wraps lines	1.0		4.0
nowrap	Prevents line wrapping	1.0		4.0
Colors and Backgrounds	**Styles applied to element colors and element backgrounds**			
background	The background attribute is a shorthand application of background styles using the syntax {background: *background-color background-image background-repeat background-attachment background-position*}.	1.0	4.0	
background-attachment	The background-attachment attribute attaches a background image to the element.	1.0	4.0	
fixed	Fixes the image regardless of element scrolling	1.0	4.0	
scroll	Scrolls the image with the element	1.0	4.0	
background-color	The background-color attribute controls the element's background color.	1.0	3.0	4.0
color	Specifies a color name or value	1.0	3.0	4.0
transparent	Specifies the use of a transparent color	1.0	4.0	
background-image	The background-image attribute specifies the element's background image.	1.0	4.0	4.0
url(*filename*)	Uses the image from the *filename* graphic file	1.0	4.0	4.0
none	Uses no background image	1.0	4.0	4.0
background-position	The background-position attribute controls the position of the background image within the element.	1.0	4.0	
x y	Places the image at the (x, y) coordinate, where x and y are measured in a unit of length	1.0	4.0	
x% y%	Places the image at a point $x\%$ of the element's width to the right, and $y\%$ of the element's height down	1.0	4.0	
keywordx keywordy	The first keyword places the image horizontally at the top, center, or bottom; the second keyword places the image vertically at the left, center, or right.	1.0	4.0	

ATTRIBUTES AND VALUES	DESCRIPTION	CSS	IE	NET-SCAPE
Colors and Backgrounds	**Styles applied to element colors and element backgrounds**			
background-repeat	The background-repeat attributes control the tiling of the background image within the element.	1.0	4.0	4.0
no-repeat	Does not repeat the image	1.0	4.0	4.0
repeat	Repeats the image horizontally and vertically	1.0	4.0	4.0
repeat-x	Repeats the image horizontally	1.0	4.0	4.0
repeat-y	Repeats the image vertically	1.0	4.0	4.0
color	The color attribute controls the foreground color of the element.	1.0	3.0	4.0
color	Specifies a color name or value	1.0	3.0	4.0
Fonts	**Styles applied to fonts used in the document**			
font	The font attribute is a shorthand application of text and font styles using the syntax {font: *font-family font-size font-style font-weight font-variant text-tranform text-decoration*}.	1.0	4.0	
font-family	The font-family attribute is used to display text in a generic or specific font.	1.0	3.0	4.0
font-name	Displays text with the *font-name* font	1.0	3.0	4.0
cursive	Uses a cursive font	1.0	4.0	
fantasy	Uses a fantasy font	1.0	4.0	
monospace	Uses a monospace font	1.0	3.0	4.0
serif	Uses a serif font	1.0	3.0	4.0
sans-serif	Uses a sans-serif font	1.0	3.0	4.0
font-size	The font-size attribute controls the size of the font.	1.0	3.0	4.0
value	Uses a relative length, absolute length, or a length keyword	1.0	varies	varies
font-style	The font-style attribute controls the style of the font.	1.0	3.0	4.0
normal	Uses a normal style	1.0	3.0	4.0
italic	Uses italics	1.0	4.0	4.0
oblique	Uses an oblique style	1.0	4.0	
font-variant	The font-variant attribute applies a variant to the font's appearance.	1.0	4.0	
normal	Displays normal text	1.0	4.0	
small-caps	Displays text in small capital letters	1.0	5.0	
font-weight	The font-weight attribute controls the weight, or boldness, of the font.	1.0	4.0	4.0
100-900	Uses a value from 100 (the lightest) to 900 (the boldest)	1.0	4.0	4.0
bold	Displays text in bold	1.0	3.0	4.0
bolder	Displays text bolder than normal	1.0	4.0	
lighter	Displays text lighter than normal	1.0	4.0	
normal	Displays text with normal weight	1.0	4.0	4.0

ATTRIBUTES AND VALUES	DESCRIPTION	CSS	IE	NET-SCAPE
Layout	Styles that control the layout of elements on the page			
bottom	The bottom attribute defines the vertical coordinate for the element, relative to the lower edge. See the position attribute for the type of coordinates to be used.	2.0		
y	Defines the bottom coordinate value, y, in absolute units, relative units, or as a percentage of the block's height	2.0		
clear	The clear attribute places the element on the page only after the left or right margin of the parent element is clear.	1.0	4.0	
both	Places the element after both margins are clear	1.0	4.0	
left	Places the element after the left margin is clear	1.0	4.0	
none	Places the element regardless of whether margins are clear	1.0	4.0	
right	Places the element after the right margin is clear	1.0	4.0	
clip	The clip attribute defines what portion of an element's rendered content is visible. By default, the clipping region has the same size and shape as the element box.	2.0	5.0	
auto	Sets the clipping region to the same size as the element box	2.0	5.0	
rect(top, right, bottom, left)	Defines the dimensions of the clipping rectangle, where top, right, bottom, and left are the offsets from the sides of the box	2.0	5.0	
float	The float attribute aligns the element with the left or right margin of the parent element, causing other elements to flow around it.	1.0	4.0	4.0
left	Aligns the element with the left margin	1.0	4.0	4.0
none	Does not align the element with either margin	1.0	4.0	4.0
right	Aligns the element with the right margin	1.0	4.0	4.0
left	The left attribute defines the horizontal coordinate for the element, relative to the left edge. See the position attribute for the type of coordinates to be used.	2.0	4.0	4.0
x	Defines the left coordinate value, x, in absolute units, relative units, or as a percentage of the block's width	2.0	4.0	4.0
overflow	The overflow attribute determines the element's behavior when the content does not fit into the element box.	2.0	5.0	
auto	Allows the browser to handle the overflow region	2.0	5.0	
hidden	Hides the overflow content	2.0	5.0	
scroll	Provides scroll bars to view the overflow content	2.0	5.0	
visible	Displays the overflow content outside the box	2.0	5.0	
position	The position attribute defines the position of an element relative to other elements on the page.	2.0	4.0	
absolute	Places the element at a defined position within the parent block, independent from the positions of other elements within the block	2.0	4.0	
fixed	Places the element at a fixed position in the display window, not allowing the element to scroll with other elements on the page; placement is determined using absolute coordinates.	2.0		
relative	Places the element relative to its natural position in the flow of the document	2.0	4.0	
static	Places the element in its natural position in the flow of the document	2.0	4.0	

ATTRIBUTES AND VALUES	DESCRIPTION	CSS	IE	NET-SCAPE
Layout	**Styles that control the layout of elements on the page**			
right	The right attribute defines the horizontal coordinate for the element, relative to the right edge. See the position attribute for the type of coordinates to be used.	2.0		
x	Defines the right coordinate value, x, in absolute units, relative units, or as a percentage of the block's width	2.0		
top	The top attribute defines the vertical coordinate for the element, relative to the upper edge. See the position attribute for the type of coordinates to be used.	2.0	4.0	4.0
y	Defines the top coordinate value, y, in absolute units, relative units, or as a percentage of the block's height	2.0	4.0	4.0
visibility	The visibility attribute determines whether an element is visible.	2.0	4.0	
hidden	Hides the element	2.0	4.0	
inherit	Inherits the visibility state from the parent element	2.0	4.0	
visible	Makes the element visible	2.0	4.0	
z-index	The z-index attribute defines how overlapping elements are to be layered on the page.	2.0	5.0	4.0
auto	Displays the layers in the order of the document flow	2.0	5.0	4.0
n	Displays the layer in the nth position, with higher numbers layered above lower numbers	2.0	5.0	4.0
Lists	**Styles applied to ordered and unordered lists**			
list-style	The list-style attribute is a shorthand application of the different list style attributes using the syntax {list-style: list-style-type list-style-image list-style-position}.	1.0	4.0	
list-style-image	The list-style-image attribute is used to display an inline image as the list label.	1.0	4.0	
url(filename)	Displays the inline image from the filename graphic file	1.0	4.0	
none	Displays no inline image	1.0	4.0	
list-style-type	The list-style-type attribute is used to determine the label for ordered and unordered lists.	1.0	4.0	4.0
circle	Displays an open circle label	1.0	4.0	4.0
decimal	Displays a sequence of integers (1, 2, 3, ...)	1.0	4.0	4.0
disc	Displays a black dot label	1.0	4.0	4.0
lower-alpha	Displays lowercase letters (a, b, c, ...)	1.0	4.0	4.0
lower-roman	Displays lowercase roman numerals (i, ii, iii, ...)	1.0	4.0	4.0
none	Displays no labels	1.0	4.0	4.0
square	Displays a square label	1.0	4.0	4.0
upper-alpha	Displays uppercase letters (A, B, C, ...)	1.0	4.0	4.0
upper-roman	Displays uppercase roman numerals (I, II, III, ...)	1.0	4.0	4.0

ATTRIBUTES AND VALUES	DESCRIPTION	CSS	IE	NET-SCAPE
Lists	**Styles applied to ordered and unordered lists**			
list-style-position	The list-style-position attribute is used to place the label relative to the position of the list's block-level box.	1.0	4.0	
inside	Places labels inside the box	1.0	4.0	
outside	Places labels outside the box	1.0	4.0	
Miscellaneous	**Miscellaneous style terms**			
/* comment */	Used for inserting a *comment* into a style sheet	1.0	3.0	4.0
! important	Specifies that the style declaration takes precedence over any conflicting style	1.0	5.0	
Text	**Styles applied to text**			
letter-spacing	The letter-spacing attribute specifies the amount of space between letters in the text.	1.0	4.0	
length	Sets the *length* between letters in absolute or relative units	1.0	4.0	
normal	Uses normal letter spacing	1.0	4.0	
line-height	The line-height attribute controls the space between lines in a block-level element.	1.0	3.0	4.0
length	Specifies the *length* of the line height in absolute units, relative units, or as a percentage of the font size of the element	1.0	3.0	4.0
normal	Uses a normal line height	1.0	3.0	4.0
text-align	The text-align attribute controls the alignment of text within the element.	1.0	3.0	4.0
center	Centers the text	1.0	3.0	4.0
justify	Displays the text flush with the left and right margins of the element	1.0	5.0	4.0
left	Displays the text aligned with the left margin	1.0	3.0	4.0
right	Displays the text aligned with the right margin	1.0	3.0	4.0
text-decoration	The text-decoration attribute applies a decoration to the text's appearance.	1.0	3.0	4.0
blink	Displays blinking text	1.0		4.0
line-through	Displays the text with a line through it	1.0	3.0	4.0
none	Applies no decoration to the text	1.0	3.0	4.0
overline	Displays the text with a line over it	1.0	4.0	
underline	Underlines the text	1.0	3.0	4.0
text-indent	The text-indent attribute controls the indent of the first line of a block-level element.	1.0	3.0	4.0
length	Specifies the *length* of the indent in absolute units, relative units, or as a percentage of the width of the block-level element	1.0	3.0	4.0
text-transform	The text-transform attribute transforms the appearance of the text in the element.	1.0	4.0	4.0
capitalize	Capitalizes the text	1.0	4.0	4.0
lowercase	Displays the text in lowercase letters	1.0	4.0	4.0
none	Applies no transformation to the text	1.0	4.0	4.0
uppercase	Displays the text in uppercase letters	1.0	4.0	4.0

ATTRIBUTES AND VALUES	DESCRIPTION	CSS	IE	NET-SCAPE
Text	**Styles applied to text**			
vertical-align	The vertical-align attribute controls the vertical alignment of text with respect to the following text.	1.0	4.0	
baseline	Aligns the text with the baseline	1.0	4.0	
bottom	Aligns the text with the bottom of the line	1.0		
middle	Aligns the text with the middle of the surrounding text	1.0		
sub	Aligns the text as a subscript of the surrounding text	1.0	4.0	
super	Aligns the text as a superscript of the surrounding text	1.0	4.0	
text-bottom	Aligns the text with the bottom of the surrounding text	1.0		
text-top	Aligns the text with the top of the surrounding text	1.0		
top	Aligns the text with the top of the line	1.0		
p%	Vertically aligns the text at p% of the line height of the surrounding text	1.0		
word-spacing	The word-spacing attribute specifies the amount of space between words in the text.	1.0	4.0	
length	Sets the length between words in absolute or relative units	1.0	4.0	
normal	Uses normal word spacing	1.0	4.0	

Pseudo-elements and Pseudo-classes

Pseudo-elements are elements that do not exist in HTML code, but whose attributes can be set with CSS. Many pseudo-elements were introduced in CSS2 and are not widely supported by browsers.

PSEUDO-ELEMENTS	DESCRIPTION	CSS	IE	NET-SCAPE
E:after {content:"text"}	Text content, text, that is inserted at the end of a block-level element E	2.0		
E:before {content:"text"}	Text content, text, that is inserted at the beginning of a block-level element E	2.0		
E:first-child	An element, E, that is the first child of its parent element	2.0		
E:first-letter	The first letter in the block-level element E	1.0		
E:first-line	The first line in the block-level element E	1.0		
E:lang(lang)	An element, E, whose contents are shown in the language lang	2.0		

Pseudo-classes are classes of HTML elements that define the condition or state of the element in the Web page. Many pseudo-classes were introduced in CSS2 and are not widely supported by browsers.

PSEUDO-CLASSES	DESCRIPTION	CSS	IE	NET-SCAPE
A:active	An active link in the document	1.0	4.0	
A:hover	A link with the mouse pointer hovering over it	2.0	5.0	
A:link	An unvisited link in the document	1.0	4.0	4.0
A:visited	A previously visited link in the document	1.0	4.0	4.0
E:focus	An element, E, in a Web page form that has received the focus	2.0		

Creating Cookies with JavaScript

Introducing Cookies

A **cookie** is a piece of information stored in a text file that the Web browser places on a user's computer. Cookies typically store data that will be accessed the next time the user visits a particular Web site. For example, many online stores use cookies to store address and credit card information for the user. The next time the user makes a purchase at the online store, the pertinent information can be quickly accessed from the cookie, freeing the user from reentering this material.

Where the browser places the cookie file depends on the type of browser. Netscape stores all cookies in a single text file named "cookie.txt." Internet Explorer stores each cookie in a separate text file, typically in the Windows/Cookies folder. Browsers limit each cookie to 4 kilobytes in size, and there cannot be more than 300 cookies stored at one time on the user's computer. If the browser tries to store additional cookies, the extra cookies are deleted, starting with the oldest ones.

Cookies, the Web Server, and CGI Scripts

The first implementation of cookies was with a CGI script running on a Web server. The CGI script retrieves the cookie information and performs some action based on whatever information was in the file. The process works as follows:

1. The user accesses the Web site and sends a request to the CGI script on the Web server (either by filling out an order form or by some other process that calls the CGI script).

2. The CGI script tests whether a cookie exists for the user.

3. If there is no cookie, the Web server sends a form or page in which the user can enter the information needed by the cookie. This information is then sent to the CGI script for processing.

4. If there is a cookie, the CGI script retrieves that information and creates a new page, or modifies the current page, based on the information in the cookie.

Information is exchanged using the same hypertext transfer protocol used for retrieving the contents of the Web page. This is because each transfer includes a header section that contains information about the document (such as its MIME data type), and allows for general information in the form:

field-name: field-value

It is these field-name/field-value pairs that contain information that can be stored in the user's cookie.

To store this information on the Web server, the Web programmer has to add the Set-Cookie statement to the header section of the CGI script. The Set-Cookie statement is used the first time the user accesses the page. There are four parameters that are often always set with cookies: name, expires, path, and domain. The syntax is:

```
Set-Cookie: name=text; expires=date; path=text; domain=text;
secure
```

where the name parameter defines the name of the cookie. The value of the name parameter cannot contain any spaces, commas, or semicolons. The expire parameter indicates the date that the information will expire. If no expire parameter is included, the cookie will expire when the user's browsing session ends. The path parameter indicates the URL path portion to which that cookie applies. Setting this value to "/" allows the cookie to be accessed from any folder within the Web site. The domain parameter specifies the URL domain portion to which the cookie applies (usually the domain name of the current document). Finally, the secure parameter indicates that the data should be transferred over a secure link—one that uses file encryption.

Once the initial cookie is created, the next time the user accesses the Web page the browser sends the Cookie statement in the header section of the transfer. The syntax of this statement is:

```
Cookie: name1:value1; name2;value2; ...
```

where *name1* is the first field name (whatever that might be) and *value1* is the value of the first field. There can be as many field/value pairs as needed by the Web page, as long as the total size of the cookie doesn't exceed 4 kilobytes.

Once the Web server retrieves the cookie field names and values, it is the CGI script that has to process them. Because CGI programming is beyond the scope of this book, you will focus on working with cookies on the client side with JavaScript.

Working with the Cookie Property

JavaScript uses the cookie property of the document object to retrieve and update cookie information. The cookie property is simply a long text string containing all of the field/value pairs used by the cookie, with each pair separated by a semicolon. To set a value for a cookie, you would use the document.cookie property as follows:

```
document.cookie='cookie1=OrderForm; expires=Mon, 08-Apr-2002
12:00:00 GMT; path="/"; secure';
```

where the cookie has the cookie1 field with the value "OrderForm". This particular cookie expires at noon on Monday, April 8, 2002. Since the path value equals "/", this cookie would be accessible from any folder within the Web site. The secure property has been set, so that any transfer of information involving this cookie will use file encryption. Note that this is a long text string, with the string value enclosed in single quotation marks.

If your Web page had an online form named "Orders", you could create additional field/value pairs using the form names and values as follows:

```
document.cookie='cookie1=OrderForm;
name='+document.Orders.Name.value+';
custid=+'document.Orders.CustId.value;
```

Here, two additional fields have been added to the cookie: name and custid. The values for these fields are respectively taken from the Name field and the CustId field in the Orders form.

Reading a Cookie

One of the challenges of working with cookies in JavaScript is reading the cookie information. To do this you need to withdraw the appropriate information from the cookie's text string and place that information in the appropriate JavaScript variables. You can use several of JavaScript's string functions to help you with this task. To start, create a function named "readCookie(fname)" where "fname" is the name of the field whose value you want to retrieve. The initial code would look as follows:

```
function readCookie(fname) {
    var cookies=document.cookie;
}
```

where the text string of the cookie is stored in the "cookies" variable. In the text string, each field name is followed by an equal sign, so you can use the indexOf( ) method (see Appendix D) to locate the occurrence of the text string "*fname=*," where *fname* is the field name you want to retrieve. You'll store this location in a variable named "startname." The command is:

```
startname=cookies.indexOf(fname+"=");
```

For example, if fname="custid" in the text string below, startname would have a value of 33, since "custid" starts the 33rd character in the text string.

```
cookie1=OrderForm; name=Brooks; custid=20010; type=clothes
```

What if the field name is not found in the cookie? In that case, startname will have a value of -1, and you can create an If...Else conditional statement to handle this contingency. To simplify things, you'll assume that this is not a concern and continue.

Next you have to locate the field's value. This value will be placed after the equal sign, and will continue until you reach a semicolon indicating the end of the field's value, or until you reach the end of the text string. The field's value then starts one space after the first equal sign after the field's name. You'll locate the beginning of the field value using the same indexOf( ) method, and store that location in the startvalue variable. The command is:

```
startvalue=cookies.indexOf("=", startname)+1;
```

Here, you locate the text string "=", starting at the point, "startname" in the cookies text string. You add one to whatever value is returned by the indexOf( ) method. In this text string:

```
cookie1=OrderForm; name=Brooks; custid=20010; type=clothes
```

the value of the startvalue variable would be 40, since the "2" in "20010" is the 40th character in the string.

Now you locate the end of the field's value. This will be the first semicolon after the startvalue character. If the field is the last value in the text string, there will be no semicolon at the end, so the indexOf( ) method returns a value of -1. If that occurs, you'll use the length of the text string to locate the value's end. Once again, using the indexOf( ) method, you'll store this value in the endvalue variable. The JavaScript command is:

```
endvalue=cookies.indexOf(";",startvalue);
if(endvalue==-1) {
    endvalue=cookies.length;
}
```

In the text string below, the value of the endvalue variable for the custid field would be 45.

```
cookie1=OrderForm; name=Brooks; custid=20010; type=clothes
```

To extract the field's value and store it in a variable named "fvalue," use the substring( ) method (see Appendix D) as follows:

```
fvalue=cookies.substring(startvalue, endvalue);
```

where the startvalue indicates the start of the substring, and the endvalue marks the substring's end. The complete readCookie(fname) function would therefore look as follows:

```
function readCookie(fname) {
      var cookies=document.cookie;
      var startname=cookies.indexOf(fname+"=");
      var startvalue=cookies.indexOf("=", startname)+1;
      var endvalue=cookies.indexOf(";",startvalue);
      if(endvalue==-1) {
         endvalue=cookies.length;
      }
      var fvalue=cookies.substring(startvalue, endvalue);
   return fvalue;
   }
```

So, in a JavaScript program, calling the following function:

```
readCookie("custid");
```

will return a value of 20010, which is the customer id value stored in the cookie file. You should review this example carefully, paying close attention to the use of the indexOf( ) method and the substring( ) method.

Encoding Cookies

Values in the cookie text string cannot contain any spaces, semicolons, or commas. This can be a problem if you are trying to store phrases or sentences that contain many words. The solution to this problem is to encode the value, using the same type of encoding scheme that is used in URL's (which also cannot contain spaces, commas, and semicolons) or in the MAILTO action. JavaScript includes the escape( ) method for encoding your text strings. Encoding replaces blank spaces, semicolons, and commas with special characters. For example, if you want to insert an Address field in your cookie that contains a street number and address, you could use the following JavaScript command:

```
document.cookie='Address='+escape(document.Orders.Address.value);
```

To read a text string that has been encoded, you use JavaScript's unescape() method. For example, you could replace the command that stores the field value in the fvalue variable in the readCookie() function with the following command:

```
var fvalue=unescape(cookies.substring(startvalue, endvalue));
```

and this command will remove any encoding characters, replacing them with the appropriate spaces, semicolons, commas, and so forth.

HTML Tags and Properties

The following is a list of the major HTML tags and properties. The three columns at the right indicate the earliest versions of HTML, Netscape, and Internet Explorer that support these tags. For example, a version number of 3.0 for Internet Explorer indicates that versions of Internet Explorer 3.0 *and above* support the tag or attribute. Both opening and closing tags are given where they are required (for example, <TABLE> … </TABLE>). A single tag means that no closing tag is needed.

You can view more detailed information about the latest HTML specifications at *http://www.w3.org*. Additional information about browser support for different HTML tags is available at *http://www.htmlcompendium.org/*.

Because the World Wide Web changes constantly, you should check this information against the current browser versions.

Properties are of the following types:

- *Character*   A single text character
- *Color*   A recognized color name or color value
- *CGI Script*   The name of a CGI script on the Web server
- *Document*   The file name or URL of a file
- *List*   List of items separated by commas, usually enclosed in double quotation marks
- *Mime-Type*   A MIME data type, such as "text/css", "audio/wav", or "video/x-msvideo"
- *Options*   Limited to a specific set of values (values are shown below the property)
- *Text*   Any text string
- *URL*   The URL for a Web page or file
- *Value*   A number, usually an integer

HTML supports six properties that are common to nearly all HTML tags.

COMMON PROPERTIES	DESCRIPTION	HTML	IE	NETSCAPE
CLASS=*Text*	The CLASS property is used to indicate the class or group to which a particular tag belongs.	4.0	3.0	4.0
DIR=*Option* (LTR I RTL)	The DIR property indicates the text direction as related to the LANG property. The LTR property value displays text from left to right, the RTL displays text from right to left.	4.0		
ID=*Text*	The ID property specifies a unique identifier to be associated with each tag. Unlike the CLASS property, an ID value can be associated with only a single tag.	4.0	3.0	4.0
LANG=*Text*	The LANG property identifies the language being used for the page content.	4.0	4.0	
STYLE="*Style declarations*"	The STYLE property is used to define an inline style for the tag.	4.0	3.0	4.0
TITLE=*Text*	The TITLE property is used to provide information about the tag and to identify the tag for scripts.	2.0	4.0	

TAGS AND PROPERTIES	DESCRIPTION	HTML	IE	NETSCAPE
Document-level Tags	Document-level tags are tags that specify the structure of the HTML file or control its operations and interactions with the Web server.			
<!>	The <!> tag is used for comments to document the features of your HTML file.	1.0	1.0	1.0

TAGS AND PROPERTIES	DESCRIPTION	HTML	IE	NETSCAPE
<BASE>	The <BASE> tag allows you to specify the URL for the HTML document. It is used by some browsers to interpret relative hyperlinks.	1.0	2.0	1.0
HREF=*URL*	Specifies the URL from which all relative hyperlinks should be based	1.0	2.0	4.0
TARGET=*Text*	Specifies the default target window or frame for every hyperlink in the document	4.0	3.0	2.0
<BASEFONT>	The <BASEFONT> tag specifies the default appearance of text in the document.	3.2	2.0	1.0
COLOR=*Color*	The color name or value of the text	4.0	1.0	
FACE=*List*	The font face of the text. Multiple font faces can be specified, separated by commas. The browser will try to render the text in the order specified by the list.	4.0	1.0	3.0
SIZE=*Value*	The size, in points, of the text font	3.2	2.0	1.1
<BODY> ... </BODY>	The <BODY> tag encloses all text, images and other elements on the Web page that will be visible to the user.	1.0	1.0	1.0
ALINK=*Color*	Color of activated hypertext links, links the user has pressed with the mouse button, but has not yet released	1.0	2.0	1.1
BACKGROUND=*Document*	The graphic image file used for the Web page background	1.0	2.0	1.1
BGCOLOR=*Color*	The color of the Web page background	3.2	2.0	1.1
BGPROPERTIES=FIXED	Keeps the background image fixed so that it does not scroll with the Web page		2.0	
BOTTOMMARGIN=*Value*	Specifies the size of the bottom margin, in pixels		4.0	
LEFTMARGIN=*Value*	Specifies the size of the left margin, in pixels		4.0	
LINK=*Color*	Color of all unvisited links	1.0	2.0	1.1
RIGHTMARGIN=*Value*	Specifies the size of the right margin, in pixels		4.0	
SCROLL=*Option* ("NO" | "YES")	Turns the scroll bars on and off (the default value is "YES")		4.0	
TEXT=*Color*	Color of all text in the document	1.0	2.0	1.1
TOPMARGIN=*Value*	Specifies the size of the top margin, in pixels		4.0	
VLINK=*Color*	Color of previously visited links	1.0	2.0	1.1
<HEAD> ... </HEAD>	The <HEAD> tag encloses code that provides information about the document.	1.0	1.0	1.0
<HTML> ... </HTML>	The <HTML> tag indicates the beginning and end of the HTML document.	1.0	1.0	1.0
<ISINDEX>	The <ISINDEX> tag identifies the file as a searchable document.	1.0	2.0	1.0
ACTION=*CGI Script*	Sends the submitted text to the program identified by *CGI Script*		2.0	2.0
PROMPT=*Text*	The text that should be placed before the index's text-input field	3.0	2.0	1.1

TAGS AND PROPERTIES	DESCRIPTION	HTML	IE	NETSCAPE
<LINK>	The <LINK> tag specifies the relationship between the document and other objects.	1.0	2.0	3.0
DISABLED	Disables the link relationship		4.0	
HREF=*URL*	The URL of the LINK tag, moves the user to the specified document	1.0	2.0	4.0
MEDIA=*Option* (ALL | AURAL | BRAILLE | PRINT | PROJECTION | SCREEN)	Specifies the destination medium for any linked information	4.0	4.0	
REL=*Option* (ALTERNATE | BOOKMARK | CHAPTER | CONTENTS | COPYRIGHT | GLOSSARY | HELP | INDEX | NEXT | PREV | SECTION | START | STYLESHEET | SUBSECTION)	Indicates the relationship type between the linked document and the current document	2.0	3.0	4.0
REV=*Option* (ALTERNATE | BOOKMARK | CHAPTER | CONTENTS | COPYRIGHT | GLOSSARY | HELP | INDEX | NEXT |PREV | SECTION | START | STYLESHEET | SUBSECTION)	Indicates the relationship type between the current document and the document specified by the HREF property	2.0	4.0	
TYPE=*Mime-Type*	The data type of the linked document (use "text/css" for linked style sheets)	1.0	2.0	4.0
<META>	The <META> tag is used to insert information about the document not defined by other HTML tags and properties. It can include special instructions for the Web server to perform.	1.0	1.0	1.0
CONTENT=*Text*	Contains information associated with the NAME or HTTP-EQUIV properties	1.0	2.0	1.1
HTTP-EQUIV=*Text*	Directs the browser to request the server to perform different HTTP operations	2.0	2.0	1.1
NAME=*Text*	The type of information specified in the CONTENT property	2.0	2.0	1.1
<STYLE> ... </STYLE>	The <STYLE> tag is used to enclose style declarations for the document.	4.0	3.0	4.0
DISABLED	Disables the style declarations		4.0	
MEDIA=*Option* (ALL | AURAL | BRAILLE | PRINT | PROJECTION | SCREEN)	Specifies the destination medium for the style information	4.0	4.0	
<TITLE> ... </TITLE>	The <TITLE> tag is used to specify the text that appears in the Web browser's title bar.	2.0	2.0	1.1
Block-level Tags	Block-level tags are used to format the appearance of large blocks of text.			
<ADDRESS> ... </ADDRESS>	The <ADDRESS> tag is used for information such as addresses and authorship. The text is usually italicized, and in some browsers it is indented.	2.0	2.0	1.0

TAGS AND PROPERTIES	DESCRIPTION	HTML	IE	NETSCAPE
\<BDO\> ... \</BDO\>	The \<BDO\> tag overrides the current direction of text.	4.0	5.0	
DIR=*Option* (LTR | RTL)	Specifies the text direction, LTR (left to right), or RTL (right to left)	4.0	5.0	
\<BLOCKQUOTE\> ... \</BLOCKQUOTE\>	The \<BLOCKQUOTE\> tag is used to set off long quotes or citations, usually by indenting the enclosed text on both sides. Some browsers italicize the text as well.	2.0	2.0	1.0
\<BR\>	The \<BR\> tag forces a line break in the text.	2.0	2.0	1.0
CLEAR=*Option* (LEFT | RIGHT | ALL | NONE)	Causes the next line to start at the spot in which the specified margin is clear	3.0	2.0	1.0
\<CENTER\> ... \</CENTER\>	The \<CENTER\> tag centers the enclosed text or image horizontally.	3.2	2.0	1.1
\<DFN\> ... \</DFN\>	The \<DFN\> tag is used for the defining instance of a term, that is, the first time the term is used. The enclosed text is usually italicized.	2.0		2.0
\<DIV\> ... \</DIV\>	The \<DIV\> tag indicates a block of document content.	3.0	2.0	3.0
ALIGN=*Option* (LEFT | CENTER | JUSTIFY | RIGHT)	Horizontal alignment of the text within the \<DIV\> tag	3.0	3.0	3.0
\<HR\>	The \<HR\> tag creates a horizontal line.	1.0	2.0	1.0
ALIGN=*Option* (LEFT | CENTER | RIGHT)	Alignment of the horizontal line (the default is CENTER)	3.2	2.0	1.1
COLOR=*Color*	Specifies a color for the line		3.0	
NOSHADE	Removes 3D shading from the line	3.0	3.0	1.1
SIZE=*Value*	The size (height) of the line, in pixels	3.2	2.0	1.1
WIDTH=*Value*	The width (length) of the line, either in pixels or as a percentage of the display area	3.2	2.0	1.1
\<H1\> ... \</H1\> \<H2\> ... \</H2\> \<H3\> ... \</H3\> \<H4\> ... \</H4\> \<H5\> ... \</H5\> \<H6\> ... \</H6\>	The \<H1\> – \<H6\> tags are used to display the six levels of text headings, ranging from the largest (\<H1\>), to the smallest (\<H6\>). Text headings appear in a boldface font.	1.0	1.0	1.0
ALIGN=*Option* (LEFT | RIGHT | CENTER)	The alignment of the heading	3.0	2.0	4.0
\<LISTING\> ... \</LISTING\>	The \<LISTING\> tag displays text in a fixed width font resembling a typewriter or computer printout. This tag has been rendered obsolete by some newer tags.	2.0	3.0	1.0
\<NOBR\> ... \</NOBR\>	The \<NOBR\> tag prevents line breaks for the enclosed text. This tag is not often used.		2.0	1.1
\<P\> ... \</P\>	The \<P\> tag defines the beginning and end of a paragraph of text.	2.0	2.0	1.0
ALIGN=*Option* (LEFT | CENTER | RIGHT)	The alignment of the text in the paragraph	2.0	3.0	1.1

TAGS AND PROPERTIES	DESCRIPTION	HTML	IE	NETSCAPE
<PLAINTEXT> ... </PLAINTEXT>	The <PLAINTEXT> tag displays text in a fixed width font. It is supported by some earlier versions of Netscape, but in an erratic way, so authors should avoid using it.	2.0	2.0	1.0
<PRE> ... </PRE>	The <PRE> tag retains the preformatted appearance of the text in the HTML file, including any line breaks or spaces. Text usually appears in a fixed width font.	2.0	2.0	1.0
<WBR> ... </WBR>	The <WBR> tag, used in conjunction with the <NOBR> tag, overrides other tags that may preclude the creation of line breaks and directs the browser to insert a line break if necessary. This tag is not often used.		2.0	1.1
<XMP> ... </XMP>	The <XMP> tag displays blocks of text in a fixed width font. This tag is obsolete and should not be used.	2.0	2.0	1.0
In-line Tags	Inline tags modify the appearance of individual characters, words, or sentences from that of the surrounding text. Inline tags usually appear nested within block-level tags.			
<A> ... </A>	The <A> tag marks the beginning and end of a hypertext link.	1.0	1.0	1.0
ACCESSKEY=*Character*	Specifies an accelerator key for the element, which can be accessed by pressing the *Character* key along with the Alt key	4.0	4.0	
COORDS=*Value 1, value 2…*	The coordinates of the hotspot when the <A> tag is applied to an inline image; the coordinates depend on the shape of the hotspot	4.0		
Rectangle: COORDS=*x_left, y_upper, x_right, y_lower*				
Circle: COORDS= *x_center, y_center, radius*				
Polygon: COORDS= $x_1, y_1, x_2, y_2, x_3, y_3, …$				
HREF=*URL*	Indicates the target, filename, or URL, to which the hypertext points	1.0	1.0	1.0
NAME=*Text*	Specifies a name for the enclosed text, allowing it to be a target of a hyperlink	1.0	2.0	1.0
REL=*Text*	Specifies the relationship between the current page and the link specified by the HREF property	1.0	2.0	
REV=*Text*	Specifies a reverse relationship between the current page and the link specified by the HREF property	1.0	2.0	
SHAPE=*Option* (RECT | CIRCLE | POLY)	The shape of the hotspot when the <A> tag is applied to an inline image	4.0		
TABINDEX=*Value*	Specifies the tab order in the form	4.0	4.0	
TARGET=*Text*	Specifies the default target window or frame for the hyperlink	4.0	3.0	1.0

TAGS AND PROPERTIES	DESCRIPTION	HTML	IE	NETSCAPE
TITLE=*Text*	Provides a title for the document whose address is given by the HREF property	1.0	2.0	
TYPE=*Mime-Type*	The data type of the linked document	4.0		
<ABBR> ... </ABBR>	The <ABBR> tag indicates text in an abbreviated form (for example, WWW, HTTP, URL).	4.0		
<ACRONYM> ... </ACRONYM>	The <ACRONYM> tag indicates a text acronym (for example, WAC, radar).	4.0	4.0	
<B> ... </B>	The <B> tag displays the enclosed text in bold type.	2.0	2.0	1.0
<BIG> ... </BIG>	The <BIG> tag increases the size of the enclosed text. The exact appearance of the text depends on the browser and the default font size.	3.2	2.0	2.0
<BLINK> ... </BLINK>	The <BLINK> tag causes the enclosed text to blink on and off.			1.0
<CITE> ... </CITE>	The <CITE> tag is used for citations. The text usually appears in italics.	1.0	2.0	1.0
<CODE> ... </CODE>	The <CODE> tag is used for text taken from the code for a computer program. The text usually appears in a fixed width font.	1.0	1.0	1.0
<DEL> ... </DEL>	The <DEL> tag is used to indicate that the text has been deleted from the document. Deleted text usually appears as strikethrough text.	4.0	4.0	
CITE=*URL*	Specifies the URL for a document that has additional information about the deleted text	4.0	4.0	
DATETIME=*Date*	Specifies the date and time of the deletion	4.0	4.0	
<EM> ... </EM>	The <EM> tag is used to emphasize text. The enclosed text usually appears in italics.	1.0	2.0	1.0
<FONT> ... </FONT>	The <FONT> tag is used to control the appearance of the text it encloses.	3.0	2.0	1.1
COLOR=*Color*	The color of the enclosed text	3.0	2.0	2.0
FACE=*List*	The font face of the text. Multiple font faces can be specified, separated by commas. The browser will try to render the text in the order specified by the list.	3.0	2.0	3.0
POINT-SIZE=*Value*	Point size of the text (used with downloadable fonts)			4.0
SIZE=*Value*	Size of the font in points, it can be absolute or relative. Specifying SIZE=5 sets the font size to 5 points. Specifying SIZE=+5 sets the font size 5 points larger than the size specified in the <BASEFONT> tag.	3.0	2.0	4.0
WEIGHT=*Value*	The weight of the font, ranging from 100 (the lightest) to 900 (the heaviest)			4.0
<I> ... </I>	The <I> tag italicizes the enclosed text.	1.0	1.0	1.0
<INS> ... </INS>	The <INS> tag is used to indicate that the text has been inserted into the document.	4.0	4.0	
CITE=*URL*	Specifies the URL for a document that has additional information about the inserted text	4.0	4.0	
DATETIME=*Date*	Specifies the date and time of the insertion	4.0	4.0	

TAGS AND PROPERTIES	DESCRIPTION	HTML	IE	NETSCAPE
<KBD> ... </KBD>	The <KBD> tag is used for text that appears as if it came from a typewriter or keyboard. Text is shown in a fixed width font.	1.0	2.0	1.0
<Q> ... </Q>	The <Q> tag indicates the enclosed text is a short quotation.	4.0	4.0	
CITE=*URL*	Specifies the URL for a document that has additional information about the quoted text	4.0	4.0	
<S> ... </S>	The <S> tag displays the enclosed text with a horizontal line striking through it.	4.0	2.0	3.0
<SAMP> ... </SAMP>	The <SAMP> tag displays text in a fixed width font.	1.0	2.0	1.0
<SMALL> ... </SMALL>	The <SMALL> tag decreases the size of the enclosed text. The exact appearance of the text depends on the browser and the default font size.	3.0	3.0	2.0
<SPAN> ... </SPAN>	The <SPAN> tag acts as a container for inline content.	4.0	3.0	4.0
DATAFLD=*Text*	Specifies the column of a data source that supplies bound data for use with the spanned text		4.0	
DATAFORMATAS=*Option* (TEXT | HTML)	Specifies whether the data in the data source column is formatted as plain text or as HTML code		4.0	
DATASRC=*Text*	Specifies the ID of the data source that is to be used with the spanned text		4.0	
<STRIKE> ... </STRIKE>	The <STRIKE> tag displays the enclosed text with a horizontal line striking through it. The <STRIKE> tag is being phased out in favor of the more-concise <S> tag.	3.2	2.0	3.0
<STRONG> ... </STRONG>	The <STRONG> tag is used to strongly emphasize the enclosed text, usually in a bold font.	1.0	1.0	1.0
<SUB> ... </SUB>	The <SUB> tag displays the enclosed text as a subscript.	1.0	3.0	2.0
<SUP> ... </SUP>	The <SUP> tag displays the enclosed text as a superscript.	1.0	3.0	2.0
<TT> ... </TT>	The <TT> tag displays text in a fixed width, teletype-style font.	1.0	1.0	1.0
<U> ... </U>	The <U> tag underlines the enclosed text. The <U> tag should be avoided because it can be confused with hypertext, which is typically underlined.	1.0	2.0	3.0
<VAR> ... </VAR>	The <VAR> tag is used for text that represents a variable. The text usually appears in italics.	1.0	1.0	1.1
In-line Object Tags	Inline object tags are used for inline objects such as graphics, multimedia files, and applets.			
<APPLET> ... </APPLET>	The <APPLET> tag, supported by all Java-enabled browsers, allows Web authors to embed a Java applet in an HTML document. It has been deprecated in favor of the <OBJECT> tag in HTML 4.0.	3.2	3.0	2.0

TAGS AND PROPERTIES	DESCRIPTION	HTML	IE	NETSCAPE
ALIGN=*Option* (ABSMIDDLE | ABSBOTTOM | ABSMIDDLE | BASELINE | BOTTOM | CENTER | LEFT | MIDDLE | RIGHT | TEXTTOP | TOP)	Specifies the alignment of the applet with the surrounding text	3.2	3.0	2.0
ALT=*Text*	Specifies alternate text to be shown in place of the Java applet	3.2	3.0	3.0
ARCHIVE=*URL*	Specifies the URL of an archive containing classes and other resources that will be preloaded for use with the Java applet	4.0		3.0
CODEBASE=*URL*	Specifies the base URL for the applet. If not specified, the browser assumes the same location as the current document.	3.2	3.0	2.0
CODE=*Text*	Specifies the name of the CLASS file that contains the Java applet	3.2	3.0	2.0
DATAFLD=*Text*	Specifies the column from a data source that supplies bound data for use with the applet		4.0	
DATASRC=*Text*	Specifies the ID of the data source that is to be used with the applet		4.0	
HEIGHT=*Value*	Specifies the height of the applet, in pixels	3.2	3.0	2.0
HSPACE=*Value*	Specifies the horizontal space around the applet, in pixels	3.2	3.0	2.0
MAYSCRIPT	Allows access to an applet by programs embedded in the document			4.0
NAME=*Text*	The name assigned to the Java applet	3.2	3.0	2.0
OBJECT=*Text*	Specifies a resource containing a serialized representation of an applet's state. It is interpreted relative to the applet's code base. The serialized data contains the applet's class name, but not the implementation. The class name is used to retrieve the implementation from a class file or archive.	4.0		
VSPACE=*Value*	Specifies the vertical space around the applet, in pixels	3.2	3.0	2.0
WIDTH=*Value*	The width of the applet, in pixels	3.2	3.0	2.0
<AREA>	The <AREA> tag defines the type and coordinates of a hotspot within an image map.	3.2	2.0	1.0
COORDS=*Value 1, Value 2…* Rectangle: COORDS=*x_left, y_upper, x_right, y_lower* Circle: COORDS= *x_center, y_center, radius* Polygon: COORDS= $x_1, y_1, x_2, y_2, x_3, y_3, …$	The hotspot coordinates, which depend on the shape of the hotspot.	3.2	2.0	1.0
HREF=*URL*	Indicates the target, filename or URL to which the hotspot points	3.2	2.0	1.0

TAGS AND PROPERTIES	DESCRIPTION	HTML	IE	NETSCAPE
SHAPE=*Option* (RECT | CIRCLE | POLY)	The shape of the hotspot	3.2	2.0	1.0
TARGET=*Text*	Specifies the default target window or frame for the hotspot	4.0	3.0	2.0
<BGSOUND>	The <BGSOUND> tag is used to play a background sound clip when the page is first opened.		2.0	
BALANCE=*Value*	Defines how the volume will be divided between two speakers, where *Value* is an integer between -10,000 and 10,000		4.0	
LOOP=*Value*	Specifies the number of times the sound clip should be played. LOOP can either be a digit or INFINITE.		3.0	
SRC=*Document*	The sound file used for the sound clip		2.0	
VOLUME=*Value*	Defines the volume of the background sound, where *Value* is an integer between -10,000 and 0		4.0	
<EMBED> ... </EMBED>	The <EMBED> tag is used to specify an object to be embedded in the document.		3.0	1.0
AUTOSTART=*Option* (TRUE | FALSE)	Specifies whether the embedded object should be started automatically when the page is loaded		3.0	1.0
ALIGN=*Option* (BOTTOM | LEFT | RIGHT | TOP)	Specifies the alignment of the embedded object with the surrounding text		3.0	1.0
ALT=*Text*	Text to display if the browser cannot display the embedded object		3.0	1.0
BORDER=*Value*	The size of the border around the embedded object, in pixels		3.0	1.0
HEIGHT=*Value*	The height of the embedded object, in pixels		3.0	1.0
HIDDEN=*Option* (TRUE | FALSE)	Specifies whether the embedded object is hidden or not			4.0
HSPACE=*Value*	The amount of space to the left and right of the image, in pixels		4.0	
TYPE=*Mime-Type*	Specifies the data type of the embedded object			4.0
UNITS=*Option* (EN | PIXELS)	Specifies the unit of measurement to be used with the embedded object			4.0
VSPACE=*Value*	The amount of space above and below the embedded object, in pixels		4.0	
WIDTH=*Value*	The width of the embedded object, in pixels		3.0	1.0
<IMG>	The <IMG> tag is used to insert an inline image into the document.	1.0	2.0	1.0
ALIGN=*Option* (LEFT | RIGHT | TOP | TEXTTOP | MIDDLE | ABSMIDDLE | BASELINE | BOTTOM | ABSBOTTOM)	Specifies the alignment of the image. Specifying an alignment of LEFT or RIGHT aligns the image with the left or right page margin. The other alignment options align the image with surrounding text.	1.0	2.0	1.1
ALT=*Text*	Text to display if the browser cannot display the image	2.0	2.0	1.1
BORDER=*Value*	The size of the border around the image, in pixels	3.2	2.0	1.1
CONTROLS	Displays VCR-like controls under moving images (used in conjunction with the DYNSRC property)		2.0	

TAGS AND PROPERTIES	DESCRIPTION	HTML	IE	NETSCAPE
DYNSRC=*Document*	Specifies the file of a video, AVI clip, or VRML worlds shown inside the page		2.0	
HEIGHT=*Value*	The height of the image, in pixels	3.0	2.0	1.1
HSPACE=*Value*	The amount of space to the left and right of the image, in pixels	3.0	2.0	1.1
ISMAP	Identifies the graphic as an image map (for use with server-side image maps)	3.0	2.0	2.0
LONGDESC=*URL*	The URL of a document that contains a long description of the image (used in conjunction with the ALT property)	4.0		
LOOP=*Value*	Specifies the number of times a moving image should be played (the value must be either a digit or INFINITE)		2.0	
LOWSRC=*Document*	A low-resolution version of the graphic that the browser should initially display before loading the high-resolution version		4.0	1.0
SRC=*Document*	The source file of the inline image	1.0	2.0	1.0
START=*Item* (FILEOPEN | MOUSEOVER)	Tells the browser when to start displaying a moving image file. FILEOPEN directs the browser to start when the file is open. MOUSEOVER directs the browser to start when the mouse pointer moves over the image.		2.0	
SUPPRESS=*Option* (TRUE | FALSE)	Suppresses the placeholder icon and any ALT text until the image is located (if SUPPRESS=TRUE)			4.0
USEMAP=*#Map_Namet*	Identifies the graphic as an image map and specifies the name of image map definition to use with the graphic (for use with client-side image maps)	3.2	2.0	2.0
VSPACE=*Value*	The amount of space above and below the image, in pixels	3.2	2.0	1.1
WIDTH=*Value*	The width of the image, in pixels	3.0	2.0	1.1
<MAP> ... </MAP>	The <MAP> tag specifies information about a client-side image map (note that it must enclose <AREA> tags).	3.2	2.0	1.0
NAME=*Text*	The name of the image map	3.2	2.0	2.0
<MARQUEE> ... </MARQUEE>	The <MARQUEE> tag is used to create an area containing scrolling text.		2.0	
ALIGN=*Option* (TOP | MIDDLE | BOTTOM)	The alignment of the scrolling text within the marquee		2.0	
BEHAVIOR=*Option* (SCROLL | SLIDE | ALTERNATE)	Controls the behavior of the text in the marquee. SCROLL causes the text to repeatedly scroll across the page. SLIDE causes the text to slide onto the page and stop at the margin. ALTERNATE causes the text to bounce from margin to margin.		2.0	
BGCOLOR=*Color*	The background color of the marquee		2.0	
DATFLD=*Text*	The column name in the data source that is bound to the marquee		4.0	
DATAFORMATAS=*Option* (TEXT | HTML)	Indicates the format of the bound data		4.0	

TAGS AND PROPERTIES	DESCRIPTION	HTML	IE	NETSCAPE
DIRECTION=*Option* (LEFT | RIGHT)	The direction that the text scrolls on the page		2.0	
HEIGHT=*Value*	The height of the marquee, either in pixels or as a percentage of the display area		2.0	
HSPACE=*Value*	The amount of space to the left and right of the marquee, in pixels		2.0	
LOOP=*Value*	The number of times the marquee will be scrolled (the value must be either a digit or INFINITE)		2.0	
SCROLLAMOUNT=*Value*	The amount of space between successive draws of the text in the marquee		2.0	
SCROLLDELAY=*Value*	The amount of time between scrolling actions, in milliseconds		2.0	
TRUESPEED	Indicates that the SCROLLDELAY property value should be honored for its exact value, otherwise any value less than 60 milliseconds is rounded up		4.0	
VSPACE=*Value*	The amount of space above and below the marquee, in pixels		2.0	
WIDTH=*Value*	The width of the marquee, in either pixels or as a percentage of the display area		2.0	
<NOEMBED> … </NOEMBED>	The <NOEMBED> tag is used to display alternate content for older browsers that do not support the <EMBED> tag.		3.0	1.0
<OBJECT> … </OBJECT>	The <OBJECT> tag allows authors to control whether data should be rendered externally or by a program, specified by the author, that renders the data within the user agent. (Most user browsers have built-in mechanisms for rendering common data types such as text, GIF images, colors, fonts, and a handful of graphic elements. To render data types not supported natively, user agents generally run external applications.)	2.0	1.0	1.1
ACCESSKEY=*Character*	Specifies an accelerator key for the object, which can be accessed by pressing the *Character* key along with the Alt key		4.0	
ARCHIVE=*URL*	Specifies the URL of an archive containing classes and other resources that will be preloaded for use with the object	4.0		
ALIGN=*Option* (TOP | BOTTOM | MIDDLE | LEFT | RIGHT)	Specifies the alignment of the embedded object, relative to the surrounding text	4.0	3.0	2.0
BORDER=*Value*	Specifies the width of the embedded object's border, in pixels	4.0	3.0	
CLASSID=*URL*	Specifies the URL of the embedded object	4.0	3.0	4.0
CODEBASE=*URL*	Specifies the base path used to resolve relative references within the embedded object	4.0	3.0	2.0
CODETYPE=*Text*	Specifies the type of data object	4.0	3.0	

TAGS AND PROPERTIES	DESCRIPTION	HTML	IE	NETSCAPE
DATA=*URL*	Specifies the location of data for the embedded object	4.0	3.0	2.0
DATAFLD=*Text*	Specifies the column from a data source that supplies bound data for use with the object		4.0	
DATASRC=*Text*	Specifies the ID of the data source that is to be used with the object		4.0	
DECLARE	Declares the object without installing it in the page	4.0		
HEIGHT=*Value*	Specifies the height of the embedded object, in pixels	4.0	3.0	2.0
HSPACE=*Value*	Specifies the horizontal space around the embedded object, in pixels	4.0	3.0	2.0
NAME=*Text*	Specifies the name of the embedded object	4.0	3.0	
STANDBY=*Text*	Specifies a message the browser should display while rendering the embedded object	4.0	3.0	
TABINDEX=*Value*	Specifies the tab order of the object when it is placed within a form	4.0	4.0	
TYPE=*Mime-Type*	Specifies the data type of the object	4.0	3.0	4.0
USEMAP=*URL*	The URL of the image map to be used with the object	4.0		
VSPACE=*Value*	Specifies the vertical space around the embedded object, in pixels	4.0	3.0	2.0
WIDTH=*Value*	Specifies the width of the embedded object, in pixels	4.0	3.0	2.0
<PARAM> ... </PARAM>	<PARAM> tags specify a set of values that might be required by an object at run-time. Any number of PARAM elements may appear in the content of an <OBJECT> or <APPLET> tag, in any order, but they must be placed at the start of the content of the enclosing <OBJECT> or <APPLET> tag.	3.2	3.0	1.0
DATAFLD=*Text*	Specifies the column name in the data source that is bound to the parameter's value		4.0	
DATAFORMATAS=*Option* (TEXT | HTML)	Specifies whether the data in the data source column is formatted as plain text or as HTML code		4.0	
DATASRC=*URL*	Specifies the URL of the data source from which to draw the data		4.0	
NAME=*Text*	Specifies the name of the parameter	3.2	3.0	2.0
VALUE=*Text*	Specifies the value of the parameter	3.2	3.0	2.0
VALUETYPE=*Option* (DATA | REF | OBJECT)	Specifies the type of the value attribute	4.0	3.0	
Form Tags	Form tags are used to create user entry forms.			
<BUTTON> ... </BUTTON>	Buttons created with the <BUTTON> tag function just like buttons created with the <INPUT> tag, but they offer richer rendering possibilities. For example, the BUTTON element may have content.	4.0	4.0	4.0
ACCESSKEY=*Character*	Specifies an accelerator key for the element, which can be accessed by pressing the *Character* key along with the Alt key	4.0	4.0	
DISABLED	Disables the button	4.0	4.0	

TAGS AND PROPERTIES	DESCRIPTION	HTML	IE	NETSCAPE
NAME=*Text*	Specifies the button name	4.0	5.0	
VALUE=*Text*	Specifies the initial value of the button	4.0	5.0	
TABINDEX=*Value*	Specifies the tab order in the form	4.0	5.0	
TYPE=*Option* (SUBMIT | RESET | BUTTON)	Specifies the type of button. Setting the type to BUTTON creates a pushbutton for use with client-side scripts.	4.0	4.0	
<FIELDSET> ... </FIELDSET>	<The FIELDSET> tag allows authors to group form controls and labels. Grouping controls makes it easier for users to understand the control's purpose, and simultaneously facilitates moving between fields.	4.0	4.0	
ALIGN=*Option* (TOP | BOTTOM | MIDDLE | LEFT | RIGHT)	Specifies the alignment of the legend with respect to the field set (see the <LEGEND> tag for more information)	4.0	4.0	
<FORM> ... </FORM>	The <FORM> tag marks the beginning and end of a Web page form.	1.0	1.0	1.0
ACTION=*URL*	Specifies the URL to which the contents of the form are to be sent	1.0	2.0	2.0
ENCTYPE=*Text*	Specifies the encoding type used to submit the data to the server	2.0	2.0	2.0
METHOD=*Option* (POST | GET)	Specifies the method of accessing the URL indicated in the ACTION property	2.0	2.0	2.0
TARGET=*Text*	The frame or window that displays the form's results	4.0	3.0	2.0
<INPUT> ... </INPUT>	The <INPUT> tag creates an input object for use in a Web page form.	1.0	2.0	1.0
ACCESSKEY=*Character*	Specifies an accelerator key for the element, which can be accessed by pressing the *Character* key along with the Alt key	4.0	4.0	
ALIGN=*Option* (LEFT | RIGHT | TOP | TEXTTOP | MIDDLE | ABSMIDDLE | BASELINE | BOTTOM | ABSBOTTOM)	Specifies the alignment of an input image (similar to the ALIGN option with the <IMG> tag)	1.0	2.0	1.1
ALT=*Text*	Alternate text description of image buttons for browsers that do not support inline images	4.0	4.0	
CHECKED	Specifies that an input check box or input radio button is selected	1.0	2.0	2.0
DISABLED	Disables the control	4.0	4.0	
MAXLENGTH=*Value*	Specifies the maximum number of characters that can be inserted into an input text box	1.0	2.0	2.0
NAME=*Text*	The label given to the input object	1.0	2.0	2.0
READONLY	Prevents the control's value from being modified	4.0	4.0	
SIZE=*Value*	The visible size, in characters, of an input text box	1.0	2.0	2.0
SRC=*Document*	The source file of the graphic used for an input image object	1.0	2.0	2.0
TABINDEX=*Value*	Specifies the tab order in the form	4.0	4.0	

TAGS AND PROPERTIES	DESCRIPTION	HTML	IE	NETSCAPE
TYPE=*Option* (CHECKBOX | HIDDEN | IMAGE | PASSWORD | RADIO | RESET | SUBMIT | TEXT | TEXTAREA)	Specifies the type of input object. CHECKBOX creates a check box. HIDDEN creates a hidden object. IMAGE creates an image object. PASSWORD creates a text box that hides the text as the user enters it. RADIO creates a radio button. RESET creates a button that resets the form's fields when pressed. SUBMIT creates a button that submits the form when pressed. TEXT creates a text box. TEXTAREA creates a text box with multiple line entry fields.	1.0	2.0	2.0
USEMAP=*#Map_Name*	Identifies the input image as an image map (similar to the USEMAP property used with the <IMG> tag)	1.0	2.0	2.0
VALUE=*Value*	Specifies the information that initially appears in the input object	2.0	2.0	2.0
WIDTH=*Value*	The width of the input image, in pixels	1.0	2.0	2.0
<LABEL> ... </LABEL>	The <LABEL> tag is used to create labels for form controls.	4.0	4.0	
ACCESSKEY=*Character*	Specifies an accelerator key for the element, which can be accessed by pressing the *Character* key along with the Alt key	4.0	4.0	
DATAFLD=*Text*	Specifies the column from a data source that supplies bound data for use with the label		4.0	
DATAFORMATAS=*Option* (TEXT | HTML)	Specifies whether the data in the data source column is formatted as plain text or as HTML code		4.0	
DATASRC=*Text*	Specifies the ID of the data source that is to be used with the label		4.0	
FOR=*Text*	Indicates the name or ID of the element to which the label is applied	4.0	4.0	
<LEGEND> ... </LEGEND>	The <LEGEND> tag allows authors to assign a caption to a FIELDSET (see the <FIELDSET> tag above).	4.0	4.0	
ACCESSKEY=*Character*	Specifies an accelerator key for the element, which can be accessed by pressing the *Character* key along with the Alt key	4.0	4.0	
ALIGN=*Option* (TOP | BOTTOM | LEFT | RIGHT)	Specifies the position of the legend with respect to the field set	4.0	4.0	
<OPTGROUP> ... </OPTGROUP>	The <OPTGROUP> tag is used to create a grouping of items in a selection list, as defined by the <OPTION> tag.	4.0		
DISABLED	Disables the group of option items	4.0		
LABEL=*Text*	Specifies a label for the option group	4.0		
<OPTION> ... </OPTION>	The <OPTION> tag is used for each item in a selection list. This tag must be placed within <SELECT> tags.	1.0	1.0	1.0
DISABLED	Disables the option item	4.0	4.0	
SELECTED	The default or selected option in the selection list	1.0	2.0	2.0
VALUE=*Value*	The value returned to the server when the user selects this option	2.0	2.0	2.0

TAGS AND PROPERTIES	DESCRIPTION	HTML	IE	NETSCAPE
<SELECT> ... </SELECT>	The <SELECT> tag encloses a set of <OPTION> tags for use in creating selection lists.	1.0	2.0	2.0
ACCESSKEY=*Character*	Specifies an accelerator key for the element, which can be accessed by pressing the *Character* key along with the Alt key	4.0	4.0	
ALIGN=*Option* (LEFT | RIGHT | TOP | TEXTTOP | MIDDLE | ABSMIDDLE | BASELINE | BOTTOM | ABSBOTTOM)	Specifies the alignment of an input image (similar to the ALIGN option with the <IMG> tag)	1.0	2.0	1.1
DISABLED	Disables the selection list	4.0	4.0	
MULTIPLE	Allows the user to select multiple options from the selection list	2.0	2.0	2.0
NAME=*Text*	The name assigned to the selection list	1.0	2.0	2.0
SIZE=*Value*	The number of visible items in the selection list	2.0	2.0	2.0
TABINDEX=*Value*	Specifies the tab order in the form	4.0	4.0	
<TEXTAREA> ... </TEXTAREA>	The <TEXTAREA> tag creates a text box.	1.0	2.0	1.0
ACCESSKEY=*Character*	Specifies an accelerator key for the element, which can be accessed by pressing the *Character* key along with the Alt key	4.0	4.0	
ALIGN=*Option* (LEFT | RIGHT | TOP | TEXTTOP | MIDDLE | ABSMIDDLE | BASELINE | BOTTOM | ABSBOTTOM)	Specifies the alignment of an input image (similar to the ALIGN option with the <IMG> tag)	1.0	2.0	1.1
COLS=*Value*	Specifies the height of the text box, in characters	1.0	2.0	2.0
DISABLED	Disables the text area	4.0	4.0	
NAME=*Text*	Specifies the name assigned to the text box	1.0	2.0	1.0
READONLY	Prevents the text area's value from being modified	4.0	4.0	
ROWS=*Value*	Specifies the width of the text box, in characters	1.0	2.0	2.0
TABINDEX=*Value*	Specifies the tab order in the form	4.0	4.0	
WRAP=*Option* (OFF | VIRTUAL | PHYSICAL)	Specifies how text should be wrapped within the text box. OFF turns off text wrapping. VIRTUAL wraps the text, but sends the text to the server as a single line. PHYSICAL wraps the text and sends the text to the server as it appears in the text box.		2.0	2.0
Frame Tags	Frame tags are used for creating and formatting frames.			
<FRAME>	The <FRAME> tag defines a single frame within a set of frames.	4.0	3.0	2.0
BORDERCOLOR=*Color*	Specifies the color of the frame border		4.0	3.0
FRAMEBORDER=*Option* (YES | NO)	Specifies whether the frame border is visible	4.0	3.0	3.0
FRAMESPACING=*Value*	Specifies the amount of space between frames, in pixels		3.0	
LONGDESC=*URL*	Specifies the URL of a document that contains a long description of the frame's content (used in conjunction with the TITLE property)	4.0		

TAGS AND PROPERTIES	DESCRIPTION	HTML	IE	NETSCAPE
MARGINHEIGHT=*Value*	Specifies the amount of space above and below the frame object and the frame borders	4.0	3.0	2.0
MARGINWIDTH=*Value*	Specifies the amount of space to the left and right of the frame object, in pixels	4.0	3.0	2.0
NAME=*Text*	Label assigned to the frame	4.0	3.0	2.0
NORESIZE	Prevents users from resizing the frame	4.0	3.0	2.0
SCROLLING=*Option* (YES | NO | AUTO)	Specifies whether scroll bars are visible (AUTO, the default, displays scroll bars only as needed)	4.0	3.0	2.0
SRC=*Document*	Specifies the document or URL of the object to be displayed in the frame	4.0	3.0	2.0
<FRAMESET> ... </FRAMESET>	The <FRAMESET> tag marks the beginning and the end of a set of frames.	4.0	3.0	2.0
BORDER=*Value*	The size of the frame's borders, in pixels		3.0	3.0
BORDERCOLOR=*Color*	The color of the frame borders		3.0	3.0
COLS=*List*	The size of each column in a set of frames. Columns can be specified either in pixels, as a percentage of the display area, or with an asterisk (*) indicating that any remaining space be allotted to that column (for example, COLS="40,25%,*").	4.0	3.0	2.0
FRAMEBORDER=*Option* (YES | NO)	Specifies whether the frame borders are visible		3.0	3.0
FRAMESPACING=*Value*	Specifies the amount of space between frames, in pixels		3.0	
ROWS=*List*	The size of each row in a set of frames. Rows can be specified either in pixels, as a percentage of the display area, or with an asterisk (*) indicating that any remaining space be allotted to that column (for example, ROWS="40,25%,*").	4.0	3.0	2.0
<IFRAME> ... </IFRAME>	The <IFRAME> tag allows authors to insert a frame within a block of text. Inserting an inline frame within a section of text allows you to insert one HTML document in the middle of another; both can be aligned with surrounding text.	4.0	3.0	
ALIGN=*Option* (ABSBOTTOM | ABSMIDDLE | BASELINE JUSTIFY | LEFT | MIDDLE | RIGHT | TEXTTOP)	Specifies the alignment of the floating frame	4.0	3.0	
FRAMEBORDER=*Option* (YES | NO)	Specifies whether the frame borders are visible	4.0	3.0	
HEIGHT=*Value*	Specifies the height of the floating frame, in pixels	4.0	3.0	
HSPACE=*Value*	Specifies the horizontal space around the inline frame, in pixels		3.0	
MARGINHEIGHT=*Value*	Specifies the amount of space above and below the frame object and the frame borders	4.0	3.0	
MARGINWIDTH=*Value*	Specifies the amount of space to the left and right of the frame object, in pixels	4.0	3.0	
NAME=*Text*	Label assigned to the frame	4.0	3.0	

TAGS AND PROPERTIES	DESCRIPTION	HTML	IE	NETSCAPE
NORESIZE	Prevents users from resizing the frame		3.0	
SCROLLING=Option (YES | NO | AUTO)	Specifies whether scroll bars are visible (AUTO, the default, displays scroll bars only as needed)	4.0	3.0	
SRC=Document	Specifies the document or URL of the object to be displayed in the frame	4.0	3.0	
VSPACE=Value	Specifies the vertical space around the inline frame, in pixels		3.0	
WIDTH=Value	Specifies the width of the floating frame, in pixels	4.0	3.0	
<NOFRAMES> … </NOFRAMES>	The <NOFRAMES> tag enables browsers that do not support frames to display a page that uses frames (the tag encloses the <BODY> tag).	4.0	3.0	2.0
Layer Tags	Layer tags are used to create overlapping content layers.			
<ILAYER> … </ILAYER>	The <ILAYER> tag is used to create an inflow layer with a relative position and which appears where it naturally would in the document.			4.0
ABOVE=Text	Specifies the name of the layer to be displayed above the current layer			4.0
BACKGROUND=URL	Specifies the URL of the layer's background image			4.0
BELOW=Text	Specifies the name of the layer to be displayed below the current layer			4.0
BGCOLOR=Color	Specifies the background color of the layer			4.0
CLIP=top_x, left_y, bottom_x, right_y	Specifies the coordinates of the viewable region of the layer			4.0
HEIGHT=Value	The height of the layer in pixels			4.0
LEFT=Value	Specifies the horizontal offset of the layer, in pixels			4.0
PAGEX=Value	Specifies the horizontal position of the layer			4.0
PAGEY=Value	Specifies the vertical position of the layer			4.0
SRC=URL	Specifies the URL of the document displayed in the layer			4.0
TOP=Value	Specifies the vertical offset of the layer, in pixels			4.0
VISIBILITY=Option (HIDE | INHERIT | SHOW)	Specifies whether the layer is hidden, shown, or inherits its visibility from the layer that contains it			4.0
WIDTH=Value	The width of the layer, in pixels			4.0
Z-INDEX=Value	Specifies the stacking order of the layer, relative to the other layers			4.0
<LAYER> … </LAYER>	The <LAYER> tag is used to create an inflow layer with an absolutely defined position in the document.			4.0
ABOVE=Text	Specifies the name of the layer to be displayed above the current layer			4.0
BACKGROUND=URL	Specifies the URL of the layer's background image			4.0
BELOW=Text	Specifies the name of the layer to be displayed below the current layer			4.0
BGCOLOR=Color	Specifies the background color of the layer			4.0

TAGS AND PROPERTIES	DESCRIPTION	HTML	IE	NETSCAPE
CLIP=*top_x, left_y, bottom_x, right_y*	Specifies the coordinates of the viewable region of the layer			4.0
HEIGHT=*Value*	The height of the layer, in pixels			4.0
LEFT=*Value*	Specifies the horizontal offset of the layer, in pixels			4.0
PAGEX=*Value*	Specifies the horizontal position of the layer			4.0
PAGEY=*Value*	Specifies the vertical position of the layer			4.0
SRC=*URL*	Specifies the URL of the document displayed in the layer			4.0
TOP=*Value*	Specifies the vertical offset of the layer, in pixels			4.0
VISIBILITY=*Option* (HIDE | INHERIT | SHOW)	Specifies whether the layer is hidden, shown, or inherits its visibility from the layer that contains it			4.0
WIDTH=*Value*	The width of the layer, in pixels			4.0
Z-INDEX=*Value*	Specifies the stacking order of the layer, relative to the other layers			4.0
List Tags	List tags are used to create a variety of different kinds of lists.			
<DD>	The <DD> tag formats text to be used as relative definitions in a <DL> list.	1.0	2.0	1.0
<DIR> ... </DIR>	The <DIR> tag encloses an unordered list of <LI> items formatted in narrow columns.	1.0	2.0	1.0
COMPACT	Reduces the whitespace between list items	2.0		
TYPE=*Option* (CIRCLE | DISC | SQUARE)	Specifies the type of bullet used for displaying each <LI> item in the <DIR> list			2.0
<DL> ... </DL>	The <DL> tag encloses a definition list in which the <DD> definition term is left-aligned, and the <DT> relative definition is indented.	1.0	2.0	1.0
COMPACT	Reduces the whitespace between list items	2.0	4.0	1.0
<DT>	The <DT> tag is used to format the definition term in a <DL> list.	1.0	2.0	1.0
<LI>	The <LI> tag identifies list items in a <DIR>, <MENU>, <OL>, or <UL> list.	1.0	2.0	1.0
TYPE=*Option* (A | a | I | i | 1)	Specifies how the list item is to be marked. A = uppercase letters, a = lowercase letters, I = uppercase Roman numerals, i = lowercase Roman numerals, and 1 = digits. The default is 1.	3.0	1.0	1.0
<MENU> ... </MENU>	The <MENU> tag encloses an unordered list of items, similar to a <UL> or <DIR> list.	1.0	2.0	1.0
COMPACT	Reduces the whitespace between menu items	2.0		
<OL> ... </OL>	The <OL> tag encloses an ordered list of <LI> items. Typically, ordered lists are rendered as numbered lists.	1.0	1.0	1.0
COMPACT	Reduces the whitespace between ordered list items	2.0		
START=*Value*	The value of the starting number in the ordered list	3.2	2.0	2.0

TAGS AND PROPERTIES	DESCRIPTION	HTML	IE	NETSCAPE
TYPE=*Option* (A | a | I | i | 1)	Specifies how ordered items are to be marked. A = uppercase letters, a = lowercase letters, I = uppercase Roman numerals, i = lowercase Roman numerals, and 1 = digits. The default is 1.	3.2	2.0	2.0
<UL> ... </UL>	The <UL> tag encloses an unordered list of <LI> items. Typically, unordered lists are rendered as bulleted lists.	1.0	1.0	1.0
COMPACT	Reduces the whitespace between unordered list items	2.0		
Type=*Option* (CIRCLE | DISK | SQUARE)	Specifies the type of bullet used for displaying each <LI> item in the <UL> list	3.2		2.0
Script Tags	Script tags are used for client-side scripts, including JavaScript and VBScript.			
<NOSCRIPT> ... </NOSCRIPT>	The <NOSCRIPT> tag is used to enclose HTML tags for browsers that do not support client-side scripts.	4.0	3.0	3.0
<SCRIPT> ... </SCRIPT>	The <SCRIPT> tag places a client-side script within a document. This element may appear any number of times in the HEAD or BODY of an HTML document.	3.2	3.0	3.0
DEFER	Specifies that the browser should defer executing the script	4.0		
EVENT=*Text*	Specifies an event that the script should be run in reaction to (this property must be used in conjunction with the FOR property)	4.0	4.0	
FOR=*Text*	Indicates the name or ID of the element to which an event, defined by the EVENT property, is applied	4.0	4.0	
LANGUAGE=*Text*	Specifies the language of the client-side script (see JavaScript for JavaScript commands)	4.0	3.0	3.0
SRC=*URL*	Specifies the source of the external script file	4.0	3.0	3.0
TYPE=*Mime-Type*	Specifies the data type of the scripting language (use text/javascript for JavaScript commands)	4.0	4.0	
Table Tags	Table tags are used to define the structure and appearance of graphical tables.			
<CAPTION> ... </CAPTION>	The <CAPTION> tag encloses the table caption.	3.0	2.0	1.1
ALIGN=*Option* (LEFT | RIGHT | CENTER | TOP | BOTTOM)	Specifies the alignment of the caption with respect to the table (the LEFT, RIGHT and CENTER options are supported only by Internet Explorer 3.0)	3.0	2.0	2.0
VALIGN=*Option* (TOP | BOTTOM)	Specifies the vertical alignment of the caption with respect to the table		2.0	
<COL> ... </COL>	The <COL> tag specifies the default settings for a column or group of columns.	4.0	3.0	
ALIGN=*Option* (CHAR | CENTER | JUSTIFY | LEFT | RIGHT)	Specifies the horizontal alignment of text within a column	4.0	4.0	
SPAN=*Value*	Specifies the columns modified by the <COL> tag	4.0	3.0	

TAGS AND PROPERTIES	DESCRIPTION	HTML	IE	NETSCAPE
VALIGN=*Option* (TOP | MIDDLE | BOTTOM)	Specifies the vertical alignment of text within a column	4.0	4.0	
WIDTH= *Value*	Specifies the width for each column or column group	4.0	3.0	
<COLGROUP> … <COLGROUP>	The <COLGROUP> tag encloses a group of <COL> tags, and groups columns together to set their alignment properties.	3.0	4.0	
ALIGN=*Option* (CHAR | CENTER | JUSTIFY | LEFT | RIGHT)	Specifies the horizontal alignment of text within a column group	4.0	4.0	
CHAR=*Character*	Specifies a character with which to align the values in the column (a period usually is used to align monetary values)	4.0		
CHAROFF=*Value*	Specifies the number of characters to offset the column data from the alignment character specified in the CHAR property	4.0		
SPAN=*Value*	Specifies the columns within the column group	4.0	4.0	
VALIGN=*Option* (TOP | MIDDLE | BOTTOM)	Specifies the vertical alignment of text within a column group	4.0	4.0	
WIDTH= *Value*	Specifies the width of each column for the column group	4.0	3.0	
<TABLE> … </TABLE>	The <TABLE> tag is used to specify the beginning and end of a table.	1.0	1.0	1.1
ALIGN=*Option* (CHAR | LEFT | CENTER | RIGHT)	Specifies the horizontal alignment of the table on the page (only LEFT and RIGHT are supported by Netscape 3.0 and Internet Explorer 3.0)	3.0	3.0	2.0
BACKGROUND=*Document*	Specifies a background image for the table		3.0	4.0
BGCOLOR=*Color*	Specifies a background color for the table	4.0	2.0	3.0
BORDER=*Value*	Specifies the width of the table border, in pixels	3.0	2.0	2.0
BORDERCOLOR=*Color*	Specifies the color of the table border		2.0	4.0
BORDERCOLORDARK=*Color*	Specifies the color of the shaded edge of the table border		2.0	
BORDERCOLORLIGHT=*Color*	Specifies the color of the unshaded edge of the table border		2.0	
CELLPADDING=*Value*	Specifies the space between table cells, in pixels	3.2	2.0	2.0
CELLSPACING=*Value*	Specifies the space between cell text and the cell border, in pixels	3.2	2.0	2.0
COLS=*Value*	Specifies the number of columns in the table, used for quickly calculating the size of the table		3.0	4.0
DATAPAGESIZE=*Value*	Specifies the number of rows that can be displayed in the table when data binding is used	4.0	4.0	
DATASRC=*URL*	Specifies the URL of the table's data source		4.0	

TAGS AND PROPERTIES	DESCRIPTION	HTML	IE	NETSCAPE
FRAME=*Option* (ABOVE | BELOW | BOX | HSIDES | LHS | RHS | VOID | VSIDES)	Specifies the display of table borders. ABOVE = top border only. BELOW = bottom border only. BOX = borders on all four sides. HSIDES = top and bottom borders. LHS = left side border. RHS = right side border. VOID = no borders. VSIDES = left and right side borders.	3.0	3.0	
HEIGHT=*Value*	The height of the table, in pixels or as a percentage of the display area		4.0	4.0
HSPACE=*Value*	Specifies the horizontal space, in pixels, between the table and the surrounding text			4.0
RULES=*Option* (ALL | COLS | NONE | ROWS)	Specifies the display of internal table borders. ALL = borders between every row and column. COLS = borders between every column. NONE = no internal table borders. ROWS = borders between every row.	4.0	3.0	
VSPACE=*Value*	Specifies the vertical space, in pixels, between the table and the surrounding text			4.0
WIDTH=*Value*	The width of the table, in pixels or as a percentage of the display area	3.0	2.0	2.0
<TBODY> ... </TBODY>	The <TBODY> tag identifies text that appears in the table body, as opposed to text in the table header (<THEAD> tag) or in the table footer (<TBODY> tag).	4.0	4.0	
ALIGN=*Option* (CHAR | LEFT | CENTER |RIGHT)	The horizontal alignment of text in the cells of the table body	4.0	4.0	
BGCOLOR=*Color*	Specifies a background color of the table body		4.0	
CHAR=*Character*	Specifies a character with which to align the values in the column (a period usually is used to align monetary values)	4.0		
CHAROFF=*Value*	Specifies the number of characters to offset the column data from the alignment character specified in the CHAR property	4.0		
VALIGN=*Option* (TOP | MIDDLE | BOTTOM)	The vertical alignment of text in the cells in the table body	4.0	4.0	
<TD> ... </TD>	The <TD> tag encloses the text that will appear in an individual table cell.	1.0	2.0	1.1
ABBR=*Text*	Specifies an abbreviated name for the header cell, used when displaying large tables on small screens	4.0		
ALIGN=*Option* (LEFT | CENTER | RIGHT)	Specifies the horizontal alignment of cell text	1.0	2.0	2.0
AXIS=*Text*	Specifies a name for a group of related table headers	4.0		
BACKGROUND=*Document*	Specifies a background image for the cell		4.0	4.0
BGCOLOR=*Color*	Specifies a background color for the cell	4.0	2.0	3.0
BORDERCOLOR=*Color*	Specifies the color of the cell border		2.0	
BORDERCOLORDARK=*Color*	Specifies the color of the shaded edge of the cell border		2.0	

TAGS AND PROPERTIES	DESCRIPTION	HTML	IE	NETSCAPE
BORDERCOLORLIGHT=*Color*	Specifies the color of the unshaded edge of the cell border		2.0	
COLSPAN=*Value*	Specifies the number of columns the cell should span	3.2	2.0	2.0
HEIGHT=*Value*	The height of the cell, in pixels or as a percentage of the display area	3.2	2.0	2.0
NOWRAP	Prohibits the browser from wrapping text in the cell	3.0	2.0	2.0
ROWSPAN=*Value*	Specifies the number of rows the cell should span	3.2	2.0	2.0
SCOPE=*Option* (COL | COLGROUP | ROW | ROWGROUP)	Specifies the table cells for which the current cell provides header information. A SCOPE value of COL indicates that the cell is a header for the rest of the column, a value of COLGROUP indicates that the cell is a header for the current column group, a value of ROW indicates that the cell is a header for the current row, and a value of ROWGROUP indicates that the cell is a header for the current row group.	4.0		
VALIGN=*Option* (TOP | MIDDLE | BOTTOM)	Specifies the vertical alignment of cell text	3.0	2.0	2.0
WIDTH= *Value*	The width of the cell, in pixels or as a percentage of the width of the table	3.2	2.0	2.0
<TFOOT> ... </TFOOT>	The <TFOOT> tag encloses footer information that will be displayed in the table footer when the table is printed on multiple pages.	4.0	4.0	
ALIGN=*Option* (CHAR | CENTER | LEFT | RIGHT)	The horizontal alignment of the table footer	4.0	4.0	
BGCOLOR=*Color*	Specifies a background color for the table footer		4.0	
CHAR=*Character*	Specifies a character with which to align the values in the column (a period is usually used to align monetary values)	4.0		
CHAROFF=*Value*	Specifies the number of characters to offset the column data from the alignment character specified in the CHAR property	4.0		
VALIGN=*Option* (TOP | MIDDLE | BOTTOM)	The vertical alignment of the table footer	4.0	4.0	
<TH> ... </TH>	The <TH> tag encloses the text that will appear in an individual table header cell.	1.0	2.0	1.1
ABBR=*Text*	Specifies an abbreviated name for the header cell, and used when displaying large tables on small screens	4.0		
ALIGN=*Option* (CENTER | CHAR | LEFT | RIGHT)	Specifies the horizontal alignment of header cell text	1.0	2.0	2.0
BACKGROUND=*Document*	Specifies a background image for the header cell		4.0	4.0
BGCOLOR=*Color*	Specifies a background color for the header cell	4.0	2.0	3.0
BORDERCOLOR=*Color*	Specifies the color of the header cell border		2.0	
BORDERCOLORDARK=*Color*	Specifies the color of the shaded edge of the header cell border		3.0	
BORDERCOLORLIGHT=*Color*	Specifies the color of the unshaded edge of the header cell border		3.0	

TAGS AND PROPERTIES	DESCRIPTION	HTML	IE	NETSCAPE
CHAR=*Character*	Specifies a character with which to align the values in the column (a period is usually used to align monetary values)	4.0		
CHAROFF=*Value*	Specifies the number of characters to offset the column data from the alignment character specified in the CHAR property	4.0		
COLSPAN=*Value*	Specifies the number of columns the header cell should span	1.0	2.0	2.0
HEADERS=*List*	Specifies of list of ID values that correspond to the header cells related to this cell	4.0		
HEIGHT=*Value*	The height of the header cell, in pixels or as a percentage of the display area	3.2	2.0	2.0
NOWRAP	Prohibits the browser from wrapping text in the header cell	3.0	2.0	2.0
ROWSPAN=*Value*	Specifies the number of rows the header cell should span	3.0	2.0	2.0
SCOPE=*Option* (COL | COLGROUP | ROW | ROWGROUP)	Specifies the table cells for which the current cell provides header information. A SCOPE value of COL indicates that the cell is a header for the rest of the column, a value of COLGROUP indicates that the cell is a header for the current column group, a value of ROW indicates that the cell is a header for the current row, and a value of ROWGROUP indicates that the cell is a header for the current row group.	4.0		
VALIGN=*Option* (TOP | MIDDLE | BOTTOM)	Specifies the vertical alignment of header cell text	3.0	2.0	2.0
WIDTH= *Value*	The width of the header cell in pixels or as a percentage of the width of the table	3.2	2.0	2.0
<THEAD> ... </THEAD>	The <THEAD> tag encloses header information that will be displayed in the table header when the table is printed on multiple pages.	3.0	3.0	
ALIGN=*Option* (LEFT | CENTER | RIGHT)	The horizontal alignment of the table header	3.0	3.0	
BGCOLOR=*Color*	Specifies a background color for the table cells within the <THEAD> tags		4.0	
CHAR=*Character*	Specifies a character with which to align the values in the table header columns (a period is usually used to align monetary values)	4.0		
CHAROFF=*Value*	Specifies the number of characters to offset the column data from the alignment character specified in the CHAR property	4.0		
VALIGN=*Option* (TOP | MIDDLE | BOTTOM)	The vertical alignment of the table header	3.0	3.0	

TAGS AND PROPERTIES	DESCRIPTION	HTML	IE	NETSCAPE
<TR> ... </TR>	The <TR> tag encloses table cells within a single row.	3.0	2.0	1.1
ALIGN=*Option* (LEFT | CENTER | RIGHT)	Specifies the horizontal alignment of text in the row	3.0	2.0	2.0
BGCOLOR=*Color*	Specifies a background color for the header cell	4.0	2.0	3.0
BORDERCOLOR=*Color*	Specifies the color of the header cell border		2.0	
BORDERCOLORDARK=*Color*	Specifies the color of the shaded edge of the header cell border		2.0	
BORDERCOLORLIGHT=*Color*	Specifies the color of the unshaded edge of the header cell border		2.0	
CHAR=*Character*	Specifies a character with which to align the values in the table row (a period is usually used to align monetary values)	4.0		
CHAROFF=*Value*	Specifies the number of characters to offset the column data from the alignment character specified in the CHAR property	4.0		
VALIGN=*Option* (TOP | MIDDLE | BOTTOM)	The vertical alignment of the text in the table row	3.0	2.0	2.0

HTML File Finder

Tutorial	Location in Tutorial	Name and Location of Data file	Student Saves File As...	Student Creates New File
Tutorial 1	Session 1.1			Resume.htm
Tutorial 1	Session 1.2	Tutorial.01\ Resume.htm	Resume.htm	
Tutorial 1	Session 1.3	Tutorial.01\Resume.htm (Saved from last session) Tutorial.01\Taylor.jpg	Resume.htm	
Tutorial 1	Review Assignment	Tutorial.01\ Resume.htm (Saved from last session)	Resume2.htm	
Tutorial 1	Case Problem 1	Tutorial.01\Cases\LVB.jpg		Ludwig.htm
Tutorial 1	Case Problem 2	Tutorial.01\Cases\Eulertxt.htm	Euler.htm	
Tutorial 1	Case Problem 3	Tutorial.01\Cases\Diamonds.jpg Tutorial.01\Cases\Chester.jpg Tutorial.01\Cases\Chestertxt.htm	Chester.htm	
Tutorial 1	Case Problem 4			MyResume.htm
Tutorial 2	Session 2.1	Tutorial.02\Resumetxt.htm	Resume.htm	
Tutorial 2	Session 2.2	Tutorial.02\Resume.htm (Saved from last session) Tutorial.02\Refertxt.htm Tutorial.02\Comtxt.htm	Resume.htm Refer.htm Comments.htm	
Tutorial 2	Session 2.3	Tutorial.02\Resume.htm	Resume.htm	
Tutorial 2	Review Assignment	Tutorial.02\Resume.htm	Resume.htm (save in Review folder)	
Tutorial 2	Case Problem 1			Depart.htm
Tutorial 2	Case Problem 2	Tutorial.02\Cases\Move1A.htm Tutorial.02\Cases\Move2A.htm Tutorial.02\Cases\Move2A.htm Tutorial.02\Cases\Move3A.htm	Move1.htm Move2.htm Move3.htm Move4.htm	
Tutorial 2	Case Problem 3	Tutorial.03\Cases\SMtxt.htm Tutorial.03\Cases\Factstxt.htm Tutorial.03\Cases\FAQtxt.htm	Scanner.htm Facts.htm FAQ.htm	
Tutorial 2	Case Problem 4			Myhome.htm
Tutorial 3	Session 3.1	Tutorial.03\Expotext.htm Tutorial.03\Space.jpg	Expo.htm	
Tutorial 3	Session 3.2	Tutorial.03\Expo.htm (Saved from last session) Tutorial.03\Logo.gif Tutorial.03\Center.jpg Tutorial.03\Logoanim.gif	Expo.htm	
Tutorial 3	Session 3.3	Tutorial.03\Expo.htm (Saved from last session) Tutorial.03\Mitchell.htm Tutorial.03\Brinkman.htm Tutorial.03\Bryd.htm Tutorial.03\Layout.gif	Expo.htm	
Tutorial 3	Review Assignment	Tutorial.03\Review\Mitchtxt.htm Tutorial.03\Review\Stars.jpg Tutorial.03\Review\Brydtxt.htm Tutorial.03\Review\Brinktxt.htm Tutorial.03\Review\Equip.jpg Tutorial.03\Review\Expotxt.htm Tutorial.03\Review\Class.htm	Mitchell.htm Bryd.htm Brinkman.htm Expo.htm (save in Review folder)	
Tutorial 3	Case Problem 1	Tutorial.03\Cases\Newtext.htm Tutorial.03\Cases\Bars.jpg Tutorial.03\Cases\Product.jpg Tutorial.03\Cases\Scantext.htm Tutorial.03\Cases\Printext.htm Tutorial.03\Cases\PStext.htm	Jackson.htm Scanner.htm Printer.htm PS150.htm	

HTML File Finder

Tutorial	Location in Tutorial	Name and Location of Data file	Student Saves File As...	Student Creates New File
Tutorial 3	Case Problem 2	Tutorial.03\Cases\Forsttxt.htm Tutorial.03\Cases\Forrest.jpg Tutorial.03\Cases\Charntxt.htm Tutorial.03\Cases\Unwintxt.htm Tutorial.03\Cases\SFSFtxt.htm Tutorial.03\Cases\SFSF.gif Tutorial.03\Cases\Guests.jpg	Forrest.htm Charnas.htm Unwin.htm SFSF.htm	
Tutorial 3	Case Problem 3	Tutorial.03\Cases\Breaktxt.htm Tutorial.03\Cases\Tan.jpg Tutorial.03\Cases\Breakfst.jpg Tutorial.03\Cases\Lunchtxt.htm Tutorial.03\Cases\Dinnrtxt.htm Tutorial.03\Cases\Dinner.jpg	Breakfst.htm Lunch.htm Dinner.htm	
Tutorial 3	Case Problem 4	Tutorial.03\Cases\House.jpg Tutorial.03\Cases\Tristate.gif Tutorial.03\Cases\Listings.gif Tutorial.03\Cases\TSBack.gif		Tristate.htm
Tutorial 4	Session 4.1	Tutorial.04\MAA.htm Tutorial.04\MAA2.htm	MAAtext.htm MAAtable.htm	
Tutorial 4	Session 4.2	Tutorial.04\MAAtable.htm (Saved from last session)	MAAtable.htm	
Tutorial 4	Session 4.3	Tutorial.04\Ghome.htm Tutorial.04\Links.htm Tutorial.04\Glogo.jpg Tutorial.04\Oneil.htm Tutorial.04\Gnotes.htm Tutorial.04\Cassini.htm	Gargoyle.htm	
Tutorial 4	Review Assignment	Tutorial.04\Review\MAA4.htm Tutorial.04\Review\MAA3.htm Tutorial.04\Review\Ghome2.htm	GTable.htm GText.htm GCollect.htm	
Tutorial 4	Case Problem 1	Tutorial.04\Cases\Avalon.htm	May_List.htm	
Tutorial 4	Case Problem 2	Tutorial.04\Cases\WMTZ.htm	TVList.htm	
Tutorial 4	Case Problem 3	Tutorial.04\Cases\DRCtext.htm Tutorial.04\Cases\Welcome.htm Tutorial.04\Cases\Dlogo.gif Tutorial.04\Cases\Dunston.jpg Tutorial.04\Cases\Nextweek.htm Tutorial.04\Cases\Letter.htm Tutorial.04\Cases\Upcoming.htm	Dunston.htm	
Tutorial 4	Case Problem 4			TW.htm
Tutorial 5	Session 5.1	Tutorial.05\COLtext.htm Tutorial.05\Head.htm Tutorial.05\Links.htm Tutorial.05\TCE.htm Tutorial.05\Linktext.htm	Colorado.htm	
Tutorial 5	Session 5.2	Tutorial.05\Colorado.htm (Saved from last session) Tutorial.05\Links.htm Tutorial.05\Tours.htm Tutorial.05\Tourtext.htm Tutorial.05\Noframes.htm	Colorado.htm	
Tutorial 5	Review Assignment	Tutorial.05\Review\Stafftxt.htm Tutorial.05\Review\Return.htm Tutorial.05\Review\Photos.htm Tutorial.05\Review\StaffNF.htm Tutorial.05\Review\Retrntxt.htm Tutorial.05\Review\Colorado.htm Tutorial.05\Links.htm Tutorial.05\Tours.htm	Staff.htm Return.htm	

HTML File Finder

Tutorial	Location in Tutorial	Name and Location of Data file	Student Saves File As...	Student Creates New File
Tutorial 5	Case Problem 1	Tutorial.05\Cases\DCCtxt.htm Tutorial.05\Cases\Head.htm Tutorial.05\Cases\Map.htm Tutorial.05\Cases\Report.htm Tutorial.05\Cases\Maptxt.htm	DCC.htm Map.htm	
Tutorial 5	Case Problem 2	Tutorial.05\Cases\Scottxt.htm Tutorial.05\Cases\TSLogo.htm Tutorial.05\Cases\Laketour.htm Tutorial.05\Cases\TSList.htm Tutorial.05\Cases\TStxt.htm Tutorial.05\Cases\Laketour.htm Tutorial.05\Cases\Casttour.htm Tutorial.05\Cases\Hightour.htm Tutorial.05\Cases\Hebdtour.htm	Scotland.htm TSList.htm	
Tutorial 5	Case Problem 3	Tutorial.05\Cases\Sontxt.htm Tutorial.05\Cases\Eng220.htm Tutorial.05\Cases\SonTOC.htm Tutorial.05\Cases\Blank.htm Tutorial.05\Cases\SnTOCtxt.htm Tutorial.05\Cases\JDtxt.htm Tutorial.05\Cases\SonJD1.htm Tutorial.05\Cases\SonJD5.htm Tutorial.05\Cases\SonJD10.htm Tutorial.05\Cases\WStxt.htm Tutorial.05\Cases\SonWS12.htm Tutorial.05\Cases\SonWS18.htm Tutorial.05\Cases\SonWS116.htm Tutorial.05\Cases\SonWS130.htm Tutorial.05\Cases\EStxt.htm Tutorial.05\Cases\SonES54.htm Tutorial.05\Cases\SonES64.htm Tutorial.05\Cases\SonES79.htm	Sonnet.htm SonTOC.htm SonnetJD.htm SonnetWS.htm SonnetES.htm	
Tutorial 5	Case Problem 4			WTOC.htm Warner.htm
Tutorial 6	Session 6.1	Tutorial.06\Regtext.htm	Register.htm	
Tutorial 6	Session 6.2	Tutorial.06\Register.htm (Saved from last session)	Register.htm	
Tutorial 6	Session 6.3	Tutorial.06\Register.htm (Saved from last session)	Register.htm	
Tutorial 6	Review Assignment	Tutorial.06\Review\Regtext.htm	Register.htm	
Tutorial 6	Case Problem 1	Tutorial.06\Cases\Adstext.htm Tutorial.06\Cases\Search.gif Tutorial.06\Cases\Help.gif Tutorial.06\Cases\Cancel.gif	Ads.htm	
Tutorial 6	Case Problem 2	Tutorial.06\Cases\Travltxt.htm	Travel.htm	
Tutorial 6	Case Problem 3	Tutorial.06\Cases\NBtext.htm	Newborn.htm	
Tutorial 6	Case Problem 4			Computer.htm
Tutorial 7	Session 7.1	Tutorial.07\Astrotxt.htm Tutorial.07\Chemtxt.htm	Astro.htm MWS.css Chem.htm	
Tutorial 7	Session 7.2	Tutorial.07\MWS.css (Saved from last session) Tutorial.07\Astro.htm (Saved from last session)	MWS.css Astro.htm	
Tutorial 7	Session 7.3	Tutorial.07\MWS.css (Saved from last session) Tutorial.07\Astro.htm (Saved from last session)	MWS.css Astro.htm	

HTML File Finder

Tutorial	Location in Tutorial	Name and Location of Data file	Student Saves File As...	Student Creates New File
Tutorial 7	Review Assignments	Tutorial.07\Review\Physicstxt.htm Tutorial.07\Review\Engtxt.htm Tutorial.07\Review\Electtxt.htm Tutorial.07\Review\MWSPtxt.css Tutorial.07\Review\Review.jpg	Physics.htm Eng.htm Elect.htm MWSP.css	
Tutorial 7	Case Problem 1	Tutorial.07\Cases\Stufftxt.htm	Stuff.htm	
Tutorial 7	Case Problem 2	Tutorial.07\Cases\Leetxt.htm	Lee.htm	
Tutorial 7	Case Problem 3	Tutorial.07\Cases\H01txt.htm through Tutorial.07\Cases\H18txt.htm	H01.htm through H18.htm	Willet.css
Tutorial 7	Case Problem 4	Tutorial.07\Cases\BizetBio.txt Tutorial.07\Cases\BizetList.txt Tutorial.07\Cases\Bizet.jpg Tutorial.07\Cases\MozartBio.txt Tutorial.07\Cases\MozartList.txt Tutorial.07\Cases\Mozart.jpg Tutorial.07\Cases\PucciniBio.txt Tutorial.07\Cases\PucciniList.txt Tutorial.07\Cases\Puccini.jpg Tutorial.07\Cases\VerdiBio.txt Tutorial.07\Cases\VerdiList.txt Tutorial.07\Cases\Verdi.jpg Tutorial.07\Cases\WagnerBio.txt Tutorial.07\Cases\WagnerList.txt Tutorial.07\Cases\Wagner.jpg		Your file name.htm Opera.css
Tutorial 8	Session 8.1	Tutorial.08\NPNtext.htm	NPN.htm	
Tutorial 8	Session 8.2	Tutorial.08\NPN.htm (Saved from last session)	NPN.htm	
Tutorial 8	Session 8.3	Tutorial.08\NPN.htm (Saved from last session)	NPN.htm	
Tutorial 8	Review Assignment	Tutorial.08\Review\NPNtext2.htm	NPN2.htm	
Tutorial 8	Case Problem 1	Tutorial.08\Cases\Menutext.htm	Menu.htm	
Tutorial 8	Case Problem 2	Tutorial.08\Cases\Twaintxt.htm	Twain.htm	
Tutorial 8	Case Problem 3	Tutorial.08\Cases\Trigtext.htm	Trig.htm	
Tutorial 8	Case Problem 4	Tutorial.08\Cases\November.htm		Avalon.htm
Tutorial 9	Session 9.1	Tutorial.09\Studytxt.htm	Study.htm	
Tutorial 9	Session 9.2	Tutorial.09\Study.htm (Saved from last session)	Study.htm	
Tutorial 9	Session 9.3	Tutorial.09\Study.htm (Saved from last session)	Study.htm	
Tutorial 9	Review Assignment	Tutorial.09\Review\Studtxt2.htm	Study2.htm	
Tutorial 9	Case Problem 1	Tutorial.09\Cases\PSText.htm	PS500.htm	
Tutorial 9	Case Problem 2	Tutorial.09\Cases\MPLtext.htm	MPL.htm	
Tutorial 9	Case Problem 3	Tutorial.09\Cases\CPtext.htm	CP.htm	
Tutorial 9	Case Problem 4			Mortgage.htm
Tutorial 10	Session 10.1	Tutorial.10\Raintxt.htm Tutorial.10\AF2000.wav Tutorial.10\AF2000.au	Rainier.htm Rainier2.htm	
Tutorial 10	Session 10.2	Tutorial.10\Rainier.htm (Saved from last session) Tutorial.10\Rainier2.htm (Saved from last session) Tutorial.10\MRIM.avi Tutorial.10\MRIM.mov	Rainier.htm Rainier2.htm	

HTML File Finder

Tutorial	Location in Tutorial	Name and Location of Data file	Student Saves File As...	Student Creates New File
Tutorial 10	Session 10.3	Tutorial.10\CRoll.txt Tutorial.10\Rainier2.htm	Rainier2.htm	
Tutorial 10	Review Assignment	Tutorial.10\Review\Raintxt3.htm Tutorial.10\Review\Raintxt4.htm Tutorial.10\Review\AF2000b.wav Tutorial.10\Review\AF2000b.au Tutorial.10\Review\MRIM2.avi Tutorial.10\Review\MRIM2.mov Tutorial.10\Review\Welcome.wav Tutorial.10\Review\Welcome.au	Rainier3.htm Rainier4.htm	
Tutorial 10	Case Problem 1	Tutorial.10\Cases\LMNHtext.htm Tutorial.10\Cases\Dino.avi Tutorial.10\Cases\Dino.mov Tutorial.10\Cases\Dino.wav Tutorial.10\Cases\Dino.au	LMNH.htm	
Tutorial 10	Case Problem 2	Tutorial.10\Cases\RFtext.htm Tutorial.10\Cases\Sound.gif Tutorial.10\Cases\FireIce.wav Tutorial.10\Cases\FireIce.au Tutorial.10\Cases\Devotion.wav Tutorial.10\Cases\Devotion.au Tutorial.10\Cases\Button.class	RF.htm	
Tutorial 10	Case Problem 3	Tutorial.10\Cases\Fracttext.htm Tutorial.10\Cases\Mandel.avi Tutorial.10\Cases\Mandel.mov Tutorial.10\Cases\Mandel.class	Fractal.htm	
Tutorial 10	Case Problem 4	Tutorial.10\Cases\CreditRoll.class		MyMedia.htm

Dynamic HTML File Finder

Tutorial	Location in Tutorial	Name and Location of Data file	Student Saves File As...	Student Creates New File
Tutorial 1	Session 1.1	Tutorial.01D\ABtext.htm Tutorial.01D\AB.jpg Tutorial.01D\Fiction.jpg Tutorial.01D\NFiction.jpg	Avalon.htm	
Tutorial 1	Session 1.2			Avalon.js
Tutorial 1	Session 1.3	Tutorial.01D\Avalon.htm (saved from the first session)	Avalon.htm	
Tutorial 1	Review Assignments	Tutorial.01D\Review\indextxt.htm Tutorial.01D\Review\ABJStext.js Tutorial.01D\Review\AB2text.htm	index.htm Avalon2.js Avalon2.htm	
Tutorial 1	Case Problem 1	Tutorial.01D\Cases\Golftext.htm Tutorial.01D\Cases\Ball.gif Tutorial.01D\Cases\BallPath.txt	GolfPage.htm	
Tutorial 1	Case Problem 2	Tutorial.01D\Cases\CCCtext.htm	CCC.htm	
Tutorial 1	Case Problem 3	Tutorial.01D\Cases\AJACtext.htm Tutorial.01D\Cases\JBall.gif Tutorial.01D\Cases\TossPath.txt	AJAC.htm	
Tutorial 1	Case Problem 4	Tutorial.01D\Cases\Bug.jpg Tutorial.01D\Cases\BugDead.jpg Tutorial.01D\Cases\Shoe.jpg Tutorial.01D\Cases\Bugs.txt		index.htm Bug.htm

Dynamic HTML File Finder

Tutorial	Location in Tutorial	Name and Location of Data File	Student Saves File As...	Student Creates New File
Tutorial 2	Session 2.1	Tutorial.02D\Pixaltxt.htm Tutorial.02D\DC100.htm Tutorial.02D\DC250.htm Tutorial.02D\DC500.htm	Pixal.htm	
Tutorial 2	Session 2.2	Tutorial.02D\StylesIE.htm Tutorial.02D\ClassIE.htm Tutorial.02D\SheetsIE.htm Tutorial.02D\DC100txt.htm Tutorial.02D\Pixal.htm (saved from the first session)	DC100_IE.htm	
Tutorial 2	Session 2.3	Tutorial.02D\StylesNS.htm Tutorial.02D\DC100txt.htm Tutorial.02D\Pixal.htm (saved from the first session)	DC100_NS.htm	
Tutorial 2	Review Assignments	Tutorial.02D\Review\Specxtxt.htm	Specs.htm	
Tutorial 2	Case Problem 1	Tutorial.02D\Cases\Frtxt.htm	French.htm	
Tutorial 2	Case Problem 2	Tutorial.02D\Cases\HQuiztxt.htm Tutorial.02D\Cases\blank.htm Tutorial.02D\Cases\Marne.htm	HQuiz.htm	
Tutorial 2	Case Problem 3	Tutorial.02D\Cases\TOCtxt.htm	TOC.htm	
Tutorial 2	Case Problem 4	Tutorial.02D\Cases\Dream.htm		Dream_IE.htm Dream_NS.htm
Tutorial 3	Session 3.1	Tutorial.03D\WStext.htm Tutorial.03D\PlaysOut.gif Tutorial.03D\PlaysOver.gif Tutorial.03D\SonOut.gif Tutorial.03D\SonOver.gif Tutorial.03D\BioOut.gif Tutorial.03D\BioOver.gif Tutorial.03D\GlobeOut.gif Tutorial.03D\GlobeOver.gif Tutorial.03D\StratOut.gif Tutorial.03D\StratOver.gif	WS.htm	
Tutorial 3	Session 3.2	Tutorial.03D\Playstxt.htm Tutorial.03D\APItext.js	Plays.htm API.js	
Tutorial 3	Session 3.3	Tutorial.03D\Plays.htm (saved from the second session) Tutorial.03D\TransTour.htm Tutorial.03D\WS.htm (saved from the first session)	Plays.htm WS.htm	
Tutorial 3	Review Assignments	Tutorial.03D\Review\Temptxt.htm Tutorial.03D\Review\PlaysOut.gif Tutorial.03D\Review\PlaysOver.gif Tutorial.03D\Review\SonOut.gif Tutorial.03D\Review\SonOver.gif Tutorial.03D\Review\BioOut.gif Tutorial.03D\Review\BioOver.gif Tutorial.03D\Review\GlobeOut.gif Tutorial.03D\Review\GlobeOver.gif Tutorial.03D\Review\StratOut.gif Tutorial.03D\Review\StratOver.gif Tutorial.03D\Review\Links1.gif Tutorial.03D\Review\Links2.gif Tutorial.03D\Review\Caliban.gif	Tempest.htm	

Dynamic HTML File Finder

Tutorial	Location in Tutorial	Name and Location of Data File	Student Saves File As...	Student Creates New File
Tutorial 3	Case Problem 1	Tutorial.03D\Cases\Housetxt.htm Tutorial.03D\Cases\RUp.gif Tutorial.03D\Cases\RDown.gif Tutorial.03D\Cases\LUp.gif Tutorial.03D\Cases\LDown.gif Tutorial.03D\Cases\Slide00.jpg through Slide.11.jpg	House.htm	
Tutorial 3	Case Problem 2	Tutorial.03D\Cases\Tilestxt.htm Tutorial.03D\Cases\Tiles.js Tutorial.03D\Cases\Image1.jpg through Image8.jpg	Tiles.htm	
Tutorial 3	Case Problem 3	Tutorial.03D\Cases\Scavtxt.htm	Scav.htm	
Tutorial 3	Case Problem 4	Tutorial.03D\Cases\Scantxt.htm Tutorial.03D\Cases\Printtxt.htm Tutorial.03D\Cases\PS150txt.htm Tutorial.03D\Cases\SM1.gif Tutorial.03D\Cases\LP1.gif Tutorial.03D\Cases\PS1.gif Tutorial.03D\Cases\SM2.gif Tutorial.03D\Cases\LP2.gif Tutorial.03D\Cases\PS2.gif		Scanner.htm Printer.htm PS150.htm
Tutorial 4	Session 4.1	Tutorial.04D\Gamestxt.htm Tutorial.04D\Gamestxt.js Tutorial.04D\CursorN.htm Tutorial.04D\CursorIE.htm	Games.htm GamesAPI.js	
Tutorial 4	Session 4.2	Tutorial.04D\Games.htm (saved from the first session) Tutorial.04D\GamesAPI.js (saved from the first session)	Games.htm GamesAPI.js	
Tutorial 4	Session 4.3	Tutorial.04D\Games.htm (saved from the second session) Tutorial.04D\GamesAPI.js (saved from the second session)	Games.htm GamesAPI.js	
Tutorial 4	Review Assignments	Tutorial.04D\Review\Puzzletxt.js Tutorial.04D\Review\Puzzletxt.htm Tutorial.04D\Review\Image1.jpg through Image24.jpg Tutorial.04D\Review\Random.js	Puzzle.js Puzzle.htm	
Tutorial 4	Case Problem 1	Tutorial.04D\Cases\Operatxt.js Tutorial.04D\Cases\Operatxt.htm Tutorial.04D\Cases\Bizet.jpg Tutorial.04D\Cases\Mozart.jpg Tutorial.04D\Cases\Puccini.jpg Tutorial.04D\Cases\Verdi.jpg Tutorial.04D\Cases\Wagner.jpg	OperaAPI.js Opera.htm	
Tutorial 4	Case Problem 2	Tutorial.04D\Cases\Surveytxt.htm	Survey.htm	
Tutorial 4	Case Problem 3	Tutorial.04D\Cases\Demotxt.htm	Demo.htm	
Tutorial 4	Case Problem 4			Produce.htm Produce.js
Tutorial 5	Session 5.1	Tutorial.05D\Defaulttxt.htm Tutorial.05D\indextxt.htm	Default.htm index.htm	

Dynamic HTML File Finder

Tutorial	Location in Tutorial	Name and Location of Data File	Student Saves File As...	Student Creates New File
Tutorial 5	Session 5.2	Tutorial.05D\PopupDemo.htm Tutorial.05D\Concertotxt.htm Tutorial.05D\Sonatatxt.htm Tutorial.05D\Symphonytxt.htm Tutorial.05D\Lesson3txt.htm Tutorial.05D\PopupDemo2.htm Tutorial.05D\Quiztxt.htm	Concerto.htm Sonata.htm Symphony.htm Lesson3.htm Quiz.htm	
Tutorial 5	Session 5.3	Tutorial.05D\navtxt.htm Tutorial.05D\Terms.htm Tutorial.05D\BlockDemo.htm Tutorial.05D\Default.htm (saved from the first session)	nav.htm Default.htm	
Tutorial 5	Review Assignments	Tutorial.05D\Review\Defaulttxt.htm Tutorial.05D\Review\atempotxt.htm Tutorial.05D\Review\Quiztxt.htm Tutorial.05D\Review\Quiz2txt.htm Tutorial.05D\Review\maintxt.htm Tutorial.05D\Review\bottomtxt.htm	Default.htm atempo.htm Quiz.htm Quiz.htm main.htm bottom.htm	
Tutorial 5	Case Problem 1	Tutorial.05D\Cases\CWJtxt.htm Tutorial.05D\Cases\Cover.htm Tutorial.05D\Cases\Form.htm	CWJ.htm	
Tutorial 5	Case Problem 2	Tutorial.05D\Cases\Braintxt.htm Tutorial.05D\Cases\Brain.css Tutorial.05D\Cases\Brain.jpg	Brain.htm	
Tutorial 5	Case Problem 3	Tutorial.05D\Cases\Sourcetxt.htm Tutorial.05D\Cases\Demo.htm Tutorial.05D\Cases\Blank.htm	Source.htm	
Tutorial 5	Case Problem 4	Tutorial.05D\Cases\UBtxt.htm Tutorial.05D\Cases\PS300.jpg Tutorial.05D\Cases\UBLogo.jpg		UB.htm